The Instant Mortgage-Equity Technique

The Instant Mortgage-Equity Technique

Totally Precomputed Over-All
Rates for the Valuation of
Income Property

Irvin E. Johnson

Published for the Society of Real Estate Appraisers

Lexington Books
D.C. Heath and Company
Lexington, Massachusetts
Toronto   London

Johnson, Irvin E.
The Instant Mortgage-Equity Technique.

1. Real property—Valuation. I. Title.
HD1387.J64   333.3'32   72-6464
ISBN 0-669-84749-6

Published simultaneously in Canada.

Printed in the United States of America.

International Standard Book Number: 0-669-84749-6

Library of Congress Catalog Card Number: 72-6464

To a three-year-old
mini-hurricane named
Cheryl Anne . . .
without whose help
the writing of this book
would not have been
so great a challenge!

Contents

viii

Introduction

The single purpose of this book is to uncomplicate the complicated.

Because the mortgage-equity technique of the income approach to value has been around for so many years without shedding its aura of mystery and complexity, I decided to do something about it. Here are the results . . . in this book.

Out of the Ivory Tower and into the Workshop

This is an age of "instants" . . . coffee, mashed potatoes, even antiques. So, why not mortgage-equity? The *sine qua non* of this new approach consists of the OAR Tables . . . totally precomputed Over-All Rates . . . nearly 150,000 of them. These are not ordinary capitalization rates. Each OAR has built into it all of the variable elements that motivate and concern the contemporary investor: relatively high rate of yield on equity; low down payment; big loan on favorable terms; cash flow; a limited period of ownership before resale, exchange, or refinancing; equity growth through both loan amortization and appreciation of property value.

The appraiser or analyst merely selects from the OAR Tables the rate that matches the variables in his problem, divides the OAR into estimated net annual income, and—*presto*—instant indicator of value! For example, he determines that the subject property can be financed for 75% of value on a loan at 8% interest to be amortized in 20 years by monthly payments. He finds that the typical investor projects a 10-year period of ownership, anticipates appreciation in market value of 20% within this holding period, and expects a *yield of 14% on his equity* (on his down payment of 25%). Net annual income, after reasonable allowances for all expenses, is estimated to be $42,000 a year. What is property value as indicated by the mortgage-equity technique? Page 243 of the OAR Tables lists the rate that matches all variables in the problem: .0879. Value = $42,000 ÷ .0879, or $477,816; say $477,800. Easy does it all the way!

Mortgage-equity tells the appraiser and the investor something no other technique of the income approach does: the investor's rate of yield on equity, on his actual cash investment. In this illustration, if the purchaser pays $477,800 for the property under the terms and conditions noted, he will earn a full 14% yield on his down payment of $119,450, assuming the reliability of his short-term projections.

Note that the appraiser merely *selects* the Over-All Rate. There is no need to *compute* the rate . . . no call for algebra, equations, or special symbols. And therein lies the difference between the *instant* mortgage-equity technique and any other version of it.

It may be unorthodox to place a problem and solution in the introduction to a specialized appraisal book, but we want to show the reader before he begins that instant mortgage-equity works and how it works.

New Routes to Old Objectives

Most of the books that probe and measure the time-value of money have been written by mathematicians for mathematicians. *The Instant Mortgage-Equity Technique* has been prepared by an appraiser for appraisers and other nonmathematicians. It is designed to express rather than impress and is more practical than profound.

Just as there are often alternate trails to the top of the mountain, there may be more than one mathematical technique leading to the computation of mortgage-equity over-all rates and related procedures of income property valuation and investment analysis. "Mortgage-equity" is frequently equated with *Ellwood*. The appraisal profession owes a debt of gratitude to L. W. Ellwood, M.A.I., for his pioneering in this field and for his scholarly work built around the *Ellwood Tables*.

Our version of "mortgage-equity" provides a new (and, we believe, easier and faster) route to old objectives. Totally precomputed rates and patterned procedures in *The Instant Mortgage-Equity Technique* are based on extended discounted cash flow calculations, in which the net reversion at the end of an investment holding period is considered as the terminal segment of the total income stream. While this approach differs in mathematical concept from the adjusted band-of-investment method of deriving an over-all rate, the results are identical. There is no single setting of a microscope or telescope to accommodate every eye. The Instant Mortgage-Equity Technique may help some students and practicing appraisers bring into focus what might otherwise have been blurred, confusing, and complex.

Here's How

Sequence of presentation in *The Instant Mortgage-Equity Technique* treats mortgage-equity theory first in Chapters 1 and 2. Chapter 3 outlines procedural practice in illustrated pattern format. It also contains a section of work sheets, with explanatory notes. A case study of income property valuation and investment analysis is given in Chapter 4. Three types of tables appear in Chapter 5: compound interest and annuity tables of present worth and amortization, the OAR Tables of precomputed mortgage-equity over-all rates, and supplemental tables of loan balances and loan constants.

Here are a few suggestions for programming your study:

- Go through Chapters 1 and 2 in order.
- Study Chapter 3 by topics, according to the priorities of your interests. Relate the discussions in Section 1 to the procedures and illustrations in Section 2. (Both sections in Chapter 3 are arranged alphabetically under the same general headings.)
- Work through the case study in Chapter 4, relating it to the pertinent specific procedures in Chapter 3 and to the three types of tables in Chapter 5.
- Whenever factors and over-all rates are used in the text, verify by locating them in the tables. You may note slight differences due to rounding in illustrations.
- Make the actual calculations shown in the examples, and check for accuracy.
- Use an electronic calculator or slide rule, if available, for ease and speed in computation.
- If calculation is a "by hand" operation, rounding factors and over-all rates to three significant decimal places simplifies your arithmetic.
- Make some trial runs, solving your own problems of appraisal and investment analysis by following the appropriate methods outlined and illustrated in Chapter 3, Section 2.

The Instant Mortgage-Equity Technique has been prepared for use in appraisal, not just for study, and certainly not for "once over lightly" speed-reading. An exploratory survey of the "Ready Reference Roster" in Chapter 3, Section 2, will indicate the many types of computations the appraiser, using this book as a tool, can make with confidence, speed, and efficiency. Chapter 3, Section 2, listing the "Mortgage-Equity Procedures," and Chapter 5, containing the compound interest, over-all rate, and supplemental tables, have been designed for quick reference and constitute the actual working parts of the book. Pages in these two areas of the text will, through continued reference and use by the appraiser, experience the greatest degree of physical depreciation; however, we foresee no probability of accelerated functional obsolescence.

Check and Double Check

While every attempt has been made to ensure accuracy in the text and tables, we cannot claim nor guarantee complete freedom from fault. Variance in "rounding" factors and rates in numerous steps of computation might account for slight differences between our calculations and yours. However, appraisal practice and the realities of the market allow a reasonable range of tolerance in "rounding" any indicator of value. If you discover a significant mistake, kindly do two things:

a. Let us know.
b. Consider that such an error has added the human touch to *The Instant Mortgage-Equity Technique*.

Where Credit Is Due

Production of this book has been expedited and sponsored by the Society of Real Estate Appraisers. Officers of the Society particularly active in implementing publication include: William W. Abelmann, S.R.E.A., M.A.I., 1972 President; James W. Law, S.R.E.A., District Governor; James A. Hueser, General Manager; Jerry C. Davis, Director of Publications.

Recognition must also be given to Edwin B. Shriner, C.A.E., Assessor of Ventura County, California; and to Walter C. Hunter, A.S.A., M.G.A., Assistant Assessor. These officials maintain an office atmosphere conducive to creative thinking and the development of progressive procedures. Personnel from this department, whose extracurricular activities assisted the author in his work include: Richard B. Tanner, Appraiser Analyst, who programmed the EDP runs of rates and factors; Richard Laquess, Senior Appraiser, who developed the form for deriving an Over-All Rate from the market; and Charlene Espinosa-Pettit, secretary, who translated longhand into legibility.

Portions of the text, tables, and procedures in *The Instant Mortgage-Equity Technique* appear in the author's book *Mini-Math for Appraisers*, published by the International Association of Assessing Officers, Chicago, Illinois. These sections are used here by special permission of the I.A.A.O.

It's All Yours!

The instant mortgage-equity technique is easier than you think. It's also easier *if* you think. Now, *go to it*!

Irvin E. Johnson
Ventura, California
July 1, 1972

The Instant Mortgage-
Equity Technique

1

The Investor's Language: Mortgage-Equity

The mortgage-equity technique of the income approach to value talks the investor's language. It answers his most significant questions . . . tells him what he wants to know.

An investor in the current marketplace focuses on three major matters:

1. What he puts into an investment.
2. What he gets out of the investment in dollars (future net benefits).
3. The yield rate on the dollar amount he invests.

The mortgage-equity technique, applied by the appraiser, zeroes in on that topical trio.

Basic Concepts

The Mortgage-Equity Technique, widely used in both feasibility studies and appraisals for market value, gives particular consideration to areas of major concern to contemporary investors.

- Income property is usually purchased on a relatively "low" down payment and "high" loan. Today's real-estate market is not a cash market.
- The investor using leverage has two purposes in mind: (1) hopefully, to maximize his projected gains; (2) as a safety measure, to minimize unexpected but possible losses.
- The investor plans to hold the property for a limited time. Since deductible interest paid on the mortgage declines period by period and nondeductible payments on principal increase accordingly, a turnover point is reached, in spite of allowable depreciation. Income tax considerations won't allow a lengthy term of ownership. Few investors project a holding period in excess of ten years before selling, refinancing, or exchanging the property.
- Within the holding period either appreciation, stability, or depreciation in market value is anticipated.
- Investor's equity at the time of purchase is his down payment, his initial cash investment.
- Investor's equity at the end of the holding period (or any point in time) is

1

the resale value less the loan balance. (Note the graph "Profile of an Equity.")

- Even though a piece of property may depreciate in value within the holding period, the investor's equity may increase because of loan amortization.
- The income stream consists of an annuity and a reversion, representing both a return on capital and a recovery of original equity (capital investment).
- A portion of yield is received periodically as it is earned. The balance is deferred yield, received or receivable at the end of the holding period.
- Yield on equity (the initial cash investment) is of greater significance to the investor than yield on purchase price. Most investors require a yield of from 12% to 20% on equity, depending primarily on risk and loan ratio.

The Essence of Mortgage-Equity

A short definition provides a foundation for the mathematics of the mortgage-equity technique: *Value is the present worth of future net benefits.*

An analysis of a bond illustrates this definitive equation. For example: a ten-year bond for $5,000 bears an interest rate of 8%. Interest is paid semiannually, and the face amount of $5,000 is due on maturity, at the end of 10 years. The investor who pays $5,000 for the bond has acquired, in appraisal terms, *future benefits* consisting of *two segments*:

- An annuity or level income stream of interest payments for 10 years: $200 twice a year for 20 semiannual periods. ($5,000 x .08 = $400 annual interest. $400 ÷ 2 = $200 interest paid semiannually.)
- A reversion, or single future income payment of $5,000 to be received at the end of 10 years.

We will go back to our definition of value, express it as an equation, expand it, and apply it to prove that the value or present worth of the future benefits generated by the bond is precisely $5,000. As a simple equation, our definition states:

Value = The present worth of future net benefits.

By substitution in our bond illustration:

Value = The present worth of $200 each period for 20 semiannual periods PLUS the present worth of $5,000 to be received at the end of 20 semiannual periods, or 10 years.

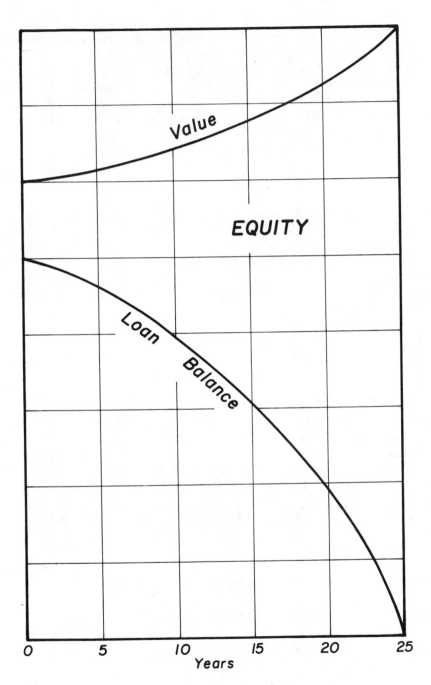

PROFILE OF AN EQUITY

4

A computation of the present worth of the periodic payment (the annuity) of $200 calls for the use of the Present Worth of 1 Per Period factor (the Inwood Coefficient) at 8% (the interest rate on the bond) for 20 semiannual periods, or 10 years (the term of the bond). The present worth of the $5,000 single payment (the reversion) to be received at the end of 20 semiannual periods or 10 years can be calculated by using the Present Worth of 1 factor at 8% for 20 semiannual periods.

Our equation can be expressed more concisely in this way:

Value = (Annuity x PW 1/P) + (Reversion x PW 1)

From the Compound Interest Tables we select two factors[1] :

PW 1/P, 8%, 20 semiannual periods: 13.590326
PW 1, 8%, 20 semiannual periods: .456387

In the equation above, use these factors, $200 for the annuity, and $5,000 for the reversion. By substitution:

Value = ($200 x 13.590326) + ($5,000 x .456387)
= $2,718.07 + 2,281.93
= $5,000

This calculation proves that the value of the $5,000 bond, at an 8% yield rate, is actually $5,000. To look at it another way: If an investor pays $5,000 for a bond and the bond generates future benefits of an annuity of $200 paid semiannually for 10 years and $5,000 paid at the end of 10 years, the purchaser would receive a yield of 8% on his capital, compounded semi-annually, plus a return of his capital. The combined value or present worth of the annuity and the reversion is precisely $5,000.

Let's make a switch from bonds to real estate, using the same definition and equation of value. We are actually working backwards to explain the structure of mortgage-equity and what makes it tick.

An analysis of an attractive, well located community shopping center indicates that the investor could anticipate these future net benefits:

— An annuity of $32,800 cash flow for 10 years.

[1]Since this text lists the compound interest factors only for *monthly* and *annual* compounding periods, use annual PW 1/P and PW 1 factors at 4% for 20 years. This substitution is identical to the use of semiannual factors for 20 semiannual periods at a nominal rate of 8% per annum, since 4% each six-month interval corresponds to 8% each year.

— A net reversion of $1,089,600 at the end of 10 years (the net reversion being the difference between the resale value at the end of 10 years and the loan balance at that time.)

Our problem at this point is as follows: The purchaser expects a yield of 14% on his actual cash investment. What is the value or present worth to him of the future net benefits he anticipates? The solution calls for the equation:

Value = (Annuity x PW 1/P) + (Reversion x PW 1). Factors at 14% for 10 years (annual periods) are:

PW 1/P: 5.216116
PW 1:   .269744

Substituting in the equation:

Value = ($32,800 x 5.216116) + ($1,089,600 x .269744)
      = $171,089 + $293,913
      = $465,002, round to $465,000

An investment of $465,000 which generates cash flow of $32,800 a year for 10 years and a reversion or single income payment of $1,089,600 at the end of 10 years would produce a yield of 14% on the investment and provide a return of the investment. The value or present worth of the future net benefits is $465,000, at a yield rate of 14%.

Note that the investor receives both *current* yield ($32,800 a year) and *deferred* yield ($1,089,600 less $465,000 return of capital, or $624,600). *Current yield* is $32,800 ÷ $465,000, or 7.054%. However, *yield to maturity* is 14%, as we have demonstrated. Yield to maturity includes both current and deferred yield.

To reiterate: An investor is concerned primarily with 3 matters:

1. What he puts into an investment.
2. What he gets out of the investment in dollars (future net benefits).
3. The yield rate on the dollar amount he invests.

The segment of an appraisal problem we have worked has answered those three questions and has proven the yield rate. Now let's go back to the beginning, look at the total problem, and solve it by the mortgage-equity technique. We will then discover how and why we arrived at the total income stream, consisting of a net annuity of $32,800 for 10 years and a net reversion of $1,089,600 at the end of 10 years, generated by an initial investment of $465,000 and made on a projection of a yield rate of 14%.

Here is the entire problem: An investor is considering the purchase of a small, five-year-old, established community shopping center in a growing area. Income from short- and long-term leases has been carefully analyzed, and a realistic expense statement has been constructed. Net annual income is calculated to be $150,000 and is not expected to decline during the economic life of the center.

The investor finds that he can finance his purchase of the property through an institutional loan for 70% of market value. The loan would be written at 9% interest with monthly payments to amortize in 20 years. His down payment or original equity would be 30% of value. The prospective purchaser anticipates that he will hold the property as an investment for 10 years before reselling, refinancing, or exchanging it. He estimates that the shopping center should appreciate 20% in market value during the 10-year holding period. A yield rate of 14% on equity is the investor's prime requirement. Based on the data and projections given, compute the following:

1. The Over-All Rate which would have these six variables built in: 10-year holding period, 14% yield on equity, 70% loan ratio, 20-year loan term, 9% interest rate, 20% appreciation.
2. Property value by the mortgage-equity technique.
3. Amount of down payment (original equity).
4. Principal amount of loan.
5. Loan balance at the end of 10 years.
6. Property value at the end of 10 years.
7. Amount of net reversion.
8. Annual debt service (12 times monthly loan payment).
9. Annual "cash flow" after debt service.
10. Present worth of the "cash flow" and net reversion at 14% yield. (This calculation will "prove" the correctness of the OAR and all computations)

Appraisal for indicated market value and investment analysis encompassing all ten points listed can be computed with ease, speed, and precision by the instant mortgage-equity technique. The appraiser or analyst as a craftsman will select the proper tools from the precomputed OAR Tables and Supplemental Tables to use in making his calculations and conclusions:

1. OAR, from the tables: .09675
2. Value = Income ÷ Rate
   Substituting:
   Value = $150,000 ÷ .09675
   = $1,550,388, say $1,550,350
3. Down payment (equity ratio) is 30%.
   Down payment: .3 x $1,550,350 = $465,100
4. Loan ratio is given as 70%.

Original principal: .7 x $1,550,350 = $1,085,250

5. Loan balance at the end of 10 years, as shown in the Supplemental Tables, is .71026 times the original principal.

Substituting:

Loan balance = .71026 x $1,085,250
$$= \$770,800$$

6. Property value at the end of 10 years, based on a projection of 20% appreciation is:

1.2 x $1,550,350 = $1,860,400

7. Reversion, net = Resale value less loan balance
$$= \$1,860,400 - \$770,800$$
$$= \$1,089,600$$

8. Annual debt service can be found by multiplying the original principal amount by the loan constant given in the Supplemental Tables.

Annual debt service = .108 x $1,085,250
$$= \$117,207, \text{ say } \$117,200$$

9. Cash flow = $150,000 − $117,200
$$= \$32,800$$

10. Value of the Original Equity = (Annuity x PW 1/P) + (Net Reversion x PW 1)
$$= (\$32,800 \text{ x } 5.216116) + (\$1,089,600 \text{ x } .269744)$$
$$= \$171,089 + \$293,913$$
$$= \$465,002, \text{ say } \$465,000$$

Factors used are PW 1/P and PW 1 at 14% for 10 years. The "target figure" in this calculation is the down payment or original equity, which is $465,100. This computation of present worth is within $100 of the figure, a slight differential attributable to rounding of numbers and factors in various steps.

Now, we are back where we started, with the investor who put in $465,000 and got out an annuity of $32,800 a year for 10 years and a reversion or lump sum of $1,089,600 at the end of 10 years. Current yield and deferred yield generated 14% return on the original investment; the net reversion included also a return of the original investment.

Returning to our basic definition, we note that value equals the present worth of the future net benefits. We have demonstrated in this investment analysis that the future benefits of the annuity and the reversion have a present worth of $465,000 at a yield rate of 14%. Therefore, the investor is justified in paying $465,000 as a down payment on a total purchase price of $1,550,350. His investment decision is based on income analysis, loan data, and reasonable assumptions and projections of holding period, appreciation, and equity yield.

Our placing of the proof before the problem has been a backward approach to a straightforward explanation of the mathematics of the instant mortgage-equity technique—a simple procedure that produces sophisticated results.

The Traditional and the Contemporary

We believe it is time to question some traditional concepts of the income approach. Are the residual techniques realistic in today's investment market? Is the straight line declining income method appropriate to the usual current valuation problem; or is it, for general use, becoming as outdated as the buggy whip? Is it possible that appraisers have been coming up with approximately the right valuations but by unrealistic procedures?

There are a few points of similarity between the mortgage-equity technique and the residual techniques of the income approach:

- The validity of each depends on a reasonably accurate projection and processing of annual income to the point at which it can be capitalized.
- Both the mortgage-equity and the residual techniques process income into an indicator of value.
- The mortgage-equity technique is more closely related to the property residual or reversion technique than to the building or land residual—even more closely allied to direct capitalization.

But there are more significant differences than similarities.

- The old "tried and true" residual techniques are all *summation* approaches: land value plus improvement value. Value by summation is not regarded as the best appraisal practice, if another technique can be used; for the value of the whole is not necessarily equal to the sum of its parts. A typical investor doesn't purchase land + improvement + personal property. He buys a total income-producing package. The mortgage equity technique is allied with the *total property* or *unit appraisal* concept.
- Mortgage-equity makes no segregation of income attributable to land and income attributable to improvements.
- Mortgage-equity does not assume that land is to be valued separately "as if vacant."
- It is not assumed that the property is "free and clear." It is assumed to be encumbered by new maximum institutional financing, the purchaser paying cash to the loan. Adjustment to a "cash equivalent" is thus built into the appraisal.
- There is no estimate of remaining economic life called for; hence, subjective judgment of depreciation is minimized.
- Projection of the size and shape of the income stream extends through a

relatively short term holding period of possibly 10 years—not 40 or 50.

- The mortgage-equity technique assumes an annuity or converts a graduated annuity to a level annuity equivalent. It is not concerned with a questionable straight line declining or curvilinear declining concept.
- Recapture is provided for at the end of a realistically limited holding period, rather than being spread over 25 to 50 years.
- The mortgage-equity technique gives full consideration not only to current yield but also to deferred yield at the time of reversion—growth of equity resulting from both loan amortization and appreciation.
- The mortgage-equity technique answers the investor's most meaningful question: "What is the yield on my equity, my actual cash investment?" The residual techniques all sidestep and ignore the issue.
- Calculation of value by mortgage-equity is a simple, one-step computation: Income divided by Over-All Rate.

The appraiser may not wish to dispense with the residual techniques. But neither should he ignore the mortgage-equity technique that speaks the investor's language and gives him the answers he seeks.

Glad You Asked . . .

A few "how about" or "what if" questions might be raised—and answered—concerning appraisal by the mortgage-equity technique:

- How about the fact that equity increases with each periodic loan payment on principal? Answer: Equity growth is "locked in" until the time of reversion (resale, refinancing, or exchange). Therefore, it must be considered as *deferred yield*. Amounts applied to principal are not additional investments, but additional earnings from the income-producing property. *Yield to maturity* on equity is computed on the original equity—the initial investment or down payment, and recognizes both current and deferred yield.
- What if the investor doesn't intend to sell or refinance at the end of a projected holding period? How does his retaining the property indefinitely affect valuation by mortgage-equity? Answer: The appraisal, based on sound data and generally accepted market assumptions, would still be valid. Market value is still there at the end of a time period, regardless of the owner's disposition or retention of the property.
- How about mortgage-equity and inflation? Answer: A projection of possible appreciation is made by percent, and is translated into dollars, not purchasing power. If inflation continues for a projected ten-year holding

period, as it did from 1961 to 1971, appreciation of 35% would just keep up with it—no more. One of the prime reasons for investing in real estate is to provide a hedge against inflation. If an investor actually believes the property under consideration will decline in dollar value over a relatively short term, will he invest in it at all? In general, in dealing with economically feasible income property, well located, wouldn't it be more realistic to project appreciation of possibly 20% than stability or depreciation over a typical ten-year holding period?

— How is the mortgage-equity approach related to the market? Answer: Yield rates and over-all rates are obtained from analysis of market sales. Economic rents are determined by the market. Financing data is found in the money market.

— How do income taxes affect yield on equity? Answer: The best explanation may be an illustration. See the analysis on pages 81 to 84 of the Casa Linda Apartments case study. Mortgage-equity appraisal for market value is made without a calculation of "typical" income tax levies. Indicated yield on equity is the rate of yield *before* income taxes. On any type of investment, other than tax-free municipal bonds, after-tax yield is obviously less than before-tax yield. This is one of the economic facts of life. While *appraisal* by mortgage-equity indicates yield *before* income taxes, *analysis* by mortgage-equity can calculate yield *after* taxes. Real estate as an investment offers several specific tax advantages over most other types of investments: particularly, allowable depreciation and long-term capital gains. For tax purposes, there is no relationship between permissable depreciation and actual depreciation or appreciation in market value. Accelerated depreciation, which may be taken on certain types of property, may provide totally tax-sheltered income in the initial years of a holding period. Further, it may convert a portion of current yield to deferred yield, taxable at the time of resale at half the rate on ordinary income. The taxpayer has the advantage of the use of this money—his deferred income taxes—until resale of the property. The time-value of money is working for him. Tax loopholes—or doors to opportunity? It may depend upon who is using them!

Market Value v. Investment Value

Mortgage-equity is a multipurpose appraisal procedure. Varied objectives it serves for analyst and investor include:

1. Appraisal for market value.
2. Appraisal for investment value or value in use.
3. Establishing a band of value for purchase price negotiations.

4. Projecting a possible range of yield on equity before and after income taxes as a basis for decision-making.
5. Investment analysis of present or prospective holdings, with the focus on equity yield rate.

The appraiser, analyst, or advisor recognizes the difference between a feasibility study and an appraisal for market value. The feasibility study to calculate investment value or value in use for a particular client considers such points as income tax position, possible unorthodox high-leverage financing with two or more mortgages, the investor's individual objectives, et cetera. An appraisal for market value assumes the property to be encumbered by a new maximum institutional loan at current interest rates. It is also assumed that the buyer pays cash to the new loan, thereby automatically adjusting market price to a cash equivalent. Market value is considered to be the value to persons in general, without being related to income tax brackets or unusual financing.

Bands of value and ranges of yield rates are as significant as specific points. The band may set upper and lower limits of possible value, within which there may be a meeting of minds by purchaser and seller. Or, it may project a range of indicated yield on equity, based on such assumptions as possible 20% depreciation or 20% appreciation within a holding period. Besides telling the analyst the market value or investment value of the property and a possible rate of yield on equity, the use of this technique may also point out properties that are not economic units. It may help the investor avoid mistakes and may set up criteria that will minimize losses as well as maximizing and retaining gains.

Mortgage-equity talks straight. The investor listens, understands, and profits.

2 The Instant Mortgage-Equity Technique: an Appraisal Tool

Text, Tables, and Tools

Appraisal is an art. It is also a craft. The appraiser, as a craftsman, requires efficient tools of the trade.

Few craftsmen in any line have either the time or skill to fashion their own tools, yet they may be very proficient in using them.

This text has been designed as a tool—or more correctly, a kit of many tools. Each Over-All Rate is a separate tool with a specific application—ready-made— ready to use. There is no call to slave over a hot calculator at a desk piled high with equations, symbols, formulas, and factors to manufacture your own mortgage-equity tools—over-all rates, that is.

The Instant Mortgage-Equity Technique is a specialized book. It is not a complete basic appraisal text, nor does it cover all principles and methods of the income approach to value. The author presumes that the student or appraiser is acquainted with the fundamentals, that he can knowledgeably process income to the point at which it can be capitalized, that possibly he has used the residual techniques of the income approach, and that with a little skill and a lot of good judgment he is ready to use the tools and techniques of mortgage-equity.

Procedures are outlined, explained, and illustrated in Chapter 3, Sections 1 and 2, and in Chapter 4, the Case Study. Tools in the form of rates and factors are tabulated in Chapter 5.

Major mortgage-equity methods of Chapter 3, used most frequently, include these calculations: Value of income-producing property, when equity yield rate is specified; rate of yield on equity when value is given; derivation of an Over-All Rate from the market and its conversion to an equity yield rate; percent of appreciation required to generate a specified yield on equity; and investment analysis.

Other procedures of a supplemental nature relate to such areas as processing of income, cash flow, trust deed analysis, secondary financing, etc.

On Reading Tables

Chapter 5 lists three categories of factors and rates in tabular form: Compound Interest Tables; Supplemental Tables of Loan Balances and Loan Constants; and OAR Tables of Mortgage-Equity Over-All Rates. In the Compound Interest

Tables appear three types of factors: The Present Worth of 1 (PW 1); The Present Worth of 1 Per Period (PW 1/P); and The Periodic Repayment (PR). Range of interest rates is from 3% to 30%. Monthly factors are given up to 360 months, and annual factors to 40 years. Many of the functions of the compound interest tables are explained and illustrated in other sections of the book. Both the Supplemental and the OAR Tables have been derived from these basic, versatile factors that contain built-in computations of the time-value of money.

The compound interest factors are percents, expressed as decimals. They either add compound interest to present worth or subtract compound interest from future worth. Factors are usually used as multipliers or divisors. They may also serve as "target figures" in the calculation of rate or time.

The Supplemental Tables provide shortcut computations of loan balances at the end of a 5, 10, or 15-year holding period. They also list loan constants for calculating annual debt service. To illustrate:

- On an 8% loan with monthly payments to amortize in 25 years, 80.763% (.80763) of the original principal balance is unpaid at the end of 10 years (See page 116.)
- The monthly payments to amortize an 8% loan in 25 years would amount annually to 9.262% of the original principal amount. The loan constant is 9.262% (.09262). (See page 118.)

Built into each precomputed Over-All Rate in the OAR Tables are six variables:

Holding Period: 5,10, or 15 years
Equity Yield Rate: 2% to 50%
Loan Ratio: 60% to 90%
Loan Term: 10 to 30 years
Interest Rate: 5% to 12%
Appreciation or Depreciation: +40% to −40%

All OAR's for a 5-year holding period appear first, then the 10-year period, followed by the 15.

The first three variables identify the page on which to find the OAR you are seeking. Look for the right holding period, next the equity yield rate, then the loan ratio. On the proper page go down to the loan term, across to the pertinent loan interest rate, and up or down to the percent of projected appreciation or depreciation. To illustrate: Your analysis show that these variables would pertain to a piece of property you are appraising:

Holding Period: 10 years
Equity Yield Rate: 14%

Loan Ratio: 75%
Loan Term: 25 years
Interest Rate: 8%
Appreciation: +10%

A search for holding period, equity yield rate, and loan ratio leads you to page 243. Down to 25 years, across to 8% interest rate and up to 10% appreciation, and you have an Over-All Rate of .091831. You've got it! Now, divide—and conquer the problem!

Variations on a Theme

The appraiser, using the mortgage-equity technique, should not be overwhelmed by the realization that there is an almost infinite number of possible combinations of variable factors. However, he should comprehend the effect of each type of variable on *value* and on the *rate of yield on equity*.

We will illustrate the influence on *value* by altering each of the following variables (making, however, only one change at a time): equity yield rate, holding period, loan ratio, loan term, interest rate, and appreciation.

Given: Holding period: 10 years
          Equity yield rate: 12%
          Loan ratio: 75%
          Loan term: 20 years, monthly payments
          Interest rate: 8%
          Appreciation: 0%
          Net annual income: $150,000
          Based on this data, the OAR is .09201.
          Indicated value: $150,000 ÷ .09201 = $1,630,257

Note the change in OAR and consequently in value by altering each variable, making only one modification at a time in the given situation (all other data remaining constant):

Holding period: 5 years
   OAR: .09055
   Value: $150,00 ÷ .09055 = $1,656,543
Equity yield rate: 15%
   OAR is now .10131
   Value: $150,000 ÷ .10131 = $1,480,604
Loan ratio: 60%
   OAR: .0976
   Value: $150,000 ÷ .0976 = $1,536,885

Loan term: 30 years
   OAR: .0908
   Value: $150,000 ÷ .0908 = $1,651,982
Interest rate: 7%
   OAR: .08558
   Value: $150,000 ÷ .08558 = $1,752,746
Appreciation: +40%
   OAR: .0692
   Value: $150,000 ÷ .0692 = $2,167,004

Note that all six variables affect value. Changes in holding period and loan term appear less critical than the other four components of the OAR, when only one variable is altered. A shift of two or more variables simultaneously will compound the differences in value conclusions and equity yield rates.

In the preceding illustration, we will consider as constants net income of $150,000, OAR of .09201, and consequently value of $1,630,257. Note the effect on *equity yield rate*, as we change a few of the variables in the given data:

Loan ratio: Increasing from 75% to 90% raises equity yield to 16% plus. (OAR, .09124)

Interest rate: Changing from 8% to 9% lowers equity yield rate to about 10% (OAR, .09235)

Appreciation: Projecting 20% appreciation raises indicated equity yield to a little over 15%. (OAR, .09146)

Variables in the mortgage-equity technique concern the investor and the appraiser. The investment analyst can, by changing variables he considers most meaningful, establish *bands of value and ranges of equity yield for decision-making*. The appraiser, seeking market value, must, however, determine a specific point within a band. Accurate data and reasonable assumptions, processed by precise procedures and good judgment, will be reflected in valid value conclusions.

Let's Talk Terms

The following is a glossary of appraisal terms defined or explained in the context of the instant mortgage-equity technique:*

Adjusted sales price. Nominal sales price, from which may be deducted the value of excess land or the value of personal property, when using the sale as a comparable in appraising other real property by the market approach or in deriving an over-all or equity yield rate from the market. Other allowances may

*For definitions of some of these terms as they apply more generally in appraisal and analysis, see The Society of Real Estate Appraisers' *Real Estate Appraisal Principles and Terminology*, 2nd ed., 1971.

be made: e.g., computing the cash equivalent of trust deeds or other noncash items involved in the transaction to adjust sales price for terms.

Amortization. Return or recapture of a capital investment over a period of time. Also, paying off a debt by periodic instalments, principal and interest included.

Annuity. A level terminal income stream or its equivalent. An *ordinary annuity* is one in which equal payments are received or assumed to be received at the *end* of each period. An *annuity due* or annuity in advance calls for payments at the *beginning* of each period. When rent is received monthly in advance, the appraiser, investor, or analyst may, in most cases, consider it to constitute an ordinary annuity. Since certain major expenses, such as property taxes, are paid on an annual or semiannual basis, net income is more realistically calculated as a yearly rather than a monthly sum. A net-net-net lease, paid annually in advance, clearly constitutes an annuity due, and should be so treated.

Variations of the income stream include a graduated step-up or step-down annuity, an annuity with a deferred start, an increasing or decreasing annuity, or a totally irregular income stream. Net annual income processed by the mortgage-equity technique is considered to be an *ordinary annuity*. Methods are given in the procedural section of this book for converting an annuity due or any type of variable annuity to an ordinary annuity equivalent for purposes of capitalization. Net annual income before loan payments can be termed the investor's *gross annuity*, and net income after debt service as the *net annuity* (cash flow.).

Appraisal. An estimate or opinion of value, arrived at and substantiated by a knowledgeable collection and processing of all pertinent data.

Appreciation. Increase in market value. It is measured in dollars, not in purchasing power, and may be offset in varying degrees by inflation.

Approaches to value. The three traditional approaches: cost of replacement or reproduction, market or comparative sales, and income. Theoretically, the cost approach usually sets the upper limit of value; and the income approach, the lower limit. Correlation of value indicators is considered to be a matter of judgment in arriving at a value conclusion, a point within the limits of the indicated range.

Balloon payment. A single lump sum payment, usually in the amount of unpaid principal balance owing at a time specified in a note, secured by a mortgage or trust deed. (Don't believe the wag who says a balloon payment is a perfect example of inflation.)

Capitalization: Any mathematical procedure which converts an income stream to a capital sum or value.

Cash equivalent. The cash value of noncash items, given as consideration in the purchase of property. If a purchaser pays cash down to a loan made at current interest rates by a lending institution, the cash equivalent of the mortgage or trust deed is its face value, and the cash equivalent of the sale is the full sales price. In a common type of situation, a portion of the sales price is a purchase money mortgage carried by the seller. Whether a "first" or a "second," the cash equivalent of such a mortgage is its value, discounted to a yield rate that would make it saleable on the open market to another investor. The computation of cash equivalent is one step in the market approach in adjusting sales price for terms. It is also important in the mortgage-equity technique of the income approach in order to derive current, realistic over-all rates.

Cash flow. Net annual income after annual loan payments but before income taxes. Positive cash flow is current yield on equity. If loan payments exceed net annual income, a negative cash flow or expenditure results. While this is generally not a feasible situation, it may be warranted under certain circumstances, all yield being deferred until the time of reversion or resale. An example would be a situation in which an investor elects to finance his purchase for a very short term, choosing to own his property "free and clear" as soon as possible. (See the procedure "Rate of Yield on Equity Investment in Non-Producing Property," pages 58-59.)

Compound interest and annuity tables. Six "standard" tables of factors that can be used as multipliers or divisors in calculating future or present worth of a single lump sum amounts or a series of periodic payments. Compound interest (the time value of money) is built into the factor. The function of the factor is to add or subtract compound interest. Names of the tables vary. The following is representative and recommended. Principal use is also given: Future Worth of 1 (growth of a single sum or value at compound interest). Future Worth of 1 Per Period (growth of a level series of deposits or investments at compound interest). Sinking Fund (amount to be deposited periodically, which will grow to a stated future amount). Present Worth of 1 (present worth of a single future income payment or value). Present Worth of 1 Per Period (present worth of a future series of income payments). Periodic Repayment (periodic payment required to amortize a capital sum, interest and return of principal included). This book provides a limited number of factors from the last three tables named.

Contract rent. Rent agreed upon by owner and tenant or lessor and lessee. It is the rent actually paid, and may be greater or less than economic rent.

Current yield. Cash flow. Within the framework of mortgage-equity, the total periodic income stream can be considered current yield on equity, if the amount of net reversion equals or exceeds the original equity or down payment.

However, in the event the net reversion is less than the original equity, a portion of cash flow is attributable to a partial recovery of capital, thereby decreasing current yield on capital. In a typical situation in which the net reversion exceeds the original equity, all of the cash flow can be considered as current yield. Recapture of capital investment occurs at the end of the holding period (time of resale). The net reversion may also include deferred yield after providing a return of capital investment. In such a case, yield to maturity (which includes both current and deferred yield) will exceed the current yield rate. Current yield is considered to be *compoundable* by reinvestment.

Debt service. Total loan payments made in one year.

Deferred yield. Yield generated by loan amortization and property appreciation. It is locked in until the time of reversion, and is thus *compounded*. As a dollar amount, it is calculated by subtracting the original equity or down payment from the net reversion.

Depreciation. Loss in market value for any reason. It is not to be equated with allowable depreciation used in income tax calculations.

Economic rent. The rent the property would bring, if offered for rent or lease on the current market. It may correspond to contract rent, or may deviate from it.

Effective gross income. Estimated annual gross income less a percentage allowance for vacancies and collection losses.

Equity. Original equity is the down payment. Equity at the end of a holding period or at any point in time is the difference between market value and loan balance.

Equity ratio. Original equity ratio is the down payment divided by the sales price. It is also 100% less the loan ratio. For example: If sales price is $100,000 and down payment is $30,000, equity ratio is $30,000 divided by $100,000 or 30% (.30). If loan ratio is 80%, equity ratio is 100% less 80%, or 20% (.20). Terminal equity ratio may be computed in two ways: (1) It is net reversion divided by resale price or value at end of holding period. For example: At the end of a 15-year holding period, resale price is $1,000,000, and loan balance is $300,000. Net reversion is $1,000,000 less $300,000, or $700,000. Equity ratio is $700,000 divided by $1,000,000, or 70% (.70). (2) Another concept relates terminal equity or net reversion to original value. For example, property pruchased for $600,000 has appreciated in a 10-year holding period to $800,000. Original loan of $400,000 has been reduced to $300,000. Terminal equity or net reversion is $800,000 less $300,000, or $500,000. Original equity ratio was $200,000 divided by $600,000, or 33%. Terminal equity ratio, as related to original value, is $500,000 divided by $600,000 or 83%. Related to resale value, it is $500,000 ÷ $800,000 or 62.5%.

Equity yield rate. Percent of yield to maturity on original equity or down payment. It is calculated on a combination of current yield and deferred yield. The rate of yield on equity is one of the investor's most significant considerations in decision-making. The instant mortgage-equity technique calculates the rate of yield on equity when value is known, or computes an estimate of value when a rate of yield on equity is stipulated. Equity yield rate should always be calculated and expressed as an annual rate, compounded.

Factors. As used in the context of *The Instant Mortgage-Equity Technique*, factors are percents, expressed as decimals, and appear in the compound interest and annuity tables. Factors are used as multipliers or divisors to compute present or future worth of dollar values. Factors also serve as target figures in solving for rate or time. Multiplying or dividing by a compound interest factor either computes and adds compound interest to present worth, or it calculates and subtracts compound interest from future worth. Calculation of compound interest (the time-value of money) is built into the factor. A comprehensive, easy-to-understand survey of the derivations, interrelationships, and functions of the standard compound interest tables, appears in the author's textbook, *Mini-Math for Appraisers*, published by the International Association of Assessing Officers, Chicago, Illinois.

Feasibility study. An appraisal for investment value or value in use. In contrast to an appraisal for market value, its purpose is a determination of value to a specific individual, rather than to persons in general. Such a study considers the client's income tax position, his personal objectives, specially tailored terms, etc. It frequently determines, by means of the mortgage-equity technique, ranges of value for bargaining, or ranges of potential yield on equity as the basis for decision-making.

Gross income. An estimate of gross annual income, before deductions for vacancies and collection losses or allowable expenses.

Holding period. A limited term of ownership between time of purchase and resale, exchange, or refinancing of the property. It is often determined by income tax considerations. In the case of a relatively substantial loan ratio, the holding period is normally about 10 years. While this text lists Over-All Rates for holding periods of 5, 10, and 15 years, interpolation by simple proportion can be made to any intermediate point in time.

Income stream. The size, shape, and duration of net annual income generated by a property determine the measurable flow of income produced. Mortgage-equity considers the income stream to consist of two segments: (1) a level, terminal ordinary annuity or its calculated equivalent; and (2) a single terminal lump sum payment (net reversion). An estimate of value is made by dividing the net annual income stream by the mortgage-equity Over-All Rate.

Interest rate. A *stipulated, fixed rate* agreed upon by borrower and lender. It is not to be confused with a *yield rate*, which is an investor's *anticipated* rate.

Investment value. Worth to an individual, considering his personal income tax situation, objectives, etc. It may differ from market value, which is considered to be value to persons in general.

Lease. An agreement in writing between owner (the lessor) and tenant (the lessee), conveying to the lessee the right to the occupancy and use of property under specified terms for a stipulated period of time.

Lease fee. The lessor's interest, consisting of the rights of receiving rents from the lessee and the reversionary rights of repossession of the property upon termination of the lease.

Leasehold interest. The lessee's interest, produced and measured by: (1) The excess of economic rent over contract rent, or (2) If improvements are erected by the lessee, the difference between economic rent of the total property and contract rent paid on the ground lease.

Loan constant. The amount paid annually on a loan (principal and interest included) as a percent of original principal. (See page 28 and "Supplemental Tables," page 118.)

Loan ratio. Original principal amount of a loan as a percent of value. For example, if property is purchased for $500,000 and is financed by a bank loan for $300,000, the loan ratio is $300,000 divided by $500,000 or 60% (.60).

Loan term. Length of a loan in years.

Market value. Value to persons in general; the most probable selling price.

Mortgage (or trust deed). Legal document making property security for the repayment of a loan, terms of which are stipulated in a promissory note.

Mortgage-equity technique. A method of converting an income stream into an indicator of value by dividing an Over-All Rate into net annual income. In computing the Over-All Rate, full consideration is given to loan and equity ratios, loan terms, holding period, projected appreciation or depreciation, and anticipated yield on equity. The *instant mortgage-equity technique* provides totally precomputed over-all rates, especially designed forms, and patterned procedures for quick calculations in income property appraisal and investment analysis.

Net income. Annual income after allowable expenses but before debt service, income taxes, or recapture.

Over-All Rate. Net income divided by value. The mortgage-equity over-all rate has built into it six variables: the holding period, the anticipated equity yield rate, loan ratio, interest rate, loan term, and projected appreciation or depreciation. An indicator of property value is found by dividing Over-All Rate into net annual income.

Periodic Repayment (PR). The PR factor is the loan amortization factor, sometimes known as the Partial Payment factor. At any given rate of interest, for any stipulated period of time, the PR factor multiplied by the original principal amount of a loan computes the level periodic payment (principal and interest included) to amortize a loan. Calculation of interest on a declining principal balance is built into the factor. The PR factor is the reciprocal of the Present Worth of 1 Per Period factor. It is also the Sinking Fund factor plus the interest rate.

Present worth. As an amount, present worth of an income stream or single income payment due in the future is future worth less compound interest. It is the original capital amount or value that will generate the future income stream at an anticipated yield rate within a specified period of time.

Present Worth of 1 (PW 1). The PW 1 factor, sometimes called the reversionary factor, multiplied by a single future income payment or value (reversion), automatically computes and deducts compound interest from future worth. The PW 1 factor is a percent, expressed as a decimal, "1" representing one dollar.

Present Worth of 1 Per Period (PW 1/P). The PW 1/P factor is the Inwood Coefficient or annuity factor. The PW 1/P multiplied by one payment of a level terminal series of income payments computes the present worth of the future income stream at a given yield or interest rate. The mortgage-equity concept considers the investor's total income stream or future net benefits to be both an annuity (annual cash flow) and a reversion (resale value less loan balance). Both PW 1 and PW 1/P factors are used in valuing the equity investment.

Recapture. A return of capital. In the residual techniques of the income approach, the allocated value of improvements (usually buildings) is calculated to be returned to or recaptured by the investor in annual increments over the estimated remaining economic life of the wasting assets. Allowance for recapture (also termed amortization) is built into the capitalization rate or is provided for in the annuity factor. The mortgage-equity technique usually provides for total recapture at the end of the holding period (time of resale, exchange, or refinancing). No allowance is made for periodic recapture. If, however, the net reversion is less than the original equity (down payment) it must be presumed that such a deficiency has been recovered periodically from cash flow, in which case yield to maturity would be less than current yield.

Reciprocal. The reciprocal of any number can be found by dividing it into 1. The product of two reciprocal numbers is always 1. Identical results are achieved by multiplying by a number or by dividing by the reciprocal of the number. Thus, one factor can substitute for another. In the compound interest and annuity tables there are three sets of reciprocal factors: Future Worth of 1 and Present Worth of 1; Future Worth of 1 Per Period and Sinking Fund; Present Worth of 1 Per Period and Periodic Repayment. Example of reciprocal numbers: 5 and .2. $(1 \div 5 = .2)$ Note that $5 \times 8 = 40$, and $8 \div .2 = 40$.

Reversion. A single future terminal income sum or value to be received by the investor. In the case of a lease, the owner receives a reversion of the property upon expiration of the lease. In the mortgage-equity concept, the *gross* reversion at the end of a holding period is the resale value. The *net* reversion is the resale value less the loan balance. In *The Instant Mortgage-Equity Technique*, unless otherwise specified, the term "reversion" refers to the *net* reversion. The excess of net reversion (terminal equity) over down payment (original equity) indicates equity growth (deferred yield) through appreciation in value and/or loan reduction by periodic amortization.

"Rule of 72." Divide any yield or interest rate into 72 to determine the approximate number of years required to double an investment at a rate compounded annually. For example, money at 8% compounded annually will double in 9 years $(72 \div 8 = 9)$. Currently most investors are seeking *yield on equity* investments in real estate of from 12% to 18%. A magic number seems to be 14%, an investment doubling at that rate in about 5 years. The range of 12% to 18% provides for doubling in from 4 to 6 years. In selecting mortgage-equity over-all rates for computations of market value, the appraiser will usually work within this band.

Secondary (junior) financing. Loans secured by a mortgage or trust deed, which are subordinate to a first mortgage or trust deed. Included in this category are seconds, thirds, etc. In using the mortgage-equity technique to appraise for market value, the appraiser assumes that the property is encumbered with a new maximum conventional loan at current interest rates and that the purchaser pays cash to the loan. In an appraisal for investment value to an individual, the appraiser may show the feasibility of paying a higher purchase price in view of particularly favorable secondary financing. Procedures are given in this text for making adjustments in computing over-all rate or rate of yield on equity.

Value. A definition most applicable to any technique of the income approach: Value is the present worth of future net benefits. Value is not necessarily equal to either *cost* or *price*. In *The Mortgage-Equity Technique* market value of the property is considered equal to the sum of the loan plus the equity (down payment). Pertinent equations of value are: Value = Income ÷ Rate, and Value of the Equity = Present Worth of the Cash Flow + Present Worth of the Net Reversion.

Yield rate. An anticipated rate of yield on future income, or a calculated rate of yield on present or past income. It is not to be confused with a fixed interest rate on a loan. Yield rate in the instant mortgage-equity technique is yield on equity, not on total property value.

Yield to maturity. Yield rate on equity, calculated on both cash flow and net reversion. It includes current yield and deferred yield.

3

Section 1: Patterned Procedures — The Appraiser's Edge

Chapters 1 and 2 have discussed theory. Now let's get down to practice. *The Instant Mortgage-Equity Technique* is an appraisal tool. Patterned procedures of Chapter 3, together with rates and factors from Chapter 5, constitute the cutting edge. Over 40 primary and secondary methods are outlined, explained and illustrated in Chapter 3, Section 2, the "how-to-do-it" section of this manual.

Preview of Procedures

Procedures are arranged alphabetically under these general headings: Annuities, Present Worth Of; and Level Ordinary Annuity Equivalent; Appreciation Required to Generate a Specified Rate of Yield on Equity; Cash Flow; Extension of the Compound Interest Tables; Income Required to Meet Equity Demands; Income Tax, Effect Of, On Yield Rate; Interpolation By Simple Proportion; Investment Analysis; Loan Constant; Mortgage or Trust Deed Calculations; Over-All Rate; Proof of OAR, Valuation, Yield Rate; Rate of Yield on Equity; Rate of Yield on Equity Investment in Non-Producing Property Held For Appreciation; Rate of Yield on 100% Equity; Reversion, Dollar Amount Of; Reversion, Present Worth Of; Secondary (Junior or Multiple Financing, Adjustment For; Value of Income Property As Indicated By the Mortgage-Equity Technique; Value of Property When Loan Ratio Is Unknown.

The appraiser should relate the topical discussions that follow to the corresponding procedures outlined in Chapter 3, Section 2. Explanatory material in Section 1 has been segregated purposely from the techniques of Section 2 in order to keep the "Mortgage-Equity Procedures" as compact as possible.

Annuities

The mathematics of mortgage-equity requires that the terminal income stream to be processed consist of a level, ordinary annuity, or be converted to a level, ordinary annuity equivalent. Averaging an irregular income stream projected for the duration of the holding period will produce approximate but not precise calculations. The appraiser must use reasonable judgment and attempt to look through the eyes of a knowledgeable investor in estimating the size, shape, and quality of the income stream for the anticipated holding period. If the stream so delineated is not an ordinary annuity, he must by proper procedures make the conversion before capitalization.

Appreciation Required

An anticipated rate of yield on equity may demand a degree of appreciation in market value, as well as loan amortization and a projected annuity, in order to generate the returns expected on the down payment, the actual cash investment. One of the variables built into the Over-All Rate is appreciation or depreciation calculated as a percent of original value or purchase price. In this type of problem, all elements, including value, are known, except the percent of appreciation. Two procedures, using either the OAR Tables or the Compound Interest Tables, may be used to calculate the unknown and answer the question: How much must the property appreciate within the holding period to produce the desired yield on equity?

Cash Flow

The difference between net annual income and debt service measures the dollar amount of cash flow. Note that this may be either a positive or a negative quantity. Easy procedures show how to make the calculation as a dollar amount or as a percent of value.

Under certain circumstances, income tax allowances may convert a negative to a positive cash flow.

An investor might justify a negative cash flow on the basis of accelerated loan amortization. In such a case he considers out-of-pocket expenditures as additional periodic investments. All yield is deferred yield, generated by loan amortization and appreciation in value.

In the mortgage-equity concept, "cash flow" as a net annuity is one of two future benefits the investor anticipates, the second segment being the net reversion.

Extension of the Compound Interest Tables

In *The Instant Mortgage-Equity Technique* a limited number of compound interest and annuity factors is given. Two circumstances would require the extension of the tables by means of the techniques provided: (1) If annual factors for time periods in excess of 40 years or monthly factors in excess of 360 months are needed. (2) If a monthly factor is to be used for a time period greater than one year and for a term of months which does not correspond to an exact whole number of years—for example, twelve years seven months, or 151 months.

Extension of the Present Worth Of 1 table is made directly; and of the Present Worth Of 1 Per Period and Periodic Repayment, by indirect means, as shown in the procedures.

Income Required To Meet Equity Demands

When value is known and mortgage-equity Over-All Rate is determined, net annual income required to generate the anticipated yield on equity can be calculated readily: Income = Rate x Value.

Income Tax, Effect Of, On Yield Rate

In an appraisal for market value, the appraiser assumes that the market has already adjusted for income tax consideration. In preparing a feasibility study, on the other hand, the analyst makes a determination for his client of after-tax cash flow and after-tax yield on equity. (Cross-reference is made to the example in the Case Study, pages 81-84.)

Interpolation By Simple Proportion

The number of possible combinations of mortgage-equity variables seems almost infinite. While precomputed rates from the OAR Tables will match most usual situations, it may on occasion be necessary to adjust Over-All Rates to allow for variables in holding period, interest rate, percent of appreciation, etc., lying at intermediate points.

The same procedures shown are applicable also to the Compound Interest and Supplemental Tables.

Adjustment of rates and factors by simple proportion is approximate, not precise. It is usually quite accurate to three decimal places.

Investment Analysis and Proof of Computations

The special worksheets, covering 14 analytical points, with explanatory notes, appear on pages 72-75. An illustration of a completed analysis is given in the Case Study, pages 78-79.

Loan Constant

This simple concept that is sometimes confusing can be clarified in three areas of the text: the explanation in the "Glossary of Terms," page 21, the "Mortgage-Equity Procedures," page 47, and the "Supplemental Tables," page 118.

Mortgage or Trust Deed Calculations

Loan analysis must be made by the appraiser to calculate several pertinent points in mortgage-equity: (1) the discounted present worth of secondary financing (cash equivalent) to adjust sales price for terms in deriving Over-All Rates from market sales; (2) the annual amount of cash flow; (3) the net reversion at the end of a holding period; and (4) various adjustments for secondary financing when computing over-all rate or rate of yield on equity. Compound interest tables and programmed procedures provide ways and means.

Over-All Rate

The OAR Tables of precomputed mortgage-equity rates furnish the key to the streamlined *instant mortgage-equity technique*. Six variables are built into each rate: holding period; equity yield rate; loan ratio, interest rate, and term; and projected appreciation or depreciation. Interpolation by simple proportion can be made to take care of most variables that differ from those in the OAR Tables. For unusual situations, outside the scope of precomputation, the appraiser can follow Procedure 2 and make a calculation of rate by using the compound interest tables.

An over-all rate may be derived from the market by dividing net income by adjusted sales price.

The OAR is used in three ways in mortgage-equity techniques: (1) As a *multiplier* in calculating income required to generate a specified rate of yield on equity; (2) As a *divisor* in estimating value; and (3) As a *target figure* in computing rate of yield on equity.

If property taxes are not deducted as an expense item but are built into the capitalization rate as an annual percentage of value, such an allowance can be added to the OAR without distortion. The annuity to be capitalized under this method consists of net annual income *before* property taxes. For example: Assume the tax rate in an area to be $12 per hundred dollars of assessed value; and assessed value, 25% of market value. Tax allowance as an annual percentage of market value is 12 x .25, or 3% (.03). If the mortgage-equity OAR in this illustration were .08553, total capitalization rate would be .08553 plus .03, or .11553. Net annual income, estimated before property taxes, divided by the *adjusted* OAR, calculates an indicator of value by the mortgage-equity technique. The rationale of this procedure is that a knowledge of the tax rate, assessment ratio, and dollar amount of taxes implies a foregone value conclusion. The method described, generally used by property tax assessors, is being adopted as a working procedure by many fee appraisers.

Proof of OAR, Valuation, Yield Rate

One of the basic equations of value spells out the primary procedure of proof: Value = (Annuity x PW 1/P) + (Reversion x PW 1). In this calculation the original equity or down payment is "Value," the target figure. A wide variance from the target figure will indicate an error in computation or a mistake in the selection of rates or factors. Note examples of proof throughout the procedures and in Chapter 4, the case study. See also notes in the mortgage-equity worksheet section.

Rate of Yield on Equity

Two procedures are given, and either may be used by the appraiser in converting an Over-All Rate derived from market analysis to an indicated rate of yield on equity. In both procedures, the six variables of mortgage-equity must be determined for the subject property and related to the Over-All Rate. A relatively high rate of yield on equity is perhaps the most important single requirement of the contemporary investor.

Rate of Yield On Equity Investment In Nonproducing Property Held for Appreciation

This procedure is particularly applicable to an investment in nonproducing land. Holding costs, consisting of loan payments and property taxes, will create a negative cash flow. The purchaser makes an initial investment (down payment) and a series of periodic investments (debt service and taxes) until the end of the projected holding period, the time of resale. All yield is deferred yield. Both return on capital and return of capital are anticipated from the net reversion.

Computation of rate of yield on equity is based on both the initial investment and the subsequent periodic payments of principal, interest, taxes, and any other holding expenses. This calculation gives full consideration to the time-value of money. It points up the erosion of an anticipated yield on equity if a holding period is extended without a corresponding increase in market value.

Rate of Yield on 100% Equity

Mortgage-equity implies a mortgage as well as an equity. However, certain concepts and calculations are applicable to the analysis of cash transactions. Procedures outlined and illustrated cover stable, increasing, and decreasing market values. Obviously, if there is neither appreciation nor depreciation within a holding period, equity yield rate and over-all rate coincide. The procedure given for calculating rate of yield if either appreciation or depreciation is projected, utilizes present worth factors from the Compound Interest Tables.

Reversion, Dollar Amount Of

In *The Instant Mortgage-Equity Technique* the term "reversion" is used in the sense of a *net reversion*: value at the end of a holding period less loan balance. The Supplemental Tables will facilitate making this computation. The net reversion is the second segment of the investor's anticipated future benefits, assuming the investment has produced a positive cash flow. If there is no cash flow, all yield has been deferred and is contained in the net reversion.

If th⁀ net reversion exceeds the down payment and any subsequent additional investments in the property, the net reversion represents both a return of capital and return on capital. If net reversion is less than the down payment, it is assumed that the difference has been recaptured periodically from cash flow; however, in the event of no cash flow, the conclusion is there has been a loss of some capital invested and that no yield has been generated.

Reversion, Present Worth Of

This is a mathematical computation, made by multiplying the dollar amount of net reversion by the Present Worth Of 1 factor at the equity yield rate for the term of the holding period. The factor computes and deducts compound interest from future worth.

Secondary (Junior or Multiple) Financing, Adjustment For

Calculations of over-all-rate or rate of yield on equity, based on loans that involve such nonconventional financing as second deeds of trust, are used in feasibility studies. However, if the purpose of the analysis is an appraisal for market value, existing financing and the possibility of obtaining new secondary financing are disregarded. The appraiser assumes, instead, that the property is encumbered with a new maximum conventional first mortgage or deed of trust.

In general, sales prices of properties sold under nonconventional financing terms are adjusted downward to a cash equivalent.

Value of Income Property as Indicated By the Mortgage-Equity Technique

This computation is the simplest procedure—and the most significant—of *The Instant Mortgage-Equity Technique*: Value equals Net Annual Income divided by precomputed Over-All Rate. The value indicator is only as valid as the income projection and the determination of the six mortgage-equity variables.

Mortgage-equity, used in an appraisal, tells the investor something no other technique can: the price he can pay for the property, under a determined set of variables that will presumably produce the rate of yield he seeks on his equity investment.

Value of Property When Loan Ratio is Unknown

This procedure, which breaks a problem in algebra down into simple steps in arithmetic, can assist an investor in determining the price he can offer for an owner's equity, if an existing loan can be assumed. Or, it can be used to calculate mortgage-equity property value when the dollar amount of available new financing is known but not tied to a specific percent of value.

Positive Explanation of a Negative OAR

The OAR Tables of precomputed rates show a few minus signs. For example, there is given an OAR of $-.00679$ for this set of variables: 5-year holding period, 6% equity yield rate, 70% loan ratio, 7% interest rate, 10-year loan term, and 40% appreciation.

At first glance the negative OAR might be quite puzzling. An explanation and illustration will clarify. An OAR of $-.00679$ does not indicate a minus property value. Nor should it be assumed that only a negative OAR means a negative cash flow. In the example a rate of minus .00679 does mean that there could be a negative annual income before debt service of .679% of property value, and still generate a yield of 6% under the given set of variables. Obviously, the total negative cash flow would be in excess of debt service.

Translated into a specific example, here is what the negative OAR of $-.00679$ actually shows:

Assume property value of $100,000
Principal amount of loan: .7 x $100,000 = $70,000

Down payment (equity): .3 x 100,000 = 30,000
Debt service (see Supplemental Tables): .13933 x $70,000 = $9,753
Loan balance, end of 5 years
  (see Supplemental Tables): .58637 x 70,000 = $41,046
Resale value: 1.4 x $100,000 = $140,000
Net reversion: $140,000 − $41,046 = $98,954
Negative net annual income *before*
  debt service: −.00679 x $100,000 = −$679
  (Note: Income = OAR x Value)
Negative cash flow *after*
  debt service: −$9,753 − $679 = −$10,432

At this point it must be noted that income from the property is not sufficient to meet any of the annual debt service payments of $9,753, and is $679 short of paying operating expenses.

It must be assumed that the owner has made an initial investment of $30,000 and is saddled with a series of annual investments of $10,432 for 5 years. If the property appreciates 40% within 5 years, the investor will have earned 6% on his total investment.

Here's proof (see procedure "Rate of Yield on Equity Investment in Non-Producing Property Held for Appreciation," Step *d*, page 58.):

$$\$10,432 \div (.2374 - .06) = \qquad \$58,805 \ (PR - i, 6\%, 5 \text{ years})$$
$$30,000 \div .74726 \qquad = \qquad \underline{\ \ 40,147\ } \ (PW\ 1, 6\%, 5 \text{ years}$$
$$\$98,952$$

Target figure is $98,954, the calculated net reversion. Let's explain it further in this way: An initial investment of $30,000 and a series of annual investments of $10,432 would grow in 5 years to $98,952 at 6% interest compounded annually. From another point of view, −$679 ÷ −.00679 = $100,000. (Value = Negative Income ÷ Negative Rate.)

In practice, a negative OAR would be used only in analysis of an existing investment that has apparently turned sour. A determination can be made of actual yield on equity, or the degree of appreciation required to rescue the investor. (This explanation will justify the computation of Over-All Rates down to a microscopic 2% yield on equity.)

Now, Take Ten

The Instant Mortgage-Equity Technique is designed to help the appraiser in his quest for value. Here is a list of suggestions, applicable to the solution of a typical problem in appraisal and analysis:

1. Gather, evaluate, organize, and outline the pertinent data: net annual income as a level annuity equivalent; loan terms; investor's projections of holding period, appreciation or depreciation, and rate of yield on equity.
2. Spell out the specific question or questions to be answered. What are the unknowns? Is the purpose of the appraisal to determine market value to persons in general or investment value to a specific client?
3. If you are dealing with a lengthy, complex problem, break it up into a number of smaller, component problems.
4. Arrange the individual segments of the total problem in logical sequence.
5. Consult the "Mortgage-Equity Procedures" to find the applicable method for each separate part of the problem and for the whole problem.
6. Study the suggested solution of a similar problem.
7. Select, list, and label the proper rates and factors from the Compound Interest, OAR, and Supplemental Tables.
8. Follow the applicable procedures, step by step, relating rates and factors to the data given in order to find the unknown for which you are solving.
9. Check and prove your calculations.
10. Look again at the problem and your solution. Ask yourself, "Is it a reasonable answer?"

Section 2: Mortgage-Equity Procedures

Patterned Procedures

In the spirit of simplicity, the instant mortgage-equity methods avoid equations and special symbols. Instead, each step in calculation by simple arithmetic is spelled out in proper sequence. The format for each type of computation includes three parts: the procedure, an illustrative problem, and a sample solution. In some cases a fourth element is added: proof. Each procedure could be expressed in equation form, but that phase will be left to the appraiser as an optional do-it-yourself project.

The following sequence in studying each procedure is suggested. First, read the sample problem; then go back to the procedure itself and relate each step to the calculations in the suggested solution. Check the computation made and check each factor and rate used against those in the tables.

The number of mortgage-equity procedures may seem formidable (there are over forty), and some of the multistep methods may appear complex. However, the basic use of the instant mortgage-equity technique is a simple, one-step operation: select the proper rate from the OAR Tables and divide net annual income by it to compute an indicator of value.

In making more difficult calculations and a detailed analysis, don't attempt to remember the procedures—just know where to find the patterned procedures when you need them. The Ready Reference Roster of mortgage-equity methods will serve as a guide and a reminder.

Ready Reference Roster

Annuities, Present Worth of; and Level Ordinary Annuity Equivalent
    Annuity, ordinary.
    Annuity due.
    Annuity with a deferred start.
    Graduated (step-up or step-down) annuity.
    Irregular annual income stream.
    Level ordinary annuity equivalent:
    1. Annuity due, annuity with a deferred start, graduated annuity, or irregular income stream.
    2. Decreasing annuity.
    3. Increasing annuity.

35

Appreciation Required to Generate a Specified Rate of Yield on Equity
  1. From the OAR Tables.
  2. From the Compound Interest Tables.
Cash Flow
  1. Dollar amount of annual cash flow.
  2. Annual cash flow as a percent of property value.
Extension of the Compound Interest Tables
Income Required to Meet Equity Demands
Income Tax, Effect Of, On Yield Rate
  (See Case Study, pages 81-84)
Interpolation By Simple Proportion
Investment Analysis
  (See Case Study, pages 78-79. Also, see Worksheets and notes, pages 72-75.)
Loan Constant
  (See also Supplemental Tables, page 118.)
Mortgage or Trust Deed Calculations
  Balloon payment.
  Payment, periodic, to amortize a loan.
  Payment, periodic, to amortize a specified percent of principal in a stipulated
    period of time.
  Present worth of a mortgage or trust deed, discounted to a yield rate higher
    or lower than the interest rate.
  Principal balance unpaid, amount of, at any time on an amortized loan.
  Principal balance unpaid, percent of, at any time on an amortized loan. (See
    also Supplemental Tables, pages 113-118.)
  Principal paid off, amount of, at any time on an amortized loan.
  Principal paid off, percent of, at any time on an amortized loan.
  Time required to amortize a loan.
Over-All Rate:
  1. From the OAR Tables, if value is not known.
  2. From the Compound Interest Tables, if value is not known.
  3. If value is known.
Proof of OAR, Valuation, Yield Rate
Rate of Yield on Equity:
  1. Using OAR Tables.
  2. Using Compound Interest Tables.
Rate of Yield on Equity Investment in Non-Producing Property Held For
Appreciation
Rate of Yield on 100% Equity:
  1. If neither appreciation nor depreciation is assumed within a holding
    period.
  2. If either appreciation or depreciation is projected within a holding period.

Reversion, Dollar Amount of
Reversion, Present Worth of
Secondary (Junior or Multiple) Financing, Adjustment For
  Over-All Rate:
  1. Using OAR Tables.
  2. Using Compound Interest Tables.
  Rate of yield on equity.
Value of Income Property As Indicated By the Mortgage-Equity Technique
Value of Property When Loan Ratio Is Unknown
Worksheets
  Data required in the computation or selection of mortgage-equity over-all
    rate.
  (Also see example, page 54.)
  Computation of value estimate.
  (Also see example, page 68.)
  OAR from market, and equity yield rate and property value from OAR.
  (Also see example, page 57.)
  Investment analysis and proof of computations.
  (Also see example, pages 78-79.)
  Notes.

Mortgage-Equity Procedures Outlined and Illustrated

Annuities, Present Worth of; and Level Ordinary Annuity Equivalent

Annuity, ordinary (payment made, or assumed to be made, at the *end* of each
period):

● Procedure:
Multiply periodic income payment by PW 1/P.

Problem:
Find the present worth of an annuity of $75,000 for 12 years at a yield rate of
9%, assuming payment to be made at the end of each year.

Solution:

$$\$75,000 \times 7.160725 = \$537,054 \text{ (PW 1/P, 9\%, 12 years)}$$

Annuity due (payment made at the *beginning* of each period):

● Procedure:
  a. Add 1.0 to the PW 1/P factor for the next-to-the-final period.

    b. Multiply the periodic income payment by the adjusted factor computed in *a*.

Problem:
A lease calls for annual net rental payments of $75,000 at the *beginning* of each year for 12 years. Find present worth at a yield rate of 9%.

Solution:
    a. 6.805191 + 1.0 = 7.805191 (PW 1/P, 9%, 11 years)
    b. $75,000 x 7.805191 = $585,389

Annuity with a deferred start:

● Procedure:
    1. a. Subtract PW 1/P factor for period immediately preceding start from PW 1/P for final period.
       b. Multiply periodic income payment by the adjusted factor computed in *a*.
    2. (Alternate)
       a. Multiply PW 1/P factor, selected as though there were no deferred start, by the PW 1 factor for period immediately preceding start.
       b. Multiply periodic income payment by the adjusted factor computed in *a*.

Problem:
An annuity of $30,000 per year runs for 7 years, starting 3 years hence. Calculate present worth at a yield rate of 10%.

Solution (Procedure 1):
    a. 6.144567 − 2.486852 = 3.657715 (PW 1/P, 10%, 10 years, 3 years)
    b. $30,000 x 3.657715 = $109,731

Solution (Procedure 2):
    a. 4.868419 x .751315 = 3.657716 (PW 1/P, 10%, 7 years x PW 1, 10%, 3 years)
    b. $30,000 x 3.657716 = $109,731

Graduated (step-up or step-down) annuity:

● Procedure:
    a. Multiply periodic payment in first level series of payments by the PW 1/P factor for the final period in the first series.
    b. Subtract factor in *a* from PW 1/P for final period in next level series of payments. (Use same method in adjusting PW 1/P factors for each additional series of payments.)

c. Multiply adjusted factor(s) from *b* by periodic payment(s).
d. Add *a* and *c*.

Problem:
A 15-year lease specifies $40,000 per year the first 3 years, $50,000 the next 7 years, and $60,000 per year for the final 5 years. What is the present worth at a 10% yield rate?

Solution:
  a. $40,000 x 2.486851 = $99,474 (PW 1/P, 10%, 3 years)
  b. Adjusted factor for years 4–10:
    6.144567 – 2.486851 = 3.657716 (PW 1/P, 10%, 10 years, 3 years)

    Adjusted factor for years 11–15:
    7.606080 – 6.144567 = 1.461513 (PW 1/P, 10%, 15 years, 10 years)
  c. $50,000 x 3.657716 = $182,886
    $60,000 x 1.461513 = $87,691
  d. Years 1–3: $ 99,474
    Years 4–10: 182,886
    Years 11–15:   87,691
              $370,051

Irregular annual income stream:

● Procedure:
  a. Multiply each annual income payment by PW 1.
  b. Add the products calculated in *a*.

Problem:
Net annual income from residential income property is expected to increase over the next three years, then decline for the following two years because of anticipated expenses. Projections for this five-year period are:

1st year:	$40,000
2nd year:	45,000
3rd year:	47,000
4th year:	42,000
5th year:	39,000

Calculate present worth at a yield rate of 12%

Solution:
  a. $40,000 x .892857 = $35,714 (PW 1, 12%, 1 year)
    45,000 x .797194 = 35,874 (PW 1, 12%, 2 years)
    47,000 x .711780 = 33,454 (PW 1, 12%, 3 years)

42,000 x .635518 = 26,692 (PW 1, 12%, 4 years)
39,000 x .567427 = 22,130 (PW 1, 12%, 5 years)
    b. Present worth: $153,864

Level ordinary annuity equivalent:

● Procedure:
    1. *Annuity due*, annuity with a *deferred start, graduated* annuity, or *irregular*
       income stream:
       a. Compute the present worth of the total income stream.
       b. Multiply the present worth calculated in *a* by the PR factor at the yield
          rate for the full term.

Problem:
In a preceding problem, terms of a 15-year lease were given as follows: $40,000
per year the first 3 years, $50,000 a year for the next 7 years, and $60,000 per
year for the final 5 years. Payments were assumed to be made at the end of each
year. Present worth was calculated in the solution to be $370,051 at a yield rate
of 10%. Convert this graduated annuity to a level annuity equivalent.

Solution:
    a. Present worth = $370,051 (Given)
    b. $370,051 x .131474 = $48,652 (PR, 10%, 15 years)

Proof:
    $48,652 x 7.60608 = $370,051 (PW 1/P, 10%, 15 years)

    2. *Decreasing annuity* (income stream declining annually by a specified uniform
       dollar amount):
       a. Multiply the amount of decline per period by the total number of periods.
       b. Subtract *a* from income payment received the first period.
       c. Multiply *b* by the PW 1/P factor.
       d. Subtract PW 1/P from the number of periods.
       e. Multiply *d* by the amount of decline per period.
       f. Divide *e* by the yield rate.
       g. Add *c* and *f*.
          (The sum is the present worth of the income stream.)
       h. Multiply *g* by the PR factor.
          (The product is the level annuity equivalent.)

Problem:
It is estimated that net annual income of $40,000, generated by an apartment
house, will decline (straight line) at the rate of 3% per annum, or $1,200 per

year, for each of the next ten years. At a *yield* rate of 12%, compute the present worth of the income stream and the level annuity equivalent.

Solution:
a. $1,200 x 10 = $12,000
b. $40,000 – $12,000 = $28,000
c. $28,000 x 5.65 = $158,200 (PW 1/P, 12%, 10 years)
d. 10 – 5.65 = 4.35 (PW 1/P, 12%, 10 years)
e. $1,200 x 4.35 = $5,220
f. $5,220 ÷ .12 = $43,500
g. $158,200 + 43,500 = $201,700
h. $201,700 x .177 = $35,700 (PR, 12%, 10 years)

Proof:
$35,700 x 5.65 = $201,705 (PW 1/P, 12%, 10 years)
(Adjust $5 for rounding factors.)

3. *Increasing Annuity* (income stream increasing annually by a specified uniform dollar amount):
a. Multiply the amount of periodic increase by the total number of periods.
b. Add the amount of income payment received the first period to *a*.
c. Multiply *b* by the PW 1/P factor.
d. Subtract PW 1/P from the number of periods.
e. Multiply *d* by the amount of increase per period.
f. Divide *e* by the yield rate.
g. Subtract *f* from *c*.
(Difference is the present worth of the income stream.)
h. Multiply *g* by the PR factor.
(The product is the level annuity equivalent.)

Problem:
Net annual income of $300,000 from a new shopping center is expected to increase $50,000 a year for each of the next four years, at which time it is projected to level off at $500,000 per year. Compute the level annuity equivalent of the first four years' anticipated income; use a 10% yield rate.

Solution:
a. $50,000 x 4 = $200,000
b. $300,000 + $200,000 = $500,000
c. $500,000 x 3.17 = $1,585,000 (PW 1/P, 10%, 4 years)
d. 4 – 3.17 = .83 (PW 1/P, 10%, 4 years)
e. $50,000 x .83 = $41,500
f. $41,500 ÷ .10 = $415,000

g. $1,585,000 − $415,000 = $1,170,000

h. $1,170,000 x .3155 = $369,135 (PR, 10%, 4 years)

Proof:

$369,135 x 3.17 = $1,170,158 (PW 1/P, 10%, 4 years)

(Adjust $158 for rounding factors.)

Appreciation Required to Generate a Specified Rate of Yield on Equity

● Procedure:

1. From the OAR Tables, when property value and/or Over-All Rate are known:
   a. Compute Over-All Rate by dividing property value into net annual income.
   b. Find percent of appreciation in OAR Tables by search and interpolation.
2. From the Compound Interest and Annuity Tables (alternate procedure):

Steps in Computation	Factor Selection	
	Rate	Term
a. Multiply Loan Ratio by Loan Constent.		
b. Subtract *a* from OAR.		
c. Multiply *b* by PW 1/P.	Equity Yield	Holding Period
d. Multiply Loan Ratio by Percent of Loan unpaid at end of holding period.		
e. Multiply *d* by PW 1.	Equity Yield	Holding Period
f. Add Equity Ratio to *e*.		
g. Subtract *c* from *f*.		
h. Divide *g* by PW 1.	Equity Yield	Holding Period
i. Subtract 1.0 from *h*. Difference is plus or minus percent of appreciation.		

Problem:

Given:

Loan data:

Loan ratio:	80%
Interest rate:	9%
Term:	20 years
Holding period:	15 years
Anticipated equity yield:	10%
Property value:	$400,000
Net annual income:	$ 31,800

What percent of appreciation would be required in order to generate a yield of 10% in equity?

Solution (Procedure 1):
  a. OAR = $31,800 ÷ $400,000
         = .0795
  b. From the OAR Tables:
      10% equity yield, 15-year holding period, 80% loan ratio, 9% interest rate,
      20-year loan term:
          OAR at + 40% appreciation: .07952
      Appreciation of 40% would thus be required to generate a yield of 10% on
      equity under this set of variables.

Problem:
Income property under consideration by an investor can be financed on a
25-year loan, 8% interest rate, for 60% of market value. Market analysis shows
that comparable property in the area is bought and sold on an over-all rate of
.0856. Based on this data, compute the percent of appreciation required to
produce a yield of 12% on equity within a 10-year holding period.

Solution (Procedure 2):
  a. .6 x .09262 = .0556
  b. .0856 − .0556 = .03
  c. .03 x 5.65 = .1695 (PW 1/P, 12%, 10 years)
  d. .6 x .80763 = .48458
  e. .48458 x .322 = .156 (PW 1, 12%, 10 years)
  f. .4 + .156 = .556
  g. .556 − .1695 = .3865
  h. .3865 ÷ .322 = 1.2 (PW 1, 12%, 10 years)
  i. 1.2 − 1.0 = .2, or 20%

Cash Flow:

● Procedure:
  1. Dollar amount of annual cash flow:
      a. Multiply original principal amount of loan by the loan constant (from
          Supplemental Tables).
      b. Subtract *a* from net annual income.
  2. Annual cash flow as a percent of property value:
      a. Multiply given loan ratio by loan constant (from Supplemental Tables).
      b. Subtract *a* from Over-All Rate.

Problem:
Property valued at $800,000 can be financed on a 20-year loan at 8% for 70% of
value. The purchaser anticipates a 10-year holding period, 0% appreciation, and

14% yield on equity. Net annual income is $80,816. Compute the annual cash flow.

Solution (Procedure 1):
- a. Original principal amount of loan:
  - .70 x $800,000 = $560,000
  - $560,000 x .10037 = $56,207
- b. $80,816 – 56,207 = $24,609

Problem:

Given (as in preceding problem):

Loan data:

Loan ratio:	70%
Interest rate:	8%
Loan term:	20 years
Holding period:	10 years
Projected appreciation:	0%
Anticipated yield on equity:	14 %

Calculate annual cash flow as a percent of property value (after allowable expenses and debt service).

Solution (Procedure 2):
- a. .7 x .10037 = .07026
- b. OAR: .10102
  - .10102 – .070259 = .03076,
  - or 3.076%

Note: In the preceding problem (Procedure 1), $24,609 is 3.076% of $800,000. Conversely, .03076 x $800,000 = $24,608. If Loan Constant x Loan Ratio is less than the OAR, there will be a positive cash flow. If it is greater than the OAR, there will be a negative cash flow.

Extension of the Compound Interest Tables

● Procedure:
1. Present Worth Of 1 (PW 1):
   Multiply PW 1 factors for any two or more time periods whose sum equals the period for which a factor is sought.
2. Present Worth Of 1 Per Period (PW 1/P):
   - a. Compute corresponding PW 1 factor by extension.
   - b. Subtract factor in *a* from 1.0.

c. Divide *b* by the interest rate.
Note: PW 1/P = (1.0 − PW 1) ÷ i
3. Periodic Repayment (**PR**):
    a. Compute corresponding PW 1 factor by extension.
    b. Subtract factor in *a* from 1.0.
    c. Divide the interest rate by *b*.
    Note: PR = i ÷ (1.0 − PW 1)

Problem:
By extension, compute the monthly PW 1 factor at 9% nominal annual interest rate for 8 years 4 months.

Solution (Procedure 1):
    From the Compound Interest Tables, select the following factors:
        .97055 (PW 1, 9%, 4 months)
        .48806 (PW 1, 9%, 96 months)
    Multiplying: .97055 x .48806 = .47369

Problem:
Calculate the annual PW 1/P factor at 6% for 75 years.

Solution (Procedure 2):
    a. .09722 x .13011 = .01265 (PW 1, 6%, 40 years and 35 years)
    b. 1.0 − .01265 = .98735
    c. .98735 ÷ .06 = 16.4558
    Note: In Step *a*, the PW 1 factors for any two or more factors for periods adding up to 75 could have been used, such as PW 1 factors for Years 37 and 38; or 20, 40, and 15.

Problem:
As in the prior example, compute the annual PR factor at 6% for 75 years.

Solution (Procedure 3):
    a. .09722 x .13011 = .01265 (PW 1, 6%, 40 years and 35 years)
    b. 1.0 − .01265 = .98735
    c. .06 ÷ .98735 = .060769

Income Required to Meet Equity Demands

● Procedure:
    Multiply value by Over-All Rate.

Problem:
Property valued at $650,000 can be financed at 8 1/2% for 20 years and for 75% of value. The prospective investor projects 20% appreciation within a 10-year holding period. What net annual income before debt service would be required in order to produce a yield of 15% on equity?

Solution:

OAR = .09467
Income = Rate x Value
= .09467 x $650,000
= $61,535.50

Income Tax, Effect of, on Yield Rate

(See Case Study, pages 81-84.)

Interpolation by Simple Proportion

● Procedure:
1. If the unknown Over-All Rate or factor lies at a point midway between two given rates or factors:
   a. Add the two rates or factors that bracket the unknown.
   b. Divide the sum in Step *a* by 2. The quotient is the rate or factor sought.
2. If the position of the unknown Over-All Rate or factor is other than midway between the two closest given rates or factors:
   a. Find the difference between the two rates or time periods that establish the upper and lower limits of the range bracketing the subject rate.
   b. Determine the difference between the subject for which a rate or factor is sought and the lower limit of the range.
   c. Divide *b* by *a*. The quotient indicates the proportionate position of the subject in its established range.
   d. Locate the Over-All Rates or factors for each interest or yield rate used in Step *a*, and compute the difference (distance) between them.
   e. Multiply *c* by *d*.
   f. Add *e* to the Over-All Rate or factor for the lower limit of the range.

Problem:
Calculate the OAR for which the following variables are given: 10-year holding period, 15% equity yield rate, 70% loan ratio, 20-year loan term, 0% appreciation, 8 3/4% loan interest rate.

Solution (Procedure 1):
   a. OAR at 8.5%: .107552
      OAR at 9.0%: <u>.110588</u>
                .218140
   b. .21814 ÷ 2 = .10907

Problem:
Given the following: 12% equity yield rate, 75% loan ratio, 9% interest rate, 20-year loan term, 0% appreciation. Compute the OAR, assuming a holding period of 8 years.

Solution (Procedure 2):
   a. 10 years − 5 years = 5 years
   b. 8 years − 5 years = 3 years
   c. 3÷5 = .6 or 60%
   d. OAR for 10 years: .098592
      OAR for 5 years: <u>−.097643</u>
                    .000949
   e. .000949 x .6 = .00057
   f. .097643 + .00057 = .098213

(Note: The appraiser can interpolate in the OAR Tables for varying holding periods, interest rates, term of the loan, loan ratios, percent of appreciation or depreciation, and equity yield rates. Interpolation by simple proportion may also be applied to the Compound Interest and Supplemental Tables. The procedure follows the same basic format in all cases.)

    This type of calculation is approximate, not precise. However, it is accurate enough for the major portion of practical applications. For example: If the OAR in this problem were computed with accuracy from the compound interest tables (see procedure on page 53) it would be calculated to be .09825, compared to .098213 as found by interpolation. If these two Over-All Rates were each used to capitalize net annual income of $200,000, the indicated values would be $2,035,623 and $2,036,390, respectively. The difference of less than a thousand dollars is so slight in relation to total value as to be absorbed entirely by rounding either figure by a reasonable amount.

Investment Analysis

   (See Case Study, pages 78-79.)

Loan Constant:

● Procedure:
   1. Annual PR factor as a percent, or

2. Monthly PR factor multiplied by 12, or
3. Annual loan payment divided by original principal, or
4. Any stipulated percent in excess of the annual interest rate:

Illustrations:

1. On a 7% loan for 15 years with annual payments, the PR factor is .1098. Therefore, the loan constant is .1098, or 10.98%.
2. If a loan is made at 7 1/2% with monthly payments for 30 years, the loan constant is 12 x .006992, or .0839 (8.39%).
3. On a loan of $75,000, annual payments of $7,000 until paid, the loan constant is $7,000 ÷ $75,000, or .0933 (9.33%).
4. An 8% loan might be set up with a loan constant of 9.5% to amortize. On a loan of $100,000 annual payments would be $9,500, including principal and interest.

Mortgage or Trust Deed Calculations

Balloon Payment, Computation of

● Procedure:
   a. Multiply periodic payment by PW 1/P for final period.
   b. Subtract product computed in Step *a* from the original principal amount.
   c. Divide the difference by PW 1 for the final period.

Problem:
Terms of a loan for $600,000 at 7 1/2% call for monthly payments of $5,500 for 8 years, with the unpaid balance due and payable at the end of 8 years. Compute the balloon payment.

Solution:
   a. $5,500 x 72.026024 = $396,143 (PW 1/P, 7 1/2%, 96 months)
   b. $600,000 − $396,143 = $203,857
   c. $203,857 ÷ .549837 = $370,759 (PW 1, 7 1/2%, 96 months)
      Balloon payment: $370,759, in addition to $5,500 payment for month 96. (Equity build-up through loan amortization has been $600,000 − $370,759, or $229,241.)

Payment, Periodic, to Amortize a Loan:

● Procedure:
   Multiply the principal amount by the PR factor.

Problem:
Compute the monthly payment to amortize a loan of $425,000 at 8½% in 30 years.

Solution:
$425,000 x .00769 = $3,268.25 (PR, 8½%, 360 months)

Payment, Periodic, to Amortize a Specified Percent of Principal in a Stipulated Period of Time:

● Procedure:
    a. Subtract the effective periodic interest rate from the PR factor.
    b. Multiply the difference calculated in a by the percent to be amortized.
    c. Add the effective periodic interest rate to the product computed in b.
    d. Multiply the original principal amount by the adjusted PR factor, as determined by Step c.

Problem:
A loan on a commercial building is made on the following terms: Principal amount: $800,000. Interest rate: 9%. Term: 15 years. Payment schedule: Monthly payments to amortize 60% of the principal amount by maturity; balance of 40% due as a balloon payment at the end of 15 years. Compute the monthly payment required.

Solution:
    a. Nominal 9%, interest rate is .0075 per month.
       .010143 − .0075 = .002643 (PR, 9%, 180 months)
    b. .6 x .002643 = .0015858
    c. .0015858 + .0075 = .0090858
    d. $800,000 x .0090858 = $7,268.64
       Monthly payment of $7,268.64 will keep all interest current and reduce the principal amount by $480,000, leaving $320,000 due as a balloon payment at the end of 15 years.

Present Worth of a mortgage or trust deed discounted to a yield rate higher or lower than the interest rate

● Procedure:
    a. Determine current yield rate as indicated by the mortgage market.
    b. Multiply the periodic payment by the PW 1/P.
    c. Multiply balloon payment by PW 1.
    d. Add b and c.

Problem:

An apartment house has sold for $800,000 on these terms:

    Down payment: $75,000

    First trust deed (institutional loan) assumed by purchaser: $500,000

    Second trust deed, carried by seller: $225,000

The note, secured by the second trust deed, is written at 8% interest and calls for monthly payments of $2,250 for 9 years and a balloon payment of $106,928 at the end of 9 years. Your problem is to calculate the cash equivalent of the sales price by computing the present worth of the second trust deed, discounted to a yield rate that would make it saleable in the open mortgage market. Your survey of the current local mortgage market indicates that the subject second trust deed would attract a buyer if it were discounted to yield 15%. What is the present worth of the second trust deed, discounted to yield 15%? By adjusting the sales price for terms, estimate the cash equivalent of the sale.

Solution:

  a. Yield rate, as determined by the market: 15%

  b. $2,250 x 59.08651 = $132,945 (PW 1/P, 15%, 108 months)

  c. $106,928 x .26142 = $27,953 (PW 1, 15%, 108 months)

  d. $132,945 + $27,953 = $160,898, round to $160,900

    Cash equivalent of sales price (adjusted for terms):

Down Payment:	$ 75,000
1st Trust Deed:	500,000
2nd Trust Deed, Discounted to Yield 15%:	160,900
Total	$735,900

(Note: (1) If loan is set up on a fully amortized schedule with *no* balloon payment, Steps *a* and *b* only are required. (2) In deriving mortgage-equity over-all rates from market sales and rental analysis, sales prices should be adjusted for terms which are other than conventional. Usually, this involves discounting purchase money trust deeds, carried by the seller. For a more complete explanation of this point and additional related procedures, see the author's *Mini-Math for Appraisers*, published by the International Association of Assessing Officers, Chicago, Illinois.)

Principal Balance Unpaid, Amount of, at Any Time on an Amortized Loan:

• Procedure:

    Multiply the periodic payment by PW 1/P for the number of periods remaining unpaid in the full schedule.

Problem:

On a 25-year loan of $150,000 at 8 1/2%, annual payments of $14,657, what is the principal balance remaining unpaid after 10 years?

Solution:

    $14,657 x 8.30424 = $121,715 (PW 1/P, 8 1/2%, 15 years)

Principal Balance Unpaid, Percent of, at Any Time on an Amortized Loan:

● Procedure:

Multiply the PR factor for the full term by the PW 1/P factor for the number of periods remaining unpaid.
(See also Supplemental Tables for precomputed loan balance percentages.)

Problem:
Calculate the percent of principal unpaid at the end of 10 years on a 9% loan with monthly payments to amortize in 25 years.

Solution:
PR factor at 9% for 300 months: .00839
PW 1/P factor at 9% for 180 months: 98.59341
.00839 x 98.59341 = .827, or 82.7%

Principal Paid Off, Amount of, at Any Time on an Amortized Loan:

● Procedure:

a. Multiply periodic payment by PW 1/P for number of periods remaining unpaid.
b. Subtract product from original principal.

Problem:
Annual payments to amortize a loan of $80,000 at 8 1/2% in 15 years amount to $9,634. What has been applied to principal by the end of 12 years?

Solution:
a. $9,634 x 2.55402 = $24,605 (PW 1/P, 8 1/2%, 3 years)
b. $80,000 − $24,605 = $55,395

Principal Paid Off, Percent of, at Any Time on an Amortized Loan:

● Procedure:

a. Multiply the PR factor for the full term by the PW 1/P factor for the number of periods remaining unpaid.
b. Subtract a from 1.0.

Problem:
On a loan at 8% with monthly payments to amortize in 20 years, what percent of principal has been paid off at the end of 15 years?

Solution:
  a. PR, 8%, 240 months: .00836
      PW 1/P, 8%, 60 months: 49.31843
      .00836 x 49.31843 = .412
  b. 1.0 − .412 = .588, or 58.8%

Time required to Amortize a Loan:

- Procedure:
  1. If all other terms of the loan are known:
      a. Divide the original principal amount by the periodic payment.
      b. Locate the quotient calculated in Step *a* in the PW 1/P tables, interpolating, if necessary.
  2. If dollar amounts are not given but loan constant and other variables are known (monthly payments assumed):
      a. Divide the loan constant by 12.
      b. Locate the quotient from Step *a* in the PR tables; interpolating, if necessary.

Problem:
A loan of $82,000 at 8% interest calls for monthly payments of $641 to amortize. What is the term of the loan?

Solution (Procedure 1):
  a. 82,000 ÷ 641 = 127.92512
  b. PW 1/P factor at 8% for 24 years (288 months) is 127.868388, indicating the loan runs for 24 years, the final payment being slightly larger than the preceding 287 monthly payments.

Problem:
A loan is set up at an interest rate of 7 1/2% and a loan constant of .09667, monthly payments to amortize. Calculate the term of the loan.

Solution (Procedure 2):
  a. .09667 ÷ 12 = .008056
  b. A search in the vertical column of monthly PR factors at 7 1/2% shows the factor for 20 years (240 months) to be .008056. The loan term: 20 years.

(Note: If a loan specifies an annual amortization schedule and a loan constant is given, find the PR factor that corresponds the closest to the loan constant to calculate term. E.g., if the loan constant is .12 on a 9% loan with annual payment, a search shows the annual PR factor at 9% for 16 years to be .1203, indicating a loan term of 16 years.)

Over-All Rate:

● Procedure:
  1. If value is not known:
     Select the rate from the OAR Tables, interpolating if necessary.
  2. If value is not known (alternate procedure using compound interest tables):

Steps in Computation	Factor Selection		
	Rate	Term	Period
a. Multiply Loan Ratio by Loan Constant.	Interest	Total	Monthly or Annual
b. Multiply Step *a* by PW 1/P.	Interest	Total less Holding Period	Monthly ÷ 12 or Annual
c. Express projected resale price as a percent of purchase price and subtract Step *b*.			
d. Multiply Step *a* by PW 1/P.	Equity Yield	Holding Period	Annual
e. Multiply Step *c* by PW 1.	Equity Yield	Holding Period	Annual
f. Subtract Step *e* from Step *d*.			
g. Add Equity Ratio to Step *f*.			
h. Divide Step *g* by PW 1/P. Quotient is Over-All Rate.	Equity Yield	Holding Period	Annual

  3. If value is known:
     Divide net annual income by property value. $(R = I \div V)$

Problem:
Given:
    Loan data:

Loan ratio:	80%
Interest rate:	8 1/2%
Term:	20 years, monthly payments
Holding period:	10 years
Anticipated depreciation:	20%
Required equity yield:	10%

What is the indicated Over-All Rate, based on these data and assumptions?

Solution (Procedure 1):
    From the OAR Tables, 10% equity yield, 10-year holding period, 80% loan ratio, 20-year term, 20% depreciation: .1008 OAR.

**Data Required
In the Computation or Selection of
Mortgage-Equity Over-All Rate**

Holding Period:	10 yrs.
Equity Yield Rate:	10%
Mortgage Specifications:	
Loan Ratio:	80%
Interest Rate:	8-1/2%
Term:	20 yrs.
Amortization Interval:	monthly
Equity Ratio:	20%
Appreciation/Depreciation	−20%
Over-All Rate:	.1008

Note: All variables are built into the OAR. This form can serve as a check list of data to be gathered by the appraiser.

Problem:
Given:

Loan specifications:	
Loan ratio:	80%
Interest rate:	9%
Loan term:	30 years, monthly payments
Holding period:	10 years
Anticipated appreciation:	20%
Required equity yield:	14%

Compute the OAR.

Solution (Procedure 2):
- a. .8 x .09656 = .077248
- b. .077248 x (111.144954 ÷ 12) = .715477 (PW 1/P, 9%, 240 months)
- c. 1.2 − .715477 = .484523
- d. .077248 x 5.216116 = .40293 (PW 1/P, 14%, 10 years)
- e. .484523 x .269744 = .1307 (PW 1, 14%, 10 years)
- f. .40293 − .1307 = .27223
- g. .2 + .27223 = .47223
- h. .47223 ÷ 5.216116 = .09053 (PW 1/P, 14%, 10 years)

Problem:
Property was sold for $740,000. Net annual income is $61,725.
What is the Over-All Rate?

Solution (Procedure 3):
  OAR = $61,725 ÷ $750,000
      = .0823

Proof of OAR, Valuation, Yield Rate

  (See Case Study, pages 78-79.)

Rate of Yield on Equity:

● Procedure:
  1. Using OAR Tables:
     a. Compute over-all rate by dividing property value into net income. (Rate =
        Income ÷ Value)
     b. Find rate in OAR Tables by search and interpolation.
  2. Using Compound Interest Tables:
     (Equity yield rate derived from an over-all rate and loan data)
     a. Multiply the loan ratio by the loan constant.
     b. Subtract *a* from the over-all rate.
     c. Multiply the loan ratio by the percent of loan remaining unpaid at the end
        of the holding period.
     d. Subtract *c* from estimated value at end of holding period expressed as a
        percent of purchase price.
     e. Make the following considerations:
          Step *b* computes the *annuity.*
          Step *d* gives the *reversion.*
          Value (the "target figure") is the equity ratio.
        Use the following equation in a dual "cut and try" operation to bracket
        the equity yield rate:
          Value = Annuity x PW 1/P + Reversion x PW 1
          (Select PW 1/P and PW 1 factors at estimated equity yield rates for
          term of holding period.)
        "Zero in" on equity yield rate by interpolation.

Problem:
Given:
        Loan data:
          Loan ratio: 75%

Interest rate:	9%
Term:	20 years
Holding period	10 years
Anticipated appreciation:	0%
Property value:	$650,000
Net annual income after property taxes:	$70,000

What is the equity yield rate?

Solution (Procedure 1):
   a. OAR = $70,000 ÷ $650,000 = .1077
   b. From the tables: OAR, 10-year holding period, 75% loan ratio, 9% interest rate, 20-year term:
      At 15% Equity Yield: .107773 OAR
   Actual OAR of .1077 indicates equity yield is about 15%.

Problem:
You are deriving equity yield rates from the market on comparable apartment houses in a given area of the city. Your analysis of sales and rents indicates an Over-All Rate of .1038. Data from lending institutions shows that residential income properties of this age, quality and type, and in this location, would support a new maximum loan for 75% of appraised value at 9% interest rate for a term of 25 years. Based on these data and on a projected holding period of 10 years, compute *equity yield rates*:
   1. Assuming 0% appreciation within the holding period.
   2. Assuming 10% depreciation.

Solution (1) Assuming 0% appreciation (Procedure 2):
   a. .75 x .10071 = .0755 (loan constant from Supplemental Tables)
   b. .1038 − .0755 = .0283
   c. .75 x .82740 = .62055 (% loan balance, Supplemental Tables)
   d. 1.0 − .62055 = .37945
   e. Try 15%:

.0283 x 5.01877	= .14203 (PW 1/P, 15%, 10 years)
.37945 x .24718	= .09379 (PW 1, 15%, 10 years)
	.23582

   Try 13%:

.0283 x 5.42624	= .15356 (PW 1/P, 13%, 10 years)
.37945 x .29459	= .11178 (PW 1, 13%, 10 years)
	.26534

Target figure is .25, the equity ratio. By interpolation between .23582 and .26534, equity yield rate is computed to be 14%, assuming 0% appreciation during the 10-year holding period.

Solution (2) Assuming 10% depreciation (Procedure 2):

- a. .75 x .10071 = .0755
- b. .1038 − .0755 = .0283
- c. .75 x .82740 = .62055
- d. .90 − .62055 = .27945
- e. Try 12%:

.0283 x 5.6502   = .1599 (PW 1/P, 12%, 10 years)

.27945 x .32197   = .0900 (PW 1, 12%, 10 years)

                       .2499

Since computed .2499 is so close to the target figure of .25, there is no need for an additional estimate of rate, nor for bracketing and interpolation. Equity yield rate is 12%, assuming 10% depreciation in value during the 10-year holding period.

OAR From Market

Sale Number	I	II	III	IV
Date of Sale	12/10/71	7/1/72	4/25/72	8/17/71
Location	Brookside	College Heights	Mar Vista	Glenview
Adjusted Sales Price	925,000	650,000	840,000	780,000
Gross Income	168,000	122,700	155,000	147,600
Eff. Gr. @ 5% Vac Fac	159,600	116,565	147,250	140,220
Expenses or Expense Ratio	63,900	42%	61,250	59,000
Net Income	95,700	67,500	86,000	81,220
Comparability	Good	Good	Fair	Good
OAR	.1034	.1038	.1023	.1041

Equity Yield Rate and Property Value from OAR

Holding Period:	10 yrs.	
Mortgage Specifications:		
Loan Ratio:	75%	
Interest Rate:	9%	
Term:	25 yrs.	
Amortization Interval:	Monthly	
OAR:	.1038	
Appreciation/Depreciation:	a. 0%	b. −10%
Equity Yield Rate:*	a. 14%	b. 12%
Net Annual Income:	74,400	

Indicated Value: $\underline{74,400 \div .1038 = 716,760}$

                        (Income) (OAR)

*Calculated from OAR Tables or Compound Interest Tables.

Rate of Yield on Equity Investment in Nonproducing Property Held for Appreciation:

- Procedure:
    a. Compute average annual expense payment.
    b. Estimate equity at anticipated time of resale (future worth) by subtracting loan balance from expected sales price.
    c. Estimate 2 yield rates: one above and one below the true yield rate to be determined.
    d. Let "Future worth" represent equity (target figure) at time of resale. At each yield rate from Step c, solve equation:

    Future worth = (Original cash investment ÷ PW 1) + [Annual Expense ÷ (PR – i)]

    e. Compare final equity (the target figure) with the 2 future worth values from Step d. Interpolate to find indicated yield rate.

Problem:

An investor is considering a syndicate proposal to purchase nonproducing acreage, zoned commercial. Plans are to hold the parcel for a period of 5 years in anticipation of appreciation, then resell. Terms of the proposed purchase are as follows:

Sales price:	$1,500,000
Down payment:	$ 500,000
First trust deed, carried by seller:	
Principal:	$1,000,000
Interest rate:	7%
Payment schedule:	

Annual interest payments of $70,000 for 12 years
Principal amount of $1,000,000 due as a balloon payment
at the end of 12 years.

Annual property taxes are estimated at $30,000. If the client invests $10,000, his pro-rata share (1/50 or 2%) of the yearly "call" for payment of taxes and interest would amount to $2,000. Compute the yield rate if the land is held for 5 years and is sold for $2,500,000. How would the yield rate be affected if the holding period were extended to 7 years, all other data remaining the same?

Solution:
    a. Annual call: $2,000 (given)
    b. Equity at time of resale: $2,500,000 – $1,000,000 = $1,500,000
    1/50 or 2% interest = .02 x $1,500,000 = $30,000
    c. If holding period is 5 years, try 12% and 10%; if 7 years, try 5% and 4½%.
    d,e. Holding period of 5 years:
    Try 12% (use 12% PW 1 and PR factors for 5 years):

Future worth = ($10,000 ÷ .56743) + [$2,000 ÷ (.27741 − .12)]
= $17,623 + ($2,000 ÷ .15741)
= $17,623 + 12,706
= $30,329

Try 10% (use 10% PW 1 and PR factors for 5 years):

Future worth = ($10,000 ÷ .62092) + [$2,000 ÷ (.26380 − .10)]
= $16,105 + ($2,000 ÷ .1638)
= $16,105 + 12,210
= $28,315

By interpolation: About 11.67% yield on equity

Holding period of 7 years:
Try 5% (use 5% PW 1 and PR factors for 7 years):

Future worth = ($10,000 ÷ .71068) + [$2,000 ÷ (.17282 − .05)]
= $14,071 + ($2,000 ÷ .12282)
= $14,071 + 16,284
= $30,355

Try 4 1/2% (use 4 1/2% PW 1 and PR factors for 7 years):

Future worth = ($10,000 ÷ .73483) + [$2,000 ÷ (.1697 − .045)]
= $13,609 + ($2,000 ÷ .1247)
= $13,609 + 16,039
= $29,648

By interpolation: About 4 3/4% yield on equity.

(Note: If the appraiser has access to and is using the six standard compound interest tables, he can substitute the following equation for the one given in Step *d* of the procedure:

Future worth = (Original cash investment x Future Worth of 1) +
(Annual expense x Future Worth of 1 Per Period)

The example used in this procedure illustrates vividly the time value of money.)

Rate of Yield on 100% Equity:

● Procedure:
1. If neither appreciation nor depreciation is assumed within a holding period:
   Divide net annual income by value.
   (Note: In this case, the Over-All Rate and the Equity Yield Rate coincide.)
2. If either appreciation or depreciation is projected within a holding period:
   a. Estimate 2 yield rates: one above and one below the true yield rate sought.
   b. Multiply net annual income by PW 1/P, making 2 calculations, using 2 rates from *a*, for the term of the holding period.

c. Multiply estimated value at end of holding period by PW 1 at each rate from *a*.
d. At each rate, add computations from *b* and *c*.
e. Use original value (equity) as a target figure and interpolate.
(Note: This procedure is an example of the use of the basic equation: Value = Annuity x PW 1/P + Reversion x PW 1. Net annual income is the annuity. Value at the end of the holding period is the reversion.)

Problem:
An investor pays $600,000 cash for a commercial building. Net annual income is $54,000. Stability of both value and income are projected for a 10-year holding period. What is the rate of yield on the purchaser's 100% equity position?

Solution (Procedure 1):
    $54,000 ÷ $600,000 = .09, or 9%
    (Over-All Rate and Equity Yield Rate correspond.)
    Proof: Use the equation:
      Value = Annuity x PW 1/P + Reversion x PW 1
        $54,000 x 6.41766 = $346,554 (PW 1/P, 9%, 10 years)
        $600,000 x .42241 = 253,446 (PW 1, 9%, 10 years)
                              $600,000

Problem:
An apartment complex, purchased for $1,500,000 cash, generates net annual income of $127,500. A holding period of 12 years is anticipated, during which time net income is expected to remain stable. Compute the rate of yield on equity, assuming:
    a. Depreciation of 20% within the 12-year holding period.
    b. Appreciation of 30% within the 12-year holding period.

Solution: (Procedure 2):
    Assuming 20% depreciation:
    a. Try 7% and 8%.
    b. At 7%:
        $127,500 x 7.94269 = $1,012,693 (PW 1/P, 7%, 12 years)
      At 8%:
        $127,500 x 7.53608 = $960,850 (PW 1/P, 8%, 12 years)
    c. Estimated value at end of holding period:
        .8 x $1,500,000 = $1,200,000
      At 7%:
        $1,200,000 x .44401 = $532,812 (PW 1, 7%, 12 years)
      At 8%:
        $1,200,000 x .39711 = $476,532 (PW 1, 8%, 12 years)

d. At 7%:

$1,012,693 + $532,812 = $1,545,505

At 8%:

$960,850 + $476,532 = $1,437,382

e. Target figure is the original value or original 100% equity:
$1,500,000

By interpolation: Equity yield rate is about 7.42%

Assuming 30% appreciation:

a. Try 9% and 10%

b. At 9%:

$127,500 x 7.16073 = $912,993 (PW 1/P, 9%, 12 years)

At 10%:

$127,500 x 6.81369 = $868,745 (PW 1/P, 10%, 12 years)

c. Estimated value at end of holding period:

1.3 x $1,500,000 = $1,950,000

At 9%:

$1,950,000 x .35553 = $693,284 (PW 1, 9%, 12 years)

At 10%:

$1,950,000 x .31863 = $621,329 (PW 1, 10%, 12 years)

d. At 9%:

$912,993 + $693,284 = $1,606,277

At 10%:

$868,745 + $621,329 + $1,490,074

e. Target figure: $1,500,000

By interpolation: Equity yield rate is about 9.9%.

(Note: If depreciation is anticipated, Over-All Rate exceeds Equity Yield Rate; if appreciation is projected, Equity Yield Rate exceeds Over-All Rate. Over-All Rate is the rate of current yield; Equity Yield Rate is yield to maturity.)

Reversion, Dollar Amount of:

● Procedure:

a. Calculate estimated property value at end of holding period.

b. Compute loan balance at end of holding period.

c. Subtract *b* from *a*.

Problem:

A shopping center acquired for $4,500,000 is expected to appreciate 25% within a ten-year projected holding period. The center is financed on a 70% loan for 20 years at 8% interest. What is the amount of anticipated reversion at the end of 10 years?

Solution:
  a. At 25% appreciation, property would be worth 125% of original purchase price:

      1.25 x $4,500,000 = $5,625,000
  b. Original loan (70% loan ratio):

      .7 x $4,500,000 = $3,150,000

    Loan balance at end of 10 years:

      .68941 x $3,150,000 = $2,171,642 (See Supplemental Tables)
  c. Reversion: $5,625,000 − 2,171,642 = $3,453,358

Reversion, Present Worth of

● Procedure:
  Multiply single future income payment or projected future value by PW 1.

Problem:
A net reversion at the end of an 8-year holding period is estimated at $275,000. What is its present worth at a yield rate of 14%?

Solution:
  $275,000 x .350559 = $96,404 (PW 1, 14%, 8 years).

Secondary (Junior or Multiple) Financing, Adjustment for:

Over-All Rate

● Procedure:
  1. By use of precomputed OAR Tables:
    a. Add the loan ratios for all mortgages or trust deeds on the property.
    b. Compute each loan ratio separately as a percent of *a*.
    c. Determine the combined interest rate as a weighted average, using ratios from Step *b*.
    d. Find the combined loan constant by calculating the weighted average.
    e. Interpolate to find the term, using the Supplemental Loan Constant Tables.
    f. Using the weighted average loan interest rate from *c* and the weighted average loan term from *e*, find the OAR in the precomputed tables by search, bracket, and interpolation.

Problem:
Income property being analyzed is encumbered by a first trust deed, which

secures a loan for 60% of value at 9% for 30 years. The seller will carry a second trust deed for 30% of value at 12% interest for 15 years. Assume 0% appreciation during a 10-year holding period. Net annual income is $75,000. The prospective purchaser anticipates a yield rate of 20% on his thin equity position. Based on this data, compute the mortgage-equity OAR and the indicated property value.

Solution:

a. Loan ratio of 1st. T.D.: .60
   Loan ratio of 2nd T.D.: .30
   Combined loan ratio: .90

b. .60 ÷ .90 = .6667
   .30 ÷ .90 = .3333

c. .6667 x .09 = .06
   .333 x .12 = .04
   Weighted average interest rate: .10

d. .6667 x .09656 = .06438
   .3333 x .14402 = .048
   Weighted average loan constant: .11238

e. Loan constant, 10%, 20 years: .11580
   Loan constant, 10%, 25 years: .10905
   By interpolation, loan constant computed in Step *d* indicates loan term of 22 1/2 years.

f. OAR, 20% equity yield, 90% loan ratio, 10-year holding period, 0% appreciation, 10% interest rate:
   20-year loan term: .11487
   25-year loan term: .11279
   $\overline{.22766}$

   OAR, 22 1/2 years: .1138, by interpolation
   Value: $75,000 ÷ .1138 = $659,000

Check and Proof (See Supplemental Tables):
   Equity: .10 x $659,000 = $ 65,900
   1st TD: .60 x $659,000 = 395,400
   2nd TD: .30 x $659,000 = 197,700
   Annual payments on 1st TD: .09656 x $395,400 = $38,180
   Annual payments on 2nd TD: .14402 x $197,700 = 28,473
                                                     $66,653

Cash flow: $75,000 − $66,653 = $8,347
Loan balance, 1st TD, end of 10 years:
          .8943 x $395,400   = $353,606
Loan balance, 2nd TD, end of 10 years:
          .53954 x $197,700   = 106,667
                                $460,273

Reversion:

$$\$659,000 - \$460,273 = \$198,727$$

Value of Original Equity = Annuity x PW 1/P + Reversion x PW 1

Substituting (use PW 1/P, PW 1, 20%, 10 years):

Value = ($8,347 x 4.1925) + ($198,727 x .161506)
= $34,995 + $32,095
= $67,090

Target figure is $65,900, the down payment. Value calculations by weighted averages are approximate, not precise.

Over-All Rate
● Procedure (alternate):
2. By the Compound Interest Tables:

Steps in Computation	Factor Selection		
	Rate	Term	Period
a. Multiply each Loan Ratio by its corresponding Loan Constant.	Interest	Total	Monthly or Annual
b. Multiply each product in Step *a* by its corresponding PW 1/P.	Interest	Total – Holding Period	Monthly ÷ 12 or Annual
c. Express projected resale value as a percent of purchase price and subtract the sum of the products in Step *b*.			
d. Multiply the sum of the products in Step *a* by PW 1/P.	Equity Yield	Holding Period	Annual
e. Multiply Step *c* by PW 1.	Equity Yield	Holding Period	Annual
f. Subtract Step *e* from Step *d*.			
g. Add Equity Ratio to Step *f*.			
h. Divide Step *g* by PW 1/P. Quotient is Over-All Rate.	Equity Yield	Holding Period	Annual

Problem:

Compute the mortgage-equity Over-All Rate and the indicated property value by Procedure 2, using all data from the prior problem.

Solution (Procedure 2):
a. .6 x .09656 = .057936 (Loan Constant, 9%, 360 months, or 30 years)
.3 x .14402 = .043206 (Loan Constant, 12%, 180 months, or 15 years)
b. .057936 x (111.14495 ÷ 12) = .5366 (PW 1/P, 9%, 240 months)
.043206 x (44.95504 ÷ 12) = .16186 (PW 1/P, 12%, 60 months)
c. 1.0 – (.5366 + .16186) = .30154

d. .057936 + .043206 = .101142

.101142 x 4.19247 = .424035   (PW 1/P, 20%, 10 years)

e. .30154 x .16151 = .0487   (PW 1, 20%, 10 years)

f. .424035 − .0487 = .375335

g. .375335 + .1 = .475335   (Equity Ratio: 10%, or .1)

h. .475335 ÷ 4.19247 = .113378   (PW 1/P, 20%, 10 years)

Over-All Rate = 11.3378%, or .113378

Value: $75,000 ÷ .113378 = $661,504, rounded to $661,500.

Proof:

Equity (down payment):	.10 x $661,500 = $ 66,150
1st Trust Deed:	.60 x 661,500 = 396,900
2nd Trust Deed:	.30 x 661,500 = 198,450
Purchase price:	$661,500

Annual loan payments (12 x monthly):

1st Trust Deed:	.09656 x $396,900 = $38,325
2nd Trust Deed:	.14402 x 198,450 = 28,581
Total:	$66,906

Cash Flow: $75,000 − $66,906 = $8,094

Loan balances (end of 10 years):

1st Trust Deed:	.89430 x $396,900 = $354,948
2nd Trust Deed:	.53954 x 198,450 = 107,072
Total:	$462,020

Reversion (net): $661,500 − $462,020 = $199,480

Value of Equity = (Cash Flow x PW 1/P) + (Net Reversion x PW 1)

               = ($8,094 x 4.19247) + ($199,480 x .16151)   (Factors,

                                        20%, 10 years)

               = $33,934 + $32,218

               = $66,152

Target figure is original equity or down payment: $66,150.

Close enough—almost a bull's-eye.

(Note: Value by this precise computation, using Compound Interest Tables in Procedure 2, is within $2,500 of the calculation by weighted averages and interpolation within the OAR Tables, as shown in Procedure 1: $661,500 v. $659,000.)

Rate of Yield on Equity:

● Procedure:

a. Compute Over-All Rate by dividing property value into net income.

b. Multiply each Loan Ratio by its corresponding Loan Constant.

c. Add the products calculated in Step b.

d. Subtract c from a.

e. Multiply each loan ratio by the corresponding percent of loan remaining unpaid at end of holding period.
f. Add the products calculated in *e*.
g. Subtract *f* from estimated value at end of holding period, expressed as a percent of purchase price.
h. Make the following considerations:

> Step *d* computes the *annuity*.
> Step *g* gives the *net reversion*.
> *Value* (the "target figure") is the *equity ratio*.

Use the following equation in a dual "cut and try" calculation to bracket the equity yield rate:

> Value = (Annuity x PW 1/P) + (Reversion x PW 1)

(Select PW 1/P and PW 1 factors at estimated equity yield rates for term of the holding period.)
Zero in on equity yield rate by interpolation.

Problem:

Property valued at $400,000 produces net annual income of $39,200. It is offered to a prospective purchaser on these terms:

Down payment: 10% of purchase price.
1st Trust Deed: 65% loan ratio, 8% interest rate, monthly payments to amortize in 25 years.
2nd Trust Deed: 25% loan ratio, 9% interest rate, monthly payments to amortize in 15 years.

Assume a 10-year holding period and 10% depreciation. Compute the equity yield rate.

Solution:

a. OAR: $39,200 ÷ $400,000 = .098
b. .65 x .09262 = .060203 (Loan Constant, 8%, 25 years)
   .25 x .12171 = .0304275 (Loan Constant, 9%, 15 years)
c.   .0906305
d. .098 − .0906305 = .0073695
e. .65 x .80763 = .5249595 (Loan Balances, from Supplemental Tables)
   .25 x .48861 = .1221525
f.   .6471120
g. .9 − .647112 = .252888 (100% − 10% Depreciation)
h. Try 15%:

.0073695 x 5.018769 =	.03698581	(PW 1/P, 15%, 10 years)
.252888 x .247185 =	.06251012	(PW 1, 15%, 10 years)
	.09949593	

Try 14%:

.0073695 x 5.216116 =	.03844016	(PW 1/P, 14%, 10 years)

.252888 x .269744 =   .06821502 (PW 1, 14%, 10 years)
                          .10665518

Target figure is .10, the equity ratio.

By observation, rate of yield on equity is slightly less than 15%; by interpolation, about 14.93%.

Proof:
   1st Trust Deed:
      Principal: .65 x $400,000 = $260,000
      Annual Payments: .09262 x $260,000 = $24,081
      Loan Balance (at end of 10-year holding period):
               .80763 x $260,000 = $209,984
   2nd Trust Deed:
      Principal: .25 x $400,000 − $100,000
      Annual Payments: .12171 x $100,000 = $12,171
      Loan Balance: .48861 x $100,000 = $48,861
  Cash Flow = $39,200 − ($24,081 + $12,171)
       = $ 2,948
  Reversion (Net) = (.9 x $400,000) − ($209,984 + $48,861)
           = $360,000 − $258,845
           = $101,155
  Equity: .10 x $400,000 = $40,000 (down payment)
  At 15%:
     $ 2,948 x 5.018769 = $14,795
     $101,155 x   .247185 =   25,004
                    $39,799
   At 14%:
     $ 2,948 x 5.216116 = $15,377
     $101,155 x   .269744 =   27,286
                    $42,663

Target figure is $40,000, the original equity.

By interpolation: About 14.93% yield on equity.

*Value of Income Property as Indicated by the
Mortgage-Equity Technique:*

● Procedure:
   Divide net annual income by OAR. (Value = Income ÷ Rate)

Problem:

Apartment house data given and assumed:
   Loan specifications:
      Loan ratio: 75%

Interest rate:	8%
Term:	25 years, monthly payments
Holding period:	10 years
Anticipated Appreciation:	20%
Required equity yield rate:	15%
Net annual income:	$38,400

Estimate value by the mortgage-equity technique.

Solution:
OAR (from the tables): .09001
$38,400 ÷ .09001 = $426,600 (rounded).

Computation of Value Estimate
Mortgage-Equity Technique

Data Required:	
Holding Period:	10 yrs.
Equity Yield Rate:	15%
Mortgage Specifications:	
Loan Ratio:	75%
Interest Rate:	8%
Term:	25 yrs.
Amortization Interval:	monthly
Equity Ratio:	25%
Appreciation/Depreciation:	+20%
Net Annual Income*:	$38,400
Valuation:	
Over-All Rate:	.09001
Value = Income ÷ Rate	
= $38,400 ÷ .09001	
= $426,600	

*Use net annual income processed to the point at which it can be capitalized as a level ordinary annuity.

Value of Property When Loan Ratio is Unknown:

● Procedure:
   a. Calculate annual cash flow.
   b. Compute loan balance at end of holding period.
   c. Multiply annual cash flow by PW 1/P.
   d. Add c to original amount of loan.
   e. Multiply loan balance at end of holding period by PW 1.
   f. Subtract e from d.

g. Express value at end of holding period as a percent of original value and multiply by PW 1.

h. Subtract *g* from 1.0.

i. Divide *f* by *h*.

(Note: Present Worth *factors* in steps *c, e*, and *g* are selected at *equity yield rates* for the term of the holding period.)

Problem:

A commercial building produces net annual income of $45,000. The property can be financed by a loan of $320,000 at 8% for 25 years, monthly payments to amortize. The prospective purchaser projects a holding period of 10 years, 10% appreciation in market value, and 14% yield on equity. What is the indicated value of the property, based on data and assumptions given?

Solution:

a. Annual debt service   = Loan Constant x Principal

                                = .09262 x $320,000

                                = $29,639

   Cash flow = $45,000 – $29,639

              = $15,361

b. Loan balance = .80763 x $320,000

                = $258,442

c. $15,361 x 5.216116 = $80,125 (PW 1/P, 14%, 10 years)

d. $80,125 + $320,000 = $400,125

e. $258,442 x .269744 = $69,713 (PW 1, 14%, 10 years)

f. $400,125 – $69,713 = $330,412

g. 1.1 x .269744 = .2967184   (PW 1, 14%, 10 years)

h. 1.0 – .2967184 = .7032816

i. $330,412 ÷ .7032816 = $469,815.

Proof:

Equity (down payment)	= $469,815 – $320,000
	= $149,815
Annuity (cash flow)	= $15,361
Reversion	= (1.1 x $469,815) – $258,442
	= $516,797 – $258,442
	= $258,355
Value of Equity	= ($15,361 x 5.216116) + ($258,355 x .269744)
	= $80,125 + $69,690
	= $149,815, which corresponds precisely with the "target figure"–the original equity or down payment.

Special Note: Procedure as outlined for the computation of value actually gives in arithmetic steps the calculations involved in solving the equation:

$$\text{Equity} = (\text{Net Income} - \text{Debt Service}) \times \text{PW } 1/P$$
$$+ (\text{Resale Value} - \text{Loan Balance}) \times \text{PW } 1$$

Original value is "x" the unknown in the equation. Equity and Resale Value should be expressed in terms of "x."

Mortgage-Equity Worksheets

The following suggested forms may serve as guidelines in the gathering and processing of data:

- "Data Required in the Computation or Selection of Mortgage-Equity Over-All Rate."
  See example of completed form: page 54.
- "Computation of Value Estimate."
  Example: page 68.
- "OAR From Market" and "Equity Yield Rate and Property Value From OAR."
  Example: page 57.
- "Investment Analysis and Proof of Computations."
  Example: pages 78-79.

Data Required
In the Computation or Selection of
Mortgage-Equity Over-All Rate

Holding Period:	_____
Equity Yield Rate:	_____
Mortgage Specifications:	
Loan Ratio:	_____
Interest Rate:	_____
Term:	_____
Amortization Interval:	_____
Equity Ratio:	_____
Appreciation/Depreciation:	_____
Over-All Rate:	_____

(Note: All variables are built into the OAR. This form can serve as a checklist of data to be gathered by the appraiser.)

Computation of Value Estimate
Mortgage-Equity Technique

Data Required:

Holding Period: _____

Equity Yield Rate: _____

Mortgage Specifications:

    Loan Ratio: _____

    Interest Rate: _____

    Term: _____

    Amortization Interval: _____

Equity Ratio: _____

Appreciation/Depreciation: _____

Net Annual Income*: _____

Valuation:

    Over-All Rate: _____

    Value = Income ÷ Rate

    = _____ ÷ _____

    = _____

*Use net annual income processed to the point at which it can be capitalized as a level ordinary annuity.

OAR From Market

Sale Number	I	II	III	IV
Date of Sale				
Location				
Adjusted Sales Price				
Gross Income				
Eff. Gr. @ % VAC FAC				
Expenses or Expense Ratio				
Net Income				
Comparability				
OAR				

Equity Yield Rate and Property Value from OAR

Holding Period: _____

Mortgage Specifications:

    Loan Ratio: _____

    Interest Rate: _____

    Term: _____

    Amortization Interval: _____

OAR: _____

Appreciation/Depreciation: a. _____ b. _____

Equity Yield Rate:*   a. _____ b. _____

Net Annual Income:

Indicated Value: _____ ÷ _____ = _____
              (Income)   (OAR)

*Calculated from OAR Tables or Compound Interest Tables.
See Alternate Procedures.

Investment Analysis and Proof of Computations
Fourteen-Point Summary of Calculations

1. Over-All Rate (selected from OAR Tables or computed):   _____

2. Property Value: _____ ÷ _____ = _____
          (Income)   (OAR)

3. Original Equity: _____ x _____ = _____
  (Down Payment) (Equity Ratio)   (Value)

4. Amount of Loan: _____ x _____ = _____
  (Original Principal) (Loan Ratio)   (Value)

5. Debt Service: _____ x _____ = _____
  (Yearly Payments) (Loan Constant)   (Principal)

6. Cash Flow: _____ − _____ = _____
  (Annuity)   (Net Income)   (Debt Service)

7. Rate of Current Yield
On Equity: _____ ÷ _____ = _____
        (Cash Flow)   (Original Equity)

8. Loan Balance: _____ x _____ = _____
  (End Holding Period) (% Unpaid)   (Principal)

9. Resale Value as %
of Original Value: 1.0   ± _____ = _____
     (Orig. Value as a %) (% Appr./Dep.)

10. Resale Value as a
Dollar Amount: _____ x _____ = _____
     (Resale Value as a%) (Original Value)

11. Reversion, Net: _____ − _____ = _____
  (Terminal Equity) (Resale Value)   (Loan Balance)

12. Deferred Yield: _____ − _____ = _____
  (Amount)   (Reversion, Net) (Down Payment)

13. Terminal Equity Ratio: _____ ÷ _____ = _____
     (Reversion, Net)   (Resale Value)

14. Proof of Yield on Equity:

    Factor Selection (from Compound Interest Tables):

        Equity Yield Rate:_____ .   Term in Years:_____ .
                  (Percent)   (Holding Period)

        Present Worth of 1 Per Period: _____
                               (PW 1/P)

        Present Worth of 1:   _____
                               (PW 1)

    Equation of Proof:

        Present Worth = (_____ x _____) + (_____ x_____)
                  (Cash Flow) (PW 1/P)   (Net Reversion) (PW 1)

                =_____ + _____

                =_____

    Final Check:

        Target Figure =   _____
                   (Down Payment,
                   Original Equity)

        Adjustment for Rounding = _____ – _____
                            (Present Worth)   (Target Figure)

                     = _____

               OR

                     = _____ – _____
                        (Target Figure)   (Present Worth)

                     = _____

(Note: For calculations in Items 5 and 8 above, select from the Supplemental Tables the following precomputed factors:
- Loan Constant.
- Percent of loan unpaid at the end of the holding period.)

Investment Analysis and Proof of Computations

Fourteen-Point Summary of Calculations

Notes:

1. The Over-All Rate should be expressed as a decimal. Selection or computation of the OAR must consider all variables. (See Data Required form, page 70.)
2. Income to be capitalized is *net annual income* after allowable expenses (fixed, operating, and reserves for replacements), but before debt service and "recapture."
3. The *original equity* is the *down payment. Equity ratio* is the difference between 100% and the loan ratio. If the loan ratio is 80% of property value, the equity ratio is 100% less 80%, or 20%. Equity ratio and loan ratio add up to 100% of value.

4. *Loan ratio* is 100% less the equity ratio. It is the dollar amount of the loan divided by property value. Value at the time of purchase is the sum of the original equity or down payment and the principal amount of the loan.

5. The *loan constant* is the percent of the original principal amount of the loan which is paid annually to amortize the loan, principal and interest included. If payments are made monthly, the loan constant is 12 times the monthly PR factor. The Supplemental Tables prepared for the instant mortgage-equity technique contain a section of precomputed loan constants for quick reference. *Debt Service* is the annual dollar amount of loan payments to be made.

6. In the mortgage-equity technique, income projected for the holding period is considered to be a level income stream, an ordinary annuity. If irregular it can be processed easily into a level ordinary annuity equivalent. (See Annuity section of mortgage-equity procedures, pages 37 to 42.)

7. The *amount of current yield* is the cash flow: net income less debt service. The *rate of current yield on equity* is found by dividing cash flow by original equity (down payment). The yield rate so computed may be low compared with the desired or required total yield on equity. Full equity yield is actually yield to maturity and includes both current and deferred yield. It is more significant to the knowledgeable investor than current yield, which does not include equity build-up through loan amortization and appreciation.

8. Supplemental Tables provide computations of the *percent of principal remaining unpaid* at the end of a projected holding period. (See also the procedure Principal Balance Unpaid, Percent Of, page 51.)

9. Original value is considered to be 100% or 1.0, to which a percent of appreciation can be added or from which a percent of depreciation can be subtracted. For example: at 20% appreciation, resale value as a percent of original value is 1.0 + .20, or 1.20; at 20% depreciation it is 1.0 −.20, or .80.

10. Resale value as a dollar amount is calculated as of the *end of the holding period.*

11. "Reversion" as generally used in appraisal literature is equated with total resale or terminal value. However, in the mortgage-equity procedures in this text we refer to a *net* reversion as being the seller's calculated and presumed *net* proceeds or terminal equity—resale value less loan balance at the end of the holding period.

12. The net reversion on an economically sound investment consists of two elements: a return to the investor of his original equity or down payment, plus equity growth through loan amortization and possibly appreciation as well. The amount by which the net reversion exceeds the original equity should be considered as *deferred yield on equity.*

13. *Terminal equity ratio* relates net reversion to resale value. In the Case Study, Chapter 4, note that equity ratio at the end of the holding period is 48.8%, compared to an initial equity position of 30%. Another concept relates net reversion to original value: in the sample problem, $612,214 as a percent of $1,044,870—58.6% equity ratio.

14. Proof of the accuracy of the OAR, related calculations, and specified yield on equity can be made by computing the *present worth of the total income stream*, including cash flow and reversion. Present worth factors are selected at the equity yield rate for the term of the holding period. Calculated present worth should equal the original equity or down payment, which is the "target figure." Slight variances will occur because of rounding factors and dollar amounts.

4

Case Study: Casa
Linda Apartments

A garden apartment-complex, nearing completion, is offered for sale by the owner-builder. It is architecturally attractive and is well planned functionally. Construction specifications are average or better. Sixty % of the units in Casa Linda Apartments have been reserved in advance by prospective tenants, indicating a favorable rental market. Plans for a new regional shopping center, about one mile north of the subject property, have just been approved by the city planning commission. The state department of education is negotiating for the purchase of a new state college site a half-mile west of Casa Linda.

A prospective buyer has engaged your services to appraise the property for market value as the basis for negotiating a purchase price. You have determined that a loan can be obtained for 70% of market value at 8% interest with monthly payments to amortize in 30 years. The investor projects a holding period of 10 years before resale, refinancing, or exchange. Based on the economic outlook for the area, scarcity of comparable building sites, market demands, and inflationary trends, he believes that anticipation of 20% appreciation in market value within the holding period would be conservative and realistic. The investor expects a yield of 12% on his equity before income taxes.

As an appraiser, you have constructed a comprehensive operating statement of income and expenses. Allowances have been made for vacancy and collection losses, fixed expenses, operating expenses (including management), and reserves for replacements. You have projected net income over the next 10 years to be an annuity of $85,000 per year. Your task now includes the following computations:

1. Property value, as indicated by the mortgage-equity technique.
2. Investment analysis and proof of equity yield.
3. After income tax analysis and yield on equity.

Suggested solutions to your appraisal problem follow.

Computation of Value Estimate
Mortgage-Equity Technique

Data Required:	
Holding Period:	10 yrs.
Equity Yield Rate:	12%

77

Computation of Value Estimate
Mortgage-Equity Technique
(cont.)

Mortgage Specifications:	
Loan Ratio:	70%
Interest Rate:	8%
Term:	30 yrs.
Amortization Interval:	monthly
Equity Ratio:	30%
Appreciation/Depreciation:	+20%
Net Annual Income*:	$85,000
Valuation:	
Over-All Rate:	.08135
Value = Income ÷ Rate	
= $85,000 ÷ .08135	
= $1,044,870	

*Use net annual income processed to the point at which it can be capitalized as a level ordinary annuity.

Investment Analysis and Proof of Computations
Fourteen-Point Summary of Calculations

1. Over-All Rate (selected from OAR Tables or computed):   .08135

2. Property Value:	$85,000	÷	.08135	=	$1,044,870	
	(Income)		(OAR)			
3. Original Equity:	.30	x	$1,044,870	=	313,460	
(Down Payment)	(Equity Ratio)		(Value)			
4. Amount of Loan:	.70	x	1,044,870	=	731,410	
(Original Principal)	(Loan Ratio)		(Value)			
5. Debt Service:	.08805	x	731,410	=	64,400	
(Yearly Payments)	(Loan Constant)		(Principal)			
6. Cash Flow:	85,000	−	64,400	=	20,600	
(Annuity)	(Net Income)		(Debt Service)			
7. Rate of Current Yield On Equity:	20,600	÷	313,460	=	.0657	
	(Cash Flow)		(Original Equity)			
8. Loan Balance:	.87725	x	731,410	=	641,630	
(End Holding Period)	(% Unpaid)		(Principal)			
9. Resale Value as % of Original Value:	1.0	±	+.20	=	1.20	
	(Orig. Value as a %)		(% Appr./Dep.)			
10. Resale Value as a Dollar Amount:	1.20	x	1,044,870	=	1,253,844	
	(Resale Value as a %)		(Original Value)			
11. Reversion, Net:	1,253,844	−	641,630	=	612,214	
(Terminal Equity)	(Resale Value)		(Loan Balance)			

Investment of Analysis and Proof of Computations
Fourteen-Point Summary of Calculations
(cont.)

---

12. Deferred Yield: $\dfrac{612,214}{\text{(Reversion, Net)}}$ $-\dfrac{313,460}{\text{(Down Payment)}}$ $=$ 298,754
   (Amount)

13. Terminal Equity Ratio: $\dfrac{612,214}{\text{(Reversion, Net)}}$ $\div\dfrac{1,253,844}{\text{(Resale Value)}}$ $=$ .4882

14. Proof of Yield on Equity:
    Factor Selection (from Compound Interest Tables):

        Equity Yield Rate: $\dfrac{12\%}{\text{(Percent)}}$.   Term in Years: $\dfrac{10}{\text{(Holding Period)}}$

        Present Worth of 1 Per Period: $\dfrac{5.65022}{\text{(PW 1/P)}}$

        Present Worth of 1: $\dfrac{.32197}{\text{(PW 1)}}$

    Equation of Proof:

        Present Worth: $\;=\;\underset{\text{(Cash Flow) (PW 1/P)}}{(\$20,600 \times 5.65022)} + \underset{\text{(Net Reversion) (PW 1)}}{(\$612,214 \times .32197)}$

                 $=\;\underline{\$116,395} + \underline{\$197,115}$

                 $=\;\$313,510$

    Final Check:

        Target Figure $=\;\underline{\$313,460}$
                (Down Payment,
                Original Equity)

        Adjustment for Rounding $=\;\underset{\text{(Present Worth)}}{\$313,510} - \underset{\text{(Target Figure)}}{\$313,460}$

                     $=\;\underline{\$50}$

           OR

                   $=\;\underset{\text{(Target Figure)}}{\underline{\hspace{2cm}}} - \underset{\text{(Present Worth)}}{\underline{\hspace{2cm}}}$

                   $=\;\underline{\hspace{2cm}}$

More Proof

It is axiomatic that three factors are of primary significance to the investor. By way of emphasis, we repeat that he is concerned with: (1) What he puts into an investment (down payment); (2) What he gets out of an investment (future net benefits); and (3) The relationship between Points 1 and 2 in terms of yield rate, with full consideration to the time-value of money.

Looking at the valuation problem in the case study and its fourteen-point analysis, we note:

1. What the buyer puts into the investment:
    $313,460 (original equity or down payment).
2. What the investor gets out of the investment:
    $20,600 (cash flow) a year for 10 years,

$612,214 (net reversion) at the end of 10 years. His capital investment of $313,460 is returned, along with an additional $298,754 deferred yield, generated by loan amortization and appreciation of property value.

3. The yield rate was determined to be 12%, relating Points 1 and 2. Proof of this yield on equity was given in Item 14 of the analysis by use of the present worth factors.

To convince the Doubting Thomas from Missouri, we take another approach and offer additional proof of 12% yield on equity, plus a return of capital. The following schedule shows the buildup of equity from $313,460 to $612,214. This results from the fact that *current yield* is *less* than 12% (actually, it is 6.57%) and that only through consideration of *deferred yield* can *12% yield to maturity* be generated. Yield *earned* annually exceeds yield *received* annually.

Look at it this way: The investor requires an anticipated 12% yield on his investment of $313,460. Twelve % of $313,460, if paid by the end of the first year of ownership, would amount to $37,615 cash flow. However, actual cash flow (current yield) is only $20,600, which the investor receives. The result is a shortage of $17,015 ($37,615–$20,600). This deficit is then *added* to the outstanding capital investment of $313,460. The total unrecovered capital amount at the beginning of the second year of ownership is now $330,475 ($313,460 + $17,015). For Year 2, the expected yield is 12% of $330,475, or $39,657. Again, $20,600 yield is received; $19,057 yield is deferred and is added to the prior capital balance of $330,475, for a new outstanding amount of $349,532. Note in the following complete schedule that this routine continues, building up to $612,214 by the end of 10 years. (Slight adjustment is made for rounding of factors, rates, and amounts in all calculations of the investment analysis.) According to projections and computations, the investor's net reversion will amount to $612,214. His original capital investment of $313,460 will then have been returned, and the deferred yield received will have brought the total *yield to maturity* up to a full 12%.

Proof of 12% Yield on Equity
(To Maturity)

Original Equity (down payment): $313,460

Cash Flow (per annum): $20,600

Reversion (net) at end of 10 years: $612,214

Year	Earned	Yield at 12% Received	Deferred	Capital Outstanding (Unrecovered)
0	–	–	–	$313,460
1	$37,615	$20,600	$17,015	330,475
2	39,657	20,600	19,057	349,532

Proof of 12% Yield on Equity
(To Maturity)
(cont.)

3	41,944	20,600	21,344	370,876
4	44,505	20,600	23,905	394,781
5	47,374	20,600	26,774	421,555
6	50,587	20,600	29,987	451,542
7	54,185	20,600	33,585	485,127
8	58,215	20,600	37,615	522,742
9	62,729	20,600	42,129	564,871
10	67,785	20,600	47,185	612,056
	Add adjustment for rounding:		158	612,214
10	Reversion:	612,214		0

A parallel reference to a typical loan situation might help to clarify the concept of deferred yield and outstanding capital buildup. Presume you borrow $50,000 from a friend for five years at 6% interest. You agree to pay interest only at the end of each year, with the entire principal amount due and payable at the end of five years. At the end of the first year $3,000 interest is due (.06 x $50,000). However, you can pay only $2,000 at that time. The lender is willing to accept your payment, even though there is a shortage of $1,000. He says, "We will add the $1,000 which is due but unpaid to the principal amount of $50,000. You now owe $51,000. Six percent interest for the second year will be computed on $51,000, and will amount to $3,060." Procedures in this illustration and in the proof of the mortgage-equity case study are identical; both adjust for the time-value of money.

In our mortgage-equity problem, the investment generates a true 12% yield compounded annually for the full ten-year term. Current yield or cash flow of $20,600 received annually is compoundable. It is cash in hand, which can be reinvested at presumably the same rate of anticipated returns. Yield which is deferred annually is not compoundable, for it is locked in until the time of reversion, the end of the holding period. However, it is compounded, as shown in the prepared schedule of proof. To summarize the point: current yield is *compoundable* yield; deferred yield is *compounded* yield.

After Income Tax Analysis and Yield on Equity (Casa Linda Apartments)

It is assumed that an allocation to land and to improvements is made as follows:

Land:	$ 244,870
Improvements:	800,000
Value:	$1,044,870

Economic life of improvements is estimated to be 40 years. Salvage value is presumed to be an amount sufficient to cover costs of demolition and removal.

The investor elects to use accelerated depreciation of 150%, declining balance, or 3.75% per year (1.5 x .025). He is currently in the 50% tax bracket. Subject to changes in economic status of the investor and in tax legislation, the top tax levy on capital gains is projected as of the end of the holding period: 25% on the first $50,000 and 35% thereafter.

Based on these assumptions, the following suggested analysis is given:

	Year				
	1	2	3	4	5
1. Net Income	85,000	85,000	85,000	85,000	85,000
2. Loan Payment	64,400	64,400	64,400	64,400	64,400
3. Before Tax Cash Flow (1 minus 2)	20,600	20,600	20,600	20,600	20,600
4. Loan Amortization	6,107	6,619	7,168	7,760	8,404
5. Interest	58,293	57,781	57,232	56,640	55,996
6. Depreciation*	30,000	28,875	27,792	26,750	25,747
7. Total Allowable Deductions (5 plus 6)	88,293	86,656	85,024	83,390	81,743
8. Taxable Income (1 minus 7)	<3,293>	<1,656>	<24>	1,610	3,257
9. Income Taxes (50%)	<1,646>	<828>	<12>	805	1,629
10. After Tax Cash Flow (3 minus 9)	22,246	21,428	20,612	19,795	18,971
11. Loan Balance	725,303	718,684	711,516	703,756	695,352
12. Undepreciated Balance	770,000	741,125	713,333	686,583	660,836
13. % Principal Unpaid	.99165	.98260	.97280	.96219	.95070
14. % Paid Off in Year	.00835	.00905	.00980	.01061	.01149
15. Cumulative % Principal	.00835	.01740	.02720	.03781	.04930

*Depreciation is made at the rate of 3.75% per year on a declining balance, starting with a base of $800,000 improvement value the first year.

	Year				
	6	7	8	9	10
1. Net Income	85,000	85,000	85,000	85,000	85,000
2. Loan Payment	64,400	64,400	64,000	64,400	64,400
3. Before Tax Cash Flow (1 minus 2)	20,600	20,600	20,600	20,600	20,600
4. Loan Amortization	9,106	9,859	10,671	11,564	12,522
5. Interest	55,294	54,541	53,729	52,836	51,878
6. Depreciation	24,781	23,852	22,958	22,097	21,268
7. Total Allowable Deductions (5 plus 6)	80,075	78,393	76,687	74,933	73,146

8. Taxable Income (1 minus 7)	4,925	6,607	8,313	10,067	11,854
9. Income Taxes	2,463	3,304	4,157	5,034	5,927
10. After Tax Cash Flow (3 minus 9)	18,137	17,296	16,443	15,566	14,673
11. Loan Balance	686,246	676,387	665,716	654,152	641,630
12. Undepreciated Balance	636,055	612,203	589,245	567,148	545,880
13. % Principal Unpaid	.93825	.92477	.91018	.89437	.87725
14. % Paid Off in Year	.01245	.01348	.01459	.01581	.01712
15. Cumulative % Principal Paid Off	.06175	.07523	.08982	.10563	.12275

Capital Gains Tax Computation:

Undepreciated balance, end of 10 years:
Improvements: $ 545,880
Land: 244,870
                                               $ 790,750
Capital gains:
Resale value: $1,253,844
Less undepreciated balance: 790,750
                                               $ 463,094
Capital gains tax (long term):
$50,000 x .25 = $ 12,500
$413,094 x .35 =   144,583
                                               $ 157,083
Net reversion before tax:
Resale value: $1,253,844
Less loan balance: 641,630
                                               $ 612,214
Net reversion after tax:
Net reversion before tax: $ 612,214
Less capital gains tax: 157,083
                                               $ 455,131

Present Worth of After-Tax Cash Flow
At 12% (Equity Yield Rate)

Year	After Tax Cash Flow	PW 1	Present Worth
1	22,246	x .89286 =	$ 19,863
2	21,428	x .79719 =	17,082
3	20,612	x .71178 =	14,671

Present Worth of After-Tax Cash Flow
At 12% (Equity Yield Rate)
(cont.)

4	19,795	x .63552 =	12,580
5	18,971	x .56743 =	10,765
6	18,137	x .50663 =	9,189
7	17,296	x .45235 =	7,824
8	16,443	x .40388 =	6,641
9	15,566	x .36061 =	5,613
10	14,673	x .32197 =	4,724
			$108,952

Level Annuity Equivalent of After-Tax Cash Flow

Computation:

$108,952 x .176984 = $19,283 (PR, 12%, 10 years)

Proof:

$19,283 x 5.650223 = $108,953 (PW 1/P, 12%, 10 years)

Rate of Yield on Equity, After Tax

Annuity equivalent, after tax: $ 19,283
Reversion, net, after tax: 455,131

Equation:
    Value of original equity = (Annuity x PW 1/P) + (Net Reversion x PW 1)
Target figure: $313,460 (Original equity or down payment)

At 10%:
    $ 19,283 x 6.14457 = $118,486 (PW 1/P, 10%, 10 years)
      455,131 x   .385543 = 175,473 (PW 1, 10%, 10 years)
                                        $293,959

At 9%:
    $ 19,283 x 6.41766 = $123,752 (PW 1/P, 9%, 10 years)
      455,131 x   .42241 = 192,252 (PW 1, 9%, 10 years)
                                      $316,004

Equity yield rate, after taxes: About 9.12%

Ending the Endless

So there you have it—*The Instant Mortgage-Equity Technique.* Now, indeed, any appraiser can! The serious student and the professional appraiser will find the mathematics of mortgage-equity valuation and analysis to be a rewarding, challenging, not too difficult, continuing study. For while there is a last letter in the alphabet, and the last word is sometimes spoken, there is no last number. It's up to you to "turn the tables" that follow in Chapter 5. They are your tools.

5 Tables

Compound Interest and Annuity Tables

3% – 30%

Monthly Periods: 1–360 Months (30 Years)
Annual Periods: 1–40 Periods (40 Years)

Abbreviation	Represents
PW 1	Present Worth Of 1 (Reversion)
PW 1/P	Present Worth Of 1 Per Period (Inwood Coefficient; Annuity)
PR	Periodic Repayment (Partial Payment; Amortization)

Note: The three types of compound interest factors not given in these tables can be calculated from the PW 1 and PR factors as follows:

Future Worth (Amount) Of $1 = 1.0 \div PW\ 1$
Future Worth (Amount) Of 1 Per Period $= 1.0 \div (PR - i)$
Sinking Fund $= PR - i$

("1" represents one dollar, and "i" is the interest rate.)

The PW 1 and PR factors given can do double or triple duty in these ways:

- Dividing by the Present Worth Of 1 factor produces the same answer as multiplying by the Future Worth Of 1 factor.
- Subtract the interest rate from the Periodic Repayment factor and divide by it to make the same computation as multiplying by the Future Worth Of 1 Per Period factor.
- Subtract the interest rate from the Periodic Repayment factor, and you have calculated the Sinking Fund factor.

3.0 PERCENT NOMINAL ANNUAL RATE   3.5 PERCENT NOMINAL ANNUAL RATE

.250 PERCENT EFFECTIVE MONTHLY RATE   .292 PERCENT EFFECTIVE MONTHLY RATE

MONTHS	PW 1	PW 1/P	PR	PW 1	PW 1/P	PR	MONTHS
1	.99751	.99751	1.00250	.99709	.99709	1.00292	1
2	.99502	1.99252	.50188	.99419	1.99128	.50219	2
3	.99254	2.98506	.33500	.99130	2.98258	.33528	3
4	.99006	3.97512	.25156	.98842	3.97100	.25183	4
5	.98759	4.96272	.20150	.98554	4.95655	.20175	5
6	.98513	5.94785	.16813	.98268	5.93922	.16837	6
7	.98267	6.93052	.14429	.97982	6.91904	.14453	7
8	.98022	7.91074	.12641	.97697	7.89601	.12665	8
9	.97778	8.88852	.11250	.97413	8.87014	.11274	9
10	.97534	9.86386	.10138	.97130	9.84144	.10161	10
11	.97291	10.83677	.09228	.96847	10.80991	.09251	11
12	.97048	11.80725	.08469	.96565	11.77556	.08492	12

YEARS

MONTHS	PW 1	PW 1/P	PR	YR	PW 1	PW 1/P	PR	MONTHS
12	.97048	11.80725	.08469	1	.96565	11.77556	.08492	12
24	.94184	23.26598	.04298	2	.93249	23.14669	.04320	24
36	.91403	34.38647	.02908	3	.90046	34.12727	.02930	36
48	.88705	45.17869	.02213	4	.86954	44.73072	.02236	48
60	.86087	55.65236	.01797	5	.83967	54.96999	.01819	60
72	.83546	65.81686	.01519	6	.81083	64.85759	.01542	72
84	.81080	75.68132	.01321	7	.78298	74.40559	.01344	84
96	.78686	85.25460	.01173	8	.75609	83.62566	.01196	96
108	.76364	94.54530	.01058	9	.73012	92.52907	.01081	108
120	.74110	103.56175	.00966	10	.70505	101.12669	.00989	120
132	.71922	112.31206	.00890	11	.68083	109.42901	.00914	132
144	.69799	120.80407	.00828	12	.65745	117.44619	.00851	144
156	.67739	129.04541	.00775	13	.63487	125.18802	.00799	156
168	.65739	137.04349	.00730	14	.61306	132.66395	.00754	168
180	.63799	144.80547	.00691	15	.59201	139.88312	.00715	180
192	.61915	152.33834	.00656	16	.57167	146.85434	.00681	192
204	.60088	159.64885	.00626	17	.55204	153.58613	.00651	204
216	.58314	166.74357	.00600	18	.53308	160.08672	.00625	216
228	.56593	173.62886	.00576	19	.51477	166.36404	.00601	228
240	.54922	180.31091	.00555	20	.49709	172.42577	.00580	240
252	.53301	186.79573	.00535	21	.48002	178.27930	.00561	252
264	.51728	193.08912	.00518	22	.46353	183.93179	.00544	264
276	.50201	199.19674	.00502	23	.44761	189.39014	.00528	276
288	.48719	205.12408	.00488	24	.43224	194.66103	.00514	288
300	.47281	210.87645	.00474	25	.41739	199.75088	.00501	300
312	.45885	216.45903	.00462	26	.40306	204.66592	.00489	312
324	.44531	221.87681	.00451	27	.38921	209.41215	.00478	324
336	.43216	227.13468	.00440	28	.37585	213.99538	.00467	336
348	.41941	232.23734	.00431	29	.36294	218.42118	.00458	348
360	.40703	237.18938	.00422	30	.35047	222.69498	.00449	360

4.0 PERCENT NOMINAL ANNUAL RATE			4.5 PERCENT NOMINAL ANNUAL RATE			
.333 PERCENT EFFECTIVE MONTHLY RATE			.375 PERCENT EFFECTIVE MONTHLY RATE			
MONTHS	PW 1	PW 1/P	PR	PW 1	PW 1/P	PR	MONTHS

MONTHS	PW 1	PW 1/P	PR	PW 1	PW 1/P	PR	MONTHS
1	.99668	.99668	1.00333	.99626	.99626	1.00375	1
2	.99337	1.99004	.50250	.99254	1.98881	.50281	2
3	.99007	2.98011	.33556	.98883	2.97764	.33584	3
4	.98678	3.96689	.25209	.98514	3.96278	.25235	4
5	.98350	4.95039	.20200	.98146	4.94424	.20226	5
6	.98023	5.93062	.16862	.97779	5.92203	.16886	6
7	.97697	6.90759	.14477	.97414	6.89617	.14501	7
8	.97373	7.88132	.12688	.97050	7.86667	.12712	8
9	.97049	8.85182	.11297	.96687	8.83354	.11320	9
10	.96727	9.81908	.10184	.96326	9.79681	.10207	10
11	.96406	10.78314	.09274	.95966	10.75647	.09297	11
12	.96085	11.74399	.08515	.95608	11.71255	.08538	12

YEARS

MONTHS	PW 1	PW 1/P	PR	YEARS	PW 1	PW 1/P	PR	MONTHS
12	.96085	11.74399	.08515	1	.95608	11.71255	.08538	12
24	.92324	23.02825	.04342	2	.91409	22.91066	.04365	24
36	.88710	33.87077	.02952	3	.87394	33.61692	.02975	36
48	.85237	44.28883	.02258	4	.83555	43.85294	.02280	48
60	.81900	54.29907	.01842	5	.79885	53.63938	.01864	60
72	.78694	63.91744	.01565	6	.76377	62.99598	.01587	72
84	.75614	73.15928	.01367	7	.73022	71.94161	.01390	84
96	.72654	82.03933	.01219	8	.69815	80.49434	.01242	96
108	.69809	90.57176	.01104	9	.66748	88.67141	.01128	108
120	.67077	98.77017	.01012	10	.63817	96.48932	.01036	120
132	.64451	106.64765	.00938	11	.61014	103.96386	.00962	132
144	.61928	114.21674	.00876	12	.58334	111.11010	.00900	144
156	.59503	121.48954	.00823	13	.55772	117.94247	.00848	156
168	.57174	128.47762	.00778	14	.53322	124.47474	.00803	168
180	.54936	135.19215	.00740	15	.50980	130.72010	.00765	180
192	.52785	141.64382	.00706	16	.48741	136.69115	.00732	192
204	.50719	147.84294	.00676	17	.46600	142.39994	.00702	204
216	.48734	153.79938	.00650	18	.44553	147.85799	.00676	216
228	.46826	159.52264	.00627	19	.42596	153.07632	.00653	228
240	.44993	165.02186	.00606	20	.40725	158.06544	.00633	240
252	.43231	170.30580	.00587	21	.38937	162.83543	.00614	252
264	.41539	175.38289	.00570	22	.37227	167.39591	.00597	264
276	.39913	180.26124	.00555	23	.35591	171.75608	.00582	276
288	.38350	184.94861	.00541	24	.34028	175.92475	.00568	288
300	.36849	189.45248	.00528	25	.32534	179.91032	.00556	300
312	.35407	193.78005	.00516	26	.31105	183.72084	.00544	312
324	.34021	197.93820	.00505	27	.29739	187.36399	.00534	324
336	.32689	201.93358	.00495	28	.28432	190.84713	.00524	336
348	.31409	205.77255	.00486	29	.27184	194.17728	.00515	348
360	.30180	209.46124	.00477	30	.25990	197.36116	.00507	360

91

5.0 PERCENT NOMINAL ANNUAL RATE   5.5 PERCENT NOMINAL ANNUAL RATE

.417 PERCENT EFFECTIVE MONTHLY RATE   .458 PERCENT EFFECTIVE MONTHLY RATE

MONTHS	PW 1	PW 1/P	PR	PW 1	PW 1/P	PR	MONTHS
1	.99585	.99585	1.00417	.99544	.99544	1.00458	1
2	.99172	1.98757	.50313	.99090	1.98633	.50344	2
3	.98760	2.97517	.33611	.98638	2.97271	.33639	3
4	.98351	3.95868	.25261	.98187	3.95458	.25287	4
5	.97942	4.93810	.20251	.97740	4.93198	.20276	5
6	.97536	5.91346	.16911	.97294	5.90491	.16935	6
7	.97131	6.88478	.14525	.96850	6.87341	.14549	7
8	.96728	7.85206	.12736	.96408	7.83749	.12759	8
9	.96327	8.81533	.11344	.95968	8.79717	.11367	9
10	.95927	9.77460	.10231	.95530	9.75247	.10254	10
11	.95529	10.72989	.09320	.95094	10.70341	.09343	11
12	.95133	11.68122	.08561	.94660	11.65002	.08584	12

YEARS

MONTHS	PW 1	PW 1/P	PR	YEARS	PW 1	PW 1/P	PR	MONTHS
12	.95133	11.68122	.08561	1	.94660	11.65002	.08584	12
24	.90503	22.79390	.04387	2	.89606	22.67797	.04410	24
36	.86098	33.36570	.02997	3	.84821	33.11708	.03020	36
48	.81907	43.42296	.02303	4	.80292	42.99878	.02326	48
60	.77921	52.99071	.01887	5	.76005	52.35284	.01910	60
72	.74128	62.09278	.01610	6	.71947	61.20743	.01634	72
84	.70520	70.75183	.01413	7	.68105	69.58922	.01437	84
96	.67088	78.98944	.01266	8	.64468	77.52345	.01290	96
108	.63822	86.82611	.01152	9	.61026	85.03403	.01176	108
120	.60716	94.28135	.01061	10	.57768	92.14358	.01085	120
132	.57761	101.37373	.00986	11	.54683	98.87351	.01011	132
144	.54950	108.12092	.00925	12	.51763	105.24408	.00950	144
156	.52275	114.53970	.00873	13	.48999	111.27450	.00899	156
168	.49731	120.64608	.00829	14	.46383	116.98291	.00855	168
180	.47310	126.45524	.00791	15	.43906	122.38652	.00817	180
192	.45008	131.98167	.00758	16	.41562	127.50160	.00784	192
204	.42817	137.23911	.00729	17	.39343	132.34355	.00756	204
216	.40733	142.24066	.00703	18	.37242	136.92696	.00730	216
228	.38751	146.99878	.00680	19	.35253	141.26564	.00708	228
240	.36864	151.52531	.00660	20	.33371	145.37265	.00688	240
252	.35070	155.83153	.00642	21	.31589	149.26036	.00670	252
264	.33363	159.92816	.00625	22	.29902	152.94048	.00654	264
276	.31739	163.82540	.00610	23	.28306	156.42411	.00639	276
288	.30195	167.53295	.00597	24	.26794	159.72171	.00626	288
300	.28725	171.06005	.00585	25	.25364	162.84325	.00614	300
312	.27327	174.41548	.00573	26	.24009	165.79810	.00603	312
324	.25997	177.60759	.00563	27	.22727	168.59518	.00593	324
336	.24732	180.64434	.00554	28	.21514	171.24290	.00584	336
348	.23528	183.53328	.00545	29	.20365	173.74925	.00576	348
360	.22383	186.28162	.00537	30	.19278	176.12176	.00568	360

6.0 PERCENT NOMINAL ANNUAL RATE

6.5 PERCENT NOMINAL ANNUAL RATE

.500 PERCENT EFFECTIVE MONTHLY RATE

.542 PERCENT EFFECTIVE MONTHLY RATE

MONTHS	PW 1	PW 1/P	PR	PW 1	PW 1/P	PR	MONTHS
1	.99502	.99502	1.00500	.99461	.99461	1.00542	1
2	.99007	1.98510	.50375	.98925	1.98387	.50407	2
3	.98515	2.97025	.33667	.98392	2.96779	.33695	3
4	.98025	3.95050	.25313	.97862	3.94641	.25339	4
5	.97537	4.92587	.20301	.97335	4.91977	.20326	5
6	.97052	5.89638	.16960	.96811	5.88787	.16984	6
7	.96569	6.86207	.14573	.96289	6.85076	.14597	7
8	.96089	7.82296	.12783	.95770	7.80847	.12807	8
9	.95610	8.77906	.11391	.95254	8.76101	.11414	9
10	.95135	9.73041	.10277	.94741	9.70843	.10300	10
11	.94661	10.67703	.09366	.94231	10.65073	.09389	11
12	.94191	11.61893	.08607	.93723	11.58797	.08630	12

YEARS

MONTHS	PW 1	PW 1/P	PR		PW 1	PW 1/P	PR	MONTHS
12	.94191	11.61893	.08607	1	.93723	11.58797	.08630	12
24	.88719	22.56287	.04432	2	.87840	22.44858	.04455	24
36	.83564	32.87102	.03042	3	.82327	32.62749	.03065	36
48	.78710	42.58032	.02349	4	.77159	42.16749	.02371	48
60	.74137	51.72556	.01933	5	.72316	51.10868	.01957	60
72	.69830	60.33951	.01657	6	.67777	59.48865	.01681	72
84	.65773	68.45304	.01461	7	.63523	67.34262	.01485	84
96	.61952	76.09522	.01314	8	.59536	74.70362	.01339	96
108	.58353	83.29342	.01201	9	.55799	81.60258	.01225	108
120	.54963	90.07345	.01110	10	.52296	88.06850	.01135	120
132	.51770	96.45960	.01037	11	.49014	94.12857	.01062	132
144	.48763	102.47474	.00976	12	.45937	99.80826	.01002	144
156	.45930	108.14044	.00925	13	.43054	105.13145	.00951	156
168	.43262	113.47699	.00881	14	.40351	110.12051	.00908	168
180	.40748	118.50351	.00844	15	.37819	114.79641	.00871	180
192	.38381	123.23803	.00811	16	.35445	119.17882	.00839	192
204	.36151	127.69749	.00783	17	.33220	123.28615	.00811	204
216	.34051	131.89788	.00758	18	.31135	127.13567	.00787	216
228	.32073	135.85425	.00736	19	.29181	130.74357	.00765	228
240	.30210	139.58077	.00716	20	.27349	134.12500	.00746	240
252	.28455	143.09081	.00699	21	.25632	137.29419	.00728	252
264	.26802	146.39693	.00683	22	.24023	140.26446	.00713	264
276	.25245	149.51098	.00669	23	.22516	143.04828	.00699	276
288	.23778	152.44412	.00656	24	.21102	145.65737	.00687	288
300	.22397	155.20686	.00644	25	.19778	148.10269	.00675	300
312	.21095	157.80911	.00634	26	.18536	150.39453	.00665	312
324	.19870	160.26017	.00624	27	.17373	152.54251	.00656	324
336	.18716	162.56884	.00615	28	.16282	154.55566	.00647	336
348	.17628	164.74339	.00607	29	.15260	156.44246	.00639	348
360	.16604	166.79161	.00600	30	.14302	158.21082	.00632	360

7.0 PERCENT NOMINAL ANNUAL RATE   7.5 PERCENT NOMINAL ANNUAL RATE

.583 PERCENT EFFECTIVE MONTHLY RATE   .625 PERCENT EFFECTIVE MONTHLY RATE

MONTHS	PW 1	PW 1/P	PR	PW 1	PW 1/P	PR	MONTHS
1	.99420	.99420	1.00583	.99379	.99379	1.00625	1
2	.98843	1.98264	.50438	.98762	1.98141	.50469	2
3	.98270	2.96534	.33723	.98148	2.96289	.33751	3
4	.97700	3.94234	.25366	.97539	3.93827	.25392	4
5	.97134	4.91368	.20351	.96933	4.90760	.20377	5
6	.96570	5.87938	.17009	.96331	5.87091	.17033	6
7	.96010	6.83948	.14621	.95732	6.82823	.14645	7
8	.95453	7.79402	.12830	.95138	7.77961	.12854	8
9	.94900	8.74302	.11438	.94547	8.72508	.11461	9
10	.94350	9.68651	.10324	.93960	9.66467	.10347	10
11	.93802	10.62454	.09412	.93376	10.59843	.09435	11
12	.93258	11.55712	.08653	.92796	11.52639	.08676	12

YEARS

MONTHS	PW 1	PW 1/P	PR	YEARS	PW 1	PW 1/P	PR	MONTHS
12	.93258	11.55712	.08653	1	.92796	11.52639	.08676	12
24	.86971	22.33510	.04477	2	.86111	22.22242	.04500	24
36	.81108	32.38646	.03088	3	.79908	32.14791	.03111	36
48	.75640	41.76020	.02395	4	.74151	41.35837	.02418	48
60	.70541	50.50199	.01980	5	.68809	49.90531	.02004	60
72	.65785	58.65444	.01705	6	.63852	57.83652	.01729	72
84	.61350	66.25729	.01509	7	.59252	65.19638	.01534	84
96	.57214	73.34757	.01363	8	.54984	72.02602	.01388	96
108	.53357	79.95985	.01251	9	.51023	78.36367	.01276	108
120	.49760	86.12635	.01161	10	.47347	84.24474	.01187	120
132	.46405	91.87713	.01088	11	.43936	89.70215	.01115	132
144	.43277	97.24022	.01028	12	.40771	94.76640	.01055	144
156	.40359	102.24174	.00978	13	.37834	99.46583	.01005	156
168	.37638	106.90607	.00935	14	.35108	103.82671	.00963	168
180	.35101	111.25596	.00899	15	.32579	107.87343	.00927	180
192	.32734	115.31259	.00867	16	.30232	111.62862	.00896	192
204	.30527	119.09573	.00840	17	.28054	115.11329	.00869	204
216	.28469	122.62383	.00816	18	.26033	118.34693	.00845	216
228	.26550	125.91408	.00794	19	.24158	121.34762	.00824	228
240	.24760	128.98251	.00775	20	.22417	124.13213	.00806	240
252	.23091	131.84407	.00758	21	.20802	126.71605	.00789	252
264	.21534	134.51272	.00743	22	.19304	129.11382	.00775	264
276	.20082	137.00146	.00730	23	.17913	131.33886	.00761	276
288	.18729	139.32242	.00718	24	.16623	133.40361	.00750	288
300	.17466	141.48690	.00707	25	.15425	135.31961	.00739	300
312	.16288	143.50547	.00697	26	.14314	137.09759	.00729	312
324	.15190	145.38795	.00688	27	.13283	138.74748	.00721	324
336	.14166	147.14351	.00680	28	.12326	140.27851	.00713	336
348	.13211	148.78073	.00672	29	.11438	141.69924	.00706	348
360	.12321	150.30757	.00665	30	.10614	143.01763	.00699	360

8.0 PERCENT NOMINAL ANNUAL RATE   8.5 PERCENT NOMINAL ANNUAL RATE

.667 PERCENT EFFECTIVE MONTHLY RATE   .708 PERCENT EFFECTIVE MONTHLY RATE

MONTHS	PW 1	PW 1/P	PR	PW 1	PW 1/P	PR	MONTHS
1	.99338	.99338	1.00667	.99297	.99297	1.00708	1
2	.98680	1.98018	.50501	.98598	1.97895	.50532	2
3	.98026	2.96044	.33779	.97905	2.95800	.33807	3
4	.97377	3.93421	.25418	.97216	3.93016	.25444	4
5	.96732	4.90154	.20402	.96532	4.89548	.20427	5
6	.96092	5.86245	.17058	.95853	5.85402	.17082	6
7	.95455	6.81701	.14669	.95179	6.80581	.14693	7
8	.94823	7.76524	.12878	.94510	7.75091	.12902	8
9	.94195	8.70719	.11485	.93845	8.68936	.11508	9
10	.93571	9.64290	.10370	.93185	9.62121	.10394	10
11	.92952	10.57242	.09459	.92530	10.54650	.09482	11
12	.92336	11.49578	.08699	.91879	11.46529	.08722	12

YEARS

MONTHS	PW 1	PW 1/P	PR		PW 1	PW 1/P	PR	MONTHS
12	.92336	11.49578	.08699	1	.91879	11.46529	.08722	12
24	.85260	22.11054	.04523	2	.84417	21.99945	.04546	24
36	.78725	31.91181	.03134	3	.77561	31.67811	.03157	36
48	.72692	40.96191	.02441	4	.71262	40.57074	.02465	48
60	.67121	49.31843	.02028	5	.65475	48.74118	.02052	60
72	.61977	57.03452	.01753	6	.60158	56.24808	.01778	72
84	.57227	64.15926	.01559	7	.55272	63.14532	.01584	84
96	.52841	70.73797	.01414	8	.50783	69.48243	.01439	96
108	.48792	76.81250	.01302	9	.46659	75.30488	.01328	108
120	.45052	82.42148	.01213	10	.42870	80.65447	.01240	120
132	.41600	87.60060	.01142	11	.39388	85.56961	.01169	132
144	.38411	92.38280	.01082	12	.36189	90.08558	.01110	144
156	.35468	96.79850	.01033	13	.33250	94.23480	.01061	156
168	.32749	100.87578	.00991	14	.30550	98.04705	.01020	168
180	.30240	104.64059	.00956	15	.28069	101.54969	.00985	180
192	.27922	108.11687	.00925	16	.25789	104.76788	.00954	192
204	.25782	111.32673	.00898	17	.23695	107.72471	.00928	204
216	.23806	114.29060	.00875	18	.21771	110.44141	.00905	216
228	.21982	117.02731	.00855	19	.20003	112.93748	.00885	228
240	.20297	119.55429	.00836	20	.18378	115.23084	.00868	240
252	.18742	121.88761	.00820	21	.16886	117.33795	.00852	252
264	.17305	124.04210	.00806	22	.15514	119.27393	.00838	264
276	.15979	126.03148	.00793	23	.14254	121.05269	.00826	276
288	.14754	127.86839	.00782	24	.13097	122.68699	.00815	288
300	.13624	129.56452	.00772	25	.12033	124.18857	.00805	300
312	.12580	131.13067	.00763	26	.11056	125.56820	.00796	312
324	.11615	132.57679	.00754	27	.10158	126.83579	.00788	324
336	.10725	133.91208	.00747	28	.09333	128.00043	.00781	336
348	.09903	135.14503	.00740	29	.08575	129.07049	.00775	348
360	.09144	136.28349	.00734	30	.07879	130.05364	.00769	360

9.0 PERCENT NOMINAL ANNUAL RATE   10.0 PERCENT NOMINAL ANNUAL RATE

.750 PERCENT EFFECTIVE MONTHLY RATE   .833 PERCENT EFFECTIVE MONTHLY RATE

MONTHS	PW 1	PW 1/P	PR		PW 1	PW 1/P	PR	MONTHS
1	.99256	.99256	1.00750		.99174	.99174	1.00833	1
2	.98517	1.97772	.50563		.98354	1.97527	.50626	2
3	.97783	2.95556	.33835		.97541	2.95069	.33890	3
4	.97055	3.92611	.25471		.96735	3.91804	.25523	4
5	.96333	4.88944	.20452		.95936	4.87739	.20503	5
6	.95616	5.84560	.17107		.95143	5.82882	.17156	6
7	.94904	6.79464	.14717		.94356	6.77238	.14766	7
8	.94198	7.73661	.12926		.93577	7.70815	.12973	8
9	.93496	8.67158	.11532		.92803	8.63618	.11579	9
10	.92800	9.59958	.10417		.92036	9.55654	.10464	10
11	.92109	10.52067	.09505		.91276	10.46930	.09552	11
12	.91424	11.43491	.08745		.90521	11.37451	.08792	12

YEARS

MONTHS	PW 1	PW 1/P	PR		PW 1	PW 1/P	PR	MONTHS
12	.91424	11.43491	.08745	1	.90521	11.37451	.08792	12
24	.83583	21.88915	.04568	2	.81941	21.67085	.04614	24
36	.76415	31.44681	.03180	3	.74174	30.99124	.03227	36
48	.69861	40.18478	.02489	4	.67143	39.42816	.02536	48
60	.63870	48.17337	.02076	5	.60779	47.06537	.02125	60
72	.58392	55.47685	.01803	6	.55018	53.97867	.01853	72
84	.53385	62.15396	.01609	7	.49803	60.23667	.01660	84
96	.48806	68.25844	.01465	8	.45082	65.90149	.01517	96
108	.44620	73.83938	.01354	9	.40809	71.02935	.01408	108
120	.40794	78.94169	.01267	10	.36941	75.67116	.01322	120
132	.37295	83.60642	.01196	11	.33439	79.87299	.01252	132
144	.34097	87.87109	.01138	12	.30270	83.67653	.01195	144
156	.31172	91.77002	.01090	13	.27400	87.11954	.01148	156
168	.28499	95.33456	.01049	14	.24803	90.23620	.01108	168
180	.26055	98.59341	.01014	15	.22452	93.05744	.01075	180
192	.23820	101.57277	.00985	16	.20324	95.61126	.01046	192
204	.21778	104.29661	.00959	17	.18397	97.92301	.01021	204
216	.19910	106.78686	.00936	18	.16654	100.01563	.01000	216
228	.18202	109.06353	.00917	19	.15075	101.90990	.00981	228
240	.16641	111.14495	.00900	20	.13646	103.62462	.00965	240
252	.15214	113.04787	.00885	21	.12353	105.17680	.00951	252
264	.13909	114.78759	.00871	22	.11182	106.58186	.00938	264
276	.12716	116.37811	.00859	23	.10122	107.85373	.00927	276
288	.11626	117.83222	.00849	24	.09162	109.00504	.00917	288
300	.10629	119.16162	.00839	25	.08294	110.04723	.00909	300
312	.09717	120.37701	.00831	26	.07508	110.99063	.00901	312
324	.08884	121.48817	.00823	27	.06796	111.84461	.00894	324
336	.08122	122.50403	.00816	28	.06152	112.61764	.00888	336
348	.07425	123.43278	.00810	29	.05569	113.31739	.00882	348
360	.06789	124.28187	.00805	30	.05041	113.95082	.00878	360

11.0 PERCENT NOMINAL ANNUAL RATE   12.0 PERCENT NOMINAL ANNUAL RATE

.917 PERCENT EFFECTIVE MONTHLY RATE   1.000 PERCENT EFFECTIVE MONTHLY RATE

MONTHS	PW 1	PW 1/P	PR	PW 1	PW 1/P	PR	MONTHS
1	.99092	.99092	1.00917	.99010	.99010	1.01000	1
2	.98192	1.97283	.50689	.98030	1.97040	.50751	2
3	.97300	2.94583	.33946	.97059	2.94099	.34002	3
4	.96416	3.90999	.25576	.96098	3.90197	.25628	4
5	.95540	4.86539	.20553	.95147	4.85343	.20604	5
6	.94672	5.81211	.17205	.94205	5.79548	.17255	6
7	.93812	6.75023	.14814	.93272	6.72819	.14863	7
8	.92960	7.67983	.13021	.92348	7.65168	.13069	8
9	.92116	8.60099	.11627	.91434	8.56602	.11674	9
10	.91279	9.51378	.10511	.90529	9.47130	.10558	10
11	.90450	10.41828	.09599	.89632	10.36763	.09645	11
12	.89628	11.31456	.08838	.88745	11.25508	.08885	12

YEARS

MONTHS	PW 1	PW 1/P	PR	YEARS	PW 1	PW 1/P	PR	MONTHS
12	.89628	11.31456	.08838	1	.88745	11.25508	.08885	12
24	.80332	21.45562	.04661	2	.78757	21.24339	.04707	24
36	.72001	30.54487	.03274	3	.69892	30.10751	.03321	36
48	.64533	38.69142	.02585	4	.62026	37.97396	.02633	48
60	.57840	45.99303	.02174	5	.55045	44.95504	.02224	60
72	.51841	52.53735	.01903	6	.48850	51.15039	.01955	72
84	.46464	58.40290	.01712	7	.43352	56.64845	.01765	84
96	.41645	63.66010	.01571	8	.38472	61.52770	.01625	96
108	.37326	68.37204	.01463	9	.34142	65.85779	.01518	108
120	.33454	72.59528	.01378	10	.30299	69.70052	.01435	120
132	.29985	76.38049	.01309	11	.26889	73.11075	.01368	132
144	.26875	79.77311	.01254	12	.23863	76.13716	.01313	144
156	.24087	82.81386	.01208	13	.21177	78.82294	.01269	156
168	.21589	85.53923	.01169	14	.18794	81.20643	.01231	168
180	.19350	87.98194	.01137	15	.16678	83.32166	.01200	180
192	.17343	90.17129	.01109	16	.14801	85.19882	.01174	192
204	.15544	92.13358	.01085	17	.13135	86.86471	.01151	204
216	.13932	93.89234	.01065	18	.11657	88.34309	.01132	216
228	.12487	95.46868	.01047	19	.10345	89.65509	.01115	228
240	.11192	96.88154	.01032	20	.09181	90.81942	.01101	240
252	.10031	98.14786	.01019	21	.08147	91.85270	.01089	252
264	.08991	99.28284	.01007	22	.07230	92.76968	.01078	264
276	.08058	100.30010	.00997	23	.06417	93.58346	.01069	276
288	.07222	101.21185	.00988	24	.05694	94.30565	.01060	288
300	.06473	102.02904	.00980	25	.05053	94.94655	.01053	300
312	.05802	102.76148	.00973	26	.04485	95.51532	.01047	312
324	.05200	103.41795	.00967	27	.03980	96.02007	.01041	324
336	.04661	104.00633	.00961	28	.03532	96.46802	.01037	336
348	.04177	104.53369	.00957	29	.03134	96.86555	.01032	348
360	.03744	105.00635	.00952	30	.02782	97.21833	.01029	360

13.0 PERCENT NOMINAL ANNUAL RATE   14.0 PERCENT NOMINAL ANNUAL RATE

1.083 PERCENT EFFECTIVE MONTHLY RATE   1.167 PERCENT EFFECTIVE MONTHLY RATE

MONTHS	PW 1	PW 1/P	PR	PW 1	PW 1/P	PR	MONTHS
1	.98928	.98928	1.01083	.98847	.98847	1.01167	1
2	.97868	1.96796	.50814	.97707	1.96554	.50877	2
3	.96819	2.93615	.34058	.96580	2.93134	.34114	3
4	.95782	3.89397	.25681	.95466	3.88600	.25733	4
5	.94755	4.84152	.20655	.94365	4.82966	.20705	5
6	.93740	5.77892	.17304	.93277	5.76243	.17354	6
7	.92735	6.70626	.14911	.92201	6.68444	.14960	7
8	.91741	7.62367	.13117	.91138	7.59582	.13165	8
9	.90758	8.53125	.11722	.90087	8.49670	.11769	9
10	.89785	9.42910	.10605	.89048	9.38718	.10653	10
11	.88823	10.31733	.09692	.88021	10.26739	.09740	11
12	.87871	11.19604	.08932	.87006	11.13746	.08979	12

YEARS

MONTHS	PW 1	PW 1/P	PR	YRS	PW 1	PW 1/P	PR	MONTHS
12	.87871	11.19604	.08932	1	.87006	11.13746	.08979	12
24	.77213	21.03411	.04754	2	.75701	20.82774	.04801	24
36	.67848	29.67892	.03369	3	.65865	29.25890	.03418	36
48	.59619	37.27519	.02683	4	.57306	36.59455	.02733	48
60	.52387	43.95011	.02275	5	.49860	42.97702	.02327	60
72	.46033	49.81542	.02007	6	.43381	48.53017	.02061	72
84	.40450	54.96933	.01819	7	.37745	53.36176	.01874	84
96	.35544	59.49812	.01681	8	.32840	57.56555	.01737	96
108	.31233	63.47760	.01575	9	.28573	61.22311	.01633	108
120	.27444	66.97442	.01493	10	.24860	64.40542	.01553	120
132	.24116	70.04710	.01428	11	.21630	67.17423	.01489	132
144	.21191	72.74710	.01375	12	.18820	69.58327	.01437	144
156	.18620	75.11961	.01331	13	.16374	71.67928	.01395	156
168	.16362	77.20436	.01295	14	.14247	73.50295	.01360	168
180	.14377	79.03625	.01265	15	.12395	75.08965	.01332	180
192	.12634	80.64595	.01240	16	.10785	76.47019	.01308	192
204	.11101	82.06041	.01219	17	.09383	77.67134	.01287	204
216	.09755	83.30331	.01200	18	.08164	78.71641	.01270	216
228	.08572	84.39545	.01185	19	.07103	79.62570	.01256	228
240	.07532	85.35513	.01172	20	.06180	80.41683	.01244	240
252	.06618	86.19841	.01160	21	.05377	81.10516	.01233	252
264	.05816	86.93941	.01150	22	.04679	81.70406	.01224	264
276	.05110	87.59053	.01142	23	.04071	82.22514	.01216	276
288	.04490	88.16268	.01134	24	.03542	82.67851	.01210	288
300	.03946	88.66543	.01128	25	.03082	83.07297	.01204	300
312	.03467	89.10720	.01122	26	.02681	83.41617	.01199	312
324	.03047	89.49539	.01117	27	.02333	83.71478	.01195	324
336	.02677	89.83649	.01113	28	.02030	83.97459	.01191	336
348	.02352	90.13623	.01109	29	.01766	84.20064	.01188	348
360	.02067	90.39961	.01106	30	.01536	84.39732	.01185	360

15.0 PERCENT NOMINAL ANNUAL RATE   16.0 PERCENT NOMINAL ANNUAL RATE

1.250 PERCENT EFFECTIVE MONTHLY RATE   1.333 PERCENT EFFECTIVE MONTHLY RATE

MONTHS	PW 1	PW 1/P	PR	PW 1	PW 1/P	PR	MONTHS
1	.98765	.98765	1.01250	.98684	.98684	1.01333	1
2	.97546	1.96312	.50939	.97386	1.96070	.51002	2
3	.96342	2.92653	.34170	.96104	2.92174	.34226	3
4	.95152	3.87806	.25786	.94840	3.87014	.25839	4
5	.93978	4.81784	.20756	.93592	4.80606	.20807	5
6	.92817	5.74601	.17403	.92360	5.72966	.17453	6
7	.91672	6.66273	.15009	.91145	6.64112	.15058	7
8	.90540	7.56812	.13213	.89946	7.54058	.13262	8
9	.89422	8.46234	.11817	.88762	8.42820	.11865	9
10	.88318	9.34553	.10700	.87594	9.30414	.10748	10
11	.87228	10.21780	.09787	.86442	10.16856	.09834	11
12	.86151	11.07931	.09026	.85305	11.02161	.09073	12

YEARS

MONTHS	PW 1	PW 1/P	PR		PW 1	PW 1/P	PR	MONTHS
12	.86151	11.07931	.09026	1	.85305	11.02161	.09073	12
24	.74220	20.62423	.04849	2	.72769	20.42354	.04896	24
36	.63941	28.84727	.03467	3	.62075	28.44381	.03516	36
48	.55086	35.93148	.02783	4	.52953	35.28547	.02834	48
60	.47457	42.03459	.02379	5	.45171	41.12171	.02432	60
72	.40884	47.29247	.02115	6	.38533	46.10028	.02169	72
84	.35222	51.82219	.01930	7	.32870	50.34723	.01986	84
96	.30344	55.72457	.01795	8	.28040	53.97008	.01853	96
108	.26142	59.08651	.01692	9	.23919	57.06052	.01753	108
120	.22521	61.98285	.01613	10	.20404	59.69682	.01675	120
132	.19402	64.47807	.01551	11	.17406	61.94569	.01614	132
144	.16715	66.62772	.01501	12	.14848	63.86409	.01566	144
156	.14400	68.47967	.01460	13	.12666	65.50056	.01527	156
168	.12406	70.07513	.01427	14	.10805	66.89655	.01495	168
180	.10688	71.44964	.01400	15	.09217	68.08739	.01469	180
192	.09208	72.63379	.01377	16	.07862	69.10323	.01447	192
204	.07933	73.65395	.01358	17	.06707	69.96979	.01429	204
216	.06834	74.53282	.01342	18	.05721	70.70900	.01414	216
228	.05888	75.28998	.01328	19	.04881	71.33959	.01402	228
240	.05072	75.94228	.01317	20	.04163	71.87750	.01391	240
252	.04370	76.50424	.01307	21	.03552	72.33637	.01382	252
264	.03765	76.98837	.01299	22	.03030	72.72780	.01375	264
276	.03243	77.40546	.01292	23	.02584	73.06171	.01369	276
288	.02794	77.76478	.01286	24	.02205	73.34655	.01363	288
300	.02407	78.07434	.01281	25	.01881	73.58953	.01359	300
312	.02074	78.34102	.01276	26	.01604	73.79681	.01355	312
324	.01787	78.57078	.01273	27	.01369	73.97362	.01352	324
336	.01539	78.76871	.01270	28	.01167	74.12445	.01349	336
348	.01326	78.93924	.01267	29	.00996	74.25312	.01347	348
360	.01142	79.08614	.01264	30	.00849	74.36288	.01345	360

18.0 PERCENT NOMINAL ANNUAL RATE   20.0 PERCENT NOMINAL ANNUAL RATE

1.500 PERCENT EFFECTIVE MONTHLY RATE   1.667 PERCENT EFFECTIVE MONTHLY RATE

MONTHS	PW 1	PW 1/P	PR		PW 1	PW 1/P	PR	MONTHS
1	.98522	.98522	1.01500		.98361	.98361	1.01667	1
2	.97066	1.95588	.51128		.96748	1.95109	.51253	2
3	.95632	2.91220	.34338		.95162	2.90271	.34451	3
4	.94218	3.85438	.25944		.93602	3.83873	.26050	4
5	.92826	4.78264	.20909		.92068	4.75941	.21011	5
6	.91454	5.69719	.17553		.90558	5.66499	.17652	6
7	.90103	6.59821	.15156		.89074	6.55573	.15254	7
8	.88771	7.48593	.13358		.87614	7.43186	.13456	8
9	.87459	8.36052	.11961		.86177	8.29364	.12057	9
10	.86167	9.22218	.10843		.84765	9.14128	.10939	10
11	.84893	10.07112	.09929		.83375	9.97503	.10025	11
12	.83639	10.90751	.09168		.82008	10.79511	.09263	12

YEARS

MONTHS	PW 1	PW 1/P	PR	YEARS	PW 1	PW 1/P	PR	MONTHS
12	.83639	10.90751	.09168	1	.82008	10.79511	.09263	12
24	.69954	20.03041	.04992	2	.67253	19.64799	.05090	24
36	.58509	27.66068	.03615	3	.55153	26.90806	.03716	36
48	.48936	34.04255	.02937	4	.45230	32.86192	.03043	48
60	.40930	39.38027	.02539	5	.37092	37.74456	.02649	60
72	.34233	43.84467	.02281	6	.30419	41.74873	.02395	72
84	.28632	47.57863	.02102	7	.24946	45.03247	.02221	84
96	.23947	50.70168	.01972	8	.20458	47.72541	.02095	96
108	.20029	53.31375	.01876	9	.16777	49.93383	.02003	108
120	.16752	55.49845	.01802	10	.13758	51.74492	.01933	120
132	.14011	57.32571	.01744	11	.11283	53.23017	.01879	132
144	.11719	58.85401	.01699	12	.09253	54.44818	.01837	144
156	.09802	60.13226	.01663	13	.07588	55.44706	.01804	156
168	.08198	61.20137	.01634	14	.06223	56.26622	.01777	168
180	.06857	62.09556	.01610	15	.05103	56.93799	.01756	180
192	.05735	62.84345	.01591	16	.04185	57.48891	.01739	192
204	.04797	63.46898	.01576	17	.03432	57.94070	.01726	204
216	.04012	63.99216	.01563	18	.02815	58.31120	.01715	216
228	.03355	64.42974	.01552	19	.02308	58.61505	.01706	228
240	.02806	64.79573	.01543	20	.01893	58.86423	.01699	240
252	.02347	65.10184	.01536	21	.01552	59.06857	.01693	252
264	.01963	65.35787	.01530	22	.01273	59.23616	.01688	264
276	.01642	65.57200	.01525	23	.01044	59.37359	.01684	276
288	.01373	65.75110	.01521	24	.00856	59.48629	.01681	288
300	.01149	65.90090	.01517	25	.00702	59.57872	.01678	300
312	.00961	66.02619	.01515	26	.00576	59.65451	.01676	312
324	.00804	66.13098	.01512	27	.00472	59.71667	.01675	324
336	.00672	66.21862	.01510	28	.00387	59.76765	.01673	336
348	.00562	66.29193	.01508	29	.00318	59.80945	.01672	348
360	.00470	66.35324	.01507	30	.00260	59.84374	.01671	360

25.0 PERCENT NOMINAL ANNUAL RATE   30.0 PERCENT NOMINAL ANNUAL RATE

2.083 PERCENT EFFECTIVE MONTHLY RATE   2.500 PERCENT EFFECTIVE MONTHLY RATE

MONTHS	PW 1	PW 1/P	PR	PW 1	PW 1/P	PR	MONTHS
1	.97959	.97959	1.02083	.97561	.97561	1.02500	1
2	.95960	1.93919	.51568	.95181	1.92742	.51883	2
3	.94002	2.87921	.34732	.92860	2.85602	.35014	3
4	.92083	3.80004	.26316	.90595	3.76197	.26582	4
5	.90204	4.70208	.21267	.88385	4.64583	.21525	5
6	.88363	5.58571	.17903	.86230	5.50813	.18155	6
7	.86560	6.45131	.15501	.84127	6.34939	.15750	7
8	.84793	7.29924	.13700	.82075	7.17014	.13947	8
9	.83063	8.12987	.12300	.80073	7.97087	.12546	9
10	.81368	8.94355	.11181	.78120	8.75206	.11426	10
11	.79707	9.74062	.10266	.76214	9.51421	.10511	11
12	.78080	10.52142	.09504	.74356	10.25776	.09749	12

YEARS

MONTHS	PW 1	PW 1/P	PR		PW 1	PW 1/P	PR	MONTHS
12	.78080	10.52142	.09504	1	.74356	10.25776	.09749	12
24	.60965	18.73658	.05337	2	.55288	17.88499	.05591	24
36	.47602	25.15102	.03976	3	.41109	23.55625	.04245	36
48	.37168	30.15943	.03316	4	.30567	27.77315	.03601	48
60	.29021	34.07001	.02935	5	.22728	30.90866	.03235	60
72	.22660	37.12341	.02694	6	.16900	33.24008	.03008	72
84	.17693	39.50752	.02531	7	.12566	34.97362	.02859	84
96	.13814	41.36904	.02417	8	.09343	36.26261	.02758	96
108	.10786	42.82252	.02335	9	.06947	37.22104	.02687	108
120	.08422	43.95741	.02275	10	.05166	37.93369	.02636	120
132	.06576	44.84353	.02230	11	.03841	38.46358	.02600	132
144	.05135	45.53541	.02196	12	.02856	38.85759	.02574	144
156	.04009	46.07564	.02170	13	.02124	39.15055	.02554	156
168	.03130	46.49745	.02151	14	.01579	39.36839	.02540	168
180	.02444	46.82681	.02136	15	.01174	39.53036	.02530	180
192	.01908	47.08397	.02124	16	.00873	39.65080	.02522	192
204	.01490	47.28476	.02115	17	.00649	39.74035	.02516	204
216	.01163	47.44154	.02108	18	.00483	39.80693	.02512	216
228	.00908	47.56395	.02102	19	.00359	39.85644	.02509	228
240	.00709	47.65953	.02098	20	.00267	39.89326	.02507	240
252	.00554	47.73416	.02095	21	.00198	39.92063	.02505	252
264	.00432	47.79243	.02092	22	.00148	39.94099	.02504	264
276	.00338	47.83793	.02090	23	.00110	39.95612	.02503	276
288	.00264	47.87345	.02089	24	.00082	39.96737	.02502	288
300	.00206	47.90119	.02088	25	.00061	39.97574	.02502	300
312	.00161	47.92285	.02087	26	.00045	39.98196	.02501	312
324	.00125	47.93976	.02086	27	.00034	39.98659	.02501	324
336	.00098	47.95297	.02085	28	.00025	39.99003	.02501	336
348	.00077	47.96328	.02085	29	.00019	39.99258	.02500	348
360	.00060	47.97133	.02085	30	.00014	39.99449	.02500	360

	3.0 PERCENT			3.5 PERCENT			
PERIOD	PW 1	PW 1/P	PR	PW 1	PW 1/P	PR	PERIOD
1	.97087	.97087	1.03000	.96618	.96618	1.03500	1
2	.94260	1.91347	.52261	.93351	1.89969	.52640	2
3	.91514	2.82861	.35353	.90194	2.80164	.35693	3
4	.88849	3.71710	.26903	.87144	3.67308	.27225	4
5	.86261	4.57971	.21835	.84197	4.51505	.22148	5
6	.83748	5.41719	.18460	.81350	5.32855	.18767	6
7	.81309	6.23028	.16051	.78599	6.11454	.16354	7
8	.78941	7.01969	.14246	.75941	6.87396	.14548	8
9	.76642	7.78611	.12843	.73373	7.60769	.13145	9
10	.74409	8.53020	.11723	.70892	8.31661	.12024	10
11	.72242	9.25262	.10808	.68495	9.00155	.11109	11
12	.70138	9.95400	.10046	.66178	9.66333	.10348	12
13	.68095	10.63496	.09403	.63940	10.30274	.09706	13
14	.66112	11.29607	.08853	.61778	10.92052	.09157	14
15	.64186	11.93794	.08377	.59689	11.51741	.08683	15
16	.62317	12.56110	.07961	.57671	12.09412	.08268	16
17	.60502	13.16612	.07595	.55720	12.65132	.07904	17
18	.58739	13.75351	.07271	.53836	13.18968	.07582	18
19	.57029	14.32380	.06981	.52016	13.70984	.07294	19
20	.55368	14.87747	.06722	.50257	14.21240	.07036	20
21	.53755	15.41502	.06487	.48557	14.69797	.06804	21
22	.52189	15.93692	.06275	.46915	15.16712	.06593	22
23	.50669	16.44361	.06081	.45329	15.62041	.06402	23
24	.49193	16.93554	.05905	.43796	16.05837	.06227	24
25	.47761	17.41315	.05743	.42315	16.48151	.06067	25
26	.46369	17.87684	.05594	.40884	16.89035	.05921	26
27	.45019	18.32703	.05456	.39501	17.28536	.05785	27
28	.43708	18.76411	.05329	.38165	17.66702	.05660	28
29	.42435	19.18845	.05211	.36875	18.03577	.05545	29
30	.41199	19.60044	.05102	.35628	18.39205	.05437	30
31	.39999	20.00043	.05000	.34423	18.73628	.05337	31
32	.38834	20.38877	.04905	.33259	19.06887	.05244	32
33	.37703	20.76579	.04816	.32134	19.39021	.05157	33
34	.36604	21.13184	.04732	.31048	19.70068	.05076	34
35	.35538	21.48722	.04654	.29998	20.00066	.05000	35
36	.34503	21.83225	.04580	.28983	20.29049	.04928	36
37	.33498	22.16724	.04511	.28003	20.57053	.04861	37
38	.32523	22.49246	.04446	.27056	20.84109	.04798	38
39	.31575	22.80822	.04384	.26141	21.10250	.04739	39
40	.30656	23.11477	.04326	.25257	21.35507	.04683	40

	4.0 PERCENT				4.5 PERCENT		
PERIOD	PW 1	PW 1/P	PR	PW 1	PW 1/P	PR	PERIOD
1	.96154	.96154	1.04000	.95694	.95694	1.04500	1
2	.92456	1.88609	.53020	.91573	1.87267	.53400	2
3	.88900	2.77509	.36035	.87630	2.74896	.36377	3
4	.85480	3.62990	.27549	.83856	3.58753	.27874	4
5	.82193	4.45182	.22463	.80245	4.38998	.22779	5
6	.79031	5.24214	.19076	.76790	5.15787	.19388	6
7	.75992	6.00205	.16661	.73483	5.89270	.16970	7
8	.73069	6.73274	.14853	.70319	6.59589	.15161	8
9	.70259	7.43533	.13449	.67290	7.26879	.13757	9
10	.67556	8.11090	.12329	.64393	7.91272	.12638	10
11	.64958	8.76048	.11415	.61620	8.52892	.11725	11
12	.62460	9.38507	.10655	.58966	9.11858	.10967	12
13	.60057	9.98565	.10014	.56427	9.68285	.10328	13
14	.57748	10.56312	.09467	.53997	10.22283	.09782	14
15	.55526	11.11839	.08994	.51672	10.73955	.09311	15
16	.53391	11.65230	.08582	.49447	11.23402	.08902	16
17	.51337	12.16567	.08220	.47318	11.70719	.08542	17
18	.49363	12.65930	.07899	.45280	12.15999	.08224	18
19	.47464	13.13394	.07614	.43330	12.59329	.07941	19
20	.45639	13.59033	.07358	.41464	13.00794	.07688	20
21	.43883	14.02916	.07128	.39679	13.40472	.07460	21
22	.42196	14.45112	.06920	.37970	13.78442	.07255	22
23	.40573	14.85684	.06731	.36335	14.14777	.07068	23
24	.39012	15.24696	.06559	.34770	14.49548	.06899	24
25	.37512	15.62208	.06401	.33273	14.82821	.06744	25
26	.36069	15.98277	.06257	.31840	15.14661	.06602	26
27	.34682	16.32959	.06124	.30469	15.45130	.06472	27
28	.33348	16.66306	.06001	.29157	15.74287	.06352	28
29	.32065	16.98371	.05888	.27902	16.02189	.06241	29
30	.30832	17.29203	.05783	.26700	16.28889	.06139	30
31	.29646	17.58849	.05686	.25550	16.54439	.06044	31
32	.28506	17.87355	.05595	.24450	16.78889	.05956	32
33	.27409	18.14765	.05510	.23397	17.02286	.05874	33
34	.26355	18.41120	.05431	.22390	17.24676	.05798	34
35	.25342	18.66461	.05358	.21425	17.46101	.05727	35
36	.24367	18.90828	.05289	.20503	17.66604	.05661	36
37	.23430	19.14258	.05224	.19620	17.86224	.05598	37
38	.22529	19.36786	.05163	.18775	18.04999	.05540	38
39	.21662	19.58448	.05106	.17967	18.22966	.05486	39
40	.20829	19.79277	.05052	.17193	18.40158	.05434	40

	5.0 PERCENT				5.5 PERCENT		
PERIOD	PW 1	PW 1/P	PR	PW 1	PW 1/P	PR	PERIOD
1	.95238	.95238	1.05000	.94787	.94787	1.05500	1
2	.90703	1.85941	.53780	.89845	1.84632	.54162	2
3	.86384	2.72325	.36721	.85161	2.69793	.37065	3
4	.82270	3.54595	.28201	.80722	3.50515	.28529	4
5	.78353	4.32948	.23097	.76513	4.27028	.23418	5
6	.74622	5.07569	.19702	.72525	4.99553	.20018	6
7	.71068	5.78637	.17282	.68744	5.68297	.17596	7
8	.67684	6.46321	.15472	.65160	6.33457	.15786	8
9	.64461	7.10782	.14069	.61763	6.95220	.14384	9
10	.61391	7.72173	.12950	.58543	7.53763	.13267	10
11	.58468	8.30641	.12039	.55491	8.09254	.12357	11
12	.55684	8.86325	.11283	.52598	8.61852	.11603	12
13	.53032	9.39357	.10646	.49856	9.11708	.10968	13
14	.50507	9.89864	.10102	.47257	9.58965	.10428	14
15	.48102	10.37966	.09634	.44793	10.03758	.09963	15
16	.45811	10.83777	.09227	.42458	10.46216	.09558	16
17	.43630	11.27407	.08870	.40245	10.86461	.09204	17
18	.41552	11.68959	.08555	.38147	11.24607	.08892	18
19	.39573	12.08532	.08275	.36158	11.60765	.08615	19
20	.37689	12.46221	.08024	.34273	11.95038	.08368	20
21	.35894	12.82115	.07800	.32486	12.27524	.08146	21
22	.34185	13.16300	.07597	.30793	12.58317	.07947	22
23	.32557	13.48857	.07414	.29187	12.87504	.07767	23
24	.31007	13.79864	.07247	.27666	13.15170	.07604	24
25	.29530	14.09394	.07095	.26223	13.41393	.07455	25
26	.28124	14.37519	.06956	.24856	13.66250	.07319	26
27	.26785	14.64303	.06829	.23560	13.89810	.07195	27
28	.25509	14.89813	.06712	.22332	14.12142	.07081	28
29	.24295	15.14107	.06605	.21168	14.33310	.06977	29
30	.23138	15.37245	.06505	.20064	14.53375	.06881	30
31	.22036	15.59281	.06413	.19018	14.72393	.06792	31
32	.20987	15.80268	.06328	.18027	14.90420	.06710	32
33	.19987	16.00255	.06249	.17087	15.07507	.06633	33
34	.19035	16.19290	.06176	.16196	15.23703	.06563	34
35	.18129	16.37419	.06107	.15352	15.39055	.06497	35
36	.17266	16.54685	.06043	.14552	15.53607	.06437	36
37	.16444	16.71129	.05984	.13793	15.67400	.06380	37
38	.15661	16.86789	.05928	.13074	15.80474	.06327	38
39	.14915	17.01704	.05876	.12392	15.92866	.06278	39
40	.14205	17.15909	.05828	.11746	16.04612	.06232	40

	6.0 PERCENT			6.5 PERCENT			
PERIOD	PW 1	PW 1/P	PR	PW 1	PW 1/P	PR	PERIOD
1	.94340	.94340	1.06000	.93897	.93897	1.06500	1
2	.89000	1.83339	.54544	.88166	1.82063	.54926	2
3	.83962	2.67301	.37411	.82785	2.64848	.37758	3
4	.79209	3.46511	.28859	.77732	3.42580	.29190	4
5	.74726	4.21236	.23740	.72988	4.15568	.24063	5
6	.70496	4.91732	.20336	.68533	4.84101	.20657	6
7	.66506	5.58238	.17914	.64351	5.48452	.18233	7
8	.62741	6.20979	.16104	.60423	6.08875	.16424	8
9	.59190	6.80169	.14702	.56735	6.65610	.15024	9
10	.55839	7.36009	.13587	.53273	7.18883	.13910	10
11	.52679	7.88687	.12679	.50021	7.68904	.13006	11
12	.49697	8.38384	.11928	.46968	8.15873	.12257	12
13	.46884	8.85268	.11296	.44102	8.59974	.11628	13
14	.44230	9.29498	.10758	.41410	9.01384	.11094	14
15	.41727	9.71225	.10296	.38883	9.40267	.10635	15
16	.39365	10.10590	.09895	.36510	9.76776	.10238	16
17	.37136	10.47726	.09544	.34281	10.11058	.09891	17
18	.35034	10.82760	.09236	.32189	10.43247	.09585	18
19	.33051	11.15812	.08962	.30224	10.73471	.09316	19
20	.31180	11.46992	.08718	.28380	11.01851	.09076	20
21	.29416	11.76408	.08500	.26648	11.28498	.08861	21
22	.27751	12.04158	.08305	.25021	11.53520	.08669	22
23	.26180	12.30338	.08128	.23494	11.77014	.08496	23
24	.24698	12.55036	.07968	.22060	11.99074	.08340	24
25	.23300	12.78336	.07823	.20714	12.19788	.08198	25
26	.21981	13.00317	.07690	.19450	12.39237	.08069	26
27	.20737	13.21053	.07570	.18263	12.57500	.07952	27
28	.19563	13.40616	.07459	.17148	12.74648	.07845	28
29	.18456	13.59072	.07358	.16101	12.90749	.07747	29
30	.17411	13.76483	.07265	.15119	13.05868	.07658	30
31	.16425	13.92909	.07179	.14196	13.20063	.07575	31
32	.15496	14.08404	.07100	.13329	13.33393	.07500	32
33	.14619	14.23023	.07027	.12516	13.45909	.07430	33
34	.13791	14.36814	.06960	.11752	13.57661	.07366	34
35	.13011	14.49825	.06897	.11035	13.68696	.07306	35
36	.12274	14.62099	.06839	.10361	13.79057	.07251	36
37	.11579	14.73678	.06786	.09729	13.88786	.07201	37
38	.10924	14.84602	.06736	.09135	13.97921	.07153	38
39	.10306	14.94907	.06689	.08578	14.06499	.07110	39
40	.09722	15.04630	.06646	.08054	14.14553	.07069	40

	7.0 PERCENT			7.5 PERCENT			
PERIOD	PW 1	PW 1/P	PR	PW 1	PW 1/P	PR	PERIOD
1	.93458	.93458	1.07000	.93023	.93023	1.07500	1
2	.87344	1.80802	.55309	.86533	1.79557	.55693	2
3	.81630	2.62432	.38105	.80496	2.60053	.38454	3
4	.76290	3.38721	.29523	.74880	3.34933	.29857	4
5	.71299	4.10020	.24389	.69656	4.04588	.24716	5
6	.66634	4.76654	.20980	.64796	4.69385	.21304	6
7	.62275	5.38929	.18555	.60275	5.29660	.18880	7
8	.58201	5.97130	.16747	.56070	5.85730	.17073	8
9	.54393	6.51523	.15349	.52158	6.37889	.15677	9
10	.50835	7.02358	.14238	.48519	6.86408	.14569	10
11	.47509	7.49867	.13336	.45134	7.31542	.13670	11
12	.44401	7.94269	.12590	.41985	7.73528	.12928	12
13	.41496	8.35765	.11965	.39056	8.12584	.12306	13
14	.38782	8.74547	.11434	.36331	8.48915	.11780	14
15	.36245	9.10791	.10979	.33797	8.82712	.11329	15
16	.33873	9.44665	.10586	.31439	9.14151	.10939	16
17	.31657	9.76322	.10243	.29245	9.43396	.10600	17
18	.29586	10.05909	.09941	.27205	9.70601	.10303	18
19	.27651	10.33560	.09675	.25307	9.95908	.10041	19
20	.25842	10.59401	.09439	.23541	10.19449	.09809	20
21	.24151	10.83553	.09229	.21899	10.41348	.09603	21
22	.22571	11.06124	.09041	.20371	10.61719	.09419	22
23	.21095	11.27219	.08871	.18950	10.80669	.09254	23
24	.19715	11.46933	.08719	.17628	10.98297	.09105	24
25	.18425	11.65358	.08581	.16398	11.14695	.08971	25
26	.17220	11.82578	.08456	.15254	11.29948	.08850	26
27	.16093	11.98671	.08343	.14190	11.44138	.08740	27
28	.15040	12.13711	.08239	.13200	11.57338	.08641	28
29	.14056	12.27767	.08145	.12279	11.69617	.08550	29
30	.13137	12.40904	.08059	.11422	11.81039	.08467	30
31	.12277	12.53181	.07980	.10625	11.91664	.08392	31
32	.11474	12.64656	.07907	.09884	12.01548	.08323	32
33	.10723	12.75379	.07841	.09194	12.10742	.08259	33
34	.10022	12.85401	.07780	.08553	12.19295	.08201	34
35	.09366	12.94767	.07723	.07956	12.27251	.08148	35
36	.08754	13.03521	.07672	.07401	12.34652	.08099	36
37	.08181	13.11702	.07624	.06885	12.41537	.08055	37
38	.07646	13.19347	.07580	.06404	12.47941	.08013	38
39	.07146	13.26493	.07539	.05958	12.53899	.07975	39
40	.06678	13.33171	.07501	.05542	12.59441	.07940	40

	8.0 PERCENT				8.5 PERCENT			
PERIOD	PW 1	PW 1/P	PR	PW 1	PW 1/P	PR	PERIOD
1	.92593	.92593	1.08000	.92166	.92166	1.08500	1
2	.85734	1.78326	.56077	.84946	1.77111	.56462	2
3	.79383	2.57710	.38803	.78291	2.55402	.39154	3
4	.73503	3.31213	.30192	.72157	3.27560	.30529	4
5	.68058	3.99271	.25046	.66505	3.94064	.25377	5
6	.63017	4.62288	.21632	.61295	4.55359	.21961	6
7	.58349	5.20637	.19207	.56493	5.11851	.19537	7
8	.54027	5.74664	.17401	.52067	5.63918	.17733	8
9	.50025	6.24689	.16008	.47988	6.11906	.16342	9
10	.46319	6.71008	.14903	.44229	6.56135	.15241	10
11	.42888	7.13896	.14008	.40764	6.96898	.14349	11
12	.39711	7.53608	.13270	.37570	7.34469	.13615	12
13	.36770	7.90378	.12652	.34627	7.69095	.13002	13
14	.34046	8.24424	.12130	.31914	8.01010	.12484	14
15	.31524	8.55948	.11683	.29414	8.30424	.12042	15
16	.29189	8.85137	.11298	.27110	8.57533	.11661	16
17	.27027	9.12164	.10963	.24986	8.82519	.11331	17
18	.25025	9.37189	.10670	.23028	9.05548	.11043	18
19	.23171	9.60360	.10413	.21224	9.26772	.10790	19
20	.21455	9.81815	.10185	.19562	9.46334	.10567	20
21	.19866	10.01680	.09983	.18029	9.64363	.10370	21
22	.18394	10.20074	.09803	.16617	9.80980	.10194	22
23	.17032	10.37106	.09642	.15315	9.96295	.10037	23
24	.15770	10.52876	.09498	.14115	10.10410	.09897	24
25	.14602	10.67478	.09368	.13009	10.23419	.09771	25
26	.13520	10.80998	.09251	.11990	10.35409	.09658	26
27	.12519	10.93516	.09145	.11051	10.46460	.09556	27
28	.11591	11.05108	.09049	.10185	10.56645	.09464	28
29	.10733	11.15841	.08962	.09387	10.66033	.09381	29
30	.09938	11.25778	.08883	.08652	10.74684	.09305	30
31	.09202	11.34980	.08811	.07974	10.82658	.09237	31
32	.08520	11.43500	.08745	.07349	10.90008	.09174	32
33	.07889	11.51389	.08685	.06774	10.96781	.09118	33
34	.07305	11.58693	.08630	.06243	11.03024	.09066	34
35	.06763	11.65457	.08580	.05754	11.08778	.09019	35
36	.06262	11.71719	.08534	.05303	11.14081	.08976	36
37	.05799	11.77518	.08492	.04888	11.18969	.08937	37
38	.05369	11.82887	.08454	.04505	11.23474	.08901	38
39	.04971	11.87858	.08419	.04152	11.27625	.08868	39
40	.04603	11.92461	.08386	.03827	11.31452	.08838	40

	9.0 PERCENT			10.0 PERCENT			
PERIOD	PW 1	PW 1/P	PR	PW 1	PW 1/P	PR	PERIOD
1	.91743	.91743	1.09000	.90909	.90909	1.10000	1
2	.84168	1.75911	.56847	.82645	1.73554	.57619	2
3	.77218	2.53129	.39505	.75131	2.48685	.40211	3
4	.70843	3.23972	.30867	.68301	3.16987	.31547	4
5	.64993	3.88965	.25709	.62092	3.79079	.26380	5
6	.59627	4.48592	.22292	.56447	4.35526	.22961	6
7	.54703	5.03295	.19869	.51316	4.86842	.20541	7
8	.50187	5.53482	.18067	.46651	5.33493	.18744	8
9	.46043	5.99525	.16680	.42410	5.75902	.17364	9
10	.42241	6.41766	.15582	.38554	6.14457	.16275	10
11	.38753	6.80519	.14695	.35049	6.49506	.15396	11
12	.35553	7.16073	.13965	.31863	6.81369	.14676	12
13	.32618	7.48690	.13357	.28966	7.10336	.14078	13
14	.29925	7.78615	.12843	.26333	7.36669	.13575	14
15	.27454	8.06069	.12406	.23939	7.60608	.13147	15
16	.25187	8.31256	.12030	.21763	7.82371	.12782	16
17	.23107	8.54363	.11705	.19784	8.02155	.12466	17
18	.21199	8.75563	.11421	.17986	8.20141	.12193	18
19	.19449	8.95011	.11173	.16351	8.36492	.11955	19
20	.17843	9.12855	.10955	.14864	8.51356	.11746	20
21	.16370	9.29224	.10762	.13513	8.64869	.11562	21
22	.15018	9.44243	.10590	.12285	8.77154	.11401	22
23	.13778	9.58021	.10438	.11168	8.88322	.11257	23
24	.12640	9.70661	.10302	.10153	8.98474	.11130	24
25	.11597	9.82258	.10181	.09230	9.07704	.11017	25
26	.10639	9.92897	.10072	.08391	9.16095	.10916	26
27	.09761	10.02658	.09973	.07628	9.23722	.10826	27
28	.08955	10.11613	.09885	.06934	9.30657	.10745	28
29	.08215	10.19828	.09806	.06304	9.36961	.10673	29
30	.07537	10.27365	.09734	.05731	9.42691	.10608	30
31	.06915	10.34280	.09669	.05210	9.47901	.10550	31
32	.06344	10.40624	.09610	.04736	9.52638	.10497	32
33	.05820	10.46444	.09556	.04306	9.56943	.10450	33
34	.05339	10.51784	.09508	.03914	9.60857	.10407	34
35	.04899	10.56682	.09464	.03558	9.64416	.10369	35
36	.04494	10.61176	.09424	.03235	9.67651	.10334	36
37	.04123	10.65299	.09387	.02941	9.70592	.10303	37
38	.03783	10.69082	.09354	.02673	9.73265	.10275	38
39	.03470	10.72552	.09324	.02430	9.75696	.10249	39
40	.03184	10.75736	.09296	.02209	9.77905	.10226	40

	11.0 PERCENT				12.0 PERCENT		
PERIOD	PW 1	PW 1/P	PR	PW 1	PW 1/P	PR	PERIOD
1	.90090	.90090	1.11000	.89286	.89286	1.12000	1
2	.81162	1.71252	.58393	.79719	1.69005	.59170	2
3	.73119	2.44371	.40921	.71178	2.40183	.41635	3
4	.65873	3.10245	.32233	.63552	3.03735	.32923	4
5	.59345	3.69590	.27057	.56743	3.60478	.27741	5
6	.53464	4.23054	.23638	.50663	4.11141	.24323	6
7	.48166	4.71220	.21222	.45235	4.56376	.21912	7
8	.43393	5.14612	.19432	.40388	4.96764	.20130	8
9	.39092	5.53705	.18060	.36061	5.32825	.18768	9
10	.35218	5.88923	.16980	.32197	5.65022	.17698	10
11	.31728	6.20652	.16112	.28748	5.93770	.16842	11
12	.28584	6.49236	.15403	.25668	6.19437	.16144	12
13	.25751	6.74987	.14815	.22917	6.42355	.15568	13
14	.23199	6.98187	.14323	.20462	6.62817	.15087	14
15	.20900	7.19087	.13907	.18270	6.81086	.14682	15
16	.18829	7.37916	.13552	.16312	6.97399	.14339	16
17	.16963	7.54879	.13247	.14564	7.11963	.14046	17
18	.15282	7.70162	.12984	.13004	7.24967	.13794	18
19	.13768	7.83929	.12756	.11611	7.36578	.13576	19
20	.12403	7.96333	.12558	.10367	7.46944	.13388	20
21	.11174	8.07507	.12384	.09256	7.56200	.13224	21
22	.10067	8.17574	.12231	.08264	7.64465	.13081	22
23	.09069	8.26643	.12097	.07379	7.71843	.12956	23
24	.08170	8.34814	.11979	.06588	7.78432	.12846	24
25	.07361	8.42174	.11874	.05882	7.84314	.12750	25
26	.06631	8.48806	.11781	.05252	7.89566	.12665	26
27	.05974	8.54780	.11699	.04689	7.94255	.12590	27
28	.05382	8.60162	.11626	.04187	7.98442	.12524	28
29	.04849	8.65011	.11561	.03738	8.02181	.12466	29
30	.04368	8.69379	.11502	.03338	8.05518	.12414	30
31	.03935	8.73315	.11451	.02980	8.08499	.12369	31
32	.03545	8.76860	.11404	.02661	8.11159	.12328	32
33	.03194	8.80054	.11363	.02376	8.13535	.12292	33
34	.02878	8.82932	.11326	.02121	8.15656	.12260	34
35	.02592	8.85524	.11293	.01894	8.17550	.12232	35
36	.02335	8.87859	.11263	.01691	8.19241	.12206	36
37	.02104	8.89963	.11236	.01510	8.20751	.12184	37
38	.01896	8.91859	.11213	.01348	8.22099	.12164	38
39	.01708	8.93567	.11191	.01204	8.23303	.12146	39
40	.01538	8.95105	.11172	.01075	8.24378	.12130	40

	13.0 PERCENT			14.0 PERCENT			
PERIOD	PW 1	PW 1/P	PR	PW 1	PW 1/P	PR	PERIOD
1	.88496	.88496	1.13000	.87719	.87719	1.14000	1
2	.78315	1.66810	.59948	.76947	1.64666	.60729	2
3	.69305	2.36115	.42352	.67497	2.32163	.43073	3
4	.61332	2.97447	.33619	.59208	2.91371	.34320	4
5	.54276	3.51723	.28431	.51937	3.43308	.29128	5
6	.48032	3.99755	.25015	.45559	3.88867	.25716	6
7	.42506	4.42261	.22611	.39964	4.28830	.23319	7
8	.37616	4.79877	.20839	.35056	4.63886	.21557	8
9	.33288	5.13166	.19487	.30751	4.94637	.20217	9
10	.29459	5.42624	.18429	.26974	5.21612	.19171	10
11	.26070	5.68694	.17584	.23662	5.45273	.18339	11
12	.23071	5.91765	.16899	.20756	5.66029	.17667	12
13	.20416	6.12181	.16335	.18207	5.84236	.17116	13
14	.18068	6.30249	.15867	.15971	6.00207	.16661	14
15	.15989	6.46238	.15474	.14010	6.14217	.16281	15
16	.14150	6.60388	.15143	.12289	6.26506	.15962	16
17	.12522	6.72909	.14861	.10780	6.37286	.15692	17
18	.11081	6.83991	.14620	.09456	6.46742	.15462	18
19	.09806	6.93797	.14413	.08295	6.55037	.15266	19
20	.08678	7.02475	.14235	.07276	6.62313	.15099	20
21	.07680	7.10155	.14081	.06383	6.68696	.14954	21
22	.06796	7.16951	.13948	.05599	6.74294	.14830	22
23	.06014	7.22966	.13832	.04911	6.79206	.14723	23
24	.05323	7.28288	.13731	.04308	6.83514	.14630	24
25	.04710	7.32998	.13643	.03779	6.87293	.14550	25
26	.04168	7.37167	.13565	.03315	6.90608	.14480	26
27	.03689	7.40856	.13498	.02908	6.93515	.14419	27
28	.03264	7.44120	.13439	.02551	6.96066	.14366	28
29	.02889	7.47009	.13387	.02237	6.98304	.14320	29
30	.02557	7.49565	.13341	.01963	7.00266	.14280	30
31	.02262	7.51828	.13301	.01722	7.01988	.14245	31
32	.02002	7.53830	.13266	.01510	7.03498	.14215	32
33	.01772	7.55602	.13234	.01325	7.04823	.14188	33
34	.01568	7.57170	.13207	.01162	7.05985	.14165	34
35	.01388	7.58557	.13183	.01019	7.07005	.14144	35
36	.01228	7.59785	.13162	.00894	7.07899	.14126	36
37	.01087	7.60872	.13143	.00784	7.08683	.14111	37
38	.00962	7.61833	.13126	.00688	7.09371	.14097	38
39	.00851	7.62684	.13112	.00604	7.09975	.14085	39
40	.00753	7.63438	.13099	.00529	7.10504	.14075	40

	15.0 PERCENT			16.0 PERCENT			
PERIOD	PW 1	PW 1/P	PR	PW 1	PW 1/P	PR	PERIOD
1	.86957	.86957	1.15000	.86207	.86207	1.16000	1
2	.75614	1.62571	.61512	.74316	1.60523	.62296	2
3	.65752	2.28323	.43798	.64066	2.24589	.44526	3
4	.57175	2.85498	.35027	.55229	2.79818	.35738	4
5	.49718	3.35216	.29832	.47611	3.27429	.30541	5
6	.43233	3.78448	.26424	.41044	3.68474	.27139	6
7	.37594	4.16042	.24036	.35383	4.03857	.24761	7
8	.32690	4.48732	.22285	.30503	4.34359	.23022	8
9	.28426	4.77158	.20957	.26295	4.60654	.21708	9
10	.24718	5.01877	.19925	.22668	4.83323	.20690	10
11	.21494	5.23371	.19107	.19542	5.02864	.19886	11
12	.18691	5.42062	.18448	.16846	5.19711	.19241	12
13	.16253	5.58315	.17911	.14523	5.34233	.18718	13
14	.14133	5.72448	.17469	.12520	5.46753	.18290	14
15	.12289	5.84737	.17102	.10793	5.57546	.17936	15
16	.10686	5.95423	.16795	.09304	5.66850	.17641	16
17	.09293	6.04716	.16537	.08021	5.74870	.17395	17
18	.08081	6.12797	.16319	.06914	5.81785	.17188	18
19	.07027	6.19823	.16134	.05961	5.87746	.17014	19
20	.06110	6.25933	.15976	.05139	5.92884	.16867	20
21	.05313	6.31246	.15842	.04430	5.97314	.16742	21
22	.04620	6.35866	.15727	.03819	6.01133	.16635	22
23	.04017	6.39884	.15628	.03292	6.04425	.16545	23
24	.03493	6.43377	.15543	.02838	6.07263	.16467	24
25	.03038	6.46415	.15470	.02447	6.09709	.16401	25
26	.02642	6.49056	.15407	.02109	6.11818	.16345	26
27	.02297	6.51353	.15353	.01818	6.13636	.16296	27
28	.01997	6.53351	.15306	.01567	6.15204	.16255	28
29	.01737	6.55088	.15265	.01351	6.16555	.16219	29
30	.01510	6.56598	.15230	.01165	6.17720	.16189	30
31	.01313	6.57911	.15200	.01004	6.18724	.16162	31
32	.01142	6.59053	.15173	.00866	6.19590	.16140	32
33	.00993	6.60046	.15150	.00746	6.20336	.16120	33
34	.00864	6.60910	.15131	.00643	6.20979	.16104	34
35	.00751	6.61661	.15113	.00555	6.21534	.16089	35
36	.00653	6.62314	.15099	.00478	6.22012	.16077	36
37	.00568	6.62881	.15086	.00412	6.22424	.16066	37
38	.00494	6.63375	.15074	.00355	6.22779	.16057	38
39	.00429	6.63805	.15065	.00306	6.23086	.16049	39
40	.00373	6.64178	.15056	.00264	6.23350	.16042	40

	18.0 PERCENT			20.0 PERCENT			
PERIOD	PW 1	PW 1/P	PR	PW 1	PW 1/P	PR	PERIOD
1	.84746	.84746	1.18000	.83333	.83333	1.20000	1
2	.71818	1.56564	.63872	.69444	1.52778	.65455	2
3	.60863	2.17427	.45992	.57870	2.10648	.47473	3
4	.51579	2.69006	.37174	.48225	2.58873	.38629	4
5	.43711	3.12717	.31978	.40188	2.99061	.33438	5
6	.37043	3.49760	.28591	.33490	3.32551	.30071	6
7	.31393	3.81153	.26236	.27908	3.60459	.27742	7
8	.26604	4.07757	.24524	.23257	3.83716	.26061	8
9	.22546	4.30302	.23239	.19381	4.03097	.24808	9
10	.19106	4.49409	.22251	.16151	4.19247	.23852	10
11	.16192	4.65601	.21478	.13459	4.32706	.23110	11
12	.13722	4.79322	.20863	.11216	4.43922	.22526	12
13	.11629	4.90951	.20369	.09346	4.53268	.22062	13
14	.09855	5.00806	.19968	.07789	4.61057	.21689	14
15	.08352	5.09158	.19640	.06491	4.67547	.21388	15
16	.07078	5.16235	.19371	.05409	4.72956	.21144	16
17	.05998	5.22233	.19149	.04507	4.77463	.20944	17
18	.05083	5.27316	.18964	.03756	4.81219	.20781	18
19	.04308	5.31624	.18810	.03130	4.84350	.20646	19
20	.03651	5.35275	.18682	.02608	4.86958	.20536	20
21	.03094	5.38368	.18575	.02174	4.89132	.20444	21
22	.02622	5.40990	.18485	.01811	4.90943	.20369	22
23	.02222	5.43212	.18409	.01509	4.92453	.20307	23
24	.01883	5.45095	.18345	.01258	4.93710	.20255	24
25	.01596	5.46691	.18292	.01048	4.94759	.20212	25
26	.01352	5.48043	.18247	.00874	4.95632	.20176	26
27	.01146	5.49189	.18209	.00728	4.96360	.20147	27
28	.00971	5.50160	.18177	.00607	4.96967	.20122	28
29	.00823	5.50983	.18149	.00506	4.97472	.20102	29
30	.00697	5.51681	.18126	.00421	4.97894	.20085	30
31	.00591	5.52272	.18107	.00351	4.98245	.20070	31
32	.00501	5.52773	.18091	.00293	4.98537	.20059	32
33	.00425	5.53197	.18077	.00244	4.98781	.20049	33
34	.00360	5.53557	.18065	.00203	4.98984	.20041	34
35	.00305	5.53862	.18055	.00169	4.99154	.20034	35
36	.00258	5.54120	.18047	.00141	4.99295	.20028	36
37	.00219	5.54339	.18039	.00118	4.99412	.20024	37
38	.00186	5.54525	.18033	.00098	4.99510	.20020	38
39	.00157	5.54682	.18028	.00082	4.99592	.20016	39
40	.00133	5.54815	.18024	.00068	4.99660	.20014	40

| | 25.0 PERCENT | | | 30.0 PERCENT | | | |
PERIOD	PW 1	PW 1/P	PR	PW 1	PW 1/P	PR	PERIOD
1	.80000	.80000	1.25000	.76923	.76923	1.30000	1
2	.64000	1.44000	.69444	.59172	1.36095	.73478	2
3	.51200	1.95200	.51230	.45517	1.81611	.55063	3
4	.40960	2.36160	.42344	.35013	2.16624	.46163	4
5	.32768	2.68928	.37185	.26933	2.43557	.41058	5
6	.26214	2.95142	.33882	.20718	2.64275	.37839	6
7	.20972	3.16114	.31634	.15937	2.80211	.35687	7
8	.16777	3.32891	.30040	.12259	2.92470	.34192	8
9	.13422	3.46313	.28876	.09430	3.01900	.33124	9
10	.10737	3.57050	.28007	.07254	3.09154	.32346	10
11	.08590	3.65640	.27349	.05580	3.14734	.31773	11
12	.06872	3.72512	.26845	.04292	3.19026	.31345	12
13	.05498	3.78010	.26454	.03302	3.22328	.31024	13
14	.04398	3.82408	.26150	.02540	3.24867	.30782	14
15	.03518	3.85926	.25912	.01954	3.26821	.30598	15
16	.02815	3.88741	.25724	.01503	3.28324	.30458	16
17	.02252	3.90993	.25576	.01156	3.29480	.30351	17
18	.01801	3.92794	.25459	.00889	3.30369	.30269	18
19	.01441	3.94235	.25366	.00684	3.31053	.30207	19
20	.01153	3.95388	.25292	.00526	3.31579	.30159	20
21	.00922	3.96311	.25233	.00405	3.31984	.30122	21
22	.00738	3.97049	.25186	.00311	3.32296	.30094	22
23	.00590	3.97639	.25148	.00239	3.32535	.30072	23
24	.00472	3.98111	.25119	.00184	3.32719	.30055	24
25	.00378	3.98489	.25095	.00142	3.32861	.30043	25
26	.00302	3.98791	.25076	.00109	3.32970	.30033	26
27	.00242	3.99033	.25061	.00084	3.33054	.30025	27
28	.00193	3.99226	.25048	.00065	3.33118	.30019	28
29	.00155	3.99381	.25039	.00050	3.33168	.30015	29
30	.00124	3.99505	.25031	.00038	3.33206	.30011	30
31	.00099	3.99604	.25025	.00029	3.33235	.30009	31
32	.00079	3.99683	.25020	.00023	3.33258	.30007	32
33	.00063	3.99746	.25016	.00017	3.33275	.30005	33
34	.00051	3.99797	.25013	.00013	3.33289	.30004	34
35	.00041	3.99838	.25010	.00010	3.33299	.30003	35
36	.00032	3.99870	.25008	.00008	3.33307	.30002	36
37	.00026	3.99896	.25006	.00006	3.33313	.30002	37
38	.00021	3.99917	.25005	.00005	3.33318	.30001	38
39	.00017	3.99934	.25004	.00004	3.33321	.30001	39
40	.00013	3.99947	.25003	.00003	3.33324	.30001	40

Supplemental Tables

Supplemental Tables

Loan Balances:
      End of holding periods: 5, 10, and 15 years
      Loan term: 10, 15, 20, 25, and 30 years
      Interest rates: 5 to 12%

Loan Constants:
      Loan term: 10, 15, 20, 25, and 30 years
      Interest rates: 5 to 12%
      Payment frequency: monthly, annual

Note: As a conservative measure the loan constant has been rounded up to 5 decimal places from the corresponding PR factor when the subsequent digit (sixth decimal place) has been *3* or more.

Loan Balance Owing at End of 5 Years as a Percent of Original Principal

Loan Term and Payment Frequency	5%	5 1/2%	6%	6 1/2%	7%	7 1/2%	8%
				Interest Rate			
10 Years							
Monthly	.56205	.56817	.57426	.58033	.58637	.59238	.59837
Annual	.56069	.56653	.57233	.57808	.58378	.58943	.59503
15 Years							
Monthly	.74557	.75289	.76022	.76717	.77413	.78096	.78766
Annual	.74393	.75094	.75782	.76455	.77120	.77761	.78394
20 Years							
Monthly	.83455	.84188	.84900	.85589	.86257	.86902	.87526
Annual	.83289	.83994	.84676	.85335	.85972	.86587	.87180
25 Years							
Monthly	.88580	.89272	.89932	.90562	.91162	.91733	.92274
Annual	.88422	.89089	.89726	.90332	.90908	.91456	.91975
30 Years							
Monthly	.91829	.92461	.93054	.93611	.94132	.94618	.95070
Annual	.91683	.92295	.92871	.93408	.93912	.94383	.94821

Loan Term and Payment Frequency	8 1/2%	9%	9 1/2%	10%	10 1/2%	11%	12%
				Interest Rate			
10 Years							
Monthly	.60432	.61024	.61612	.62197	.62778	.63355	.64497
Annual	.60058	.60609	.61154	.61693	.62228	.62756	.63799
15 Years							
Monthly	.79424	.80068	.80699	.81317	.81921	.82505	.83652
Annual	.79012	.79617	.80208	.80785	.81349	.81899	.82959
20 Years							
Monthly	.88127	.88707	.89266	.89802	.90319	.90806	.91744
Annual	.87752	.88302	.88832	.89341	.89830	.90300	.91183
25 Years							
Monthly	.92787	.93273	.93731	.94164	.94563	.94954	.95651
Annual	.92468	.92934	.93376	.93792	.94185	.94557	.95235
30 Years							
Monthly	.95490	.95880	.96241	.96574	.96878	.97162	.97662
Annual	.95230	.95610	.95962	.96290	.96591	.96871	.97368

Loan Balance Owing at End of 10 Years as a Percent of Original Principal

Loan Term and Payment Frequency	Interest Rate						
	5%	5 1/2%	6%	6 1/2%	7%	7 1/2%	8%
15 Years							
Monthly	.41905	.42777	.43649	.44521	.45393	.46263	.47131
Annual	.41711	.42543	.43372	.44197	.45018	.45835	.46647
20 Years							
Monthly	.62222	.63384	.64531	.65662	.66774	.67867	.68941
Annual	.61961	.63074	.64169	.65243	.66298	.67331	.68344
25 Years							
Monthly	.73924	.75156	.76352	.77512	.78634	.79718	.80763
Annual	.73646	.74830	.75976	.77085	.78155	.79189	.80184
30 Years							
Monthly	.81342	.82541	.83686	.84776	.85813	.86795	.87725
Annual	.81068	.82225	.83328	.84377	.85373	.86318	.87212

Loan Term and Payment Frequency	Interest Rate						
	8 1/2%	9%	9 1/2%	10%	10 1/2%	11%	12%
15 Years							
Monthly	.47998	.48861	.49721	.50577	.51429	.52271	.53954
Annual	.47454	.48255	.49050	.49839	.50621	.51397	.52927
20 Years							
Monthly	.69994	.71026	.72036	.73024	.73990	.74926	.76747
Annual	.69335	.70303	.71250	.72174	.73075	.73954	.75645
25 Years							
Monthly	.81771	.82740	.83670	.84561	.85408	.86231	.87754
Annual	.81142	.82063	.82947	.83795	.84607	.85384	.86839
30 Years							
Monthly	.88603	.89430	.90208	.90938	.91618	.92260	.93417
Annual	.88057	.88854	.89605	.90312	.90975	.91598	.92729

Loan Balance Owing at End of 15 Years as a Percent of Original Principal

Loan Term and Payment Frequency	Interest Rate						
	5%	5 1/2%	6%	6 1/2%	7%	7 1/2%	8%
20 Years							
Monthly	.34972	.36013	.37058	.38105	.39154	.40203	.41252
Annual	.34741	.35733	.36725	.37716	.38703	.39687	.40667
25 Years							
Monthly	.55116	.56584	.58034	.59465	.60872	.62256	.63614
Annual	.54788	.56193	.57576	.58935	.60270	.61578	.62859
30 Years							
Monthly	.67884	.69490	.71049	.72559	.74019	.75427	.76782
Annual	.67521	.69064	.70560	.72003	.73397	.74740	.76032

Loan Term and Payment Frequency	Interest Rate						
	8 1/2%	9%	9 1/2%	10%	10 1/2%	11%	12%
20 Years							
Monthly	.42299	.43343	.44383	.45419	.46449	.47469	.49500
Annual	.41641	.42610	.43572	.44527	.45473	.46412	.48261
25 Years							
Monthly	.64945	.66248	.67521	.68762	.69967	.71151	.73409
Annual	.64112	.65336	.66530	.67694	.68826	.69938	.72040
30 Years							
Monthly	.78083	.79331	.80524	.81665	.82748	.83785	.85705
Annual	.77272	.78460	.79598	.80685	.81722	.82713	.84553

Loan Constant as an Annual Percent of Original Principal

Loan Term and Payment Frequency	Interest Rate						
	5%	5 1/2%	6%	6 1/2%	7%	7 1/2%	8%
10 Years							
Monthly	.12728	.13023	.13323	.13626	.13933	.14244	.14559
Annual	.12951	.13267	.13587	.13911	.14238	.14569	.14903
15 Years							
Monthly	.09490	.09805	.10127	.10454	.10786	.11124	.11468
Annual	.09634	.09963	.10296	.10635	.10980	.11329	.11683
20 Years							
Monthly	.07920	.08255	.08597	.08947	.09304	.09667	.10037
Annual	.08024	.08368	.08719	.09076	.09439	.09809	.10185
25 Years							
Monthly	.07015	.07369	.07732	.08103	.08482	.08868	.09262
Annual	.07095	.07455	.07823	.08198	.08581	.08971	.09368
30 Years							
Monthly	.06442	.06814	.07195	.07585	.07984	.08391	.08805
Annual	.06505	.06881	.07265	.07658	.08059	.08467	.08883

Loan Term and Payment Frequency	Interest Rate						
	8 1/2%	9%	9 1/2%	10%	10 1/2%	11%	12%
10 Years							
Monthly	.14878	.15201	.15528	.15858	.16192	.16530	.17217
Annual	.15241	.15582	.15927	.16275	.16626	.16980	.17699
15 Years							
Monthly	.11817	.12171	.12531	.12895	.13265	.13638	.14402
Annual	.12042	.12406	.12775	.13148	.13525	.13907	.14683
20 Years							
Monthly	.10414	.10800	.11186	.11580	.11981	.12385	.13213
Annual	.10567	.10955	.11348	.11746	.12149	.12558	.13388
25 Years							
Monthly	.09663	.10071	.10485	.10905	.11329	.11761	.12639
Annual	.09771	.10181	.10596	.11017	.11443	.11874	.12750
30 Years							
Monthly	.09227	.09656	.10091	.10531	.10977	.11428	.12343
Annual	.09305	.09734	.10168	.10608	.11053	.11503	.12415

OAR Tables
(Precomputed Mortgage-Equity Over-All Rates)

Holding Periods: 5, 10, and 15 years

Equity Yield Rates: 2, 4, 6, 8, 10, 12, 14, 15, 18, 20, 25, 30, 40, and 50%

Loan Ratios: 60, 66.7, 70, 75, 80, and 90%

Loan Term: 10, 15, 20, 25, and 30 years

Interest Rates: 5, 5½, 6, 6½, 7, 7½, 8, 8½, 9, 9½, 10, 11, and 12%

Appreciation/Depreciation: 40, 30, 20, 10, 0, −10, −20, −30, and −40%

INTEREST RATE

TERM YEARS	APPR DEP	5.0	5.5	6.0	6.5	7.0	7.5	8.0	8.5	9.0	9.5	10.0	11.0	12.0
10	.40	-.042990	-.040513	-.038014	-.035495	-.032955	-.030394	-.027814	-.025213	-.022594	-.019956	-.017300	-.011933	-.006497
	.30	-.023774	-.021297	-.018798	-.016279	-.013739	-.011178	-.008598	-.005998	-.003378	-.000740	.001916	.007283	.012719
	.20	-.004558	-.002061	.000417	.002937	.005477	.008038	.010618	.013218	.015837	.018476	.021132	.026499	.031935
	.10	.014658	.017135	.019633	.022153	.024693	.027253	.029834	.032434	.035053	.037691	.040348	.045715	.051151
	0.00	.033089	.036351	.038849	.041369	.043909	.046469	.049050	.051650	.054269	.056907	.059564	.064931	.070366
	-.10	.053089	.055566	.058065	.060584	.063125	.065685	.068266	.070866	.073485	.076123	.078780	.084146	.089582
	-.20	.072505	.074782	.077281	.079800	.082340	.084901	.087481	.090082	.092701	.095339	.097995	.103362	.108798
	-.30	.091521	.093998	.096497	.099014	.101556	.104117	.106697	.109297	.111917	.114555	.117211	.122578	.128014
	-.40	.110737	.113214	.115712	.118232	.120772	.123333	.125913	.128513	.131133	.133771	.136427	.141794	.147230
15	.40	-.041261	-.038524	-.035766	-.032988	-.030190	-.027373	-.024538	-.021686	-.018817	-.015932	-.013033	-.007192	-.001299
	.30	-.022645	-.019308	-.016550	-.013772	-.010974	-.008157	-.005322	-.002470	.000399	.003284	.006183	.012024	.017917
	.20	-.002829	-.000092	.002666	.005444	.008242	.011059	.013894	.016746	.019615	.022499	.025399	.031240	.037132
	.10	.016387	.019124	.021882	.024660	.027458	.030275	.033110	.035962	.038831	.041715	.044615	.050456	.056348
	0.00	.035603	.038339	.041097	.043876	.046674	.049491	.052326	.055178	.058046	.060931	.063831	.069672	.075564
	-.10	.054819	.057555	.060313	.063092	.065890	.068706	.071541	.074394	.077262	.080147	.083046	.088888	.094780
	-.20	.074034	.076771	.079529	.082307	.085105	.087922	.090757	.093609	.096478	.099363	.102262	.108103	.113996
	-.30	.093250	.095987	.098745	.101523	.104321	.107138	.109973	.112825	.115694	.118579	.121548	.127319	.133212
	-.40	.112466	.115203	.117961	.120739	.123537	.126354	.129189	.132041	.134910	.137794	.140694	.146535	.152427
20	.40	-.040422	-.037566	-.034690	-.031797	-.028887	-.025962	-.023022	-.020069	-.017103	-.014126	-.011139	-.005137	.000896
	.30	-.021206	-.018350	-.015474	-.012581	-.009671	-.006746	-.003806	-.000853	.002113	.005089	.008077	.014079	.020112
	.20	-.001991	.000866	.003741	.006635	.009544	.012470	.015410	.018363	.021328	.024305	.027293	.033295	.039328
	.10	.017225	.020082	.022957	.025850	.028760	.031686	.034625	.037579	.040544	.043521	.046508	.052511	.058544
	0.00	.036441	.039298	.042173	.045066	.047976	.050901	.053841	.056795	.059760	.062737	.065724	.071726	.077760
	-.10	.055657	.058513	.061389	.064282	.067192	.070117	.073057	.076010	.078976	.081953	.084940	.090942	.096976
	-.20	.074873	.077729	.080605	.083498	.086408	.089333	.092273	.095226	.098192	.101169	.104156	.110158	.116192
	-.30	.094089	.096945	.099821	.102714	.105624	.108549	.111489	.114442	.117408	.120384	.123372	.129374	.135407
	-.40	.113304	.116161	.119036	.121930	.124839	.127765	.130705	.133658	.136623	.139600	.142588	.148590	.154623
25	.40	-.039939	-.037016	-.034081	-.031130	-.028165	-.025188	-.022200	-.019203	-.016198	-.013185	-.010166	-.004112	.001957
	.30	-.020724	-.017803	-.014866	-.011914	-.008949	-.005972	-.002985	.000013	.003018	.006031	.009050	.015104	.021173
	.20	-.001508	.001413	.004350	.007302	.010267	.013244	.016231	.019228	.022234	.025247	.028266	.034320	.040389
	.10	.017708	.020629	.023566	.026518	.029483	.032460	.035447	.038444	.041450	.044463	.047482	.053536	.059605
	0.00	.036924	.039845	.042782	.045734	.048699	.051675	.054663	.057660	.060666	.063678	.066698	.072751	.078820
	-.10	.056140	.059061	.061998	.064949	.067914	.070891	.073879	.076876	.079881	.082894	.085913	.091967	.098036
	-.20	.075356	.078277	.081214	.084165	.087130	.090107	.093095	.096092	.099097	.102110	.105129	.111183	.117252
	-.30	.094572	.097492	.100429	.103381	.106346	.109323	.112311	.115308	.118313	.121326	.124345	.130399	.136468
	-.40	.113787	.116708	.119645	.122597	.125562	.128539	.131526	.134523	.137529	.140542	.143561	.149615	.155684
30	.40	-.039633	-.036675	-.033704	-.030721	-.027728	-.024726	-.021717	-.018701	-.015681	-.012656	-.009628	-.003565	.002503
	.30	-.020417	-.017459	-.014488	-.011505	-.008512	-.005510	-.002501	.000515	.003535	.006560	.009588	.015651	.021718
	.20	-.001202	.001757	.004728	.007711	.010704	.013706	.016715	.019731	.022751	.025776	.028804	.034867	.040934
	.10	.018014	.020972	.023944	.026927	.029920	.032922	.035931	.038946	.041967	.044992	.048020	.054082	.060150
	0.00	.037230	.040188	.043160	.046143	.049136	.052138	.055147	.058162	.061183	.064208	.067236	.073298	.079366
	-.10	.056446	.059404	.062375	.065359	.068352	.071353	.074363	.077378	.080399	.083423	.086451	.092513	.098582
	-.20	.075662	.078620	.081591	.084574	.087567	.090569	.093579	.096594	.099615	.102639	.105667	.111730	.117798
	-.30	.094878	.097836	.100807	.103790	.106783	.109785	.112794	.115810	.118830	.121855	.124883	.130946	.137013
	-.40	.114093	.117052	.120023	.123006	.125999	.129001	.132010	.135026	.138046	.141071	.144099	.150162	.156229

5.0 YEAR HOLDING PERIOD
.020 EQUITY YIELD RATE
.667 LOAN RATIO

INTEREST RATE

TERM YEARS	APPR DEP	5.0	5.5	6.0	6.5	7.0	7.5	8.0	8.5	9.0	9.5	10.0	11.0	12.0
10	.40	-.041448	-.038696	-.035920	-.033120	-.030298	-.027453	-.024586	-.021697	-.018786	-.015855	-.012903	-.006940	-.000500
	.30	-.022232	-.019480	-.016704	-.013905	-.011082	-.008237	-.005370	-.002481	.000430	.003361	.006312	.012276	.018315
	.20	-.003017	-.000264	.002512	.005311	.008134	.010979	.013846	.016735	.019645	.022577	.025528	.031491	.037531
	.10	.016199	.018952	.021728	.024527	.027350	.030195	.033062	.035951	.038861	.041792	.044744	.050707	.056747
	0.00	.035415	.038167	.040943	.043743	.046565	.049410	.052278	.055167	.058077	.061008	.063960	.069923	.075963
	-.10	.054631	.057383	.060159	.062959	.065781	.068626	.071494	.074383	.077293	.080224	.083176	.089139	.095179
	-.20	.073807	.076599	.079375	.082175	.084997	.087842	.090709	.093598	.096509	.099440	.102392	.108355	.114395
	-.30	.093063	.095815	.098591	.101390	.104213	.107058	.109925	.112814	.115725	.118656	.121608	.127571	.133610
	-.40	.112278	.115031	.117807	.120606	.123429	.126274	.129141	.132030	.134940	.137872	.140823	.146787	.152826
15	.40	-.039527	-.036486	-.033422	-.030335	-.027226	-.024096	-.020946	-.017777	-.014589	-.011384	-.008162	-.001672	.004875
	.30	-.020311	-.017270	-.014206	-.011119	-.008010	-.004880	-.001730	.001439	.004627	.007832	.011053	.017544	.024091
	.20	-.001095	.001946	.005010	.008097	.011206	.014336	.017486	.020655	.023842	.027047	.030269	.036559	.043306
	.10	.018121	.021161	.024226	.027313	.030422	.033552	.036702	.039871	.043058	.046263	.049485	.055975	.062522
	0.00	.037336	.040377	.043442	.046529	.049638	.052767	.055917	.059087	.062274	.065479	.068701	.075191	.081738
	-.10	.056552	.059593	.062657	.065745	.068853	.071983	.075133	.078302	.081490	.084695	.087917	.094407	.100954
	-.20	.075768	.078809	.081873	.084960	.088069	.091199	.094349	.097518	.100706	.103911	.107133	.113623	.120170
	-.30	.094984	.098025	.101089	.104176	.107285	.110415	.113565	.116734	.119922	.123127	.126348	.132839	.139386
	-.40	.114200	.117241	.120305	.123392	.126501	.129631	.132781	.135950	.139137	.142342	.145564	.152054	.158602
20	.40	-.038595	-.035421	-.032227	-.029012	-.025779	-.022528	-.019262	-.015980	-.012685	-.009378	-.006058	.000611	.007315
	.30	-.019380	-.016206	-.013011	-.009796	-.006563	-.003312	-.000046	.003235	.006531	.009838	.013157	.019827	.026530
	.20	-.000164	.003010	.006210	.009420	.012653	.015903	.019170	.022451	.025746	.029054	.032373	.039042	.045746
	.10	.019052	.022226	.025421	.028636	.031869	.035119	.038386	.041667	.044962	.048270	.051589	.058258	.064952
	0.00	.038268	.041442	.044637	.047852	.051085	.054335	.057602	.060883	.064178	.067486	.070805	.077474	.084178
	-.10	.057484	.060658	.063853	.067067	.070301	.073551	.076817	.080099	.083394	.086702	.090021	.096690	.103394
	-.20	.076700	.079874	.083068	.086283	.089516	.092767	.096033	.099315	.102610	.105917	.109237	.115906	.122610
	-.30	.095915	.099089	.102284	.105499	.108732	.111983	.115249	.118531	.121826	.125133	.128453	.135122	.141825
	-.40	.115131	.118305	.121500	.124715	.127948	.131199	.134465	.137746	.141041	.144349	.147668	.154338	.161041
25	.40	-.038059	-.034813	-.031550	-.028270	-.024976	-.021668	-.018349	-.015019	-.011679	-.008332	-.004977	.001750	.008493
	.30	-.018843	-.015598	-.012334	-.009055	-.005760	-.002452	.000867	.004197	.007537	.010884	.014239	.020965	.027709
	.20	.000373	.003618	.006882	.010161	.013456	.016763	.020083	.023413	.026753	.030100	.033455	.040181	.046925
	.10	.019589	.022834	.026098	.029377	.032672	.035979	.039299	.042629	.045968	.049316	.052671	.059397	.066141
	0.00	.038805	.042050	.045313	.048593	.051887	.055195	.058515	.061845	.065184	.068532	.071886	.078613	.085356
	-.10	.058020	.061266	.064529	.067809	.071103	.074411	.077730	.081061	.084400	.087748	.091102	.097829	.104572
	-.20	.077236	.080482	.083745	.087025	.090319	.093627	.096946	.100276	.103616	.106963	.110318	.117045	.123788
	-.30	.096452	.099698	.102961	.106241	.109535	.112843	.116162	.119492	.122832	.126179	.129534	.136260	.143004
	-.40	.115668	.118913	.122177	.125456	.128751	.132058	.135378	.138708	.142048	.145395	.148750	.155468	.162220
30	.40	-.037719	-.034432	-.031130	-.027816	-.024490	-.021155	-.017811	-.014461	-.011104	-.007744	-.004379	.002357	.009099
	.30	-.018503	-.015216	-.011914	-.008600	-.005274	-.001939	.001405	.004755	.008111	.011472	.014837	.021573	.028315
	.20	.000713	.004000	.007301	.010616	.013942	.017277	.020621	.023971	.027327	.030688	.034052	.040789	.047531
	.10	.019929	.023216	.026517	.029832	.033157	.036493	.039836	.043187	.046543	.049904	.053268	.060005	.066747
	0.00	.039145	.042432	.045734	.049048	.052373	.055709	.059052	.062403	.065759	.069120	.072484	.079221	.085962
	-.10	.058361	.061648	.064950	.068264	.071589	.074924	.078268	.081619	.084975	.088336	.091700	.098436	.105178
	-.20	.077576	.080863	.084165	.087479	.090805	.094140	.097484	.100834	.104191	.107551	.110916	.117652	.124394
	-.30	.096792	.100079	.103381	.106695	.110021	.113356	.116700	.120050	.123406	.126767	.130132	.136868	.143610
	-.40	.116008	.119295	.122596	.125911	.129237	.132572	.135916	.139266	.142622	.145983	.149348	.156084	.162826

5.0 YEAR HOLDING PERIOD
.020 EQUITY YIELD RATE
.700 LOAN RATIO

INTEREST RATE

TERM YEARS	APPR DEP	5.0	5.5	6.0	6.5	7.0	7.5	8.0	8.5	9.0	9.5	10.0	11.0	12.0
10	.40	-.040678	-.037788	-.034873	-.031933	-.028970	-.025983	-.022972	-.019939	-.016883	-.013805	-.010706	-.004444	.001897
	.30	-.021462	-.018572	-.015657	-.012718	-.009754	-.006767	-.003756	-.000723	.002333	.005411	.008510	.014772	.021113
	.20	-.002246	.000644	.003559	.006498	.009462	.012449	.015460	.018493	.021549	.024627	.027726	.033987	.040329
	.10	.016970	.019860	.022775	.025714	.028678	.031665	.034676	.037709	.040765	.043843	.046942	.053203	.059545
	0.00	.036186	.039076	.041991	.044930	.047894	.050881	.053891	.056925	.059981	.063058	.066158	.072419	.078761
	-.10	.055402	.058292	.061206	.064146	.067109	.070097	.073107	.076141	.079197	.082274	.085374	.091635	.097977
	-.20	.074617	.077507	.080422	.083362	.086325	.089312	.092323	.095357	.098412	.101490	.104589	.110851	.117192
	-.30	.093833	.096723	.099638	.102577	.105541	.108528	.111539	.114572	.117628	.120706	.123805	.130067	.136408
	-.40	.113049	.115939	.118854	.121793	.124757	.127744	.130755	.133788	.136844	.139922	.143021	.149282	.155624
15	.40	-.038660	-.035467	-.032250	-.029008	-.025744	-.022458	-.019150	-.015823	-.012476	-.009110	-.005728	.001087	.007961
	.30	-.019444	-.016251	-.013034	-.009793	-.006528	-.003242	-.000066	.003393	.006740	.010105	.013488	.020303	.027177
	.20	-.000228	.002964	.006182	.009423	.012688	.015974	.019281	.022609	.025956	.029321	.032704	.039519	.046393
	.10	.018987	.022180	.025398	.028639	.031903	.035190	.038497	.041825	.045172	.048537	.051920	.058734	.065609
	0.00	.038203	.041396	.044614	.047855	.051119	.054406	.057713	.061041	.064388	.067753	.071136	.077950	.084825
	-.10	.057419	.060612	.063829	.067071	.070335	.073622	.076929	.080257	.083603	.086969	.090351	.097166	.104041
	-.20	.076635	.079828	.083045	.086287	.089551	.092837	.096145	.099472	.102819	.106185	.109567	.116382	.123256
	-.30	.095851	.099044	.102261	.105503	.108767	.112053	.115361	.118688	.122035	.125400	.128783	.135598	.142472
	-.40	.115067	.118259	.121477	.124718	.127983	.131269	.134576	.137904	.141251	.144616	.147999	.154814	.151688
20	.40	-.037682	-.034350	-.030995	-.027619	-.024225	-.020812	-.017382	-.013936	-.010477	-.007034	-.003518	.003484	.010523
	.30	-.018466	-.015134	-.011779	-.008404	-.005009	-.001596	.001834	.005279	.008739	.012212	.015697	.022700	.029739
	.20	.000750	.004082	.007437	.010812	.014207	.017620	.021050	.024495	.027955	.031428	.034913	.041916	.048955
	.10	.019965	.023298	.026653	.030028	.033423	.036836	.040266	.043711	.047171	.050644	.054129	.061132	.068171
	0.00	.039181	.042514	.045869	.049244	.052639	.056052	.059482	.062927	.066387	.069850	.073345	.080348	.087386
	-.10	.058397	.061730	.065084	.068460	.071855	.075268	.078697	.082143	.085603	.089076	.092561	.099563	.106602
	-.20	.077613	.080946	.084300	.087676	.091070	.094483	.097913	.101359	.104818	.108291	.111777	.118779	.125818
	-.30	.096829	.100161	.103516	.106891	.110286	.113699	.117129	.120574	.124034	.127507	.130993	.137995	.145034
	-.40	.116045	.119377	.122732	.126107	.129502	.132915	.136345	.139790	.143250	.146723	.150208	.157211	.164250
25	.40	-.037119	-.033711	-.030284	-.026841	-.023382	-.019909	-.016423	-.012927	-.009420	-.005905	-.002383	.004680	.011761
	.30	-.017903	-.014495	-.011069	-.007625	-.004166	-.000693	.002793	.006289	.009796	.013311	.016833	.023896	.030976
	.20	.001313	.004721	.008147	.011591	.015050	.018523	.022008	.025505	.029012	.032526	.036049	.043112	.050192
	.10	.020529	.023937	.027363	.030807	.034266	.037739	.041224	.044721	.048227	.051742	.055265	.062327	.069408
	0.00	.039745	.043152	.046579	.050022	.053482	.056955	.060440	.063937	.067443	.070958	.074480	.081543	.088624
	-.10	.058961	.062368	.065795	.069238	.072697	.076170	.079656	.083153	.086659	.090174	.093696	.100759	.107840
	-.20	.078176	.081584	.085011	.088454	.091913	.095386	.098872	.102368	.105875	.109390	.112912	.119975	.127056
	-.30	.097392	.100800	.104226	.107670	.111129	.114602	.118088	.121584	.125091	.128606	.132128	.139191	.146271
	-.40	.116608	.120016	.123442	.126886	.130345	.133818	.137304	.140800	.144307	.147822	.151344	.158407	.165487
30	.40	-.036762	-.033310	-.029844	-.026364	-.022872	-.019369	-.015859	-.012341	-.008817	-.005288	-.001755	.005318	.012397
	.30	-.017546	-.014095	-.010628	-.007148	-.003656	-.000154	.003357	.006875	.010399	.013928	.017465	.024534	.031613
	.20	.001670	.005121	.008588	.012068	.015560	.019062	.022573	.026091	.029615	.033144	.036676	.043750	.050829
	.10	.020886	.024337	.027804	.031284	.034776	.038278	.041789	.045307	.048831	.052360	.055892	.062965	.070044
	0.00	.040102	.043553	.047020	.050500	.053992	.057494	.061005	.064523	.068047	.071575	.075108	.082181	.089260
	-.10	.059318	.062769	.066235	.069716	.073208	.076710	.080220	.083738	.087262	.090791	.094324	.101397	.108476
	-.20	.078533	.081985	.085451	.088931	.092423	.095926	.099436	.102954	.106478	.110007	.113540	.120613	.127692
	-.30	.097749	.101200	.104667	.108147	.111639	.115141	.118652	.122170	.125694	.129223	.132756	.139829	.146908
	-.40	.116965	.120416	.123883	.127363	.130855	.134357	.137868	.141386	.144910	.148439	.151971	.159045	.166124

5.0 YEAR HOLDING PERIOD
.020 EQUITY YIELD RATE
.750 LOAN RATIO

INTEREST RATE

TERM YEARS	APPR DEP	5.0	5.5	6.0	6.5	7.0	7.5	8.0	8.5	9.0	9.5	10.0	11.0	12.0
10	.40	-.039521	-.036425	-.033302	-.030153	-.026977	-.023777	-.020551	-.017301	-.014027	-.010729	-.007409	-.000700	.006695
	.30	-.020306	-.017209	-.014086	-.010937	-.007762	-.004561	-.001335	.001915	.005189	.008487	.011807	.018516	.025510
	.20	-.001090	.002007	.005130	.008279	.011455	.014655	.017881	.021131	.024405	.027702	.031023	.037732	.044526
	.10	.018126	.021222	.024345	.027495	.030670	.033871	.037096	.040346	.043621	.046918	.050239	.056947	.063742
	0.00	.037342	.040438	.043561	.046711	.049886	.053087	.056312	.059562	.062836	.066134	.069455	.076163	.082558
	-.10	.056558	.059654	.062777	.065926	.069102	.072302	.075528	.078778	.082052	.085350	.088671	.095379	.102174
	-.20	.075774	.078870	.081993	.085142	.088318	.091518	.094744	.097994	.101268	.104566	.107886	.114595	.121390
	-.30	.094989	.098086	.101209	.104358	.107533	.110734	.113960	.117210	.120484	.123782	.127102	.133811	.140605
	-.40	.114205	.117302	.120425	.123574	.126749	.129950	.133176	.136426	.139700	.142997	.146318	.153027	.159821
15	.40	-.037360	-.033939	-.030492	-.027019	-.023521	-.020000	-.016456	-.012891	-.009305	-.005700	-.002075	.005226	.012552
	.30	-.018144	-.014723	-.011276	-.007803	-.004305	-.000784	.002759	.006325	.009911	.013516	.017141	.024442	.031808
	.20	.001072	.004493	.007940	.011403	.014910	.018432	.021975	.025540	.029126	.032732	.036357	.043658	.051023
	.10	.020288	.023708	.027156	.030629	.034126	.037647	.041191	.044756	.048342	.051948	.055572	.062874	.070239
	0.00	.039503	.042924	.046372	.049845	.053342	.056863	.060407	.063972	.067558	.071164	.074788	.082090	.089455
	-.10	.058719	.062140	.065588	.069060	.072558	.076079	.079623	.083188	.086771	.090380	.094004	.101305	.108671
	-.20	.077935	.081356	.084803	.088276	.091774	.095295	.098839	.102404	.105990	.109595	.113220	.120521	.127887
	-.30	.097151	.100572	.104019	.107492	.110990	.114511	.118054	.121620	.125206	.128811	.132436	.139737	.147103
	-.40	.116367	.119788	.123235	.126708	.130206	.133727	.137270	.140836	.144421	.148027	.151652	.158953	.166318
20	.40	-.036312	-.032741	-.029147	-.025531	-.021893	-.018237	-.014562	-.010870	-.007163	-.003442	.000292	.007795	.015336
	.30	-.017096	-.013526	-.009931	-.006315	-.002677	.000979	.004654	.008346	.012053	.015774	.019508	.027011	.034552
	.20	.002120	.005690	.009285	.012901	.016538	.020195	.023870	.027561	.031268	.034990	.038724	.046226	.053768
	.10	.021336	.024906	.028500	.032117	.035754	.039411	.043086	.046777	.050484	.054205	.057940	.065442	.072984
	0.00	.040551	.044122	.047716	.051333	.054970	.058627	.062302	.065993	.069700	.073421	.077155	.084658	.092200
	-.10	.059767	.063338	.066932	.070549	.074186	.077843	.081517	.085209	.088916	.092637	.096371	.103874	.111416
	-.20	.078983	.082554	.086148	.089764	.093402	.097059	.100733	.104425	.108132	.111853	.115587	.123090	.130631
	-.30	.098199	.101770	.105364	.108980	.112618	.116274	.119949	.123641	.127348	.131069	.134803	.142306	.149847
	-.40	.117415	.120985	.124580	.128196	.131833	.135490	.139165	.142856	.146563	.150285	.154019	.161521	.169063
25	.40	-.035708	-.032057	-.028386	-.024696	-.020990	-.017269	-.013535	-.009788	-.006031	-.002265	.001509	.009076	.016662
	.30	-.016493	-.012841	-.009170	-.005481	-.001774	.001947	.005681	.009428	.013184	.016950	.020724	.028292	.035878
	.20	.002723	.006374	.010046	.013735	.017441	.021163	.024897	.028643	.032400	.036166	.039940	.047508	.055094
	.10	.021939	.025590	.029262	.032951	.036657	.040378	.044113	.047859	.051616	.055382	.059156	.066723	.074310
	0.00	.041155	.044806	.048477	.052167	.055873	.059594	.063329	.067075	.070832	.074598	.078372	.085939	.093526
	-.10	.060371	.064022	.067693	.071383	.075089	.078810	.082545	.086291	.090048	.093814	.097588	.105155	.112741
	-.20	.079587	.083238	.086909	.090599	.094305	.098026	.101760	.105507	.109264	.113030	.116804	.124371	.131957
	-.30	.098803	.102454	.106125	.109814	.113521	.117242	.120976	.124723	.128480	.132246	.136019	.143587	.151173
	-.40	.118018	.121669	.125341	.129030	.132736	.136458	.140192	.143938	.147695	.151461	.155235	.162803	.170389
30	.40	-.035326	-.031628	-.027914	-.024185	-.020444	-.016691	-.012930	-.009161	-.005385	-.001604	.002181	.009759	.017344
	.30	-.016110	-.012412	-.008698	-.004969	-.001228	.002525	.006286	.010055	.013831	.017612	.021397	.028975	.036560
	.20	.003106	.006804	.010518	.014247	.017988	.021740	.025502	.029271	.033047	.036828	.040613	.048191	.055776
	.10	.022322	.026019	.029734	.033463	.037204	.040956	.044718	.048487	.052263	.056044	.059829	.067403	.074992
	0.00	.041538	.045235	.048950	.052678	.056420	.060172	.063934	.067703	.071479	.075260	.079044	.086603	.094207
	-.10	.060753	.064451	.068165	.071894	.075636	.079388	.083149	.086919	.090694	.094475	.098260	.105839	.113423
	-.20	.079969	.083667	.087381	.091110	.094851	.098604	.102365	.106135	.109910	.113691	.117476	.125055	.132635
	-.30	.099185	.102883	.106597	.110326	.114067	.117820	.121581	.125350	.129126	.132907	.136691	.144270	.151855
	-.40	.118401	.122099	.125813	.129542	.133283	.137035	.140797	.144566	.148342	.152123	.155908	.163486	.171071

5.0 YEAR HOLDING PERIOD
.020 EQUITY YIELD RATE
.800 LOAN RATIO

INTEREST RATE

TERM YEARS	APPR DEP	5.0	5.5	6.0	6.5	7.0	7.5	8.0	8.5	9.0	9.5	10.0	11.0	12.0
10	.40	-.038365	-.035063	-.031731	-.028372	-.024985	-.021571	-.018130	-.014664	-.011171	-.007654	-.004112	.003044	.010292
	.30	-.019149	-.015847	-.012515	-.009156	-.005769	-.002355	.001086	.004552	.008045	.011552	.015104	.022260	.029508
	.20	-.000066	.003369	.006700	.010060	.013447	.016861	.020301	.023768	.027261	.030778	.034320	.041476	.048723
	.10	.019282	.022585	.025916	.029276	.032662	.036077	.039517	.042984	.046476	.049994	.053536	.060692	.067936
	0.00	.038498	.041801	.045132	.048491	.051878	.055292	.058733	.062200	.065692	.069210	.072752	.079907	.087155
	-.10	.057714	.061017	.064348	.067707	.071094	.074508	.077949	.081416	.084908	.088426	.091968	.099123	.106371
	-.20	.076930	.080232	.083564	.086923	.090310	.093724	.097165	.100631	.104124	.107641	.111183	.118339	.125587
	-.30	.096146	.099448	.102780	.106139	.109526	.112940	.116381	.119847	.123340	.126857	.130399	.137505	.144803
	-.40	.115361	.118664	.121995	.125355	.128742	.132156	.135596	.139063	.142556	.146073	.149615	.156771	.164019
15	.40	-.036060	-.032411	-.028734	-.025029	-.021298	-.017543	-.013763	-.009960	-.006135	-.002289	.001577	.009366	.017222
	.30	-.016844	-.013195	-.009518	-.005813	-.002083	.001673	.005453	.009256	.013081	.016927	.020793	.028581	.036438
	.20	.002372	.006021	.009698	.013403	.017133	.020889	.024669	.028472	.032297	.036143	.040009	.047797	.055654
	.10	.021588	.025237	.028914	.032619	.036349	.040105	.043885	.047688	.051513	.055359	.059225	.067013	.074870
	0.00	.040804	.044453	.048130	.051834	.055565	.059321	.063101	.066904	.070729	.074575	.078441	.086229	.094085
	-.10	.060019	.063668	.067346	.071050	.074781	.078537	.082317	.086119	.089945	.093791	.097657	.105445	.113301
	-.20	.079235	.082884	.086562	.090266	.093997	.097752	.101532	.105335	.109160	.113006	.116847	.124661	.132517
	-.30	.098451	.102100	.105777	.109482	.113212	.116968	.120748	.124551	.128376	.132222	.136088	.143876	.151733
	-.40	.117667	.121316	.124993	.128698	.132428	.136184	.139964	.143767	.147592	.151438	.155304	.163092	.170949
20	.40	-.034942	-.031133	-.027299	-.023442	-.019562	-.015661	-.011742	-.007804	-.003850	.000119	.004102	.012105	.020150
	.30	-.015726	-.011917	-.008083	-.004226	-.000346	.003554	.007474	.011412	.015366	.019335	.023318	.031321	.039366
	.20	.003490	.007298	.011132	.014990	.018870	.022770	.026690	.030628	.034582	.038551	.042534	.050537	.058581
	.10	.022706	.026514	.030348	.034206	.038086	.041986	.045906	.049843	.053798	.057767	.061750	.069753	.077797
	0.00	.041921	.045730	.049564	.053422	.057301	.061202	.065122	.069059	.073013	.076983	.080966	.088969	.097013
	-.10	.061137	.064946	.068780	.072637	.076517	.080418	.084338	.088275	.092229	.096198	.100182	.108184	.116229
	-.20	.080353	.084162	.087996	.091853	.095733	.099634	.103553	.107491	.111445	.115414	.119397	.127400	.135445
	-.30	.099569	.103378	.107212	.111069	.114949	.118849	.122769	.126707	.130661	.134630	.138613	.146616	.154661
	-.40	.118785	.122593	.126427	.130285	.134165	.138065	.141985	.145923	.149877	.153846	.157829	.165832	.173876
25	.40	-.034298	-.030403	-.026487	-.022552	-.018599	-.014629	-.010646	-.006650	-.002643	.001375	.005400	.013472	.021564
	.30	-.015082	-.011188	-.007272	-.003336	.000617	.004586	.008570	.012566	.016573	.020590	.024616	.032688	.040780
	.20	.004134	.008028	.011944	.015880	.019833	.023802	.027786	.031782	.035789	.039806	.043832	.051903	.059996
	.10	.023350	.027244	.031160	.035096	.039049	.043018	.047002	.050998	.055005	.059022	.063048	.071119	.079211
	0.00	.042565	.046460	.050376	.054311	.058265	.062234	.066217	.070213	.074221	.078238	.082263	.090335	.098427
	-.10	.061781	.065676	.069592	.073527	.077481	.081450	.085433	.089429	.093437	.097454	.101475	.109551	.117643
	-.20	.080997	.084892	.088808	.092743	.096696	.100666	.104649	.108645	.112656	.116670	.120695	.128763	.136855
	-.30	.100213	.104107	.108023	.111959	.115912	.119881	.123865	.127861	.131868	.135885	.139911	.147983	.156075
	-.40	.119429	.123323	.127239	.131175	.135128	.139097	.143081	.147077	.151084	.155101	.159127	.167198	.175291
30	.40	-.033890	-.029946	-.025984	-.022006	-.018016	-.014013	-.010001	-.005980	-.001953	.002080	.006117	.014201	.022291
	.30	-.014674	-.010730	-.006768	-.002791	.001200	.005203	.009215	.013236	.017263	.021296	.025333	.033417	.041507
	.20	.004542	.008486	.012448	.016425	.020416	.024418	.028431	.032451	.036479	.040512	.044549	.052633	.060723
	.10	.023758	.027702	.031664	.035641	.039632	.043634	.047647	.051667	.055695	.059728	.063765	.071849	.079939
	0.00	.042973	.046918	.050380	.054857	.058848	.062850	.066862	.070883	.074910	.078943	.082981	.091064	.099155
	-.10	.062189	.066134	.070095	.074073	.078064	.082066	.086078	.090099	.094126	.098159	.102197	.110280	.118370
	-.20	.081405	.085349	.089311	.093289	.097279	.101282	.105294	.109315	.113342	.117375	.121412	.129496	.137586
	-.30	.100621	.104565	.108527	.112504	.116495	.120498	.124510	.128531	.132558	.136591	.140628	.148712	.156802
	-.40	.119837	.123781	.127743	.131720	.135711	.139714	.143726	.147746	.151807	.155807	.159844	.167928	.176018

124

5.0 YEAR HOLDING PERIOD
.020 EQUITY YIELD RATE
.900 LOAN RATIO

INTEREST RATE

TERM YEARS	APPR DEP	5.0	5.5	6.0	6.5	7.0	7.5	8.0	8.5	9.0	9.5	10.0	11.0	12.0
10	.40	-.036053	-.032337	-.028590	-.024811	-.021000	-.017159	-.013289	-.009389	-.005460	-.001502	.002482	.010533	.018686
	.30	-.016837	-.013122	-.009374	-.005595	-.001784	.002056	.005927	.009827	.013756	.017713	.021698	.029748	.037902
	.20	.002379	.006094	.009843	.013621	.017431	.021272	.025143	.029043	.032972	.036929	.040914	.048964	.057118
	.10	.021594	.025310	.029058	.032837	.036647	.040488	.044359	.048259	.052188	.056145	.060130	.068180	.076334
	0.00	.040810	.044526	.048274	.052053	.055863	.059704	.063575	.067475	.071404	.075361	.079346	.087396	.095550
	-.10	.060026	.063742	.067489	.071269	.075079	.078920	.082790	.086691	.090620	.094577	.098562	.106612	.114765
	-.20	.079242	.082958	.086705	.090484	.094295	.098136	.102006	.105906	.109835	.113793	.117777	.125828	.133981
	-.30	.098458	.102173	.105921	.109700	.113511	.117351	.121122	.125122	.129051	.133008	.136993	.145043	.153197
	-.40	.117674	.121389	.125137	.128916	.132726	.136567	.140438	.144338	.148267	.152224	.156209	.164259	.172413
15	.40	-.033459	-.029354	-.025217	-.021050	-.016853	-.012628	-.008375	-.004097	.000206	.004533	.008882	.017644	.026483
	.30	-.014243	-.010138	-.006001	-.001834	.002363	.006588	.010841	.015119	.019422	.023749	.028098	.036860	.045699
	.20	.004972	.009077	.013215	.017382	.021579	.025804	.030057	.034335	.038638	.042965	.047314	.056076	.064914
	.10	.024188	.028293	.032430	.036598	.040795	.045020	.049272	.053551	.057854	.062181	.066530	.075292	.084130
	0.00	.043404	.047509	.051646	.055814	.060011	.064236	.068488	.072767	.077070	.081397	.085746	.094508	.103346
	-.10	.062620	.066725	.070862	.075029	.079226	.083452	.087704	.091982	.096286	.100612	.104962	.113723	.122562
	-.20	.081836	.085941	.090078	.094245	.098442	.102668	.106920	.111198	.115501	.119828	.124178	.132939	.141778
	-.30	.101052	.105157	.109294	.113461	.117658	.121883	.126136	.130414	.134717	.139044	.143393	.152155	.160994
	-.40	.120267	.124373	.128510	.132674	.136874	.141099	.145352	.149630	.153933	.158260	.162609	.171371	.180209
20	.40	-.032202	-.027917	-.023604	-.019264	-.014899	-.010511	-.006101	-.001672	.002777	.007242	.011723	.020726	.029776
	.30	-.012986	-.008701	-.004388	-.000048	.004317	.008705	.013114	.017544	.021993	.026458	.030939	.039942	.048992
	.20	.006230	.010515	.014828	.019168	.023532	.027921	.032330	.036760	.041208	.045674	.050155	.059158	.068208
	.10	.025446	.029731	.034044	.038384	.042748	.047136	.051546	.055976	.060424	.064890	.069371	.078374	.087424
	0.00	.044662	.048946	.053260	.057599	.061984	.066352	.070762	.075192	.079640	.084105	.088586	.097590	.106640
	-.10	.063877	.068162	.072475	.076815	.081180	.085568	.089978	.094408	.098856	.103321	.107802	.116806	.125856
	-.20	.083093	.087378	.091691	.096031	.100396	.104784	.109194	.113623	.118072	.122537	.127018	.136021	.145071
	-.30	.102309	.106594	.110907	.115247	.119612	.124000	.128410	.132839	.137288	.141753	.146234	.155237	.164287
	-.40	.121525	.125810	.130123	.134463	.138827	.143216	.147625	.152055	.156503	.160969	.165450	.174453	.183503
25	.40	-.031477	-.027096	-.022691	-.018263	-.013816	-.009350	-.004869	-.000373	.004135	.008654	.013183	.022264	.031367
	.30	-.012262	-.007880	-.003475	.000953	.005400	.009866	.014347	.018843	.023351	.027870	.032399	.041480	.050583
	.20	.006954	.011336	.015741	.020169	.024616	.029081	.033563	.038058	.042567	.047086	.051615	.060695	.069799
	.10	.026170	.030552	.034957	.039384	.043832	.048297	.052779	.057274	.061783	.066302	.070831	.079911	.089015
	0.00	.045386	.049767	.054173	.058600	.063048	.067513	.071995	.076490	.080998	.085518	.090046	.099127	.108231
	-.10	.064602	.068983	.073389	.077816	.082264	.086729	.091210	.095706	.100214	.104733	.109262	.118343	.127447
	-.20	.083818	.088199	.092605	.097032	.101479	.105945	.110426	.114922	.119430	.123949	.128478	.137559	.146652
	-.30	.103034	.107415	.111820	.116248	.120695	.125161	.129642	.134138	.138646	.143165	.147694	.156878	.165878
	-.40	.122249	.126631	.131036	.135464	.139911	.144376	.148858	.153354	.157862	.162381	.166910	.175990	.185034
30	.40	-.031018	-.026581	-.022124	-.017649	-.013160	-.008657	-.004143	.000380	.004911	.009448	.013990	.023084	.032136
	.30	-.011802	-.007365	-.002908	.001566	.006056	.010559	.015073	.019596	.024127	.028664	.033206	.042300	.051401
	.20	.007413	.011851	.016308	.020782	.025272	.029775	.034289	.038812	.043343	.047880	.052422	.061516	.070617
	.10	.026629	.031067	.035524	.039998	.044488	.048991	.053504	.058028	.062558	.067095	.071638	.080732	.089843
	0.00	.045845	.050282	.054739	.059214	.063704	.068206	.072720	.077243	.081774	.086311	.090853	.099947	.109000
	-.10	.065061	.069498	.073955	.078430	.082920	.087422	.091936	.096459	.100990	.105527	.110069	.119163	.128265
	-.20	.084277	.088714	.093171	.097646	.102135	.106638	.111152	.115675	.120206	.124743	.129285	.138379	.147481
	-.30	.103493	.107930	.112387	.116862	.121351	.125854	.130368	.134891	.139422	.143959	.148501	.157595	.166696
	-.40	.122708	.127146	.131603	.136077	.140567	.145070	.149584	.154107	.158638	.163175	.167717	.176811	.185912

5.0 YEAR HOLDING PERIOD
.040 EQUITY YIELD RATE
.600 LOAN RATIO

INTEREST RATE

TERM YEARS	APPR DEP	5.0	5.5	6.0	6.5	7.0	7.5	8.0	8.5	9.0	9.5	10.0	11.0	12.0
10	.40	-.029998	-.027549	-.025078	-.022586	-.020073	-.017540	-.014986	-.012413	-.009820	-.007209	-.004579	.000736	.006120
	.30	-.011536	-.009086	-.006615	-.004123	-.001610	.000923	.003477	.006050	.008642	.011254	.013884	.019198	.024583
	.20	.006927	.009377	.011847	.014340	.016852	.019386	.021939	.024512	.027105	.029716	.032347	.037661	.043045
	.10	.025390	.027839	.030310	.032802	.035315	.037848	.040402	.042975	.045568	.048179	.050809	.056124	.061508
	0.00	.043853	.046302	.048773	.051265	.053778	.056311	.058865	.061438	.064030	.066642	.069272	.074586	.079971
	-.10	.062315	.064765	.067236	.069728	.072241	.074774	.077327	.079901	.082493	.085105	.087735	.093049	.098433
	-.20	.080778	.083227	.085698	.088190	.090703	.093237	.095790	.098363	.100956	.103567	.106197	.111512	.116896
	-.30	.099241	.101690	.104161	.106653	.109166	.111699	.114253	.116826	.119419	.122030	.124660	.129975	.135359
	-.40	.117703	.120153	.122624	.125116	.127629	.130162	.132715	.135289	.137881	.140493	.143123	.148437	.153821
15	.40	-.029098	-.026395	-.023669	-.020923	-.018156	-.015370	-.012566	-.009743	-.006904	-.004048	-.001176	.004611	.010452
	.30	-.010636	-.007932	-.005207	-.002460	.000306	.003092	.005897	.008719	.011559	.014415	.017287	.023074	.028915
	.20	.007827	.010531	.013256	.016002	.018769	.021555	.024360	.027182	.030022	.032878	.035749	.041537	.047377
	.10	.026290	.028993	.031719	.034465	.037232	.040018	.042822	.045645	.048484	.051340	.054212	.059999	.065840
	0.00	.044752	.047456	.050181	.052928	.055694	.058480	.061285	.064108	.066947	.069803	.072675	.078462	.084303
	-.10	.063215	.065919	.068644	.071391	.074157	.076943	.079748	.082570	.085410	.088266	.091138	.096925	.102765
	-.20	.081678	.084382	.087107	.089853	.092620	.095406	.098210	.101033	.103873	.106729	.109600	.115387	.121228
	-.30	.100141	.102844	.105570	.108316	.111083	.113868	.116673	.119496	.122335	.125191	.128063	.133850	.139691
	-.40	.118603	.121307	.124032	.126779	.129545	.132331	.135136	.137958	.140798	.143654	.146526	.152313	.158154
20	.40	-.028662	-.025839	-.022995	-.020133	-.017254	-.014358	-.011446	-.008520	-.005580	-.002629	.000334	.006291	.012282
	.30	-.010199	-.007376	-.004533	-.001671	.001209	.004105	.007017	.009943	.012882	.015834	.018797	.024753	.030745
	.20	.008263	.011087	.013930	.016792	.019672	.022568	.025480	.028406	.031345	.034297	.037260	.043216	.049207
	.10	.026726	.029549	.032393	.035255	.038134	.041031	.043942	.046868	.049808	.052759	.055722	.061679	.067670
	0.00	.045189	.048012	.050855	.053717	.056597	.059493	.062405	.065331	.068270	.071222	.074185	.080142	.086133
	-.10	.063651	.066475	.069318	.072180	.075060	.077956	.080868	.083794	.086733	.089685	.092648	.098604	.104596
	-.20	.082114	.084938	.087781	.090643	.093523	.096419	.099330	.102256	.105196	.108147	.111111	.117067	.123058
	-.30	.100577	.103400	.106244	.109106	.111985	.114881	.117793	.120719	.123658	.126610	.129573	.135530	.141521
	-.40	.119040	.121863	.124706	.127568	.130448	.133344	.136256	.139182	.142121	.145073	.148036	.153992	.159984
25	.40	-.028411	-.025521	-.022614	-.019691	-.016753	-.013802	-.010839	-.007865	-.004881	-.001889	.001110	.007128	.013166
	.30	-.009948	-.007058	-.004151	-.001228	.001710	.004661	.007624	.010598	.013581	.016574	.019573	.025591	.031629
	.20	.008515	.011404	.014311	.017235	.020172	.023124	.026087	.029061	.032044	.035036	.038036	.044054	.050091
	.10	.026977	.029867	.032774	.035697	.038635	.041586	.044549	.047523	.050507	.053499	.056499	.062517	.068554
	0.00	.045440	.048330	.051237	.054160	.057098	.060049	.063012	.065986	.068970	.071962	.074961	.080979	.087017
	-.10	.063903	.066792	.069700	.072623	.075561	.078512	.081475	.084449	.087432	.090424	.093424	.099442	.105480
	-.20	.082365	.085255	.088162	.091085	.094023	.096974	.099938	.102911	.105895	.108887	.111887	.117905	.123942
	-.30	.100828	.103718	.106625	.109548	.112486	.115437	.118400	.121374	.124358	.127350	.130349	.136367	.142405
	-.40	.119291	.122181	.125088	.128011	.130949	.133900	.136863	.139837	.142820	.145813	.148812	.154830	.160868
30	.40	-.028252	-.025322	-.022377	-.019419	-.016450	-.013470	-.010431	-.007485	-.004482	-.001473	.001539	.007576	.013621
	.30	-.009789	-.006859	-.003915	-.000957	.002013	.004993	.007981	.010978	.013981	.016989	.020020	.026038	.032083
	.20	.008674	.011604	.014548	.017506	.020476	.023455	.026444	.029441	.032444	.035452	.038465	.044501	.050546
	.10	.027137	.030066	.033011	.035969	.038938	.041918	.044907	.047903	.050906	.053915	.056928	.062964	.069009
	0.00	.045599	.048529	.051474	.054431	.057401	.060381	.063370	.066366	.069369	.072377	.075390	.081426	.087472
	-.10	.064062	.066992	.069936	.072894	.075864	.078844	.081832	.084829	.087832	.090840	.093853	.099889	.105993
	-.20	.082525	.085454	.088399	.091357	.094326	.097306	.100295	.103291	.106294	.109303	.112316	.118352	.124397
	-.30	.100987	.103917	.106862	.109820	.112789	.115769	.118758	.121754	.124757	.127766	.130778	.136815	.142860
	-.40	.119450	.122380	.125324	.128282	.131252	.134232	.137220	.140217	.143220	.146228	.149241	.155277	.161323

5.0 YEAR HOLDING PERIOD
.040 EQUITY YIELD RATE
.667 LOAN RATIO

INTEREST RATE

TERM YEARS	APPR DEP	5.0	5.5	6.0	6.5	7.0	7.5	8.0	8.5	9.0	9.5	10.0	11.0	12.0
10	.40	-.029570	-.026849	-.024103	-.021334	-.018542	-.015727	-.012890	-.010031	-.007150	-.004249	-.001326	.004579	.010561
	.30	-.011107	-.008386	-.005640	-.002871	-.000079	.002735	.005573	.008432	.011312	.014214	.017137	.023042	.029024
	.20	.007355	.010077	.012822	.015591	.018383	.021198	.024035	.026895	.029775	.032677	.035599	.041504	.047487
	.10	.025818	.028539	.031285	.034054	.036846	.039661	.042498	.045357	.048238	.051140	.054063	.059949	.065949
	0.00	.044281	.047002	.049748	.052554	.055309	.058124	.060961	.063820	.066701	.069602	.072525	.078430	.084412
	-.10	.062743	.065465	.068210	.070979	.073771	.076586	.079424	.082283	.085163	.088065	.090987	.096892	.102875
	-.20	.081206	.083928	.086673	.089442	.092234	.095049	.097886	.100745	.103626	.106528	.109450	.115355	.121337
	-.30	.099669	.102390	.105136	.107905	.110697	.113512	.116363	.119208	.122089	.124990	.127913	.133818	.139800
	-.40	.118131	.120853	.123599	.126367	.129160	.131974	.134812	.137671	.140551	.143453	.146375	.152280	.158263
15	.40	-.028570	-.025566	-.022538	-.019487	-.016413	-.013317	-.010201	-.007065	-.003909	-.000736	.002455	.008885	.015375
	.30	-.010108	-.007104	-.004075	-.001024	.002050	.005146	.008262	.011398	.014553	.017727	.020917	.027348	.033837
	.20	.008355	.011359	.014387	.017439	.020513	.023608	.026725	.029861	.033016	.036189	.039380	.045810	.052300
	.10	.026818	.029822	.032850	.035902	.038976	.042071	.045187	.048324	.051479	.054652	.057843	.064273	.070763
	0.00	.045281	.048285	.051313	.054364	.057438	.060534	.063650	.066786	.069941	.073115	.076306	.082736	.089226
	-.10	.063743	.066747	.069776	.072827	.075901	.078997	.082113	.085249	.088404	.091578	.094768	.101198	.107688
	-.20	.082206	.085210	.088238	.091290	.094364	.097459	.100575	.103712	.106867	.110040	.113231	.119661	.126151
	-.30	.100669	.103673	.106701	.109752	.112826	.115922	.119038	.122174	.125330	.128503	.131694	.138124	.144614
	-.40	.119131	.122135	.125164	.128215	.131289	.134385	.137501	.140637	.143792	.146966	.150156	.156587	.163076
20	.40	-.028086	-.024948	-.021789	-.018609	-.015410	-.012191	-.008956	-.005705	-.002439	.000840	.004133	.010751	.017408
	.30	-.009623	-.006480	-.003327	-.000146	.003053	.006271	.009506	.012758	.016024	.019303	.022595	.029214	.035871
	.20	.008840	.011977	.015136	.018316	.021516	.024734	.027969	.031220	.034486	.037766	.041058	.047677	.054334
	.10	.027303	.030440	.033599	.036779	.039979	.043197	.046432	.049683	.052949	.056229	.059521	.066139	.072796
	0.00	.045765	.048902	.052062	.055242	.058441	.061659	.064895	.068146	.071412	.074691	.077984	.084602	.091259
	-.10	.064228	.067365	.070524	.073704	.076904	.080122	.083357	.086608	.089874	.093154	.096446	.103065	.109722
	-.20	.082691	.085828	.088987	.092167	.095367	.098585	.101820	.105071	.108337	.111617	.114909	.121527	.128184
	-.30	.101153	.104291	.107450	.110630	.113829	.117048	.120283	.123534	.126800	.130079	.133372	.139990	.146647
	-.40	.119616	.122753	.125912	.129093	.132292	.135510	.138745	.141997	.145263	.148542	.151834	.158453	.165110
25	.40	-.027806	-.024596	-.021365	-.018117	-.014853	-.011574	-.008282	-.004977	-.001662	.001662	.004995	.011682	.018390
	.30	-.009344	-.006133	-.002903	.000345	.003610	.006889	.010181	.013485	.016800	.020125	.023458	.030145	.036853
	.20	.009119	.012330	.015560	.018808	.022072	.025351	.028644	.031948	.035263	.038588	.041921	.048607	.055316
	.10	.027582	.030793	.034023	.037271	.040535	.043814	.047106	.050411	.053726	.057050	.060383	.067070	.073779
	0.00	.046045	.049255	.052485	.055733	.058998	.062277	.065569	.068874	.072189	.075513	.078846	.085533	.092241
	-.10	.064508	.067718	.070948	.074196	.077460	.080739	.084032	.087336	.090651	.093976	.097309	.103996	.110704
	-.20	.082970	.086181	.089411	.092659	.095923	.099202	.102495	.105799	.109114	.112439	.115771	.122458	.129157
	-.30	.101433	.104643	.107874	.111122	.114386	.117665	.120957	.124262	.127577	.130901	.134234	.140921	.147629
	-.40	.119895	.123106	.126336	.129584	.132849	.136128	.139420	.142724	.146039	.149364	.152697	.159384	.166092
30	.40	-.027629	-.024374	-.021102	-.017816	-.014516	-.011205	-.007884	-.004555	-.001218	.002124	.005472	.012179	.018836
	.30	-.009167	-.005911	-.002640	.000647	.003946	.007257	.010578	.013908	.017244	.020587	.023935	.030641	.037358
	.20	.009296	.012551	.015823	.019110	.022409	.025720	.029041	.032370	.035707	.039050	.042397	.049104	.055821
	.10	.027759	.031014	.034286	.037572	.040872	.044183	.047504	.050833	.054170	.057512	.060860	.067567	.074284
	0.00	.046222	.049477	.052748	.056035	.059335	.062645	.065966	.069296	.072632	.075975	.079323	.086030	.092746
	-.10	.064684	.067939	.071211	.074498	.077797	.081108	.084429	.087758	.091095	.094438	.097785	.104492	.111209
	-.20	.083147	.086402	.089674	.092960	.096260	.099571	.102892	.106221	.109558	.112900	.116248	.122955	.129672
	-.30	.101610	.104865	.108137	.111423	.114723	.118034	.121355	.124684	.128021	.131363	.134711	.141418	.148135
	-.40	.120072	.123327	.126599	.129886	.133185	.136496	.139817	.143147	.146483	.149826	.153174	.159880	.166597

127

5.0 YEAR HOLDING PERIOD
.040 EQUITY YIELD RATE
.700 LOAN RATIO

INTEREST RATE

TERM YEARS	APPR DEP	12.0	11.0	10.0	9.5	9.0	8.5	8.0	7.5	7.0	6.5	6.0	5.5	5.0
10	.40	.012782	.006500	.000300	-.002759	-.005815	-.008840	-.011842	-.014821	-.017777	-.020708	-.023616	-.026499	-.029356
	.30	.031244	.024963	.018763	.015634	.012647	.009623	.006621	.003642	.000686	-.002246	-.005153	-.008036	-.010893
	.20	.049707	.043425	.037225	.034157	.031110	.028085	.025083	.022104	.019149	.016217	.013310	.010427	.007569
	.10	.068170	.061888	.055688	.052620	.049573	.046548	.043546	.040567	.037611	.034680	.031772	.028890	.026034
	0.00	.086632	.080351	.074151	.071082	.068035	.065011	.062009	.059030	.056074	.053142	.050235	.047352	.044495
	-.10	.105095	.098814	.092613	.089545	.086498	.083474	.080471	.077492	.074537	.071605	.068698	.065815	.062957
	-.20	.123558	.117276	.111076	.108008	.104961	.101936	.098934	.095955	.093000	.090068	.087160	.084278	.081420
	-.30	.142021	.135739	.129539	.126470	.123424	.120399	.117397	.114418	.111462	.108531	.105623	.102740	.099883
	-.40	.160483	.154202	.148002	.144933	.141886	.138862	.135860	.132881	.129925	.126993	.124086	.121203	.118345
15	.40	.017836	.011021	.004270	.000920	-.002412	-.005725	-.009018	-.012290	-.015541	-.018768	-.021972	-.025152	-.028306
	.30	.036298	.029484	.022732	.019382	.016050	.012737	.009444	.006172	.002922	-.000306	-.003510	-.006689	-.009844
	.20	.054761	.047947	.041195	.037845	.034513	.031200	.027907	.024635	.021385	.018157	.014953	.011773	.008619
	.10	.073224	.066410	.059658	.056308	.052976	.049663	.046370	.043098	.039847	.036620	.033416	.030236	.027082
	0.00	.091687	.084872	.078121	.074770	.071438	.068125	.064833	.061560	.058310	.055082	.051878	.048699	.045545
	-.10	.110149	.103335	.096583	.093233	.089901	.086588	.083295	.080023	.076773	.073545	.070341	.067161	.064007
	-.20	.128612	.121798	.115046	.111696	.108364	.105051	.101758	.098486	.095236	.092004	.088804	.085624	.082470
	-.30	.147075	.140260	.133509	.130159	.126827	.123514	.120221	.116949	.113698	.110471	.107267	.104087	.100933
	-.40	.165537	.158723	.151971	.148621	.145289	.141976	.138683	.135411	.132161	.128933	.125729	.122550	.119395
20	.40	.019971	.012981	.006032	.002575	-.000869	-.004298	-.007712	-.011109	-.014488	-.017847	-.021186	-.024503	-.027797
	.30	.038434	.031444	.024494	.021038	.017594	.014165	.010751	.007354	.003975	.000616	-.002724	-.006041	-.009335
	.20	.056896	.049906	.042957	.039500	.036057	.032627	.029214	.025817	.022438	.019078	.015739	.012422	.009128
	.10	.075359	.068369	.061420	.057963	.054519	.051090	.047676	.044280	.040901	.037541	.034202	.030885	.027591
	0.00	.093822	.086832	.079883	.076426	.072982	.069553	.066139	.062742	.059363	.056004	.052665	.049347	.046054
	-.10	.112284	.105295	.098345	.094888	.091445	.088016	.084602	.081205	.077826	.074466	.071127	.067810	.064516
	-.20	.130747	.123757	.116808	.113351	.109908	.106478	.103065	.099668	.096289	.092929	.089590	.086273	.082979
	-.30	.149210	.142220	.135271	.131814	.128370	.124941	.121527	.118130	.114751	.111392	.108053	.104736	.101442
	-.40	.167673	.160683	.153733	.150277	.146833	.143404	.139990	.136593	.133214	.129855	.126515	.123198	.119904
25	.40	.021002	.013958	.006937	.003438	-.000053	-.003534	-.007003	-.010460	-.013903	-.017331	-.020741	-.024133	-.027504
	.30	.039465	.032421	.025400	.021901	.018410	.014929	.011459	.008002	.004559	.001132	-.002278	-.005670	-.009041
	.20	.057928	.050884	.043863	.040363	.036872	.033392	.029922	.026465	.023022	.019595	.016184	.012793	.009422
	.10	.076390	.069347	.062325	.058826	.055335	.051854	.048385	.044928	.041485	.038057	.034647	.031255	.027884
	0.00	.094853	.087809	.080788	.077289	.073798	.070317	.066847	.063390	.059948	.056520	.053110	.049718	.046347
	-.10	.113316	.106272	.099251	.095751	.092261	.088780	.085311	.081853	.078410	.074983	.071572	.068181	.064809
	-.20	.131778	.124735	.117713	.114215	.110723	.107242	.103773	.100316	.096873	.093445	.090035	.086643	.083272
	-.30	.150241	.143197	.136176	.132677	.129186	.125705	.122236	.118779	.115336	.111908	.108498	.105106	.101735
	-.40	.168704	.161660	.154639	.151139	.147649	.144168	.140698	.137241	.133798	.130371	.126960	.123569	.120198
30	.40	.021533	.014480	.007438	.003923	.000413	-.003090	-.006586	-.010073	-.013550	-.017014	-.020465	-.023900	-.027318
	.30	.039995	.032943	.025901	.022385	.018876	.015372	.011876	.008390	.004913	.001448	-.002002	-.005438	-.008856
	.20	.058458	.051405	.044363	.040848	.037339	.033835	.030339	.026852	.023376	.019911	.016460	.013025	.009607
	.10	.076921	.069868	.062826	.059311	.055801	.052298	.048802	.045315	.041838	.038374	.034923	.031488	.028070
	0.00	.095383	.088331	.081289	.077774	.074264	.070760	.067265	.063778	.060301	.056837	.053386	.049950	.046533
	-.10	.113846	.106793	.099752	.096236	.092727	.089223	.085727	.082240	.078764	.075299	.071848	.068413	.064995
	-.20	.132309	.125256	.118214	.114699	.111189	.107686	.104190	.100703	.097227	.093762	.090311	.086876	.083458
	-.30	.150772	.143719	.136677	.133162	.129652	.126149	.122653	.119166	.115689	.112225	.108774	.105339	.101921
	-.40	.169234	.162182	.155140	.151624	.148115	.144611	.141115	.137628	.134152	.130687	.127237	.123801	.120383

5.0 YEAR HOLDING PERIOD
.040 EQUITY YIELD RATE
.750 LOAN RATIO

INTEREST RATE

TERM YEARS	APPR DEP	5.0	5.5	6.0	6.5	7.0	7.5	8.0	8.5	9.0	9.5	10.0	11.0	12.0
10	.40	-.029035	-.025973	-.022885	-.019770	-.016629	-.013462	-.010270	-.007054	-.003813	-.000548	.002739	.009382	.016112
	.30	-.010572	-.007511	-.004422	-.001307	.001834	.005001	.008193	.011409	.014650	.017914	.021202	.027845	.034575
	.20	.007890	.010952	.014041	.017156	.020297	.023464	.026655	.029872	.033113	.036377	.039665	.046308	.053038
	.10	.026353	.029415	.032503	.035618	.038760	.041926	.045118	.048335	.051575	.054840	.058127	.064770	.071501
	0.00	.044816	.047877	.050966	.054081	.057222	.060389	.063581	.066797	.070038	.073302	.076590	.083233	.089963
	-.10	.063278	.066340	.069429	.072544	.075685	.078852	.082044	.085260	.088501	.091765	.095053	.101696	.108426
	-.20	.081741	.084803	.087891	.091007	.094148	.097314	.100506	.103723	.106963	.110228	.113515	.120158	.126889
	-.30	.100204	.103266	.106354	.109469	.112610	.115777	.118969	.122185	.125426	.128691	.131978	.138621	.145351
	-.40	.118667	.121728	.124817	.127932	.131073	.134240	.137432	.140648	.143889	.147153	.150441	.157084	.163814
15	.40	-.027910	-.024531	-.021124	-.017691	-.014233	-.010750	-.007245	-.003716	-.000167	.003403	.006993	.014227	.021528
	.30	-.009448	-.006068	-.002661	.000772	.004230	.007712	.011218	.014746	.018296	.021866	.025455	.032689	.039990
	.20	.009015	.012395	.015801	.019234	.022693	.026175	.029681	.033209	.036759	.040329	.043918	.051152	.058453
	.10	.027478	.030857	.034264	.037697	.041155	.044638	.048144	.051672	.055221	.058791	.062381	.069615	.076916
	0.00	.045941	.049320	.052727	.056160	.059618	.063100	.066606	.070134	.073684	.077254	.080844	.088077	.095378
	-.10	.064403	.067783	.071190	.074622	.078081	.081563	.085069	.088597	.092147	.095717	.099306	.106540	.113841
	-.20	.082866	.086246	.089652	.093085	.096543	.100026	.103532	.107060	.110609	.114179	.117769	.125003	.132304
	-.30	.101329	.104708	.108115	.111548	.115006	.118489	.121994	.125523	.129072	.132642	.136232	.143466	.150767
	-.40	.119791	.123171	.126578	.130011	.133469	.136951	.140457	.143985	.147535	.151105	.154694	.161928	.169229
20	.40	-.027365	-.023836	-.020282	-.016704	-.013104	-.009484	-.005845	-.002187	.001487	.005177	.008881	.016326	.023815
	.30	-.008902	-.005373	-.001819	.001759	.005358	.008979	.012618	.016276	.019950	.023639	.027343	.034789	.042278
	.20	.009560	.013090	.016644	.020221	.023821	.027441	.031081	.034738	.038413	.042102	.045806	.053252	.060741
	.10	.028023	.031552	.035107	.038684	.042284	.045904	.049544	.053201	.056875	.060565	.064269	.071714	.079203
	0.00	.046486	.050015	.053569	.057147	.060746	.064367	.068006	.071664	.075338	.079028	.082731	.090177	.097666
	-.10	.064949	.068478	.072032	.075610	.079209	.082829	.086469	.090126	.093801	.097490	.101194	.108640	.116129
	-.20	.083411	.086941	.090495	.094072	.097672	.101292	.104932	.108589	.112263	.115953	.119657	.127102	.134592
	-.30	.101874	.105403	.108957	.112535	.116135	.119755	.123394	.127052	.130726	.134416	.138119	.145565	.153054
	-.40	.120337	.123866	.127420	.130998	.134597	.138218	.141857	.145515	.149189	.152878	.156582	.164028	.171517
25	.40	-.027051	-.023439	-.019605	-.016151	-.012479	-.008790	-.005086	-.001368	.002361	.006101	.009851	.017373	.024920
	.30	-.008588	-.004976	-.001342	.002312	.005984	.009673	.013377	.017094	.020824	.024564	.028314	.035836	.043383
	.20	.009875	.013487	.017121	.020775	.024447	.028136	.031840	.035557	.039287	.043027	.046776	.054299	.061846
	.10	.028337	.031949	.035583	.039237	.042910	.046599	.050302	.054020	.057749	.061489	.065239	.072761	.080308
	0.00	.046800	.050412	.054046	.057700	.061372	.065061	.068765	.072483	.076212	.079952	.083702	.091224	.098771
	-.10	.065263	.068875	.072509	.076163	.079835	.083524	.087228	.090945	.094675	.098415	.102164	.109687	.117234
	-.20	.083725	.087338	.090971	.094625	.098298	.101987	.105691	.109408	.113137	.116878	.120627	.128150	.135697
	-.30	.102188	.105800	.109434	.113088	.116760	.120449	.124153	.127871	.131600	.135340	.139090	.146612	.154159
	-.40	.120651	.124263	.127897	.131551	.135223	.138912	.142616	.146333	.150063	.153803	.157552	.165075	.172622
30	.40	-.026852	-.023190	-.019509	-.015812	-.012100	-.008375	-.004639	-.000893	.002860	.006621	.010387	.017932	.025489
	.30	-.008389	-.004727	-.001046	.002651	.006363	.010088	.013824	.017569	.021323	.025084	.028850	.036395	.043951
	.20	.010074	.013736	.017416	.021114	.024826	.028551	.032287	.036032	.039786	.043546	.047312	.054858	.062414
	.10	.028536	.032198	.035879	.039577	.043289	.047013	.050749	.054495	.058249	.062009	.065775	.073320	.080877
	0.00	.046999	.050661	.054342	.058039	.061751	.065476	.069212	.072958	.076711	.080472	.084238	.091783	.099340
	-.10	.065462	.069124	.072805	.076502	.080214	.083939	.087675	.091420	.095174	.098934	.102701	.110246	.117802
	-.20	.083925	.087587	.091267	.094965	.098677	.102401	.106137	.109883	.113637	.117397	.121163	.128708	.136255
	-.30	.102387	.106049	.109730	.113427	.117139	.120864	.124600	.128346	.132099	.135860	.139627	.147171	.154728
	-.40	.120850	.124512	.128193	.131890	.135602	.139327	.143063	.146808	.150562	.154323	.158089	.165634	.173130

5.0 YEAR HOLDING PERIOD
.040 EQUITY YIELD RATE
.800 LOAN RATIO

INTEREST RATE

TERM YEARS	APPR DEP	5.0	5.5	6.0	6.5	7.0	7.5	8.0	8.5	9.0	9.5	10.0	11.0	12.0
10	.40	-.028714	-.025448	-.022154	-.018831	-.015480	-.012103	-.008698	-.005267	-.001810	.001672	.005179	.012264	.019443
	.30	-.010251	-.006986	-.003691	-.000368	.002982	.006360	.009765	.013196	.016652	.020134	.023641	.030727	.037906
	.20	.008211	.011477	.014772	.018094	.021445	.024823	.028227	.031658	.035115	.038597	.042104	.049190	.056369
	.10	.026674	.029900	.033234	.036557	.039908	.043286	.046690	.050121	.053578	.057060	.060567	.067653	.074831
	0.00	.045137	.048403	.051697	.055020	.058370	.061748	.065153	.068584	.072041	.075523	.079029	.086115	.093294
	-.10	.063599	.066865	.070160	.073483	.076833	.080211	.083616	.087047	.090503	.093985	.097492	.104578	.111757
	-.20	.082062	.085328	.088623	.091945	.095296	.098674	.102078	.105509	.108966	.112448	.115955	.123041	.130220
	-.30	.100525	.103791	.107085	.110408	.113759	.117136	.120541	.123972	.127429	.130911	.134418	.141503	.148682
	-.40	.118988	.122253	.125548	.128871	.132221	.135599	.139004	.142435	.145891	.149373	.152880	.159966	.167145
15	.40	-.027514	-.023909	-.020276	-.016614	-.012925	-.009210	-.005471	-.001707	.002079	.005887	.009716	.017432	.025220
	.30	-.009052	-.005447	-.001813	.001849	.005538	.009252	.012992	.016755	.020541	.024349	.028178	.035894	.043682
	.20	.009411	.013016	.016650	.020312	.024000	.027715	.031455	.035218	.039004	.042812	.046641	.054357	.062145
	.10	.027874	.031479	.035113	.038774	.042463	.046178	.049917	.053681	.057467	.061275	.065104	.072820	.080608
	0.00	.046337	.049941	.053575	.057237	.060926	.064640	.068380	.072143	.075930	.079738	.083566	.091283	.099070
	-.10	.064799	.068404	.072038	.075700	.079389	.083103	.086843	.090606	.094392	.098200	.102029	.109745	.117533
	-.20	.083262	.086867	.090501	.094163	.097851	.101566	.105305	.109069	.112855	.116663	.120492	.128208	.135996
	-.30	.101725	.105330	.108963	.112625	.116314	.120029	.123768	.127532	.131318	.135126	.138955	.146671	.154458
	-.40	.120187	.123792	.127426	.131088	.134777	.138491	.142231	.145994	.149780	.153588	.157417	.165133	.172921
20	.40	-.026933	-.023168	-.019377	-.015561	-.011721	-.007860	-.003978	-.000076	.003843	.007779	.011729	.019671	.027660
	.30	-.008470	-.004705	-.000914	.002902	.006741	.010603	.014485	.018387	.022306	.026241	.030192	.038134	.046122
	.20	.009993	.013757	.017548	.021364	.025204	.029066	.032948	.036849	.040768	.044704	.048655	.056597	.064585
	.10	.028456	.032220	.036011	.039827	.043667	.047528	.051411	.055312	.059231	.063167	.067117	.075059	.083048
	0.00	.046918	.050683	.054474	.058290	.062130	.065991	.069873	.073775	.077694	.081629	.085580	.093522	.101511
	-.10	.065381	.069145	.072937	.076753	.080592	.084454	.088336	.092237	.096157	.100092	.104043	.111985	.119973
	-.20	.083844	.087608	.091399	.095215	.099055	.102917	.106799	.110700	.114619	.118555	.122506	.130448	.138436
	-.30	.102306	.106071	.109862	.113678	.117518	.121379	.125261	.129163	.133082	.137018	.140968	.148910	.156899
	-.40	.120769	.124534	.128325	.132141	.135980	.139842	.143724	.147626	.151545	.155480	.159431	.167373	.175361
25	.40	-.026597	-.022745	-.018868	-.014971	-.011054	-.007119	-.003168	.000797	.004775	.008765	.012764	.020788	.028838
	.30	-.008135	-.004282	-.000406	.003492	.007409	.011344	.015295	.019260	.023238	.027227	.031227	.039251	.047301
	.20	.010328	.014181	.018057	.021955	.025872	.029807	.033757	.037723	.041701	.045690	.049690	.057714	.065764
	.10	.028791	.032644	.036520	.040417	.044334	.048269	.052220	.056185	.060163	.064153	.068152	.076176	.084227
	0.00	.047253	.051106	.054982	.058880	.062797	.066732	.070683	.074648	.078626	.082616	.086615	.094639	.102689
	-.10	.065716	.069569	.073445	.077343	.081260	.085195	.089146	.093111	.097089	.101078	.105078	.113101	.121152
	-.20	.084179	.088032	.091908	.095805	.099723	.103657	.107608	.111573	.115552	.119541	.123540	.131565	.139615
	-.30	.102642	.106494	.110371	.114268	.118185	.122120	.126071	.130036	.134014	.138004	.142003	.150027	.158077
	-.40	.121104	.124957	.128833	.132731	.136648	.140583	.144534	.148499	.152477	.156466	.160466	.168490	.176540
30	.40	-.026385	-.022479	-.018553	-.014609	-.010650	-.006676	-.002691	.001304	.005308	.009319	.013336	.021384	.029444
	.30	-.007922	-.004016	-.000090	.003854	.007813	.011786	.015771	.019767	.023771	.027782	.031799	.039847	.047907
	.20	.010540	.014447	.018373	.022316	.026276	.030249	.034234	.038229	.042233	.046244	.050262	.058310	.066370
	.10	.029003	.032909	.036835	.040779	.044739	.048712	.052697	.056692	.060696	.064707	.068724	.076772	.084833
	0.00	.047466	.051372	.055298	.059242	.063201	.067174	.071159	.075155	.079159	.083170	.087187	.095235	.103295
	-.10	.065928	.069835	.073761	.077705	.081664	.085637	.089622	.093617	.097621	.101633	.105650	.113698	.121758
	-.20	.084391	.088297	.092223	.096167	.100127	.104100	.108085	.112080	.116084	.120095	.124113	.132161	.140221
	-.30	.102854	.106760	.110686	.114630	.118589	.122563	.126548	.130543	.134547	.138558	.142575	.150623	.158683
	-.40	.121317	.125223	.129149	.133093	.137052	.141025	.145010	.149006	.153010	.157021	.161038	.169086	.177146

5.0 YEAR HOLDING PERIOD
.040 EQUITY YIELD RATE
.900 LOAN RATIO

INTEREST RATE

TERM YEARS	APPR DEP	5.0	5.5	6.0	6.5	7.0	7.5	8.0	8.5	9.0	9.5	10.0	11.0	12.0
10	.40	-.028072	-.024398	-.020692	-.016953	-.013184	-.009384	-.005554	-.001694	.002195	.006112	.010057	.018029	.026105
	.30	-.009609	-.005935	-.002229	.001509	.005279	.009079	.012909	.016769	.020657	.024575	.028520	.036492	.044568
	.20	.008853	.012527	.016234	.019972	.023741	.027541	.031372	.035231	.039120	.043037	.046983	.054954	.063031
	.10	.027316	.030990	.034697	.038435	.042204	.046004	.049834	.053694	.057583	.061500	.065445	.073417	.081493
	0.00	.045779	.049453	.053159	.056897	.060667	.064467	.068297	.072157	.076046	.079963	.083908	.091880	.099956
	-.10	.064242	.067916	.071622	.075360	.079129	.082929	.086760	.090619	.094508	.098426	.102371	.110342	.118419
	-.20	.082704	.086378	.090085	.093823	.097592	.101392	.105222	.109082	.112971	.116888	.120833	.128805	.136881
	-.30	.101167	.104841	.108547	.112280	.116055	.119855	.123685	.127545	.131434	.135351	.139296	.147268	.155344
	-.40	.119630	.123304	.127010	.130748	.134518	.138318	.142148	.146008	.149896	.153814	.157759	.165731	.173807
15	.40	-.026722	-.022667	-.018579	-.014459	-.010309	-.006130	-.001923	.002310	.006570	.010854	.015161	.023842	.032603
	.30	-.008259	-.004204	-.000116	.004004	.008153	.012332	.016539	.020773	.025033	.029317	.033624	.042305	.051066
	.20	.010203	.014259	.018347	.022466	.026616	.030795	.035002	.039236	.043495	.047779	.052087	.060767	.069529
	.10	.028666	.032721	.036809	.040929	.045079	.049258	.053465	.057699	.061958	.066242	.070550	.079230	.087991
	0.00	.047129	.051184	.055272	.059392	.063542	.067721	.071928	.076161	.080421	.084705	.089012	.097693	.106454
	-.10	.065591	.069647	.073735	.077854	.082004	.086183	.090390	.094624	.098883	.103168	.107475	.116156	.124927
	-.20	.084054	.088110	.092198	.096317	.100467	.104646	.108853	.113087	.117346	.121630	.125938	.134618	.143380
	-.30	.102517	.106572	.110660	.114780	.118930	.123109	.127316	.131549	.135809	.140093	.144401	.153081	.161842
	-.40	.120979	.125035	.129123	.133243	.137392	.141571	.145778	.150012	.154272	.158556	.162863	.171544	.180305
20	.40	-.026068	-.021833	-.017568	-.013275	-.008955	-.004611	-.000243	.004146	.008555	.012982	.017427	.026362	.035348
	.30	-.007605	-.003370	.000895	.005188	.009508	.013852	.018219	.022608	.027017	.031445	.035889	.044824	.053811
	.20	.010858	.015093	.019358	.023651	.027970	.032315	.036682	.041071	.045440	.049908	.054352	.063287	.072274
	.10	.029320	.033555	.037820	.042113	.046433	.050777	.055145	.059534	.063943	.068370	.072815	.081750	.090737
	0.00	.047783	.052018	.056283	.060576	.064896	.069240	.073607	.077997	.082406	.086833	.091278	.100212	.109199
	-.10	.066246	.070481	.074746	.079039	.083358	.087703	.092070	.096459	.100868	.105296	.109740	.118675	.127662
	-.20	.084709	.088944	.093208	.097502	.101821	.106165	.110533	.114922	.119331	.123758	.128203	.137138	.146125
	-.30	.103171	.107406	.111671	.115964	.120284	.124628	.128996	.133385	.137794	.142221	.146666	.155601	.164587
	-.40	.121634	.125869	.130134	.134427	.138747	.143091	.147458	.151847	.156256	.160684	.165128	.174063	.183050
25	.40	-.025691	-.021356	-.016996	-.012611	-.008204	-.003777	.000667	.005128	.009604	.014092	.018591	.027618	.036675
	.30	-.007228	-.002894	.001467	.005852	.010259	.014685	.019130	.023591	.028066	.032554	.037054	.046081	.055137
	.20	.011235	.015569	.019930	.024315	.028721	.033148	.037593	.042054	.046529	.051017	.055517	.064544	.073600
	.10	.029697	.034032	.038393	.042777	.047184	.051611	.056055	.060516	.064992	.069480	.073979	.083006	.092063
	0.00	.048160	.052495	.056855	.061240	.065647	.070073	.074518	.078979	.083454	.087943	.092442	.101469	.110525
	-.10	.066623	.070957	.075318	.079703	.084110	.088536	.092981	.097442	.101917	.106405	.110905	.119932	.128988
	-.20	.085085	.089420	.093781	.098165	.102572	.106999	.111444	.115904	.120380	.124868	.129367	.138394	.147451
	-.30	.103548	.107883	.112243	.116628	.121035	.125462	.129906	.134367	.138843	.143331	.147830	.156857	.165914
	-.40	.122011	.126345	.130706	.135091	.139498	.143924	.148369	.152830	.157305	.161793	.166293	.175320	.184376
30	.40	-.025452	-.021057	-.016641	-.012204	-.007749	-.003280	.001204	.005698	.010203	.014715	.019235	.028289	.037356
	.30	-.006989	-.002595	.001822	.006259	.010713	.015183	.019666	.024161	.028665	.033197	.037697	.046751	.055819
	.20	.011474	.015868	.020285	.024722	.029176	.033646	.038129	.042624	.047128	.051641	.056160	.065214	.074282
	.10	.029936	.034331	.038748	.043184	.047639	.052109	.056592	.061086	.065591	.070103	.074623	.083677	.092745
	0.00	.048399	.052793	.057210	.061647	.066101	.070571	.075054	.079549	.084053	.088566	.093085	.102140	.111207
	-.10	.066862	.071256	.075673	.080112	.084564	.089034	.093517	.098012	.102516	.107029	.111548	.120602	.129670
	-.20	.085324	.089719	.094136	.098572	.103027	.107497	.111980	.116475	.120979	.125492	.130011	.139065	.148133
	-.30	.103787	.108182	.112598	.117035	.121490	.125959	.130443	.134937	.139442	.143954	.148474	.157528	.166595
	-.40	.122250	.126644	.131061	.135498	.139952	.144422	.148905	.153400	.157904	.162417	.166936	.175990	.185058

131

5.0 YEAR HOLDING PERIOD
.060 EQUITY YIELD RATE
.600 LOAN RATIO

INTEREST RATE

TERM YEARS	APPR DEP	5.0	5.5	6.0	6.5	7.0	7.5	8.0	8.5	9.0	9.5	10.0	11.0	12.0
10	.40	-.017206	-.014763	-.012339	-.009873	-.007386	-.004879	-.002351	.000196	.002763	.005349	.007954	.013218	.018552
	.30	.000534	.002957	.005401	.007867	.010353	.012861	.015388	.017936	.020502	.023088	.025693	.030957	.036292
	.20	.018273	.020696	.023141	.025606	.028093	.030600	.033128	.035675	.038242	.040828	.043433	.048697	.054032
	.10	.036013	.038456	.040880	.043346	.045833	.048340	.050867	.053415	.055982	.058568	.061172	.066437	.071771
	0.00	.053753	.056175	.058620	.061086	.063572	.066080	.068607	.071154	.073721	.076307	.078912	.084176	.089511
	-.10	.071492	.073915	.076360	.078825	.081312	.083819	.086347	.088894	.091461	.094047	.096652	.101916	.107251
	-.20	.089236	.091655	.094099	.096565	.099052	.101559	.104086	.106634	.109201	.111787	.114391	.119656	.124990
	-.30	.106971	.109394	.111839	.114305	.116791	.119299	.121826	.124373	.126940	.129526	.132131	.137395	.142730
	-.40	.124711	.127134	.129578	.132044	.134531	.137038	.139566	.142113	.144680	.147266	.149871	.155135	.160469
15	.40	-.017102	-.014430	-.011736	-.009021	-.006284	-.003528	-.000752	.002042	.004853	.007682	.010527	.016262	.022053
	.30	.000637	.003309	.006003	.008719	.011455	.014212	.016987	.019781	.022593	.025422	.028266	.034002	.039793
	.20	.018377	.021049	.023743	.026459	.029195	.031951	.034727	.037521	.040333	.043161	.046006	.051741	.057533
	.10	.036117	.038789	.041483	.044198	.046935	.049691	.052467	.055261	.058072	.060901	.063746	.069481	.075272
	0.00	.053856	.056528	.059222	.061938	.064674	.067431	.070206	.073000	.075812	.078641	.081485	.087221	.093012
	-.10	.071596	.074268	.076962	.079678	.082414	.085170	.087946	.090740	.093552	.096380	.099225	.104960	.110752
	-.20	.089336	.092007	.094701	.097417	.100154	.102910	.105685	.108480	.111291	.114120	.116965	.122700	.128491
	-.30	.107075	.109747	.112441	.115157	.117893	.120650	.123425	.126219	.129031	.131859	.134704	.140440	.146231
	-.40	.124815	.127487	.130181	.132896	.135633	.138389	.141165	.143959	.146770	.149599	.152444	.158179	.163971
20	.40	-.017052	-.014260	-.011448	-.008616	-.005765	-.002897	-.000012	.002888	.005802	.008729	.011669	.017582	.023532
	.30	.000688	.003479	.006292	.009124	.011974	.014843	.017727	.020627	.023541	.026469	.029409	.035321	.041272
	.20	.018427	.021219	.024031	.026863	.029714	.032582	.035467	.038367	.041281	.044208	.047148	.053061	.059012
	.10	.036167	.038958	.041771	.044603	.047454	.050322	.053207	.056106	.059021	.061948	.064888	.070800	.076751
	0.00	.053907	.056698	.059510	.062343	.065193	.068062	.070946	.073846	.076760	.079688	.082627	.088540	.094491
	-.10	.071646	.074438	.077250	.080082	.082933	.085801	.088686	.091586	.094500	.097427	.100367	.106280	.112231
	-.20	.089386	.092177	.094990	.097822	.100673	.103541	.106425	.109325	.112240	.115167	.118107	.124019	.129970
	-.30	.107125	.109917	.112729	.115562	.118412	.121281	.124165	.127065	.129979	.132907	.135846	.141759	.147710
	-.40	.124865	.127657	.130469	.133301	.136152	.139020	.141905	.144805	.147719	.150646	.153586	.159499	.165450
25	.40	-.017023	-.014163	-.011285	-.008389	-.005477	-.002551	.000389	.003340	.006303	.009275	.012256	.018240	.024247
	.30	.000717	.003576	.006455	.009351	.012437	.015189	.018128	.021080	.024043	.027015	.029996	.035979	.041987
	.20	.018456	.021316	.024194	.027090	.030002	.032928	.035868	.038820	.041782	.044754	.047735	.053719	.059726
	.10	.036196	.039056	.041934	.044830	.047742	.050668	.053608	.056559	.059522	.062494	.065475	.071459	.077466
	0.00	.053935	.056795	.059674	.062569	.065481	.068408	.071347	.074299	.077261	.080234	.083214	.089198	.095206
	-.10	.071675	.074535	.077413	.080309	.083221	.086147	.089087	.092039	.095001	.097973	.100954	.106938	.112945
	-.20	.089415	.092274	.095153	.098049	.100961	.103887	.106827	.109778	.112741	.115713	.118694	.124677	.130685
	-.30	.107154	.110014	.112893	.115788	.118700	.121627	.124566	.127518	.130480	.133453	.136433	.142417	.148424
	-.40	.124894	.127754	.130632	.133528	.136440	.139366	.142306	.145258	.148220	.151192	.154173	.160157	.166164
30	.40	-.017005	-.014103	-.011184	-.008250	-.005303	-.002344	.000625	.003603	.006589	.009532	.012580	.018591	.024614
	.30	.000735	.003637	.006556	.009490	.012437	.015395	.018365	.021343	.024329	.027322	.030330	.036330	.042354
	.20	.018475	.021377	.024296	.027229	.030176	.033135	.036104	.039082	.042068	.045061	.048060	.054070	.060094
	.10	.036214	.039116	.042035	.044969	.047916	.050875	.053844	.056822	.059808	.062801	.065799	.071810	.077833
	0.00	.053954	.056856	.059775	.062709	.065656	.068614	.071584	.074562	.077548	.080540	.083539	.089549	.095572
	-.10	.071693	.074596	.077514	.080448	.083395	.086354	.089323	.092301	.095287	.098280	.101279	.107289	.113313
	-.20	.089433	.092335	.095254	.098188	.101135	.104094	.107063	.110041	.113027	.116020	.119018	.125029	.131052
	-.30	.107173	.110075	.112994	.115927	.118874	.121833	.124802	.127781	.130767	.133759	.136759	.142768	.148792
	-.40	.124912	.127815	.130733	.133667	.136614	.139573	.142542	.145520	.148506	.151499	.154497	.160508	.166531

132

INTEREST RATE

TERM YEARS	APPR DEP	5.0	5.5	6.0	6.5	7.0	7.5	8.0	8.5	9.0	9.5	10.0	11.0	12.0
10	.40	-.017900	-.015208	-.012492	-.009752	-.006989	-.004203	-.001395	.001435	.004287	.007161	.010055	.015904	.021931
	.30	-.000161	-.002532	-.005248	-.007987	-.010750	-.013536	-.016345	-.019175	-.022027	-.024900	-.027795	-.033644	-.039571
	.20	-.017579	-.020271	-.022987	-.025727	-.028490	-.031276	-.034084	-.036915	-.039767	-.042640	-.045534	-.051383	-.057311
	.10	-.035319	-.038011	-.040727	-.043467	-.046230	-.049016	-.051824	-.054654	-.057506	-.060380	-.063274	-.069123	-.075050
	0.00	-.053058	-.055750	-.058467	-.061206	-.063969	-.066755	-.069563	-.072394	-.075246	-.078119	-.081014	-.086863	-.092790
	-.10	-.070798	-.073490	-.076206	-.078946	-.081709	-.084495	-.087303	-.090134	-.092986	-.095859	-.098753	-.104602	-.110530
	-.20	-.088538	-.091230	-.093946	-.096686	-.099449	-.102234	-.105043	-.107873	-.110725	-.113599	-.116493	-.122342	-.128269
	-.30	-.106277	-.108969	-.111685	-.114425	-.117188	-.119974	-.122782	-.125613	-.128465	-.131338	-.134232	-.140082	-.146809
	-.40	-.124017	-.126709	-.129425	-.132165	-.134928	-.137714	-.140522	-.143352	-.146205	-.149078	-.151972	-.157821	-.163749
15	.40	-.017785	-.014816	-.011623	-.008805	-.005765	-.002702	.000382	.003486	.006610	.009753	.012914	.019287	.025722
	.30	-.000045	-.002923	-.005917	-.008934	-.011975	-.015037	-.018121	-.021226	-.024350	-.027493	-.030654	-.037026	-.043461
	.20	-.017694	-.020663	-.023657	-.026674	-.029714	-.032777	-.035861	-.038965	-.042090	-.045233	-.048393	-.054766	-.061201
	.10	-.035434	-.038403	-.041396	-.044414	-.047454	-.050517	-.053601	-.056705	-.059829	-.062972	-.066133	-.072506	-.078941
	0.00	-.053174	-.056142	-.059136	-.062153	-.065194	-.068256	-.071340	-.074445	-.077569	-.080712	-.083873	-.090245	-.096680
	-.10	-.070913	-.073882	-.076876	-.079893	-.082933	-.085996	-.089080	-.092184	-.095309	-.098451	-.101612	-.107985	-.114420
	-.20	-.088653	-.091622	-.094615	-.097633	-.100673	-.103736	-.106820	-.109924	-.113048	-.116191	-.119352	-.125725	-.132155
	-.30	-.106393	-.109361	-.112355	-.115372	-.118413	-.121475	-.124559	-.127664	-.130788	-.133931	-.137092	-.143464	-.149899
	-.40	-.124132	-.127101	-.130094	-.133112	-.136152	-.139215	-.142299	-.145403	-.148527	-.151670	-.154831	-.161204	-.167639
20	.40	-.017729	-.014627	-.011502	-.008356	-.005188	-.002001	.001204	.004426	.007664	.010917	.014183	.020753	.027365
	.30	-.000011	-.003112	-.006237	-.009384	-.012552	-.015738	-.018944	-.022166	-.025404	-.028656	-.031923	-.038492	-.045105
	.20	-.017750	-.020852	-.023977	-.027124	-.030291	-.033478	-.036683	-.039905	-.043143	-.046396	-.049663	-.056232	-.062844
	.10	-.035490	-.038592	-.041716	-.044863	-.048031	-.051218	-.054423	-.057645	-.060883	-.064136	-.067402	-.073972	-.080584
	0.00	-.053229	-.056331	-.059456	-.062603	-.065770	-.068957	-.072162	-.075385	-.078623	-.081875	-.085142	-.091711	-.098324
	-.10	-.070969	-.074071	-.077196	-.080343	-.083510	-.086697	-.089902	-.093124	-.096362	-.099615	-.102881	-.109451	-.116063
	-.20	-.088709	-.091811	-.094935	-.098082	-.101250	-.104437	-.107642	-.110864	-.114102	-.117355	-.120621	-.127191	-.133803
	-.30	-.106448	-.109550	-.112675	-.115822	-.118989	-.122176	-.125381	-.128604	-.131842	-.135094	-.138361	-.144930	-.151542
	-.40	-.124188	-.127290	-.130415	-.133562	-.136729	-.139916	-.143121	-.146343	-.149581	-.152834	-.156100	-.162670	-.169282
25	.40	-.017697	-.014520	-.011321	-.008104	-.004868	-.001617	.001650	.004929	.008221	.011523	.014835	.021484	.028159
	.30	-.000043	-.003220	-.006418	-.009636	-.012871	-.016123	-.019389	-.022669	-.025961	-.029263	-.032575	-.039224	-.045898
	.20	-.017783	-.020960	-.024158	-.027376	-.030611	-.033863	-.037129	-.040409	-.043700	-.047003	-.050315	-.056963	-.063638
	.10	-.035522	-.038699	-.041898	-.045115	-.048351	-.051602	-.054869	-.058148	-.061440	-.064742	-.068054	-.074703	-.081378
	0.00	-.053262	-.056439	-.059637	-.062855	-.066090	-.069342	-.072608	-.075888	-.079180	-.082482	-.085794	-.092443	-.099117
	-.10	-.071001	-.074179	-.077377	-.080595	-.083830	-.087082	-.090348	-.093627	-.096919	-.100222	-.103534	-.110182	-.116857
	-.20	-.088741	-.091918	-.095117	-.098334	-.101570	-.104821	-.108087	-.111367	-.114659	-.117961	-.121273	-.127922	-.134597
	-.30	-.106481	-.109658	-.112856	-.116074	-.119309	-.122561	-.125827	-.129107	-.132398	-.135701	-.139013	-.145662	-.152336
	-.40	-.124220	-.127398	-.130596	-.133814	-.137049	-.140300	-.143567	-.146846	-.150138	-.153441	-.156763	-.163401	-.170076
30	.40	-.017677	-.014452	-.011209	-.007949	-.004675	-.001387	.001912	.005221	.008539	.011864	.015196	.021874	.028567
	.30	-.000063	-.003288	-.006531	-.009791	-.013065	-.016353	-.019652	-.022961	-.026279	-.029604	-.032936	-.039604	-.046307
	.20	-.017803	-.021027	-.024271	-.027530	-.030805	-.034092	-.037391	-.040700	-.044018	-.047344	-.050675	-.057354	-.064046
	.10	-.035542	-.038767	-.042010	-.045270	-.048544	-.051832	-.055131	-.058440	-.061758	-.065083	-.068415	-.075093	-.081786
	0.00	-.053282	-.056507	-.059750	-.063010	-.066284	-.069572	-.072871	-.076180	-.079498	-.082823	-.086155	-.092833	-.099526
	-.10	-.071022	-.074246	-.077489	-.080749	-.084024	-.087311	-.090610	-.093919	-.097237	-.100563	-.103894	-.110572	-.117265
	-.20	-.088761	-.091986	-.095229	-.098489	-.101763	-.105051	-.108350	-.111659	-.114977	-.118302	-.121634	-.128312	-.135005
	-.30	-.106501	-.109726	-.112969	-.116228	-.119503	-.122790	-.126090	-.129399	-.132717	-.136042	-.139373	-.146052	-.152745
	-.40	-.124241	-.127465	-.130708	-.133968	-.137243	-.140530	-.143829	-.147138	-.150456	-.153781	-.157113	-.163791	-.170484

5.0 YEAR HOLDING PERIOD
.060 EQUITY YIELD RATE
.700 LOAN RATIO

INTEREST RATE

TERM YEARS	APPR DEP	5.0	5.5	6.0	6.5	7.0	7.5	8.0	8.5	9.0	9.5	10.0	11.0	12.0
10	.40	-.018247	-.015421	-.012569	-.009692	-.006791	-.003866	-.000917	.002055	.005050	.008067	.011106	.017247	.023471
	.30	-.000508	.002319	.005171	.008048	.010949	.013874	.016823	.019795	.022789	.025806	.028845	.034987	.041210
	.20	.017232	.020059	.022911	.025787	.028688	.031614	.034562	.037534	.040529	.043546	.046585	.052726	.058950
	.10	.034972	.037798	.040650	.043527	.046428	.049353	.052302	.055274	.058269	.061286	.064324	.070466	.076690
	0.00	.052711	.055538	.058390	.061267	.064168	.067093	.070042	.073014	.076008	.079025	.082064	.088206	.094429
	-.10	.070451	.073278	.076130	.079006	.081907	.084833	.087781	.090753	.093748	.096765	.099804	.105945	.112169
	-.20	.088191	.091017	.093869	.096746	.099647	.102572	.105521	.108493	.111488	.114505	.117543	.123685	.129909
	-.30	.105930	.108757	.111609	.114485	.117387	.120312	.123261	.126232	.129227	.132244	.135283	.141425	.147648
	-.40	.123670	.126497	.129348	.132225	.135126	.138051	.141000	.143972	.146967	.149934	.153023	.159164	.165388
15	.40	-.018126	-.015009	-.011806	-.008698	-.005505	-.002289	.000949	.004208	.007489	.010789	.014108	.020799	.027555
	.30	-.000387	.002731	.005874	.009042	.012234	.015450	.018688	.021948	.025228	.028528	.031847	.038539	.045295
	.20	.017353	.020470	.023613	.026782	.029974	.033190	.036428	.039688	.042968	.046268	.049587	.056278	.063035
	.10	.035093	.038210	.041353	.044521	.047714	.050929	.054168	.057427	.060708	.064008	.067327	.074018	.080774
	0.00	.052832	.055950	.059093	.062261	.065453	.068669	.071907	.075167	.078447	.081747	.085066	.091757	.098514
	-.10	.070572	.073689	.076832	.080001	.083193	.086409	.089647	.092907	.096187	.099487	.102806	.109497	.116254
	-.20	.088312	.091429	.094572	.097740	.100933	.104148	.107387	.110646	.113927	.117227	.120546	.127237	.133993
	-.30	.106051	.109168	.112312	.115480	.118672	.121888	.125126	.128386	.131666	.134966	.138285	.144976	.151733
	-.40	.123791	.126908	.130051	.133219	.136412	.139628	.142866	.146125	.149406	.152706	.156025	.162716	.169473
20	.40	-.018068	-.014811	-.011530	-.008225	-.004900	-.001553	.001812	.005195	.008595	.012010	.015440	.022338	.029281
	.30	-.000328	.002929	.006210	.009514	.012840	.016186	.019552	.022935	.026335	.029750	.033180	.040078	.047021
	.20	.017412	.020668	.023950	.027254	.030580	.033926	.037291	.040675	.044074	.047490	.050919	.057818	.064760
	.10	.035151	.038408	.041689	.044993	.048319	.051666	.055031	.058414	.061814	.065229	.068659	.075557	.082500
	0.00	.052891	.056148	.059429	.062733	.066059	.069405	.072771	.076154	.079554	.082969	.086399	.093297	.100240
	-.10	.070631	.073887	.077169	.080473	.083799	.087145	.090510	.093893	.097293	.100709	.104138	.111036	.117979
	-.20	.088370	.091627	.094908	.098212	.101538	.104884	.108250	.111633	.115033	.118448	.121878	.128776	.135719
	-.30	.106110	.109367	.112648	.115952	.119278	.122624	.125989	.129373	.132773	.136188	.139618	.146516	.153458
	-.40	.123850	.127106	.130387	.133692	.137017	.140364	.143729	.147112	.150512	.153928	.157357	.164255	.171198
25	.40	-.018034	-.014698	-.011339	-.007961	-.004564	-.001150	.002280	.005724	.009180	.012647	.016125	.023106	.030115
	.30	-.000294	.003042	.006401	.009779	.013176	.016590	.020020	.023463	.026919	.030387	.033865	.040846	.047854
	.20	.017445	.020782	.024140	.027518	.030916	.034330	.037759	.041203	.044659	.048127	.051604	.058585	.065594
	.10	.035185	.038521	.041880	.045258	.048655	.052069	.055499	.058943	.062399	.065866	.069344	.076325	.083333
	0.00	.052925	.056261	.059619	.062998	.066395	.069809	.073239	.076682	.080138	.083606	.087084	.094065	.101073
	-.10	.070664	.074001	.077359	.080737	.084134	.087549	.090978	.094422	.097878	.101346	.104823	.111804	.118813
	-.20	.088404	.091740	.095099	.098477	.101874	.105288	.108718	.112161	.115618	.119085	.122563	.129544	.136552
	-.30	.106144	.109480	.112838	.116217	.119614	.123028	.126457	.129901	.133357	.136825	.140302	.147283	.154292
	-.40	.123883	.127220	.130578	.133956	.137353	.140768	.144197	.147641	.151097	.154564	.158042	.165023	.172032
30	.40	-.018012	-.014627	-.011221	-.007799	-.004360	-.000908	.002556	.006030	.009514	.013005	.016504	.023516	.030543
	.30	-.000273	.003113	.006518	.009941	.013379	.016831	.020295	.023770	.027253	.030745	.034243	.041255	.048283
	.20	.017467	.020853	.024258	.027681	.031119	.034571	.038035	.041509	.044993	.048485	.051983	.058995	.066022
	.10	.035207	.038592	.041998	.045420	.048859	.052310	.055774	.059249	.062733	.066224	.069722	.076735	.083762
	0.00	.052946	.056332	.059737	.063160	.066598	.070050	.073514	.076989	.080472	.083964	.087462	.094474	.101502
	-.10	.070686	.074072	.077477	.080899	.084338	.087790	.091254	.094728	.098212	.101704	.105202	.112214	.119241
	-.20	.088425	.091811	.095217	.098639	.102077	.105529	.108993	.112468	.115952	.119443	.122941	.129954	.136981
	-.30	.106165	.109551	.112956	.116379	.119817	.123269	.126733	.130208	.133691	.137183	.140681	.147693	.154721
	-.40	.123905	.127291	.130696	.134118	.137557	.141009	.144473	.147947	.151431	.154922	.158420	.165433	.172460

5.0 YEAR HOLDING PERIOD
.060 EQUITY YIELD RATE
.750 LOAN RATIO

INTEREST RATE

TERM YEARS	APPR DEP	5.0	5.5	6.0	6.5	7.0	7.5	8.0	8.5	9.0	9.5	10.0	11.0	12.0
10	.40	-.018768	-.015739	-.012684	-.009602	-.006493	-.003359	-.000200	.002985	.006193	.009426	.012682	.019262	.025930
	.30	-.001028	-.002200	-.005056	-.008138	-.011246	-.014381	-.017540	.020724	.023933	.027165	.030421	.037001	.043670
	.20	-.016711	-.019740	-.022796	-.025878	-.028986	-.032120	-.035280	.038464	.041672	.044905	.048161	.054741	.061409
	.10	-.034451	-.037480	-.040535	-.043617	-.046726	-.049860	-.053019	.056203	.059412	.062645	.065900	.072481	.079149
	0.00	-.052191	-.055219	-.058275	-.061357	-.064465	-.067599	-.070759	.073943	.077152	.080384	.083640	.090220	.096889
	-.10	-.069930	-.072959	-.076015	-.079097	-.082205	-.085339	-.088499	.091683	.094891	.098124	.101380	.107960	.114628
	-.20	-.087670	-.090699	-.093754	-.096836	-.099945	-.103079	-.106238	.109422	.112631	.115863	.119119	.125700	.132368
	-.30	-.105410	-.108438	-.111494	-.114576	-.117684	-.120818	-.123978	.127162	.130371	.133603	.136859	.143439	.150108
	-.40	-.123149	-.126178	-.129233	-.132316	-.135424	-.138558	-.141717	.144902	.148110	.151343	.154599	.161179	.167847
15	.40	-.018638	-.015298	-.011931	-.008536	-.005116	-.001670	.001799	.005292	.008806	.012342	.015898	.023067	.030386
	.30	-.000899	-.002441	-.005809	-.009203	-.012624	-.016069	-.019539	.023031	.026546	.030082	.033638	.040807	.048046
	.20	-.016841	-.020181	-.023549	-.026943	-.030364	-.033809	-.037278	.040771	.044286	.047821	.051377	.058786	.065786
	.10	-.034581	-.037921	-.041288	-.044683	-.048103	-.051549	-.055018	.058511	.062025	.065561	.069117	.076286	.083525
	0.00	-.052320	-.055660	-.059028	-.062422	-.065843	-.069288	-.072758	.076250	.079765	.083301	.086857	.094026	.101265
	-.10	-.070060	-.073400	-.076768	-.080162	-.083583	-.087028	-.090497	.093990	.097505	.101040	.104596	.111765	.119005
	-.20	-.087800	-.091139	-.094507	-.097902	-.101322	-.104768	-.108237	.111730	.115244	.118780	.122336	.129505	.136744
	-.30	-.105539	-.108879	-.112247	-.115641	-.119062	-.122507	-.125977	.129469	.132984	.136520	.140076	.147245	.154484
	-.40	-.123279	-.126619	-.129986	-.133381	-.136801	-.140247	-.143716	.147209	.150723	.154259	.157815	.164984	.172224
20	.40	-.018575	-.015086	-.011570	-.008030	-.004467	-.000882	.002724	.006349	.009992	.013651	.017326	.024717	.032155
	.30	-.000836	-.002654	-.006169	-.009709	-.013273	-.016858	-.020464	.024089	.027731	.031391	.035065	.042456	.049895
	.20	-.016940	-.020393	-.023909	-.027449	-.031013	-.034598	-.038203	.041828	.045471	.049130	.052805	.060196	.067635
	.10	-.034644	-.038133	-.041648	-.045189	-.048752	-.052337	-.055943	.059568	.063211	.066870	.070545	.077936	.085374
	0.00	-.052383	-.055873	-.059388	-.062928	-.066492	-.070077	-.073683	.077308	.080950	.084610	.088284	.095675	.103114
	-.10	-.070123	-.073612	-.077128	-.080668	-.084231	-.087817	-.091422	.095047	.098690	.102349	.106024	.113415	.120853
	-.20	-.087862	-.091352	-.094867	-.098408	-.101971	-.105556	-.109162	.112787	.116430	.120089	.123764	.131154	.138593
	-.30	-.105602	-.109092	-.112607	-.116147	-.119711	-.123296	-.126902	.130527	.134169	.137829	.141503	.148894	.156333
	-.40	-.123342	-.126831	-.130347	-.133887	-.137450	-.141036	-.144641	.148266	.151909	.155568	.159243	.166634	.174072
25	.40	-.018539	-.014965	-.011367	-.007747	-.004107	-.000449	.003226	.006915	.010618	.014334	.018060	.025539	.033048
	.30	-.000777	-.002775	-.006373	-.009993	-.013633	-.017291	-.020965	.024358	.028358	.032073	.035799	.043279	.050788
	.20	-.016940	-.020515	-.024113	-.027733	-.031372	-.035030	-.038705	.042394	.046098	.049813	.053539	.061018	.068528
	.10	-.034680	-.038254	-.041852	-.045472	-.049112	-.052770	-.056445	.060134	.063837	.067552	.071278	.078758	.086267
	0.00	-.052419	-.055994	-.059592	-.063212	-.066852	-.070510	-.074184	.077874	.081577	.085292	.089018	.096498	.104007
	-.10	-.070159	-.073734	-.077332	-.080951	-.084591	-.088249	-.091924	.095613	.099316	.103032	.106758	.114237	.121747
	-.20	-.087899	-.091473	-.095071	-.098691	-.102331	-.105989	-.109663	.113353	.117056	.120771	.124497	.131977	.139486
	-.30	-.105638	-.109213	-.112811	-.116431	-.120071	-.123729	-.127403	.131093	.134796	.138511	.142238	.149717	.157226
	-.40	-.123378	-.126952	-.130551	-.134170	-.137810	-.141468	-.145143	.148832	.152535	.156251	.159977	.167456	.174956
30	.40	-.018516	-.014889	-.011240	-.007573	-.003889	-.000191	.003521	.007244	.010976	.014717	.018465	.025978	.033508
	.30	-.000777	-.002551	-.006500	-.010167	-.013851	-.017549	-.021260	.024983	.028716	.032457	.036205	.043718	.051247
	.20	-.016963	-.020591	-.024239	-.027906	-.031590	-.035289	-.039000	.042723	.046455	.050196	.053944	.061457	.068987
	.10	-.034703	-.038330	-.041979	-.045646	-.049330	-.053028	-.056749	.060462	.064195	.067936	.071684	.079197	.086726
	0.00	-.052442	-.056070	-.059719	-.063386	-.067069	-.070768	-.074479	.078202	.081935	.085676	.089424	.096937	.104466
	-.10	-.070182	-.073810	-.077458	-.081125	-.084809	-.088508	-.092219	.095942	.099674	.103415	.107163	.114676	.122206
	-.20	-.087922	-.091549	-.095198	-.098865	-.102549	-.106247	-.109959	.113681	.117414	.121155	.124903	.132416	.139945
	-.30	-.105661	-.109289	-.112937	-.116605	-.120288	-.123987	-.127698	.131421	.135154	.138895	.142643	.150156	.157685
	-.40	-.123401	-.127029	-.130677	-.134344	-.138028	-.141727	-.145438	.149161	.152893	.156634	.160382	.167895	.175425

5.0 YEAR HOLDING PERIOD
.060 EQUITY YIELD RATE
.800 LOAN RATIO

INTEREST RATE

TERM YEARS	APPR DEP	5.0	5.5	6.0	6.5	7.0	7.5	8.0	8.5	9.0	9.5	10.0	11.0	12.0
10	.40	-.019288	-.016058	-.012799	-.009911	-.006195	-.002852	.000518	.003914	.007337	.010785	.014258	.021277	.028389
	.30	-.001549	.001682	.004941	.007829	.011544	.014887	.018257	.021654	.025076	.028524	.031997	.039016	.046129
	.20	.016191	.019421	.022680	.025568	.029284	.032627	.035997	.039393	.042816	.046264	.049737	.056756	.063869
	.10	.033930	.037161	.040420	.043308	.047023	.050366	.053736	.057133	.060555	.064003	.067476	.074445	.081608
	0.00	.051670	.054901	.058160	.061048	.064763	.068106	.071476	.074873	.078295	.081743	.085216	.092235	.099348
	-.10	.069410	.072640	.075899	.078787	.082503	.085846	.089216	.092612	.096035	.099483	.102956	.109975	.117088
	-.20	.087149	.090380	.093639	.096527	.100242	.103585	.106955	.110352	.113774	.117222	.120695	.127714	.134827
	-.30	.104889	.108119	.111379	.114266	.117982	.121325	.124695	.128092	.131514	.134962	.138435	.145454	.152567
	-.40	.122629	.125859	.129118	.132406	.135722	.139065	.142435	.145831	.149254	.152702	.156175	.163194	.170306
15	.40	-.019150	-.015588	-.011996	-.008375	-.004726	-.001051	.002650	.006375	.010124	.013896	.017689	.025336	.033057
	.30	-.001411	.002152	.005744	.009365	.013013	.016689	.020389	.024115	.027864	.031635	.035428	.043075	.050797
	.20	.016329	.019892	.023484	.027105	.030753	.034428	.038129	.041854	.045603	.049375	.053168	.060815	.068537
	.10	.034069	.037631	.041223	.044844	.048493	.052168	.055869	.059594	.063343	.067114	.070908	.078555	.086276
	0.00	.051808	.055371	.058963	.062584	.066232	.069908	.073608	.077334	.081083	.084854	.088647	.096294	.104016
	-.10	.069548	.073111	.076703	.080324	.083972	.087647	.091348	.095073	.098822	.102594	.106387	.114034	.121756
	-.20	.087288	.090850	.094442	.098063	.101712	.105387	.109088	.112813	.116562	.120333	.124126	.131774	.139495
	-.30	.105027	.108590	.112182	.115803	.119451	.123126	.126827	.130553	.134301	.138073	.141866	.149513	.157235
	-.40	.122767	.126329	.129922	.133542	.137191	.140866	.144567	.148292	.152041	.155813	.159606	.167253	.174975
20	.40	-.019083	-.015361	-.011611	-.007835	-.004034	-.000210	.003636	.007503	.011389	.015292	.019211	.027095	.035029
	.30	-.001344	.002379	.006128	.009905	.013706	.017530	.021376	.025243	.029128	.033031	.036951	.044835	.052769
	.20	.016396	.020118	.023868	.027644	.031445	.035270	.039116	.042982	.046868	.050771	.054690	.062574	.070509
	.10	.034136	.037858	.041608	.045384	.049185	.053009	.056855	.060722	.064607	.068511	.072430	.080314	.088248
	0.00	.051875	.055597	.059347	.063124	.066924	.070749	.074595	.078461	.082347	.086250	.090170	.098053	.105988
	-.10	.069615	.073337	.077087	.080863	.084664	.088488	.092335	.096201	.100087	.103990	.107910	.115793	.123728
	-.20	.087355	.091077	.094827	.098603	.102404	.106228	.110074	.113941	.117826	.121730	.125649	.133533	.141467
	-.30	.105094	.108816	.112566	.116342	.120143	.123968	.127814	.131680	.135566	.139469	.143389	.151272	.159207
	-.40	.122834	.126556	.130306	.134082	.137883	.141707	.145553	.149420	.153306	.157209	.161129	.169012	.176947
25	.40	-.019045	-.015232	-.011394	-.007533	-.003650	.000252	.004171	.008107	.012057	.016020	.019994	.027972	.035982
	.30	-.001305	.002508	.006346	.010207	.014089	.017991	.021911	.025846	.029796	.033759	.037734	.045712	.053722
	.20	.016435	.020248	.024086	.027947	.031829	.035731	.039650	.043586	.047536	.051499	.055473	.063452	.071461
	.10	.034174	.037987	.041825	.045686	.049569	.053471	.057390	.061326	.065276	.069239	.073213	.081191	.089201
	0.00	.051914	.055727	.059565	.063426	.067308	.071210	.075130	.079065	.083015	.086978	.090953	.098931	.106941
	-.10	.069654	.073466	.077305	.081166	.085048	.088950	.092869	.096805	.100755	.104718	.108692	.116671	.124680
	-.20	.087393	.091206	.095044	.098905	.102788	.106690	.110609	.114545	.118495	.122457	.126432	.134410	.142420
	-.30	.105133	.108946	.112784	.116645	.120527	.124429	.128349	.132284	.136234	.140197	.144172	.152150	.160160
	-.40	.122873	.126685	.130523	.134385	.138267	.142169	.146088	.150024	.153974	.157937	.161911	.169890	.177899
30	.40	-.019020	-.015151	-.011259	-.007347	-.003418	.000527	.004486	.008457	.012438	.016429	.020427	.028441	.036472
	.30	-.001280	.002589	.006481	.010392	.014322	.018267	.022226	.026197	.030178	.034168	.038166	.046180	.054212
	.20	.016459	.020329	.024221	.028132	.032061	.036007	.039965	.043936	.047918	.051908	.055906	.063920	.071951
	.10	.034199	.038068	.041960	.045872	.049801	.053746	.057705	.061676	.065657	.069648	.073646	.081660	.089691
	0.00	.051938	.055808	.059700	.063611	.067541	.071486	.075445	.079416	.083397	.087387	.091385	.099399	.107431
	-.10	.069678	.073548	.077439	.081351	.085280	.089225	.093184	.097155	.101137	.105127	.109125	.117139	.125170
	-.20	.087418	.091287	.095179	.099091	.103020	.106965	.110924	.114895	.118876	.122867	.126865	.134878	.142910
	-.30	.105157	.109027	.112919	.116830	.120760	.124705	.128664	.132635	.136616	.140606	.144604	.152618	.160649
	-.40	.122897	.126767	.130658	.134570	.138499	.142444	.146403	.150374	.154356	.158346	.162344	.170358	.178389

5.0 YEAR HOLDING PERIOD
.060 EQUITY YIELD RATE
.900 LOAN RATIO

INTEREST RATE

TERM YEARS	APPR DEP	5.0	5.5	6.0	6.5	7.0	7.5	8.0	8.5	9.0	9.5	10.0	11.0	12.0
10	.40	-.020330	-.016695	-.013029	-.009330	-.005600	-.001839	.001952	.005773	.009623	.013502	.017410	.025306	.033318
	.30	-.002590	-.001044	.004711	.008840	.012140	.015900	.019692	.023513	.027363	.031242	.035149	.043046	.051047
	.20	.015150	.018784	.022451	.026149	.029879	.033640	.037431	.041252	.045103	.048982	.052889	.060785	.068737
	.10	.032889	.036523	.040190	.043889	.047619	.051380	.055171	.058992	.062842	.066721	.070628	.078525	.086627
	0.00	.050629	.054263	.057930	.061628	.065358	.069119	.072911	.076732	.080582	.084461	.088368	.096264	.104256
	-.10	.068369	.072003	.075669	.079368	.083098	.086859	.090650	.094471	.098322	.102201	.106108	.114004	.122006
	-.20	.086108	.089742	.093409	.097108	.100838	.104599	.108390	.112211	.116061	.119940	.123847	.131744	.139746
	-.30	.103848	.107482	.111149	.114847	.118577	.122338	.126130	.129951	.133801	.137680	.141587	.149483	.157485
	-.40	.121587	.125222	.128888	.132587	.136317	.140078	.143869	.147690	.151541	.155420	.159327	.167223	.175225
15	.40	-.020174	-.016166	-.012125	-.008052	-.003947	.000187	.004351	.008542	.012759	.017002	.021270	.029872	.038559
	.30	-.002435	-.001573	.005615	.009688	.013793	.017927	.022090	.026281	.030499	.034742	.039009	.047612	.056299
	.20	.015305	.019313	.023354	.027428	.031532	.035667	.039830	.044021	.048239	.052482	.056749	.065352	.074039
	.10	.033045	.037053	.041094	.045167	.049272	.053406	.057570	.061761	.065978	.070221	.074488	.083091	.091778
	0.00	.050784	.054792	.058833	.062907	.067011	.071146	.075309	.079500	.083718	.087961	.092228	.100831	.109518
	-.10	.068524	.072532	.076573	.080647	.084751	.088886	.093049	.097240	.101458	.105700	.109968	.118571	.127258
	-.20	.086264	.090272	.094313	.098386	.102491	.106625	.110789	.114980	.119197	.123440	.127707	.136310	.144997
	-.30	.104003	.108011	.112052	.116126	.120230	.124365	.128528	.132719	.136937	.141180	.145447	.154050	.162737
	-.40	.121743	.125751	.129792	.133865	.137970	.142105	.146268	.150459	.154676	.158919	.163187	.171790	.180477
20	.40	-.020099	-.015911	-.011693	-.007445	-.003169	.001134	.005461	.009811	.014182	.018573	.022983	.031852	.040778
	.30	-.002359	-.001828	.006047	.010295	.014571	.018873	.023200	.027550	.031922	.036313	.040722	.049591	.058518
	.20	.015381	.019568	.023786	.028035	.032311	.036613	.040940	.045290	.049661	.054052	.058462	.067331	.076257
	.10	.033120	.037307	.041526	.045774	.050050	.054353	.058680	.063030	.067401	.071792	.076202	.085071	.093997
	0.00	.050860	.055047	.059266	.063514	.067790	.072092	.076419	.080769	.085140	.089532	.093941	.102810	.111737
	-.10	.068599	.072787	.077005	.081254	.085530	.089832	.094159	.098509	.102680	.107271	.111681	.120550	.129476
	-.20	.086339	.090526	.094745	.098993	.103269	.107572	.111899	.116248	.120620	.125011	.129421	.138289	.147216
	-.30	.104079	.108266	.112485	.116733	.121009	.125311	.129638	.133988	.138359	.142751	.147160	.156029	.164955
	-.40	.121818	.126006	.130224	.134473	.138749	.143051	.147378	.151728	.156099	.160490	.164900	.173769	.182695
25	.40	-.020055	-.015706	-.011448	-.007104	-.002737	.001653	.006062	.010490	.014934	.019392	.023863	.032839	.041850
	.30	-.002316	-.001974	.006292	.010635	.015003	.019393	.023802	.028230	.032673	.037132	.041603	.050578	.059589
	.20	.015424	.019713	.024031	.028375	.032743	.037132	.041542	.045969	.050413	.054871	.059342	.068318	.077329
	.10	.033164	.037453	.041771	.046115	.050482	.054872	.059281	.063709	.068153	.072611	.077082	.086058	.095069
	0.00	.050903	.055193	.059510	.063854	.068222	.072612	.077021	.081448	.085892	.090350	.094822	.103797	.112808
	-.10	.068643	.072932	.077250	.081594	.085962	.090351	.094761	.099188	.103632	.108090	.112561	.121537	.130548
	-.20	.086383	.090672	.094990	.099334	.103701	.108091	.112500	.116928	.121371	.125830	.130301	.139277	.148288
	-.30	.104122	.108412	.112729	.117073	.121441	.125830	.130240	.134667	.139111	.143569	.148041	.157016	.166027
	-.40	.121862	.126151	.130469	.134813	.139180	.143570	.147980	.152407	.156851	.161309	.165780	.174756	.183767
30	.40	-.020028	-.015675	-.011296	-.006890	-.002475	.001963	.006417	.010884	.015363	.019852	.024350	.033366	.042401
	.30	-.002288	-.002065	.006443	.010860	.015264	.019703	.024156	.028624	.033103	.037592	.042089	.051105	.060140
	.20	.015451	.019805	.024183	.028584	.033004	.037442	.041896	.046363	.050842	.055331	.059829	.068845	.077880
	.10	.033191	.037544	.041923	.046323	.050744	.055182	.059636	.064103	.068582	.073071	.077569	.086584	.095620
	0.00	.050931	.055284	.059662	.064063	.068483	.072922	.077375	.081843	.086322	.090811	.095308	.104324	.113359
	-.10	.068670	.073024	.077402	.081802	.086223	.090661	.095115	.099582	.104061	.108550	.113048	.122064	.131099
	-.20	.086410	.090763	.095142	.099542	.103963	.108401	.112855	.117322	.121801	.126290	.130788	.139803	.148839
	-.30	.104150	.108503	.112881	.117282	.121702	.126140	.130594	.135061	.139541	.144030	.148527	.157543	.166578
	-.40	.121889	.126243	.130621	.135021	.139442	.143880	.148334	.152801	.157280	.161769	.166267	.175283	.184318

5.0 YEAR HOLDING PERIOD
.080 EQUITY YIELD RATE
.600 LOAN RATIO

INTEREST RATE

TERM YEARS	APPR DEP	5.0	5.5	6.0	6.5	7.0	7.5	8.0	8.5	9.0	9.5	10.0	11.0	12.0
10	.40	-.004606	-.002209	.000210	.002651	.005112	.007594	.010097	.012619	.015162	.017723	.020304	.025520	.030807
	.30	.012439	.014837	.017256	.019696	.022158	.024640	.027143	.029665	.032207	.034769	.037349	.042565	.047852
	.20	.029485	.031882	.034301	.036742	.039203	.041686	.044188	.046711	.049253	.051814	.054395	.059611	.064898
	.10	.046531	.048928	.051347	.053787	.056249	.058731	.061234	.063756	.066299	.068860	.071441	.076657	.081949
	0.00	.063576	.065974	.068393	.070833	.073295	.075777	.078279	.080802	.083344	.085906	.088486	.093702	.098989
	-.10	.080622	.083019	.085438	.087879	.090340	.092823	.095325	.097848	.100390	.102951	.105532	.110748	.116035
	-.20	.097667	.100065	.102484	.104924	.107386	.109868	.112371	.114893	.117436	.119997	.122577	.127793	.133081
	-.30	.114713	.117111	.119530	.121970	.124432	.126914	.129416	.131939	.134481	.137043	.139623	.144839	.150126
	-.40	.131759	.134156	.136575	.139016	.141477	.143959	.146462	.148985	.151527	.154088	.156669	.161885	.167172
15	.40	-.005267	-.002625	.000039	.002725	.005432	.008160	.010908	.013674	.016459	.019262	.022081	.027766	.033510
	.30	.011779	.014420	.017084	.019770	.022478	.025206	.027953	.030720	.033505	.036307	.039126	.044812	.050556
	.20	.028824	.031466	.034130	.036816	.039524	.042251	.044999	.047766	.050551	.053353	.056172	.061858	.067601
	.10	.045870	.048511	.051176	.053862	.056569	.059297	.062045	.064811	.067596	.070399	.073218	.078903	.084647
	0.00	.062916	.065557	.068221	.070907	.073615	.076343	.079090	.081857	.084642	.087444	.090263	.095949	.101693
	-.10	.079961	.082603	.085267	.087953	.090661	.093388	.096136	.098903	.101688	.104490	.107309	.112995	.118738
	-.20	.097007	.099648	.102313	.104999	.107706	.110434	.113182	.115948	.118733	.121536	.124355	.130040	.135784
	-.30	.114053	.116694	.119358	.122044	.124752	.127480	.130227	.132994	.135779	.138581	.141400	.147086	.152830
	-.40	.131098	.133740	.136404	.139090	.141797	.144525	.147273	.150040	.152824	.155627	.158446	.164131	.169875
20	.40	-.005587	-.002826	-.000043	.002760	.005583	.008424	.011283	.014158	.017048	.019952	.022870	.028740	.034652
	.30	.011459	.014220	.017002	.019806	.022629	.025470	.028329	.031204	.034094	.036998	.039915	.045786	.051698
	.20	.028504	.031265	.034048	.036851	.039674	.042515	.045374	.048249	.051139	.054043	.056961	.062831	.068744
	.10	.045550	.048311	.051094	.053897	.056720	.059561	.062420	.065295	.068185	.071089	.074006	.079877	.085789
	0.00	.062595	.065356	.068139	.070943	.073766	.076607	.079466	.082340	.085231	.088135	.091052	.096923	.102835
	-.10	.079641	.082402	.085185	.087989	.090812	.093653	.096512	.099386	.102277	.105181	.108098	.113969	.119881
	-.20	.096686	.099447	.102230	.105034	.107857	.110698	.113557	.116431	.119322	.122226	.125143	.131014	.136926
	-.30	.113732	.116493	.119276	.122080	.124903	.127744	.130603	.133477	.136367	.139272	.142189	.148060	.153972
	-.40	.130778	.133539	.136322	.139125	.141948	.144790	.147648	.150523	.153413	.156317	.159235	.165105	.171017
25	.40	-.005772	-.002941	-.000089	.002780	.005667	.008569	.011486	.014417	.017359	.020312	.023275	.029226	.035204
	.30	.011274	.014105	.016956	.019826	.022712	.025615	.028532	.031462	.034405	.037358	.040321	.046271	.052250
	.20	.028320	.031151	.034002	.036871	.039758	.042661	.045578	.048508	.051450	.054403	.057366	.063317	.069295
	.10	.045365	.048196	.051047	.053917	.056804	.059706	.062623	.065554	.068496	.071449	.074412	.080363	.086341
	0.00	.062411	.065242	.068093	.070962	.073849	.076752	.079669	.082599	.085542	.088495	.091458	.097408	.103386
	-.10	.079457	.082288	.085139	.088008	.090895	.093798	.096715	.099645	.102588	.105541	.108504	.114454	.120432
	-.20	.096502	.099333	.102184	.105054	.107941	.110843	.113760	.116691	.119633	.122586	.125549	.131500	.137478
	-.30	.113548	.116379	.119230	.122099	.124986	.127889	.130806	.133736	.136679	.139632	.142594	.148545	.154523
	-.40	.130594	.133424	.136275	.139145	.142032	.144935	.147852	.150782	.153724	.156677	.159640	.165591	.171569
30	.40	-.005888	-.003013	-.000118	.002792	.005717	.008656	.011606	.014567	.017537	.020514	.023499	.029485	.035488
	.30	.011157	.014033	.016927	.019838	.022763	.025702	.028652	.031613	.034582	.037560	.040545	.046531	.052533
	.20	.028203	.031079	.033973	.036884	.039809	.042747	.045698	.048659	.051628	.054606	.057590	.063576	.069579
	.10	.045248	.048124	.051018	.053929	.056854	.059793	.062743	.065704	.068674	.071651	.074636	.080622	.086625
	0.00	.062294	.065170	.068064	.070975	.073900	.076838	.079789	.082749	.085719	.088697	.091682	.097667	.103670
	-.10	.079340	.082216	.085110	.088021	.090946	.093884	.096835	.099795	.102765	.105743	.108728	.114713	.120716
	-.20	.096385	.099261	.102155	.105066	.107991	.110930	.113880	.116841	.119811	.122788	.125773	.131759	.137761
	-.30	.113431	.116307	.119201	.122112	.125037	.127975	.130926	.133886	.136856	.139834	.142819	.148804	.154807
	-.40	.130477	.133353	.136247	.139157	.142083	.145021	.147971	.150932	.153902	.156879	.159864	.165850	.171853

5.0 YEAR HOLDING PERIOD
.080 EQUITY YIELD RATE
.667 LOAN RATIO

INTEREST RATE

TERM YEARS	APPR DEP	5.0	5.5	6.0	6.5	7.0	7.5	8.0	8.5	9.0	9.5	10.0	11.0	12.0
10	.40	-.006431	-.003768	-.001080	.001632	.004367	.007125	.009906	.012709	.015533	.018379	.021247	.027042	.032917
	.30	.010614	.013278	.015966	.018678	.021413	.024471	.026951	.029754	.032579	.035425	.038292	.044088	.049962
	.20	.027660	.030324	.033012	.035723	.038458	.041216	.043997	.046800	.049625	.052471	.055338	.061133	.067008
	.10	.044706	.047369	.050057	.052769	.055504	.058262	.061043	.063846	.066670	.069516	.072383	.078179	.084054
	0.00	.061751	.064415	.067103	.069815	.072550	.075308	.078088	.080891	.083716	.086562	.089429	.095225	.101059
	-.10	.078797	.081461	.084149	.086860	.089595	.092353	.095134	.097937	.100762	.103608	.106475	.112270	.118145
	-.20	.095843	.098506	.101194	.103906	.106641	.109399	.112180	.114982	.117807	.120653	.123520	.129316	.135191
	-.30	.112888	.115552	.118240	.120951	.123687	.126445	.129225	.132028	.134853	.137699	.140566	.146362	.152236
	-.40	.129934	.132598	.135285	.137997	.140732	.143490	.146271	.149074	.151898	.154745	.157612	.163407	.169282
15	.40	-.007165	-.004230	-.001270	.001715	.004723	.007754	.010807	.013881	.016975	.020089	.023221	.029538	.035921
	.30	.009880	.012815	.015776	.018760	.021768	.024799	.027852	.030926	.034021	.037134	.040267	.046584	.052966
	.20	.026926	.029861	.032821	.035806	.038814	.041845	.044898	.047972	.051066	.054180	.057312	.063630	.070012
	.10	.043972	.046907	.049867	.052851	.055860	.058891	.061944	.065018	.068112	.071226	.074358	.080675	.087057
	0.00	.061017	.063952	.066912	.069897	.072905	.075936	.078989	.082063	.085158	.088271	.091404	.097721	.104103
	-.10	.078063	.080998	.083958	.086943	.089951	.092982	.096035	.099109	.102203	.105317	.108449	.114767	.121149
	-.20	.095109	.098044	.101004	.103988	.106997	.110028	.113081	.116155	.119249	.122363	.125495	.131812	.138194
	-.30	.112154	.115089	.118049	.121034	.124042	.127073	.130126	.133200	.136295	.139408	.142541	.148858	.155240
	-.40	.129200	.132135	.135095	.138080	.141088	.144119	.147172	.150246	.153340	.156454	.159586	.165904	.172286
20	.40	-.007521	-.004453	-.001361	.001754	.004890	.008047	.011224	.014418	.017629	.020856	.024098	.030620	.037190
	.30	.009525	.012592	.015684	.018799	.021936	.025093	.028269	.031464	.034675	.037902	.041143	.047666	.054235
	.20	.026570	.029638	.032730	.035845	.038982	.042139	.045315	.048509	.051720	.054947	.058189	.064712	.071281
	.10	.043616	.046684	.049776	.052891	.056027	.059184	.062361	.065555	.068766	.071993	.075235	.081757	.088326
	0.00	.060662	.063729	.066821	.069936	.073073	.076230	.079406	.082601	.085812	.089039	.092280	.098803	.105372
	-.10	.077707	.080775	.083867	.086982	.090119	.093276	.096452	.099646	.102857	.106084	.109326	.115849	.122418
	-.20	.094753	.097821	.100913	.104028	.107164	.110321	.113498	.116692	.119903	.123130	.126371	.132894	.139463
	-.30	.111798	.114866	.117958	.121073	.124210	.127367	.130543	.133737	.136949	.140176	.143417	.149940	.156509
	-.40	.128844	.131912	.135004	.138119	.141255	.144413	.147589	.150783	.153994	.157221	.160463	.166986	.173555
25	.40	-.007726	-.004581	-.001413	.001776	.004983	.008208	.011450	.014706	.017975	.021256	.024548	.031160	.037813
	.30	.009320	.012465	.015633	.018821	.022029	.025254	.028495	.031751	.035020	.038302	.041594	.048206	.054848
	.20	.026365	.029511	.032678	.035867	.039075	.042300	.045541	.048797	.052066	.055347	.058639	.065251	.071894
	.10	.043411	.046556	.049724	.052913	.056120	.059345	.062587	.065843	.069112	.072393	.075685	.082297	.088939
	0.00	.060457	.063602	.066770	.069958	.073166	.076391	.079632	.082888	.086157	.089439	.092731	.099343	.105985
	-.10	.077502	.080648	.083815	.087004	.090211	.093437	.096678	.099934	.103203	.106484	.109776	.116388	.123031
	-.20	.094548	.097693	.100861	.104050	.107257	.110482	.113724	.116979	.120249	.123530	.126822	.133434	.140076
	-.30	.111594	.114739	.117907	.121095	.124303	.127528	.130769	.134025	.137294	.140576	.143868	.150480	.157122
	-.40	.128639	.131785	.134952	.138141	.141348	.144574	.147815	.151071	.154340	.157621	.160913	.167525	.174158
30	.40	-.007856	-.004660	-.001445	.001789	.005040	.008305	.011583	.014872	.018172	.021481	.024797	.031448	.038118
	.30	.009190	.012385	.015601	.018835	.022085	.025350	.028628	.031918	.035218	.038526	.041843	.048494	.055163
	.20	.026235	.029431	.032646	.035880	.039131	.042396	.045674	.048964	.052264	.055572	.058888	.065539	.072209
	.10	.043281	.046476	.049692	.052926	.056176	.059442	.062720	.066009	.069309	.072618	.075934	.082585	.089255
	0.00	.060327	.063522	.066738	.069972	.073222	.076487	.079765	.083055	.086355	.089663	.092980	.099631	.106300
	-.10	.077372	.080568	.083783	.087017	.090268	.093533	.096811	.100101	.103400	.106709	.110025	.116676	.123346
	-.20	.094418	.097613	.100829	.104063	.107313	.110578	.113857	.117146	.120446	.123755	.127071	.133722	.140392
	-.30	.111464	.114659	.117875	.121108	.124359	.127624	.130902	.134192	.137492	.140800	.144117	.150768	.157437
	-.40	.128509	.131705	.134920	.138154	.141405	.144670	.147948	.151238	.154537	.157846	.161162	.167813	.174483

5.0 YEAR HOLDING PERIOD
.080 EQUITY YIELD RATE
.700 LOAN RATIO

INTEREST RATE

TERM YEARS	APPR DEP	5.0	5.5	6.0	6.5	7.0	7.5	8.0	8.5	9.0	9.5	10.0	11.0	12.0
10	.40	-.007344	-.004547	-.001724	.001123	.003995	.006890	.009810	.012753	.015719	.018707	.021718	.027803	.033972
	.30	.009702	.012499	.015321	.018168	.021040	.023936	.026856	.029799	.032765	.035753	.038764	.044849	.051017
	.20	.026748	.029545	.032367	.035214	.038086	.040982	.043901	.046844	.049810	.052799	.055809	.061895	.068063
	.10	.043793	.046590	.049412	.052260	.055131	.058027	.060947	.063890	.066856	.069844	.072855	.078940	.085108
	0.00	.060839	.063636	.066458	.069305	.072177	.075073	.077993	.080936	.083902	.086890	.089901	.095986	.102154
	-.10	.077885	.080681	.083504	.086351	.089223	.092119	.095038	.097981	.100947	.103936	.106946	.113032	.119200
	-.20	.094930	.097727	.100549	.103397	.106268	.109164	.112084	.115027	.117993	.120981	.123992	.130077	.136245
	-.30	.111976	.114773	.117595	.120442	.123314	.126210	.129130	.132073	.135039	.138027	.141037	.147123	.153291
	-.40	.129021	.131818	.134641	.137488	.140360	.143256	.146175	.149118	.152084	.155073	.158083	.164168	.170337
15	.40	-.008114	-.005033	-.001924	.001209	.004368	.007551	.010756	.013984	.017233	.020502	.023791	.030424	.037126
	.30	.008931	.012013	.015121	.018255	.021414	.024596	.027802	.031030	.034279	.037548	.040837	.047470	.054171
	.20	.025977	.029059	.032167	.035301	.038459	.041642	.044847	.048075	.051324	.054594	.057883	.064516	.071217
	.10	.043023	.046104	.049213	.052346	.055505	.058688	.061893	.065121	.068370	.071639	.074928	.081561	.088263
	0.00	.060068	.063150	.066258	.069392	.072551	.075733	.078939	.082167	.085416	.088685	.091974	.098607	.105308
	-.10	.077114	.080196	.083304	.086438	.089596	.092779	.095984	.099212	.102461	.105731	.109020	.115653	.122354
	-.20	.094160	.097241	.100349	.103483	.106642	.109824	.113030	.116258	.119507	.122776	.126065	.132698	.139399
	-.30	.111205	.114287	.117395	.120529	.123688	.126870	.130076	.133303	.136552	.139822	.143111	.149744	.156445
	-.40	.128251	.131333	.134441	.137575	.140733	.143916	.147121	.150349	.153598	.156868	.160156	.166790	.173491
20	.40	-.008488	-.005267	-.002020	.001251	.004544	.007859	.011194	.014548	.017920	.021308	.024712	.031560	.038458
	.30	.008558	.011779	.015026	.018296	.021590	.024905	.028240	.031594	.034965	.038354	.041757	.048606	.055504
	.20	.025603	.028825	.032071	.035342	.038635	.041950	.045285	.048639	.052011	.055399	.058803	.065652	.072549
	.10	.042649	.045870	.049117	.052388	.055681	.058996	.062331	.065685	.069057	.072445	.075848	.082697	.089595
	0.00	.059695	.062916	.066162	.069433	.072727	.076041	.079377	.082731	.086102	.089491	.092894	.099743	.106641
	-.10	.076740	.079962	.083208	.086479	.089772	.093087	.096422	.099776	.103148	.106536	.109940	.116789	.123686
	-.20	.093786	.097007	.100254	.103524	.106818	.110133	.113468	.116822	.120194	.123582	.126985	.133834	.140732
	-.30	.110832	.114053	.117299	.120570	.123864	.127178	.130513	.133868	.137239	.140627	.144031	.150880	.157778
	-.40	.127877	.131098	.134345	.137616	.140909	.144224	.147559	.150913	.154285	.157673	.161077	.167926	.174823
25	.40	-.008703	-.005400	-.002074	.001274	.004642	.008028	.011431	.014850	.018283	.021728	.025185	.032127	.039102
	.30	.008343	.011645	.014971	.018319	.021687	.025074	.028477	.031896	.035328	.038774	.042230	.049173	.056147
	.20	.025388	.028691	.032017	.035365	.038733	.042119	.045523	.048941	.052374	.055819	.059276	.066218	.073193
	.10	.042434	.045737	.049063	.052411	.055779	.059165	.062568	.065987	.069420	.072865	.076321	.083264	.090239
	0.00	.059480	.062782	.066108	.069456	.072824	.076211	.079614	.083033	.086465	.089910	.093367	.100310	.107284
	-.10	.076525	.079828	.083154	.086502	.089870	.093256	.096660	.100078	.103511	.106956	.110413	.117355	.124330
	-.20	.093571	.096873	.100200	.103548	.106915	.110302	.113705	.117124	.120556	.124002	.127458	.134401	.141376
	-.30	.110616	.113919	.117245	.120593	.123961	.127348	.130751	.134169	.137602	.141047	.144504	.151447	.158421
	-.40	.127662	.130965	.134291	.137639	.141007	.144393	.147796	.151215	.154648	.158093	.161550	.168492	.175467
30	.40	-.008839	-.005494	-.002108	.001288	.004701	.008129	.011571	.015025	.018490	.021964	.025446	.032429	.039433
	.30	.008206	.011561	.014938	.018333	.021746	.025175	.028617	.032071	.035536	.039010	.042492	.049475	.056478
	.20	.025252	.028607	.031983	.035379	.038792	.042220	.045662	.049116	.052581	.056055	.059537	.066521	.073524
	.10	.042297	.045653	.049029	.052425	.055838	.059266	.062708	.066162	.069627	.073101	.076583	.083566	.090570
	0.00	.059343	.062698	.066075	.069470	.072883	.076312	.079754	.083208	.086672	.090147	.093629	.100612	.107615
	-.10	.076389	.079744	.083120	.086516	.089929	.093357	.096799	.100253	.103718	.107192	.110674	.117658	.124661
	-.20	.093434	.096790	.100166	.103562	.106975	.110403	.113845	.117299	.120764	.124238	.127720	.134703	.141707
	-.30	.110480	.113835	.117212	.120607	.124020	.127449	.130891	.134345	.137809	.141283	.144765	.151749	.158752
	-.40	.127526	.130881	.134257	.137653	.141066	.144494	.147936	.151390	.154855	.158329	.161811	.168795	.175798

5.0 YEAR HOLDING PERIOD
.080 EQUITY YIELD RATE
.750 LOAN RATIO

INTEREST RATE

TERM YEARS	APPR DEP	5.0	5.5	6.0	6.5	7.0	7.5	8.0	8.5	9.0	9.5	10.0	11.0	12.0
10	.40	-.008712	-.005716	-.002692	.000359	.003436	.006539	.009667	.012820	.015998	.019200	.022425	.028945	.035554
	.30	.008333	.011330	.014354	.017404	.020481	.023584	.026712	.029866	.033043	.036245	.039471	.045991	.052600
	.20	.025379	.028376	.031400	.034450	.037527	.040630	.043758	.046911	.050089	.053291	.056516	.063036	.069645
	.10	.042425	.045421	.048445	.051496	.054573	.057675	.060804	.063957	.067135	.070337	.073562	.080082	.086691
	0.00	.059470	.062467	.065491	.068541	.071618	.074721	.077849	.081003	.084180	.087382	.090608	.097128	.103737
	-.10	.076516	.079513	.082536	.085587	.088664	.091767	.094895	.098048	.101226	.104428	.107653	.114173	.120782
	-.20	.093562	.096558	.099582	.102633	.105710	.108812	.111941	.115094	.118272	.121474	.124699	.131219	.137828
	-.30	.110607	.113604	.116628	.119678	.122755	.125858	.128986	.132140	.135317	.138519	.141745	.148265	.154873
	-.40	.127653	.130650	.133673	.136724	.139801	.142904	.146032	.149185	.152363	.155565	.158790	.165310	.171919
15	.40	-.009538	-.006236	-.002906	.000452	.003836	.007246	.010680	.014139	.017620	.021123	.024647	.031754	.038933
	.30	.007508	.010809	.014140	.017497	.020882	.024291	.027726	.031184	.034665	.038168	.041692	.048799	.055979
	.20	.024553	.027855	.031185	.034543	.037927	.041337	.044772	.048230	.051711	.055214	.058738	.065845	.073025
	.10	.041599	.044901	.048231	.051589	.054973	.058383	.061817	.065276	.068757	.072260	.075784	.082890	.090070
	0.00	.058645	.061946	.065277	.068634	.072019	.075428	.078863	.082321	.085802	.089305	.092829	.099936	.107116
	-.10	.075690	.078992	.082322	.085680	.089064	.092474	.095909	.099367	.102848	.106351	.109875	.116982	.124152
	-.20	.092736	.096038	.099368	.102726	.106110	.109520	.112954	.116413	.119894	.123397	.126920	.134027	.141207
	-.30	.109782	.113083	.116414	.119771	.123155	.126565	.130000	.133458	.136939	.140442	.143966	.151073	.158253
	-.40	.126827	.130129	.133459	.136817	.140201	.143611	.147046	.150504	.153985	.157488	.161012	.168119	.175238
20	.40	-.009938	-.006487	-.003008	.000496	.004024	.007576	.011149	.014743	.018356	.021986	.025633	.032971	.040351
	.30	.007107	.010559	.014037	.017541	.021070	.024622	.028195	.031789	.035401	.039031	.042678	.050016	.057417
	.20	.024153	.027604	.031083	.034587	.038116	.041667	.045241	.048834	.052447	.056077	.059724	.067062	.074452
	.10	.041199	.044650	.048128	.051633	.055161	.058713	.062286	.065880	.069493	.073123	.076770	.084108	.091488
	0.00	.058244	.061696	.065174	.068678	.072207	.075759	.079332	.082926	.086538	.090168	.093815	.101153	.108544
	-.10	.075290	.078741	.082219	.085724	.089253	.092804	.096378	.099971	.103584	.107214	.110861	.118199	.125539
	-.20	.092336	.095787	.099265	.102770	.106298	.109850	.113423	.117017	.120629	.124260	.127906	.135245	.142635
	-.30	.109381	.112833	.116311	.119815	.123344	.126896	.130469	.134063	.137675	.141305	.144952	.152290	.159630
	-.40	.126427	.129878	.133357	.136861	.140390	.143941	.147515	.151108	.154721	.158351	.161998	.169336	.176726
25	.40	-.010169	-.006630	-.003067	.000521	.004129	.007757	.011403	.015067	.018744	.022436	.026139	.033578	.041051
	.30	.006877	.010415	.013979	.017566	.021175	.024803	.028449	.032112	.035790	.039481	.043185	.050623	.058036
	.20	.023922	.027461	.031025	.034612	.038220	.041849	.045495	.049158	.052836	.056527	.060231	.067669	.075142
	.10	.040968	.044507	.048070	.051657	.055266	.058894	.062541	.066204	.069881	.073573	.077276	.084715	.092188
	0.00	.058014	.061552	.065116	.068703	.072312	.075940	.079586	.083249	.086927	.090618	.094322	.101760	.109233
	-.10	.075059	.078598	.082162	.085749	.089357	.092986	.096632	.100295	.103973	.107664	.111368	.118806	.126279
	-.20	.092105	.095644	.099207	.102794	.106403	.110031	.113678	.117340	.121018	.124710	.128413	.135852	.143324
	-.30	.109151	.112689	.116253	.119840	.123449	.127077	.130723	.134386	.138064	.141755	.145459	.152897	.160369
	-.40	.126196	.129735	.133299	.136886	.140494	.144122	.147769	.151432	.155110	.158801	.162504	.169943	.177416
30	.40	-.010315	-.006720	-.003103	.000536	.004192	.007866	.011553	.015254	.018967	.022689	.026419	.033902	.041405
	.30	.006731	.010326	.013943	.017581	.021238	.024911	.028599	.032300	.036012	.039734	.043465	.050947	.058451
	.20	.023776	.027371	.030989	.034627	.038284	.041957	.045645	.049346	.053058	.056780	.060511	.067993	.075496
	.10	.040822	.044417	.048034	.051673	.055329	.059002	.062690	.066391	.070103	.073826	.077556	.085039	.092542
	0.00	.057868	.061462	.065080	.068718	.072375	.076048	.079736	.083437	.087149	.090871	.094602	.102084	.109538
	-.10	.074913	.078508	.082126	.085764	.089421	.093094	.096782	.100483	.104195	.107917	.111648	.119130	.126633
	-.20	.091959	.095554	.099171	.102810	.106466	.110139	.113827	.117528	.121240	.124963	.128693	.136175	.143679
	-.30	.109005	.112599	.116217	.119855	.123512	.127185	.130873	.134574	.138286	.142008	.145739	.153221	.160725
	-.40	.126050	.129645	.133263	.136901	.140557	.144231	.147919	.151619	.155332	.159054	.162785	.170267	.177770

5.0 YEAR HOLDING PERIOD
.080 EQUITY YIELD RATE
.800 LOAN RATIO

INTEREST RATE

TERM YEARS	APPR DEP	12.0	11.0	10.0	9.5	9.0	8.5	8.0	7.5	7.0	6.5	6.0	5.5	5.0
10	.40	.037136	.030087	.023132	.019692	.016276	.012887	.009523	.006187	.002877	-.000405	-.003059	-.006884	-.010081
	.30	.054182	.047133	.040178	.036737	.033322	.029932	.026569	.023232	.019923	.016641	.013387	.010161	.006965
	.20	.071228	.064178	.057224	.053783	.050368	.046978	.043615	.040278	.036968	.033686	.030432	.027207	.024010
	.10	.088273	.081224	.074269	.070829	.067413	.064024	.060660	.057324	.054014	.050732	.047478	.044252	.041056
	0.00	.105319	.098270	.091315	.087874	.084459	.081069	.077706	.074369	.071060	.067778	.064524	.061298	.058102
	-.10	.122365	.115315	.108361	.104920	.101505	.098115	.094752	.091415	.088105	.084823	.081569	.078344	.075147
	-.20	.139410	.132361	.125406	.121956	.118550	.115161	.111797	.108460	.105151	.101869	.098615	.095389	.092193
	-.30	.156466	.149406	.142452	.139011	.135596	.132206	.128843	.125506	.122196	.118914	.115660	.112435	.109239
	-.40	.173502	.166452	.159497	.156057	.152642	.149252	.145889	.142552	.139242	.135960	.132706	.129481	.126284
15	.40	.040741	.033083	.025502	.021743	.018007	.014293	.010605	.006941	.003304	-.000306	-.003888	-.007440	-.010962
	.30	.057787	.050128	.042548	.038739	.035052	.031339	.027650	.023987	.020350	.016740	.013158	.009606	.006084
	.20	.074832	.067174	.059593	.055834	.052098	.048385	.044696	.041032	.037395	.033785	.030204	.026652	.023130
	.10	.091879	.084220	.076639	.072830	.069144	.065430	.061742	.058078	.054441	.050831	.047249	.043697	.040175
	0.00	.108924	.101265	.093684	.089926	.086189	.082476	.078787	.075124	.071486	.067877	.064295	.060743	.057221
	-.10	.125969	.118311	.110730	.106971	.103235	.099522	.095833	.092169	.088532	.084922	.081341	.077788	.074267
	-.20	.143015	.135356	.127775	.124017	.120280	.116567	.112878	.109215	.105577	.101968	.098386	.094834	.091312
	-.30	.160061	.152402	.144821	.141053	.137326	.133613	.129924	.126261	.122623	.119014	.115432	.111880	.108358
	-.40	.177106	.169448	.161867	.158108	.154372	.150659	.146970	.143306	.139669	.136059	.132478	.128925	.125404
20	.40	.042264	.034381	.026554	.022654	.018791	.014938	.011105	.007293	.003505	-.000259	-.003997	-.007707	-.011389
	.30	.059309	.051427	.043599	.039709	.035837	.031984	.028151	.024339	.020551	.016787	.013049	.009338	.005657
	.20	.076355	.068472	.060645	.056755	.052883	.049029	.045196	.041385	.037596	.033832	.030094	.026384	.022703
	.10	.093401	.085518	.077691	.073801	.069928	.066075	.062242	.058430	.054642	.050878	.047140	.043430	.039748
	0.00	.110446	.102563	.094736	.090846	.086974	.083121	.079287	.075476	.071688	.067924	.064186	.060475	.056794
	-.10	.127492	.119609	.111782	.107892	.104020	.100166	.096333	.092522	.088733	.084969	.081231	.077521	.073840
	-.20	.144538	.136653	.128827	.124938	.121065	.117212	.113379	.109567	.105779	.102015	.098277	.094567	.090885
	-.30	.161583	.153700	.145873	.141983	.138111	.134258	.130424	.126613	.122824	.119061	.115323	.111612	.107931
	-.40	.178629	.170746	.162919	.159029	.155157	.151303	.147470	.143659	.139870	.136106	.132368	.128658	.124977
25	.40	.042999	.035028	.027094	.023144	.019206	.015283	.011376	.007487	.003616	-.000233	-.004059	-.007860	-.011635
	.30	.060045	.052074	.044140	.040189	.036252	.032329	.028422	.024532	.020662	.016813	.012987	.009186	.005411
	.20	.077091	.069120	.061185	.057235	.053298	.049375	.045467	.041578	.037708	.033859	.030033	.026231	.022457
	.10	.094136	.086165	.078231	.074281	.070343	.066420	.062513	.058624	.054753	.050904	.047078	.043277	.039502
	0.00	.111182	.103211	.095277	.091326	.087389	.083466	.079559	.075669	.071799	.067950	.064124	.060322	.056548
	-.10	.128228	.120257	.112322	.108372	.104434	.100512	.096604	.092715	.088845	.084996	.081170	.077368	.073594
	-.20	.145273	.137302	.129368	.125418	.121480	.117557	.113650	.109761	.105890	.102041	.098215	.094414	.090639
	-.30	.162319	.154348	.146414	.142463	.138526	.134603	.130696	.126806	.122936	.119087	.115261	.111459	.107685
	-.40	.179365	.171394	.163459	.159509	.155571	.151648	.147741	.143852	.139982	.136133	.132306	.128505	.124731
30	.40	.043378	.035374	.027393	.023413	.019443	.015483	.011536	.007602	.003684	-.000216	-.004097	-.007956	-.011790
	.30	.060423	.052420	.044438	.040459	.036489	.032529	.028581	.024648	.020730	.016829	.012948	.009090	.005255
	.20	.077469	.069465	.061484	.057505	.053534	.049575	.045627	.041693	.037875	.033875	.029994	.026135	.022301
	.10	.094515	.086511	.078530	.074550	.070580	.066620	.062673	.058739	.054821	.050920	.047040	.043181	.039346
	0.00	.111560	.103557	.095575	.091596	.087626	.083666	.079714	.075785	.071867	.067966	.064085	.060227	.056392
	-.10	.128606	.120606	.112620	.108642	.104671	.100711	.096764	.092830	.088912	.085012	.081131	.077272	.073438
	-.20	.145652	.137648	.129667	.125687	.121717	.117757	.113810	.109876	.105958	.102057	.098177	.094318	.090483
	-.30	.162697	.154694	.146712	.142733	.138763	.134803	.130855	.126922	.123004	.119103	.115222	.111364	.107529
	-.40	.179743	.171739	.163758	.159779	.155808	.151849	.147901	.143967	.140049	.136148	.132268	.128409	.124575

5.0 YEAR HOLDING PERIOD
.080 EQUITY YIELD RATE
.900 LOAN RATIO

INTEREST RATE

TERM YEARS	APPR DEP	5.0	5.5	6.0	6.5	7.0	7.5	8.0	8.5	9.0	9.5	10.0	11.0	12.0
10	.40	-.012818	-.009222	-.005594	-.001933	.001759	.005483	.009237	.013021	.016834	.020676	.024547	.032371	.040301
	.30	.004227	.007823	.011452	.015113	.018805	.022528	.026282	.030066	.033879	.037722	.041592	.049416	.057347
	.20	.021273	.024869	.028498	.032158	.035851	.039574	.043328	.047112	.050925	.054767	.058638	.066462	.074393
	.10	.038319	.041915	.045543	.049204	.052896	.056620	.060374	.064158	.067971	.071813	.075684	.083508	.091438
	0.00	.055364	.058960	.062589	.066250	.069942	.073665	.077419	.081203	.085016	.088859	.092729	.100553	.108484
	-.10	.072410	.076006	.079635	.083295	.086988	.090711	.094465	.098249	.102062	.105904	.109775	.117599	.125529
	-.20	.089456	.093052	.096680	.100341	.104033	.107757	.111511	.115294	.119108	.122950	.126821	.134645	.142575
	-.30	.106501	.110097	.113726	.117387	.121079	.124802	.128556	.132340	.136153	.139996	.143866	.151690	.159621
	-.40	.123547	.127143	.130772	.134432	.138125	.141848	.145602	.149386	.153199	.157041	.160912	.168736	.176666
15	.40	-.013809	-.009847	-.005851	-.001821	.002240	.006332	.010453	.014603	.018780	.022984	.027212	.035741	.044356
	.30	.003237	.007199	.011195	.015224	.019285	.023377	.027499	.031649	.035826	.040029	.044258	.052787	.061402
	.20	.020282	.024244	.028241	.032270	.036331	.040423	.044544	.048694	.052872	.057075	.061304	.069832	.078448
	.10	.037328	.041290	.045286	.049315	.053377	.057468	.061590	.065740	.069917	.074121	.078349	.086878	.095493
	0.00	.054374	.058336	.062332	.066361	.070423	.074514	.078636	.082786	.086963	.091166	.095395	.103923	.112539
	-.10	.071419	.075381	.079378	.083407	.087468	.091560	.095681	.099831	.104008	.108212	.112441	.120969	.129585
	-.20	.088465	.092427	.096423	.100452	.104514	.108605	.112727	.116877	.121054	.125258	.129486	.138015	.146630
	-.30	.105510	.109473	.113469	.117498	.121559	.125651	.129772	.133922	.138100	.142303	.146532	.155060	.163676
	-.40	.122556	.126518	.130514	.134544	.138605	.142697	.146818	.150968	.155145	.159349	.163578	.172106	.180722
20	.40	-.014289	-.010148	-.005974	-.001769	.002466	.006728	.011016	.015328	.019663	.024020	.028396	.037201	.046070
	.30	.002756	.006898	.011072	.015277	.019512	.023774	.028061	.032374	.036709	.041065	.045441	.054247	.063115
	.20	.019802	.023943	.028118	.032323	.036557	.040819	.045107	.049419	.053755	.058111	.062487	.071293	.080161
	.10	.036848	.040989	.045163	.049368	.053603	.057865	.062153	.066465	.070800	.075156	.079533	.088338	.097207
	0.00	.053893	.058035	.062209	.066414	.070648	.074910	.079198	.083511	.087846	.092202	.096578	.105384	.114258
	-.10	.070939	.075080	.079255	.083460	.087694	.091956	.096244	.100556	.104891	.109248	.113624	.122430	.131298
	-.20	.087984	.092126	.096300	.100505	.104740	.109002	.113290	.117602	.121937	.126293	.130669	.139475	.148344
	-.30	.105030	.109172	.113346	.117551	.121785	.126047	.130335	.134648	.138983	.143339	.147715	.156520	.165389
	-.40	.122076	.126217	.130391	.134597	.138831	.143093	.147381	.151693	.156028	.160385	.164761	.173567	.182435
25	.40	-.014566	-.010320	-.006043	-.001739	.002591	.006945	.011321	.015716	.020130	.024559	.029004	.037930	.046857
	.30	.002480	.006726	.011002	.015307	.019637	.023991	.028367	.032762	.037175	.041605	.046049	.054975	.063943
	.20	.019525	.023772	.028048	.032352	.036683	.041037	.045412	.049808	.054221	.058651	.063095	.072021	.080988
	.10	.036571	.040817	.045094	.049398	.053728	.058082	.062458	.066853	.071267	.075696	.080141	.089067	.098034
	0.00	.053617	.057863	.062139	.066444	.070774	.075128	.079504	.083899	.088312	.092742	.097186	.106112	.115080
	-.10	.070662	.074908	.079185	.083489	.087820	.092174	.096549	.100945	.105358	.109788	.114232	.123158	.132125
	-.20	.087708	.091954	.096231	.100535	.104865	.109219	.113595	.117990	.122404	.126833	.131278	.140204	.149171
	-.30	.104753	.108999	.113276	.117581	.121911	.126265	.130640	.135036	.139449	.143879	.148323	.157249	.166217
	-.40	.121799	.126045	.130322	.134626	.138957	.143310	.147686	.152082	.156495	.160925	.165369	.174295	.183262
30	.40	-.014741	-.010428	-.006086	-.001721	.002667	.007075	.011501	.015942	.020396	.024863	.029340	.038319	.047323
	.30	.002304	.006618	.010959	.015325	.019713	.024121	.028546	.032987	.037442	.041909	.046385	.055364	.064368
	.20	.019350	.023664	.028005	.032371	.036759	.041166	.045592	.050033	.054488	.058954	.063431	.072410	.081414
	.10	.036395	.040709	.045050	.049416	.053804	.058212	.062638	.067079	.071533	.076000	.080477	.089456	.098460
	0.00	.053441	.057755	.062096	.066462	.070850	.075258	.079683	.084124	.088579	.093046	.097522	.106501	.115505
	-.10	.070487	.074801	.079142	.083508	.087896	.092303	.096729	.101170	.105625	.110091	.114568	.123547	.132551
	-.20	.087532	.091846	.096187	.100553	.104941	.109349	.113774	.118216	.122670	.127137	.131614	.140592	.149597
	-.30	.104578	.108892	.113233	.117599	.121987	.126395	.130820	.135261	.139716	.144182	.148659	.157638	.166642
	-.40	.121624	.125938	.130279	.134644	.139032	.143440	.147866	.152307	.156762	.161228	.165705	.174684	.183688

143

5.0 YEAR HOLDING PERIOD
.100 EQUITY YIELD RATE
.600 LOAN RATIO

TERM YEARS	APPR DEP	5.0	5.5	6.0	6.5	7.0	7.5	8.0	8.5	9.0	9.5	10.0	11.0	12.0
10	.40	.007807	.010180	.012575	.014991	.017428	.019886	.022365	.024864	.027383	.029921	.032478	.037647	.042889
	.30	.024187	.026560	.028954	.031371	.033808	.036266	.038745	.041244	.043762	.046300	.048857	.054027	.059268
	.20	.040566	.042939	.045334	.047750	.050188	.052646	.055125	.057623	.060142	.062680	.065237	.070407	.075648
	.10	.056940	.059319	.061714	.064130	.066568	.069026	.071504	.074003	.076522	.079060	.081617	.086787	.092028
	0.00	.073326	.075699	.078094	.080510	.082947	.085405	.087884	.090383	.092902	.095440	.097997	.103166	.108408
	-.10	.089706	.092079	.094473	.096890	.099327	.101785	.104264	.106763	.109281	.111819	.114376	.119546	.124787
	-.20	.106065	.108458	.110853	.113269	.115707	.118165	.120644	.123142	.125661	.128199	.130756	.135926	.141167
	-.30	.122465	.124838	.127233	.129649	.132087	.134545	.137023	.139522	.142041	.144579	.147136	.152306	.157547
	-.40	.138845	.141218	.143613	.146029	.148466	.150924	.153403	.155902	.158421	.160959	.163516	.168685	.173927
15	.40	.006413	.009025	.011661	.014319	.016998	.019699	.022420	.025160	.027919	.030696	.033491	.039149	.044827
	.30	.022793	.025405	.028041	.030698	.033378	.036079	.038800	.041540	.044299	.047076	.049871	.055508	.061207
	.20	.039173	.041785	.044420	.047078	.049758	.052458	.055179	.057920	.060679	.063456	.066250	.071888	.077586
	.10	.055552	.058165	.060800	.063458	.066138	.068838	.071559	.074299	.077058	.079836	.082630	.088268	.093966
	0.00	.071932	.074544	.077180	.079838	.082517	.085218	.087939	.090679	.093438	.096215	.099010	.104648	.110346
	-.10	.088312	.090924	.093560	.096217	.098897	.101598	.104318	.107059	.109818	.112595	.115390	.121027	.126726
	-.20	.104692	.107304	.109939	.112597	.115277	.117977	.120698	.123439	.126198	.128975	.131770	.137407	.143105
	-.30	.121071	.123684	.126319	.128977	.131657	.134357	.137078	.139818	.142577	.145355	.148149	.153787	.159485
	-.40	.137451	.140063	.142699	.145357	.148036	.150737	.153458	.156198	.158957	.161734	.164529	.170167	.175865
20	.40	.005738	.008469	.011224	.013999	.016796	.019611	.022445	.025296	.028163	.031045	.033941	.039771	.045646
	.30	.022117	.024849	.027603	.030379	.033175	.035991	.038825	.041676	.044542	.047424	.050320	.056150	.062025
	.20	.038497	.041229	.043983	.046759	.049555	.052371	.055205	.058055	.060922	.063804	.066700	.072530	.078405
	.10	.054877	.057608	.060363	.063139	.065935	.068751	.071584	.074435	.077302	.080184	.083080	.088910	.094785
	0.00	.071257	.073988	.076743	.079518	.082315	.085130	.087964	.090815	.093682	.096564	.099460	.105290	.111165
	-.10	.087636	.090368	.093122	.095898	.098694	.101510	.104344	.107195	.110061	.112943	.115839	.121669	.127544
	-.20	.104016	.106748	.109502	.112278	.115074	.117890	.120724	.123574	.126441	.129323	.132219	.138049	.143924
	-.30	.120396	.123127	.125882	.128658	.131454	.134270	.137103	.139954	.142821	.145703	.148599	.154429	.160304
	-.40	.136775	.139507	.142262	.145037	.147834	.150649	.153483	.156334	.159201	.162083	.164979	.170809	.176684
25	.40	.005348	.008152	.010976	.013821	.016683	.019563	.022459	.025369	.028291	.031226	.034172	.040091	.046041
	.30	.021728	.024531	.027356	.030200	.033063	.035943	.038838	.041748	.044671	.047606	.050551	.056471	.062421
	.20	.038108	.040911	.043736	.046580	.049443	.052323	.055218	.058128	.061051	.063986	.066931	.072850	.078801
	.10	.054488	.057291	.060115	.062960	.065823	.068702	.071598	.074508	.077431	.080365	.083311	.089230	.095180
	0.00	.070867	.073671	.076495	.079340	.082202	.085082	.087978	.090888	.093810	.096745	.099691	.105610	.111560
	-.10	.087247	.090050	.092875	.095719	.098582	.101462	.104357	.107267	.110190	.113125	.116070	.121989	.127940
	-.20	.103627	.106430	.109255	.112099	.114962	.117842	.120737	.123647	.126570	.129505	.132450	.138369	.144320
	-.30	.120007	.122810	.125634	.128479	.131342	.134221	.137117	.140027	.142950	.145884	.148830	.154749	.160699
	-.40	.136386	.139190	.142014	.144859	.147721	.150601	.153497	.156407	.159329	.162264	.165210	.171129	.177079
30	.40	.005102	.007952	.010823	.013711	.016615	.019535	.022467	.025411	.028365	.031328	.034299	.040262	.046245
	.30	.021481	.024332	.027202	.030091	.032995	.035914	.038847	.041790	.044745	.047708	.050679	.056641	.062624
	.20	.037861	.040712	.043582	.046470	.049375	.052294	.055226	.058170	.061124	.064088	.067059	.073021	.075384
	.10	.054241	.057091	.059962	.062850	.065755	.068674	.071606	.074550	.077504	.080467	.083439	.089401	.095384
	0.00	.070621	.073471	.076342	.079230	.082134	.085054	.087986	.090930	.093884	.096847	.099818	.105781	.111764
	-.10	.087000	.089851	.092721	.095610	.098514	.101433	.104366	.107309	.110264	.113227	.116198	.122160	.128143
	-.20	.103380	.106231	.109101	.111989	.114894	.117813	.120745	.123689	.126643	.129607	.132578	.138540	.144523
	-.30	.119760	.122610	.125481	.128369	.131274	.134193	.137125	.140069	.143023	.145986	.148958	.154920	.160903
	-.40	.136140	.138991	.141861	.144749	.147653	.150573	.153505	.156449	.159403	.162366	.165337	.171403	.177283

5.0 YEAR HOLDING PERIOD
.100 EQUITY YIELD RATE
.667 LOAN RATIO

INTEREST RATE

TERM YEARS	APPR DEP	5.0	5.5	6.0	6.5	7.0	7.5	8.0	8.5	9.0	9.5	10.0	11.0	12.0
10	.40	.004843	.007480	.010141	.012825	.015533	.018265	.021019	.023795	.026594	.029414	.032255	.037999	.043823
	.30	.021223	.023859	.026520	.029205	.031913	.034645	.037399	.040175	.042974	.045794	.048635	.054379	.060203
	.20	.037603	.040239	.042900	.045585	.048293	.051024	.053778	.056555	.059353	.062173	.065014	.070759	.076582
	.10	.053982	.056619	.059280	.061964	.064673	.067404	.070158	.072935	.075733	.078553	.081394	.087138	.092962
	0.00	.070362	.072999	.075659	.078344	.081052	.083784	.086538	.089314	.092113	.094933	.097774	.103518	.109342
	-.10	.086742	.089378	.092039	.094724	.097432	.100164	.102918	.105694	.108493	.111313	.114154	.119898	.125722
	-.20	.103122	.105758	.108419	.111104	.113812	.116543	.119297	.122074	.124872	.127692	.130533	.136278	.142101
	-.30	.119501	.122138	.124799	.127483	.130192	.132923	.135677	.138454	.141252	.144072	.146913	.152657	.158481
	-.40	.135881	.138518	.141178	.143863	.146571	.149303	.152057	.154833	.157632	.160452	.163293	.169037	.174861
15	.40	.003294	.006197	.009125	.012078	.015056	.018056	.021080	.024124	.027190	.030276	.033381	.039645	.045976
	.30	.019674	.022577	.025505	.028458	.031436	.034436	.037459	.040504	.043570	.046656	.049761	.056025	.062356
	.20	.036054	.038957	.041885	.044838	.047815	.050816	.053839	.056884	.059950	.063035	.066140	.072405	.078736
	.10	.052434	.055336	.058264	.061218	.064195	.067196	.070219	.073264	.076329	.079415	.082520	.088784	.095116
	0.00	.068813	.071716	.074644	.077597	.080575	.083575	.086599	.089643	.092709	.095795	.098900	.105164	.111495
	-.10	.085193	.088096	.091024	.093977	.096955	.099955	.102978	.106023	.109089	.112175	.115280	.121544	.127875
	-.20	.101573	.104475	.107404	.110357	.113334	.116335	.119358	.122403	.125469	.128554	.131659	.137924	.144255
	-.30	.117953	.120855	.123783	.126737	.129714	.132715	.135738	.138783	.141848	.144934	.148039	.154303	.160635
	-.40	.134332	.137235	.140163	.143116	.146094	.149094	.152118	.155162	.158228	.161314	.164419	.170683	.177024
20	.40	.002544	.005579	.008639	.011724	.014831	.017959	.021108	.024275	.027461	.030663	.033881	.040358	.046886
	.30	.018923	.021959	.025019	.028104	.031211	.034339	.037487	.040655	.043840	.047043	.050260	.056738	.063266
	.20	.035303	.038338	.041399	.044483	.047590	.050719	.053867	.057035	.060220	.063422	.066640	.073118	.079646
	.10	.051683	.054718	.057779	.060863	.063970	.067098	.070247	.073414	.076600	.079802	.083020	.089498	.096025
	0.00	.068063	.071098	.074158	.077243	.080350	.083478	.086627	.089794	.092980	.096182	.099400	.105877	.112405
	-.10	.084443	.087478	.090538	.093622	.096729	.099858	.103006	.106174	.109359	.112562	.115779	.122257	.128785
	-.20	.100822	.103857	.106918	.110002	.113109	.116238	.119386	.122554	.125739	.128941	.132159	.138637	.145165
	-.30	.117202	.120237	.123298	.126382	.129489	.132617	.135766	.138933	.142119	.145321	.148539	.155017	.161544
	-.40	.133582	.136617	.139677	.142762	.145869	.148997	.152146	.155313	.158499	.161701	.164918	.171396	.177924
25	.40	.002111	.005226	.008364	.011525	.014706	.017906	.021123	.024356	.027604	.030865	.034137	.040714	.047326
	.30	.018491	.021606	.024744	.027905	.031086	.034285	.037503	.040736	.043983	.047244	.050517	.057094	.063705
	.20	.034871	.037985	.041124	.044284	.047465	.050665	.053882	.057115	.060363	.063624	.066897	.073474	.080085
	.10	.051250	.054365	.057504	.060664	.063845	.067045	.070262	.073495	.076743	.080004	.083277	.089853	.096465
	0.00	.067630	.070745	.073883	.077044	.080225	.083425	.086642	.089875	.093123	.096383	.099656	.106233	.112845
	-.10	.084010	.087125	.090263	.093424	.096605	.099804	.103022	.106255	.109502	.112763	.116036	.122613	.129224
	-.20	.100390	.103504	.106643	.109803	.112984	.116184	.119401	.122634	.125882	.129143	.132416	.138993	.145604
	-.30	.116769	.119884	.123023	.126183	.129364	.132564	.135781	.139014	.142262	.145523	.148796	.155372	.161984
	-.40	.133149	.136264	.139402	.142563	.145744	.148944	.152161	.155394	.158642	.161902	.165175	.171752	.178364
30	.40	.001837	.005004	.008194	.011403	.014630	.017874	.021132	.024403	.027685	.030978	.034279	.040904	.047552
	.30	.018217	.021384	.024573	.027783	.031010	.034253	.037512	.040783	.044065	.047358	.050659	.057284	.063931
	.20	.034597	.037764	.040953	.044162	.047390	.050633	.053891	.057162	.060445	.063737	.067039	.073664	.080311
	.10	.050976	.054144	.057333	.060542	.063769	.067013	.070271	.073542	.076825	.080117	.083419	.090043	.096691
	0.00	.067356	.070523	.073713	.076922	.080149	.083393	.086651	.089922	.093204	.096497	.099798	.106423	.113071
	-.10	.083736	.086903	.090092	.093302	.096529	.099772	.103031	.106302	.109584	.112877	.116178	.122803	.129450
	-.20	.100116	.103283	.106472	.109681	.112909	.116152	.119410	.122681	.125964	.129256	.132558	.139183	.145830
	-.30	.116495	.119663	.122852	.126061	.129288	.132532	.135790	.139061	.142344	.145636	.148938	.155562	.162210
	-.40	.132875	.136042	.139232	.142441	.145668	.148912	.152170	.155441	.158723	.162016	.165317	.171942	.178590

5.0 YEAR HOLDING PERIOD
.100 EQUITY YIELD RATE
.700 LOAN RATIO

INTEREST RATE

TERM YEARS	APPR DEP	5.0	5.5	6.0	6.5	7.0	7.5	8.0	8.5	9.0	9.5	10.0	11.0	12.0
10	.40	.003361	.006130	.008924	.011743	.014586	.017454	.020346	.023261	.026199	.029160	.032144	.038175	.044290
	.30	.019741	.022503	.025303	.028122	.030966	.033834	.036726	.039641	.042579	.045540	.048523	.054555	.060670
	.20	.036121	.038889	.041683	.044502	.047346	.050214	.053105	.056021	.058959	.061920	.064903	.070934	.077749
	.10	.052501	.055269	.058063	.060882	.063725	.066593	.069485	.072400	.075339	.078300	.081283	.087314	.093429
	0.00	.068880	.071649	.074443	.077262	.080105	.082973	.085865	.088780	.091718	.094679	.097663	.103694	.109809
	-.10	.085260	.088028	.090822	.093641	.096485	.099353	.102245	.105160	.108098	.111059	.114042	.120074	.126189
	-.20	.101640	.104408	.107202	.110021	.112865	.115733	.118624	.121540	.124478	.127439	.130422	.136453	.142568
	-.30	.118020	.120788	.123582	.126401	.129244	.132112	.135004	.137919	.140858	.143819	.146802	.152833	.158948
	-.40	.134399	.137168	.139962	.142781	.145624	.148492	.151384	.154299	.157237	.160198	.163182	.169213	.175328
15	.40	.001735	.004783	.007857	.010958	.014084	.017235	.020410	.023607	.026826	.030056	.033326	.039903	.046551
	.30	.018115	.021163	.024237	.027338	.030464	.033615	.036789	.039986	.043205	.046445	.049706	.056283	.062931
	.20	.034495	.037542	.040617	.043718	.046844	.049995	.053169	.056366	.059585	.062825	.066085	.072663	.079311
	.10	.050875	.053922	.056997	.060098	.063224	.066374	.069549	.072746	.075965	.079205	.082465	.089042	.095690
	0.00	.067254	.070302	.073376	.076477	.079603	.082754	.085929	.089126	.092345	.095585	.098845	.105422	.112070
	-.10	.083634	.086682	.089756	.092857	.095983	.099134	.102308	.105505	.108724	.111964	.115225	.121802	.128450
	-.20	.100014	.103061	.106136	.109237	.112363	.115514	.118688	.121885	.125104	.128344	.131604	.138182	.144830
	-.30	.116394	.119441	.122516	.125617	.128743	.131893	.135068	.138265	.141484	.144724	.147984	.154561	.161210
	-.40	.132773	.135821	.138895	.141996	.145122	.148273	.151448	.154645	.157864	.161104	.164364	.170941	.177589
20	.40	.000947	.004134	.007347	.010586	.013848	.017133	.020439	.023765	.027110	.030472	.033850	.040652	.047506
	.30	.017327	.020514	.023727	.026966	.030228	.033513	.036819	.040145	.043489	.046852	.050230	.057032	.063886
	.20	.033706	.036893	.040107	.043345	.046608	.049893	.053199	.056524	.059869	.063231	.066610	.073412	.080266
	.10	.050086	.053273	.056487	.059725	.062987	.066272	.069578	.072904	.076249	.079611	.082990	.089791	.096646
	0.00	.066466	.069653	.072866	.076105	.079367	.082652	.085958	.089284	.092629	.095991	.099369	.106171	.113025
	-.10	.082846	.086033	.089246	.092485	.095747	.099032	.102338	.105664	.109008	.112371	.115749	.122551	.129405
	-.20	.099225	.102412	.105626	.108864	.112127	.115412	.118718	.122043	.125388	.128750	.132129	.138931	.145785
	-.30	.115605	.118792	.122006	.125244	.128506	.131791	.135097	.138423	.141768	.145130	.148509	.155310	.162165
	-.40	.131985	.135172	.138385	.141624	.144886	.148171	.151477	.154803	.158148	.161510	.164888	.171690	.178544
25	.40	.000493	.003763	.007059	.010377	.013717	.017077	.020455	.023850	.027260	.030684	.034120	.041026	.047968
	.30	.016873	.020143	.023438	.026757	.030097	.033457	.036835	.040230	.043640	.047053	.050500	.057406	.064348
	.20	.033252	.036523	.039818	.043137	.046477	.049836	.053215	.056609	.060019	.063443	.066880	.073785	.080727
	.10	.049632	.052903	.056198	.059516	.062856	.066216	.069594	.072989	.076399	.079823	.083259	.090165	.097107
	0.00	.066012	.069282	.072578	.075896	.079236	.082596	.085974	.089369	.092779	.096203	.099639	.106545	.113487
	-.10	.082392	.085662	.088957	.092276	.095616	.098976	.102354	.105749	.109159	.112582	.116019	.122925	.129867
	-.20	.098771	.102042	.105337	.108656	.111996	.115355	.118733	.122128	.125538	.128962	.132399	.139304	.146246
	-.30	.115151	.118422	.121717	.125035	.128375	.131735	.135113	.138508	.141918	.145342	.148778	.155684	.162626
	-.40	.131531	.134801	.138097	.141415	.144755	.148115	.151493	.154888	.158298	.161722	.165158	.172064	.179006
30	.40	.000205	.003531	.006879	.010249	.013638	.017043	.020464	.023899	.027346	.030803	.034269	.041225	.048205
	.30	.016585	.019910	.023259	.026629	.030018	.033423	.036844	.040279	.043725	.047182	.050649	.057605	.064585
	.20	.032964	.036290	.039639	.043009	.046397	.049803	.053224	.056658	.060105	.063552	.067029	.073985	.080965
	.10	.049344	.052670	.056019	.059388	.062777	.066183	.069604	.073038	.076485	.079942	.083408	.090364	.097344
	0.00	.065724	.069050	.072398	.075768	.079157	.082562	.085983	.089418	.092865	.096322	.099788	.106744	.113724
	-.10	.082104	.085429	.088778	.092148	.095537	.098942	.102363	.105798	.109244	.112701	.116168	.123124	.130104
	-.20	.098483	.101809	.105158	.108528	.111916	.115322	.118743	.122177	.125624	.129081	.132548	.139504	.146484
	-.30	.114863	.118189	.121538	.124907	.128296	.131702	.135123	.138557	.142004	.145461	.148927	.155883	.162863
	-.40	.131243	.134569	.137917	.141287	.144676	.148081	.151502	.154937	.158384	.161841	.165307	.172263	.179243

5.0 YEAR HOLDING PERIOD
.100 EQUITY YIELD RATE
.750 LOAN RATIO

INTEREST RATE

TERM YEARS	APPR DEP	5.0	5.5	6.0	6.5	7.0	7.5	8.0	8.5	9.0	9.5	10.0	11.0	12.0
10	.40	.001138	.004105	.007098	.010118	.013165	.016238	.019336	.022460	.025608	.028780	.031977	.038439	.044991
	.30	.017518	.020484	.023478	.026498	.029545	.032618	.035716	.038839	.041988	.045160	.048356	.054819	.061377
	.20	.033898	.036864	.039858	.042878	.045925	.048997	.052096	.055219	.058367	.061540	.064736	.071198	.077751
	.10	.050278	.053244	.056237	.059258	.062304	.065377	.068475	.071599	.074747	.077920	.081116	.087578	.094131
	0.00	.066657	.069624	.072617	.075637	.078684	.081757	.084855	.087979	.091127	.094299	.097496	.103958	.110511
	-.10	.083037	.086003	.088997	.092017	.095064	.098137	.101235	.104358	.107507	.110679	.113875	.120338	.126883
	-.20	.099417	.102383	.105377	.108397	.111444	.114516	.117615	.120738	.123886	.127059	.130255	.136717	.143269
	-.30	.115797	.118763	.121756	.124777	.127823	.130896	.133994	.137118	.140266	.143439	.146635	.153097	.159643
	-.40	.132176	.135143	.138136	.141156	.144203	.147276	.150374	.153498	.156646	.159818	.163015	.169477	.176023
15	.40	-.000604	.002662	.005956	.009278	.012628	.016003	.019404	.022830	.026279	.029750	.033243	.040291	.047413
	.30	.015776	.019041	.022336	.025658	.029007	.032383	.035784	.039210	.042659	.046130	.049623	.056670	.063793
	.20	.032156	.035421	.038715	.042038	.045387	.048763	.052164	.055589	.059038	.062510	.066003	.073050	.080173
	.10	.048536	.051801	.055095	.058417	.061767	.065143	.068544	.071969	.075418	.078889	.082383	.089430	.096553
	0.00	.064915	.068181	.071475	.074797	.078147	.081522	.084923	.088349	.091798	.095269	.098762	.105810	.112932
	-.10	.081295	.084560	.087854	.091177	.094526	.097902	.101303	.104729	.108178	.111649	.115142	.122189	.129312
	-.20	.097675	.100940	.104234	.107557	.110906	.114282	.117683	.121108	.124557	.128029	.131522	.138569	.145692
	-.30	.114055	.117320	.120614	.123936	.127286	.130662	.134063	.137488	.140937	.144408	.147902	.154949	.162072
	-.40	.130434	.133700	.136994	.140316	.143666	.147041	.150442	.153868	.157317	.160788	.164281	.171329	.178451
20	.40	-.001448	.001966	.005409	.008879	.012374	.015894	.019436	.023000	.026583	.030186	.033805	.041093	.048437
	.30	.014931	.018346	.021789	.025259	.028754	.032274	.035816	.039379	.042963	.046565	.050185	.057473	.064817
	.20	.031311	.034726	.038169	.041639	.045134	.048653	.052196	.055759	.059343	.062945	.066565	.073853	.081196
	.10	.047691	.051106	.054548	.058018	.061514	.065033	.068575	.072139	.075722	.079325	.082945	.090232	.097576
	0.00	.064071	.067485	.070928	.074398	.077893	.081413	.084955	.088519	.092102	.095705	.099324	.106612	.113956
	-.10	.080450	.083865	.087308	.090778	.094273	.097793	.101335	.104898	.108482	.112084	.115704	.122992	.130336
	-.20	.096830	.100245	.103688	.107158	.110653	.114172	.117715	.121278	.124862	.128464	.132084	.139372	.146715
	-.30	.113210	.116625	.120067	.123537	.127033	.130552	.134094	.137658	.141241	.144844	.148464	.155751	.163095
	-.40	.129590	.133004	.136447	.139917	.143412	.146932	.150474	.154038	.157621	.161224	.164843	.172131	.179475
25	.40	-.001935	.001569	.005100	.008655	.012234	.015834	.019453	.023090	.026744	.030412	.034094	.041493	.048931
	.30	.014445	.017949	.021480	.025035	.028614	.032214	.035833	.039470	.043124	.046792	.050474	.057873	.065311
	.20	.030825	.034329	.037859	.041415	.044994	.048593	.052213	.055850	.059503	.063172	.066854	.074253	.081691
	.10	.047204	.050708	.054239	.057795	.061373	.064973	.068592	.072230	.075883	.079552	.083234	.090633	.098070
	0.00	.063584	.067088	.070619	.074174	.077753	.081353	.084972	.088609	.092263	.095931	.099613	.107012	.114450
	-.10	.079964	.083468	.086999	.090554	.094133	.097733	.101352	.104989	.108643	.112311	.115993	.123392	.130830
	-.20	.096344	.099848	.103378	.106934	.110512	.114112	.117732	.121369	.125022	.128691	.132373	.139772	.147210
	-.30	.112723	.116227	.119758	.123314	.126892	.130492	.134111	.137749	.141402	.145071	.148753	.156152	.163589
	-.40	.129103	.132607	.136138	.139693	.143272	.146872	.150491	.154128	.157782	.161450	.165132	.172531	.179969
30	.40	-.002243	.001320	.004908	.008518	.012149	.015798	.019463	.023143	.026836	.030540	.034254	.041707	.049185
	.30	.014136	.017700	.021288	.024898	.028529	.032178	.035843	.039523	.043216	.046920	.050634	.058087	.065565
	.20	.030516	.034080	.037667	.041278	.044908	.048557	.052223	.055903	.059595	.063299	.067014	.074466	.081945
	.10	.046896	.050459	.054047	.057658	.061288	.064937	.068602	.072282	.075975	.079679	.083393	.090846	.098325
	0.00	.063276	.066839	.070427	.074037	.077668	.081317	.084982	.088662	.092355	.096059	.099773	.107226	.114704
	-.10	.079655	.083219	.086807	.090417	.094048	.097697	.101362	.105042	.108735	.112439	.116153	.123606	.131084
	-.20	.096035	.099599	.103186	.106797	.110427	.114076	.117742	.121422	.125114	.128818	.132533	.139985	.147464
	-.30	.112415	.115978	.119566	.123177	.126807	.130456	.134121	.137801	.141494	.145198	.148912	.156365	.163844
	-.40	.128795	.132358	.135946	.139556	.143187	.146836	.150501	.154181	.157874	.161578	.165292	.172745	.180223

5.0 YEAR HOLDING PERIOD
.100 EQUITY YIELD RATE
.800 LOAN RATIO

INTEREST RATE

TERM YEARS	APPR DEP	5.0	5.5	6.0	6.5	7.0	7.5	8.0	8.5	9.0	9.5	10.0	11.0	12.0
10	.40	-.001084	.002080	.005273	.008494	.011744	.015022	.018327	.021658	.025016	.028400	.031810	.038703	.045691
	.30	.015295	.018459	.021652	.024874	.028124	.031401	.034706	.038038	.041396	.044780	.048189	.055082	.062071
	.20	.031675	.034839	.038032	.041254	.044504	.047781	.051086	.054418	.057776	.061160	.064569	.071462	.078451
	.10	.048055	.051219	.054412	.057633	.060883	.064161	.067466	.070798	.074156	.077540	.080949	.087842	.094830
	0.00	.064435	.067599	.070792	.074013	.077263	.080541	.083846	.087177	.090535	.093919	.097329	.104222	.111210
	-.10	.080814	.083978	.087171	.090393	.093643	.096920	.100225	.103557	.106915	.110299	.113708	.120601	.127590
	-.20	.097194	.100358	.103551	.106773	.110023	.113300	.116605	.119937	.123295	.126679	.130088	.136981	.143970
	-.30	.113574	.116738	.119931	.123152	.126402	.129680	.132985	.136317	.139675	.143059	.146468	.153361	.160349
	-.40	.129954	.133118	.136311	.139532	.142782	.146060	.149365	.152696	.156054	.159438	.162848	.169741	.176729
15	.40	-.002943	-.000540	.004054	.007598	.011171	.014772	.018399	.022053	.025732	.029435	.033161	.040678	.048275
	.30	.013437	.016920	.020434	.023978	.027550	.031151	.034779	.038433	.042112	.045815	.049541	.057058	.064655
	.20	.029817	.033300	.036814	.040357	.043930	.047531	.051159	.054813	.058492	.062194	.065920	.073437	.081035
	.10	.046197	.049679	.053193	.056737	.060310	.063911	.067539	.071192	.074871	.078574	.082300	.089817	.097415
	0.00	.062576	.066059	.069573	.073117	.076690	.080291	.083918	.087572	.091251	.094954	.098680	.106197	.113794
	-.10	.078956	.082439	.085953	.089497	.093069	.096670	.100298	.103952	.107631	.111334	.115060	.122587	.130174
	-.20	.095336	.098819	.102333	.105876	.109449	.113050	.116678	.120332	.124010	.127713	.131439	.138956	.146554
	-.30	.111716	.115198	.118712	.122256	.125829	.129430	.133058	.136711	.140390	.144093	.147819	.155336	.162934
	-.40	.128095	.131578	.135092	.138636	.142209	.145810	.149437	.153091	.156770	.160473	.164199	.171716	.179313
20	.40	-.003844	-.000201	.003471	.007172	.010901	.014655	.018433	.022234	.026057	.029893	.033760	.041534	.049367
	.30	.012536	.016178	.019851	.023552	.027280	.031034	.034813	.038614	.042436	.046273	.050140	.057914	.065747
	.20	.028916	.032558	.036231	.039932	.043660	.047414	.051193	.054994	.058816	.062659	.066520	.074293	.082127
	.10	.045296	.048938	.052610	.056312	.060040	.063794	.067572	.071373	.075196	.079033	.082900	.090673	.098506
	0.00	.061675	.065318	.068990	.072691	.076420	.080174	.083952	.087753	.091576	.095418	.099279	.107053	.114886
	-.10	.078055	.081697	.085370	.089071	.092799	.096553	.100332	.104133	.107955	.111798	.115659	.123433	.131266
	-.20	.094435	.098077	.101750	.105451	.109179	.112933	.116712	.120513	.124335	.128178	.132039	.139812	.147646
	-.30	.110815	.114457	.118129	.121831	.125559	.129313	.133091	.136892	.140715	.144557	.148419	.156192	.164025
	-.40	.127194	.130837	.134509	.138210	.141939	.145693	.149471	.153272	.157095	.160937	.164798	.172572	.180405
25	.40	-.004363	-.000625	.003141	.006934	.010751	.014591	.018451	.022331	.026228	.030141	.034069	.041961	.049855
	.30	.012017	.015755	.019521	.023313	.027131	.030970	.034831	.038711	.042608	.046521	.050448	.058341	.066274
	.20	.028397	.032135	.035901	.039693	.043511	.047350	.051211	.055091	.058988	.062901	.066828	.074720	.082654
	.10	.044777	.048514	.052280	.056073	.059890	.063730	.067591	.071470	.075367	.079281	.083208	.091100	.099034
	0.00	.061156	.064894	.068660	.072453	.076270	.080110	.083970	.087850	.091747	.095660	.099588	.107480	.115414
	-.10	.077536	.081274	.085040	.088832	.092650	.096489	.100350	.104230	.108127	.112040	.115967	.123860	.131793
	-.20	.093916	.097654	.101420	.105212	.109029	.112869	.116730	.120610	.124507	.128420	.132347	.140239	.148173
	-.30	.110296	.114033	.117799	.121592	.125409	.129249	.133091	.136990	.140886	.144793	.148727	.156619	.164553
	-.40	.126675	.130413	.134179	.137972	.141789	.145629	.149489	.153369	.157266	.161173	.165107	.172999	.180933
30	.40	-.004692	-.000891	.002936	.006787	.010660	.014552	.018462	.022387	.026326	.030277	.034239	.042189	.050166
	.30	.011688	.015489	.019316	.023167	.027040	.030932	.034842	.038767	.042706	.046657	.050619	.058568	.066545
	.20	.028068	.031869	.035696	.039547	.043420	.047312	.051222	.055147	.059086	.063037	.066998	.074948	.082925
	.10	.044448	.048249	.052076	.055927	.059799	.063692	.067601	.071526	.075465	.079417	.083378	.091328	.099305
	0.00	.060827	.064628	.068455	.072306	.076179	.080071	.083981	.087906	.091845	.095795	.099758	.107708	.115685
	-.10	.077207	.081008	.084835	.088686	.092559	.096451	.100361	.104286	.108225	.112175	.116138	.124087	.132064
	-.20	.093587	.097388	.101215	.105066	.108939	.112831	.116741	.120666	.124605	.128555	.132517	.140467	.148444
	-.30	.109967	.113768	.117595	.121446	.125318	.129211	.133120	.137045	.140984	.144936	.148897	.156847	.164824
	-.40	.126346	.130147	.133974	.137826	.141698	.145590	.149500	.153425	.157364	.161315	.165277	.173227	.181204

5.0 YEAR HOLDING PERIOD
.100 EQUITY YIELD RATE
.900 LOAN RATIO

INTEREST RATE

TERM YEARS	APPR DEP	5.0	5.5	6.0	6.5	7.0	7.5	8.0	8.5	9.0	9.5	10.0	11.0	12.0
10	.40	-.005530	-.001971	.001621	.005246	.008902	.012589	.016307	.020055	.023833	.027640	.031476	.039230	.047063
	.30	-.010850	-.014409	.018001	.021626	.025282	.028969	.032687	.036435	.040213	.044020	.047856	.055610	.063472
	.20	-.027229	.030789	.034381	.038005	.041661	.045349	.049067	.052815	.056593	.060400	.064235	.071990	.079852
	.10	-.043069	.047169	.050761	.054385	.058041	.061728	.065446	.069195	.072973	.076780	.080615	.088370	.096232
	0.00	.059989	.063548	.067140	.070765	.074421	.078108	.081826	.085574	.089352	.093159	.096995	.104749	.112612
	-.10	.076369	.079928	.083520	.087145	.090801	.094488	.098206	.101954	.105732	.109539	.113375	.121129	.128991
	-.20	.092748	.096308	.099900	.103524	.107180	.110868	.114586	.118334	.122112	.125919	.129755	.137509	.145371
	-.30	.109128	.112688	.116280	.119904	.123560	.127247	.130965	.134714	.138492	.142299	.146134	.153889	.161751
	-.40	.125508	.129067	.132659	.136284	.139940	.143627	.147345	.151093	.154871	.158678	.162514	.170268	.178131
15	.40	-.007621	-.003702	.000251	.004238	.008257	.012308	.016389	.020500	.024638	.028804	.032996	.041452	.050000
	.30	-.008759	.012677	.016630	.020617	.024637	.028688	.032769	.036879	.041018	.045184	.049375	.057832	.066380
	.20	.025139	.029057	.033010	.036997	.041016	.045067	.049149	.053259	.057398	.061564	.065755	.074212	.082759
	.10	.041519	.045437	.049390	.053377	.057396	.061447	.065528	.069639	.073778	.077943	.082135	.090592	.099139
	0.00	.057898	.061817	.065770	.069756	.073776	.077827	.081908	.086019	.090157	.094323	.098515	.106971	.115519
	-.10	.074278	.078196	.082149	.086136	.090156	.094207	.098288	.102398	.106537	.110703	.114894	.123351	.131899
	-.20	.090658	.094576	.098529	.102516	.106535	.110586	.114668	.118778	.122917	.127083	.131274	.139731	.148278
	-.30	.107038	.110956	.114909	.118896	.122915	.126966	.131047	.135158	.139297	.143462	.147654	.156111	.164658
	-.40	.123417	.127336	.131289	.135275	.139295	.143346	.147427	.151538	.155676	.159842	.164034	.172490	.181038
20	.40	-.008634	-.004537	-.000405	.003759	.007953	.012176	.016427	.020703	.025004	.029326	.033670	.042415	.051228
	.30	-.007746	.011843	.015975	.020138	.024333	.028556	.032807	.037083	.041383	.045706	.050050	.058795	.067608
	.20	.024125	.028223	.032355	.036518	.040713	.044936	.049187	.053463	.057763	.062086	.066430	.075175	.083987
	.10	.040505	.044603	.048734	.052898	.057092	.061316	.065566	.069843	.074143	.078466	.082810	.091555	.100367
	0.00	.056885	.060982	.065114	.069278	.073472	.077695	.081946	.086222	.090523	.094845	.099189	.107934	.116747
	-.10	.073265	.077362	.081494	.085657	.089852	.094075	.098326	.102602	.106902	.111225	.115569	.124314	.133127
	-.20	.089644	.093742	.097873	.102037	.106232	.110455	.114706	.118982	.123282	.127605	.131949	.140694	.149506
	-.30	.106024	.110122	.114253	.118417	.122611	.126835	.131085	.135362	.139662	.143985	.148329	.157074	.165886
	-.40	.122404	.126501	.130633	.134797	.138991	.143214	.147465	.151741	.156042	.160364	.164708	.173453	.182266
25	.40	-.009218	-.005013	-.000776	.003490	.007785	.012104	.016448	.020812	.025197	.029599	.034017	.042896	.051821
	.30	-.007162	.011367	.015603	.019870	.024164	.028441	.032827	.037192	.041576	.045979	.050397	.059276	.068201
	.20	.023541	.027747	.031983	.036250	.040544	.044864	.049207	.053572	.057956	.062358	.066777	.075655	.084581
	.10	.039921	.044126	.048363	.052630	.056924	.061244	.065587	.069952	.074336	.078738	.083156	.092035	.100961
	0.00	.056301	.060506	.064743	.069009	.073304	.077623	.081967	.086331	.090716	.095118	.099536	.108415	.117340
	-.10	.072681	.076886	.081123	.085389	.089683	.094003	.098346	.102711	.107095	.111497	.115916	.124795	.133720
	-.20	.089060	.093265	.097502	.101769	.106063	.110383	.114726	.119091	.123475	.127877	.132296	.141174	.150100
	-.30	.105440	.109645	.113882	.118149	.122443	.126763	.131106	.135471	.139855	.144257	.148675	.157554	.166480
	-.40	.121820	.126025	.130262	.134528	.138823	.143142	.147486	.151850	.156235	.160637	.165055	.173934	.182859
30	.40	-.009588	-.005312	-.001007	.003326	.007683	.012061	.016460	.020876	.025307	.029752	.034209	.043152	.052126
	.30	-.006792	.011068	.015373	.019706	.024062	.028441	.032839	.037255	.041687	.046132	.050588	.059532	.068506
	.20	.023171	.027447	.031753	.036085	.040442	.044821	.049219	.053635	.058066	.062511	.066968	.075912	.084886
	.10	.039551	.043827	.048133	.052465	.056822	.061201	.065599	.070015	.074446	.078891	.083348	.092291	.101266
	0.00	.055931	.060207	.064512	.068845	.073202	.077580	.081979	.086395	.090826	.095271	.099728	.108671	.117645
	-.10	.072311	.076587	.080892	.085225	.089581	.093960	.098358	.102774	.107206	.111651	.116107	.125051	.134025
	-.20	.088690	.092966	.097272	.101604	.105961	.110340	.114738	.119154	.123585	.128030	.132487	.141431	.150405
	-.30	.105070	.109346	.113652	.117984	.122341	.126720	.131118	.135534	.139965	.144410	.148867	.157810	.166785
	-.40	.121450	.125726	.130031	.134364	.138721	.143099	.147498	.151914	.156345	.160790	.165247	.174190	.183164

149

5.0 YEAR HOLDING PERIOD
.120 EQUITY YIELD RATE
.600 LOAN RATIO

INTEREST RATE

TERM YEARS	APPR DEP	5.0	5.5	6.0	6.5	7.0	7.5	8.0	8.5	9.0	9.5	10.0	11.0	12.0
10	.40	.020041	.022390	.024761	.027154	.029569	.032004	.034460	.036936	.039431	.041947	.044481	.049607	.054804
	.30	.035782	.038131	.040502	.042895	.045310	.047745	.050201	.052677	.055172	.057688	.060222	.065343	.070545
	.20	.051523	.053872	.056243	.058636	.061051	.063486	.065942	.068418	.070913	.073429	.075963	.081089	.086286
	.10	.067264	.069613	.071984	.074377	.076792	.079227	.081683	.084159	.086658	.089170	.091704	.096830	.102027
	0.00	.083004	.085354	.087725	.090118	.092533	.094968	.097424	.099900	.102395	.104911	.107445	.112571	.117768
	-.10	.098745	.101095	.103466	.105859	.108274	.110709	.113165	.115641	.118136	.120652	.123186	.128312	.133509
	-.20	.114486	.116836	.119207	.121600	.124015	.126450	.128906	.131382	.133877	.136393	.138927	.144053	.149250
	-.30	.130227	.132577	.134948	.137341	.139755	.142191	.144647	.147123	.149618	.152134	.154668	.159794	.164991
	-.40	.145968	.148318	.150689	.153082	.155496	.157932	.160388	.162864	.165359	.167875	.170409	.175535	.180732
15	.40	.017943	.020528	.023135	.025766	.028419	.031094	.033789	.036504	.039238	.041991	.044762	.050354	.055089
	.30	.033684	.036269	.038876	.041507	.044160	.046834	.049530	.052245	.054979	.057732	.060503	.066095	.071749
	.20	.049425	.052010	.054617	.057248	.059901	.062571	.065271	.067986	.070720	.073473	.076244	.081836	.087490
	.10	.065166	.067751	.070358	.072989	.075642	.078316	.081012	.083727	.086461	.089214	.091985	.097577	.103231
	0.00	.080907	.083491	.086099	.088730	.091383	.094057	.096753	.099468	.102202	.104955	.107726	.113318	.118972
	-.10	.096648	.099232	.101840	.104471	.107124	.109798	.112494	.115209	.117943	.120696	.123467	.129059	.134713
	-.20	.112389	.114973	.117581	.120212	.122865	.125539	.128235	.130950	.133684	.136437	.139208	.144800	.150454
	-.30	.128130	.130714	.133322	.135953	.138606	.141280	.143975	.146691	.149425	.152178	.154949	.160541	.166195
	-.40	.143871	.146455	.149063	.151694	.154347	.157021	.159716	.162432	.165166	.167919	.170690	.176282	.181936
20	.40	.016927	.019630	.022357	.025107	.027878	.030668	.033478	.036306	.039151	.042011	.044886	.050678	.056517
	.30	.032668	.035371	.038098	.040848	.043619	.046409	.049219	.052047	.054892	.057752	.060627	.066419	.072258
	.20	.048409	.051112	.053839	.056589	.059360	.062150	.064960	.067788	.070633	.073493	.076368	.082160	.087999
	.10	.064150	.066853	.069580	.072330	.075101	.077891	.080701	.083529	.086374	.089234	.092109	.097901	.103740
	0.00	.079891	.082594	.085321	.088071	.090842	.093632	.096442	.099270	.102115	.104975	.107850	.113642	.119481
	-.10	.095632	.098335	.101062	.103812	.106583	.109373	.112183	.115011	.117856	.120716	.123591	.129383	.135222
	-.20	.111373	.114076	.116803	.119553	.122324	.125114	.127924	.130752	.133596	.136457	.139332	.145124	.150963
	-.30	.127114	.129817	.132544	.135294	.138065	.140855	.143665	.146493	.149337	.152198	.155073	.160865	.166704
	-.40	.142855	.145558	.148285	.151035	.153805	.156596	.159406	.162234	.165078	.167939	.170814	.176606	.182445
25	.40	.016341	.019118	.021917	.024737	.027577	.030435	.033310	.036200	.039104	.042022	.044950	.050839	.056763
	.30	.032082	.034859	.037658	.040478	.043318	.046176	.049051	.051941	.054845	.057763	.060691	.066580	.072504
	.20	.047823	.050600	.053399	.056219	.059059	.061917	.064792	.067682	.070586	.073503	.076432	.082321	.088245
	.10	.063564	.066341	.069140	.071960	.074800	.077658	.080533	.083423	.086327	.089244	.092173	.098062	.103986
	0.00	.079305	.082082	.084881	.087701	.090541	.093399	.096274	.099164	.102068	.104985	.107914	.113803	.119727
	-.10	.095046	.097823	.100622	.103442	.106282	.109140	.112015	.114905	.117809	.120726	.123655	.129544	.135468
	-.20	.110787	.113564	.116363	.119183	.122023	.124881	.127756	.130646	.133550	.136467	.139396	.145285	.151209
	-.30	.126528	.129305	.132104	.134924	.137764	.140622	.143497	.146387	.149291	.152208	.155137	.161026	.166950
	-.40	.142269	.145046	.147845	.150665	.153505	.156363	.159238	.162128	.165032	.167949	.170878	.176767	.182691
30	.40	.015970	.018796	.021644	.024511	.027395	.030296	.033211	.036139	.039078	.042027	.044986	.050926	.056889
	.30	.031711	.034537	.037385	.040252	.043136	.046037	.048952	.051880	.054819	.057768	.060727	.066666	.072630
	.20	.047452	.050278	.053126	.055993	.058877	.061778	.064693	.067621	.070560	.073509	.076468	.082407	.088371
	.10	.063193	.066019	.068867	.071734	.074618	.077519	.080434	.083362	.086301	.089250	.092209	.098148	.104112
	0.00	.078934	.081760	.084608	.087475	.090359	.093260	.096175	.099103	.102042	.104991	.107950	.113889	.119853
	-.10	.094675	.097501	.100349	.103216	.106100	.109001	.111916	.114844	.117783	.120732	.123691	.129630	.135594
	-.20	.110416	.113242	.116090	.118957	.121841	.124742	.127657	.130585	.133524	.136473	.139432	.145371	.151335
	-.30	.126157	.128983	.131831	.134698	.137582	.140483	.143398	.146325	.149265	.152214	.155173	.161112	.167076
	-.40	.141898	.144724	.147572	.150439	.153323	.156224	.159139	.162066	.165006	.167955	.170914	.176853	.182817

5.0 YEAR HOLDING PERIOD
.120 EQUITY YIELD RATE
.667 LOAN RATIO

INTEREST RATE

TERM YEARS	APPR DEP	5.0	5.5	6.0	6.5	7.0	7.5	8.0	8.5	9.0	9.5	10.0	11.0	12.0
10	.40	.015930	.018540	.021175	.023834	.026517	.029222	.031951	.034702	.037475	.040270	.043086	.048781	.054557
	.30	.031671	.034281	.036916	.039575	.042258	.044963	.047692	.050443	.053216	.056011	.058827	.064522	.070297
	.20	.047412	.050022	.052657	.055316	.057999	.060704	.063433	.066184	.068957	.071752	.074568	.080263	.086038
	.10	.063153	.065763	.068398	.071057	.073740	.076445	.079174	.081925	.084698	.087493	.090309	.096004	.101779
	0.00	.078894	.081504	.084139	.086798	.089480	.092186	.094915	.097666	.100439	.103234	.106050	.111745	.117520
	-.10	.094635	.097245	.099880	.102539	.105221	.107927	.110656	.113407	.116180	.118975	.121791	.127486	.133261
	-.20	.110376	.112986	.115621	.118280	.120962	.123668	.126397	.129148	.131921	.134716	.137532	.143227	.149002
	-.30	.126117	.128727	.131362	.134021	.136703	.139409	.142138	.144889	.147662	.150457	.153273	.158968	.164743
	-.40	.141858	.144468	.147103	.149762	.152444	.155150	.157879	.160630	.163403	.166198	.169014	.174709	.180484
15	.40	.013600	.016471	.019368	.022292	.025239	.028211	.031205	.034222	.037261	.040320	.043398	.049611	.055894
	.30	.029341	.032212	.035109	.038032	.040980	.043952	.046946	.049963	.053002	.056060	.059139	.065352	.071635
	.20	.045082	.047953	.050850	.053773	.056721	.059693	.062687	.065704	.068743	.071801	.074880	.081093	.087376
	.10	.060823	.063694	.066591	.069514	.072462	.075434	.078428	.081445	.084484	.087542	.090620	.096834	.103117
	0.00	.076564	.079435	.082332	.085255	.088203	.091175	.094169	.097186	.100225	.103283	.106362	.112575	.118858
	-.10	.092305	.095176	.098073	.100996	.103944	.106916	.109910	.112927	.115966	.119024	.122103	.128316	.134599
	-.20	.108045	.110917	.113814	.116737	.119685	.122657	.125651	.128668	.131706	.134765	.137844	.144057	.150340
	-.30	.123786	.126658	.129555	.132478	.135426	.138398	.141392	.144409	.147447	.150506	.153585	.159798	.166081
	-.40	.139527	.142399	.145296	.148219	.151167	.154139	.157133	.160150	.163188	.166247	.169326	.175539	.181822
20	.40	.012470	.015474	.018504	.021559	.024638	.027739	.030861	.034003	.037163	.040342	.043536	.049971	.056460
	.30	.028211	.031215	.034245	.037300	.040379	.043479	.046602	.049744	.052904	.056083	.059277	.065712	.072200
	.20	.043952	.046956	.049986	.053041	.056120	.059220	.062343	.065484	.068645	.071824	.075018	.081453	.087941
	.10	.059693	.062697	.065727	.068782	.071861	.074961	.078083	.081225	.084386	.087565	.090759	.097194	.103682
	0.00	.075434	.078438	.081468	.084523	.087601	.090702	.093824	.096966	.100127	.103306	.106500	.112935	.119423
	-.10	.091175	.094179	.097209	.100264	.103342	.106443	.109565	.112707	.115868	.119046	.122241	.128676	.135164
	-.20	.106916	.109920	.112950	.116005	.119083	.122184	.125306	.128448	.131609	.134787	.137982	.144417	.150905
	-.30	.122657	.125661	.128691	.131746	.134824	.137925	.141047	.144189	.147350	.150528	.153723	.160158	.166646
	-.40	.138398	.141402	.144432	.147487	.150565	.153666	.156788	.159930	.163091	.166269	.169464	.175899	.182387
25	.40	.011819	.014904	.018015	.021148	.024304	.027479	.030674	.033885	.037112	.040353	.043608	.050151	.056733
	.30	.027560	.030645	.033756	.036889	.040045	.043220	.046415	.049626	.052853	.056094	.059349	.065892	.072473
	.20	.043301	.046386	.049497	.052630	.055786	.058961	.062156	.065367	.068594	.071835	.075090	.081633	.088214
	.10	.059042	.062127	.065238	.068371	.071527	.074702	.077896	.081108	.084335	.087576	.090830	.097374	.103955
	0.00	.074783	.077868	.080979	.084112	.087268	.090443	.093637	.096849	.100076	.103317	.106571	.113115	.119696
	-.10	.090524	.093609	.096720	.099853	.103009	.106184	.109378	.112590	.115817	.119058	.122312	.128856	.135437
	-.20	.106265	.109350	.112461	.115594	.118750	.121925	.125119	.128331	.131558	.134799	.138053	.144597	.151178
	-.30	.122006	.125091	.128202	.131335	.134491	.137666	.140860	.144072	.147299	.150540	.153794	.160338	.166919
	-.40	.137747	.140832	.143943	.147076	.150232	.153407	.156601	.159813	.163040	.166281	.169535	.176079	.182660
30	.40	.011407	.014547	.017711	.020897	.024102	.027325	.030563	.033817	.037082	.040360	.043647	.050247	.056873
	.30	.027148	.030288	.033452	.036638	.039843	.043066	.046304	.049558	.052823	.056101	.059388	.065988	.072614
	.20	.042889	.046029	.049193	.052379	.055584	.058807	.062045	.065299	.068564	.071842	.075129	.081728	.088355
	.10	.058630	.061770	.064934	.068120	.071325	.074548	.077786	.081039	.084305	.087583	.090870	.097469	.104096
	0.00	.074371	.077511	.080675	.083861	.087066	.090289	.093527	.096780	.100046	.103324	.106611	.113210	.119837
	-.10	.090112	.093252	.096416	.099602	.102807	.106030	.109268	.112521	.115787	.119065	.122352	.128951	.135578
	-.20	.105853	.108993	.112157	.115343	.118548	.121771	.125009	.128262	.131528	.134805	.138093	.144692	.151319
	-.30	.121594	.124734	.127898	.131084	.134289	.137511	.140750	.144003	.147269	.150546	.153834	.160433	.167060
	-.40	.137634	.140475	.143639	.146825	.150030	.153252	.156491	.159744	.163010	.166287	.169575	.176174	.182801

151

5.0 YEAR HOLDING PERIOD
.120 EQUITY YIELD RATE
.700 LOAN RATIO

INTEREST RATE

TERM YEARS	APPR DEP	5.0	5.5	6.0	6.5	7.0	7.5	8.0	8.5	9.0	9.5	10.0	11.0	12.0
10	.40	.013875	.016616	.019382	.022174	.024991	.027832	.030697	.033585	.036497	.039432	.042389	.048369	.054433
	.30	.029616	.032357	.035123	.037915	.040732	.043573	.046438	.049326	.052238	.055173	.058130	.064110	.070174
	.20	.045357	.048098	.050864	.053656	.056473	.059314	.062179	.065067	.067979	.070914	.073871	.079851	.085914
	.10	.061098	.063839	.066605	.069397	.072214	.075055	.077920	.080808	.083720	.086656	.089612	.095592	.101655
	0.00	.076839	.079580	.082346	.085138	.087955	.090796	.093661	.096549	.099461	.102396	.105353	.111333	.117396
	-.10	.092580	.095321	.098087	.100879	.103696	.106537	.109402	.112290	.115202	.118137	.121094	.127073	.133137
	-.20	.108321	.111062	.113828	.116620	.119437	.122278	.125143	.128031	.130943	.133878	.136835	.142814	.148878
	-.30	.124061	.126803	.129569	.132361	.135178	.138019	.140884	.143772	.146684	.149619	.152576	.158555	.164619
	-.40	.139802	.142544	.145310	.148102	.150919	.153760	.156625	.159513	.162425	.165360	.168317	.174296	.180360
15	.40	.011428	.014443	.017485	.020554	.023650	.026770	.029914	.033082	.036272	.039484	.042716	.049240	.055837
	.30	.027169	.030184	.033226	.036295	.039391	.042511	.045655	.048823	.052013	.055225	.058457	.064981	.071578
	.20	.042910	.045925	.048967	.052036	.055132	.058252	.061396	.064564	.067754	.070966	.074198	.080722	.087319
	.10	.058651	.061666	.064708	.067777	.070872	.073993	.077137	.080305	.083495	.086707	.089939	.096453	.103060
	0.00	.074392	.077407	.080449	.083518	.086613	.089734	.092878	.096046	.099236	.102448	.105680	.112204	.118801
	-.10	.090133	.093148	.096190	.099259	.102354	.105475	.108619	.111787	.114977	.118189	.121421	.127945	.134542
	-.20	.105874	.108889	.111931	.115000	.118095	.121216	.124360	.127528	.130718	.133930	.137162	.143686	.150283
	-.30	.121615	.124630	.127672	.130741	.133836	.136957	.140101	.143269	.146459	.149671	.152903	.159427	.166024
	-.40	.137356	.140371	.143413	.146482	.149577	.152698	.155842	.159010	.162200	.165412	.168644	.175168	.181765
20	.40	.010242	.013396	.016578	.019785	.023018	.026274	.029552	.032851	.036170	.039507	.042862	.049618	.056431
	.30	.025983	.029137	.032319	.035526	.038759	.042015	.045293	.048592	.051911	.055248	.058603	.065359	.072172
	.20	.041724	.044878	.048060	.051267	.054500	.057756	.061034	.064333	.067652	.070989	.074344	.081100	.087913
	.10	.057465	.060619	.063801	.067008	.070241	.073497	.076775	.080074	.083393	.086730	.090084	.096841	.103654
	0.00	.073206	.076360	.079542	.082749	.085982	.089238	.092516	.095815	.099134	.102471	.105825	.112582	.119395
	-.10	.088947	.092101	.095283	.098490	.101723	.104979	.108257	.111556	.114875	.118212	.121566	.128323	.135136
	-.20	.104688	.107842	.111024	.114231	.117464	.120720	.123998	.127297	.130616	.133953	.137307	.144064	.150877
	-.30	.120429	.123583	.126765	.129972	.133205	.136461	.139739	.143038	.146357	.149694	.153048	.159805	.166617
	-.40	.136170	.139324	.142505	.145713	.148946	.152202	.155480	.158779	.162098	.165435	.168789	.175546	.182358
25	.40	.009559	.012798	.016064	.019354	.022667	.026002	.029356	.032727	.036116	.039519	.042936	.049807	.056717
	.30	.025300	.028539	.031805	.035095	.038408	.041743	.045097	.048468	.051857	.055260	.058677	.065548	.072458
	.20	.041040	.044280	.047546	.050836	.054149	.057484	.060838	.064209	.067598	.071001	.074418	.081288	.088199
	.10	.056781	.060021	.063287	.066577	.069890	.073225	.076578	.079950	.083339	.086742	.090159	.097029	.103940
	0.00	.072522	.075762	.079028	.082318	.085631	.088966	.092320	.095691	.099080	.102483	.105900	.112770	.119681
	-.10	.088263	.091503	.094769	.098059	.101372	.104707	.108060	.111432	.114821	.118224	.121641	.128511	.135422
	-.20	.104004	.107244	.110510	.113800	.117113	.120448	.123801	.127173	.130562	.133965	.137382	.144252	.151163
	-.30	.119745	.122985	.126251	.129541	.132854	.136189	.139542	.142914	.146303	.149706	.153123	.159993	.166904
	-.40	.135486	.138726	.141992	.145282	.148595	.151930	.155283	.158655	.162044	.165447	.168864	.175734	.182645
30	.40	.009125	.012423	.015745	.019090	.022455	.025839	.029240	.032656	.036085	.039526	.042977	.049907	.056865
	.30	.024866	.028164	.031486	.034831	.038196	.041580	.044981	.048397	.051826	.055267	.058718	.065648	.072606
	.20	.040607	.043905	.047227	.050572	.053937	.057321	.060722	.064138	.067567	.071108	.074459	.081389	.088347
	.10	.056348	.059646	.062968	.066313	.069678	.073062	.076463	.079879	.083308	.086749	.090200	.097130	.104088
	0.00	.072089	.075387	.078709	.082054	.085419	.088803	.092204	.095620	.099049	.102490	.105941	.112871	.119829
	-.10	.087830	.091128	.094450	.097795	.101160	.104544	.107945	.111361	.114790	.118231	.121682	.128612	.135570
	-.20	.103571	.106869	.110191	.113536	.116901	.120285	.123686	.127102	.130531	.133972	.137423	.144353	.151311
	-.30	.119312	.122610	.125932	.129277	.132642	.136026	.139427	.142843	.146272	.149713	.153164	.160094	.167052
	-.40	.135053	.138351	.141673	.145018	.148383	.151767	.155168	.158583	.162013	.165454	.168905	.175835	.182793

152

5.0 YEAR HOLDING PERIOD
.120 EQUITY YIELD RATE
.750 LOAN RATIO

INTEREST RATE

TERM YEARS	APPR DEP	5.0	5.5	6.0	6.5	7.0	7.5	8.0	8.5	9.0	9.5	10.0	11.0	12.0
10	.40	.010792	.013729	.016093	.019684	.022702	.025746	.028815	.031910	.035030	.038175	.041343	.047750	.054247
	.30	.026533	.029470	.032434	.035425	.038443	.041487	.044556	.047651	.050771	.053916	.057084	.063490	.069988
	.20	.042274	.045211	.048175	.051166	.054184	.057228	.060297	.063392	.066512	.069657	.072825	.079231	.085729
	.10	.058015	.060952	.063916	.066907	.069925	.072969	.076038	.079133	.082253	.085397	.088566	.094972	.101469
	0.00	.073756	.076692	.079657	.082648	.085666	.088710	.091779	.094874	.097994	.101138	.104307	.110713	.117210
	-.10	.089497	.092433	.095398	.098389	.101407	.104451	.107520	.110615	.113735	.116879	.120048	.126454	.132951
	-.20	.105238	.108174	.111139	.114130	.117148	.120192	.123261	.126356	.129476	.132620	.135789	.142195	.148692
	-.30	.120979	.123915	.126880	.129871	.132889	.135933	.139002	.142097	.145217	.148361	.151530	.157936	.164433
	-.40	.136720	.139656	.142621	.145612	.148630	.151674	.154743	.157838	.160958	.164102	.167271	.173677	.180174
15	.40	.008170	.011400	.014660	.017949	.021265	.024608	.027977	.031371	.034789	.038230	.041693	.048683	.055752
	.30	.023911	.027141	.030401	.033690	.037006	.040349	.043718	.047112	.050530	.053971	.057434	.064424	.071493
	.20	.039652	.042882	.046142	.049431	.052747	.056090	.059459	.062853	.066271	.069712	.073175	.080165	.087234
	.10	.055393	.058623	.061883	.065172	.068488	.071831	.075200	.078594	.082012	.085453	.088916	.095906	.102975
	0.00	.071134	.074364	.077624	.080913	.084229	.087572	.090941	.094335	.097753	.101194	.104657	.111647	.118716
	-.10	.086875	.090105	.093365	.096653	.099970	.103313	.106682	.110076	.113494	.116935	.120398	.127388	.134456
	-.20	.102616	.105846	.109106	.112394	.115711	.119054	.122423	.125817	.129235	.132676	.136139	.143129	.150197
	-.30	.118357	.121587	.124847	.128135	.131452	.134795	.138164	.141558	.144976	.148417	.151880	.158870	.165938
	-.40	.134098	.137328	.140588	.143876	.147193	.150536	.153905	.157299	.160717	.164158	.167621	.174611	.181679
20	.40	.006899	.010279	.013588	.017125	.020588	.024076	.027589	.031123	.034679	.038255	.041849	.049088	.056387
	.30	.022640	.026020	.029429	.032866	.036329	.039817	.043330	.046864	.050420	.053996	.057590	.064829	.072128
	.20	.038381	.041761	.045170	.048607	.052070	.055558	.059071	.062605	.066161	.069737	.073331	.080570	.087869
	.10	.054122	.057502	.060911	.064348	.067811	.071299	.074812	.078346	.081902	.085478	.089072	.096311	.103610
	0.00	.069863	.073243	.076652	.080088	.083552	.087040	.090553	.094087	.097643	.101219	.104813	.112052	.119351
	-.10	.085604	.088984	.092393	.095829	.099293	.102781	.106294	.109828	.113384	.116960	.120554	.127793	.135092
	-.20	.101345	.104725	.108134	.111570	.115034	.118522	.122035	.125569	.129125	.132701	.136295	.143534	.150833
	-.30	.117086	.120466	.123875	.127311	.130775	.134263	.137776	.141310	.144866	.148442	.152036	.159275	.166574
	-.40	.132827	.136207	.139616	.143052	.146516	.150004	.153517	.157051	.160607	.164183	.167777	.175016	.182315
25	.40	.006167	.009638	.013137	.016663	.020213	.023785	.027378	.030991	.034621	.038268	.041929	.049290	.056695
	.30	.021908	.025379	.028878	.032404	.035953	.039526	.043119	.046732	.050362	.054009	.057670	.065031	.072436
	.20	.037649	.041120	.044019	.048145	.051694	.055267	.058860	.062473	.066103	.069750	.073411	.080772	.088177
	.10	.053390	.056861	.060360	.063886	.067435	.071008	.074601	.078214	.081844	.085491	.089152	.096513	.103917
	0.00	.069131	.072602	.076101	.079627	.083176	.086749	.090342	.093955	.097585	.101232	.104893	.112254	.119658
	-.10	.084872	.088343	.091842	.095368	.098917	.102490	.106083	.109696	.113326	.116973	.120634	.127995	.135399
	-.20	.100613	.104084	.107583	.111109	.114658	.118231	.121824	.125437	.129067	.132714	.136375	.143736	.151140
	-.30	.116354	.119825	.123324	.126850	.130399	.133972	.137565	.141178	.144808	.148455	.152116	.159477	.166881
	-.40	.132095	.135566	.139065	.142590	.146140	.149713	.153306	.156919	.160549	.164196	.167857	.175218	.182622
30	.40	.005703	.009236	.012796	.016380	.019985	.023611	.027255	.030914	.034588	.038275	.041973	.049398	.056853
	.30	.021444	.024977	.028537	.032121	.035726	.039352	.042996	.046655	.050329	.054016	.057714	.065139	.072553
	.20	.037185	.040718	.044278	.047861	.051467	.055093	.058737	.062396	.066070	.069757	.073455	.080880	.088334
	.10	.052926	.056459	.060019	.063602	.067208	.070834	.074477	.078137	.081811	.085498	.089196	.096621	.104075
	0.00	.068667	.072200	.075760	.079343	.082949	.086575	.090218	.093878	.097552	.101239	.104937	.112362	.119816
	-.10	.084408	.087941	.091501	.095084	.098690	.102316	.105959	.109619	.113293	.116980	.120678	.128103	.135557
	-.20	.100149	.103682	.107242	.110825	.114431	.118057	.121700	.125360	.129034	.132721	.136419	.143844	.151258
	-.30	.115890	.119423	.122983	.126566	.130172	.133798	.137441	.141101	.144775	.148462	.152160	.159585	.167039
	-.40	.131631	.135164	.138724	.142307	.145913	.149539	.153182	.156842	.160516	.164203	.167901	.175326	.182780

5.0 YEAR HOLDING PERIOD
.120 EQUITY YIELD RATE
.800 LOAN RATIO

INTEREST RATE

TERM YEARS	APPR DEP	5.0	5.5	6.0	6.5	7.0	7.5	8.0	8.5	9.0	9.5	10.0	11.0	12.0
10	.40	.007709	.010841	.014003	.017194	.020413	.023660	.026934	.030235	.033563	.036917	.040297	.047130	.054061
	.30	.023450	.026582	.029744	.032935	.036154	.039401	.042675	.045976	.049304	.052658	.056038	.062871	.069802
	.20	.039191	.042323	.045485	.048676	.051895	.055142	.058416	.061717	.065045	.068359	.071779	.078612	.085542
	.10	.054932	.058064	.061226	.064417	.067636	.070883	.074157	.077458	.080786	.084140	.087520	.094353	.101284
	0.00	.070673	.073805	.076967	.080158	.083377	.086624	.089898	.093199	.096527	.099881	.103261	.110094	.117024
	-.10	.086414	.089546	.092708	.095899	.099118	.102365	.105639	.108940	.112268	.115622	.119002	.125835	.132765
	-.20	.102155	.105287	.108449	.111640	.114859	.118106	.121380	.124681	.128009	.131363	.134742	.141576	.148506
	-.30	.117896	.121028	.124190	.127381	.130600	.133847	.137121	.140422	.143750	.147104	.150483	.157317	.164247
	-.40	.133637	.136769	.139931	.143122	.146341	.149588	.152862	.156163	.159491	.162845	.166224	.173058	.179988
15	.40	.004913	.008358	.011835	.015343	.018880	.022446	.026040	.029660	.033306	.036976	.040671	.048127	.055666
	.30	.020654	.024099	.027576	.031084	.034621	.038187	.041781	.045401	.049047	.052717	.056412	.063868	.071407
	.20	.036395	.039840	.043317	.046825	.050362	.053928	.057521	.061142	.064788	.068458	.072153	.079609	.087148
	.10	.052136	.055581	.059058	.062566	.066103	.069669	.073262	.076883	.080529	.084199	.087894	.095350	.102889
	0.00	.067876	.071322	.074799	.078307	.081844	.085410	.089003	.092624	.096270	.099940	.103635	.111091	.118630
	-.10	.083617	.087063	.090540	.094048	.097585	.101151	.104744	.108365	.112011	.115681	.119375	.126831	.134371
	-.20	.099358	.102804	.106281	.109789	.113326	.116892	.120485	.124106	.127752	.131422	.135116	.142572	.150112
	-.30	.115099	.118545	.122022	.125530	.129067	.132633	.136226	.139847	.143492	.147163	.150857	.158313	.165853
	-.40	.130840	.134286	.137763	.141271	.144808	.148374	.151967	.155588	.159233	.162904	.166598	.174054	.181594
20	.40	.003557	.007162	.010798	.014464	.018158	.021879	.025626	.029396	.033189	.037003	.040837	.048558	.056344
	.30	.019298	.022903	.026539	.030205	.033899	.037620	.041367	.045137	.048930	.052744	.056578	.064299	.072085
	.20	.035039	.038644	.042280	.045946	.049640	.053361	.057108	.060878	.064671	.068435	.072319	.080040	.087826
	.10	.050780	.054385	.058021	.061687	.065381	.069102	.072849	.076619	.080412	.084226	.088060	.095781	.103567
	0.00	.066521	.070126	.073762	.077428	.081122	.084843	.088590	.092360	.096153	.099957	.103801	.111522	.119308
	-.10	.082262	.085867	.089503	.093169	.096863	.100584	.104330	.108101	.111894	.115708	.119541	.127263	.135049
	-.20	.098003	.101608	.105244	.108910	.112604	.116325	.120071	.123842	.127635	.131449	.135282	.143004	.150790
	-.30	.113744	.117349	.120985	.124651	.128345	.132066	.135812	.139583	.143376	.147190	.151024	.158745	.166531
	-.40	.129485	.133090	.136726	.140392	.144086	.147807	.151553	.155324	.159117	.162931	.166764	.174702	.182272
25	.40	.002776	.006478	.010211	.013971	.017758	.021568	.025401	.029255	.033127	.037017	.040922	.048774	.056672
	.30	.018517	.022219	.025952	.029712	.033499	.037309	.041142	.044996	.048868	.052758	.056663	.064515	.072413
	.20	.034258	.037960	.041693	.045453	.049240	.053050	.056883	.060737	.064609	.068499	.072404	.080256	.088154
	.10	.049999	.053701	.057434	.061194	.064981	.068791	.072624	.076478	.080350	.084240	.088146	.095997	.103895
	0.00	.065740	.069442	.073175	.076935	.080722	.084532	.088365	.092219	.096091	.099981	.103887	.111738	.119636
	-.10	.081481	.085183	.088916	.092676	.096462	.100273	.104106	.107960	.111832	.115722	.119627	.127479	.135377
	-.20	.097222	.100924	.104657	.108417	.112203	.116014	.119847	.123701	.127573	.131463	.135368	.143220	.151118
	-.30	.112963	.116665	.120398	.124158	.127944	.131755	.135588	.139442	.143314	.147203	.151156	.158961	.166859
	-.40	.128704	.132406	.136139	.139899	.143685	.147496	.151329	.155183	.159055	.162944	.166850	.174702	.182600
30	.40	.002281	.006050	.009846	.013669	.017515	.021383	.025269	.029173	.033092	.037024	.040969	.048889	.056840
	.30	.018022	.021791	.025587	.029410	.033256	.037124	.041010	.044914	.048833	.052765	.056710	.064630	.072581
	.20	.033763	.037532	.041328	.045151	.048997	.052865	.056751	.060655	.064574	.068506	.072451	.080371	.088322
	.10	.049504	.053273	.057069	.060892	.064738	.068605	.072492	.076396	.080315	.084247	.088192	.096112	.104063
	0.00	.065245	.069014	.072810	.076633	.080479	.084347	.088233	.092137	.096056	.099988	.103933	.111853	.119804
	-.10	.080986	.084755	.088551	.092374	.096220	.100087	.103974	.107878	.111797	.115729	.119674	.127594	.135545
	-.20	.096727	.100495	.104292	.108115	.111961	.115828	.119715	.123619	.127538	.131470	.135415	.143334	.151286
	-.30	.112468	.116236	.120033	.123856	.127702	.131569	.135456	.139360	.143279	.147211	.151156	.159075	.167027
	-.40	.128209	.131977	.135774	.139597	.143443	.147310	.151197	.155101	.159020	.162952	.166897	.174816	.182768

5.0 YEAR HOLDING PERIOD
.120 EQUITY YIELD RATE
.900 LOAN RATIO

INTEREST RATE

TERM YEARS	APPR DEP	5.0	5.5	6.0	6.5	7.0	7.5	8.0	8.5	9.0	9.5	10.0	11.0	12.0
10	.40	.001543	.005067	.008624	.012214	.015835	.019488	.023171	.026885	.030629	.034402	.038204	.045892	.053689
	.30	.017284	.020808	.024365	.027955	.031576	.035229	.038912	.042626	.046370	.050143	.053945	.061633	.069430
	.20	.033025	.036549	.040106	.043696	.047317	.050970	.054653	.058367	.062111	.065884	.069686	.077374	.085171
	.10	.048766	.052290	.055847	.059437	.063058	.066711	.070394	.074108	.077852	.081625	.085427	.093115	.100912
	0.00	.064507	.068031	.071588	.075178	.078799	.082452	.086135	.089849	.093593	.097366	.101168	.108856	.116653
	-.10	.080248	.083772	.087329	.090918	.094540	.098193	.101876	.105590	.109334	.113107	.116909	.124597	.132394
	-.20	.095989	.099513	.103070	.106659	.110281	.113934	.117617	.121331	.125075	.128848	.132650	.140338	.148135
	-.30	.111730	.115254	.118811	.122400	.126022	.129674	.133358	.137072	.140816	.144589	.148391	.156079	.163875
	-.40	.127471	.130995	.134552	.138141	.141763	.145415	.149099	.152813	.156557	.160330	.164132	.171820	.179616
15	.40	-.001603	.002273	.006185	.010131	.014111	.018122	.022165	.026238	.030339	.034469	.038625	.047013	.055495
	.30	.014138	.018014	.021926	.025872	.029852	.033863	.037906	.041979	.046080	.050210	.054366	.062754	.071236
	.20	.029879	.033755	.037667	.041613	.045593	.049604	.053647	.057720	.061821	.065951	.070107	.078495	.086977
	.10	.045620	.049496	.053408	.057354	.061333	.065345	.069388	.073461	.077562	.081692	.085848	.094236	.102718
	0.00	.061361	.065237	.069149	.073095	.077074	.081086	.085129	.089202	.093303	.097433	.101589	.109977	.118459
	-.10	.077102	.080978	.084890	.088836	.092815	.096827	.100870	.104943	.109044	.113174	.117330	.125718	.134200
	-.20	.092843	.096719	.100631	.104577	.108556	.112568	.116611	.120684	.124785	.128915	.133071	.141459	.149941
	-.30	.108584	.112460	.116372	.120318	.124297	.128309	.132352	.136425	.140526	.144656	.148812	.157200	.165682
	-.40	.124325	.128201	.132113	.136059	.140038	.144050	.148093	.152166	.156267	.160397	.164553	.172941	.181423
20	.40	-.003128	.000927	.005018	.009142	.013298	.017485	.021699	.025941	.030208	.034499	.038812	.047499	.056258
	.30	.012613	.016668	.020759	.024883	.029039	.033226	.037440	.041682	.045949	.050240	.054553	.063240	.071999
	.20	.028354	.032409	.036500	.040624	.044780	.048966	.053181	.057423	.061690	.065981	.070294	.078981	.087740
	.10	.044095	.048150	.052241	.056365	.060521	.064707	.068922	.073164	.077431	.081722	.086035	.094722	.103481
	0.00	.059836	.063891	.067982	.072106	.076262	.080448	.084663	.088905	.093172	.097463	.101776	.110463	.119222
	-.10	.075577	.079632	.083723	.087847	.092003	.096189	.100404	.104646	.108913	.113204	.117517	.126204	.134963
	-.20	.091318	.095373	.099464	.103588	.107744	.111930	.116145	.120387	.124654	.128945	.133258	.141945	.150704
	-.30	.107059	.111114	.115205	.119329	.123485	.127671	.131886	.136128	.140395	.144685	.148999	.157685	.166445
	-.40	.122800	.126855	.130946	.135070	.139226	.143412	.147627	.151869	.156136	.160426	.164739	.173426	.182185
25	.40	-.004006	.000159	.004358	.008588	.012848	.017135	.021447	.025782	.030138	.034514	.038908	.047741	.056626
	.30	.011735	.015900	.020099	.024329	.028589	.032876	.037188	.041523	.045879	.050255	.054649	.063482	.072367
	.20	.027475	.031641	.035840	.040070	.044330	.048617	.052929	.057264	.061620	.065996	.070390	.079223	.088108
	.10	.043210	.047382	.051580	.055811	.060071	.064358	.068670	.073005	.077361	.081737	.086131	.094964	.103849
	0.00	.058957	.063123	.067321	.071552	.075812	.080099	.084411	.088746	.093102	.097478	.101872	.110705	.119590
	-.10	.074698	.078864	.083063	.087293	.091553	.095840	.100152	.104487	.108843	.113219	.117613	.126446	.135331
	-.20	.090439	.094605	.098803	.103034	.107294	.111581	.115893	.120228	.124584	.128960	.133354	.142187	.151072
	-.30	.106180	.110345	.114544	.118775	.123035	.127322	.131634	.135969	.140325	.144701	.149094	.157928	.166813
	-.40	.121921	.126086	.130285	.134516	.138776	.143063	.147375	.151710	.156066	.160442	.164835	.173669	.182554
30	.40	-.004563	-.000324	.003948	.008248	.012575	.016926	.021298	.025690	.030099	.034523	.038961	.047870	.056816
	.30	.011178	.015417	.019689	.023989	.028316	.032667	.037039	.041431	.045840	.050264	.054702	.063611	.072557
	.20	.026919	.031158	.035430	.039730	.044057	.048408	.052780	.057172	.061581	.066005	.070443	.079352	.088298
	.10	.042660	.046899	.051171	.055471	.059798	.064149	.068521	.072913	.077322	.081746	.086184	.095093	.104039
	0.00	.058401	.062640	.066912	.071212	.075539	.079890	.084262	.088654	.093063	.097487	.101925	.110834	.119780
	-.10	.074142	.078381	.082653	.086953	.091280	.095631	.100003	.104395	.108804	.113228	.117666	.126575	.135521
	-.20	.089883	.094122	.098394	.102694	.107021	.111372	.115744	.120136	.124545	.128969	.133407	.142316	.151262
	-.30	.105624	.109863	.114135	.118435	.122762	.127113	.131485	.135877	.140286	.144710	.149148	.158057	.167003
	-.40	.121364	.125604	.129876	.134176	.138503	.142854	.147226	.151618	.156027	.160451	.164889	.173798	.182744

5.0 YEAR HOLDING PERIOD
.140 EQUITY YIELD RATE
.600 LOAN RATIO

INTEREST RATE

TERM YEARS	APPR DEP	5.0	5.5	6.0	6.5	7.0	7.5	8.0	8.5	9.0	9.5	10.0	11.0	12.0
10	.40	.032101	.034428	.036677	.039148	.041540	.043953	.046386	.048840	.051315	.053808	.056321	.061404	.066560
	.30	.047229	.049556	.051905	.054276	.056668	.059081	.061515	.063969	.066443	.068937	.071450	.076533	.081688
	.20	.062358	.064685	.067034	.069404	.071796	.074209	.076643	.079097	.081571	.084065	.086578	.091661	.096817
	.10	.077486	.079813	.082162	.084533	.086925	.089338	.091771	.094225	.096700	.099193	.101707	.106789	.111945
	0.00	.092614	.094941	.097290	.099661	.102053	.104466	.106900	.109354	.111828	.114322	.116835	.121918	.127073
	-.10	.107743	.110070	.112419	.114789	.117181	.119594	.122028	.124482	.126956	.129450	.131963	.137046	.142202
	-.20	.122871	.125198	.127547	.129918	.132310	.134723	.137156	.139611	.142085	.144578	.147092	.152174	.157330
	-.30	.137999	.140326	.142675	.145046	.147438	.149851	.152285	.154739	.157213	.159707	.162220	.167303	.172458
	-.40	.153128	.155455	.157804	.160174	.162566	.164979	.167413	.169867	.172341	.174835	.177348	.182431	.187587
15	.40	.029329	.031886	.034468	.037072	.039700	.042349	.045020	.047711	.050421	.053151	.055899	.061447	.067060
	.30	.044458	.047015	.049596	.052201	.054828	.057477	.060148	.062839	.065550	.068280	.071028	.076576	.082188
	.20	.059586	.062143	.064724	.067329	.069956	.072606	.075276	.077967	.080678	.083408	.086156	.091704	.097317
	.10	.074714	.077271	.079853	.082457	.085085	.087734	.090405	.093096	.095806	.098536	.101284	.106832	.112445
	0.00	.089843	.092400	.094981	.097586	.100213	.102863	.105533	.108224	.110935	.113665	.116413	.121961	.127573
	-.10	.104971	.107528	.110119	.112714	.115342	.117991	.120661	.123352	.126063	.128793	.131541	.137089	.142702
	-.20	.120099	.122657	.125238	.127843	.130470	.133119	.135790	.138481	.141192	.143921	.146669	.152217	.157830
	-.30	.135228	.137785	.140366	.142971	.145598	.148248	.150918	.153609	.156320	.159050	.161798	.167346	.172958
	-.40	.150356	.152913	.155495	.158099	.160727	.163376	.166046	.168737	.171448	.174178	.176926	.182474	.188087
20	.40	.027985	.030662	.033363	.036087	.038833	.041600	.044387	.047193	.050016	.052856	.055712	.061466	.067271
	.30	.043114	.045790	.048491	.051215	.053962	.056729	.059516	.062321	.065145	.067985	.070840	.076594	.082399
	.20	.058242	.060919	.063620	.066344	.069090	.071857	.074644	.077450	.080273	.083113	.085969	.091723	.097528
	.10	.073370	.076047	.078748	.081472	.084218	.086985	.089772	.092578	.095401	.098241	.101097	.106851	.112656
	0.00	.088499	.091175	.093876	.096600	.099347	.102114	.104901	.107706	.110530	.113370	.116225	.121979	.127785
	-.10	.103627	.106304	.109005	.111729	.114475	.117242	.120029	.122835	.125658	.128498	.131354	.137108	.142913
	-.20	.118755	.121432	.124133	.126857	.129603	.132370	.135157	.137963	.140786	.143626	.146482	.152236	.158041
	-.30	.133884	.136560	.139261	.141986	.144732	.147499	.150286	.153091	.155915	.158755	.161610	.167364	.173170
	-.40	.149012	.151689	.154390	.157114	.159860	.162627	.165414	.168220	.171043	.173883	.176739	.182493	.188298
25	.40	.027221	.029963	.032738	.035535	.038353	.041190	.044044	.046916	.049802	.052702	.055615	.061475	.067373
	.30	.042340	.045091	.047866	.050663	.053481	.056318	.059173	.062044	.064930	.067831	.070744	.076604	.082501
	.20	.057468	.060219	.062994	.065791	.068609	.071446	.074301	.077172	.080059	.082959	.085872	.091732	.097630
	.10	.072596	.075348	.078123	.080920	.083738	.086575	.089429	.092301	.095187	.098088	.101001	.106860	.112758
	0.00	.087725	.090476	.093251	.096048	.098866	.101703	.104558	.107429	.110316	.113216	.116129	.121989	.127887
	-.10	.102853	.105604	.108379	.111177	.113994	.116831	.119686	.122557	.125444	.128344	.131257	.137117	.143015
	-.20	.117981	.120733	.123508	.126305	.129123	.131960	.134815	.137686	.140572	.143473	.146386	.152245	.158143
	-.30	.133110	.135861	.138636	.141433	.144251	.147088	.149943	.152814	.155701	.158601	.161514	.167374	.173272
	-.40	.148238	.150989	.153764	.156562	.159379	.162216	.165071	.167943	.170829	.173729	.176642	.182502	.188400
30	.40	.026721	.029524	.032350	.035196	.038062	.040944	.043843	.046755	.049680	.052616	.055562	.061480	.067426
	.30	.041849	.044652	.047478	.050325	.053190	.056073	.058971	.061883	.064808	.067744	.070691	.076609	.082554
	.20	.056977	.059781	.062606	.065453	.068318	.071201	.074099	.077012	.079937	.082873	.085819	.091737	.097682
	.10	.072106	.074909	.077735	.080581	.083447	.086329	.089228	.092140	.095065	.098001	.100947	.106865	.112811
	0.00	.087234	.090037	.092863	.095710	.098575	.101458	.104356	.107268	.110193	.113129	.116076	.121994	.127939
	-.10	.102362	.105166	.107991	.110838	.113703	.116586	.119484	.122397	.125322	.128258	.131204	.137122	.143067
	-.20	.117491	.120294	.123120	.125966	.128832	.131714	.134613	.137525	.140450	.143386	.146332	.152250	.158196
	-.30	.132619	.135422	.138248	.141095	.143960	.146843	.149741	.152653	.155578	.158514	.161461	.167379	.173324
	-.40	.147748	.150551	.153376	.156223	.159088	.161971	.164869	.167782	.170707	.173643	.176589	.182507	.188452

INTEREST RATE

TERM YEARS	APPR DEP	5.0	5.5	6.0	6.5	7.0	7.5	8.0	8.5	9.0	9.5	10.0	11.0	12.0
10	.40	.026836	.029421	.032031	.034665	.037323	.040004	.042708	.045435	.048184	.050955	.053747	.059395	.065124
	.30	.041964	.044549	.047159	.049794	.052451	.055133	.057837	.060563	.063313	.066083	.068876	.074523	.080252
	.20	.057092	.059678	.062288	.064922	.067580	.070261	.072965	.075692	.078441	.081212	.084404	.089652	.095380
	.10	.072221	.074806	.077416	.080050	.082708	.085389	.088093	.090820	.093569	.096340	.099133	.104780	.110509
	0.00	.087349	.089935	.092545	.095179	.097836	.100518	.103222	.105949	.108698	.111469	.114261	.119908	.125637
	-.10	.102477	.105063	.107673	.110307	.112965	.115646	.118350	.121077	.123826	.126597	.129389	.135037	.140765
	-.20	.117606	.120191	.122801	.125435	.128093	.130774	.133478	.136205	.138954	.141725	.144515	.150165	.155894
	-.30	.132734	.135320	.137930	.140564	.143221	.145903	.148607	.151334	.154083	.156854	.159646	.165293	.171022
	-.40	.147862	.150448	.153058	.155692	.158350	.161031	.163735	.166462	.169211	.171982	.174774	.180422	.186150
15	.40	.023756	.026597	.029465	.032359	.035279	.038223	.041190	.044180	.047192	.050225	.053278	.059443	.065679
	.30	.038884	.041726	.044594	.047488	.050407	.053351	.056318	.059308	.062320	.065353	.068407	.074571	.080807
	.20	.054013	.056854	.059722	.062616	.065536	.068479	.071446	.074437	.077448	.080482	.083535	.089700	.095936
	.10	.069141	.071982	.074850	.077745	.080664	.083608	.086575	.089565	.092577	.095610	.098663	.104828	.111064
	0.00	.084269	.087111	.089979	.092873	.095792	.098736	.101703	.104693	.107705	.110738	.113792	.119956	.126192
	-.10	.099398	.102239	.105107	.108001	.110921	.113864	.116832	.119822	.122834	.125867	.128920	.135085	.141321
	-.20	.114526	.117367	.120235	.123130	.126049	.128993	.131960	.134950	.137962	.140995	.144048	.150213	.156449
	-.30	.129654	.132496	.135364	.138258	.141177	.144121	.147088	.150078	.153090	.156123	.159177	.165341	.171578
	-.40	.144783	.147624	.150492	.153386	.156306	.159249	.162217	.165207	.168219	.171252	.174305	.180470	.186706
20	.40	.022263	.025237	.028238	.031265	.034316	.037391	.040487	.043605	.046742	.049897	.053070	.059464	.065914
	.30	.037391	.040365	.043366	.046393	.049444	.052519	.055615	.058733	.061870	.065025	.068198	.074592	.081042
	.20	.052519	.055494	.058499	.061521	.064573	.067647	.070744	.073861	.076998	.080154	.083327	.089720	.096170
	.10	.067648	.070622	.073623	.076650	.079701	.082776	.085872	.088990	.092127	.095282	.098455	.104849	.111299
	0.00	.082776	.085750	.088751	.091778	.094829	.097904	.101001	.104118	.107255	.110411	.113583	.119977	.126427
	-.10	.097905	.100879	.103880	.106906	.109958	.113032	.116129	.119246	.122383	.125539	.128712	.135105	.141556
	-.20	.113033	.116007	.119008	.122035	.125086	.128161	.131257	.134375	.137512	.140667	.143840	.150234	.156684
	-.30	.128161	.131135	.134136	.137163	.140214	.143289	.146386	.149503	.152640	.155796	.158969	.165362	.171812
	-.40	.143290	.146264	.149265	.152292	.155343	.158417	.161514	.164631	.167768	.170924	.174097	.180490	.186941
25	.40	.021403	.024460	.027543	.030651	.033782	.036934	.040106	.043297	.046504	.049726	.052963	.059474	.066027
	.30	.036531	.039588	.042671	.045779	.048910	.052062	.055235	.058426	.061632	.064855	.068091	.074602	.081155
	.20	.051659	.054716	.057800	.060908	.064039	.067191	.070363	.073553	.076760	.079983	.083220	.089731	.096284
	.10	.066788	.069845	.072928	.076036	.079167	.082319	.085491	.088682	.091889	.095111	.098348	.104859	.111412
	0.00	.081916	.084973	.088056	.091164	.094295	.097448	.100620	.103810	.107017	.110240	.113476	.119987	.126541
	-.10	.097044	.100101	.103185	.106293	.109424	.112576	.115748	.118938	.122145	.125368	.128605	.135116	.141669
	-.20	.112173	.115230	.118313	.121421	.124552	.127704	.130876	.134067	.137274	.140496	.143733	.150244	.156797
	-.30	.127301	.130358	.133442	.136549	.139680	.142833	.146005	.149195	.152402	.155625	.158861	.165372	.171926
	-.40	.142429	.145486	.148570	.151678	.154809	.157961	.161133	.164323	.167531	.170753	.173990	.180501	.187054
30	.40	.020857	.023972	.027112	.030275	.033459	.036662	.039882	.043118	.046368	.049630	.052904	.059479	.066085
	.30	.035986	.039101	.042240	.045403	.048587	.051790	.055010	.058246	.061496	.064759	.068032	.074608	.081214
	.20	.051114	.054229	.057369	.060531	.063715	.066918	.070139	.073375	.076624	.079887	.083161	.089736	.096342
	.10	.066243	.069357	.072497	.075660	.078844	.082047	.085267	.088503	.091753	.095015	.098289	.104864	.111470
	0.00	.081371	.084486	.087625	.090788	.093972	.097175	.100395	.103631	.106881	.110144	.113417	.119993	.126599
	-.10	.096499	.099614	.102754	.105917	.109100	.112303	.115524	.118760	.122010	.125272	.128546	.135121	.141727
	-.20	.111628	.114742	.117882	.121046	.124229	.127432	.130652	.133888	.137138	.140400	.143674	.150250	.156856
	-.30	.126756	.129871	.133010	.136173	.139357	.142560	.145780	.149016	.152266	.155529	.158802	.165378	.171984
	-.40	.141884	.144999	.148139	.151302	.154485	.157688	.160909	.164145	.167395	.170657	.173931	.180506	.187112

5.0 YEAR HOLDING PERIOD
.140 EQUITY YIELD RATE
.700 LOAN RATIO

INTEREST RATE

TERM YEARS	APPR DEP	5.0	5.5	6.0	6.5	7.0	7.5	8.0	8.5	9.0	9.5	10.0	11.0	12.0
10	.40	.024203	.026918	.029659	.032424	.035215	.038030	.040870	.043733	.046619	.049529	.052461	.058391	.064405
	.30	.039332	.042046	.044787	.047553	.050343	.053159	.055998	.058861	.061748	.064657	.067589	.073519	.079534
	.20	.054460	.057175	.059915	.062681	.065472	.068287	.071126	.073989	.076876	.079785	.082717	.088647	.094662
	.10	.069588	.072303	.075044	.077809	.080600	.083415	.086255	.089118	.092004	.094914	.097846	.103776	.109791
	0.00	.084717	.087431	.090172	.092938	.095728	.098544	.101383	.104246	.107133	.110042	.112974	.118904	.124919
	-.10	.099845	.102560	.105300	.108066	.110857	.113672	.116511	.119375	.122261	.125170	.128102	.134032	.140047
	-.20	.114973	.117688	.120429	.123194	.125985	.128800	.131640	.134503	.137389	.140299	.143231	.149161	.155176
	-.30	.130102	.132817	.135557	.138323	.141113	.143929	.146768	.149631	.152518	.155427	.158359	.164269	.170304
	-.40	.145230	.147945	.150685	.153451	.156242	.159057	.161896	.164760	.167646	.170556	.173487	.179417	.185432
15	.40	.020970	.023953	.026965	.030003	.033069	.036160	.039275	.042415	.045577	.048762	.051968	.058441	.064989
	.30	.036098	.039081	.042093	.045132	.048197	.051288	.054404	.057543	.060706	.063890	.067096	.073569	.080117
	.20	.051226	.054210	.057221	.060260	.063325	.066416	.069532	.072671	.075834	.079019	.082225	.088697	.095245
	.10	.066355	.069338	.072350	.075388	.078454	.081545	.084660	.087800	.090962	.094147	.097353	.103826	.110374
	0.00	.081483	.084466	.087478	.090517	.093582	.096673	.099789	.102928	.106091	.109275	.112481	.118954	.125502
	-.10	.096611	.099595	.102606	.105645	.108710	.111801	.114917	.118056	.121219	.124404	.127610	.134083	.140631
	-.20	.111740	.114723	.117735	.120774	.123839	.126930	.130046	.133185	.136347	.139532	.142738	.149211	.155759
	-.30	.126868	.129851	.132863	.135902	.138967	.142058	.145174	.148313	.151476	.154660	.157866	.164339	.170887
	-.40	.141996	.144980	.147991	.151030	.154095	.157186	.160302	.163441	.166604	.169789	.172995	.179468	.186016
20	.40	.019402	.022525	.025676	.028854	.032058	.035286	.038537	.041811	.045104	.048418	.051749	.058463	.065235
	.30	.034530	.037653	.040804	.043982	.047186	.050414	.053666	.056939	.060233	.063546	.066878	.073591	.080364
	.20	.049659	.052781	.055932	.059111	.062314	.065543	.068794	.072067	.075361	.078675	.082006	.088719	.095492
	.10	.064787	.067910	.071061	.074239	.077443	.080671	.083922	.087196	.090490	.093803	.097134	.103848	.110620
	0.00	.079915	.083038	.086189	.089367	.092571	.095799	.099051	.102324	.105618	.108931	.112263	.118976	.125749
	-.10	.095044	.098166	.101317	.104496	.107699	.110928	.114179	.117452	.120746	.124060	.127391	.134104	.140877
	-.20	.110172	.113295	.116446	.119624	.122828	.126056	.129307	.132581	.135875	.139188	.142519	.149223	.156005
	-.30	.125300	.128423	.131574	.134752	.137956	.141184	.144436	.147709	.151003	.154316	.157648	.164361	.171134
	-.40	.140429	.143551	.146703	.149881	.153085	.156313	.159564	.162837	.166131	.169445	.172776	.179489	.186262
25	.40	.018499	.021709	.024946	.028209	.031497	.034807	.038137	.041487	.044855	.048238	.051637	.058473	.065354
	.30	.033627	.036837	.040074	.043338	.046625	.049935	.053266	.056616	.059983	.063367	.066765	.073602	.080483
	.20	.048755	.051965	.055203	.058466	.061754	.065063	.068394	.071744	.075111	.078495	.081894	.088750	.095611
	.10	.063884	.067094	.070331	.073595	.076882	.080192	.083522	.086872	.090240	.093623	.097022	.103858	.110739
	0.00	.079012	.082350	.085460	.088723	.092010	.095320	.098651	.102001	.105368	.108752	.112150	.118987	.125868
	-.10	.094141	.097350	.100588	.103851	.107139	.110449	.113779	.117129	.120496	.123880	.127279	.134115	.140996
	-.20	.109269	.112479	.115716	.118980	.122267	.125577	.128907	.132257	.135625	.139009	.142407	.149243	.156124
	-.30	.124397	.127607	.130845	.134108	.137395	.140705	.144036	.147386	.150753	.154137	.157535	.164372	.171253
	-.40	.139526	.142735	.145973	.149236	.152524	.155834	.159164	.162514	.165882	.169265	.172664	.179500	.186381
30	.40	.017926	.021197	.024493	.027814	.031157	.034521	.037902	.041300	.044712	.048138	.051575	.058479	.065415
	.30	.033055	.036325	.039622	.042943	.046286	.049649	.053030	.056428	.059840	.063266	.066703	.073608	.080544
	.20	.048183	.051453	.054750	.058071	.061414	.064777	.068159	.071556	.074969	.078394	.081832	.088736	.095672
	.10	.063311	.066582	.069879	.073199	.076542	.079906	.083287	.086685	.090097	.093523	.096960	.103864	.110800
	0.00	.078440	.081710	.085007	.088328	.091671	.095034	.098415	.101813	.105225	.108651	.112088	.118993	.125929
	-.10	.093568	.096839	.100135	.103456	.106799	.110162	.113544	.116941	.120354	.123779	.127217	.134121	.141057
	-.20	.108696	.111967	.115264	.118585	.121928	.125291	.128672	.132070	.135482	.138908	.142345	.149249	.156186
	-.30	.123825	.127095	.130392	.133713	.137056	.140419	.143800	.147198	.150610	.154036	.157473	.164378	.171314
	-.40	.138953	.142224	.145520	.148841	.152184	.155547	.158929	.162326	.165738	.169162	.172602	.179506	.186442

5.0 YEAR HOLDING PERIOD
.140 EQUITY YIELD RATE
.750 LOAN RATIO

INTEREST RATE

TERM YEARS	APPR DEP	5.0	5.5	6.0	6.5	7.0	7.5	8.0	8.5	9.0	9.5	10.0	11.0	12.0
10	.40	.020254	.023163	.026099	.029063	.032053	.035069	.038111	.041179	.044272	.047389	.050530	.056884	.063328
	.30	.035383	.038292	.041228	.044191	.047181	.050197	.053240	.056307	.059400	.062517	.065659	.072012	.074457
	.20	.050511	.053420	.056356	.059319	.062309	.065326	.068368	.071436	.074528	.077646	.080787	.087140	.093585
	.10	.065639	.068548	.071484	.074448	.077438	.080464	.083496	.086564	.089657	.092774	.095915	.102269	.108713
	0.00	.080768	.083677	.086613	.089576	.092566	.095582	.098625	.101692	.104785	.107902	.111044	.117397	.123842
	-.10	.095896	.098805	.101741	.104705	.107695	.110711	.113753	.116821	.119913	.123031	.126172	.132525	.138970
	-.20	.111025	.113933	.116870	.119833	.122823	.125839	.128881	.131949	.135042	.138159	.141300	.147654	.154058
	-.30	.126153	.129062	.131998	.134961	.137951	.140968	.144010	.147077	.150170	.153287	.156429	.162782	.169227
	-.40	.141281	.144190	.147126	.150090	.153080	.156096	.159138	.162206	.165298	.168416	.171557	.177911	.184355
15	.40	.016790	.019986	.023213	.026469	.029753	.033065	.036403	.039767	.043155	.046567	.050002	.056937	.063953
	.30	.031918	.035115	.038341	.041597	.044881	.048193	.051531	.054895	.058283	.061696	.065131	.072066	.079082
	.20	.047047	.050243	.053470	.056726	.060010	.063321	.066660	.070023	.073412	.076824	.080259	.087217	.094210
	.10	.062175	.065371	.068598	.071854	.075138	.078450	.081788	.085152	.088540	.091952	.095387	.102323	.109338
	0.00	.077303	.080500	.083726	.086982	.090267	.093578	.096916	.100280	.103669	.107081	.110516	.117451	.124467
	-.10	.092432	.095628	.098855	.102111	.105395	.108707	.112045	.115409	.118797	.122209	.125644	.132580	.139595
	-.20	.107560	.110756	.113983	.117239	.120523	.123835	.127173	.130537	.133925	.137337	.140772	.147708	.154723
	-.30	.122688	.125885	.129111	.132367	.135652	.138963	.142301	.145665	.149054	.152466	.155901	.162836	.169852
	-.40	.137817	.141013	.144240	.147496	.150780	.154092	.157430	.160794	.164182	.167594	.171029	.177964	.184980
20	.40	.015110	.018456	.021832	.025237	.028670	.032129	.035612	.039119	.042649	.046199	.049768	.056961	.064247
	.30	.030238	.033564	.036960	.040366	.043798	.047257	.050741	.054248	.057777	.061327	.064896	.072089	.079346
	.20	.045367	.048713	.052089	.055494	.058927	.062385	.065869	.069376	.072905	.076455	.080025	.087217	.094474
	.10	.060495	.063841	.067217	.070622	.074055	.077514	.080997	.084505	.088034	.091584	.095153	.102346	.109602
	0.00	.075623	.078969	.082345	.085751	.089183	.092642	.096126	.099633	.103162	.106712	.110282	.117474	.124731
	-.10	.090752	.094098	.097474	.100879	.104312	.107771	.111254	.114761	.118290	.121840	.125410	.132603	.139859
	-.20	.105880	.109226	.112602	.116007	.119440	.122899	.126383	.129890	.133419	.136969	.140538	.147731	.154987
	-.30	.121009	.124354	.127731	.131136	.134568	.138027	.141511	.145018	.148547	.152097	.155667	.162859	.170116
	-.40	.136137	.139483	.142859	.146264	.149697	.153156	.156639	.160146	.163675	.167225	.170795	.177988	.185244
25	.40	.014142	.017582	.021050	.024547	.028069	.031615	.035184	.038773	.042381	.046006	.049648	.056972	.064345
	.30	.029271	.032710	.036179	.039675	.043197	.046744	.050312	.053901	.057509	.061135	.064776	.072101	.079473
	.20	.044399	.047838	.051307	.054804	.058326	.061872	.065441	.069030	.072638	.076263	.079904	.087229	.094601
	.10	.059528	.062967	.066435	.069932	.073454	.077000	.080569	.084158	.087766	.091391	.095033	.102357	.109730
	0.00	.074656	.078095	.081504	.085060	.088582	.092129	.095697	.099286	.102894	.106520	.110161	.117486	.124858
	-.10	.089784	.093223	.096692	.100189	.103711	.107257	.110826	.114415	.118023	.121648	.125289	.132614	.139987
	-.20	.104913	.108352	.111821	.115317	.118839	.122385	.125954	.129543	.133151	.136777	.140418	.147743	.155115
	-.30	.120041	.123480	.126949	.130445	.133968	.137514	.141082	.144671	.148279	.151905	.155546	.162871	.170243
	-.40	.135169	.138608	.142077	.145577	.149096	.152642	.156211	.159800	.163408	.167033	.170675	.177999	.185372
30	.40	.013529	.017033	.020565	.024124	.027705	.031309	.034932	.038572	.042228	.045898	.049581	.056979	.064410
	.30	.028658	.032162	.035694	.039252	.042834	.046437	.050060	.053700	.057356	.061027	.064710	.072107	.079539
	.20	.043786	.047290	.050822	.054380	.057962	.061565	.065188	.068829	.072485	.076155	.079838	.087235	.094667
	.10	.058914	.062418	.065950	.069509	.073090	.076694	.080317	.083957	.087613	.091283	.094966	.102364	.109795
	0.00	.074043	.077547	.081079	.084637	.088219	.091822	.095445	.099085	.102742	.106412	.110095	.117492	.124924
	-.10	.089171	.092675	.096207	.099765	.103347	.106950	.110573	.114214	.117870	.121540	.125223	.132620	.140052
	-.20	.104299	.107803	.111336	.114894	.118475	.122079	.125702	.129342	.132998	.136669	.140351	.147749	.155130
	-.30	.119428	.122932	.126464	.130022	.133604	.137207	.140830	.144470	.148127	.151797	.155480	.162877	.170309
	-.40	.134556	.138060	.141592	.145150	.148732	.152336	.155958	.159599	.163255	.166925	.170608	.178005	.185437

5.0 YEAR HOLDING PERIOD
.140 EQUITY YIELD RATE
.800 LOAN RATIO

INTEREST RATE

TERM YEARS	APPR DEP	5.0	5.5	6.0	6.5	7.0	7.5	8.0	8.5	9.0	9.5	10.0	11.0	12.0
10	.40	.016306	.019408	.022540	.025701	.028891	.032108	.035353	.038625	.041924	.045249	.048600	.055377	.062251
	.30	.031434	.034537	.037669	.040830	.044019	.047236	.050481	.053753	.057052	.060377	.063728	.070505	.077379
	.20	.046562	.049665	.052797	.055958	.059147	.062365	.065610	.068882	.072181	.075506	.078857	.085634	.092508
	.10	.061691	.064793	.067925	.071086	.074276	.077493	.080738	.084010	.087309	.090634	.093985	.100762	.107636
	0.00	.076819	.079922	.083054	.086215	.089404	.092621	.095866	.099138	.102437	.105762	.109113	.115890	.122764
	-.10	.091947	.095050	.098182	.101343	.104532	.107750	.110995	.114267	.117566	.120891	.124242	.131019	.137893
	-.20	.107076	.110178	.113310	.116471	.119661	.122878	.126123	.129395	.132694	.136019	.139370	.146147	.153021
	-.30	.122204	.125307	.128439	.131600	.134789	.138006	.141251	.144524	.147822	.151147	.154498	.161275	.168150
	-.40	.137332	.140435	.143567	.146728	.149917	.153135	.156380	.159652	.162951	.166276	.169627	.176404	.183278
15	.40	.012610	.016020	.019461	.022934	.026438	.029970	.033531	.037119	.040733	.044373	.048037	.055434	.062918
	.30	.027738	.031148	.034590	.038063	.041566	.045098	.048659	.052247	.055861	.059501	.063165	.070563	.078046
	.20	.042867	.046276	.049718	.053191	.056694	.060227	.063787	.067375	.070990	.074629	.078293	.085691	.093174
	.10	.057995	.061405	.064846	.068319	.071823	.075355	.078916	.082504	.086118	.089758	.093422	.100819	.108303
	0.00	.073123	.076533	.079975	.083448	.086951	.090483	.094044	.097632	.101246	.104886	.108550	.115948	.123431
	-.10	.088252	.091661	.095103	.098576	.102079	.105612	.109172	.112760	.116375	.120014	.123679	.131076	.138559
	-.20	.103380	.106790	.110232	.113704	.117208	.120740	.124301	.127889	.131503	.135143	.138807	.146204	.153688
	-.30	.118509	.121918	.125360	.128833	.132336	.135868	.139429	.143017	.146631	.150271	.153935	.161333	.168816
	-.40	.133637	.137046	.140488	.143961	.147464	.150997	.154557	.158146	.161760	.165400	.169064	.176461	.183944
20	.40	.010818	.014387	.017988	.021621	.025282	.028972	.032687	.036428	.040193	.043979	.047787	.055459	.063199
	.30	.025947	.029516	.033117	.036749	.040410	.044100	.047816	.051557	.055321	.059108	.062915	.070587	.078328
	.20	.041075	.044644	.048245	.051877	.055539	.059228	.062944	.066685	.070449	.074236	.078044	.085716	.093456
	.10	.056203	.059772	.063373	.067006	.070667	.074357	.078073	.081813	.085578	.089364	.093172	.100844	.108584
	0.00	.071332	.074901	.078502	.082134	.085796	.089485	.093201	.096942	.100706	.104493	.108300	.115972	.123713
	-.10	.086460	.090029	.093630	.097262	.100924	.104613	.108329	.112070	.115835	.119621	.123429	.131101	.138841
	-.20	.101588	.105157	.108759	.112391	.116052	.119742	.123458	.127198	.130963	.134750	.138557	.146229	.153969
	-.30	.116717	.120286	.123887	.127519	.131181	.134870	.138586	.142327	.146091	.149878	.153685	.161358	.169098
	-.40	.131845	.135414	.139015	.142647	.146309	.149998	.153714	.157455	.161220	.165006	.168814	.176486	.184226
25	.40	.009786	.013455	.017155	.020884	.024641	.028424	.032230	.036059	.039907	.043774	.047658	.055471	.063335
	.30	.024915	.028583	.032283	.036013	.039770	.043552	.047359	.051187	.055036	.058903	.062787	.070600	.078464
	.20	.040043	.043711	.047411	.051141	.054898	.058681	.062487	.066315	.070164	.074031	.077915	.085729	.093592
	.10	.055171	.058840	.062540	.066269	.070026	.073809	.077615	.081444	.085292	.089159	.093044	.100857	.108720
	0.00	.070300	.073968	.077668	.081398	.085155	.088937	.092744	.096572	.100421	.104268	.108172	.115985	.123849
	-.10	.085428	.089096	.092796	.096526	.100283	.104066	.107872	.111700	.115549	.119416	.123300	.131113	.138977
	-.20	.100556	.104225	.107925	.111654	.115411	.119194	.123000	.126829	.130677	.134545	.138429	.146242	.154105
	-.30	.115685	.119353	.123053	.126783	.130540	.134322	.138129	.141957	.145806	.149673	.153557	.161370	.169234
	-.40	.130813	.134481	.138181	.141911	.145668	.149451	.153257	.157086	.160934	.164801	.168685	.176498	.184362
30	.40	.009132	.012870	.016637	.020433	.024253	.028097	.031961	.035844	.039744	.043659	.047587	.055478	.063405
	.30	.024260	.027998	.031766	.035561	.039382	.043225	.047090	.050973	.054873	.058788	.062716	.070606	.078534
	.20	.039389	.043126	.046894	.050689	.054510	.058354	.062218	.066101	.070001	.073916	.077844	.085735	.093662
	.10	.054517	.058255	.062022	.065818	.069638	.073482	.077346	.081229	.085129	.089044	.092973	.100863	.108790
	0.00	.069645	.073383	.077151	.080946	.084767	.088610	.092475	.096358	.100258	.104173	.108101	.115992	.123919
	-.10	.084774	.088511	.092279	.096074	.099896	.103739	.107603	.111486	.115386	.119301	.123229	.131120	.139047
	-.20	.099902	.103640	.107407	.111203	.115023	.118867	.122731	.126614	.130514	.134429	.138358	.146248	.154175
	-.30	.115031	.118768	.122536	.126331	.130152	.133995	.137860	.141743	.145643	.149558	.153486	.161377	.169304
	-.40	.130159	.133896	.137664	.141460	.145280	.149124	.152988	.156871	.160771	.164686	.168614	.176505	.184432

5.0 YEAR HOLDING PERIOD
.140 EQUITY YIELD RATE
.900 LOAN RATIO

TERM YEARS	APPR DEP	5.0	5.5	6.0	6.5	7.0	7.5	8.0	8.5	9.0	9.5	10.0	11.0	12.0
10	.40	.008408	.011898	.015422	.018978	.022556	.026186	.029836	.033517	.037229	.040969	.044739	.052363	.060097
	.30	.023536	.027027	.030550	.034106	.037694	.041314	.044965	.048646	.052357	.056098	.059867	.067491	.075225
	.20	.038665	.042155	.045679	.049235	.052823	.056442	.060093	.063774	.067485	.071226	.074996	.082620	.090353
	.10	.053793	.057284	.060807	.064363	.067951	.071571	.075221	.078902	.082614	.086354	.090124	.097748	.105482
	0.00	.068921	.072412	.075935	.079491	.083079	.086699	.090350	.094031	.097742	.101483	.105252	.112876	.120610
	-.10	.084050	.087540	.091064	.094620	.098208	.101827	.105478	.109159	.112870	.116611	.120381	.128005	.135738
	-.20	.099178	.102669	.106132	.109748	.113336	.116956	.120606	.124287	.127999	.131739	.135509	.143133	.150867
	-.30	.114306	.117797	.121320	.124876	.128464	.132084	.135735	.139416	.143127	.146868	.150637	.158262	.165995
	-.40	.129435	.132925	.136449	.140005	.143593	.147212	.150863	.154544	.158255	.161996	.165766	.173390	.181123
15	.40	.004250	.008086	.011958	.015865	.019806	.023780	.027786	.031823	.035889	.039983	.044106	.052428	.060847
	.30	.019379	.023215	.027087	.030994	.034935	.038909	.042915	.046951	.051017	.055112	.059234	.067556	.075975
	.20	.034507	.038343	.042215	.046122	.050063	.054037	.058043	.062079	.066146	.070240	.074362	.082684	.091103
	.10	.049636	.053471	.057343	.061250	.065191	.069165	.073171	.077208	.081274	.085369	.089491	.097813	.106232
	0.00	.064764	.068600	.072472	.076379	.080320	.084294	.088300	.092336	.096402	.100497	.104619	.112941	.121350
	-.10	.079892	.083728	.087600	.091507	.095448	.099422	.103428	.107464	.111531	.115625	.119747	.128069	.136498
	-.20	.095021	.098856	.102728	.106635	.110577	.114550	.118556	.122593	.126659	.130754	.134876	.143198	.151617
	-.30	.110149	.113985	.117857	.121764	.125705	.129679	.133685	.137721	.141787	.145882	.150004	.158336	.166745
	-.40	.125277	.129113	.132985	.136892	.140833	.144807	.148813	.152850	.156916	.161010	.165132	.173454	.181873
20	.40	.002235	.006250	.010301	.014387	.018507	.022657	.026838	.031046	.035281	.039541	.043824	.052456	.061163
	.30	.017363	.021378	.025430	.029516	.033635	.037786	.041966	.046174	.050409	.054669	.058953	.067584	.076292
	.20	.032491	.036506	.040558	.044644	.048763	.052914	.057094	.061303	.065538	.069798	.074081	.082712	.091420
	.10	.047620	.051635	.055686	.059772	.063892	.068042	.072223	.076431	.080666	.084926	.089209	.097841	.106548
	0.00	.062748	.066763	.070815	.074901	.079020	.083171	.087351	.091559	.095794	.100054	.104338	.112969	.121677
	-.10	.077877	.081892	.085943	.090029	.094148	.098299	.102479	.106688	.110923	.115183	.119466	.128097	.136805
	-.20	.093005	.097020	.101071	.105157	.109277	.113427	.117608	.121816	.126051	.130311	.134595	.143226	.151933
	-.30	.108133	.112148	.116200	.120286	.124405	.128556	.132736	.136945	.141180	.145439	.149723	.158354	.167062
	-.40	.123262	.127277	.131328	.135414	.139533	.143684	.147864	.152073	.156308	.160568	.164851	.173482	.182190
25	.40	.001074	.005201	.009363	.013559	.017786	.022041	.026323	.030630	.034960	.039310	.043680	.052470	.061316
	.30	.016202	.020329	.024492	.028687	.032914	.037169	.041452	.045759	.050088	.054439	.058808	.067598	.076445
	.20	.031330	.035457	.039620	.043816	.048043	.052298	.056580	.060887	.065217	.069567	.073937	.082726	.091573
	.10	.046459	.050586	.054748	.058944	.063171	.067426	.071708	.076015	.080345	.084695	.089065	.097855	.106701
	0.00	.061587	.065714	.069877	.074072	.078299	.082554	.086837	.091144	.095473	.099824	.104193	.112983	.121830
	-.10	.076715	.080842	.085002	.089201	.093427	.097663	.101965	.106272	.110602	.114952	.119322	.128111	.136958
	-.20	.091844	.095971	.100133	.104329	.108556	.112811	.117093	.121400	.125730	.130080	.134450	.143240	.152087
	-.30	.106972	.111099	.115262	.119457	.123684	.127940	.132222	.136529	.140858	.145209	.149578	.158368	.167215
	-.40	.122100	.126227	.130390	.134586	.138812	.143068	.147350	.151657	.155987	.160337	.164707	.173496	.182343
30	.40	.000638	.004543	.008781	.013051	.017349	.021673	.026021	.030389	.034776	.039181	.043600	.052477	.061395
	.30	.015466	.019671	.023910	.028179	.032477	.036801	.041149	.045517	.049905	.054309	.058728	.067605	.076523
	.20	.030594	.034799	.039038	.043308	.047606	.051930	.056277	.060646	.065033	.069437	.073857	.082734	.091652
	.10	.045723	.049928	.054166	.058436	.062734	.067058	.071406	.075774	.080161	.084566	.088985	.097862	.106780
	0.00	.060851	.065056	.069295	.073564	.077863	.082187	.086534	.090902	.095290	.099694	.104113	.112990	.121909
	-.10	.075979	.080184	.084423	.088693	.092991	.097315	.101662	.106031	.110418	.114823	.119242	.128119	.137037
	-.20	.091108	.095313	.099551	.103821	.108119	.112443	.116791	.121159	.125547	.129951	.134370	.143247	.152165
	-.30	.106236	.110441	.114680	.118949	.123248	.127572	.131919	.136287	.140675	.145079	.149499	.158376	.167294
	-.40	.121365	.125569	.129808	.134078	.138376	.142700	.147047	.151416	.155803	.160208	.164627	.173504	.182442

5.0 YEAR HOLDING PERIOD
.150 EQUITY YIELD RATE
.600 LOAN RATIO

INTEREST RATE

TERM YEARS	APPR DEP	5.0	5.5	6.0	6.5	7.0	7.5	8.0	8.5	9.0	9.5	10.0	11.0	12.0
10	.40	.038068	.040384	.042722	.045082	.047463	.049866	.052289	.054732	.057196	.059679	.062182	.067244	.072379
	.30	.052900	.055216	.057554	.059914	.062295	.064697	.067120	.069564	.072027	.074511	.077013	.082076	.087211
	.20	.067731	.070047	.072385	.074745	.077126	.079529	.081952	.084395	.086859	.089342	.091845	.096907	.102042
	.10	.082563	.084879	.087217	.089577	.091958	.094360	.096783	.099227	.101691	.104174	.106677	.111739	.116874
	0.00	.097394	.099710	.102048	.104408	.106790	.109192	.111615	.114058	.116522	.119005	.121508	.126570	.131706
	-.10	.112226	.114542	.116880	.119240	.121621	.124023	.126447	.128890	.131354	.133837	.136340	.141402	.146537
	-.20	.127057	.129373	.131712	.134071	.136453	.138855	.141278	.143722	.146185	.148669	.151171	.156233	.161369
	-.30	.141889	.144205	.146543	.148903	.151284	.153687	.156110	.158553	.161017	.163500	.166003	.171065	.176200
	-.40	.156720	.159037	.161375	.163734	.166116	.168518	.170941	.173385	.175848	.178332	.180834	.185896	.191032
15	.40	.034969	.037514	.040082	.042674	.045289	.047926	.050585	.053264	.055964	.058682	.061419	.066946	.072538
	.30	.049801	.052345	.054914	.057506	.060121	.062758	.065417	.068096	.070795	.073514	.076251	.081777	.087370
	.20	.064633	.067177	.069745	.072337	.074952	.077589	.080248	.082927	.085627	.088345	.091082	.096609	.102201
	.10	.079464	.082008	.084577	.087169	.089784	.092421	.095080	.097759	.100458	.103177	.105914	.111441	.117033
	0.00	.094296	.096840	.099408	.102000	.104615	.107253	.109911	.112590	.115290	.118008	.120745	.126272	.131864
	-.10	.109127	.111671	.114240	.116832	.119447	.122084	.124743	.127422	.130121	.132840	.135577	.141104	.146696
	-.20	.123959	.126503	.129071	.131664	.134279	.136916	.139574	.142254	.144953	.147671	.150408	.155935	.161528
	-.30	.138790	.141335	.143903	.146495	.149110	.151747	.154406	.157085	.159784	.162503	.165240	.170767	.176359
	-.40	.153622	.156166	.158735	.161327	.163942	.166579	.169237	.171917	.174616	.177335	.180072	.185598	.191191
20	.40	.033467	.036131	.038819	.041531	.044265	.047021	.049797	.052592	.055405	.058235	.061081	.066817	.072605
	.30	.048299	.050962	.053651	.056362	.059097	.061852	.064628	.067423	.070236	.073066	.075912	.081648	.087437
	.20	.063130	.065794	.068482	.071194	.073928	.076684	.079460	.082255	.085068	.087898	.090744	.096480	.102268
	.10	.077962	.080625	.083314	.086026	.088760	.091515	.094291	.097086	.099899	.102729	.105575	.111311	.117100
	0.00	.092793	.095457	.098145	.100857	.103591	.106347	.109123	.111918	.114731	.117561	.120407	.126143	.131932
	-.10	.107625	.110289	.112977	.115689	.118423	.121179	.123954	.126749	.129562	.132392	.135238	.140975	.146763
	-.20	.122457	.125120	.127808	.130520	.133254	.136010	.138786	.141581	.144394	.147224	.150070	.155806	.161595
	-.30	.137288	.139952	.142640	.145352	.148086	.150842	.153617	.156412	.159225	.162055	.164901	.170638	.176426
	-.40	.152120	.154783	.157472	.160183	.162918	.165673	.168449	.171244	.174057	.176887	.179733	.185469	.191258
25	.40	.032602	.035341	.038104	.040890	.043697	.046524	.049369	.052231	.055109	.058001	.060907	.066752	.072638
	.30	.047433	.050172	.052936	.055722	.058529	.061356	.064201	.067063	.069941	.072833	.075738	.081584	.087469
	.20	.062265	.065004	.067767	.070553	.073360	.076187	.079032	.081894	.084772	.087664	.090570	.096415	.102301
	.10	.077097	.079836	.082599	.085385	.088192	.091019	.093864	.096726	.099604	.102496	.105401	.111247	.117132
	0.00	.091928	.094667	.097430	.100216	.103023	.105850	.108695	.111558	.114435	.117327	.120233	.126079	.131964
	-.10	.106760	.109499	.112262	.115048	.117855	.120682	.123527	.126389	.129267	.132159	.135064	.140910	.146796
	-.20	.121591	.124330	.127093	.129879	.132686	.135513	.138359	.141221	.144098	.146991	.149896	.155742	.161627
	-.30	.136423	.139162	.141925	.144711	.147518	.150345	.153190	.156052	.158930	.161822	.164727	.170573	.176459
	-.40	.151254	.153993	.156757	.159542	.162350	.165176	.168022	.170884	.173762	.176654	.179559	.185405	.191290
30	.40	.032053	.034845	.037661	.040497	.043353	.046227	.049118	.052022	.054940	.057870	.060810	.066718	.072654
	.30	.046885	.049677	.052492	.055329	.058185	.061059	.063949	.066854	.069772	.072702	.075642	.081549	.087486
	.20	.061716	.064508	.067324	.070160	.073016	.075890	.078781	.081685	.084603	.087533	.090474	.096381	.102318
	.10	.076548	.079340	.082155	.084992	.087848	.090722	.093612	.096517	.099435	.102365	.105305	.111213	.117149
	0.00	.091380	.094172	.096987	.099823	.102680	.105554	.108444	.111349	.114267	.117196	.120137	.126044	.131981
	-.10	.106211	.109003	.111818	.114655	.117511	.120385	.123275	.126180	.129098	.132028	.134968	.140876	.146812
	-.20	.121043	.123835	.126650	.129486	.132343	.135217	.138107	.141011	.143930	.146859	.149800	.155707	.161644
	-.30	.135874	.138666	.141481	.144318	.147174	.150048	.152938	.155843	.158761	.161691	.164631	.170539	.176476
	-.40	.150706	.153498	.156313	.159150	.162006	.164880	.167770	.170675	.173593	.176523	.179463	.185370	.191307

162

5.0 YEAR HOLDING PERIOD
.150 EQUITY YIELD RATE
.667 LOAN RATIO

INTEREST RATE

TERM YEARS	APPR DEP	5.0	5.5	6.0	6.5	7.0	7.5	8.0	8.5	9.0	9.5	10.0	11.0	12.0
10	.40	.032223	.034796	.037394	.040016	.042662	.045331	.048024	.050739	.053476	.056235	.059016	.064641	.070347
	.30	.047054	.049628	.052226	.054848	.057493	.060163	.062855	.065570	.068307	.071067	.073848	.079472	.085178
	.20	.061886	.064459	.067057	.069679	.072325	.074994	.077687	.080402	.083139	.085898	.088679	.094304	.100010
	.10	.076717	.079291	.081889	.084511	.087157	.089826	.092518	.095233	.097971	.100730	.103511	.109135	.114841
	0.00	.091549	.094122	.096720	.099342	.101988	.104657	.107350	.110065	.112802	.115561	.118342	.123967	.129673
	-.10	.106380	.108954	.111552	.114174	.116820	.119489	.122181	.124896	.127634	.130393	.133174	.138798	.144504
	-.20	.121212	.123785	.126383	.129005	.131651	.134321	.137013	.139728	.142465	.145224	.148005	.153630	.159336
	-.30	.136043	.138617	.141215	.143837	.146483	.149152	.151844	.154559	.157297	.160056	.162837	.168461	.174167
	-.40	.150875	.153448	.156046	.158668	.161314	.163984	.166676	.169391	.172128	.174888	.177668	.183293	.188999
15	.40	.028780	.031607	.034461	.037341	.040246	.043176	.046130	.049107	.052107	.055127	.058168	.064309	.070523
	.30	.043611	.046438	.049292	.052172	.055078	.058008	.060962	.063939	.066938	.069959	.073000	.079141	.085355
	.20	.058443	.061270	.064124	.067004	.069909	.072840	.075794	.078771	.081770	.084790	.087832	.093972	.100186
	.10	.073274	.076101	.078955	.081835	.084741	.087671	.090625	.093602	.096601	.099622	.102663	.108804	.115018
	0.00	.088106	.090933	.093787	.096667	.099572	.102503	.105457	.108434	.111433	.114453	.117495	.123636	.129849
	-.10	.102938	.105764	.108618	.111498	.114404	.117334	.120288	.123265	.126264	.129285	.132326	.138467	.144681
	-.20	.117769	.120596	.123450	.126330	.129236	.132166	.135120	.138097	.141096	.144117	.147158	.153299	.159512
	-.30	.132601	.135428	.138281	.141162	.144067	.146997	.149951	.152928	.155928	.158948	.161989	.168130	.174344
	-.40	.147432	.150259	.153113	.155993	.158899	.161829	.164783	.167760	.170759	.173780	.176821	.182962	.189175
20	.40	.027111	.030070	.033057	.036070	.039108	.042170	.045254	.048360	.051486	.054630	.057792	.064166	.070598
	.30	.041942	.044902	.047889	.050902	.053940	.057003	.060086	.063191	.066317	.069462	.072624	.078997	.085429
	.20	.056774	.059733	.062720	.065733	.068772	.071833	.074918	.078023	.081149	.084293	.087455	.093829	.100261
	.10	.071605	.074565	.077552	.080565	.083603	.086665	.089749	.092855	.095980	.099125	.102287	.108660	.115092
	0.00	.086437	.089396	.092383	.095397	.098435	.101496	.104581	.107686	.110812	.113956	.117119	.123492	.129924
	-.10	.101268	.104228	.107215	.110228	.113266	.116328	.119412	.122518	.125643	.128788	.131950	.138324	.144755
	-.20	.116100	.119059	.122046	.125060	.128098	.131160	.134244	.137349	.140475	.143619	.146782	.153155	.159587
	-.30	.130931	.133891	.136878	.139891	.142929	.145991	.149075	.152181	.155306	.158451	.161613	.167987	.174418
	-.40	.145763	.148723	.151710	.154723	.157761	.160823	.163907	.167012	.170138	.173282	.176445	.182818	.189250
25	.40	.026149	.029192	.032263	.035358	.038477	.041618	.044780	.047960	.051157	.054371	.057599	.064094	.070634
	.30	.040981	.044024	.047094	.050190	.053309	.056450	.059611	.062791	.065989	.069202	.072431	.078926	.085465
	.20	.055812	.058856	.061926	.065021	.068140	.071281	.074443	.077623	.080820	.084034	.087262	.093757	.100297
	.10	.070644	.073687	.076757	.079853	.082972	.086113	.089274	.092454	.095652	.098865	.102094	.108589	.115128
	0.00	.085475	.088519	.091589	.094684	.097803	.100944	.104106	.107286	.110484	.113697	.116925	.123420	.129960
	-.10	.100307	.103350	.106421	.109516	.112635	.115776	.118937	.122118	.125315	.128529	.131757	.138252	.144791
	-.20	.115138	.118182	.121252	.124348	.127467	.130608	.133769	.136949	.140147	.143360	.146588	.153084	.159623
	-.30	.129970	.133013	.136084	.139179	.142298	.145439	.148600	.151781	.154978	.158192	.161420	.167915	.174455
	-.40	.144802	.147845	.150915	.154011	.157130	.160271	.163432	.166612	.169810	.173023	.176251	.182747	.189286
30	.40	.025540	.028642	.031770	.034922	.038095	.041289	.044500	.047728	.050970	.054225	.057492	.064056	.070652
	.30	.040371	.043473	.046601	.049753	.052927	.056120	.059331	.062559	.065801	.069057	.072324	.078888	.085434
	.20	.055203	.058305	.061433	.064585	.067758	.070952	.074163	.077391	.080633	.083888	.087155	.093719	.100315
	.10	.070034	.073137	.076265	.079416	.082590	.085783	.088995	.092222	.095464	.098720	.101987	.108551	.115147
	0.00	.084866	.087968	.091096	.094248	.097421	.100615	.103826	.107054	.110296	.113551	.116818	.123382	.129978
	-.10	.099697	.102800	.105928	.109079	.112253	.115446	.118658	.121885	.125128	.128383	.131650	.138214	.144810
	-.20	.114529	.117631	.120759	.123911	.127085	.130278	.133489	.136717	.139959	.143214	.146481	.153045	.159641
	-.30	.129361	.132463	.135591	.138743	.141916	.145109	.148321	.151548	.154791	.158046	.161313	.167877	.174473
	-.40	.144192	.147294	.150422	.153574	.156748	.159941	.163152	.166380	.169622	.172878	.176145	.182708	.189305

5.0 YEAR HOLDING PERIOD
.150 EQUITY YIELD RATE
.700 LOAN RATIO

INTEREST RATE

TERM YEARS	APPR DEP	5.0	5.5	6.0	6.5	7.0	7.5	8.0	8.5	9.0	9.5	10.0	11.0	12.0
10	.40	.029900	.032002	.034730	.037483	.040262	.043064	.045891	.048742	.051616	.054513	.057433	.063339	.069330
	.30	.044132	.046834	.049562	.052315	.055093	.057896	.060723	.063574	.066448	.069345	.072265	.078171	.084162
	.20	.058963	.061666	.064393	.067147	.069925	.072727	.075554	.078405	.081279	.084177	.087096	.093002	.098993
	.10	.073795	.076497	.079225	.081978	.084756	.087559	.090386	.093237	.096111	.099008	.101928	.107834	.113825
	0.00	.088627	.091329	.094056	.096810	.099588	.102391	.105217	.108068	.110942	.113840	.116759	.122665	.128657
	-.10	.103458	.106160	.108888	.111641	.114419	.117222	.120049	.122900	.125774	.128671	.131591	.137497	.143488
	-.20	.118290	.120992	.123720	.126473	.129251	.132054	.134881	.137731	.140606	.143503	.146423	.152328	.158320
	-.30	.133121	.135823	.138551	.141304	.144082	.146885	.149712	.152563	.155437	.158334	.161260	.167160	.173151
	-.40	.147953	.150655	.153383	.156136	.158914	.161717	.164544	.167394	.170269	.173166	.176086	.181991	.187983
15	.40	.025685	.028654	.031650	.034674	.037725	.040802	.043903	.047029	.050179	.053350	.056543	.062991	.069516
	.30	.040517	.043485	.046482	.049506	.052557	.055633	.058735	.061861	.065010	.068182	.071375	.077823	.084347
	.20	.055349	.058317	.061313	.064337	.067388	.070465	.073567	.076692	.079842	.083013	.086206	.092654	.099179
	.10	.070180	.073148	.076145	.079169	.082220	.085296	.088398	.091524	.094673	.097845	.101038	.107486	.114010
	0.00	.085012	.087980	.090976	.094001	.097051	.100128	.103230	.106356	.109505	.112676	.115870	.122317	.128842
	-.10	.099843	.102811	.105808	.108832	.111883	.114960	.118061	.121187	.124336	.127508	.130701	.137149	.143673
	-.20	.114675	.117643	.120640	.123664	.126714	.129791	.132893	.136019	.139168	.142339	.145533	.151981	.158505
	-.30	.129506	.132474	.135471	.138495	.141546	.144623	.147724	.150850	.153999	.157171	.160364	.166812	.173336
	-.40	.144338	.147306	.150303	.153327	.156378	.159454	.162556	.165682	.168831	.172003	.175196	.181644	.188168
20	.40	.023933	.027040	.030177	.033340	.036530	.039745	.042984	.046244	.049526	.052828	.056148	.062841	.069594
	.30	.038764	.041872	.045008	.048172	.051362	.054577	.057815	.061076	.064358	.067650	.070980	.077672	.084425
	.20	.053596	.056703	.059840	.063004	.066194	.069408	.072647	.075908	.079189	.082491	.085812	.092504	.099257
	.10	.068427	.071535	.074671	.077835	.081025	.084240	.087478	.090739	.094021	.097323	.100643	.107335	.114089
	0.00	.083259	.086367	.089503	.092667	.095857	.099071	.102310	.105571	.108853	.112154	.115475	.122167	.128920
	-.10	.098091	.101198	.104334	.107498	.110688	.113903	.117141	.120402	.123684	.126986	.130306	.136998	.143752
	-.20	.112922	.116030	.119166	.122330	.125520	.128735	.131973	.135234	.138516	.141817	.145138	.151830	.158583
	-.30	.127754	.130861	.133998	.137161	.140351	.143566	.146805	.150065	.153347	.156649	.159969	.166661	.173415
	-.40	.142585	.145693	.148829	.151993	.155183	.158398	.161636	.164897	.168179	.171480	.174801	.181493	.188246
25	.40	.022923	.026119	.029342	.032593	.035868	.039166	.042485	.045824	.049182	.052556	.055945	.062765	.069632
	.30	.037755	.040950	.044174	.047424	.050699	.053997	.057317	.060656	.064013	.067387	.070777	.077597	.084463
	.20	.052586	.055782	.059006	.062256	.065530	.068829	.072148	.075487	.078845	.082219	.085609	.092428	.099295
	.10	.067418	.070613	.073837	.077087	.080362	.083660	.086980	.090319	.093676	.097051	.100440	.107260	.114126
	0.00	.082249	.085445	.088669	.091919	.095194	.098492	.101811	.105150	.108508	.111882	.115272	.122092	.128958
	-.10	.097081	.100277	.103500	.106751	.110025	.113323	.116643	.119982	.123339	.126714	.130103	.136923	.143789
	-.20	.111913	.115108	.118332	.121582	.124857	.128155	.131474	.134814	.138171	.141545	.144935	.151755	.158621
	-.30	.126744	.129940	.133163	.136414	.139689	.142987	.146306	.149645	.153003	.156377	.159766	.166586	.173453
	-.40	.141576	.144771	.147995	.151245	.154520	.157818	.161138	.164477	.167834	.171208	.174598	.181418	.188284
30	.40	.022283	.025541	.028825	.032134	.035467	.038820	.042191	.045580	.048985	.052403	.055833	.062725	.069651
	.30	.037115	.040372	.043657	.046966	.050298	.053651	.057023	.060412	.063816	.067234	.070665	.077557	.084483
	.20	.051946	.055204	.058468	.061797	.065130	.068483	.071855	.075244	.078648	.082066	.085496	.092388	.099314
	.10	.066778	.070035	.073320	.076629	.079961	.083314	.086686	.090075	.093479	.096898	.100328	.107220	.114146
	0.00	.081610	.084867	.088151	.091461	.094793	.098146	.101518	.104907	.108311	.111729	.115159	.122051	.128977
	-.10	.096441	.099698	.102983	.106292	.109624	.112977	.116349	.119738	.123143	.126561	.129991	.136883	.143809
	-.20	.111273	.114530	.117814	.121124	.124456	.127809	.131181	.134570	.137974	.141392	.144823	.151715	.158641
	-.30	.126104	.129361	.132646	.135955	.139287	.142640	.146012	.149401	.152806	.156224	.159654	.166546	.173472
	-.40	.140936	.144193	.147477	.150787	.154119	.157472	.160844	.164233	.167637	.171055	.174486	.181378	.188304

5.0 YEAR-HOLDING PERIOD
.150 EQUITY YIELD RATE
.750 LOAN RATIO

INTEREST RATE

TERM YEARS	APPR DEP	5.0	5.5	6.0	6.5	7.0	7.5	8.0	8.5	9.0	9.5	10.0	11.0	12.0
10	.40	.024916	.027812	.030734	.033684	.036661	.039664	.042692	.045747	.048826	.051931	.055059	.061387	.067806
	.30	.039748	.042643	.045566	.048516	.051492	.054495	.057524	.060578	.063658	.066762	.069890	.076218	.082637
	.20	.054580	.057475	.060397	.063357	.066324	.069327	.072356	.075410	.078489	.081594	.084722	.091050	.097469
	.10	.069411	.072306	.075229	.078179	.081155	.084158	.087187	.090242	.093321	.096425	.099554	.105881	.112300
	0.00	.084243	.087138	.090061	.093010	.095987	.098990	.102019	.105073	.108153	.111257	.114385	.120713	.127132
	-.10	.099074	.101969	.104892	.107842	.110818	.113821	.116850	.119905	.122984	.126088	.129217	.135544	.141964
	-.20	.113906	.116801	.119724	.122673	.125650	.128653	.131682	.134736	.137816	.140920	.144048	.150376	.156795
	-.30	.128737	.131633	.134555	.137505	.140482	.143485	.146513	.149568	.152647	.155751	.158880	.165207	.171627
	-.40	.143569	.146464	.149387	.152237	.155313	.158316	.161345	.164399	.167479	.170583	.173711	.180039	.186458
15	.40	.021043	.024224	.027434	.030674	.033943	.037240	.040563	.043912	.047286	.050684	.054105	.061014	.068004
	.30	.035875	.039055	.042266	.045506	.048775	.052071	.055394	.058743	.062118	.065516	.068937	.075846	.082836
	.20	.050706	.053887	.057097	.060337	.063606	.066903	.070226	.073575	.076949	.080347	.083768	.090677	.097667
	.10	.065538	.068718	.071929	.075169	.078438	.081734	.085057	.088407	.091781	.095179	.098600	.105509	.112499
	0.00	.080370	.083550	.086760	.090001	.093269	.096566	.099889	.103238	.106612	.110010	.113432	.120340	.127331
	-.10	.095201	.098381	.101592	.104832	.108101	.111397	.114721	.118070	.121444	.124842	.128263	.135172	.142162
	-.20	.110033	.113213	.116424	.119664	.122932	.126229	.129552	.132901	.136275	.139673	.143095	.150003	.156994
	-.30	.124864	.128044	.131255	.134495	.137764	.141060	.144384	.147733	.151107	.154505	.157926	.164835	.171825
	-.40	.139696	.142876	.146087	.149327	.152596	.155892	.159215	.162564	.165938	.169337	.172758	.179666	.186657
20	.40	.019166	.022495	.025855	.029245	.032663	.036107	.039577	.043071	.046587	.050125	.053682	.060852	.068088
	.30	.033997	.037327	.040687	.044077	.047495	.050939	.054409	.057902	.061419	.064956	.068514	.075684	.082920
	.20	.048829	.052158	.055519	.058908	.062326	.065771	.069240	.072734	.076250	.079788	.083345	.090516	.097751
	.10	.063660	.066990	.070350	.073740	.077158	.080602	.084072	.087566	.091082	.094619	.098177	.105347	.112583
	0.00	.078492	.081821	.085182	.088571	.091989	.095434	.098903	.102397	.105913	.109451	.113010	.120179	.127414
	-.10	.093323	.096653	.100013	.103403	.106821	.110265	.113735	.117229	.120745	.124283	.127840	.135010	.142246
	-.20	.108155	.111484	.114845	.118235	.121652	.125097	.128567	.132060	.135577	.139114	.142672	.149842	.157078
	-.30	.122986	.126316	.129676	.133066	.136484	.139928	.143398	.146892	.150408	.153946	.157503	.164673	.171909
	-.40	.137818	.141147	.144508	.147898	.151315	.154760	.158230	.161723	.165240	.168777	.172335	.179505	.186741
25	.40	.018084	.021508	.024902	.028444	.031953	.035487	.039043	.042621	.046218	.049833	.053465	.060772	.068129
	.30	.032915	.036339	.039793	.043276	.046785	.050318	.053875	.057452	.061049	.064665	.068296	.075603	.082960
	.20	.047747	.051171	.054625	.058107	.061616	.065150	.068706	.072284	.075881	.079496	.083128	.090435	.097792
	.10	.062579	.066002	.069456	.072939	.076448	.079981	.083538	.087115	.090713	.094328	.097959	.105267	.112623
	0.00	.077410	.080834	.084288	.087770	.091279	.094813	.098369	.101947	.105544	.109159	.112791	.120098	.127455
	-.10	.092242	.095665	.099119	.102602	.106111	.109644	.113201	.116778	.120376	.123991	.127623	.134930	.142286
	-.20	.107073	.110497	.113951	.117433	.120942	.124476	.128032	.131610	.135207	.138822	.142454	.149761	.157118
	-.30	.121905	.125329	.128783	.132265	.135774	.139307	.142864	.146441	.150039	.153654	.157286	.164593	.171950
	-.40	.136736	.140160	.143614	.147097	.150605	.154139	.157695	.161273	.164870	.168486	.172117	.179424	.186781
30	.40	.017398	.020888	.024407	.027953	.031523	.035116	.038728	.042360	.046007	.049669	.053345	.060729	.068150
	.30	.032230	.035720	.039239	.042785	.046355	.049947	.053560	.057191	.060839	.064501	.068176	.075560	.082981
	.20	.047061	.050551	.054070	.057616	.061186	.064779	.068392	.072023	.075670	.079332	.083008	.090392	.097813
	.10	.061893	.065383	.068902	.072448	.076018	.079610	.083223	.086854	.090502	.094164	.097839	.105224	.112644
	0.00	.076725	.080214	.083733	.087279	.090849	.094442	.098055	.101686	.105333	.108995	.112671	.120055	.127476
	-.10	.091556	.095046	.098565	.102111	.105681	.109273	.112886	.116517	.120165	.123827	.127502	.134887	.142307
	-.20	.106388	.109878	.113397	.116942	.120513	.124105	.127718	.131349	.134996	.138659	.142334	.149718	.157139
	-.30	.121219	.124709	.128228	.131774	.135344	.138937	.142549	.146180	.149828	.153490	.157165	.164550	.171970
	-.40	.136051	.139541	.143060	.146605	.150176	.153768	.157381	.161012	.164659	.168322	.171997	.179381	.186802

5.0 YEAR HOLDING PERIOD
.150 EQUITY YIELD RATE
.800 LOAN RATIO

INTEREST RATE

TERM YEARS	APPR DEP	5.0	5.5	6.0	6.5	7.0	7.5	8.0	8.5	9.0	9.5	10.0	11.0	12.0
10	.40	.020533	.023621	.026738	.029885	.033060	.036263	.039494	.042752	.046037	.049348	.052685	.059434	.066281
	.30	.035364	.038452	.041570	.044716	.047891	.051094	.054325	.057583	.060868	.064179	.067516	.074266	.081113
	.20	.050196	.053284	.056401	.059548	.062723	.065926	.069157	.072415	.075700	.079011	.082348	.089097	.095944
	.10	.065027	.068115	.071233	.074379	.077554	.080758	.083988	.087246	.090531	.093842	.097179	.103929	.110776
	0.00	.079859	.082947	.086065	.089211	.092386	.095589	.098820	.102078	.105363	.108674	.112011	.118760	.125607
	-.10	.094690	.097779	.100896	.104043	.107218	.110421	.113652	.116916	.120194	.123505	.126842	.133592	.140439
	-.20	.109522	.112610	.115728	.118874	.122049	.125252	.128483	.131741	.135026	.138337	.141674	.148423	.155271
	-.30	.124354	.127442	.130559	.133706	.136881	.140084	.143315	.146573	.149857	.153169	.156505	.163255	.170102
	-.40	.139185	.142273	.145391	.148537	.151712	.154915	.158146	.161404	.164689	.168000	.171337	.178087	.184934
15	.40	.016401	.019794	.023218	.026674	.030161	.033677	.037222	.040794	.044393	.048018	.051668	.059037	.066493
	.30	.031233	.034625	.038050	.041506	.044993	.048509	.052054	.055626	.059225	.062850	.066499	.073868	.081325
	.20	.046064	.049457	.052881	.056337	.059824	.063340	.066885	.070458	.074057	.077681	.081331	.088700	.096156
	.10	.060896	.064288	.067713	.071169	.074656	.078172	.081717	.085289	.088888	.092513	.096162	.103531	.110988
	0.00	.075728	.079120	.082544	.086001	.089487	.093003	.096548	.100121	.103720	.107344	.110994	.118363	.125819
	-.10	.090559	.093951	.097376	.100832	.104319	.107835	.111380	.114952	.118551	.122176	.125825	.133194	.140651
	-.20	.105391	.108783	.112208	.115664	.119151	.122667	.126211	.129784	.133383	.137008	.140657	.148026	.155482
	-.30	.120222	.123614	.127039	.130495	.133982	.137498	.141043	.144615	.148214	.151839	.155488	.162858	.170314
	-.40	.135054	.138446	.141871	.145327	.148813	.152330	.155874	.159447	.163046	.166671	.170320	.177689	.185145
20	.40	.014398	.017950	.021534	.025150	.028796	.032470	.036171	.039897	.043648	.047421	.051216	.058864	.066582
	.30	.029230	.032781	.036366	.039981	.043627	.047301	.051002	.054729	.058480	.062253	.066048	.073696	.081414
	.20	.044061	.047613	.051197	.054813	.058459	.062132	.065834	.069561	.073311	.077085	.080879	.088527	.096246
	.10	.058893	.062444	.066029	.069645	.073290	.076964	.080665	.084392	.088143	.091916	.095711	.103359	.111077
	0.00	.073725	.077276	.080860	.084476	.088122	.091796	.095497	.099224	.102974	.106748	.110542	.118191	.125909
	-.10	.088556	.092108	.095692	.099308	.102953	.106628	.110329	.114055	.117806	.121579	.125374	.133016	.140740
	-.20	.103388	.106939	.110523	.114139	.117785	.121459	.125160	.128887	.132637	.136411	.140206	.147854	.155552
	-.30	.118219	.121771	.125355	.128971	.132617	.136291	.139992	.143718	.147469	.151242	.155037	.162685	.170403
	-.40	.133051	.136602	.140187	.143802	.147448	.151122	.154823	.158550	.162301	.166074	.169869	.177517	.185235
25	.40	.013245	.016897	.020581	.024295	.028038	.031807	.035601	.039417	.043254	.047110	.050984	.058778	.066626
	.30	.028076	.031728	.035412	.039127	.042870	.046639	.050433	.054249	.058086	.061942	.065816	.073610	.081457
	.20	.042908	.046560	.050244	.053958	.057701	.061470	.065264	.069080	.072917	.076773	.080647	.088441	.096289
	.10	.057739	.061391	.065075	.068789	.072532	.076301	.080095	.083912	.087749	.091605	.095479	.103273	.111120
	0.00	.072571	.076223	.079907	.083622	.087364	.091134	.094927	.098743	.102580	.106437	.110310	.118105	.125952
	-.10	.087402	.091054	.094739	.098453	.102196	.105965	.109759	.113575	.117412	.121268	.125142	.132936	.140783
	-.20	.102234	.105886	.109570	.113285	.117028	.120797	.124590	.128407	.132244	.136100	.139845	.147768	.155615
	-.30	.117065	.120717	.124402	.128116	.131859	.135628	.139422	.143238	.147075	.150931	.154805	.162599	.170447
	-.40	.131897	.135549	.139233	.142948	.146691	.150460	.154253	.158070	.161907	.165763	.169637	.177431	.185278
30	.40	.012513	.016236	.019989	.023772	.027580	.031412	.035265	.039139	.043029	.046936	.050856	.058733	.066648
	.30	.027345	.031067	.034821	.038603	.042411	.046243	.050097	.053970	.057861	.061767	.065688	.073564	.081480
	.20	.042176	.045899	.049653	.053435	.057243	.061075	.064929	.068802	.072692	.076599	.080519	.088396	.096311
	.10	.057008	.060731	.064484	.068267	.072074	.075906	.079760	.083633	.087524	.091430	.095351	.103227	.111143
	0.00	.071839	.075562	.079316	.083098	.086906	.090738	.094592	.098465	.102355	.106262	.110182	.118059	.125974
	-.10	.086671	.090394	.094147	.097930	.101738	.105570	.109423	.113296	.117187	.121093	.125014	.132890	.140806
	-.20	.101503	.105225	.108979	.112761	.116569	.120401	.124255	.128128	.132019	.135925	.139845	.147722	.155637
	-.30	.116334	.120057	.123810	.127592	.131401	.135233	.139086	.142959	.146850	.150756	.154677	.162553	.170469
	-.40	.131166	.134889	.138642	.142424	.146232	.150064	.153918	.157791	.161682	.165588	.169508	.177385	.185300

166

5.0 YEAR HOLDING PERIOD
.150 EQUITY YIELD RATE
.900 LOAN RATIO

INTEREST RATE

TERM YEARS	APPR DEP	5.0	5.5	6.0	6.5	7.0	7.5	8.0	8.5	9.0	9.5	10.0	11.0	12.0
10	.40	.011765	.015239	.018746	.022286	.025858	.029462	.033096	.036761	.040457	.044182	.047936	.055529	.063232
	.30	.026597	.030071	.033578	.037118	.040690	.044293	.047928	.051593	.055288	.059013	.062767	.070361	.078064
	.20	.041428	.044902	.048410	.051949	.055521	.059125	.062759	.066425	.070120	.073845	.077599	.085142	.092895
	.10	.056260	.059734	.063241	.066781	.070353	.073956	.077591	.081256	.084952	.088677	.092431	.100024	.107727
	0.00	.071091	.074565	.078073	.081612	.085184	.088788	.092422	.096088	.099783	.103508	.107262	.114855	.122558
	-.10	.085923	.089397	.092904	.096444	.100016	.103619	.107254	.110919	.114615	.118340	.122094	.129687	.137390
	-.20	.100754	.104229	.107736	.111276	.114847	.118451	.122086	.125751	.129446	.133171	.136925	.144518	.152221
	-.30	.115586	.119060	.122567	.126107	.129679	.133282	.136917	.140582	.144278	.148003	.151757	.159350	.167053
	-.40	.130417	.133892	.137399	.140939	.144511	.148114	.151749	.155414	.159109	.162834	.166588	.174182	.181885
15	.40	.007117	.010934	.014786	.018674	.022597	.026553	.030541	.034560	.038608	.042686	.046792	.055082	.063470
	.30	.021949	.025765	.029618	.033506	.037428	.041384	.045372	.049391	.053440	.057518	.061623	.069914	.078302
	.20	.036780	.040597	.044449	.048338	.052260	.056216	.060204	.064223	.068272	.072349	.076455	.084745	.093134
	.10	.051612	.055428	.059281	.063169	.067091	.071047	.075035	.079054	.083103	.087181	.091286	.099577	.107965
	0.00	.066443	.070260	.074113	.078001	.081923	.085879	.089867	.093886	.097935	.102012	.106118	.114408	.122797
	-.10	.081275	.085091	.088944	.092832	.096755	.100710	.104698	.108717	.112766	.116844	.120950	.129240	.137628
	-.20	.096107	.099923	.103776	.107664	.111586	.115542	.119530	.123549	.127598	.131676	.135781	.144071	.152460
	-.30	.110938	.114754	.118607	.122495	.126418	.130374	.134361	.138380	.142429	.146507	.150613	.158903	.167291
	-.40	.125770	.129586	.133439	.137327	.141249	.145205	.149193	.153212	.157261	.161339	.165444	.173734	.182123
20	.40	.004864	.008859	.012892	.016959	.021061	.025194	.029358	.033550	.037770	.042015	.046284	.054888	.063571
	.30	.019695	.023691	.027723	.031791	.035892	.040026	.044190	.048382	.052601	.056847	.061116	.069720	.078403
	.20	.034527	.038522	.042555	.046623	.050724	.054857	.059021	.063213	.067433	.071678	.075947	.084551	.093234
	.10	.049359	.053354	.057386	.061454	.065556	.069689	.073853	.078045	.082265	.086510	.090779	.099383	.108066
	0.00	.064190	.068186	.072218	.076286	.080387	.084520	.086684	.092877	.097096	.101341	.105610	.114241	.122897
	-.10	.079022	.083017	.087049	.091117	.095219	.099352	.103516	.107708	.111928	.116173	.120446	.129046	.137729
	-.20	.093853	.097849	.101881	.105949	.110050	.114184	.118347	.122540	.126759	.131004	.135273	.143878	.152560
	-.30	.108685	.112680	.116713	.120780	.124882	.129015	.133179	.137371	.141591	.145836	.150105	.158709	.167392
	-.40	.123516	.127512	.131544	.135612	.139713	.143847	.148010	.152203	.156422	.160667	.164936	.173541	.182224
25	.40	.003566	.007674	.011819	.015998	.020209	.024449	.028717	.033010	.037327	.041665	.046023	.054792	.063620
	.30	.018397	.022506	.026651	.030830	.035040	.039281	.043548	.047842	.052158	.056497	.060855	.069623	.078451
	.20	.033229	.037338	.041482	.045661	.049872	.054112	.058380	.062673	.066990	.071328	.075686	.084455	.093283
	.10	.048061	.052169	.056314	.060493	.064703	.068944	.073212	.077505	.081821	.086160	.090518	.099286	.108114
	0.00	.062892	.067001	.071145	.075324	.079535	.083775	.088043	.092336	.096653	.100991	.105349	.114118	.122946
	-.10	.077724	.081832	.085977	.090156	.094367	.098607	.102875	.107168	.111485	.115823	.120181	.128946	.137777
	-.20	.092555	.096664	.100809	.104987	.109198	.113438	.117706	.121999	.126316	.130654	.135012	.143781	.152609
	-.30	.107387	.111495	.115640	.119819	.124030	.128270	.132538	.136831	.141148	.145486	.149844	.158612	.167441
	-.40	.122218	.126327	.130472	.134651	.138861	.143102	.147369	.151663	.155979	.160317	.164675	.173444	.182272
30	.40	.002743	.006931	.011154	.015409	.019693	.024004	.028339	.032697	.037074	.041468	.045879	.054740	.063645
	.30	.017575	.021763	.025965	.030240	.034525	.038836	.043171	.047528	.051905	.056300	.060710	.069572	.078474
	.20	.032406	.036594	.040817	.045072	.049356	.053667	.058003	.062360	.066737	.071131	.075542	.084403	.093308
	.10	.047238	.051426	.055649	.059903	.064188	.068499	.072834	.077191	.081568	.085963	.090373	.099235	.108139
	0.00	.062069	.066257	.070480	.074735	.079019	.083330	.087666	.092023	.096400	.100795	.105205	.114066	.122971
	-.10	.076901	.081089	.085312	.089567	.093851	.098162	.102497	.106854	.111231	.115626	.120037	.128898	.137802
	-.20	.091733	.095920	.100143	.104398	.108682	.112993	.117329	.121686	.126063	.130458	.134868	.143729	.152634
	-.30	.106564	.110752	.114975	.119230	.123514	.127825	.132160	.136518	.140895	.145289	.149700	.158561	.167466
	-.40	.121396	.125584	.129806	.134061	.138346	.142657	.146992	.151349	.155726	.160121	.164531	.173392	.182297

5.0 YEAR HOLDING PERIOD
.180 EQUITY YIELD RATE
.600 LOAN RATIO

INTEREST RATE

TERM YEARS	APPR DEP	5.0	5.5	6.0	6.5	7.0	7.5	8.0	8.5	9.0	9.5	10.0	11.0	12.0
10	.40	.055726	.058011	.060318	.062647	.064997	.067369	.069761	.072174	.074608	.077061	.079533	.084536	.089613
	.30	.069704	.071989	.074296	.076625	.078975	.081347	.083739	.086152	.088585	.091038	.093511	.098514	.103591
	.20	.083682	.085967	.088274	.090603	.092953	.095324	.097717	.100130	.102563	.105016	.107489	.112492	.117569
	.10	.097660	.099945	.102252	.104580	.106931	.109302	.111695	.114108	.116541	.118994	.121467	.126470	.131546
	0.00	.111638	.113922	.116229	.118558	.120908	.123280	.125672	.128085	.130519	.132972	.135445	.140447	.145524
	-.10	.125615	.127900	.130207	.132536	.134886	.137258	.139650	.142063	.144496	.146950	.149422	.154425	.159502
	-.20	.139593	.141878	.144185	.146514	.148864	.151236	.153628	.156041	.158474	.160927	.163400	.168403	.173480
	-.30	.153571	.155856	.158163	.160491	.162842	.165213	.167606	.170019	.172452	.174905	.177378	.182381	.187458
	-.40	.167549	.169834	.172140	.174469	.176820	.179191	.181584	.183997	.186430	.188883	.191356	.196359	.201435
15	.40	.051688	.054195	.056728	.059282	.061861	.064464	.067088	.069733	.072400	.075086	.077791	.083257	.088791
	.30	.065666	.068172	.070704	.073260	.075839	.078441	.081066	.083711	.086377	.089064	.091769	.097235	.102769
	.20	.079643	.082150	.084682	.087238	.089817	.092419	.095043	.097689	.100355	.103041	.105747	.111212	.116746
	.10	.093621	.096128	.098660	.101215	.103795	.106397	.109021	.111667	.114333	.117019	.119725	.125190	.130724
	0.00	.107599	.110106	.112637	.115193	.117772	.120375	.122999	.125645	.128311	.130997	.133702	.139168	.144702
	-.10	.121577	.124083	.126615	.129171	.131750	.134352	.136977	.139622	.142289	.144975	.147680	.153146	.158680
	-.20	.135555	.138061	.140593	.143149	.145728	.148330	.150954	.153600	.156266	.158953	.161658	.167124	.172657
	-.30	.149532	.152039	.154571	.157126	.159706	.162308	.164932	.167578	.170244	.172930	.175636	.181101	.186635
	-.40	.163510	.166017	.168548	.171104	.173684	.176286	.178910	.181556	.184222	.186908	.189614	.195079	.200613
20	.40	.049730	.052356	.055008	.057684	.060384	.063107	.065851	.068615	.071398	.074200	.077018	.082702	.088443
	.30	.063708	.066334	.068985	.071662	.074362	.077085	.079828	.082593	.085376	.088177	.090996	.096680	.102421
	.20	.077685	.080311	.082963	.085640	.088340	.091062	.093806	.096570	.099354	.102155	.104974	.110658	.116399
	.10	.091663	.094289	.096941	.099618	.102318	.105040	.107784	.110548	.113331	.116133	.118951	.124636	.130377
	0.00	.105641	.108267	.110919	.113595	.116295	.119018	.121762	.124526	.127309	.130111	.132929	.138614	.144354
	-.10	.119619	.122245	.124897	.127573	.130273	.132996	.135740	.138504	.141287	.144088	.146907	.152591	.158332
	-.20	.133597	.136223	.138874	.141551	.144251	.146973	.149717	.152482	.155265	.158066	.160885	.166569	.172310
	-.30	.147574	.150200	.152852	.155529	.158229	.160951	.163695	.166459	.169243	.172044	.174863	.180547	.186288
	-.40	.161552	.164178	.166830	.169506	.172207	.174929	.177673	.180437	.183220	.186022	.188840	.194525	.200266
25	.40	.048602	.051306	.054035	.056789	.059565	.062363	.065180	.068016	.070869	.073737	.076621	.082426	.088275
	.30	.062580	.065283	.068013	.070766	.073543	.076340	.079158	.081994	.084847	.087715	.090598	.096404	.102253
	.20	.076557	.079261	.081991	.084744	.087521	.090318	.093136	.095971	.098824	.101693	.104576	.110381	.116231
	.10	.090535	.093239	.095968	.098722	.101498	.104296	.107113	.109949	.112802	.115671	.118554	.124359	.130209
	0.00	.104513	.107217	.109946	.112700	.115476	.118274	.121091	.123927	.126780	.129649	.132532	.138337	.144187
	-.10	.118491	.121194	.123924	.126677	.129454	.132252	.135069	.137905	.140758	.143626	.146510	.152315	.158164
	-.20	.132469	.135172	.137902	.140655	.143432	.146229	.149047	.151883	.154736	.157604	.160487	.166293	.172142
	-.30	.146446	.149150	.151879	.154633	.157409	.160207	.163025	.165860	.168713	.171582	.174465	.180270	.186120
	-.40	.160424	.163128	.165857	.168611	.171387	.174185	.177002	.179838	.182691	.185560	.188443	.194248	.200098
30	.40	.047887	.050647	.053431	.056239	.059069	.061918	.064785	.067668	.070566	.073478	.076401	.082278	.088189
	.30	.061865	.064624	.067409	.070217	.073047	.075896	.078763	.081646	.084544	.087456	.090379	.096256	.102167
	.20	.075843	.078602	.081387	.084195	.087025	.089874	.092741	.095624	.098522	.101433	.104357	.110234	.116145
	.10	.089820	.092580	.095365	.098173	.101002	.103851	.106719	.109602	.112500	.115411	.118334	.124212	.130123
	0.00	.103798	.106558	.109343	.112151	.114980	.117829	.120696	.123580	.126478	.129389	.132312	.138189	.144100
	-.10	.117776	.120536	.123320	.126128	.128958	.131807	.134674	.137557	.140455	.143367	.146290	.152167	.158078
	-.20	.131754	.134513	.137298	.140106	.142936	.145785	.148652	.151535	.154433	.157345	.160268	.166145	.172056
	-.30	.145732	.148491	.151276	.154084	.156913	.159763	.162630	.165513	.168411	.171322	.174246	.180123	.186034
	-.40	.159709	.162469	.165254	.168062	.170891	.173740	.176607	.179491	.182389	.185300	.188223	.194101	.200011

168

INTEREST RATE

TERM 10 YEARS

APPR DEP	5.0	5.5	6.0	6.5	7.0	7.5	8.0	8.5	9.0	9.5	10.0	11.0	12.0
.40	.048130	.050669	.053232	.055820	.058431	.061066	.063725	.066406	.069109	.071835	.074583	.080141	.085782
.30	.062108	.064647	.067210	.069798	.072409	.075044	.077702	.080383	.083087	.085813	.088560	.094119	.099760
.20	.076086	.078625	.081188	.083775	.086387	.089022	.091680	.094361	.097065	.099791	.102538	.108097	.113738
.10	.090064	.092602	.095166	.097753	.100365	.103000	.105658	.108339	.111043	.113768	.116516	.122075	.127716
0.00	.104041	.106580	.109143	.111731	.114342	.116977	.119636	.122317	.125020	.127746	.130494	.136052	.141593
-.10	.118019	.120558	.123121	.125709	.128320	.130955	.133613	.136295	.138998	.141724	.144472	.150030	.155571
-.20	.131997	.134536	.137099	.139686	.142298	.144933	.147591	.150272	.152976	.155702	.158449	.164008	.169549
-.30	.145975	.148513	.151077	.153664	.156276	.158911	.161569	.164250	.166954	.169680	.172427	.177986	.183527
-.40	.159953	.162491	.165054	.167642	.170253	.172889	.175547	.178228	.180932	.183657	.186405	.191964	.197505

TERM 15 YEARS

APPR DEP	5.0	5.5	6.0	6.5	7.0	7.5	8.0	8.5	9.0	9.5	10.0	11.0	12.0
.40	.043643	.046428	.049241	.052081	.054947	.057838	.060754	.063694	.066656	.069641	.072647	.078720	.084369
.30	.057621	.060406	.063219	.066059	.068925	.071816	.074732	.077671	.080634	.083619	.086625	.092698	.098346
.20	.071598	.074384	.077197	.080036	.082902	.085794	.088710	.091649	.094612	.097596	.100602	.106675	.112324
.10	.085576	.088361	.091174	.094014	.096880	.099772	.102687	.105627	.108590	.111574	.114580	.120653	.126302
0.00	.099554	.102339	.105152	.107992	.110858	.113749	.116665	.119605	.122567	.125552	.128558	.134631	.140280
-.10	.113532	.116317	.119130	.121970	.124836	.127727	.130643	.133583	.136545	.139530	.142536	.148609	.154257
-.20	.127510	.130295	.133108	.135948	.138814	.141705	.144621	.147560	.150523	.153508	.156514	.162586	.168235
-.30	.141487	.144273	.147086	.149925	.152791	.155683	.158598	.161538	.164501	.167485	.170492	.176564	.182213
-.40	.155465	.158250	.161063	.163903	.166769	.169660	.172576	.175516	.178478	.181463	.184469	.190542	.196191

TERM 20 YEARS

APPR DEP	5.0	5.5	6.0	6.5	7.0	7.5	8.0	8.5	9.0	9.5	10.0	11.0	12.0
.40	.041467	.044385	.047332	.050306	.053306	.056331	.059379	.062451	.065543	.068656	.071788	.078104	.084482
.30	.055445	.058363	.061309	.064283	.067283	.070308	.073357	.076428	.079521	.082634	.085766	.092081	.098460
.20	.069423	.072341	.075287	.078261	.081261	.084286	.087335	.090406	.093499	.096612	.099743	.106059	.112438
.10	.083401	.086318	.089265	.092239	.095239	.098264	.101313	.104384	.107477	.110589	.113721	.120037	.126416
0.00	.097378	.100296	.103243	.106217	.109217	.112242	.115291	.118362	.121454	.124567	.127699	.134015	.140394
-.10	.111356	.114274	.117221	.120194	.123195	.126220	.129268	.132340	.135432	.138545	.141677	.147993	.154371
-.20	.125334	.128252	.131198	.134172	.137172	.140197	.143246	.146317	.149410	.152523	.155654	.161970	.168349
-.30	.139312	.142230	.145176	.148150	.151150	.154175	.157224	.160295	.163388	.166500	.169632	.175948	.182327
-.40	.153290	.156207	.159154	.162128	.165128	.168153	.171202	.174273	.177366	.180478	.183610	.189926	.196305

TERM 25 YEARS

APPR DEP	5.0	5.5	6.0	6.5	7.0	7.5	8.0	8.5	9.0	9.5	10.0	11.0	12.0
.40	.040214	.043218	.046251	.049310	.052395	.055504	.058634	.061785	.064955	.068143	.071346	.077796	.084296
.30	.054192	.057196	.060229	.063288	.066373	.069482	.072612	.075763	.078933	.082120	.085324	.091774	.098274
.20	.068170	.071174	.074206	.077266	.080351	.083459	.086590	.089741	.092911	.096098	.099302	.105752	.112252
.10	.082147	.085151	.088184	.091244	.094329	.097437	.100568	.103719	.106889	.110076	.113280	.119730	.126229
0.00	.096125	.099129	.102162	.105222	.108306	.111415	.114545	.117696	.120866	.124054	.127257	.133707	.140207
-.10	.110103	.113107	.116140	.119199	.122284	.125393	.128523	.131674	.134844	.138032	.141235	.147685	.154185
-.20	.124081	.127085	.130117	.133177	.136262	.139370	.142501	.145652	.148822	.152009	.155213	.161663	.168163
-.30	.138059	.141063	.144095	.147155	.150240	.153348	.156479	.159630	.162800	.165987	.169191	.175641	.182141
-.40	.152036	.155040	.158073	.161133	.164218	.167326	.170457	.173608	.176777	.179965	.183168	.189619	.196118

TERM 30 YEARS

APPR DEP	5.0	5.5	6.0	6.5	7.0	7.5	8.0	8.5	9.0	9.5	10.0	11.0	12.0
.40	.039420	.042486	.045580	.048700	.051844	.055010	.058196	.061399	.064619	.067854	.071102	.077632	.084200
.30	.053398	.056464	.059558	.062678	.065822	.068988	.072173	.075377	.078597	.081832	.085080	.091610	.098178
.20	.067375	.070442	.073536	.076656	.079800	.082965	.086151	.089355	.092575	.095810	.099058	.105588	.112156
.10	.081353	.084419	.087514	.090634	.093778	.096943	.100129	.103333	.106553	.109787	.113035	.119566	.126133
0.00	.095331	.098397	.101491	.104611	.107755	.110921	.114107	.117310	.120530	.123765	.127013	.133544	.140111
-.10	.109309	.112375	.115469	.118589	.121733	.124899	.128084	.131288	.134508	.137743	.140991	.147521	.154089
-.20	.123286	.126353	.129447	.132567	.135711	.138877	.142062	.145266	.148486	.151721	.154969	.161499	.168067
-.30	.137264	.140330	.143425	.146545	.149689	.152854	.156040	.159244	.162464	.165699	.168947	.175477	.182045
-.40	.151242	.154308	.157402	.160523	.163666	.166832	.170018	.173221	.176442	.179676	.182924	.189455	.196022

5.0 YEAR HOLDING PERIOD
.180 EQUITY YIELD RATE
.700 LOAN RATIO

INTEREST RATE

TERM YEARS	APPR DEP	5.0	5.5	6.0	6.5	7.0	7.5	8.0	8.5	9.0	9.5	10.0	11.0	12.0
10	.40	.044333	.046998	.049690	.052407	.055149	.057915	.060707	.063522	.066361	.069223	.072108	.077944	.083867
	.30	.058311	.060976	.063668	.066384	.069126	.071893	.074684	.077500	.080338	.083200	.086085	.091922	.097845
	.20	.072268	.074954	.077645	.080362	.083104	.085871	.088662	.091477	.094316	.097178	.100063	.105900	.111823
	.10	.086660	.088932	.091623	.094340	.097082	.099849	.102640	.105455	.108294	.111156	.114041	.119878	.125800
	0.00	.100624	.102909	.105601	.108318	.111060	.113827	.116618	.119433	.122272	.125134	.128019	.133855	.139778
	-.10	.114222	.116887	.119579	.122290	.125038	.127804	.130596	.133411	.136250	.139112	.141996	.147833	.153756
	-.20	.128199	.130865	.133556	.136273	.139015	.141782	.144573	.147389	.150227	.153089	.155974	.161811	.167734
	-.30	.142177	.144843	.147534	.150251	.152993	.155760	.158551	.161366	.164205	.167067	.169952	.175789	.181712
	-.40	.156115	.158821	.161512	.164229	.166971	.169738	.172529	.175344	.178183	.181045	.183930	.189766	.195685
15	.40	.039621	.042546	.045499	.048481	.051490	.054526	.057588	.060674	.063785	.066919	.070075	.076452	.082908
	.30	.053599	.056523	.059477	.062459	.065468	.068504	.071565	.074652	.077763	.080897	.084053	.090429	.096885
	.20	.067577	.070501	.073455	.076436	.079446	.082482	.085543	.088630	.091740	.094874	.098031	.104407	.110863
	.10	.081554	.084479	.087432	.090414	.093423	.096459	.099521	.102608	.105718	.108852	.112008	.118385	.124841
	0.00	.095532	.098457	.101410	.104392	.107401	.110437	.113499	.116585	.119696	.122830	.125986	.132363	.138819
	-.10	.109510	.112434	.115388	.118370	.121379	.124415	.127477	.130563	.133674	.136808	.139964	.146340	.152797
	-.20	.123488	.126412	.129366	.132348	.135357	.138393	.141454	.144541	.147652	.150785	.153942	.160318	.166774
	-.30	.137466	.140390	.143344	.146325	.149335	.152370	.155432	.158519	.161629	.164763	.167920	.174296	.180752
	-.40	.151443	.154368	.157321	.160303	.163312	.166348	.169410	.172496	.175607	.178741	.181897	.188274	.194730
20	.40	.037537	.040400	.043494	.046617	.049767	.052943	.056144	.059369	.062616	.065885	.069173	.075805	.082502
	.30	.051314	.054378	.057472	.060595	.063745	.066921	.070122	.073347	.076594	.079362	.083151	.089782	.096480
	.20	.065292	.068356	.071450	.074572	.077722	.080899	.084100	.087325	.090572	.093840	.097129	.103760	.110458
	.10	.079270	.082334	.085428	.088550	.091700	.094878	.098078	.101302	.104550	.107818	.111106	.117738	.124436
	0.00	.093248	.096311	.099405	.102528	.105678	.108854	.112055	.115280	.118527	.121796	.125084	.131716	.138414
	-.10	.107226	.110289	.113383	.116506	.119656	.122832	.126033	.129258	.132505	.135774	.139062	.145694	.152391
	-.20	.121203	.124267	.127361	.130483	.133634	.136810	.140011	.143236	.146483	.149751	.153040	.159671	.166369
	-.30	.135181	.138245	.141339	.144461	.147611	.150788	.153989	.157214	.160461	.163729	.167017	.173649	.180347
	-.40	.149159	.152223	.155316	.158439	.161589	.164765	.167967	.171191	.174439	.177707	.180995	.187627	.194325
25	.40	.036021	.039175	.042359	.045572	.048811	.052075	.055362	.058670	.061999	.065346	.068709	.075482	.082307
	.30	.049999	.053153	.056337	.059550	.062789	.066053	.069340	.072648	.075977	.079323	.082687	.089460	.096284
	.20	.063976	.067131	.070315	.073527	.076767	.080030	.083317	.086626	.089954	.093301	.096665	.103438	.110262
	.10	.077954	.081108	.084293	.087505	.090744	.094008	.097295	.100604	.103932	.107279	.110643	.117435	.124240
	0.00	.091932	.095086	.098270	.101483	.104722	.107986	.111273	.114582	.117910	.121257	.124620	.131393	.138218
	-.10	.105910	.109064	.112248	.115461	.118700	.121964	.125251	.128559	.131888	.135235	.138598	.145371	.152191
	-.20	.119887	.123042	.126226	.129439	.132678	.135942	.139229	.142537	.145866	.149212	.152576	.159349	.166173
	-.30	.133865	.137019	.140204	.143416	.146655	.149919	.153206	.156515	.159843	.163190	.166554	.173326	.180151
	-.40	.147843	.150997	.154182	.157394	.160633	.163897	.167184	.170493	.173821	.177168	.180532	.187304	.194129
30	.40	.035187	.038406	.041655	.044931	.048232	.051556	.054901	.058265	.061646	.065043	.068453	.075310	.082206
	.30	.049165	.052384	.055633	.058909	.062210	.065534	.068879	.072243	.075624	.079020	.082431	.089288	.096184
	.20	.063142	.066362	.069611	.072887	.076188	.079512	.082857	.086221	.089602	.092998	.096409	.103286	.110161
	.10	.077120	.080340	.083589	.086865	.090166	.093490	.096835	.100198	.103579	.106976	.110386	.117243	.124139
	0.00	.091098	.094317	.097566	.100842	.104143	.107467	.110812	.114176	.117557	.120954	.124364	.131221	.138117
	-.10	.105076	.108295	.111544	.114820	.118121	.121445	.124790	.128153	.131535	.134932	.138342	.145199	.152095
	-.20	.119053	.122273	.125522	.128798	.132099	.135423	.138768	.142132	.145513	.148909	.152320	.159176	.166073
	-.30	.133031	.136251	.139500	.142776	.146077	.149401	.152746	.156110	.159491	.162887	.166298	.173154	.180050
	-.40	.147009	.150229	.153477	.156754	.160055	.163379	.166723	.170087	.173468	.176863	.180275	.187132	.194028

5.0 YEAR HOLDING PERIOD
.180 EQUITY YIELD RATE
.750 LOAN RATIO

INTEREST RATE

TERM YEARS	APPR DEP	5.0	5.5	6.0	6.5	7.0	7.5	8.0	8.5	9.0	9.5	10.0	11.0	12.0
10	.40	.038636	.041492	.044376	.047286	.050224	.053189	.056179	.059196	.062237	.065304	.068395	.074648	.080934
	.30	.052614	.055470	.058354	.061264	.064202	.067167	.070157	.073174	.076215	.079282	.082373	.088626	.094912
	.20	.066592	.069448	.072332	.075242	.078180	.081145	.084135	.087152	.090193	.093260	.096351	.102604	.108890
	.10	.080570	.083426	.086310	.089220	.092158	.095123	.098113	.101130	.104171	.107238	.110329	.116582	.122868
	0.00	.094548	.097404	.100288	.103198	.106136	.109101	.112091	.115108	.118149	.121216	.124307	.130560	.136846
	-.10	.108526	.111382	.114266	.117176	.120114	.123079	.126069	.129086	.132127	.135194	.138285	.144538	.150824
	-.20	.122504	.125360	.128244	.131154	.134092	.137057	.140047	.143064	.146105	.149172	.152263	.158516	.164802
	-.30	.136482	.139338	.142222	.145132	.148070	.151035	.154025	.157042	.160083	.163150	.166241	.172494	.178780
	-.40	.150460	.153316	.156200	.159110	.162048	.165013	.168003	.171020	.174061	.177128	.180219	.186472	.192758
15	.40	.033588	.036721	.039886	.043080	.046304	.049557	.052838	.056145	.059477	.062835	.066217	.073049	.079956
	.30	.047566	.050699	.053864	.057058	.060282	.063535	.066816	.070123	.073455	.076813	.080195	.087027	.093934
	.20	.061544	.064677	.067842	.071036	.074260	.077513	.080794	.084101	.087433	.090791	.094173	.101005	.107912
	.10	.075522	.078655	.081820	.085014	.088238	.091491	.094772	.098079	.101411	.104769	.108151	.114983	.121890
	0.00	.089500	.092633	.095798	.098992	.102216	.105469	.108750	.112057	.115389	.118747	.122129	.128961	.135868
	-.10	.103478	.106611	.109776	.112970	.116194	.119447	.122728	.126035	.129367	.132725	.136107	.142939	.149846
	-.20	.117456	.120589	.123754	.126948	.130172	.133425	.136706	.140013	.143345	.146703	.150085	.156917	.163824
	-.30	.131434	.134567	.137732	.140926	.144150	.147403	.150684	.153991	.157323	.160681	.164063	.170895	.177802
	-.40	.145412	.148545	.151710	.154904	.158128	.161381	.164662	.167969	.171301	.174659	.178041	.184873	.191780
20	.40	.031140	.034423	.037737	.041083	.044458	.047861	.051291	.054746	.058225	.061727	.065250	.072356	.079532
	.30	.045118	.048401	.051715	.055061	.058436	.061839	.065269	.068724	.072203	.075705	.079228	.086334	.093510
	.20	.059096	.062379	.065693	.069039	.072414	.075817	.079247	.082702	.086181	.089683	.093206	.100312	.107488
	.10	.073074	.076357	.079671	.083017	.086392	.089795	.093225	.096680	.100159	.103661	.107184	.114290	.121466
	0.00	.087052	.090335	.093649	.096995	.100370	.103773	.107203	.110658	.114137	.117639	.121162	.128268	.135444
	-.10	.101030	.104313	.107627	.110973	.114348	.117751	.121181	.124636	.128115	.131617	.135140	.142246	.149422
	-.20	.115008	.118291	.121605	.124951	.128326	.131729	.135159	.138614	.142093	.145595	.149118	.156224	.163400
	-.30	.128986	.132269	.135583	.138929	.142304	.145707	.149137	.152592	.156071	.159573	.163096	.170202	.177378
	-.40	.142964	.146247	.149561	.152907	.156282	.159685	.163115	.166570	.170049	.173551	.177074	.184180	.191356
25	.40	.029730	.033110	.036521	.039964	.043434	.046931	.050453	.053998	.057564	.061150	.064754	.072010	.079322
	.30	.043708	.047088	.050499	.053942	.057412	.060909	.064431	.067976	.071542	.075128	.078732	.085988	.093300
	.20	.057686	.061066	.064477	.067920	.071390	.074887	.078409	.081954	.085520	.089106	.092710	.099966	.107278
	.10	.071664	.075044	.078455	.081898	.085368	.088865	.092387	.095932	.099498	.103084	.106688	.113944	.121256
	0.00	.085642	.089022	.092433	.095876	.099346	.102843	.106365	.109910	.113476	.117062	.120666	.127922	.135234
	-.10	.099620	.103000	.106411	.109854	.113324	.116821	.120343	.123888	.127454	.131040	.134644	.141900	.149212
	-.20	.113598	.116978	.120389	.123832	.127302	.130799	.134321	.137866	.141432	.145018	.148622	.155878	.163190
	-.30	.127576	.130956	.134367	.137810	.141280	.144777	.148299	.151844	.155410	.158996	.162600	.169856	.177168
	-.40	.141554	.144934	.148345	.151788	.155258	.158755	.162277	.165822	.169388	.172974	.176578	.183834	.191146
30	.40	.026637	.032286	.035767	.039277	.042814	.046375	.049959	.053563	.057186	.060825	.064479	.071826	.079214
	.30	.040615	.046264	.049745	.053255	.056792	.060353	.063937	.067541	.071164	.074803	.078457	.085804	.093192
	.20	.054593	.060242	.063723	.067233	.070770	.074331	.077915	.081519	.085142	.088781	.092435	.099782	.107170
	.10	.068571	.074220	.077701	.081211	.084748	.088309	.091893	.095497	.099120	.102759	.106413	.113760	.121148
	0.00	.082549	.088198	.091679	.095189	.098726	.102287	.105871	.109475	.113098	.116737	.120391	.127738	.135126
	-.10	.096527	.102176	.105657	.109167	.112704	.116265	.119849	.123453	.127076	.130715	.134369	.141716	.149104
	-.20	.110505	.116154	.119635	.123145	.126682	.130243	.133827	.137431	.141054	.144693	.148347	.155694	.163082
	-.30	.124483	.130132	.133613	.137123	.140660	.144221	.147805	.151409	.155032	.158671	.162325	.169672	.177060
	-.40	.138461	.144110	.147591	.151101	.154638	.158199	.161783	.165387	.169010	.172649	.176303	.183650	.191038

171

5.0 YEAR HOLDING PERIOD
.180 EQUITY YIELD RATE
.800 LOAN RATIO

INTEREST RATE

TERM YEARS	APPR DEP	5.0	5.5	6.0	6.5	7.0	7.5	8.0	8.5	9.0	9.5	10.0	11.0	12.0
10	.40	.032939	.035985	.039061	.042166	.045300	.048462	.051652	.054869	.058114	.061385	.064682	.071352	.078121
	.30	.046941	.049963	.053039	.056144	.059278	.062440	.065630	.068847	.072092	.075362	.078659	.085330	.092099
	.20	.060895	.063941	.067017	.070122	.073256	.076418	.079608	.082825	.086069	.089340	.092637	.099308	.106077
	.10	.074872	.077919	.080995	.084100	.087233	.090395	.093585	.096803	.100047	.103318	.106615	.113285	.120055
	0.00	.088850	.091697	.094972	.098077	.101211	.104373	.107563	.110781	.114025	.117296	.120593	.127263	.134032
	-.10	.102028	.105697	.108950	.112055	.115189	.118351	.121541	.124758	.128003	.131274	.134571	.141241	.148010
	-.20	.116806	.119852	.122928	.126033	.129167	.132329	.135519	.138736	.141980	.145251	.148548	.155219	.161988
	-.30	.130784	.133830	.136906	.140011	.143145	.146307	.149497	.152714	.155958	.159229	.162526	.169197	.175966
	-.40	.144761	.147808	.150884	.153989	.157122	.160284	.163474	.166692	.169936	.173207	.176504	.183174	.189943
15	.40	.027554	.030896	.034272	.037680	.041119	.044588	.048087	.051615	.055170	.058752	.062359	.069646	.077025
	.30	.041532	.044874	.048250	.051658	.055097	.058566	.062065	.065593	.069148	.072729	.076337	.083624	.091002
	.20	.055510	.058852	.062228	.065635	.069074	.072544	.076043	.079570	.083126	.086707	.090314	.097602	.104980
	.10	.069488	.072830	.076205	.079613	.083052	.086522	.090021	.093548	.097103	.100685	.104292	.111580	.118958
	0.00	.083465	.086808	.090183	.093591	.097030	.100500	.103999	.107526	.111081	.114663	.118270	.125558	.132936
	-.10	.097443	.100785	.104161	.107569	.111008	.114477	.117976	.121504	.125059	.128640	.132248	.139535	.146914
	-.20	.111421	.114763	.118139	.121546	.124986	.128455	.131954	.135482	.139037	.142618	.146225	.153513	.160892
	-.30	.125399	.128741	.132116	.135524	.138963	.142433	.145932	.149459	.153014	.156596	.160203	.167491	.174869
	-.40	.139376	.142719	.146094	.149502	.152941	.156411	.159910	.163437	.166992	.170574	.174181	.181468	.188847
20	.40	.024943	.028445	.031981	.035549	.039149	.042779	.046438	.050123	.053835	.057570	.061328	.068907	.076561
	.30	.038921	.042423	.045958	.049527	.053127	.056757	.060416	.064101	.067812	.071548	.075306	.082885	.090539
	.20	.052899	.056400	.059936	.063505	.067105	.070735	.074394	.078079	.081790	.085525	.089283	.096862	.104517
	.10	.066877	.070378	.073914	.077483	.081083	.084713	.088371	.092057	.095768	.099503	.103261	.110840	.118495
	0.00	.080855	.084356	.087892	.091460	.095061	.098691	.102349	.106035	.109746	.113481	.117239	.124818	.132473
	-.10	.094832	.098334	.101870	.105438	.109038	.112668	.116327	.120012	.123723	.127459	.131217	.138796	.146450
	-.20	.108810	.112312	.115847	.119416	.123016	.126646	.130305	.133990	.137701	.141436	.145195	.152774	.160428
	-.30	.122788	.126289	.129825	.133394	.136994	.140624	.144282	.147968	.151679	.155414	.159172	.166751	.174406
	-.40	.136766	.140267	.143803	.147372	.150972	.154602	.158260	.161946	.165657	.169392	.173150	.180729	.188384
25	.40	.023440	.027044	.030684	.034355	.038057	.041787	.045544	.049325	.053129	.056954	.060798	.068538	.076338
	.30	.037417	.041022	.044661	.048333	.052035	.055765	.059522	.063303	.067107	.070931	.074776	.082516	.090315
	.20	.051395	.055000	.058639	.062311	.066013	.069743	.073499	.077280	.081084	.084909	.088753	.096494	.104293
	.10	.065373	.068978	.072617	.076289	.079990	.083721	.087477	.091258	.095062	.098887	.102731	.110471	.118271
	0.00	.079351	.082956	.086595	.090266	.093968	.097698	.101455	.105236	.109040	.112865	.116709	.124449	.132249
	-.10	.093329	.096933	.100573	.104244	.107946	.111676	.115433	.119214	.123018	.126843	.130687	.138427	.146227
	-.20	.107306	.110911	.114550	.118222	.121924	.125654	.129410	.133192	.136996	.140820	.144665	.152404	.160204
	-.30	.121284	.124889	.128528	.132200	.135901	.139632	.143388	.147169	.150973	.154798	.158642	.166383	.174182
	-.40	.135262	.138867	.142506	.146177	.149879	.153609	.157366	.161147	.164951	.168776	.172620	.180360	.188160
30	.40	.022486	.026166	.029879	.033623	.037396	.041195	.045017	.048862	.052726	.056607	.060505	.068341	.076223
	.30	.036464	.040144	.043857	.047601	.051373	.055172	.058995	.062839	.066703	.070585	.074483	.082319	.090200
	.20	.050442	.054121	.057835	.061579	.065351	.069150	.072973	.076817	.080681	.084563	.088461	.096297	.104178
	.10	.064420	.068099	.071812	.075556	.079329	.083128	.086951	.090795	.094659	.098541	.102438	.110275	.118156
	0.00	.078398	.082077	.085790	.089534	.093307	.097106	.100928	.104773	.108637	.112519	.116416	.124252	.132134
	-.10	.092375	.096055	.099768	.103512	.107285	.111083	.114906	.118751	.122615	.126496	.130394	.138230	.146112
	-.20	.106353	.110033	.113746	.117490	.121262	.125061	.128884	.132728	.136592	.140474	.144371	.152208	.160089
	-.30	.120331	.124010	.127723	.131468	.135240	.139039	.142862	.146706	.150570	.154452	.158349	.166186	.174067
	-.40	.134309	.137988	.141701	.145445	.149218	.153016	.156840	.160684	.164548	.168430	.172327	.180164	.188045

INTEREST RATE

TERM YEARS	APPR DEP	5.0	5.5	6.0	6.5	7.0	7.5	8.0	8.5	9.0	9.5	10.0	11.0	12.0
10	.40	.021545	.024972	.028433	.031926	.035451	.039009	.042597	.046217	.049867	.053547	.057256	.064760	.072375
	.30	.035523	.038950	.042411	.045904	.049429	.052987	.056575	.060195	.063845	.067524	.071234	.078738	.086363
	.20	.049501	.052928	.056388	.059882	.063407	.066964	.070553	.074173	.077822	.081502	.085211	.092716	.100331
	.10	.063479	.066906	.070366	.073859	.077385	.080942	.084531	.088150	.091800	.095480	.099189	.106693	.114309
	0.00	.077456	.080884	.084344	.087837	.091363	.094920	.098509	.102128	.105778	.109458	.113167	.120671	.128286
	-.10	.091434	.094861	.098322	.101815	.105340	.108898	.112486	.116106	.119756	.123436	.127145	.134649	.142264
	-.20	.105412	.108839	.112300	.115793	.119318	.122876	.126464	.130084	.133734	.137413	.141102	.148627	.156242
	-.30	.119390	.122817	.126277	.129770	.133296	.136853	.140442	.144061	.147711	.151391	.155100	.162060	.170220
	-.40	.133368	.136795	.140255	.143748	.147274	.150831	.154420	.158039	.161689	.165369	.169078	.176582	.184197
15	.40	.015487	.019247	.023045	.026879	.030748	.034651	.038587	.042556	.046555	.050584	.054643	.062841	.071142
	.30	.029465	.033225	.037023	.040856	.044725	.048629	.052565	.056533	.060533	.064562	.068620	.076819	.085119
	.20	.043443	.047203	.051000	.054834	.058703	.062606	.066543	.070511	.074511	.078540	.082598	.090796	.099097
	.10	.057421	.061181	.064978	.068812	.072681	.076584	.080521	.084489	.088488	.092518	.096576	.104774	.113075
	0.00	.071399	.075159	.078956	.082790	.086659	.090562	.094496	.098467	.102466	.106496	.110554	.118752	.127053
	-.10	.085376	.089136	.092934	.096768	.100637	.104540	.108476	.112445	.116444	.120473	.124531	.132730	.141131
	-.20	.099354	.103114	.106912	.110745	.114614	.118518	.122454	.126422	.130422	.134451	.138509	.146708	.155108
	-.30	.113332	.117092	.120889	.124723	.128592	.132495	.136432	.140400	.144400	.148429	.152467	.160685	.169086
	-.40	.127310	.131070	.134867	.138701	.142570	.146473	.150410	.154378	.158377	.162407	.166465	.174663	.182964
20	.40	.012550	.016489	.020467	.024482	.028532	.032616	.036732	.040878	.045053	.049255	.053483	.062009	.070621
	.30	.026528	.030467	.034445	.038460	.042510	.046594	.050709	.054856	.059031	.063233	.067460	.075987	.084598
	.20	.040506	.044445	.048423	.052437	.056488	.060571	.064687	.068833	.073008	.077210	.081438	.089965	.098576
	.10	.054484	.058423	.062400	.066415	.070465	.074549	.078665	.082811	.086986	.091188	.095416	.103942	.112554
	0.00	.068461	.072400	.076378	.080393	.084443	.088527	.092643	.096789	.100964	.105166	.109394	.117920	.126532
	-.10	.082439	.086378	.090356	.094371	.098421	.102505	.106620	.110767	.114942	.119144	.123372	.131898	.140509
	-.20	.096417	.100356	.104334	.108349	.112399	.116482	.120598	.124744	.128919	.133122	.137349	.145876	.154487
	-.30	.110395	.114334	.118312	.122326	.126377	.130460	.134576	.138722	.142897	.147099	.151327	.159854	.168465
	-.40	.124373	.128312	.132289	.136304	.140354	.144438	.148554	.152700	.156875	.161077	.165305	.173831	.182443
25	.40	.010058	.014914	.019008	.023138	.027303	.031499	.035726	.039979	.044259	.048562	.052887	.061594	.070369
	.30	.024836	.028892	.032986	.037116	.041281	.045477	.049703	.053957	.058237	.062540	.066864	.075572	.084247
	.20	.038814	.042869	.046964	.051094	.055259	.059455	.063681	.067935	.072214	.076517	.080842	.089528	.098224
	.10	.052792	.056847	.060941	.065072	.069236	.073433	.077659	.081913	.086193	.090497	.094802	.103528	.112202
	0.00	.066770	.070825	.074919	.079050	.083214	.087411	.091637	.095891	.100170	.104473	.108798	.117505	.126280
	-.10	.080747	.084803	.088897	.093027	.097192	.101388	.105615	.109868	.114148	.118451	.122775	.131483	.140258
	-.20	.094725	.098781	.102875	.107005	.111170	.115366	.119592	.123846	.128129	.132429	.136753	.145461	.154258
	-.30	.108703	.112758	.116852	.120983	.125147	.129344	.133570	.137824	.142103	.146406	.150731	.159439	.168213
	-.40	.122681	.126736	.130830	.134961	.139125	.143322	.147548	.151802	.156081	.160384	.164709	.173417	.182191
30	.40	.009786	.013926	.018103	.022315	.026559	.030833	.035133	.039458	.043805	.048172	.052557	.061373	.070239
	.30	.023764	.027903	.032080	.036293	.040537	.044811	.049111	.053436	.057783	.062150	.066535	.075351	.084217
	.20	.037742	.041881	.046058	.050270	.054515	.058798	.063089	.067414	.071761	.076128	.080513	.089328	.098195
	.10	.051719	.055859	.060036	.064248	.068492	.072766	.077067	.081392	.085739	.090106	.094490	.103306	.112173
	0.00	.065697	.069837	.074014	.078226	.082470	.086744	.091044	.095369	.099716	.104083	.108468	.117284	.126150
	-.10	.079675	.083814	.087992	.092204	.096448	.100722	.105022	.109347	.113694	.118061	.122446	.131262	.140128
	-.20	.093653	.097792	.101969	.106182	.110426	.114699	.119022	.123325	.127672	.132039	.136424	.145240	.154106
	-.30	.107631	.111770	.115947	.120159	.124404	.128677	.132978	.137303	.141650	.146017	.150402	.159217	.168084
	-.40	.121608	.125748	.129925	.134137	.138381	.142655	.146956	.151281	.155628	.159995	.164379	.173195	.182062

5.0 YEAR HOLDING PERIOD
.200 EQUITY YIELD RATE
.600 LOAN RATIO

INTEREST RATE

TERM YEARS	APPR DEP	5.0	5.5	6.0	6.5	7.0	7.5	8.0	8.5	9.0	9.5	10.0	11.0	12.0
10	.40	.067304	.069509	.071856	.074165	.076496	.078848	.081221	.083615	.086029	.088463	.090917	.095882	.100922
	.30	.080742	.083007	.085294	.087603	.089934	.092286	.094659	.097053	.099467	.101901	.104355	.103320	.114360
	.20	.094180	.096445	.098732	.101041	.103372	.105724	.108097	.110491	.112905	.115339	.117793	.122758	.127798
	.10	.107618	.109883	.112170	.114479	.116810	.119162	.121535	.123929	.126343	.128777	.131231	.136196	.141236
	0.00	.121056	.123321	.125608	.127917	.130248	.132600	.134973	.137367	.139781	.142215	.144669	.149634	.154674
	-.10	.134494	.130759	.139046	.141355	.143688	.146038	.148411	.150805	.153219	.155653	.158107	.163372	.168112
	-.20	.147932	.150197	.152484	.154793	.157124	.159476	.161849	.164243	.166657	.169091	.171545	.176510	.181550
	-.30	.161370	.163635	.165922	.168231	.170562	.172914	.175287	.177681	.180095	.182529	.184983	.189948	.194988
	-.40	.174808	.177073	.179360	.181669	.184000	.186352	.188725	.191119	.193533	.195967	.198421	.203386	.208428
15	.40	.062671	.065154	.067662	.070195	.072752	.075332	.077935	.080559	.083205	.085870	.088556	.093983	.099479
	.30	.076109	.078592	.081100	.083633	.086190	.088770	.091373	.093987	.096642	.099308	.101946	.107421	.112917
	.20	.089547	.092030	.094538	.097071	.099628	.102208	.104811	.107435	.110080	.112746	.115432	.120858	.126355
	.10	.102985	.105468	.107976	.110509	.113066	.115646	.118249	.120873	.123518	.126184	.128870	.134296	.139793
	0.00	.116423	.118906	.121414	.123947	.126504	.129084	.131687	.134311	.136956	.139622	.142308	.147734	.153231
	-.10	.129861	.132344	.134852	.137385	.139942	.142522	.145125	.147749	.150394	.153060	.155746	.161172	.166669
	-.20	.143299	.145782	.148290	.150823	.153380	.155960	.158563	.161187	.163832	.166498	.169184	.174610	.180107
	-.30	.156737	.159220	.161728	.164261	.166818	.169398	.172001	.174625	.177270	.179936	.182621	.188048	.193545
	-.40	.170175	.172658	.175166	.177699	.180256	.182836	.185439	.188063	.190708	.193374	.196059	.201486	.206983
20	.40	.060425	.063027	.065656	.068310	.070989	.073690	.076414	.079159	.081923	.084706	.087505	.093159	.098870
	.30	.073863	.076465	.079094	.081748	.084427	.087128	.089852	.092597	.095361	.098144	.100946	.106597	.112308
	.20	.087301	.089903	.092532	.095186	.097865	.100566	.103290	.106035	.108799	.111582	.114384	.120035	.125746
	.10	.100739	.103341	.105970	.108624	.111303	.114004	.116728	.119473	.122237	.125020	.127822	.133473	.139184
	0.00	.114177	.116779	.119408	.122062	.124741	.127442	.130166	.132911	.135675	.138458	.141259	.146911	.152622
	-.10	.127615	.130217	.132846	.135500	.138179	.140880	.143604	.146348	.149113	.151896	.154697	.160349	.166060
	-.20	.141053	.143655	.146284	.148938	.151616	.154318	.157042	.159786	.162551	.165334	.168135	.173787	.179498
	-.30	.154491	.157093	.159722	.162376	.165054	.167756	.170480	.173224	.175989	.178772	.181573	.187225	.192936
	-.40	.167929	.170531	.173160	.175814	.178492	.181194	.183918	.186662	.189427	.192210	.195011	.200663	.206374
25	.40	.059131	.061812	.064520	.067254	.070010	.072790	.075590	.078409	.081246	.084100	.086969	.092748	.098576
	.30	.072569	.075250	.077958	.080691	.083448	.086228	.089028	.091847	.094684	.097538	.100407	.106186	.112013
	.20	.086007	.088688	.091396	.094129	.096886	.099666	.102465	.105285	.108122	.110976	.113845	.119624	.125451
	.10	.099445	.102126	.104834	.107567	.110324	.113104	.115903	.118723	.121560	.124414	.127283	.133062	.138889
	0.00	.112883	.115564	.118272	.121005	.123762	.126541	.129341	.132161	.134998	.137852	.140721	.146500	.152327
	-.10	.126321	.129002	.131710	.134443	.137200	.139979	.142779	.145599	.148436	.151290	.154159	.159938	.165765
	-.20	.139759	.142440	.145148	.147881	.150638	.153417	.156217	.159037	.161874	.164728	.167597	.173376	.179203
	-.30	.153197	.155878	.158586	.161319	.164076	.166855	.169655	.172475	.175312	.178166	.181035	.186814	.192641
	-.40	.166635	.169316	.172024	.174757	.177514	.180293	.183093	.185913	.188750	.191604	.194473	.200252	.206079
30	.40	.058311	.061050	.063816	.066650	.069418	.072252	.075104	.077974	.080859	.083759	.086671	.092529	.098424
	.30	.071749	.074488	.077254	.080044	.082856	.085690	.088542	.091412	.094297	.097197	.100109	.105967	.111862
	.20	.085187	.087926	.090692	.093482	.096294	.099128	.101980	.104850	.107735	.110635	.113547	.119405	.125300
	.10	.098625	.101364	.104130	.106920	.109732	.112566	.115418	.118288	.121173	.124073	.126985	.132843	.138738
	0.00	.112063	.114802	.117568	.120358	.123170	.126004	.128856	.131726	.134611	.137511	.140423	.146281	.152176
	-.10	.125501	.128240	.131005	.133796	.136608	.139442	.142294	.145164	.148049	.150949	.153861	.159719	.165614
	-.20	.138939	.141678	.144443	.147234	.150046	.152880	.155732	.158602	.161487	.164387	.167299	.173157	.179052
	-.30	.152377	.155118	.157883	.160671	.163484	.166318	.169170	.172040	.174925	.177825	.180737	.186595	.192490
	-.40	.165815		.171319					.176578		.181263		.200073	

174

5.0 YEAR HOLDING PERIOD
.200 EQUITY YIELD RATE
.667 LOAN RATIO

INTEREST RATE

TERM YEARS	APPR DEP	5.0	5.5	6.0	6.5	7.0	7.5	8.0	8.5	9.0	9.5	10.0	11.0	12.0
10	.40	.058532	.061049	.063590	.066156	.068746	.071359	.073996	.076655	.079338	.082042	.084769	.090286	.095886
	.30	.071970	.074487	.077028	.079594	.082184	.084797	.087434	.090093	.092776	.095480	.098207	.103724	.109324
	.20	.085408	.087925	.090466	.093032	.095622	.098235	.100872	.103531	.106214	.108918	.111645	.117162	.122762
	.10	.098846	.101363	.103904	.106470	.109060	.111673	.114310	.116969	.119652	.122356	.125083	.130600	.136200
	0.00	.112284	.114801	.117342	.119908	.122497	.125111	.127748	.130407	.133090	.135794	.138521	.144038	.149608
	-.10	.125722	.128239	.130780	.133346	.135935	.138549	.141186	.143845	.146528	.149232	.151959	.157476	.163076
	-.20	.139160	.141677	.144218	.146784	.149373	.151987	.154624	.157283	.159966	.162670	.165397	.170914	.176524
	-.30	.152598	.155115	.157656	.160222	.162811	.165425	.168062	.170721	.173404	.176108	.178835	.184352	.189952
	-.40	.166036	.168553	.171094	.173660	.176249	.178863	.181500	.184159	.186842	.189546	.192273	.197790	.203390
15	.40	.053384	.056143	.058930	.061745	.064586	.067452	.070344	.073260	.076199	.079161	.082145	.088175	.094283
	.30	.066822	.069581	.072368	.075183	.078024	.080890	.083782	.086698	.089637	.092599	.095583	.101613	.107721
	.20	.080260	.083019	.085806	.088621	.091462	.094328	.097220	.100136	.103075	.106037	.109021	.115051	.121159
	.10	.093698	.096457	.099244	.102059	.104900	.107766	.110658	.113574	.116513	.119475	.122459	.128489	.134597
	0.00	.107136	.109895	.112682	.115497	.118337	.121204	.124096	.127012	.129951	.132913	.135897	.141927	.148035
	-.10	.120574	.123333	.126120	.128934	.131775	.134642	.137534	.140450	.143389	.146351	.149335	.155365	.161473
	-.20	.134012	.136771	.139558	.142372	.145213	.148080	.150972	.153888	.156827	.159789	.162773	.168803	.174911
	-.30	.147450	.150209	.152996	.155810	.158651	.161518	.164410	.167326	.170265	.173227	.176211	.182241	.188348
	-.40	.160888	.163647	.166434	.169248	.172089	.174956	.177848	.180764	.183703	.186665	.189649	.195679	.201786
20	.40	.050889	.053780	.056701	.059650	.062626	.065628	.068654	.071704	.074776	.077868	.080981	.087260	.093605
	.30	.064327	.067218	.070139	.073088	.076064	.079066	.082092	.085142	.088214	.091306	.094419	.100698	.107043
	.20	.077765	.080656	.083577	.086526	.089502	.092504	.095530	.098580	.101651	.104744	.107856	.114136	.120481
	.10	.091202	.094094	.097015	.099964	.102940	.105942	.108968	.112018	.115089	.118182	.121294	.127574	.133919
	0.00	.104646	.107532	.110453	.113402	.116378	.119380	.122406	.125456	.128527	.131620	.134732	.141012	.147357
	-.10	.118078	.120970	.123891	.126840	.129816	.132818	.135844	.138894	.141965	.145058	.148170	.154450	.160795
	-.20	.131516	.134408	.137329	.140278	.143254	.146256	.149282	.152332	.155403	.158496	.161608	.167888	.174233
	-.30	.144954	.147846	.150767	.153716	.156692	.159694	.162720	.165770	.168841	.171934	.175046	.181326	.187671
	-.40	.158392	.161284	.164205	.167154	.170130	.173132	.176158	.179208	.182279	.185372	.188484	.194764	.201109
25	.40	.049451	.052433	.055439	.058476	.061539	.064627	.067738	.070871	.074023	.077194	.080382	.086804	.093278
	.30	.062889	.065868	.068877	.071914	.074977	.078065	.081176	.084309	.087461	.090632	.093820	.100242	.106716
	.20	.076327	.079306	.082315	.085352	.088415	.091503	.094614	.097747	.100899	.104070	.107258	.113680	.120154
	.10	.089765	.092744	.095753	.098790	.101853	.104941	.108052	.111185	.114337	.117508	.120696	.127118	.133592
	0.00	.103203	.106182	.109191	.112228	.115291	.118379	.121490	.124623	.127775	.130946	.134134	.140556	.147030
	-.10	.116641	.119620	.122629	.125666	.128729	.131817	.134928	.138061	.141213	.144384	.147572	.153994	.160458
	-.20	.130079	.133058	.136067	.139104	.142167	.145255	.148366	.151499	.154651	.157822	.161010	.167432	.173906
	-.30	.143517	.146496	.149505	.152542	.155605	.158693	.161804	.164936	.168089	.171260	.174448	.180870	.187344
	-.40	.156955	.159934	.162943	.165980	.169043	.172131	.175242	.178374	.181527	.184698	.187886	.194308	.200782
30	.40	.048540	.051583	.054656	.057756	.060881	.064029	.067199	.070387	.073593	.076815	.080051	.086560	.093110
	.30	.061978	.065021	.068094	.071194	.074319	.077467	.080637	.083825	.087031	.090253	.093489	.099998	.106548
	.20	.075416	.078459	.081532	.084632	.087757	.090905	.094075	.097263	.100469	.103691	.106927	.113436	.119986
	.10	.088854	.091897	.094970	.098070	.101195	.104343	.107513	.110701	.113907	.117129	.120365	.126874	.133424
	0.00	.102292	.105335	.108408	.111508	.114633	.117781	.120951	.124139	.127345	.130567	.133803	.140312	.146862
	-.10	.115730	.118773	.121846	.124946	.128071	.131219	.134389	.137577	.140783	.144005	.147241	.153750	.160300
	-.20	.129167	.132211	.135284	.138384	.141509	.144657	.147827	.151015	.154221	.157443	.160679	.167188	.173738
	-.30	.142605	.145649	.148722	.151822	.154947	.158095	.161265	.164453	.167659	.170881	.174117	.180626	.187176
	-.40	.156043	.159087	.162160	.165260	.168385	.171533	.174703	.177891	.181097	.184319	.187555	.194064	.200614

175

5.0 YEAR HOLDING PERIOD
.200 EQUITY YIELD RATE
.700 LOAN RATIO

INTEREST RATE

TERM YEARS	APPR DEP	5.0	5.5	6.0	6.5	7.0	7.5	8.0	8.5	9.0	9.5	10.0	11.0	12.0
10	.40	.054147	.056789	.059458	.062152	.064871	.067615	.070384	.073176	.075993	.078832	.081695	.087488	.093368
	.30	.067585	.070227	.072896	.075590	.078309	.081053	.083822	.086614	.089431	.092270	.095133	.100926	.106806
	.20	.081023	.083665	.086334	.089028	.091747	.094491	.097259	.100052	.102869	.105708	.108571	.114364	.120244
	.10	.094461	.097103	.099772	.102466	.105185	.107929	.110697	.113490	.116307	.119146	.122009	.127802	.133682
	0.00	.107899	.110541	.113210	.115904	.118623	.121367	.124135	.126928	.129745	.132534	.135447	.141240	.147120
	-.10	.121337	.123979	.126648	.129342	.132061	.134805	.137573	.140366	.143183	.146022	.148885	.154678	.160558
	-.20	.134775	.137417	.140086	.142780	.145499	.148243	.151011	.153804	.156621	.159460	.162323	.168116	.173996
	-.30	.148213	.150855	.153524	.156218	.158937	.161681	.164449	.167242	.170058	.172898	.175761	.181554	.187434
	-.40	.161651	.164293	.166962	.169655	.172375	.175119	.177887	.180680	.183496	.186336	.189199	.194992	.200872
15	.40	.048742	.051639	.054565	.057520	.060503	.063513	.066549	.069611	.072697	.075807	.078940	.085272	.091685
	.30	.062180	.065076	.068003	.070958	.073941	.076951	.079987	.083049	.086135	.089245	.092378	.098710	.105123
	.20	.075618	.078514	.081441	.084396	.087379	.090389	.093425	.096487	.099573	.102683	.105816	.112148	.118561
	.10	.089056	.091952	.094879	.097834	.100817	.103827	.106863	.109925	.113011	.116121	.119254	.125586	.131999
	0.00	.102494	.105390	.108317	.111272	.114255	.117265	.120301	.123363	.126449	.129559	.132692	.139024	.145437
	-.10	.115932	.118828	.121755	.124710	.127693	.130703	.133739	.136801	.139887	.142997	.146130	.152461	.158875
	-.20	.129370	.132266	.135193	.138148	.141131	.144141	.147177	.150239	.153325	.156435	.159568	.165899	.172313
	-.30	.142808	.145704	.148631	.151586	.154569	.157579	.160615	.163677	.166763	.169873	.173006	.179337	.185750
	-.40	.156245	.159142	.162069	.165024	.168007	.171017	.174053	.177115	.180201	.183311	.186444	.192775	.199188
20	.40	.046121	.049157	.052224	.055321	.058445	.061597	.064775	.067977	.071202	.074450	.077718	.084311	.090974
	.30	.059559	.062595	.065662	.068759	.071883	.075035	.078213	.081415	.084640	.087888	.091155	.097749	.104412
	.20	.072997	.076033	.079100	.082196	.085321	.088473	.091651	.094853	.098078	.101325	.104593	.111187	.117850
	.10	.086435	.089471	.092538	.095634	.098759	.101911	.105089	.108291	.111516	.114763	.118031	.124625	.131288
	0.00	.099873	.102909	.105976	.109072	.112197	.115349	.118527	.121729	.124954	.128201	.131469	.138063	.144725
	-.10	.113311	.116347	.119414	.122510	.125635	.128787	.131965	.135167	.138392	.141639	.144907	.151501	.158163
	-.20	.126749	.129785	.132852	.135948	.139073	.142225	.145403	.148605	.151830	.155077	.158345	.164939	.171601
	-.30	.140187	.143223	.146290	.149386	.152511	.155663	.158841	.162043	.165268	.168515	.171783	.178377	.185039
	-.40	.153625	.156661	.159728	.162824	.165949	.169101	.172279	.175481	.178706	.181953	.185221	.191815	.198477
25	.40	.044612	.047740	.050899	.054088	.057304	.060547	.063813	.067102	.070412	.073742	.077089	.083832	.090630
	.30	.058050	.061178	.064337	.067526	.070742	.073985	.077251	.080540	.083850	.087180	.090527	.097270	.104068
	.20	.071487	.074616	.077775	.080964	.084180	.087422	.090689	.093978	.097288	.100618	.103965	.110708	.117506
	.10	.084925	.088054	.091213	.094402	.097618	.100860	.104127	.107416	.110726	.114056	.117403	.124146	.130944
	0.00	.098363	.101492	.104651	.107840	.111056	.114298	.117565	.120854	.124164	.127494	.130841	.137584	.144382
	-.10	.111801	.114929	.118089	.111278	.114494	.127736	.131003	.134292	.137602	.140932	.144279	.151022	.157820
	-.20	.125239	.128367	.131527	.134716	.137932	.141174	.144441	.147730	.151040	.154370	.157717	.164450	.171258
	-.30	.138677	.141805	.144965	.148154	.151370	.154612	.157879	.161168	.164478	.167808	.171155	.177898	.184696
	-.40	.152115	.155243	.158403	.161592	.164808	.168050	.171317	.174606	.177916	.181245	.184593	.191336	.198134
30	.40	.043655	.046850	.050077	.053332	.056613	.059919	.063247	.066595	.069961	.073344	.076742	.083576	.090453
	.30	.057093	.060288	.063515	.066770	.070051	.073357	.076685	.080033	.083399	.086782	.090180	.097014	.103891
	.20	.070531	.073726	.076953	.080208	.083489	.086795	.090123	.093471	.096837	.100220	.103618	.110452	.117329
	.10	.083969	.087164	.090391	.093646	.096927	.100233	.103561	.106909	.110275	.113658	.117056	.123890	.130767
	0.00	.097407	.100602	.103829	.107084	.110365	.113671	.116999	.120347	.123713	.127096	.130494	.137328	.144205
	-.10	.110845	.114040	.117267	.120522	.123803	.127109	.130437	.133785	.137151	.140534	.143932	.150766	.157643
	-.20	.124283	.127478	.130705	.133960	.137241	.140547	.143875	.147223	.150589	.153972	.157370	.164204	.171081
	-.30	.137721	.140916	.144143	.147398	.150679	.153985	.157313	.160661	.164027	.167410	.170808	.177642	.184519
	-.40	.151159	.154354	.157581	.160826	.164117	.167423	.170808	.174098	.177465	.180848	.184246	.191080	.197957

.200 EQUITY YIELD RATE
.750 LOAN RATIO

INTEREST RATE

TERM YEARS	APPR DEP	5.0	5.5	6.0	6.5	7.0	7.5	8.0	8.5	9.0	9.5	10.0	11.0	12.0
10	.40	.047568	.050399	.053258	.056145	.059058	.061998	.064965	.067957	.070974	.074017	.077084	.083291	.089591
	.30	.061006	.063837	.066696	.069583	.072496	.075436	.078403	.081395	.084412	.087455	.090522	.096729	.103329
	.20	.074444	.077275	.080134	.083021	.085934	.088874	.091841	.094833	.097850	.100893	.103960	.110167	.116467
	.10	.087882	.090713	.093572	.096459	.099372	.102312	.105279	.108271	.111288	.114331	.117398	.123603	.129905
	0.00	.101320	.104151	.107010	.109897	.112810	.115750	.118717	.121709	.124726	.127769	.130836	.137043	.143343
	-.10	.114758	.117589	.120448	.123335	.126248	.129188	.132154	.135147	.138164	.141207	.144274	.150481	.156781
	-.20	.128196	.131027	.133886	.136773	.139686	.142626	.145592	.148585	.151602	.154645	.157712	.163919	.170219
	-.30	.141634	.144465	.147324	.150211	.153124	.156064	.159030	.162023	.165040	.168083	.171150	.177357	.183657
	-.40	.155072	.157903	.160762	.163649	.166562	.169502	.172468	.175461	.178478	.181521	.184588	.190795	.197095
15	.40	.041777	.044881	.048016	.051182	.054378	.057603	.060856	.064137	.067444	.070776	.074133	.080916	.087787
	.30	.055215	.058319	.061454	.064620	.067816	.071041	.074294	.077575	.080882	.084214	.087571	.094354	.101225
	.20	.068653	.071757	.074892	.078058	.081254	.084479	.087732	.091013	.094320	.097652	.101009	.107792	.114663
	.10	.082091	.085195	.088330	.091496	.094692	.097917	.101170	.104451	.107758	.111090	.114446	.121230	.128101
	0.00	.095529	.098633	.101768	.104934	.108130	.111355	.114608	.117889	.121195	.124528	.127884	.134668	.141539
	-.10	.108967	.112071	.115206	.118372	.121568	.124793	.128046	.131327	.134633	.137966	.141322	.148106	.154977
	-.20	.122405	.125509	.128644	.131810	.135006	.138231	.141484	.144765	.148071	.151404	.154760	.161544	.168415
	-.30	.135843	.138946	.142082	.145248	.148444	.151669	.154922	.158203	.161509	.164842	.168198	.174982	.181853
	-.40	.149281	.152384	.155520	.158686	.161882	.165107	.168360	.171641	.174947	.178280	.181636	.188420	.195291
20	.40	.038969	.042222	.045508	.048826	.052174	.055551	.058955	.062386	.065842	.069321	.072822	.079887	.087025
	.30	.052407	.055660	.058946	.062264	.065612	.068989	.072393	.075824	.079280	.082759	.086260	.093325	.100463
	.20	.065845	.069098	.072384	.075702	.079050	.082427	.085831	.089262	.092718	.096197	.099698	.106763	.113901
	.10	.079283	.082536	.085822	.089140	.092488	.095865	.099269	.102700	.106156	.109635	.113136	.120201	.127339
	0.00	.092721	.095974	.099260	.102578	.105926	.109303	.112707	.116138	.119594	.123073	.126574	.133639	.140777
	-.10	.106159	.109412	.112698	.116016	.119364	.122741	.126145	.129576	.133032	.136511	.140012	.147077	.154215
	-.20	.119597	.122850	.126136	.129454	.132802	.136179	.139583	.143014	.146470	.149949	.153453	.160515	.167653
	-.30	.133035	.136288	.139574	.142892	.146240	.149617	.153021	.156452	.159908	.163387	.166888	.173953	.181091
	-.40	.146473	.149726	.153012	.156329	.159678	.163055	.166459	.169890	.173346	.176825	.180326	.187391	.194529
25	.40	.037352	.040703	.044088	.047505	.050951	.054425	.057925	.061449	.064995	.068563	.072149	.079374	.086657
	.30	.050790	.054141	.057526	.060943	.064389	.067863	.071363	.074887	.078433	.082001	.085587	.092812	.100095
	.20	.064228	.067579	.070964	.074381	.077827	.081301	.084801	.088325	.091871	.095439	.099025	.106250	.113533
	.10	.077666	.081017	.084402	.087819	.091265	.094739	.098239	.101763	.105309	.108877	.112463	.119687	.126571
	0.00	.091104	.094455	.097840	.101257	.104703	.108177	.111677	.115201	.118747	.122315	.125901	.133125	.140409
	-.10	.104542	.107893	.111278	.114695	.118141	.121615	.125115	.128639	.132185	.135753	.139339	.146563	.153847
	-.20	.117980	.121331	.124716	.128133	.131579	.135053	.138553	.142077	.145623	.149191	.152777	.160001	.167285
	-.30	.131418	.134769	.138154	.141571	.145017	.148491	.151991	.155515	.159061	.162628	.166215	.173439	.180723
	-.40	.144856	.148207	.151592	.155009	.158455	.161929	.165429	.168953	.172499	.176066	.179653	.186877	.194161
30	.40	.036327	.039751	.043208	.046695	.050211	.053753	.057318	.060905	.064512	.068136	.071777	.079100	.086468
	.30	.049765	.053189	.056645	.060133	.063649	.067191	.070756	.074343	.077950	.081574	.085215	.092538	.099906
	.20	.063203	.066627	.070083	.073571	.077087	.080629	.084194	.087781	.091388	.095012	.098653	.105976	.113344
	.10	.076641	.080064	.083521	.087009	.090525	.094067	.097632	.101219	.104826	.108450	.112091	.119414	.126782
	0.00	.090079	.093502	.096959	.100447	.103963	.107505	.111070	.114657	.118264	.121888	.125529	.132851	.140220
	-.10	.103517	.106940	.110397	.113885	.117401	.120942	.124508	.128095	.131702	.135326	.138967	.146289	.153658
	-.20	.116954	.120378	.123835	.127323	.130839	.134380	.137946	.141533	.145140	.148764	.152405	.159727	.167096
	-.30	.130392	.133816	.137273	.140761	.144277	.147818	.151384	.154971	.158578	.162202	.165843	.173165	.180534
	-.40	.143830	.147254	.150711	.154199	.157715	.161256	.164822	.168409	.172016	.175640	.179281	.186603	.193972

5.0 YEAR HOLDING PERIOD
.200 EQUITY YIELD RATE
.800 LOAN RATIO

INTEREST RATE

TERM YEARS	APPR DEP	5.0	5.5	6.0	6.5	7.0	7.5	8.0	8.5	9.0	9.5	10.0	11.0	12.0
10	.40	.040990	.044010	.047059	.050038	.053246	.056382	.059546	.062737	.065956	.069202	.072473	.079094	.085814
	.30	.054428	.057448	.060497	.063570	.066684	.069820	.072984	.076175	.079394	.082640	.085911	.092532	.099252
	.20	.067866	.070886	.073935	.077014	.080122	.083258	.086422	.089613	.092832	.096078	.099349	.105970	.112690
	.10	.081304	.084323	.087373	.090452	.093559	.096696	.099860	.103051	.106270	.109516	.112787	.119408	.126128
	0.00	.094741	.097761	.100811	.103890	.106997	.110134	.113298	.116489	.119708	.122954	.126225	.132846	.139566
	-.10	.108179	.111199	.114249	.117328	.120435	.123572	.126736	.129927	.133146	.136392	.139663	.146284	.153003
	-.20	.121617	.124637	.127687	.130766	.133873	.137009	.140174	.143365	.146584	.149830	.153101	.159722	.166441
	-.30	.135055	.138075	.141125	.144204	.147311	.150447	.153612	.156803	.160022	.163267	.166539	.173160	.179879
	-.40	.148493	.151513	.154563	.157642	.160749	.163885	.167049	.170241	.173460	.176705	.179977	.186598	.193317
15	.40	.034612	.038123	.041467	.044844	.048254	.051694	.055164	.058663	.062190	.065744	.069325	.076561	.083890
	.30	.048250	.051561	.054905	.058282	.061692	.065132	.068602	.072101	.075628	.079182	.082763	.089999	.097328
	.20	.061888	.064999	.068343	.071720	.075129	.078570	.082040	.085539	.089066	.092620	.096201	.103437	.110766
	.10	.075126	.078437	.081781	.085158	.088567	.092008	.095478	.098977	.102504	.106058	.109639	.116875	.124204
	0.00	.088564	.091875	.095219	.098596	.102008	.105445	.108916	.112415	.115942	.119496	.123077	.130313	.137642
	-.10	.102002	.105313	.108657	.112034	.115443	.118883	.122354	.125853	.129380	.132934	.136515	.143751	.151080
	-.20	.115440	.118751	.122095	.125472	.128881	.132321	.135791	.139291	.142818	.146372	.149953	.157189	.164518
	-.30	.128878	.132189	.135533	.138910	.142319	.145759	.149229	.152729	.156256	.159810	.163391	.170626	.177956
	-.40	.142316	.145627	.148971	.152348	.155757	.159197	.162667	.166167	.169694	.173248	.176829	.184064	.191394
20	.40	.031817	.035287	.038792	.042351	.045902	.049504	.053136	.056795	.060481	.064193	.067927	.075463	.083077
	.30	.045255	.048725	.052230	.055769	.059340	.062942	.066574	.070233	.073919	.077631	.081365	.088901	.096515
	.20	.058693	.062163	.065668	.069207	.072778	.076380	.080012	.083671	.087357	.091069	.094803	.102339	.109953
	.10	.072131	.075601	.079106	.082645	.086216	.089818	.093450	.097109	.100795	.104507	.108241	.115777	.123391
	0.00	.085569	.089039	.092544	.096083	.099654	.103256	.106888	.110547	.114233	.117944	.121679	.129215	.136829
	-.10	.099007	.102477	.105982	.109521	.113092	.116694	.120326	.123985	.127671	.131382	.135117	.142653	.150267
	-.20	.112445	.115915	.119420	.122959	.126530	.130132	.133764	.137423	.141109	.144820	.148555	.156091	.163705
	-.30	.125883	.129353	.132858	.136397	.139968	.143570	.147202	.150861	.154547	.158258	.161993	.169529	.177143
	-.40	.139321	.142791	.146296	.149835	.153406	.157008	.160640	.164299	.167985	.171696	.175431	.182967	.190581
25	.40	.030092	.033667	.037278	.040922	.044598	.048303	.052037	.055796	.059579	.063384	.067209	.074915	.082685
	.30	.043530	.047105	.050716	.054360	.058036	.061741	.065475	.069234	.073017	.076822	.080647	.088353	.096123
	.20	.056968	.060543	.064154	.067798	.071474	.075179	.078913	.082672	.086455	.090260	.094085	.101791	.109561
	.10	.070406	.073981	.077592	.081236	.084912	.088617	.092351	.096110	.099893	.103698	.107523	.115229	.122999
	0.00	.083844	.087419	.091030	.094674	.098350	.102055	.105789	.109548	.113330	.117136	.120961	.128667	.136437
	-.10	.097282	.100857	.104468	.108112	.111788	.115493	.119227	.122986	.126768	.130574	.134399	.142105	.149875
	-.20	.110720	.114295	.117905	.121550	.125226	.128931	.132664	.136423	.140206	.144011	.147837	.155543	.163312
	-.30	.124158	.127733	.131343	.134988	.138664	.142369	.146102	.149861	.153644	.157449	.161275	.168981	.176750
	-.40	.137596	.141171	.144781	.148426	.152102	.155807	.159540	.163299	.167082	.170887	.174713	.182419	.190188
30	.40	.028999	.032651	.036338	.040058	.043808	.047586	.051389	.055216	.059063	.062929	.066812	.074623	.082483
	.30	.042437	.046089	.049776	.053496	.057246	.061024	.064827	.068654	.072501	.076367	.080250	.088061	.095921
	.20	.055875	.059527	.063214	.066934	.070684	.074462	.078265	.082092	.085939	.089805	.093688	.101499	.109359
	.10	.069312	.072965	.076652	.080372	.084122	.087900	.091703	.095530	.099377	.103243	.107126	.114937	.122797
	0.00	.082750	.086403	.090090	.093810	.097560	.101338	.105141	.108968	.112815	.116681	.120564	.128375	.136235
	-.10	.096188	.099841	.103528	.107248	.110998	.114776	.118579	.122406	.126253	.130119	.134002	.141813	.149673
	-.20	.109626	.113279	.116966	.120686	.124436	.128214	.132017	.135844	.139691	.143557	.147440	.155251	.163111
	-.30	.123064	.126712	.130404	.134124	.137874	.141652	.145455	.149261	.153129	.156995	.160878	.168683	.176549

178

5.0 YEAR HOLDING PERIOD
.200 EQUITY YIELD RATE
.900 LOAN RATIO

INTEREST RATE

TERM YEARS	APPR DEP	5.0	5.5	6.0	6.5	7.0	7.5	8.0	8.5	9.0	9.5	10.0	11.0	12.0
10	.40	.027832	.031230	.034660	.038124	.041620	.045148	.048708	.052299	.055920	.059571	.063252	.070700	.078259
	.30	.041270	.044668	.048098	.051562	.055058	.058586	.062146	.065737	.069358	.073009	.076690	.084137	.091697
	.20	.054708	.058106	.061536	.065000	.068496	.072024	.075584	.079174	.082796	.086447	.090128	.097575	.105135
	.10	.068146	.071544	.074974	.078438	.081934	.085462	.089022	.092612	.096234	.099885	.103566	.111013	.118573
	0.00	.081584	.084982	.088412	.091876	.095372	.098900	.102460	.106050	.109672	.113323	.117003	.124465	.132011
	-.10	.095022	.098420	.101850	.105314	.108810	.112338	.115898	.119488	.123110	.126761	.130441	.137889	.145449
	-.20	.108460	.111858	.115288	.118752	.122248	.125776	.129336	.132926	.136548	.140199	.143879	.151327	.158887
	-.30	.121898	.125296	.128726	.132190	.135686	.139214	.142774	.146364	.149985	.153637	.157317	.164765	.172325
	-.40	.135336	.138733	.142164	.145628	.149124	.152662	.156212	.159802	.163423	.167075	.170755	.178203	.185763
15	.40	.020883	.024607	.028370	.032169	.036004	.039874	.043778	.047715	.051683	.055681	.059709	.067850	.076095
	.30	.034321	.038045	.041808	.045607	.049442	.053312	.057216	.061153	.065121	.069119	.073147	.081288	.089533
	.20	.047759	.051483	.055246	.059045	.062880	.066750	.070654	.074591	.078559	.082557	.086585	.094726	.102971
	.10	.061197	.064921	.068684	.072483	.076318	.080188	.084092	.088029	.091997	.095995	.100023	.108164	.116409
	0.00	.074635	.078359	.082122	.085921	.089756	.093626	.097530	.101466	.105435	.109433	.113461	.121602	.129847
	-.10	.088073	.091797	.095559	.099359	.103194	.107064	.110968	.114904	.118873	.122871	.126899	.135040	.143285
	-.20	.101511	.105235	.108997	.112797	.116632	.120502	.124406	.128342	.132311	.136309	.140337	.148478	.156723
	-.30	.114949	.118673	.122435	.126235	.130070	.133940	.137844	.141780	.145749	.149747	.153775	.161916	.170161
	-.40	.128386	.132111	.135873	.139673	.143508	.147378	.151282	.155218	.159186	.163185	.167213	.175354	.183599
20	.40	.017513	.021417	.025360	.029341	.033359	.037411	.041497	.045614	.049761	.053936	.058137	.066615	.075181
	.30	.030951	.034855	.038798	.042779	.046797	.050849	.054935	.059052	.063199	.067374	.071575	.080053	.088619
	.20	.044389	.048293	.052236	.056217	.060235	.064287	.068373	.072490	.076637	.080812	.085013	.093491	.102057
	.10	.057827	.061731	.065674	.069655	.073673	.077725	.081811	.085928	.090075	.094250	.098451	.106929	.115495
	0.00	.071265	.075169	.079112	.083093	.087111	.091163	.095249	.099366	.103513	.107688	.111889	.120367	.128933
	-.10	.084703	.088607	.092550	.096531	.100549	.104601	.108687	.112804	.116950	.121126	.125327	.133805	.142371
	-.20	.098141	.102045	.105988	.109969	.113987	.118039	.122125	.126242	.130388	.134563	.138765	.147242	.155809
	-.30	.111579	.115483	.119426	.123407	.127425	.131477	.135563	.139680	.143826	.148001	.152203	.160680	.169247
	-.40	.125017	.128921	.132864	.136845	.140863	.144915	.149001	.153118	.157264	.161439	.165641	.174118	.182685
25	.40	.015573	.019594	.023656	.027756	.031892	.036060	.040260	.044489	.048745	.053026	.057329	.065999	.074739
	.30	.029010	.033032	.037094	.041194	.045330	.049498	.053698	.057927	.062183	.066464	.070767	.079437	.088177
	.20	.042448	.046470	.050532	.054632	.058768	.062936	.067136	.071365	.075621	.079902	.084205	.092875	.101615
	.10	.055886	.059908	.063970	.068070	.072206	.076374	.080574	.084803	.089059	.093340	.097643	.106313	.115053
	0.00	.069324	.073346	.077408	.081508	.085644	.089812	.094012	.098241	.102497	.106778	.111081	.119751	.128491
	-.10	.082762	.086784	.090846	.094946	.099081	.103250	.107450	.111679	.115935	.120215	.124519	.133189	.141929
	-.20	.096200	.100222	.104284	.108384	.112519	.116688	.120888	.125117	.129373	.133653	.137957	.146626	.155367
	-.30	.109638	.113660	.117722	.121822	.125957	.130126	.134326	.138555	.142811	.147091	.151395	.160064	.168805
	-.40	.123076	.127098	.131160	.135260	.139395	.143564	.147764	.151993	.156249	.160529	.164833	.173502	.182243
30	.40	.014342	.018451	.022599	.026784	.031003	.035254	.039532	.043837	.048165	.052514	.056883	.065670	.074512
	.30	.027780	.031889	.036037	.040222	.044441	.048691	.052970	.057275	.061603	.065952	.070321	.079108	.087950
	.20	.041218	.045327	.049475	.053660	.057879	.062129	.066408	.070713	.075041	.079390	.083759	.092546	.101388
	.10	.054656	.058765	.062913	.067098	.071317	.075567	.079846	.084151	.088479	.092828	.097197	.105984	.114826
	0.00	.068094	.072203	.076351	.080536	.084755	.089005	.093284	.097589	.101917	.106266	.110635	.119422	.128264
	-.10	.081532	.085641	.089789	.093974	.098193	.102443	.106722	.111026	.115355	.119704	.124073	.132860	.141702
	-.20	.094970	.099079	.103227	.107412	.111631	.115881	.120160	.124464	.128793	.133142	.137511	.146298	.155140
	-.30	.108408	.112517	.116665	.120850	.125069	.129319	.133598	.137902	.142231	.146580	.150949	.159736	.168578
	-.40	.121846	.125955	.130103	.134288	.138507	.142757	.147036	.151340	.155668	.160018	.164387	.173174	.182016

5.0 YEAR HOLDING PERIOD
.250 EQUITY YIELD RATE
.600 LOAN RATIO

INTEREST RATE

TERM YEARS	APPR DEP	5.0	5.5	6.0	6.5	7.0	7.5	8.0	8.5	9.0	9.5	10.0	11.0	12.0
10	.40	.095611	.097830	.100071	.102335	.104620	.106927	.109255	.111604	.113973	.116363	.118773	.123651	.128605
	.30	.107795	.110014	.112256	.114519	.116804	.119111	.121439	.123788	.126158	.128548	.130958	.135836	.140790
	.20	.119980	.122199	.124440	.126704	.128989	.131296	.133624	.135973	.138343	.140732	.143142	.148021	.152974
	.10	.132165	.134384	.136625	.138889	.141174	.143481	.145809	.148158	.150527	.152917	.155327	.160205	.165159
	0.00	.144349	.146568	.148810	.151073	.153358	.155665	.157993	.160342	.162712	.165102	.167512	.172390	.177344
	-.10	.156534	.158753	.160994	.163258	.165543	.167850	.170178	.172527	.174897	.177287	.179696	.184575	.189529
	-.20	.168719	.170938	.173179	.175443	.177728	.180035	.182363	.184712	.187081	.189471	.191881	.196759	.201713
	-.30	.180903	.183122	.185364	.187627	.189913	.192219	.194547	.196896	.199266	.201656	.204066	.208944	.213898
	-.40	.193088	.195307	.197548	.199812	.202097	.204404	.206732	.209081	.211451	.213841	.216250	.221129	.226083
15	.40	.089598	.092026	.094480	.096959	.099464	.101993	.104545	.107120	.109717	.112335	.114974	.120311	.125722
	.30	.101782	.104210	.106664	.109144	.111649	.114177	.116729	.119304	.121901	.124520	.127158	.132496	.137907
	.20	.113967	.116395	.118849	.121329	.123833	.126362	.128914	.131489	.134086	.136704	.139343	.144680	.150091
	.10	.126152	.128580	.131034	.133513	.136018	.138547	.141099	.143674	.146271	.148889	.151528	.156865	.162276
	0.00	.138336	.140764	.143218	.145698	.148203	.150731	.153283	.155858	.158455	.161074	.163713	.169050	.174461
	-.10	.150521	.152949	.155403	.157883	.160387	.162916	.165468	.168043	.170640	.173258	.175897	.181234	.186645
	-.20	.162706	.165134	.167588	.170067	.172572	.175101	.177653	.180228	.182825	.185443	.188082	.193419	.198830
	-.30	.174890	.177318	.179772	.182252	.184757	.187285	.189837	.192412	.195009	.197628	.200266	.205604	.211015
	-.40	.187075	.189503	.191957	.194437	.196941	.199470	.202022	.204597	.207194	.209812	.212451	.217788	.223199
20	.40	.086682	.089229	.091805	.094407	.097035	.099688	.102365	.105065	.107786	.110527	.113288	.118863	.124504
	.30	.098867	.101414	.103989	.106592	.109220	.111873	.114550	.117249	.119970	.122712	.125472	.131048	.136689
	.20	.111052	.113599	.116174	.118776	.121405	.124058	.126735	.129434	.132155	.134896	.137657	.143232	.148873
	.10	.123236	.125783	.128359	.130961	.133589	.136242	.138919	.141618	.144340	.147081	.149842	.155417	.161058
	0.00	.135421	.137968	.140543	.143146	.145774	.148427	.151104	.153803	.156524	.159266	.162026	.167602	.173243
	-.10	.147606	.150153	.152728	.155330	.157959	.160612	.163289	.165988	.168709	.171450	.174211	.179786	.185427
	-.20	.159790	.162337	.164913	.167515	.170143	.172796	.175473	.178173	.180894	.183635	.186396	.191972	.197612
	-.30	.171975	.174522	.177097	.179700	.182328	.184981	.187658	.190357	.193078	.195820	.198580	.204156	.209797
	-.40	.184160	.186707	.189282	.191884	.194513	.197166	.199843	.202542	.205263	.208004	.210765	.216341	.221981
25	.40	.085003	.087632	.090291	.092976	.095688	.098424	.101184	.103964	.106765	.109584	.112421	.118141	.123916
	.30	.097188	.099817	.102475	.105161	.107873	.110609	.113368	.116149	.118950	.121769	.124606	.130326	.136100
	.20	.109372	.112002	.114660	.117346	.120058	.122794	.125553	.128334	.131134	.133954	.136790	.142510	.148285
	.10	.121557	.124186	.126845	.129530	.132242	.134978	.137738	.140518	.143319	.146138	.148975	.154695	.160470
	0.00	.133742	.136371	.139029	.141715	.144427	.147163	.149922	.152703	.155504	.158323	.161160	.166880	.172654
	-.10	.145926	.148556	.151214	.153900	.156612	.159348	.162107	.164888	.167688	.170508	.173344	.179064	.184839
	-.20	.158111	.160740	.163399	.166084	.168796	.171533	.174292	.177072	.179873	.182692	.185529	.191249	.197024
	-.30	.170296	.172925	.175583	.178269	.180981	.183717	.186476	.189257	.192058	.194877	.197714	.203434	.209208
	-.40	.182480	.185110	.187768	.190454	.193166	.195902	.198661	.201442	.204242	.207062	.209898	.215618	.221393
30	.40	.083939	.086630	.089351	.092099	.094873	.097670	.100488	.103326	.106182	.109055	.111942	.117756	.123613
	.30	.096123	.098815	.101536	.104284	.107057	.109854	.112673	.115511	.118367	.121239	.124127	.129940	.135798
	.20	.108308	.111000	.113720	.116469	.119242	.122039	.124857	.127695	.130552	.133424	.136311	.142125	.147982
	.10	.120493	.123184	.125905	.128653	.131427	.134224	.137042	.139880	.142736	.145609	.148609	.154310	.160167
	0.00	.132677	.135369	.138090	.140838	.143611	.146408	.149227	.152065	.154921	.157793	.160681	.166494	.172352
	-.10	.144862	.147554	.150274	.153023	.155796	.158593	.161411	.164249	.167106	.169978	.172865	.178679	.184536
	-.20	.157047	.159738	.162459	.165207	.167981	.170778	.173596	.176434	.179290	.182163	.185050	.190864	.196721
	-.30	.169231	.171923	.174644	.177392	.180166	.182962	.185781	.188619	.191475	.194347	.197235	.203048	.208906
	-.40	.181416	.184108	.186829	.189577	.192350	.195147	.197965	.200803	.203660	.206532	.209419	.215233	.221090

5.0 YEAR HOLDING PERIOD
.250 EQUITY YIELD RATE
.667 LOAN RATIO

INTEREST RATE

TERM YEARS	APPR DEP	12.0	11.0	10.0	9.5	9.0	8.5	8.0	7.5	7.0	6.5	6.0	5.5	5.0
10	.40	.120532	.115027	.109607	.106930	.104274	.101641	.099031	.096444	.093881	.091342	.088827	.086337	.083871
	.30	.132717	.127212	.121792	.119114	.116459	.113826	.111216	.108629	.106066	.103527	.101012	.098521	.096056
	.20	.144501	.139337	.133976	.131299	.128643	.126011	.123401	.120814	.118251	.115711	.113196	.110706	.108241
	.10	.157086	.151581	.146161	.143484	.140828	.138195	.135585	.132998	.130435	.127896	.125381	.122891	.120425
	0.00	.169271	.163766	.158346	.155668	.153013	.150380	.147770	.145183	.142620	.140081	.137566	.135075	.132610
	-.10	.181455	.175951	.170531	.167853	.165197	.162565	.159955	.157368	.154805	.152265	.149750	.147260	.144795
	-.20	.193640	.188135	.182715	.180038	.177382	.174749	.172139	.169553	.166989	.164450	.161935	.159445	.156979
	-.30	.205825	.200320	.194900	.192222	.189567	.186934	.184324	.181737	.179174	.176635	.174120	.171629	.169164
	-.40	.218009	.212505	.207085	.204407	.201752	.199119	.196509	.193922	.191359	.188819	.186304	.183814	.181349
15	.40	.117328	.111316	.105386	.102454	.099544	.096659	.093798	.090962	.088152	.085370	.082615	.079888	.077190
	.30	.129513	.123501	.117571	.114638	.111729	.108844	.105983	.103147	.100337	.097554	.094799	.092072	.089375
	.20	.141698	.135685	.129755	.126823	.123914	.121028	.118167	.115331	.112522	.109739	.106984	.104257	.101559
	.10	.153882	.147870	.141940	.139008	.136098	.133213	.130352	.127516	.124707	.121924	.119169	.116442	.113744
	0.00	.166067	.160055	.154125	.151192	.148283	.145398	.142537	.139701	.136891	.134108	.131353	.128626	.125929
	-.10	.178252	.172239	.166309	.163377	.160468	.157582	.154721	.151886	.149076	.146293	.143538	.140811	.138113
	-.20	.190436	.184424	.178494	.175562	.172652	.169767	.166906	.164070	.161261	.158478	.155723	.152996	.150298
	-.30	.202621	.196609	.190679	.187746	.184837	.181952	.179091	.176255	.173445	.170662	.167907	.165180	.162483
	-.40	.214806	.208793	.202863	.199931	.197022	.194136	.191275	.188440	.185630	.182847	.180092	.177365	.174667
20	.40	.115975	.109707	.103512	.100445	.097399	.094376	.091376	.088402	.085454	.082534	.079642	.076781	.073951
	.30	.128160	.121892	.115697	.112629	.109583	.106560	.103561	.100587	.097639	.094718	.091827	.088966	.086135
	.20	.140344	.134077	.127882	.124814	.121768	.118745	.115746	.112771	.109823	.106903	.104012	.101150	.098320
	.10	.152529	.146261	.140066	.136999	.133953	.130930	.127930	.124956	.122008	.119088	.116196	.113335	.110505
	0.00	.164714	.158446	.152251	.149183	.146137	.143114	.140115	.137141	.134193	.131272	.128381	.125520	.122690
	-.10	.176898	.170631	.164436	.161368	.158322	.155299	.152300	.149325	.146377	.143457	.140566	.137704	.134874
	-.20	.189083	.182815	.176620	.173553	.170507	.167484	.164484	.161510	.158562	.155642	.152750	.149889	.147059
	-.30	.201258	.195000	.188805	.185737	.182692	.179668	.176669	.173695	.170747	.167826	.164935	.162074	.159243
	-.40	.213452	.207185	.200990	.197922	.194876	.191853	.188854	.185879	.182931	.180011	.177120	.174258	.171428
25	.40	.115321	.108905	.102549	.099398	.096265	.093153	.090063	.086998	.083957	.080944	.077960	.075006	.072085
	.30	.127505	.121090	.114734	.111582	.108450	.105338	.102248	.099182	.096142	.093129	.090145	.087191	.084269
	.20	.139631	.133274	.126919	.123767	.120634	.117522	.114433	.111367	.108327	.105313	.102329	.099375	.096454
	.10	.151875	.145459	.139103	.135952	.132819	.129707	.126617	.123552	.120511	.117498	.114514	.111560	.108639
	0.00	.164040	.157644	.151288	.148136	.145004	.141892	.138802	.135736	.132696	.129683	.126699	.123745	.120823
	-.10	.176245	.169828	.163473	.160321	.157188	.154076	.150987	.147921	.144881	.141868	.138883	.135930	.133008
	-.20	.188429	.182013	.175657	.172506	.169373	.166261	.163171	.160106	.157065	.154052	.151068	.148114	.145193
	-.30	.200614	.194198	.187842	.184690	.181558	.178446	.175356	.172290	.169250	.166237	.163253	.160299	.157377
	-.40	.212799	.206382	.200027	.196875	.193742	.190630	.187541	.184475	.181435	.178422	.175437	.172484	.169562
30	.40	.114985	.108477	.102017	.098809	.095617	.092444	.089290	.086159	.083051	.079970	.076916	.073893	.070902
	.30	.127170	.120662	.114202	.110994	.107802	.104629	.101475	.098344	.095236	.092154	.089101	.086077	.083087
	.20	.139354	.132846	.126386	.123178	.119987	.116813	.113660	.110528	.107421	.104339	.101285	.098262	.095271
	.10	.151539	.145031	.138571	.135363	.132171	.128998	.125844	.122713	.119605	.116524	.113470	.110447	.107456
	0.00	.163724	.157216	.150756	.147548	.144356	.141183	.138029	.134898	.131790	.128708	.125655	.122631	.119641
	-.10	.175908	.169400	.162941	.159732	.156541	.153367	.150214	.147082	.143975	.140893	.137839	.134816	.131825
	-.20	.188093	.181585	.175125	.171917	.168725	.165552	.162398	.159267	.156159	.153078	.150024	.147001	.144010
	-.30	.200278	.193770	.187310	.184102	.180910	.177737	.174583	.171452	.168344	.165262	.162209	.159185	.156195
	-.40	.212462	.205954	.199495	.196286	.193095	.189921	.186768	.183636	.180529	.177447	.174393	.171370	.168379

181

5.0 YEAR HOLDING PERIOD
.250 EQUITY YIELD RATE
.700 LOAN RATIO

INTEREST RATE

TERM YEARS	APPR DEP	5.0	5.5	6.0	6.5	7.0	7.5	8.0	8.5	9.0	9.5	10.0	11.0	12.0
10	.40	.078002	.080591	.083206	.085847	.088513	.091204	.093920	.096661	.099425	.102213	.105025	.110716	.116496
	.30	.090187	.092776	.095391	.098031	.100698	.103389	.106105	.108845	.111610	.114398	.117210	.122901	.128680
	.20	.102372	.104960	.107575	.110216	.112882	.115574	.118290	.121030	.123795	.126583	.129394	.135085	.140865
	.10	.114556	.117145	.119760	.122401	.125067	.127758	.130474	.133215	.135979	.138767	.141579	.147270	.153050
	0.00	.126741	.129330	.131945	.134585	.137252	.139943	.142659	.145399	.148164	.150952	.153764	.159455	.165234
	-.10	.138926	.141514	.144129	.146770	.149436	.152128	.154844	.157584	.160349	.163137	.165948	.171640	.177419
	-.20	.151110	.153699	.156314	.158955	.161621	.164312	.167028	.169769	.172533	.175321	.178133	.183824	.189604
	-.30	.163295	.165884	.168499	.171139	.173806	.176497	.179213	.181953	.184718	.187506	.190318	.196009	.201789
	-.40	.175480	.178068	.180683	.183324	.185990	.188682	.191398	.194138	.196903	.199631	.202502	.208194	.213973
15	.40	.070987	.073820	.076083	.079576	.082498	.085448	.088425	.091429	.094459	.097514	.100593	.106819	.113132
	.30	.083172	.086004	.088867	.091760	.094682	.097632	.100610	.103614	.106644	.109698	.112777	.119004	.125317
	.20	.095356	.098189	.101052	.103945	.106867	.109817	.112795	.115799	.118828	.121883	.124962	.131188	.137501
	.10	.107541	.110374	.113237	.116130	.119052	.122002	.124979	.127983	.131013	.134068	.137147	.143373	.149686
	0.00	.119726	.122558	.125421	.128314	.131236	.134186	.137164	.140168	.143198	.146252	.149331	.155558	.161871
	-.10	.131910	.134743	.137606	.140499	.143421	.146371	.149349	.152353	.155382	.158437	.161516	.167742	.174055
	-.20	.144095	.146928	.149791	.152684	.155606	.158556	.161533	.164537	.167567	.170622	.173701	.179927	.186240
	-.30	.156280	.159112	.161976	.164868	.167790	.170740	.173718	.176722	.179752	.182807	.185885	.192112	.198425
	-.40	.168464	.171297	.174160	.177053	.179975	.182925	.185903	.188907	.191936	.194991	.198070	.204296	.210609
20	.40	.067586	.070557	.073562	.076598	.079664	.082760	.085883	.089032	.092206	.095404	.098625	.105130	.111711
	.30	.079770	.082742	.085747	.088783	.091849	.094944	.098067	.101216	.104391	.107589	.110810	.117315	.123896
	.20	.091955	.094927	.097931	.100967	.104034	.107129	.110252	.113401	.116576	.119774	.122995	.129499	.136080
	.10	.104140	.107111	.110116	.113152	.116218	.119314	.122437	.125586	.128760	.131959	.135179	.141684	.148266
	0.00	.116324	.119296	.122301	.125337	.128403	.131498	.134621	.137771	.140945	.144143	.147364	.153869	.160450
	-.10	.128509	.131481	.134485	.137521	.140588	.143683	.146806	.149955	.153130	.156328	.159549	.166053	.172634
	-.20	.140694	.143666	.146670	.149706	.152772	.155868	.158991	.162140	.165314	.168513	.171733	.178238	.184819
	-.30	.152879	.155850	.158855	.161891	.164957	.168052	.171175	.174325	.177499	.180697	.183918	.190423	.197004
	-.40	.165063	.168035	.171039	.174075	.177142	.180237	.183360	.186509	.189684	.192882	.196103	.202607	.209188
25	.40	.065627	.068694	.071795	.074929	.078093	.081285	.084504	.087748	.091016	.094305	.097614	.104288	.111025
	.30	.077811	.080879	.083980	.087114	.090277	.093470	.096689	.099933	.103200	.106490	.109799	.116472	.123209
	.20	.089996	.093063	.096165	.099298	.102462	.105654	.108873	.112118	.115385	.118674	.121984	.128657	.135394
	.10	.102181	.105248	.108349	.111483	.114647	.117839	.121058	.124302	.127570	.130859	.134168	.140842	.147579
	0.00	.114305	.117433	.120534	.123668	.126831	.130024	.133243	.136487	.139754	.143044	.146353	.153026	.159763
	-.10	.126550	.129617	.132719	.135852	.139016	.142208	.145427	.148672	.151939	.155228	.158538	.165211	.171948
	-.20	.138735	.141802	.144903	.148037	.151201	.154393	.157612	.160856	.164124	.167413	.170722	.177396	.184133
	-.30	.150919	.153987	.157088	.160222	.163385	.166578	.169797	.173041	.176308	.179598	.182907	.189580	.196317
	-.40	.163104	.166171	.169273	.172406	.175570	.178762	.181981	.185226	.188493	.191782	.195092	.201765	.208502
30	.40	.064385	.067525	.070699	.073906	.077141	.080404	.083692	.087004	.090336	.093687	.097055	.103838	.110672
	.30	.076569	.079710	.082884	.086090	.089326	.092589	.095877	.099188	.102520	.105872	.109240	.116023	.122856
	.20	.088754	.091894	.095069	.098275	.101511	.104774	.108062	.111373	.114705	.118056	.121425	.128207	.135041
	.10	.100939	.104079	.107253	.110460	.113695	.116958	.120246	.123558	.126890	.130241	.133609	.140392	.147226
	0.00	.113124	.116264	.119438	.122644	.125880	.129143	.132431	.135742	.139074	.142426	.145794	.152577	.159410
	-.10	.125308	.128448	.131623	.134829	.138065	.141328	.144616	.147927	.151259	.154610	.157979	.164761	.171595
	-.20	.137493	.140633	.143807	.147014	.150249	.153512	.156801	.160112	.163444	.166795	.170164	.176946	.183780
	-.30	.149678	.152818	.155992	.159198	.162434	.165697	.168985	.172296	.175628	.178980	.182348	.189131	.195964
	-.40	.161862	.165002	.168177	.171383	.174619	.177882	.181170	.184481	.187813	.191164	.194533	.201316	.208149

INTEREST RATE

TERM YEARS	APPR DEP	5.0	5.5	6.0	6.5	7.0	7.5	8.0	8.5	9.0	9.5	10.0	11.0	12.0
10	.40	.069198	.071972	.074773	.077603	.080459	.083343	.086253	.089189	.092151	.095139	.098151	.104249	.110441
	.30	.081383	.084156	.086958	.089787	.092644	.095528	.098438	.101374	.104336	.107323	.110336	.116433	.122626
	.20	.093567	.096343	.099143	.101972	.104829	.107712	.110622	.113559	.116521	.119508	.122520	.128618	.134810
	.10	.105752	.108526	.111327	.114157	.117013	.119897	.122807	.125743	.128705	.131693	.134705	.140803	.146995
	0.00	.117937	.120710	.123512	.126341	.129198	.132082	.134992	.137928	.140890	.143877	.146890	.152987	.159180
	-.10	.130121	.132895	.135697	.138526	.141383	.144266	.147176	.150113	.153075	.156062	.159074	.165172	.171364
	-.20	.142306	.145080	.147882	.150711	.153567	.156451	.159361	.162297	.165259	.168247	.171259	.177357	.183549
	-.30	.154491	.157264	.160066	.162896	.165752	.168636	.171546	.174482	.177444	.180431	.183444	.189541	.195734
	-.40	.166675	.169449	.172251	.175080	.177937	.180820	.183730	.186667	.189629	.192616	.195628	.201726	.207918
15	.40	.061682	.064717	.067784	.070884	.074015	.077175	.080366	.083584	.086830	.090103	.093402	.100073	.106837
	.30	.073866	.076901	.079969	.083069	.086360	.089360	.092550	.095769	.099015	.102288	.105587	.112258	.119022
	.20	.086051	.089086	.092154	.095253	.098384	.101545	.104735	.107954	.111200	.114473	.117771	.124443	.131206
	.10	.098236	.101271	.104338	.107438	.110569	.113729	.116920	.120138	.123384	.126657	.129956	.136627	.143391
	0.00	.110420	.113455	.116523	.119623	.122753	.125914	.129104	.132323	.135569	.138842	.142141	.148812	.155576
	-.10	.122605	.125640	.128708	.131807	.134938	.138099	.141289	.144508	.147754	.151027	.154325	.160997	.167760
	-.20	.134790	.137825	.140892	.143992	.147123	.150283	.153474	.156692	.159938	.163211	.166510	.173181	.179945
	-.30	.146974	.150009	.153077	.156177	.159307	.162468	.165658	.168877	.172123	.175396	.178695	.185366	.192130
	-.40	.159159	.162194	.165262	.168361	.171492	.174653	.177843	.181062	.184308	.187581	.190879	.197551	.204315
20	.40	.058038	.061221	.064441	.067693	.070979	.074295	.077641	.081015	.084417	.087843	.091294	.098264	.105315
	.30	.070222	.073406	.076625	.079878	.083163	.086480	.089826	.093200	.096601	.100028	.103479	.110448	.117499
	.20	.082407	.085591	.088810	.092063	.095348	.098665	.102011	.105385	.108786	.112213	.115664	.122633	.129684
	.10	.094592	.097776	.100995	.104248	.107533	.110849	.114195	.117569	.120971	.124397	.127848	.134818	.141869
	0.00	.106776	.109960	.113179	.116432	.119718	.123034	.126380	.129754	.133155	.136582	.140033	.147002	.154053
	-.10	.118961	.122145	.125364	.128617	.131902	.135219	.138565	.141939	.145340	.148767	.152218	.159187	.166238
	-.20	.131146	.134330	.137549	.140802	.144087	.147403	.150750	.154123	.157525	.160951	.164402	.171372	.178423
	-.30	.143330	.146514	.149733	.152986	.156272	.159588	.162934	.166309	.169709	.173136	.176587	.183556	.190607
	-.40	.155515	.158699	.161918	.165171	.168456	.171773	.175119	.178493	.181894	.185321	.188772	.195741	.202792
25	.40	.055938	.059225	.062548	.065905	.069295	.072715	.076164	.079640	.083141	.086665	.090211	.097361	.104579
	.30	.068123	.071410	.074733	.078090	.081480	.084900	.088349	.091825	.095326	.098850	.102396	.109546	.116764
	.20	.080308	.083594	.086917	.090275	.093664	.097085	.100534	.104009	.107510	.111034	.114580	.121730	.128949
	.10	.092492	.095779	.099102	.102459	.105849	.109269	.112718	.116194	.119695	.123219	.126765	.133915	.141133
	0.00	.104677	.107964	.111287	.114644	.118034	.121454	.124903	.128379	.131880	.135404	.138950	.146100	.153318
	-.10	.116862	.120148	.123471	.126829	.130218	.133639	.137088	.140564	.144064	.147589	.151134	.158284	.165503
	-.20	.129046	.132333	.135656	.139013	.142403	.145823	.149272	.152748	.156249	.159773	.163319	.170469	.177637
	-.30	.141231	.144518	.147841	.151198	.154588	.158008	.161457	.164933	.168434	.171958	.175504	.182654	.189872
	-.40	.153416	.156702	.160025	.163383	.166772	.170193	.173642	.177118	.180618	.184143	.187688	.194838	.202057
30	.40	.054608	.057972	.061374	.064809	.068276	.071772	.075295	.078842	.082412	.086003	.089612	.096879	.104201
	.30	.066793	.070157	.073558	.076993	.080460	.083956	.087479	.091027	.094597	.098188	.101797	.109064	.116386
	.20	.078977	.082342	.085743	.089178	.092645	.096141	.099664	.103212	.106782	.110372	.113982	.121249	.128570
	.10	.091162	.094526	.097928	.101363	.104830	.108326	.111849	.115396	.118966	.122557	.126166	.133433	.140755
	0.00	.103347	.106711	.110112	.113548	.117014	.120510	.124033	.127581	.131151	.134742	.138351	.145618	.152914
	-.10	.115531	.118896	.122297	.125732	.129199	.132695	.136218	.139766	.143336	.146926	.150536	.157803	.165124
	-.20	.127716	.131080	.134482	.137917	.141384	.144880	.148403	.151956	.155520	.159111	.162700	.169987	.177309
	-.30	.139901	.143265	.146666	.150102	.153568	.157064	.160587	.164135	.167705	.171296	.174905	.182172	.189494
	-.40	.152085	.155450	.158851	.162286	.165753	.169249	.172772	.176320	.179890	.183480	.187090	.194357	.201678

5.0 YEAR HOLDING PERIOD
.250 EQUITY YIELD RATE
.800 LOAN RATIO

INTEREST RATE

TERM YEARS	APPR DEP	5.0	5.5	6.0	6.5	7.0	7.5	8.0	8.5	9.0	9.5	10.0	11.0	12.0
10	.40	.060394	.063352	.066341	.069359	.072406	.075482	.078580	.081718	.084877	.088064	.091277	.097781	.104386
	.30	.072579	.075526	.078526	.081544	.084591	.087666	.090765	.093903	.097062	.100248	.103462	.109966	.116571
	.20	.084763	.087722	.090710	.093728	.096775	.099851	.102955	.106087	.109247	.112433	.115646	.122150	.128756
	.10	.096948	.099906	.102895	.105913	.108960	.112036	.115140	.118272	.121431	.124618	.127831	.134335	.140940
	0.00	.109133	.112091	.115080	.118098	.121144	.124220	.127325	.130456	.133616	.136802	.140016	.146520	.153125
	-.10	.121317	.124276	.127264	.130282	.133329	.136405	.139509	.142641	.145801	.148987	.152200	.158704	.165310
	-.20	.133502	.136461	.139449	.142467	.145514	.148590	.151694	.154826	.157985	.161172	.164385	.170889	.177494
	-.30	.145687	.148645	.151634	.154652	.157699	.160774	.163879	.167011	.170170	.173356	.176570	.183074	.189679
	-.40	.157871	.160830	.163818	.166836	.169883	.172959	.176063	.179195	.182355	.185541	.188754	.195259	.201864
15	.40	.052376	.055614	.058886	.062192	.065531	.068903	.072306	.075739	.079202	.082693	.086211	.093327	.100542
	.30	.064561	.067798	.071071	.074377	.077716	.081088	.084490	.087924	.091386	.094877	.098396	.105512	.112727
	.20	.076746	.079983	.083255	.086561	.089901	.093272	.096675	.100108	.103571	.107062	.110581	.117697	.124912
	.10	.088930	.092168	.095440	.098746	.102085	.105457	.108860	.112293	.115756	.119247	.122765	.129881	.137096
	0.00	.101115	.104352	.107625	.110931	.114270	.117642	.121045	.124477	.127940	.131431	.134950	.142066	.149281
	-.10	.113300	.116537	.119809	.123115	.126455	.129826	.133229	.136662	.140125	.143616	.147135	.154251	.161466
	-.20	.125484	.128722	.131994	.135300	.138639	.142011	.145414	.148847	.152310	.155801	.159319	.166435	.173650
	-.30	.137669	.140906	.144179	.147485	.150824	.154196	.157599	.161031	.164494	.167985	.171504	.178620	.185835
	-.40	.149854	.153091	.156363	.159669	.163009	.166380	.169783	.173216	.176679	.180170	.183689	.190805	.198020
20	.40	.048489	.051885	.055319	.058789	.062293	.065831	.069400	.072999	.076627	.080282	.083963	.091397	.098518
	.30	.060674	.064070	.067504	.070974	.074478	.078015	.081584	.085184	.088812	.092467	.096148	.103582	.111103
	.20	.072859	.076255	.079689	.083158	.086663	.090200	.093769	.097368	.100996	.104651	.108332	.115766	.123288
	.10	.085043	.088440	.091873	.095343	.098847	.102385	.105954	.109553	.113181	.116836	.120517	.127951	.135472
	0.00	.097228	.100624	.104058	.107528	.111032	.114569	.118139	.121738	.125366	.129021	.132702	.140136	.147657
	-.10	.109413	.112809	.116243	.119712	.123217	.126754	.130323	.133922	.137550	.141205	.144886	.152320	.159842
	-.20	.121597	.124994	.128427	.131897	.135401	.138939	.142508	.146107	.149735	.153390	.157071	.164505	.172026
	-.30	.133782	.137178	.140612	.144082	.147586	.151123	.154693	.158292	.161920	.165575	.169256	.176690	.184211
	-.40	.145967	.149363	.152797	.156266	.159771	.163308	.166877	.170476	.174104	.177759	.181440	.188874	.196396
25	.40	.046650	.049756	.053300	.056881	.060497	.064146	.067825	.071532	.075266	.079025	.082808	.090434	.098134
	.30	.058435	.061941	.065485	.069066	.072682	.076330	.080009	.083717	.087451	.091210	.094992	.102619	.110318
	.20	.070200	.074125	.077670	.081251	.084867	.088515	.092194	.095901	.099636	.103395	.107177	.114804	.122503
	.10	.082004	.086310	.089854	.093435	.097051	.100700	.104379	.108086	.111820	.115579	.119362	.126988	.134688
	0.00	.094989	.098495	.102039	.105620	.109236	.112884	.116563	.120271	.124005	.127764	.131546	.139173	.146872
	-.10	.107174	.110679	.114224	.117805	.121421	.125069	.128748	.132455	.136190	.139949	.143731	.151358	.159057
	-.20	.119358	.122864	.126408	.129989	.133605	.137254	.140933	.144640	.148374	.152133	.155916	.163542	.171242
	-.30	.131543	.135049	.138593	.142174	.145790	.149438	.153117	.156825	.160559	.164318	.168100	.175727	.183426
	-.40	.143728	.147233	.150778	.154359	.157975	.161623	.165302	.169009	.172744	.176503	.180285	.187912	.195611
30	.40	.044631	.048420	.052048	.055712	.059410	.063139	.066897	.070681	.074489	.078319	.082169	.089921	.097730
	.30	.057016	.060605	.064232	.067897	.071595	.075324	.079082	.082866	.086674	.090504	.094354	.102105	.109915
	.20	.069200	.072789	.076417	.080081	.083779	.087508	.091266	.095050	.098858	.102688	.106538	.114290	.122100
	.10	.081385	.084974	.088602	.092266	.095964	.099693	.103451	.107235	.111043	.114873	.118723	.126475	.134284
	0.00	.093570	.097159	.100786	.104451	.108149	.111878	.115636	.119420	.123228	.127058	.130908	.138659	.146469
	-.10	.105754	.109343	.112971	.116635	.120333	.124062	.127820	.131604	.135413	.139242	.143092	.150844	.158654
	-.20	.117939	.121528	.125156	.128820	.132518	.136247	.140005	.143789	.147597	.151427	.155277	.163029	.170838
	-.30	.130124	.133713	.137340	.141005	.144703	.148432	.152190	.155974	.159782	.163612	.167462	.175213	.183023
	-.40	.142308	.145897	.149525	.153189	.156887	.160617	.164374	.168158	.171967	.175797	.179646	.187398	.195208

5.0 YEAR HOLDING PERIOD
.250 EQUITY YIELD RATE
.900 LOAN RATIO

INTEREST RATE

TERM YEARS	APPR DEP	5.0	5.5	6.0	6.5	7.0	7.5	8.0	8.5	9.0	9.5	10.0	11.0	12.0
10	.40	.042785	.046114	.049476	.052871	.056299	.059759	.063251	.066775	.070329	.073914	.077529	.084846	.092277
	.30	.054970	.058299	.061661	.065056	.068484	.071944	.075436	.078960	.082514	.086099	.089713	.097031	.104462
	.20	.067155	.070483	.073845	.077240	.080668	.084129	.087621	.091144	.094699	.098283	.101808	.109145	.116646
	.10	.079339	.082668	.086030	.089425	.092853	.096313	.099805	.103329	.106883	.110468	.114083	.121400	.128831
	0.00	.091524	.094853	.098215	.101610	.105038	.108498	.111990	.115514	.119068	.122653	.126267	.133585	.141016
	-.10	.103709	.107037	.110399	.113794	.117222	.120683	.124175	.127698	.131253	.134837	.138452	.145769	.152200
	-.20	.115893	.119222	.122584	.125979	.129407	.132867	.136359	.139883	.143437	.147022	.150637	.157954	.165385
	-.30	.128078	.131407	.134769	.138164	.141592	.145052	.148544	.152068	.155622	.159207	.162822	.170139	.177570
	-.40	.140263	.143591	.146953	.150348	.153776	.157237	.160729	.164252	.167807	.171391	.175006	.182323	.189754
15	.40	.033766	.037408	.041089	.044808	.048565	.052358	.056186	.060049	.063944	.067872	.071630	.079836	.087952
	.30	.045950	.049592	.053274	.056993	.060743	.064543	.068371	.072233	.076129	.080056	.083815	.092020	.100137
	.20	.058135	.061777	.065458	.069177	.072935	.076728	.080556	.084418	.088314	.092241	.096199	.104205	.112322
	.10	.070320	.073962	.077643	.081362	.085119	.088912	.092740	.096603	.100498	.104426	.108384	.116390	.124506
	0.00	.082504	.086146	.089828	.093547	.097304	.101097	.104925	.108787	.112683	.116610	.120569	.128574	.136691
	-.10	.094689	.098331	.102012	.105732	.109489	.113282	.117110	.120972	.124868	.128795	.132753	.140759	.148876
	-.20	.106874	.110516	.114197	.117916	.121673	.125466	.129294	.133157	.137052	.140980	.144938	.152944	.161060
	-.30	.119059	.122700	.126382	.130101	.133858	.137651	.141479	.145341	.149237	.153164	.157123	.165128	.173245
	-.40	.131243	.134885	.138566	.142286	.146043	.149836	.153664	.157526	.161422	.165349	.169307	.177313	.185430
20	.40	.029393	.033214	.037076	.040980	.044922	.048902	.052917	.056966	.061048	.065160	.069301	.077664	.086125
	.30	.041577	.045398	.049261	.053165	.057107	.061087	.065102	.069151	.073232	.077344	.081485	.089849	.098310
	.20	.053762	.057583	.061446	.065350	.069292	.073271	.077286	.081336	.085417	.089529	.093670	.102033	.110495
	.10	.065947	.069768	.073630	.077534	.081476	.085456	.089471	.093520	.097602	.101714	.105855	.114218	.122679
	0.00	.078131	.081952	.085815	.089719	.093661	.097641	.101656	.105705	.109786	.113898	.118039	.126403	.134864
	-.10	.090316	.094137	.098000	.101903	.105846	.109825	.113840	.117890	.121971	.126083	.130224	.138587	.147040
	-.20	.102501	.106322	.110184	.114088	.118030	.122010	.126025	.130074	.134156	.138268	.142409	.150772	.159233
	-.30	.114686	.118506	.122369	.126273	.130215	.134195	.138210	.142259	.146340	.150452	.154594	.162957	.171418
	-.40	.126870	.130691	.134554	.138457	.142400	.146379	.150395	.154444	.158525	.162637	.166748	.175141	.183603
25	.40	.026674	.030818	.034805	.038834	.042902	.047006	.051145	.055316	.059517	.063746	.068001	.076581	.085243
	.30	.039059	.043002	.046990	.051019	.055086	.059191	.063330	.067501	.071702	.075932	.080186	.088766	.097427
	.20	.051243	.055187	.059175	.063203	.067271	.071375	.075514	.079685	.083886	.088115	.092370	.100950	.109612
	.10	.063428	.067372	.071359	.075388	.079456	.083560	.087699	.091870	.096071	.100300	.104555	.113135	.121797
	0.00	.075613	.079556	.083544	.087573	.091640	.095745	.099884	.104055	.108256	.112485	.116740	.125320	.133981
	-.10	.087797	.091741	.095729	.099757	.103825	.107929	.112068	.116239	.120440	.124669	.128924	.137504	.146166
	-.20	.099982	.103926	.107913	.111942	.116010	.120114	.124253	.128424	.132625	.136854	.141109	.149689	.158351
	-.30	.112167	.116110	.120098	.124127	.128194	.132299	.136438	.140609	.144810	.149039	.153294	.161874	.170535
	-.40	.124351	.128295	.132283	.136311	.140379	.144483	.148622	.152793	.156994	.161223	.165478	.174058	.182720
30	.40	.025277	.029315	.033396	.037518	.041679	.045874	.050101	.054358	.058643	.062951	.067282	.076003	.084789
	.30	.037462	.041499	.045581	.049703	.053863	.058059	.062286	.066543	.070827	.075136	.079467	.088188	.096974
	.20	.049647	.053684	.057765	.061888	.066048	.070243	.074471	.078728	.083012	.087321	.091652	.100372	.109158
	.10	.061831	.065869	.069950	.074072	.078233	.082428	.086655	.090913	.095197	.099505	.103836	.112557	.121343
	0.00	.074016	.078053	.082135	.086257	.090417	.094613	.098840	.103097	.107381	.111690	.116021	.124742	.133528
	-.10	.086201	.090238	.094319	.098442	.102602	.106797	.111025	.115282	.119566	.123875	.128206	.136926	.145712
	-.20	.098385	.102423	.106504	.110626	.114787	.118982	.123209	.127467	.131751	.136059	.140390	.149111	.157897
	-.30	.110570	.114607	.118689	.122811	.126971	.131167	.135394	.139651	.143935	.148244	.152575	.161296	.170082
	-.40	.122755	.126792	.130873	.134996	.139156	.143351	.147579	.151836	.156120	.160429	.164760	.173480	.182256

5.0 YEAR HOLDING PERIOD
.300 EQUITY YIELD RATE
.600 LOAN RATIO

TERM YEARS	APPR DEP	5.0	5.5	6.0	6.5	7.0	7.5	8.0	8.5	9.0	9.5	10.0	11.0	12.0
10	.40	.123077	.125255	.127455	.129677	.131922	.134188	.136475	.138784	.141114	.143464	.145834	.150634	.155511
	.30	.134135	.136513	.138513	.140735	.142980	.145246	.147534	.149842	.152172	.154522	.156892	.161692	.166569
	.20	.145193	.147371	.149571	.151793	.154038	.156304	.158592	.160901	.163230	.165580	.167950	.172750	.177627
	.10	.156251	.158429	.160629	.162852	.165096	.167362	.169650	.171959	.174288	.176638	.179009	.183609	.188685
	0.00	.167310	.169487	.171687	.173910	.176154	.178420	.180708	.183017	.185346	.187696	.190067	.194867	.199744
	-.10	.178368	.180545	.182746	.184968	.187212	.189479	.191766	.194075	.196405	.198755	.201125	.205935	.210802
	-.20	.189426	.191603	.193804	.196026	.198271	.200537	.202824	.205133	.207463	.209813	.212183	.216983	.221860
	-.30	.200484	.202662	.204862	.207084	.209329	.211595	.213883	.216191	.218521	.220871	.223241	.228041	.232918
	-.40	.211542	.213720	.215920	.218142	.220387	.222653	.224941	.227249	.229579	.231929	.234299	.239099	.243976
15	.40	.115623	.118202	.120607	.123039	.125497	.127979	.130486	.133016	.135570	.138146	.140743	.145999	.151333
	.30	.126682	.129260	.131666	.134097	.136555	.139037	.141544	.144075	.146628	.149204	.151801	.157057	.162391
	.20	.137940	.140318	.142724	.145155	.147613	.150095	.152602	.155133	.157686	.160262	.162859	.168115	.173449
	.10	.148998	.151376	.153782	.156214	.158671	.161154	.163660	.166191	.168744	.171320	.173917	.179173	.184507
	0.00	.160056	.162435	.164840	.167272	.169730	.172212	.174719	.177249	.179802	.182378	.184975	.190232	.195566
	-.10	.171114	.173493	.175898	.178330	.180787	.183270	.185777	.188307	.190861	.193436	.196034	.201290	.206624
	-.20	.182172	.184551	.186956	.189388	.191846	.194328	.196835	.199365	.201919	.204494	.207092	.212348	.217682
	-.30	.193231	.195609	.198014	.200446	.202903	.205386	.207893	.210424	.212977	.215553	.218150	.223406	.228740
	-.40	.204289	.206667	.209073	.211504	.213962	.216444	.218951	.221482	.224035	.226611	.229208	.234464	.239798
20	.40	.112307	.114804	.117331	.119887	.122470	.125080	.127714	.130373	.133055	.135759	.138483	.143990	.149568
	.30	.123365	.125862	.128390	.130945	.133528	.136138	.138773	.141431	.144113	.146817	.149541	.155048	.160626
	.20	.134423	.136921	.139448	.142003	.144587	.147196	.149831	.152489	.155171	.157875	.160599	.166106	.171684
	.10	.145481	.147979	.150506	.153062	.155645	.158254	.160889	.163548	.166229	.168933	.171657	.177165	.182742
	0.00	.156539	.159037	.161564	.164120	.166703	.169312	.171947	.174606	.177288	.179991	.182716	.188223	.193801
	-.10	.167597	.170095	.172622	.175178	.177761	.180371	.183005	.185664	.188346	.191049	.193774	.199281	.204859
	-.20	.178656	.181153	.183680	.186236	.188819	.191429	.194063	.196722	.199404	.202107	.204832	.210339	.215917
	-.30	.189714	.192211	.194739	.197294	.199877	.202487	.205122	.207780	.210462	.213166	.215890	.221397	.226971
	-.40	.200772	.203270	.205797	.208352	.210936	.213545	.216180	.218838	.221520	.224224	.226948	.232455	.238033
25	.40	.110281	.112863	.115477	.118120	.120792	.123489	.126212	.128958	.131726	.134514	.137322	.142988	.148715
	.30	.121339	.123922	.126535	.129179	.131850	.134548	.137270	.140016	.142784	.145572	.148380	.154046	.159774
	.20	.132397	.134980	.137593	.140237	.142908	.145606	.148328	.151074	.153842	.156630	.159438	.165104	.170832
	.10	.143455	.146038	.148652	.151295	.153966	.156664	.159386	.162132	.164900	.167689	.170496	.176163	.181890
	0.00	.154514	.157096	.159710	.162353	.165024	.167722	.170445	.173191	.175958	.178747	.181554	.187221	.192948
	-.10	.165572	.168154	.170768	.173411	.176082	.178780	.181503	.184249	.187017	.189805	.192613	.198279	.204006
	-.20	.176630	.179212	.181826	.184469	.187141	.189838	.192561	.195307	.198075	.200863	.203670	.209337	.215064
	-.30	.187688	.190271	.192884	.195527	.198199	.200896	.203619	.206365	.209133	.211921	.214729	.220395	.226123
	-.40	.198746	.201329	.203942	.206586	.209257	.211955	.214677	.217423	.220191	.222979	.225787	.231453	.237181
30	.40	.108997	.111646	.114327	.117037	.119776	.122540	.125327	.128137	.130967	.133815	.136680	.142453	.148277
	.30	.120055	.122704	.125385	.128095	.130834	.133598	.136385	.139195	.142025	.144873	.147738	.153512	.159335
	.20	.131113	.133762	.136443	.139154	.141893	.144656	.147444	.150253	.153083	.155931	.158796	.164570	.170393
	.10	.142171	.144820	.147501	.150212	.152950	.155714	.158502	.161311	.164141	.166989	.169854	.175628	.181452
	0.00	.153230	.155878	.158559	.161270	.164008	.166772	.169560	.172370	.175199	.178047	.180912	.186686	.192510
	-.10	.164288	.166937	.169617	.172328	.175066	.177830	.180618	.183428	.186257	.189106	.191970	.197744	.203568
	-.20	.175346	.177995	.180676	.183386	.186124	.188888	.191676	.194486	.197316	.200164	.203029	.208802	.214626
	-.30	.186404	.189053	.191734	.194444	.197183	.199947	.202734	.205544	.208374	.211222	.214087	.219861	.225684
	-.40	.197462	.200111	.202792	.205502	.208241	.211005	.213793	.216602	.219432	.222280	.225145	.230919	.236742

5.0 YEAR HOLDING PERIOD
.300 EQUITY YIELD RATE
.667 LOAN RATIO

INTEREST RATE

TERM YEARS	APPR DEP	5.0	5.5	6.0	6.5	7.0	7.5	8.0	8.5	9.0	9.5	10.0	11.0	12.0
10	.40	.108333	.110752	.113197	.115666	.118160	.120678	.123220	.125785	.128374	.130985	.133619	.138952	.144371
	.30	.119391	.121811	.124255	.126725	.129218	.131736	.134278	.136844	.139432	.142043	.144677	.150010	.155429
	.20	.130449	.132869	.135313	.137783	.140277	.142795	.145336	.147902	.150490	.153101	.155737	.161068	.166487
	.10	.141507	.143927	.146372	.148841	.151335	.153853	.156395	.158960	.161548	.164160	.166793	.172126	.177545
	0.00	.152565	.154985	.157430	.159899	.162393	.164911	.167453	.170018	.172606	.175218	.177851	.183185	.188603
	-.10	.163624	.166043	.168488	.170957	.173451	.175969	.178511	.181076	.183665	.186276	.188910	.194243	.199661
	-.20	.174682	.177101	.179546	.182015	.184509	.187027	.189569	.192134	.194723	.197334	.199968	.205301	.210720
	-.30	.185740	.188160	.190604	.193074	.195567	.198085	.200627	.203192	.205781	.208392	.211026	.216359	.221778
	-.40	.196798	.199218	.201662	.204132	.206626	.209144	.211685	.214251	.216839	.219450	.222084	.227417	.232836
15	.40	.100273	.102916	.105589	.108291	.111021	.113780	.116565	.119377	.122214	.125076	.127962	.133802	.139729
	.30	.111331	.113974	.116647	.119349	.122080	.124838	.127623	.130435	.133272	.136134	.139020	.144860	.150787
	.20	.122390	.125032	.127705	.130407	.133138	.135896	.138681	.141493	.144330	.147192	.150078	.155918	.161845
	.10	.133448	.136091	.138763	.141465	.144196	.146954	.149740	.152551	.155388	.158250	.161136	.166976	.172903
	0.00	.144506	.147149	.149821	.152523	.155254	.158012	.160798	.163609	.166447	.169308	.172194	.178034	.183961
	-.10	.155564	.158207	.160880	.163582	.166312	.169071	.171856	.174668	.177505	.180367	.183252	.189093	.195019
	-.20	.166622	.169265	.171938	.174640	.177370	.180129	.182914	.185726	.188563	.191425	.194310	.200151	.206078
	-.30	.177680	.180323	.182996	.185698	.188428	.191187	.193972	.196784	.199621	.202483	.205369	.211209	.217136
	-.40	.188739	.191381	.194054	.196756	.199487	.202245	.205030	.207842	.210679	.213541	.216427	.222267	.228194
20	.40	.096366	.099141	.101949	.104789	.107659	.110558	.113486	.116440	.119419	.122424	.125451	.131570	.137768
	.30	.107424	.110199	.113007	.115847	.118717	.121616	.124544	.127498	.130478	.133482	.136509	.142628	.148826
	.20	.118482	.121257	.124065	.126905	.129775	.132675	.135602	.138556	.141536	.144540	.147567	.153686	.159884
	.10	.129540	.132315	.135123	.137963	.140833	.143733	.146660	.149614	.152594	.155598	.158625	.164744	.170942
	0.00	.140598	.143374	.146182	.149021	.151891	.154791	.157718	.160672	.163652	.166656	.169683	.175802	.182000
	-.10	.151657	.154432	.157240	.160079	.162950	.165849	.168776	.171731	.174710	.177714	.180741	.186861	.193058
	-.20	.162715	.165490	.168298	.171138	.174008	.176907	.179835	.182789	.185768	.188772	.191800	.197919	.204116
	-.30	.173773	.176548	.179356	.182196	.185066	.187965	.190893	.193847	.196827	.199831	.202858	.208977	.215175
	-.40	.184831	.187606	.190414	.193254	.196124	.199023	.201951	.204905	.207885	.210889	.213916	.220035	.222233
25	.40	.094115	.096984	.099889	.102826	.105794	.108791	.111816	.114867	.117943	.121041	.124160	.130456	.136820
	.30	.105173	.108043	.110947	.113884	.116852	.119849	.122874	.125925	.129001	.132099	.135218	.141515	.147878
	.20	.116231	.119101	.122005	.124942	.127910	.130907	.133933	.136984	.140059	.143157	.146277	.152573	.158937
	.10	.127289	.130159	.133063	.136000	.138968	.141966	.144991	.148042	.151117	.154215	.157335	.163631	.169995
	0.00	.138348	.141221	.144121	.147058	.150026	.153024	.156049	.159100	.162175	.165274	.168393	.174689	.181053
	-.10	.149406	.152275	.155179	.158116	.161084	.164082	.167107	.170158	.173234	.176332	.179451	.185747	.192111
	-.20	.160464	.163333	.166237	.169174	.172143	.175140	.178165	.181216	.184292	.187390	.190509	.196805	.203169
	-.30	.171522	.174392	.177296	.180233	.183201	.186198	.189223	.192274	.195350	.198448	.201567	.207864	.214227
	-.40	.182580	.185450	.188354	.191291	.194259	.197256	.200281	.203333	.206408	.209506	.212625	.218922	.225285
30	.40	.092688	.095632	.098610	.101622	.104665	.107736	.110833	.113955	.117099	.120264	.123447	.129862	.136333
	.30	.103747	.106690	.109668	.112680	.115723	.118794	.121891	.125013	.128157	.131322	.134505	.140921	.147391
	.20	.114805	.117748	.120727	.123738	.126781	.129852	.132950	.136071	.139216	.142380	.145563	.151979	.158449
	.10	.125863	.128806	.131785	.134796	.137839	.140910	.144008	.147130	.150274	.153438	.156621	.163037	.169508
	0.00	.136921	.139864	.142843	.145855	.148897	.151968	.155066	.158188	.161332	.164496	.167680	.174095	.180566
	-.10	.147979	.150922	.153901	.156913	.159955	.163026	.166124	.169246	.172390	.175555	.178738	.185153	.191624
	-.20	.159037	.161981	.164959	.167971	.171014	.174085	.177182	.180304	.183448	.186613	.189796	.196211	.202682
	-.30	.170095	.173039	.176017	.179029	.182072	.185143	.188240	.191362	.194506	.197671	.200854	.207269	.213740
	-.40	.181154	.184097	.187075	.190087	.193130	.196201	.199299	.202420	.205565	.208729	.211912	.218328	.224798

5.0 YEAR HOLDING PERIOD
.300 EQUITY YIELD RATE
.700 LOAN RATIO

INTEREST RATE

TERM YEARS	APPR DEP	5.0	5.5	6.0	6.5	7.0	7.5	8.0	8.5	9.0	9.5	10.0	11.0	12.0
10	.40	.109962	.103502	.106069	.108662	.111281	.113925	.116593	.119287	.122005	.124747	.127512	.133112	.138801
	.30	.112020	.114561	.117127	.119720	.122339	.124983	.127652	.130345	.133063	.135805	.138570	.144170	.149860
	.20	.123078	.125619	.128186	.130778	.133397	.136041	.138710	.141403	.144121	.146863	.149628	.155228	.160918
	.10	.136136	.136677	.139244	.141837	.144455	.147099	.149768	.152420	.155179	.157921	.160686	.166286	.171976
	0.00	.145194	.147735	.150302	.152895	.155513	.158157	.160826	.163520	.166237	.168979	.171745	.177345	.183034
	-.10	.156253	.158793	.161360	.163953	.166571	.169215	.171884	.174578	.177296	.180037	.182803	.188403	.194092
	-.20	.167311	.169851	.172418	.175011	.177630	.180273	.182942	.185636	.188354	.191096	.193861	.199461	.205150
	-.30	.178369	.180910	.183478	.186069	.188688	.191332	.194001	.196694	.199412	.202154	.204919	.210519	.216209
	-.40	.189427	.191968	.194535	.197127	.199746	.202390	.205059	.207752	.210470	.213212	.215977	.221577	.227267
15	.40	.092499	.095274	.098081	.100918	.103785	.106681	.109606	.112558	.115537	.118542	.121572	.127704	.133927
	.30	.103558	.106332	.109139	.111976	.114843	.117739	.120664	.123616	.126595	.129600	.132630	.138762	.144985
	.20	.114616	.117391	.120197	.123034	.125901	.128797	.131722	.134674	.137653	.140658	.143688	.149821	.156044
	.10	.125674	.128449	.131255	.134092	.136959	.139856	.142780	.145732	.148711	.151716	.154746	.160879	.167102
	0.00	.136732	.139507	.142313	.145150	.148017	.150914	.153838	.156791	.159770	.162774	.165805	.171937	.178160
	-.10	.147790	.150565	.153371	.156209	.159076	.161972	.164897	.167849	.170828	.173833	.176863	.182995	.189218
	-.20	.158848	.161623	.164430	.167267	.170134	.173030	.175955	.178907	.181886	.184891	.187921	.194053	.200276
	-.30	.169907	.172681	.175488	.178325	.181192	.184088	.187013	.189965	.192944	.195949	.198979	.205111	.211334
	-.40	.180965	.183740	.186546	.189383	.192250	.195146	.198071	.201023	.204002	.207007	.210037	.216169	.222392
20	.40	.088397	.091310	.094259	.097240	.100254	.103299	.106372	.109474	.112603	.115757	.118936	.125361	.131868
	.30	.099455	.102369	.105317	.108299	.111312	.114357	.117430	.120532	.123661	.126815	.129994	.136419	.142926
	.20	.110513	.113427	.116375	.119357	.122370	.125415	.128489	.131590	.134719	.137873	.141052	.147477	.153984
	.10	.121571	.124485	.127433	.130415	.133429	.136473	.139547	.142649	.145777	.148932	.152110	.158535	.165043
	0.00	.132629	.135543	.138491	.141473	.144487	.147531	.150605	.153707	.156835	.159990	.163168	.169593	.176101
	-.10	.143687	.146601	.149550	.152531	.155545	.158589	.161663	.164765	.167894	.171048	.174226	.180651	.187159
	-.20	.154745	.157659	.160608	.163589	.166603	.169647	.172721	.175823	.178952	.182106	.185284	.191709	.198217
	-.30	.165804	.168717	.171666	.174648	.177661	.180706	.183779	.186881	.190010	.193164	.196343	.202768	.209275
	-.40	.176862	.179776	.182724	.185706	.188719	.191764	.194838	.197939	.201068	.204222	.207401	.213826	.220333
25	.40	.086033	.089046	.092095	.095179	.098296	.101443	.104619	.107823	.111052	.114305	.117581	.124192	.130873
	.30	.097091	.100104	.103154	.106237	.109354	.112501	.115678	.118881	.122110	.125363	.128639	.135250	.141932
	.20	.108150	.111162	.114212	.117296	.120412	.123559	.126736	.129939	.133169	.136422	.139697	.146308	.152990
	.10	.119208	.122221	.125270	.128354	.131470	.134618	.137794	.140998	.144227	.147480	.150755	.157366	.164048
	0.00	.130266	.133279	.136328	.139412	.142528	.145676	.148852	.152056	.155285	.158538	.161813	.168424	.175106
	-.10	.141324	.144337	.147386	.150470	.153586	.156734	.159910	.163114	.166343	.169596	.172871	.179482	.186164
	-.20	.152382	.155395	.158444	.161528	.164645	.167792	.170968	.174172	.177401	.180654	.183930	.190541	.197222
	-.30	.163440	.166453	.169503	.172586	.175703	.178850	.182027	.185230	.188459	.191712	.194988	.201599	.208281
	-.40	.174498	.177511	.180561	.183644	.186761	.189908	.193085	.196288	.199518	.202771	.206046	.212657	.219339
30	.40	.084535	.087626	.090753	.093916	.097110	.100335	.103587	.106865	.110167	.113489	.116832	.123568	.130362
	.30	.095593	.098684	.101811	.104974	.108168	.111393	.114645	.117923	.121225	.124548	.127890	.134626	.141420
	.20	.106652	.109742	.112870	.116032	.119227	.122451	.125704	.128982	.132283	.135606	.138948	.145684	.152478
	.10	.117710	.120800	.123928	.127090	.130285	.133509	.136762	.140040	.143341	.146664	.150006	.156742	.163536
	0.00	.128768	.131858	.134986	.138148	.141343	.144568	.147820	.151098	.154399	.157722	.161064	.167800	.174595
	-.10	.139826	.142916	.146044	.149206	.152401	.155626	.158878	.162156	.165457	.168780	.172122	.178859	.185653
	-.20	.150884	.153975	.157102	.160264	.163459	.166684	.169936	.173214	.176516	.179838	.183181	.189917	.196711
	-.30	.161942	.165033	.168160	.171323	.174517	.177742	.180994	.184272	.187574	.190896	.194239	.200975	.207769
	-.40	.173000	.176091	.179218	.182381	.185575	.188800	.192053	.195330	.198632	.201955	.205297	.212033	.218827

INTEREST RATE

TERM YEARS	APPR DEP	5.0	5.5	6.0	6.5	7.0	7.5	8.0	8.5	9.0	9.5	10.0	11.0	12.0
10	.40	.089904	.092626	.095377	.098155	.100960	.103793	.106652	.109538	.112450	.115388	.118351	.124351	.130447
	.30	.100962	.103685	.106435	.109213	.112018	.114851	.117711	.120597	.123509	.126446	.129409	.135409	.141005
	.20	.112021	.114743	.117493	.120271	.123077	.125909	.128769	.131655	.134567	.137504	.140467	.146467	.152563
	.10	.123079	.125801	.128551	.131329	.134135	.136967	.139827	.142713	.145625	.148562	.151525	.157525	.163621
	0.00	.134137	.136859	.139609	.142387	.145193	.148026	.150885	.153771	.156683	.159621	.162583	.168583	.174679
	-.10	.145195	.147917	.150667	.153445	.156251	.159084	.161943	.164829	.167741	.170679	.173642	.179642	.185738
	-.20	.156253	.158975	.161726	.164504	.167309	.170142	.173001	.175887	.178799	.181737	.184700	.190700	.196796
	-.30	.167311	.170033	.172784	.175562	.178367	.181200	.184060	.186945	.189857	.192795	.195758	.201758	.207854
	-.40	.178370	.181092	.183842	.186620	.189425	.192258	.195118	.198004	.200916	.203853	.206816	.212816	.218912
15	.40	.080837	.083811	.086817	.089857	.092929	.096032	.099166	.102329	.105520	.108740	.111987	.118557	.125224
	.30	.091896	.094869	.097876	.100915	.103987	.107090	.110224	.113387	.116579	.119798	.123045	.129615	.136283
	.20	.102954	.105927	.108934	.111973	.115045	.118148	.121282	.124445	.127637	.130856	.134103	.140673	.147341
	.10	.114012	.116985	.119992	.123032	.126103	.129207	.132340	.135503	.138695	.141915	.145161	.151731	.158399
	0.00	.125070	.128043	.131050	.134090	.137162	.140265	.143398	.146561	.149753	.152973	.156219	.162789	.169457
	-.10	.136128	.139101	.142108	.145148	.148220	.151323	.154456	.157619	.160811	.164031	.167277	.173848	.180515
	-.20	.147186	.150159	.153166	.156206	.159278	.162381	.165515	.168678	.171869	.175089	.178335	.184906	.191573
	-.30	.158245	.161218	.164224	.167264	.170336	.173439	.176573	.179736	.182928	.186147	.189394	.195964	.202631
	-.40	.169303	.172276	.175283	.178322	.181394	.184497	.187631	.190794	.193986	.197205	.200452	.207022	.213690
20	.40	.076441	.079563	.082722	.085917	.089146	.092408	.095701	.099025	.102377	.105756	.109162	.116046	.123018
	.30	.087500	.090622	.093781	.096975	.100204	.103466	.106759	.110083	.113435	.116814	.120220	.127104	.134076
	.20	.098558	.101680	.104839	.108033	.111262	.114524	.117817	.121141	.124493	.127873	.131278	.138162	.145135
	.10	.109616	.112738	.115897	.119092	.122321	.125582	.128876	.132199	.135551	.138931	.142336	.149220	.156193
	0.00	.120674	.123796	.126955	.130150	.133379	.136640	.139934	.143257	.146609	.149989	.153394	.160278	.167251
	-.10	.131732	.134854	.138013	.141208	.144437	.147699	.150992	.154315	.157668	.161047	.164453	.171337	.178339
	-.20	.142790	.145912	.149071	.152266	.155495	.158757	.162050	.165374	.168726	.172105	.175511	.182395	.189367
	-.30	.153849	.156971	.160130	.163324	.166553	.169815	.173108	.176432	.179784	.183163	.186569	.193453	.200425
	-.40	.164907	.168029	.171188	.174382	.177611	.180873	.184166	.187490	.190842	.194222	.197627	.204511	.211483
25	.40	.073909	.077137	.080405	.083709	.087048	.090420	.093823	.097256	.100715	.104201	.107710	.114793	.121952
	.30	.084967	.088196	.091463	.094767	.098106	.101478	.104881	.108314	.111774	.115259	.118768	.125851	.133011
	.20	.096026	.099254	.102521	.105825	.109164	.112536	.115939	.119372	.122832	.126317	.129826	.136910	.144069
	.10	.107084	.110312	.113579	.116883	.120222	.123594	.126998	.130430	.133890	.137375	.140885	.147968	.155127
	0.00	.118142	.121370	.124637	.127941	.131280	.134653	.138056	.141488	.144948	.148434	.151943	.159026	.166185
	-.10	.129200	.132428	.135695	.138999	.142339	.145711	.149114	.152546	.156006	.159492	.163001	.170084	.177243
	-.20	.140258	.143486	.146753	.150058	.153397	.156769	.160172	.163605	.167064	.170550	.174059	.181142	.188301
	-.30	.151316	.154545	.157812	.161116	.164455	.167827	.171230	.174663	.178123	.181608	.185117	.192200	.199360
	-.40	.162375	.165603	.168870	.172174	.175513	.178885	.182288	.185721	.189181	.192666	.196175	.203259	.210418
30	.40	.072304	.075616	.078966	.082355	.085778	.089233	.092717	.096229	.099767	.103327	.106908	.114125	.121404
	.30	.083363	.086674	.090025	.093443	.096836	.100291	.103775	.107248	.110825	.114385	.117966	.125183	.132463
	.20	.094421	.097736	.101083	.104471	.107894	.111349	.114834	.118346	.121883	.125443	.129024	.136241	.143521
	.10	.105479	.108790	.112141	.115529	.118952	.122407	.125892	.129404	.132941	.136501	.140082	.147299	.154579
	0.00	.116537	.119848	.123199	.126587	.130010	.133465	.136950	.140462	.143999	.147559	.151140	.158358	.165637
	-.10	.127595	.130906	.134257	.137645	.141068	.144523	.148008	.151520	.155057	.158617	.162198	.169416	.176695
	-.20	.138653	.141964	.145315	.148704	.152127	.155582	.159066	.162578	.166115	.169676	.173257	.180474	.187753
	-.30	.149711	.153023	.156374	.159762	.163185	.166640	.170124	.173636	.177174	.180734	.184315	.191532	.198812
	-.40	.160770	.164081	.167432	.170820	.174243	.177698	.181183	.184695	.188232	.191792	.195373	.202590	.209870

5.0 YEAR HOLDING PERIOD
.300 EQUITY YIELD RATE
.800 LOAN RATIO

INTEREST RATE

TERM YEARS	APPR DEP	5.0	5.5	6.0	6.5	7.0	7.5	8.0	8.5	9.0	9.5	10.0	11.0	12.0
10	.40	.078847	.081750	.084684	.087047	.090640	.093661	.096711	.099790	.102896	.106029	.109190	.115590	.122092
	.30	.089905	.092806	.095742	.098705	.101698	.104719	.107770	.110848	.113954	.117038	.120248	.126648	.133150
	.20	.100963	.103867	.106800	.109763	.112756	.115778	.118828	.121906	.125012	.128146	.131306	.137706	.144208
	.10	.112021	.114925	.117858	.120822	.123814	.126836	.129886	.132964	.136070	.139204	.142364	.148764	.155267
	0.00	.123079	.125983	.128916	.131880	.134872	.137894	.140944	.144022	.147129	.150262	.153422	.159822	.166325
	-.10	.134138	.137041	.139975	.142938	.145931	.148952	.152002	.155081	.158187	.161320	.164481	.170880	.177383
	-.20	.145199	.148099	.151033	.153996	.156989	.160010	.163060	.166139	.169245	.172378	.175539	.181939	.188441
	-.30	.156254	.159157	.162091	.165054	.168047	.171068	.174119	.177197	.180303	.183436	.186597	.192997	.199499
	-.40	.167312	.170216	.173149	.176112	.179105	.182127	.185177	.188255	.191361	.194495	.197655	.204055	.210557
15	.40	.069175	.072347	.075554	.078796	.082073	.085383	.088726	.092099	.095504	.098938	.102401	.109410	.116522
	.30	.080234	.083405	.086612	.089855	.093131	.096441	.099784	.103158	.106562	.109996	.113459	.120468	.127580
	.20	.091292	.094463	.097670	.100913	.104189	.107499	.110842	.114216	.117620	.121055	.124517	.131526	.138638
	.10	.102350	.105521	.108728	.111971	.115248	.118558	.121900	.125274	.128678	.132113	.135576	.142584	.149696
	0.00	.113408	.116579	.119787	.123029	.126306	.129616	.132958	.136332	.139737	.143171	.146634	.153642	.160754
	-.10	.124466	.127638	.130845	.134087	.137364	.140674	.144016	.147390	.150795	.154229	.157692	.164700	.171812
	-.20	.135524	.138696	.141903	.145145	.148422	.151732	.155074	.158448	.161853	.165287	.168750	.175758	.182870
	-.30	.146583	.149754	.152961	.156204	.159480	.162790	.166133	.169507	.172911	.176345	.179808	.186817	.193929
	-.40	.157641	.160812	.164019	.167262	.170538	.173848	.177191	.180565	.183969	.187403	.190866	.197875	.204987
20	.40	.064468	.067817	.071186	.074594	.078038	.081517	.085030	.088575	.092151	.095756	.099388	.106731	.114168
	.30	.075545	.078875	.082244	.085652	.089096	.092575	.096088	.099633	.103209	.106814	.110446	.117789	.125226
	.20	.086603	.089933	.093302	.096710	.100154	.103634	.107146	.110691	.114267	.117672	.121504	.128847	.136285
	.10	.097661	.100991	.104361	.107768	.111212	.114692	.118205	.121750	.125325	.128930	.132563	.139905	.147343
	0.00	.108719	.112049	.115419	.118826	.122271	.125750	.129263	.132808	.136383	.139988	.143621	.150964	.158401
	-.10	.119777	.123107	.126477	.129885	.133329	.136808	.140321	.143866	.147442	.151046	.154679	.162022	.169459
	-.20	.130835	.134165	.137535	.140943	.144387	.147866	.151379	.154924	.158500	.162105	.165737	.173080	.180517
	-.30	.141894	.145224	.148593	.152001	.155445	.158924	.162437	.165982	.169558	.173163	.176795	.184138	.191575
	-.40	.152952	.156282	.159651	.163059	.166503	.169982	.173495	.177040	.180616	.184221	.187853	.195196	.202633
25	.40	.061785	.065229	.068714	.072238	.075800	.079397	.083027	.086688	.090379	.094096	.097840	.105395	.113031
	.30	.072844	.076287	.079772	.083296	.086858	.090455	.094085	.097746	.101437	.105155	.108898	.116453	.124090
	.20	.083902	.087345	.090830	.094354	.097916	.101513	.105143	.108804	.112495	.116213	.119956	.127511	.135148
	.10	.094960	.098403	.101888	.105413	.108974	.112571	.116201	.119863	.123553	.127271	.131014	.138570	.146206
	0.00	.106018	.109461	.112946	.116471	.120032	.123629	.127259	.130921	.134611	.138329	.142072	.149628	.157264
	-.10	.117076	.120520	.124004	.127529	.131091	.134687	.138318	.141979	.145669	.149387	.153130	.160686	.168322
	-.20	.128134	.131578	.135063	.138587	.142149	.145746	.149376	.153037	.156728	.160445	.164189	.171744	.179380
	-.30	.139193	.142636	.146121	.149645	.153207	.156804	.160434	.164095	.167786	.171504	.175247	.182802	.190439
	-.40	.150251	.153694	.157179	.160703	.164265	.167862	.171492	.175153	.178844	.182562	.186305	.193860	.201497
30	.40	.060074	.063605	.067180	.070794	.074445	.078130	.081847	.085594	.089367	.093164	.096984	.104682	.112447
	.30	.071132	.074664	.078238	.081852	.085503	.089188	.092905	.096652	.100425	.104222	.108042	.115740	.123505
	.20	.082190	.085722	.089296	.092910	.096561	.100247	.103964	.107710	.111483	.115280	.119100	.126798	.134563
	.10	.093248	.096780	.100354	.103968	.107619	.111305	.115022	.118768	.122541	.126338	.130158	.137857	.145621
	0.00	.104306	.107838	.111412	.115026	.118677	.122363	.126080	.129826	.133599	.137397	.141216	.148915	.156680
	-.10	.115364	.118896	.122471	.126085	.129736	.133421	.137138	.140884	.144657	.148455	.152274	.159973	.167738
	-.20	.126422	.129954	.133529	.137143	.140794	.144479	.148196	.151942	.155715	.159513	.163331	.171031	.178796
	-.30	.137481	.141012	.144587	.148201	.151852	.155537	.159254	.163001	.166774	.170571	.174391	.182089	.189854
	-.40	.148539	.152071	.155645	.159259	.162910	.166596	.170313	.174059	.177832	.181629	.185449	.193147	.200912

5.0 YEAR HOLDING PERIOD
.300 EQUITY YIELD RATE
.900 LOAN RATIO

INTEREST RATE

TERM YEARS	APPR DEP	5.0	5.5	6.0	6.5	7.0	7.5	8.0	8.5	9.0	9.5	10.0	11.0	12.0
10	.40	.056732	.059998	.063298	.066632	.069999	.073398	.076829	.080293	.083787	.087312	.090868	.098067	.105383
	.30	.067790	.071056	.074357	.077690	.081057	.084456	.087888	.091351	.094845	.098370	.101926	.109126	.116441
	.20	.078848	.082114	.085415	.088748	.092115	.095514	.098946	.102409	.105903	.109428	.112984	.120184	.127499
	.10	.089906	.093173	.096473	.099807	.103173	.106573	.110004	.113467	.116961	.120487	.124042	.131242	.138557
	0.00	.100964	.104231	.107531	.110865	.114231	.117631	.121062	.124525	.128020	.131545	.135100	.142300	.149615
	-.10	.112023	.115289	.118589	.121923	.125290	.128689	.132120	.135583	.139078	.142603	.146158	.153358	.160673
	-.20	.123081	.126347	.129647	.132981	.136348	.139747	.143178	.146642	.150136	.153661	.157217	.164416	.171732
	-.30	.134139	.137405	.140705	.144039	.147406	.150805	.154237	.157700	.161194	.164719	.168275	.175475	.182790
	-.40	.145197	.148463	.151764	.155097	.158464	.161863	.165295	.168758	.172252	.175777	.179333	.186533	.193848
15	.40	.045851	.049419	.053027	.056675	.060361	.064085	.067845	.071641	.075471	.079335	.083230	.091115	.099116
	.30	.056910	.060477	.064086	.067733	.071419	.075143	.078903	.082699	.086529	.090393	.094289	.102173	.110174
	.20	.067968	.071535	.075144	.078791	.082478	.086201	.089962	.093757	.097587	.101451	.105347	.113231	.121232
	.10	.079026	.082594	.086202	.089850	.093536	.097259	.101020	.104815	.108646	.112509	.116405	.124289	.132290
	0.00	.090084	.093652	.097260	.100908	.104594	.108318	.112078	.115874	.119704	.123567	.127463	.135347	.143348
	-.10	.101142	.104710	.108318	.111966	.115652	.119376	.123136	.126932	.130762	.134625	.138521	.146406	.154407
	-.20	.112200	.115768	.119376	.123024	.126710	.130434	.134194	.137990	.141820	.145684	.149579	.157464	.165465
	-.30	.123259	.126826	.130434	.134082	.137768	.141492	.145252	.149048	.152878	.156742	.160637	.168522	.176523
	-.40	.134317	.137884	.141493	.145140	.148827	.152550	.156311	.160106	.163936	.167800	.171696	.179580	.187581
20	.40	.040576	.044323	.048114	.051947	.055822	.059736	.063688	.067676	.071699	.075754	.079841	.088101	.096468
	.30	.051634	.055381	.059172	.063005	.066880	.070794	.074746	.078734	.082757	.086812	.090899	.099160	.107527
	.20	.062693	.066439	.070230	.074063	.077938	.081852	.085804	.089792	.093815	.097870	.101957	.110218	.118585
	.10	.073751	.077497	.081288	.085122	.088996	.092910	.096862	.100851	.104873	.108929	.113015	.121276	.129643
	0.00	.084809	.088555	.092346	.096180	.100054	.103969	.107921	.111909	.115931	.119987	.124073	.132334	.140701
	-.10	.095867	.099613	.103404	.107238	.111113	.115027	.118979	.122967	.126989	.131045	.135132	.143392	.151759
	-.20	.106925	.110672	.114462	.118296	.122171	.126085	.130037	.134025	.138048	.142103	.146190	.154450	.162817
	-.30	.117983	.121730	.125521	.129354	.133229	.137143	.141095	.145083	.149106	.153161	.157248	.165509	.173875
	-.40	.129042	.132788	.136579	.140412	.144287	.148201	.152153	.156141	.160164	.164219	.168306	.176567	.184934
25	.40	.037538	.041411	.045332	.049297	.053304	.057350	.061434	.065553	.069705	.073888	.078099	.086599	.095190
	.30	.048596	.052470	.056390	.060355	.064362	.068449	.072492	.076611	.080763	.084946	.089157	.097657	.106248
	.20	.059654	.063528	.067448	.071413	.075420	.079467	.083551	.087670	.091821	.096004	.100215	.108715	.117306
	.10	.070712	.074586	.078506	.082471	.086478	.090525	.094609	.098728	.102880	.107062	.111273	.119773	.128364
	0.00	.081770	.085644	.089565	.093530	.097536	.101583	.105667	.109786	.113938	.118120	.122331	.130831	.139422
	-.10	.092828	.096702	.100623	.104588	.108595	.112641	.116725	.120844	.124996	.129178	.133389	.141889	.150480
	-.20	.103887	.107760	.111681	.115646	.119653	.123699	.127783	.131902	.136054	.140237	.144448	.152947	.161538
	-.30	.114945	.118819	.122739	.126704	.130711	.134757	.138841	.142960	.147112	.151295	.155506	.164006	.172597
	-.40	.126003	.129877	.133797	.137762	.141769	.145816	.149900	.154019	.158170	.162353	.166564	.175064	.183655
30	.40	.035012	.039585	.043606	.047672	.051780	.055926	.060107	.064322	.068566	.072839	.077136	.085796	.094532
	.30	.046070	.050643	.054664	.058730	.062838	.066984	.071165	.075380	.079625	.083897	.088194	.096855	.105590
	.20	.057128	.061701	.065723	.069788	.073896	.078042	.082224	.086438	.090683	.094955	.099252	.107913	.116648
	.10	.068186	.072760	.076781	.080847	.084954	.089100	.093282	.097496	.101741	.106013	.110310	.118971	.127706
	0.00	.079244	.083818	.087839	.091905	.096013	.100158	.104340	.108554	.112799	.117071	.121368	.130029	.138765
	-.10	.090303	.094876	.098897	.102963	.107070	.111216	.115398	.119613	.123857	.128129	.132427	.141087	.149823
	-.20	.101361	.105934	.109955	.114021	.118129	.122275	.126456	.130671	.134915	.139187	.143485	.152145	.160881
	-.30	.112419	.116992	.121013	.125079	.129187	.133333	.137514	.141729	.145973	.150246	.154543	.163204	.171939
	-.40	.123477	.128050	.132072	.136137	.140245	.144391	.148573	.152787	.157032	.161304	.165601	.174262	.182997

5.0 YEAR HOLDING PERIOD
.400 EQUITY YIELD RATE
.600 LOAN RATIO

INTEREST RATE

TERM YEARS	APPR DEP	5.0	5.5	6.0	6.5	7.0	7.5	8.0	8.5	9.0	9.5	10.0	11.0	12.0
10	.40	.175816	.177923	.180053	.182205	.184380	.186577	.188795	.191036	.193297	.195579	.197882	.202548	.207293
	.30	.184952	.187059	.189189	.191341	.193516	.195713	.197932	.200172	.202433	.204715	.207018	.211684	.216430
	.20	.194088	.196195	.198325	.200477	.202652	.204849	.207068	.209308	.211569	.213851	.216154	.220821	.225566
	.10	.203224	.205331	.207461	.209614	.211788	.213985	.216204	.218444	.220705	.222987	.225290	.229957	.234702
	0.00	.212360	.214467	.216597	.218750	.220924	.223121	.225340	.227580	.229841	.232123	.234426	.239093	.243838
	-.10	.221496	.223603	.225733	.227886	.230060	.232257	.234476	.236716	.238977	.241260	.243562	.248229	.252974
	-.20	.230632	.232739	.234869	.237022	.239197	.241393	.243612	.245852	.248113	.250396	.252699	.257365	.262110
	-.30	.239768	.241876	.244005	.246158	.248333	.250529	.252748	.254988	.257250	.259532	.261835	.266501	.271246
	-.40	.248905	.251012	.253142	.255294	.257469	.259666	.261884	.264124	.266386	.268668	.270971	.275637	.280382
15	.40	.166440	.168740	.171062	.173412	.175790	.178193	.180623	.183078	.185557	.188060	.190586	.195704	.200907
	.30	.175582	.177876	.180198	.182549	.184926	.187330	.189759	.192214	.194693	.197196	.199722	.204840	.210043
	.20	.184718	.187012	.189335	.191685	.194062	.196466	.198895	.201350	.203829	.206332	.208858	.213976	.219179
	.10	.193854	.196148	.198471	.200821	.203198	.205602	.208031	.210486	.212965	.215468	.217994	.223112	.228315
	0.00	.202990	.205284	.207607	.209957	.212334	.214738	.217167	.219622	.222101	.224604	.227130	.232248	.237451
	-.10	.212126	.214420	.216743	.219093	.221470	.223874	.226303	.228758	.231237	.233740	.236266	.241385	.246587
	-.20	.221262	.223556	.225879	.228229	.230606	.233010	.235440	.237894	.240373	.242876	.245402	.250521	.255723
	-.30	.230398	.232693	.235015	.237365	.239742	.242146	.244576	.247030	.249509	.252012	.254538	.259657	.264859
	-.40	.239535	.241829	.244151	.246501	.248878	.251282	.253712	.256166	.258645	.261148	.263674	.268793	.273995
20	.40	.161903	.164316	.166761	.169237	.171744	.174279	.176841	.179431	.182045	.184685	.187347	.192738	.198208
	.30	.171039	.173452	.175897	.178373	.180880	.183415	.185977	.188567	.191182	.193821	.196483	.201874	.207344
	.20	.180175	.182588	.185033	.187510	.190016	.192551	.195113	.197703	.200318	.202957	.205619	.211010	.216481
	.10	.189311	.191724	.194169	.196646	.199152	.201687	.204250	.206839	.209454	.212093	.214756	.220146	.225617
	0.00	.198447	.200860	.203306	.205782	.208288	.210823	.213386	.215975	.218590	.221229	.223892	.229282	.234753
	-.10	.207583	.209996	.212442	.214918	.217424	.219959	.222522	.225111	.227726	.230365	.233028	.238418	.243889
	-.20	.216720	.219133	.221578	.224054	.226560	.229095	.231658	.234247	.236862	.239501	.242164	.247554	.253025
	-.30	.225856	.228269	.230714	.233190	.235696	.238231	.240794	.243383	.245998	.248637	.251300	.256690	.262161
	-.40	.234992	.237405	.239850	.242326	.244832	.247367	.249930	.252519	.255134	.257773	.260436	.265826	.271297
25	.40	.159286	.161789	.164326	.166897	.169499	.172131	.174791	.177478	.180190	.182925	.185683	.191258	.196905
	.30	.168422	.170925	.173463	.176033	.178635	.181267	.183927	.186614	.189326	.192361	.194819	.200394	.206041
	.20	.177558	.180061	.182599	.185169	.187771	.190403	.193063	.195750	.198462	.201198	.203955	.209530	.215177
	.10	.186694	.189197	.191735	.194305	.196907	.199539	.202200	.204886	.207598	.210334	.213091	.218666	.224313
	0.00	.195831	.198333	.200871	.203441	.206043	.208675	.211336	.214022	.216734	.219470	.222227	.227803	.233449
	-.10	.204967	.207469	.210007	.212578	.215180	.217812	.220472	.223159	.225870	.228606	.231363	.236939	.242585
	-.20	.214103	.216606	.219143	.221714	.224316	.226948	.229608	.232295	.235007	.237742	.240499	.246075	.251722
	-.30	.223239	.225742	.228279	.230850	.233452	.236084	.238744	.241431	.244143	.246878	.249636	.255211	.260858
	-.40	.232375	.234878	.237415	.239986	.242588	.245220	.247880	.250567	.253279	.256014	.258772	.264347	.269994
30	.40	.157628	.160204	.162816	.165462	.168141	.170849	.173584	.176345	.179130	.181937	.184763	.190469	.196235
	.30	.166764	.169340	.171952	.174598	.177277	.179985	.182720	.185481	.188266	.191073	.193899	.199605	.205371
	.20	.175900	.178476	.181088	.183734	.186413	.189121	.191856	.194618	.197402	.200209	.203035	.208741	.214507
	.10	.185036	.187612	.190224	.192871	.195549	.198257	.200992	.203754	.206538	.209345	.212171	.217877	.223643
	0.00	.194172	.196748	.199360	.202007	.204685	.207393	.210129	.212890	.215674	.218481	.221307	.227013	.232779
	-.10	.203308	.205884	.208496	.211143	.213821	.216529	.219265	.222026	.224811	.227617	.230443	.236149	.241915
	-.20	.212444	.215020	.217632	.220279	.222957	.225665	.228401	.231162	.233947	.236753	.239579	.245285	.251051
	-.30	.221580	.224156	.226769	.229415	.232093	.234801	.237537	.240298	.243083	.245889	.248716	.254421	.260187
	-.40	.230716	.233292	.235905	.238551	.241229	.243937	.246673	.249434	.252219	.255025	.257852	.263557	.269324

192

5.0 YEAR HOLDING PERIOD
.400 EQUITY YIELD RATE
.667 LOAN RATIO

INTEREST RATE

TERM YEARS	APPR DEP	5.0	5.5	6.0	6.5	7.0	7.5	8.0	8.5	9.0	9.5	10.0	11.0	12.0
10	.40	.154966	.157307	.159674	.162065	.164482	.166923	.169388	.171877	.174389	.176925	.179484	.184669	.189941
	.30	.164102	.166443	.168810	.171201	.173618	.176059	.178524	.181013	.183526	.186061	.188620	.193805	.199077
	.20	.173238	.175579	.177946	.180337	.182754	.185195	.187660	.190149	.192662	.195197	.197756	.202941	.208213
	.10	.182374	.184715	.187082	.189474	.191890	.194331	.196796	.199285	.201798	.204334	.206892	.212077	.217349
	0.00	.191510	.193851	.196218	.198610	.201026	.203467	.205932	.208421	.210934	.213470	.216028	.221213	.226486
	-.10	.200646	.202988	.205354	.207746	.210162	.212603	.215068	.217557	.220070	.222606	.225164	.230349	.235622
	-.20	.209782	.212124	.214490	.216882	.219298	.221739	.224204	.226693	.229206	.231742	.234301	.239485	.244758
	-.30	.218919	.221260	.223626	.226018	.228434	.230875	.233340	.235829	.238342	.240878	.243437	.248622	.253894
	-.40	.228055	.230396	.232762	.235154	.237570	.240011	.242477	.244966	.247478	.250014	.252573	.257758	.263030
15	.40	.144555	.147104	.149684	.152296	.154937	.157608	.160307	.163035	.165789	.168570	.171377	.177064	.182845
	.30	.153691	.156240	.158820	.161432	.164073	.166744	.169443	.172171	.174925	.177706	.180513	.186200	.191981
	.20	.162827	.165376	.167956	.170568	.173209	.175880	.178579	.181307	.184061	.186842	.189649	.195336	.201117
	.10	.171963	.174512	.177093	.179704	.182345	.185016	.187716	.190443	.193197	.195978	.198785	.204472	.210253
	0.00	.181099	.183648	.186229	.188840	.191481	.194152	.196852	.199579	.202334	.205115	.207921	.213608	.219389
	-.10	.190235	.192784	.195365	.197976	.200617	.203288	.205988	.208715	.211470	.214251	.217057	.222745	.228525
	-.20	.199371	.201920	.204501	.207112	.209753	.212424	.215124	.217851	.220606	.223387	.226193	.231881	.237661
	-.30	.208507	.211056	.213637	.216248	.218890	.221560	.224260	.226987	.229742	.232523	.235330	.241017	.246797
	-.40	.217644	.220192	.222773	.225384	.228026	.230696	.233396	.236123	.238878	.241659	.244466	.250153	.255933
20	.40	.139507	.142188	.144905	.147656	.150441	.153258	.156105	.158982	.161888	.164820	.167779	.173768	.179847
	.30	.148643	.151324	.154041	.156793	.159577	.162394	.165241	.168118	.171024	.173956	.176915	.182904	.188983
	.20	.157779	.160460	.163177	.165929	.168713	.171530	.174377	.177255	.180160	.183092	.186051	.192040	.198119
	.10	.166915	.169597	.172313	.175065	.177849	.180666	.183514	.186391	.189296	.192229	.195187	.201176	.207255
	0.00	.176051	.178733	.181449	.184201	.186985	.189802	.192650	.195527	.198432	.201365	.204323	.210312	.216391
	-.10	.185188	.187869	.190586	.193337	.196122	.198938	.201786	.204663	.207568	.210501	.213459	.219449	.225527
	-.20	.194324	.197005	.199722	.202473	.205258	.208074	.210922	.213799	.216704	.219637	.222595	.228585	.234663
	-.30	.203460	.206141	.208858	.211609	.214394	.217210	.220058	.222935	.225840	.228773	.231731	.237721	.243799
	-.40	.212596	.215277	.217994	.220745	.223530	.226347	.229194	.232071	.234977	.237909	.240867	.246857	.252935
25	.40	.136600	.139380	.142200	.145056	.147947	.150872	.153827	.156813	.159826	.162865	.165929	.172124	.178398
	.30	.145736	.148517	.151336	.154192	.157083	.160008	.162964	.165949	.168962	.172002	.175065	.181260	.187535
	.20	.154872	.157653	.160472	.163328	.166220	.169144	.172100	.175085	.178098	.181138	.184202	.190396	.196671
	.10	.164008	.166789	.169608	.172464	.175356	.178280	.181236	.184221	.187234	.190274	.193338	.199532	.205807
	0.00	.173144	.175925	.178744	.181600	.184492	.187416	.190372	.193357	.196370	.199410	.202474	.208669	.214943
	-.10	.182280	.185061	.187880	.190737	.193628	.196552	.199508	.202493	.205507	.208546	.211610	.217805	.224079
	-.20	.191416	.194197	.197016	.199873	.202764	.205688	.208644	.211629	.214643	.217682	.220746	.226941	.233215
	-.30	.200552	.203333	.206153	.209009	.211900	.214824	.217780	.220765	.223779	.226818	.229882	.236077	.242351
	-.40	.209688	.212469	.215289	.218145	.221036	.223960	.226916	.229902	.232915	.235954	.239018	.245213	.251487
30	.40	.134757	.137619	.140521	.143462	.146438	.149447	.152486	.155554	.158648	.161767	.164907	.171247	.177654
	.30	.143893	.146755	.149658	.152598	.155574	.158583	.161622	.164690	.167785	.170903	.174043	.180383	.186790
	.20	.153029	.155891	.158794	.161734	.164710	.167719	.170758	.173826	.176921	.180039	.183179	.189519	.195926
	.10	.162165	.165027	.167930	.170870	.173846	.176855	.179895	.182963	.186057	.189175	.192315	.198655	.205062
	0.00	.171301	.174163	.177066	.180006	.182982	.185991	.189031	.192099	.195193	.198311	.201452	.207791	.214198
	-.10	.180437	.183299	.186202	.189142	.192118	.195127	.198167	.201235	.204329	.207447	.210588	.216927	.223334
	-.20	.189573	.192435	.195338	.198278	.201254	.204263	.207303	.210371	.213465	.216583	.219724	.226063	.232470
	-.30	.198709	.201572	.204474	.207415	.210390	.213399	.216439	.219507	.222601	.225719	.228860	.235200	.241606
	-.40	.207845	.210708	.213610	.216551	.219527	.222535	.225575	.228643	.231737	.234856	.237996	.244336	.250743

193

5.0 YEAR HOLDING PERIOD
.400 EQUITY YIELD RATE
.700 LOAN RATIO

INTEREST RATE

TERM YEARS	APPR DEP	5.0	5.5	6.0	6.5	7.0	7.5	8.0	8.5	9.0	9.5	10.0	11.0	12.0
10	.40	.144543	.147001	.149486	.151997	.154534	.157097	.159685	.162299	.164937	.167600	.170286	.175730	.181266
	.30	.153679	.156137	.158622	.161133	.163670	.166233	.168822	.171435	.174073	.176736	.179422	.184867	.190402
	.20	.162815	.165273	.167758	.170269	.172806	.175369	.177958	.180571	.183209	.185872	.188559	.194003	.199595
	.10	.171951	.174409	.176894	.179405	.181942	.184505	.187094	.189707	.192345	.195008	.197695	.203139	.208675
	0.00	.181087	.183545	.186030	.188541	.191078	.193641	.196230	.198843	.201481	.204144	.206831	.212275	.217811
	-.10	.190223	.192681	.195166	.197677	.200215	.202778	.205366	.207979	.210618	.213280	.215967	.221411	.226947
	-.20	.199351	.201817	.204302	.206813	.209351	.211914	.214502	.217115	.219754	.222416	.225103	.230547	.236083
	-.30	.208495	.210953	.213438	.215949	.218487	.221050	.223638	.226252	.228890	.231552	.234239	.239683	.245219
	-.40	.217631	.220090	.222574	.225086	.227623	.230186	.232774	.235388	.238026	.240688	.243375	.248619	.254355
15	.40	.133611	.136287	.138997	.141739	.144512	.147316	.150151	.153015	.155907	.158827	.161774	.167745	.173815
	.30	.142747	.145423	.148133	.150875	.153648	.156453	.159287	.162151	.165043	.167963	.170910	.176882	.182951
	.20	.151883	.154559	.157269	.160011	.162784	.165589	.168423	.171287	.174179	.177099	.180046	.186018	.192087
	.10	.161019	.163696	.166405	.169147	.171920	.174725	.177559	.180423	.183315	.186235	.189182	.195154	.201223
	0.00	.170155	.172832	.175541	.178283	.181056	.183861	.186695	.189559	.192451	.195371	.198318	.204290	.210359
	-.10	.179291	.181968	.184677	.187419	.190193	.192997	.195831	.198695	.201587	.204507	.207454	.213426	.219495
	-.20	.188427	.191104	.193813	.196555	.199329	.202133	.204967	.207831	.210723	.213644	.216590	.222562	.228632
	-.30	.197564	.200240	.202949	.205691	.208465	.211269	.214104	.216967	.219860	.222780	.225727	.231698	.237768
	-.40	.206700	.209376	.212086	.214827	.217601	.220405	.223240	.226103	.228996	.231916	.234863	.240834	.246904
20	.40	.128311	.131126	.133979	.136868	.139791	.142749	.145739	.148760	.151810	.154890	.157996	.164285	.170667
	.30	.137447	.140262	.143115	.146004	.148928	.151885	.154875	.157896	.160947	.164026	.167132	.173421	.179803
	.20	.146583	.149398	.152251	.155140	.158064	.161021	.164011	.167032	.170083	.173162	.176268	.182557	.188939
	.10	.155719	.158534	.161387	.164276	.167200	.170157	.173147	.176168	.179219	.182298	.185404	.191693	.198075
	0.00	.164855	.167670	.170523	.173412	.176336	.179293	.182283	.185304	.188355	.191434	.194540	.200829	.207212
	-.10	.173991	.176807	.179659	.182548	.185472	.188429	.191419	.194440	.197491	.200570	.203676	.209965	.216348
	-.20	.183127	.185943	.188795	.191684	.194608	.197566	.200555	.203576	.206627	.209706	.212812	.219101	.225484
	-.30	.192264	.195079	.197931	.200820	.203744	.206702	.209692	.212712	.215763	.218842	.221948	.228237	.234620
	-.40	.201400	.204215	.207067	.209956	.212880	.215838	.218828	.221849	.224899	.227978	.231085	.237373	.243756
25	.40	.125258	.128178	.131138	.134137	.137173	.140244	.143347	.146482	.149646	.152837	.156054	.162559	.169147
	.30	.134394	.137314	.140274	.143273	.146309	.149380	.152483	.155618	.158782	.161973	.165190	.171695	.178283
	.20	.143530	.146450	.149410	.152409	.155445	.158516	.161619	.164754	.167918	.171109	.174326	.180831	.187419
	.10	.152666	.155586	.158547	.161546	.164581	.167652	.170755	.173890	.177054	.180245	.183462	.189967	.196555
	0.00	.161802	.164722	.167683	.170682	.173717	.176788	.179892	.183026	.186190	.189381	.192598	.199103	.205691
	-.10	.170938	.173858	.176819	.179818	.182854	.185924	.189028	.192162	.195326	.198517	.201735	.208239	.214827
	-.20	.180074	.182994	.185955	.188954	.191990	.195060	.198164	.201298	.204462	.207654	.210871	.217375	.223963
	-.30	.189211	.192130	.195091	.198090	.201126	.204196	.207300	.210434	.213598	.216790	.220007	.226511	.233099
	-.40	.198347	.201267	.204227	.207226	.210262	.213332	.216436	.219571	.222734	.225926	.229143	.235647	.242235
30	.40	.123323	.126328	.129376	.132463	.135588	.138747	.141939	.145160	.148409	.151683	.154981	.161638	.168365
	.30	.132459	.135464	.138512	.141599	.144724	.147883	.151075	.154296	.157545	.160819	.164117	.170774	.177501
	.20	.141595	.144600	.147648	.150736	.153860	.157020	.160211	.163432	.166681	.169956	.173253	.179910	.186637
	.10	.150731	.153737	.156784	.159872	.162996	.166156	.169347	.172569	.175817	.179092	.182389	.189046	.195773
	0.00	.159867	.162873	.165920	.169008	.172132	.175292	.178483	.181705	.184954	.188228	.191525	.198182	.204909
	-.10	.169003	.172009	.175056	.178144	.181268	.184428	.187619	.190841	.194090	.197364	.200661	.207318	.214045
	-.20	.178139	.181145	.184193	.187280	.190405	.193564	.196755	.199977	.203226	.206500	.209797	.216454	.223181
	-.30	.187276	.190281	.193329	.196416	.199541	.202700	.205892	.209113	.212362	.215636	.218933	.225590	.232317
	-.40	.196412	.199417	.202465	.205552	.208677	.211836	.215028	.218250	.221498	.224772	.228070	.234726	.241453

5.0 YEAR HOLDING PERIOD
.400 EQUITY YIELD RATE
.750 LOAN RATIO

INTEREST RATE

TERM YEARS	APPR DEP	5.0	5.5	6.0	6.5	7.0	7.5	8.0	8.5	9.0	9.5	10.0	11.0	12.0
10	.40	.128906	.131540	.134202	.136893	.139611	.142357	.145130	.147931	.150757	.153610	.156489	.162322	.168253
	.30	.138042	.140676	.143338	.146029	.148747	.151493	.154267	.157067	.159893	.162746	.165625	.171458	.177389
	.20	.147178	.149812	.152474	.155165	.157883	.160629	.163403	.166203	.169029	.171882	.174761	.180594	.186525
	.10	.156314	.158948	.161610	.164301	.167019	.169765	.172539	.175339	.178165	.181018	.183897	.189730	.195661
	0.00	.165450	.168084	.170746	.173437	.176155	.178902	.181675	.184475	.187302	.190154	.193033	.198866	.204797
	-.10	.174586	.177220	.179883	.182573	.185292	.188038	.190811	.193611	.196438	.199290	.202169	.208002	.213933
	-.20	.183722	.186356	.189019	.191709	.194428	.197174	.199947	.202747	.205574	.208427	.211305	.217138	.223069
	-.30	.192859	.195492	.198155	.200845	.203564	.206310	.209083	.211883	.214710	.217563	.220441	.226274	.232206
	-.40	.201995	.204628	.207291	.209981	.212700	.215446	.218219	.221019	.223846	.226699	.229577	.235410	.241342
15	.40	.117193	.120061	.122964	.125902	.128873	.131878	.134915	.137983	.141082	.144211	.147368	.153766	.160269
	.30	.126329	.129197	.132100	.135038	.138009	.141014	.144051	.147119	.150218	.153347	.156504	.162902	.169405
	.20	.135466	.138333	.141236	.144174	.147145	.150150	.153187	.156255	.159354	.162483	.165640	.172038	.178541
	.10	.144602	.147469	.150372	.153310	.156282	.159286	.162323	.165391	.168490	.171619	.174776	.181174	.187678
	0.00	.153738	.156605	.159508	.162446	.165418	.168422	.171459	.174528	.177626	.180755	.183912	.190311	.196814
	-.10	.162874	.165741	.168644	.171582	.174554	.177558	.180595	.183664	.186762	.189891	.193049	.199447	.205950
	-.20	.172010	.174878	.177781	.180718	.183690	.186694	.189731	.192800	.195899	.199027	.202185	.208583	.215086
	-.30	.181146	.184014	.186917	.189854	.192826	.195831	.198867	.201936	.205035	.208163	.211321	.217719	.224222
	-.40	.190282	.193150	.196053	.198990	.201962	.204967	.208004	.211072	.214171	.217299	.220457	.226855	.233358
20	.40	.111515	.114531	.117588	.120683	.123815	.126984	.130188	.133424	.136693	.139992	.143320	.150058	.156897
	.30	.120651	.123667	.126724	.129819	.132952	.136120	.139324	.142560	.145829	.149128	.152456	.159194	.166033
	.20	.129787	.132803	.135860	.138955	.142088	.145256	.148460	.151696	.154965	.158264	.161592	.168330	.175169
	.10	.138923	.141939	.144996	.148091	.151224	.154393	.157596	.160833	.164101	.167400	.170728	.177467	.184305
	0.00	.148059	.151075	.154132	.157227	.160360	.163529	.166732	.169969	.173237	.176536	.179865	.186603	.193441
	-.10	.157195	.160212	.163268	.166363	.169496	.172665	.175868	.179105	.182373	.185672	.189001	.195739	.202577
	-.20	.166331	.169348	.172404	.175499	.178632	.181801	.185004	.188241	.191510	.194809	.198137	.204875	.211713
	-.30	.175467	.178484	.181540	.184635	.187768	.190937	.194140	.197377	.200646	.203945	.207273	.214011	.220649
	-.40	.184604	.187620	.190676	.193772	.196904	.200073	.203276	.206513	.209782	.213081	.216409	.223147	.229985
25	.40	.108244	.111372	.114544	.117757	.121010	.124300	.127625	.130984	.134374	.137793	.141240	.148209	.155267
	.30	.117380	.120508	.123680	.126894	.130146	.133436	.136761	.140120	.143510	.146929	.150376	.157345	.164403
	.20	.126516	.129644	.132816	.136030	.139282	.142572	.145897	.149256	.152646	.156065	.159512	.166481	.173540
	.10	.135652	.138781	.141952	.145166	.148418	.151708	.155033	.158392	.161782	.165201	.168648	.175617	.182676
	0.00	.144788	.147917	.151089	.154302	.157554	.160844	.164170	.167528	.170918	.174337	.177784	.184753	.191812
	-.10	.153924	.157053	.160225	.163438	.166690	.169980	.173306	.176664	.180054	.183473	.186920	.193889	.200948
	-.20	.163060	.166189	.169361	.172574	.175827	.179116	.182442	.185800	.189190	.192609	.196056	.203025	.210084
	-.30	.172196	.175325	.178497	.181710	.184963	.188253	.191578	.194936	.198326	.201745	.205192	.212161	.219220
	-.40	.181333	.184461	.187633	.190846	.194099	.197389	.200714	.204072	.207462	.210882	.214328	.221298	.228356
30	.40	.106171	.109391	.112656	.115964	.119312	.122697	.126116	.129568	.133049	.136557	.140090	.147222	.154430
	.30	.115307	.118527	.121792	.125100	.128448	.131833	.135252	.138704	.142185	.145693	.149226	.156358	.163566
	.20	.124443	.127663	.130928	.134236	.137584	.140969	.144388	.147840	.151321	.154829	.158362	.165494	.172702
	.10	.133579	.136799	.140064	.143372	.146720	.150105	.153525	.156976	.160457	.163965	.167498	.174630	.181838
	0.00	.142715	.145935	.149200	.152508	.155856	.159241	.162661	.166112	.169593	.173101	.176634	.183766	.190974
	-.10	.151851	.155071	.158336	.161644	.164992	.168377	.171797	.175248	.178729	.182237	.185770	.192902	.200110
	-.20	.160987	.164207	.167473	.170781	.174128	.177513	.180933	.184384	.187865	.191373	.194906	.202038	.209246
	-.30	.170123	.173343	.176609	.179917	.183264	.186649	.190069	.193520	.197001	.200509	.204042	.211175	.218382
	-.40	.179259	.182479	.185745	.189053	.192401	.195786	.199205	.202656	.206137	.209646	.213179	.220311	.227518

5.0 YEAR HOLDING PERIOD
.400 EQUITY YIELD RATE
.800 LOAN RATIO

INTEREST RATE

TERM YEARS	APPR DEP	5.0	5.5	6.0	6.5	7.0	7.5	8.0	8.5	9.0	9.5	10.0	11.0	12.0
10	.40	.113269	.116079	.118919	.121788	.124688	.127617	.130575	.133562	.136577	.139620	.142691	.148913	.155239
	.30	.122405	.125215	.128055	.130925	.133824	.136753	.139711	.142698	.145713	.148756	.151827	.158049	.164375
	.20	.131541	.134351	.137191	.140061	.142960	.145889	.148848	.151834	.154849	.157892	.160963	.167185	.173512
	.10	.140677	.143487	.146327	.149197	.152096	.155026	.157984	.160970	.163986	.167029	.170099	.176321	.182648
	0.00	.149814	.152623	.155463	.158333	.161233	.164162	.167120	.170107	.173122	.176165	.179235	.185457	.191784
	-.10	.158950	.161759	.164599	.167469	.170369	.173298	.176256	.179243	.182258	.185331	.188371	.194593	.200920
	-.20	.168086	.170895	.173735	.176605	.179505	.182434	.185392	.188379	.191394	.194437	.197507	.203729	.210056
	-.30	.177222	.180031	.182871	.185741	.188641	.191570	.194528	.197515	.200530	.203573	.206643	.212865	.219192
	-.40	.186358	.189167	.192007	.194877	.197777	.200706	.203664	.206651	.209666	.212709	.215780	.222001	.228328
15	.40	.100776	.103835	.106931	.110065	.113234	.116439	.119679	.122952	.126257	.129594	.132962	.139787	.146723
	.30	.109912	.112971	.116067	.119201	.122371	.125575	.128815	.132088	.135393	.138730	.142098	.148923	.155860
	.20	.119048	.122107	.125203	.128337	.131507	.134712	.137951	.141224	.144529	.147866	.151234	.158059	.164996
	.10	.128184	.131243	.134340	.137473	.140643	.143848	.147087	.150360	.153665	.157003	.160371	.167195	.174132
	0.00	.137320	.140379	.143476	.146609	.149779	.152984	.156223	.159496	.162801	.166139	.169507	.176331	.183268
	-.10	.146456	.149515	.152612	.155745	.158915	.162120	.165359	.168632	.171938	.175275	.178643	.185467	.192404
	-.20	.155592	.158651	.161748	.164881	.168051	.171256	.174495	.177768	.181074	.184411	.187779	.194603	.201540
	-.30	.164729	.167787	.170884	.174017	.177187	.180392	.183631	.186904	.190210	.193547	.196915	.203740	.210676
	-.40	.173865	.176923	.180020	.183154	.186323	.189528	.192767	.196040	.199346	.202683	.206051	.212876	.219812
20	.40	.094719	.097936	.101196	.104498	.107839	.111219	.114636	.118089	.121575	.125094	.128644	.135832	.143126
	.30	.103855	.107072	.110332	.113634	.116976	.120356	.123773	.127225	.130712	.134231	.137781	.144968	.152262
	.20	.112991	.116208	.119469	.122770	.126112	.129492	.132909	.136361	.139848	.143367	.146917	.154104	.161398
	.10	.122127	.125344	.128605	.131906	.135248	.138628	.142045	.145497	.148984	.152503	.156053	.163240	.170534
	0.00	.131263	.134480	.137741	.141042	.144384	.147764	.151181	.154633	.158120	.161639	.165189	.172376	.179670
	-.10	.140399	.143617	.146877	.150178	.153520	.156900	.160317	.163769	.167256	.170775	.174325	.181512	.188806
	-.20	.149535	.152753	.156013	.159314	.162656	.166036	.169453	.172906	.176392	.179911	.183461	.190648	.197942
	-.30	.158671	.161889	.165149	.168451	.171792	.175172	.178589	.182042	.185528	.189047	.192597	.199784	.207079
	-.40	.167807	.171025	.174285	.177587	.180928	.184308	.187725	.191178	.194664	.198183	.201733	.208920	.216215
25	.40	.091230	.094567	.097950	.101378	.104847	.108356	.111903	.115486	.119101	.122749	.126425	.133859	.141388
	.30	.100366	.103703	.107086	.110514	.113983	.117492	.121039	.124622	.128237	.131885	.135562	.142995	.150524
	.20	.109502	.112839	.116222	.119650	.123119	.126628	.130175	.133758	.137374	.141021	.144697	.152131	.159660
	.10	.118638	.121975	.125358	.128786	.132255	.135764	.139311	.142894	.146510	.150157	.153834	.161267	.168796
	0.00	.127774	.131111	.134494	.137922	.141391	.144901	.148447	.152030	.155646	.159293	.162969	.170403	.177932
	-.10	.136910	.140247	.143630	.147058	.150527	.154037	.157584	.161166	.164782	.168429	.172106	.179540	.187068
	-.20	.146046	.149383	.152767	.156194	.159664	.163173	.166720	.170302	.173918	.177565	.181242	.188676	.196205
	-.30	.155182	.158519	.161903	.165330	.168800	.172309	.175856	.179438	.183054	.186701	.190378	.197812	.205341
	-.40	.164318	.167655	.171039	.174466	.177936	.181445	.184992	.188574	.192190	.195837	.199514	.206947	.214477
30	.40	.089018	.092453	.095936	.099465	.103036	.106646	.110294	.113975	.117688	.121430	.125199	.132806	.140495
	.30	.098154	.101589	.105072	.108601	.112172	.115782	.119430	.123111	.126824	.130566	.134335	.141942	.149631
	.20	.107290	.110725	.114208	.117737	.121308	.124918	.128566	.132247	.135960	.139702	.143471	.151079	.158767
	.10	.116427	.119861	.123344	.126873	.130444	.134054	.137702	.141383	.145096	.148838	.152607	.160215	.167903
	0.00	.125563	.128997	.132480	.136009	.139580	.143191	.146838	.150519	.154233	.157974	.161743	.169351	.177039
	-.10	.134699	.138133	.141616	.145145	.148716	.152327	.155974	.159656	.163369	.167111	.170879	.178487	.186175
	-.20	.143835	.147269	.150753	.154281	.157852	.161463	.165110	.168792	.172505	.176247	.180015	.187623	.195311
	-.30	.152971	.156406	.159889	.163417	.166988	.170599	.174246	.177928	.181641	.185383	.189151	.196759	.204447
	-.40	.162107	.165542	.169025	.172553	.176124	.179735	.183382	.187064	.190777	.194519	.198287	.205895	.213583

5.0 YEAR HOLDING PERIOD
.400 EQUITY YIELD RATE
.900 LOAN RATIO

INTEREST RATE

TERM YEARS	APPR DEP	5.0	5.5	6.0	6.5	7.0	7.5	8.0	8.5	9.0	9.5	10.0	11.0	12.0
10	.40	.081996	.085157	.088351	.091580	.094842	.098137	.101465	.104826	.108218	.111641	.115095	.122095	.129212
	.30	.091132	.094293	.097487	.100716	.103978	.107274	.110601	.113962	.117354	.120777	.124231	.131231	.138348
	.20	.100268	.103429	.106624	.109852	.113114	.116546	.119738	.123098	.126490	.129913	.133367	.140367	.147485
	.10	.109404	.112565	.115760	.118988	.122250	.125546	.128874	.132234	.135626	.139049	.142503	.149503	.156621
	0.00	.118540	.121701	.124896	.128124	.131387	.134682	.138010	.141370	.144762	.148185	.151640	.158639	.165757
	-.10	.127676	.130837	.134032	.137261	.140523	.143818	.147146	.150506	.153898	.157321	.160776	.167775	.174893
	-.20	.136812	.139973	.143168	.146397	.149659	.152954	.156282	.159642	.163034	.166457	.169912	.176911	.184029
	-.30	.145949	.149109	.152304	.155533	.158795	.162090	.165418	.168778	.172170	.175594	.179048	.186047	.193165
	-.40	.155085	.158245	.161440	.164669	.167931	.171226	.174554	.177914	.181306	.184730	.188184	.195183	.202301
15	.40	.067941	.071382	.074866	.078391	.081957	.085562	.089207	.092889	.096607	.100362	.104151	.111828	.119632
	.30	.077077	.080518	.084002	.087527	.091093	.094698	.098343	.102025	.105743	.109498	.113287	.120964	.128768
	.20	.086213	.089654	.093138	.096663	.100229	.103835	.107479	.111161	.114879	.118634	.122423	.130100	.137904
	.10	.095349	.098790	.102274	.105799	.109365	.112971	.116615	.120297	.124016	.127770	.131559	.139237	.147040
	0.00	.104485	.107926	.111410	.114935	.118501	.122107	.125751	.129433	.133152	.136906	.140695	.148373	.155176
	-.10	.113621	.117063	.120546	.124071	.127637	.131243	.134887	.138569	.142288	.146042	.149831	.157509	.163312
	-.20	.122758	.126199	.129682	.133207	.136773	.140379	.144023	.147705	.151424	.155178	.158967	.166645	.174448
	-.30	.131894	.135335	.138818	.142344	.145909	.149515	.153159	.156841	.160560	.164314	.168103	.175781	.183585
	-.40	.141030	.144471	.147954	.151480	.155046	.158651	.162295	.165977	.169696	.173450	.177239	.184917	.192721
20	.40	.061127	.064746	.068414	.072128	.075887	.079690	.083534	.087418	.091340	.095299	.099293	.107379	.115585
	.30	.070263	.073882	.077550	.081264	.085024	.088826	.092670	.096554	.100477	.104435	.108429	.116515	.124721
	.20	.079399	.083018	.086686	.090400	.094160	.097962	.101806	.105690	.109613	.113571	.117565	.125651	.133857
	.10	.088535	.092154	.095822	.099536	.103296	.107098	.110942	.114826	.118749	.122708	.126701	.134787	.142993
	0.00	.097671	.101291	.104958	.108673	.112432	.116234	.120078	.123963	.127885	.131844	.135837	.143923	.152129
	-.10	.106807	.110427	.114094	.117809	.121568	.125370	.129215	.133099	.137021	.140980	.144974	.153059	.161265
	-.20	.115943	.119563	.123230	.126945	.130704	.134507	.138351	.142235	.146157	.150116	.154110	.162195	.170401
	-.30	.125079	.128699	.132367	.136081	.139840	.143643	.147487	.151371	.155293	.159252	.163246	.171331	.179537
	-.40	.134215	.137835	.141503	.145217	.148976	.152779	.156623	.160507	.164429	.168388	.172382	.180467	.188673
25	.40	.057201	.060956	.064762	.068618	.072521	.076469	.080459	.084489	.088557	.092660	.096796	.105159	.113630
	.30	.066338	.070092	.073898	.077754	.081657	.085605	.089595	.093625	.097693	.101796	.105933	.114296	.122766
	.20	.075474	.079228	.083034	.086890	.090793	.094741	.098731	.102761	.106829	.110932	.115069	.123432	.131902
	.10	.084610	.088364	.092170	.096026	.099929	.103877	.107867	.111898	.115965	.120069	.124205	.132568	.141038
	0.00	.093746	.097500	.101306	.105162	.109065	.113013	.117003	.121034	.125101	.129205	.133341	.141704	.150174
	-.10	.102882	.106636	.110442	.114298	.118201	.122149	.126140	.130170	.134238	.138341	.142477	.150840	.159310
	-.20	.112018	.115772	.119578	.123434	.127337	.131285	.135276	.139306	.143374	.147477	.151613	.159976	.168446
	-.30	.121154	.124908	.128715	.132570	.136474	.140421	.144412	.148442	.152510	.156613	.160749	.169112	.177582
	-.40	.130290	.134044	.137851	.141706	.145610	.149558	.153548	.157578	.161646	.165749	.169885	.178248	.186718
30	.40	.054714	.058578	.062496	.066466	.070483	.074545	.078648	.082790	.086967	.091177	.095417	.103975	.112624
	.30	.063850	.067714	.071632	.075602	.079619	.083681	.087784	.091926	.096103	.100313	.104553	.113111	.121760
	.20	.072986	.076850	.080768	.084738	.088755	.092817	.096921	.101062	.105240	.109449	.113689	.122247	.130897
	.10	.082122	.085986	.089904	.093874	.097891	.101953	.106057	.110198	.114376	.118585	.122825	.131383	.140033
	0.00	.091258	.095122	.099040	.103010	.107027	.111089	.115193	.119335	.123512	.127721	.131961	.140520	.149169
	-.10	.100394	.104258	.108177	.112146	.116163	.120225	.124329	.128471	.132648	.136857	.141097	.149656	.158305
	-.20	.109530	.113394	.117313	.121282	.125300	.129362	.133465	.137607	.141784	.145994	.150233	.158792	.167441
	-.30	.118666	.122530	.126449	.130418	.134436	.138498	.142601	.146743	.150920	.155130	.159369	.167928	.176577
	-.40	.127802	.131666	.135585	.139554	.143572	.147634	.151737	.155879	.160056	.164266	.168505	.177064	.185713

5.0 YEAR HOLDING PERIOD
.500 EQUITY YIELD RATE
.600 LOAN RATIO

INTEREST RATE

TERM YEARS	APPR DEP	5.0	5.5	6.0	6.5	7.0	7.5	8.0	8.5	9.0	9.5	10.0	11.0	12.0
10	.40	.226110	.228160	.230233	.232329	.234447	.236588	.238751	.240935	.243142	.245369	.247617	.252176	.256814
	.30	.233693	.235743	.237816	.239912	.242030	.244171	.246334	.248518	.250725	.252952	.255200	.259759	.264397
	.20	.241276	.243326	.245399	.247495	.249613	.251754	.253917	.256101	.258308	.260535	.262783	.267342	.271580
	.10	.248858	.250909	.252982	.255078	.257196	.259337	.261500	.263684	.265890	.268118	.270366	.274925	.279563
	0.00	.256441	.258491	.260565	.262660	.264779	.266920	.269083	.271267	.273473	.275701	.277949	.282508	.287146
	-.10	.264024	.266074	.268148	.270243	.272362	.274503	.276666	.278850	.281056	.283284	.285532	.290091	.294229
	-.20	.271607	.273657	.275730	.277826	.279945	.282086	.284248	.286433	.288639	.290867	.293115	.297673	.302312
	-.30	.279190	.281240	.283313	.285409	.287528	.289669	.291831	.294016	.296222	.298450	.300698	.305256	.309895
	-.40	.286773	.288823	.290896	.292992	.295111	.297252	.299414	.301599	.303805	.306033	.308281	.312839	.317478
15	.40	.215029	.217255	.219511	.221795	.224107	.226447	.228814	.231208	.233627	.236071	.238539	.243546	.248643
	.30	.222612	.224838	.227094	.229378	.231690	.234030	.236397	.238791	.241210	.243654	.246122	.251129	.256225
	.20	.230195	.232421	.234677	.236961	.239273	.241613	.243980	.246374	.248793	.251237	.253705	.258712	.263808
	.10	.237778	.240004	.242259	.244544	.246856	.249196	.251503	.253957	.256376	.258820	.261288	.266295	.271361
	0.00	.245361	.247587	.249842	.252127	.254439	.256779	.259146	.261539	.263959	.266403	.268871	.273878	.278974
	-.10	.252944	.255170	.257425	.259710	.262022	.264362	.266729	.269122	.271542	.273986	.276454	.281461	.286557
	-.20	.260527	.262753	.265008	.267292	.269605	.271945	.274312	.276705	.279124	.281569	.284037	.289044	.294140
	-.30	.268110	.270336	.272591	.274875	.277188	.279528	.281895	.284288	.286707	.289151	.291620	.296627	.301723
	-.40	.275693	.277919	.280174	.282458	.284771	.287111	.289478	.291871	.294290	.296734	.299203	.304210	.309306
20	.40	.209657	.212002	.214381	.216793	.219237	.221712	.224216	.226750	.229310	.231898	.234510	.239806	.245190
	.30	.217240	.219585	.221964	.224376	.226820	.229295	.231799	.234333	.236893	.239481	.242093	.247389	.252773
	.20	.224823	.227168	.229547	.231959	.234403	.236878	.239382	.241916	.244476	.247064	.249676	.254972	.260356
	.10	.232406	.234751	.237130	.239542	.241986	.244461	.246965	.249498	.252059	.254647	.257259	.262555	.267939
	0.00	.239989	.242334	.244713	.247125	.249569	.252043	.254548	.257081	.259642	.262229	.264842	.270138	.275522
	-.10	.247572	.249917	.252296	.254708	.257152	.259626	.262131	.264664	.267225	.269812	.272425	.277721	.283105
	-.20	.255155	.257500	.259879	.262291	.264734	.267209	.269714	.272247	.274808	.277395	.280008	.285304	.290688
	-.30	.262738	.265083	.267462	.269873	.272317	.274792	.277297	.279830	.282391	.284978	.287591	.292887	.298271
	-.40	.270321	.272666	.275044	.277456	.279900	.282375	.284880	.287413	.289974	.292561	.295174	.300470	.305854
25	.40	.206563	.209001	.211477	.213989	.216535	.219114	.221724	.224363	.227030	.229722	.232439	.237941	.243523
	.30	.214146	.216584	.219060	.221572	.224118	.226697	.229307	.231946	.234612	.237305	.240022	.245524	.251106
	.20	.221729	.224167	.226643	.229155	.231701	.234280	.236890	.239529	.242195	.244888	.247605	.253107	.258689
	.10	.229312	.231750	.234226	.236738	.239284	.241863	.244473	.247112	.249778	.252471	.255188	.260690	.266272
	0.00	.236895	.239333	.241809	.244321	.246867	.249446	.252056	.254695	.257361	.260054	.262771	.268273	.273854
	-.10	.244478	.246916	.249392	.251904	.254450	.257029	.259639	.262278	.264944	.267637	.270354	.275856	.281437
	-.20	.252061	.254499	.256975	.259487	.262033	.264612	.267221	.269860	.272527	.275220	.277937	.283439	.289020
	-.30	.259644	.262082	.264558	.267070	.269616	.272195	.274804	.277443	.280110	.282803	.285520	.291022	.296603
	-.40	.267226	.269665	.272141	.274653	.277199	.279778	.282387	.285026	.287693	.290386	.293103	.298604	.304186
30	.40	.204602	.207119	.209676	.212270	.214900	.217563	.220256	.222978	.225727	.228499	.231295	.236946	.242665
	.30	.212185	.214702	.217259	.219853	.222483	.225146	.227839	.230561	.233310	.236082	.238878	.244528	.250248
	.20	.219768	.222285	.224842	.227436	.230066	.232729	.235422	.238144	.240893	.243665	.246461	.252111	.257831
	.10	.227350	.229868	.232425	.235019	.237649	.240312	.243005	.245727	.248475	.251248	.254044	.259694	.265414
	0.00	.234933	.237451	.240008	.242602	.245232	.247895	.250588	.253310	.256058	.258831	.261627	.267277	.272997
	-.10	.242516	.245033	.247590	.250185	.252815	.255478	.258171	.260893	.263641	.266414	.269209	.274860	.280580
	-.20	.250099	.252616	.255173	.257768	.260398	.263060	.265754	.268476	.271224	.273997	.276792	.282443	.288163
	-.30	.257682	.260199	.262756	.265351	.267981	.270643	.273337	.276059	.278807	.281580	.284375	.290026	.295746
	-.40	.265265	.267782	.270339	.272934	.275564	.278226	.280920	.283642	.286390	.289163	.291958	.297609	.303249

5.0 YEAR HOLDING PERIOD
.500 EQUITY YIELD RATE
.667 LOAN RATIO

INTEREST RATE

TERM YEARS	APPR DEP	5.0	5.5	6.0	6.5	7.0	7.5	8.0	8.5	9.0	9.5	10.0	11.0	12.0
10	.40	.199046	.201324	.203628	.205956	.208310	.210689	.213092	.215519	.217971	.220446	.222944	.228009	.233153
	.30	.206629	.208907	.211211	.213539	.215893	.218272	.220675	.223102	.225554	.228029	.230527	.235592	.240746
	.20	.214212	.216490	.218793	.221122	.223476	.225855	.228258	.230685	.233137	.235612	.238110	.243175	.248329
	.10	.221795	.224073	.226376	.228705	.231059	.233438	.235841	.238268	.240720	.243194	.245693	.250758	.255912
	0.00	.229378	.231656	.233959	.236288	.238642	.241021	.243424	.245851	.248303	.250777	.253276	.258341	.263495
	-.10	.236961	.239239	.241542	.243871	.246225	.248604	.251007	.253434	.255885	.258360	.260859	.265924	.271078
	-.20	.244544	.246822	.249125	.251454	.253808	.256187	.258590	.261017	.263468	.265943	.268441	.273506	.278661
	-.30	.252127	.254405	.256708	.259037	.261391	.263769	.266173	.268600	.271051	.273526	.276024	.281089	.286243
	-.40	.259710	.261988	.264291	.266620	.268974	.271352	.273756	.276183	.278634	.281109	.283607	.288672	.293826
15	.40	.186735	.189208	.191714	.194252	.196821	.199421	.202051	.204711	.207399	.210114	.212857	.218420	.224033
	.30	.194318	.196791	.199297	.201835	.204404	.207004	.209634	.212294	.214982	.217697	.220440	.226003	.231666
	.20	.201901	.204374	.206880	.209418	.211987	.214587	.217217	.219877	.222565	.225280	.228023	.233586	.239249
	.10	.209484	.211957	.214463	.217001	.219570	.222170	.224800	.227460	.230147	.232863	.235606	.241169	.246832
	0.00	.217067	.219540	.222046	.224584	.227153	.229753	.232383	.235043	.237730	.240446	.243189	.248752	.254415
	-.10	.224650	.227123	.229629	.232167	.234736	.237336	.239966	.242625	.245313	.248030	.250772	.256335	.261998
	-.20	.232232	.234706	.237212	.239750	.242319	.244919	.247549	.250208	.252896	.255612	.258355	.263918	.269581
	-.30	.239815	.242289	.244795	.247333	.249902	.252502	.255132	.257791	.260479	.263195	.265938	.271501	.277163
	-.40	.247398	.249872	.252377	.254915	.257485	.260085	.262715	.265374	.268062	.270778	.273521	.279084	.284746
20	.40	.180766	.183371	.186014	.188694	.191410	.194160	.196943	.199757	.202603	.205477	.208380	.214265	.220247
	.30	.188349	.190954	.193597	.196277	.198993	.201743	.204526	.207340	.210186	.213060	.215963	.221848	.227830
	.20	.195932	.198537	.201180	.203860	.206576	.209325	.212108	.214923	.217769	.220643	.223546	.229431	.235413
	.10	.203515	.206120	.208763	.211443	.214159	.216908	.219691	.222506	.225352	.228226	.231129	.237014	.242996
	0.00	.211098	.213703	.216346	.219026	.221742	.224491	.227274	.230089	.232934	.235809	.238712	.244597	.250579
	-.10	.218681	.221286	.223929	.226609	.229324	.232074	.234857	.237672	.240517	.243392	.246295	.252180	.258162
	-.20	.226264	.228869	.231512	.234192	.236907	.239657	.242440	.245255	.248100	.250975	.253878	.259763	.265745
	-.30	.233846	.236452	.239095	.241775	.244490	.247240	.250023	.252838	.255683	.258558	.261461	.267345	.273328
	-.40	.241429	.244035	.246678	.249358	.252073	.254823	.257606	.260421	.263266	.266141	.269044	.274928	.280911
25	.40	.177328	.180037	.182788	.185579	.188408	.191273	.194173	.197105	.200068	.203060	.206079	.212192	.218394
	.30	.184911	.187620	.190371	.193162	.195991	.198856	.201756	.204688	.207651	.210643	.213662	.219775	.225977
	.20	.192493	.195203	.197954	.200745	.203574	.206439	.209339	.212271	.215234	.218226	.221245	.227358	.233560
	.10	.200076	.202786	.205537	.208328	.211157	.214022	.216922	.219854	.222817	.225809	.228828	.234941	.241143
	0.00	.207659	.210369	.213120	.215911	.218740	.221605	.224505	.227437	.230400	.233392	.236411	.242524	.248726
	-.10	.215242	.217952	.220703	.223494	.226323	.229188	.232088	.235020	.237983	.240975	.243994	.250107	.256309
	-.20	.222825	.225535	.228286	.231077	.233906	.236771	.239671	.242603	.245566	.248558	.251577	.257690	.263892
	-.30	.230408	.233117	.235869	.238660	.241489	.244354	.247254	.250186	.253149	.256141	.259160	.265273	.271475
	-.40	.237991	.240700	.243451	.246242	.249072	.251937	.254837	.257769	.260732	.263724	.266743	.272856	.279058
30	.40	.175148	.177945	.180786	.183669	.186591	.189550	.192542	.195567	.198621	.201702	.204808	.211086	.217441
	.30	.182731	.185528	.188369	.191252	.194174	.197133	.200125	.203150	.206204	.209285	.212390	.218669	.225024
	.20	.190314	.193111	.195952	.198835	.201757	.204716	.207708	.210733	.213787	.216867	.219973	.226252	.232607
	.10	.197897	.200694	.203535	.206418	.209340	.212298	.215291	.218316	.221369	.224450	.227556	.233835	.240190
	0.00	.205480	.208277	.211118	.214001	.216923	.219881	.222874	.225899	.228952	.232033	.235139	.241418	.247773
	-.10	.213063	.215860	.218701	.221584	.224506	.227464	.230457	.233482	.236535	.239616	.242722	.249001	.255356
	-.20	.220646	.223443	.226284	.229167	.232089	.235047	.238040	.241064	.244118	.247199	.250305	.256584	.262939
	-.30	.228229	.231026	.233867	.236750	.239672	.242630	.245623	.248647	.251701	.254782	.257888	.264167	.270522
	-.40	.235812	.238609	.241450	.244333	.247255	.250213	.253206	.256230	.259284	.262365	.265471	.271750	.278105

5.0 YEAR HOLDING PERIOD
.500 EQUITY YIELD RATE
.700 LOAN RATIO

INTEREST RATE

TERM YEARS	APPR DEP	5.0	5.5	6.0	6.5	7.0	7.5	8.0	8.5	9.0	9.5	10.0	11.0	12.0
10	.40	.185517	.187908	.190327	.192772	.195244	.197741	.200265	.202813	.205387	.207986	.210609	.215927	.221339
	.30	.193110	.195491	.197910	.200355	.202827	.205324	.207848	.210396	.212970	.215569	.218192	.223510	.228922
	.20	.200682	.203074	.205493	.207938	.210410	.212907	.215430	.217979	.220553	.223152	.225775	.231093	.236505
	.10	.208265	.210657	.213076	.215521	.217993	.220490	.223013	.225562	.228136	.230735	.233358	.238676	.244088
	0.00	.215848	.218240	.220659	.223104	.225575	.228073	.230596	.233145	.235719	.238318	.240941	.246259	.251671
	-.10	.223431	.225823	.228242	.230687	.233158	.235656	.238179	.240728	.243302	.245901	.248524	.253842	.259254
	-.20	.231014	.233406	.235825	.238270	.240741	.243239	.245762	.248311	.250885	.253483	.256107	.261425	.266837
	-.30	.238597	.240989	.243408	.245853	.248324	.250822	.253345	.255894	.258468	.261066	.263690	.269008	.274419
	-.40	.246180	.248572	.250990	.253436	.255907	.258405	.260928	.263477	.266051	.268649	.271272	.276591	.282002
15	.40	.172590	.175187	.177818	.180483	.183180	.185910	.188672	.191464	.194287	.197138	.200018	.205859	.211805
	.30	.180173	.182769	.185401	.188066	.190763	.193493	.196255	.199047	.201870	.204721	.207601	.213442	.219388
	.20	.187756	.190352	.192984	.195648	.198346	.201076	.203838	.206630	.209452	.212304	.215184	.221025	.226971
	.10	.195338	.197935	.200567	.203231	.205929	.208659	.211421	.214213	.217035	.219887	.222767	.228608	.234554
	0.00	.202921	.205518	.208149	.210814	.213512	.216242	.219004	.221796	.224618	.227470	.230350	.236191	.242137
	-.10	.210504	.213101	.215732	.218397	.221095	.223825	.226587	.229379	.232201	.235053	.237933	.243774	.249720
	-.20	.218087	.220684	.223315	.225980	.228678	.231408	.234170	.236962	.239784	.242636	.245515	.251357	.257303
	-.30	.225670	.228267	.230898	.233563	.236261	.238991	.241753	.244545	.247367	.250219	.253098	.258940	.264886
	-.40	.233253	.235850	.238481	.241146	.243844	.246574	.249336	.252128	.254950	.257802	.260681	.266523	.272468
20	.40	.166322	.169058	.171833	.174647	.177498	.180386	.183308	.186263	.189251	.192269	.195317	.201496	.207777
	.30	.173905	.176641	.179416	.182230	.185081	.187969	.190891	.193846	.196834	.199852	.202900	.209079	.215360
	.20	.181488	.184224	.186999	.189813	.192664	.195552	.198474	.201429	.204417	.207435	.210483	.216662	.222943
	.10	.189071	.191807	.194582	.197396	.200247	.203134	.206057	.209012	.212000	.215018	.218066	.224245	.230526
	0.00	.196654	.199390	.202165	.204979	.207830	.210717	.213639	.216595	.219583	.222601	.225649	.231828	.238109
	-.10	.204237	.206972	.209748	.212562	.215413	.218300	.221222	.224178	.227166	.230184	.233232	.239411	.245692
	-.20	.211820	.214555	.217331	.220145	.222996	.225883	.228805	.231761	.234748	.237767	.240815	.246994	.253275
	-.30	.219403	.222138	.224914	.227728	.230579	.233466	.236388	.239344	.242331	.245350	.248398	.254577	.260858
	-.40	.226986	.229721	.232497	.235311	.238162	.241049	.243971	.246927	.249914	.252933	.255981	.262160	.268441
25	.40	.162712	.165557	.168445	.171376	.174347	.177355	.180400	.183479	.186590	.189731	.192901	.199320	.205832
	.30	.170295	.173140	.176028	.178959	.181929	.184938	.187983	.191062	.194173	.197314	.200484	.206903	.213415
	.20	.177878	.180723	.183611	.186542	.189512	.192521	.195566	.198644	.201756	.204897	.208067	.214486	.220998
	.10	.185461	.188306	.191194	.194125	.197095	.200104	.203149	.206227	.209339	.212480	.215650	.222069	.228581
	0.00	.193044	.195889	.198777	.201708	.204678	.207687	.210732	.213810	.216921	.220063	.223233	.229652	.236164
	-.10	.200627	.203472	.206360	.209291	.212261	.215270	.218314	.221393	.224504	.227646	.230816	.237234	.243746
	-.20	.208210	.211054	.213943	.216874	.219844	.222853	.225897	.228976	.232087	.235229	.238399	.244817	.251329
	-.30	.215793	.218637	.221526	.224457	.227427	.230436	.233480	.236559	.239670	.242812	.245982	.252400	.258912
	-.40	.223376	.226220	.229109	.232039	.235010	.238019	.241063	.244142	.247253	.250395	.253565	.259983	.266495
30	.40	.160424	.163361	.166344	.169371	.172439	.175545	.178688	.181863	.185070	.188305	.191566	.198158	.204831
	.30	.168007	.170944	.173927	.176954	.180022	.183128	.186270	.189446	.192653	.195888	.199149	.205741	.212414
	.20	.175590	.178526	.181510	.184537	.187605	.190711	.193853	.197029	.200236	.203471	.206732	.213324	.219997
	.10	.183173	.186109	.189093	.192119	.195187	.198294	.201436	.204612	.207819	.211054	.214315	.220907	.227580
	0.00	.190756	.193692	.196675	.199702	.202770	.205877	.209019	.212195	.215401	.218636	.221898	.228490	.235163
	-.10	.198339	.201275	.204258	.207285	.210353	.213460	.216602	.219778	.222984	.226219	.229481	.236073	.242746
	-.20	.205922	.208858	.211841	.214868	.217936	.221043	.224185	.227361	.230567	.233802	.237064	.243656	.250329
	-.30	.213505	.216441	.219424	.222451	.225519	.228626	.231768	.234944	.238150	.241385	.244646	.251239	.257912
	-.40	.221087	.224024	.227007	.230034	.233102	.236209	.239351	.242527	.245733	.248968	.252229	.258822	.265495

5.0 YEAR HOLDING PERIOD
.500 EQUITY YIELD RATE
.750 LOAN RATIO

INTEREST RATE

TERM YEARS	APPR DEP	5.0	5.5	6.0	6.5	7.0	7.5	8.0	8.5	9.0	9.5	10.0	11.0	12.0
10	.40	.165220	.167783	.170374	.172994	.175642	.178318	.181021	.183752	.186510	.189294	.192105	.197803	.203601
	.30	.172803	.175366	.177957	.180577	.183225	.185901	.188604	.191335	.194093	.196877	.199688	.205386	.211184
	.20	.180386	.182948	.185540	.188160	.190808	.193484	.196187	.198918	.201676	.204460	.207271	.212969	.218767
	.10	.187969	.190531	.193123	.195743	.198391	.201067	.203770	.206501	.209259	.212043	.214854	.220552	.226350
	0.00	.195552	.198114	.200706	.203326	.205974	.208650	.211353	.214084	.216842	.219626	.222436	.228134	.233933
	-.10	.203135	.205697	.208289	.210909	.213557	.216233	.218936	.221667	.224425	.227209	.230019	.235717	.241516
	-.20	.210718	.213280	.215872	.218491	.221140	.223816	.226519	.229250	.232008	.234792	.237602	.243300	.249099
	-.30	.218301	.220863	.223455	.226074	.228723	.231399	.234102	.236833	.239591	.242375	.245185	.250883	.256682
	-.40	.225884	.228446	.231037	.233657	.236305	.238981	.241685	.244416	.247174	.249958	.252768	.258466	.264265
15	.40	.151370	.154152	.156971	.159826	.162717	.165642	.168601	.171593	.174616	.177672	.180757	.187016	.193386
	.30	.158953	.161735	.164554	.167409	.170300	.173225	.176184	.179176	.182199	.185255	.188340	.194599	.200969
	.20	.166536	.169318	.172137	.174992	.177883	.180808	.183767	.186758	.189782	.192837	.195923	.202182	.208552
	.10	.174119	.176901	.179720	.182575	.185466	.188391	.191350	.194341	.197365	.200420	.203506	.209765	.216135
	0.00	.181702	.184484	.187303	.190158	.193049	.195974	.198933	.201924	.204948	.208003	.211089	.217348	.223718
	-.10	.189284	.192067	.194886	.197741	.200632	.203557	.206516	.209507	.212531	.215586	.218672	.224931	.231301
	-.20	.196867	.199650	.202469	.205324	.208215	.211140	.214099	.217090	.220114	.223169	.226255	.232514	.238884
	-.30	.204450	.207233	.210052	.212907	.215798	.218723	.221681	.224673	.227697	.230752	.233838	.240097	.246467
	-.40	.212033	.214816	.217635	.220490	.223380	.226306	.229264	.232256	.235280	.238335	.241421	.247679	.254350
20	.40	.144655	.147586	.150659	.153574	.156629	.159723	.162853	.166020	.169221	.172455	.175721	.182341	.189071
	.30	.152238	.155169	.158142	.161157	.164212	.167306	.170436	.173603	.176804	.180038	.183304	.189924	.196654
	.20	.159821	.162751	.165725	.168740	.171795	.174888	.178019	.181186	.184387	.187621	.190887	.197507	.204237
	.10	.167404	.170334	.173308	.176323	.179378	.182471	.185602	.188769	.191970	.195204	.198469	.205090	.211820
	0.00	.174986	.177917	.180891	.183906	.186961	.190054	.193185	.196352	.199553	.202787	.206052	.212673	.219403
	-.10	.182569	.185500	.188474	.191489	.194544	.197637	.200768	.203935	.207136	.210370	.213635	.220256	.226986
	-.20	.190152	.193083	.196057	.199072	.202127	.205220	.208351	.211518	.214719	.217953	.221218	.227839	.234568
	-.30	.197735	.200666	.203640	.206655	.209710	.212803	.215934	.219101	.222302	.225536	.228801	.235421	.242151
	-.40	.205318	.208249	.211223	.214238	.217293	.220386	.223517	.226684	.229885	.233119	.236384	.243004	.249734
25	.40	.140787	.143835	.146930	.150069	.153252	.156476	.159738	.163036	.166370	.169736	.173132	.180009	.186986
	.30	.148370	.151418	.154512	.157652	.160835	.164059	.167321	.170619	.173953	.177319	.180715	.187592	.194569
	.20	.155953	.159000	.162095	.165235	.168418	.171641	.174904	.178202	.181536	.184902	.188298	.195175	.202152
	.10	.163535	.166583	.169678	.172818	.176001	.179224	.182487	.185785	.189119	.192485	.195881	.202758	.209735
	0.00	.171118	.174166	.177261	.180401	.183584	.186807	.190069	.193368	.196702	.200067	.203464	.210341	.217318
	-.10	.178701	.181749	.184844	.187984	.191167	.194390	.197652	.200951	.204285	.207650	.211047	.217924	.224901
	-.20	.186284	.189332	.192427	.195567	.198750	.201973	.205235	.208534	.211867	.215233	.218630	.225507	.232484
	-.30	.193867	.196915	.200010	.203150	.206333	.209556	.212818	.216117	.219450	.222816	.226213	.233090	.240067
	-.40	.201450	.204498	.207593	.210733	.213916	.217139	.220401	.223700	.227033	.230399	.233796	.240673	.247650
30	.40	.138335	.141481	.144678	.147921	.151208	.154536	.157903	.161306	.164741	.168207	.171701	.178765	.185914
	.30	.145918	.149064	.152261	.155504	.158791	.162119	.165486	.168889	.172324	.175790	.179284	.186348	.193497
	.20	.153501	.156647	.159844	.163087	.166374	.169702	.173069	.176472	.179907	.183373	.186867	.193931	.201080
	.10	.161084	.164230	.167426	.170670	.173957	.177285	.180652	.184054	.187490	.190956	.194450	.201514	.208663
	0.00	.168667	.171813	.175009	.178253	.181540	.184868	.188235	.191637	.195073	.198539	.202033	.209097	.216246
	-.10	.176250	.179396	.182592	.185835	.189123	.192451	.195818	.199220	.202656	.206122	.209616	.216680	.223829
	-.20	.183833	.186979	.190175	.193418	.196706	.200034	.203401	.206803	.210239	.213705	.217199	.224262	.231412
	-.30	.191416	.194562	.197758	.201001	.204289	.207617	.210984	.214386	.217822	.221288	.224782	.231845	.238995
	-.40	.198999	.202145	.205341	.208584	.211871	.215200	.218567	.221969	.225405	.228871	.232365	.239428	.246578

5.0 YEAR HOLDING PERIOD
.500 EQUITY YIELD RATE
.800 LOAN RATIO

INTEREST RATE

TERM YEARS	APPR DEP	5.0	5.5	6.0	6.5	7.0	7.5	8.0	8.5	9.0	9.5	10.0	11.0	12.0
10	.40	.144923	.147657	.150421	.153216	.156040	.158895	.161778	.164691	.167633	.170603	.173600	.179678	.185863
	.30	.152506	.155240	.158004	.160799	.163623	.166478	.169361	.172274	.175216	.178186	.181183	.187261	.193446
	.20	.160089	.162823	.165587	.168381	.171206	.174060	.176944	.179857	.182799	.185769	.188766	.194844	.201029
	.10	.167672	.170406	.173170	.175964	.178789	.181643	.184527	.187440	.190382	.193351	.196349	.202427	.208612
	0.00	.175255	.177989	.180753	.183547	.186372	.189226	.192110	.195023	.197965	.200934	.203932	.210010	.216195
	-.10	.182838	.185572	.188336	.191130	.193955	.196809	.199693	.202606	.205547	.208517	.211515	.217593	.223778
	-.20	.190421	.193155	.195919	.198713	.201538	.204392	.207276	.210189	.213130	.216100	.219098	.225176	.231361
	-.30	.198004	.200737	.203502	.206296	.209121	.211975	.214859	.217772	.220713	.223683	.226681	.232759	.238944
	-.40	.205587	.208320	.211085	.213879	.216704	.219558	.222442	.225355	.228296	.231266	.234264	.240342	.246527
15	.40	.130150	.133118	.136125	.139170	.142254	.145374	.148530	.151721	.154946	.158205	.161496	.168172	.174967
	.30	.137733	.140701	.143708	.146753	.149837	.152957	.156113	.159304	.162529	.165788	.169079	.175755	.182550
	.20	.145316	.148284	.151291	.154336	.157419	.160540	.163696	.166887	.170112	.173371	.176662	.183338	.190133
	.10	.152899	.155867	.158874	.161919	.165002	.168122	.171279	.174470	.177695	.180954	.184245	.190921	.197716
	0.00	.160482	.163449	.166457	.169502	.172585	.175705	.178861	.182053	.185278	.188537	.191828	.198504	.205299
	-.10	.168065	.171032	.174039	.177085	.180168	.183288	.186444	.189636	.192861	.196120	.199411	.206087	.212882
	-.20	.175648	.178615	.181622	.184668	.187751	.190871	.194027	.197219	.200444	.203703	.206994	.213670	.220465
	-.30	.183230	.186198	.189205	.192251	.195334	.198454	.201610	.204801	.208027	.211286	.214577	.221253	.228048
	-.40	.190813	.193781	.196788	.199834	.202917	.206037	.209193	.212384	.215610	.218869	.222160	.228836	.235631
20	.40	.122987	.126113	.129285	.132501	.135760	.139060	.142399	.145777	.149191	.152641	.156124	.163186	.170364
	.30	.130570	.133696	.136868	.140084	.143343	.146642	.149982	.153360	.156774	.160224	.163707	.170769	.177947
	.20	.138153	.141279	.144451	.147667	.150926	.154225	.157565	.160943	.164357	.167807	.171290	.178352	.185530
	.10	.145736	.148862	.152034	.155250	.158509	.161808	.165148	.168526	.171940	.175390	.178873	.185935	.193113
	0.00	.153319	.156445	.159617	.162833	.166091	.169391	.172731	.176109	.179523	.182973	.186456	.193517	.200696
	-.10	.160902	.164028	.167200	.170416	.173674	.176974	.180314	.183692	.187106	.190556	.194039	.201100	.208279
	-.20	.168485	.171611	.174783	.177999	.181257	.184557	.187897	.191275	.194689	.198138	.201622	.208683	.215862
	-.30	.176068	.179194	.182366	.185582	.188840	.192140	.195480	.198857	.202272	.205721	.209205	.216266	.223445
	-.40	.183651	.186777	.189949	.193165	.196423	.199723	.203063	.206440	.209855	.213304	.216788	.223849	.231028
25	.40	.118861	.122112	.125414	.128763	.132158	.135596	.139076	.142594	.146150	.149740	.153363	.160699	.168141
	.30	.126444	.129695	.132997	.136346	.139741	.143179	.146659	.150177	.153733	.157323	.160946	.168281	.175724
	.20	.134027	.137278	.140580	.143929	.147324	.150762	.154242	.157760	.161316	.164906	.168529	.175864	.183307
	.10	.141610	.144861	.148162	.151512	.154907	.158345	.161825	.165343	.168899	.172489	.176112	.183447	.190890
	0.00	.149193	.152444	.155745	.159095	.162489	.165928	.169407	.172926	.176482	.180072	.183695	.191030	.198473
	-.10	.156776	.160027	.163328	.166678	.170072	.173511	.176990	.180509	.184065	.187655	.191278	.198613	.206056
	-.20	.164359	.167610	.170911	.174260	.177655	.181094	.184573	.188092	.191648	.195238	.198861	.206196	.213638
	-.30	.171942	.175193	.178494	.181843	.185238	.188677	.192156	.195675	.199230	.202821	.206444	.213779	.221221
	-.40	.179525	.182776	.186077	.189426	.192821	.196260	.199739	.203258	.206813	.210404	.214027	.221362	.228804
30	.40	.116246	.119602	.123012	.126471	.129977	.133528	.137119	.140748	.144413	.148110	.151837	.159371	.166997
	.30	.123829	.127185	.130595	.134054	.137560	.141111	.144702	.148331	.151996	.155693	.159420	.166954	.174580
	.20	.131412	.134768	.138178	.141637	.145143	.148693	.152285	.155914	.159579	.163276	.167003	.174537	.182163
	.10	.138995	.142351	.145760	.149220	.152726	.156276	.159868	.163497	.167162	.170859	.174586	.182120	.189746
	0.00	.146578	.149934	.153343	.156803	.160309	.163859	.167451	.171080	.174745	.178442	.182169	.189703	.197329
	-.10	.154161	.157517	.160926	.164386	.167892	.171442	.175034	.178663	.182327	.186025	.189752	.197286	.204912
	-.20	.161744	.165100	.168509	.171969	.175475	.179025	.182616	.186246	.189910	.193608	.197335	.204869	.212495
	-.30	.169327	.172683	.176092	.179552	.183058	.186608	.190199	.193829	.197493	.201190	.204918	.212452	.220078
	-.40	.176910	.180266	.183675	.187134	.190641	.194191	.197782	.201412	.205076	.208773	.212500	.220035	.227661

5.0 YEAR HOLDING PERIOD
.500 EQUITY YIELD RATE
.900 LOAN RATIO

INTEREST RATE

TERM YEARS	APPR DEP	5.0	5.5	6.0	6.5	7.0	7.5	8.0	8.5	9.0	9.5	10.0	11.0	12.0
10	.40	.104330	.107405	.110515	.113659	.116837	.120048	.123292	.126569	.129878	.133219	.136592	.143430	.150388
	.30	.111913	.114988	.118098	.121242	.124420	.127631	.130875	.134152	.137461	.140802	.144175	.151013	.157971
	.20	.119496	.122571	.125681	.128825	.132003	.135214	.138458	.141735	.145044	.148385	.151758	.158556	.165553
	.10	.127079	.130154	.133264	.136408	.139586	.142797	.146041	.149318	.152627	.155968	.159341	.166178	.173136
	0.00	.134662	.137737	.140847	.143991	.147168	.150380	.153624	.156901	.160210	.163551	.166924	.173761	.180719
	-.10	.142245	.145320	.148430	.151574	.154751	.157963	.161207	.164484	.167793	.171134	.174507	.181344	.188302
	-.20	.149828	.152903	.156013	.159157	.162334	.165546	.168790	.172067	.175376	.178717	.182090	.188927	.195885
	-.30	.157411	.160486	.163596	.166740	.169917	.173128	.176373	.179650	.182959	.186300	.189673	.196510	.203468
	-.40	.164994	.168069	.171179	.174322	.177500	.180711	.183956	.187233	.190542	.193883	.197256	.204093	.211051
15	.40	.087710	.091049	.094432	.097858	.101327	.104837	.108387	.111977	.115606	.119272	.122975	.130485	.138130
	.30	.095293	.098632	.102015	.105441	.108910	.112420	.115970	.119560	.123189	.126855	.130558	.138068	.145713
	.20	.102876	.106215	.109598	.113024	.116493	.120003	.123553	.127143	.130772	.134438	.138141	.145659	.153296
	.10	.110459	.113798	.117181	.120607	.124076	.127586	.131136	.134726	.138355	.142021	.145724	.153234	.160879
	0.00	.118042	.121381	.124764	.128190	.131658	.135169	.138719	.142309	.145938	.149604	.153307	.160817	.168461
	-.10	.125625	.128964	.132347	.135773	.139241	.142752	.146302	.149892	.153521	.157187	.160890	.168404	.176044
	-.20	.133208	.136547	.139929	.143356	.146824	.150334	.153885	.157475	.161104	.164770	.168472	.175983	.183527
	-.30	.140791	.144129	.147512	.150939	.154407	.157917	.161468	.165058	.168687	.172353	.176055	.183566	.191210
	-.40	.148374	.151712	.155095	.158522	.161990	.165500	.169051	.172641	.176270	.179936	.183638	.191149	.198793
20	.40	.079652	.083169	.086737	.090355	.094021	.097733	.101490	.105290	.109132	.113012	.116931	.124875	.132951
	.30	.087235	.090752	.094320	.097938	.101604	.105316	.109073	.112873	.116715	.120595	.124514	.132458	.140534
	.20	.094818	.098335	.101903	.105521	.109187	.112899	.116656	.120456	.124297	.128178	.132097	.140041	.148117
	.10	.102401	.105918	.109486	.113104	.116770	.120482	.124239	.128039	.131880	.135761	.139680	.147624	.155700
	0.00	.109984	.113501	.117069	.120687	.124353	.128065	.131822	.135622	.139463	.143344	.147263	.155207	.163283
	-.10	.117567	.121084	.124652	.128270	.131936	.135648	.139405	.143205	.147046	.150927	.154846	.162790	.170866
	-.20	.125150	.128667	.132235	.135853	.139519	.143231	.146988	.150788	.154629	.158510	.162429	.170373	.178449
	-.30	.132733	.136250	.139818	.143436	.147102	.150814	.154571	.158371	.162212	.166093	.170012	.177956	.186032
	-.40	.140316	.143833	.147401	.151019	.154685	.158397	.162154	.165954	.169795	.173676	.177595	.185539	.193615
25	.40	.075010	.078668	.082382	.086150	.089969	.093837	.097752	.101710	.105710	.109749	.113825	.122077	.130450
	.30	.082593	.086251	.089965	.093733	.097552	.101420	.105335	.109293	.113293	.117332	.121408	.129660	.138033
	.20	.090176	.093834	.097548	.101316	.105135	.109003	.112918	.116876	.120876	.124915	.128991	.137243	.145616
	.10	.097759	.101417	.105131	.108898	.112718	.116586	.120500	.124459	.128459	.132498	.136574	.144826	.153199
	0.00	.105342	.109000	.112714	.116481	.120301	.124168	.128083	.132042	.136042	.140081	.144157	.152409	.160782
	-.10	.112925	.116583	.120296	.124064	.127884	.131752	.135666	.139625	.143625	.147664	.151740	.159992	.168365
	-.20	.120508	.124166	.127879	.131647	.135467	.139335	.143249	.147208	.151208	.155247	.159323	.167575	.175948
	-.30	.128091	.131748	.135462	.139230	.143049	.146918	.150832	.154791	.158791	.162830	.166905	.175158	.183530
	-.40	.135674	.139331	.143045	.146813	.150632	.154501	.158415	.162374	.166374	.170413	.174488	.182741	.191113
30	.40	.072068	.075844	.079680	.083571	.087516	.091510	.095550	.099633	.103756	.107915	.112108	.120584	.129164
	.30	.079651	.083427	.087262	.091154	.095099	.099093	.103133	.107216	.111339	.115498	.119691	.128167	.136747
	.20	.087234	.091010	.094845	.098737	.102682	.106676	.110716	.114799	.118922	.123081	.127274	.135750	.144330
	.10	.094817	.098593	.102428	.106320	.110265	.114259	.118299	.122382	.126505	.130664	.134857	.143333	.151512
	0.00	.102401	.106176	.110011	.113903	.117848	.121842	.125882	.129965	.134088	.138247	.142442	.150916	.159495
	-.10	.109983	.113759	.117594	.121486	.125431	.129425	.133465	.137548	.141671	.145830	.150023	.158499	.167078
	-.20	.117566	.121342	.125177	.129069	.133014	.137008	.141048	.145131	.149253	.153413	.157606	.166082	.174661
	-.30	.125149	.128925	.132760	.136652	.140597	.144591	.148631	.152714	.156836	.160996	.165189	.173665	.182244
	-.40	.132732	.136508	.140343	.144235	.148179	.152174	.156214	.160297	.164419	.168579	.172772	.181248	.189827

```
10.0  YEAR HOLDING PERIOD
 .020 EQUITY YIELD RATE
 .600 LOAN RATIO
```

INTEREST RATE

TERM YEARS	APPR DEP	5.0	5.5	6.0	6.5	7.0	7.5	8.0	8.5	9.0	9.5	10.0	11.0	12.0
10	.40	-.006959	-.005188	-.003392	-.001572	.000272	.002139	.004029	.005943	.007880	.009840	.011822	.015853	.019973
	.30	.002173	.003945	.005741	.007561	.009404	.011271	.013162	.015076	.017013	.018972	.020955	.024986	.029105
	.20	.011306	.013078	.014874	.016693	.018537	.020404	.022295	.024208	.026145	.028105	.030087	.034119	.038238
	.10	.020439	.022210	.024006	.025826	.027670	.029537	.031427	.033341	.035278	.037238	.039220	.043251	.047371
	0.00	.029571	.031343	.033139	.034959	.036802	.038669	.040560	.042474	.044411	.046370	.048353	.052384	.056503
	-.10	.038704	.040476	.042271	.044091	.045935	.047802	.049693	.051606	.053543	.055503	.057485	.061517	.065636
	-.20	.047837	.049608	.051404	.053224	.055067	.056935	.058825	.060739	.062676	.064636	.066618	.070649	.074768
	-.30	.056969	.058741	.060537	.062357	.064200	.066067	.067958	.069872	.071809	.073768	.075751	.079782	.083901
	-.40	.066102	.067874	.069669	.071489	.073333	.075220	.077091	.079004	.080941	.082901	.084883	.088915	.093034
15	.40	-.003427	-.001057	.001349	.003789	.006262	.008769	.011306	.013875	.016474	.019102	.021759	.027153	.032650
	.30	.005705	.008076	.010482	.012922	.015395	.017901	.020439	.023008	.025607	.028235	.030892	.036286	.041783
	.20	.014838	.017209	.019614	.022054	.024528	.027034	.029572	.032141	.034740	.037368	.040024	.045419	.050915
	.10	.023971	.026341	.028747	.031187	.033660	.036166	.038704	.041273	.043872	.046500	.049157	.054551	.060048
	0.00	.033103	.035474	.037880	.040320	.042793	.045299	.047837	.050406	.053005	.055633	.058290	.063684	.069181
	-.10	.042236	.044607	.047012	.049452	.051926	.054432	.056970	.059539	.062138	.064766	.067422	.072817	.078313
	-.20	.051369	.053739	.056145	.058585	.061058	.063564	.066102	.068671	.071270	.073898	.076555	.081949	.087446
	-.30	.060501	.062872	.065278	.067718	.070191	.072697	.075235	.077804	.080403	.083031	.085688	.091082	.096579
	-.40	.069634	.072005	.074410	.076850	.079324	.081830	.084368	.086937	.089536	.092164	.094820	.100215	.105711
20	.40	-.001715	.000933	.003617	.006335	.009084	.011865	.014674	.017511	.020373	.023260	.026169	.032051	.038006
	.30	.007418	.010066	.012750	.015467	.018217	.020997	.023806	.026643	.029506	.032392	.035302	.041183	.047138
	.20	.016550	.019199	.021882	.024600	.027350	.030130	.032939	.035776	.038638	.041525	.044435	.050316	.056271
	.10	.025683	.028331	.031015	.033733	.036482	.039262	.042072	.044908	.047771	.050658	.053567	.059449	.065403
	0.00	.034816	.037464	.040148	.042865	.045615	.048395	.051204	.054041	.056904	.059790	.062700	.068581	.074536
	-.10	.043948	.046597	.049280	.051998	.054748	.057528	.060337	.063174	.066036	.068923	.071833	.077714	.083669
	-.20	.053081	.055729	.058413	.061130	.063880	.066660	.069470	.072306	.075169	.078056	.080965	.086847	.092801
	-.30	.062214	.064862	.067546	.070263	.073013	.075793	.078602	.081439	.084302	.087188	.090098	.095979	.101934
	-.40	.071346	.073995	.076678	.079396	.082145	.084926	.087735	.090572	.093434	.096321	.099231	.105112	.111067
25	.40	-.000728	.002070	.004901	.007761	.010649	.013563	.016499	.019457	.022433	.025427	.028436	.034493	.040593
	.30	.008404	.011203	.014034	.016894	.019782	.022695	.025632	.028589	.031566	.034560	.037569	.043626	.049725
	.20	.017537	.020336	.023166	.026027	.028915	.031828	.034765	.037722	.040699	.043692	.046701	.052759	.058858
	.10	.026670	.029468	.032299	.035159	.038047	.040961	.043897	.046855	.049831	.052825	.055834	.061891	.067990
	0.00	.035802	.038601	.041432	.044292	.047180	.050093	.053030	.055987	.058964	.061957	.064967	.071024	.077123
	-.10	.044935	.047733	.050564	.053424	.056313	.059226	.062162	.065120	.068097	.071090	.074099	.080157	.086256
	-.20	.054067	.056866	.059697	.062557	.065445	.068359	.071295	.074253	.077229	.080223	.083232	.089289	.095388
	-.30	.063200	.065999	.068830	.071690	.074578	.077491	.080428	.083385	.086362	.089356	.092365	.098422	.104521
	-.40	.072333	.075131	.077962	.080823	.083711	.086624	.089560	.092518	.095495	.098488	.101497	.107555	.113654
30	.40	-.000103	.002783	.005697	.008636	.011597	.014577	.017574	.020586	.023610	.026645	.029689	.035797	.041923
	.30	.009029	.011916	.014830	.017769	.020730	.023710	.026707	.029718	.032743	.035778	.038822	.044930	.051055
	.20	.018162	.021049	.023963	.026902	.029862	.032842	.035839	.038851	.041875	.044910	.047954	.054062	.060188
	.10	.027295	.030181	.033095	.036034	.038995	.041975	.044972	.047984	.051008	.054043	.057087	.063195	.069321
	0.00	.036427	.039314	.042228	.045166	.048128	.051108	.054105	.057116	.060141	.063176	.066219	.072327	.078453
	-.10	.045560	.048447	.051361	.054299	.057260	.060240	.063237	.066249	.069273	.072308	.075352	.081460	.087586
	-.20	.054693	.057579	.060493	.063432	.066393	.069373	.072370	.075382	.078406	.081441	.084485	.090593	.096719
	-.30	.063825	.066712	.069626	.072565	.075526	.078506	.081503	.084514	.087539	.090574	.093618	.099725	.105851
	-.40	.072958	.075844	.078759	.081697	.084658	.087638	.090635	.093647	.096671	.099706	.102750	.108858	.114984

10.0 YEAR HOLDING PERIOD
.020 EQUITY YIELD RATE
.667 LOAN RATIO

INTEREST RATE

TERM YEARS	APPR DEP	5.0	5.5	6.0	6.5	7.0	7.5	8.0	8.5	9.0	9.5	10.0	11.0	12.0
10	.40	-.005896	-.003927	-.001932	-.000090	.002139	.004213	.006314	.008440	.010592	.012770	.014972	.019452	.024029
	.30	.003237	.005205	.007201	.009223	.011271	.013346	.015447	.017573	.019725	.021903	.024105	.028585	.033161
	.20	.012369	.014338	.016333	.018355	.020404	.022479	.024579	.026706	.028857	.031035	.033238	.037717	.042294
	.10	.021502	.023471	.025466	.027488	.029537	.031611	.033712	.035838	.037990	.040168	.042370	.046850	.051427
	0.00	.030635	.032603	.034599	.036621	.038669	.040744	.042845	.044971	.047123	.049301	.051503	.055983	.060559
	-.10	.039767	.041736	.043731	.045753	.047802	.049876	.051977	.054104	.056256	.058433	.060636	.065115	.069692
	-.20	.048900	.050869	.052864	.054886	.056934	.059009	.061110	.063236	.065388	.067566	.069768	.074248	.078825
	-.30	.058033	.060001	.061997	.064019	.066067	.068142	.070242	.072369	.074521	.076698	.078901	.083380	.087957
	-.40	.067165	.069134	.071129	.073151	.075200	.077274	.079375	.081502	.083654	.085831	.088034	.092513	.097090
15	.40	-.001971	.000663	.003336	.006047	.008795	.011580	.014400	.017254	.020142	.023062	.026014	.032007	.038115
	.30	.007161	.009795	.012468	.015179	.017928	.020712	.023532	.026387	.029274	.032195	.035146	.041140	.047247
	.20	.016294	.018928	.021601	.024312	.027060	.029845	.032665	.035519	.038407	.041327	.044279	.050273	.056380
	.10	.025427	.028061	.030734	.033445	.036193	.038978	.041798	.044652	.047540	.050460	.053412	.059405	.065513
	0.00	.034559	.037193	.039866	.042577	.045326	.048110	.050930	.053785	.056672	.059593	.062544	.068538	.074645
	-.10	.043692	.046326	.048999	.051710	.054458	.057243	.060063	.062917	.065805	.068725	.071677	.077671	.083777
	-.20	.052825	.055459	.058132	.060843	.063591	.066376	.069196	.072050	.074938	.077858	.080810	.086803	.092911
	-.30	.061957	.064591	.067264	.069975	.072724	.075508	.078328	.081182	.084070	.086990	.089942	.095936	.102043
	-.40	.071090	.073724	.076397	.079108	.081856	.084641	.087461	.090315	.093203	.096123	.099075	.105069	.111176
20	.40	-.000069	.002874	.005856	.008875	.011930	.015020	.018141	.021293	.024474	.027681	.030914	.037449	.044065
	.30	.009064	.012007	.014988	.018008	.021063	.024152	.027274	.030426	.033606	.036814	.040047	.046582	.053198
	.20	.018197	.021139	.024121	.027141	.030196	.033285	.036406	.039558	.042739	.045947	.049179	.055714	.062331
	.10	.027329	.030272	.033254	.036273	.039328	.042418	.045539	.048691	.051872	.055079	.058312	.064847	.071463
	0.00	.036462	.039405	.042386	.045406	.048461	.051550	.054672	.057824	.061005	.064212	.067445	.073980	.080596
	-.10	.045595	.048537	.051519	.054539	.057594	.060683	.063804	.066956	.070137	.073344	.076577	.083112	.089729
	-.20	.054727	.057670	.060652	.063671	.066726	.069816	.072937	.076089	.079270	.082477	.085710	.092245	.098861
	-.30	.063860	.066803	.069784	.072804	.075859	.078948	.082070	.085222	.088402	.091610	.094843	.101377	.107994
	-.40	.072993	.075935	.078917	.081936	.084992	.088081	.091202	.094354	.097535	.100742	.103975	.110510	.117127
25	.40	.001027	.004137	.007282	.010461	.013670	.016907	.020169	.023456	.026763	.030089	.033433	.040163	.046940
	.30	.010160	.013270	.016415	.019593	.022802	.026039	.029302	.032588	.035896	.039222	.042565	.049296	.056073
	.20	.019293	.022402	.025548	.028726	.031935	.035172	.038435	.041721	.045028	.048355	.051698	.058428	.065205
	.10	.028425	.031535	.034680	.037859	.041068	.044305	.047567	.050854	.054161	.057487	.060831	.067561	.074338
	0.00	.037558	.040668	.043813	.046991	.050201	.053437	.056700	.059986	.063293	.066620	.069963	.076694	.083470
	-.10	.046691	.049800	.052946	.056124	.059333	.062570	.065833	.069119	.072426	.075753	.079096	.085826	.092603
	-.20	.055823	.058933	.062078	.065257	.068466	.071703	.074965	.078251	.081559	.084885	.088229	.094959	.101736
	-.30	.064956	.068066	.071211	.074389	.077598	.080835	.084098	.087384	.090691	.094018	.097361	.104090	.110868
	-.40	.074089	.077198	.080344	.083522	.086731	.089968	.093231	.096517	.099824	.103150	.106494	.113224	.120001
30	.40	.001722	.004929	.008167	.011433	.014722	.018034	.021364	.024710	.028070	.031443	.034825	.041611	.048418
	.30	.010855	.014062	.017300	.020566	.023855	.027166	.030496	.033843	.037203	.040575	.043957	.050744	.057551
	.20	.019967	.023195	.026433	.029698	.032988	.036299	.039629	.042975	.046336	.049708	.053090	.059877	.066683
	.10	.029120	.032327	.035565	.038831	.042120	.045432	.048762	.052108	.055468	.058841	.062223	.069009	.075816
	0.00	.038253	.041460	.044698	.047963	.051253	.054564	.057894	.061241	.064601	.067973	.071355	.078142	.084949
	-.10	.047385	.050593	.053831	.057096	.060386	.063697	.067027	.070373	.073734	.077106	.080488	.087275	.094081
	-.20	.056518	.059725	.062963	.066229	.069518	.072830	.076160	.079506	.082866	.086239	.089621	.096407	.103214
	-.30	.065651	.068858	.072096	.075361	.078651	.081962	.085292	.088639	.091999	.095371	.098753	.105540	.112347
	-.40	.074783	.077991	.081229	.084494	.087784	.091095	.094425	.097771	.101132	.104504	.107886	.114673	.121479

10.0 YEAR HOLDING PERIOD
.020 EQUITY YIELD RATE
.700 LOAN RATIO

INTEREST RATE

TERM YEARS	APPR DEP	5.0	5.5	6.0	6.5	7.0	7.5	8.0	8.5	9.0	9.5	10.0	11.0	12.0
10	.40	-.005364	-.003297	-.001202	.000921	.003072	.005250	.007456	.009689	.011948	.014235	.016547	.021251	.026056
	.30	.003769	.005836	.007931	.010054	.012205	.014383	.016589	.018821	.021081	.023367	.025680	.030383	.035189
	.20	.012901	.014968	.017063	.019186	.021337	.023516	.025721	.027954	.030214	.032500	.034813	.039516	.044322
	.10	.022034	.024101	.026196	.028319	.030470	.032648	.034854	.037087	.039346	.041633	.043946	.048649	.053454
	0.00	.031166	.033234	.035329	.037452	.039603	.041781	.043987	.046219	.048479	.050765	.053078	.057781	.062587
	-.10	.040299	.042366	.044461	.046584	.048735	.050914	.053119	.055352	.057612	.059898	.062211	.066914	.071720
	-.20	.049432	.051499	.053594	.055717	.057868	.060046	.062252	.064485	.066744	.069031	.071343	.076047	.080852
	-.30	.058564	.060631	.062727	.064850	.067001	.069179	.071385	.073617	.075877	.078163	.080476	.085179	.089985
	-.40	.067697	.069764	.071859	.073982	.076133	.078312	.080517	.082750	.085010	.087296	.089609	.094312	.099118
15	.40	-.001243	.001522	.004329	.007176	.010061	.012985	.015946	.018943	.021975	.025041	.028141	.034434	.040847
	.30	.007889	.010655	.013462	.016308	.019194	.022118	.025079	.028076	.031108	.034174	.037273	.043567	.049979
	.20	.017022	.019788	.022594	.025441	.028327	.031250	.034211	.037208	.040240	.043307	.046406	.052699	.059112
	.10	.026155	.028920	.031727	.034574	.037459	.040383	.043344	.046341	.049373	.052439	.055539	.061832	.068245
	0.00	.035287	.038053	.040860	.043706	.046592	.049516	.052477	.055474	.058506	.061572	.064671	.070965	.077377
	-.10	.044420	.047186	.049992	.052839	.055725	.058648	.061609	.064606	.067638	.070705	.073804	.080097	.086510
	-.20	.053552	.056318	.059125	.061971	.064857	.067781	.070742	.073739	.076771	.079837	.082937	.089230	.095643
	-.30	.062685	.065451	.068258	.071104	.073990	.076914	.079875	.082872	.085904	.088970	.092069	.098363	.104775
	-.40	.071818	.074584	.077390	.080237	.083122	.086046	.089007	.092004	.095036	.098103	.101202	.107495	.113908
20	.40	.000754	.003844	.006975	.010145	.013353	.016597	.019875	.023184	.026524	.029892	.033286	.040148	.047095
	.30	.009887	.012977	.016108	.019278	.022486	.025730	.029007	.032317	.035656	.039024	.042419	.049280	.056228
	.20	.019020	.022109	.025240	.028411	.031618	.034862	.038140	.041449	.044789	.048157	.051551	.058413	.065360
	.10	.028152	.031242	.034373	.037543	.040751	.043995	.047273	.050582	.053922	.057290	.060684	.067546	.074493
	0.00	.037285	.040375	.043506	.046676	.049884	.053128	.056405	.059715	.063054	.066422	.069817	.076678	.083625
	-.10	.046418	.049507	.052638	.055809	.059017	.062260	.065538	.068847	.072187	.075555	.078949	.085811	.092758
	-.20	.055550	.058640	.061771	.064941	.068149	.071393	.074670	.077980	.081320	.084687	.088082	.094944	.101891
	-.30	.064683	.067773	.070904	.074074	.077282	.080526	.083803	.087113	.090452	.093820	.097215	.104076	.111023
	-.40	.073816	.076905	.080036	.083207	.086415	.089658	.092936	.096245	.099585	.102953	.106347	.113209	.120156
25	.40	.001905	.005170	.008473	.011810	.015179	.018578	.022004	.025455	.028927	.032420	.035931	.042997	.050113
	.30	.011038	.014303	.017606	.020943	.024312	.027711	.031137	.034587	.038060	.041553	.045063	.052130	.059246
	.20	.020171	.023436	.026738	.030075	.033445	.036844	.040270	.043720	.047193	.050685	.054196	.061263	.068378
	.10	.029303	.032568	.035871	.039208	.042577	.045976	.049402	.052853	.056325	.059818	.063329	.070395	.077511
	0.00	.038436	.041701	.045003	.048341	.051710	.055109	.058535	.061985	.065458	.068951	.072461	.079528	.086644
	-.10	.047569	.050834	.054136	.057473	.060843	.064242	.067667	.071118	.074591	.078083	.081594	.088661	.095776
	-.20	.056701	.059966	.063269	.066606	.069975	.073374	.076800	.080251	.083723	.087216	.090726	.097793	.104909
	-.30	.065834	.069099	.072401	.075739	.079108	.082507	.085933	.089383	.092856	.096349	.099859	.106926	.114042
	-.40	.074966	.078232	.081534	.084871	.088241	.091640	.095065	.098516	.101989	.105481	.108992	.116059	.123174
30	.40	.002635	.006002	.009402	.012831	.016285	.019762	.023258	.026772	.030300	.033841	.037392	.044518	.051665
	.30	.011767	.015135	.018535	.021963	.025418	.028894	.032391	.035905	.039433	.042974	.046525	.053651	.060798
	.20	.020900	.024268	.027667	.031096	.034550	.038027	.041523	.045037	.048566	.052106	.055658	.062783	.069930
	.10	.030033	.033400	.036800	.040229	.043683	.047160	.050656	.054170	.057698	.061239	.064790	.071916	.079063
	0.00	.039165	.042533	.045933	.049361	.052815	.056292	.059789	.063303	.066831	.070372	.073923	.081049	.088196
	-.10	.048298	.051666	.055065	.058494	.061948	.065425	.068921	.072435	.075964	.079504	.083055	.090181	.097328
	-.20	.057431	.060798	.064198	.067627	.071081	.074558	.078054	.081568	.085096	.088637	.092188	.099314	.106461
	-.30	.066563	.069931	.073331	.076759	.080213	.083690	.087187	.090700	.094229	.097770	.101321	.108447	.115594
	-.40	.075696	.079064	.082463	.085892	.089346	.092823	.096319	.099833	.103361	.106902	.110453	.117579	.124726

10.0 YEAR HOLDING PERIOD
.020 EQUITY YIELD RATE
.750 LOAN RATIO

INTEREST RATE

TERM YEARS	APPR DEP	5.0	5.5	6.0	6.5	7.0	7.5	8.0	8.5	9.0	9.5	10.0	11.0	12.0
10	.40	-.004567	-.002352	-.000107	.002168	.004472	.006806	.009169	.011562	.013983	.016432	.018910	.023950	.029098
	.30	.004566	.006781	.009026	.011300	.013605	.015939	.018302	.020694	.023115	.025565	.028043	.033082	.038231
	.20	.013699	.015913	.018158	.020433	.022737	.025071	.027435	.029827	.032248	.034698	.037175	.042215	.047364
	.10	.022831	.025046	.027291	.029566	.031870	.034204	.036567	.038960	.041381	.043830	.046308	.051347	.056496
	0.00	.031964	.034179	.036424	.038698	.041003	.043337	.045700	.048092	.050513	.052963	.055441	.060480	.065629
	-.10	.041097	.043311	.045556	.047831	.050135	.052469	.054833	.057225	.059646	.062096	.064573	.069613	.074762
	-.20	.050229	.052444	.054689	.056964	.059268	.061602	.063965	.066358	.068779	.071228	.073706	.078745	.083894
	-.30	.059362	.061577	.063822	.066096	.068401	.070735	.073098	.075490	.077911	.080361	.082839	.087878	.093027
	-.40	.068495	.070709	.072954	.075229	.077533	.079867	.082231	.084623	.087044	.089494	.091971	.097011	.102160
15	.40	-.000151	.002812	.005819	.008869	.011961	.015093	.018266	.021477	.024726	.028011	.031331	.038074	.044945
	.30	.008981	.011944	.014952	.018002	.021093	.024226	.027398	.030609	.033858	.037143	.040464	.047207	.054078
	.20	.018114	.021077	.024084	.027134	.030226	.033359	.036531	.039742	.042991	.046276	.049597	.056340	.063210
	.10	.027246	.030210	.033217	.036267	.039359	.042491	.045664	.048875	.052123	.055409	.058729	.065472	.072343
	0.00	.036379	.039342	.042350	.045399	.048491	.051624	.054796	.058007	.061256	.064541	.067862	.074605	.081476
	-.10	.045512	.048475	.051482	.054532	.057624	.060757	.063929	.067140	.070389	.073674	.076995	.083738	.090608
	-.20	.054644	.057608	.060615	.063665	.066757	.069889	.073062	.076273	.079521	.082807	.086127	.092870	.099741
	-.30	.063777	.066740	.069747	.072797	.075889	.079022	.082194	.085405	.088654	.091939	.095260	.102003	.108874
	-.40	.072910	.075873	.078880	.081930	.085022	.088155	.091327	.094538	.097787	.101072	.104393	.111136	.118006
20	.40	.001989	.005299	.008654	.012051	.015488	.018963	.022475	.026021	.029599	.033207	.036844	.044196	.051640
	.30	.011122	.014432	.017787	.021184	.024621	.028096	.031608	.035153	.038732	.042340	.045977	.053329	.060772
	.20	.020254	.023565	.026919	.030316	.033753	.037229	.040740	.044286	.047864	.051473	.055110	.062461	.069905
	.10	.029387	.032697	.036052	.039449	.042886	.046361	.049873	.053419	.056997	.060605	.064242	.071594	.079037
	0.00	.038520	.041830	.045185	.048581	.052019	.055494	.059006	.062551	.066130	.069738	.073375	.080727	.088170
	-.10	.047652	.050963	.054317	.057714	.061151	.064627	.068138	.071684	.075262	.078871	.082508	.089859	.097303
	-.20	.056785	.060095	.063450	.066847	.070284	.073759	.077271	.080817	.084395	.088003	.091640	.098992	.106435
	-.30	.065918	.069228	.072583	.075979	.079417	.082892	.086403	.089949	.093528	.097136	.100773	.108125	.115568
	-.40	.075050	.078361	.081715	.085112	.088549	.092025	.095536	.099082	.102660	.106269	.109906	.117257	.124701
25	.40	.003222	.006720	.010259	.013834	.017444	.021086	.024757	.028454	.032174	.035916	.039678	.047249	.054873
	.30	.012355	.015853	.019391	.022967	.026577	.030219	.033889	.037586	.041307	.045049	.048811	.056382	.064006
	.20	.021487	.024986	.028524	.032100	.035710	.039351	.043022	.046719	.050440	.054182	.057943	.065515	.073139
	.10	.030620	.034118	.037657	.041232	.044842	.048484	.052155	.055852	.059572	.063314	.067076	.074647	.082271
	0.00	.039753	.043251	.046789	.050365	.053975	.057617	.061287	.064984	.068705	.072447	.076208	.083780	.091404
	-.10	.048885	.052384	.055922	.059498	.063108	.066749	.070420	.074117	.077838	.081580	.085341	.092913	.100537
	-.20	.058018	.061516	.065055	.068630	.072240	.075882	.079553	.083250	.086970	.090712	.094474	.102045	.109669
	-.30	.067151	.070649	.074187	.077763	.081373	.085015	.088685	.092382	.096103	.099845	.103606	.111178	.118802
	-.40	.076283	.079782	.083320	.086896	.090506	.094147	.097818	.101515	.105236	.108978	.112739	.120311	.127935
30	.40	.004004	.007612	.011254	.014928	.018629	.022354	.026100	.029865	.033645	.037439	.041244	.048879	.056536
	.30	.013136	.016745	.020387	.024061	.027761	.031487	.035233	.038998	.042778	.046572	.050376	.058011	.065669
	.20	.022269	.025877	.029520	.033193	.036894	.040619	.044366	.048130	.051911	.055704	.059509	.067144	.074801
	.10	.031402	.035010	.038652	.042326	.046027	.049752	.053498	.057263	.061043	.064837	.068642	.076277	.083934
	0.00	.040534	.044142	.047785	.051459	.055159	.058885	.062631	.066396	.070176	.073970	.077774	.085409	.093067
	-.10	.049667	.053275	.056918	.060591	.064292	.068017	.071764	.075528	.079309	.083102	.086907	.094542	.102199
	-.20	.058800	.062408	.066050	.069724	.073425	.077150	.080896	.084661	.088441	.092235	.096040	.103675	.111332
	-.30	.067932	.071540	.075183	.078857	.082557	.086283	.090029	.093793	.097574	.101368	.105172	.112807	.120465
	-.40	.077065	.080673	.084316	.087989	.091690	.095415	.099161	.102926	.106707	.110500	.114305	.121940	.129597

207

10.0 YEAR HOLDING PERIOD
.020 EQUITY YIELD RATE
.800 LOAN RATIO

INTEREST RATE

TERM YEARS	APPR DEP	5.0	5.5	6.0	6.5	7.0	7.5	8.0	8.5	9.0	9.5	10.0	11.0	12.0
10	.40	-.003769	-.001407	.000988	.003414	.005872	.008362	.010883	.013434	.016017	.018630	.021273	.026648	.032140
	.30	.005364	.007726	.010121	.012547	.015005	.017495	.020015	.022567	.025150	.027762	.030406	.035781	.041273
	.20	.014496	.016859	.019253	.021680	.024138	.026627	.029148	.031700	.034282	.036895	.039538	.044913	.050406
	.10	.023629	.025991	.028386	.030812	.033270	.035760	.038281	.040832	.043415	.046028	.048671	.054046	.059538
	0.00	.032762	.035124	.037518	.039945	.042403	.044892	.047413	.049965	.052548	.055160	.057803	.063179	.068671
	-.10	.041894	.044257	.046651	.049077	.051536	.054025	.056546	.059098	.061680	.064293	.066936	.072311	.077804
	-.20	.051027	.053389	.055784	.058210	.060668	.063158	.065679	.068230	.070813	.073426	.076069	.081444	.086936
	-.30	.060160	.062522	.064916	.067343	.069801	.072290	.074811	.077363	.079945	.082558	.085201	.090577	.096069
	-.40	.069292	.071655	.074049	.076475	.078934	.081423	.083944	.086496	.089078	.091691	.094334	.099709	.105201
15	.40	.000940	.004101	.007309	.010562	.013860	.017202	.020585	.024011	.027476	.030980	.034522	.041715	.049043
	.30	.010073	.013234	.016442	.019695	.022993	.026334	.029718	.033143	.036609	.040113	.043655	.050847	.058176
	.20	.019206	.022367	.025574	.028827	.032125	.035467	.038851	.042276	.045741	.049246	.052788	.059980	.067309
	.10	.028338	.031499	.034707	.037960	.041258	.044600	.047983	.051409	.054874	.058378	.061920	.069113	.076441
	0.00	.037471	.040632	.043840	.047093	.050391	.053732	.057116	.060541	.064007	.067511	.071053	.078245	.085574
	-.10	.046604	.049765	.052972	.056225	.059523	.062865	.066249	.069674	.073139	.076643	.080185	.087378	.094707
	-.20	.055736	.058897	.062105	.065358	.068656	.071997	.075381	.078807	.082272	.085776	.089318	.096511	.103839
	-.30	.064869	.068030	.071237	.074491	.077789	.081130	.084514	.087939	.091405	.094909	.098451	.105643	.112972
	-.40	.074002	.077163	.080370	.083623	.086921	.090263	.093647	.097072	.100537	.104041	.107583	.114776	.122105
20	.40	.003264	.006755	.010333	.013956	.017623	.021330	.025075	.028858	.032674	.036523	.040403	.048244	.056184
	.30	.012356	.015887	.019466	.023089	.026755	.030462	.034208	.037990	.041807	.045656	.049535	.057377	.065317
	.20	.021489	.025020	.028598	.032222	.035888	.039595	.043341	.047123	.050940	.054789	.058668	.066510	.074450
	.10	.030622	.034153	.037731	.041354	.045020	.048728	.052473	.056255	.060072	.063921	.067801	.075642	.083582
	0.00	.039754	.043285	.046864	.050487	.054153	.057860	.061606	.065388	.069205	.073054	.076933	.084775	.092715
	-.10	.048887	.052418	.055996	.059620	.063286	.066993	.070739	.074521	.078338	.082137	.086066	.093908	.101847
	-.20	.058020	.061551	.065129	.068752	.072418	.076125	.079871	.083653	.087470	.091319	.095199	.103040	.110980
	-.30	.067152	.070683	.074262	.077885	.081551	.085258	.089004	.092786	.096603	.100452	.104331	.112173	.120113
	-.40	.076285	.079816	.083394	.087018	.090684	.094391	.098137	.101919	.105735	.109585	.113464	.121306	.129245
25	.40	.004539	.008270	.012045	.015859	.019709	.023594	.027509	.031453	.035421	.039413	.043425	.051501	.059634
	.30	.013672	.017403	.021177	.024991	.028842	.032727	.036642	.040585	.044554	.048546	.052558	.060634	.068766
	.20	.022804	.026536	.030310	.034124	.037975	.041859	.045774	.049718	.053687	.057678	.061690	.069767	.077899
	.10	.031937	.035668	.039443	.043257	.047107	.050992	.054907	.058850	.062819	.066811	.070823	.078899	.087032
	0.00	.041070	.044801	.048575	.052389	.056240	.060125	.064040	.067983	.071952	.075944	.079956	.088032	.096164
	-.10	.050202	.053934	.057708	.061522	.065373	.069257	.073172	.077116	.081085	.085076	.089088	.097165	.105297
	-.20	.059335	.063066	.066841	.070655	.074505	.078390	.082305	.086248	.090217	.094209	.098221	.106297	.114429
	-.30	.068468	.072199	.075973	.079787	.083638	.087522	.091438	.095381	.099350	.103342	.107354	.115430	.123562
	-.40	.077600	.081332	.085106	.088920	.092771	.096655	.100570	.104514	.108483	.112474	.116486	.124563	.132695
30	.40	.005373	.009221	.013107	.017025	.020973	.024946	.028942	.032958	.036990	.041037	.045095	.053239	.061407
	.30	.014505	.018354	.022239	.026158	.030105	.034079	.038075	.042091	.046123	.050170	.054228	.062372	.070540
	.20	.023638	.027487	.031372	.035290	.039238	.043212	.047208	.051223	.055256	.059302	.063361	.071505	.079673
	.10	.032771	.036619	.040505	.044423	.048371	.052344	.056340	.060356	.064388	.068435	.072493	.080637	.088805
	0.00	.041903	.045752	.049637	.053556	.057503	.061477	.065473	.069489	.073521	.077568	.081626	.089770	.097938
	-.10	.051036	.054885	.058770	.062688	.066636	.070610	.074606	.078621	.082654	.086700	.090770	.098903	.107071
	-.20	.060168	.064017	.067902	.071821	.075769	.079742	.083738	.087754	.091786	.095833	.099891	.108035	.116203
	-.30	.069301	.073150	.077035	.080954	.084901	.088875	.092871	.096887	.100919	.104966	.109024	.117168	.125336
	-.40	.078434	.082283	.086168	.090086	.094034	.098007	.102004	.106019	.110052	.114098	.118157	.126301	.134469

10.0 YEAR HOLDING PERIOD
.020 EQUITY YIELD RATE
.900 LOAN RATIO

INTEREST RATE

TERM YEARS	APPR DEP	5.0	5.5	6.0	6.5	7.0	7.5	8.0	8.5	9.0	9.5	10.0	11.0	12.0
10	.40	-.002174	.000484	.003178	.005907	.008673	.011473	.014309	.017180	.020085	.023025	.025998	.032046	.038224
	.30	.006959	.009617	.012310	.015040	.017805	.020606	.023442	.026313	.029218	.032158	.035131	.041178	.047357
	.20	.016092	.018749	.021443	.024173	.026938	.029739	.032575	.035445	.038351	.041290	.044264	.050311	.056489
	.10	.025224	.027882	.030576	.033305	.036071	.038871	.041707	.044578	.047483	.050423	.053396	.059443	.065622
	0.00	.034357	.037015	.039708	.042438	.045203	.048004	.050840	.053711	.056616	.059555	.062529	.068576	.074755
	-.10	.043490	.046147	.048841	.051571	.054336	.057137	.059973	.062843	.065749	.068688	.071662	.077709	.083887
	-.20	.052622	.055280	.057974	.060703	.063469	.066269	.069105	.071976	.074881	.077821	.080794	.086841	.093020
	-.30	.061755	.064412	.067106	.069836	.072601	.075402	.078238	.081109	.084014	.086953	.089927	.095974	.102153
	-.40	.070887	.073545	.076239	.078969	.081734	.084535	.087371	.090241	.093147	.096086	.099060	.105107	.111285
15	.40	.003124	.006680	.010289	.013949	.017659	.021418	.025225	.029078	.032977	.036919	.040904	.048995	.057240
	.30	.012257	.015813	.019421	.023081	.026792	.030551	.034358	.038211	.042109	.046052	.050036	.058128	.066373
	.20	.021390	.024946	.028554	.032214	.035924	.039683	.043490	.047344	.051242	.055184	.059169	.067261	.075506
	.10	.030522	.034078	.037687	.041347	.045057	.048816	.052623	.056476	.060375	.064317	.068302	.076393	.084638
	0.00	.039655	.043211	.046819	.050479	.054190	.057949	.061756	.065609	.069507	.073450	.077435	.085526	.093771
	-.10	.048788	.052344	.055952	.059612	.063322	.067081	.070888	.074742	.078640	.082582	.086567	.094659	.102903
	-.20	.057920	.061476	.065085	.068745	.072455	.076214	.080021	.083874	.087773	.091715	.095700	.103791	.112036
	-.30	.067053	.070609	.074217	.077877	.081587	.085347	.089154	.093007	.096905	.100848	.104832	.112924	.121169
	-.40	.076186	.079742	.083350	.087010	.090720	.094479	.098286	.102140	.106038	.109980	.113965	.122056	.130301
20	.40	.005693	.009665	.013691	.017767	.021892	.026062	.030276	.034531	.038825	.043155	.047519	.056341	.065274
	.30	.014826	.018798	.022824	.026900	.031024	.035195	.039409	.043664	.047958	.052288	.056652	.065474	.074406
	.20	.023958	.027931	.031956	.036032	.040157	.044327	.048541	.052796	.057090	.061420	.065785	.074607	.083539
	.10	.033091	.037063	.041089	.045165	.049290	.053460	.057674	.061929	.066223	.070553	.074917	.083739	.092672
	0.00	.042224	.046196	.050222	.054298	.058422	.062593	.066807	.071062	.075355	.079686	.084050	.092872	.101804
	-.10	.051356	.055329	.059354	.063430	.067555	.071725	.075939	.080194	.084488	.088818	.093183	.102005	.110937
	-.20	.060489	.064461	.068487	.072563	.076688	.080858	.085072	.089327	.093621	.097951	.102315	.111137	.120069
	-.30	.069622	.073594	.077620	.081696	.085820	.089991	.094205	.098460	.102753	.107084	.111448	.120270	.129202
	-.40	.078754	.082727	.086752	.090828	.094953	.099123	.103337	.107592	.111886	.116216	.120581	.129403	.138335
25	.40	.007173	.011371	.015617	.019907	.024240	.028609	.033014	.037450	.041915	.046406	.050919	.060005	.069154
	.30	.016305	.020503	.024749	.029040	.033372	.037742	.042147	.046583	.051048	.055539	.060052	.069138	.078287
	.20	.025438	.029636	.033882	.038173	.042505	.046875	.051279	.055716	.060181	.064671	.069185	.078271	.087419
	.10	.034571	.038769	.043015	.047305	.051637	.056007	.060412	.064848	.069313	.073804	.078317	.087403	.096552
	0.00	.043703	.047901	.052147	.056438	.060770	.065140	.069545	.073981	.078446	.082936	.087450	.096536	.105685
	-.10	.052836	.057034	.061280	.065571	.069903	.074273	.078677	.083114	.087579	.092069	.096583	.105669	.114817
	-.20	.061969	.066167	.070413	.074703	.079035	.083405	.087810	.092246	.096711	.101202	.105716	.114802	.123950
	-.30	.071101	.075299	.079545	.083836	.088168	.092538	.096943	.101379	.105844	.110334	.114848	.123934	.133083
	-.40	.080234	.084432	.088678	.092969	.097301	.101671	.106075	.110512	.114977	.119467	.123981	.133067	.142215
30	.40	.008110	.012440	.016812	.021220	.025661	.030131	.034626	.039144	.043681	.048233	.052799	.061961	.071150
	.30	.017243	.021573	.025944	.030352	.034793	.039263	.043759	.048277	.052813	.057366	.061931	.071093	.080282
	.20	.026376	.030706	.035077	.039485	.043926	.048396	.052892	.057409	.061946	.066498	.071064	.080226	.089415
	.10	.035508	.039838	.044209	.048618	.053059	.057529	.062024	.066542	.071078	.075631	.080197	.089359	.098548
	0.00	.044641	.048971	.053342	.057750	.062191	.066661	.071157	.075675	.080211	.084764	.089329	.098491	.107680
	-.10	.053774	.058104	.062475	.066883	.071324	.075794	.080290	.084807	.089344	.093896	.098462	.107624	.116813
	-.20	.062906	.067236	.071607	.076016	.080457	.084927	.089422	.093940	.098476	.103029	.107595	.116757	.125945
	-.30	.072039	.076369	.080740	.085148	.089589	.094059	.098555	.103073	.107609	.112162	.116727	.125889	.135078
	-.40	.081172	.085502	.089873	.094281	.098722	.103192	.107688	.112205	.116742	.121294	.125860	.135022	.144211

209

10.0 YEAR HOLDING PERIOD
.040 EQUITY YIELD RATE
.600 LOAN RATIO

INTEREST RATE

TERM YEARS	APPR DEP	5.0	5.5	6.0	6.5	7.0	7.5	8.0	8.5	9.0	9.5	10.0	11.0	12.0
10	.40	.009076	.010848	.012644	.014464	.016307	.018174	.020065	.021979	.023916	.025875	.027858	.031889	.036008
	.30	.017405	.019177	.020973	.022793	.024636	.026503	.028394	.030308	.032245	.034204	.036187	.040218	.044337
	.20	.025734	.027506	.029302	.031122	.032965	.034833	.036723	.038637	.040574	.042533	.044516	.048547	.052666
	.10	.034064	.035835	.037631	.039451	.041294	.043162	.045052	.046966	.048903	.050863	.052845	.056876	.060995
	0.00	.042393	.044164	.045960	.047780	.049624	.051491	.053381	.055295	.057232	.059192	.061174	.065205	.069325
	-.10	.050722	.052493	.054289	.056109	.057953	.059820	.061710	.063624	.065561	.067521	.069503	.073535	.077654
	-.20	.059051	.060823	.062618	.064438	.066282	.068149	.070039	.071953	.073890	.075850	.077832	.081864	.085983
	-.30	.067380	.069152	.070947	.072767	.074611	.076478	.078369	.080282	.082219	.084179	.086161	.090193	.094312
	-.40	.075709	.077481	.079277	.081096	.082940	.084807	.086698	.088612	.090548	.092508	.094490	.098522	.102641
15	.40	.010588	.012917	.015280	.017678	.020109	.022574	.025070	.027597	.030154	.032741	.035356	.040669	.046084
	.30	.018917	.021246	.023609	.026007	.028439	.030903	.033399	.035926	.038483	.041070	.043685	.048998	.054413
	.20	.027246	.029575	.031938	.034336	.036768	.039232	.041728	.044255	.046812	.049399	.052014	.057327	.062742
	.10	.035575	.037904	.040267	.042665	.045097	.047561	.050057	.052584	.055141	.057728	.060343	.065656	.071072
	0.00	.043904	.046233	.048597	.050994	.053426	.055890	.058386	.060913	.063471	.066057	.068672	.073985	.079401
	-.10	.052233	.054562	.056926	.059324	.061755	.064219	.066715	.069242	.071800	.074386	.077002	.082314	.087730
	-.20	.060562	.062891	.065255	.067653	.070084	.072548	.075044	.077571	.080129	.082715	.085331	.090643	.096059
	-.30	.068892	.071220	.073584	.075982	.078413	.080877	.083373	.085900	.088458	.091045	.093660	.098972	.104388
	-.40	.077221	.079549	.081913	.084311	.086742	.089206	.091702	.094230	.096787	.099374	.101989	.107301	.112717
20	.40	.011321	.013913	.016541	.019204	.021900	.024628	.027386	.030171	.032984	.035322	.038684	.044474	.050341
	.30	.019650	.022242	.024870	.027533	.030230	.032957	.035715	.038501	.041313	.044151	.047013	.052803	.058670
	.20	.027979	.030571	.033200	.035863	.038559	.041286	.044044	.046830	.049642	.052480	.055342	.061132	.066999
	.10	.036308	.038900	.041529	.044192	.046888	.049615	.052373	.055159	.057971	.060810	.063671	.069461	.075328
	0.00	.044637	.047229	.049858	.052521	.055217	.057944	.060702	.063488	.066301	.069139	.072001	.077790	.083657
	-.10	.052966	.055558	.058187	.060850	.063546	.066273	.069031	.071817	.074630	.077468	.080330	.086119	.091986
	-.20	.061295	.063888	.066516	.069180	.071875	.074603	.077360	.080146	.082959	.085797	.088659	.094448	.100315
	-.30	.069624	.072217	.074845	.077508	.080204	.082932	.085689	.088475	.091288	.094126	.096988	.102777	.108645
	-.40	.077954	.080546	.083174	.085837	.088533	.091261	.094018	.096804	.099617	.102455	.105317	.111106	.116974
25	.40	.011743	.014482	.017255	.020060	.022894	.025755	.028641	.031550	.034480	.037429	.040395	.046371	.052397
	.30	.020072	.022811	.025584	.028389	.031223	.034084	.036970	.039879	.042809	.045758	.048724	.054700	.060726
	.20	.028401	.031140	.033914	.036718	.039552	.042413	.045299	.048208	.051138	.054087	.057053	.063030	.069055
	.10	.036730	.039470	.042243	.045047	.047881	.050742	.053628	.056537	.059467	.062416	.065382	.071359	.077384
	0.00	.045059	.047799	.050572	.053376	.056210	.059071	.061957	.064866	.067796	.070745	.073711	.079688	.085713
	-.10	.053388	.056128	.058901	.061705	.064539	.067400	.070286	.073195	.076125	.079074	.082040	.088017	.094043
	-.20	.061718	.064457	.067230	.070035	.072868	.075729	.078616	.081524	.084454	.087403	.090369	.096346	.102372
	-.30	.070047	.072786	.075559	.078364	.081198	.084059	.086945	.089854	.092783	.095732	.098698	.104675	.110701
	-.40	.078376	.081115	.083888	.086693	.089527	.092388	.095274	.098183	.101113	.104061	.107027	.113004	.119030
30	.40	.012011	.014839	.017698	.020584	.023495	.026428	.029380	.032350	.035334	.038331	.041340	.047384	.053454
	.30	.020340	.023168	.026027	.028914	.031824	.034757	.037709	.040679	.043663	.046661	.049669	.055713	.061783
	.20	.028669	.031498	.034356	.037243	.040153	.043086	.046038	.049008	.051992	.054990	.057998	.064042	.070113
	.10	.036998	.039827	.042686	.045572	.048482	.051415	.054367	.057337	.060321	.063319	.066327	.072371	.078442
	0.00	.045327	.048156	.051015	.053901	.056812	.059744	.062697	.065666	.068650	.071648	.074656	.080701	.086771
	-.10	.053656	.056485	.059344	.062230	.065141	.068073	.071026	.073995	.076979	.079977	.082986	.089030	.095100
	-.20	.061985	.064814	.067673	.070559	.073470	.076402	.079353	.082324	.085309	.088306	.091315	.097359	.103429
	-.30	.070314	.073143	.076002	.078888	.081799	.084732	.087684	.090653	.093638	.096635	.099644	.105688	.111758
	-.40	.078643	.081472	.084331	.087217	.090128	.093061	.096013	.098982	.101967	.104964	.107973	.114017	.120087

10.0 YEAR HOLDING PERIOD
.040 EQUITY YIELD RATE
.667 LOAN RATIO

INTEREST RATE

TERM YEARS	APPR DEP	5.0	5.5	6.0	6.5	7.0	7.5	8.0	8.5	9.0	9.5	10.0	11.0	12.0
10	.40	.009342	.011311	.013306	.015328	.017376	.019451	.021552	.023678	.025830	.028008	.030210	.034690	.039257
	.30	.017671	.019640	.021635	.023657	.025706	.027780	.029881	.032007	.034159	.036337	.038539	.043019	.047596
	.20	.026000	.027969	.029964	.031986	.034035	.036109	.038210	.040336	.042489	.044666	.046869	.051348	.055925
	.10	.034329	.036298	.038293	.040315	.042364	.044438	.046539	.048666	.050818	.052995	.055198	.059677	.064254
	0.00	.042658	.044627	.046622	.048644	.050693	.052768	.054868	.056995	.059147	.061324	.063527	.068006	.072583
	-.10	.050988	.052956	.054952	.056974	.059022	.061097	.063197	.065324	.067476	.069653	.071856	.076335	.080912
	-.20	.059317	.061285	.063281	.065303	.067351	.069426	.071526	.073653	.075805	.077982	.080185	.084664	.089241
	-.30	.067646	.069614	.071610	.073632	.075680	.077755	.079855	.081982	.084134	.086311	.088514	.092993	.097570
	-.40	.075975	.077943	.079939	.081961	.084009	.086084	.088185	.090311	.092463	.094641	.096843	.101323	.105899
15	.40	.011022	.013609	.016235	.018900	.021601	.024339	.027113	.029921	.032762	.035636	.038542	.044445	.050462
	.30	.019351	.021938	.024564	.027229	.029930	.032668	.035442	.038250	.041091	.043965	.046871	.052774	.058791
	.20	.027680	.030267	.032894	.035558	.038259	.040997	.043771	.046579	.049420	.052294	.055200	.061103	.067120
	.10	.036009	.038596	.041223	.043887	.046589	.049327	.052100	.054908	.057749	.060624	.063529	.069432	.075450
	0.00	.044338	.046925	.049552	.052216	.054918	.057656	.060429	.063237	.066078	.068953	.071858	.077761	.083779
	-.10	.052667	.055255	.057881	.060545	.063247	.065985	.068758	.071566	.074408	.077282	.080188	.086090	.092108
	-.20	.060996	.063584	.066210	.068874	.071576	.074314	.077087	.079895	.082737	.085611	.088517	.094419	.100437
	-.30	.069325	.071913	.074539	.077203	.079905	.082643	.085416	.088224	.091066	.093940	.096846	.102748	.108766
	-.40	.077654	.080242	.082868	.085532	.088234	.090972	.093745	.096553	.099395	.102269	.105175	.111078	.117095
20	.40	.011836	.014716	.017637	.020596	.023591	.026622	.029686	.032781	.035907	.039060	.042240	.048673	.055192
	.30	.020165	.023045	.025966	.028925	.031920	.034951	.038015	.041110	.044236	.047389	.050569	.057002	.063521
	.20	.028494	.031375	.034295	.037254	.040249	.043280	.046344	.049440	.052565	.055718	.058898	.065331	.071850
	.10	.036823	.039704	.042624	.045583	.048579	.051609	.054673	.057769	.060894	.064047	.067227	.073660	.080179
	0.00	.045152	.048033	.050953	.053912	.056908	.059938	.063002	.066098	.069223	.072376	.075556	.081989	.088508
	-.10	.053482	.056362	.059282	.062241	.065237	.068267	.071331	.074427	.077552	.080706	.083885	.090318	.096837
	-.20	.061811	.064691	.067611	.070570	.073566	.076596	.079660	.082756	.085881	.089035	.092215	.098647	.105166
	-.30	.070140	.073020	.075940	.078899	.081895	.084926	.087990	.091085	.094210	.097364	.100544	.106976	.113495
	-.40	.078469	.081349	.084270	.087228	.090224	.093255	.096319	.099414	.102539	.105693	.108873	.115305	.121825
25	.40	.012305	.015349	.018430	.021546	.024695	.027874	.031081	.034313	.037568	.040845	.044141	.050781	.057477
	.30	.020634	.023678	.026759	.029875	.033024	.036203	.039410	.042642	.045897	.049174	.052470	.059110	.065806
	.20	.028963	.032007	.035088	.038204	.041353	.044532	.047739	.050971	.054227	.057503	.060799	.067440	.074135
	.10	.037292	.040336	.043417	.046534	.049682	.052861	.056068	.059300	.062556	.065832	.069128	.075769	.082464
	0.00	.045622	.048665	.051746	.054863	.058011	.061190	.064397	.067629	.070885	.074161	.077457	.084098	.090793
	-.10	.053951	.056994	.060075	.063192	.066341	.069520	.072726	.075958	.079214	.082490	.085786	.092427	.099122
	-.20	.062280	.065323	.068405	.071521	.074670	.077849	.081055	.084288	.087543	.090819	.094115	.100756	.107451
	-.30	.070609	.073652	.076734	.079851	.083000	.086179	.089384	.092617	.095872	.099149	.102444	.109085	.115780
	-.40	.078938	.081982	.085063	.088179	.091328	.094507	.097714	.100946	.104201	.107478	.110773	.117414	.124109
30	.40	.012602	.015746	.018922	.022129	.025363	.028622	.031902	.035201	.038518	.041848	.045191	.051907	.058651
	.30	.020932	.024075	.027251	.030458	.033692	.036951	.040231	.043531	.046847	.050177	.053520	.060236	.066981
	.20	.029261	.032404	.035580	.038787	.042021	.045280	.048560	.051860	.055176	.058506	.061849	.068565	.075310
	.10	.037590	.040733	.043909	.047116	.050351	.053609	.056889	.060189	.063505	.066835	.070178	.076894	.083639
	0.00	.045919	.049062	.052239	.055445	.058680	.061938	.065218	.068518	.071834	.075164	.078507	.085223	.091968
	-.10	.054248	.057391	.060568	.063775	.067009	.070267	.073548	.076847	.080163	.083494	.086836	.093552	.100297
	-.20	.062577	.065720	.068897	.072104	.075338	.078596	.081877	.085176	.088492	.091823	.095166	.101881	.108626
	-.30	.070906	.074049	.077226	.080433	.083667	.086926	.090206	.093505	.096821	.100152	.103495	.110210	.116955
	-.40	.079235	.082378	.085555	.088762	.091996	.095255	.098535	.101834	.105150	.108481	.111824	.118539	.125284

10.0 YEAR HOLDING PERIOD
.040 EQUITY YIELD RATE
.700 LOAN RATIO

INTEREST RATE

TERM YEARS	APPR DEP	5.0	5.5	6.0	6.5	7.0	7.5	8.0	8.5	9.0	9.5	10.0	11.0	12.0
10	.40	.009475	.011542	.013637	.015760	.017911	.020089	.022295	.024528	.026788	.029074	.031387	.036090	.040856
	.30	.017804	.019871	.021966	.024089	.026240	.028419	.030624	.032857	.035117	.037403	.039716	.044419	.049225
	.20	.026133	.028200	.030295	.032418	.034569	.036748	.038953	.041186	.043446	.045732	.048045	.052748	.057554
	.10	.034462	.036529	.038624	.040748	.042898	.045077	.047282	.049515	.051775	.054061	.056374	.061077	.065883
	0.00	.042791	.044858	.046954	.049077	.051227	.053406	.055612	.057844	.060104	.062390	.064703	.069406	.074212
	-.10	.051120	.053188	.055283	.057406	.059557	.061735	.063941	.066173	.068433	.070719	.073032	.077735	.082541
	-.20	.059450	.061517	.063612	.065735	.067886	.070064	.072270	.074503	.076762	.079048	.081361	.086065	.090870
	-.30	.067779	.069846	.071941	.074064	.076215	.078393	.080599	.082832	.085091	.087378	.089690	.094394	.099199
	-.40	.076108	.078175	.080270	.082393	.084544	.086722	.088928	.091161	.093420	.095707	.098019	.102723	.107528
15	.40	.011239	.013955	.016713	.019510	.022347	.025222	.028134	.031082	.034066	.037084	.040135	.046333	.052651
	.30	.019568	.022284	.025042	.027840	.030676	.033551	.036463	.039411	.042395	.045413	.048464	.054662	.060980
	.20	.027897	.030614	.033371	.036169	.039005	.041880	.044792	.047740	.050724	.053742	.056793	.062991	.069309
	.10	.036226	.038943	.041700	.044498	.047334	.050209	.053121	.056070	.059053	.062071	.065122	.071320	.077638
	0.00	.044555	.047272	.050029	.052827	.055663	.058538	.061450	.064399	.067382	.070400	.073451	.079649	.085967
	-.10	.052884	.055601	.058358	.061156	.063993	.066867	.069779	.072728	.075711	.078729	.081780	.087978	.094296
	-.20	.061213	.063930	.066687	.069485	.072322	.075196	.078109	.081057	.084040	.087058	.090109	.096307	.102626
	-.30	.069542	.072259	.075017	.077814	.080651	.083526	.086438	.089386	.092370	.095387	.098439	.104636	.110955
	-.40	.077871	.080588	.083346	.086143	.088980	.091855	.094767	.097715	.100699	.103717	.106768	.112965	.119284
20	.40	.012094	.015118	.018184	.021291	.024437	.027619	.030836	.034086	.037368	.040679	.044018	.050772	.057617
	.30	.020423	.023447	.026513	.029620	.032766	.035948	.039165	.042415	.045697	.049008	.052347	.059101	.065946
	.20	.028752	.031776	.034843	.037949	.041095	.044277	.047494	.050744	.054026	.057337	.060676	.067430	.074275
	.10	.037081	.040105	.043172	.046278	.049424	.052606	.055823	.059073	.062355	.065666	.069005	.075759	.082604
	0.00	.045410	.048434	.051501	.054608	.057753	.060935	.064152	.067402	.070684	.073995	.077334	.084088	.090933
	-.10	.053739	.056763	.059830	.062937	.066082	.069264	.072481	.075732	.079013	.082324	.085663	.092417	.099263
	-.20	.062068	.065092	.068159	.071266	.074411	.077593	.080810	.084061	.087342	.090653	.093992	.100746	.107592
	-.30	.070397	.073422	.076488	.079595	.082740	.085922	.089139	.092390	.095671	.098982	.102321	.109076	.115921
	-.40	.078726	.081751	.084817	.087924	.091069	.094251	.097469	.100719	.104000	.107311	.110650	.117405	.124250
25	.40	.012586	.015782	.019017	.022289	.025596	.028933	.032300	.035694	.039112	.042553	.046013	.052986	.060016
	.30	.020915	.024111	.027346	.030618	.033925	.037263	.040630	.044023	.047442	.050882	.054342	.061315	.068345
	.20	.029244	.032440	.035675	.038948	.042254	.045592	.048959	.052352	.055771	.059211	.062671	.069644	.076674
	.10	.037573	.040769	.044005	.047277	.050583	.053921	.057288	.060682	.064100	.067540	.071000	.077973	.085003
	0.00	.045903	.049098	.052334	.055606	.058912	.062250	.065617	.069011	.072429	.075869	.079330	.086302	.093332
	-.10	.054232	.057428	.060663	.063935	.067241	.070579	.073946	.077340	.080758	.084198	.087659	.094631	.101661
	-.20	.062561	.065757	.068992	.072264	.075570	.078908	.082275	.085669	.089087	.092527	.095988	.102961	.109991
	-.30	.070890	.074086	.077321	.080593	.083899	.087237	.090604	.093998	.097416	.100856	.104317	.111290	.118320
	-.40	.079219	.082415	.085650	.088922	.092228	.095566	.098933	.102327	.105745	.109186	.112646	.119619	.126649
30	.40	.012898	.016199	.019534	.022901	.026297	.029719	.033163	.036627	.040109	.043606	.047116	.054168	.061250
	.30	.021227	.024528	.027863	.031230	.034626	.038048	.041492	.044956	.048438	.051935	.055445	.062497	.069579
	.20	.029557	.032857	.036192	.039559	.042955	.046377	.049821	.053285	.056767	.060264	.063774	.070826	.077908
	.10	.037886	.041186	.044521	.047889	.051284	.054706	.058150	.061615	.065096	.068593	.072103	.079155	.086237
	0.00	.046215	.049515	.052850	.056218	.059614	.063035	.066479	.069944	.073425	.076922	.080433	.087484	.094566
	-.10	.054544	.057844	.061180	.064547	.067943	.071364	.074808	.078273	.081755	.085252	.088762	.095813	.102895
	-.20	.062873	.066173	.069509	.072876	.076272	.079693	.083137	.086602	.090084	.093581	.097091	.104142	.111224
	-.30	.071202	.074506	.077838	.081205	.084601	.088022	.091467	.094931	.098413	.101910	.105420	.112471	.119553
	-.40	.079531	.082831	.086167	.089534	.092930	.096351	.099796	.103260	.106742	.110239	.113749	.120800	.127882

10.0 YEAR HOLDING PERIOD
.040 EQUITY YIELD RATE
.750 LOAN RATIO

INTEREST RATE

TERM YEARS	APPR DEP	5.0	5.5	6.0	6.5	7.0	7.5	8.0	8.5	9.0	9.5	10.0	11.0	12.0
10	.40	.009674	.011889	.014134	.016409	.018713	.021047	.023410	.025803	.028224	.030673	.033151	.038190	.043339
	.30	.018003	.020218	.022463	.024738	.027042	.029376	.031739	.034132	.036553	.039002	.041480	.046520	.051668
	.20	.026333	.028547	.030792	.033067	.035371	.037705	.040068	.042461	.044882	.047331	.049809	.054849	.059997
	.10	.034662	.036876	.039121	.041396	.043700	.046034	.048398	.050790	.053211	.055660	.058138	.063178	.068327
	0.00	.042991	.045205	.047450	.049725	.052029	.054363	.056727	.059119	.061540	.063990	.066467	.071507	.075656
	-.10	.051320	.053535	.055779	.058054	.060359	.062692	.065056	.067448	.069869	.072319	.074797	.079836	.084985
	-.20	.059649	.061864	.064108	.066383	.068688	.071022	.073385	.075777	.078198	.080648	.083126	.088165	.093314
	-.30	.067978	.070193	.072438	.074712	.077017	.079351	.081714	.084106	.086527	.088977	.091455	.096494	.101643
	-.40	.076307	.078522	.080767	.083041	.085346	.087680	.090043	.092435	.094856	.097306	.099784	.104823	.109972
15	.40	.011564	.014475	.017429	.020427	.023466	.026546	.029666	.032825	.036022	.039255	.042524	.049165	.055934
	.30	.019893	.022804	.025758	.028756	.031795	.034875	.037995	.041154	.044351	.047584	.050853	.057494	.064263
	.20	.028222	.031133	.034087	.037085	.040124	.043204	.046324	.049483	.052680	.055913	.059182	.065823	.072593
	.10	.036551	.039462	.042417	.045414	.048453	.051533	.054653	.057812	.061009	.064242	.067512	.074152	.080922
	0.00	.044880	.047791	.050746	.053743	.056782	.059862	.062983	.066141	.069338	.072572	.075841	.082481	.089251
	-.10	.053209	.056120	.059075	.062072	.065111	.068191	.071312	.074471	.077667	.080901	.084170	.090810	.097580
	-.20	.061539	.064449	.067404	.070401	.073440	.076521	.079641	.082800	.085996	.089230	.092499	.099139	.105909
	-.30	.069868	.072778	.075733	.078730	.081770	.084850	.087970	.091129	.094325	.097559	.100828	.107468	.114238
	-.40	.078197	.081107	.084062	.087059	.090099	.093179	.096299	.099458	.102655	.105888	.109157	.115797	.122567
20	.40	.012480	.015720	.019006	.022335	.025705	.029114	.032561	.036043	.039559	.043107	.046684	.053921	.061255
	.30	.020809	.024049	.027335	.030664	.034034	.037443	.040890	.044373	.047888	.051436	.055013	.062250	.069584
	.20	.029138	.032379	.035664	.038993	.042363	.045772	.049219	.052702	.056218	.059765	.063343	.070579	.077913
	.10	.037467	.040708	.043993	.047322	.050692	.054101	.057548	.061031	.064547	.068094	.071672	.078908	.086242
	0.00	.045796	.049037	.052322	.055651	.059021	.062430	.065877	.069360	.072876	.076423	.080001	.087237	.094572
	-.10	.054126	.057366	.060651	.063980	.067350	.070760	.074206	.077689	.081205	.084752	.088330	.095567	.102901
	-.20	.062455	.065695	.068980	.072309	.075679	.079089	.082536	.086018	.089534	.093082	.096659	.103896	.111230
	-.30	.070784	.074024	.077309	.080638	.084008	.087418	.090865	.094347	.097863	.101411	.104988	.112225	.119559
	-.40	.079113	.082353	.085639	.088967	.092337	.095747	.099194	.102676	.106192	.109740	.113317	.120554	.127888
25	.40	.013008	.016432	.019898	.023404	.026946	.030523	.034130	.037766	.041429	.045115	.048822	.056293	.063825
	.30	.021337	.024761	.028227	.031733	.035276	.038852	.042459	.046096	.049758	.053444	.057152	.064622	.072155
	.20	.029666	.033090	.036556	.040062	.043605	.047181	.050788	.054425	.058087	.061773	.065481	.072952	.080484
	.10	.037995	.041419	.044886	.048391	.051934	.055510	.059118	.062754	.066416	.070102	.073810	.081231	.088813
	0.00	.046324	.049748	.053215	.056720	.060263	.063839	.067447	.071083	.074745	.078431	.082139	.089610	.097142
	-.10	.054653	.058077	.061544	.065049	.068592	.072168	.075776	.079412	.083074	.086760	.090468	.097939	.105471
	-.20	.062982	.066406	.069873	.073379	.076921	.080497	.084105	.087741	.091403	.095089	.098797	.106268	.113800
	-.30	.071311	.074736	.078202	.081708	.085250	.088826	.092434	.096070	.099732	.103419	.107126	.114597	.122129
	-.40	.079641	.083065	.086531	.090037	.093579	.097155	.100763	.104399	.108062	.111748	.115455	.122926	.130458
30	.40	.013342	.016878	.020452	.024060	.027698	.031364	.035054	.038766	.042497	.046243	.050004	.057559	.065147
	.30	.021671	.025207	.028781	.032389	.036027	.039693	.043383	.047095	.050826	.054573	.058333	.065888	.073476
	.20	.030000	.033536	.037110	.040718	.044356	.048022	.051712	.055424	.059155	.062902	.066662	.074217	.081805
	.10	.038330	.041866	.045439	.049047	.052685	.056351	.060042	.063763	.067484	.071231	.074991	.082547	.090134
	0.00	.046659	.050195	.053768	.057376	.061014	.064680	.068371	.072082	.075813	.079560	.083321	.090876	.098463
	-.10	.054988	.058524	.062097	.065705	.069344	.073009	.076700	.080412	.084142	.087889	.091650	.099205	.106793
	-.20	.063317	.066853	.070427	.074034	.077673	.081339	.085029	.088741	.092471	.096218	.099979	.107534	.115122
	-.30	.071646	.075182	.078756	.082363	.086002	.089668	.093358	.097070	.100800	.104547	.108308	.115863	.123451
	-.40	.079975	.083511	.087085	.090692	.094331	.097997	.101687	.105399	.109129	.112876	.116637	.124192	.131780

213

10.0 YEAR HOLDING PERIOD
.040 EQUITY YIELD RATE
.800 LOAN RATIO

INTEREST RATE

TERM YEARS	APPR DEP	5.0	5.5	6.0	6.5	7.0	7.5	8.0	8.5	9.0	9.5	10.0	11.0	12.0
10	.40	.009874	.012236	.014631	.017057	.019515	.022005	.024525	.027077	.029660	.032273	.034916	.040291	.045783
	.30	.018203	.020565	.022960	.025356	.027844	.030334	.032854	.035406	.037989	.040602	.043245	.048620	.054112
	.20	.026532	.028894	.031289	.033715	.036173	.038663	.041184	.043735	.046318	.048931	.051574	.056949	.062441
	.10	.034861	.037223	.039618	.042044	.044502	.046992	.049513	.052064	.054647	.057260	.059903	.065278	.070770
	0.00	.043190	.045552	.047947	.050373	.052831	.055321	.057842	.060394	.062976	.065589	.068232	.073607	.079099
	-.10	.051519	.053882	.056276	.058702	.061160	.063650	.066171	.068723	.071305	.073918	.076561	.081936	.087428
	-.20	.059848	.062211	.064605	.067031	.069490	.071979	.074500	.077052	.079634	.082247	.084890	.090255	.095758
	-.30	.068177	.070540	.072934	.075361	.077819	.080308	.082829	.085381	.087963	.090576	.093219	.098555	.104087
	-.40	.076507	.078869	.081263	.083690	.086148	.088637	.091158	.093710	.096292	.098905	.101548	.106924	.112416
15	.40	.011889	.014994	.018146	.021343	.024585	.027870	.031198	.034568	.037978	.041427	.044914	.051997	.059218
	.30	.020218	.023323	.026475	.029672	.032914	.036199	.039527	.042897	.046307	.049756	.053243	.060326	.067547
	.20	.028548	.031652	.034804	.038001	.041243	.044528	.047857	.051226	.054636	.058085	.061572	.068655	.075876
	.10	.036877	.039981	.043133	.046330	.049572	.052858	.056186	.059555	.062965	.066414	.069901	.076984	.084205
	0.00	.045206	.048311	.051462	.054659	.057901	.061187	.064515	.067884	.071294	.074743	.078230	.085313	.092534
	-.10	.053535	.056640	.059791	.062988	.066230	.069516	.072844	.076213	.079623	.083072	.086559	.093642	.100863
	-.20	.061864	.064969	.068120	.071317	.074559	.077845	.081173	.084542	.087952	.091401	.094888	.101971	.109192
	-.30	.070193	.073298	.076449	.079647	.082888	.086174	.089502	.092871	.096281	.099730	.103217	.110300	.117521
	-.40	.078522	.081627	.084778	.087976	.091217	.094503	.097831	.101201	.104610	.108059	.111546	.118530	.125851
20	.40	.012867	.016323	.019827	.023378	.026973	.030609	.034286	.038001	.041751	.045535	.049351	.057070	.064893
	.30	.021196	.024652	.028156	.031707	.035302	.038939	.042615	.046330	.050080	.053864	.057680	.065399	.073222
	.20	.029525	.032981	.036486	.040036	.043631	.047268	.050944	.054659	.058409	.062193	.066009	.073728	.081551
	.10	.037854	.041310	.044815	.048365	.051960	.055597	.059273	.062988	.066738	.070522	.074338	.082057	.089881
	0.00	.046183	.049639	.053144	.056694	.060289	.063926	.067603	.071317	.075067	.078852	.082667	.090387	.098210
	-.10	.054512	.057968	.061473	.065023	.068618	.072255	.075932	.079646	.083397	.087181	.090997	.098716	.106539
	-.20	.062841	.066297	.069802	.073353	.076947	.080584	.084261	.087975	.091726	.095510	.099326	.107045	.114868
	-.30	.071170	.074626	.078131	.081682	.085276	.088913	.092590	.096306	.100055	.103839	.107655	.115374	.123197
	-.40	.079499	.082956	.086460	.090011	.093605	.097242	.100919	.104633	.108384	.112168	.115984	.123703	.131526
25	.40	.013429	.017082	.020779	.024519	.028297	.032112	.035960	.039839	.043745	.047677	.051632	.059601	.067635
	.30	.021759	.025411	.029108	.032848	.036626	.040441	.044289	.048168	.052074	.056006	.059961	.067930	.075964
	.20	.030088	.033740	.037437	.041177	.044955	.048770	.052618	.056497	.060403	.064335	.068290	.076259	.084293
	.10	.038417	.042069	.045767	.049506	.053285	.057099	.060947	.064826	.068732	.072664	.076619	.084588	.092622
	0.00	.046746	.050398	.054096	.057835	.061614	.065428	.069276	.073155	.077062	.080993	.084948	.092917	.100951
	-.10	.055075	.058727	.062425	.066164	.069943	.073757	.077606	.081484	.085391	.089322	.093277	.101246	.109280
	-.20	.063404	.067056	.070754	.074493	.078272	.082087	.085935	.089813	.093720	.097652	.101606	.109575	.117609
	-.30	.071733	.075385	.079083	.082822	.086601	.090416	.094264	.098142	.102049	.105981	.109935	.117904	.125939
	-.40	.080062	.083715	.087412	.091151	.094930	.098745	.102593	.106471	.110378	.114310	.118264	.126233	.134268
30	.40	.013786	.017558	.021370	.025218	.029099	.033009	.036946	.040905	.044884	.048881	.052892	.060951	.069045
	.30	.022115	.025887	.029699	.033547	.037428	.041338	.045275	.049234	.053213	.057210	.061221	.069280	.077374
	.20	.030444	.034216	.038028	.041876	.045757	.049668	.053604	.057563	.061542	.065539	.069550	.077609	.085703
	.10	.038773	.042545	.046357	.050205	.054086	.057997	.061933	.065892	.069871	.073868	.077880	.085938	.094032
	0.00	.047103	.050874	.054686	.058534	.062415	.066326	.070262	.074221	.078201	.082197	.086209	.094267	.102361
	-.10	.055432	.059203	.063015	.066864	.070745	.074655	.078591	.082550	.086530	.090526	.094538	.102596	.110690
	-.20	.063762	.067533	.071344	.075193	.079074	.082984	.086921	.090879	.094859	.098855	.102867	.110926	.119019
	-.30	.072090	.075862	.079673	.083522	.087403	.091313	.095249	.099209	.103188	.107184	.111196	.119255	.127348
	-.40	.080419	.084191	.088003	.091851	.095732	.099642	.103578	.107538	.111517	.115514	.119525	.127584	.135677

10.0 YEAR HOLDING PERIOD
.040 EQUITY YIELD RATE
.900 LOAN RATIO

INTEREST RATE

TERM YEARS	APPR DEP	5.0	5.5	6.0	6.5	7.0	7.5	8.0	8.5	9.0	9.5	10.0	11.0	12.0
10	.40	.010273	.012930	.015624	.018354	.021119	.023920	.026756	.029626	.032532	.035471	.038445	.044492	.050670
	.30	.018602	.021259	.023953	.026683	.029448	.032249	.035085	.037955	.040861	.043800	.046774	.052821	.058999
	.20	.026931	.029588	.032282	.035012	.037775	.040578	.043414	.046285	.049190	.052129	.055103	.061150	.067329
	.10	.035260	.037917	.040611	.043341	.046106	.048907	.051743	.054614	.057519	.060458	.063432	.069479	.075658
	0.00	.043589	.046247	.048940	.051670	.054435	.057236	.060072	.062943	.065848	.068788	.071761	.077808	.083987
	-.10	.051918	.054576	.057269	.059999	.062764	.065565	.068401	.071272	.074177	.077117	.080090	.086137	.092316
	-.20	.060247	.062905	.065598	.068328	.071093	.073894	.076730	.079601	.082506	.085446	.088419	.094466	.100645
	-.30	.068576	.071234	.073928	.076657	.079423	.082223	.085059	.087930	.090835	.093775	.096748	.102795	.108974
	-.40	.076905	.079563	.082257	.084986	.087752	.090552	.093388	.096259	.099164	.102104	.105077	.111125	.117303
15	.40	.012540	.016033	.019578	.023175	.026822	.030519	.034263	.038053	.041889	.045770	.049692	.057661	.065785
	.30	.020869	.024362	.027907	.031504	.035151	.038848	.042592	.046382	.050218	.054099	.058021	.065990	.074114
	.20	.029198	.032691	.036237	.039833	.043481	.047177	.050921	.054712	.058548	.062428	.066351	.074319	.082443
	.10	.037527	.041020	.044566	.048163	.051810	.055506	.059250	.063041	.066877	.070757	.074680	.082648	.090772
	0.00	.045856	.049349	.052895	.056492	.060139	.063835	.067579	.071370	.075206	.079086	.083009	.090977	.099101
	-.10	.054186	.057678	.061224	.064821	.068468	.072164	.075908	.079699	.083535	.087415	.091338	.099306	.107430
	-.20	.062515	.066008	.069553	.073150	.076797	.080493	.084237	.088028	.091864	.095744	.099667	.107636	.115759
	-.30	.070844	.074337	.077382	.081479	.085126	.088822	.092566	.096357	.100193	.104073	.107996	.115965	.124088
	-.40	.079173	.082666	.086211	.089808	.093455	.097151	.100895	.104686	.108522	.112402	.116325	.124294	.132417
20	.40	.013639	.017528	.021470	.025465	.029509	.033600	.037736	.041915	.046134	.050392	.054684	.063369	.072170
	.30	.021968	.025857	.029799	.033794	.037838	.041929	.046066	.050244	.054464	.058721	.063014	.071698	.080459
	.20	.030298	.034186	.038128	.042123	.046167	.050258	.054395	.058574	.062793	.067050	.071343	.080027	.088828
	.10	.038627	.042515	.046458	.050452	.054496	.058587	.062724	.066903	.071122	.075379	.079672	.088356	.097157
	0.00	.046956	.050844	.054787	.058781	.062825	.066917	.071053	.075232	.079451	.083708	.088001	.096685	.105466
	-.10	.055285	.059173	.063116	.067110	.071154	.075246	.079382	.083561	.087780	.092037	.096330	.105014	.113815
	-.20	.063614	.067502	.071445	.075439	.079483	.083575	.087711	.091890	.096109	.100366	.104659	.113343	.122144
	-.30	.071943	.075831	.079774	.083768	.087812	.091904	.096040	.100219	.104438	.108695	.112988	.121672	.130473
	-.40	.080272	.084160	.088103	.092098	.096142	.100233	.104369	.108548	.112767	.117024	.121317	.130001	.138802
25	.40	.014673	.018382	.022541	.026748	.030999	.035291	.039620	.043983	.048378	.052801	.057250	.066215	.075254
	.30	.022602	.026711	.030870	.035077	.039328	.043620	.047949	.052312	.056707	.061130	.065579	.074544	.083583
	.20	.030931	.035040	.039199	.043406	.047657	.051949	.056278	.060641	.065036	.069459	.073908	.082873	.091912
	.10	.039260	.043369	.047528	.051735	.055986	.060278	.064607	.068970	.073365	.077788	.082237	.091203	.100241
	0.00	.047589	.051698	.055858	.060064	.064315	.068607	.072936	.077299	.081694	.086118	.090567	.099532	.108570
	-.10	.055918	.060027	.064187	.068394	.072644	.076936	.081265	.085628	.090023	.094447	.098896	.107861	.116899
	-.20	.064247	.068356	.072516	.076723	.080974	.085265	.089594	.093958	.098352	.102776	.107225	.116190	.125228
	-.30	.072576	.076685	.080845	.085052	.089303	.093594	.097923	.102287	.106681	.111105	.115554	.124519	.133557
	-.40	.080905	.085014	.089174	.093381	.097632	.101923	.106252	.110616	.115011	.119434	.123883	.132848	.141887
30	.40	.014674	.018917	.023206	.027535	.031901	.036300	.040728	.045183	.049659	.054155	.058668	.067734	.076840
	.30	.023003	.027246	.031535	.035864	.040230	.044629	.049058	.053512	.057988	.062484	.066997	.076064	.085169
	.20	.031332	.035575	.039864	.044193	.048559	.052958	.057387	.061841	.066317	.070814	.075327	.084393	.093498
	.10	.039661	.043905	.048193	.052522	.056888	.061287	.065716	.070170	.074646	.079143	.083656	.092722	.101827
	0.00	.047990	.052234	.056522	.060851	.065217	.069616	.074045	.078499	.082976	.087472	.091985	.101051	.110155
	-.10	.056319	.060563	.064851	.069180	.073546	.077946	.082374	.086828	.091305	.095801	.100314	.109380	.118485
	-.20	.064649	.068892	.073180	.077509	.081876	.086275	.090703	.095157	.099634	.104130	.108643	.117709	.126814
	-.30	.072978	.077221	.081509	.085839	.090205	.094604	.099032	.103486	.107963	.112459	.116972	.126038	.135143
	-.40	.081307	.085550	.089838	.094168	.098534	.102933	.107361	.111815	.116292	.120788	.125301	.134367	.143473

10.0 YEAR HOLDING PERIOD
.060 EQUITY YIELD RATE
.600 LOAN RATIO

INTEREST RATE

TERM YEARS	APPR DEP	12.0	11.0	10.0	9.5	9.0	8.5	8.0	7.5	7.0	6.5	6.0	5.5	5.0
10	.40	.051431	.047312	.043281	.041298	.039339	.037402	.035488	.033597	.031730	.029887	.028067	.026271	.024499
	.30	.059018	.054899	.050867	.048885	.046925	.044989	.043075	.041184	.039317	.037473	.035654	.033858	.032080
	.20	.066605	.062486	.058454	.056472	.054512	.052575	.050662	.048771	.046904	.045060	.043240	.041445	.039673
	.10	.074192	.070072	.066041	.064059	.062099	.060162	.058248	.056358	.054491	.052647	.050827	.049031	.047260
	0.00	.081778	.077659	.073628	.071645	.069686	.067749	.065835	.063944	.062077	.060234	.058414	.056618	.054846
	-.10	.089365	.085246	.081215	.079232	.077273	.075336	.073422	.071531	.069664	.067821	.066001	.064205	.062433
	-.20	.096952	.092833	.088801	.086819	.084859	.082923	.081009	.079118	.077251	.075407	.073588	.071792	.070020
	-.30	.104533	.100420	.096388	.094406	.092446	.090509	.088595	.086707	.084838	.082994	.081174	.079379	.077607
	-.40	.112125	.108006	.103975	.101993	.100033	.098096	.096182	.094292	.092425	.090581	.088761	.086965	.085194
15	.40	.059104	.053763	.048527	.045949	.043401	.040882	.038394	.035936	.033511	.031118	.028759	.026434	.024145
	.30	.066691	.061350	.056113	.053536	.050988	.048469	.045980	.043523	.041098	.038705	.036346	.034021	.031731
	.20	.074278	.068937	.063700	.061123	.058575	.056056	.053567	.051110	.048684	.046292	.043933	.041608	.039318
	.10	.081865	.076524	.071287	.068710	.066161	.063642	.061154	.058697	.056271	.053879	.051519	.049195	.046905
	0.00	.089451	.084110	.078874	.076257	.073748	.071229	.068741	.066283	.063858	.061465	.059106	.056781	.054492
	-.10	.097038	.091697	.086460	.083883	.081335	.078816	.076327	.073870	.071445	.069052	.066693	.064368	.062079
	-.20	.104625	.099284	.094047	.091470	.088922	.086403	.083914	.081457	.079032	.076639	.074280	.071955	.069665
	-.30	.112212	.106871	.101634	.099057	.096509	.093990	.091501	.089044	.086618	.084226	.081867	.079542	.077252
	-.40	.119799	.114458	.109221	.106644	.104095	.101576	.099088	.096631	.094205	.091813	.089453	.087129	.084839
20	.40	.062346	.056659	.050855	.048037	.045244	.042477	.039738	.037028	.034349	.031703	.029090	.026513	.023973
	.30	.069933	.064146	.058442	.055624	.052831	.050064	.047325	.044615	.041936	.039290	.036677	.034100	.031559
	.20	.077519	.071733	.066028	.063211	.060417	.057651	.054912	.052202	.049523	.046877	.044264	.041687	.039146
	.10	.085106	.079320	.073615	.070797	.068004	.065237	.062498	.059789	.057110	.054463	.051851	.049273	.046733
	0.00	.092693	.086906	.081202	.078384	.075591	.072824	.070085	.067376	.064697	.062050	.059437	.056860	.054320
	-.10	.100280	.094493	.088789	.085971	.083178	.080411	.077672	.074962	.072283	.069637	.067024	.064447	.061907
	-.20	.107867	.102080	.096376	.093558	.090765	.087998	.085259	.082549	.079870	.077224	.074611	.072034	.069493
	-.30	.115453	.109667	.103962	.101145	.098351	.095585	.092846	.090136	.087457	.084811	.082198	.079621	.077080
	-.40	.123040	.117254	.111549	.108731	.105938	.103171	.100432	.097723	.095044	.092397	.089785	.087207	.084667
25	.40	.063912	.057954	.052051	.049125	.046218	.043331	.040467	.037627	.034815	.032031	.029278	.026558	.023874
	.30	.071498	.065541	.059638	.056712	.053805	.050918	.048054	.045214	.042401	.039618	.036865	.034145	.031460
	.20	.079085	.073127	.067225	.064299	.061391	.058505	.055640	.052801	.049988	.047204	.044451	.041732	.039047
	.10	.086672	.080714	.074812	.071886	.068978	.066091	.063227	.060388	.057575	.054791	.052038	.049318	.046634
	0.00	.094259	.088301	.082399	.079472	.076565	.073678	.070814	.067975	.065162	.062378	.059625	.056905	.054221
	-.10	.101846	.095888	.089985	.087059	.084152	.081265	.078401	.075561	.072749	.069965	.067212	.064492	.061807
	-.20	.109432	.103475	.097572	.094646	.091738	.088852	.085988	.083148	.080335	.077552	.074799	.072079	.069395
	-.30	.117019	.111061	.105159	.102233	.099325	.096439	.093574	.090735	.087922	.085138	.082385	.079666	.076981
	-.40	.124606	.118648	.112746	.109820	.106912	.104025	.101161	.098322	.095509	.092725	.089972	.087252	.084568
30	.40	.064717	.058698	.052713	.049737	.046774	.043826	.040896	.037985	.035096	.032232	.029394	.026586	.023811
	.30	.072304	.066285	.060300	.057324	.054361	.051413	.048483	.045572	.042683	.039818	.036981	.034173	.031398
	.20	.079890	.073872	.067886	.064910	.061948	.059000	.056070	.053159	.050270	.047405	.044568	.041760	.038984
	.10	.087477	.081458	.075473	.072497	.069534	.066587	.063656	.060746	.057857	.054992	.052154	.049347	.046571
	0.00	.095064	.089045	.083060	.080084	.077121	.074174	.071243	.068332	.065443	.062579	.059741	.056933	.054158
	-.10	.102651	.096632	.090647	.087671	.084708	.081760	.078830	.075919	.073030	.070166	.067328	.064520	.061745
	-.20	.110238	.104219	.098234	.095258	.092295	.089347	.086417	.083506	.080617	.077752	.074915	.072107	.069332
	-.30	.117824	.111806	.105820	.102844	.099882	.096934	.094004	.091093	.088204	.085339	.082502	.079694	.076918
	-.40	.125411	.119392	.113407	.110431	.107469	.104521	.101590	.098680	.095791	.092926	.090088	.087281	.084505

10.0 YEAR HOLDING PERIOD
.060 EQUITY YIELD RATE
.667 LOAN RATIO

INTEREST RATE

TERM YEARS	APPR DEP	5.0	5.5	6.0	6.5	7.0	7.5	8.0	8.5	9.0	9.5	10.0	11.0	12.0
10	.40	.023927	.025895	.027891	.029913	.031961	.034036	.036136	.038263	.040415	.042592	.044795	.049274	.053851
	.30	.031513	.033482	.035477	.037499	.039548	.041622	.043723	.045850	.048002	.050179	.052382	.056861	.061438
	.20	.039100	.041069	.043064	.045086	.047135	.049209	.051310	.053436	.055588	.057766	.059968	.064448	.069025
	.10	.046687	.048656	.050651	.052673	.054721	.056796	.058897	.061023	.063175	.065353	.067555	.072035	.076611
	0.00	.054274	.056242	.058238	.060260	.062308	.064383	.066483	.068610	.070762	.072939	.075142	.079621	.084198
	-.10	.061861	.063829	.065825	.067847	.069895	.071970	.074070	.076197	.078349	.080526	.082729	.087208	.091785
	-.20	.069447	.071416	.073411	.075433	.077482	.079556	.081657	.083784	.085936	.088113	.090316	.094795	.099372
	-.30	.077034	.079003	.080998	.083020	.085069	.087143	.089244	.091370	.093522	.095700	.097902	.102382	.106959
	-.40	.084621	.086590	.088585	.090607	.092655	.094730	.096831	.098957	.101109	.103287	.105489	.109969	.114545
15	.40	.023532	.026077	.028660	.031281	.033939	.036634	.039365	.042130	.044929	.047760	.050624	.056442	.062377
	.30	.031119	.033663	.036247	.038868	.041526	.044221	.046952	.049717	.052515	.055347	.058210	.064029	.069964
	.20	.038706	.041250	.043834	.046455	.049113	.051808	.054538	.057303	.060102	.062934	.065797	.071616	.077550
	.10	.046293	.048837	.051420	.054041	.056700	.059395	.062125	.064890	.067689	.070521	.073384	.079203	.085137
	0.00	.053880	.056424	.059007	.061628	.064287	.066981	.069712	.072477	.075276	.078107	.080971	.086790	.092724
	-.10	.061466	.064011	.066594	.069215	.071873	.074568	.077299	.080064	.082863	.085694	.088558	.094376	.100311
	-.20	.069053	.071597	.074181	.076802	.079460	.082155	.084886	.087651	.090449	.093281	.096144	.101963	.107898
	-.30	.076640	.079184	.081767	.084389	.087047	.089742	.092472	.095237	.098036	.100868	.103731	.109550	.115484
	-.40	.084227	.086771	.089354	.091975	.094634	.097329	.100059	.102824	.105623	.108455	.111318	.117137	.123071
20	.40	.023341	.026164	.029028	.031931	.034871	.037848	.040859	.043902	.046976	.050080	.053211	.059549	.065978
	.30	.030928	.033751	.036615	.039518	.042458	.045435	.048445	.051489	.054563	.057667	.060798	.067136	.073565
	.20	.038515	.041338	.044201	.047104	.050045	.053021	.056032	.059076	.062150	.065253	.068384	.074723	.081152
	.10	.046102	.048924	.051788	.054691	.057632	.060608	.063619	.066662	.069737	.072840	.075971	.082309	.088739
	0.00	.053689	.056511	.059375	.062278	.065219	.068195	.071206	.074249	.077323	.080427	.083558	.089896	.096326
	-.10	.061275	.064098	.066962	.069865	.072805	.075782	.078793	.081836	.084910	.088014	.091145	.097483	.103912
	-.20	.068862	.071685	.074549	.077452	.080392	.083369	.086379	.089423	.092497	.095600	.098732	.105070	.111499
	-.30	.076449	.079272	.082135	.085038	.087979	.090955	.093966	.097010	.100084	.103187	.106318	.112657	.119086
	-.40	.084036	.086858	.089722	.092625	.095566	.098542	.101553	.104596	.107671	.110774	.113905	.120243	.126673
25	.40	.023231	.026214	.029236	.032295	.035388	.038514	.041669	.044851	.048058	.051289	.054540	.061098	.067718
	.30	.030818	.033801	.036823	.039882	.042975	.046100	.049255	.052438	.055645	.058876	.062127	.068685	.075205
	.20	.038405	.041388	.044410	.047469	.050562	.053687	.056842	.060024	.063232	.066462	.069714	.076272	.082892
	.10	.045992	.048974	.051996	.055055	.058149	.061274	.064429	.067611	.070819	.074049	.077301	.083859	.090479
	0.00	.053579	.056561	.059583	.062642	.065735	.068861	.072016	.075198	.078406	.081636	.084488	.091446	.098065
	-.10	.061165	.064148	.067170	.070229	.073322	.076448	.079602	.082785	.085992	.089223	.092474	.099032	.105652
	-.20	.068752	.071735	.074757	.077816	.080909	.084034	.087189	.090372	.093579	.096810	.100061	.106619	.113239
	-.30	.076339	.079322	.082344	.085403	.088496	.091621	.094776	.097958	.101166	.104396	.107648	.114206	.120826
	-.40	.083926	.086908	.089930	.092989	.096083	.099208	.102363	.105545	.108753	.111983	.115235	.121793	.128413
30	.40	.023162	.026245	.029365	.032518	.035701	.038911	.042145	.045401	.048676	.051968	.055275	.061925	.068613
	.30	.030748	.033832	.036952	.040105	.043288	.046498	.049732	.052988	.056263	.059555	.062862	.069512	.076200
	.20	.038335	.041419	.044539	.047692	.050875	.054085	.057319	.060575	.063850	.067142	.070449	.077099	.083787
	.10	.045922	.049006	.052126	.055279	.058462	.061671	.064906	.068162	.071437	.074729	.078036	.084686	.091373
	0.00	.053509	.056561	.059713	.062865	.066048	.069258	.072493	.075748	.079024	.082316	.085622	.092273	.098960
	-.10	.061096	.064179	.067299	.070452	.073635	.076845	.080079	.083335	.086610	.089902	.093209	.099859	.106547
	-.20	.068682	.071766	.074886	.078039	.081222	.084432	.087666	.090922	.094197	.097489	.100796	.107446	.114134
	-.30	.076269	.079353	.082473	.085626	.088809	.092019	.095253	.098509	.101784	.105076	.108383	.115033	.121721
	-.40	.083856	.086940	.090060	.093213	.096396	.099605	.102840	.106096	.109371	.112663	.115970	.122620	.129307

217

10.0 YEAR HOLDING PERIOD
.060 EQUITY YIELD RATE
.700 LOAN RATIO

INTEREST RATE

TERM YEARS	APPR DEP	5.0	5.5	6.0	6.5	7.0	7.5	8.0	8.5	9.0	9.5	10.0	11.0	12.0
10	.40	.023640	.025707	.027802	.029926	.032076	.034255	.036460	.038693	.040953	.043239	.045552	.050255	.055061
	.30	.031227	.033294	.035389	.037512	.039663	.041842	.044047	.046280	.048540	.050826	.053139	.057842	.062648
	.20	.038814	.040881	.042976	.045099	.047250	.049428	.051634	.053867	.056126	.058413	.060725	.065429	.070234
	.10	.046401	.048468	.050563	.052686	.054837	.057015	.059221	.061454	.063713	.066000	.068312	.073016	.077821
	0.00	.053987	.056055	.058150	.060273	.062424	.064602	.066808	.069040	.071300	.073536	.075899	.080602	.085408
	-.10	.061574	.063641	.065736	.067860	.070010	.072189	.074394	.076627	.078887	.081173	.083486	.088189	.092995
	-.20	.069161	.071228	.073323	.075446	.077597	.079776	.081981	.084214	.086474	.088760	.091073	.095776	.100582
	-.30	.076748	.078815	.080910	.083033	.085184	.087362	.089568	.091801	.094060	.096347	.098659	.103363	.108168
	-.40	.084335	.086402	.088497	.090620	.092771	.094949	.097155	.099388	.101647	.103934	.106246	.110950	.115755
15	.40	.023226	.025898	.028610	.031362	.034154	.036983	.039850	.042754	.045692	.048666	.051672	.057782	.064013
	.30	.030813	.033485	.036197	.038949	.041741	.044570	.047437	.050340	.053279	.056252	.059259	.065368	.071600
	.20	.038400	.041071	.043784	.046536	.049327	.052157	.055024	.057927	.060866	.063839	.066846	.072955	.079186
	.10	.045987	.048658	.051371	.054123	.056914	.059744	.062611	.065514	.068453	.071426	.074433	.080542	.086773
	0.00	.053574	.056245	.058957	.061710	.064501	.067331	.070197	.073101	.076040	.079013	.082019	.088129	.094360
	-.10	.061160	.063832	.066544	.069296	.072088	.074917	.077784	.080688	.083626	.086599	.089606	.095716	.101947
	-.20	.068747	.071419	.074131	.076883	.079675	.082504	.085371	.088274	.091213	.094186	.097193	.103302	.109534
	-.30	.076334	.079005	.081718	.084470	.087261	.090091	.092958	.095861	.098800	.101773	.104780	.110889	.117120
	-.40	.083921	.086592	.089304	.092057	.094848	.097678	.100545	.103448	.106387	.109360	.112366	.118476	.124707
20	.40	.023026	.025990	.028997	.032045	.035132	.038258	.041419	.044614	.047842	.051101	.054389	.061044	.067795
	.30	.030613	.033576	.036583	.039631	.042719	.045844	.049006	.052201	.055429	.058688	.061975	.068630	.075381
	.20	.038199	.041163	.044170	.047218	.050306	.053431	.056592	.059788	.063016	.066275	.069562	.076217	.082968
	.10	.045786	.048750	.051757	.054805	.057893	.061018	.064179	.067375	.070603	.073861	.077149	.083804	.090555
	0.00	.053373	.056337	.059344	.062392	.065479	.068605	.071766	.074962	.078190	.081448	.084736	.091391	.098142
	-.10	.060960	.063924	.066931	.069979	.073066	.076192	.079353	.082548	.085776	.089035	.092322	.098978	.105729
	-.20	.068547	.071510	.074517	.077565	.080653	.083778	.086940	.090135	.093363	.096622	.099909	.106564	.113315
	-.30	.076133	.079097	.082104	.085152	.088240	.091365	.094526	.097722	.100950	.104209	.107496	.114151	.120902
	-.40	.083720	.086684	.089691	.092739	.095827	.098952	.102113	.105309	.108537	.111795	.115083	.121738	.128489
25	.40	.022910	.026042	.029215	.032427	.035675	.038957	.042269	.045611	.048979	.052371	.055785	.062671	.069621
	.30	.030497	.033629	.036802	.040014	.043262	.046543	.049856	.053197	.056565	.059957	.063371	.070257	.077208
	.20	.038084	.041216	.044389	.047601	.050849	.054130	.057443	.060784	.064152	.067544	.070958	.077844	.084795
	.10	.045671	.048803	.051976	.055187	.058435	.061717	.065030	.068371	.071739	.075131	.078545	.085431	.092382
	0.00	.053257	.056389	.059562	.062774	.066022	.069304	.072616	.075958	.079326	.082718	.086132	.093018	.099969
	-.10	.060844	.063976	.067149	.070361	.073609	.076891	.080203	.083545	.086913	.090305	.093719	.100605	.107555
	-.20	.068431	.071563	.074736	.077948	.081196	.084477	.087790	.091131	.094499	.097891	.101305	.108191	.115142
	-.30	.076018	.079150	.082323	.085535	.088783	.092064	.095377	.098718	.102086	.105478	.108892	.115778	.122729
	-.40	.083605	.086737	.089910	.093121	.096369	.099651	.102964	.106305	.109673	.113065	.116479	.123365	.130316
30	.40	.022837	.026075	.029351	.032662	.036004	.039374	.042770	.046189	.049628	.053084	.056556	.063539	.070561
	.30	.030424	.033662	.036938	.040249	.043590	.046961	.050357	.053775	.057214	.060671	.064143	.071126	.078148
	.20	.038011	.041249	.044525	.047835	.051177	.054548	.057943	.061362	.064801	.068258	.071730	.078712	.085734
	.10	.045597	.048835	.052111	.055422	.058764	.062134	.065530	.068949	.072388	.075845	.079317	.086299	.093321
	0.00	.053184	.056422	.059698	.063009	.066351	.069721	.073117	.076536	.079975	.083431	.086903	.093886	.100908
	-.10	.060771	.064009	.067285	.070595	.073938	.077308	.080704	.084123	.087561	.091018	.094490	.101473	.108495
	-.20	.068358	.071596	.074872	.078182	.081524	.084895	.088291	.091709	.095148	.098605	.102077	.109060	.116082
	-.30	.075945	.079183	.082459	.085769	.089111	.092482	.095878	.099296	.102735	.106192	.109664	.116646	.123668
	-.40	.083531	.086769	.090045	.093356	.096698	.100068	.103464	.106883	.110322	.113778	.117251	.124233	.131255

10.0 YEAR HOLDING PERIOD
.060 EQUITY YIELD RATE
.750 LOAN RATIO

INTEREST RATE

TERM YEARS	APPR DEP	5.0	5.5	6.0	6.5	7.0	7.5	8.0	8.5	9.0	9.5	10.0	11.0	12.0
10	.40	.023211	.025425	.027670	.029945	.032249	.034583	.036947	.039339	.041760	.044210	.046688	.051727	.055876
	.30	.030798	.033012	.035257	.037532	.039836	.042170	.044533	.046926	.049347	.051796	.054274	.059314	.064462
	.20	.038384	.040599	.042844	.045119	.047423	.049757	.052120	.054513	.056934	.059383	.061861	.066900	.072049
	.10	.045971	.048186	.050431	.052705	.055010	.057344	.059707	.062100	.064520	.066970	.069448	.074487	.079636
	0.00	.053558	.055773	.058017	.060292	.062597	.064931	.067294	.069686	.072107	.074557	.077035	.082074	.087223
	-.10	.061145	.063359	.065604	.067879	.070183	.072517	.074881	.077273	.079694	.082144	.084621	.089661	.094810
	-.20	.068732	.070946	.073191	.075466	.077770	.080104	.082467	.084860	.087281	.089730	.092208	.097248	.102396
	-.30	.076318	.078533	.080778	.083053	.085357	.087691	.090054	.092447	.094868	.097317	.099795	.104834	.109983
	-.40	.083905	.086120	.088365	.090639	.092944	.095278	.097641	.100033	.102454	.104904	.107382	.112421	.117570
15	.40	.022767	.025630	.028536	.031484	.034475	.037507	.040579	.043689	.046838	.050024	.053245	.059791	.066467
	.30	.030354	.033216	.036122	.039071	.042062	.045094	.048165	.051276	.054425	.057610	.060832	.067378	.074054
	.20	.037941	.040803	.043709	.046658	.049649	.052681	.055752	.058863	.062012	.065197	.068419	.074964	.081641
	.10	.045528	.048390	.051296	.054245	.057236	.060267	.063339	.066450	.069598	.072784	.076005	.082551	.089227
	0.00	.053115	.055977	.058883	.061832	.064822	.067854	.070926	.074037	.077185	.080371	.083592	.090138	.096814
	-.10	.060701	.063563	.066470	.069418	.072409	.075441	.078513	.081623	.084772	.087958	.091179	.097725	.104401
	-.20	.068288	.071150	.074056	.077005	.079996	.083028	.086099	.089210	.092359	.095544	.098766	.105312	.111988
	-.30	.075875	.078737	.081643	.084592	.087583	.090615	.093686	.096797	.099946	.103131	.106353	.112898	.119575
	-.40	.083462	.086324	.089230	.092179	.095170	.098201	.101273	.104384	.107532	.110718	.113939	.120485	.127161
20	.40	.022553	.025728	.028950	.032215	.035524	.038872	.042259	.045683	.049142	.052633	.056155	.063286	.070519
	.30	.030139	.033315	.036536	.039802	.043110	.046459	.049846	.053270	.056728	.060220	.063742	.070873	.078106
	.20	.037726	.040902	.044123	.047389	.050697	.054046	.057433	.060857	.064315	.067807	.071329	.078459	.085693
	.10	.045313	.048488	.051710	.054976	.058284	.061633	.065020	.068443	.071902	.075393	.078916	.086046	.093279
	0.00	.052900	.056075	.059297	.062563	.065871	.069219	.072607	.076030	.079489	.082980	.086503	.093633	.100866
	-.10	.060486	.063662	.066884	.070150	.073458	.076806	.080193	.083617	.087076	.090567	.094089	.101220	.108453
	-.20	.068073	.071249	.074470	.077736	.081044	.084393	.087780	.091204	.094662	.098154	.101676	.108807	.116040
	-.30	.075660	.078836	.082057	.085323	.088631	.091980	.095367	.098791	.102249	.105741	.109263	.116393	.123627
	-.40	.083247	.086422	.089644	.092910	.096218	.099567	.102954	.106377	.109836	.113327	.116850	.123980	.131213
25	.40	.022429	.025819	.029184	.032625	.036105	.039621	.043170	.046751	.050359	.053993	.057651	.065029	.072476
	.30	.030015	.033371	.036771	.040212	.043692	.047208	.050757	.054337	.057946	.061580	.065238	.072616	.080063
	.20	.037602	.040958	.044358	.047799	.051279	.054795	.058344	.061924	.065533	.069167	.072825	.080203	.087650
	.10	.045189	.048545	.051944	.055386	.058866	.062381	.065931	.069511	.073119	.076754	.080412	.087789	.095237
	0.00	.052775	.056131	.059531	.062972	.066452	.069968	.073518	.077098	.080706	.084340	.087998	.095376	.102823
	-.10	.060363	.063718	.067118	.070559	.074039	.077555	.081104	.084685	.088293	.091927	.095585	.102963	.110410
	-.20	.067949	.071305	.074705	.078146	.081626	.085142	.088691	.092271	.095880	.099514	.103172	.110550	.117997
	-.30	.075536	.078892	.082292	.085733	.089213	.092729	.096278	.099858	.103467	.107101	.110759	.118137	.125584
	-.40	.083123	.086479	.089878	.093320	.096800	.100315	.103865	.107445	.111053	.114688	.118346	.125723	.133171
30	.40	.022350	.025819	.029329	.032876	.036457	.040068	.043707	.047370	.051054	.054758	.058478	.065959	.073433
	.30	.029937	.033406	.036916	.040463	.044044	.047655	.051294	.054957	.058641	.062345	.066065	.073546	.081020
	.20	.037524	.040993	.044503	.048050	.051631	.055242	.058880	.062543	.066228	.069931	.073651	.081133	.088656
	.10	.045111	.048580	.052090	.055637	.059218	.062829	.066467	.070130	.073815	.077518	.081238	.088720	.096243
	0.00	.052697	.056167	.059677	.063224	.066804	.070416	.074054	.077717	.081401	.085105	.088825	.096306	.103830
	-.10	.060284	.063753	.067263	.070810	.074391	.078002	.081641	.085304	.088988	.092692	.096412	.103893	.111417
	-.20	.067871	.071340	.074850	.078397	.081978	.085589	.089228	.092891	.096575	.100279	.103999	.111480	.119004
	-.30	.075458	.078927	.082437	.085984	.089565	.093176	.096815	.100477	.104162	.107865	.111585	.119067	.126590
	-.40	.083045	.086514	.090024	.093571	.097152	.100763	.104401	.108064	.111749	.115452	.119172	.126654	.134177

10.0 YEAR HOLDING PERIOD
.060 EQUITY YIELD RATE
.800 LOAN RATIO

INTEREST RATE

TERM YEARS	APPR DEP	5.0	5.5	6.0	6.5	7.0	7.5	8.0	8.5	9.0	9.5	10.0	11.0	12.0
10	.40	.022781	.025144	.027538	.029965	.032423	.034912	.037433	.039985	.042567	.045180	.047823	.053138	.058691
	.30	.030368	.032730	.035125	.037551	.040009	.042499	.045020	.047572	.050154	.052767	.055410	.060785	.066277
	.20	.037955	.040317	.042712	.045138	.047596	.050086	.052607	.055158	.057741	.060354	.062997	.068372	.073864
	.10	.045542	.047904	.050299	.052725	.055183	.057673	.060193	.062745	.065328	.067940	.070584	.075959	.081451
	0.00	.053129	.055491	.057885	.060312	.062770	.065259	.067780	.070332	.072914	.075527	.078170	.083546	.089038
	-.10	.060715	.063078	.065472	.067898	.070357	.072846	.075367	.077919	.080501	.083114	.085757	.091132	.096625
	-.20	.068302	.070665	.073059	.075485	.077943	.080433	.082954	.085505	.088088	.090701	.093344	.098734	.104211
	-.30	.075889	.078251	.080646	.083072	.085530	.088020	.090541	.093092	.095675	.098288	.100931	.106306	.111798
	-.40	.083476	.085838	.088232	.090659	.093117	.095607	.098127	.100679	.103262	.105874	.108518	.113893	.119385
15	.40	.022308	.025361	.028461	.031607	.034797	.038031	.041307	.044625	.047984	.051382	.054818	.061800	.068921
	.30	.029895	.032948	.036048	.039193	.042384	.045617	.048894	.052212	.055570	.058968	.062405	.069387	.076508
	.20	.037482	.040535	.043635	.046780	.049970	.053204	.056481	.059799	.063157	.066555	.069991	.076984	.084095
	.10	.045069	.048122	.051222	.054367	.057557	.060791	.064067	.067386	.070744	.074142	.077578	.084560	.091682
	0.00	.052656	.055709	.058808	.061954	.065144	.068378	.071654	.074972	.078331	.081729	.085165	.092147	.099269
	-.10	.060243	.063296	.066395	.069541	.072731	.075965	.079241	.082559	.085918	.089316	.092752	.099734	.106855
	-.20	.067829	.070882	.073982	.077127	.080318	.083551	.086828	.090146	.093504	.096902	.100339	.107321	.114442
	-.30	.075416	.078469	.081569	.084714	.087904	.091138	.094415	.097733	.101091	.104489	.107925	.114908	.122029
	-.40	.083003	.086056	.089156	.092301	.095491	.098725	.102001	.105320	.108678	.112076	.115512	.122494	.129616
20	.40	.022079	.025466	.028903	.032286	.035915	.039487	.043100	.046752	.050441	.054165	.057922	.065528	.073243
	.30	.029666	.033053	.036490	.039973	.043502	.047074	.050687	.054339	.058028	.061752	.065509	.073115	.080830
	.20	.037253	.040640	.044076	.047560	.051089	.054660	.058273	.061925	.065614	.069339	.073096	.080702	.088417
	.10	.044840	.048227	.051663	.055147	.058675	.062247	.065860	.069512	.073201	.076925	.080683	.088288	.096004
	0.00	.052426	.055814	.059250	.062733	.066262	.069834	.073447	.077099	.080788	.084512	.088269	.095875	.103591
	-.10	.060013	.063401	.066837	.070320	.073849	.077421	.081034	.084686	.088375	.092099	.095856	.103462	.111177
	-.20	.067600	.070987	.074424	.077907	.081436	.085008	.088621	.092273	.095962	.099686	.103443	.111049	.118764
	-.30	.075187	.078574	.082010	.085494	.089023	.092594	.096207	.099859	.103548	.107273	.111030	.118636	.126351
	-.40	.082774	.086161	.089597	.093081	.096609	.100181	.103794	.107446	.111135	.114859	.118617	.126222	.133938
25	.40	.021947	.025526	.029153	.032823	.036535	.040286	.044072	.047890	.051739	.055616	.059518	.067387	.075331
	.30	.029534	.033113	.036740	.040411	.044122	.047872	.051658	.055477	.059326	.063203	.067105	.074974	.082918
	.20	.037121	.040700	.044326	.047997	.051709	.055459	.059245	.063064	.066913	.070790	.074691	.082561	.090505
	.10	.044707	.048287	.051913	.055584	.059296	.063046	.066832	.070651	.074500	.078376	.082278	.090148	.098092
	0.00	.052294	.055874	.059500	.063171	.066882	.070633	.074419	.078237	.082087	.085963	.089865	.097735	.105678
	-.10	.059881	.063460	.067087	.070757	.074469	.078219	.082006	.085824	.089673	.093550	.097452	.105321	.113265
	-.20	.067468	.071047	.074674	.078344	.082056	.085806	.089592	.093411	.097260	.101137	.105038	.112908	.120852
	-.30	.075055	.078634	.082260	.085931	.089643	.093393	.097179	.100998	.104847	.108724	.112626	.120439	.128439
	-.40	.082641	.086221	.089847	.093518	.097230	.100980	.104766	.108585	.112434	.116310	.120212	.128082	.136026
30	.40	.021863	.025564	.029308	.033091	.036911	.040763	.044644	.048551	.052481	.056431	.060400	.068380	.076405
	.30	.029450	.033151	.036895	.040678	.044498	.048350	.052231	.056138	.060068	.064018	.067986	.075966	.083992
	.20	.037037	.040738	.044481	.048265	.052084	.055936	.059817	.063724	.067655	.071605	.075573	.083553	.091578
	.10	.044624	.048324	.052068	.055852	.059671	.063523	.067404	.071311	.075241	.079192	.083160	.091140	.099165
	0.00	.052211	.055911	.059655	.063438	.067258	.071110	.074991	.078898	.082828	.086779	.090747	.098727	.106752
	-.10	.059797	.063498	.067242	.071025	.074845	.078697	.082578	.086485	.090415	.094365	.098334	.106314	.114339
	-.20	.067384	.071085	.074829	.078612	.082432	.086283	.090165	.094072	.098002	.101952	.105920	.113900	.121925
	-.30	.074971	.078671	.082415	.086199	.090018	.093870	.097751	.101658	.105589	.109539	.113507	.121487	.129512
	-.40	.082558	.086258	.090002	.093786	.097605	.101457	.105338	.109245	.113175	.117126	.121094	.129074	.137099

10.0 YEAR HOLDING PERIOD
.060 EQUITY YIELD RATE
.900 LOAN RATIO

INTEREST RATE

TERM YEARS	APPR DEP	5.0	5.5	6.0	6.5	7.0	7.5	8.0	8.5	9.0	9.5	10.0	11.0	12.0
10	.40	.021922	.024580	.027274	.030003	.032769	.035570	.038405	.041276	.044181	.047121	.050094	.056142	.062320
	.30	.029509	.032167	.034861	.037590	.040356	.043156	.045992	.048863	.051768	.054708	.057681	.063728	.069907
	.20	.037096	.039754	.042447	.045177	.047942	.050743	.053579	.056450	.059355	.062295	.065268	.071315	.077494
	.10	.044683	.047340	.050034	.052764	.055529	.058330	.061166	.064037	.066942	.069881	.072855	.078902	.085081
	0.00	.052270	.054927	.057621	.060351	.063116	.065917	.068753	.071623	.074529	.077468	.080442	.086489	.092667
	-.10	.059856	.062514	.065208	.067937	.070703	.073504	.076339	.079210	.082115	.085055	.088028	.094094	.100254
	-.20	.067443	.070101	.072795	.075524	.078290	.081090	.083926	.086797	.089702	.092642	.095615	.101662	.107841
	-.30	.075030	.077688	.080381	.083111	.085876	.088677	.091513	.094384	.097289	.100229	.103202	.109249	.115428
	-.40	.082617	.085274	.087968	.090698	.093463	.096264	.099100	.101971	.104876	.107815	.110789	.116836	.123015
15	.40	.021390	.024825	.028312	.031851	.035440	.039078	.042764	.046497	.050275	.054098	.057963	.065818	.073830
	.30	.028977	.032412	.035899	.039438	.043027	.046665	.050351	.054083	.057862	.061685	.065550	.073405	.081417
	.20	.036564	.039999	.043486	.047024	.050613	.054251	.057937	.061670	.065449	.069271	.073137	.080992	.089004
	.10	.044151	.047585	.051073	.054611	.058200	.061838	.065524	.069257	.073035	.076858	.080724	.088579	.096590
	0.00	.051738	.055172	.058659	.062198	.065787	.069425	.073111	.076844	.080622	.084445	.088311	.096166	.104177
	-.10	.059324	.062759	.066246	.069785	.073374	.077012	.080698	.084431	.088209	.092032	.095897	.103752	.111764
	-.20	.066911	.070346	.073833	.077372	.080960	.084599	.088285	.092017	.095796	.099618	.103484	.111339	.119351
	-.30	.074498	.077933	.081420	.084958	.088547	.092185	.095871	.099604	.103383	.107205	.111071	.118926	.126938
	-.40	.082085	.085519	.089007	.092545	.096134	.099772	.103458	.107191	.110969	.114792	.118658	.126513	.134524
20	.40	.021132	.024943	.028809	.032728	.036698	.040716	.044781	.048889	.053039	.057229	.061456	.070012	.078692
	.30	.028719	.032530	.036396	.040315	.044285	.048303	.052367	.056476	.060626	.064816	.069043	.077599	.086279
	.20	.036306	.040117	.043983	.047902	.051871	.055890	.059954	.064063	.068213	.072403	.076629	.085186	.093866
	.10	.043893	.047703	.051569	.055488	.059458	.063476	.067541	.071650	.075800	.079989	.084216	.092773	.101453
	0.00	.051480	.055290	.059156	.063075	.067045	.071063	.075128	.079236	.083387	.087576	.091803	.100360	.109039
	-.10	.059066	.062877	.066743	.070662	.074632	.078650	.082715	.086823	.090973	.095163	.099390	.107946	.116626
	-.20	.066653	.070464	.074330	.078249	.082219	.086237	.090301	.094410	.098560	.102750	.106977	.115533	.124213
	-.30	.074240	.078051	.081917	.085836	.089805	.093824	.097888	.101997	.106147	.110337	.114563	.123120	.131800
	-.40	.081827	.085637	.089503	.093422	.097392	.101410	.105475	.109584	.113734	.117923	.122150	.130707	.139387
25	.40	.020984	.025011	.029090	.033220	.037396	.041615	.045874	.050170	.054500	.058861	.063251	.072104	.081041
	.30	.028571	.032597	.036677	.040806	.044982	.049202	.053461	.057757	.062087	.066448	.070838	.079691	.088628
	.20	.036157	.040184	.044264	.048393	.052569	.056788	.061048	.065344	.069674	.074035	.078424	.087278	.096215
	.10	.043744	.047771	.051851	.055980	.060156	.064375	.068634	.072930	.077261	.081622	.086011	.094865	.103801
	0.00	.051331	.055358	.059437	.063567	.067743	.071962	.076221	.080517	.084847	.089209	.093598	.102451	.111388
	-.10	.058918	.062944	.067024	.071154	.075330	.079549	.083808	.088104	.092434	.096795	.101185	.110038	.118975
	-.20	.066505	.070531	.074611	.078740	.082916	.087136	.091395	.095691	.100021	.104382	.108772	.117625	.126562
	-.30	.074091	.078118	.082198	.086327	.090503	.094722	.098982	.103278	.107608	.111969	.116358	.125212	.134149
	-.40	.081678	.085705	.089785	.093914	.098090	.102309	.106568	.110864	.115195	.119556	.123945	.132799	.141735
30	.40	.020890	.025053	.029265	.033521	.037818	.042151	.046518	.050913	.055335	.059779	.064243	.073221	.082249
	.30	.028476	.032640	.036851	.041108	.045405	.049738	.054104	.058500	.062921	.067366	.071830	.080807	.089836
	.20	.036063	.040226	.044438	.048695	.052992	.057325	.061691	.066087	.070508	.074952	.079417	.088394	.097422
	.10	.043650	.047813	.052025	.056281	.060578	.064912	.069278	.073674	.078095	.082539	.087003	.095981	.105009
	0.00	.051237	.055400	.059612	.063868	.068165	.072499	.076865	.081260	.085682	.090126	.094590	.103568	.112596
	-.10	.058824	.062987	.067199	.071455	.075752	.080085	.084452	.088847	.093269	.097713	.102177	.111155	.120183
	-.20	.066410	.070574	.074785	.079042	.083339	.087672	.092038	.096434	.100855	.105300	.109764	.118741	.127769
	-.30	.073997	.078160	.082372	.086629	.090926	.095259	.099625	.104021	.108442	.112886	.117350	.126328	.135356
	-.40	.081584	.085747	.089959	.094215	.098512	.102846	.107212	.111608	.116029	.120473	.124937	.133915	.142943

221

10.0 YEAR HOLDING PERIOD
.080 EQUITY YIELD RATE
.600 LOAN RATIO

INTEREST RATE

TERM YEARS	APPR DEP	5.0	5.5	6.0	6.5	7.0	7.5	8.0	8.5	9.0	9.5	10.0	11.0	12.0
10	.40	.039338	.041109	.042905	.044725	.046569	.048436	.050326	.052240	.054177	.056137	.058119	.062151	.066270
	.30	.046241	.048012	.049808	.051628	.053472	.055339	.057229	.059143	.061080	.063040	.065022	.069053	.073173
	.20	.053144	.054915	.056711	.058531	.060375	.062242	.064132	.066046	.067983	.069943	.071925	.075956	.080075
	.10	.060047	.061818	.063614	.065434	.067277	.069145	.071035	.072946	.074886	.076846	.078828	.082859	.086978
	0.00	.066949	.068721	.070517	.072337	.074180	.076048	.077938	.079852	.081789	.083749	.085731	.089762	.093881
	-.10	.073852	.075624	.077420	.079240	.081083	.082951	.084841	.086755	.088692	.090651	.092634	.096665	.100784
	-.20	.080755	.082527	.084323	.086143	.087986	.089853	.091744	.093658	.095595	.097554	.099537	.103568	.107687
	-.30	.087658	.089430	.091226	.093046	.094889	.096756	.098647	.100561	.102498	.104457	.106440	.110471	.114590
	-.40	.094561	.096333	.098129	.099949	.101792	.103659	.105550	.107464	.109401	.111360	.113343	.117374	.121493
15	.40	.037264	.039510	.041807	.044130	.046487	.048876	.051298	.053751	.056235	.058748	.061290	.066457	.071729
	.30	.044167	.046421	.048710	.051033	.053390	.055779	.058201	.060654	.063138	.065651	.068193	.073360	.078632
	.20	.051070	.053324	.055612	.057936	.060293	.062682	.065104	.067557	.070041	.072554	.075096	.080263	.085535
	.10	.057972	.060226	.062515	.064839	.067196	.069585	.072007	.074460	.076944	.079457	.081999	.087166	.092438
	0.00	.064875	.067129	.069418	.071742	.074099	.076488	.078910	.081363	.083846	.086360	.088902	.094069	.099341
	-.10	.071778	.074032	.076321	.078645	.081001	.083391	.085813	.088266	.090749	.093263	.095805	.100972	.106244
	-.20	.078681	.080935	.083224	.085548	.087905	.090294	.092716	.095169	.097652	.100165	.102708	.107875	.113147
	-.30	.085584	.087838	.090127	.092451	.094807	.097197	.099619	.102072	.104555	.107068	.109610	.114777	.120050
	-.40	.092487	.094741	.097030	.099353	.101710	.104100	.106522	.108975	.111458	.113971	.116513	.121680	.126953
20	.40	.036258	.038751	.041281	.043847	.046448	.049082	.051748	.054444	.057168	.059920	.062697	.068323	.074035
	.30	.043161	.045654	.048184	.050750	.053351	.055985	.058651	.061347	.064071	.066823	.069600	.075226	.080938
	.20	.050064	.052557	.055087	.057653	.060254	.062888	.065503	.068250	.070974	.073726	.076503	.082129	.087841
	.10	.056967	.059460	.061990	.064556	.067157	.069791	.072457	.075152	.077877	.080629	.083406	.089032	.094744
	0.00	.063870	.066363	.068893	.071459	.074060	.076694	.079360	.082055	.084780	.087531	.090309	.095935	.101647
	-.10	.070773	.073265	.075796	.078362	.080963	.083597	.086263	.088958	.091683	.094434	.097211	.102843	.108550
	-.20	.077676	.080168	.082699	.085265	.087866	.090500	.093166	.095861	.098586	.101337	.104115	.109741	.115453
	-.30	.084579	.087071	.089602	.092168	.094769	.097403	.100068	.102764	.105489	.108240	.111018	.116644	.122356
	-.40	.091482	.093974	.096505	.099071	.101672	.104306	.106971	.109667	.112392	.115143	.117921	.123547	.129259
25	.40	.035679	.038313	.040983	.043689	.046427	.049195	.051992	.054814	.057661	.060531	.063420	.069254	.075149
	.30	.042582	.045216	.047886	.050592	.053330	.056098	.058895	.061717	.064564	.067434	.070323	.076157	.082052
	.20	.049485	.052119	.054789	.057398	.060233	.063001	.065798	.068620	.071467	.074337	.077226	.083060	.088955
	.10	.056388	.059022	.061692	.064398	.067136	.069904	.072700	.075523	.078370	.081239	.084129	.089963	.095858
	0.00	.063291	.065925	.068595	.071301	.074039	.076807	.079603	.082426	.085273	.088142	.091032	.096866	.102761
	-.10	.070194	.072827	.075498	.078204	.080941	.083710	.086506	.089329	.092176	.095045	.097935	.103769	.109664
	-.20	.077097	.079730	.082401	.085107	.087844	.090613	.093409	.096232	.099079	.101948	.104838	.110672	.116567
	-.30	.083999	.086633	.089304	.092009	.094747	.097516	.100312	.103135	.105982	.108851	.111741	.117575	.123470
	-.40	.090902	.093536	.096207	.098912	.101650	.104419	.107215	.110038	.112885	.115754	.118644	.124478	.130373
30	.40	.035312	.038038	.040799	.043592	.046414	.049262	.052135	.055029	.057943	.060874	.063820	.069751	.075722
	.30	.042215	.044941	.047702	.050495	.053317	.056165	.059038	.061932	.064846	.067777	.070723	.076654	.082625
	.20	.049118	.051844	.054605	.057398	.060220	.063068	.065941	.068835	.071749	.074680	.077626	.083557	.089528
	.10	.056021	.058747	.061508	.064301	.067123	.069971	.072844	.075738	.078652	.081583	.084529	.090460	.096431
	0.00	.062923	.065650	.068411	.071204	.074026	.076874	.079747	.082641	.085555	.088486	.091432	.097363	.103334
	-.10	.069826	.072553	.075314	.078106	.080929	.083777	.086650	.089544	.092458	.095389	.098335	.104266	.110237
	-.20	.076729	.079456	.082217	.085009	.087831	.090680	.093553	.096447	.099361	.102292	.105238	.111169	.117140
	-.30	.083632	.086359	.089119	.091912	.094734	.097583	.100456	.103350	.106264	.109195	.112141	.118071	.124043
	-.40	.090535	.093261	.096022	.098815	.101637	.104486	.107359	.110253	.113167	.116098	.119044	.124974	.130946

222

10.0 YEAR HOLDING PERIOD
.080 EQUITY YIELD RATE
.667 LOAN RATIO

INTEREST RATE

TERM YEARS	APPR DEP	5.0	5.5	6.0	6.5	7.0	7.5	8.0	8.5	9.0	9.5	10.0	11.0	12.0
10	.40	.037888	.039856	.041852	.043874	.045922	.047997	.050097	.052224	.054376	.056553	.058756	.063235	.067812
	.30	.044791	.046759	.048755	.050777	.052825	.054900	.057000	.059127	.061279	.063456	.065659	.070138	.074715
	.20	.051693	.053662	.055657	.057679	.059728	.061803	.063903	.066030	.068182	.070359	.072562	.077041	.081618
	.10	.058596	.060565	.062560	.064582	.066631	.068705	.070806	.072933	.075085	.077262	.079465	.083944	.088521
	0.00	.065499	.067468	.069463	.071485	.073534	.075608	.077709	.079836	.081988	.084165	.086368	.090847	.095424
	-.10	.072402	.074371	.076366	.078388	.080437	.082511	.084612	.086739	.088891	.091068	.093271	.097750	.102327
	-.20	.079305	.081274	.083269	.085291	.087340	.089414	.091515	.093641	.095794	.097971	.100174	.104653	.109230
	-.30	.086208	.088177	.090172	.092194	.094243	.096317	.098418	.100544	.102696	.104874	.107076	.111556	.116133
	-.40	.093111	.095080	.097075	.099097	.101146	.103220	.105321	.107447	.109599	.111777	.113979	.118459	.123036
15	.40	.035583	.038087	.040631	.043212	.045831	.048486	.051177	.053903	.056662	.059454	.062279	.068020	.073878
	.30	.042486	.044990	.047534	.050115	.052734	.055389	.058080	.060806	.063565	.066357	.069182	.074923	.080781
	.20	.049389	.051893	.054437	.057018	.059637	.062292	.064983	.067709	.070468	.073260	.076085	.081826	.087684
	.10	.056292	.058796	.061340	.063921	.066540	.069195	.071886	.074611	.077371	.080163	.082988	.088729	.094587
	0.00	.063195	.065699	.068243	.070824	.073443	.076098	.078789	.081514	.084274	.087066	.089891	.095632	.101490
	-.10	.070098	.072602	.075146	.077727	.080346	.083001	.085692	.088417	.091177	.093969	.096794	.102535	.108393
	-.20	.077001	.079505	.082048	.084630	.087249	.089904	.092595	.095320	.098080	.100872	.103697	.109438	.115296
	-.30	.083904	.086408	.088951	.091533	.094152	.096807	.099498	.102223	.104983	.107775	.110600	.116341	.122199
	-.40	.090807	.093311	.095854	.098436	.101055	.103710	.106401	.109126	.111886	.114678	.117502	.123244	.129102
20	.40	.034466	.037235	.040047	.042898	.045788	.048715	.051677	.054672	.057699	.060757	.063843	.070094	.076441
	.30	.041369	.044138	.046950	.049801	.052691	.055618	.058580	.061575	.064602	.067660	.070745	.076997	.083344
	.20	.048272	.051041	.053853	.056704	.059594	.062521	.065483	.068478	.071505	.074562	.077648	.083900	.090246
	.10	.055175	.057944	.060756	.063607	.066497	.069424	.072386	.075381	.078408	.081465	.084551	.090803	.097149
	0.00	.062078	.064847	.067659	.070510	.073400	.076327	.079289	.082284	.085311	.088368	.091454	.097706	.104052
	-.10	.068980	.071750	.074562	.077413	.080303	.083230	.086191	.089187	.092214	.095271	.098357	.104609	.110955
	-.20	.075883	.078653	.081464	.084316	.087206	.090133	.093094	.096090	.099117	.102174	.105260	.111512	.117858
	-.30	.082786	.085556	.088367	.091219	.094109	.097035	.099997	.102993	.106020	.109077	.112163	.118414	.124761
	-.40	.089689	.092459	.095270	.098122	.101012	.103938	.106900	.109896	.112923	.115980	.119066	.125317	.131664
25	.40	.033822	.036749	.039716	.042722	.045764	.048840	.051948	.055084	.058247	.061435	.064646	.071128	.077678
	.30	.040725	.043652	.046619	.049625	.052667	.055743	.058850	.061987	.065150	.068338	.071549	.078031	.084581
	.20	.047628	.050555	.053522	.056528	.059570	.062646	.065753	.068890	.072053	.075241	.078452	.084934	.091484
	.10	.054531	.057458	.060425	.063431	.066473	.069549	.072656	.075793	.078956	.082144	.085355	.091837	.098387
	0.00	.061434	.064360	.067328	.070334	.073376	.076452	.079559	.082696	.085859	.089047	.092258	.098740	.105290
	-.10	.068337	.071263	.074231	.077237	.080279	.083355	.086462	.089599	.092762	.095950	.099161	.105643	.112193
	-.20	.075240	.078166	.081134	.084140	.087182	.090258	.093365	.096502	.099665	.102853	.106064	.112546	.119096
	-.30	.082143	.085069	.088037	.091043	.094085	.097161	.100268	.103405	.106568	.109756	.112967	.119449	.125999
	-.40	.089046	.091972	.094940	.097946	.100988	.104064	.107171	.110308	.113471	.116659	.119870	.126352	.132902
30	.40	.033414	.036443	.039511	.042614	.045750	.048915	.052107	.055323	.058560	.061817	.065090	.071680	.078315
	.30	.040317	.043346	.046414	.049517	.052653	.055818	.059010	.062226	.065463	.068720	.071993	.078583	.085218
	.20	.047220	.050249	.053317	.056420	.059556	.062721	.065913	.069129	.072366	.075623	.078896	.085486	.092121
	.10	.054123	.057152	.060220	.063323	.066459	.069624	.072816	.076032	.079269	.082526	.085799	.092389	.099024
	0.00	.061026	.064055	.067123	.070226	.073362	.076527	.079719	.082935	.086172	.089429	.092702	.099292	.105927
	-.10	.067929	.070958	.074026	.077129	.080265	.083430	.086622	.089838	.093075	.096332	.099605	.106195	.112830
	-.20	.074832	.077861	.080929	.084032	.087168	.090333	.093525	.096741	.099978	.103235	.106508	.113098	.119733
	-.30	.081735	.084764	.087832	.090935	.094071	.097236	.100428	.103644	.106881	.110138	.113411	.120001	.126636
	-.40	.088638	.091667	.094735	.097838	.100974	.104139	.107331	.110546	.113784	.117040	.120314	.126904	.133539

10.0 YEAR HOLDING PERIOD
.080 EQUITY YIELD RATE
.700 LOAN RATIO

INTEREST RATE

TERM YEARS	APPR DEP	5.0	5.5	6.0	6.5	7.0	7.5	8.0	8.5	9.0	9.5	10.0	11.0	12.0
10	.40	.037163	.039230	.041325	.043448	.045599	.047777	.049983	.052216	.054475	.056762	.059074	.063778	.068583
	.30	.044066	.046133	.048228	.050351	.052502	.054680	.056886	.059118	.061378	.063664	.065977	.070681	.075486
	.20	.050968	.053036	.055131	.057254	.059405	.061583	.063789	.066021	.068281	.070567	.072880	.077583	.082389
	.10	.057871	.059938	.062034	.064157	.066308	.068486	.070692	.072924	.075184	.077470	.079783	.084486	.089292
	0.00	.064774	.066841	.068937	.071060	.073210	.075389	.077595	.079827	.082087	.084373	.086686	.091389	.096195
	-.10	.071677	.073744	.075840	.077963	.080113	.082292	.084497	.086730	.088990	.091276	.093589	.098292	.103098
	-.20	.078580	.080647	.082742	.084866	.087016	.089195	.091400	.093633	.095893	.098179	.100492	.105195	.110001
	-.30	.085483	.087550	.089645	.091769	.093919	.096098	.098303	.100536	.102796	.105082	.107395	.112098	.116904
	-.40	.092386	.094453	.096548	.098671	.100822	.103001	.105206	.107439	.109699	.111985	.114298	.119001	.123807
15	.40	.034743	.037373	.040043	.042753	.045503	.048291	.051110	.053978	.056876	.059808	.062773	.068802	.074952
	.30	.041646	.044275	.046946	.049656	.052406	.055194	.058019	.060881	.063779	.066711	.069676	.075705	.081855
	.20	.048549	.051178	.053849	.056559	.059309	.062097	.064922	.067784	.070682	.073614	.076579	.082607	.088758
	.10	.055452	.058081	.060752	.063462	.066212	.069000	.071825	.074687	.077585	.080517	.083482	.089510	.095661
	0.00	.062355	.064984	.067655	.070365	.073115	.075903	.078728	.081590	.084488	.087420	.090385	.096413	.102564
	-.10	.069258	.071887	.074558	.077268	.080018	.082806	.085631	.088493	.091390	.094322	.097288	.103316	.109467
	-.20	.076161	.078790	.081461	.084171	.086921	.089709	.092534	.095396	.098293	.101225	.104191	.110219	.116370
	-.30	.083063	.085693	.088364	.091074	.093824	.096612	.099437	.102299	.105196	.108128	.111094	.117122	.123273
	-.40	.089966	.092596	.095267	.097977	.100727	.103515	.106340	.109202	.112099	.115031	.117997	.124025	.130176
20	.40	.033570	.036478	.039430	.042424	.045458	.048531	.051641	.054786	.057965	.061175	.064415	.070979	.077643
	.30	.040473	.043381	.046333	.049327	.052361	.055434	.058544	.061689	.064868	.068078	.071318	.077882	.084546
	.20	.047376	.050284	.053236	.056230	.059264	.062337	.065447	.068592	.071771	.074981	.078221	.084785	.091449
	.10	.054279	.057187	.060139	.063133	.066167	.069240	.072350	.075495	.078674	.081884	.085124	.091688	.098352
	0.00	.061181	.064090	.067042	.070036	.073070	.076143	.079253	.082398	.085577	.088787	.092027	.098591	.105255
	-.10	.068084	.070993	.073945	.076939	.079973	.083046	.086156	.089301	.092479	.095690	.098930	.105494	.112158
	-.20	.074987	.077896	.080847	.083841	.086876	.089949	.093059	.096204	.099382	.102593	.105833	.112397	.119061
	-.30	.081890	.084798	.087750	.090744	.093779	.096852	.099962	.103107	.106285	.109496	.112736	.119300	.125964
	-.40	.088793	.091701	.094653	.097647	.100682	.103755	.106865	.110010	.113188	.116399	.119639	.126203	.132867
25	.40	.032894	.035967	.039083	.042239	.045433	.048663	.051925	.055219	.058540	.061888	.065259	.072065	.078943
	.30	.039797	.042870	.045986	.049142	.052336	.055566	.058828	.062122	.065443	.068791	.072162	.078968	.085846
	.20	.046700	.049773	.052889	.056045	.059239	.062469	.065731	.069025	.072346	.075694	.079065	.085871	.092749
	.10	.053603	.056676	.059791	.062948	.066142	.069372	.072634	.075928	.079249	.082597	.085968	.092774	.099652
	0.00	.060506	.063579	.066694	.069851	.073045	.076275	.079537	.082830	.086152	.089499	.092871	.099677	.106555
	-.10	.067409	.070482	.073597	.076754	.079948	.083178	.086440	.089733	.093055	.096402	.099774	.106580	.113458
	-.20	.074312	.077384	.080500	.083657	.086851	.090081	.093343	.096636	.099958	.103305	.106677	.113483	.120361
	-.30	.081215	.084287	.087403	.090560	.093754	.096983	.100246	.103539	.106861	.110208	.113580	.120386	.127263
	-.40	.088117	.091190	.094306	.097463	.100657	.103886	.107149	.110442	.113764	.117111	.120483	.127289	.134166
30	.40	.032466	.035646	.038867	.042126	.045418	.048741	.052093	.055470	.058869	.062288	.065725	.072645	.079611
	.30	.039369	.042549	.045770	.049029	.052321	.055644	.058996	.062373	.065772	.069191	.072628	.079548	.086514
	.20	.046271	.049452	.052673	.055932	.059224	.062547	.065899	.069276	.072675	.076094	.079531	.086450	.093417
	.10	.053174	.056355	.059576	.062834	.066127	.069450	.072802	.076178	.079578	.082997	.086434	.093353	.100320
	0.00	.060077	.063258	.066479	.069737	.073030	.076353	.079705	.083081	.086481	.089900	.093337	.100256	.107223
	-.10	.066980	.070161	.073382	.076640	.079933	.083256	.086608	.089984	.093384	.096803	.100240	.107159	.114126
	-.20	.073883	.077064	.080285	.083543	.086836	.090159	.093511	.096887	.100287	.103706	.107143	.114062	.121029
	-.30	.080786	.083967	.087188	.090446	.093739	.097062	.100414	.103790	.107190	.110609	.114046	.120965	.127932
	-.40	.087689	.090870	.094091	.097349	.100642	.103965	.107317	.110693	.114093	.117512	.120949	.127868	.134835

10.0 YEAR HOLDING PERIOD
.080 EQUITY YIELD RATE
.750 LOAN RATIO

INTEREST RATE

TERM YEARS	APPR DEP	5.0	5.5	6.0	6.5	7.0	7.5	8.0	8.5	9.0	9.5	10.0	11.0	12.0
10	.40	.036075	.038290	.040535	.042809	.045114	.047448	.049811	.052203	.054624	.057074	.059552	.064591	.069740
	.30	.042978	.045193	.047437	.049712	.052017	.054351	.056714	.059106	.061527	.063977	.066455	.071494	.076643
	.20	.049881	.052096	.054340	.056615	.058920	.061254	.063617	.066009	.068430	.070880	.073358	.078397	.083546
	.10	.056784	.058999	.061243	.063518	.065823	.068157	.070520	.072912	.075333	.077783	.080261	.085300	.090449
	0.00	.063687	.065902	.068146	.070421	.072726	.075059	.077423	.079815	.082236	.084686	.087164	.092203	.097352
	-.10	.070590	.072804	.075049	.077324	.079628	.081962	.084326	.086718	.089139	.091589	.094066	.099106	.104255
	-.20	.077493	.079707	.081952	.084227	.086531	.088865	.091229	.093621	.096042	.098492	.100969	.106009	.111158
	-.30	.084396	.086610	.088855	.091130	.093434	.095768	.098132	.100524	.102945	.105395	.107872	.112912	.118061
	-.40	.091299	.093513	.095758	.098033	.100337	.102671	.105035	.107427	.109848	.112297	.114775	.119815	.124964
15	.40	.033482	.036300	.039161	.042065	.045011	.047998	.051026	.054092	.057196	.060338	.063515	.069974	.076564
	.30	.040385	.043203	.046064	.048968	.051914	.054901	.057929	.060995	.064099	.067241	.070418	.076877	.083467
	.20	.047288	.050106	.052967	.055871	.058817	.061804	.064832	.067898	.071002	.074144	.077321	.083780	.090370
	.10	.054191	.057009	.059870	.062774	.065720	.068707	.071735	.074801	.077905	.081047	.084224	.090683	.097273
	0.00	.061094	.063912	.066773	.069677	.072623	.075610	.078637	.081704	.084808	.087950	.091127	.097586	.104176
	-.10	.067997	.070815	.073676	.076580	.079526	.082513	.085540	.088607	.091711	.094852	.098030	.104489	.111079
	-.20	.074900	.077718	.080579	.083483	.086429	.089416	.092443	.095510	.098614	.101755	.104933	.111392	.117982
	-.30	.081803	.084621	.087482	.090386	.093332	.096319	.099346	.102413	.105517	.108658	.111836	.118295	.124885
	-.40	.088706	.091524	.094385	.097289	.100235	.103222	.106249	.109315	.112420	.115561	.118739	.125198	.131788
20	.40	.032226	.035341	.038504	.041712	.044963	.048256	.051588	.054957	.058363	.061803	.065274	.072307	.079447
	.30	.039128	.042244	.045407	.048615	.051866	.055159	.058491	.061860	.065266	.068706	.072177	.079210	.086350
	.20	.046031	.049147	.052310	.055518	.058769	.062062	.065394	.068763	.072169	.075608	.079080	.086113	.093253
	.10	.052934	.056050	.059213	.062421	.065672	.068965	.072297	.075666	.079072	.082511	.085983	.093016	.100156
	0.00	.059837	.062953	.066116	.069324	.072575	.075867	.079200	.082569	.085975	.089414	.092886	.099919	.107059
	-.10	.066740	.069856	.073019	.076227	.079478	.082770	.086102	.089472	.092878	.096317	.099789	.106822	.113962
	-.20	.073643	.076759	.079922	.083130	.086381	.089673	.093005	.096375	.099781	.103220	.106692	.113725	.120865
	-.30	.080546	.083662	.086825	.090033	.093284	.096576	.099908	.103278	.106684	.110123	.113595	.120628	.127768
	-.40	.087449	.090565	.093728	.096936	.100187	.103479	.106811	.110181	.113587	.117026	.120498	.127531	.134671
25	.40	.031501	.034794	.038132	.041514	.044936	.048397	.051892	.055421	.058980	.062566	.066178	.073471	.080840
	.30	.038404	.041697	.045035	.048417	.051839	.055300	.058795	.062324	.065883	.069469	.073081	.080373	.087743
	.20	.045307	.048600	.051938	.055320	.058742	.062203	.065698	.069227	.072786	.076372	.079984	.087276	.094645
	.10	.052210	.055503	.058841	.062223	.065645	.069106	.072601	.076130	.079688	.083275	.086887	.094179	.101548
	0.00	.059113	.062406	.065744	.069126	.072548	.076009	.079504	.083033	.086591	.090178	.093790	.101082	.108451
	-.10	.066016	.069309	.072647	.076029	.079451	.082912	.086407	.089936	.093494	.097081	.100693	.107985	.115354
	-.20	.072919	.076212	.079550	.082932	.086354	.089815	.093310	.096839	.100397	.103984	.107596	.114888	.122257
	-.30	.079822	.083114	.086453	.089835	.093257	.096718	.100213	.103742	.107300	.110887	.114499	.121791	.129160
	-.40	.086725	.090017	.093356	.096738	.100160	.103620	.107116	.110644	.114203	.117790	.121402	.128694	.136063
30	.40	.031043	.034450	.037902	.041393	.044920	.048481	.052072	.055690	.059332	.062995	.066678	.074091	.081556
	.30	.037945	.041353	.044804	.048296	.051823	.055384	.058975	.062593	.066235	.069898	.073581	.080994	.088459
	.20	.044848	.048256	.051707	.055199	.058726	.062287	.065878	.069496	.073138	.076801	.080484	.087897	.095362
	.10	.051751	.055159	.058610	.062101	.065629	.069190	.072781	.076399	.080041	.083704	.087387	.094800	.102265
	0.00	.058654	.062062	.065513	.069004	.072532	.076093	.079684	.083302	.086944	.090607	.094290	.101703	.109167
	-.10	.065557	.068965	.072416	.075907	.079435	.082996	.086587	.090205	.093847	.097510	.101193	.108606	.116070
	-.20	.072460	.075868	.079319	.082810	.086338	.089899	.093490	.097107	.100749	.104413	.108096	.115509	.122973
	-.30	.079363	.082771	.086222	.089713	.093241	.096802	.100392	.104010	.107652	.111316	.114999	.122412	.129876
	-.40	.086266	.089674	.093125	.096616	.100144	.103705	.107295	.110913	.114555	.118219	.121902	.129315	.136779

225

10.0 YEAR HOLDING PERIOD
.080 EQUITY YIELD RATE
.800 LOAN RATIO

INTEREST RATE

TERM YEARS	APPR DEP	5.0	5.5	6.0	6.5	7.0	7.5	8.0	8.5	9.0	9.5	10.0	11.0	12.0
10	.40	.034988	.037350	.039744	.042171	.044629	.047118	.049639	.052191	.054773	.057386	.060029	.065405	.070897
	.30	.041890	.044253	.046647	.049074	.051532	.054021	.056542	.059094	.061676	.064289	.066932	.072308	.077800
	.20	.048793	.051156	.053550	.055977	.058435	.060924	.063445	.065997	.068579	.071192	.073835	.079211	.084703
	.10	.055696	.058059	.060453	.062880	.065338	.067827	.070348	.072900	.075482	.078095	.080738	.086113	.091606
	0.00	.062599	.064962	.067356	.069782	.072241	.074730	.077251	.079803	.082385	.084998	.087641	.093016	.098509
	-.10	.069502	.071865	.074259	.076685	.079143	.081633	.084154	.086706	.089288	.091901	.094544	.099919	.105411
	-.20	.076405	.078768	.081162	.083588	.086046	.088536	.091057	.093609	.096191	.098804	.101447	.106822	.112314
	-.30	.083308	.085670	.088065	.090491	.092949	.095439	.097960	.100512	.103094	.105707	.108350	.113725	.119217
	-.40	.090211	.092573	.094968	.097394	.099852	.102342	.104863	.107414	.109997	.112610	.115253	.120628	.126120
15	.40	.032222	.035227	.038279	.041377	.044520	.047706	.050935	.054205	.057517	.060868	.064257	.071146	.078176
	.30	.039125	.042130	.045182	.048280	.051423	.054609	.057838	.061108	.064420	.067771	.071160	.078049	.085079
	.20	.046028	.049033	.052085	.055183	.058325	.061512	.064741	.068011	.071323	.074674	.078063	.084952	.091982
	.10	.052931	.055936	.058989	.062086	.065228	.068415	.071644	.074966	.078226	.081577	.084966	.091855	.098885
	0.00	.059834	.062839	.065891	.068989	.072131	.075318	.078547	.081817	.085129	.088479	.091869	.098758	.105788
	-.10	.066737	.069742	.072794	.075892	.079034	.082221	.085450	.088720	.092032	.095382	.098772	.105661	.112691
	-.20	.073640	.076645	.079697	.082795	.085937	.089123	.092352	.095623	.098935	.102285	.105675	.112564	.119594
	-.30	.080543	.083548	.086600	.089698	.092840	.096026	.099255	.102526	.105837	.109138	.112578	.119467	.126497
	-.40	.087446	.090451	.093503	.096601	.099743	.102929	.106158	.109429	.112740	.116091	.119481	.126370	.133399
20	.40	.030881	.034205	.037579	.041000	.044468	.047980	.051534	.055129	.058761	.062430	.066133	.073635	.081251
	.30	.037784	.041108	.044482	.047903	.051371	.054883	.058437	.062032	.065664	.069333	.073036	.080538	.088154
	.20	.044687	.048011	.051384	.054806	.058274	.061786	.065340	.068935	.072567	.076236	.079939	.087441	.095057
	.10	.051590	.054914	.058287	.061709	.065177	.068689	.072243	.075838	.079470	.083139	.086842	.094344	.101960
	0.00	.058493	.061817	.065190	.068612	.072080	.075592	.079146	.082741	.086373	.090042	.093745	.101247	.108863
	-.10	.065396	.068720	.072093	.075515	.078983	.082495	.086049	.089643	.093276	.096945	.100648	.108150	.115766
	-.20	.072299	.075623	.078996	.082418	.085886	.089398	.092952	.096546	.100179	.103848	.107551	.115053	.122669
	-.30	.079202	.082526	.085899	.089321	.092789	.096301	.099855	.103449	.107082	.110751	.114454	.121955	.129572
	-.40	.086105	.089429	.092802	.096224	.099692	.103204	.106758	.110352	.113985	.117654	.121357	.128858	.136475
25	.40	.030109	.033621	.037182	.040789	.044440	.048131	.051859	.055623	.059419	.063245	.067098	.074876	.082736
	.30	.037012	.040524	.044085	.047692	.051343	.055034	.058762	.062526	.066322	.070148	.074001	.081779	.089639
	.20	.043915	.047427	.050988	.054595	.058245	.061937	.065665	.069429	.073225	.077051	.080904	.088682	.096542
	.10	.050818	.054330	.057891	.061498	.065149	.068839	.072568	.076332	.080128	.083954	.087807	.095585	.103445
	0.00	.057721	.061233	.064794	.068401	.072051	.075742	.079471	.083235	.087031	.090857	.094710	.102488	.110348
	-.10	.064624	.068136	.071697	.075304	.078954	.082645	.086374	.090138	.093934	.097759	.101612	.109391	.117251
	-.20	.071527	.075039	.078600	.082207	.085857	.089548	.093277	.097041	.100837	.104662	.108515	.116294	.124154
	-.30	.078430	.081942	.085502	.089110	.092760	.096451	.100180	.103944	.107740	.111565	.115418	.123197	.131057
	-.40	.085333	.088844	.092405	.096013	.099663	.103354	.107083	.110847	.114643	.118468	.122321	.130100	.137960
30	.40	.029619	.033254	.036936	.040660	.044422	.048221	.052051	.055910	.059795	.063703	.067631	.075538	.083500
	.30	.036522	.040157	.043839	.047563	.051325	.055123	.058954	.062813	.066698	.070606	.074534	.082441	.090403
	.20	.043425	.047060	.050742	.054466	.058228	.062026	.065857	.069716	.073601	.077508	.081437	.089344	.097306
	.10	.050328	.053963	.057645	.061368	.065131	.068929	.072760	.076619	.080504	.084411	.088340	.096247	.104209
	0.00	.057231	.060866	.064548	.068271	.072034	.075832	.079663	.083522	.087406	.091314	.095243	.103150	.111112
	-.10	.064134	.067769	.071450	.075174	.078937	.082735	.086565	.090425	.094309	.098217	.102146	.110053	.118015
	-.20	.071037	.074672	.078353	.082077	.085840	.089638	.093468	.097328	.101212	.105120	.109048	.116956	.124918
	-.30	.077940	.081575	.085256	.088980	.092743	.096541	.100371	.104230	.108115	.112023	.115951	.123859	.131821
	-.40	.084843	.088478	.092159	.095883	.099646	.103444	.107274	.111133	.115018	.118326	.122854	.130762	.138724

10.0 YEAR HOLDING PERIOD
.080 EQUITY YIELD RATE
.900 LOAN RATIO

INTEREST RATE

TERM YEARS	APPR DEP	5.0	5.5	6.0	6.5	7.0	7.5	8.0	8.5	9.0	9.5	10.0	11.0	12.0
10	.40	.032812	.035470	.038164	.040893	.043659	.046460	.049295	.052166	.055072	.058011	.060984	.067032	.073210
	.30	.039715	.042373	.045067	.047796	.050562	.053363	.056198	.059069	.061974	.064914	.067887	.073935	.080113
	.20	.046618	.049276	.051970	.054699	.057465	.060265	.063101	.065972	.068877	.071817	.074790	.080838	.087016
	.10	.053521	.056179	.058873	.061602	.064368	.067168	.070004	.072875	.075780	.078720	.081693	.087741	.093919
	0.00	.060424	.063082	.065776	.068505	.071271	.074071	.076907	.079778	.082683	.085623	.088596	.094643	.100822
	-.10	.067327	.069985	.072679	.075408	.078174	.080974	.083810	.086681	.089586	.092526	.095499	.101546	.107725
	-.20	.074230	.076888	.079582	.082311	.085077	.087877	.090713	.093584	.096489	.099429	.102402	.108449	.114628
	-.30	.081133	.083791	.086484	.089214	.091979	.094780	.097616	.100487	.103392	.106332	.109305	.115352	.121531
	-.40	.088036	.090694	.093387	.096117	.098882	.101683	.104519	.107390	.110295	.113235	.116208	.122255	.128434
15	.40	.029701	.033082	.036516	.040001	.043536	.047120	.050753	.054433	.058158	.061928	.065741	.073491	.081399
	.30	.036604	.039985	.043419	.046904	.050439	.054023	.057656	.061336	.065061	.068831	.072644	.080394	.088302
	.20	.043507	.046888	.050322	.053807	.057342	.060926	.064559	.068239	.071964	.075734	.079547	.087297	.095205
	.10	.050410	.053791	.057225	.060710	.064245	.067829	.071462	.075141	.078867	.082636	.086449	.094200	.102108
	0.00	.057313	.060694	.064128	.067613	.071148	.074732	.078365	.082044	.085770	.089539	.093352	.101103	.109011
	-.10	.064216	.067597	.071031	.074515	.078051	.081635	.085268	.088947	.092673	.096442	.100255	.108006	.115914
	-.20	.071119	.074500	.077933	.081418	.084954	.088538	.092171	.095850	.099576	.103345	.107158	.114909	.122817
	-.30	.078022	.081403	.084836	.088321	.091857	.095441	.099074	.102753	.106479	.110248	.114061	.121812	.129720
	-.40	.084925	.088306	.091739	.095224	.098760	.102344	.105977	.109656	.113381	.117151	.120964	.128715	.136623
20	.40	.028193	.031932	.035727	.039577	.043478	.047429	.051428	.055471	.059558	.063685	.067851	.076291	.084859
	.30	.035096	.038835	.042630	.046480	.050381	.054332	.058331	.062374	.066461	.070588	.074754	.083194	.091762
	.20	.041999	.045738	.049533	.053383	.057284	.061235	.065234	.069277	.073364	.077491	.081657	.090097	.098665
	.10	.048902	.052641	.056436	.060286	.064187	.068138	.072136	.076180	.080267	.084394	.088560	.097000	.105568
	0.00	.055805	.059544	.063339	.067189	.071090	.075041	.079039	.083083	.087170	.091297	.095463	.103902	.112471
	-.10	.062708	.066447	.070242	.074092	.077993	.081944	.085942	.089986	.094073	.098200	.102366	.110805	.119374
	-.20	.069611	.073350	.077145	.080994	.084896	.088847	.092845	.096889	.100976	.105103	.109269	.117708	.126276
	-.30	.076514	.080253	.084048	.087897	.091799	.095750	.099748	.103792	.107879	.112006	.116172	.124611	.133179
	-.40	.083417	.087156	.090951	.094800	.098702	.102653	.106651	.110695	.114782	.118909	.123075	.131514	.140082
25	.40	.027324	.031275	.035281	.039339	.043446	.047598	.051793	.056027	.060298	.064602	.068936	.077687	.086530
	.30	.034227	.038178	.042184	.046242	.050349	.054501	.058696	.062930	.067201	.071505	.075839	.084590	.093433
	.20	.041130	.045081	.049087	.053145	.057252	.061404	.065599	.069833	.074104	.078408	.082742	.091493	.100336
	.10	.048033	.051984	.055990	.060048	.064155	.068307	.072502	.076736	.081007	.085311	.089645	.098396	.107239
	0.00	.054936	.058887	.062893	.066951	.071058	.075210	.079405	.083639	.087910	.092214	.096548	.105299	.114142
	-.10	.061839	.065790	.069796	.073854	.077961	.082113	.086308	.090542	.094813	.099117	.103451	.112202	.121045
	-.20	.068742	.072693	.076699	.080757	.084864	.089016	.093211	.097445	.101716	.106020	.110354	.119105	.127948
	-.30	.075645	.079596	.083602	.087660	.091767	.095919	.100114	.104348	.108619	.112922	.117257	.126008	.134851
	-.40	.082548	.086499	.090505	.094563	.098670	.102822	.107017	.111251	.115521	.119825	.124160	.132911	.141754
30	.40	.026773	.030863	.035004	.039193	.043427	.047700	.052009	.056350	.060721	.065117	.069536	.078432	.087289
	.30	.033676	.037766	.041907	.046096	.050330	.054603	.058912	.063253	.067623	.072020	.076439	.085335	.094292
	.20	.040579	.044669	.048810	.052999	.057232	.061505	.065814	.070156	.074526	.078923	.083342	.092238	.101195
	.10	.047482	.051572	.055713	.059902	.064135	.068408	.072717	.077059	.081429	.085826	.090245	.099141	.108098
	0.00	.054385	.058475	.062616	.066805	.071038	.075311	.079620	.083962	.088332	.092729	.097148	.106044	.115001
	-.10	.061288	.065377	.069519	.073708	.077941	.082214	.086523	.090865	.095235	.099632	.104051	.112947	.121904
	-.20	.068191	.072280	.076422	.080611	.084844	.089117	.093426	.097768	.102138	.106535	.110954	.119850	.128807
	-.30	.075094	.079183	.083325	.087514	.091747	.096020	.100329	.104671	.109041	.113437	.117857	.126753	.135710
	-.40	.081997	.086086	.090228	.094447	.098650	.102923	.107232	.111574	.115944	.120340	.124760	.133656	.142613

10.0 YEAR HOLDING PERIOD
.100 EQUITY YIELD RATE
.600 LOAN RATIO

INTEREST RATE

TERM YEARS	APPR DEP	5.0	5.5	6.0	6.5	7.0	7.5	8.0	8.5	9.0	9.5	10.0	11.0	12.0
10	.40	.053622	.055394	.057189	.059009	.060853	.062720	.064610	.066524	.068461	.070421	.072403	.076435	.080554
	.30	.059896	.061668	.063464	.065284	.067127	.068994	.070885	.072799	.074736	.076695	.078678	.082709	.086828
	.20	.066171	.067943	.069738	.071558	.073402	.075269	.077160	.079073	.081010	.082970	.084952	.088984	.093103
	.10	.072445	.074217	.076013	.077833	.079676	.081543	.083434	.085348	.087285	.089244	.091227	.095258	.099377
	0.00	.078720	.080492	.082288	.084107	.085951	.087818	.089709	.091622	.093559	.095519	.097501	.101533	.105652
	-.10	.084994	.086766	.088562	.090382	.092225	.094093	.095983	.097897	.099834	.101794	.103776	.107807	.111926
	-.20	.091269	.093041	.094837	.096656	.098500	.100367	.102258	.104172	.106108	.108068	.110050	.114082	.118201
	-.30	.097544	.099315	.101111	.102931	.104774	.106642	.108532	.110446	.112383	.114343	.116325	.120356	.124475
	-.40	.103818	.105590	.107386	.109205	.111049	.112916	.114807	.116721	.118657	.120617	.122599	.126631	.130750
15	.40	.049968	.052189	.054445	.056735	.059059	.061416	.063805	.066226	.068676	.071157	.073667	.078770	.083979
	.30	.056242	.058463	.060719	.063010	.065334	.067691	.070080	.072500	.074951	.077432	.079941	.085044	.090253
	.20	.062517	.064738	.066994	.069284	.071608	.073965	.076354	.078775	.081226	.083706	.086216	.091319	.096528
	.10	.068791	.071012	.073269	.075559	.077883	.080240	.082629	.085049	.087500	.089981	.092491	.097593	.102802
	0.00	.075066	.077287	.079543	.081833	.084157	.086514	.088903	.091324	.093775	.096255	.098765	.103868	.109077
	-.10	.081340	.083562	.085818	.088108	.090432	.092789	.095178	.097598	.100049	.102530	.105040	.110143	.115351
	-.20	.087615	.089836	.092092	.094383	.096707	.099063	.101452	.103873	.106324	.108804	.111314	.116417	.121626
	-.30	.093889	.096111	.098367	.100657	.102981	.105338	.107727	.110147	.112598	.115079	.117589	.122692	.127901
	-.40	.100164	.102385	.104641	.106932	.109256	.111612	.114001	.116422	.118873	.121354	.123863	.128966	.134175
20	.40	.048196	.050645	.053132	.055656	.058215	.060807	.063433	.066089	.068774	.071488	.074228	.079782	.085426
	.30	.054471	.056920	.059406	.061930	.064489	.067082	.069707	.072363	.075049	.077762	.080502	.086057	.091700
	.20	.060745	.063194	.065681	.068205	.070764	.073356	.075982	.078638	.081323	.084037	.086777	.092331	.097975
	.10	.067020	.069469	.071956	.074479	.077038	.079631	.082256	.084912	.087598	.090311	.093051	.098606	.104249
	0.00	.073294	.075743	.078230	.080754	.083313	.085906	.088531	.091187	.093872	.096586	.099326	.104880	.110524
	-.10	.079569	.082018	.084505	.087028	.089587	.092180	.094805	.097461	.100147	.102860	.105600	.111155	.116798
	-.20	.085843	.088292	.090779	.093303	.095862	.098455	.101080	.103736	.106421	.109135	.111875	.117429	.123073
	-.30	.092118	.094567	.097054	.099577	.102136	.104729	.107354	.110010	.112696	.115409	.118150	.123704	.129347
	-.40	.098392	.100841	.103328	.105852	.108411	.111004	.113629	.116285	.118970	.121684	.124424	.129978	.135622
25	.40	.047176	.049763	.052389	.055050	.057746	.060473	.063231	.066015	.068826	.071660	.074516	.080287	.086125
	.30	.053450	.056038	.058663	.061325	.064021	.066748	.069505	.072290	.075100	.077935	.080791	.086561	.092399
	.20	.059725	.062312	.064938	.067599	.070295	.073022	.075780	.078564	.081375	.084209	.087065	.092836	.098674
	.10	.065999	.068587	.071212	.073874	.076570	.079297	.082054	.084839	.087649	.090484	.093340	.099110	.104948
	0.00	.072274	.074861	.077487	.080149	.082844	.085572	.088329	.091113	.093924	.096758	.099614	.105385	.111223
	-.10	.078548	.081136	.083761	.086423	.089119	.091846	.094603	.097388	.100198	.103033	.105889	.111660	.117497
	-.20	.084823	.087410	.090036	.092698	.095393	.098121	.100878	.103663	.106473	.109307	.112163	.117934	.123772
	-.30	.091097	.093685	.096310	.098972	.101668	.104395	.107152	.109937	.112748	.115582	.118438	.124209	.130046
	-.40	.097372	.099959	.102585	.105247	.107942	.110670	.113427	.116212	.119022	.121856	.124712	.130483	.136321
30	.40	.046529	.049210	.051928	.054679	.057462	.060274	.063112	.065973	.068855	.071757	.074675	.080556	.086484
	.30	.052803	.055484	.058202	.060954	.063737	.066549	.069386	.072247	.075130	.078031	.080950	.086831	.092759
	.20	.059078	.061759	.064477	.067228	.070011	.072823	.075661	.078522	.081404	.084306	.087224	.093105	.099033
	.10	.065352	.068033	.070751	.073503	.076286	.079098	.081935	.084796	.087679	.090580	.093499	.099380	.105308
	0.00	.071627	.074308	.077026	.079778	.082561	.085372	.088210	.091071	.093953	.096855	.099774	.105654	.111582
	-.10	.077901	.080583	.083300	.086052	.088835	.091647	.094484	.097345	.100228	.103130	.106048	.111929	.117857
	-.20	.084176	.086857	.089575	.092327	.095110	.097921	.100759	.103620	.106502	.109404	.112323	.118203	.124131
	-.30	.090451	.093132	.095849	.098601	.101384	.104196	.107033	.109895	.112777	.115679	.118597	.124478	.130406
	-.40	.096725	.099406	.102124	.104876	.107659	.110470	.113308	.116169	.119051	.121953	.124872	.130753	.136680

10.0 YEAR HOLDING PERIOD
.100 EQUITY YIELD RATE
.667 LOAN RATIO

INTEREST RATE

TERM YEARS	APPR DEP	5.0	5.5	6.0	6.5	7.0	7.5	8.0	8.5	9.0	9.5	10.0	11.0	12.0
10	.40	.051257	.053226	.055221	.057243	.059292	.061366	.063467	.065593	.067745	.069923	.072125	.076605	.081182
	.30	.057532	.059500	.061496	.063518	.065566	.067641	.069741	.071868	.074020	.076197	.078400	.082879	.087456
	.20	.063806	.065775	.067770	.069792	.071841	.073915	.076016	.078142	.080295	.082472	.084675	.089154	.093731
	.10	.070081	.072049	.074045	.076067	.078115	.080190	.082291	.084417	.086569	.088747	.090949	.095449	.100005
	0.00	.076355	.078324	.080319	.082341	.084390	.086464	.088565	.090692	.092844	.095021	.097224	.101703	.106280
	-.10	.082630	.084599	.086594	.088616	.090664	.092739	.094840	.096966	.099118	.101296	.103498	.107978	.112554
	-.20	.088904	.090873	.092868	.094890	.096939	.099013	.101114	.103241	.105393	.107570	.109773	.114252	.118829
	-.30	.095179	.097148	.099143	.101165	.103213	.105288	.107389	.109515	.111667	.113845	.116047	.120527	.125103
	-.40	.101454	.103422	.105418	.107440	.109488	.111563	.113663	.115790	.117942	.120119	.122322	.126801	.131378
15	.40	.047197	.049665	.052172	.054717	.057299	.059918	.062572	.065261	.067985	.070741	.073530	.079200	.084987
	.30	.053472	.055940	.058446	.060991	.063573	.066192	.068847	.071536	.074259	.077016	.079804	.085474	.091252
	.20	.059746	.062214	.064721	.067266	.069848	.072467	.075121	.077811	.080534	.083290	.086079	.091749	.097536
	.10	.066021	.068489	.070995	.073540	.076123	.078741	.081396	.084085	.086808	.089565	.092353	.098023	.103811
	0.00	.072295	.074763	.077270	.079815	.082397	.085016	.087670	.090360	.093083	.095839	.098628	.104298	.110085
	-.10	.078570	.081038	.083545	.086089	.088672	.091290	.093945	.096634	.099357	.102114	.104902	.110572	.116350
	-.20	.084844	.087312	.089819	.092364	.094946	.097565	.100220	.102909	.105632	.108388	.111177	.116847	.122635
	-.30	.091119	.093587	.096094	.098638	.101221	.103839	.106494	.109183	.111907	.114663	.117451	.123121	.128909
	-.40	.097393	.099861	.102368	.104913	.107495	.110114	.112768	.115458	.118181	.120937	.123726	.129396	.135184
20	.40	.045229	.047950	.050713	.053517	.056360	.059241	.062158	.065109	.068093	.071108	.074153	.080324	.086595
	.30	.051503	.054224	.056987	.059792	.062635	.065516	.068433	.071384	.074368	.077383	.080427	.086599	.092870
	.20	.057778	.060499	.063262	.066066	.068909	.071790	.074707	.077658	.080642	.083657	.086702	.092873	.099144
	.10	.064052	.066773	.069537	.072341	.075184	.078065	.080982	.083933	.086917	.089932	.092977	.099148	.105419
	0.00	.070327	.073048	.075811	.078615	.081458	.084339	.087256	.090207	.093191	.096206	.099251	.105422	.111693
	-.10	.076601	.079322	.082086	.084890	.087733	.090614	.093531	.096482	.099466	.102481	.105526	.111697	.117968
	-.20	.082876	.085597	.088360	.091164	.094008	.096888	.099805	.102757	.105741	.108756	.111800	.117972	.124242
	-.30	.089150	.091871	.094635	.097439	.100282	.103163	.106080	.109031	.112015	.115030	.118075	.124246	.130517
	-.40	.095425	.098146	.100909	.103713	.106557	.109438	.112354	.115306	.118290	.121305	.124349	.130521	.136791
25	.40	.044095	.046970	.049887	.052845	.055840	.058870	.061934	.065028	.068151	.071300	.074473	.080885	.087372
	.30	.050369	.053244	.056162	.059119	.062114	.065145	.068208	.071302	.074425	.077574	.080748	.087160	.093646
	.20	.056644	.059519	.062436	.065394	.068389	.071419	.074483	.077577	.080700	.083849	.087022	.093434	.099921
	.10	.062918	.065793	.068711	.071668	.074663	.077694	.080757	.083851	.086974	.090123	.093297	.099709	.106195
	0.00	.069193	.072068	.074985	.077943	.080938	.083968	.087032	.090126	.093249	.096398	.099571	.105983	.112470
	-.10	.075467	.078342	.081260	.084217	.087212	.090243	.093306	.096401	.099523	.102672	.105846	.112258	.118744
	-.20	.081742	.084617	.087534	.090492	.093487	.096517	.099581	.102675	.105798	.108947	.112120	.118532	.125019
	-.30	.088017	.090892	.093809	.096766	.099761	.102792	.105855	.108950	.112072	.115222	.118395	.124807	.131293
	-.40	.094291	.097166	.100083	.103041	.106036	.109066	.112130	.115224	.118347	.121496	.124670	.131081	.137568
30	.40	.043376	.046355	.049375	.052432	.055525	.058649	.061801	.064981	.068183	.071407	.074650	.081184	.087771
	.30	.049651	.052630	.055649	.058707	.061799	.064923	.068076	.071255	.074458	.077682	.080925	.087459	.094046
	.20	.055925	.058904	.061924	.064981	.068074	.071198	.074351	.077530	.080732	.083956	.087199	.093734	.100320
	.10	.062200	.065179	.068198	.071256	.074348	.077472	.080625	.083804	.087007	.090231	.093474	.100008	.106595
	0.00	.068474	.071453	.074473	.077530	.080623	.083747	.086900	.090079	.093282	.096506	.099748	.106283	.112869
	-.10	.074749	.077728	.080747	.083805	.086897	.090021	.093174	.096353	.099556	.102780	.106023	.112557	.119144
	-.20	.081023	.084002	.087022	.090080	.093172	.096296	.099449	.102628	.105831	.109055	.112297	.118832	.125418
	-.30	.087298	.090277	.093297	.096354	.099446	.102570	.105723	.108902	.112105	.115329	.118572	.125106	.131693
	-.40	.093572	.096551	.099571	.102629	.105721	.108845	.111998	.115177	.118380	.121604	.124847	.131381	.137967

229

10.0 YEAR HOLDING PERIOD
.100 EQUITY YIELD RATE
.700 LOAN RATIO

INTEREST RATE

TERM YEARS	APPR DEP	5.0	5.5	6.0	6.5	7.0	7.5	8.0	8.5	9.0	9.5	10.0	11.0	12.0
10	.40	.050075	.052142	.054237	.056360	.058511	.060690	.062895	.065128	.067388	.069674	.071987	.076690	.081496
	.30	.056350	.058417	.060512	.062635	.064786	.066964	.069170	.071403	.073662	.075949	.078261	.082965	.087770
	.20	.062624	.064691	.066786	.068909	.071060	.073239	.075444	.077677	.079937	.082223	.084536	.089239	.094045
	.10	.068899	.070966	.073061	.075184	.077335	.079513	.081719	.083952	.086211	.088498	.090810	.095514	.100319
	0.00	.075173	.077240	.079335	.081459	.083609	.085788	.087993	.090226	.092486	.094772	.097085	.101788	.106594
	-.10	.081448	.083515	.085610	.087733	.089884	.092062	.094268	.096501	.098760	.101047	.103359	.108063	.112868
	-.20	.087722	.089789	.091885	.094008	.096158	.098337	.100542	.102775	.105035	.107321	.109634	.114337	.119143
	-.30	.093997	.096064	.098159	.100282	.102433	.104611	.106817	.109050	.111309	.113596	.115908	.120612	.125417
	-.40	.100271	.102338	.104434	.106557	.108708	.110886	.113092	.115324	.117584	.119870	.122183	.126886	.131692
15	.40	.045812	.048403	.051035	.053708	.056419	.059169	.061956	.064779	.067639	.070533	.073461	.079415	.085492
	.30	.052087	.054678	.057310	.059982	.062693	.065443	.068230	.071054	.073913	.076808	.079736	.085689	.091766
	.20	.058361	.060952	.063585	.066257	.068968	.071718	.074505	.077329	.080148	.083082	.086010	.091964	.098041
	.10	.064636	.067227	.069859	.072531	.075243	.077992	.080779	.083603	.086463	.089357	.092285	.098238	.104315
	0.00	.070910	.073501	.076134	.078806	.081517	.084267	.087054	.089878	.092737	.095631	.098559	.104513	.110590
	-.10	.077185	.079776	.082408	.085080	.087792	.090541	.093328	.096152	.099012	.101906	.104834	.110787	.116864
	-.20	.083459	.086051	.088683	.091355	.094066	.096816	.099603	.102427	.105286	.108180	.111108	.117062	.123139
	-.30	.089734	.092325	.094957	.097629	.100341	.103090	.105878	.108701	.111561	.114455	.117383	.123336	.129413
	-.40	.096008	.098600	.101232	.103904	.106615	.109365	.112152	.114976	.117835	.120729	.123657	.129611	.135688
20	.40	.043745	.046602	.049504	.052448	.055433	.058458	.061521	.064620	.067753	.070919	.074115	.080595	.087180
	.30	.050020	.052877	.055778	.058722	.061708	.064733	.067796	.070894	.074027	.077193	.080390	.086870	.093454
	.20	.056294	.059151	.062053	.064997	.067982	.071007	.074070	.077169	.080302	.083468	.086665	.093144	.099729
	.10	.062569	.065426	.068327	.071272	.074257	.077282	.080345	.083443	.086576	.089742	.092939	.099419	.106003
	0.00	.068843	.071700	.074602	.077546	.080532	.083556	.086619	.089718	.092851	.096017	.099214	.105694	.112278
	-.10	.075118	.077975	.080876	.083821	.086806	.089831	.092894	.095992	.099126	.102291	.105488	.111968	.118552
	-.20	.081392	.084249	.087151	.090095	.093081	.096106	.099168	.102267	.105400	.108566	.111763	.118243	.124827
	-.30	.087667	.090524	.093425	.096370	.099355	.102380	.105443	.108542	.111675	.114840	.118037	.124517	.131101
	-.40	.093941	.096798	.099700	.102644	.105630	.108655	.111717	.114816	.117949	.121115	.124312	.130792	.137376
25	.40	.042555	.045573	.048637	.051742	.054887	.058069	.061285	.064534	.067813	.071120	.074452	.081184	.087995
	.30	.048829	.051848	.054911	.058016	.061161	.064343	.067560	.070809	.074088	.077394	.080726	.087459	.094270
	.20	.055104	.058122	.061186	.064291	.067436	.070618	.073834	.077083	.080362	.083669	.087001	.093733	.100544
	.10	.061378	.064397	.067460	.070565	.073710	.076892	.080109	.083358	.086637	.089943	.093275	.100008	.106819
	0.00	.067653	.070671	.073735	.076840	.079985	.083167	.086383	.089632	.092911	.096218	.099550	.106282	.113093
	-.10	.073927	.076946	.080009	.083115	.086259	.089441	.092658	.095907	.099186	.102492	.105824	.112557	.119368
	-.20	.080202	.083221	.086284	.089389	.092534	.095716	.098933	.102181	.105460	.108767	.112099	.118832	.125642
	-.30	.086476	.089495	.092558	.095664	.098808	.101990	.105207	.108456	.111735	.115041	.118374	.125106	.131917
	-.40	.092751	.095770	.098833	.101938	.105083	.108265	.111482	.114731	.118009	.121316	.124648	.131381	.138191
30	.40	.041800	.044928	.048099	.051309	.054556	.057836	.061147	.064485	.067847	.071233	.074638	.081499	.088414
	.30	.048075	.051202	.054373	.057583	.060830	.064111	.067421	.070759	.074122	.077507	.080912	.087773	.094689
	.20	.054349	.057477	.060648	.063858	.067105	.070385	.073696	.077034	.080397	.083782	.087187	.094048	.100963
	.10	.060624	.063751	.066922	.070133	.073379	.076660	.079970	.083308	.086671	.090056	.093461	.100322	.107238
	0.00	.066898	.070026	.073197	.076407	.079654	.082934	.086245	.089583	.092946	.096331	.099736	.106597	.113513
	-.10	.073173	.076301	.079471	.082682	.085928	.089209	.092519	.095857	.099220	.102605	.106010	.112871	.119787
	-.20	.079447	.082575	.085746	.088956	.092203	.095483	.098794	.102132	.105495	.108880	.112285	.119146	.126062
	-.30	.085722	.088850	.092020	.095231	.098478	.101758	.105068	.108406	.111769	.115154	.118559	.125420	.132336
	-.40	.091996	.095124	.098295	.101505	.104752	.108032	.111343	.114681	.118044	.121429	.124834	.131695	.138611

INTEREST RATE

TERM YEARS	APPR DEP	5.0	5.5	6.0	6.5	7.0	7.5	8.0	8.5	9.0	9.5	10.0	11.0	12.0
10	.40	.048302	.050516	.052761	.055036	.057340	.059674	.062038	.064430	.066851	.069301	.071778	.076818	.081967
	.30	.054576	.056791	.059036	.061311	.063615	.065949	.068312	.070704	.073126	.075575	.078053	.083092	.088241
	.20	.060851	.063066	.065310	.067585	.069890	.072223	.074587	.076979	.079400	.081850	.084328	.089367	.094516
	.10	.067125	.069340	.071585	.073860	.076164	.078498	.080861	.083254	.085675	.088124	.090602	.095641	.100790
	0.00	.073400	.075615	.077859	.080134	.082439	.084773	.087136	.089528	.091949	.094399	.096877	.101916	.107065
	-.10	.079674	.081889	.084134	.086409	.088713	.091047	.093410	.095803	.098224	.100673	.103151	.108191	.113339
	-.20	.085949	.088164	.090408	.092683	.094988	.097322	.099685	.102077	.104498	.106948	.109426	.114465	.119614
	-.30	.092224	.094438	.096683	.098958	.101262	.103596	.105959	.108352	.110773	.113222	.115700	.120740	.125888
	-.40	.098498	.100713	.102958	.105232	.107537	.109871	.112234	.114626	.117047	.119497	.121975	.127014	.132163
15	.40	.043734	.046511	.049331	.052194	.055099	.058045	.061031	.064056	.067120	.070221	.073358	.079737	.086248
	.30	.050009	.052785	.055605	.058468	.061373	.064319	.067306	.070331	.073395	.076496	.079633	.086011	.092523
	.20	.056283	.059060	.061880	.064743	.067648	.070594	.073580	.076606	.079669	.082770	.085907	.092286	.098797
	.10	.062558	.065334	.068154	.071017	.073922	.076868	.079855	.082880	.085944	.089045	.092182	.098561	.105072
	0.00	.068832	.071609	.074429	.077292	.080197	.083143	.086129	.089155	.092218	.095319	.098456	.104835	.111346
	-.10	.075107	.077883	.080703	.083566	.086471	.089417	.092404	.095429	.098493	.101594	.104731	.111110	.117621
	-.20	.081381	.084158	.086978	.089841	.092746	.095692	.098678	.101704	.104767	.107868	.111005	.117384	.123895
	-.30	.087656	.090432	.093252	.096115	.099020	.101967	.104953	.107978	.111042	.114143	.117280	.123659	.130170
	-.40	.093930	.096707	.099527	.102390	.105295	.108241	.111227	.114253	.117316	.120417	.123554	.129933	.136444
20	.40	.041520	.044581	.047689	.050844	.054043	.057284	.060565	.063885	.067242	.070634	.074059	.081002	.088057
	.30	.047794	.050855	.053964	.057119	.060317	.063558	.066840	.070160	.073517	.076909	.080334	.087277	.094331
	.20	.054069	.057130	.060239	.063393	.066592	.069833	.073114	.076434	.079791	.083183	.086608	.093551	.100606
	.10	.060343	.063404	.066513	.069668	.072866	.076107	.079389	.082709	.086066	.089458	.092883	.099826	.106880
	0.00	.066618	.069679	.072788	.075942	.079141	.082382	.085663	.088983	.092340	.095732	.099157	.106101	.113155
	-.10	.072892	.075953	.079062	.082217	.085415	.088656	.091938	.095258	.098615	.102007	.105432	.112375	.119429
	-.20	.079167	.082228	.085337	.088491	.091690	.094931	.098212	.101533	.104889	.108281	.111707	.118649	.125704
	-.30	.085441	.088503	.091611	.094766	.097965	.101206	.104487	.107807	.111164	.114556	.117981	.124924	.131978
	-.40	.091716	.094777	.097886	.101040	.104239	.107480	.110762	.114082	.117439	.120830	.124256	.131198	.138253
25	.40	.040244	.043478	.046760	.050088	.053457	.056866	.060313	.063794	.067307	.070850	.074420	.081633	.088930
	.30	.046519	.049753	.053035	.056362	.059732	.063141	.066587	.070068	.073581	.077124	.080694	.087908	.095205
	.20	.052793	.056027	.059310	.062637	.066006	.069415	.072862	.076343	.079856	.083399	.086969	.094182	.101479
	.10	.059068	.062302	.065584	.068911	.072281	.075690	.079136	.082617	.086130	.089673	.093243	.100457	.107754
	0.00	.065342	.068577	.071859	.075186	.078555	.081964	.085411	.088892	.092405	.095948	.099518	.106731	.114028
	-.10	.071617	.074851	.078133	.081460	.084830	.088239	.091685	.095166	.098679	.102222	.105792	.113006	.120303
	-.20	.077891	.081126	.084408	.087735	.091104	.094514	.097960	.101441	.104954	.108497	.112067	.119280	.126578
	-.30	.084166	.087400	.090682	.094009	.097379	.100788	.104234	.107715	.111229	.114771	.118341	.125555	.132852
	-.40	.090440	.093675	.096957	.100284	.103653	.107063	.110509	.113990	.117503	.121046	.124615	.131829	.139127
30	.40	.039436	.042787	.046184	.049624	.053103	.056617	.060164	.063744	.067344	.070971	.074619	.081970	.089380
	.30	.045710	.049061	.052459	.055898	.059377	.062892	.066439	.070015	.073618	.077245	.080893	.088244	.095654
	.20	.051985	.055336	.058733	.062173	.065652	.069166	.072713	.076290	.079893	.083520	.087168	.094519	.101929
	.10	.058259	.061610	.065008	.068447	.071926	.075441	.078988	.082564	.086167	.089794	.093442	.100793	.108203
	0.00	.064534	.067885	.071282	.074722	.078201	.081715	.085262	.088833	.092442	.096069	.099717	.107068	.114478
	-.10	.070808	.074160	.077557	.080996	.084475	.087990	.091537	.095113	.098716	.102343	.105991	.113342	.120752
	-.20	.077083	.080434	.083831	.087271	.090750	.094264	.097811	.101388	.104991	.108618	.112266	.119617	.127027
	-.30	.083357	.086709	.090106	.093546	.097024	.100539	.104086	.107662	.111265	.114892	.118541	.125892	.133301
	-.40	.089632	.092983	.096380	.099820	.103299	.106813	.110360	.113937	.117540	.121167	.124815	.132166	.139576

10.0 YEAR HOLDING PERIOD
.100 EQUITY YIELD RATE
.800 LOAN RATIO

INTEREST RATE

TERM YEARS	APPR DEP	5.0	5.5	6.0	6.5	7.0	7.5	8.0	8.5	9.0	9.5	10.0	11.0	12.0
10	.40	.046528	.048891	.051285	.053712	.056170	.058659	.061180	.063732	.066314	.068927	.071570	.076946	.082438
	.30	.052803	.055165	.057560	.059986	.062444	.064934	.067455	.070006	.072589	.075202	.077845	.083220	.088712
	.20	.059077	.061440	.063834	.066261	.068719	.071208	.073729	.076281	.078863	.081476	.084119	.089495	.094987
	.10	.065352	.067714	.070109	.072535	.074993	.077483	.080004	.082555	.085138	.087751	.090394	.095769	.101261
	0.00	.071627	.073989	.076383	.078810	.081268	.083757	.086278	.088830	.091412	.094025	.096668	.102044	.107536
	-.10	.077901	.080263	.082658	.085084	.087542	.090032	.092553	.095104	.097687	.100300	.102943	.108318	.113810
	-.20	.084176	.086538	.088932	.091359	.093817	.096306	.098827	.101379	.103962	.106574	.109217	.114593	.120085
	-.30	.090450	.092813	.095207	.097633	.100091	.102581	.105102	.107654	.110236	.112649	.115492	.120867	.126359
	-.40	.096725	.099087	.101482	.103908	.106366	.108856	.111376	.113928	.116511	.119123	.121767	.127142	.132634
15	.40	.041656	.044618	.047626	.050680	.053778	.056921	.060106	.063333	.066601	.069909	.073255	.080059	.087004
	.30	.047931	.050892	.053900	.056954	.060053	.063195	.066381	.069608	.072876	.076184	.079530	.086334	.093279
	.20	.054205	.057167	.060175	.063229	.066328	.069470	.072655	.075883	.079150	.082458	.085804	.092608	.099553
	.10	.060480	.063441	.066450	.069503	.072602	.075745	.078930	.082157	.085425	.088733	.092079	.098883	.105828
	0.00	.066754	.069716	.072724	.075778	.078877	.082019	.085204	.088432	.091700	.095007	.098353	.105157	.112103
	-.10	.073029	.075991	.078999	.082053	.085151	.088294	.091479	.094706	.097974	.101282	.104628	.111432	.118377
	-.20	.079304	.082265	.085273	.088327	.091426	.094568	.097754	.100981	.104249	.107556	.110902	.117706	.124652
	-.30	.085578	.088540	.091548	.094602	.097700	.100843	.104028	.107255	.110523	.113831	.117177	.123981	.130926
	-.40	.091853	.094814	.097822	.100876	.103975	.107117	.110303	.113530	.116798	.120105	.123452	.130256	.137201
20	.40	.039294	.042559	.045875	.049240	.052652	.056109	.059609	.063151	.066732	.070350	.074003	.081409	.088934
	.30	.045569	.048834	.052150	.055515	.058927	.062384	.065884	.069425	.073006	.076624	.080278	.087683	.095208
	.20	.051843	.055108	.058424	.061789	.065201	.068658	.072159	.075700	.079281	.082899	.086552	.093958	.101483
	.10	.058118	.061383	.064699	.068064	.071476	.074933	.078433	.081974	.085555	.089173	.092827	.100232	.107757
	0.00	.064392	.067657	.070973	.074338	.077750	.081207	.084708	.088249	.091830	.095448	.099101	.106507	.114032
	-.10	.070667	.073932	.077248	.080613	.084025	.087482	.090982	.094524	.098104	.101722	.105376	.112781	.120306
	-.20	.076941	.080207	.083523	.086887	.090299	.093756	.097257	.100798	.104379	.107997	.111650	.119056	.126581
	-.30	.083216	.086481	.089797	.093162	.096574	.100031	.103531	.107073	.110653	.114271	.117925	.125330	.132855
	-.40	.089491	.092756	.096072	.099437	.102848	.106306	.109806	.113347	.116928	.120546	.124199	.131605	.139130
25	.40	.037934	.041383	.044884	.048433	.052027	.055664	.059340	.063053	.066800	.070579	.074387	.082082	.089866
	.30	.044208	.047658	.051159	.054708	.058302	.061938	.065615	.069328	.073075	.076854	.080662	.088356	.096140
	.20	.050483	.053933	.057433	.060982	.064576	.068213	.071889	.075602	.079350	.083128	.086937	.094631	.102415
	.10	.056757	.060207	.063708	.067257	.070851	.074488	.078164	.081877	.085624	.089403	.093211	.100905	.108689
	0.00	.063032	.066482	.069983	.073531	.077126	.080762	.084438	.088151	.091899	.095678	.099486	.107180	.114964
	-.10	.069306	.072756	.076257	.079806	.083400	.087037	.090713	.094426	.098173	.101952	.105760	.113454	.121238
	-.20	.075581	.079031	.082532	.086080	.089675	.093311	.096987	.100700	.104448	.108227	.112035	.119729	.127513
	-.30	.081855	.085305	.088806	.092355	.095949	.099586	.103262	.106975	.110722	.114501	.118309	.126004	.133787
	-.40	.088130	.091580	.095081	.098630	.102224	.105860	.109536	.113249	.116997	.120776	.124584	.132278	.140062
30	.40	.037071	.040646	.044270	.047939	.051649	.055398	.059181	.062996	.066840	.070708	.074600	.082441	.090345
	.30	.043346	.046920	.050544	.054213	.057924	.061673	.065456	.069271	.073114	.076983	.080874	.088716	.096619
	.20	.049620	.053195	.056819	.060488	.064198	.067947	.071731	.075546	.079389	.083258	.087149	.094990	.102894
	.10	.055895	.059469	.063093	.066762	.070473	.074222	.078005	.081820	.085663	.089532	.093424	.101265	.109168
	0.00	.062169	.065744	.069368	.073037	.076747	.080496	.084280	.088094	.091938	.095807	.099698	.107539	.115443
	-.10	.068444	.072019	.075642	.079311	.083022	.086771	.090554	.094369	.098212	.102081	.105973	.113814	.121717
	-.20	.074718	.078293	.081917	.085586	.089296	.093045	.096829	.100644	.104487	.108356	.112247	.120088	.127992
	-.30	.080993	.084568	.088191	.091860	.095571	.099320	.103103	.106918	.110762	.114630	.118522	.126363	.134267
	-.40	.087267	.090842	.094466	.098135	.101845	.105594	.109378	.113193	.117037	.120905	.124796	.132637	.140541

10.0 YEAR HOLDING PERIOD
.100 EQUITY YIELD RATE
.900 LOAN RATIO

INTEREST RATE

TERM YEARS	APPR DEP	5.0	5.5	6.0	6.5	7.0	7.5	8.0	8.5	9.0	9.5	10.0	11.0	12.0
10	.40	.042982	.045639	.048333	.051063	.053828	.056629	.059465	.062336	.065241	.068180	.071154	.077201	.083380
	.30	.049256	.051914	.054608	.057337	.060103	.062903	.065739	.068610	.071515	.074455	.077428	.083476	.089654
	.20	.055531	.058188	.060882	.063612	.066377	.069178	.072014	.074885	.077790	.080729	.083703	.089750	.095929
	.10	.061805	.064463	.067157	.069886	.072652	.075453	.078288	.081159	.084064	.087004	.089977	.096025	.102203
	.00	.068080	.070738	.073431	.076161	.078926	.081727	.084563	.087434	.090339	.093279	.096252	.102299	.108478
	-.10	.074354	.077012	.079706	.082435	.085201	.088002	.090837	.093708	.096614	.099553	.102526	.108574	.114752
	-.20	.080629	.083287	.085980	.088710	.091475	.094276	.097112	.099983	.102888	.105828	.108801	.114848	.121027
	-.30	.086904	.089561	.092255	.094985	.097750	.100551	.103387	.106257	.109163	.112102	.115076	.121123	.127301
	-.40	.093178	.095836	.098529	.101259	.104024	.106825	.109661	.112532	.115437	.118377	.121350	.127397	.133576
15	.40	.037501	.040832	.044216	.047652	.051138	.054673	.058257	.061887	.065564	.069285	.073049	.080704	.088517
	.30	.043775	.047107	.050491	.053927	.057413	.060948	.064531	.068162	.071838	.075559	.079324	.086978	.094792
	.20	.050050	.053381	.056766	.060201	.063687	.067222	.070806	.074436	.078113	.081834	.085599	.093253	.101066
	.10	.056324	.059656	.063040	.066476	.069962	.073497	.077080	.080711	.084387	.088109	.091873	.099528	.107341
	.00	.062599	.065930	.069315	.072750	.076236	.079771	.083355	.086986	.090662	.094383	.098148	.105802	.113615
	-.10	.068873	.072205	.075589	.079025	.082511	.086046	.089630	.093260	.096936	.100658	.104422	.112077	.119890
	-.20	.075148	.078480	.081864	.085299	.088785	.092321	.095904	.099535	.103211	.106932	.110697	.118351	.126164
	-.30	.081422	.084754	.088138	.091574	.095060	.098595	.102179	.105809	.109486	.113207	.116972	.124626	.132439
	-.40	.087697	.091029	.094413	.097848	.101334	.104870	.108453	.112084	.115760	.119481	.123246	.130900	.138714
20	.40	.034843	.038517	.042247	.046033	.049871	.053760	.057698	.061682	.065710	.069781	.073891	.082222	.090688
	.30	.041118	.044791	.048522	.052307	.056145	.060035	.063972	.067957	.071985	.076055	.080165	.088497	.096962
	.20	.047392	.051066	.054796	.058582	.062420	.066309	.070247	.074231	.078259	.082330	.086440	.094771	.103237
	.10	.053667	.057340	.061071	.064856	.068695	.072584	.076521	.080506	.084534	.088604	.092714	.101046	.109511
	.00	.059941	.063615	.067345	.071131	.074969	.078858	.082796	.086780	.090808	.094879	.098989	.107320	.115786
	-.10	.066216	.069889	.073620	.077405	.081244	.085133	.089071	.093055	.097083	.101153	.105263	.113595	.122060
	-.20	.072490	.076164	.079894	.083680	.087518	.091407	.095345	.099329	.103358	.107428	.111538	.119869	.128335
	-.30	.078765	.082438	.086169	.089954	.093793	.097682	.101620	.105604	.109632	.113702	.117813	.126144	.134609
	-.40	.085040	.088713	.092443	.096229	.100067	.103956	.107894	.111878	.115907	.119977	.124087	.132418	.140884
25	.40	.033312	.037194	.041132	.045125	.049168	.053259	.057395	.061572	.065788	.070039	.074323	.082979	.091736
	.30	.039587	.043468	.047407	.051399	.055443	.059534	.063669	.067847	.072062	.076314	.080598	.089254	.098011
	.20	.045862	.049743	.053681	.057674	.061717	.065808	.069944	.074121	.078337	.082588	.086872	.095528	.104285
	.10	.052136	.056017	.059956	.063948	.067992	.072083	.076218	.080396	.084611	.088863	.093147	.101803	.110560
	.00	.058411	.062292	.066230	.070223	.074266	.078357	.082493	.086670	.090886	.095137	.099421	.108077	.116834
	-.10	.064685	.068566	.072505	.076497	.080541	.084632	.088768	.092945	.097160	.101412	.105696	.114352	.123109
	-.20	.070960	.074841	.078779	.082772	.086815	.090906	.095042	.099219	.103435	.107686	.111970	.120627	.129383
	-.30	.077234	.081115	.085054	.089046	.093090	.097181	.101317	.105494	.109710	.113961	.118245	.126901	.135658
	-.40	.083509	.087390	.091328	.095321	.099364	.103456	.107591	.111768	.115984	.120235	.124520	.133176	.141932
30	.40	.032342	.036364	.040440	.044568	.048743	.052960	.057216	.061508	.065832	.070184	.074562	.083383	.092275
	.30	.038617	.042638	.046715	.050843	.055017	.059235	.063491	.067783	.072107	.076459	.080837	.089658	.098550
	.20	.044891	.048913	.052990	.057117	.061292	.065509	.069766	.074057	.078381	.082733	.087111	.095932	.104824
	.10	.051166	.055187	.059264	.063392	.067566	.071784	.076040	.080332	.084656	.089008	.093386	.102207	.111099
	.00	.057440	.061462	.065539	.069666	.073841	.078058	.082315	.086606	.090930	.095282	.099660	.108482	.117373
	-.10	.063715	.067736	.071813	.075941	.080115	.084333	.088589	.092881	.097205	.101557	.105935	.114756	.123648
	-.20	.069990	.074011	.078088	.082215	.086390	.090607	.094864	.099155	.103479	.107832	.112209	.121031	.129922
	-.30	.076264	.080286	.084362	.088490	.092664	.096882	.101138	.105430	.109754	.114106	.118484	.127305	.136197
	-.40	.082539	.086560	.090637	.094764	.098939	.103156	.107413	.111705	.116028	.120381	.124759	.133580	.142471

10.0 YEAR HOLDING PERIOD
.120 EQUITY YIELD RATE
.600 LOAN RATIO

INTEREST RATE

TERM YEARS	APPR DEP	5.0	5.5	6.0	6.5	7.0	7.5	8.0	8.5	9.0	9.5	10.0	11.0	12.0
10	.40	.067383	.069155	.070951	.072770	.074614	.076481	.078372	.080286	.082222	.084182	.086164	.090196	.094315
	.30	.073081	.074853	.076649	.078469	.080312	.082180	.084070	.085984	.087921	.089880	.091863	.095994	.100013
	.20	.078780	.080552	.082347	.084167	.086011	.087878	.089769	.091682	.093619	.095579	.097561	.101593	.105712
	.10	.084478	.086250	.088046	.089866	.091709	.093576	.095467	.097381	.099318	.101277	.103260	.107291	.111410
	0.00	.090177	.091948	.093744	.095564	.097408	.099275	.101165	.103079	.105016	.106976	.108958	.112990	.117109
	-.10	.095875	.097647	.099443	.101262	.103106	.104973	.106864	.108778	.110714	.112674	.114656	.118688	.122807
	-.20	.101574	.103345	.105141	.106961	.108804	.110672	.112562	.114476	.116413	.118373	.120355	.124386	.128505
	-.30	.107272	.109044	.110840	.112659	.114503	.116370	.118261	.120174	.122111	.124071	.126053	.130085	.134204
	-.40	.112970	.114742	.116538	.118358	.120201	.122068	.123959	.125873	.127810	.129769	.131752	.135783	.139902
15	.40	.062280	.064471	.066697	.068958	.071251	.073578	.075937	.078328	.080749	.083200	.085680	.090724	.095875
	.30	.067979	.070170	.072396	.074656	.076950	.079277	.081636	.084026	.086447	.088898	.091378	.096422	.101573
	.20	.073677	.075868	.078094	.080354	.082648	.084975	.087334	.089724	.092146	.094597	.097077	.102121	.107272
	.10	.079376	.081567	.083793	.086053	.088347	.090673	.093032	.095423	.097844	.100295	.102775	.107819	.112970
	0.00	.085074	.087265	.089491	.091751	.094045	.096372	.098731	.101121	.103542	.105993	.108473	.113518	.118669
	-.10	.090772	.092963	.095189	.097450	.099744	.102070	.104429	.106820	.109241	.111692	.114172	.119216	.124367
	-.20	.096471	.098662	.100888	.103148	.105442	.107769	.110128	.112518	.114939	.117390	.119870	.124915	.130065
	-.30	.102169	.104360	.106586	.108846	.111140	.113467	.115826	.118217	.120638	.123089	.125569	.130613	.135764
	-.40	.107868	.110059	.112285	.114545	.116839	.119166	.121525	.123915	.126336	.128787	.131267	.136311	.141462
20	.40	.059806	.062215	.064662	.067147	.069668	.072223	.074811	.077430	.080080	.082759	.085465	.090953	.096534
	.30	.065505	.067914	.070361	.072846	.075366	.077921	.080509	.083129	.085779	.088457	.091163	.096651	.102232
	.20	.071203	.073612	.076059	.078544	.081064	.083619	.086207	.088827	.091477	.094156	.096862	.102350	.107931
	.10	.076902	.079310	.081758	.084242	.086763	.089318	.091906	.094526	.097175	.099854	.102560	.108048	.113629
	0.00	.082600	.085009	.087456	.089941	.092461	.095016	.097604	.100224	.102874	.105552	.108258	.113747	.119328
	-.10	.088299	.090707	.093155	.095639	.098160	.100715	.103303	.105922	.108572	.111251	.113957	.119445	.125026
	-.20	.093997	.096406	.098853	.101338	.103858	.106413	.109001	.111621	.114271	.116949	.119655	.125144	.130724
	-.30	.099695	.102104	.104551	.107036	.109557	.112112	.114700	.117319	.119969	.122648	.125354	.130842	.136423
	-.40	.105394	.107802	.110250	.112734	.115255	.117810	.120398	.123018	.125668	.128346	.131052	.136540	.142121
25	.40	.058381	.060926	.063511	.066132	.068789	.071479	.074200	.076950	.079727	.082529	.085354	.091067	.096852
	.30	.064080	.066625	.069209	.071831	.074488	.077177	.079898	.082648	.085425	.088227	.091053	.096766	.102551
	.20	.069778	.072323	.074907	.077529	.080186	.082876	.085597	.088347	.091124	.093926	.096751	.102464	.108249
	.10	.075477	.078022	.080606	.083228	.085884	.088574	.091295	.094045	.096822	.099624	.102449	.108162	.113948
	0.00	.081175	.083720	.086304	.088926	.091583	.094273	.096994	.099744	.102521	.105323	.108148	.113861	.119646
	-.10	.086874	.089418	.092003	.094624	.097281	.099971	.102692	.105442	.108219	.111021	.113846	.119559	.125344
	-.20	.092572	.095117	.097701	.100323	.102980	.105670	.108390	.111140	.113917	.116719	.119545	.125258	.131043
	-.30	.098270	.100815	.103400	.106021	.108678	.111368	.114089	.116839	.119616	.122418	.125243	.130956	.136741
	-.40	.103969	.106514	.109098	.111720	.114376	.117066	.119787	.122537	.125314	.128116	.130942	.136655	.142440
30	.40	.057478	.060118	.062796	.065510	.068257	.071035	.073840	.076671	.079525	.082400	.085293	.091128	.097016
	.30	.063177	.065816	.068494	.071209	.073956	.076733	.079539	.082370	.085224	.088098	.090992	.096827	.102714
	.20	.068875	.071515	.074193	.076907	.079654	.082432	.085237	.088068	.090922	.093797	.096690	.102525	.108413
	.10	.074573	.077213	.079891	.082605	.085353	.088130	.090936	.093767	.096620	.099495	.102388	.108223	.114111
	0.00	.080272	.082911	.085590	.088304	.091051	.093829	.096634	.099465	.102319	.105193	.108087	.113922	.119810
	-.10	.085970	.088610	.091288	.094002	.096749	.099527	.102332	.105163	.108017	.110892	.113786	.119620	.125508
	-.20	.091669	.094308	.096987	.099701	.102448	.105225	.108031	.110862	.113716	.116590	.119484	.125319	.131207
	-.30	.097367	.100007	.102685	.105399	.108146	.110924	.113729	.116560	.119414	.122289	.125182	.131017	.136905
	-.40	.103066	.105705	.108383	.111097	.113845	.116622	.119428	.122259	.125112	.127987	.130880	.136715	.142603

10.0 YEAR HOLDING PERIOD
.120 EQUITY YIELD RATE
.667 LOAN RATIO

INTEREST RATE

TERM YEARS	APPR DEP	5.0	5.5	6.0	6.5	7.0	7.5	8.0	8.5	9.0	9.5	10.0	11.0	12.0
10	.40	.064069	.066038	.068033	.070055	.072104	.074178	.076279	.078405	.080557	.082735	.084937	.089417	.093994
	.30	.069768	.071736	.073732	.075754	.077802	.079877	.081977	.084104	.086256	.088433	.090636	.095115	.099692
	.20	.075466	.077435	.079430	.081452	.083500	.085575	.087676	.089802	.091954	.094132	.096334	.100814	.105390
	.10	.081164	.083133	.085128	.087150	.089199	.091273	.093374	.095501	.097653	.099830	.102033	.106512	.111089
	0.00	.086863	.088831	.090827	.092849	.094897	.096972	.099073	.101199	.103351	.105529	.107731	.112211	.116787
	-.10	.092561	.094530	.096525	.098547	.100596	.102670	.104771	.106897	.109050	.111227	.113430	.117909	.122486
	-.20	.098260	.100228	.102224	.104246	.106294	.108369	.110469	.112596	.114748	.116925	.119128	.123607	.128184
	-.30	.103958	.105927	.107922	.109944	.111992	.114067	.116168	.118294	.120446	.122624	.124826	.129306	.133883
	-.40	.109656	.111625	.113620	.115642	.117691	.119766	.121866	.123993	.126145	.128322	.130525	.135004	.139581
15	.40	.058400	.060834	.063307	.065819	.068367	.070953	.073574	.076230	.078920	.081643	.084399	.090004	.095727
	.30	.064098	.066532	.069006	.071517	.074066	.076651	.079272	.081928	.084618	.087342	.090097	.095702	.101425
	.20	.069796	.072231	.074704	.077215	.079764	.082350	.084971	.087627	.090317	.093040	.095796	.101401	.107124
	.10	.075495	.077929	.080403	.082914	.085463	.088048	.090669	.093325	.096015	.098739	.101494	.107099	.112822
	0.00	.081193	.083628	.086101	.088612	.091161	.093746	.096368	.099024	.101714	.104437	.107193	.112797	.118521
	-.10	.086892	.089326	.091799	.094311	.096860	.099445	.102066	.104722	.107412	.110135	.112891	.118496	.124219
	-.20	.092590	.095024	.097498	.100009	.102558	.105143	.107764	.110420	.113111	.115834	.118590	.124194	.129918
	-.30	.098288	.100723	.103196	.105708	.108256	.110842	.113463	.116119	.118809	.121532	.124288	.129893	.135616
	-.40	.103987	.106421	.108895	.111406	.113955	.116540	.119161	.121817	.124507	.127231	.129986	.135591	.141314
20	.40	.055651	.058327	.061046	.063807	.066608	.069447	.072322	.075233	.078177	.081153	.084160	.090258	.096459
	.30	.061349	.064025	.066745	.069505	.072306	.075145	.078021	.080931	.083876	.086852	.089859	.095957	.102158
	.20	.067048	.069724	.072443	.075204	.078004	.080843	.083719	.086630	.089574	.092550	.095557	.101655	.107856
	.10	.072746	.075422	.078142	.080902	.083703	.086542	.089417	.092328	.095272	.098249	.101255	.107353	.113555
	0.00	.078444	.081121	.083840	.086601	.089401	.092240	.095116	.098027	.100971	.103947	.106954	.113052	.119253
	-.10	.084143	.086819	.089538	.092299	.095100	.097939	.100814	.103725	.106669	.109646	.112652	.118750	.124951
	-.20	.089841	.092518	.095237	.097998	.100798	.103637	.106513	.109423	.112368	.115344	.118351	.124449	.130650
	-.30	.095540	.098216	.100935	.103696	.106497	.109335	.112211	.115122	.118066	.121042	.124049	.130147	.136348
	-.40	.101238	.103914	.106634	.109394	.112195	.115034	.117909	.120820	.123765	.126741	.129747	.135846	.142047
25	.40	.054067	.056895	.059767	.062679	.065631	.068620	.071644	.074699	.077785	.080898	.084037	.090385	.096613
	.30	.059766	.062593	.065465	.068378	.071330	.074319	.077342	.080398	.083483	.086597	.089736	.096083	.102511
	.20	.065464	.068292	.071163	.074076	.077028	.080017	.083040	.086096	.089182	.092295	.095434	.101782	.108210
	.10	.071163	.073990	.076862	.079775	.082727	.085716	.088739	.091794	.094880	.097993	.101133	.107480	.113908
	0.00	.076861	.079689	.082560	.085473	.088425	.091414	.094437	.097493	.100578	.103692	.106831	.113179	.119607
	-.10	.082559	.085387	.088259	.091172	.094124	.097112	.100136	.103191	.106277	.109390	.112529	.118877	.125305
	-.20	.088258	.091086	.093957	.096870	.099822	.102811	.105834	.108890	.111975	.115089	.118228	.124576	.131003
	-.30	.093956	.096784	.099655	.102568	.105520	.108509	.111533	.114588	.117674	.120787	.123926	.130274	.136702
	-.40	.099655	.102482	.105354	.108267	.111219	.114208	.117231	.120286	.123372	.126485	.129625	.135972	.142400
30	.40	.053064	.055997	.058972	.061988	.065041	.068127	.071244	.074389	.077560	.080755	.083969	.090453	.096395
	.30	.058762	.061695	.064671	.067687	.070739	.073825	.076942	.080088	.083259	.086453	.089668	.096151	.102593
	.20	.064461	.067394	.070369	.073385	.076437	.079524	.082641	.085786	.088957	.092151	.095366	.101850	.108392
	.10	.070159	.073092	.076068	.079083	.082136	.085222	.088339	.091485	.094656	.097850	.101065	.107548	.114090
	0.00	.075857	.078790	.081766	.084782	.087834	.090921	.094038	.097183	.100354	.103548	.106763	.113246	.119789
	-.10	.081556	.084489	.087465	.090480	.093533	.096619	.099736	.102882	.106053	.109247	.112461	.118945	.125487
	-.20	.087254	.090187	.093163	.096179	.099231	.102317	.105435	.108580	.111751	.114945	.118160	.124643	.131185
	-.30	.092953	.095886	.098861	.101877	.104929	.108016	.111133	.114278	.117449	.120643	.123858	.130342	.136884
	-.40	.098651	.101584	.104560	.107575	.110628	.113714	.116831	.119977	.123148	.126342	.129557	.136040	.142582

10.0 YEAR HOLDING PERIOD
.120 EQUITY YIELD RATE
.700 LOAN RATIO

INTEREST RATE

TERM YEARS	APPR DEP	5.0	5.5	6.0	6.5	7.0	7.5	8.0	8.5	9.0	9.5	10.0	11.0	12.0
10	.40	.062412	.064479	.066575	.068698	.070849	.073027	.075233	.077465	.079725	.082011	.084324	.089027	.093833
	.30	.068111	.070178	.072273	.074396	.076547	.078725	.080931	.083164	.085423	.087710	.090022	.094726	.099531
	.20	.073809	.075876	.077971	.080095	.082245	.084424	.086629	.088862	.091122	.093408	.095721	.100424	.105230
	.10	.079508	.081575	.083670	.085793	.087944	.090122	.092328	.094561	.096820	.099107	.101419	.106123	.110928
	0.00	.085206	.087273	.089368	.091491	.093642	.095821	.098026	.100259	.102519	.104805	.107118	.111821	.116627
	-.10	.090905	.092972	.095067	.097190	.099341	.101519	.103725	.105957	.108217	.110503	.112816	.117520	.122325
	-.20	.096603	.098670	.100765	.102888	.105039	.107217	.109423	.111656	.113916	.116202	.118515	.123218	.128024
	-.30	.102301	.104368	.106465	.108587	.110737	.112916	.115122	.117354	.119614	.121900	.124213	.128916	.133722
	-.40	.108000	.110067	.112162	.114285	.116436	.118614	.120820	.123053	.125312	.127599	.129911	.134615	.139420
15	.40	.056459	.059016	.061612	.064249	.066926	.069640	.072392	.075181	.078006	.080865	.083759	.089644	.095653
	.30	.062158	.064714	.067311	.069948	.072624	.075339	.078091	.080880	.083704	.086564	.089457	.095342	.101351
	.20	.067856	.070412	.073009	.075646	.078322	.081037	.083789	.086578	.089403	.092262	.095156	.101041	.107050
	.10	.073555	.076111	.078708	.081345	.084021	.086735	.089488	.092276	.095101	.097961	.100854	.106739	.112748
	0.00	.079253	.081809	.084406	.087043	.089719	.092434	.095186	.097975	.100799	.103659	.106552	.112437	.118447
	-.10	.084952	.087508	.090105	.092742	.095418	.098132	.100884	.103673	.106498	.109357	.112251	.118136	.124145
	-.20	.090650	.093206	.095803	.098440	.101116	.103831	.106583	.109372	.112196	.115056	.117949	.123834	.129844
	-.30	.096348	.098904	.101501	.104138	.106815	.109529	.112281	.115070	.117895	.120754	.123648	.129533	.135542
	-.40	.102047	.104603	.107200	.109837	.112513	.115228	.117980	.120769	.123593	.126453	.129346	.135231	.141240
20	.40	.053573	.056383	.059239	.062137	.065078	.068059	.071078	.074134	.077226	.080351	.083508	.089911	.096422
	.30	.059272	.062082	.064937	.067836	.070776	.073757	.076776	.079833	.082924	.086049	.089206	.095609	.102120
	.20	.064970	.067780	.070635	.073534	.076475	.079455	.082475	.085531	.088623	.091748	.094905	.101308	.107819
	.10	.070668	.073479	.076334	.079232	.082173	.085154	.088173	.091230	.094321	.097446	.100603	.107006	.113517
	0.00	.076367	.079177	.082032	.084931	.087871	.090852	.093872	.096928	.100020	.103145	.106302	.112704	.119216
	-.10	.082065	.084875	.087731	.090629	.093570	.096551	.099570	.102626	.105718	.108843	.112000	.118403	.124914
	-.20	.087764	.090574	.093429	.096328	.099268	.102249	.105269	.108325	.111416	.114541	.117698	.124101	.130612
	-.30	.093462	.096272	.099127	.102026	.104967	.107948	.110967	.114023	.117115	.120254	.123397	.129800	.136311
	-.40	.099161	.101971	.104826	.107725	.110665	.113646	.116665	.119722	.122813	.125938	.129095	.135498	.142009
25	.40	.051911	.054880	.057895	.060953	.064053	.067191	.070366	.073574	.076814	.080083	.083379	.090044	.096793
	.30	.057609	.060578	.063593	.066652	.069751	.072890	.076064	.079272	.082512	.085781	.089077	.095742	.102492
	.20	.063307	.066277	.069292	.072350	.075450	.078588	.081762	.084971	.088211	.091480	.094776	.101441	.108190
	.10	.069006	.071975	.074990	.078049	.081148	.084588	.087461	.090669	.093909	.097178	.100474	.107139	.113889
	0.00	.074704	.077673	.080688	.083747	.086847	.089985	.093159	.096368	.099607	.102876	.106173	.112838	.119587
	-.10	.080403	.083372	.086387	.089445	.092545	.095683	.098858	.102066	.105306	.108575	.111871	.118536	.125285
	-.20	.086101	.089070	.092085	.095144	.098243	.101382	.104556	.107764	.111004	.114273	.117569	.124235	.130984
	-.30	.091800	.094769	.097784	.100842	.103942	.107080	.110255	.113463	.116703	.119972	.123268	.129933	.136682
	-.40	.097498	.100467	.103482	.106541	.109640	.112778	.115953	.119161	.122401	.125670	.128966	.135631	.142381
30	.40	.050857	.053936	.057061	.060227	.063432	.066673	.069946	.073249	.076578	.079932	.083308	.090115	.096984
	.30	.056555	.059635	.062759	.065926	.069131	.072371	.075644	.078947	.082277	.085630	.089006	.095814	.102683
	.20	.062254	.065333	.068458	.071624	.074829	.078070	.081343	.084646	.087975	.091329	.094704	.101512	.108381
	.10	.067952	.071032	.074156	.077323	.080528	.083768	.087041	.090344	.093674	.097027	.100403	.107210	.114080
	0.00	.073651	.076730	.079855	.083021	.086226	.089467	.092740	.096042	.099372	.102726	.106101	.112909	.119778
	-.10	.079349	.082428	.085553	.088719	.091925	.095165	.098438	.101741	.105070	.108424	.111798	.118607	.125476
	-.20	.085047	.088127	.091251	.094418	.097623	.100864	.104137	.107439	.110769	.114124	.117498	.124306	.131175
	-.30	.090746	.093825	.096950	.100116	.103321	.106562	.109835	.113138	.116467	.119821	.123197	.130004	.136873
	-.40	.096444	.099524	.102648	.105815	.109020	.112260	.115533	.118836	.122166	.125519	.128895	.135702	.142572

10.0 YEAR HOLDING PERIOD
.120 EQUITY YIELD RATE
.750 LOAN RATIO

INTEREST RATE

TERM YEARS	APPR DEP	5.0	5.5	6.0	6.5	7.0	7.5	8.0	8.5	9.0	9.5	10.0	11.0	12.0
10	.40	.059927	.062142	.064387	.066661	.068966	.071300	.073663	.076055	.078476	.080926	.083404	.088443	.093552
	.30	.065626	.067840	.070085	.072360	.074664	.076998	.079361	.081754	.084175	.086624	.089102	.094142	.099250
	.20	.071324	.073539	.075783	.078058	.080363	.082697	.085060	.087452	.089873	.092323	.094801	.099840	.104969
	.10	.077022	.079237	.081482	.083757	.086061	.088395	.090758	.093151	.095572	.098021	.100499	.105538	.110667
	0.00	.082721	.084936	.087180	.089455	.091760	.094093	.096457	.098849	.101270	.103720	.106198	.111237	.116366
	-.10	.088419	.090634	.092879	.095153	.097458	.099792	.102155	.104547	.106968	.109418	.111896	.116935	.122084
	-.20	.094118	.096332	.098577	.100852	.103156	.105490	.107854	.110246	.112667	.115117	.117594	.122634	.127763
	-.30	.099816	.102031	.104276	.106550	.108855	.111189	.113552	.115944	.118365	.120815	.123293	.128332	.133481
	-.40	.105515	.107729	.109974	.112249	.114553	.116887	.119250	.121643	.124064	.126513	.128991	.134031	.139179
15	.40	.053549	.056288	.059070	.061895	.064763	.067671	.070620	.073608	.076634	.079698	.082798	.089104	.095542
	.30	.059247	.061986	.064768	.067594	.070461	.073370	.076318	.079306	.082333	.085396	.088497	.094802	.101241
	.20	.064946	.067684	.070467	.073292	.076160	.079068	.082017	.085005	.088031	.091095	.094195	.100500	.106939
	.10	.070644	.073383	.076165	.078991	.081858	.084766	.087715	.090703	.093730	.096793	.099893	.106199	.112637
	0.00	.076343	.079081	.081864	.084689	.087556	.090465	.093414	.096402	.099428	.102492	.105592	.111897	.118336
	-.10	.082041	.084780	.087562	.090387	.093255	.096163	.099112	.102100	.105126	.108190	.111290	.117596	.124034
	-.20	.087739	.090478	.093261	.096086	.098953	.101862	.104810	.107798	.110825	.113889	.116989	.123294	.129733
	-.30	.093438	.096177	.098959	.101784	.104652	.107560	.110509	.113497	.116523	.119587	.122687	.128992	.135431
	-.40	.099136	.101875	.104657	.107483	.110350	.113259	.116207	.119195	.122222	.125285	.128386	.134691	.141129
20	.40	.050457	.053467	.056527	.059632	.062783	.065977	.069212	.072486	.075799	.079147	.082529	.089390	.096366
	.30	.056155	.059166	.062225	.065331	.068481	.071675	.074910	.078185	.081497	.084845	.088228	.095088	.102064
	.20	.061853	.064864	.067923	.071029	.074180	.077374	.080609	.083883	.087196	.090544	.093926	.100787	.107763
	.10	.067552	.070563	.073622	.076728	.079878	.083072	.086307	.089582	.092894	.096242	.099625	.106485	.113461
	0.00	.073250	.076261	.079320	.082426	.085577	.088770	.092005	.095280	.098592	.101941	.105323	.112183	.119160
	-.10	.078949	.081959	.085019	.088124	.091275	.094469	.097704	.100978	.104291	.107639	.111021	.117882	.124858
	-.20	.084647	.087658	.090717	.093823	.096973	.100167	.103402	.106677	.109989	.113337	.116720	.123580	.130556
	-.30	.090345	.093356	.096415	.099521	.102672	.105866	.109101	.112375	.115688	.119036	.122418	.129279	.136255
	-.40	.096044	.099055	.102114	.105220	.108370	.111564	.114799	.118074	.121386	.124734	.128117	.134977	.141953
25	.40	.048675	.051856	.055087	.058364	.061685	.065047	.068448	.071886	.075357	.078860	.082391	.089532	.096764
	.30	.054374	.057555	.060785	.064062	.067383	.070746	.074147	.077584	.081055	.084558	.088090	.095231	.102452
	.20	.060072	.063253	.066484	.069761	.073082	.076444	.079845	.083283	.086754	.090256	.093788	.100929	.108151
	.10	.065770	.068952	.072182	.075459	.078780	.082142	.085544	.088981	.092452	.095955	.099486	.106628	.113859
	0.00	.071469	.074650	.077880	.081157	.084478	.087841	.091242	.094680	.098151	.101653	.105185	.112326	.119557
	-.10	.077167	.080348	.083579	.086856	.090177	.093539	.096940	.100378	.103849	.107352	.110883	.118025	.125256
	-.20	.082866	.086047	.089277	.092554	.095875	.099238	.102639	.106076	.109548	.113050	.116582	.123723	.130954
	-.30	.088564	.091745	.094976	.098253	.101574	.104936	.108337	.111775	.115246	.118749	.122280	.129421	.136653
	-.40	.094263	.097444	.100674	.103951	.107272	.110635	.114036	.117473	.120944	.124447	.127979	.135120	.142351
30	.40	.047546	.050846	.054193	.057586	.061020	.064492	.067999	.071537	.075105	.078698	.082315	.089609	.096968
	.30	.053245	.056544	.059892	.063284	.066718	.070190	.073697	.077236	.080803	.084397	.088013	.095307	.102667
	.20	.058943	.062243	.065590	.068983	.072417	.075889	.079396	.082934	.086502	.090095	.093712	.101005	.108365
	.10	.064641	.067941	.071289	.074681	.078115	.081587	.085094	.088633	.092200	.095793	.099410	.106704	.114064
	0.00	.070340	.073639	.076987	.080380	.083814	.087286	.090793	.094331	.097899	.101492	.105109	.112402	.119762
	-.10	.076038	.079338	.082686	.086078	.089512	.092984	.096491	.100030	.103597	.107190	.110807	.118101	.125461
	-.20	.081737	.085036	.088384	.091777	.095211	.098683	.102189	.105728	.109295	.112889	.116505	.123799	.131159
	-.30	.087435	.090735	.094082	.097475	.100909	.104381	.107888	.111426	.114994	.118587	.122204	.129498	.136857
	-.40	.093134	.096433	.099781	.103173	.106607	.110079	.113586	.117125	.120692	.124286	.127902	.135196	.142556

10.0 YEAR HOLDING PERIOD
.120 EQUITY YIELD RATE
.800 LOAN RATIO

INTEREST RATE

TERM YEARS	APPR DEP	5.0	5.5	6.0	6.5	7.0	7.5	8.0	8.5	9.0	9.5	10.0	11.0	12.0
10	.40	.057442	.059804	.062199	.064625	.067083	.069573	.072093	.074645	.077228	.079841	.082484	.087859	.093351
	.30	.063140	.065503	.067897	.070323	.072782	.075271	.077792	.080344	.082926	.085539	.088182	.093557	.099050
	.20	.068839	.071201	.073596	.076022	.078480	.080970	.083490	.086042	.088625	.091237	.093881	.099256	.104748
	.10	.074537	.076899	.079294	.081720	.084178	.086668	.089189	.091741	.094323	.096936	.099579	.104954	.110446
	0.00	.080236	.082598	.084992	.087419	.089877	.092366	.094887	.097439	.100021	.102634	.105277	.110653	.116145
	-.10	.085934	.088296	.090691	.093117	.095575	.098065	.100586	.103137	.105720	.108333	.110976	.116351	.121843
	-.20	.091632	.093995	.096389	.098816	.101274	.103763	.106284	.108836	.111418	.114031	.116674	.122050	.127542
	-.30	.097331	.099693	.102088	.104514	.106972	.109462	.111982	.114534	.117117	.119730	.122373	.127748	.133240
	-.40	.103029	.105392	.107786	.110212	.112670	.115160	.117681	.120233	.122815	.125428	.128071	.133446	.138938
15	.40	.050638	.053560	.056528	.059541	.062600	.065702	.068847	.072035	.075263	.078531	.081838	.088563	.095431
	.30	.056337	.059258	.062226	.065240	.068298	.071401	.074546	.077733	.080961	.084229	.087536	.094262	.101130
	.20	.062035	.064957	.067924	.070938	.073997	.077099	.080244	.083432	.086660	.089928	.093234	.099960	.106828
	.10	.067734	.070655	.073623	.076637	.079695	.082797	.085944	.089130	.092358	.095626	.098933	.105659	.112526
	0.00	.073432	.076353	.079321	.082335	.085393	.088496	.091641	.094828	.098057	.101325	.104631	.111357	.118225
	-.10	.079131	.082052	.085020	.088033	.091092	.094194	.097340	.100527	.103755	.107023	.110330	.117055	.123923
	-.20	.084829	.087750	.090718	.093732	.096790	.099893	.103038	.106225	.109453	.112721	.116028	.122754	.129622
	-.30	.090527	.093449	.096417	.099430	.102489	.105591	.108736	.111924	.115152	.118420	.121727	.128452	.135320
	-.40	.096226	.099147	.102115	.105129	.108187	.111290	.114435	.117622	.120850	.124118	.127425	.134151	.141018
20	.40	.047340	.050551	.053815	.057127	.060488	.063895	.067345	.070838	.074372	.077943	.081551	.088869	.096310
	.30	.053038	.056250	.059513	.062826	.066186	.069593	.073044	.076537	.080070	.083641	.087249	.094557	.102008
	.20	.058737	.061948	.065211	.068524	.071885	.075292	.078742	.082235	.085768	.089340	.092948	.100265	.107707
	.10	.064435	.067647	.070910	.074223	.077583	.080990	.084441	.087934	.091467	.095038	.098646	.105964	.113405
	0.00	.070134	.073345	.076608	.079921	.083282	.086688	.090139	.093632	.097165	.100737	.104345	.111662	.119104
	-.10	.075832	.079044	.082307	.085619	.088980	.092387	.095838	.099330	.102864	.106435	.110043	.117361	.124802
	-.20	.081530	.084742	.088005	.091318	.094679	.098085	.101536	.105029	.108562	.112133	.115741	.123059	.130500
	-.30	.087229	.090440	.093703	.097016	.100377	.103784	.107234	.110727	.114260	.117832	.121440	.128758	.136199
	-.40	.092927	.096139	.099402	.102715	.106075	.109482	.112933	.116426	.119959	.123530	.127138	.134456	.141897
25	.40	.045440	.048833	.052279	.055774	.059317	.062903	.066531	.070198	.073900	.077637	.081404	.089021	.096734
	.30	.051138	.054531	.057977	.061473	.065015	.068602	.072230	.075896	.079599	.083335	.087102	.094719	.102433
	.20	.056837	.060230	.063676	.067171	.070714	.074300	.077928	.081595	.085297	.089033	.092800	.100418	.108131
	.10	.062535	.065928	.069374	.072870	.076412	.079998	.083626	.087293	.090996	.094732	.098499	.106197	.113830
	0.00	.068234	.071627	.075072	.078568	.082110	.085697	.089325	.092991	.096694	.100430	.104197	.111815	.119528
	-.10	.073932	.077325	.080771	.084266	.087809	.091395	.095023	.098690	.102393	.106129	.109896	.117513	.125226
	-.20	.079630	.083024	.086469	.089965	.093507	.097100	.100722	.104388	.108091	.111827	.115594	.123211	.130925
	-.30	.085329	.088722	.092168	.095663	.099206	.102792	.106420	.110087	.113789	.117525	.121292	.128910	.136623
	-.40	.091027	.094420	.097866	.101362	.104904	.108491	.112119	.115785	.119488	.123224	.126991	.134608	.142322
30	.40	.044236	.047755	.051326	.054945	.058608	.062311	.066052	.069826	.073631	.077464	.081322	.089102	.096953
	.30	.049934	.053453	.057024	.060643	.064306	.068010	.071750	.075525	.079330	.083163	.087021	.094801	.102651
	.20	.055632	.059152	.062723	.066342	.070005	.073708	.077449	.081223	.085028	.088861	.092719	.100499	.108349
	.10	.061331	.064850	.068421	.072040	.075703	.079406	.083147	.086921	.090727	.094560	.098417	.106197	.114048
	0.00	.067029	.070549	.074120	.077738	.081401	.085105	.088845	.092620	.096425	.100258	.104116	.111896	.119746
	-.10	.072728	.076247	.079818	.083437	.087100	.090803	.094544	.098318	.102123	.105956	.109814	.117594	.125445
	-.20	.078426	.081945	.085516	.089135	.092798	.096502	.100242	.104017	.107822	.111655	.115513	.123293	.131143
	-.30	.084124	.087644	.091215	.094834	.098497	.102200	.105941	.109715	.113520	.117353	.121211	.128991	.136841
	-.40	.089823	.093342	.096913	.100532	.104195	.107898	.111639	.115414	.119220	.123052	.126909	.134689	.142540

10.0 YEAR HOLDING PERIOD
.120 EQUITY YIELD RATE
.900 LOAN RATIO

INTEREST RATE

TERM YEARS	APPR DEP	5.0	5.5	6.0	6.5	7.0	7.5	8.0	8.5	9.0	9.5	10.0	11.0	12.0
10	.40	.052471	.055129	.057823	.060552	.063318	.066118	.068954	.071825	.074730	.077670	.080643	.086691	.092869
	.30	.058170	.060827	.063521	.066251	.069016	.071817	.074653	.077524	.080429	.083368	.086342	.092389	.098568
	.20	.063868	.066526	.069220	.071949	.074715	.077515	.080351	.083222	.086127	.089067	.092040	.098087	.104266
	.10	.069567	.072224	.074918	.077648	.080413	.083214	.086050	.088920	.091826	.094765	.097739	.103786	.109964
	0.00	.075265	.077923	.080616	.083346	.086111	.088912	.091748	.094619	.097524	.100464	.103437	.109484	.115663
	-.10	.080963	.083621	.086315	.089044	.091810	.094611	.097446	.100317	.103223	.106162	.109135	.115183	.121361
	-.20	.086662	.089319	.092013	.094743	.097508	.100309	.103145	.106016	.108921	.111860	.114834	.120881	.127060
	-.30	.092360	.095018	.097712	.100441	.103207	.106007	.108843	.111714	.114619	.117559	.120532	.126580	.132758
	-.40	.098059	.100716	.103410	.106140	.108905	.111706	.114542	.117412	.120318	.123257	.126231	.132278	.138457
15	.40	.044817	.048104	.051443	.054833	.058274	.061764	.065303	.068888	.072520	.076196	.079917	.087483	.095239
	.30	.050516	.053802	.057141	.060532	.063972	.067463	.071001	.074587	.078218	.081895	.085615	.093181	.100938
	.20	.056214	.059501	.062840	.066230	.069671	.073161	.076699	.080285	.083917	.087593	.091313	.098880	.106636
	.10	.061913	.065199	.068538	.071928	.075369	.078859	.082398	.085984	.089615	.093292	.097012	.104578	.112304
	0.00	.067611	.070898	.074236	.077627	.081068	.084558	.088096	.091682	.095314	.098990	.102710	.110277	.118003
	-.10	.073310	.076596	.079935	.083325	.086766	.090256	.093795	.097380	.101012	.104689	.108409	.115975	.123701
	-.20	.079008	.082294	.085633	.089024	.092464	.095955	.099493	.103079	.106710	.110387	.114107	.121673	.129400
	-.30	.084706	.087993	.091332	.094722	.098163	.101653	.105192	.108777	.112409	.116085	.119805	.127372	.135098
	-.40	.090405	.093691	.097030	.100421	.103861	.107351	.110890	.114476	.118107	.121784	.125504	.133070	.140797
20	.40	.041107	.044720	.048391	.052117	.055898	.059731	.063613	.067542	.071517	.075535	.079594	.087826	.096198
	.30	.046805	.050418	.054089	.057816	.061597	.065429	.069311	.073241	.077216	.081233	.085292	.093525	.101896
	.20	.052503	.056116	.059787	.063514	.067295	.071128	.075010	.078939	.082914	.086932	.090991	.099223	.107595
	.10	.058202	.061815	.065486	.069213	.072993	.076826	.080708	.084638	.088612	.092630	.096689	.104922	.113293
	0.00	.063900	.067513	.071184	.074911	.078692	.082524	.086406	.090336	.094311	.098329	.102388	.110620	.118991
	-.10	.069599	.073212	.076883	.080610	.084390	.088223	.092105	.096034	.100009	.104027	.108086	.116318	.124690
	-.20	.075297	.078910	.082581	.086308	.090089	.093921	.097803	.101733	.105708	.109726	.113784	.122017	.130388
	-.30	.080995	.084608	.088279	.092006	.095787	.099620	.103502	.107431	.111406	.115424	.119483	.127715	.136087
	-.40	.086694	.090307	.093978	.097705	.101486	.105318	.109200	.113130	.117104	.121122	.125181	.133414	.141785
25	.40	.038969	.042786	.046663	.050595	.054580	.058615	.062697	.066822	.070987	.075190	.079428	.087998	.096675
	.30	.044667	.048485	.052361	.056294	.060279	.064314	.068395	.072520	.076686	.080889	.085127	.093696	.102374
	.20	.050366	.054183	.058060	.061992	.065977	.070012	.074094	.078219	.082384	.086587	.090825	.099394	.108072
	.10	.056064	.059882	.063758	.067690	.071676	.075711	.079792	.083917	.088082	.092286	.096523	.105093	.113771
	0.00	.061763	.065580	.069456	.073389	.077374	.081409	.085490	.089615	.093781	.097984	.102222	.110791	.119469
	-.10	.067461	.071278	.075155	.079087	.083073	.087107	.091189	.095314	.099479	.103682	.107920	.116490	.125167
	-.20	.073160	.076977	.080853	.084786	.088771	.092806	.096887	.101012	.105178	.109381	.113619	.122188	.130866
	-.30	.078858	.082675	.086552	.090484	.094469	.098504	.102586	.106711	.110876	.115079	.119317	.127887	.136564
	-.40	.084556	.088374	.092250	.096183	.100168	.104203	.108284	.112409	.116575	.120778	.125016	.133585	.142263
30	.40	.037614	.041574	.045591	.049662	.053783	.057949	.062157	.066404	.070685	.074997	.079337	.088089	.096921
	.30	.043313	.047272	.051289	.055360	.059481	.063648	.067856	.072102	.076383	.080695	.085035	.093787	.102619
	.20	.049011	.052970	.056988	.061059	.065180	.069346	.073554	.077801	.082081	.086393	.090733	.099486	.108318
	.10	.054709	.058669	.062686	.066757	.070878	.075044	.079253	.083499	.087780	.092092	.096432	.105184	.114016
	0.00	.060408	.064367	.068385	.072456	.076576	.080743	.084951	.089197	.093478	.097790	.102130	.110883	.119715
	-.10	.066106	.070066	.074083	.078154	.082275	.086441	.090650	.094896	.099177	.103489	.107829	.116581	.125413
	-.20	.071805	.075764	.079781	.083853	.087973	.092140	.096348	.100594	.104875	.109187	.113527	.122280	.131111
	-.30	.077503	.081462	.085480	.089551	.093671	.097838	.102046	.106293	.110573	.114885	.119226	.127978	.136810
	-.40	.083202	.087161	.091178	.095249	.099370	.103537	.107745	.111991	.116272	.120584	.124924	.133676	.142508

239

10.0 YEAR HOLDING PERIOD
.140 EQUITY YIELD RATE
.600 LOAN RATIO

INTEREST RATE

TERM YEARS	APPR DEP	5.0	5.5	6.0	6.5	7.0	7.5	8.0	8.5	9.0	9.5	10.0	11.0	12.0
10	.40	.080654	.082425	.084221	.086041	.087685	.089752	.091642	.093556	.095493	.097453	.099435	.103466	.107586
	.30	.085825	.087597	.089393	.091212	.093056	.094923	.096813	.098728	.100664	.102624	.104606	.108538	.112757
	.20	.090996	.092768	.094564	.096384	.098227	.100094	.101985	.103899	.105836	.107795	.109778	.113809	.117928
	.10	.096168	.097939	.099735	.101555	.103399	.105266	.107156	.109070	.111007	.112967	.114949	.118981	.123100
	0.00	.101339	.103111	.104907	.106726	.108570	.110437	.112328	.114242	.116178	.118138	.120120	.124152	.128271
	-.10	.106510	.108282	.110078	.111898	.113741	.115609	.117499	.119413	.121350	.123309	.125292	.129323	.133442
	-.20	.111682	.113454	.115249	.117069	.118913	.120780	.122670	.124584	.126521	.128481	.130463	.134495	.138614
	-.30	.116853	.118625	.120421	.122240	.124084	.125951	.127842	.129756	.131692	.133652	.135634	.139666	.143785
	-.40	.122024	.123796	.125592	.127412	.129255	.131123	.133013	.134927	.136864	.138824	.140806	.144837	.148956
15	.40	.074226	.076389	.078588	.080820	.083087	.085386	.087717	.090080	.092474	.094898	.097351	.102342	.107439
	.30	.079397	.081561	.083759	.085992	.088258	.090557	.092889	.095252	.097646	.100069	.102522	.107513	.112611
	.20	.084569	.086732	.088930	.091163	.093429	.095729	.098060	.100423	.102817	.105241	.107694	.112684	.117782
	.10	.089740	.091903	.094102	.096334	.098601	.100900	.103231	.105594	.107988	.110412	.112865	.117856	.122953
	0.00	.094911	.097075	.099273	.101506	.103772	.106071	.108403	.110766	.113160	.115583	.118036	.123027	.128125
	-.10	.100083	.102246	.104444	.106677	.108943	.111243	.113574	.115937	.118331	.120755	.123208	.128198	.133296
	-.20	.105254	.107417	.109616	.111848	.114115	.116414	.118745	.121109	.123502	.125926	.128379	.133370	.138467
	-.30	.110425	.112589	.114787	.117020	.119286	.121585	.123917	.126280	.128674	.131097	.133551	.138541	.143639
	-.40	.115597	.117760	.119958	.122191	.124457	.126757	.129088	.131451	.133845	.136269	.138722	.143712	.148810
20	.40	.071109	.073481	.075892	.078341	.080827	.083347	.085901	.088488	.091105	.093751	.096426	.101854	.107378
	.30	.076281	.078653	.081064	.083513	.085998	.088518	.091072	.093659	.096276	.098923	.101597	.107025	.112549
	.20	.081452	.083824	.086235	.088684	.091169	.093690	.096244	.098830	.101447	.104094	.106769	.112197	.117720
	.10	.086624	.088995	.091406	.093855	.096341	.098861	.101415	.104002	.106619	.109265	.111940	.117368	.122892
	0.00	.091795	.094167	.096578	.099027	.101512	.104032	.106587	.109173	.111790	.114437	.117112	.122539	.128063
	-.10	.096966	.099338	.101749	.104198	.106683	.109204	.111758	.114344	.116961	.119608	.122283	.127711	.133234
	-.20	.102138	.104509	.106921	.109370	.111855	.114375	.116929	.119516	.122133	.124780	.127454	.132882	.138406
	-.30	.107309	.109681	.112092	.114541	.117026	.119547	.122101	.124687	.127304	.129951	.132626	.138053	.143577
	-.40	.112480	.114852	.117263	.119712	.122197	.124718	.127272	.129858	.132476	.135122	.137797	.143225	.148748
25	.40	.069314	.071820	.074367	.076952	.079573	.082229	.084917	.087635	.090381	.093154	.095951	.101611	.107348
	.30	.074486	.076992	.079538	.082123	.084744	.087400	.090088	.092806	.095552	.098325	.101122	.106782	.112519
	.20	.079657	.082163	.084709	.087294	.089916	.092571	.095259	.097977	.100724	.103496	.106293	.111954	.117690
	.10	.084828	.087334	.089881	.092466	.095087	.097743	.100431	.103149	.105895	.108668	.111465	.117125	.122862
	0.00	.090000	.092506	.095052	.097637	.100258	.102914	.105602	.108320	.111066	.113839	.116636	.122296	.128033
	-.10	.095171	.097677	.100224	.102808	.105430	.108085	.110773	.113491	.116238	.119010	.121807	.127468	.133205
	-.20	.100342	.102848	.105395	.107980	.110601	.113257	.115945	.118663	.121409	.124182	.126979	.132639	.138376
	-.30	.105514	.108020	.110566	.113151	.115773	.118428	.121116	.123834	.126581	.129353	.132150	.137810	.143547
	-.40	.110685	.113191	.115738	.118323	.120944	.123600	.126287	.129006	.131752	.134525	.137322	.142982	.148719
30	.40	.068177	.070778	.073420	.076100	.078814	.081561	.084337	.087140	.089968	.092818	.095688	.101481	.107732
	.30	.073348	.075950	.078592	.081271	.083986	.086732	.089508	.092311	.095139	.097989	.100859	.106652	.112504
	.20	.078519	.081121	.083763	.086443	.089157	.091903	.094680	.097483	.100310	.103160	.106031	.111824	.117675
	.10	.083691	.086292	.088934	.091614	.094328	.097075	.099851	.102654	.105482	.108332	.111202	.116995	.122846
	0.00	.088862	.091464	.094106	.096785	.099500	.102246	.105022	.107825	.110653	.113503	.116373	.122167	.128018
	-.10	.094033	.096635	.099277	.101957	.104671	.107418	.110194	.112997	.115824	.118674	.121545	.127338	.133189
	-.20	.099205	.101806	.104448	.107128	.109842	.112589	.115365	.118168	.120996	.123846	.126716	.132509	.138361
	-.30	.104376	.106978	.109620	.112299	.115014	.117760	.120536	.123339	.126167	.129017	.131887	.137681	.143532
	-.40	.109547	.112149	.114791	.117471	.120185	.122932	.125708	.128511	.131338	.134189	.137059	.142852	.148703

INTEREST RATE

TERM YEARS	APPR DEP	5.0	5.5	6.0	6.5	7.0	7.5	8.0	8.5	9.0	9.5	10.0	11.0	12.0
10	.40	.076358	.078326	.080322	.082344	.084392	.086467	.088567	.090694	.092846	.095023	.097226	.101705	.106282
	.30	.081529	.083498	.085493	.087515	.089564	.091638	.093739	.095865	.098017	.100195	.102397	.106887	.111454
	.20	.086700	.088669	.090664	.092686	.094735	.096810	.098910	.101037	.103189	.105366	.107569	.112048	.116625
	.10	.091872	.093840	.095836	.097858	.099906	.101981	.104082	.106208	.108360	.110538	.112740	.117220	.121796
	0.00	.097043	.099012	.101007	.103029	.105078	.107152	.109253	.111379	.113531	.115709	.117911	.122391	.126968
	-.10	.102215	.104183	.106179	.108201	.110279	.112324	.114424	.116551	.118703	.120880	.123083	.127562	.132139
	-.20	.107386	.109354	.111350	.113372	.115420	.117495	.119596	.121722	.123874	.126052	.128254	.132734	.137310
	-.30	.112557	.114526	.116521	.118543	.120592	.122666	.124767	.126893	.129046	.131223	.133426	.137905	.142482
	-.40	.117729	.119697	.121693	.123715	.125763	.127838	.129938	.132065	.134217	.136394	.138597	.143076	.147653
15	.40	.069216	.071620	.074062	.076543	.079061	.081616	.084206	.086832	.089492	.092185	.094911	.100456	.106120
	.30	.074387	.076791	.079234	.081714	.084232	.086787	.089378	.092003	.094663	.097356	.100082	.105627	.111291
	.20	.079558	.081962	.084405	.086886	.089404	.091958	.094549	.097175	.099834	.102528	.105253	.110798	.116463
	.10	.084730	.087134	.089576	.092057	.094575	.097130	.099720	.102346	.105006	.107699	.110425	.115970	.121634
	0.00	.089901	.092305	.094748	.097228	.099746	.102301	.104892	.107517	.110177	.112870	.115596	.121141	.126805
	-.10	.095073	.097476	.099919	.102400	.104918	.107473	.110063	.112689	.115349	.118042	.120767	.126312	.131977
	-.20	.100244	.102648	.105090	.107571	.110089	.112644	.115235	.117860	.120520	.123213	.125939	.131484	.137148
	-.30	.105415	.107819	.110262	.112742	.115261	.117815	.120406	.123031	.125691	.128384	.131110	.136655	.142319
	-.40	.110587	.112990	.115433	.117914	.120432	.122977	.125577	.128203	.130863	.133556	.136281	.141826	.147491
20	.40	.065753	.068388	.071067	.073788	.076550	.079350	.082188	.085062	.087970	.090911	.093883	.099914	.106051
	.30	.070924	.073560	.076239	.078960	.081721	.084522	.087360	.090233	.093141	.096082	.099054	.105085	.111223
	.20	.076096	.078731	.081410	.084131	.086893	.089693	.092531	.095405	.098313	.101254	.104226	.110257	.116394
	.10	.081267	.083903	.086582	.089303	.092064	.094864	.097702	.100576	.103484	.106425	.109397	.115428	.121565
	0.00	.086438	.089074	.091753	.094474	.097235	.100036	.102874	.105748	.108656	.111596	.114568	.120599	.126737
	-.10	.091610	.094245	.096924	.099645	.102407	.105207	.108045	.110919	.113827	.116768	.119740	.125771	.131908
	-.20	.096781	.099417	.102096	.104817	.107578	.110379	.113216	.116090	.118998	.121939	.124911	.130942	.137079
	-.30	.101953	.104588	.107267	.109988	.112749	.115550	.118388	.121262	.124170	.127110	.130082	.136113	.142251
	-.40	.107124	.109759	.112438	.115159	.117921	.120721	.123559	.126433	.129341	.132282	.135254	.141285	.147422
25	.40	.063758	.066543	.069372	.072244	.075157	.078108	.081094	.084115	.087166	.090247	.093355	.099644	.106018
	.30	.068930	.071714	.074544	.077416	.080328	.083279	.086266	.089286	.092337	.095418	.098526	.104815	.111189
	.20	.074101	.076886	.079715	.082587	.085500	.088451	.091437	.094457	.097509	.100589	.103697	.109986	.116361
	.10	.079273	.082057	.084886	.087759	.090671	.093622	.096608	.099629	.102680	.105761	.108869	.115158	.121532
	0.00	.084444	.087228	.090058	.092930	.095842	.098793	.101780	.104800	.107851	.110932	.114040	.120329	.126703
	-.10	.089615	.092400	.095229	.098101	.101014	.103965	.106951	.109971	.113023	.116104	.119211	.125500	.131875
	-.20	.094787	.097571	.100400	.103273	.106185	.109136	.112122	.115141	.118194	.121275	.124383	.130672	.137046
	-.30	.099958	.102742	.105572	.108444	.111357	.114307	.117294	.120314	.123366	.126446	.129554	.135843	.142218
	-.40	.105129	.107914	.110743	.113615	.116528	.119479	.122465	.125485	.128537	.131618	.134725	.141015	.147389
30	.40	.062494	.065385	.068321	.071298	.074314	.077366	.080450	.083565	.086707	.089873	.093063	.099499	.106001
	.30	.067666	.070556	.073492	.076469	.079485	.082537	.085622	.088736	.091878	.095045	.098234	.104671	.111172
	.20	.072837	.075728	.078663	.081641	.084657	.087708	.090793	.093908	.097049	.100216	.103405	.109842	.116344
	.10	.078008	.080899	.083835	.086812	.089828	.092880	.095964	.099079	.102221	.105388	.108577	.115014	.121515
	0.00	.083180	.086070	.089006	.091983	.094999	.098051	.101136	.104250	.107392	.110559	.113748	.120185	.126686
	-.10	.088351	.091242	.094177	.097155	.100171	.103222	.106307	.109422	.112563	.115730	.118919	.125356	.131858
	-.20	.093522	.096413	.099349	.102326	.105342	.108394	.111478	.114593	.117735	.120902	.124091	.130528	.137029
	-.30	.098694	.101584	.104520	.107497	.110513	.113565	.116650	.119764	.122906	.126073	.129262	.135699	.142200
	-.40	.103865	.106756	.109691	.112669	.115685	.118737	.121821	.124936	.128078	.131244	.134433	.140870	.147372

241

10.0 YEAR HOLDING PERIOD
.140 EQUITY YIELD RATE
.700 LOAN RATIO

INTEREST RATE

TERM YEARS	APPR DEP	5.0	5.5	6.0	6.5	7.0	7.5	8.0	8.5	9.0	9.5	10.0	11.0	12.0
10	.40	.074210	.076277	.078372	.080495	.082646	.084825	.087030	.089263	.091523	.093809	.096122	.100825	.105631
	.30	.079381	.081449	.083544	.085567	.087818	.089996	.092202	.094434	.096694	.098980	.101293	.105996	.110802
	.20	.084553	.086620	.088715	.090838	.092989	.095167	.097373	.099606	.101865	.104152	.106464	.111168	.115973
	.10	.089724	.091791	.093886	.096009	.098160	.100339	.102544	.104777	.107037	.109323	.111636	.116339	.121145
	0.00	.094896	.096963	.099058	.101181	.103332	.105510	.107716	.109949	.112208	.114494	.116807	.121511	.126316
	-.10	.100067	.102134	.104229	.106352	.108503	.110681	.112887	.115120	.117380	.119666	.121978	.126682	.131487
	-.20	.105238	.107305	.109400	.111524	.113674	.115853	.118058	.120291	.122551	.124837	.127150	.131853	.136659
	-.30	.110410	.112477	.114572	.116846	.118846	.121024	.123230	.125463	.127722	.130009	.132321	.137025	.141830
	-.40	.115581	.117648	.119743	.121866	.124017	.126195	.128401	.130634	.132894	.135180	.137493	.142196	.147002
15	.40	.066711	.069235	.071800	.074405	.077049	.079731	.082451	.085208	.088001	.090829	.093690	.099513	.105460
	.30	.071882	.074406	.076971	.079576	.082220	.084902	.087623	.090379	.093172	.096000	.098862	.104684	.110631
	.20	.077054	.079578	.082142	.084747	.087391	.090074	.092794	.095551	.098344	.101171	.104033	.109855	.115803
	.10	.082225	.084749	.087314	.089919	.092563	.095245	.097965	.100722	.103515	.106343	.109204	.115027	.120974
	0.00	.087396	.089920	.092485	.095090	.097734	.100416	.103137	.105893	.108686	.111514	.114376	.120198	.126146
	-.10	.092568	.095092	.097657	.100261	.102905	.105588	.108308	.111065	.113858	.116685	.119547	.125369	.131317
	-.20	.097739	.100263	.102828	.105433	.108077	.110759	.113479	.116236	.119029	.121857	.124719	.130541	.136488
	-.30	.102911	.105435	.107999	.110604	.113248	.115931	.118651	.121408	.124200	.127028	.129890	.135712	.141660
	-.40	.108082	.110606	.113171	.115775	.118419	.121102	.123822	.126579	.129372	.132199	.135061	.140884	.146831
20	.40	.063075	.065842	.068655	.071512	.074412	.077352	.080332	.083350	.086403	.089491	.092611	.098944	.105388
	.30	.068247	.071014	.073827	.076684	.079583	.082524	.085504	.088521	.091574	.094662	.097783	.104115	.110559
	.20	.073418	.076185	.078998	.081855	.084755	.087695	.090675	.093692	.096746	.099634	.102954	.109287	.115731
	.10	.078589	.081357	.084169	.087026	.089926	.092866	.095846	.098864	.101917	.105005	.108125	.114458	.120902
	0.00	.083761	.086528	.089341	.092198	.095097	.098038	.101018	.104035	.107089	.110176	.113297	.119629	.126074
	-.10	.088932	.091699	.094512	.097369	.100269	.103209	.106189	.109206	.112260	.115348	.118468	.124801	.131245
	-.20	.094103	.096871	.099683	.102540	.105440	.108381	.111360	.114378	.117431	.120519	.123639	.129972	.136416
	-.30	.099275	.102042	.104855	.107712	.110611	.113552	.116532	.119549	.122603	.125690	.128811	.135143	.141588
	-.40	.104446	.107213	.110026	.112883	.115783	.118723	.121703	.124720	.127774	.130862	.133982	.140315	.146759
25	.40	.060981	.063905	.066875	.069891	.072949	.076048	.079184	.082355	.085559	.088794	.092057	.098660	.105353
	.30	.066152	.069076	.072047	.075063	.078121	.081219	.084355	.087526	.090730	.093965	.097228	.103832	.110525
	.20	.071324	.074247	.077218	.080234	.083292	.086390	.089526	.092697	.095901	.099136	.102399	.109003	.115696
	.10	.076495	.079419	.082390	.085405	.088463	.091562	.094698	.097869	.101073	.104308	.107571	.114174	.120867
	0.00	.081666	.084590	.087561	.090577	.093635	.096733	.099869	.103040	.106244	.109479	.112742	.119346	.126039
	-.10	.086838	.089761	.092732	.095748	.098806	.101904	.105040	.108211	.111416	.114650	.117914	.124517	.131210
	-.20	.092009	.094933	.097904	.100919	.103978	.107076	.110212	.113383	.116587	.119822	.123085	.129688	.136381
	-.30	.097180	.100104	.103075	.106091	.109149	.112247	.115383	.118554	.121758	.124993	.128256	.134860	.141553
	-.40	.102352	.105275	.108246	.111262	.114320	.117419	.120554	.123726	.126930	.130164	.133428	.140031	.146724
30	.40	.059654	.062689	.065771	.068897	.072064	.075268	.078507	.081777	.085077	.088402	.091750	.098509	.105335
	.30	.064825	.067860	.070942	.074069	.077236	.080440	.083679	.086949	.090248	.093573	.096922	.103680	.110507
	.20	.069996	.073031	.076114	.079240	.082407	.085611	.088850	.092120	.095419	.098744	.102093	.108852	.115678
	.10	.075168	.078203	.081285	.084411	.087578	.090783	.094021	.097292	.100591	.103916	.107264	.114023	.120849
	0.00	.080339	.083374	.086457	.089583	.092750	.095954	.099193	.102463	.105762	.109187	.112436	.119194	.126021
	-.10	.085510	.088546	.091628	.094754	.097921	.101125	.104364	.107634	.110933	.114258	.117607	.124366	.131192
	-.20	.090682	.093717	.096799	.099925	.103092	.106297	.109535	.112806	.116105	.119430	.122779	.129537	.136363
	-.30	.095853	.098888	.101971	.105097	.108264	.111468	.114707	.117977	.121276	.124601	.127950	.134708	.141535
	-.40	.101024	.104060	.107142	.110268	.113435	.116639	.119878	.123148	.126447	.129772	.133121	.139880	.146706

10.0 YEAR HOLDING PERIOD
.140 EQUITY YIELD RATE
.750 LOAN RATIO

INTEREST RATE

TERM YEARS	APPR DEP	5.0	5.5	6.0	6.5	7.0	7.5	8.0	8.5	9.0	9.5	10.0	11.0	12.0
10	.40	.070988	.073203	.075448	.077723	.080027	.082361	.084724	.087117	.089538	.091987	.094465	.099504	.104653
	.30	.076160	.078374	.080619	.082994	.085198	.087532	.089896	.092288	.094709	.097159	.099636	.104676	.109825
	.20	.081331	.083546	.085791	.088065	.090370	.092704	.095067	.097459	.099880	.102330	.104808	.109847	.114996
	.10	.086502	.088717	.090962	.093237	.095541	.097875	.100238	.102631	.105052	.107501	.109979	.115019	.120157
	0.00	.091674	.093888	.096133	.098408	.100712	.103046	.105410	.107802	.110223	.112673	.115151	.120361	.125339
	-.10	.096845	.099060	.101305	.103579	.105884	.108218	.110581	.112973	.115394	.117844	.120322	.125361	.130510
	-.20	.102017	.104231	.106476	.108751	.111055	.113389	.115752	.118145	.120566	.123015	.125493	.130533	.135631
	-.30	.107188	.109403	.111647	.113922	.116227	.118560	.120924	.123316	.125737	.128187	.130665	.135704	.140853
	-.40	.112359	.114574	.116819	.119093	.121398	.123732	.126095	.128487	.130908	.133358	.135836	.140875	.146024
15	.40	.062954	.065658	.068406	.071197	.074030	.076904	.079818	.082772	.085764	.088794	.091860	.098098	.104471
	.30	.068125	.070829	.073577	.076368	.079201	.082075	.084989	.087943	.090935	.093965	.097031	.103270	.109642
	.20	.073296	.076001	.078749	.081539	.084372	.087246	.090161	.093115	.096107	.099137	.102203	.108441	.114813
	.10	.078468	.081172	.083920	.086711	.089544	.092418	.095332	.098286	.101278	.104308	.107374	.113612	.119985
	0.00	.083639	.086343	.089091	.091882	.094715	.097590	.100503	.103457	.106450	.109479	.112546	.118784	.125156
	-.10	.088810	.091515	.094263	.097053	.099886	.102760	.105675	.108629	.111621	.114651	.117717	.123955	.130327
	-.20	.093982	.096686	.099434	.102225	.105058	.107932	.110846	.113800	.116792	.119822	.122888	.129126	.135499
	-.30	.099153	.101857	.104605	.107396	.110229	.113103	.116018	.118971	.121964	.124993	.128060	.134298	.140670
	-.40	.104324	.107029	.109777	.112568	.115400	.118274	.121189	.124143	.127135	.130165	.133231	.139469	.145841
20	.40	.059058	.062023	.065037	.068098	.071205	.074355	.077548	.080781	.084052	.087361	.090704	.097489	.104333
	.30	.064230	.067194	.070208	.073269	.076376	.079526	.082719	.085952	.089224	.092532	.095875	.102660	.109555
	.20	.069401	.072366	.075380	.078441	.081547	.084698	.087890	.091123	.094395	.097703	.101047	.107832	.114736
	.10	.074572	.077537	.080551	.083612	.086719	.089869	.093062	.096295	.099566	.102875	.106218	.113003	.119907
	0.00	.079744	.082708	.085722	.088783	.091890	.095041	.098233	.101466	.104738	.108046	.111389	.118174	.125079
	-.10	.084915	.087880	.090894	.093955	.097061	.100212	.103405	.106638	.109909	.113217	.116561	.123346	.130250
	-.20	.090086	.093051	.096065	.099126	.102233	.105383	.108576	.111809	.115080	.118389	.121732	.128517	.135421
	-.30	.095258	.098223	.101236	.104297	.107404	.110555	.113747	.116980	.120252	.123560	.126903	.133688	.140593
	-.40	.100429	.103394	.106408	.109469	.112575	.115726	.118919	.122152	.125423	.128731	.132075	.138860	.145764
25	.40	.056814	.059947	.063130	.066361	.069638	.072957	.076317	.079715	.083148	.086613	.090110	.097185	.104356
	.30	.061986	.065118	.068301	.071532	.074809	.078129	.081488	.084886	.088319	.091785	.095281	.102356	.109527
	.20	.067157	.070289	.073472	.076704	.079980	.083300	.086660	.090057	.093490	.096956	.100452	.107528	.114699
	.10	.072328	.075461	.078644	.081875	.085152	.088471	.091831	.095228	.098662	.102128	.105624	.112699	.119870
	0.00	.077500	.080632	.083815	.087046	.090323	.093643	.097002	.100400	.103833	.107299	.110795	.117870	.125041
	-.10	.082671	.085803	.088987	.092218	.095494	.098814	.102174	.105571	.109004	.112470	.115967	.123042	.130213
	-.20	.087843	.090975	.094158	.097389	.100666	.103985	.107345	.110743	.114176	.117642	.121138	.128213	.135384
	-.30	.093014	.096146	.099329	.102560	.105837	.109157	.112517	.115914	.119347	.122813	.126309	.133384	.140556
	-.40	.098185	.101318	.104501	.107732	.111008	.114328	.117688	.121086	.124518	.127984	.131481	.138556	.145727
30	.40	.055392	.058644	.061947	.065296	.068689	.072122	.075592	.079096	.082631	.086194	.089781	.097023	.104337
	.30	.060563	.063815	.067118	.070467	.073860	.077294	.080764	.084268	.087802	.091365	.094953	.102194	.109508
	.20	.065735	.068987	.072289	.075639	.079032	.082465	.085935	.089439	.092974	.096536	.100124	.107365	.114680
	.10	.070906	.074158	.077461	.080810	.084203	.087636	.091106	.094610	.098145	.101708	.105295	.112537	.119851
	0.00	.076077	.079330	.082632	.085982	.089375	.092808	.096278	.099782	.103316	.106879	.110467	.117708	.125022
	-.10	.081249	.084501	.087803	.091153	.094546	.097979	.101449	.104953	.108488	.112050	.115638	.122879	.130194
	-.20	.086420	.089672	.092975	.096324	.099717	.103150	.106621	.110124	.113659	.117222	.120809	.128051	.135365
	-.30	.091591	.094844	.098146	.101496	.104889	.108322	.111792	.115296	.118830	.122393	.125981	.133222	.140536
	-.40	.096763	.100015	.103317	.106667	.110060	.113493	.116963	.120467	.124002	.127564	.131152	.138394	.145708

10.0 YEAR HOLDING PERIOD
.140 EQUITY YIELD RATE
.800 LOAN RATIO

INTEREST RATE

TERM YEARS	APPR DEP	5.0	5.5	6.0	6.5	7.0	7.5	8.0	8.5	9.0	9.5	10.0	11.0	12.0
10	.40	.067767	.070129	.072523	.074950	.077408	.079897	.082418	.084970	.087552	.090165	.092808	.098184	.103676
	.30	.072938	.075300	.077695	.080121	.082579	.085069	.087590	.090141	.092724	.095337	.097980	.103355	.108847
	.20	.078109	.080472	.082866	.085293	.087751	.090240	.092761	.095313	.097895	.100508	.103151	.108526	.114019
	.10	.083281	.085643	.088037	.090464	.092922	.095412	.097932	.100484	.103067	.105679	.108323	.113698	.119190
	0.00	.088452	.090814	.093209	.095635	.098093	.100583	.103104	.105655	.108238	.110851	.113494	.118869	.124361
	-.10	.093623	.095986	.098380	.100807	.103265	.105754	.108275	.110827	.113409	.116022	.118665	.124041	.129533
	-.20	.098795	.101157	.103552	.105978	.108436	.110926	.113446	.115998	.118581	.121194	.123837	.129212	.134704
	-.30	.103966	.106328	.108723	.111149	.113607	.116097	.118618	.121169	.123752	.126365	.129008	.134383	.139875
	-.40	.109137	.111500	.113894	.116321	.118779	.121268	.123789	.126341	.128923	.131536	.134179	.139555	.145047
15	.40	.059196	.062081	.065012	.067989	.071011	.074076	.077185	.080336	.083527	.086759	.090030	.096684	.103481
	.30	.064368	.067252	.070183	.073160	.076182	.079248	.082356	.085507	.088699	.091930	.095201	.101855	.108652
	.20	.069539	.072424	.075355	.078332	.081353	.084419	.087528	.090678	.093870	.097102	.100373	.107027	.113824
	.10	.074710	.077595	.080526	.083503	.086525	.089590	.092699	.095850	.099041	.102273	.105544	.112198	.118995
	0.00	.079882	.082766	.085697	.088674	.091696	.094762	.097870	.101021	.104213	.107445	.110715	.117369	.124166
	-.10	.085053	.087938	.090869	.093846	.096867	.099933	.103042	.106192	.109384	.112616	.115887	.122541	.129338
	-.20	.090224	.093109	.096040	.099017	.102039	.105104	.108213	.111364	.114556	.117787	.121058	.127712	.134509
	-.30	.095396	.098280	.101211	.104188	.107210	.110276	.113384	.116535	.119727	.122959	.126229	.132883	.139680
	-.40	.100567	.103452	.106383	.109360	.112381	.115447	.118556	.121706	.124898	.128130	.131401	.138055	.144852
20	.40	.055041	.058204	.061418	.064683	.067997	.071358	.074763	.078212	.081701	.085230	.088797	.096034	.103399
	.30	.060212	.063375	.066590	.069855	.073169	.076529	.079935	.083383	.086873	.090402	.093968	.101205	.108570
	.20	.065384	.068546	.071761	.075026	.078340	.081701	.085106	.088555	.092044	.095573	.099139	.106377	.113741
	.10	.070555	.073718	.076932	.080198	.083511	.086872	.090277	.093726	.097216	.100744	.104311	.111548	.118913
	0.00	.075726	.078889	.082104	.085369	.088683	.092043	.095448	.098897	.102387	.105916	.109482	.116719	.124084
	-.10	.080898	.084060	.087275	.090540	.093854	.097215	.100620	.104069	.107558	.111087	.114653	.121891	.129255
	-.20	.086069	.089232	.092446	.095712	.099025	.102386	.105791	.109240	.112730	.116258	.119825	.127062	.134427
	-.30	.091241	.094403	.097618	.100883	.104197	.107557	.110963	.114411	.117901	.121430	.124996	.132233	.139598
	-.40	.096412	.099574	.102789	.106054	.109368	.112729	.116134	.119583	.123072	.126601	.130167	.137405	.144769
25	.40	.052648	.055989	.059384	.062831	.066326	.069867	.073451	.077075	.080737	.084433	.088163	.095710	.103359
	.30	.057819	.061160	.064555	.068002	.071497	.075038	.078622	.082246	.085908	.089605	.093334	.100681	.108530
	.20	.062990	.066332	.069727	.073173	.076669	.080209	.083793	.087417	.091079	.094776	.098505	.106052	.113702
	.10	.068162	.071503	.074898	.078345	.081840	.085381	.088965	.092589	.096251	.099947	.103677	.111224	.118873
	0.00	.073333	.076674	.080070	.083516	.087011	.090552	.094136	.097760	.101422	.105119	.108848	.116395	.124044
	-.10	.078504	.081846	.085241	.088688	.092183	.095723	.099307	.102931	.106593	.110290	.114020	.121566	.129216
	-.20	.083676	.087017	.090412	.093859	.097354	.100894	.104479	.108103	.111765	.115461	.119191	.126738	.134387
	-.30	.088847	.092188	.095584	.099030	.102525	.106066	.109650	.113274	.116936	.120633	.124362	.131909	.139558
	-.40	.094018	.097360	.100755	.104202	.107697	.111238	.114821	.118446	.122107	.125804	.129534	.137080	.144730
30	.40	.051131	.054599	.058122	.061695	.065314	.068976	.072678	.076415	.080185	.083985	.087812	.095537	.103338
	.30	.056302	.059771	.063293	.066866	.070485	.074148	.077849	.081586	.085357	.089157	.092984	.100708	.108510
	.20	.061473	.064942	.068465	.072038	.075657	.079319	.083020	.086758	.090528	.094328	.098155	.105879	.113681
	.10	.066645	.070113	.073636	.077209	.080828	.084490	.088192	.091929	.095699	.099499	.103326	.111051	.118852
	0.00	.071816	.075285	.078807	.082380	.086000	.089662	.093363	.097100	.100871	.104671	.108498	.116222	.124024
	-.10	.076987	.080456	.083979	.087552	.091171	.094833	.098534	.102272	.106042	.109842	.113669	.121393	.129195
	-.20	.082159	.085628	.089150	.092723	.096342	.100004	.103706	.107443	.111213	.115014	.118842	.126565	.134366
	-.30	.087330	.090799	.094322	.097894	.101514	.105176	.108877	.112615	.116385	.120185	.124012	.131736	.139538
	-.40	.092501	.095970	.099493	.103066	.106685	.110347	.114048	.117786	.121556	.125356	.129183	.136907	.144709

244

10.0 YEAR HOLDING PERIOD
.140 EQUITY YIELD RATE
.900 LOAN RATIO

INTEREST RATE

TERM YEARS	APPR DEP	5.0	5.5	6.0	6.5	7.0	7.5	8.0	8.5	9.0	9.5	10.0	11.0	12.0
10	.40	.061323	.063981	.066675	.069404	.072170	.074970	.077806	.080677	.083582	.086522	.089495	.095542	.101721
	.30	.066495	.069152	.071846	.074576	.077341	.080142	.082978	.085848	.088754	.091693	.094667	.100714	.106892
	.20	.071666	.074323	.077017	.079747	.082512	.085343	.088149	.091020	.093925	.096864	.099838	.105885	.112064
	.10	.076637	.079495	.082189	.084918	.087684	.090484	.093320	.096191	.099096	.102036	.105009	.111056	.117235
	0.00	.082009	.084666	.087360	.090090	.092855	.095656	.098492	.101362	.104268	.107207	.110181	.116228	.122406
	-.10	.087180	.089838	.092531	.095261	.098026	.100827	.103663	.106534	.109439	.112379	.115352	.121399	.127579
	-.20	.092351	.095009	.097703	.100432	.103198	.105998	.108834	.111705	.114610	.117550	.120523	.126571	.132749
	-.30	.097523	.100180	.102874	.105604	.108369	.111170	.114006	.116876	.119782	.122721	.125695	.131742	.137920
	-.40	.102694	.105352	.108045	.110775	.113540	.116341	.119177	.122048	.124953	.127893	.130866	.136913	.143092
15	.40	.051681	.054927	.058224	.061573	.064973	.068421	.071919	.075463	.079054	.082690	.086369	.093855	.101502
	.30	.056853	.060098	.063395	.066744	.070144	.073593	.077090	.080635	.084225	.087861	.091541	.099026	.106673
	.20	.062024	.065269	.068567	.071916	.075315	.078764	.082261	.085806	.089397	.093032	.096712	.104198	.111844
	.10	.067196	.070441	.073738	.077087	.080487	.083936	.087433	.090977	.094568	.098204	.101883	.109369	.117016
	0.00	.072367	.075612	.078910	.082259	.085658	.089107	.092604	.096149	.099739	.103375	.107055	.114540	.122187
	-.10	.077538	.080783	.084081	.087430	.090829	.094278	.097776	.101320	.104911	.108546	.112226	.119712	.127359
	-.20	.082710	.085955	.089252	.092601	.096001	.099450	.102947	.106491	.110082	.113718	.117397	.124883	.132530
	-.30	.087881	.091126	.094424	.097773	.101172	.104621	.108118	.111663	.115253	.118889	.122569	.130055	.137701
	-.40	.093052	.096297	.099595	.102944	.106343	.109792	.113290	.116834	.120425	.124061	.127740	.135226	.142873
20	.40	.047007	.050565	.054181	.057855	.061583	.065363	.069194	.073074	.077000	.080970	.084982	.093124	.101409
	.30	.052178	.055736	.059353	.063026	.066754	.070535	.074366	.078245	.082171	.086141	.090153	.098295	.106580
	.20	.057350	.060907	.064524	.068197	.071925	.075706	.079537	.083417	.087343	.091313	.095325	.103466	.111752
	.10	.062521	.066079	.069695	.073369	.077097	.080877	.084708	.088588	.092514	.096484	.100496	.108638	.116923
	0.00	.067692	.071250	.074867	.078540	.082268	.086049	.089880	.093759	.097685	.101655	.105667	.113809	.122095
	-.10	.072864	.076421	.080038	.083711	.087439	.091220	.095051	.098931	.102857	.106827	.110839	.118981	.127266
	-.20	.078035	.081593	.085209	.088883	.092611	.096391	.100223	.104102	.108028	.111998	.116010	.124152	.132437
	-.30	.083206	.086764	.090381	.094054	.097782	.101563	.105394	.109273	.113199	.117169	.121181	.129323	.137609
	-.40	.088378	.091936	.095552	.099225	.102953	.106734	.110565	.114445	.118371	.122341	.126353	.134495	.142780
25	.40	.044314	.048073	.051893	.055770	.059702	.063686	.067718	.071795	.075914	.080073	.084269	.092759	.101364
	.30	.049486	.053244	.057064	.060942	.064874	.068857	.072889	.076966	.081086	.085245	.089440	.097930	.106536
	.20	.054657	.058416	.062236	.066113	.070045	.074028	.078060	.082137	.086257	.090416	.094611	.103102	.111707
	.10	.059828	.063587	.067407	.071284	.075216	.079200	.083232	.087309	.091428	.095587	.099783	.108273	.116878
	0.00	.065000	.068759	.072578	.076456	.080388	.084371	.088403	.092480	.096600	.100759	.104954	.113444	.122050
	-.10	.070171	.073930	.077750	.081627	.085559	.089542	.093574	.097652	.101771	.105930	.110126	.118616	.127221
	-.20	.075342	.079101	.082921	.086798	.090730	.094714	.098746	.102823	.106942	.111101	.115297	.123787	.132392
	-.30	.080514	.084273	.088092	.091970	.095902	.099885	.103917	.107994	.112114	.116273	.120468	.128958	.137564
	-.40	.085685	.089444	.093264	.097141	.101073	.105057	.109088	.113166	.117285	.121444	.125640	.134130	.142735
30	.40	.042608	.046510	.050473	.054492	.058564	.062684	.066848	.071053	.075294	.079569	.083875	.092564	.101341
	.30	.047779	.051681	.055644	.059664	.063735	.067855	.072019	.076224	.080466	.084741	.089046	.097736	.106513
	.20	.052950	.056853	.060816	.064835	.068907	.073027	.077191	.081395	.085637	.089912	.094217	.102907	.111684
	.10	.058122	.062024	.065987	.070006	.074078	.078198	.082362	.086567	.090808	.095083	.099389	.108078	.116855
	0.00	.063293	.067195	.071158	.075178	.079249	.083369	.087533	.091738	.095980	.100255	.104560	.113250	.122027
	-.10	.068464	.072367	.076330	.080349	.084421	.088541	.092705	.096909	.101151	.105426	.109731	.118421	.127198
	-.20	.073636	.077538	.081501	.085521	.089592	.093712	.097876	.102081	.106322	.110597	.114903	.123592	.132369
	-.30	.078807	.082709	.086672	.090692	.094764	.098883	.103047	.107252	.111494	.115769	.120074	.128764	.137541
	-.40	.083978	.087881	.091844	.095863	.099935	.104055	.108219	.112423	.116665	.120940	.125246	.133935	.142712

10.0 YEAR HOLDING PERIOD
.150 EQUITY YIELD RATE
.600 LOAN RATIO

INTEREST RATE

TERM YEARS	APPR DEP	5.0	5.5	6.0	6.5	7.0	7.5	8.0	8.5	9.0	9.5	10.0	11.0	12.0
10	.40	.087115	.088887	.090683	.092502	.094346	.096213	.098104	.100018	.101954	.103914	.105896	.109928	.114047
	.30	.092040	.093812	.095608	.097428	.099271	.101138	.103029	.104943	.106880	.108839	.110822	.114853	.118972
	.20	.096966	.098737	.100533	.102353	.104196	.106064	.107954	.109868	.111805	.113765	.115747	.119778	.123897
	.10	.101891	.103662	.105458	.107278	.109122	.110989	.112879	.114793	.116730	.118690	.120672	.124704	.128823
	0.00	.106816	.108588	.110384	.112203	.114047	.115914	.117805	.119718	.121655	.123615	.125597	.129629	.133748
	-.10	.111741	.113513	.115309	.117129	.118972	.120839	.122730	.124644	.126581	.128540	.130522	.134554	.138673
	-.20	.116666	.118438	.120234	.122054	.123897	.125764	.127655	.129569	.131506	.133465	.135448	.139479	.143598
	-.30	.121592	.123363	.125159	.126979	.128822	.130690	.132580	.134494	.136431	.138391	.140373	.144404	.148523
	-.40	.126517	.128289	.130084	.131904	.133748	.135615	.137505	.139419	.141356	.143316	.145298	.149330	.153449
15	.40	.080068	.082219	.084404	.086624	.088878	.091164	.093483	.095833	.098214	.100625	.103066	.108031	.113104
	.30	.084994	.087144	.089330	.091549	.093803	.096089	.098408	.100758	.103139	.105550	.107991	.112956	.118029
	.20	.089919	.092069	.094255	.096475	.098728	.101014	.103333	.105683	.108064	.110476	.112916	.117881	.122954
	.10	.094844	.096995	.099180	.101400	.103653	.105940	.108258	.110609	.112990	.115401	.117841	.122807	.127880
	0.00	.099769	.101920	.104105	.106325	.108578	.110865	.113184	.115534	.117915	.120326	.122766	.127732	.132805
	-.10	.104694	.106845	.109030	.111250	.113504	.115790	.118109	.120459	.122840	.125251	.127692	.132657	.137730
	-.20	.109620	.111770	.113956	.116175	.118429	.120715	.123034	.125384	.127765	.130176	.132617	.137582	.142655
	-.30	.114545	.116695	.118881	.121101	.123354	.125641	.127959	.130309	.132690	.135102	.137542	.142507	.147580
	-.40	.119470	.121621	.123806	.126026	.128279	.130566	.132884	.135235	.137616	.140027	.142467	.147433	.152506
20	.40	.076652	.079007	.081401	.083833	.086302	.088806	.091344	.093915	.096517	.099149	.101809	.107209	.112706
	.30	.081577	.083932	.086326	.088758	.091227	.093731	.096270	.098840	.101442	.104074	.106734	.112114	.117631
	.20	.086502	.088857	.091251	.093683	.096152	.098657	.101195	.103766	.106368	.108999	.111659	.117059	.122556
	.10	.091428	.093782	.096176	.098609	.101078	.103582	.106120	.108691	.111293	.113925	.116585	.121984	.127481
	0.00	.096353	.098708	.101102	.103534	.106003	.108507	.111045	.113616	.116218	.118850	.121510	.126910	.132406
	-.10	.101278	.103633	.106027	.108459	.110928	.113432	.115970	.118541	.121143	.123775	.126435	.131835	.137332
	-.20	.106203	.108558	.110952	.113384	.115853	.118357	.120896	.123466	.126068	.128700	.131360	.136760	.142257
	-.30	.111128	.113483	.115877	.118309	.120778	.123283	.125821	.128392	.130994	.133625	.136286	.141685	.147182
	-.40	.116054	.118408	.120802	.123235	.125704	.128208	.130746	.133317	.135919	.138551	.141211	.146610	.152107
25	.40	.074684	.077172	.079701	.082268	.084873	.087513	.090185	.092889	.095621	.098379	.101163	.106799	.112513
	.30	.079609	.082097	.084626	.087194	.089798	.092438	.095110	.097814	.100546	.103305	.106089	.111724	.117438
	.20	.084534	.087022	.089551	.092119	.094724	.097363	.100036	.102739	.105471	.108230	.111014	.116649	.122364
	.10	.089460	.091947	.094476	.097044	.099649	.102288	.104961	.107664	.110396	.113155	.115939	.121574	.127289
	0.00	.094385	.096873	.099401	.101969	.104574	.107214	.109886	.112589	.115321	.118080	.120864	.126500	.132214
	-.10	.099310	.101798	.104327	.106894	.109499	.112139	.114811	.117515	.120247	.123005	.125789	.131425	.137139
	-.20	.104235	.106723	.109252	.111820	.114424	.117064	.119736	.122440	.125172	.127931	.130715	.136350	.142064
	-.30	.109160	.111648	.114177	.116745	.119350	.121989	.124662	.127365	.130097	.132856	.135640	.141275	.146990
	-.40	.114086	.116573	.119102	.121670	.124275	.126914	.129587	.132290	.135022	.137781	.140565	.146200	.151915
30	.40	.073437	.076021	.078646	.081309	.084008	.086740	.089503	.092293	.095108	.097947	.100806	.106580	.112414
	.30	.078362	.080946	.083571	.086234	.088934	.091666	.094428	.097218	.100034	.102872	.105732	.111505	.117339
	.20	.083287	.085871	.088496	.091160	.093859	.096591	.099353	.102143	.104959	.107797	.110657	.116430	.122265
	.10	.088212	.090796	.093421	.096085	.098784	.101516	.104278	.107068	.109884	.112723	.115582	.121356	.127190
	0.00	.093138	.095721	.098347	.101010	.103709	.106441	.109204	.111994	.114809	.117648	.120507	.126281	.132115
	-.10	.098063	.100647	.103272	.105935	.108634	.111366	.114129	.116919	.119734	.122573	.125432	.131206	.137040
	-.20	.102988	.105572	.108197	.110860	.113560	.116292	.119054	.121844	.124660	.127498	.130358	.136131	.141965
	-.30	.107913	.110497	.113122	.115786	.118485	.121217	.123979	.126769	.129585	.132423	.135283	.141056	.146891
	-.40	.112838	.115422	.118047	.120711	.123410	.126142	.128904	.131695	.134510	.137349	.140208	.145982	.151816

10.0 YEAR HOLDING PERIOD
.150 EQUITY YIELD RATE
.667 LOAN RATIO

INTEREST RATE

TERM YEARS	APPR DEP	5.0	5.5	6.0	6.5	7.0	7.5	8.0	8.5	9.0	9.5	10.0	11.0	12.0
10	.40	.082317	.084285	.086281	.088303	.090351	.092426	.094526	.096653	.098805	.100982	.103185	.107664	.112241
	.30	.087242	.089210	.091206	.093228	.095276	.097351	.099452	.101578	.103730	.105908	.108110	.112560	.117166
	.20	.092167	.094136	.096131	.098153	.100201	.102276	.104377	.106503	.108655	.110833	.113035	.117515	.122092
	.10	.097092	.099061	.101056	.103078	.105127	.107201	.109302	.111428	.113581	.115758	.117961	.122440	.127017
	0.00	.102017	.103986	.105981	.108003	.110052	.112127	.114227	.116354	.118506	.120683	.122886	.127365	.131942
	-.10	.106943	.108911	.110907	.112929	.114977	.117052	.119152	.121279	.123431	.125608	.127811	.132290	.136867
	-.20	.111868	.113836	.115832	.117854	.119902	.121977	.124078	.126204	.128356	.130534	.132736	.137216	.141792
	-.30	.116793	.118762	.120757	.122779	.124827	.126902	.129003	.131129	.133281	.135459	.137661	.142141	.146718
	-.40	.121718	.123687	.125682	.127704	.129753	.131827	.133928	.136054	.138207	.140384	.142587	.147066	.151643
15	.40	.074487	.076676	.079305	.081771	.084275	.086816	.089392	.092003	.094649	.097328	.100039	.105557	.111193
	.30	.079412	.081802	.084230	.086696	.089200	.091741	.094317	.096928	.099574	.102253	.104965	.110482	.116119
	.20	.084337	.086727	.089155	.091622	.094125	.096666	.099242	.101854	.104499	.107178	.109890	.115407	.121044
	.10	.089263	.091652	.094080	.096547	.099051	.101591	.104167	.106779	.109424	.112104	.114815	.120332	.125969
	0.00	.094188	.096557	.099006	.101472	.103976	.106516	.109093	.111704	.114350	.117029	.119740	.125257	.130894
	-.10	.099113	.101502	.103931	.106397	.108901	.111442	.114018	.116629	.119275	.121954	.124665	.130183	.135819
	-.20	.104038	.106428	.108856	.111322	.113826	.116367	.118943	.121554	.124200	.126879	.129591	.135108	.140745
	-.30	.108963	.111353	.113781	.116248	.118751	.121292	.123868	.126480	.129125	.131804	.134516	.140033	.145670
	-.40	.113889	.116278	.118706	.121173	.123677	.126217	.128793	.131405	.134051	.136730	.139441	.144958	.150595
20	.40	.070691	.073307	.075967	.078670	.081413	.084196	.087016	.089872	.092763	.095688	.098643	.104643	.110751
	.30	.075616	.078232	.080893	.083595	.086338	.089121	.091941	.094798	.097689	.100613	.103569	.109568	.115676
	.20	.080541	.083158	.085818	.088520	.091263	.094046	.096866	.099723	.102614	.105538	.108494	.114494	.120601
	.10	.085467	.088083	.090743	.093445	.096189	.098971	.101792	.104648	.107539	.110463	.113419	.119419	.125526
	0.00	.090392	.093008	.095668	.098371	.101114	.103896	.106717	.109573	.112464	.115388	.118344	.124344	.130452
	-.10	.095317	.097933	.100593	.103296	.106039	.108822	.111642	.114498	.117390	.120314	.123269	.129269	.135377
	-.20	.100242	.102858	.105519	.108221	.110964	.113747	.116567	.119424	.122315	.125239	.128195	.134194	.140302
	-.30	.105167	.107784	.110444	.113146	.115890	.118672	.121492	.124349	.127240	.130164	.133120	.139120	.145227
	-.40	.110093	.112709	.115369	.118071	.120815	.123597	.126418	.129274	.132165	.135089	.138045	.144045	.150152
25	.40	.068504	.071268	.074078	.076931	.079826	.082759	.085728	.088732	.091767	.094833	.097926	.104187	.110537
	.30	.073429	.076194	.079003	.081857	.084751	.087684	.090653	.093657	.096692	.099758	.102851	.109113	.115452
	.20	.078355	.081119	.083929	.086782	.089676	.092609	.095578	.098582	.101618	.104683	.107776	.114038	.120377
	.10	.083280	.086044	.088854	.091707	.094601	.097534	.100504	.103507	.106543	.109608	.112701	.118963	.125312
	0.00	.088205	.090969	.093779	.096632	.099526	.102459	.105429	.108432	.111468	.114533	.117627	.123888	.130238
	-.10	.093130	.095894	.098704	.101557	.104452	.107385	.110354	.113358	.116393	.119459	.122552	.128814	.135163
	-.20	.098055	.100820	.103629	.106483	.109377	.112310	.115279	.118283	.121318	.124384	.127477	.133739	.140088
	-.30	.102981	.105745	.108555	.111408	.114302	.117235	.120204	.123208	.126244	.129309	.132402	.138664	.145013
	-.40	.107906	.110670	.113480	.116333	.119227	.122160	.125130	.128133	.131169	.134234	.137327	.143589	.149939
30	.40	.067118	.069989	.072906	.075866	.078865	.081900	.084970	.088070	.091198	.094352	.097529	.103944	.110427
	.30	.072044	.074915	.077831	.080791	.083790	.086825	.089895	.092995	.096123	.099277	.102454	.108870	.115352
	.20	.076969	.079840	.082757	.085716	.088715	.091751	.094820	.097920	.101048	.104202	.107380	.113795	.120277
	.10	.081894	.084765	.087682	.090641	.093640	.096676	.099745	.102845	.105974	.109128	.112305	.118720	.125203
	0.00	.086819	.089690	.092607	.095566	.098565	.101601	.104670	.107771	.110899	.114053	.117230	.123645	.130128
	-.10	.091744	.094615	.097532	.100492	.103491	.106526	.109596	.112696	.115824	.118978	.122155	.128570	.135053
	-.20	.096670	.099541	.102457	.105417	.108416	.111451	.114521	.117621	.120749	.123903	.127080	.133496	.139978
	-.30	.101595	.104466	.107383	.110342	.113341	.116377	.119446	.122546	.125675	.128829	.132006	.138421	.144903
	-.40	.106520	.109391	.112308	.115267	.118266	.121302	.124371	.127471	.130600	.133754	.136931	.143346	.149829

10.0 YEAR HOLDING PERIOD
.150 EQUITY YIELD RATE
.700 LOAN RATIO

INTEREST RATE

TERM YEARS	APPR DEP	5.0	5.5	6.0	6.5	7.0	7.5	8.0	8.5	9.0	9.5	10.0	11.0	12.0
10	.40	.079918	.081985	.084080	.086203	.088354	.090532	.092738	.094971	.097230	.099517	.101829	.106533	.111338
	.30	.084843	.086990	.089005	.091128	.093279	.095457	.097663	.099896	.102156	.104442	.106755	.111458	.116264
	.20	.089768	.091835	.093930	.096053	.098204	.100383	.102588	.104821	.107081	.109367	.111680	.116383	.121189
	.10	.094693	.096760	.098856	.100979	.103129	.105308	.107514	.109746	.112006	.114292	.116605	.121308	.126114
	0.00	.099619	.101686	.103781	.105904	.108055	.110233	.112439	.114672	.116931	.119218	.121530	.126234	.131039
	-.10	.104544	.106611	.108706	.110829	.112980	.115158	.117364	.119597	.121856	.124143	.126455	.131159	.135964
	-.20	.109469	.111536	.113631	.115754	.117905	.120083	.122289	.124522	.126782	.129068	.131381	.136084	.140890
	-.30	.114394	.116461	.118556	.120679	.122830	.125009	.127214	.129447	.131707	.133993	.136306	.141009	.145815
	-.40	.119319	.121386	.123482	.125605	.127756	.129934	.132140	.134372	.136632	.138918	.141231	.145934	.150740
15	.40	.071697	.074206	.076755	.079345	.081974	.084642	.087347	.090089	.092867	.095679	.098527	.104320	.110238
	.30	.076622	.079131	.081681	.084270	.086899	.089567	.092272	.095014	.097792	.100605	.103452	.109245	.115163
	.20	.081547	.084056	.086606	.089195	.091824	.094492	.097197	.099939	.102717	.105530	.108377	.114170	.120089
	.10	.086472	.088981	.091531	.094121	.096750	.099417	.102122	.104864	.107642	.110455	.113302	.119095	.125014
	0.00	.091397	.093906	.096456	.099046	.101675	.104342	.107048	.109789	.112567	.115380	.118227	.124020	.129939
	-.10	.096323	.098832	.101381	.103971	.106600	.109268	.111973	.114715	.117493	.120306	.123153	.128946	.134864
	-.20	.101248	.103757	.106307	.108896	.111525	.114193	.116898	.119640	.122418	.125231	.128078	.133871	.139789
	-.30	.106173	.108682	.111232	.113822	.116451	.119118	.121823	.124565	.127343	.130156	.133003	.138796	.144715
	-.40	.111098	.113607	.116157	.118747	.121376	.124043	.126748	.129490	.132268	.135031	.137928	.143721	.149640
20	.40	.067711	.070458	.073251	.076089	.078969	.081891	.084852	.087851	.090887	.093957	.097061	.103360	.109773
	.30	.072636	.075383	.078176	.081014	.083894	.086816	.089777	.092776	.095812	.098832	.101986	.108286	.114699
	.20	.077561	.080308	.083101	.085939	.088819	.091741	.094702	.097702	.100737	.103808	.106911	.113211	.119624
	.10	.082486	.085234	.088027	.090864	.093745	.096666	.099628	.102627	.105663	.108733	.111836	.118136	.124549
	0.00	.087412	.090159	.092952	.095789	.098670	.101592	.104553	.107552	.110588	.113658	.116762	.123061	.129474
	-.10	.092337	.095084	.097877	.100715	.103595	.106517	.109478	.112477	.115513	.118583	.121687	.127986	.134399
	-.20	.097262	.100009	.102802	.105640	.108520	.111442	.114403	.117403	.120438	.123509	.126612	.132912	.139325
	-.30	.102187	.104934	.107728	.110565	.113446	.116367	.119328	.122328	.125363	.128434	.131537	.137837	.144250
	-.40	.107112	.109860	.112653	.115490	.118371	.121292	.124254	.127253	.130289	.133359	.136462	.142762	.149175
25	.40	.065415	.068317	.071267	.074263	.077302	.080382	.083500	.086653	.089841	.093059	.096307	.102882	.109549
	.30	.070340	.073242	.076193	.079188	.082227	.085307	.088425	.091579	.094766	.097985	.101233	.107807	.114474
	.20	.075265	.078168	.081118	.084114	.087153	.090232	.093350	.096504	.099691	.102910	.106158	.112732	.119399
	.10	.080190	.083093	.086043	.089039	.092078	.095157	.098275	.101429	.104616	.107835	.111083	.117658	.124324
	0.00	.085116	.088018	.090968	.093964	.097003	.100083	.103200	.106354	.109542	.112760	.116008	.122583	.129250
	-.10	.090041	.092943	.095894	.098889	.101928	.105008	.108126	.111279	.114467	.117686	.120933	.127508	.134175
	-.20	.094966	.097868	.100819	.103815	.106853	.109933	.113051	.116204	.119392	.122611	.125859	.132433	.139100
	-.30	.099891	.102794	.105744	.108740	.111779	.114858	.117976	.121130	.124317	.127536	.130784	.137358	.144025
	-.40	.104816	.107719	.110669	.113665	.116704	.119783	.122901	.126055	.129242	.132461	.135709	.142284	.148950
30	.40	.063960	.066974	.070037	.073144	.076293	.079481	.082703	.085958	.089243	.092555	.095891	.102627	.109433
	.30	.068885	.071899	.074962	.078069	.081218	.084406	.087629	.090884	.094168	.097480	.100816	.107552	.114359
	.20	.073810	.076825	.079887	.082995	.086144	.089331	.092554	.095809	.099094	.102405	.105741	.112477	.119284
	.10	.078735	.081750	.084812	.087920	.091069	.094256	.097479	.100734	.104019	.107331	.110667	.117402	.124209
	0.00	.083660	.086675	.089738	.092845	.095994	.099181	.102404	.105659	.108944	.112256	.115592	.122328	.129134
	-.10	.088586	.091600	.094663	.097770	.100919	.104107	.107329	.110585	.113869	.117181	.120517	.127253	.134059
	-.20	.093511	.096525	.099588	.102695	.105844	.109032	.112255	.115510	.118794	.122106	.125442	.132178	.138985
	-.30	.098436	.101451	.104513	.107621	.110770	.113957	.117180	.120435	.123720	.127031	.130367	.137103	.143910
	-.40	.103361	.106376	.109438	.112546	.115695	.118882	.122105	.125360	.128645	.131957	.135293	.142028	.148835

10.0 YEAR HOLDING PERIOD
.150 EQUITY YIELD RATE
.750 LOAN RATIO

INTEREST RATE

TERM YEARS	APPR DEP	5.0	5.5	6.0	6.5	7.0	7.5	8.0	8.5	9.0	9.5	10.0	11.0	12.0
10	.40	.076319	.078534	.080779	.083053	.085358	.087692	.090055	.092447	.094868	.097318	.099796	.104835	.109984
	.30	.081244	.083459	.085704	.087979	.090283	.092617	.094980	.097372	.099794	.102243	.104721	.109760	.114909
	.20	.086170	.088384	.090629	.092904	.095208	.097542	.099905	.102298	.104719	.107168	.109646	.114686	.119834
	.10	.091095	.093309	.095554	.097829	.100133	.102467	.104831	.107223	.109644	.112094	.114571	.119611	.124760
	0.00	.096020	.098235	.100480	.102754	.105059	.107393	.109756	.112148	.114569	.117019	.119497	.124536	.129685
	-.10	.100945	.103160	.105405	.107679	.109984	.112318	.114681	.117073	.119494	.121944	.124422	.129461	.134610
	-.20	.105870	.108085	.110330	.112605	.114909	.117243	.119606	.121998	.124420	.126869	.129347	.134386	.139535
	-.30	.110796	.113010	.115255	.117530	.119834	.122168	.124531	.126924	.129345	.131794	.134272	.139312	.144460
	-.40	.115721	.117935	.120180	.122455	.124759	.127093	.129457	.131849	.134270	.136720	.139197	.144237	.149386
15	.40	.067511	.070199	.072931	.075705	.078522	.081380	.084279	.087216	.090193	.093207	.096257	.102464	.108805
	.30	.072436	.075124	.077856	.080631	.083447	.086305	.089204	.092142	.095118	.098132	.101182	.107389	.113730
	.20	.077361	.080049	.082781	.085556	.088373	.091231	.094129	.097067	.100043	.103057	.106108	.112314	.118655
	.10	.082286	.084975	.087706	.090481	.093298	.096156	.099054	.101992	.104968	.107982	.111033	.117240	.123581
	0.00	.087212	.089900	.092632	.095406	.098223	.101081	.103979	.106917	.109894	.112907	.115958	.122165	.128506
	-.10	.092137	.094825	.097557	.100332	.103148	.106006	.108905	.111842	.114819	.117833	.120883	.127090	.133431
	-.20	.097062	.099750	.102482	.105257	.108074	.110932	.113830	.116768	.119744	.122758	.125808	.132015	.138356
	-.30	.101987	.104675	.107407	.110182	.112999	.115857	.118755	.121693	.124669	.127683	.130734	.136940	.143282
	-.40	.106912	.109601	.112332	.115107	.117924	.120782	.123660	.126618	.129594	.132608	.135659	.141866	.148207
20	.40	.063240	.066184	.069176	.072216	.075303	.078433	.081606	.084819	.088072	.091361	.094687	.101436	.108307
	.30	.068165	.071109	.074101	.077142	.080228	.083358	.086531	.089744	.092997	.096287	.099612	.106361	.113232
	.20	.073091	.076034	.079027	.082067	.085153	.088283	.091456	.094670	.097922	.101212	.104537	.111287	.118158
	.10	.078016	.080959	.083952	.086992	.090078	.093209	.096381	.099595	.102847	.106137	.109462	.116212	.123083
	0.00	.082941	.085884	.088877	.091917	.095003	.098134	.101307	.104520	.107773	.111062	.114387	.121137	.128008
	-.10	.087866	.090810	.093802	.096842	.099929	.103059	.106232	.109445	.112698	.115987	.119313	.126062	.132933
	-.20	.092791	.095735	.098727	.101768	.104854	.107984	.111157	.114371	.117623	.120913	.124238	.130987	.137858
	-.30	.097717	.100660	.103653	.106693	.109779	.112909	.116082	.119296	.122548	.125838	.129163	.135913	.142784
	-.40	.102642	.105585	.108578	.111618	.114704	.117835	.121007	.124221	.127473	.130763	.134088	.140838	.147709
25	.40	.060780	.063890	.067051	.070261	.073517	.076816	.080157	.083536	.086951	.090400	.093879	.100924	.108067
	.30	.065705	.068815	.071976	.075186	.078442	.081741	.085082	.088461	.091876	.095325	.098805	.105849	.112992
	.20	.070631	.073740	.076901	.080111	.083367	.086667	.090007	.093386	.096801	.100250	.103730	.110774	.117917
	.10	.075556	.078666	.081827	.085036	.088292	.091592	.094932	.098311	.101727	.105175	.108655	.115699	.122842
	0.00	.080481	.083591	.086752	.089962	.093218	.096517	.099858	.103237	.106652	.110100	.113580	.120625	.127767
	-.10	.085406	.088516	.091677	.094887	.098143	.101442	.104783	.108162	.111577	.115026	.118505	.125550	.132693
	-.20	.090331	.093441	.096602	.099812	.103068	.106367	.109708	.113087	.116502	.119951	.123431	.130475	.137618
	-.30	.095257	.098366	.101527	.104737	.107993	.111293	.114633	.118012	.121427	.124876	.128356	.135400	.142543
	-.40	.100182	.103292	.106453	.109662	.112918	.116218	.119558	.122937	.126353	.129801	.133281	.140325	.147468
30	.40	.059221	.062451	.065732	.069062	.072436	.075851	.079304	.082791	.086311	.089859	.093433	.100650	.107943
	.30	.064146	.067376	.070658	.073987	.077361	.080776	.084229	.087716	.091236	.094784	.098358	.105575	.112858
	.20	.069071	.072301	.075583	.078912	.082286	.085701	.089154	.092642	.096161	.099709	.103284	.110501	.117793
	.10	.073997	.077227	.080508	.083837	.087211	.090626	.094079	.097567	.101086	.104634	.108209	.115426	.122719
	0.00	.078922	.082152	.085433	.088763	.092136	.095551	.099004	.102492	.106011	.109560	.113134	.120351	.127644
	-.10	.083847	.087077	.090358	.093688	.097062	.100477	.103930	.107417	.110937	.114485	.118059	.125276	.132559
	-.20	.088772	.092002	.095284	.098613	.101987	.105402	.108855	.112343	.115862	.119410	.122984	.130201	.137494
	-.30	.093698	.096927	.100209	.103538	.106912	.110327	.113780	.117268	.120787	.124335	.127910	.135127	.142419
	-.40	.098623	.101853	.105134	.108463	.111837	.115252	.118705	.122193	.125712	.129261	.132835	.140052	.147345

249

10.0 YEAR HOLDING PERIOD
.150 EQUITY YIELD RATE
.800 LOAN RATIO

INTEREST RATE

TERM YEARS	APPR DEP	5.0	5.5	6.0	6.5	7.0	7.5	8.0	8.5	9.0	9.5	10.0	11.0	12.0
10	.40	.072720	.075083	.077477	.079904	.082362	.084851	.087372	.089924	.092506	.095119	.097762	.103138	.108630
	.30	.077646	.080008	.082402	.084829	.087287	.089776	.092297	.094849	.097431	.100044	.102697	.108063	.113555
	.20	.082571	.084933	.087328	.089754	.092212	.094702	.097222	.099774	.102357	.104970	.107613	.112988	.118480
	.10	.087496	.089858	.092253	.094679	.097137	.099627	.102148	.104699	.107282	.109895	.112538	.117913	.123405
	0.00	.092421	.094784	.097178	.099604	.102062	.104552	.107073	.109625	.112207	.114820	.117463	.122838	.128330
	-.10	.097346	.099709	.102103	.104530	.106988	.109477	.111998	.114550	.117132	.119745	.122388	.127764	.133256
	-.20	.102272	.104634	.107028	.109455	.111913	.114402	.116923	.119475	.122058	.124670	.127313	.132689	.138181
	-.30	.107197	.109559	.111954	.114380	.116838	.119328	.121848	.124400	.126983	.129596	.132239	.137614	.143106
	-.40	.112122	.114484	.116879	.119305	.121763	.124253	.126774	.129325	.131908	.134521	.137164	.142539	.148031
15	.40	.063325	.066192	.069106	.072066	.075070	.078119	.081211	.084344	.087519	.090734	.093988	.100608	.107372
	.30	.068250	.071117	.074031	.076991	.079996	.083044	.086136	.089269	.092444	.095659	.098913	.105533	.112297
	.20	.073175	.076043	.078957	.081916	.084921	.087969	.091061	.094195	.097369	.100584	.103838	.110459	.117223
	.10	.078100	.080968	.083882	.086842	.089846	.092895	.095986	.099120	.102295	.105509	.108763	.115384	.122148
	0.00	.083026	.085893	.088807	.091767	.094771	.097820	.100911	.104045	.107220	.110435	.113688	.120309	.127073
	-.10	.087951	.090818	.093732	.096692	.099697	.102745	.105837	.108970	.112145	.115360	.118614	.125234	.131998
	-.20	.092876	.095743	.098657	.101617	.104622	.107670	.110762	.113896	.117070	.120285	.123539	.130159	.136924
	-.30	.097801	.100669	.103583	.106542	.109547	.112595	.115687	.118821	.121995	.125210	.128464	.135085	.141849
	-.40	.102727	.105594	.108508	.111468	.114472	.117521	.120612	.123746	.126921	.130135	.133389	.140010	.146774
20	.40	.058770	.061909	.065101	.068344	.071636	.074975	.078360	.081787	.085257	.088766	.092312	.099512	.106841
	.30	.063695	.066834	.070027	.073269	.076561	.079900	.083285	.086712	.090182	.093691	.097238	.104437	.111766
	.20	.068620	.071760	.074952	.078195	.081487	.084826	.088210	.091638	.095107	.098616	.102163	.109362	.116692
	.10	.073545	.076685	.079877	.083120	.086412	.089751	.093135	.096563	.100032	.103541	.107088	.114288	.121617
	0.00	.078470	.081610	.084802	.088045	.091337	.094676	.098060	.101488	.104957	.108466	.112013	.119213	.126542
	-.10	.083396	.086535	.089727	.092970	.096262	.099601	.102986	.106413	.109883	.113392	.116938	.124138	.131467
	-.20	.088321	.091460	.094653	.097896	.101187	.104526	.107911	.111339	.114808	.118317	.121864	.129063	.136392
	-.30	.093246	.096386	.099578	.102821	.106113	.109452	.112836	.116264	.119733	.123242	.126789	.133988	.141318
	-.40	.098171	.101311	.104503	.107746	.111038	.114377	.117761	.121189	.124658	.128167	.131714	.138914	.146243
25	.40	.056146	.059463	.062834	.066258	.069731	.073251	.076814	.080418	.084061	.087740	.091451	.098965	.105585
	.30	.061071	.064388	.067760	.071183	.074656	.078176	.081739	.085343	.088986	.092665	.096377	.103891	.111510
	.20	.065996	.069313	.072685	.076109	.079582	.083101	.086664	.090269	.093911	.097590	.101302	.108816	.116435
	.10	.070921	.074238	.077610	.081034	.084507	.088026	.091590	.095194	.098837	.102515	.106227	.113741	.121360
	0.00	.075846	.079163	.082535	.085959	.089432	.092952	.096515	.100119	.103762	.107440	.111152	.118666	.126285
	-.10	.080772	.084089	.087460	.090884	.094357	.097877	.101440	.105044	.108687	.112366	.116077	.123591	.131211
	-.20	.085697	.089014	.092386	.095809	.099282	.102802	.106365	.109970	.113612	.117291	.121003	.128517	.136136
	-.30	.090622	.093939	.097311	.100735	.104208	.107727	.111290	.114895	.118537	.122216	.125928	.133442	.141061
	-.40	.095547	.098864	.102236	.105660	.109133	.112652	.116216	.119820	.123463	.127141	.130853	.138367	.145986
30	.40	.054483	.057928	.061428	.064979	.068578	.072221	.075904	.079624	.083378	.087163	.090975	.098674	.106453
	.30	.059408	.062853	.066353	.069904	.073503	.077146	.080829	.084549	.088303	.092088	.095901	.103599	.111378
	.20	.064333	.067778	.071278	.074830	.078428	.082071	.085754	.089474	.093229	.097013	.100826	.108524	.116303
	.10	.069258	.072703	.076204	.079755	.083354	.086996	.090680	.094400	.098154	.101938	.105751	.113449	.121228
	0.00	.074183	.077629	.081129	.084680	.088279	.091922	.095605	.099325	.103079	.106864	.110676	.118374	.126153
	-.10	.079109	.082554	.086054	.089605	.093204	.096847	.100530	.104250	.108004	.111789	.115602	.123300	.131079
	-.20	.084034	.087479	.090979	.094530	.098129	.101772	.105455	.109175	.112929	.116714	.120527	.128225	.136004
	-.30	.088959	.092404	.095904	.099456	.103055	.106697	.110380	.114101	.117855	.121639	.125452	.133150	.140929
	-.40	.093884	.097329	.100830	.104381	.107980	.111622	.115306	.119026	.122780	.126565	.130377	.138075	.145854

10.0 YEAR HOLDING PERIOD
.150 EQUITY YIELD RATE
.900 LOAN RATIO

INTEREST RATE

TERM YEARS	APPR DEP	5.0	5.5	6.0	6.5	7.0	7.5	8.0	8.5	9.0	9.5	10.0	11.0	12.0
10	.40	.065523	.061181	.070874	.073604	.076369	.079170	.082006	.084877	.087782	.090722	.093695	.099742	.105921
	.30	.070448	.073106	.075800	.078529	.081295	.084095	.086931	.089802	.092707	.095647	.098620	.104668	.110846
	.20	.075373	.078031	.080725	.083455	.086220	.089021	.091857	.094727	.097633	.100572	.103555	.109593	.115771
	.10	.080299	.082956	.085650	.088380	.091145	.093946	.096782	.099652	.102558	.105497	.108471	.114518	.120697
	0.00	.085224	.087882	.090575	.093305	.096070	.098871	.101707	.104578	.107483	.110423	.113396	.119443	.125622
	-.10	.090149	.092807	.095500	.098230	.100996	.103796	.106632	.109503	.112408	.115348	.118321	.124368	.130547
	-.20	.095074	.097732	.100426	.103155	.105921	.108721	.111557	.114428	.117333	.120273	.123246	.129294	.135472
	-.30	.100000	.102657	.105351	.108081	.110846	.113647	.116483	.119353	.122259	.125198	.128172	.134219	.140397
	-.40	.104925	.107582	.110276	.113006	.115771	.118572	.121408	.124279	.127184	.130123	.133097	.139144	.145323
15	.40	.054953	.058179	.061457	.064787	.068167	.071597	.075075	.078600	.082171	.085788	.089449	.096897	.104506
	.30	.059878	.063104	.066382	.069712	.073092	.076522	.080000	.083525	.087097	.090713	.094374	.101822	.109432
	.20	.064803	.068029	.071307	.074637	.078017	.081447	.084925	.088450	.092022	.095639	.099299	.106747	.114357
	.10	.069729	.072954	.076233	.079562	.082943	.086372	.089850	.093376	.096947	.100564	.104224	.111673	.119282
	0.00	.074654	.077880	.081158	.084488	.087868	.091297	.094775	.098301	.101872	.105489	.109150	.116598	.124207
	-.10	.079579	.082805	.086083	.089413	.092793	.096223	.099701	.103226	.106798	.110414	.114075	.121523	.129132
	-.20	.084504	.087730	.091008	.094338	.097718	.101148	.104626	.108151	.111723	.115339	.119000	.126448	.134058
	-.30	.089430	.092655	.095934	.099263	.102643	.106073	.109551	.113076	.116648	.120265	.123925	.131373	.138983
	-.40	.094355	.097581	.100859	.104188	.107569	.110998	.114476	.118002	.121573	.125190	.128850	.136299	.143908
20	.40	.049828	.053360	.056952	.060600	.064303	.068060	.071867	.075723	.079626	.083574	.087564	.095664	.103909
	.30	.054754	.058286	.061877	.065525	.069228	.072985	.076792	.080648	.084551	.088499	.092489	.100554	.108834
	.20	.059679	.063211	.066802	.070450	.074154	.077910	.081717	.085573	.089477	.093424	.097414	.105514	.113759
	.10	.064604	.068136	.071727	.075376	.079079	.082835	.086643	.090499	.094402	.098350	.102340	.110439	.118684
	0.00	.069529	.073061	.076652	.080301	.084004	.087761	.091568	.095424	.099327	.103275	.107265	.115364	.123610
	-.10	.074454	.077986	.081578	.085226	.088929	.092686	.096493	.100349	.104252	.108200	.112190	.120290	.128535
	-.20	.079380	.082912	.086503	.090151	.093855	.097611	.101418	.105275	.109178	.113125	.117115	.125215	.133460
	-.30	.084305	.087837	.091428	.095076	.098780	.102536	.106344	.110200	.114103	.118050	.122040	.130140	.138385
	-.40	.089230	.092762	.096353	.100000	.103705	.107461	.111269	.115125	.119028	.122976	.126966	.135065	.143310
25	.40	.046876	.050608	.054401	.058253	.062160	.066120	.070128	.074183	.078281	.082420	.086595	.095049	.103620
	.30	.051802	.055533	.059327	.063178	.067085	.071045	.075054	.079108	.083206	.087345	.091521	.099974	.108545
	.20	.056727	.060458	.064252	.068103	.072011	.075970	.079979	.084034	.088132	.092270	.096446	.104899	.113471
	.10	.061652	.065384	.069177	.073029	.076936	.080895	.084904	.088959	.093057	.097195	.101371	.109824	.118396
	0.00	.066577	.070309	.074102	.077954	.081861	.085820	.089829	.093884	.097982	.102120	.106296	.114749	.123321
	-.10	.071502	.075234	.079027	.082879	.086786	.090746	.094754	.098809	.102907	.107046	.111221	.119675	.128246
	-.20	.076428	.080159	.083953	.087804	.091711	.095671	.099680	.103734	.107832	.111971	.116147	.124600	.133171
	-.30	.081353	.085085	.088878	.092729	.096637	.100596	.104605	.108660	.112758	.116896	.121072	.129525	.138097
	-.40	.086278	.090010	.093803	.097655	.101562	.105521	.109530	.113585	.117683	.121821	.125997	.134450	.143022
30	.40	.045005	.048881	.052819	.056814	.060863	.064961	.069104	.073290	.077513	.081771	.086060	.094720	.103472
	.30	.049931	.053807	.057744	.061739	.065788	.069886	.074030	.078215	.082438	.086696	.090985	.099646	.108397
	.20	.054856	.058732	.062669	.066665	.070713	.074811	.078955	.083140	.087363	.091621	.095910	.104571	.113322
	.10	.059781	.063657	.067595	.071590	.075639	.079737	.083880	.088065	.092289	.096546	.100836	.109496	.118247
	0.00	.064706	.068582	.072520	.076515	.080564	.084662	.088805	.092991	.097214	.101472	.105761	.114421	.123173
	-.10	.069631	.073507	.077445	.081440	.085489	.089587	.093731	.097916	.102139	.106397	.110686	.119346	.128098
	-.20	.074557	.078433	.082370	.086365	.090414	.094512	.098656	.102841	.107064	.111322	.115611	.124272	.133023
	-.30	.079462	.083358	.087295	.091291	.095339	.099437	.103581	.107766	.111989	.116247	.120536	.129197	.137948
	-.40	.084407	.088283	.092221	.096216	.100265	.104363	.108506	.112691	.116915	.121172	.125462	.134122	.142873

10.0 YEAR HOLDING PERIOD
.180 EQUITY YIELD RATE
.600 LOAN RATIO

INTEREST RATE

TERM YEARS	APPR DEP	5.0	5.5	6.0	6.5	7.0	7.5	8.0	8.5	9.0	9.5	10.0	11.0	12.0
10	.40	.105853	.107624	.109420	.111240	.113083	.114951	.116841	.118755	.120692	.122652	.124634	.128565	.132784
	.30	.110104	.111876	.113672	.115491	.117335	.119202	.121093	.123007	.124943	.126903	.128885	.132917	.137036
	.20	.114355	.116127	.117923	.119743	.121586	.123454	.125344	.127258	.129195	.131155	.133137	.137168	.141287
	.10	.118607	.120379	.122175	.123994	.125838	.127705	.129596	.131509	.133446	.135406	.137388	.141509	.145539
	0.00	.122858	.124630	.126426	.128246	.130089	.131956	.133847	.135761	.137698	.139657	.141640	.145571	.149790
	-.10	.127110	.128882	.130677	.132497	.134341	.136208	.138099	.140012	.141949	.143909	.145891	.149323	.154042
	-.20	.131361	.133361	.134929	.136749	.138592	.140459	.142350	.144264	.146201	.148160	.150143	.154174	.158293
	-.30	.135613	.137385	.139180	.141000	.142844	.144711	.146601	.148515	.150452	.152412	.154394	.158426	.162545
	-.40	.139864	.141636	.143432	.145252	.147095	.148962	.150853	.152767	.154704	.156663	.158646	.162577	.166796
15	.40	.097112	.099227	.101377	.103562	.105780	.108031	.110315	.112630	.114976	.117353	.119758	.124555	.129660
	.30	.101363	.103479	.105629	.107813	.110032	.112283	.114566	.116882	.119228	.121604	.124010	.128907	.133912
	.20	.105615	.107730	.109880	.112065	.114283	.116534	.118818	.121133	.123479	.125856	.128261	.133158	.138163
	.10	.109866	.111982	.114132	.116316	.118534	.120786	.123069	.125385	.127731	.130107	.132513	.137410	.142415
	0.00	.114118	.116233	.118383	.120568	.122786	.125037	.127321	.129636	.131982	.134359	.136764	.141661	.146666
	-.10	.118369	.120484	.122635	.124819	.127037	.129289	.131572	.133887	.136234	.138610	.141016	.145913	.150918
	-.20	.122621	.124736	.126886	.129071	.131289	.133540	.135824	.138139	.140485	.142861	.145267	.150164	.155169
	-.30	.126872	.128987	.131138	.133322	.135540	.137792	.140075	.142390	.144737	.147113	.149519	.154415	.159421
	-.40	.131124	.133239	.135389	.137574	.139792	.142043	.144327	.146642	.148988	.151364	.153770	.158567	.163672
20	.40	.092874	.095182	.097530	.099916	.102340	.104800	.107295	.109823	.112383	.114974	.117595	.122917	.128341
	.30	.097126	.099433	.101781	.104168	.106591	.109052	.111546	.114075	.116635	.119226	.121846	.127169	.132592
	.20	.101377	.103685	.106033	.108419	.110843	.113303	.115798	.118326	.120886	.123477	.126097	.131420	.136844
	.10	.105629	.107936	.110284	.112670	.115094	.117555	.120049	.122578	.125138	.127729	.130349	.135672	.141095
	0.00	.109880	.112188	.114535	.116922	.119346	.121806	.124301	.126829	.129389	.131980	.134600	.139923	.145346
	-.10	.114131	.116439	.118787	.121173	.123597	.126057	.128552	.131081	.133641	.136232	.138852	.144174	.149598
	-.20	.118383	.120690	.123038	.125425	.127849	.130309	.132804	.135332	.137892	.140483	.143103	.148426	.153844
	-.30	.122634	.124942	.127290	.129676	.132100	.134560	.137055	.139583	.142144	.144735	.147355	.152577	.158101
	-.40	.126886	.129194	.131541	.133928	.136352	.138812	.141307	.143835	.146395	.148986	.151606	.156329	.162352
25	.40	.090433	.092871	.095352	.097872	.100432	.103028	.105658	.108320	.111013	.113735	.116482	.122050	.127703
	.30	.094685	.097123	.099603	.102124	.104683	.107279	.109909	.112572	.115265	.117986	.120734	.126302	.131955
	.20	.098936	.101374	.103854	.106375	.108935	.111531	.114161	.116823	.119516	.122237	.124985	.130553	.136206
	.10	.103187	.105625	.108106	.110627	.113186	.115782	.118412	.121075	.123768	.126489	.129237	.134805	.140457
	0.00	.107439	.109877	.112357	.114878	.117438	.120034	.122664	.125326	.128019	.130740	.133488	.139056	.144709
	-.10	.111690	.114128	.116609	.119130	.121689	.124285	.126915	.129578	.132271	.134992	.137740	.143308	.148960
	-.20	.115942	.118380	.120860	.123381	.125941	.128536	.131167	.133829	.136522	.139243	.141991	.147559	.153212
	-.30	.120193	.122631	.125112	.127633	.130192	.132788	.135418	.138081	.140774	.143495	.146243	.151811	.157463
	-.40	.124445	.126883	.129363	.131884	.134444	.137039	.139670	.142332	.145025	.147746	.150494	.156062	.161715
30	.40	.088886	.091421	.094000	.096620	.099277	.101969	.104694	.107449	.110231	.113038	.115868	.121588	.127375
	.30	.093137	.095673	.098252	.100871	.103528	.106221	.108945	.111700	.114482	.117289	.120119	.125839	.131627
	.20	.097389	.099924	.102503	.105123	.107780	.110472	.113197	.115951	.118734	.121541	.124371	.130091	.135878
	.10	.101640	.104176	.106755	.109374	.112031	.114724	.117448	.120203	.122985	.125792	.128622	.134342	.140130
	0.00	.105892	.108427	.111006	.113625	.116283	.118975	.121700	.124454	.127236	.130044	.132874	.138594	.144381
	-.10	.110143	.112679	.115258	.117877	.120534	.123226	.125951	.128706	.131488	.134295	.137125	.142845	.148633
	-.20	.114395	.116930	.119509	.122128	.124786	.127478	.130203	.132957	.135739	.138547	.141376	.147096	.152884
	-.30	.118646	.121182	.123760	.126380	.129037	.131729	.134454	.137209	.139991	.142798	.145628	.151348	.157136
	-.40	.122898	.125433	.128012	.130631	.133289	.135981	.138706	.141460	.144242	.147049	.149879	.155599	.161387

10.0 YEAR HOLDING PERIOD
.180 EQUITY YIELD RATE
.667 LOAN RATIO

INTEREST RATE

TERM YEARS	APPR DEP	5.0	5.5	6.0	6.5	7.0	7.5	8.0	8.5	9.0	9.5	10.0	11.0	12.0
10	.40	.099503	.101472	.103467	.105489	.107538	.109612	.111713	.113839	.115991	.118169	.120371	.124851	.129428
	.30	.103755	.105723	.107719	.109741	.111789	.113864	.115964	.118091	.120243	.122420	.124623	.129102	.133679
	.20	.108006	.109975	.111970	.113992	.116040	.118115	.120216	.122342	.124494	.126672	.128874	.133354	.137931
	.10	.112258	.114226	.116222	.118244	.120292	.122367	.124467	.126746	.128746	.130923	.133126	.137605	.142182
	0.00	.116509	.118478	.120473	.122495	.124543	.126618	.128719	.130845	.132997	.135175	.137377	.141857	.145433
	-.10	.120760	.122729	.124724	.126746	.128795	.130870	.132970	.135097	.137249	.139426	.141629	.146108	.150685
	-.20	.125012	.126981	.128976	.130998	.133046	.135121	.137222	.139348	.141500	.143678	.145880	.150360	.154936
	-.30	.129263	.131232	.133227	.135249	.137298	.139372	.141473	.143600	.145752	.147929	.150132	.154611	.159188
	-.40	.133515	.135483	.137479	.139501	.141549	.143624	.145725	.147851	.150003	.152181	.154383	.158863	.163439
15	.40	.089791	.092142	.094531	.096958	.099423	.101924	.104461	.107034	.109641	.112281	.114954	.120395	.125956
	.30	.094043	.096393	.098782	.101209	.103674	.106176	.108713	.111285	.113892	.116553	.119206	.124647	.130208
	.20	.098294	.100645	.103034	.105461	.107926	.110427	.112964	.115537	.118144	.120784	.123457	.128898	.134459
	.10	.102546	.104896	.107285	.109712	.112177	.114678	.117216	.119788	.122395	.125036	.127709	.133149	.138711
	0.00	.106797	.109147	.111537	.113964	.116429	.118930	.121467	.124040	.126647	.129287	.131960	.137401	.142962
	-.10	.111049	.113399	.115788	.118215	.120680	.123181	.125719	.128291	.130898	.133538	.136212	.141652	.147214
	-.20	.115300	.117650	.120040	.122467	.124931	.127433	.129970	.132543	.135150	.137790	.140463	.145904	.151465
	-.30	.119552	.121902	.124291	.126718	.129183	.131684	.134222	.136794	.139401	.142041	.144714	.150155	.155717
	-.40	.123803	.126153	.128542	.130970	.133434	.135936	.138473	.141046	.143652	.146293	.148966	.154407	.159968
20	.40	.085083	.087647	.090255	.092907	.095600	.098334	.101106	.103915	.106760	.109639	.112550	.118464	.124490
	.30	.089334	.091898	.094507	.097159	.099852	.102585	.105357	.108166	.111011	.113890	.116801	.122715	.128741
	.20	.093586	.096150	.098758	.101410	.104103	.106837	.109609	.112418	.115263	.118142	.121053	.126967	.132993
	.10	.097837	.100401	.103010	.105661	.108355	.111088	.113860	.116669	.119514	.122393	.125304	.131218	.137244
	0.00	.102088	.104653	.107261	.109913	.112606	.115340	.118112	.120921	.123766	.126644	.129556	.135470	.141496
	-.10	.106340	.108904	.111513	.114164	.116858	.119591	.122363	.125172	.128017	.130896	.133807	.139721	.145747
	-.20	.110591	.113156	.115764	.118416	.121109	.123843	.126615	.129424	.132269	.135147	.138059	.143973	.149999
	-.30	.114843	.117407	.120016	.122667	.125361	.128094	.130866	.133675	.136520	.139399	.142310	.148224	.154250
	-.40	.119094	.121658	.124267	.126919	.129612	.132345	.135118	.137927	.140771	.143650	.146562	.152476	.158502
25	.40	.082370	.085079	.087835	.090636	.093480	.096364	.099287	.102245	.105237	.108261	.111314	.117501	.123782
	.30	.086622	.089331	.092087	.094868	.097732	.100616	.103538	.106497	.109489	.112512	.115566	.121752	.128033
	.20	.090873	.093582	.096338	.099139	.101983	.104867	.107790	.110748	.113740	.116764	.119817	.126004	.132285
	.10	.095125	.097834	.100590	.103391	.106235	.109119	.112041	.115000	.117992	.121015	.124069	.130255	.136536
	0.00	.099376	.102085	.104841	.107642	.110486	.113370	.116293	.119251	.122243	.125267	.128320	.134507	.140788
	-.10	.103628	.106337	.109093	.111894	.114737	.117622	.120544	.123503	.126495	.129518	.132571	.138758	.145039
	-.20	.107879	.110588	.113344	.116145	.118989	.121873	.124796	.127754	.130746	.133770	.136823	.143010	.149230
	-.30	.112131	.114839	.117596	.120397	.123240	.126125	.129047	.132005	.134998	.138021	.141074	.147261	.153542
	-.40	.116382	.119091	.121847	.124648	.127492	.130376	.133299	.136257	.139249	.142273	.145326	.151512	.157793
30	.40	.080651	.083468	.086334	.089244	.092197	.095188	.098216	.101277	.104368	.107487	.110631	.116987	.123437
	.30	.084903	.087720	.090585	.093496	.096448	.099440	.102467	.105528	.108619	.111738	.114883	.121238	.127669
	.20	.089154	.091971	.094837	.097747	.100700	.103691	.106719	.109779	.112871	.115990	.119134	.125490	.131920
	.10	.093406	.096223	.099088	.101999	.104951	.107943	.110970	.114031	.117122	.120241	.123386	.129741	.136172
	0.00	.097657	.100474	.103340	.106250	.109203	.112194	.115222	.118282	.121374	.124493	.127637	.133993	.140423
	-.10	.101909	.104726	.107591	.110502	.113454	.116446	.119473	.122534	.125625	.128744	.131888	.138244	.144675
	-.20	.106160	.108977	.111843	.114753	.117706	.120697	.123725	.126785	.129877	.132996	.136140	.142496	.148926
	-.30	.110411	.113229	.116094	.119005	.121957	.124949	.127976	.131037	.134128	.137247	.140391	.146747	.153178
	-.40	.114663	.117480	.120346	.123256	.126208	.129200	.132227	.135288	.138379	.141498	.144643	.150998	.157429

10.0 YEAR HOLDING PERIOD
.180 EQUITY YIELD RATE
.700 LOAN RATIO

INTEREST RATE

TERM YEARS	APPR DEP	5.0	5.5	6.0	6.5	7.0	7.5	8.0	8.5	9.0	9.5	10.0	11.0	12.0
10	.40	.096329	.098396	.100491	.102614	.104765	.106943	.109149	.111382	.113642	.115928	.118241	.122944	.127749
	.30	.100580	.102647	.104743	.106866	.109016	.111195	.113401	.115633	.117893	.120179	.122492	.127195	.132001
	.20	.104832	.106899	.108994	.111117	.113268	.115446	.117652	.119885	.122144	.124431	.126743	.131447	.136252
	.10	.109083	.111150	.113246	.115369	.117519	.119698	.121903	.124136	.126396	.128682	.130995	.135698	.140504
	0.00	.113335	.115402	.117497	.119620	.121771	.123949	.126155	.128388	.130647	.132934	.135246	.139950	.144755
	-.10	.117586	.119653	.121748	.123872	.126022	.128201	.130406	.132639	.134899	.137185	.139498	.144201	.149007
	-.20	.121838	.123905	.126000	.128123	.130274	.132452	.134658	.136891	.139150	.141437	.143750	.148453	.153258
	-.30	.126089	.128156	.130251	.132374	.134525	.136704	.138909	.141142	.143402	.145688	.148001	.152704	.157510
	-.40	.130341	.132408	.134503	.136626	.138777	.140955	.143161	.145394	.147653	.149940	.152252	.156956	.161761
15	.40	.086132	.088599	.091108	.093657	.096244	.098871	.101535	.104236	.106973	.109746	.112552	.118265	.124105
	.30	.090383	.092851	.095359	.097908	.100496	.103122	.105787	.108488	.111225	.113997	.116804	.122517	.128356
	.20	.094634	.097102	.099611	.102159	.104747	.107374	.110038	.112739	.115476	.118249	.121055	.126768	.132608
	.10	.098886	.101354	.103862	.106411	.108999	.111625	.114289	.116991	.119728	.122500	.125307	.131020	.136859
	0.00	.103137	.105605	.108114	.110662	.113250	.115877	.118541	.121242	.123979	.126752	.129558	.135271	.141111
	-.10	.107389	.109857	.112365	.114914	.117502	.120128	.122792	.125493	.128231	.131003	.133810	.139523	.145362
	-.20	.111640	.114108	.116617	.119165	.121753	.124380	.127044	.129745	.132482	.135255	.138061	.143774	.149614
	-.30	.115892	.118360	.120868	.123417	.126005	.128631	.131295	.133996	.136734	.139506	.142313	.148026	.153865
	-.40	.120143	.122611	.125120	.127668	.130256	.132883	.135547	.138248	.140985	.143757	.146564	.152277	.158116
20	.40	.081187	.083880	.086619	.089403	.092231	.095101	.098012	.100961	.103948	.106971	.110028	.116238	.122565
	.30	.085439	.088131	.090870	.093655	.096482	.099353	.102263	.105213	.108200	.111223	.114279	.120489	.126816
	.20	.089690	.092383	.095122	.097906	.100734	.103604	.106515	.109464	.112451	.115474	.118531	.124741	.131068
	.10	.093942	.096634	.099373	.102157	.104985	.107856	.110766	.113716	.116703	.119725	.122782	.128992	.135319
	0.00	.098193	.100886	.103625	.106409	.109237	.112107	.115018	.117967	.120954	.123977	.127034	.133244	.139571
	-.10	.102445	.105137	.107876	.110660	.113488	.116358	.119269	.122219	.125206	.128228	.131285	.137495	.143822
	-.20	.106696	.109389	.112128	.114912	.117740	.120610	.123521	.126470	.129457	.132480	.135537	.141746	.148074
	-.30	.110948	.113640	.116379	.119163	.121991	.124861	.127772	.130722	.133709	.136731	.139788	.145998	.152325
	-.40	.115199	.117891	.120631	.123415	.126243	.129113	.132023	.134973	.137960	.140983	.144040	.150249	.156577
25	.40	.078340	.081184	.084078	.087019	.090005	.093033	.096102	.099208	.102350	.105525	.108730	.115226	.121821
	.30	.082591	.085435	.088329	.091270	.094256	.097285	.100353	.103460	.106601	.109776	.112982	.119478	.126073
	.20	.086842	.089687	.092581	.095522	.098508	.101536	.104605	.107711	.110853	.114028	.117233	.123729	.130324
	.10	.091094	.093938	.096832	.099773	.102759	.105788	.108856	.111962	.115104	.118279	.121485	.127981	.134576
	0.00	.095345	.098190	.101084	.104025	.107011	.110039	.113108	.116214	.119356	.122530	.125736	.132232	.138827
	-.10	.099597	.102441	.105335	.108276	.111262	.114291	.117359	.120465	.123607	.126782	.129988	.136484	.143079
	-.20	.103848	.106693	.109587	.112528	.115514	.118542	.121611	.124717	.127859	.131033	.134239	.140735	.147330
	-.30	.108100	.110944	.113838	.116779	.119765	.122794	.125862	.128968	.132110	.135285	.138491	.144987	.151581
	-.40	.112351	.115196	.118089	.121031	.124017	.127045	.130114	.133220	.136362	.139536	.142742	.149238	.155833
30	.40	.076535	.079493	.082501	.085557	.088657	.091798	.094977	.098191	.101437	.104712	.108013	.114687	.121439
	.30	.080786	.083744	.086753	.089809	.092909	.096050	.099229	.102442	.105688	.108963	.112265	.118938	.125690
	.20	.085037	.087996	.091004	.094060	.097160	.100301	.103480	.106694	.109940	.113215	.116516	.123190	.129942
	.10	.089289	.092247	.095256	.098312	.101412	.104553	.107732	.110945	.114191	.117466	.120768	.127441	.134193
	0.00	.093540	.096498	.099507	.102563	.105663	.108804	.111983	.115197	.118443	.121718	.125020	.131692	.138445
	-.10	.097792	.100750	.103759	.106815	.109915	.113056	.116235	.119448	.122694	.125969	.129271	.135944	.142696
	-.20	.102043	.105001	.108010	.111066	.114166	.117307	.120486	.123700	.126945	.130220	.133522	.140195	.146948
	-.30	.106295	.109253	.112261	.115317	.118418	.121559	.124737	.127951	.131197	.134472	.137774	.144447	.151199
	-.40	.110546	.113448	.116513	.119569	.122669	.125810	.128989	.132203	.135448	.138698	.142025	.148698	.155450

10.0 YEAR HOLDING PERIOD
.180 EQUITY YIELD RATE
.750 LOAN RATIO

INTEREST RATE

TERM YEARS	APPR DEP	5.0	5.5	6.0	6.5	7.0	7.5	8.0	8.5	9.0	9.5	10.0	11.0	12.0
10	.40	.091567	.093782	.096027	.098301	.100606	.102940	.105303	.107695	.110116	.112566	.115044	.120083	.125232
	.30	.095819	.098033	.100278	.102553	.104857	.107191	.109554	.111947	.114368	.116817	.119295	.124335	.129483
	.20	.100070	.102285	.104530	.106804	.109109	.111443	.113806	.116198	.118619	.121069	.123547	.128586	.133735
	.10	.104322	.106536	.108781	.111056	.113360	.115694	.118057	.120450	.122871	.125320	.127798	.132838	.137986
	0.00	.108573	.110788	.113032	.115307	.117612	.119946	.122309	.124701	.127122	.129572	.132050	.137089	.142238
	-.10	.112824	.115039	.117284	.119559	.121863	.124197	.126560	.128953	.131374	.133823	.136301	.141340	.146489
	-.20	.117076	.119291	.121535	.123810	.126115	.128449	.130812	.133204	.135625	.138075	.140553	.145592	.150741
	-.30	.121327	.123542	.125787	.128062	.130366	.132700	.135063	.137456	.139877	.142326	.144804	.149843	.154992
	-.40	.125579	.127794	.130038	.132313	.134618	.136951	.139315	.141707	.144128	.146578	.149056	.154095	.159244
15	.40	.080641	.083285	.085973	.088704	.091477	.094291	.097145	.100039	.102972	.105942	.108949	.115070	.121327
	.30	.084893	.087537	.090225	.092955	.095728	.098542	.101397	.104291	.107223	.110194	.113201	.119322	.125578
	.20	.089144	.091788	.094476	.097207	.099980	.102794	.105648	.108542	.111475	.114445	.117452	.123573	.129830
	.10	.093396	.096040	.098728	.101458	.104231	.107045	.109900	.112794	.115726	.118697	.121704	.127825	.134081
	0.00	.097647	.100291	.102979	.105710	.108482	.111296	.114151	.117045	.119978	.122948	.125955	.132076	.138333
	-.10	.101899	.104543	.107230	.109961	.112734	.115548	.118402	.121296	.124229	.127200	.130207	.136328	.142584
	-.20	.106150	.108794	.111482	.114213	.116985	.119799	.122654	.125548	.128481	.131451	.134458	.140579	.146836
	-.30	.110402	.113046	.115733	.118464	.121237	.124051	.126905	.129799	.132732	.135703	.138710	.144831	.151087
	-.40	.114653	.117297	.119985	.122716	.125488	.128302	.131157	.134051	.136984	.139954	.142961	.149082	.155339
20	.40	.075344	.078229	.081163	.084147	.087177	.090252	.093370	.096530	.099731	.102969	.106245	.112898	.119677
	.30	.079596	.082480	.085415	.088398	.091428	.094503	.097623	.100782	.103982	.107221	.110496	.117149	.123929
	.20	.083847	.086732	.089666	.092649	.095679	.098755	.101873	.105033	.108234	.111472	.114748	.121401	.128180
	.10	.088099	.090983	.093918	.096901	.099931	.103006	.106125	.109285	.112485	.115724	.118999	.125652	.132432
	0.00	.092350	.095235	.098169	.101152	.104182	.107257	.110376	.113536	.116737	.119975	.123250	.129904	.136683
	-.10	.096601	.099486	.102421	.105404	.108434	.111509	.114627	.117788	.120988	.124227	.127502	.134155	.140635
	-.20	.100853	.103738	.106672	.109655	.112685	.115760	.118879	.122039	.125240	.128478	.131753	.138407	.145186
	-.30	.105104	.107989	.110924	.113907	.116937	.120012	.123130	.126291	.129491	.132730	.136005	.142658	.149437
	-.40	.109356	.112240	.115175	.118158	.121188	.124263	.127382	.130542	.133743	.136981	.140256	.146981	.153689
25	.40	.072293	.075340	.078441	.081592	.084791	.088036	.091324	.094652	.098018	.101420	.104854	.111814	.118880
	.30	.076544	.079592	.082692	.085844	.089043	.092288	.095575	.098903	.102270	.105671	.109106	.116066	.123132
	.20	.080796	.083843	.086944	.090095	.093294	.096539	.099827	.103155	.106521	.109923	.113357	.120317	.127383
	.10	.085047	.088095	.091195	.094346	.097546	.100790	.104078	.107406	.110772	.114174	.117609	.124569	.131635
	0.00	.089299	.092346	.095447	.098598	.101797	.105042	.108330	.111658	.115024	.118426	.121860	.128820	.135586
	-.10	.093550	.096598	.099698	.102849	.106049	.109293	.112581	.115909	.119275	.122677	.126112	.133072	.140138
	-.20	.097802	.100849	.103950	.107101	.110300	.113545	.116833	.120161	.123527	.126928	.130363	.137323	.144389
	-.30	.102053	.105101	.108201	.111352	.114552	.117796	.121084	.124412	.127778	.131180	.134615	.141575	.148641
	-.40	.106305	.109352	.112453	.115604	.118803	.122048	.125336	.128664	.132030	.135431	.138866	.145826	.152892
30	.40	.070359	.073528	.076752	.080026	.083348	.086713	.090119	.093562	.097040	.100549	.104086	.111236	.118471
	.30	.074610	.077780	.081003	.084277	.087599	.090964	.094370	.097814	.101291	.104800	.108338	.115488	.122722
	.20	.078862	.082031	.085255	.088529	.091850	.095216	.098622	.102065	.105543	.109052	.112589	.119739	.126973
	.10	.083113	.086283	.089506	.092780	.096102	.099467	.102873	.106317	.109794	.113303	.116840	.123989	.131225
	0.00	.087365	.090534	.093758	.097032	.100353	.103719	.107125	.110568	.114046	.117555	.121092	.128242	.135576
	-.10	.091616	.094785	.098009	.101283	.104605	.107970	.111376	.114819	.118297	.121806	.125343	.132493	.139728
	-.20	.095868	.099037	.102261	.105535	.108856	.112222	.115628	.119071	.122549	.126057	.129595	.136745	.143979
	-.30	.100119	.103268	.106512	.109786	.113108	.116473	.119879	.123322	.126800	.130309	.133846	.140996	.148131
	-.40	.104371	.107540	.110763	.114038	.117359	.120725	.124131	.127574	.131051	.134560	.138098	.145248	.152482

255

10.0 YEAR HOLDING PERIOD
.180 EQUITY YIELD RATE
.800 LOAN RATIO

INTEREST RATE

TERM YEARS	APPR DEP	5.0	5.5	6.0	6.5	7.0	7.5	8.0	8.5	9.0	9.5	10.0	11.0	12.0
10	.40	.086805	.089168	.091562	.093988	.096447	.098936	.101457	.104009	.106591	.109204	.111847	.117222	.122715
	.30	.091057	.093419	.095814	.098240	.100698	.103188	.105708	.108260	.110843	.113456	.116099	.121474	.126966
	.20	.095308	.097671	.100065	.102491	.104949	.107439	.109960	.112512	.115094	.117707	.120350	.125725	.131217
	.10	.099560	.101922	.104317	.106743	.109201	.111691	.114211	.116763	.119346	.121958	.124602	.129977	.135469
	0.00	.103811	.106174	.108568	.110994	.113452	.115942	.118463	.121015	.123597	.126210	.128853	.134228	.139720
	-.10	.108063	.110425	.112819	.115246	.117704	.120193	.122714	.125266	.127848	.130461	.133104	.138480	.143972
	-.20	.112314	.114676	.117071	.119497	.121955	.124445	.126966	.129517	.132100	.134713	.137356	.142731	.148223
	-.30	.116566	.118928	.121322	.123749	.126207	.128696	.131217	.133769	.136351	.138964	.141607	.146983	.152475
	-.40	.120817	.123179	.125574	.128000	.130458	.132948	.135469	.138020	.140603	.143216	.145859	.151234	.156726
15	.40	.075151	.077972	.080838	.083751	.086709	.089710	.092755	.095842	.098970	.102139	.105347	.111876	.118549
	.30	.079403	.082223	.085090	.088003	.090960	.093962	.097007	.100094	.103222	.106390	.109598	.116127	.122801
	.20	.083654	.086474	.089341	.092255	.095212	.098213	.101258	.104345	.107473	.110642	.113849	.120378	.127052
	.10	.087906	.090726	.093593	.096506	.099463	.102465	.105510	.108597	.111725	.114893	.118101	.124630	.131304
	0.00	.092157	.094977	.097844	.100757	.103715	.106716	.109761	.112848	.115976	.119145	.122352	.128881	.135555
	-.10	.096408	.099229	.102096	.105008	.107966	.110968	.114013	.117099	.120228	.123396	.126604	.133133	.139806
	-.20	.100660	.103480	.106347	.109260	.112218	.115219	.118264	.121351	.124479	.127648	.130855	.137384	.144058
	-.30	.104911	.107732	.110599	.113511	.116469	.119471	.122515	.125602	.128731	.131899	.135107	.141636	.148309
	-.40	.109163	.111983	.114850	.117763	.120720	.123722	.126767	.129854	.132982	.136151	.139358	.145887	.152561
20	.40	.069501	.072578	.075708	.078890	.082122	.085402	.088729	.092100	.095513	.098968	.102461	.109558	.116789
	.30	.073752	.076829	.079960	.083142	.086373	.089654	.092980	.096351	.099765	.103219	.106713	.113810	.121041
	.20	.078004	.081081	.084211	.087393	.090625	.093905	.097231	.100602	.104016	.107471	.110964	.118061	.125292
	.10	.082255	.085332	.088462	.091644	.094876	.098156	.101483	.104854	.108268	.111722	.115216	.122313	.129544
	0.00	.086507	.089584	.092714	.095896	.099128	.102408	.105734	.109105	.112519	.115974	.119467	.126564	.133795
	-.10	.090758	.093835	.096965	.100147	.103379	.106659	.109986	.113357	.116771	.120225	.123719	.130815	.138047
	-.20	.095010	.098087	.101217	.104399	.107631	.110911	.114237	.117608	.121022	.124477	.127970	.135067	.142298
	-.30	.099261	.102338	.105468	.108650	.111882	.115162	.118489	.121860	.125273	.128728	.132222	.139318	.146550
	-.40	.103512	.106589	.109720	.112902	.116134	.119414	.122740	.126111	.129525	.132979	.136473	.143570	.150801
25	.40	.066246	.069497	.072804	.076165	.079578	.083039	.086546	.090096	.093686	.097315	.100978	.108402	.115939
	.30	.070498	.073748	.077055	.080417	.083829	.087290	.090797	.094347	.097938	.101566	.105230	.112654	.120191
	.20	.074749	.078000	.081307	.084668	.088081	.091542	.095049	.098599	.102189	.105818	.109481	.116905	.124442
	.10	.079000	.082251	.085558	.088920	.092332	.095793	.099300	.102850	.106441	.110069	.113733	.121157	.128694
	0.00	.083252	.086503	.089810	.093171	.096584	.100045	.103552	.107102	.110692	.114321	.117984	.125408	.132945
	-.10	.087503	.090754	.094061	.097423	.100835	.104296	.107803	.111353	.114944	.118572	.122236	.129660	.137197
	-.20	.091755	.095005	.098313	.101674	.105087	.108548	.112055	.115605	.119195	.122823	.126487	.133911	.141448
	-.30	.096006	.099257	.102564	.105926	.109338	.112799	.116306	.119856	.123447	.127075	.130739	.138163	.145700
	-.40	.100258	.103508	.106816	.110177	.113590	.117051	.120557	.124108	.127698	.131326	.134990	.142414	.149951
30	.40	.064183	.067564	.071002	.074495	.078038	.081627	.085261	.088933	.092643	.096386	.100159	.107786	.115502
	.30	.068435	.071815	.075254	.078746	.082290	.085879	.089512	.093185	.096894	.100637	.104410	.112037	.119754
	.20	.072686	.076067	.079505	.082998	.086541	.090130	.093763	.097436	.101146	.104889	.108662	.116288	.124005
	.10	.076938	.080318	.083757	.087249	.090792	.094382	.098015	.101688	.105397	.109140	.112913	.120540	.128257
	0.00	.081189	.084570	.088008	.091501	.095044	.098633	.102266	.105939	.109649	.113391	.117165	.124791	.132508
	-.10	.085440	.088821	.092260	.095752	.099295	.102885	.106518	.110191	.113900	.117643	.121416	.129043	.136760
	-.20	.089692	.093073	.096511	.100004	.103547	.107136	.110769	.114442	.118152	.121894	.125668	.133294	.141011
	-.30	.093943	.097324	.100762	.104255	.107798	.111388	.115021	.118694	.122403	.126146	.129919	.137546	.145263
	-.40	.098195	.101575	.105014	.108506	.112049	.115639	.119272	.122945	.126655	.130397	.134171	.141797	.149514

10.0 YEAR HOLDING PERIOD
.180 EQUITY YIELD RATE
.900 LOAN RATIO

INTEREST RATE

TERM YEARS	APPR DEP	5.0	5.5	6.0	6.5	7.0	7.5	8.0	8.5	9.0	9.5	10.0	11.0	12.0
10	.40	.077282	.079939	.082633	.085363	.088128	.090929	.093765	.096636	.099541	.102480	.105454	.111501	.117680
	.30	.081533	.084191	.086885	.089614	.092380	.095180	.098016	.100887	.103792	.106732	.109705	.115752	.121931
	.20	.085785	.088442	.091136	.093866	.096631	.099432	.102268	.105138	.108044	.110983	.113957	.120004	.126183
	.10	.090036	.092694	.095388	.098117	.100883	.103683	.106519	.109390	.112295	.115235	.118208	.124255	.130434
	0.00	.094288	.096945	.099639	.102369	.105134	.107935	.110771	.113641	.116547	.119486	.122460	.128507	.134685
	-.10	.098539	.101197	.103890	.106620	.109385	.112186	.115022	.117893	.120798	.123738	.126711	.132758	.138937
	-.20	.102791	.105448	.108142	.110872	.113637	.116438	.119274	.122144	.125050	.127989	.130963	.137010	.143188
	-.30	.107042	.109700	.112393	.115123	.117888	.120689	.123525	.126396	.129301	.132241	.135214	.141261	.147440
	-.40	.111293	.113951	.116645	.119374	.122140	.124941	.127776	.130647	.133553	.136492	.139465	.145513	.151691
15	.40	.064171	.067344	.070569	.073846	.077173	.080550	.083975	.087448	.090967	.094532	.098141	.105486	.112593
	.30	.068422	.071595	.074820	.078097	.081425	.084801	.088227	.091700	.095219	.098783	.102392	.109737	.117245
	.20	.072674	.075847	.079072	.082349	.085676	.089053	.092478	.095951	.099470	.103035	.106643	.113989	.121496
	.10	.076925	.080098	.083323	.086600	.089927	.093304	.096730	.100203	.103722	.107286	.110895	.118240	.125748
	0.00	.081177	.084350	.087575	.090852	.094179	.097556	.100981	.104454	.107973	.111538	.115146	.122492	.129999
	-.10	.085428	.088601	.091826	.095103	.098430	.101807	.105233	.108705	.112225	.115789	.119398	.126743	.134251
	-.20	.089680	.092852	.096078	.099355	.102682	.106059	.109484	.112957	.116476	.120041	.123649	.130995	.138502
	-.30	.093931	.097104	.100329	.103606	.106933	.110310	.113736	.117208	.120728	.124292	.127901	.135246	.142754
	-.40	.098182	.101355	.104581	.107857	.111185	.114562	.117987	.121460	.124979	.128544	.132152	.139497	.147005
20	.40	.057814	.061276	.064797	.068377	.072013	.075703	.079445	.083238	.087078	.090964	.094895	.102879	.111014
	.30	.062066	.065527	.069049	.072629	.076264	.079955	.083697	.087489	.091330	.095216	.099146	.107130	.115265
	.20	.066317	.069779	.073300	.076880	.080516	.084206	.087948	.091741	.095581	.099467	.103398	.111382	.119517
	.10	.070569	.074030	.077552	.081131	.084767	.088457	.092200	.095992	.099833	.103719	.107649	.115633	.123768
	0.00	.074620	.078282	.081803	.085383	.089019	.092709	.096451	.100244	.104084	.107970	.111901	.119885	.128020
	-.10	.079071	.082533	.086055	.089634	.093270	.096960	.100703	.104495	.108335	.112222	.116152	.124136	.132271
	-.20	.083323	.086784	.090306	.093886	.097522	.101212	.104954	.108747	.112587	.116473	.120404	.128387	.136523
	-.30	.087574	.091036	.094558	.098137	.101773	.105463	.109206	.112998	.116838	.120725	.124655	.132639	.140774
	-.40	.091826	.095287	.098809	.102389	.106025	.109715	.113457	.117249	.121090	.124976	.128906	.136890	.145026
25	.40	.054153	.057810	.061530	.065312	.069151	.073044	.076990	.080984	.085023	.089105	.093227	.101578	.110058
	.30	.058404	.062061	.065782	.069563	.073402	.077296	.081241	.085235	.089274	.093356	.097478	.105830	.114309
	.20	.062655	.066312	.070033	.073815	.077654	.081547	.085493	.089486	.093526	.097608	.101729	.110081	.118560
	.10	.066907	.070564	.074285	.078066	.081905	.085799	.089744	.093738	.097777	.101859	.105981	.114333	.122812
	0.00	.071158	.074815	.078536	.082318	.086157	.090050	.093996	.097989	.102029	.106111	.110232	.118584	.127063
	-.10	.075410	.079067	.082788	.086569	.090408	.094302	.098247	.102241	.106280	.110362	.114484	.122836	.131315
	-.20	.079661	.083318	.087039	.090820	.094660	.098553	.102499	.106492	.110532	.114614	.118735	.127087	.135566
	-.30	.083913	.087570	.091290	.095072	.098911	.102805	.106750	.110744	.114783	.118865	.122987	.131339	.139818
	-.40	.088164	.091821	.095542	.099323	.103162	.107056	.111001	.114995	.119035	.123116	.127238	.135590	.144059
30	.40	.051832	.055635	.059503	.063432	.067418	.071457	.075544	.079676	.083849	.088060	.092304	.100884	.109556
	.30	.056083	.059886	.063755	.067684	.071670	.075708	.079795	.083927	.088100	.092311	.096556	.105136	.113817
	.20	.060335	.064138	.068006	.071935	.075921	.079960	.084047	.088179	.092352	.096562	.100807	.109387	.118059
	.10	.064586	.068389	.072258	.076187	.080173	.084211	.088298	.092430	.096603	.100814	.105059	.113639	.122320
	0.00	.068838	.072641	.076509	.080438	.084424	.088463	.092550	.096682	.100855	.105065	.109310	.117890	.126572
	-.10	.073089	.076892	.080761	.084690	.088676	.092714	.096801	.100933	.105106	.109317	.113562	.122142	.130823
	-.20	.077341	.081144	.085012	.088941	.092927	.096965	.101053	.105185	.109358	.113568	.117813	.126393	.135075
	-.30	.081592	.085395	.089263	.093193	.097178	.101217	.105304	.109436	.113609	.117820	.122065	.130645	.139326
	-.40	.085843	.089647	.093515	.097444	.101430	.105468	.109556	.113687	.117861	.122071	.126316	.134896	.143578

257

10.0 YEAR HOLDING PERIOD
.200 EQUITY YIELD RATE
.600 LOAN RATIO

INTEREST RATE

TERM YEARS	APPR DEP	5.0	5.5	6.0	6.5	7.0	7.5	8.0	8.5	9.0	9.5	10.0	11.0	12.0
10	.40	.117844	.119616	.121412	.123232	.125075	.126943	.128833	.130747	.132684	.134643	.136626	.140657	.144776
	.30	.121697	.123468	.125264	.127084	.128928	.130795	.132685	.134599	.136536	.138496	.140478	.144510	.148629
	.20	.125549	.127321	.129117	.130936	.132780	.134647	.136538	.138451	.140388	.142348	.144330	.148362	.152481
	.10	.129401	.131173	.132969	.134789	.136632	.138499	.140390	.142304	.144241	.146200	.148183	.152214	.156333
	0.00	.133254	.135025	.136821	.138641	.140484	.142352	.144242	.146156	.148093	.150053	.152035	.156066	.160185
	-.10	.137106	.138878	.140673	.142493	.144337	.146204	.148094	.150008	.151945	.153905	.155887	.159919	.164038
	-.20	.140958	.142730	.144526	.146345	.148189	.150056	.151947	.153861	.155797	.157757	.159739	.163771	.167890
	-.30	.144810	.146582	.148378	.150198	.152041	.153908	.155799	.157713	.159650	.161609	.163592	.167623	.171742
	-.40	.148663	.150434	.152230	.154050	.155894	.157761	.159651	.161565	.163502	.165462	.167444	.171475	.175595
15	.40	.108100	.110194	.112324	.114487	.116685	.118915	.121178	.123472	.125798	.128154	.130539	.135395	.140360
	.30	.111952	.114047	.116176	.118340	.120537	.122767	.125030	.127325	.129650	.132006	.134391	.139247	.144212
	.20	.115805	.117899	.120028	.122192	.124389	.126620	.128883	.131177	.133502	.135858	.138243	.143100	.148065
	.10	.119657	.121751	.123881	.126044	.128242	.130472	.132735	.135029	.137355	.139710	.142096	.146952	.151917
	0.00	.123509	.125604	.127733	.129897	.132094	.134324	.136587	.138882	.141207	.143563	.145948	.150804	.155769
	-.10	.127361	.129456	.131585	.133749	.135946	.138177	.140439	.142734	.145059	.147415	.149800	.154656	.159621
	-.20	.131214	.133308	.135437	.137601	.139798	.142029	.144292	.146586	.148912	.151267	.153653	.158509	.163474
	-.30	.135066	.137160	.139290	.141453	.143651	.145881	.148144	.150438	.152764	.155120	.157505	.162361	.167326
	-.40	.138918	.141013	.143142	.145306	.147503	.149733	.151996	.154291	.156616	.158972	.161357	.166213	.171178
20	.40	.103376	.105656	.107976	.110335	.112733	.115166	.117636	.120139	.122674	.125241	.127837	.133114	.138494
	.30	.107228	.109508	.111828	.114188	.116585	.119019	.121488	.123991	.126526	.129093	.131690	.136967	.142347
	.20	.111080	.113360	.115680	.118040	.120437	.122871	.125340	.127843	.130379	.132945	.135542	.140819	.146199
	.10	.114933	.117212	.119533	.121892	.124289	.126723	.129192	.131695	.134231	.136798	.139394	.144671	.150051
	0.00	.118785	.121065	.123385	.125744	.128142	.130576	.133045	.135548	.138083	.140650	.143246	.148523	.153903
	-.10	.122637	.124917	.127237	.129597	.131994	.134428	.136897	.139400	.141936	.144502	.147099	.152376	.157756
	-.20	.126489	.128769	.131090	.133449	.135846	.138280	.140749	.143252	.145788	.148355	.150951	.156228	.161608
	-.30	.130342	.132622	.134942	.137301	.139699	.142132	.144602	.147105	.149640	.152207	.154803	.160080	.165460
	-.40	.134194	.136474	.138794	.141153	.143551	.145985	.148454	.150957	.153492	.156059	.158656	.163933	.169313
25	.40	.100654	.103063	.105515	.108008	.110540	.113110	.115715	.118354	.121023	.123722	.126449	.131977	.137593
	.30	.104507	.106915	.109367	.111860	.114393	.116963	.119568	.122206	.124876	.127575	.130301	.135829	.141445
	.20	.108359	.110767	.113219	.115712	.118245	.120815	.123420	.126058	.128728	.131427	.134153	.139681	.145298
	.10	.112211	.114620	.117072	.119565	.122097	.124667	.127272	.129911	.132580	.135279	.138006	.143534	.149150
	0.00	.116063	.118472	.120924	.123417	.125949	.128519	.131124	.133763	.136433	.139132	.141858	.147386	.153002
	-.10	.119916	.122324	.124776	.127269	.129802	.132372	.134977	.137615	.140285	.142984	.145710	.151238	.156854
	-.20	.123768	.126177	.128628	.131122	.133654	.136224	.138829	.141467	.144137	.146836	.149563	.155090	.160707
	-.30	.127620	.130029	.132481	.134974	.137506	.140076	.142681	.145320	.147989	.150688	.153415	.158943	.164559
	-.40	.131473	.133881	.136333	.138826	.141359	.143928	.146534	.149172	.151842	.154541	.157267	.162795	.168411
30	.40	.098930	.101436	.103988	.106581	.109213	.111882	.114585	.117318	.120081	.122869	.125681	.131370	.137130
	.30	.102782	.105289	.107840	.110433	.113066	.115734	.118437	.121171	.123933	.126721	.129533	.135222	.140982
	.20	.106634	.109141	.111692	.114286	.116918	.119587	.122289	.125023	.127785	.130574	.133386	.139074	.144834
	.10	.110486	.112993	.115545	.118138	.120770	.123439	.126142	.128875	.131637	.134426	.137238	.142927	.148686
	0.00	.114339	.116845	.119397	.121990	.124623	.127291	.129994	.132727	.135490	.138278	.141091	.146779	.152539
	-.10	.118191	.120698	.123249	.125842	.128475	.131144	.133846	.136580	.139342	.142130	.144943	.150631	.156391
	-.20	.122043	.124550	.127101	.129695	.132327	.134996	.137698	.140432	.143194	.145983	.148795	.154483	.160243
	-.30	.125895	.128402	.130954	.133547	.136179	.138848	.141551	.144284	.147046	.149835	.152647	.158336	.164096
	-.40	.129748	.132254	.134806	.137399	.140032	.142700	.145403	.148137	.150889	.153687	.156500	.162188	.167948

258

10.0 YEAR HOLDING PERIOD
.200 EQUITY YIELD RATE
.667 LOAN RATIO

INTEREST RATE

TERM YEARS	APPR DEP	5.0	5.5	6.0	6.5	7.0	7.5	8.0	8.5	9.0	9.5	10.0	11.0	12.0
10	.40	.110428	.112396	.114392	.116414	.118462	.120537	.122637	.124764	.126916	.129093	.131296	.135775	.140352
	.30	.114280	.116249	.118244	.120266	.122314	.124389	.126490	.128616	.130768	.132946	.135148	.139628	.144205
	.20	.118132	.120101	.122096	.124118	.126167	.128241	.130342	.132469	.134621	.136798	.139001	.143480	.148057
	.10	.121985	.123953	.125949	.127971	.130019	.132094	.134194	.136321	.138473	.140650	.142853	.147332	.151909
	0.00	.125837	.127805	.129801	.131823	.133871	.135946	.138047	.140173	.142325	.144503	.146705	.151185	.155751
	-.10	.129689	.131658	.133653	.135675	.137724	.139798	.141899	.144025	.146177	.148355	.150557	.155037	.159614
	-.20	.133541	.135510	.137505	.139527	.141576	.143650	.145751	.147878	.150030	.152207	.154410	.158889	.163466
	-.30	.137394	.139362	.141358	.143380	.145428	.147503	.149603	.151730	.153882	.156059	.158262	.162741	.167318
	-.40	.141246	.143215	.145210	.147232	.149280	.151355	.153456	.155582	.157734	.159912	.162114	.166594	.171170
15	.40	.099601	.101928	.104294	.106698	.109139	.111617	.114132	.116681	.119265	.121883	.124533	.129929	.135445
	.30	.103453	.105780	.108146	.110550	.112992	.115470	.117984	.120533	.123117	.125735	.128385	.133781	.139297
	.20	.107305	.109632	.111998	.114402	.116844	.119322	.121836	.124386	.126970	.129587	.132237	.137633	.143150
	.10	.111158	.113485	.115851	.118255	.120696	.123174	.125689	.128238	.130822	.133439	.136090	.141485	.147002
	0.00	.115010	.117337	.119703	.122107	.124548	.127027	.129541	.132090	.134674	.137292	.139942	.145338	.150854
	-.10	.118862	.121189	.123555	.125959	.128401	.130879	.133393	.135943	.138526	.141144	.143794	.149190	.154707
	-.20	.122714	.125041	.127407	.129811	.132253	.134731	.137245	.139795	.142379	.144996	.147647	.153042	.158559
	-.30	.126567	.128894	.131260	.133664	.136105	.138583	.141098	.143647	.146231	.148848	.151499	.156894	.162411
	-.40	.130419	.132746	.135112	.137516	.139957	.142436	.144950	.147499	.150083	.152701	.155351	.160747	.166263
20	.40	.094351	.096885	.099463	.102084	.104748	.107452	.110196	.112977	.115794	.118646	.121531	.127394	.133372
	.30	.098204	.100737	.103315	.105937	.108600	.111305	.114048	.116829	.119646	.122498	.125383	.131247	.137224
	.20	.102056	.104589	.107167	.109789	.112452	.115157	.117900	.120681	.123499	.126351	.129236	.135099	.141077
	.10	.105908	.108441	.111019	.113641	.116305	.119009	.121753	.124534	.127351	.130203	.133088	.138951	.144929
	0.00	.109760	.112294	.114872	.117493	.120157	.122861	.125605	.128386	.131203	.134055	.136940	.142804	.148781
	-.10	.113613	.116146	.118724	.121346	.124009	.126714	.129457	.132238	.135056	.137907	.140793	.146656	.152634
	-.20	.117465	.119998	.122576	.125198	.127862	.130566	.133309	.136091	.138908	.141760	.144645	.150508	.156486
	-.30	.121317	.123850	.126429	.129050	.131714	.134418	.137162	.139943	.142760	.145612	.148497	.154360	.160338
	-.40	.125170	.127703	.130281	.132902	.135566	.138270	.141014	.143795	.146612	.149464	.152349	.158213	.164190
25	.40	.091328	.094004	.096728	.099498	.102312	.105168	.108062	.110994	.113960	.116959	.119988	.126131	.132371
	.30	.095180	.097856	.100580	.103350	.106164	.109020	.111914	.114846	.117812	.120811	.123841	.129983	.136223
	.20	.099032	.101708	.104433	.107203	.110017	.112872	.115767	.118698	.121665	.124664	.127693	.133835	.140075
	.10	.102884	.105561	.108285	.111055	.113869	.116724	.119619	.122551	.125517	.128516	.131545	.137687	.143928
	0.00	.106737	.109413	.112137	.114907	.117721	.120577	.123471	.126403	.129369	.132368	.135397	.141540	.147780
	-.10	.110589	.113265	.115989	.118760	.121574	.124429	.127324	.130255	.133221	.136220	.139250	.145392	.151632
	-.20	.114441	.117117	.119842	.122612	.125426	.128281	.131176	.134107	.137074	.140073	.143102	.149244	.155485
	-.30	.118294	.120970	.123694	.126464	.129278	.132133	.135028	.137960	.140926	.143925	.146954	.153096	.159337
	-.40	.122146	.124822	.127546	.130316	.133130	.135986	.138880	.141812	.144778	.147777	.150807	.156949	.163189
30	.40	.089411	.092196	.095031	.097913	.100838	.103803	.106806	.109843	.112912	.116011	.119136	.125456	.131856
	.30	.093263	.096049	.098884	.101765	.104690	.107655	.110658	.113695	.116765	.119863	.122988	.129308	.135708
	.20	.097116	.099901	.102736	.105617	.108542	.111508	.114510	.117548	.120617	.123715	.126840	.133161	.139560
	.10	.100968	.103753	.106588	.109470	.112395	.115360	.118363	.121400	.124469	.127568	.130693	.137013	.143413
	0.00	.104820	.107606	.110440	.113322	.116247	.119212	.122215	.125252	.128321	.131420	.134545	.140865	.147265
	-.10	.108672	.111458	.114293	.117174	.120099	.123064	.126067	.129105	.132174	.135272	.138397	.144717	.151117
	-.20	.112525	.115310	.118145	.121026	.123951	.126917	.129919	.132957	.136026	.139124	.142249	.148570	.154970
	-.30	.116377	.119162	.121997	.124879	.127804	.130769	.133772	.136809	.139878	.142977	.146102	.152422	.158822
	-.40	.120229	.123015	.125850	.128731	.131656	.134621	.137624	.140661	.143731	.146829	.149954	.156274	.162674

10.0 YEAR HOLDING PERIOD
.200 EQUITY YIELD RATE
.700 LOAN RATIO

INTEREST RATE

TERM YEARS	APPR DEP	5.0	5.5	6.0	6.5	7.0	7.5	8.0	8.5	9.0	9.5	10.0	11.0	12.0
10	.40	.106720	.108787	.110882	.113005	.115156	.117334	.119540	.121773	.124033	.126319	.128632	.133335	.138141
	.30	.110572	.112639	.114734	.116858	.119008	.121187	.123392	.125625	.127885	.130171	.132484	.137187	.141993
	.20	.114425	.116492	.118587	.120710	.122861	.125039	.127245	.129477	.131737	.134023	.136336	.141040	.145845
	.10	.118277	.120344	.122439	.124562	.126713	.128891	.131097	.133330	.135589	.137876	.140188	.144892	.149697
	0.00	.122129	.124196	.126291	.128414	.130565	.132742	.134949	.137182	.139442	.141728	.144041	.148744	.153550
	-.10	.125981	.128048	.130144	.132267	.134417	.136596	.138802	.141034	.143294	.145580	.147893	.152596	.157402
	-.20	.129834	.131901	.133996	.136119	.138270	.140448	.142654	.144887	.147146	.149433	.151745	.156449	.161254
	-.30	.133686	.135753	.137848	.139971	.142122	.144300	.146506	.148739	.150999	.153285	.155598	.160301	.165106
	-.40	.137538	.139605	.141700	.143823	.145974	.148153	.150358	.152591	.154851	.157137	.159450	.164153	.168959
15	.40	.095352	.097795	.100279	.102804	.105367	.107969	.110609	.113286	.115999	.118747	.121530	.127196	.132988
	.30	.099204	.101647	.104132	.106656	.109219	.111821	.114461	.117138	.119851	.122600	.125383	.131048	.136840
	.20	.103056	.105500	.107984	.110508	.113072	.115674	.118314	.120991	.123704	.126452	.129235	.134900	.140693
	.10	.106908	.109352	.111836	.114360	.116924	.119526	.122166	.124843	.127556	.130304	.133087	.138753	.144545
	0.00	.110761	.113204	.115688	.118213	.120776	.123378	.126018	.128695	.131408	.134157	.136939	.142605	.148397
	-.10	.114613	.117056	.119541	.122065	.124628	.127231	.129871	.132547	.135260	.138009	.140792	.146457	.152250
	-.20	.118465	.120909	.123393	.125917	.128481	.131083	.133723	.136400	.139113	.141851	.144649	.150309	.156102
	-.30	.122318	.124761	.127245	.129769	.132333	.134935	.137575	.140252	.142965	.145713	.148496	.154162	.159954
	-.40	.126170	.128613	.131097	.133622	.136185	.138787	.141427	.144104	.146817	.149556	.152348	.158014	.163806
20	.40	.089840	.092500	.095207	.097959	.100756	.103596	.106476	.109397	.112355	.115349	.118378	.124535	.130812
	.30	.093692	.096352	.099059	.101812	.104608	.107448	.110329	.113249	.116207	.119202	.122231	.128387	.134664
	.20	.097544	.100204	.102911	.105664	.108461	.111300	.114181	.117101	.120059	.123054	.126083	.132239	.138516
	.10	.101397	.104057	.106764	.109516	.112313	.115153	.118033	.120953	.123912	.126906	.129935	.136092	.142368
	0.00	.105249	.107909	.110616	.113368	.116165	.119005	.121886	.124806	.127764	.130758	.133788	.139944	.146221
	-.10	.109101	.111761	.114468	.117221	.120018	.122857	.125738	.128658	.131616	.134611	.137640	.143796	.150073
	-.20	.112954	.115613	.118320	.121073	.123870	.126709	.129590	.132510	.135468	.138463	.141492	.147649	.153925
	-.30	.116806	.119466	.122173	.124925	.127722	.130562	.133442	.136363	.139321	.142315	.145344	.151501	.157777
	-.40	.120658	.123318	.126025	.128778	.131574	.134414	.137295	.140215	.143173	.146167	.149197	.155353	.161630
25	.40	.086665	.089475	.092235	.095244	.098199	.101197	.104236	.107314	.110429	.113578	.116759	.123208	.129760
	.30	.090517	.093327	.096188	.099096	.102051	.105049	.108088	.111167	.114281	.117430	.120611	.127060	.133612
	.20	.094370	.097179	.100040	.102949	.105903	.108901	.111941	.115019	.118133	.121282	.124463	.130912	.137465
	.10	.098222	.101032	.103892	.106801	.109755	.112754	.115793	.118871	.121986	.125135	.128315	.134765	.141317
	0.00	.102074	.104884	.107744	.110653	.113608	.116606	.119645	.122723	.125838	.128987	.132168	.138617	.145169
	-.10	.105926	.108736	.111597	.114505	.117460	.120458	.123497	.126576	.129690	.132839	.136020	.142469	.149021
	-.20	.109779	.112588	.115449	.118358	.121312	.124310	.127350	.130428	.133543	.136691	.139872	.146321	.152874
	-.30	.113631	.116441	.119301	.122210	.125165	.128163	.131202	.134280	.137395	.140544	.143725	.150174	.156726
	-.40	.117483	.120293	.123154	.126062	.129017	.132015	.135054	.138132	.141247	.144396	.147577	.154026	.160578
30	.40	.084653	.087577	.090554	.093579	.096650	.099764	.102917	.106106	.109329	.112582	.115863	.122500	.129219
	.30	.088505	.091429	.094406	.097432	.100503	.103616	.106769	.109958	.113181	.116434	.119716	.126352	.133072
	.20	.092357	.095282	.098258	.101284	.104355	.107469	.110622	.113811	.117033	.120287	.123568	.130204	.136924
	.10	.096209	.099134	.102111	.105136	.108207	.111321	.114474	.117663	.120886	.124139	.127420	.134056	.140776
	0.00	.100062	.102986	.105963	.108988	.112060	.115173	.118326	.121515	.124738	.127991	.131272	.137909	.144629
	-.10	.103914	.106839	.109815	.112841	.115912	.119025	.122178	.125368	.128590	.131843	.135125	.141761	.148481
	-.20	.107766	.110691	.113667	.116693	.119764	.122878	.126031	.129220	.132442	.135696	.138977	.145613	.152333
	-.30	.111619	.114543	.117520	.120545	.123616	.126730	.129883	.133072	.136295	.139548	.142829	.149466	.156185
	-.40	.115471	.118395	.121372	.124398	.127469	.130582	.133735	.136924	.140147	.143400	.146681	.153318	.160038

10.0 YEAR HOLDING PERIOD
.200 EQUITY YIELD RATE
.750 LOAN RATIO

INTEREST RATE

TERM YEARS	APPR DEP	5.0	5.5	6.0	6.5	7.0	7.5	8.0	8.5	9.0	9.5	10.0	11.0	12.0
10	.40	.101158	.103372	.105617	.107892	.110196	.112530	.114894	.117286	.119707	.122157	.124634	.129674	.134823
	.30	.105010	.107225	.109470	.111744	.114049	.116383	.118746	.121138	.123559	.126009	.128487	.133526	.138675
	.20	.108862	.111077	.113322	.115597	.117901	.120235	.122598	.124991	.127412	.129861	.132339	.137378	.142527
	.10	.112715	.114929	.117174	.119449	.121753	.124087	.126450	.128843	.131264	.133713	.136191	.141231	.146380
	0.00	.116567	.118782	.121026	.123301	.125606	.127940	.130303	.132695	.135116	.137566	.140044	.145083	.150232
	-.10	.120419	.122634	.124879	.127153	.129458	.131792	.134155	.136547	.138968	.141418	.143896	.148935	.154084
	-.20	.124271	.126486	.128731	.131006	.133310	.135644	.138007	.140400	.142821	.145270	.147748	.152787	.157936
	-.30	.128124	.130338	.132583	.134858	.137162	.139496	.141860	.144252	.146673	.149123	.151600	.156640	.161789
	-.40	.131976	.134191	.136435	.138710	.141015	.143349	.145712	.148104	.150525	.152975	.155453	.160492	.165641
15	.40	.088977	.091595	.094257	.096962	.099708	.102496	.105325	.108193	.111100	.114044	.117026	.123096	.129302
	.30	.092830	.095448	.098109	.100814	.103561	.106349	.109177	.112045	.114952	.117897	.120878	.126948	.133155
	.20	.096682	.099300	.101962	.104666	.107413	.110201	.113029	.115897	.118804	.121749	.124730	.130801	.137007
	.10	.100534	.103152	.105814	.108518	.111265	.114053	.116882	.119750	.122656	.125601	.128583	.134653	.140859
	0.00	.104386	.107004	.109666	.112371	.115117	.117905	.120734	.123602	.126509	.129453	.132435	.138505	.144711
	-.10	.108239	.110857	.113518	.116223	.118970	.121758	.124586	.127454	.130361	.133306	.136287	.142357	.148564
	-.20	.112091	.114709	.117371	.120075	.122822	.125610	.128438	.131306	.134213	.137158	.140140	.146210	.152416
	-.30	.115943	.118561	.121223	.123928	.126674	.129462	.132291	.135159	.138066	.141010	.143992	.150062	.156268
	-.40	.119796	.122414	.125075	.127780	.130526	.133314	.136143	.139011	.141918	.144863	.147844	.153914	.160120
20	.40	.083072	.085922	.088622	.091771	.094768	.097810	.100897	.104026	.107195	.110403	.113649	.120245	.126970
	.30	.086924	.089774	.092474	.095624	.098620	.101663	.104749	.107878	.111047	.114256	.117501	.124097	.130822
	.20	.090776	.093626	.096327	.099476	.102473	.105515	.108601	.111730	.114900	.118108	.121354	.127950	.134675
	.10	.094629	.097479	.100179	.103328	.106325	.109367	.112454	.115582	.118752	.121960	.125206	.131802	.138527
	0.00	.098481	.101331	.104031	.107180	.110177	.113219	.116306	.119435	.122604	.125812	.129058	.135654	.142379
	-.10	.102333	.105183	.107883	.111033	.114029	.117072	.120158	.123287	.126456	.129665	.132910	.139507	.146232
	-.20	.106186	.109035	.111736	.114885	.117882	.120924	.124010	.127139	.130309	.133517	.136763	.143359	.150084
	-.30	.110038	.112888	.115588	.118737	.121734	.124776	.127863	.130992	.134161	.137369	.140615	.147211	.153936
	-.40	.113890	.116740	.119440	.122590	.125586	.128629	.131715	.134844	.138013	.141222	.144467	.151063	.157788
25	.40	.079670	.082681	.085746	.088862	.092028	.095240	.098496	.101794	.105132	.108505	.111913	.118823	.125844
	.30	.083523	.086533	.089598	.092714	.095880	.099092	.102349	.105647	.108984	.112358	.115766	.122676	.129696
	.20	.087375	.090385	.093450	.096567	.099732	.102945	.106201	.109499	.112836	.116210	.119618	.126528	.133548
	.10	.091227	.094238	.097302	.100419	.103585	.106797	.110053	.113351	.116688	.120062	.123470	.130380	.137400
	0.00	.095079	.098090	.101154	.104271	.107437	.110649	.113906	.117204	.120541	.123914	.127323	.134232	.141253
	-.10	.098932	.101942	.105007	.108123	.111289	.114501	.117758	.121056	.124393	.127767	.131175	.138085	.145105
	-.20	.102784	.105794	.108859	.111976	.115141	.118354	.121610	.124908	.128245	.131619	.135027	.141937	.148957
	-.30	.106636	.109647	.112712	.115828	.118994	.122206	.125462	.128760	.132098	.135471	.138879	.145789	.152810
	-.40	.110488	.113499	.116564	.119680	.122846	.126058	.129315	.132613	.135950	.139324	.142732	.149641	.156662
30	.40	.077514	.080648	.083837	.087079	.090369	.093705	.097083	.100500	.103953	.107439	.110954	.118064	.125264
	.30	.081366	.084500	.087689	.090931	.094221	.097557	.100935	.104352	.107805	.111291	.114806	.121917	.129117
	.20	.085219	.088352	.091541	.094783	.098074	.101410	.104788	.108205	.111658	.115143	.118659	.125769	.132969
	.10	.089071	.092204	.095394	.098635	.101926	.105262	.108640	.112057	.115510	.118995	.122511	.129621	.136821
	0.00	.092923	.096057	.099246	.102488	.105778	.109114	.112492	.115909	.119362	.122848	.126363	.133474	.140673
	-.10	.096776	.099909	.103098	.106340	.109630	.112966	.116345	.119762	.123214	.126700	.130216	.137326	.144526
	-.20	.100628	.103761	.106951	.110192	.113483	.116819	.120197	.123614	.127067	.130552	.134068	.141178	.148378
	-.30	.104480	.107614	.110803	.114044	.117335	.120671	.124049	.127466	.130919	.134405	.137920	.145030	.152230
	-.40	.108332	.111466	.114655	.117897	.121187	.124523	.127901	.131318	.134771	.138257	.141772	.148883	.156083

261

10.0 YEAR HOLDING PERIOD
.200 EQUITY YIELD RATE
.800 LOAN RATIO

INTEREST RATE

TERM YEARS	APPR DEP	5.0	5.5	6.0	6.5	7.0	7.5	8.0	8.5	9.0	9.5	10.0	11.0	12.0
10	.40	.095598	.097958	.100352	.102779	.105237	.107726	.110247	.112799	.115381	.117994	.120637	.126013	.131505
	.30	.099448	.101810	.104205	.106631	.109089	.111579	.114099	.116651	.119234	.121847	.124490	.129865	.135357
	.20	.103300	.105662	.108057	.110483	.112941	.115431	.117952	.120504	.123086	.125699	.128342	.133717	.139209
	.10	.107152	.109515	.111909	.114336	.116794	.119283	.121804	.124356	.126938	.129551	.132194	.137570	.143062
	0.00	.111005	.113367	.115761	.118188	.120646	.123135	.125656	.128208	.130791	.133403	.136047	.141422	.146914
	-.10	.114857	.117219	.119614	.122040	.124498	.126988	.129509	.132060	.134643	.137256	.139899	.145274	.150766
	-.20	.118709	.121072	.123406	.125892	.128350	.130840	.133361	.135913	.138495	.141108	.143751	.149126	.154618
	-.30	.122562	.124924	.127318	.129745	.132203	.134692	.137213	.139765	.142347	.144960	.147603	.152979	.158471
	-.40	.126414	.128776	.131171	.133597	.136055	.138545	.141065	.143617	.146200	.148813	.151456	.156831	.162323
15	.40	.082603	.085396	.088235	.091120	.094049	.097023	.100040	.103100	.106200	.109341	.112522	.118996	.125616
	.30	.086455	.089248	.092087	.094972	.097902	.100876	.103893	.106952	.110053	.113194	.116374	.122849	.129469
	.20	.090308	.093100	.095939	.098824	.101754	.104728	.107745	.110804	.113905	.117046	.120226	.126701	.133321
	.10	.094160	.096953	.099792	.102676	.105606	.108580	.111597	.114657	.117757	.120898	.124078	.130553	.137173
	0.00	.098012	.100805	.103644	.106529	.109458	.112432	.115449	.118509	.121609	.124750	.127931	.134405	.141025
	-.10	.101865	.104657	.107496	.110381	.113311	.116285	.119302	.122361	.125462	.128603	.131783	.138258	.144878
	-.20	.105717	.108509	.111348	.114233	.117163	.120137	.123154	.126213	.129314	.132455	.135635	.142110	.148730
	-.30	.109569	.112362	.115201	.118086	.121015	.123989	.127006	.130066	.133166	.136307	.139488	.145962	.152582
	-.40	.113421	.116214	.119053	.121938	.124868	.127841	.130859	.133918	.137018	.140159	.143340	.149815	.156435
20	.40	.076304	.079344	.082437	.085583	.088780	.092025	.095317	.098655	.102035	.105458	.108920	.115955	.123129
	.30	.080156	.083196	.086290	.089436	.092632	.095877	.099169	.102507	.105888	.109310	.112772	.119808	.126981
	.20	.084009	.087048	.090142	.093288	.096484	.099730	.103022	.106359	.109740	.113162	.116624	.123660	.130833
	.10	.087861	.090901	.093994	.097140	.100337	.103582	.106874	.110211	.113592	.117014	.120476	.127512	.134686
	0.00	.091713	.094753	.097847	.100993	.104189	.107434	.110726	.114064	.117444	.120867	.124329	.131365	.138538
	-.10	.095565	.098605	.101699	.104845	.108041	.111286	.114579	.117916	.121297	.124719	.128181	.135217	.142390
	-.20	.099418	.102457	.105551	.108697	.111893	.115138	.118431	.121768	.125149	.128571	.132033	.139069	.146242
	-.30	.103270	.106310	.109403	.112549	.115746	.118991	.122283	.125620	.129001	.132423	.135885	.142921	.150095
	-.40	.107122	.110162	.113256	.116402	.119598	.122843	.126135	.129473	.132853	.136276	.139738	.146774	.153947
25	.40	.072676	.075887	.079156	.082480	.085857	.089283	.092757	.096275	.099834	.103433	.107068	.114439	.121927
	.30	.076528	.079739	.083008	.086332	.089709	.093136	.096609	.100127	.103687	.107285	.110921	.118291	.125779
	.20	.080380	.083591	.086860	.090185	.093561	.096988	.100461	.103979	.107539	.111138	.114773	.122143	.129632
	.10	.084232	.087444	.090713	.094037	.097414	.100840	.104314	.107832	.111391	.114990	.118625	.125996	.133484
	0.00	.088085	.091296	.094565	.097889	.101266	.104692	.108166	.111684	.115243	.118842	.122477	.129848	.137336
	-.10	.091937	.095148	.098417	.101742	.105118	.108545	.112018	.115536	.119096	.122694	.126330	.133702	.141189
	-.20	.095789	.099000	.102270	.105594	.108971	.112397	.115871	.119388	.122948	.126547	.130182	.137552	.145041
	-.30	.099641	.102853	.106122	.109446	.112823	.116249	.119723	.123241	.126800	.130399	.134034	.141405	.148893
	-.40	.103494	.106705	.109974	.113298	.116675	.120102	.123575	.127093	.130652	.134251	.137886	.145257	.152745
30	.40	.070376	.073718	.077120	.080578	.084088	.087646	.091249	.094894	.098577	.102295	.106045	.113629	.121309
	.30	.074228	.077570	.080972	.084430	.087940	.091498	.095102	.098746	.102429	.106147	.109897	.117482	.125162
	.20	.078080	.081423	.084825	.088282	.091792	.095350	.098954	.102599	.106282	.110000	.113750	.121334	.129014
	.10	.081933	.085275	.088677	.092135	.095644	.099203	.102806	.106451	.110134	.113852	.117602	.125186	.132866
	0.00	.085785	.089127	.092529	.095987	.099497	.103055	.106658	.110303	.113986	.117704	.121454	.129039	.136718
	-.10	.089637	.092979	.096381	.099839	.103349	.106907	.110511	.114155	.117838	.121556	.125306	.132891	.140571
	-.20	.093489	.096832	.100234	.103691	.107201	.110760	.114363	.118008	.121691	.125409	.129159	.136743	.144423
	-.30	.097342	.100684	.104086	.107544	.111053	.114612	.118215	.121860	.125543	.129261	.133011	.140595	.148275
	-.40	.101194	.104538	.107938	.111396	.114906	.118464	.122067	.125712	.129345	.133113	.136863	.144448	.152127

262

10.0 YEAR HOLDING PERIOD
.200 EQUITY YIELD RATE
.900 LOAN RATIO

INTEREST RATE

TERM YEARS	APPR DEP	5.0	5.5	6.0	6.5	7.0	7.5	8.0	8.5	9.0	9.5	10.0	11.0	12.0
10	.40	.084471	.087129	.089823	.092552	.095318	.098118	.100954	.103825	.106730	.109670	.112643	.118690	.124869
	.30	.088323	.090981	.093675	.096405	.099170	.101971	.104806	.107677	.110583	.113522	.116495	.122543	.128721
	.20	.092176	.094833	.097527	.100257	.103022	.105823	.108659	.111530	.114435	.117374	.120348	.126395	.132574
	.10	.096028	.098686	.101379	.104109	.106874	.109675	.112511	.115382	.118287	.121227	.124200	.130247	.136426
	0.00	.099880	.102538	.105232	.107961	.110727	.113527	.116363	.119234	.122139	.125079	.128052	.134100	.140278
	-.10	.103733	.106390	.109084	.111814	.114579	.117380	.120216	.123086	.125992	.128931	.131905	.137952	.144130
	-.20	.107585	.110242	.112936	.115666	.118431	.121232	.124068	.126939	.129844	.132783	.135757	.141804	.147983
	-.30	.111437	.114095	.116788	.119518	.122284	.125084	.127920	.130791	.133696	.136636	.139609	.145656	.151835
	-.40	.115289	.117947	.120641	.123370	.126136	.128937	.131772	.134643	.137548	.140488	.143461	.149509	.155687
15	.40	.069855	.072996	.076190	.079436	.082732	.086077	.089471	.092913	.096401	.099935	.103513	.110797	.118245
	.30	.073707	.076849	.080043	.083288	.086584	.089930	.093324	.096765	.100254	.103787	.107365	.114649	.122097
	.20	.077559	.080701	.083895	.087140	.090436	.093782	.097176	.100618	.104106	.107640	.111218	.118502	.125949
	.10	.081412	.084553	.087747	.090993	.094289	.097634	.101028	.104470	.107958	.111492	.115070	.122354	.129801
	0.00	.085264	.088405	.091599	.094845	.098141	.101486	.104881	.108322	.111811	.115344	.118922	.126206	.133654
	-.10	.089116	.092258	.095452	.098697	.101993	.105339	.108733	.112175	.115663	.119196	.122774	.130058	.137506
	-.20	.092968	.096110	.099304	.102549	.105845	.109191	.112585	.116027	.119515	.123049	.126627	.133911	.141358
	-.30	.096821	.099962	.103156	.106402	.109698	.113043	.116437	.119879	.123367	.126901	.130479	.137763	.145210
	-.40	.100673	.103815	.107008	.110254	.113550	.116896	.120290	.123731	.127220	.130753	.134331	.141615	.149063
20	.40	.062768	.066188	.069668	.073207	.076803	.080454	.084158	.087913	.091716	.095566	.099461	.107376	.115446
	.30	.066620	.070040	.073521	.077060	.080656	.084307	.088010	.091765	.095568	.099418	.103313	.111228	.119298
	.20	.070473	.073892	.077373	.080912	.084508	.088159	.091863	.095617	.099420	.103270	.107165	.115081	.123151
	.10	.074325	.077745	.081225	.084764	.088360	.092011	.095715	.099469	.103273	.107123	.111017	.118933	.127003
	0.00	.078177	.081597	.085077	.088617	.092213	.095863	.099567	.103322	.107125	.110975	.114870	.122785	.130855
	-.10	.082030	.085449	.088930	.092469	.096065	.099716	.103419	.107174	.110977	.114827	.118722	.126637	.134707
	-.20	.085882	.089302	.092782	.096321	.099917	.103568	.107272	.111026	.114829	.118680	.122574	.130490	.138560
	-.30	.089734	.093154	.096634	.100173	.103769	.107420	.111124	.114878	.118682	.122532	.126427	.134342	.142412
	-.40	.093586	.097006	.100487	.104026	.107622	.111272	.114976	.118731	.122534	.126384	.130279	.138194	.146264
25	.40	.058686	.062299	.065977	.069716	.073515	.077370	.081278	.085235	.089240	.093288	.097378	.105670	.114094
	.30	.062538	.066151	.069829	.073569	.077367	.081222	.085130	.089087	.093092	.097141	.101230	.109522	.117946
	.20	.066391	.070003	.073681	.077421	.081220	.085074	.088982	.092940	.096944	.100993	.105082	.113374	.121799
	.10	.070243	.073856	.077533	.081273	.085072	.088927	.092834	.096792	.100797	.104845	.108935	.117227	.125651
	0.00	.074095	.077708	.081386	.085125	.088924	.092779	.096687	.100644	.104649	.108697	.112787	.121079	.129503
	-.10	.077947	.081560	.085238	.088978	.092777	.096631	.100539	.104497	.108501	.112550	.116639	.124931	.133356
	-.20	.081800	.085412	.089090	.092830	.096629	.100484	.104391	.108349	.112353	.116402	.120492	.128783	.137208
	-.30	.085652	.089265	.092942	.096682	.100481	.104336	.108244	.112201	.116206	.120254	.124344	.132636	.141060
	-.40	.089504	.093117	.096795	.100535	.104333	.108188	.112096	.116053	.120058	.124106	.128196	.136488	.144912
30	.40	.056099	.059859	.063686	.067576	.071525	.075528	.079582	.083682	.087825	.092008	.096227	.104759	.113399
	.30	.059951	.063711	.067538	.071428	.075377	.079380	.083434	.087534	.091678	.095860	.100079	.108611	.117251
	.20	.063803	.067564	.071391	.075281	.079229	.083232	.087286	.091387	.095530	.099713	.103931	.112464	.121104
	.10	.067656	.071416	.075243	.079133	.083081	.087085	.091138	.095239	.099382	.103565	.107784	.116316	.124956
	0.00	.071508	.075268	.079095	.082985	.086934	.090937	.094991	.099091	.103234	.107417	.111636	.120168	.128808
	-.10	.075360	.079120	.082947	.086837	.090786	.094789	.098843	.102943	.107087	.111269	.115488	.124021	.132660
	-.20	.079212	.082973	.086800	.090690	.094638	.098641	.102695	.106796	.110939	.115122	.119340	.127873	.136513
	-.30	.083065	.086825	.090652	.094542	.098491	.102494	.106547	.110648	.114791	.118974	.123193	.131725	.140365
	-.40	.086917	.090677	.094504	.098394	.102343	.106346	.110400	.114500	.118644	.122826	.127045	.135577	.144217

10.0 YEAR HOLDING PERIOD
.250 EQUITY YIELD RATE
.600 LOAN RATIO

INTEREST RATE

TERM YEARS	APPR DEP	5.0	5.5	6.0	6.5	7.0	7.5	8.0	8.5	9.0	9.5	10.0	11.0	12.0
10	.40	.146295	.148066	.149862	.151682	.153526	.155393	.157283	.159197	.161134	.163094	.165076	.169107	.173227
	.30	.149302	.151073	.152869	.154689	.156533	.158400	.160290	.162204	.164141	.166101	.168083	.172114	.176234
	.20	.152310	.154081	.155877	.157697	.159541	.161407	.163298	.165212	.167149	.169108	.171090	.175122	.179241
	.10	.155317	.157088	.158884	.160704	.162548	.164415	.166305	.168219	.170156	.172115	.174098	.178129	.182249
	0.00	.158324	.160095	.161891	.163711	.165555	.167422	.169312	.171226	.173163	.175123	.177105	.181136	.185256
	-.10	.161331	.163102	.164898	.166718	.168562	.170429	.172319	.174233	.176170	.178130	.180112	.184144	.188263
	-.20	.164339	.166110	.167906	.169726	.171570	.173436	.175327	.177241	.179178	.181137	.183120	.187151	.191270
	-.30	.167346	.169117	.170913	.172733	.174577	.176444	.178334	.180248	.182185	.184144	.186127	.190158	.194278
	-.40	.170353	.172124	.173920	.175740	.177584	.179451	.181341	.183255	.185192	.187152	.189134	.193165	.197285
15	.40	.134426	.136476	.138561	.140680	.142834	.145020	.147239	.149489	.151771	.154083	.156425	.161195	.166075
	.30	.137433	.139483	.141568	.143687	.145841	.148027	.150246	.152496	.154778	.157090	.159432	.164202	.169082
	.20	.140441	.142490	.144575	.146695	.148848	.151034	.153253	.155504	.157785	.160097	.162439	.167209	.172089
	.10	.143448	.145498	.147583	.149702	.151855	.154042	.156261	.158511	.160793	.163105	.165447	.170217	.175096
	0.00	.146455	.148505	.150590	.152709	.154863	.157049	.159268	.161518	.163800	.166112	.168454	.173224	.178104
	-.10	.149462	.151512	.153597	.155716	.157870	.160056	.162275	.164525	.166807	.169119	.171461	.176231	.181111
	-.20	.152469	.154519	.156604	.158724	.160877	.163063	.165282	.167533	.169814	.172127	.174469	.179238	.184118
	-.30	.155477	.157527	.159612	.161731	.163884	.166071	.168289	.170540	.172822	.175134	.177476	.182246	.187125
	-.40	.158484	.160534	.162619	.164738	.166892	.169078	.171297	.173547	.175829	.178141	.180483	.185253	.190133
20	.40	.128671	.130892	.133154	.135456	.137797	.140176	.142590	.145040	.147523	.150039	.152585	.157765	.163053
	.30	.131678	.133899	.136161	.138464	.140805	.143183	.145598	.148047	.150531	.153046	.155592	.160773	.166061
	.20	.134686	.136907	.139169	.141471	.143812	.146191	.148605	.151055	.153538	.156053	.158600	.163780	.169068
	.10	.137693	.139914	.142176	.144478	.146819	.149198	.151612	.154062	.156545	.159061	.161607	.166787	.172075
	0.00	.140700	.142921	.145183	.147485	.149826	.152205	.154619	.157069	.159552	.162068	.164614	.169794	.175082
	-.10	.143707	.145928	.148191	.150493	.152834	.155212	.157627	.160076	.162560	.165075	.167621	.172802	.178090
	-.20	.146715	.148936	.151198	.153500	.155841	.158220	.160634	.163084	.165567	.168082	.170629	.175809	.181097
	-.30	.149722	.151943	.154205	.156507	.158848	.161227	.163641	.166091	.168574	.171090	.173636	.178816	.184104
	-.40	.152729	.154950	.157212	.159514	.161855	.164234	.166648	.169098	.171581	.174097	.176643	.181823	.187111
25	.40	.125357	.127703	.130094	.132528	.135004	.137519	.140071	.142658	.145279	.147931	.150612	.156055	.161594
	.30	.128364	.130710	.133101	.135535	.138011	.140526	.143078	.145665	.148286	.150938	.153619	.159062	.164601
	.20	.131371	.133717	.136108	.138543	.141018	.143533	.146085	.148672	.151293	.153945	.156626	.162069	.167608
	.10	.134378	.136724	.139116	.141550	.144026	.146540	.149093	.151680	.154300	.156952	.159634	.165077	.170616
	0.00	.137386	.139732	.142123	.144557	.147033	.149548	.152100	.154687	.157308	.159959	.162641	.168084	.173623
	-.10	.140393	.142739	.145130	.147564	.150040	.152555	.155107	.157694	.160315	.162967	.165648	.171091	.176630
	-.20	.143400	.145746	.148137	.150572	.153047	.155562	.158114	.160701	.163322	.165974	.168655	.174098	.179637
	-.30	.146407	.148753	.151145	.153579	.156055	.158569	.161122	.163709	.166329	.168981	.171663	.177106	.182645
	-.40	.149415	.151761	.154152	.156586	.159062	.161577	.164129	.166716	.169337	.171989	.174670	.180113	.185652
30	.40	.123256	.125702	.128195	.130733	.133313	.135932	.138587	.141276	.143997	.146746	.149521	.155142	.160843
	.30	.126263	.128709	.131202	.133740	.136320	.138939	.141594	.144283	.147004	.149753	.152528	.158149	.163851
	.20	.129270	.131716	.134209	.136747	.139327	.141947	.144602	.147291	.150011	.152761	.155536	.161157	.166858
	.10	.132277	.134723	.137217	.139755	.142335	.144954	.147609	.150298	.153018	.155768	.158543	.164164	.169865
	0.00	.135285	.137731	.140224	.142762	.145342	.147961	.150616	.153305	.156026	.158775	.161550	.167171	.172872
	-.10	.138292	.140738	.143231	.145769	.148349	.150968	.153623	.156313	.159033	.161782	.164557	.170178	.175880
	-.20	.141299	.143745	.146238	.148776	.151356	.153975	.156631	.159320	.162040	.164790	.167565	.173186	.178887
	-.30	.144306	.146752	.149246	.151784	.154364	.156983	.159638	.162327	.165047	.167797	.170572	.176193	.181894
	-.40	.147314	.149760	.152253	.154791	.157371	.159990	.162645	.165334	.168055	.170804	.173579	.179200	.184901

10.0-YEAR HOLDING PERIOD
.250 EQUITY YIELD RATE
.667 LOAN RATIO

INTEREST RATE

TERM YEARS	APPR DEP	5.0	5.5	6.0	6.5	7.0	7.5	8.0	8.5	9.0	9.5	10.0	11.0	12.0
10	.40	.136108	.138076	.140072	.142094	.144142	.146217	.148318	.150444	.152596	.154774	.156976	.161456	.166032
	.30	.139115	.141084	.143079	.145101	.147150	.149224	.151325	.153451	.155603	.157781	.159983	.164463	.169040
	.20	.142122	.144091	.146086	.148108	.150157	.152231	.154332	.156459	.158611	.160788	.162991	.167470	.172047
	.10	.145130	.147098	.149094	.151116	.153164	.155239	.157339	.159466	.161618	.163795	.165998	.170477	.175054
	0.00	.148137	.150105	.152101	.154123	.156171	.158246	.160347	.162473	.164625	.166803	.169005	.173485	.178061
	-.10	.151144	.153113	.155108	.157130	.159179	.161253	.163354	.165480	.167632	.169810	.172012	.176492	.181069
	-.20	.154151	.156120	.158115	.160137	.162186	.164260	.166361	.168488	.170640	.172817	.175020	.179499	.184076
	-.30	.157159	.159127	.161123	.163145	.165193	.167268	.169368	.171495	.173647	.175824	.178027	.182506	.187083
	-.40	.160166	.162135	.164130	.166152	.168200	.170275	.172376	.174502	.176654	.178832	.181034	.185514	.190090
15	.40	.122920	.125198	.127515	.129870	.132262	.134691	.137157	.139657	.142193	.144762	.147364	.152664	.158086
	.30	.125927	.128205	.130522	.132877	.135269	.137699	.140164	.142665	.145200	.147769	.150371	.155671	.161093
	.20	.128935	.131213	.133529	.135884	.138277	.140706	.143171	.145672	.148207	.150776	.153378	.158678	.164100
	.10	.131942	.134220	.136537	.138892	.141284	.143713	.146178	.148679	.151214	.153783	.156385	.161685	.167108
	0.00	.134949	.137227	.139544	.141899	.144291	.146720	.149186	.151686	.154222	.156791	.159393	.164693	.170115
	-.10	.137956	.140234	.142551	.144906	.147298	.149728	.152193	.154694	.157229	.159798	.162400	.167700	.173122
	-.20	.140964	.143242	.145558	.147913	.150306	.152735	.155200	.157701	.160236	.162805	.165407	.170707	.176129
	-.30	.143971	.146249	.148566	.150921	.153313	.155742	.158207	.160708	.163243	.165812	.168414	.173714	.179137
	-.40	.146978	.149256	.151573	.153928	.156320	.158749	.161215	.163715	.166251	.168820	.171422	.176722	.182144
20	.40	.116526	.118994	.121507	.124065	.126666	.129309	.131992	.134714	.137473	.140268	.143097	.148853	.154729
	.30	.119533	.122001	.124515	.127073	.129674	.132316	.134999	.137721	.140480	.143275	.146105	.151860	.157736
	.20	.122541	.125008	.127522	.130080	.132681	.135324	.138007	.140728	.143488	.146283	.149112	.154868	.160743
	.10	.125548	.128016	.130529	.133087	.135688	.138331	.141014	.143736	.146495	.149290	.152119	.157875	.163751
	0.00	.128555	.131023	.133536	.136094	.138695	.141338	.144021	.146743	.149502	.152297	.155126	.160882	.166758
	-.10	.131562	.134030	.136544	.139102	.141703	.144345	.147028	.149750	.152509	.155304	.158134	.163889	.169765
	-.20	.134570	.137037	.139551	.142109	.144710	.147353	.150036	.152757	.155517	.158312	.161141	.166897	.172772
	-.30	.137577	.140045	.142558	.145116	.147717	.150360	.153043	.155765	.158524	.161319	.164148	.169904	.175780
	-.40	.140584	.143052	.145565	.148123	.150724	.153367	.156050	.158772	.161531	.164326	.167155	.172911	.178787
25	.40	.112843	.115450	.118107	.120812	.123562	.126357	.129192	.132067	.134979	.137926	.140905	.146953	.153107
	.30	.115850	.118457	.121114	.123819	.126570	.129364	.132200	.135074	.137986	.140933	.143912	.149960	.156114
	.20	.118858	.121464	.124121	.126826	.129577	.132371	.135207	.138082	.140994	.143940	.146919	.152967	.159122
	.10	.121865	.124472	.127129	.129833	.132584	.135379	.138214	.141089	.144001	.146947	.149927	.155974	.162129
	0.00	.124872	.127479	.130136	.132841	.135591	.138386	.141221	.144096	.147008	.149955	.152934	.158982	.165136
	-.10	.127879	.130486	.133143	.135848	.138599	.141393	.144229	.147104	.150015	.152962	.155941	.161989	.168143
	-.20	.130887	.133493	.136150	.138855	.141606	.144400	.147236	.150111	.153023	.155969	.158948	.164996	.171151
	-.30	.133894	.136501	.139157	.141862	.144613	.147408	.150243	.153118	.156030	.158976	.161955	.168003	.174158
	-.40	.136901	.139508	.142165	.144870	.147620	.150415	.153250	.156125	.159037	.161984	.164963	.171011	.177165
30	.40	.110509	.113227	.115997	.118817	.121684	.124594	.127544	.130532	.133554	.136609	.139693	.145938	.152273
	.30	.113516	.116234	.119004	.121824	.124691	.127601	.130551	.133539	.136562	.139616	.142700	.148946	.155281
	.20	.116523	.119241	.122012	.124832	.127698	.130608	.133558	.136546	.139569	.142623	.145707	.151953	.158288
	.10	.119531	.122248	.125019	.127839	.130705	.133615	.136566	.139554	.142577	.145631	.148715	.154960	.161295
	0.00	.122538	.125256	.128026	.130846	.133713	.136623	.139573	.142561	.145583	.148638	.151722	.157968	.164302
	-.10	.125545	.128263	.131033	.133853	.136720	.139630	.142580	.145568	.148591	.151645	.154729	.160975	.167310
	-.20	.128552	.131270	.134041	.136861	.139727	.142637	.145587	.148575	.151598	.154652	.157736	.163982	.170317
	-.30	.131560	.134277	.137048	.139868	.142734	.145644	.148595	.151583	.154605	.157660	.160744	.166989	.173324
	-.40	.134567	.137285	.140055	.142875	.145742	.148652	.151602	.154590	.157612	.160667	.163751	.169997	.176331

10.0 YEAR HOLDING PERIOD
.250 EQUITY YIELD RATE
.700 LOAN RATIO

INTEREST RATE

TERM YEARS	APPR DEP	5.0	5.5	6.0	6.5	7.0	7.5	8.0	8.5	9.0	9.5	10.0	11.0	12.0
10	.40	.131015	.133082	.135177	.137300	.139451	.141630	.143835	.146068	.148328	.150614	.152927	.157630	.162436
	.30	.134022	.136090	.138185	.140308	.142459	.144637	.146843	.149075	.151335	.153621	.155934	.160637	.165443
	.20	.137030	.139097	.141192	.143315	.145466	.147644	.149850	.152083	.154342	.156629	.158941	.163645	.168450
	.10	.140037	.142104	.144199	.146322	.148473	.150651	.152857	.155090	.157350	.159636	.161952	.166652	.171458
	0.00	.143044	.145111	.147206	.149330	.151480	.153659	.155864	.158097	.160357	.162643	.164956	.169659	.174465
	-.10	.146051	.148119	.150214	.152337	.154488	.156666	.158872	.161104	.163364	.165650	.167963	.172666	.177472
	-.20	.149059	.151126	.153221	.155344	.157495	.159673	.161879	.164112	.166371	.168658	.170974	.175674	.180487
	-.30	.152066	.154133	.156228	.158351	.160502	.162680	.164886	.167119	.169379	.171665	.173978	.178681	.183487
	-.40	.155073	.157140	.159235	.161359	.163509	.165688	.167893	.170126	.172386	.174672	.176985	.181688	.186494
15	.40	.117168	.119560	.121993	.124465	.126977	.129528	.132116	.134742	.137404	.140102	.142834	.148399	.154092
	.30	.120175	.122567	.125000	.127473	.129985	.132535	.135124	.137749	.140411	.143109	.145841	.151406	.157099
	.20	.123183	.125575	.128007	.130480	.132992	.135542	.138131	.140757	.143419	.146116	.148848	.154413	.160106
	.10	.126190	.128582	.131014	.133487	.135999	.138550	.141138	.143764	.146426	.149123	.151856	.157421	.163114
	0.00	.129197	.131589	.134022	.136494	.139006	.141557	.144145	.146771	.149433	.152131	.154863	.160428	.166121
	-.10	.132204	.134596	.137029	.139502	.142014	.144564	.147153	.149778	.152440	.155138	.157870	.163435	.169128
	-.20	.135212	.137604	.140036	.142509	.145021	.147571	.150160	.152786	.155448	.158145	.160877	.166442	.172135
	-.30	.138219	.140611	.143043	.145516	.148028	.150579	.153167	.155793	.158455	.161152	.163885	.169450	.175143
	-.40	.141226	.143618	.146051	.148523	.151035	.153586	.156175	.158800	.161462	.164160	.166892	.172457	.178150
20	.40	.110455	.113046	.115685	.118371	.121102	.123877	.126694	.129552	.132449	.135383	.138354	.144398	.150567
	.30	.113462	.116053	.118692	.121378	.124109	.126884	.129701	.132559	.135456	.138391	.141361	.147405	.153574
	.20	.116469	.119060	.121699	.124385	.127116	.129891	.132708	.135566	.138463	.141398	.144369	.150412	.156582
	.10	.119476	.122067	.124707	.127392	.130123	.132898	.135715	.138573	.141470	.144405	.147376	.153424	.159589
	0.00	.122484	.125075	.127714	.130400	.133131	.135906	.138723	.141581	.144478	.147412	.150383	.156427	.162596
	-.10	.125491	.128082	.130721	.133407	.136138	.138913	.141730	.144588	.147485	.150420	.153391	.159434	.165603
	-.20	.128498	.131089	.133728	.136414	.139145	.141920	.144737	.147595	.150492	.153427	.156398	.162441	.168611
	-.30	.131505	.134096	.136736	.139421	.142152	.144927	.147744	.150602	.153499	.156434	.159405	.165449	.171618
	-.40	.134513	.137104	.139743	.142429	.145160	.147935	.150752	.153610	.156507	.159441	.162412	.168456	.174625
25	.40	.106587	.109324	.112114	.114954	.117843	.120777	.123754	.126773	.129830	.132924	.136052	.142402	.148864
	.30	.109595	.112332	.115121	.117962	.120850	.123784	.126761	.129780	.132837	.135931	.139059	.145410	.151872
	.20	.112602	.115339	.118129	.120969	.123857	.126791	.129768	.132787	.135844	.138938	.142066	.148417	.154879
	.10	.115609	.118346	.121136	.123976	.126864	.129798	.132776	.135794	.138852	.141946	.145074	.151424	.157886
	0.00	.118616	.121353	.124143	.126983	.129872	.132806	.135783	.138802	.141859	.144953	.148081	.154431	.160893
	-.10	.121624	.124361	.127150	.129991	.132879	.135813	.138790	.141808	.144866	.147960	.151088	.157439	.163901
	-.20	.124631	.127368	.130158	.132998	.135886	.138820	.141798	.144816	.147873	.150967	.154095	.160446	.166908
	-.30	.127638	.130375	.133165	.136005	.138893	.141827	.144805	.147823	.150881	.153975	.157103	.163453	.169915
	-.40	.130645	.133383	.136172	.139012	.141901	.144835	.147812	.150831	.153888	.156982	.160110	.166460	.172922
30	.40	.104136	.106990	.109899	.112860	.115870	.118925	.122023	.125160	.128334	.131541	.134779	.141337	.147989
	.30	.107144	.109997	.112906	.115867	.118877	.121932	.125030	.128168	.131341	.134549	.137787	.144345	.150996
	.20	.110151	.113005	.115913	.118874	.121884	.124939	.128038	.131175	.134349	.137556	.140794	.147352	.154003
	.10	.113158	.116012	.118921	.121882	.124892	.127947	.131045	.134182	.137356	.140563	.143801	.150359	.157011
	0.00	.116165	.119019	.121928	.124889	.127899	.130954	.134052	.137189	.140363	.143570	.146808	.153366	.160018
	-.10	.119173	.122026	.124935	.127896	.130906	.133962	.137059	.140197	.143370	.146578	.149816	.156374	.163025
	-.20	.122180	.125034	.127942	.130903	.133913	.136969	.140067	.143204	.146378	.149585	.152823	.159381	.166032
	-.30	.125187	.128041	.130950	.133911	.136921	.139976	.143074	.146211	.149385	.152592	.155830	.162388	.169040
	-.40	.128194	.131048	.133957	.136918	.139928	.142983	.146081	.149219	.152392	.155599	.158837	.165395	.172047

10.0 YEAR HOLDING PERIOD
.250 EQUITY YIELD RATE
.750 LOAN RATIO

INTEREST RATE

TERM YEARS	APPR DEP	5.0	5.5	6.0	6.5	7.0	7.5	8.0	8.5	9.0	9.5	10.0	11.0	12.0
10	.40	.123376	.125590	.127835	.130110	.132414	.134748	.137111	.139504	.141925	.144374	.146852	.151892	.157040
	.30	.126383	.128597	.130842	.133117	.135421	.137755	.140119	.142511	.144932	.147382	.149859	.154899	.160048
	.20	.129390	.131605	.133850	.136124	.138429	.140763	.143126	.145518	.147939	.150389	.152867	.157906	.163055
	.10	.132397	.134612	.136857	.139132	.141436	.143770	.146133	.148525	.150947	.153396	.155874	.160913	.166062
	0.00	.135405	.137619	.139864	.142139	.144443	.146777	.149140	.151533	.153954	.156403	.158881	.163921	.169069
	-.10	.138412	.140626	.142871	.145146	.147450	.149784	.152148	.154540	.156961	.159411	.161888	.166928	.172077
	-.20	.141419	.143634	.145879	.148153	.150458	.152792	.155155	.157547	.159968	.162418	.164896	.169935	.175084
	-.30	.144426	.146641	.148886	.151161	.153465	.155799	.158162	.160554	.162976	.165425	.167903	.172942	.178091
	-.40	.147434	.149648	.151893	.154168	.156472	.158806	.161169	.163562	.165983	.168432	.170910	.175950	.181098
15	.40	.108539	.111102	.113708	.116358	.119049	.121782	.124555	.127369	.130221	.133111	.136038	.142001	.148101
	.30	.111547	.114109	.116716	.119365	.122056	.124789	.127563	.130376	.133228	.136118	.139046	.145008	.151108
	.20	.114554	.117117	.119723	.122372	.125064	.127796	.130570	.133383	.136235	.139125	.142053	.148015	.154115
	.10	.117561	.120124	.122731	.125379	.128071	.130804	.133577	.136390	.139243	.142133	.145060	.151022	.157122
	0.00	.120568	.123131	.125737	.128387	.131078	.133811	.136584	.139398	.142250	.145140	.148067	.154030	.160130
	-.10	.123576	.126138	.128745	.131394	.134085	.136818	.139592	.142405	.145257	.148147	.151075	.157037	.163137
	-.20	.126583	.129146	.131752	.134401	.137093	.139826	.142599	.145412	.148264	.151155	.154082	.160044	.166144
	-.30	.129590	.132153	.134759	.137408	.140100	.142833	.145606	.148419	.151272	.154162	.157089	.163052	.169151
	-.40	.132597	.135160	.137766	.140416	.143107	.145840	.148613	.151427	.154279	.157169	.160096	.166059	.172159
20	.40	.101346	.104122	.106950	.109828	.112754	.115727	.118745	.121807	.124911	.128056	.131239	.137714	.144324
	.30	.104354	.107130	.109957	.112835	.115761	.118734	.121753	.124815	.127919	.131063	.134246	.140721	.147331
	.20	.107361	.110137	.112965	.115842	.118768	.121741	.124760	.127822	.130926	.134070	.137253	.143729	.150338
	.10	.110368	.113144	.115972	.118849	.121776	.124749	.127767	.130829	.133933	.137077	.140260	.146736	.153346
	0.00	.113375	.116151	.118979	.121857	.124783	.127756	.130774	.133836	.136940	.140085	.143268	.149743	.156353
	-.10	.116383	.119159	.121986	.124864	.127790	.130763	.133782	.136844	.139948	.143092	.146275	.152750	.159360
	-.20	.119390	.122166	.124994	.127871	.130797	.133770	.136789	.139851	.142955	.146099	.149282	.155758	.162368
	-.30	.122397	.125173	.128001	.130879	.133805	.136778	.139796	.142858	.145962	.149107	.152290	.158765	.165375
	-.40	.125404	.128180	.131008	.133886	.136812	.139785	.142803	.145865	.148969	.152114	.155297	.161772	.168382
25	.40	.097203	.100135	.103124	.106167	.109262	.112406	.115596	.118830	.122106	.125420	.128772	.135576	.142507
	.30	.100210	.103143	.106132	.109175	.112269	.115413	.118603	.121837	.125113	.128428	.131779	.138583	.145507
	.20	.103217	.106150	.109139	.112182	.115277	.118421	.121610	.124844	.128120	.131435	.134786	.141590	.148514
	.10	.106225	.109157	.112146	.115189	.118284	.121427	.124617	.127852	.131127	.134442	.137794	.144598	.151521
	0.00	.109232	.112164	.115153	.118196	.121291	.124435	.127625	.130859	.134134	.137449	.140801	.147605	.154529
	-.10	.112239	.115172	.118161	.121204	.124298	.127442	.130632	.133866	.137142	.140457	.143808	.150612	.157536
	-.20	.115246	.118179	.121168	.124211	.127306	.130449	.133639	.136873	.140149	.143464	.146815	.153619	.160543
	-.30	.118254	.121186	.124175	.127218	.130313	.133456	.136647	.139881	.143156	.146471	.149823	.156627	.163550
	-.40	.121261	.124193	.127182	.130225	.133320	.136464	.139654	.142888	.146164	.149478	.152830	.159634	.166558
30	.40	.094577	.097634	.100751	.103923	.107148	.110423	.113741	.117103	.120503	.123939	.127409	.134435	.141562
	.30	.097584	.100641	.103758	.106931	.110156	.113429	.116748	.120110	.123510	.126947	.130416	.137442	.144569
	.20	.100591	.103649	.106765	.109938	.113163	.116436	.119756	.123117	.126517	.129954	.133423	.140449	.147576
	.10	.103599	.106656	.109773	.112945	.116170	.119444	.122763	.126124	.129525	.132961	.136430	.143457	.150583
	0.00	.106606	.109663	.112780	.115952	.119177	.122451	.125770	.129132	.132532	.135968	.139438	.146464	.153591
	-.10	.109613	.112670	.115787	.118960	.122185	.125458	.128777	.132139	.135539	.138976	.142445	.149471	.156598
	-.20	.112620	.115678	.118794	.121967	.125192	.128466	.131785	.135146	.138546	.141983	.145452	.152478	.159605
	-.30	.115628	.118685	.121802	.124974	.128199	.131473	.134792	.138153	.141554	.144990	.148459	.155486	.162612
	-.40	.118635	.121692	.124809	.127981	.131206	.134480	.137799	.141161	.144561	.147997	.151467	.158493	.165620

10.0 YEAR HOLDING PERIOD
.250 EQUITY YIELD RATE
.800 LOAN RATIO

INTEREST RATE

TERM YEARS	APPR DEP	5.0	5.5	6.0	6.5	7.0	7.5	8.0	8.5	9.0	9.5	10.0	11.0	12.0
10	.40	.115736	.118098	.120493	.122919	.125377	.127867	.130387	.132939	.135522	.138135	.140778	.146153	.151645
	.30	.118743	.121105	.123500	.125926	.128384	.130874	.133395	.135946	.138529	.141142	.143785	.149160	.154652
	.20	.121750	.124113	.126507	.128933	.131392	.133881	.136402	.138954	.141536	.144149	.146792	.152167	.157660
	.10	.124758	.127120	.129514	.131941	.134399	.136888	.139409	.141961	.144543	.147156	.149799	.155175	.160667
	0.00	.127765	.130127	.132524	.134948	.137406	.139896	.142416	.144968	.147551	.150164	.152807	.158182	.163674
	-.10	.130772	.133134	.135529	.137955	.140413	.142903	.145424	.147975	.150558	.153171	.155814	.161189	.166681
	-.20	.133787	.136142	.138536	.140963	.143421	.145910	.148431	.150983	.153565	.156178	.158821	.164196	.169689
	-.30	.136787	.139149	.141543	.143990	.146428	.148917	.151438	.153990	.156572	.159185	.161828	.167204	.172696
	-.40	.139794	.142156	.144551	.146977	.149435	.151925	.154445	.156997	.159580	.162193	.164836	.170211	.175703
15	.40	.099911	.102644	.105424	.108250	.111121	.114036	.116994	.119995	.123037	.126120	.129243	.135603	.142109
	.30	.102918	.105651	.108432	.111257	.114128	.117043	.120002	.123002	.126045	.129128	.132250	.138610	.145116
	.20	.105925	.108659	.111439	.114265	.117136	.120051	.123009	.126010	.129052	.132135	.135257	.141617	.148124
	.10	.108932	.111666	.114446	.117272	.120143	.123058	.126016	.129017	.132059	.135142	.138265	.144624	.151131
	0.00	.111940	.114673	.117453	.120279	.123150	.126065	.129023	.132024	.135066	.138149	.141272	.147632	.154138
	-.10	.114947	.117680	.120461	.123286	.126157	.129072	.132031	.135031	.138074	.141157	.144279	.150639	.157146
	-.20	.117954	.120688	.123468	.126294	.129165	.132080	.135038	.138039	.141081	.144164	.147286	.153646	.160153
	-.30	.120961	.123695	.126475	.129301	.132172	.135087	.138045	.141046	.144088	.147171	.150294	.156654	.163160
	-.40	.123969	.126702	.129482	.132308	.135179	.138094	.141052	.144053	.147095	.150178	.153301	.159661	.166167
20	.40	.092238	.095199	.098215	.101285	.104406	.107577	.110797	.114063	.117374	.120728	.124123	.131030	.138081
	.30	.095245	.098206	.101223	.104292	.107413	.110585	.113804	.117070	.120381	.123735	.127130	.134037	.141088
	.20	.098252	.101214	.104230	.107299	.110421	.113592	.116811	.120078	.123389	.126743	.130138	.137045	.144095
	.10	.101260	.104221	.107237	.110307	.113428	.116599	.119819	.123085	.126396	.129750	.133145	.140052	.147103
	0.00	.104267	.107228	.110244	.113314	.116435	.119606	.122826	.126092	.129403	.132757	.136152	.143059	.150110
	-.10	.107274	.110235	.113252	.116321	.119442	.122614	.125833	.129099	.132410	.135764	.139160	.146066	.153117
	-.20	.110281	.113243	.116259	.119328	.122450	.125621	.128840	.132107	.135418	.138772	.142167	.149074	.156124
	-.30	.113289	.116250	.119266	.122336	.125457	.128628	.131848	.135114	.138425	.141779	.145174	.152081	.159132
	-.40	.116296	.119257	.122273	.125343	.128464	.131635	.134855	.138121	.141432	.144786	.148181	.155088	.162139
25	.40	.087818	.090946	.094135	.097381	.100681	.104035	.107437	.110887	.114381	.117917	.121492	.128750	.136135
	.30	.090826	.093954	.097142	.100388	.103689	.107042	.110445	.113894	.117388	.120924	.124499	.131757	.139142
	.20	.093833	.096961	.100150	.103395	.106696	.110049	.113452	.116902	.120396	.123932	.127507	.134764	.142149
	.10	.096840	.099968	.103156	.106402	.109703	.113056	.116459	.119909	.123403	.126939	.130514	.137771	.145157
	0.00	.099847	.102975	.106164	.109410	.112710	.116064	.119466	.122916	.126410	.129946	.133521	.140779	.148164
	-.10	.102855	.105983	.109171	.112417	.115718	.119071	.122474	.125923	.129418	.132953	.136528	.143786	.151171
	-.20	.105862	.108990	.112178	.115424	.118725	.122078	.125481	.128931	.132425	.135961	.139536	.146793	.154178
	-.30	.108869	.111997	.115185	.118431	.121732	.125085	.128488	.131938	.135432	.138968	.142543	.149800	.157186
	-.40	.111876	.115004	.118193	.121439	.124739	.128093	.131495	.134945	.138439	.141975	.145550	.152808	.160193
30	.40	.085017	.088278	.091603	.094987	.098427	.101919	.105459	.109045	.112672	.116337	.120038	.127533	.135134
	.30	.088024	.091286	.094610	.097994	.101434	.104926	.108466	.112052	.115679	.119344	.123045	.130540	.138142
	.20	.091032	.094293	.097617	.101001	.104441	.107933	.111474	.115059	.118686	.122352	.126052	.133547	.141149
	.10	.094039	.097300	.100625	.104009	.107449	.110940	.114481	.118066	.121694	.125359	.129059	.136554	.144156
	0.00	.097046	.100307	.103632	.107016	.110456	.113948	.117488	.121074	.124701	.128366	.132067	.139562	.147163
	-.10	.100053	.103315	.106639	.110023	.113463	.116955	.120495	.124081	.127708	.131373	.135074	.142569	.150171
	-.20	.103061	.106322	.109646	.113030	.116470	.119962	.123503	.127088	.130715	.134381	.138081	.145576	.153178
	-.30	.106068	.109329	.112654	.116038	.119478	.122969	.126510	.130095	.133723	.137388	.141089	.148583	.156185
	-.40	.109075	.112336	.115661	.119045	.122485	.125977	.129517	.133103	.136730	.140395	.144096	.151591	.159192

10.0 YEAR HOLDING PERIOD
.250 EQUITY YIELD RATE
.900 LOAN RATIO

INTEREST RATE

TERM YEARS	APPR DEP	5.0	5.5	6.0	6.5	7.0	7.5	8.0	8.5	9.0	9.5	10.0	11.0	12.0
10	.40	.100456	.103114	.105808	.108537	.111303	.114404	.116939	.119810	.122716	.125655	.128628	.134676	.140854
	.30	.103464	.106121	.108815	.111545	.114310	.117111	.119947	.122817	.125723	.128662	.131636	.137683	.143862
	.20	.106471	.109129	.111822	.114552	.117317	.120118	.122954	.125825	.128730	.131670	.134643	.140690	.146869
	.10	.109478	.112136	.114830	.117559	.120325	.123125	.125961	.128832	.131737	.134677	.137650	.143697	.149876
	0.00	.112485	.115143	.117837	.120567	.123332	.126133	.128968	.131839	.134745	.137684	.140657	.146705	.152883
	-.10	.115493	.118150	.120844	.123574	.126339	.129140	.131976	.134846	.137752	.140691	.143665	.149712	.155891
	-.20	.118500	.121158	.123851	.126581	.129346	.132147	.134983	.137854	.140759	.143699	.146672	.152719	.158898
	-.30	.121507	.124165	.126859	.129588	.132354	.135154	.137990	.140861	.143766	.146706	.149679	.155726	.161905
	-.40	.124514	.127172	.129866	.132596	.135361	.138162	.140998	.143868	.146774	.149713	.152687	.158734	.164912
15	.40	.082653	.085728	.088856	.092035	.095265	.098544	.101872	.105248	.108671	.112139	.115652	.122807	.130127
	.30	.085660	.088736	.091863	.095042	.098272	.101551	.104880	.108255	.111678	.115146	.118659	.125814	.133134
	.20	.088668	.091743	.094870	.098050	.101279	.104559	.107887	.111263	.114685	.118153	.121666	.128821	.136141
	.10	.091675	.094750	.097878	.101057	.104287	.107566	.110894	.114270	.117693	.121161	.124674	.131828	.139148
	0.00	.094682	.097757	.100885	.104064	.107294	.110573	.113901	.117277	.120700	.124168	.127681	.134836	.142156
	-.10	.097689	.100765	.103892	.107071	.110301	.113580	.116909	.120284	.123707	.127175	.130688	.137843	.145163
	-.20	.100697	.103772	.106899	.110079	.113308	.116588	.119916	.123292	.126714	.130182	.133695	.140850	.148170
	-.30	.103704	.106779	.109907	.113086	.116316	.119595	.122923	.126299	.129722	.133190	.136703	.143857	.151177
	-.40	.106711	.109786	.112914	.116093	.119323	.122602	.125930	.129306	.132729	.136197	.139710	.146865	.154185
20	.40	.074021	.077353	.080746	.084199	.087710	.091278	.094900	.098675	.102299	.106073	.109892	.117663	.125595
	.30	.077029	.080360	.083753	.087206	.090718	.094285	.097907	.101682	.105307	.109080	.112900	.120670	.128602
	.20	.080036	.083367	.086760	.090214	.093725	.097293	.100915	.104689	.108314	.112087	.115907	.123677	.131609
	.10	.083043	.086374	.089768	.093221	.096732	.100300	.103922	.107596	.111321	.115094	.118914	.126684	.134616
	0.00	.086050	.089382	.092775	.096228	.099739	.103307	.106929	.110604	.114328	.118102	.121921	.129692	.137624
	-.10	.089058	.092389	.095782	.099235	.102747	.106314	.109936	.113611	.117336	.121109	.124929	.132699	.140631
	-.20	.092065	.095396	.098789	.102243	.105754	.109322	.112944	.116618	.120343	.124116	.127936	.135706	.143638
	-.30	.095072	.098403	.101797	.105250	.108761	.112329	.115951	.119625	.123350	.127123	.130943	.138713	.146645
	-.40	.098079	.101411	.104804	.108257	.111769	.115336	.118958	.122633	.126357	.130131	.133950	.141721	.149653
25	.40	.069049	.072568	.076155	.079807	.083520	.087293	.091121	.095002	.098933	.102910	.106932	.115097	.123405
	.30	.072057	.075575	.079162	.082814	.086527	.090300	.094128	.098009	.101940	.105918	.109939	.118104	.126413
	.20	.075064	.078583	.082170	.085821	.089535	.093307	.097135	.101016	.104947	.108925	.112947	.121111	.129420
	.10	.078071	.081590	.085177	.088828	.092542	.096314	.100142	.104023	.107954	.111932	.115954	.124118	.132427
	0.00	.081078	.084597	.088184	.091836	.095549	.099322	.103150	.107031	.110962	.114939	.118961	.127126	.135434
	-.10	.084086	.087605	.091191	.094843	.098556	.102329	.106157	.110038	.113969	.117947	.121968	.130133	.138442
	-.20	.087093	.090612	.094199	.097850	.101564	.105336	.109164	.113045	.116976	.120954	.124976	.133140	.141449
	-.30	.090100	.093619	.097206	.100858	.104571	.108343	.112171	.116052	.119983	.123961	.127983	.136148	.144456
	-.40	.093107	.096626	.100213	.103865	.107578	.111351	.115179	.119060	.122991	.126968	.130990	.139155	.147463
30	.40	.065898	.069567	.073307	.077114	.079984	.084912	.088895	.092929	.097009	.101133	.105296	.113728	.122280
	.30	.068905	.072574	.076314	.080121	.083991	.087919	.091902	.095936	.100017	.104140	.108303	.116735	.125287
	.20	.071912	.075581	.079321	.083128	.086998	.090927	.094910	.098943	.103024	.107147	.111311	.119742	.128294
	.10	.074920	.078589	.082329	.086136	.090005	.093934	.097917	.101958	.106031	.110155	.114318	.122750	.131301
	0.00	.077927	.081596	.085336	.089143	.093013	.096941	.100924	.104958	.109038	.113162	.117325	.125757	.134309
	-.10	.080934	.084603	.088343	.092150	.096020	.099948	.103931	.107965	.112046	.116169	.120332	.128764	.137316
	-.20	.083941	.087610	.091350	.095157	.099027	.102956	.106939	.110972	.115053	.119176	.123340	.131771	.140323
	-.30	.086949	.090618	.094358	.098165	.102035	.105963	.109946	.113980	.118060	.122184	.126347	.134779	.143330
	-.40	.089956	.093625	.097365	.101172	.105042	.108970	.112953	.116987	.121067	.125191	.129354	.137786	.146338

269

10.0 YEAR HOLDING PERIOD
.300 EQUITY YIELD RATE
.600 LOAN RATIO

INTEREST RATE

TERM YEARS	APPR DEP	5.0	5.5	6.0	6.5	7.0	7.5	8.0	8.5	9.0	9.5	10.0	11.0	12.0
10	.40	.172904	.174675	.176471	.178291	.180135	.182002	.183892	.185806	.187743	.189703	.191685	.195717	.199836
	.30	.175250	.177022	.178818	.180637	.182481	.184348	.186239	.188153	.190089	.192049	.194031	.198063	.202182
	.20	.177596	.179368	.181164	.182984	.184827	.186695	.188585	.190499	.192436	.194395	.196378	.200409	.204528
	.10	.179943	.181715	.183510	.185330	.187176	.189041	.190931	.192845	.194782	.196742	.198724	.202756	.206875
	0.00	.182289	.184061	.185857	.187676	.189520	.191387	.193278	.195192	.197128	.199088	.201070	.205102	.209221
	-.10	.184635	.186407	.188203	.190023	.191866	.193734	.195624	.197538	.199475	.201435	.203417	.207448	.211567
	-.20	.186982	.188754	.190549	.192369	.194213	.196080	.197970	.199884	.201821	.203781	.205763	.209795	.213914
	-.30	.189328	.191100	.192896	.194716	.196559	.198426	.200317	.202231	.204168	.206127	.208109	.212141	.216260
	-.40	.191674	.193446	.195242	.197062	.198905	.200773	.202663	.204577	.206514	.208474	.210456	.214487	.218606
15	.40	.159373	.161389	.163439	.165524	.167643	.169794	.171979	.174195	.176442	.178720	.181028	.185731	.190544
	.30	.161719	.163735	.165786	.167870	.169989	.172141	.174325	.176541	.178789	.181067	.183375	.188077	.192891
	.20	.164066	.166081	.168132	.170217	.172335	.174487	.176671	.178888	.181135	.183413	.185721	.190424	.195237
	.10	.166412	.168428	.170478	.172563	.174682	.176833	.179018	.181234	.183481	.185759	.188067	.192770	.197583
	0.00	.168758	.170774	.172825	.174909	.177028	.179180	.181364	.183580	.185828	.188106	.190414	.195116	.199930
	-.10	.171105	.173120	.175171	.177256	.179374	.181526	.183710	.185927	.188174	.190452	.192760	.197463	.202276
	-.20	.173451	.175467	.177517	.179602	.181721	.183872	.186057	.188273	.190520	.192798	.195106	.199809	.204622
	-.30	.175797	.177813	.179864	.181948	.184067	.186219	.188403	.190619	.192867	.195145	.197453	.202155	.206969
	-.40	.178144	.180159	.182210	.184295	.186413	.188565	.190749	.192966	.195213	.197491	.199799	.204502	.209315
20	.40	.152813	.154988	.157204	.159462	.161759	.164094	.166466	.168874	.171316	.173791	.176299	.181403	.186619
	.30	.155159	.157334	.159551	.161808	.164105	.166440	.168812	.171220	.173662	.176138	.178645	.183749	.188965
	.20	.157506	.159680	.161897	.164154	.166451	.168786	.171158	.173566	.176009	.178484	.180991	.186096	.191312
	.10	.159852	.162027	.164243	.166501	.168798	.171133	.173505	.175913	.178355	.180830	.183338	.188442	.193658
	0.00	.162198	.164373	.166590	.168847	.171144	.173479	.175851	.178259	.180701	.183177	.185684	.190788	.196005
	-.10	.164545	.166719	.168936	.171193	.173490	.175825	.178197	.180605	.183048	.185523	.188030	.193135	.198351
	-.20	.166891	.169066	.171282	.173540	.175837	.178172	.180544	.182952	.185394	.187869	.190377	.195481	.200697
	-.30	.169237	.171412	.173629	.175886	.178183	.180518	.182890	.185298	.187740	.190216	.192723	.197828	.203044
	-.40	.171584	.173758	.175975	.178232	.180529	.182864	.185237	.187644	.190087	.192562	.195069	.200174	.205390
25	.40	.149034	.151331	.153675	.156064	.158495	.160967	.163477	.166025	.168607	.171222	.173868	.179245	.184723
	.30	.151381	.153678	.156021	.158410	.160841	.163313	.165824	.168371	.170953	.173568	.176214	.181591	.187069
	.20	.153727	.156024	.158368	.160756	.163187	.165659	.168170	.170717	.173299	.175914	.178560	.183937	.189416
	.10	.156073	.158370	.160714	.163103	.165534	.168006	.170516	.173064	.175646	.178251	.180907	.186284	.191762
	0.00	.158420	.160717	.163061	.165449	.167880	.170352	.172863	.175410	.177992	.180607	.183253	.188620	.194108
	-.10	.160766	.163063	.165407	.167795	.170226	.172698	.175209	.177756	.180338	.182953	.185599	.190976	.196455
	-.20	.163112	.165409	.167753	.170142	.172573	.175045	.177555	.180103	.182685	.185300	.187946	.193323	.198801
	-.30	.165459	.167756	.170100	.172488	.174919	.177391	.179902	.182449	.185031	.187646	.190292	.195669	.201148
	-.40	.167805	.170102	.172446	.174834	.177265	.179737	.182248	.184795	.187378	.189993	.192638	.198015	.203494
30	.40	.146639	.149038	.151486	.153980	.156519	.159099	.161718	.164372	.167059	.169778	.172524	.178093	.183748
	.30	.148985	.151384	.153832	.156327	.158865	.161445	.164064	.166718	.169406	.172124	.174870	.180439	.186094
	.20	.151332	.153730	.156178	.158673	.161212	.163792	.166410	.169065	.171752	.174470	.177217	.182785	.188441
	.10	.153678	.156077	.158525	.161019	.163558	.166138	.168757	.171411	.174098	.176817	.179563	.185132	.190787
	0.00	.156024	.158423	.160871	.163366	.165904	.168484	.171103	.173757	.176445	.179163	.181909	.187478	.193133
	-.10	.158371	.160769	.163217	.165712	.168251	.170831	.173449	.176104	.178791	.181509	.184256	.189824	.195480
	-.20	.160717	.163116	.165564	.168058	.170597	.173177	.175796	.178450	.181137	.183856	.186602	.192171	.197826
	-.30	.163064	.165462	.167910	.170405	.172943	.175523	.178142	.180796	.183484	.186202	.188948	.194517	.200173
	-.40	.165410	.167808	.170256	.172751	.175290	.177870	.180488	.183143	.185830	.188548	.191295	.196863	.202519

10.0 YEAR HOLDING PERIOD
.300 EQUITY YIELD RATE
.667 LOAN RATIO

INTEREST RATE

TERM YEARS	APPR DEP	5.0	5.5	6.0	6.5	7.0	7.5	8.0	8.5	9.0	9.5	10.0	11.0	12.0
10	.40	.159824	.161793	.163788	.165810	.167859	.169933	.172034	.174160	.176312	.178490	.180692	.185172	.189749
	.30	.162170	.164139	.166134	.168156	.170205	.172279	.174380	.176507	.178659	.180836	.183039	.187518	.192095
	.20	.164517	.166485	.168481	.170503	.172551	.174626	.176727	.178853	.181005	.183183	.185865	.189865	.194441
	.10	.166863	.168832	.170827	.172849	.174898	.176972	.179073	.181199	.183351	.185529	.187731	.192211	.196788
	0.00	.169209	.171178	.173173	.175195	.177244	.179319	.181419	.183546	.185698	.187875	.190078	.194557	.199134
	-.10	.171556	.173524	.175520	.177542	.179590	.181665	.183766	.185892	.188044	.190222	.192424	.196904	.201480
	-.20	.173902	.175871	.177866	.179888	.181937	.184011	.186112	.188238	.190390	.192568	.194771	.199250	.203827
	-.30	.176248	.178217	.180213	.182234	.184283	.186358	.188458	.190585	.192737	.194914	.197117	.201596	.206173
	-.40	.178595	.180563	.182559	.184581	.186629	.188704	.190805	.192931	.195083	.197261	.199463	.203943	.208519
15	.40	.144790	.147030	.149308	.151624	.153978	.156369	.158796	.161259	.163756	.166287	.168851	.174077	.179425
	.30	.147136	.149376	.151654	.153971	.156325	.158716	.161143	.163605	.166102	.168633	.171198	.176423	.181771
	.20	.149483	.151722	.154001	.156317	.158671	.161062	.163489	.165951	.168449	.170980	.173544	.178769	.184147
	.10	.151829	.154069	.156347	.158663	.161017	.163408	.165835	.168298	.170795	.173326	.175891	.181116	.186464
	0.00	.154175	.156415	.158693	.161010	.163364	.165755	.168182	.170644	.173141	.175672	.178237	.183462	.188810
	-.10	.156522	.158761	.161040	.163356	.165710	.168101	.170528	.172990	.175488	.178019	.180583	.185808	.191157
	-.20	.158868	.161108	.163386	.165702	.168056	.170447	.172874	.175337	.177834	.180365	.182930	.188155	.193503
	-.30	.161214	.163454	.165732	.168049	.170403	.172794	.175221	.177683	.180180	.182712	.185276	.190501	.195849
	-.40	.163561	.165800	.168079	.170395	.172749	.175140	.177567	.180029	.182527	.185058	.187622	.192847	.198196
20	.40	.137501	.139917	.142380	.144888	.147440	.150035	.152671	.155346	.158060	.160810	.163596	.169268	.175054
	.30	.139847	.142264	.144727	.147235	.149787	.152381	.155017	.157692	.160406	.163157	.165942	.171614	.177410
	.20	.142194	.144610	.147073	.149581	.152133	.154728	.157363	.160039	.162753	.165503	.168289	.173961	.179756
	.10	.144540	.146956	.149419	.151927	.154479	.157074	.159710	.162385	.165099	.167849	.170635	.176307	.182103
	0.00	.146886	.149303	.151766	.154274	.156826	.159420	.162056	.164732	.167445	.170196	.172981	.178653	.184449
	-.10	.149233	.151649	.154112	.156620	.159172	.161767	.164402	.167078	.169792	.172542	.175328	.181000	.186795
	-.20	.151579	.153995	.156458	.158966	.161519	.164113	.166749	.169424	.172138	.174888	.177674	.183346	.189142
	-.30	.153925	.156342	.158805	.161313	.163865	.166459	.169095	.171771	.174484	.177235	.180021	.185692	.191488
	-.40	.156272	.158688	.161151	.163659	.166211	.168806	.171441	.174117	.176831	.179581	.182367	.188039	.193834
25	.40	.133302	.135855	.138459	.141113	.143814	.146561	.149350	.152181	.155050	.157955	.160895	.166869	.172957
	.30	.135655	.138201	.140805	.143459	.146160	.148907	.151696	.154527	.157396	.160302	.163241	.169216	.175303
	.20	.137995	.140547	.143152	.145805	.148507	.151253	.154043	.156873	.159742	.162648	.165588	.171562	.177649
	.10	.140341	.142894	.145498	.148152	.150853	.153600	.156389	.159220	.162089	.164994	.167934	.173908	.179996
	0.00	.142688	.145240	.147844	.150498	.153199	.155946	.158736	.161566	.164435	.167341	.170280	.176255	.182342
	-.10	.145034	.147586	.150191	.152844	.155546	.158292	.161082	.163912	.166781	.169687	.172627	.178601	.184689
	-.20	.147380	.149933	.152537	.155191	.157892	.160639	.163428	.166259	.169128	.172033	.174973	.180948	.187035
	-.30	.149727	.152279	.154883	.157537	.160238	.162985	.165775	.168605	.171474	.174380	.177319	.183294	.189381
	-.40	.152073	.154625	.157230	.159883	.162585	.165331	.168121	.170951	.173820	.176726	.179666	.185640	.191728
30	.40	.130641	.133306	.136026	.138798	.141619	.144485	.147395	.150344	.153330	.156351	.159402	.165590	.171873
	.30	.132987	.135652	.138372	.141144	.143965	.146832	.149741	.152691	.155677	.158697	.161749	.167936	.174220
	.20	.135334	.137999	.140719	.143491	.146311	.149178	.152088	.155037	.158023	.161043	.164095	.170282	.176566
	.10	.137680	.140345	.143065	.145837	.148658	.151525	.154434	.157383	.160369	.163390	.166441	.172629	.178912
	0.00	.140026	.142691	.145411	.148183	.151004	.153871	.156780	.159730	.162716	.165736	.168788	.174975	.181259
	-.10	.142373	.145038	.147758	.150530	.153351	.156217	.159127	.162076	.165062	.168082	.171134	.177321	.183605
	-.20	.144719	.147384	.150104	.152876	.155697	.158564	.161473	.164422	.167408	.170429	.173480	.179668	.185952
	-.30	.147065	.149730	.152450	.155222	.158043	.160910	.163819	.166769	.169755	.172775	.175827	.182014	.188298
	-.40	.149412	.152077	.154797	.157569	.160390	.163256	.166166	.169115	.172101	.175121	.178173	.184360	.190644

271

16.0 YEAR HOLDING PERIOD
.300 EQUITY YIELD RATE
.700 LOAN RATIO

INTEREST RATE

TERM YEARS	APPR DEP	5.0	5.5	6.0	6.5	7.0	7.5	8.0	8.5	9.0	9.5	10.0	11.0	12.0
10	.40	.153285	.155352	.157447	.159571	.161721	.163900	.166105	.168338	.170598	.172884	.175197	.179900	.184706
	.30	.155632	.157699	.159794	.161917	.164068	.166246	.168452	.170685	.172944	.175231	.177543	.182247	.187052
	.20	.157978	.160045	.162140	.164263	.166414	.168592	.170798	.173031	.175291	.177577	.179890	.184593	.189399
	.10	.160324	.162391	.164486	.166610	.168760	.170939	.173144	.175377	.177637	.179923	.182236	.186939	.191745
	0.00	.162671	.164738	.166833	.168956	.171107	.173285	.175491	.177724	.179983	.182270	.184582	.189286	.194091
	-.10	.165017	.167084	.169179	.171302	.173453	.175631	.177837	.180070	.182330	.184616	.186929	.191632	.196438
	-.20	.167363	.169430	.171526	.173649	.175799	.177978	.180183	.182416	.184676	.186962	.189275	.193978	.198784
	-.30	.169710	.171777	.173872	.175995	.178146	.180324	.182530	.184763	.187022	.189309	.191621	.196325	.201130
	-.40	.172056	.174123	.176218	.178341	.180492	.182670	.184876	.187109	.189369	.191655	.193968	.198671	.203477
15	.40	.137499	.139851	.142243	.144676	.147147	.149658	.152206	.154792	.157414	.160071	.162764	.168250	.173866
	.30	.139846	.142197	.144590	.147022	.149494	.152004	.154552	.157138	.159760	.162418	.165110	.170597	.176212
	.20	.142192	.144544	.146936	.149368	.151840	.154350	.156899	.159484	.162106	.164764	.167457	.172943	.178559
	.10	.144539	.146890	.149282	.151715	.154186	.156697	.159245	.161831	.164453	.167110	.169803	.175289	.180905
	0.00	.146885	.149236	.151629	.154061	.156533	.159043	.161591	.164177	.166799	.169457	.172149	.177636	.183251
	-.10	.149231	.151583	.153975	.156407	.158879	.161389	.163938	.166523	.169145	.171803	.174496	.179982	.185598
	-.20	.151578	.153929	.156321	.158754	.161225	.163736	.166284	.168870	.171492	.174149	.176842	.182328	.187944
	-.30	.153924	.156275	.158668	.161100	.163572	.166082	.168630	.171216	.173838	.176496	.179188	.184675	.190290
	-.40	.156270	.158622	.161014	.163446	.165918	.168428	.170977	.173562	.176184	.178842	.181535	.187021	.192637
20	.40	.129846	.132383	.134969	.137603	.140283	.143007	.145774	.148583	.151433	.154321	.157246	.163201	.169287
	.30	.132192	.134730	.137316	.139949	.142629	.145353	.148121	.150930	.153779	.156667	.159592	.165548	.171633
	.20	.134539	.137076	.139662	.142296	.144975	.147699	.150467	.153276	.156125	.159013	.161939	.167894	.173979
	.10	.136885	.139422	.142008	.144642	.147322	.150046	.152813	.155622	.158471	.161360	.164285	.170240	.176326
	0.00	.139231	.141769	.144355	.146988	.149668	.152392	.155160	.157969	.160818	.163706	.166631	.172587	.178672
	-.10	.141578	.144115	.146701	.149335	.152014	.154739	.157506	.160315	.163164	.166052	.168978	.174933	.181018
	-.20	.143924	.146461	.149047	.151681	.154361	.157085	.159852	.162662	.165511	.168399	.171324	.177279	.183365
	-.30	.146270	.148808	.151394	.154027	.156707	.159431	.162199	.165008	.167857	.170745	.173670	.179626	.185711
	-.40	.148617	.151154	.153740	.156374	.159053	.161778	.164545	.167354	.170204	.173092	.176017	.181972	.188057
25	.40	.125437	.128117	.130852	.133638	.136475	.139359	.142288	.145260	.148272	.151323	.154410	.160683	.167075
	.30	.127784	.130464	.133198	.135985	.138821	.141705	.144634	.147606	.150618	.153669	.156756	.163029	.169421
	.20	.130130	.132810	.135545	.138331	.141167	.144051	.146980	.149952	.152965	.156016	.159102	.165376	.171767
	.10	.132476	.135157	.137891	.140677	.143514	.146398	.149327	.152299	.155311	.158362	.161449	.167722	.174114
	0.00	.134823	.137503	.140237	.143024	.145860	.148744	.151673	.154645	.157658	.160708	.163795	.170068	.176460
	-.10	.137169	.139849	.142584	.145370	.148206	.151090	.154019	.156991	.160004	.163055	.166142	.172415	.178806
	-.20	.139516	.142196	.144930	.147716	.150553	.153437	.156366	.159338	.162350	.165401	.168488	.174761	.181153
	-.30	.141862	.144542	.147276	.150063	.152899	.155783	.158712	.161684	.164697	.167747	.170834	.177107	.183499
	-.40	.144208	.146888	.149623	.152409	.155245	.158129	.161058	.164030	.167043	.170094	.173181	.179454	.185845
30	.40	.122643	.125441	.128297	.131208	.134170	.137180	.140235	.143331	.146467	.149638	.152842	.159339	.165937
	.30	.124990	.127788	.130644	.133554	.136516	.139526	.142581	.145678	.148813	.151984	.155189	.161685	.168283
	.20	.127336	.130134	.132990	.135901	.138862	.141872	.144927	.148024	.151160	.154331	.157535	.164032	.170630
	.10	.129682	.132480	.135336	.138247	.141209	.144219	.147274	.150370	.153506	.156677	.159881	.166378	.172976
	0.00	.132029	.134827	.137683	.140593	.143555	.146565	.149620	.152717	.155852	.159023	.162228	.168724	.175322
	-.10	.134375	.137173	.140029	.142940	.145902	.148912	.151966	.155063	.158199	.161370	.164574	.171071	.177669
	-.20	.136721	.139519	.142375	.145286	.148248	.151258	.154313	.157409	.160545	.163716	.166920	.173417	.180015
	-.30	.139068	.141866	.144722	.147632	.150594	.153604	.156659	.159756	.162891	.166062	.169267	.175763	.182361
	-.40	.141414	.144212	.147068	.149952	.152941	.155951	.159005	.162102	.165238	.168409	.171613	.178110	.184708

10.0 YEAR HOLDING PERIOD
.300 EQUITY YIELD RATE
.750 LOAN RATIO

TERM YEARS	APPR DEP	5.0	5.5	6.0	6.5	7.0	7.5	8.0	8.5	9.0	9.5	10.0	11.0	12.0
10	.40	.143476	.145691	.147935	.150210	.152515	.154849	.157212	.159604	.162025	.164475	.166953	.171992	.177141
	.30	.145822	.148037	.150282	.152557	.154861	.157195	.159558	.161951	.164372	.166821	.169299	.174338	.179487
	.20	.148169	.150383	.152628	.154903	.157207	.159542	.161905	.164297	.166718	.169168	.171645	.176685	.181834
	.10	.150515	.152730	.154975	.157249	.159554	.161888	.164251	.166643	.169064	.171514	.173992	.179031	.184180
	0.00	.152861	.155076	.157321	.159596	.161900	.164234	.166597	.168990	.171411	.173860	.176338	.181377	.186626
	-.10	.155208	.157422	.159667	.161942	.164246	.166580	.168944	.171336	.173757	.176207	.178684	.183724	.188823
	-.20	.157554	.159769	.162014	.164288	.166593	.168927	.171290	.173682	.176103	.178553	.181031	.186070	.191219
	-.30	.159900	.162115	.164360	.166635	.168939	.171273	.173636	.176029	.178450	.180899	.183377	.188416	.193565
	-.40	.162247	.164461	.166706	.168981	.171285	.173619	.175983	.178375	.180796	.183246	.185723	.190763	.195912
15	.40	.126563	.129082	.131645	.134251	.136900	.139589	.142320	.145090	.147899	.150747	.153632	.159510	.165527
	.30	.128909	.131429	.133992	.136598	.139246	.141936	.144666	.147436	.150246	.153093	.155978	.161856	.167843
	.20	.131255	.133775	.136338	.138944	.141592	.144282	.147012	.149783	.152592	.155440	.158324	.164203	.170219
	.10	.133602	.136121	.138684	.141290	.143939	.146628	.149359	.152129	.154938	.157786	.160671	.166549	.172566
	0.00	.135948	.138468	.141031	.143637	.146285	.148975	.151705	.154475	.157285	.160132	.163017	.168895	.174912
	-.10	.138294	.140814	.143377	.145983	.148631	.151321	.154051	.156822	.159631	.162479	.165363	.171242	.177258
	-.20	.140641	.143160	.145723	.148329	.150978	.153667	.156398	.159168	.161977	.164825	.167710	.173588	.179605
	-.30	.142987	.145507	.148070	.150676	.153324	.156014	.158744	.161514	.164324	.167171	.170056	.175934	.181951
	-.40	.145333	.147853	.150416	.153022	.155670	.158360	.161090	.163861	.166670	.169518	.172403	.178281	.184297
20	.40	.118363	.121081	.123852	.126673	.129544	.132463	.135429	.138438	.141491	.144585	.147720	.154100	.160320
	.30	.120709	.123427	.126198	.129020	.131891	.134810	.137775	.140785	.143838	.146932	.150066	.156447	.162367
	.20	.123055	.125774	.128544	.131366	.134237	.137156	.140121	.143131	.146184	.149278	.152412	.158793	.165313
	.10	.125402	.128120	.130891	.133712	.136584	.139502	.142468	.145477	.148530	.151625	.154759	.161139	.167759
	0.00	.127748	.130466	.133237	.136059	.138930	.141849	.144814	.147824	.150877	.153971	.157105	.163486	.170306
	-.10	.130094	.132813	.135584	.138405	.141276	.144195	.147160	.150170	.153223	.156317	.159451	.165832	.172352
	-.20	.132441	.135159	.137930	.140752	.143623	.146541	.149507	.152516	.155569	.158664	.161798	.168178	.174598
	-.30	.134787	.137505	.140276	.143098	.145969	.148888	.151853	.154863	.157916	.161010	.164144	.170525	.177195
	-.40	.137133	.139852	.142623	.145444	.148315	.151234	.154199	.157209	.160262	.163356	.166490	.172871	.179391
25	.40	.113639	.116511	.119940	.122426	.125465	.128555	.131693	.134877	.138105	.141374	.144681	.151402	.158260
	.30	.115985	.118857	.121787	.124772	.127811	.130901	.134039	.137223	.140451	.143720	.147027	.153748	.160597
	.20	.118332	.121203	.124133	.127119	.130157	.133247	.136386	.139570	.142798	.146066	.149374	.156095	.162943
	.10	.120678	.123550	.126479	.129465	.132504	.135594	.138732	.141916	.145144	.148413	.151720	.158441	.165289
	0.00	.123024	.125896	.128826	.131811	.134850	.137940	.141078	.144262	.147490	.150759	.154066	.160787	.167636
	-.10	.125371	.128242	.131172	.134158	.137196	.140286	.143425	.146609	.149837	.153105	.156413	.163134	.169982
	-.20	.127717	.130589	.133518	.136504	.139543	.142633	.145771	.148955	.152183	.155452	.158759	.165480	.172328
	-.30	.130063	.132935	.135865	.138851	.141889	.144979	.148117	.151302	.154529	.157798	.161105	.167826	.174675
	-.40	.132410	.135281	.138211	.141197	.144235	.147325	.150464	.153648	.156876	.160144	.163452	.170173	.177021
30	.40	.110645	.113643	.116703	.119822	.122995	.126220	.129493	.132811	.136171	.139568	.143001	.149962	.157331
	.30	.112992	.115990	.119050	.122168	.125342	.128567	.131840	.135158	.138517	.141915	.145348	.152308	.159578
	.20	.115338	.118336	.121396	.124514	.127688	.130913	.134186	.137504	.140863	.144261	.147694	.154655	.161724
	.10	.117684	.120682	.123742	.126861	.130034	.133259	.136532	.139850	.143210	.146607	.150040	.157001	.164071
	0.00	.120031	.123029	.126089	.129207	.132381	.135606	.138879	.142197	.145556	.148954	.152387	.159348	.166417
	-.10	.122377	.125375	.128435	.131553	.134727	.137952	.141225	.144543	.147902	.151300	.154733	.161694	.168763
	-.20	.124723	.127721	.130781	.133900	.137073	.140298	.143571	.146890	.150249	.153646	.157079	.164040	.171110
	-.30	.127070	.130068	.133128	.136246	.139420	.142645	.145918	.149236	.152595	.155993	.159426	.166387	.173456
	-.40	.129416	.132414	.135474	.138592	.141766	.144991	.148264	.151582	.154941	.158339	.161772	.168733	.175802

10.0 YEAR HOLDING PERIOD
.300 EQUITY YIELD RATE
.800 LOAN RATIO

INTEREST RATE

TERM YEARS	APPR DEP	5.0	5.5	6.0	6.5	7.0	7.5	8.0	8.5	9.0	9.5	10.0	11.0	12.0
10	.40	.133609	.136029	.138424	.140850	.143308	.145798	.148318	.150870	.153453	.156066	.158709	.164084	.169576
	.30	.136013	.138375	.140770	.143196	.145654	.148144	.150665	.153216	.155799	.158412	.161055	.166430	.171922
	.20	.138359	.140722	.143116	.145543	.148001	.150490	.153011	.155563	.158145	.160758	.163401	.168777	.174269
	.10	.140706	.143068	.145463	.147889	.150347	.152837	.155357	.157909	.160492	.163105	.165748	.171123	.176615
	0.00	.143052	.145414	.147809	.150235	.152693	.155183	.157704	.160256	.162838	.165451	.168094	.173469	.178961
	-.10	.145398	.147761	.150155	.152582	.155040	.157529	.160050	.162602	.165184	.167797	.170440	.175816	.181308
	-.20	.147745	.150107	.152502	.154928	.157386	.159876	.162396	.164948	.167531	.170144	.172787	.178162	.183654
	-.30	.150091	.152454	.154848	.157274	.159732	.162222	.164743	.167295	.169877	.172490	.175133	.180508	.186000
	-.40	.152438	.154800	.157194	.159621	.162079	.164568	.167089	.169641	.172223	.174836	.177479	.182855	.188347
15	.40	.115626	.118313	.121047	.123827	.126652	.129521	.132433	.135388	.138385	.141422	.144500	.150770	.157188
	.30	.117972	.120660	.123394	.126173	.128998	.131867	.134780	.137735	.140731	.143769	.146846	.153116	.159534
	.20	.120319	.123006	.125740	.128520	.131345	.134214	.137126	.140081	.143078	.146115	.149192	.155462	.161880
	.10	.122665	.125352	.128086	.130866	.133691	.136560	.139472	.142427	.145424	.148461	.151539	.157809	.164227
	0.00	.125011	.127699	.130433	.133213	.136037	.138906	.141819	.144774	.147770	.150808	.153885	.160155	.166573
	-.10	.127358	.130045	.132779	.135559	.138384	.141253	.144165	.147120	.150117	.153154	.156231	.162501	.168919
	-.20	.129704	.132391	.135125	.137905	.140730	.143599	.146511	.149466	.152463	.155500	.158578	.164848	.171266
	-.30	.132050	.134738	.137472	.140252	.143076	.145945	.148858	.151813	.154809	.157847	.160924	.167194	.173612
	-.40	.134397	.137084	.139818	.142598	.145423	.148292	.151204	.154159	.157156	.160193	.163270	.169540	.175958
20	.40	.106879	.109779	.112734	.115744	.118806	.121920	.125083	.128293	.131550	.134850	.138193	.144399	.151954
	.30	.109225	.112125	.115081	.118090	.121153	.124266	.127429	.130640	.133896	.137197	.140540	.147346	.154300
	.20	.111572	.114471	.117427	.120437	.123499	.126613	.129775	.132986	.136242	.139543	.142886	.149692	.156647
	.10	.113918	.116818	.119773	.122783	.125846	.128959	.132122	.135332	.138589	.141889	.145232	.152038	.158993
	0.00	.116264	.119164	.122120	.125129	.128192	.131305	.134468	.137679	.140935	.144236	.147579	.154385	.161339
	-.10	.118611	.121511	.124466	.127476	.130538	.133652	.136815	.140025	.143281	.146582	.149925	.156731	.163686
	-.20	.120957	.123857	.126812	.129822	.132885	.135998	.139161	.142371	.145628	.148928	.152271	.159077	.166032
	-.30	.123303	.126203	.129159	.132168	.135231	.138344	.141507	.144718	.147974	.151275	.154618	.161424	.168378
	-.40	.125650	.128550	.131505	.134515	.137577	.140691	.143854	.147064	.150320	.153621	.156964	.163770	.170725
25	.40	.101841	.104904	.108029	.111213	.114455	.117751	.121098	.124495	.127937	.131424	.134952	.142121	.149426
	.30	.104187	.107250	.110375	.113560	.116801	.120097	.123444	.126841	.130284	.133770	.137298	.144468	.151772
	.20	.106533	.109596	.112721	.115906	.119147	.122443	.125791	.129187	.132630	.136117	.139645	.146814	.154119
	.10	.108880	.111943	.115068	.118252	.121494	.124790	.128137	.131534	.134977	.138463	.141991	.149160	.156465
	0.00	.111226	.114289	.117414	.120599	.123840	.127136	.130483	.133880	.137323	.140810	.144337	.151507	.158811
	-.10	.113572	.116635	.119760	.122945	.126186	.129482	.132830	.136226	.139669	.143156	.146684	.153853	.161158
	-.20	.115919	.118982	.122107	.125291	.128533	.131829	.135176	.138573	.142016	.145502	.149030	.156199	.163504
	-.30	.118265	.121328	.124453	.127638	.130879	.134175	.137523	.140919	.144362	.147849	.151376	.158546	.165850
	-.40	.120611	.123674	.126799	.129984	.133226	.136521	.139869	.143265	.146708	.150195	.153723	.160892	.168197
30	.40	.098647	.101845	.105109	.108436	.111821	.115261	.118752	.122291	.125874	.129499	.133160	.140585	.148126
	.30	.100994	.104192	.107456	.110782	.114167	.117607	.121098	.124637	.128221	.131845	.135507	.142932	.150472
	.20	.103340	.106538	.109802	.113128	.116513	.119953	.123445	.126984	.130567	.134191	.137853	.145278	.152819
	.10	.105686	.108884	.112148	.115475	.118860	.122300	.125791	.129330	.132913	.136538	.140200	.147624	.155165
	0.00	.108033	.111231	.114495	.117821	.121206	.124646	.128137	.131676	.135260	.138884	.142546	.149971	.157511
	-.10	.110379	.113577	.116841	.120167	.123552	.126992	.130484	.134023	.137606	.141230	.144892	.152317	.159858
	-.20	.112725	.115923	.119187	.122514	.125899	.129339	.132830	.136369	.139952	.143577	.147239	.154663	.162204
	-.30	.115072	.118270	.121534	.124860	.128245	.131685	.135176	.138715	.142299	.145923	.149585	.157010	.164550
	-.40	.117418	.120616	.123880	.127206	.130591	.134031	.137523	.141062	.144645	.148269	.151931	.159356	.166897

274

INTEREST RATE

TERM YEARS	APPR DEP	5.0	5.5	6.0	6.5	7.0	7.5	8.0	8.5	9.0	9.5	10.0	11.0	12.0
10	.40	.114448	.116706	.119000	.122129	.124895	.127695	.130531	.133402	.136307	.139247	.142220	.148268	.154446
	.30	.116395	.119052	.121746	.124476	.127241	.130042	.132878	.135748	.138654	.141593	.144567	.150614	.156792
	.20	.118741	.121359	.124092	.126822	.129587	.132388	.135224	.138095	.141000	.143940	.146913	.152960	.159139
	.10	.121087	.123745	.126439	.129168	.131934	.134734	.137570	.140441	.143346	.146286	.149259	.155307	.161435
	0.00	.123434	.126091	.128785	.131515	.134280	.137081	.139917	.142787	.145693	.148632	.151606	.157653	.163832
	-.10	.125780	.128438	.131131	.133861	.136626	.139427	.142263	.145134	.148039	.150979	.153952	.159999	.166178
	-.20	.128126	.130784	.133478	.136207	.138973	.141774	.144609	.147480	.150385	.153325	.156298	.162346	.168524
	-.30	.130473	.133130	.135824	.138554	.141319	.144120	.146956	.149826	.152732	.155671	.158645	.164692	.170871
	-.40	.132819	.135477	.138170	.140900	.143665	.146466	.149302	.152173	.155078	.158018	.160991	.167038	.173217
15	.40	.093752	.096776	.099951	.102979	.106157	.109384	.112661	.115985	.119356	.122773	.126235	.133289	.140509
	.30	.096099	.099122	.102298	.105325	.108503	.111731	.115007	.118331	.121703	.125120	.128582	.135635	.142855
	.20	.098445	.101468	.104644	.107671	.110849	.114077	.117353	.120678	.124049	.127466	.130928	.137982	.145202
	.10	.100791	.103815	.106990	.110018	.113196	.116423	.119700	.123024	.126395	.129812	.133274	.140328	.147548
	0.00	.103138	.106161	.109237	.112364	.115542	.118770	.122046	.125370	.128742	.132159	.135621	.142674	.149894
	-.10	.105484	.108507	.111683	.114711	.117888	.121116	.124392	.127717	.131088	.134505	.137967	.145021	.152241
	-.20	.107830	.110854	.113930	.117057	.120235	.123462	.126739	.130063	.133434	.136851	.140313	.147367	.154537
	-.30	.110177	.113200	.116376	.119403	.122581	.125809	.129085	.132409	.135781	.139198	.142660	.149713	.156934
	-.40	.112523	.115546	.118622	.121749	.124927	.128155	.131431	.134756	.138127	.141544	.145006	.152060	.159280
20	.40	.083912	.087174	.090499	.093885	.097330	.100833	.104391	.108003	.111667	.115380	.119140	.126797	.134621
	.30	.086258	.089521	.092946	.096232	.099677	.103179	.106738	.110349	.114013	.117726	.121487	.129144	.136968
	.20	.088605	.091867	.095192	.098578	.102023	.105526	.109084	.112696	.116359	.120072	.123833	.131490	.139314
	.10	.090951	.094213	.097538	.100924	.104370	.107872	.111430	.115042	.118706	.122419	.126180	.133836	.141660
	0.00	.093298	.096560	.099885	.103271	.106716	.110219	.113777	.117388	.121052	.124765	.128526	.136183	.144007
	-.10	.095644	.098906	.102231	.105617	.109062	.112565	.116123	.119735	.123398	.127111	.130872	.138529	.146353
	-.20	.097990	.101252	.104577	.107963	.111409	.114911	.118469	.122081	.125745	.129458	.133219	.140875	.148699
	-.30	.100337	.103599	.106924	.110310	.113755	.117258	.120816	.124428	.128091	.131804	.135565	.143222	.151046
	-.40	.102683	.105945	.109270	.112656	.116101	.119604	.123162	.126774	.130437	.134150	.137911	.145568	.153392
25	.40	.078244	.081690	.085205	.088788	.092435	.096143	.099909	.103730	.107603	.111525	.115494	.123559	.131777
	.30	.080590	.084036	.087552	.091134	.094781	.098489	.102255	.106076	.109949	.113872	.117840	.125906	.134124
	.20	.082937	.086382	.089898	.093481	.097127	.100835	.104601	.108422	.112296	.116218	.120187	.128252	.136470
	.10	.085283	.088729	.092244	.095827	.099474	.103182	.106948	.110769	.114642	.118564	.122533	.130599	.138816
	0.00	.087629	.091075	.094591	.098173	.101820	.105528	.109294	.113115	.116988	.120911	.124879	.132945	.141163
	-.10	.089976	.093421	.096937	.100520	.104166	.107874	.111640	.115461	.119335	.123257	.127226	.135291	.143509
	-.20	.092322	.095768	.099283	.102866	.106513	.110221	.113987	.117808	.121681	.125603	.129572	.137638	.145855
	-.30	.094668	.098114	.101630	.105212	.108859	.112567	.116333	.120154	.124027	.127950	.131919	.139984	.148202
	-.40	.097015	.100461	.103976	.107559	.111206	.114913	.118679	.122500	.126374	.130296	.134265	.142330	.150548
30	.40	.074651	.078249	.081921	.085663	.089471	.093341	.097269	.101250	.105282	.109359	.113479	.121832	.130305
	.30	.076998	.080595	.084267	.088009	.091818	.095688	.099615	.103597	.107628	.111705	.115825	.124178	.132661
	.20	.079344	.082942	.086614	.090356	.094164	.098034	.101962	.105943	.109974	.114052	.118171	.126524	.135008
	.10	.081690	.085288	.088960	.092702	.096510	.100380	.104308	.108290	.112321	.116398	.120518	.128871	.137354
	0.00	.084037	.087634	.091306	.095049	.098857	.102727	.106654	.110636	.114667	.118744	.122864	.131217	.139700
	-.10	.086383	.089981	.093653	.097395	.101203	.105073	.109001	.112982	.117013	.121091	.125210	.133563	.142047
	-.20	.088729	.092327	.095999	.099741	.103549	.107419	.111347	.115329	.119360	.123437	.127557	.135910	.144393
	-.30	.091076	.094673	.098345	.102088	.105896	.109766	.113693	.117675	.121706	.125783	.129903	.138256	.146739
	-.40	.093422	.097020	.100692	.104434	.108242	.112112	.116040	.120021	.124052	.128130	.132249	.140602	.149036

10.0 YEAR HOLDING PERIOD
.400 EQUITY YIELD RATE
.600 LOAN RATIO

INTEREST RATE

TERM YEARS	APPR DEP	5.0	5.5	6.0	6.5	7.0	7.5	8.0	8.5	9.0	9.5	10.0	11.0	12.0
10	.40	.222043	.223815	.225611	.227431	.229274	.231141	.233032	.234946	.236883	.238842	.240825	.244856	.248975
	.30	.223476	.225247	.227043	.228863	.230707	.232574	.234464	.236378	.238315	.240275	.242257	.246289	.250408
	.20	.224908	.226680	.228476	.230295	.232139	.234006	.235897	.237811	.239747	.241707	.243689	.247721	.251840
	.10	.226340	.228112	.229908	.231728	.233571	.235439	.237329	.239243	.241180	.243140	.245122	.249153	.253272
	0.00	.227773	.229545	.231340	.233160	.235004	.236871	.238762	.240675	.242612	.244572	.246554	.250586	.254705
	-.10	.229205	.230977	.232773	.234593	.236436	.238303	.240194	.242108	.244045	.246004	.247987	.252018	.256137
	-.20	.230638	.232409	.234205	.236025	.237869	.239736	.241626	.243540	.245477	.247437	.249419	.253450	.257570
	-.30	.232070	.233842	.235638	.237457	.239301	.241168	.243059	.244973	.246909	.248869	.250851	.254883	.259002
	-.40	.233502	.235274	.237070	.238890	.240733	.242601	.244491	.246405	.248342	.250301	.252284	.256315	.260434
15	.40	.206615	.208183	.210185	.212222	.214493	.216397	.218534	.220702	.222903	.225133	.227394	.232004	.236725
	.30	.207647	.209615	.211618	.213655	.215725	.217829	.219966	.222135	.224335	.226566	.228827	.233436	.238158
	.20	.209079	.211047	.213050	.215087	.217158	.219262	.221398	.223567	.225767	.227998	.230259	.234869	.239590
	.10	.210512	.212480	.214482	.216519	.218590	.220694	.222831	.225000	.227200	.229431	.231692	.236301	.241022
	0.00	.211944	.213912	.215915	.217952	.220023	.222127	.224263	.226432	.228632	.230863	.233124	.237733	.242455
	-.10	.213377	.215344	.217347	.219384	.221455	.223559	.225696	.227864	.230065	.232295	.234556	.239166	.243887
	-.20	.214809	.216777	.218779	.220816	.222887	.224991	.227128	.229297	.231497	.233728	.235989	.240598	.245320
	-.30	.216241	.218209	.220212	.222249	.224320	.226424	.228560	.230729	.232929	.235160	.237421	.242031	.246752
	-.40	.217674	.219642	.221644	.223681	.225752	.227856	.229993	.232162	.234362	.236593	.238854	.243463	.248184
20	.40	.198540	.200651	.202805	.205001	.207236	.209512	.211825	.214175	.216561	.218931	.221434	.226434	.231550
	.30	.199973	.202084	.204238	.206433	.208669	.210944	.213257	.215607	.217993	.220413	.222866	.227866	.232983
	.20	.201405	.203516	.205670	.207865	.210101	.212376	.214690	.217040	.219425	.221845	.224298	.229298	.234415
	.10	.202838	.204949	.207102	.209298	.211534	.213809	.216122	.218472	.220858	.223278	.225731	.230731	.235847
	0.00	.204270	.206381	.208535	.210730	.212966	.215241	.217554	.219904	.222290	.224710	.227163	.232163	.237280
	-.10	.205702	.207813	.209967	.212162	.214398	.216673	.218987	.221337	.223723	.226143	.228596	.233596	.238712
	-.20	.207135	.209246	.211400	.213595	.215831	.218106	.220419	.222769	.225155	.227575	.230028	.235028	.240144
	-.30	.208567	.210678	.212832	.215027	.217263	.219538	.221852	.224202	.226587	.229007	.231460	.236460	.241577
	-.40	.210000	.212111	.214264	.216460	.218695	.220971	.223284	.225634	.228020	.230440	.232893	.237893	.243009
25	.40	.194120	.196350	.198628	.200953	.203322	.205735	.208188	.210680	.213209	.215773	.218370	.223655	.229050
	.30	.195552	.197782	.200060	.202385	.204755	.207167	.209620	.212113	.214642	.217206	.219802	.225088	.230483
	.20	.196985	.199214	.201493	.203817	.206187	.208599	.211053	.213545	.216074	.218638	.221235	.226520	.231915
	.10	.198417	.200647	.202925	.205250	.207619	.210032	.212485	.214977	.217506	.220070	.222667	.227953	.233348
	0.00	.199849	.202079	.204357	.206682	.209052	.211464	.213918	.216410	.218939	.221503	.224100	.229385	.234780
	-.10	.201282	.203512	.205790	.208115	.210484	.212897	.215350	.217842	.220371	.222935	.225532	.230817	.236212
	-.20	.202714	.204944	.207222	.209547	.211917	.214329	.216782	.219274	.221803	.224367	.226964	.232250	.237645
	-.30	.204147	.206376	.208654	.210979	.213349	.215761	.218215	.220707	.223236	.225800	.228397	.233682	.239077
	-.40	.205579	.207809	.210087	.212412	.214781	.217194	.219647	.222139	.224668	.227232	.229829	.235114	.240509
30	.40	.191318	.193651	.196036	.198471	.200953	.203479	.206047	.208653	.211295	.213970	.216677	.222173	.227765
	.30	.192750	.195083	.197468	.199903	.202385	.204911	.207479	.210085	.212727	.215403	.218109	.223605	.229197
	.20	.194183	.196516	.198901	.201336	.203818	.206344	.208911	.211517	.214160	.216835	.219542	.225038	.230630
	.10	.195615	.197948	.200333	.202768	.205250	.207776	.210344	.212950	.215592	.218258	.220974	.226470	.232062
	0.00	.197048	.199380	.201766	.204201	.206682	.209209	.211776	.214382	.217024	.219700	.222406	.227902	.233494
	-.10	.198480	.200813	.203198	.205633	.208115	.210641	.213208	.215815	.218457	.221132	.223839	.229335	.234927
	-.20	.199912	.202245	.204630	.207065	.209547	.212073	.214641	.217247	.219889	.222565	.225271	.230767	.236359
	-.30	.201345	.203677	.206063	.208498	.210980	.213506	.216073	.218679	.221322	.223997	.226703	.232199	.237792
	-.40	.202777	.205110	.207495	.209930	.212412	.214938	.217506	.220112	.222754	.225429	.228136	.233632	.239224

276

10.0 YEAR HOLDING PERIOD
.400 EQUITY YIELD RATE
.667 LOAN RATIO

INTEREST RATE

TERM YEARS	APPR DEP	5.0	5.5	6.0	6.5	7.0	7.5	8.0	8.5	9.0	9.5	10.0	11.0	12.0
10	.40	.202906	.204875	.206870	.208892	.210940	.213015	.215116	.217242	.219394	.221572	.223774	.228254	.232831
	.30	.204338	.206307	.208302	.210324	.212373	.214447	.216548	.218675	.220827	.223004	.225207	.229686	.234263
	.20	.205771	.207729	.209735	.211757	.213805	.215880	.217981	.220107	.222259	.224437	.226639	.231119	.235695
	.10	.207203	.209172	.211167	.213189	.215238	.217312	.219413	.221539	.223691	.225869	.228071	.232551	.237128
	0.00	.208636	.210604	.212600	.214622	.216670	.218745	.220845	.222972	.225124	.227301	.229504	.233983	.238560
	-.10	.210068	.212037	.214032	.216054	.218102	.220177	.222278	.224404	.226556	.228734	.230936	.235416	.239992
	-.20	.211500	.213469	.215464	.217486	.219535	.221609	.223710	.225837	.227989	.230166	.232369	.236848	.241425
	-.30	.212933	.214901	.216897	.218919	.220967	.223042	.225142	.227269	.229421	.231598	.233801	.238280	.242857
	-.40	.214365	.216334	.218329	.220351	.222400	.224474	.226575	.228701	.230853	.233031	.235233	.239713	.244290
15	.40	.185319	.187505	.189730	.191994	.194294	.196632	.199006	.201416	.203861	.206340	.208852	.213973	.219219
	.30	.186751	.188937	.191163	.193426	.195727	.198065	.200439	.202849	.205293	.207772	.210284	.215406	.220652
	.20	.188183	.190370	.192595	.194858	.197159	.199497	.201871	.204281	.206726	.209204	.211717	.216838	.222084
	.10	.189616	.191802	.194027	.196291	.198592	.200929	.203304	.205713	.208158	.210637	.213149	.218270	.223516
	0.00	.191048	.193235	.195460	.197723	.200024	.202362	.204736	.207146	.209590	.212069	.214581	.219702	.224949
	-.10	.192481	.194667	.196892	.199155	.201456	.203794	.206168	.208578	.211023	.213501	.216014	.221135	.226381
	-.20	.193913	.196099	.198325	.200588	.202889	.205227	.207601	.210010	.212455	.214934	.217446	.222568	.227814
	-.30	.195345	.197532	.199757	.202020	.204321	.206659	.209033	.211443	.213887	.216366	.218878	.224000	.229246
	-.40	.196778	.198964	.201189	.203453	.205754	.208091	.210466	.212875	.215320	.217799	.220311	.225432	.230678
20	.40	.176792	.179137	.181530	.183970	.186454	.188982	.191552	.194163	.196814	.199503	.202229	.207784	.213465
	.30	.178224	.180570	.182963	.185402	.187886	.190414	.192984	.195596	.198246	.200935	.203661	.209217	.214902
	.20	.179656	.182002	.184395	.186834	.189319	.191847	.194417	.197028	.199679	.202368	.205093	.210649	.216334
	.10	.181089	.183434	.185827	.188267	.190751	.193279	.195849	.198460	.201111	.203800	.206526	.212081	.217766
	0.00	.182521	.184867	.187260	.189699	.192183	.194711	.197282	.199893	.202544	.205233	.207958	.213514	.219199
	-.10	.183954	.186299	.188692	.191131	.193616	.196144	.198714	.201325	.203976	.206665	.209391	.214946	.220631
	-.20	.185386	.187732	.190125	.192564	.195048	.197576	.200146	.202758	.205408	.208097	.210823	.216378	.222064
	-.30	.186818	.189164	.191557	.193996	.196481	.199008	.201579	.204190	.206841	.209530	.212255	.217811	.223496
	-.40	.188251	.190596	.192989	.195429	.197913	.200441	.203011	.205622	.208273	.210962	.213688	.219243	.224928
25	.40	.171880	.174357	.176889	.179472	.182105	.184785	.187511	.190280	.193090	.195939	.198825	.204697	.210692
	.30	.173312	.175790	.178321	.180904	.183537	.186218	.188943	.191713	.194523	.197371	.200257	.206130	.212124
	.20	.174745	.177222	.179753	.182337	.184969	.187650	.190376	.193145	.195955	.198804	.201689	.207562	.213556
	.10	.176177	.178654	.181186	.183769	.186402	.189082	.191808	.194577	.197387	.200236	.203122	.208994	.214989
	0.00	.177609	.180087	.182618	.185201	.187834	.190515	.193241	.196010	.198820	.201669	.204554	.210427	.216421
	-.10	.179042	.181519	.184051	.186634	.189267	.191947	.194673	.197442	.200252	.203101	.205987	.211859	.217854
	-.20	.180474	.182952	.185483	.188066	.190699	.193380	.196105	.198874	.201685	.204533	.207419	.213291	.219286
	-.30	.181907	.184384	.186916	.189499	.192131	.194812	.197538	.200307	.203117	.205966	.208851	.214724	.220718
	-.40	.183339	.185816	.188348	.190931	.193564	.196244	.198970	.201739	.204549	.207398	.210284	.216156	.222151
30	.40	.168767	.171359	.174009	.176714	.179472	.182279	.185132	.188027	.190963	.193936	.196943	.203050	.209263
	.30	.170199	.172791	.175441	.178147	.180904	.183711	.186564	.189460	.192396	.195368	.198376	.204482	.210696
	.20	.171631	.174223	.176874	.179579	.182337	.185144	.187996	.190892	.193828	.196801	.199808	.205915	.212128
	.10	.173064	.175656	.178306	.181012	.183769	.186576	.189429	.192325	.195260	.198233	.201240	.207347	.213561
	0.00	.174496	.177088	.179738	.182444	.185202	.188008	.190861	.193757	.196693	.199666	.202673	.208779	.214993
	-.10	.175929	.178521	.181171	.183876	.186634	.189441	.192294	.195189	.198125	.201098	.204105	.210212	.216425
	-.20	.177361	.179953	.182603	.185309	.188066	.190873	.193726	.196622	.199558	.202530	.205537	.211644	.217858
	-.30	.178793	.181385	.184036	.186741	.189499	.192306	.195158	.198054	.200990	.203963	.206970	.213077	.219290
	-.40	.180226	.182818	.185468	.188173	.190931	.193738	.196591	.199487	.202422	.205395	.208402	.214509	.220722

10.0 YEAR HOLDING PERIOD
.400 EQUITY YIELD RATE
.700 LOAN RATIO

INTEREST RATE

TERM YEARS	APPR DEP	5.0	5.5	6.0	6.5	7.0	7.5	8.0	8.5	9.0	9.5	10.0	11.0	12.0
10	.40	.193339	.195540	.197501	.199624	.201775	.203953	.206159	.208392	.210651	.212938	.215250	.219954	.224759
	.30	.194771	.196972	.198933	.201156	.203207	.205386	.207591	.209824	.212084	.214370	.216683	.221386	.226192
	.20	.196204	.198404	.200366	.202489	.204640	.206818	.209024	.211257	.213516	.215802	.218115	.222819	.227624
	.10	.197636	.199837	.201798	.203921	.206072	.208250	.210456	.212689	.214949	.217235	.219548	.224251	.229057
	0.00	.199068	.201269	.203231	.205354	.207504	.209683	.211888	.214121	.216381	.218667	.220980	.225683	.230489
	-.10	.200501	.202701	.204663	.206786	.208937	.211115	.213321	.215554	.217813	.220100	.222412	.227116	.231921
	-.20	.201933	.204133	.206095	.208218	.210369	.212548	.214753	.216986	.219246	.221532	.223845	.228548	.233354
	-.30	.203365	.205565	.207528	.209651	.211802	.213980	.216186	.218418	.220678	.222964	.225277	.229980	.234786
	-.40	.204798	.206998	.208960	.211083	.213234	.215412	.217618	.219851	.222110	.224397	.226709	.231413	.236218
15	.40	.174872	.177168	.179504	.181881	.184297	.186751	.189244	.191774	.194341	.196944	.199582	.204959	.210468
	.30	.176304	.178600	.180937	.183313	.185729	.188184	.190677	.193207	.195774	.198376	.201014	.206392	.211900
	.20	.177737	.180033	.182369	.184746	.187161	.189616	.192109	.194639	.197206	.199809	.202447	.207824	.213332
	.10	.179169	.181465	.183801	.186178	.188594	.191049	.193541	.196072	.198638	.201241	.203879	.209257	.214765
	0.00	.180602	.182897	.185234	.187610	.190026	.192481	.194974	.197504	.200071	.202673	.205311	.210689	.216197
	-.10	.182034	.184330	.186666	.189043	.191459	.193913	.196406	.198936	.201503	.204106	.206744	.212121	.217630
	-.20	.183466	.185762	.188099	.190475	.192891	.195346	.197839	.200369	.202936	.205538	.208176	.213554	.219062
	-.30	.184899	.187195	.189531	.191907	.194323	.196778	.199271	.201801	.204368	.206971	.209608	.214986	.220494
	-.40	.186331	.188627	.190963	.193340	.195756	.198211	.200703	.203234	.205800	.208403	.211041	.216418	.221927
20	.40	.165919	.168382	.170894	.173456	.176064	.178718	.181417	.184159	.186942	.189766	.192628	.198461	.204430
	.30	.167351	.169814	.172327	.174888	.177496	.180151	.182850	.185591	.188375	.191198	.194060	.199893	.205863
	.20	.168784	.171246	.173759	.176320	.178929	.181583	.184282	.187024	.189807	.192630	.195492	.201326	.207295
	.10	.170216	.172679	.175191	.177753	.180361	.183016	.185714	.188456	.191239	.194063	.196925	.202758	.208727
	0.00	.171648	.174111	.176624	.179185	.181794	.184448	.187147	.189889	.192672	.195495	.198357	.204190	.210160
	-.10	.173081	.175544	.178056	.180618	.183226	.185880	.188579	.191321	.194104	.196928	.199789	.205623	.211592
	-.20	.174513	.176976	.179489	.182050	.184658	.187313	.190012	.192753	.195537	.198360	.201222	.207055	.213024
	-.30	.175946	.178408	.180921	.183482	.186091	.188745	.191444	.194186	.196969	.199792	.202654	.208487	.214457
	-.40	.177378	.179841	.182353	.184915	.187523	.190177	.192876	.195618	.198401	.201225	.204087	.209920	.215889
25	.40	.160762	.163363	.166021	.168733	.171498	.174312	.177174	.180082	.183032	.186024	.189053	.195220	.201514
	.30	.162194	.164795	.167453	.170165	.172930	.175744	.178607	.181514	.184465	.187456	.190486	.196652	.202946
	.20	.163626	.166228	.168885	.171598	.174362	.177177	.180039	.182946	.185897	.188888	.191918	.198084	.204378
	.10	.165059	.167660	.170318	.173030	.175795	.178609	.181471	.184379	.187329	.190321	.193350	.199517	.205811
	0.00	.166491	.169092	.171750	.174463	.177227	.180042	.182904	.185811	.188762	.191753	.194783	.200949	.207243
	-.10	.167923	.170525	.173183	.175895	.178659	.181474	.184336	.187244	.190194	.193185	.196215	.202381	.208676
	-.20	.169356	.171957	.174615	.177327	.180092	.182906	.185769	.188676	.191627	.194618	.197648	.203814	.210108
	-.30	.170788	.173389	.176047	.178760	.181524	.184339	.187201	.190108	.193059	.196050	.199080	.205246	.211540
	-.40	.172221	.174822	.177480	.180192	.182957	.185771	.188633	.191541	.194491	.197483	.200512	.206679	.212973
30	.40	.157493	.160214	.162997	.165838	.168733	.171680	.174676	.177716	.180799	.183920	.187078	.193490	.200014
	.30	.158925	.161647	.164429	.167270	.170166	.173113	.176108	.179149	.182231	.185353	.188510	.194922	.201446
	.20	.160357	.163079	.165862	.168702	.171598	.174545	.177541	.180581	.183664	.186785	.189943	.196355	.202879
	.10	.161790	.164511	.167294	.170135	.173030	.175978	.178973	.182014	.185096	.188218	.191375	.197787	.204311
	0.00	.163222	.165944	.168726	.171567	.174463	.177410	.180405	.183446	.186528	.189650	.192807	.199219	.205744
	-.10	.164655	.167376	.170159	.173000	.175895	.178842	.181838	.184878	.187961	.191082	.194240	.200652	.207176
	-.20	.166087	.168808	.171591	.174432	.177328	.180275	.183270	.186311	.189393	.192515	.195672	.202084	.208608
	-.30	.167519	.170241	.173024	.175864	.178760	.181707	.184703	.187743	.190826	.193947	.197105	.203517	.210041
	-.40	.168952	.171673	.174456	.177297	.180192	.183140	.186135	.189175	.192258	.195379	.198537	.204949	.211473

278

10.0 YEAR HOLDING PERIOD
.400 EQUITY YIELD RATE
.750 LOAN RATIO

INTEREST RATE

TERM YEARS	APPR DEP	5.0	5.5	6.0	6.5	7.0	7.5	8.0	8.5	9.0	9.5	10.0	11.0	12.0
10	.40	.178987	.181201	.183446	.185721	.188025	.190359	.192722	.195115	.197536	.199985	.202463	.207503	.212651
	.30	.180419	.182634	.184878	.187153	.189458	.191792	.194155	.196547	.198968	.201418	.203896	.208935	.214084
	.20	.181851	.184066	.186311	.188586	.190890	.193224	.195587	.197979	.200401	.202850	.205328	.210367	.215515
	.10	.183284	.185498	.187743	.190018	.192322	.194656	.197020	.199412	.201833	.204283	.206760	.211800	.216943
	0.00	.184716	.186931	.189176	.191450	.193755	.196089	.198452	.200844	.203265	.205715	.208193	.213232	.218381
	-.10	.186148	.188363	.190608	.192883	.195187	.197521	.199884	.202227	.204698	.207147	.209625	.214665	.219813
	-.20	.187581	.189796	.192040	.194315	.196620	.198953	.201317	.203709	.206130	.208580	.211058	.216097	.221245
	-.30	.189013	.191228	.193473	.195747	.198052	.200386	.202749	.205141	.207562	.210012	.212490	.217529	.222678
	-.40	.190446	.192660	.194905	.197180	.199484	.201818	.204181	.206574	.208995	.211444	.213922	.218962	.224111
15	.40	.159201	.161661	.164164	.166710	.169299	.171929	.174600	.177310	.180061	.182849	.185675	.191437	.197339
	.30	.160633	.163093	.165596	.168142	.170731	.173361	.176032	.178743	.181493	.184282	.187108	.192870	.198771
	.20	.162066	.164526	.167029	.169575	.172163	.174793	.177464	.180175	.182925	.185714	.188540	.194302	.200204
	.10	.163498	.165958	.168461	.171007	.173596	.176226	.178897	.181608	.184358	.187146	.189973	.195734	.201636
	0.00	.164930	.167390	.169893	.172440	.175028	.177658	.180329	.183040	.185790	.188579	.191405	.197167	.203068
	-.10	.166363	.168822	.171326	.173872	.176461	.179091	.181761	.184472	.187223	.190011	.192837	.198599	.204501
	-.20	.167795	.170255	.172758	.175304	.177893	.180523	.183194	.185905	.188655	.191444	.194270	.200032	.205933
	-.30	.169227	.171687	.174191	.176737	.179325	.181955	.184626	.187337	.190087	.192876	.195702	.201464	.207366
	-.40	.170660	.173120	.175623	.178169	.180758	.183388	.186059	.188770	.191520	.194308	.197135	.202896	.208798
20	.40	.149608	.152247	.154939	.157683	.160478	.163322	.166213	.169151	.172133	.175158	.178224	.184474	.190870
	.30	.151040	.153679	.156371	.159115	.161910	.164754	.167646	.170583	.173566	.176591	.179657	.185907	.192302
	.20	.152473	.155111	.157804	.160548	.163343	.166187	.169078	.172016	.174998	.178023	.181089	.187339	.193735
	.10	.153905	.156544	.159236	.161980	.164775	.167619	.170511	.173448	.176430	.179455	.182522	.188772	.195167
	0.00	.155338	.157976	.160669	.163413	.166207	.169051	.171943	.174881	.177863	.180888	.183954	.190204	.196600
	-.10	.156770	.159409	.162101	.164845	.167640	.170484	.173375	.176313	.179295	.182320	.185386	.191636	.198032
	-.20	.158202	.160841	.163533	.166277	.169072	.171916	.174808	.177745	.180727	.183752	.186819	.193069	.199464
	-.30	.159635	.162273	.164966	.167710	.170505	.173349	.176240	.179178	.182160	.185185	.188251	.194501	.200897
	-.40	.161067	.163706	.166398	.169142	.171937	.174781	.177672	.180610	.183592	.186617	.189684	.195933	.202329
25	.40	.144082	.146869	.149717	.152623	.155585	.158601	.161667	.164783	.167944	.171149	.174395	.181002	.187745
	.30	.145515	.148302	.151149	.154056	.157018	.160033	.163100	.166215	.169376	.172581	.175827	.182434	.189178
	.20	.146947	.149734	.152582	.155488	.158450	.161466	.164532	.167647	.170809	.174014	.177260	.183866	.190610
	.10	.148379	.151167	.154014	.156920	.159882	.162898	.165964	.169080	.172241	.175446	.178692	.185299	.192042
	0.00	.149812	.152599	.155447	.158353	.161315	.164330	.167397	.170512	.173673	.176878	.180125	.186731	.193475
	-.10	.151244	.154031	.156879	.159785	.162747	.165763	.168829	.171944	.175106	.178311	.181557	.188164	.194907
	-.20	.152677	.155464	.158311	.161217	.164180	.167195	.170262	.173377	.176538	.179743	.182989	.189596	.196340
	-.30	.154109	.156896	.159744	.162650	.165612	.168627	.171694	.174809	.177971	.181175	.184422	.191028	.197772
	-.40	.155541	.158328	.161176	.164082	.167044	.170060	.173126	.176242	.179403	.182608	.185854	.192461	.199204
30	.40	.140580	.143496	.146477	.149521	.152624	.155781	.158991	.162248	.165551	.168895	.172278	.179148	.186128
	.30	.142012	.144928	.147910	.150953	.154056	.157214	.160423	.163681	.166983	.170328	.173711	.180581	.187571
	.20	.143445	.146361	.149342	.152386	.155488	.158646	.161855	.165113	.168416	.171760	.175143	.182013	.189003
	.10	.144877	.147793	.150775	.153818	.156921	.160078	.163288	.166545	.169848	.173193	.176576	.183445	.190436
	0.00	.146310	.149225	.152207	.155251	.158353	.161511	.164720	.167978	.171280	.174625	.178008	.184878	.191868
	-.10	.147742	.150658	.153639	.156683	.159785	.162943	.166152	.169410	.172713	.176057	.179440	.186310	.193300
	-.20	.149174	.152090	.155072	.158115	.161218	.164375	.167585	.170843	.174145	.177490	.180873	.187743	.194733
	-.30	.150607	.153523	.156504	.159548	.162650	.165808	.169017	.172275	.175578	.178922	.182305	.189175	.196165
	-.40	.152039	.154955	.157936	.160980	.164083	.167240	.170450	.173707	.177010	.180354	.183737	.190607	.197598

INTEREST RATE

TERM YEARS	APPR DEP	5.0	5.5	6.0	6.5	7.0	7.5	8.0	8.5	9.0	9.5	10.0	11.0	12.0
10	.40	.164634	.166997	.169391	.171817	.174276	.176765	.179286	.181838	.184420	.187033	.189676	.195051	.200543
	.30	.166067	.168429	.170823	.173250	.175708	.178197	.180718	.183270	.185853	.188465	.191108	.196484	.201976
	.20	.167499	.169861	.172256	.174682	.177140	.179630	.182151	.184702	.187285	.189898	.192541	.197916	.203408
	.10	.168931	.171294	.173688	.176115	.178573	.181062	.183583	.186135	.188717	.191330	.193949	.199349	.204841
	0.00	.170364	.172726	.175121	.177547	.180005	.182495	.185015	.187567	.190150	.192763	.195406	.200781	.206273
	-.10	.171796	.174159	.176553	.178979	.181437	.183927	.186448	.189000	.191582	.194195	.196838	.202213	.207705
	-.20	.173229	.175591	.177985	.180412	.182870	.185359	.187880	.190432	.193014	.195627	.198270	.203646	.209138
	-.30	.174661	.177023	.179418	.181844	.184302	.186792	.189313	.191864	.194447	.197060	.199703	.205078	.210570
	-.40	.176093	.178456	.180850	.183277	.185735	.188224	.190745	.193297	.195879	.198492	.201135	.206510	.212003
15	.40	.143529	.146153	.148823	.151539	.154300	.157106	.159955	.162846	.165780	.168754	.171769	.177915	.184210
	.30	.144962	.147586	.150256	.152972	.155733	.158538	.161387	.164279	.167212	.170187	.173201	.179347	.185642
	.20	.146394	.149018	.151688	.154404	.157165	.159971	.162820	.165711	.168645	.171619	.174634	.180780	.187075
	.10	.147827	.150450	.153121	.155837	.158598	.161403	.164252	.167144	.170077	.173052	.176066	.182212	.188507
	0.00	.149259	.151883	.154553	.157269	.160030	.162835	.165684	.168576	.171509	.174484	.177499	.183645	.189940
	-.10	.150691	.153315	.155985	.158701	.161462	.164268	.167117	.170008	.172942	.175916	.178931	.185077	.191372
	-.20	.152124	.154748	.157418	.160134	.162895	.165700	.168549	.171441	.174374	.177349	.180363	.186509	.192804
	-.30	.153556	.156180	.158850	.161566	.164327	.167133	.169981	.172873	.175807	.178781	.181796	.187942	.194237
	-.40	.154989	.157612	.160282	.162998	.165760	.168565	.171414	.174306	.177239	.180214	.183228	.189374	.195669
20	.40	.133297	.136112	.138983	.141911	.144892	.147925	.151010	.154143	.157324	.160551	.163821	.170488	.177310
	.30	.134730	.137544	.140416	.143343	.146324	.149358	.152442	.155575	.158756	.161983	.165254	.171920	.178742
	.20	.136162	.138977	.141848	.144776	.147756	.150790	.153874	.157008	.160189	.163415	.166686	.173353	.180175
	.10	.137594	.140409	.143281	.146208	.149189	.152222	.155307	.158440	.161621	.164848	.168119	.174785	.181607
	0.00	.139027	.141841	.144713	.147640	.150621	.153655	.156739	.159873	.163054	.166280	.169551	.176218	.183040
	-.10	.140459	.143274	.146145	.149073	.152054	.155087	.158172	.161305	.164486	.167713	.170983	.177650	.184472
	-.20	.141891	.144706	.147578	.150505	.153486	.156520	.159604	.162737	.165918	.169145	.172416	.179082	.185904
	-.30	.143324	.146139	.149010	.151937	.154918	.157952	.161036	.164170	.167351	.170577	.173848	.180515	.187337
	-.40	.144756	.147571	.150443	.153370	.156351	.159384	.162469	.165602	.168783	.172010	.175280	.181947	.188769
25	.40	.127403	.130376	.133414	.136513	.139673	.142889	.146160	.149483	.152855	.156274	.159737	.166784	.173977
	.30	.128835	.131808	.134846	.137946	.141105	.144322	.147593	.150916	.154288	.157706	.161169	.168216	.175409
	.20	.130268	.133241	.136278	.139378	.142538	.145754	.149025	.152348	.155720	.159139	.162601	.169648	.176842
	.10	.131700	.134673	.137711	.140811	.143970	.147187	.150458	.153780	.157153	.160571	.164034	.171081	.178274
	0.00	.133133	.136106	.139143	.142243	.145402	.148619	.151890	.155213	.158585	.162004	.165466	.172513	.179707
	-.10	.134565	.137538	.140575	.143675	.146835	.150051	.153322	.156645	.160017	.163436	.166899	.173946	.181139
	-.20	.135997	.138970	.142008	.145108	.148267	.151484	.154755	.158078	.161450	.164868	.168331	.175378	.182571
	-.30	.137430	.140403	.143440	.146540	.149700	.152916	.156187	.159510	.162882	.166301	.169763	.176810	.184004
	-.40	.138862	.141835	.144873	.147972	.151132	.154349	.157620	.160942	.164314	.167733	.171196	.178243	.185436
30	.40	.123667	.126778	.129958	.133204	.136514	.139882	.143305	.146780	.150303	.153871	.157479	.164807	.172263
	.30	.125100	.128210	.131390	.134637	.137946	.141314	.144738	.148212	.151735	.155303	.158911	.166239	.173695
	.20	.126532	.129642	.132823	.136069	.139379	.142747	.146170	.149645	.153168	.156735	.160344	.167672	.175128
	.10	.127964	.131075	.134255	.137502	.140811	.144179	.147602	.151077	.154600	.158163	.161776	.169104	.175560
	0.00	.129397	.132507	.135687	.138934	.142243	.145611	.149035	.152510	.156033	.159601	.163208	.170536	.177993
	-.10	.130829	.133939	.137120	.140366	.143676	.147044	.150467	.153942	.157465	.161032	.164641	.171969	.179425
	-.20	.132262	.135372	.138552	.141799	.145108	.148476	.151900	.155374	.158897	.162465	.166073	.173401	.180857
	-.30	.133694	.136804	.139985	.143231	.146540	.149909	.153332	.156807	.160330	.163897	.167506	.174834	.182290
	-.40	.135126	.138237	.141417	.144664	.147973	.151341	.154764	.158239	.161762	.165329	.168938	.176266	.183722

10.0 YEAR HOLDING PERIOD
.400 EQUITY YIELD RATE
.900 LOAN RATIO

INTEREST RATE

TERM YEARS	APPR DEP	5.0	5.5	6.0	6.5	7.0	7.5	8.0	8.5	9.0	9.5	10.0	11.0	12.0
10	.40	.135930	.138587	.141281	.144011	.146776	.149577	.152413	.155284	.158189	.161128	.164102	.170149	.176328
	.30	.137362	.140020	.142714	.145443	.148209	.151009	.153845	.156716	.159621	.162561	.165534	.171581	.177760
	.20	.138795	.141452	.144146	.146876	.149641	.152442	.155278	.158148	.161054	.163993	.166967	.173014	.179192
	.10	.140227	.142885	.145578	.148308	.151073	.153874	.156710	.159581	.162486	.165426	.168399	.174446	.180625
	0.00	.141659	.144317	.147011	.149740	.152506	.155306	.158142	.161013	.163918	.166858	.169831	.175879	.182057
	-.10	.143092	.145749	.148443	.151173	.153938	.156739	.159575	.162445	.165351	.168290	.171264	.177311	.183490
	-.20	.144524	.147182	.149875	.152605	.155370	.158171	.161007	.163878	.166783	.169723	.172696	.178743	.184922
	-.30	.145956	.148614	.151308	.154038	.156803	.159604	.162439	.165310	.168216	.171155	.174128	.180176	.186354
	-.40	.147389	.150046	.152740	.155470	.158235	.161036	.163872	.166743	.169648	.172587	.175561	.181608	.187787
15	.40	.112167	.115139	.118143	.121198	.124304	.127460	.130665	.133918	.137219	.140565	.143956	.150871	.157953
	.30	.113619	.116571	.119575	.122630	.125737	.128893	.132098	.135351	.138651	.141997	.145389	.152303	.159385
	.20	.115052	.118003	.121007	.124063	.127169	.130325	.133530	.136783	.140083	.143430	.146821	.153735	.160817
	.10	.116484	.119436	.122440	.125495	.128601	.131757	.134962	.138216	.141516	.144862	.148254	.155168	.162250
	0.00	.117916	.120868	.123872	.126928	.130034	.133190	.136395	.139648	.142948	.146295	.149686	.156600	.163582
	-.10	.119349	.122300	.125304	.128360	.131466	.134622	.137827	.141080	.144381	.147727	.151118	.158032	.165114
	-.20	.120781	.123733	.126737	.129792	.132899	.136055	.139260	.142513	.145813	.149159	.152551	.159465	.166547
	-.30	.122214	.125165	.128169	.131225	.134331	.137487	.140692	.143945	.147245	.150592	.153983	.160897	.167979
	-.40	.123646	.126598	.129602	.132657	.135763	.138919	.142124	.145378	.148678	.152024	.155416	.162330	.169412
20	.40	.100675	.103842	.107073	.110366	.113719	.117132	.120602	.124127	.127706	.131336	.135015	.142515	.150190
	.30	.102108	.105274	.108505	.111798	.115152	.118564	.122034	.125560	.129138	.132768	.136448	.143948	.151622
	.20	.103540	.106707	.109937	.113230	.116584	.119997	.123467	.126992	.130570	.134200	.137880	.145380	.153055
	.10	.104973	.108139	.111370	.114663	.118017	.121429	.124899	.128424	.132003	.135633	.139312	.146812	.154487
	0.00	.106405	.109572	.112802	.116095	.119449	.122862	.126332	.129857	.133435	.137065	.140745	.148245	.155920
	-.10	.107837	.111004	.114235	.117528	.120881	.124294	.127764	.131289	.134868	.138498	.142177	.149677	.157352
	-.20	.109270	.112436	.115667	.118960	.122314	.125726	.129196	.132721	.136300	.139930	.143610	.151109	.158784
	-.30	.110702	.113869	.117099	.120392	.123746	.127159	.130629	.134154	.137732	.141362	.145042	.152542	.160217
	-.40	.112135	.115301	.118532	.121825	.125178	.128591	.132061	.135586	.139165	.142795	.146474	.153974	.161649
25	.40	.094045	.097389	.100806	.104294	.107848	.111467	.115147	.118885	.122679	.126524	.130420	.138348	.146440
	.30	.095477	.098822	.102239	.105726	.109281	.112899	.116579	.120317	.124111	.127957	.131852	.139780	.147873
	.20	.096909	.100254	.103671	.107158	.110713	.114332	.118011	.121750	.125543	.129389	.133285	.141213	.149305
	.10	.098342	.101686	.105104	.108591	.112145	.115764	.119444	.123182	.126976	.130822	.134717	.142645	.150737
	0.00	.099774	.103119	.106536	.110023	.113578	.117196	.120876	.124614	.128408	.132254	.136149	.144077	.152170
	-.10	.101207	.104551	.107968	.111456	.115010	.118629	.122309	.126047	.129840	.133686	.137582	.145510	.153602
	-.20	.102639	.105983	.109401	.112888	.116442	.120061	.123741	.127479	.131273	.135119	.139014	.146942	.155035
	-.30	.104071	.107416	.110833	.114320	.117875	.121493	.125173	.128912	.132705	.136551	.140447	.148375	.156467
	-.40	.105504	.108848	.112266	.115753	.119307	.122926	.126606	.130344	.134138	.137984	.141879	.149807	.157899
30	.40	.089842	.093341	.096919	.100571	.104294	.108083	.111935	.115844	.119807	.123820	.127880	.136124	.144512
	.30	.091274	.094773	.098351	.102004	.105727	.109516	.113367	.117276	.121239	.125253	.129312	.137556	.145944
	.20	.092707	.096206	.099784	.103436	.107159	.110948	.114799	.118709	.122672	.126685	.130745	.138989	.147377
	.10	.094139	.097638	.101216	.104868	.108591	.112380	.116232	.120141	.124104	.128118	.132177	.140421	.148809
	0.00	.095571	.099070	.102648	.106301	.110024	.113813	.117664	.121573	.125537	.129550	.133610	.141853	.150242
	-.10	.097004	.100503	.104081	.107733	.111456	.115245	.119096	.123006	.126969	.130982	.135042	.143286	.151674
	-.20	.098436	.101935	.105513	.109166	.112888	.116678	.120529	.124438	.128401	.132415	.136474	.144718	.153106
	-.30	.099869	.103368	.106945	.110598	.114321	.118110	.121961	.125871	.129834	.133847	.137907	.146151	.154539
	-.40	.101301	.104800	.108378	.112030	.115753	.119542	.123394	.127303	.131266	.135279	.139339	.147583	.155971

10.0 YEAR HOLDING PERIOD
.500 EQUITY YIELD RATE
.600 LOAN RATIO

INTEREST RATE

TERM YEARS	APPR DEP	5.0	5.5	6.0	6.5	7.0	7.5	8.0	8.5	9.0	9.5	10.0	11.0	12.0
10	.40	.267543	.269315	.271111	.272931	.274774	.276641	.278532	.280446	.282383	.284342	.286325	.290356	.294475
	.30	.268426	.270198	.271993	.273813	.275657	.277524	.279414	.281328	.283265	.285225	.287207	.291239	.295558
	.20	.269308	.271080	.272876	.274696	.276539	.278406	.280297	.282211	.284148	.286107	.288090	.292121	.296240
	.10	.270191	.271962	.273758	.275578	.277421	.279289	.281179	.283093	.285030	.286990	.288972	.293003	.297122
	0.00	.271073	.272845	.274640	.276460	.278304	.280171	.282062	.283975	.285912	.287872	.289854	.293886	.298005
	-.10	.271955	.273727	.275523	.277343	.279186	.281053	.282944	.284858	.286795	.288754	.290737	.294768	.298887
	-.20	.272838	.274609	.276405	.278225	.280069	.281936	.283826	.285740	.287677	.289637	.291619	.295650	.299770
	-.30	.273720	.275492	.277288	.279107	.280951	.282818	.284709	.286623	.288559	.290519	.292501	.296533	.300652
	-.40	.274602	.276374	.278170	.279990	.281833	.283701	.285591	.287505	.289442	.291401	.293384	.297415	.301534
15	.40	.250332	.252271	.254245	.256253	.258295	.260370	.262478	.264619	.266790	.268993	.271225	.275779	.280445
	.30	.251214	.253153	.255127	.257135	.259177	.261253	.263361	.265501	.267673	.269875	.272108	.276561	.281327
	.20	.252097	.254036	.256010	.258018	.260060	.262135	.264243	.266383	.268555	.270757	.272990	.277544	.282210
	.10	.252979	.254918	.256892	.258900	.260942	.263018	.265126	.267266	.269437	.271640	.273873	.278426	.283092
	0.00	.253861	.255800	.257774	.259783	.261825	.263900	.266008	.268148	.270320	.272522	.274755	.279308	.283974
	-.10	.254744	.256683	.258657	.260665	.262707	.264782	.266890	.269030	.271202	.273405	.275637	.280191	.284857
	-.20	.255626	.257565	.259539	.261547	.263589	.265665	.267773	.269913	.272084	.274287	.276520	.281073	.285739
	-.30	.256509	.258448	.260421	.262430	.264472	.266547	.268655	.270795	.272967	.275169	.277402	.281955	.286621
	-.40	.257391	.259330	.261304	.263312	.265354	.267429	.269537	.271678	.273849	.276052	.278284	.282838	.287504
20	.40	.241987	.244060	.246176	.248334	.250533	.252772	.255050	.257365	.259717	.262103	.264524	.269461	.274518
	.30	.242870	.244942	.247058	.249216	.251415	.253654	.255932	.258248	.260599	.262986	.265406	.270343	.275400
	.20	.243752	.245825	.247940	.250099	.252298	.254537	.256815	.259130	.261482	.263868	.266289	.271226	.276282
	.10	.244634	.246707	.248823	.250981	.253180	.255419	.257697	.260012	.262364	.264751	.267171	.272108	.277165
	0.00	.245517	.247589	.249705	.251863	.254062	.256302	.258579	.260895	.263246	.265633	.268053	.272990	.278047
	-.10	.246399	.248472	.250588	.252746	.254945	.257184	.259462	.261777	.264129	.266515	.268936	.273873	.278929
	-.20	.247281	.249354	.251470	.253628	.255827	.258066	.260344	.262659	.265011	.267398	.269818	.274755	.279812
	-.30	.248164	.250236	.252352	.254510	.256710	.258949	.261226	.263542	.265893	.268280	.270701	.275638	.280694
	-.40	.249046	.251119	.253235	.255393	.257592	.259831	.262109	.264424	.266776	.269162	.271583	.276520	.281577
25	.40	.237180	.239369	.241608	.243895	.246227	.248604	.251023	.253482	.255979	.258512	.261080	.266310	.271654
	.30	.238063	.240252	.242491	.244777	.247110	.249486	.251905	.254364	.256861	.259394	.261962	.267192	.272537
	.20	.238945	.241134	.243373	.245660	.247992	.250369	.252788	.255246	.257744	.260277	.262844	.268074	.273419
	.10	.239828	.242017	.244255	.246542	.248875	.251251	.253670	.256129	.258626	.261159	.263727	.268957	.274302
	0.00	.240710	.242899	.245138	.247424	.249757	.252134	.254552	.257011	.259508	.262042	.264609	.269839	.275184
	-.10	.241592	.243781	.246020	.248307	.250639	.253016	.255435	.257894	.260391	.262924	.265491	.270722	.276066
	-.20	.242475	.244664	.246902	.249189	.251522	.253898	.256317	.258776	.261273	.263806	.266374	.271604	.276949
	-.30	.243357	.245546	.247785	.250071	.252404	.254781	.257199	.259658	.262155	.264689	.267256	.272486	.277831
	-.40	.244239	.246429	.248667	.250954	.253286	.255663	.258082	.260541	.263038	.265571	.268139	.273369	.278713
30	.40	.234134	.236427	.238774	.241173	.243621	.246115	.248652	.251229	.253844	.256494	.259176	.264628	.270182
	.30	.235016	.237309	.239657	.242056	.244504	.246997	.249534	.252111	.254726	.257376	.260058	.265511	.271065
	.20	.235899	.238192	.240539	.242938	.245386	.247880	.250416	.252994	.255608	.258258	.260941	.266393	.271947
	.10	.236781	.239074	.241422	.243821	.246268	.248762	.251299	.253876	.256491	.259141	.261823	.267275	.272829
	0.00	.237663	.239956	.242304	.244703	.247151	.249644	.252181	.254758	.257373	.260023	.262705	.268158	.273712
	-.10	.238546	.240839	.243186	.245585	.248033	.250527	.253064	.255641	.258256	.260905	.263588	.269040	.274594
	-.20	.239428	.241721	.244069	.246468	.248915	.251409	.253946	.256523	.259138	.261788	.264470	.269922	.275476
	-.30	.240310	.242604	.244951	.247350	.249798	.252291	.254828	.257405	.260020	.262670	.265353	.270805	.276359
	-.40	.241193	.243486	.245833	.248232	.250680	.253174	.255711	.258288	.260903	.263553	.266235	.271687	.277241

10.0 YEAR HOLDING PERIOD
.500 EQUITY YIELD RATE
.667 LOAN RATIO

INTEREST RATE

TERM YEARS	APPR DEP	5.0	5.5	6.0	6.5	7.0	7.5	8.0	8.5	9.0	9.5	10.0	11.0	12.0
10	.40	.242106	.244074	.246070	.248092	.250140	.252215	.254315	.256442	.258594	.260771	.262974	.267453	.272030
	.30	.242988	.244957	.246952	.248974	.251023	.253097	.255198	.257324	.259476	.261654	.263856	.268336	.272913
	.20	.243871	.245839	.247835	.249857	.251905	.253980	.256080	.258207	.260359	.262536	.264739	.269218	.273795
	.10	.244753	.246722	.248717	.250739	.252787	.254862	.256963	.259089	.261241	.263419	.265621	.270101	.274677
0.00	0.00	.245635	.247604	.249599	.251621	.253670	.255744	.257845	.259971	.262124	.264301	.266504	.270983	.275560
	-.10	.246518	.248486	.250482	.252504	.254552	.256627	.258727	.260854	.263006	.265183	.267386	.271865	.276442
	-.20	.247400	.249369	.251364	.253386	.255434	.257509	.259610	.261736	.263888	.266066	.268268	.272748	.277325
	-.30	.248282	.250251	.252246	.254268	.256317	.258391	.260492	.262619	.264771	.266948	.269151	.273630	.278207
	-.40	.249165	.251133	.253129	.255151	.257199	.259274	.261375	.263501	.265653	.267831	.270033	.274513	.279089
15	.40	.222982	.225136	.227329	.229561	.231830	.234136	.236478	.238856	.241269	.243716	.246197	.251256	.256441
	.30	.223864	.226019	.228212	.230443	.232712	.235018	.237360	.239738	.242151	.244599	.247079	.252139	.257323
	.20	.224747	.226901	.229094	.231326	.233595	.235901	.238243	.240621	.243034	.245481	.247962	.253021	.258205
	.10	.225629	.227783	.229977	.232208	.234477	.236783	.239125	.241503	.243916	.246363	.248844	.253903	.259088
0.00	0.00	.226511	.228666	.230859	.233090	.235359	.237665	.240008	.242385	.244798	.247246	.249726	.254786	.259970
	-.10	.227394	.229548	.231741	.233973	.236242	.238548	.240890	.243268	.245681	.248128	.250609	.255668	.260853
	-.20	.228276	.230431	.232624	.234855	.237124	.239430	.241772	.244150	.246563	.249010	.251491	.256551	.261735
	-.30	.229158	.231313	.233506	.235738	.238006	.240312	.242655	.245033	.247446	.249893	.252374	.257433	.262617
	-.40	.230041	.232195	.234389	.236620	.238889	.241195	.243537	.245915	.248328	.250775	.253256	.258315	.263500
20	.40	.213710	.216013	.218364	.220762	.223205	.225693	.228224	.230797	.233410	.236061	.238751	.244236	.249855
	.30	.214592	.216895	.219246	.221644	.224088	.226575	.229107	.231679	.234292	.236944	.239633	.245119	.250737
	.20	.215474	.217778	.220128	.222526	.224970	.227458	.229989	.232561	.235174	.237826	.240516	.246001	.251620
	.10	.216357	.218660	.221011	.223409	.225852	.228340	.230871	.233444	.236057	.238709	.241398	.246883	.252502
0.00	0.00	.217239	.219542	.221893	.224291	.226734	.229223	.231753	.234326	.236939	.239591	.242280	.247766	.253384
	-.10	.218122	.220425	.222776	.225174	.227617	.230105	.232636	.235208	.237821	.240473	.243163	.248648	.254267
	-.20	.219004	.221307	.223658	.226056	.228499	.230987	.233518	.236091	.238704	.241356	.244045	.249531	.255149
	-.30	.219887	.222189	.224540	.226938	.229382	.231870	.234401	.236973	.239586	.242238	.244927	.250413	.256032
	-.40	.220769	.223072	.225423	.227821	.230264	.232752	.235283	.237856	.240469	.243120	.245810	.251295	.256914
25	.40	.208369	.210801	.213289	.215829	.218421	.221062	.223749	.226482	.229256	.232071	.234924	.240735	.246574
	.30	.209251	.211684	.214171	.216712	.219304	.221944	.224632	.227364	.230139	.232953	.235806	.241617	.247556
	.20	.210134	.212566	.215054	.217594	.220186	.222827	.225514	.228246	.231021	.233836	.236688	.242500	.248438
	.10	.211016	.213448	.215936	.218477	.221068	.223709	.226397	.229129	.231903	.234718	.237571	.243382	.249321
0.00	0.00	.211899	.214331	.216818	.219359	.221951	.224591	.227279	.230011	.232786	.235600	.238453	.244265	.250203
	-.10	.212781	.215213	.217701	.220241	.222833	.225474	.228161	.230894	.233668	.236483	.239336	.245147	.251085
	-.20	.213663	.216096	.218583	.221124	.223715	.226356	.229044	.231776	.234550	.237365	.240218	.246029	.251968
	-.30	.214546	.216978	.219465	.222006	.224598	.227239	.229926	.232658	.235433	.238248	.241100	.246912	.252850
	-.40	.215428	.217860	.220348	.222888	.225480	.228121	.230809	.233541	.236315	.239130	.241983	.247794	.253733
30	.40	.204984	.207532	.210140	.212806	.215525	.218296	.221115	.223978	.226884	.229828	.232808	.238867	.245038
	.30	.205866	.208414	.211022	.213688	.216408	.219179	.221997	.224861	.227766	.230711	.233691	.239749	.245920
	.20	.206749	.209297	.211905	.214570	.217290	.220061	.222880	.225743	.228649	.231593	.234573	.240631	.246802
	.10	.207631	.210179	.212787	.215453	.218172	.220943	.223762	.226626	.229531	.232475	.235456	.241514	.247685
0.00	0.00	.208513	.211061	.213670	.216335	.219055	.221826	.224644	.227508	.230413	.233358	.236338	.242396	.248567
	-.10	.209396	.211944	.214552	.217218	.219937	.222708	.225527	.228390	.231296	.234240	.237220	.243278	.249450
	-.20	.210278	.212826	.215434	.218100	.220820	.223590	.226409	.229273	.232178	.235122	.238103	.244161	.250332
	-.30	.211161	.213708	.216317	.218982	.221702	.224473	.227291	.230155	.233060	.236005	.238985	.245043	.251214
	-.40	.212043	.214591	.217199	.219865	.222584	.225355	.228174	.231037	.233943	.236887	.239868	.245926	.252097

10.0 YEAR HOLDING PERIOD
.500 EQUITY YIELD RATE
.700 LOAN RATIO

INTEREST RATE

TERM YEARS	APPR DEP	5.0	5.5	6.0	6.5	7.0	7.5	8.0	8.5	9.0	9.5	10.0	11.0	12.0
10	.40	.229389	.231456	.233551	.235674	.237825	.240003	.242209	.244442	.246701	.248988	.251300	.256004	.260809
	.30	.230271	.232338	.234433	.236557	.238707	.240886	.243091	.245324	.247584	.249870	.252183	.256886	.261692
	.20	.231154	.233221	.235316	.237439	.239590	.241768	.243974	.246207	.248466	.250753	.253065	.257769	.262574
	.10	.232036	.234103	.236198	.238321	.240472	.242650	.244856	.247089	.249349	.251635	.253948	.258651	.263457
	0.00	.232918	.234985	.237081	.239204	.241354	.243533	.245739	.247971	.250231	.252517	.254830	.259533	.264339
	-.10	.233801	.235868	.237963	.240086	.242237	.244415	.246621	.248854	.251113	.253400	.255712	.260416	.265221
	-.20	.234683	.236750	.238845	.240968	.243119	.245298	.247503	.249736	.251996	.254282	.256595	.261298	.266104
	-.30	.235566	.237633	.239728	.241851	.244002	.246180	.248386	.250618	.252878	.255164	.257477	.262180	.266986
	-.40	.236448	.238515	.240610	.242733	.244884	.247062	.249268	.251501	.253761	.256047	.258359	.263063	.267868
15	.40	.209309	.211571	.213874	.216217	.218599	.221020	.223480	.225977	.228510	.231080	.233685	.238997	.244440
	.30	.210191	.212453	.214756	.217099	.219482	.221903	.224362	.226859	.229393	.231962	.234567	.239879	.245323
	.20	.211074	.213336	.215639	.217982	.220364	.222785	.225245	.227741	.230275	.232845	.235449	.240762	.246205
	.10	.211956	.214218	.216521	.218864	.221246	.223668	.226127	.228624	.231157	.233727	.236332	.241644	.247088
	0.00	.212838	.215101	.217403	.219746	.222129	.224550	.227009	.229506	.232040	.234609	.237214	.242526	.247970
	-.10	.213721	.215983	.218286	.220629	.223011	.225432	.227892	.230388	.232922	.235492	.238097	.243409	.248853
	-.20	.214603	.216865	.219168	.221511	.223893	.226315	.228774	.231271	.233804	.236374	.238979	.244291	.249735
	-.30	.215485	.217748	.220051	.222393	.224776	.227197	.229656	.232153	.234687	.237256	.239861	.245174	.250617
	-.40	.216368	.218630	.220933	.223276	.225658	.228079	.230539	.233036	.235569	.238139	.240744	.246056	.251500
20	.40	.199573	.201991	.204460	.206978	.209543	.212156	.214813	.217514	.220258	.223042	.225866	.231626	.237525
	.30	.200455	.202874	.205342	.207860	.210426	.213038	.215695	.218397	.221140	.223925	.226748	.232508	.238408
	.20	.201338	.203756	.206225	.208742	.211308	.213920	.216578	.219279	.222023	.224807	.227631	.233391	.239290
	.10	.202220	.204639	.207107	.209625	.212190	.214803	.217460	.220161	.222905	.225689	.228513	.234273	.240173
	0.00	.203103	.205521	.207989	.210507	.213073	.215685	.218343	.221044	.223787	.226572	.229396	.235155	.241055
	-.10	.203985	.206403	.208872	.211390	.213955	.216567	.219225	.221926	.224670	.227454	.230278	.236038	.241937
	-.20	.204868	.207286	.209754	.212272	.214838	.217450	.220107	.222809	.225552	.228337	.231160	.236920	.242820
	-.30	.205750	.208168	.210637	.213154	.215720	.218332	.220990	.223691	.226434	.229219	.232043	.237803	.243702
	-.40	.206632	.209050	.211519	.214037	.216602	.219215	.221872	.224573	.227317	.230101	.232925	.238685	.244584
25	.40	.193965	.196519	.199131	.201799	.204520	.207293	.210115	.212984	.215897	.218852	.221848	.227950	.234185
	.30	.194848	.197402	.200014	.202681	.205403	.208175	.210997	.213866	.216779	.219735	.222730	.228832	.235067
	.20	.195730	.198284	.200896	.203564	.206285	.209058	.211880	.214748	.217662	.220617	.223613	.229714	.235950
	.10	.196613	.199166	.201778	.204446	.207167	.209940	.212762	.215631	.218544	.221499	.224495	.230597	.236832
	0.00	.197495	.200049	.202661	.205328	.208050	.210822	.213644	.216513	.219426	.222382	.225377	.231479	.237715
	-.10	.198377	.200931	.203543	.206211	.208932	.211705	.214527	.217395	.220309	.223264	.226260	.232361	.238597
	-.20	.199260	.201814	.204425	.207093	.209814	.212587	.215409	.218278	.221191	.224147	.227142	.233244	.239479
	-.30	.200142	.202696	.205308	.207975	.210697	.213470	.216292	.219160	.222073	.225029	.228024	.234126	.240362
	-.40	.201024	.203578	.206190	.208858	.211579	.214352	.217174	.220043	.222956	.225911	.228907	.235009	.241244
30	.40	.190411	.193086	.195825	.198624	.201480	.204389	.207349	.210355	.213406	.216497	.219627	.225988	.232467
	.30	.191293	.193969	.196707	.199506	.202362	.205271	.208231	.211238	.214288	.217380	.220509	.226870	.233350
	.20	.192176	.194851	.197590	.200389	.203244	.206154	.209113	.212120	.215171	.218262	.221392	.227752	.234232
	.10	.193058	.195734	.198472	.201271	.204127	.207036	.209996	.213002	.216053	.219145	.222274	.228635	.235115
	0.00	.193941	.196616	.199355	.202153	.205009	.207918	.210878	.213885	.216935	.220027	.223156	.229517	.235997
	-.10	.194823	.197498	.200237	.203036	.205891	.208801	.211760	.214767	.217818	.220909	.224039	.230400	.236879
	-.20	.195705	.198381	.201119	.203918	.206774	.209683	.212643	.215650	.218700	.221792	.224921	.231282	.237762
	-.30	.196588	.199263	.202002	.204801	.207656	.210566	.213525	.216532	.219583	.222674	.225803	.232164	.238644
	-.40	.197470	.200145	.202884	.205683	.208539	.211448	.214408	.217414	.220465	.223556	.226686	.233047	.239526

10.0 YEAR HOLDING PERIOD
.500 EQUITY YIELD RATE
.750 LOAN RATIO

INTEREST RATE

TERM YEARS	APPR DEP	5.0	5.5	6.0	6.5	7.0	7.5	8.0	8.5	9.0	9.5	10.0	11.0	12.0
10	.40	.210312	.212526	.214771	.217046	.219350	.221684	.224047	.226440	.228861	.231310	.233788	.238828	.243977
	.30	.211194	.213409	.215653	.217928	.220233	.222567	.224930	.227322	.229743	.232193	.234671	.239710	.244859
	.20	.212076	.214291	.216536	.218811	.221115	.223449	.225812	.228205	.230626	.233075	.235553	.240592	.245741
	.10	.212959	.215173	.217418	.219693	.221997	.224331	.226695	.229087	.231508	.233958	.236435	.241475	.246624
	0.00	.213841	.216056	.218301	.220575	.222880	.225214	.227577	.229969	.232390	.234840	.237318	.242357	.247506
	-.10	.214724	.216938	.219183	.221458	.223762	.226096	.228459	.230852	.233273	.235722	.238200	.243240	.248388
	-.20	.215606	.217821	.220065	.222340	.224645	.226979	.229342	.231734	.234155	.236605	.239083	.244122	.249271
	-.30	.216488	.218703	.220948	.223222	.225527	.227861	.230224	.232616	.235037	.237487	.239965	.245004	.250153
	-.40	.217371	.219585	.221830	.224105	.226409	.228743	.231107	.233499	.235920	.238369	.240847	.245887	.251036
15	.40	.188797	.191221	.193688	.196199	.198751	.201345	.203980	.206656	.209370	.212123	.214914	.220606	.226438
	.30	.189680	.192103	.194571	.197081	.199634	.202228	.204863	.207538	.210253	.213006	.215797	.221488	.227321
	.20	.190562	.192986	.195453	.197963	.200516	.203110	.205745	.208420	.211135	.213888	.216679	.222371	.228203
	.10	.191444	.193868	.196336	.198846	.201398	.203992	.206628	.209303	.212017	.214770	.217561	.223253	.229085
	0.00	.192327	.194751	.197218	.199728	.202281	.204875	.207510	.210185	.212900	.215653	.218444	.224135	.229968
	-.10	.193209	.195633	.198100	.200611	.203163	.205757	.208392	.211067	.213782	.216535	.219326	.225018	.230850
	-.20	.194092	.196515	.198983	.201493	.204045	.206640	.209275	.211950	.214664	.217418	.220208	.225900	.231733
	-.30	.194974	.197398	.199865	.202375	.204928	.207522	.210157	.212832	.215547	.218300	.221091	.226783	.232615
	-.40	.195856	.198280	.200747	.203258	.205810	.208404	.211039	.213715	.216429	.219182	.221973	.227665	.233497
20	.40	.178366	.180957	.183602	.186300	.189049	.191847	.194695	.197589	.200528	.203512	.206537	.212708	.219029
	.30	.179249	.181840	.184484	.187182	.189931	.192730	.195577	.198471	.201411	.204394	.207420	.213591	.219912
	.20	.180131	.182722	.185367	.188064	.190813	.193612	.196459	.199354	.202293	.205276	.208302	.214473	.220794
	.10	.181014	.183604	.186249	.188947	.191696	.194494	.197342	.200236	.203175	.206159	.209184	.215356	.221676
	0.00	.181896	.184487	.187132	.189829	.192578	.195377	.198224	.201118	.204058	.207041	.210067	.216238	.222559
	-.10	.182778	.185369	.188014	.190711	.193460	.196259	.199107	.202001	.204940	.207924	.210949	.217120	.223441
	-.20	.183661	.186251	.188896	.191594	.194343	.197142	.199989	.202883	.205823	.208806	.211831	.218003	.224324
	-.30	.184543	.187134	.189779	.192476	.195225	.198024	.200871	.203765	.206705	.209688	.212714	.218885	.225206
	-.40	.185425	.188016	.190661	.193359	.196108	.198906	.201754	.204648	.207587	.210571	.213596	.219768	.226088
25	.40	.172358	.175094	.177893	.180751	.183667	.186637	.189661	.192735	.195856	.199022	.202232	.208770	.215450
	.30	.173240	.175977	.178775	.181633	.184549	.187520	.190543	.193617	.196738	.199905	.203114	.209652	.216333
	.20	.174123	.176859	.179657	.182516	.185431	.188402	.191426	.194499	.197621	.200787	.203997	.210534	.217215
	.10	.175005	.177741	.180540	.183398	.186314	.189285	.192308	.195382	.198503	.201652	.204879	.211417	.218098
	0.00	.175887	.178624	.181422	.184280	.187196	.190167	.193190	.196264	.199385	.202552	.205761	.212299	.218980
	-.10	.176770	.179506	.182305	.185163	.188078	.191049	.194073	.197146	.200268	.203434	.206644	.213181	.219862
	-.20	.177652	.180388	.183187	.186045	.188961	.191932	.194955	.198029	.201150	.204317	.207526	.214064	.220745
	-.30	.178535	.181271	.184069	.186928	.189843	.192814	.195838	.198911	.202033	.205199	.208408	.214946	.221627
	-.40	.179417	.182153	.184952	.187810	.190726	.193696	.196720	.199794	.202915	.206081	.209291	.215829	.222509
30	.40	.168550	.171416	.174350	.177349	.180409	.183526	.186697	.189918	.193187	.196499	.199852	.206668	.213610
	.30	.169432	.172298	.175233	.178231	.181291	.184408	.187579	.190801	.194069	.197382	.200735	.207550	.214492
	.20	.170314	.173181	.176115	.179114	.182174	.185291	.188462	.191683	.194952	.198264	.201617	.208432	.215375
	.10	.171197	.174063	.176998	.179996	.183056	.186173	.189344	.192566	.195834	.199146	.202499	.209315	.216257
	0.00	.172079	.174946	.177880	.180879	.183938	.187055	.190226	.193448	.196717	.200029	.203382	.210197	.217140
	-.10	.172962	.175828	.178762	.181761	.184821	.187938	.191109	.194330	.197599	.200911	.204264	.211079	.218022
	-.20	.173844	.176710	.179645	.182643	.185703	.188820	.191991	.195213	.198481	.201794	.205146	.211962	.218904
	-.30	.174726	.177593	.180527	.183526	.186585	.189703	.192874	.196095	.199364	.202676	.206029	.212844	.219787
	-.40	.175609	.178475	.181409	.184408	.187468	.190585	.193756	.196977	.200246	.203558	.206911	.213727	.220669

285

10.0 YEAR HOLDING PERIOD
.500 EQUITY YIELD RATE
.800 LOAN RATIO

INTEREST RATE

TERM YEARS	APPR DEP	5.0	5.5	6.0	6.5	7.0	7.5	8.0	8.5	9.0	9.5	10.0	11.0	12.0
10	.40	.191234	.193597	.195991	.198418	.200876	.203365	.205886	.208438	.211020	.213633	.216276	.221651	.227144
	.30	.192117	.194479	.196874	.199300	.201758	.204248	.206768	.209320	.211903	.214515	.217159	.222534	.228026
	.20	.192999	.195361	.197756	.200182	.202640	.205130	.207651	.210202	.212785	.215398	.218041	.223416	.228908
	.10	.193881	.196244	.198638	.201065	.203523	.206012	.208533	.211085	.213667	.216280	.218923	.224299	.229791
	0.00	.194764	.197126	.199521	.201947	.204405	.206895	.209415	.211967	.214550	.217163	.219806	.225181	.230673
	-.10	.195646	.198009	.200403	.202829	.205287	.207777	.210298	.212850	.215432	.218045	.220688	.226063	.231555
	-.20	.196529	.198891	.201285	.203712	.206170	.208659	.211180	.213732	.216314	.218927	.221570	.226946	.232438
	-.30	.197411	.199773	.202168	.204594	.207052	.209542	.212063	.214614	.217197	.219810	.222453	.227828	.233320
	-.40	.198293	.200656	.203050	.205477	.207935	.210424	.212945	.215497	.218079	.220692	.223335	.228710	.234203
15	.40	.168286	.170871	.173503	.176181	.178903	.181670	.184481	.187335	.190230	.193167	.196144	.202215	.208436
	.30	.169166	.171753	.174385	.177063	.179786	.182553	.185363	.188217	.191113	.194049	.197026	.203097	.209319
	.20	.170050	.172636	.175268	.177945	.180668	.183435	.186246	.189099	.191995	.194932	.197909	.203980	.210201
	.10	.170933	.173518	.176150	.178828	.181550	.184317	.187128	.189982	.192877	.195814	.198791	.204862	.211083
	0.00	.171815	.174401	.177032	.179710	.182433	.185200	.188011	.190864	.193760	.196696	.199673	.205744	.211966
	-.10	.172698	.175283	.177915	.180592	.183315	.186082	.188893	.191746	.194642	.197579	.200556	.206627	.212848
	-.20	.173580	.176165	.178797	.181475	.184198	.186965	.189775	.192629	.195524	.198461	.201438	.207509	.213730
	-.30	.174462	.177048	.179680	.182357	.185080	.187847	.190658	.193511	.196407	.199343	.202320	.208392	.214613
	-.40	.175345	.177930	.180562	.183240	.185962	.188729	.191540	.194394	.197289	.200226	.203203	.209274	.215495
20	.40	.157159	.159923	.162744	.165622	.168554	.171539	.174576	.177663	.180799	.183981	.187208	.193791	.200533
	.30	.158042	.160805	.163627	.166504	.169436	.172422	.175459	.178546	.181681	.184863	.188091	.194673	.201416
	.20	.158924	.161688	.164509	.167386	.170318	.173304	.176341	.179428	.182564	.185746	.188973	.195556	.202298
	.10	.159807	.162570	.165391	.168269	.171201	.174186	.177223	.180311	.183446	.186628	.189855	.196438	.203180
	0.00	.160689	.163452	.166274	.169151	.172083	.175069	.178106	.181193	.184328	.187511	.190738	.197321	.204063
	-.10	.161571	.164335	.167156	.170033	.172966	.175951	.178988	.182075	.185211	.188393	.191620	.198203	.204945
	-.20	.162454	.165217	.168038	.170916	.173848	.176833	.179871	.182958	.186093	.189275	.192503	.199085	.205828
	-.30	.163336	.166100	.168921	.171798	.174730	.177716	.180753	.183840	.186976	.190158	.193385	.199968	.206710
	-.40	.164218	.166982	.169803	.172681	.175613	.178598	.181635	.184722	.187858	.191040	.194267	.200850	.207592
25	.40	.150750	.153669	.156654	.159703	.162813	.165982	.169207	.172485	.175815	.179193	.182616	.189589	.196716
	.30	.151633	.154552	.157536	.160585	.163695	.166864	.170089	.173368	.176697	.180075	.183498	.190472	.197598
	.20	.152515	.155434	.158419	.161468	.164578	.167747	.170972	.174250	.177580	.180957	.184381	.191354	.198480
	.10	.153398	.156316	.159301	.162350	.165460	.168629	.171854	.175133	.178462	.181840	.185263	.192237	.199363
	0.00	.154280	.157199	.160184	.163232	.166343	.169511	.172736	.176015	.179344	.182722	.186145	.193119	.200245
	-.10	.155162	.158081	.161066	.164115	.167225	.170394	.173619	.176897	.180227	.183604	.187028	.194001	.201128
	-.20	.156045	.158963	.161948	.164997	.168107	.171276	.174501	.177780	.181109	.184487	.187910	.194884	.202010
	-.30	.156927	.159846	.162831	.165880	.168990	.172159	.175384	.178662	.181992	.185369	.188793	.195766	.202892
	-.40	.157809	.160728	.163713	.166762	.169872	.173041	.176266	.179544	.182874	.186252	.189675	.196648	.203775
30	.40	.146688	.149746	.152876	.156074	.159338	.162663	.166045	.169482	.172968	.176501	.180078	.187347	.194753
	.30	.147571	.150628	.153758	.156957	.160220	.163545	.166928	.170364	.173850	.177384	.180960	.188230	.195635
	.20	.148453	.151511	.154640	.157839	.161103	.164428	.167810	.171246	.174733	.178266	.181842	.189112	.196517
	.10	.149335	.152393	.155523	.158721	.161985	.165310	.168693	.172129	.175615	.179148	.182725	.189994	.197400
	0.00	.150218	.153275	.156405	.159604	.162868	.166192	.169575	.173011	.176498	.180031	.183607	.190877	.198282
	-.10	.151100	.154158	.157288	.160486	.163750	.167075	.170457	.173894	.177380	.180913	.184490	.191759	.199165
	-.20	.151983	.155040	.158170	.161369	.164632	.167957	.171340	.174776	.178262	.181796	.185372	.192642	.200047
	-.30	.152865	.155922	.159052	.162251	.165515	.168840	.172222	.175658	.179145	.182678	.186254	.193524	.200929
	-.40	.153747	.156805	.159935	.163133	.166397	.169722	.173104	.176541	.180027	.183560	.187137	.194406	.201812

10.0 YEAR HOLDING PERIOD
.500 EQUITY YIELD RATE
.900 LOAN RATIO

INTEREST RATE

TERM YEARS	APPR DEP	5.0	5.5	6.0	6.5	7.0	7.5	8.0	8.5	9.0	9.5	10.0	11.0	12.0
10	.40	.153060	.155737	.158431	.161161	.163926	.166727	.169563	.172434	.175339	.178278	.181252	.187299	.193478
	.30	.153962	.156020	.159314	.162043	.164809	.167609	.170445	.173316	.176221	.179161	.182134	.188181	.194360
	.20	.154845	.157502	.160196	.162926	.165691	.168492	.171328	.174198	.177104	.180043	.183017	.189064	.195242
	.10	.155727	.158385	.161078	.163808	.166573	.169374	.172210	.175081	.177986	.180926	.183899	.189946	.196125
	0.00	.156609	.159267	.161961	.164690	.167456	.170257	.173092	.175963	.178868	.181808	.184781	.190829	.197007
	-.10	.157492	.160149	.162843	.165573	.168338	.171139	.173975	.176846	.179751	.182690	.185664	.191711	.197890
	-.20	.158374	.161032	.163725	.166455	.169221	.172021	.174857	.177728	.180633	.183573	.186546	.192593	.198772
	-.30	.159256	.161914	.164608	.167338	.170103	.172904	.175740	.178610	.181516	.184455	.187429	.193476	.199654
	-.40	.160139	.162796	.165490	.168220	.170985	.173786	.176622	.179493	.182398	.185337	.188311	.194358	.200537
15	.40	.127263	.130171	.133132	.136144	.139207	.142320	.145482	.148693	.151950	.155254	.158603	.165433	.172432
	.30	.128145	.131054	.134014	.137027	.140090	.143203	.146365	.149575	.152832	.156136	.159485	.166315	.173314
	.20	.129028	.131936	.134897	.137909	.140972	.144085	.147247	.150457	.153715	.157019	.160368	.167198	.174197
	.10	.129910	.132818	.135779	.138791	.141854	.144967	.148130	.151340	.154597	.157901	.161250	.168080	.175079
	0.00	.130792	.133701	.136661	.139674	.142737	.145850	.149012	.152222	.155480	.158783	.162133	.168962	.175961
	-.10	.131675	.134583	.137544	.140556	.143619	.146732	.149894	.153105	.156362	.159666	.163015	.169845	.176844
	-.20	.132557	.135465	.138426	.141439	.144502	.147615	.150777	.153987	.157244	.160548	.163897	.170727	.177726
	-.30	.133439	.136348	.139309	.142321	.145384	.148497	.151659	.154869	.158127	.161431	.164780	.171610	.178609
	-.40	.134322	.137230	.140191	.143203	.146266	.149379	.152541	.155752	.159009	.162313	.165662	.172492	.179491
20	.40	.114746	.117855	.121028	.124265	.127564	.130923	.134339	.137812	.141340	.144920	.148551	.155956	.163541
	.30	.115628	.118737	.121911	.125148	.128447	.131805	.135222	.138695	.142222	.145802	.149433	.156838	.164423
	.20	.116510	.119619	.122793	.126030	.129329	.132687	.136104	.139577	.143105	.146685	.150315	.157721	.165306
	.10	.117393	.120502	.123675	.126913	.130211	.133570	.136987	.140460	.143987	.147567	.151198	.158603	.166188
	0.00	.118275	.121384	.124558	.127795	.131094	.134452	.137869	.141342	.144869	.148449	.152080	.159486	.167071
	-.10	.119157	.122266	.125440	.128677	.131976	.135335	.138751	.142224	.145752	.149332	.152962	.160368	.167953
	-.20	.120040	.123149	.126323	.129560	.132858	.136217	.139634	.143107	.146634	.150214	.153845	.161250	.168835
	-.30	.120922	.124031	.127205	.130442	.133741	.137099	.140516	.143989	.147517	.151097	.154727	.162133	.169718
	-.40	.121805	.124914	.128087	.131324	.134623	.137982	.141398	.144872	.148399	.151979	.155610	.163015	.170600
25	.40	.107535	.110819	.114177	.117607	.121106	.124671	.128299	.131987	.135733	.139533	.143384	.151229	.159246
	.30	.108418	.111701	.115059	.118489	.121988	.125553	.129181	.132870	.136615	.140415	.144267	.152112	.160129
	.20	.109300	.112584	.115942	.119372	.122871	.126436	.130064	.133752	.137498	.141298	.145149	.152994	.161011
	.10	.110183	.113466	.116824	.120254	.123753	.127318	.130946	.134634	.138380	.142180	.146031	.153876	.161894
	0.00	.111065	.114348	.117707	.121136	.124635	.128200	.131828	.135517	.139262	.143062	.146914	.154759	.162776
	-.10	.111947	.115231	.118589	.122019	.125518	.129083	.132711	.136399	.140145	.143945	.147796	.155641	.163658
	-.20	.112830	.116113	.119471	.122901	.126400	.129965	.133593	.137282	.141027	.144827	.148678	.156524	.164541
	-.30	.113712	.116996	.120354	.123784	.127282	.130848	.134476	.138164	.141910	.145709	.149561	.157406	.165423
	-.40	.114594	.117878	.121236	.124666	.128165	.131730	.135358	.139047	.142792	.146592	.150443	.158288	.166305
30	.40	.102966	.106405	.109926	.113525	.117196	.120937	.124742	.128608	.132530	.136505	.140529	.148707	.157038
	.30	.103848	.107288	.110809	.114407	.118079	.121819	.125625	.129490	.133413	.137387	.141411	.149589	.157920
	.20	.104730	.108170	.111691	.115290	.118961	.122702	.126507	.130373	.134295	.138270	.142293	.150472	.158803
	.10	.105613	.109052	.112573	.116172	.119844	.123584	.127389	.131255	.135177	.139152	.143176	.151354	.159685
	0.00	.106495	.109935	.113456	.117054	.120726	.124467	.128272	.132138	.136060	.140035	.144058	.152236	.160557
	-.10	.107377	.110817	.114338	.117937	.121608	.125349	.129154	.133020	.136942	.140917	.144940	.153119	.161450
	-.20	.108260	.111699	.115221	.118819	.122491	.126231	.130036	.133902	.137825	.141799	.145823	.154001	.162332
	-.30	.109142	.112582	.116103	.119701	.123373	.127114	.130919	.134785	.138707	.142682	.146705	.154884	.163215
	-.40	.110025	.113464	.116985	.120584	.124255	.127996	.131801	.135667	.139589	.143564	.147588	.155766	.164097

15.0 YEAR HOLDING PERIOD
.020 EQUITY YIELD RATE
.600 LOAN RATIO

INTEREST RATE

TERM YEARS	APPR DEP	5.0	5.5	6.0	6.5	7.0	7.5	8.0	8.5	9.0	9.5	10.0	11.0	12.0
10	.40	.001516	.002377	.003235	.004087	.004932	.005770	.006600	.007421	.008232	.009031	.009818	.011351	.012820
	.30	.007298	.008160	.009017	.009869	.010715	.011553	.012383	.013204	.014014	.014814	.015601	.017133	.018603
	.20	.013081	.013943	.014800	.015652	.016497	.017335	.018165	.018986	.019797	.020596	.021383	.022916	.024385
	.10	.018863	.019725	.020582	.021434	.022280	.023118	.023948	.024769	.025579	.026379	.027166	.028698	.030168
	0.00	.024646	.025508	.026365	.027217	.028062	.028900	.029731	.030551	.031362	.032161	.032948	.034481	.035951
	-.10	.030428	.031290	.032147	.032999	.033845	.034683	.035513	.036334	.037145	.037944	.038731	.040263	.041733
	-.20	.036211	.037073	.037930	.038782	.039627	.040466	.041296	.042116	.042927	.043726	.044513	.046046	.047516
	-.30	.041993	.042855	.043712	.044564	.045410	.046248	.047078	.047899	.048710	.049509	.050296	.051828	.053298
	-.40	.047776	.048638	.049495	.050347	.051192	.052031	.052861	.053682	.054492	.055291	.056078	.057611	.059081
15	.40	.007112	.009005	.010932	.012894	.014890	.016919	.018981	.021076	.023202	.025359	.027546	.032010	.036587
	.30	.012894	.014787	.016715	.018677	.020673	.022702	.024764	.026858	.028984	.031141	.033329	.037792	.042369
	.20	.018677	.020570	.022497	.024459	.026455	.028485	.030547	.032641	.034767	.036924	.039111	.043575	.048152
	.10	.024459	.026352	.028280	.030242	.032238	.034267	.036329	.038423	.040549	.042706	.044894	.049357	.053934
	0.00	.030242	.032135	.034062	.036024	.038020	.040050	.042112	.044206	.046332	.048489	.050676	.055140	.059717
	-.10	.036024	.037917	.039845	.041807	.043803	.045832	.047894	.049989	.052114	.054271	.056459	.060922	.065499
	-.20	.041807	.043700	.045628	.047590	.049585	.051615	.053677	.055771	.057897	.060054	.062241	.066705	.071282
	-.30	.047589	.049482	.051410	.053372	.055368	.057397	.059459	.061554	.063680	.065837	.068024	.072487	.077064
	-.40	.053372	.055265	.057193	.059155	.061151	.063180	.065242	.067336	.069462	.071619	.073806	.078270	.082847
20	.40	.009825	.012197	.014615	.017077	.019581	.022126	.024711	.027333	.029993	.032637	.035414	.040963	.046627
	.30	.015607	.017980	.020397	.022859	.025363	.027908	.030493	.033116	.035775	.038469	.041197	.046746	.052409
	.20	.021390	.023762	.026180	.028642	.031146	.033691	.036276	.038899	.041558	.044252	.046979	.052528	.058192
	.10	.027172	.029545	.031963	.034424	.036928	.039474	.042058	.044681	.047340	.050035	.052762	.058311	.063974
	0.00	.032955	.035327	.037745	.040207	.042711	.045256	.047841	.050464	.053123	.055817	.058545	.064093	.069757
	-.10	.038738	.041110	.043528	.045989	.048493	.051039	.053623	.056246	.058905	.061600	.064327	.069876	.075539
	-.20	.044520	.046892	.049310	.051772	.054276	.056821	.059406	.062029	.064688	.067382	.070110	.075658	.081322
	-.30	.050303	.052675	.055093	.057554	.060059	.062604	.065189	.067811	.070471	.073165	.075892	.081441	.087105
	-.40	.056085	.058458	.060875	.063337	.065841	.068386	.070971	.073594	.076253	.078947	.081675	.087224	.092887
25	.40	.011388	.014021	.016699	.019421	.022182	.024982	.027816	.030684	.033581	.036507	.039458	.045429	.051477
	.30	.017170	.019803	.022482	.025203	.027965	.030764	.033599	.036466	.039364	.042290	.045241	.051211	.057259
	.20	.022953	.025586	.028265	.030986	.033748	.036547	.039382	.042249	.045147	.048072	.051023	.056994	.063042
	.10	.028735	.031369	.034047	.036768	.039530	.042329	.045164	.048031	.050929	.053855	.056806	.062777	.068824
	0.00	.034518	.037151	.039830	.042551	.045313	.048112	.050947	.053814	.056712	.059637	.062588	.068559	.074607
	-.10	.040300	.042934	.045612	.048333	.051095	.053895	.056729	.059597	.062494	.065420	.068371	.074342	.080389
	-.20	.046083	.048716	.051395	.054116	.056878	.059677	.062512	.065379	.068277	.071202	.074154	.080124	.086172
	-.30	.051865	.054499	.057177	.059899	.062660	.065460	.068294	.071162	.074059	.076985	.079936	.085907	.091954
	-.40	.057648	.060281	.062960	.065681	.068443	.071242	.074077	.076944	.079842	.082767	.085719	.091689	.097737
30	.40	.012378	.015165	.017993	.020858	.023757	.026687	.029645	.032627	.035631	.038654	.041693	.047812	.053970
	.30	.018161	.020948	.023775	.026641	.029540	.032470	.035428	.038410	.041414	.044437	.047476	.053595	.059753
	.20	.023943	.026730	.029558	.032423	.035322	.038253	.041210	.044192	.047196	.050219	.053259	.059377	.065536
	.10	.029726	.032513	.035340	.038206	.041105	.044035	.046993	.049975	.052979	.056002	.059041	.065160	.071318
	0.00	.035508	.038295	.041123	.043988	.046888	.049818	.052775	.055758	.058761	.061784	.064824	.070942	.077101
	-.10	.041291	.044078	.046905	.049771	.052670	.055600	.058558	.061540	.064544	.067567	.070606	.076725	.082883
	-.20	.047073	.049860	.052688	.055553	.058453	.061383	.064340	.067323	.070327	.073349	.076389	.082507	.088666
	-.30	.052856	.055643	.058471	.061336	.064235	.067165	.070123	.073105	.076109	.079132	.082171	.088290	.094448
	-.40	.058639	.061425	.064253	.067118	.070018	.072948	.075906	.078888	.081892	.084915	.087954	.094072	.100231

15.0 YEAR HOLDING PERIOD
.020 EQUITY YIELD RATE
.667 LOAN RATIO

INTEREST RATE

TERM YEARS	APPR DEP	5.0	5.5	6.0	6.5	7.0	7.5	8.0	8.5	9.0	9.5	10.0	11.0	12.0
10	.40	.002032	.002989	.003942	.004888	.005828	.006759	.007682	.008594	.009494	.010382	.011257	.012960	.014593
	.30	.007814	.008772	.009724	.010671	.011610	.012542	.013464	.014376	.015277	.016165	.017039	.018742	.020375
	.20	.013597	.014554	.015507	.016453	.017393	.018324	.019247	.020159	.021059	.021948	.022822	.024525	.026158
	.10	.019380	.020337	.021290	.022236	.023137	.024107	.025029	.025941	.026842	.027730	.028605	.030307	.031940
	0.00	.025162	.026120	.027072	.028019	.028958	.029889	.030812	.031724	.032624	.033513	.034387	.036090	.037723
	-.10	.030945	.031902	.032855	.033801	.034741	.035672	.036594	.037506	.038407	.039295	.040170	.041872	.043505
	-.20	.036727	.037685	.038637	.039584	.040523	.041455	.042377	.043289	.044190	.045078	.045952	.047655	.049288
	-.30	.042510	.043467	.044420	.045366	.046306	.047237	.048159	.049071	.049972	.050860	.051735	.053438	.055071
	-.40	.048292	.049250	.050202	.051149	.052088	.053020	.053942	.054854	.055755	.056643	.057517	.059220	.060853
15	.40	.008250	.010353	.012495	.014675	.016893	.019147	.021438	.023765	.026128	.028524	.030955	.035914	.041000
	.30	.014032	.016135	.018277	.020457	.022675	.024930	.027221	.029548	.031910	.034307	.036737	.041697	.046782
	.20	.019815	.021918	.024060	.026240	.028458	.030712	.033004	.035331	.037693	.040089	.042520	.047479	.052565
	.10	.025597	.027701	.029842	.032022	.034240	.036495	.038786	.041113	.043475	.045872	.048302	.053262	.058347
	0.00	.031380	.033483	.035625	.037805	.040023	.042277	.044569	.046896	.049258	.051654	.054085	.059044	.064130
	-.10	.037162	.039266	.041408	.043588	.045805	.048060	.050351	.052678	.055040	.057437	.059867	.064827	.069913
	-.20	.042945	.045048	.047190	.049370	.051588	.053843	.056134	.058461	.060823	.063220	.065650	.070609	.075695
	-.30	.048728	.050831	.052973	.055153	.057370	.059625	.061916	.064243	.066605	.069002	.071433	.076392	.081478
	-.40	.054510	.056613	.058755	.060935	.063153	.065408	.067699	.070026	.072388	.074785	.077215	.082174	.087260
20	.40	.011264	.013900	.016587	.019322	.022104	.024932	.027804	.030718	.033673	.036667	.039697	.045863	.052155
	.30	.017047	.019683	.022369	.025104	.027687	.030715	.033587	.036501	.039456	.042449	.045480	.051645	.057538
	.20	.022829	.025465	.028152	.030887	.033669	.036497	.039369	.042284	.045238	.048232	.051262	.057428	.063721
	.10	.028612	.031248	.033934	.036669	.039452	.042280	.045152	.048066	.051021	.054014	.057045	.063210	.069503
	0.00	.034395	.037030	.039717	.042452	.045234	.048062	.050934	.053849	.056803	.059797	.062828	.068993	.075286
	-.10	.040177	.042813	.045499	.048235	.051017	.053845	.056717	.059631	.062586	.065579	.068610	.074775	.081068
	-.20	.045960	.048596	.051282	.054017	.056800	.059628	.062500	.065414	.068369	.071362	.074393	.080558	.086851
	-.30	.051742	.054378	.057064	.059800	.062582	.065410	.068282	.071196	.074151	.077145	.080175	.086340	.092633
	-.40	.057525	.060161	.062847	.065582	.068365	.071193	.074065	.076979	.079934	.082927	.085958	.092123	.098416
25	.40	.013001	.015927	.018903	.021927	.024995	.028106	.031255	.034441	.037661	.040911	.044191	.050825	.057544
	.30	.018783	.021709	.024685	.027709	.030778	.033888	.037038	.040224	.043443	.046694	.049973	.056607	.063327
	.20	.024566	.027492	.030468	.033492	.036560	.039671	.042820	.046006	.049226	.052477	.055756	.062390	.069109
	.10	.030348	.033274	.036250	.039274	.042343	.045453	.048603	.051789	.055008	.058259	.061538	.068172	.074892
	0.00	.036131	.039057	.042033	.045057	.048125	.051236	.054385	.057571	.060791	.064042	.067321	.073955	.080674
	-.10	.041914	.044839	.047816	.050839	.053908	.057018	.060168	.063354	.066573	.069824	.073103	.079737	.086457
	-.20	.047696	.050622	.053598	.056622	.059690	.062801	.065950	.069136	.072356	.075607	.078886	.085520	.092240
	-.30	.053479	.056404	.059381	.062404	.065473	.068583	.071733	.074919	.078139	.081389	.084668	.091302	.098022
	-.40	.059261	.062187	.065163	.068187	.071255	.074366	.077515	.080701	.083921	.087172	.090451	.097085	.103805
30	.40	.014101	.017198	.020340	.023524	.026745	.030001	.033287	.036601	.039938	.043297	.046674	.053473	.060315
	.30	.019884	.022980	.026122	.029306	.032528	.035783	.039070	.042383	.045721	.049080	.052457	.059255	.066098
	.20	.025667	.028763	.031905	.035089	.038310	.041566	.044852	.048166	.051503	.054862	.058239	.065038	.071880
	.10	.031449	.034546	.037688	.040871	.044093	.047348	.050635	.053948	.057286	.060645	.064022	.070820	.077663
	0.00	.037232	.040328	.043470	.046654	.049875	.053131	.056417	.059731	.063069	.066427	.069804	.076603	.083445
	-.10	.043014	.046111	.049253	.052436	.055658	.058913	.062200	.065513	.068851	.072210	.075587	.082385	.089228
	-.20	.048797	.051893	.055035	.058219	.061440	.064696	.067982	.071296	.074634	.077992	.081369	.088168	.095011
	-.30	.054579	.057676	.060818	.064001	.067223	.070479	.073765	.077078	.080416	.083775	.087152	.093950	.100793
	-.40	.060362	.063458	.066600	.069784	.073005	.076261	.079547	.082861	.086199	.089557	.092934	.099733	.106576

15.0 YEAR HOLDING PERIOD
.020 EQUITY YIELD RATE
.700 LOAN RATIO

INTEREST RATE

TERM YEARS	APPR DEP	5.0	5.5	6.0	6.5	7.0	7.5	8.0	8.5	9.0	9.5	10.0	11.0	12.0
10	.40	.002690	.003295	.004295	.005289	.006276	.007254	.008222	.009180	.010125	.011058	.011976	.013764	.015479
	.30	.008601	.009078	.010078	.011072	.012058	.013036	.014005	.014962	.015908	.016841	.017759	.019547	.021261
	.20	.013855	.014860	.015861	.016854	.017841	.018819	.019787	.020745	.021691	.022623	.023541	.025329	.027044
	.10	.019638	.020643	.021643	.022637	.023623	.024601	.025570	.026527	.027473	.028406	.029324	.031112	.032826
	0.00	.025420	.026426	.027426	.028419	.029406	.030384	.031352	.032310	.033256	.034188	.035106	.036894	.038609
	-.10	.031203	.032209	.033208	.034202	.035188	.036166	.037135	.038092	.039038	.039971	.040889	.042677	.044392
	-.20	.036985	.037991	.038991	.039985	.040971	.041949	.042917	.043875	.044821	.045753	.046671	.048459	.050174
	-.30	.042768	.043774	.044773	.045767	.046754	.047732	.048700	.049657	.050603	.051536	.052454	.054242	.055957
	-.40	.046550	.049556	.050556	.051550	.052536	.053514	.054482	.055440	.056386	.057318	.058237	.060025	.061739
15	.40	.008819	.011027	.013276	.015565	.017894	.020261	.022667	.025110	.027590	.030107	.032659	.037866	.043206
	.30	.014601	.016810	.019059	.021348	.023676	.026044	.028449	.030893	.033373	.035889	.038441	.043649	.048989
	.20	.020384	.022592	.024841	.027130	.029459	.031826	.034232	.036675	.039155	.041672	.044224	.049431	.054771
	.10	.026166	.028375	.030624	.032913	.035241	.037609	.040014	.042458	.044938	.047454	.050006	.055214	.060554
	0.00	.031949	.034157	.036406	.038695	.041024	.043391	.045797	.048240	.050721	.053237	.055789	.060996	.066336
	-.10	.037731	.039940	.042189	.044478	.046806	.049174	.051579	.054023	.056503	.059020	.061572	.066779	.072119
	-.20	.043514	.045722	.047971	.050260	.052589	.054956	.057362	.059805	.062286	.064802	.067354	.072561	.077901
	-.30	.049296	.051505	.053754	.056043	.058371	.060739	.063145	.065588	.068068	.070585	.073137	.078344	.083684
	-.40	.055079	.057287	.059536	.061825	.064154	.066521	.068927	.071370	.073851	.076367	.078919	.084127	.089466
20	.40	.011984	.014752	.017572	.020444	.023366	.026335	.029351	.032411	.035513	.038656	.041838	.048312	.054919
	.30	.017767	.020534	.023355	.026227	.029148	.032118	.035133	.038193	.041296	.044439	.047621	.054095	.060702
	.20	.023549	.026317	.029137	.032009	.034931	.037900	.040916	.043976	.047078	.050221	.053404	.059877	.066485
	.10	.029332	.032099	.034920	.037792	.040713	.043683	.046698	.049758	.052861	.056004	.059186	.065660	.072267
	0.00	.035114	.037882	.040703	.043574	.046496	.049465	.052481	.055541	.058643	.061787	.064969	.071442	.078050
	-.10	.040897	.043664	.046485	.049357	.052279	.055248	.058264	.061323	.064426	.067569	.070751	.077225	.083832
	-.20	.046679	.049447	.052268	.055140	.058061	.061031	.064046	.067106	.070208	.073352	.076534	.083007	.089615
	-.30	.052462	.055230	.058050	.060922	.063844	.066813	.069829	.072889	.075991	.079134	.082316	.088790	.095397
	-.40	.058244	.061012	.063833	.066705	.069626	.072596	.075611	.078671	.081774	.084917	.088099	.094572	.101180
25	.40	.013807	.016879	.020004	.023179	.026401	.029667	.032974	.036319	.039700	.043113	.046556	.053522	.060578
	.30	.019590	.022662	.025787	.028962	.032184	.035450	.038757	.042102	.045483	.048896	.052339	.059305	.066360
	.20	.025372	.028444	.031569	.034744	.037966	.041232	.044539	.047885	.051265	.054678	.058121	.065087	.072143
	.10	.031155	.034227	.037352	.040527	.043749	.047015	.050322	.053667	.057048	.060461	.063904	.070870	.077925
	0.00	.036937	.040010	.043135	.046310	.049531	.052797	.056104	.059450	.062830	.066243	.069687	.076652	.083708
	-.10	.042720	.045792	.048917	.052092	.055314	.058580	.061887	.065232	.068613	.072026	.075469	.082435	.089490
	-.20	.048503	.051575	.054700	.057875	.061097	.064362	.067669	.071015	.074395	.077809	.081252	.088217	.095273
	-.30	.054285	.057357	.060482	.063657	.066879	.070145	.073452	.076797	.080178	.083591	.087034	.094000	.101056
	-.40	.060068	.063140	.066265	.069440	.072662	.075928	.079235	.082580	.085960	.089374	.092817	.099782	.106838
30	.40	.014963	.018214	.021513	.024856	.028239	.031657	.035108	.038587	.042092	.045518	.049164	.056302	.063487
	.30	.020745	.023997	.027296	.030639	.034021	.037440	.040890	.044370	.047874	.051301	.054947	.062085	.069270
	.20	.026528	.029779	.033078	.036421	.039804	.043222	.046673	.050152	.053657	.057083	.060729	.067868	.075052
	.10	.032311	.035562	.038861	.042204	.045586	.049005	.052455	.055935	.059439	.062866	.066512	.073650	.080835
	0.00	.038093	.041344	.044643	.047986	.051369	.054787	.058238	.061717	.065222	.068748	.072294	.079433	.086617
	-.10	.043876	.047127	.050426	.053769	.057151	.060570	.064020	.067500	.071004	.074531	.078077	.085215	.092400
	-.20	.049658	.052909	.056209	.059551	.062934	.066352	.069803	.073282	.076787	.080313	.083859	.090998	.098183
	-.30	.055441	.058692	.061991	.065334	.068716	.072135	.075586	.079065	.082569	.086096	.089642	.096780	.103965
	-.40	.061223	.064474	.067774	.071116	.074499	.077917	.081368	.084847	.088352	.091879	.095424	.102563	.109748

15.0 YEAR HOLDING PERIOD
.020 EQUITY YIELD RATE
.750 LOAN RATIO

INTEREST RATE

TERM YEARS	APPR DEP	12.0	11.0	10.0	9.5	9.0	8.5	8.0	7.5	7.0	6.5	6.0	5.5	5.0
10	.40	.016608	.014971	.013055	.012071	.011072	.010059	.009033	.007995	.006948	.005891	.004826	.003754	.002677
	.30	.022591	.020753	.018838	.017854	.016855	.015842	.014816	.013778	.012730	.011673	.010608	.009537	.008460
	.20	.028573	.026536	.024620	.023637	.022637	.021624	.020598	.019561	.018513	.017456	.016391	.015319	.014242
	.10	.034456	.032319	.030403	.029419	.028420	.027407	.026381	.025343	.024295	.023238	.022174	.021102	.020025
	0.00	.039538	.038101	.036185	.035202	.034202	.033189	.032163	.031126	.030078	.029021	.027956	.026884	.025807
	-.10	.045721	.043884	.041968	.040984	.039985	.038972	.037946	.036908	.035860	.034803	.033739	.032667	.031590
	-.20	.051103	.049666	.047750	.046767	.045768	.044754	.043728	.042691	.041643	.040586	.039521	.038450	.037372
	-.30	.057286	.055449	.053533	.052549	.051550	.050537	.049511	.048473	.047425	.046369	.045304	.044232	.043155
	-.40	.063068	.061231	.059316	.058332	.057333	.056319	.055293	.054256	.053208	.052151	.051086	.050015	.048937
15	.40	.046516	.040794	.035215	.032481	.029785	.027127	.024509	.021332	.019395	.016900	.014448	.012038	.009672
	.30	.052298	.046577	.040998	.038263	.035567	.032910	.030292	.027714	.025178	.022683	.020230	.017821	.015455
	.20	.058081	.052360	.046780	.044046	.041350	.038692	.036074	.033497	.030960	.028465	.026013	.023603	.021237
	.10	.063863	.058142	.052563	.049829	.047132	.044475	.041857	.039279	.036743	.034248	.031795	.029386	.027020
	0.00	.069646	.063925	.058345	.055611	.052915	.050257	.047640	.045062	.042525	.040031	.037578	.035168	.032802
	-.10	.075429	.069707	.064128	.061394	.058697	.056040	.053422	.050845	.048308	.045813	.043361	.040951	.038585
	-.20	.081211	.075490	.069910	.067176	.064480	.061823	.059205	.056627	.054091	.051596	.049143	.046734	.044367
	-.30	.086994	.081272	.075693	.072959	.070263	.067605	.064987	.062410	.059873	.057378	.054926	.052516	.050150
	-.40	.092776	.087055	.081476	.078741	.076045	.073388	.070770	.068192	.065656	.063161	.060708	.058299	.055933
20	.40	.059066	.051986	.045051	.041641	.038273	.034949	.031671	.028440	.025258	.022128	.019051	.016029	.013064
	.30	.064848	.057769	.050833	.047424	.044056	.040732	.037453	.034222	.031041	.027911	.024834	.021812	.018846
	.20	.070631	.063552	.056616	.053206	.049839	.046514	.043236	.040005	.036824	.033693	.030616	.027594	.024629
	.10	.076414	.069334	.062398	.058989	.055621	.052297	.049019	.045788	.042606	.039476	.036399	.033377	.030411
	0.00	.082196	.075117	.068181	.064771	.061404	.058080	.054801	.051570	.048389	.045258	.042181	.039159	.036194
	-.10	.087979	.080899	.073963	.070554	.067186	.063862	.060584	.057353	.054171	.051041	.047964	.044942	.041976
	-.20	.093761	.086682	.079746	.076336	.072969	.069645	.066366	.063135	.059954	.056823	.053746	.050724	.047759
	-.30	.099544	.092464	.085528	.082119	.078751	.075427	.072149	.068918	.065736	.062606	.059529	.056507	.053541
	-.40	.105326	.098247	.091311	.087902	.084534	.081210	.077931	.074700	.071519	.068389	.065312	.062289	.059324
25	.40	.065128	.057569	.050105	.046416	.042759	.039137	.035553	.032010	.028511	.025059	.021657	.018309	.015017
	.30	.070911	.063351	.055888	.052199	.048542	.044920	.041336	.037792	.034293	.030841	.027439	.024091	.020800
	.20	.076693	.069134	.061671	.057981	.054324	.050702	.047118	.043575	.040076	.036624	.033222	.029874	.026582
	.10	.082476	.074916	.067453	.063764	.060107	.056485	.052901	.049357	.045858	.042406	.039004	.035656	.032365
	0.00	.088258	.080699	.073236	.069547	.065890	.062267	.058683	.055140	.051641	.048189	.044787	.041439	.038147
	-.10	.094041	.086481	.079018	.075329	.071672	.068050	.064466	.060923	.057423	.053971	.050570	.047221	.043930
	-.20	.099824	.092264	.084801	.081112	.077455	.073833	.070248	.066705	.063206	.059754	.056352	.053004	.049712
	-.30	.105606	.098047	.090583	.086894	.083237	.079615	.076031	.072488	.068988	.065536	.062135	.058786	.055495
	-.40	.111389	.103829	.096366	.092677	.089020	.085398	.081813	.078270	.074771	.071319	.067917	.064569	.061277
30	.40	.068246	.060548	.052899	.049100	.045322	.041567	.037839	.034142	.030479	.026855	.023274	.019739	.016255
	.30	.074028	.066331	.058682	.054883	.051104	.047349	.043622	.039924	.036262	.032638	.029056	.025521	.022038
	.20	.079811	.072113	.064464	.060665	.056887	.053132	.049404	.045707	.042044	.038420	.034839	.031304	.027820
	.10	.085593	.077895	.070247	.066448	.062669	.058914	.055187	.051490	.047827	.044203	.040621	.037086	.033603
	0.00	.091376	.083678	.076030	.072230	.068452	.064697	.060969	.057272	.053609	.049985	.046404	.042869	.039385
	-.10	.097158	.089460	.081812	.078013	.074234	.070480	.066752	.063055	.059392	.055768	.052186	.048652	.045168
	-.20	.102941	.095243	.087595	.083796	.080017	.076262	.072534	.068837	.065175	.061550	.057969	.054434	.050951
	-.30	.108723	.101025	.093377	.089578	.085799	.082045	.078317	.074620	.070957	.067333	.063751	.060217	.056733
	-.40	.114506	.106808	.099160	.095361	.091582	.087827	.084099	.080402	.076740	.073115	.069534	.065999	.062516

15.0 YEAR HOLDING PERIOD
.020 EQUITY YIELD RATE
.800 LOAN RATIO

INTEREST RATE

TERM YEARS	APPR DEP	5.0	5.5	6.0	6.5	7.0	7.5	8.0	8.5	9.0	9.5	10.0	11.0	12.0
10	.40	.003064	.004213	.005356	.006492	.007619	.008737	.009844	.010938	.012019	.013085	.014134	.016178	.018137
	.30	.008847	.009996	.011139	.012275	.013402	.014520	.015626	.016721	.017802	.018867	.019917	.021960	.023920
	.20	.014629	.015778	.016921	.018057	.019185	.020302	.021409	.022503	.023584	.024650	.025699	.027743	.029702
	.10	.020412	.021561	.022704	.023840	.024967	.026085	.027192	.028286	.029367	.030433	.031482	.033525	.035485
	0.00	.026194	.027343	.028486	.029622	.030750	.031867	.032974	.034068	.035149	.036215	.037264	.039308	.041267
	-.10	.031977	.033126	.034269	.035405	.036532	.037650	.038757	.039851	.040932	.041998	.043047	.045090	.047050
	-.20	.037760	.038909	.040052	.041187	.042315	.043432	.044539	.045634	.046714	.047780	.048829	.050873	.052833
	-.30	.043542	.044691	.045834	.046970	.048097	.049215	.050322	.051416	.052497	.053563	.054612	.056655	.058615
	-.40	.049325	.050474	.051617	.052752	.053880	.054998	.056104	.057199	.058279	.059345	.060395	.062438	.064398
15	.40	.010526	.013049	.015620	.018236	.020897	.023603	.026352	.029144	.031979	.034855	.037772	.043723	.049826
	.30	.016308	.018832	.021402	.024018	.026679	.029385	.032135	.034927	.037762	.040638	.043554	.049505	.055608
	.20	.022091	.024615	.027185	.029801	.032462	.035168	.037917	.040710	.043544	.046420	.049337	.055288	.061391
	.10	.027873	.030397	.032967	.035583	.038245	.040950	.043700	.046492	.049327	.052203	.055119	.061070	.067173
	0.00	.033656	.036180	.038750	.041366	.044027	.046733	.049482	.052275	.055109	.057985	.060902	.066853	.072956
	-.10	.039438	.041962	.044532	.047148	.049810	.052515	.055265	.058057	.060892	.063768	.066684	.072635	.078738
	-.20	.045221	.047745	.050315	.052931	.055592	.058298	.061047	.063840	.066674	.069550	.072497	.078418	.084521
	-.30	.051003	.053527	.056098	.058714	.061375	.064080	.066830	.069622	.072457	.075333	.078249	.084201	.090303
	-.40	.056786	.059310	.061880	.064496	.067157	.069863	.072612	.075405	.078239	.081115	.084032	.089983	.096086
20	.40	.014143	.017306	.020530	.023812	.027151	.030545	.033991	.037488	.041034	.044626	.048263	.055661	.063212
	.30	.019926	.023089	.026312	.029595	.032934	.036327	.039774	.043271	.046816	.050408	.054045	.061443	.068995
	.20	.025708	.028871	.032095	.035377	.038716	.042110	.045556	.049053	.052599	.056191	.059828	.067226	.074777
	.10	.031491	.034654	.037878	.041160	.044499	.047892	.051339	.054836	.058381	.061974	.065611	.073009	.080560
	0.00	.037273	.040436	.043660	.046942	.050281	.053675	.057121	.060618	.064164	.067756	.071393	.078791	.086342
	-.10	.043056	.046219	.049443	.052725	.056064	.059457	.062904	.066401	.069946	.073539	.077175	.084574	.092125
	-.20	.048838	.052002	.055225	.058507	.061846	.065240	.068686	.072183	.075729	.079321	.082958	.090356	.097908
	-.30	.054621	.057784	.061008	.064290	.067629	.071022	.074469	.077966	.081512	.085104	.088740	.096139	.103690
	-.40	.060404	.063567	.066790	.070072	.073411	.076805	.080251	.083748	.087294	.090886	.094523	.101921	.109473
25	.40	.016227	.019738	.023309	.026938	.030620	.034353	.038132	.041955	.045819	.049719	.053654	.061615	.069679
	.30	.022009	.025520	.029092	.032720	.036403	.040135	.043915	.047738	.051601	.055502	.059437	.067398	.075461
	.20	.027792	.031303	.034874	.038503	.042185	.045918	.049697	.053520	.057384	.061285	.065220	.073180	.081244
	.10	.033575	.037086	.040657	.044285	.047968	.051700	.055480	.059303	.063166	.067067	.071002	.078963	.087026
	0.00	.039357	.042868	.046440	.050068	.053750	.057483	.061262	.065085	.068949	.072850	.076785	.084745	.092809
	-.10	.045140	.048651	.052222	.055851	.059533	.063265	.067045	.070868	.074731	.078632	.082567	.090528	.098592
	-.20	.050922	.054433	.058005	.061633	.065315	.069048	.072827	.076650	.080514	.084415	.088350	.096311	.104374
	-.30	.056705	.060216	.063787	.067416	.071098	.074830	.078610	.082433	.086296	.090197	.094132	.102093	.110157
	-.40	.062487	.065998	.069570	.073198	.076880	.080613	.084392	.088215	.092079	.095980	.099915	.107876	.115939
30	.40	.017548	.021263	.025034	.028854	.032720	.036627	.040570	.044547	.048552	.052582	.056635	.064793	.073004
	.30	.023330	.027046	.030816	.034637	.038502	.042409	.046353	.050329	.054334	.058365	.062417	.070575	.078787
	.20	.029113	.032828	.036599	.040419	.044285	.048192	.052135	.056112	.060117	.064147	.068200	.076358	.084569
	.10	.034895	.038611	.042381	.046202	.050068	.053974	.057918	.061894	.065899	.069930	.073982	.082140	.090352
	0.00	.040678	.044394	.048164	.051985	.055850	.059757	.063700	.067677	.071682	.075712	.079765	.087923	.096134
	-.10	.046460	.050176	.053946	.057767	.061633	.065539	.069483	.073459	.077465	.081495	.085547	.093706	.101917
	-.20	.052243	.055959	.059729	.063549	.067415	.071322	.075266	.079242	.083247	.087278	.091330	.099488	.107699
	-.30	.058025	.061741	.065512	.069332	.073198	.077105	.081048	.085024	.089030	.093060	.097112	.105271	.113482
	-.40	.063808	.067523	.071294	.075114	.078980	.082887	.086831	.090807	.094810	.098843	.102895	.111053	.119264

15.0 YEAR HOLDING PERIOD
.020 EQUITY YIELD RATE
.900 LOAN RATIO

INTEREST RATE

TERM YEARS	APPR DEP	5.0	5.5	6.0	6.5	7.0	7.5	8.0	8.5	9.0	9.5	10.0	11.0	12.0
10	.40	.003839	.005131	.006417	.007695	.008963	.010221	.011466	.012697	.013913	.015112	.016292	.018591	.020796
	.30	.009621	.010914	.012200	.013477	.014746	.016003	.017248	.018479	.019695	.020894	.022075	.024374	.026578
	.20	.015404	.016696	.017982	.019260	.020528	.021786	.023031	.024262	.025478	.026677	.027857	.030156	.032361
	.10	.021186	.022479	.023765	.025042	.026311	.027568	.028813	.030045	.031260	.032459	.033640	.035939	.038143
	0.00	.026969	.028261	.029547	.030825	.032093	.033351	.034596	.035827	.037043	.038242	.039422	.041721	.043926
	-.10	.032751	.034044	.035330	.036608	.037876	.039133	.040378	.041610	.042826	.044025	.045205	.047504	.049708
	-.20	.038534	.039826	.041112	.042390	.043658	.044916	.046161	.047392	.048608	.049807	.050988	.053286	.055491
	-.30	.044316	.045609	.046895	.048173	.049441	.050698	.051943	.053175	.054391	.055590	.056770	.059069	.061273
	-.40	.050099	.051392	.052677	.053955	.055224	.056481	.057726	.058957	.060173	.061372	.062553	.064851	.067056
15	.40	.012233	.015072	.017963	.020906	.023900	.026944	.030037	.033179	.036368	.039603	.042884	.049579	.056445
	.30	.018015	.020854	.023746	.026689	.029683	.032727	.035820	.038961	.042150	.045386	.048667	.055362	.062228
	.20	.023798	.026637	.029529	.032472	.035465	.038509	.041602	.044744	.047933	.051168	.054449	.061144	.068010
	.10	.029580	.032420	.035311	.038254	.041248	.044292	.047385	.050526	.053715	.056951	.060232	.066927	.073793
	0.00	.035363	.038202	.041094	.044037	.047031	.050074	.053168	.056309	.059498	.062733	.066014	.072710	.079575
	-.10	.041145	.043985	.046876	.049819	.052813	.055857	.058950	.062091	.065280	.068516	.071797	.078492	.085358
	-.20	.046928	.049767	.052659	.055602	.058596	.061640	.064733	.067874	.071063	.074298	.077580	.084275	.091140
	-.30	.052710	.055550	.058441	.061384	.064378	.067422	.070515	.073657	.076846	.080081	.083362	.090057	.096923
	-.40	.058493	.061332	.064224	.067167	.070161	.073205	.076298	.079439	.082628	.085864	.089145	.095840	.102705
20	.40	.016302	.019861	.023487	.027180	.030936	.034754	.038631	.042565	.046554	.050595	.054687	.063010	.071505
	.30	.022085	.025643	.029270	.032962	.036719	.040537	.044414	.048348	.052337	.056378	.060470	.068792	.077288
	.20	.027867	.031426	.035052	.038745	.042501	.046319	.050196	.054130	.058119	.062160	.066252	.074575	.083070
	.10	.033650	.037208	.040835	.044528	.048284	.052102	.055979	.059913	.063902	.067943	.072034	.080357	.088852
	0.00	.039432	.042991	.046618	.050310	.054066	.057884	.061761	.065695	.069684	.073726	.077817	.086140	.094635
	-.10	.045215	.048774	.052400	.056093	.059849	.063667	.067544	.071478	.075467	.079508	.083599	.091923	.100418
	-.20	.050998	.054556	.058183	.061875	.065631	.069449	.073326	.077261	.081249	.085291	.089382	.097705	.106200
	-.30	.056780	.060339	.063965	.067658	.071414	.075232	.079109	.083043	.087032	.091073	.095164	.103488	.111983
	-.40	.062563	.066121	.069748	.073440	.077197	.081014	.084891	.088826	.092815	.096856	.100947	.109270	.117765
25	.40	.018647	.022596	.026614	.030696	.034839	.039038	.043290	.047591	.051937	.056326	.060753	.069708	.078780
	.30	.024429	.028379	.032397	.036479	.040622	.044820	.049072	.053373	.057720	.062108	.066535	.075491	.084562
	.20	.030212	.034162	.038179	.042261	.046404	.050603	.054855	.059156	.063502	.067891	.072318	.081274	.090345
	.10	.035994	.039944	.043961	.048044	.052186	.056385	.060637	.064938	.069285	.073673	.078100	.087056	.096128
	0.00	.041777	.045727	.049744	.053827	.057969	.062168	.066420	.070721	.075067	.079456	.083883	.092839	.101910
	-.10	.047559	.051509	.055526	.059609	.063752	.067951	.072202	.076504	.080850	.085238	.089665	.098621	.107693
	-.20	.053342	.057292	.061309	.065392	.069534	.073733	.077985	.082286	.086633	.091021	.095448	.104404	.113475
	-.30	.059124	.063074	.067092	.071174	.075317	.079516	.083768	.088069	.092415	.096804	.101230	.110186	.119258
	-.40	.064907	.068857	.072874	.076957	.081099	.085298	.089550	.093851	.098198	.102580	.107013	.115969	.125040
30	.40	.020132	.024313	.028554	.032854	.037201	.041596	.046033	.050506	.055012	.059546	.064105	.073283	.082521
	.30	.025915	.030095	.034337	.038637	.042984	.047379	.051815	.056289	.060795	.065329	.069888	.079066	.088303
	.20	.031697	.035878	.040119	.044419	.048766	.053161	.057598	.062071	.066577	.071111	.075670	.084848	.094086
	.10	.037480	.041660	.045902	.050202	.054549	.058944	.063380	.067854	.072360	.076894	.081453	.090631	.099868
	0.00	.043263	.047443	.051684	.055982	.060331	.064726	.069163	.073636	.078142	.082677	.087235	.096413	.105651
	-.10	.049045	.053225	.057467	.061765	.066114	.070509	.074946	.079419	.083925	.088459	.093018	.102196	.111434
	-.20	.054828	.059008	.063250	.067547	.071896	.076292	.080728	.085201	.089707	.094242	.098801	.107978	.117216
	-.30	.060610	.064790	.069032	.073330	.077679	.082074	.086511	.090984	.095490	.100024	.104583	.113761	.122999
	-.40	.066393	.070573	.074815	.079113	.083462	.087857	.092293	.096767	.101272	.105807	.110366	.119544	.128781

293

15.0 YEAR HOLDING PERIOD
.040 EQUITY YIELD RATE
.600 LOAN RATIO

INTEREST RATE

TERM YEARS	APPR DEP	5.0	5.5	6.0	6.5	7.0	7.5	8.0	8.5	9.0	9.5	10.0	11.0	12.0
10	.40	.020812	.021798	.022783	.023767	.024749	.025727	.026702	.027672	.028636	.029594	.030543	.032417	.034248
	.30	.025806	.026792	.027777	.028761	.029743	.030721	.031696	.032666	.033630	.034588	.035538	.037411	.039242
	.20	.030800	.031786	.032772	.033755	.034737	.035716	.036690	.037660	.038624	.039582	.040532	.042405	.044236
	.10	.035795	.036780	.037766	.038749	.039731	.040710	.041684	.042654	.043618	.044582	.045526	.047399	.049230
	0.00	.040789	.041775	.042760	.043744	.044725	.045704	.046678	.047648	.048612	.049570	.050520	.052393	.054224
	-.10	.045783	.046769	.047754	.048738	.049719	.050698	.051673	.052642	.053607	.054564	.055514	.057387	.059218
	-.20	.050777	.051763	.052748	.053732	.054713	.055692	.056667	.057636	.058601	.059558	.060508	.062381	.064212
	-.30	.055771	.056757	.057742	.058726	.059708	.060686	.061661	.062631	.063595	.064552	.065502	.067376	.069206
	-.40	.060765	.061751	.062736	.063720	.064702	.065680	.066655	.067625	.068589	.069546	.070496	.072370	.074201
15	.40	.022996	.024889	.026817	.028779	.030775	.032804	.034866	.036960	.039086	.041243	.043430	.047894	.052471
	.30	.027990	.029883	.031811	.033773	.035769	.037798	.039860	.041954	.044080	.046237	.048425	.052888	.057465
	.20	.032984	.034877	.036805	.038767	.040763	.042792	.044854	.046948	.049074	.051231	.053419	.057882	.062459
	.10	.037978	.039871	.041799	.043761	.045757	.047786	.049848	.051942	.054068	.056225	.058413	.062876	.067453
	0.00	.042972	.044865	.046793	.048755	.050751	.052780	.054842	.056937	.059063	.061220	.063407	.067870	.072447
	-.10	.047967	.049859	.051787	.053749	.055745	.057774	.059836	.061931	.064057	.066214	.068401	.072864	.077442
	-.20	.052961	.054854	.056781	.058743	.060739	.062768	.064831	.066925	.069051	.071208	.073395	.077859	.082436
	-.30	.057955	.059848	.061775	.063737	.065733	.067763	.069825	.071919	.074045	.076202	.078389	.082853	.087430
	-.40	.062949	.064842	.066769	.068732	.070727	.072757	.074819	.076913	.079039	.081196	.083383	.087847	.092424
20	.40	.024055	.026378	.028746	.031158	.033613	.036108	.038644	.041217	.043827	.046472	.049150	.054602	.060169
	.30	.029049	.031372	.033740	.036152	.038607	.041103	.043638	.046211	.048821	.051466	.054144	.059596	.065164
	.20	.034043	.036366	.038734	.041146	.043601	.046097	.048632	.051205	.053815	.056460	.059138	.064590	.070158
	.10	.039037	.041360	.043729	.046141	.048595	.051091	.053626	.056199	.058809	.061454	.064132	.069584	.075152
	0.00	.044031	.046354	.048723	.051135	.053589	.056085	.058620	.061193	.063803	.066448	.069127	.074578	.080146
	-.10	.049025	.051348	.053717	.056129	.058583	.061079	.063614	.066187	.068797	.071442	.074121	.079572	.085140
	-.20	.054019	.056343	.058711	.061123	.063577	.066073	.068608	.071182	.073791	.076436	.079115	.084566	.090134
	-.30	.059014	.061337	.063705	.066117	.068572	.071067	.073602	.076176	.078785	.081430	.084109	.089560	.095128
	-.40	.064008	.066331	.068699	.071111	.073566	.076061	.078596	.081170	.083780	.086425	.089103	.094555	.100122
25	.40	.024665	.027228	.029838	.032492	.035187	.037921	.040691	.043496	.046332	.049197	.052090	.057947	.063888
	.30	.029659	.032223	.034833	.037486	.040181	.042915	.045686	.048490	.051326	.054191	.057084	.062941	.068882
	.20	.034653	.037217	.039827	.042480	.045175	.047909	.050680	.053484	.056320	.059186	.062078	.067936	.073876
	.10	.039647	.042211	.044821	.047474	.050170	.052903	.055674	.058478	.061314	.064180	.067072	.072930	.078871
	0.00	.044641	.047205	.049815	.052468	.055164	.057898	.060668	.063472	.066308	.069174	.072066	.077924	.083865
	-.10	.049635	.052199	.054809	.057463	.060158	.062892	.065662	.068466	.071302	.074168	.077060	.082918	.088859
	-.20	.054629	.057193	.059803	.062457	.065152	.067886	.070656	.073461	.076297	.079162	.082054	.087912	.093853
	-.30	.059623	.062187	.064797	.067451	.070146	.072880	.075650	.078455	.081291	.084156	.087049	.092906	.098847
	-.40	.064618	.067181	.069791	.072445	.075140	.077874	.080644	.083449	.086285	.089150	.092043	.097900	.103841
30	.40	.025051	.027762	.030516	.033310	.036140	.039004	.041897	.044818	.047763	.050729	.053715	.059733	.065800
	.30	.030045	.032756	.035510	.038304	.041134	.043998	.046891	.049812	.052757	.055723	.058709	.064727	.070795
	.20	.035039	.037750	.040504	.043298	.046128	.048992	.051886	.054806	.057751	.060717	.063703	.069721	.075789
	.10	.040034	.042744	.045498	.048292	.051123	.053986	.056880	.059800	.062745	.065712	.068697	.074715	.080783
	0.00	.045028	.047739	.050493	.053286	.056117	.058980	.061874	.064794	.067739	.070706	.073692	.079709	.085777
	-.10	.050022	.052733	.055487	.058280	.061111	.063974	.066868	.069789	.072733	.075700	.078685	.084703	.090771
	-.20	.055016	.057727	.060481	.063275	.066105	.068968	.071862	.074783	.077727	.080694	.083679	.089697	.095765
	-.30	.060010	.062721	.065475	.068269	.071099	.073962	.076856	.079777	.082722	.085688	.088673	.094692	.100759
	-.40	.065004	.067715	.070469	.073263	.076093	.078957	.081850	.084771	.087716	.090682	.093667	.099686	.105753

15.0 YEAR HOLDING PERIOD
.040 EQUITY YIELD RATE
.667 LOAN RATIO

INTEREST RATE

TERM YEARS	APPR DEP	5.0	5.5	6.0	6.5	7.0	7.5	8.0	8.5	9.0	9.5	10.0	11.0	12.0
10	.40	.020900	.021995	.023090	.024183	.025274	.026361	.027444	.028522	.029593	.030657	.031712	.033794	.035828
	.30	.025894	.026989	.028084	.029177	.030268	.031355	.032438	.033516	.034587	.035651	.036707	.038788	.040822
	.20	.030888	.031984	.033078	.034171	.035262	.036349	.037432	.038510	.039581	.040645	.041701	.043782	.045816
	.10	.035882	.036978	.038072	.039165	.040256	.041343	.042426	.043504	.044575	.045639	.046695	.048776	.050811
	0.00	.040876	.041972	.043066	.044160	.045250	.046338	.047420	.048498	.049569	.050633	.051689	.053770	.055805
	-.10	.045870	.046966	.048061	.049154	.050244	.051332	.052415	.053492	.054564	.055627	.056683	.058764	.060799
	-.20	.050865	.051960	.053055	.054148	.055238	.056326	.057409	.058486	.059558	.060622	.061687	.063769	.065793
	-.30	.055859	.056955	.058049	.059142	.060233	.061320	.062403	.063480	.064552	.065616	.066671	.068753	.070787
	-.40	.060853	.061948	.063043	.064136	.065227	.066314	.067397	.068475	.069546	.070610	.071665	.073747	.075781
15	.40	.023326	.025430	.027571	.029751	.031969	.034224	.036515	.038842	.041204	.043601	.046031	.050991	.056076
	.30	.028320	.030424	.032560	.034746	.036963	.039218	.041509	.043836	.046198	.048595	.051025	.055985	.061071
	.20	.033315	.035418	.037560	.039740	.041957	.044212	.046503	.048830	.051192	.053589	.056020	.060979	.066065
	.10	.038309	.040412	.042554	.044734	.046951	.049206	.051497	.053824	.056187	.058583	.061014	.065973	.071059
	0.00	.043303	.045406	.047548	.049728	.051946	.054200	.056492	.058819	.061181	.063577	.066008	.070967	.076053
	-.10	.048297	.050400	.052542	.054722	.056940	.059194	.061486	.063813	.066175	.068571	.071002	.075961	.081047
	-.20	.053291	.055394	.057536	.059716	.061934	.064189	.066480	.068807	.071169	.073566	.075996	.080955	.086041
	-.30	.058285	.060388	.062530	.064710	.066928	.069183	.071474	.073801	.076163	.078560	.080990	.085950	.091035
	-.40	.063279	.065382	.067524	.069704	.071922	.074177	.076468	.078795	.081157	.083554	.085984	.090944	.096029
20	.40	.024503	.027084	.029715	.032396	.035123	.037896	.040713	.043572	.046472	.049410	.052387	.058444	.064630
	.30	.029497	.032078	.034710	.037390	.040117	.042890	.045707	.048566	.051466	.054405	.057381	.063438	.069624
	.20	.034491	.037072	.039704	.042384	.045111	.047884	.050701	.053560	.056460	.059399	.062375	.068432	.074619
	.10	.039485	.042066	.044698	.047378	.050105	.052878	.055695	.058554	.061454	.064393	.067369	.073426	.079613
	0.00	.044479	.047060	.049692	.052372	.055099	.057872	.060689	.063548	.066448	.069387	.072363	.078420	.084607
	-.10	.049473	.052055	.054686	.057366	.060093	.062866	.065683	.068542	.071442	.074381	.077357	.083414	.089601
	-.20	.054467	.057049	.059680	.062360	.065087	.067860	.070677	.073536	.076436	.079375	.082351	.088409	.094595
	-.30	.059462	.062043	.064674	.067354	.070082	.072854	.075671	.078531	.081430	.084369	.087345	.093403	.099589
	-.40	.064456	.067037	.069668	.072348	.075076	.077849	.080665	.083525	.086425	.089363	.092339	.098397	.104583
25	.40	.025180	.028029	.030929	.033878	.036872	.039910	.042988	.046104	.049255	.052439	.055653	.062161	.068762
	.30	.030175	.033023	.035923	.038872	.041866	.044904	.047982	.051098	.054249	.057433	.060647	.067155	.073756
	.20	.035169	.038017	.040917	.043866	.046860	.049898	.052976	.056092	.059243	.062427	.065641	.072150	.078750
	.10	.040163	.043011	.045911	.048860	.051854	.054892	.057970	.061086	.064238	.067421	.070635	.077144	.083745
	0.00	.045157	.048005	.050905	.053854	.056849	.059886	.062964	.066080	.069232	.072415	.075629	.082138	.088739
	-.10	.050151	.053000	.055900	.058848	.061843	.064880	.067959	.071075	.074226	.077410	.080623	.087132	.093733
	-.20	.055145	.057994	.060894	.063842	.066837	.069874	.072953	.076069	.079220	.082404	.085618	.092126	.098727
	-.30	.060139	.062988	.065888	.068836	.071831	.074869	.077947	.081063	.084214	.087398	.090612	.097120	.103721
	-.40	.065133	.067982	.070882	.073830	.076825	.079863	.082941	.086057	.089208	.092392	.095606	.102114	.108715
30	.40	.025610	.028622	.031682	.034786	.037931	.041113	.044328	.047573	.050845	.054141	.057458	.064145	.070387
	.30	.030604	.033616	.036676	.039780	.042925	.046107	.049322	.052567	.055839	.059135	.062452	.069139	.075381
	.20	.035598	.038610	.041670	.044774	.047919	.051101	.054316	.057561	.060833	.064129	.067446	.074133	.080375
	.10	.040592	.043604	.046664	.049769	.052913	.056095	.059310	.062555	.065827	.069123	.072441	.079127	.085365
	0.00	.045586	.048598	.051658	.054763	.057907	.061089	.064304	.067549	.070822	.074118	.077435	.084122	.090363
	-.10	.050580	.053592	.056653	.059757	.062902	.066083	.069298	.072544	.075816	.079112	.082429	.089116	.095358
	-.20	.055575	.058587	.061647	.064751	.067896	.071077	.074292	.077538	.080810	.084106	.087423	.094110	.100352
	-.30	.060569	.063581	.066641	.069745	.072890	.076071	.079287	.082532	.085804	.089100	.092417	.099104	.105346
	-.40	.065563	.068575	.071635	.074739	.077884	.081066	.084281	.087526	.090798	.094094	.097411	.104098	.110340

15.0 YEAR HOLDING PERIOD
.040 EQUITY YIELD RATE
.700 LOAN RATIO

INTEREST RATE

TERM YEARS	APPR DEP	5.0	5.5	6.0	6.5	7.0	7.5	8.0	8.5	9.0	9.5	10.0	11.0	12.0
10	.40	.020944	.022094	.023243	.024391	.025536	.026678	.027815	.028947	.030071	.031189	.032297	.034482	.036618
	.30	.025938	.027088	.028237	.029385	.030530	.031672	.032809	.033941	.035066	.036183	.037291	.039476	.041613
	.20	.030932	.032082	.033231	.034379	.035525	.036666	.037803	.038935	.040060	.041177	.042285	.044471	.046607
	.10	.035926	.037076	.038225	.039373	.040519	.041660	.042797	.043929	.045054	.046171	.047279	.049465	.051601
	0.00	.040920	.042070	.043219	.044367	.045513	.046654	.047791	.048923	.050048	.051165	.052273	.054459	.056595
	-.10	.045914	.047064	.048214	.049362	.050507	.051649	.052786	.053917	.055042	.056159	.057267	.059453	.061589
	-.20	.050908	.052059	.053208	.054356	.055501	.056643	.057780	.058911	.060036	.061153	.062261	.064447	.066583
	-.30	.055903	.057053	.058202	.059350	.060495	.061637	.062774	.063905	.065030	.066147	.067256	.069441	.071577
	-.40	.060897	.062047	.063196	.064344	.065489	.066631	.067768	.068899	.070024	.071141	.072250	.074435	.076571
15	.40	.023491	.025700	.027949	.030238	.032566	.034934	.037340	.039783	.042263	.044780	.047332	.052539	.057879
	.30	.028485	.030694	.032943	.035232	.037560	.039928	.042334	.044777	.047257	.049774	.052326	.057533	.062873
	.20	.033480	.035688	.037937	.040226	.042555	.044922	.047328	.049771	.052251	.054768	.057320	.062527	.067867
	.10	.038474	.040682	.042931	.045220	.047549	.049916	.052322	.054765	.057246	.059762	.062314	.067521	.072861
	0.00	.043468	.045676	.047925	.050214	.052543	.054910	.057316	.059759	.062240	.064756	.067308	.072515	.077855
	-.10	.048462	.050671	.052920	.055209	.057537	.059904	.062310	.064753	.067234	.069750	.072302	.077509	.082849
	-.20	.053456	.055665	.057914	.060202	.062531	.064898	.067304	.069748	.072228	.074744	.077296	.082504	.087844
	-.30	.058450	.060659	.062908	.065197	.067525	.069893	.072298	.074742	.077222	.079738	.082290	.087498	.092838
	-.40	.063444	.065653	.067902	.070191	.072519	.074887	.077292	.079736	.082216	.084733	.087284	.092492	.097832
20	.40	.024727	.027437	.030200	.033014	.035878	.038789	.041747	.044749	.047794	.050880	.054005	.060365	.066860
	.30	.029721	.032431	.035194	.038008	.040872	.043783	.046741	.049743	.052788	.055874	.058999	.065359	.071854
	.20	.034715	.037425	.040188	.043002	.045866	.048777	.051735	.054737	.057782	.060868	.063993	.070353	.076848
	.10	.039709	.042419	.045182	.047996	.050860	.053771	.056729	.059731	.062776	.065862	.068987	.075347	.081842
	0.00	.044703	.047413	.050176	.052990	.055854	.058766	.061723	.064725	.067770	.070856	.073981	.080341	.086836
	-.10	.049697	.052408	.055171	.057985	.060849	.063760	.066717	.069720	.072764	.075850	.078976	.085336	.091831
	-.20	.054692	.057402	.060165	.062979	.065842	.068754	.071712	.074714	.077759	.080845	.083970	.090330	.096825
	-.30	.059685	.062396	.065159	.067973	.070836	.073748	.076706	.079708	.082753	.085838	.088963	.095324	.101819
	-.40	.064680	.067390	.070153	.072967	.075831	.078742	.081700	.084702	.087747	.090833	.093957	.100318	.106813
25	.40	.025438	.028429	.031474	.034570	.037714	.040904	.044136	.047408	.050717	.054060	.057434	.064268	.071199
	.30	.030432	.033423	.036468	.039564	.042709	.045898	.049130	.052402	.055711	.059054	.062428	.069262	.076193
	.20	.035426	.038418	.041462	.044558	.047703	.050892	.054124	.057396	.060705	.064048	.067422	.074256	.081187
	.10	.040421	.043412	.046457	.049553	.052697	.055886	.059118	.062390	.065699	.069042	.072416	.079250	.086181
	0.00	.045415	.048406	.051451	.054547	.057691	.060880	.064113	.067384	.070693	.074036	.077411	.084244	.091175
	-.10	.050409	.053400	.056445	.059541	.062685	.065875	.069107	.072378	.075687	.079030	.082405	.089239	.096170
	-.20	.055403	.058394	.061439	.064535	.067679	.070869	.074101	.077373	.080681	.084024	.087399	.094233	.101164
	-.30	.060397	.063388	.066433	.069529	.072673	.075863	.079095	.082367	.085675	.089018	.092393	.099227	.106158
	-.40	.065391	.068382	.071427	.074523	.077667	.080857	.084089	.087361	.090670	.094012	.097387	.104221	.111152
30	.40	.025889	.029052	.032265	.035524	.038826	.042167	.045543	.048950	.052386	.055847	.059330	.066351	.073430
	.30	.030883	.034046	.037259	.040518	.043820	.047161	.050537	.053944	.057380	.060841	.064324	.071345	.078424
	.20	.035877	.039040	.042253	.045513	.048815	.052155	.055531	.058939	.062374	.065835	.069318	.076339	.083418
	.10	.040871	.044034	.047247	.050507	.053809	.057149	.060525	.063933	.067368	.070829	.074312	.081333	.088412
	0.00	.045866	.049028	.052241	.055501	.058803	.062143	.065519	.068927	.072362	.075823	.079306	.086327	.093406
	-.10	.050860	.054022	.057235	.060495	.063797	.067138	.070513	.073921	.077357	.080817	.084300	.091322	.098401
	-.20	.055854	.059016	.062229	.065489	.068791	.072132	.075508	.078915	.082351	.085811	.089294	.096316	.103395
	-.30	.060848	.064011	.067224	.070483	.073785	.077126	.080502	.083909	.087345	.090806	.094288	.101310	.108389
	-.40	.065842	.069005	.072218	.075477	.078780	.082120	.085496	.088903	.092339	.095800	.099283	.106304	.113383

15.0 YEAR HOLDING PERIOD
.040 EQUITY YIELD RATE
.750 LOAN RATIO

TERM YEARS	APPR DEP	5.0	5.5	6.0	6.5	7.0	7.5	8.0	8.5	9.0	9.5	10.0	11.0	12.0
10	.40	.021009	.022242	.023473	.024703	.025930	.027153	.028372	.029584	.030789	.031986	.033173	.035515	.037304
	.30	.026004	.027236	.028467	.029697	.030924	.032147	.033366	.034578	.035783	.036980	.038162	.040503	.042798
	.20	.030998	.032230	.033461	.034691	.035918	.037141	.038360	.039572	.040777	.041979	.043162	.045503	.047792
	.10	.035992	.037224	.038456	.039685	.040912	.042136	.043354	.044566	.045771	.046968	.048156	.050497	.052786
	0.00	.040986	.042218	.043450	.044679	.045906	.047130	.048348	.049560	.050766	.051962	.053150	.055492	.057780
	-.10	.045980	.047212	.048444	.049674	.050900	.052124	.053342	.054560	.055760	.056957	.058144	.060486	.062774
	-.20	.050974	.052206	.053438	.054668	.055895	.057118	.058336	.059549	.060754	.061951	.063138	.065480	.067768
	-.30	.055968	.057201	.058432	.059662	.060889	.062112	.063330	.064543	.065748	.066945	.068132	.070474	.072763
	-.40	.060962	.062195	.063426	.064656	.065883	.067106	.068324	.069537	.070742	.071939	.073126	.075468	.077757
15	.40	.023739	.026105	.028515	.030967	.033462	.035999	.038576	.041194	.043852	.046548	.049282	.054861	.060583
	.30	.028733	.031099	.033509	.035962	.038456	.040993	.043571	.046188	.048846	.051542	.054276	.059856	.065577
	.20	.033727	.036093	.038503	.040956	.043450	.045987	.048565	.051183	.053840	.056536	.059270	.064850	.070571
	.10	.038721	.041088	.043497	.045950	.048445	.050981	.053559	.056177	.058834	.061530	.064265	.069844	.075565
	0.00	.043716	.046082	.048491	.050944	.053439	.055975	.058553	.061171	.063828	.066524	.069259	.074838	.080559
	-.10	.048710	.051076	.053485	.055938	.058433	.060969	.063547	.066165	.068822	.071519	.074253	.079832	.085553
	-.20	.053704	.056070	.058480	.060932	.063427	.065964	.068541	.071159	.073816	.076513	.079247	.084826	.090548
	-.30	.058698	.061064	.063474	.065926	.068421	.070958	.073535	.076153	.078810	.081507	.084241	.089820	.095542
	-.40	.063692	.066058	.068468	.070920	.073415	.075952	.078529	.081147	.083805	.086501	.089235	.094814	.100536
20	.40	.025063	.027967	.030927	.033992	.037010	.040130	.043299	.046515	.049777	.053084	.056432	.063246	.070206
	.30	.029057	.032961	.035921	.038936	.042004	.045124	.048293	.051509	.054772	.058078	.061426	.068240	.075200
	.20	.035051	.037955	.040915	.043930	.046998	.050118	.053287	.056503	.059760	.063072	.066420	.073234	.080594
	.10	.040045	.042949	.045909	.048924	.051992	.055112	.058281	.061497	.064760	.068066	.071414	.078229	.085588
	0.00	.045039	.047943	.050903	.053918	.056987	.060106	.063275	.066524	.069754	.073060	.076408	.083223	.090582
	-.10	.050033	.052937	.055897	.058913	.061981	.065100	.068269	.071486	.074748	.078054	.081402	.088217	.095576
	-.20	.055027	.057931	.060891	.063907	.066975	.070094	.073263	.076480	.079742	.083048	.086396	.093211	.100571
	-.30	.060021	.062925	.065886	.068901	.071969	.075088	.078257	.081474	.084736	.088042	.091391	.098205	.105565
	-.40	.065016	.067919	.070880	.073895	.076963	.080083	.083251	.086468	.089730	.093037	.096385	.103199	.110559
25	.40	.025825	.029030	.032292	.035609	.038976	.042395	.045858	.049364	.052909	.056491	.060106	.067428	.074854
	.30	.030819	.034024	.037286	.040603	.043972	.047390	.050853	.054358	.057903	.061485	.065100	.072422	.079848
	.20	.035813	.039018	.042280	.045598	.048966	.052384	.055847	.059352	.062891	.066479	.070095	.077417	.084843
	.10	.040807	.044012	.047274	.050592	.053960	.057378	.060841	.064346	.067891	.071473	.075095	.082417	.089837
	0.00	.045801	.049006	.052269	.055586	.058955	.062372	.065835	.069340	.072885	.076467	.080083	.087405	.094831
	-.10	.050796	.054000	.057263	.060580	.063949	.067366	.070829	.074334	.077880	.081461	.085077	.092399	.099825
	-.20	.055790	.058994	.062257	.065574	.068943	.072360	.075823	.079329	.082874	.086455	.090071	.097393	.104819
	-.30	.060784	.063988	.067251	.070568	.073937	.077355	.080818	.084323	.087868	.091450	.095065	.102387	.109813
	-.40	.065778	.068983	.072245	.075562	.078931	.082348	.085811	.089317	.092862	.096444	.100059	.107381	.114807
30	.40	.026308	.029697	.033139	.036631	.040169	.043749	.047366	.051017	.054698	.058406	.062137	.069660	.077245
	.30	.031302	.034691	.038133	.041626	.045163	.048743	.052360	.056011	.059692	.063400	.067131	.074654	.082239
	.20	.036296	.039685	.043127	.046620	.050158	.053737	.057354	.061005	.064686	.068394	.072126	.079648	.087233
	.10	.041290	.044679	.048122	.051614	.055152	.058731	.062348	.065999	.069680	.073388	.077120	.084642	.092227
	0.00	.046285	.049673	.053116	.056608	.060146	.063725	.067342	.070993	.074674	.078382	.082114	.089636	.097221
	-.10	.051279	.054667	.058110	.061602	.065140	.068719	.072336	.075987	.079668	.083376	.087108	.094631	.102215
	-.20	.056273	.059661	.063104	.066596	.070134	.073713	.077330	.080981	.084662	.088370	.092102	.099625	.107209
	-.30	.061267	.064655	.068098	.071590	.075128	.078707	.082324	.085975	.089656	.093364	.097096	.104619	.112203
	-.40	.066261	.069650	.073092	.076584	.080122	.083702	.087319	.090969	.094651	.098359	.102090	.109613	.117198

297

15.0 YEAR HOLDING PERIOD
.040 EQUITY YIELD RATE
.800 LOAN RATIO

INTEREST RATE

TERM YEARS	APPR DEP	5.0	5.5	6.0	6.5	7.0	7.5	8.0	8.5	9.0	9.5	10.0	11.0	12.0
10	.40	.021073	.022390	.023703	.025015	.026324	.027629	.028928	.030221	.031507	.032784	.034056	.036548	.038989
	.30	.026069	.027384	.028697	.030009	.031318	.032623	.033922	.035215	.036501	.037778	.039044	.041542	.043983
	.20	.031063	.032378	.033691	.035003	.036312	.037617	.038916	.040209	.041495	.042772	.044038	.046536	.048977
	.10	.036057	.037372	.038686	.039997	.041306	.042611	.043910	.045204	.046489	.047766	.049032	.051530	.053971
	0.00	.041052	.042366	.043680	.044991	.046300	.047605	.048905	.050198	.051483	.052760	.054027	.056524	.058966
	-.10	.046046	.047360	.048674	.049986	.051294	.052599	.053899	.055192	.056477	.057754	.059021	.061518	.063960
	-.20	.051040	.052354	.053668	.054980	.056288	.057593	.058893	.060186	.061471	.062748	.064015	.066512	.068954
	-.30	.056034	.057348	.058662	.059974	.061283	.062587	.063867	.065180	.066466	.067742	.069009	.071507	.073948
	-.40	.061028	.062342	.063656	.064968	.066277	.067581	.068881	.070174	.071460	.072736	.074003	.076501	.078942
15	.40	.023967	.026511	.029081	.031697	.034358	.037064	.039813	.042606	.045440	.048316	.051233	.057184	.063287
	.30	.028981	.031505	.034075	.036691	.039352	.042058	.044807	.047600	.050434	.053310	.056227	.062178	.068281
	.20	.033975	.036499	.039069	.041685	.044346	.047052	.049801	.052594	.055428	.058304	.061221	.067172	.073275
	.10	.038969	.041493	.044063	.046679	.049341	.052046	.054796	.057588	.060423	.063299	.066215	.072166	.078269
	0.00	.043963	.046487	.049057	.051673	.054335	.057040	.059790	.062582	.065417	.068293	.071209	.077160	.083263
	-.10	.048957	.051481	.054051	.056668	.059329	.062034	.064784	.067576	.070411	.073287	.076203	.082155	.088257
	-.20	.053952	.056475	.059046	.061662	.064323	.067029	.069778	.072570	.075405	.078281	.081197	.087149	.093251
	-.30	.058946	.061469	.064040	.066656	.069317	.072023	.074772	.077564	.080399	.083275	.086192	.092143	.098246
	-.40	.063940	.066464	.069034	.071650	.074311	.077017	.079766	.082559	.085393	.088269	.091186	.097137	.103240
20	.40	.025399	.028496	.031054	.034870	.038143	.041470	.044850	.048281	.051761	.055288	.058859	.066128	.073551
	.30	.030393	.033490	.036648	.039864	.043137	.046464	.049844	.053275	.056755	.060282	.063853	.071122	.078545
	.20	.035387	.038484	.041642	.044858	.048131	.051458	.054838	.058269	.061749	.065276	.068847	.076116	.083540
	.10	.040381	.043478	.046636	.049852	.053125	.056452	.059833	.063264	.066743	.070270	.073841	.081110	.088534
	0.00	.045375	.048472	.051630	.054846	.058119	.061446	.064827	.068258	.071738	.075264	.078835	.086104	.093528
	-.10	.050369	.053467	.056024	.059940	.063113	.066441	.069821	.073252	.076732	.080258	.083830	.091098	.098522
	-.20	.055363	.058461	.061018	.064935	.068107	.071435	.074815	.078281	.081726	.085252	.088824	.096092	.103516
	-.30	.060357	.063455	.066012	.069929	.073101	.076429	.079809	.083240	.086720	.090246	.093818	.101087	.108510
	-.40	.065351	.068449	.071607	.074823	.078095	.081423	.084803	.088234	.091714	.095241	.098812	.106081	.113504
25	.40	.026212	.029630	.033110	.036648	.040242	.043887	.047581	.051320	.055101	.058922	.062779	.070589	.078510
	.30	.031206	.034624	.038104	.041642	.045236	.048881	.052575	.056314	.060095	.063916	.067773	.075583	.083504
	.20	.036200	.039618	.043098	.046637	.050230	.053875	.057569	.061308	.065090	.068910	.072767	.080577	.088498
	.10	.041194	.044612	.048092	.051631	.055224	.058869	.062563	.066302	.070084	.073904	.077761	.085571	.093492
	0.00	.046188	.049607	.053086	.056625	.060218	.063863	.067557	.071296	.075078	.078898	.082755	.090565	.098486
	-.10	.051182	.054601	.058081	.061619	.065212	.068857	.072551	.076290	.080072	.083892	.087749	.095553	.103480
	-.20	.056176	.059595	.063075	.066613	.070206	.073852	.077545	.081285	.085066	.088887	.092743	.100553	.108474
	-.30	.061170	.064589	.068069	.071607	.075200	.078846	.082540	.086279	.090060	.093881	.097737	.105547	.113468
	-.40	.066165	.069583	.073063	.076601	.080195	.083840	.087534	.091273	.095054	.098375	.102731	.110542	.118463
30	.40	.026727	.030342	.034014	.037739	.041512	.045330	.049189	.053083	.057009	.060964	.064945	.072969	.081059
	.30	.031721	.035336	.039008	.042733	.046506	.050325	.054183	.058077	.062003	.065959	.069939	.077963	.086053
	.20	.036715	.040330	.044002	.047727	.051504	.055319	.059177	.063071	.066997	.070953	.074935	.082957	.091048
	.10	.041709	.045324	.048996	.052721	.056495	.060313	.064171	.068065	.071992	.075947	.079927	.087951	.096042
	0.00	.046704	.050318	.053990	.057715	.061489	.065307	.069165	.073059	.076986	.080941	.084921	.092946	.101036
	-.10	.051698	.055312	.058984	.062709	.066483	.070301	.074159	.078053	.081980	.085935	.089915	.097940	.106030
	-.20	.056692	.060306	.063978	.067703	.071477	.075295	.079153	.083047	.086974	.090929	.094910	.102934	.111024
	-.30	.061686	.065300	.068972	.072697	.076471	.080289	.084147	.088042	.091968	.095923	.099904	.107928	.116018
	-.40	.066680	.070294	.073996	.077692	.081465	.085283	.089141	.093036	.096962	.100317	.104498	.112922	.121012

15.0 YEAR HOLDING PERIOD
.040 EQUITY YIELD RATE
.900 LOAN RATIO

INTEREST RATE

TERM YEARS	APPR DEP	5.0	5.5	6.0	6.5	7.0	7.5	8.0	8.5	9.0	9.5	10.0	11.0	12.0
10	.40	.021207	.022685	.024163	.025639	.027111	.026679	.030041	.031496	.032942	.034379	.035603	.036613	.041360
	.30	.026201	.027679	.029157	.030633	.032105	.033573	.035035	.036490	.037936	.039373	.040798	.043607	.046354
	.20	.031195	.032674	.034151	.035627	.037100	.038567	.040029	.041484	.042930	.044367	.045792	.048602	.051348
	.10	.036189	.037668	.039146	.040621	.042094	.043562	.045023	.046478	.047925	.049361	.050786	.053596	.056342
	0.00	.041183	.042662	.044140	.045615	.047088	.048556	.050018	.051467	.052919	.054355	.055780	.058590	.061336
	-.10	.046177	.047656	.049134	.050609	.052082	.053551	.055012	.056467	.057913	.059349	.060774	.063584	.066330
	-.20	.051171	.052650	.054128	.055604	.057076	.058544	.060006	.061461	.062907	.064343	.065768	.068578	.071224
	-.30	.056165	.057644	.059122	.060598	.062070	.063538	.065000	.066455	.067901	.069337	.070762	.073572	.076319
	-.40	.061159	.062638	.064116	.065592	.067064	.068532	.069994	.071449	.072895	.074331	.075756	.078566	.081313
15	.40	.024482	.027322	.030213	.033150	.036150	.039194	.042287	.045426	.048617	.051853	.055134	.061829	.068695
	.30	.029476	.032316	.035207	.038150	.041144	.044188	.047281	.050423	.053611	.056847	.060128	.066823	.073683
	.20	.034471	.037310	.040201	.043144	.046138	.049182	.052275	.055417	.058606	.061841	.065122	.071817	.078683
	.10	.039465	.042304	.045195	.048138	.051132	.054176	.057269	.060411	.063600	.066835	.070116	.076811	.083677
	0.00	.044459	.047298	.050190	.053133	.056126	.059170	.062263	.065405	.068594	.071829	.075110	.081805	.088671
	-.10	.049453	.052292	.055184	.058127	.061121	.064164	.067258	.070399	.073588	.076823	.080104	.086800	.093665
	-.20	.054447	.057286	.060178	.063121	.066115	.069159	.072252	.075393	.078582	.081817	.085099	.091794	.098659
	-.30	.059441	.062280	.065172	.068115	.071109	.074153	.077246	.080387	.083576	.086812	.090093	.096788	.103653
	-.40	.064435	.067274	.070166	.073109	.076103	.079147	.082240	.085381	.088570	.091806	.095087	.101782	.108648
20	.40	.026670	.029555	.033107	.036726	.040407	.044151	.047954	.051813	.055728	.059696	.063713	.071891	.080242
	.30	.031665	.034549	.038102	.041720	.045402	.049145	.052948	.056808	.060722	.064690	.068708	.076885	.085236
	.20	.036659	.039544	.043096	.046714	.050396	.054139	.057942	.061802	.065716	.069684	.073702	.081879	.090231
	.10	.041653	.044537	.048090	.051708	.055390	.059133	.062936	.066796	.070711	.074678	.078696	.086873	.095225
	0.00	.046647	.049532	.053084	.056702	.060384	.064127	.067930	.071790	.075705	.079672	.083690	.091867	.100219
	-.10	.051641	.054526	.058078	.061696	.065378	.069121	.072924	.076784	.080699	.084666	.088684	.096861	.105213
	-.20	.056635	.059520	.063072	.066690	.070372	.074116	.077918	.081778	.085693	.089660	.093678	.101855	.110207
	-.30	.061629	.064514	.068066	.071684	.075366	.079110	.082912	.086772	.090687	.094654	.098672	.106850	.115201
	-.40	.066623	.069508	.073060	.076679	.080360	.084104	.087906	.091766	.095681	.099649	.103666	.111844	.120195
25	.40	.029905	.030831	.034746	.038726	.042769	.046870	.051025	.055232	.059486	.063784	.068123	.076909	.085820
	.30	.031973	.035825	.039740	.043721	.047763	.051864	.056020	.060226	.064480	.068778	.073117	.081903	.090815
	.20	.036973	.040819	.044734	.048715	.052757	.056858	.061014	.065220	.069474	.073772	.078111	.086897	.095809
	.10	.041968	.045813	.049728	.053709	.057751	.061852	.066008	.070214	.074468	.078766	.083105	.091892	.100803
	0.00	.046962	.050807	.054722	.058703	.062745	.066846	.071002	.075208	.079463	.083761	.088099	.096886	.105797
	-.10	.051956	.055801	.059716	.063697	.067740	.071840	.075996	.080203	.084457	.088755	.093093	.101880	.110791
	-.20	.056950	.060796	.064711	.068691	.072734	.076835	.080990	.085197	.089451	.093749	.098088	.106874	.115785
	-.30	.061944	.065790	.069705	.073685	.077728	.081829	.085984	.090191	.094445	.098743	.103082	.111868	.120779
	-.40	.066938	.070784	.074699	.078679	.082722	.086823	.090978	.095185	.099439	.103737	.108076	.116862	.125773
30	.40	.027565	.031631	.035762	.039953	.044198	.048494	.052834	.057215	.061632	.066082	.070560	.079587	.086689
	.30	.032559	.036625	.040756	.044947	.049193	.053488	.057828	.062209	.066627	.071076	.075554	.084581	.093683
	.20	.037553	.041620	.045751	.049941	.054187	.058482	.062822	.067203	.071621	.076071	.080548	.089576	.098677
	.10	.042547	.046614	.050745	.054935	.059181	.063476	.067816	.072197	.076615	.081064	.085542	.094570	.103671
	0.00	.047542	.051608	.055739	.059930	.064175	.068470	.072811	.077192	.081609	.086058	.090537	.099564	.108665
	-.10	.052536	.056602	.060733	.064924	.069169	.073464	.077805	.082186	.086603	.091053	.095531	.104558	.113659
	-.20	.057530	.061596	.065727	.069918	.074163	.078458	.082799	.087180	.091597	.096047	.100525	.109552	.118654
	-.30	.062524	.066590	.070721	.074912	.079157	.083453	.087793	.092174	.096591	.101041	.105519	.114546	.123648
	-.40	.067518	.071584	.075715	.079906	.084151	.088447	.092787	.097168	.101585	.106035	.110513	.119540	.123642

15.0 YEAR HOLDING PERIOD
.060 EQUITY YIELD RATE
.600 LOAN RATIO

INTEREST RATE

TERM YEARS	APPR DEP	5.0	5.5	6.0	6.5	7.0	7.5	8.0	8.5	9.0	9.5	10.0	11.0	12.0
10	.40	.038841	.039906	.041005	.042106	.043208	.044310	.045413	.046515	.047616	.048713	.049907	.051981	.054132
	.30	.043107	.044203	.045301	.046402	.047504	.048607	.049709	.050811	.051912	.053009	.054103	.056278	.058428
	.20	.047403	.048499	.049597	.050698	.051800	.052903	.054005	.055107	.056208	.057305	.058399	.060574	.062725
	.10	.051700	.052795	.053894	.054994	.056096	.057199	.058302	.059404	.060504	.061601	.062695	.064870	.067021
	0.00	.055996	.057091	.058190	.059291	.060393	.061495	.062598	.063700	.064800	.065897	.066992	.069166	.071317
	-.10	.060292	.061388	.062486	.063587	.064689	.065792	.066894	.067996	.069096	.070194	.071288	.073463	.075613
	-.20	.064588	.065684	.066783	.067883	.068985	.070088	.071191	.072292	.073392	.074490	.075584	.077759	.079910
	-.30	.068885	.069980	.071079	.072179	.073281	.074384	.075487	.076589	.077689	.078786	.079880	.082055	.084206
	-.40	.073181	.074277	.075375	.076476	.077578	.078680	.079783	.080885	.081985	.083083	.084177	.086352	.088502
15	.40	.037974	.039667	.041795	.043757	.045757	.047782	.049844	.051938	.054064	.056221	.058409	.062872	.067449
	.30	.042271	.044164	.046091	.048053	.050053	.052078	.054140	.056235	.058360	.060518	.062705	.067168	.071746
	.20	.046567	.048460	.050387	.052350	.054345	.056375	.058437	.060531	.062657	.064814	.067001	.071465	.076042
	.10	.050863	.052756	.054684	.056646	.058642	.060671	.062733	.064827	.066953	.069110	.071298	.075761	.080338
	0.00	.055159	.057052	.058980	.060942	.062938	.064967	.067026	.069124	.071250	.073407	.075594	.080057	.084634
	-.10	.059456	.061349	.063276	.065238	.067234	.069264	.071326	.073420	.075546	.077703	.079890	.084354	.088931
	-.20	.063752	.065645	.067573	.069535	.071531	.073560	.075622	.077716	.079842	.081999	.084186	.088650	.093227
	-.30	.068048	.069941	.071869	.073831	.075827	.077856	.079918	.082012	.084138	.086295	.088483	.092946	.097523
	-.40	.072345	.074237	.076165	.078127	.080123	.082152	.084214	.086309	.088435	.090592	.092779	.097242	.101820
20	.40	.037569	.039048	.042173	.044541	.046952	.049403	.051895	.054424	.056990	.059592	.062227	.067592	.073075
	.30	.041865	.044145	.046469	.048837	.051248	.053700	.056191	.058720	.061287	.063888	.066523	.071889	.077371
	.20	.046161	.048441	.050765	.053134	.055544	.057996	.060487	.063017	.065583	.068184	.070819	.076185	.081668
	.10	.050458	.052737	.055062	.057430	.059841	.062292	.064784	.067313	.069879	.072480	.075116	.080481	.085964
	0.00	.054754	.057033	.059358	.061726	.064137	.066589	.069080	.071609	.074175	.076777	.079412	.084777	.090260
	-.10	.059050	.061330	.063654	.066023	.068433	.070885	.073376	.075906	.078472	.081073	.083708	.089074	.094557
	-.20	.063347	.065626	.067951	.070319	.072729	.075181	.077672	.080202	.082768	.085369	.088004	.093370	.098853
	-.30	.067643	.069922	.072247	.074615	.077026	.079478	.081969	.084498	.087064	.089666	.092301	.097666	.103149
	-.40	.071939	.074219	.076543	.078911	.081322	.083774	.086265	.088794	.091360	.093962	.096597	.101963	.107445
25	.40	.037335	.039638	.042287	.044981	.047617	.050293	.053006	.055755	.058536	.061349	.064189	.069347	.075793
	.30	.041632	.044134	.046683	.049277	.051913	.054589	.057303	.060051	.062833	.065645	.068485	.074243	.080085
	.20	.045928	.048423	.050979	.053573	.056209	.058885	.061599	.064347	.067129	.069941	.072782	.078539	.084385
	.10	.050224	.052726	.055275	.057870	.060506	.063182	.065895	.068644	.071425	.074237	.077078	.082835	.088682
	0.00	.054520	.057016	.059572	.062166	.064802	.067478	.070191	.072940	.075722	.078533	.081374	.087132	.092978
	-.10	.058817	.061319	.063868	.066462	.069098	.071774	.074488	.077236	.080018	.082830	.085670	.091428	.097274
	-.20	.063113	.065615	.068165	.070758	.073394	.076070	.078784	.081533	.084314	.087126	.089967	.095724	.101570
	-.30	.067409	.069912	.072461	.075055	.077691	.080367	.083080	.085829	.088610	.091422	.094263	.100021	.105867
	-.40	.071706	.074208	.076757	.079351	.081987	.084663	.087376	.090125	.092907	.095719	.098559	.104317	.110163
30	.40	.037187	.039831	.042520	.045250	.048019	.050824	.053661	.056527	.059420	.062336	.065274	.071203	.077190
	.30	.041484	.044127	.046816	.049546	.052316	.055120	.057957	.060823	.063716	.066632	.069570	.075499	.081487
	.20	.045780	.048423	.051112	.053843	.056612	.059416	.062253	.065120	.068012	.070929	.073866	.079795	.085783
	.10	.050076	.052720	.055409	.058139	.060908	.063713	.066550	.069416	.072308	.075225	.078162	.084092	.090079
	0.00	.054372	.057016	.059705	.062435	.065204	.068009	.070846	.073712	.076605	.079521	.082459	.088388	.094375
	-.10	.058669	.061312	.064001	.066732	.069501	.072305	.075142	.078008	.080901	.083817	.086755	.092684	.098672
	-.20	.062965	.065609	.068297	.071024	.073797	.076602	.079438	.082305	.085197	.088114	.091051	.096981	.102968
	-.30	.067261	.069905	.072594	.075324	.078093	.080898	.083735	.086601	.089494	.092410	.095348	.101277	.107264
	-.40	.071557	.074201	.076890	.079620	.082390	.085194	.088031	.090897	.093790	.096706	.099644	.105573	.111560

15.0 YEAR HOLDING PERIOD
.060 EQUITY YIELD RATE
.667 LOAN RATIO

INTEREST RATE

TERM YEARS	APPR DEP	5.0	5.5	6.0	6.5	7.0	7.5	8.0	8.5	9.0	9.5	10.0	11.0	12.0
10	.40	.038366	.039583	.040804	.042027	.043251	.044476	.045702	.046926	.048148	.049368	.050583	.053000	.055390
	.30	.042662	.043879	.045100	.046323	.047547	.048773	.049998	.051222	.052444	.053664	.054880	.057296	.059686
	.20	.046958	.048176	.049396	.050619	.051844	.053069	.054295	.055519	.056741	.057960	.059176	.061592	.063983
	.10	.051255	.052472	.053693	.054916	.056140	.057365	.058590	.059815	.061037	.062256	.063472	.065889	.068278
	0.00	.055551	.056768	.057989	.059212	.060436	.061662	.062887	.064111	.065333	.066553	.067769	.070185	.072575
	-.10	.059847	.061065	.062285	.063508	.064733	.065958	.067183	.068407	.069629	.070849	.072065	.074481	.076871
	-.20	.064143	.065361	.066581	.067804	.069029	.070254	.071479	.072703	.073926	.075145	.076361	.078778	.081168
	-.30	.068440	.069657	.070878	.072101	.073325	.074550	.075776	.077000	.078222	.079442	.080657	.083074	.085454
	-.40	.072736	.073953	.075174	.076397	.077621	.078847	.080072	.081296	.082518	.083738	.084954	.087370	.089750
15	.40	.037437	.039540	.041682	.043802	.046079	.048334	.050625	.052952	.055314	.057711	.060142	.065101	.070137
	.30	.041733	.043836	.045978	.048098	.050376	.052630	.054921	.057248	.059611	.062007	.064438	.069397	.074433
	.20	.046029	.048132	.050274	.052394	.054672	.056927	.059218	.061545	.063907	.066304	.068734	.073693	.078779
	.10	.050325	.052429	.054570	.056691	.058968	.061223	.063514	.065841	.068203	.070600	.073030	.077990	.083075
	0.00	.054622	.056725	.058867	.060987	.063264	.065519	.067810	.070137	.072500	.074896	.077327	.082286	.087322
	-.10	.058918	.061021	.063163	.065283	.067561	.069815	.072107	.074434	.076796	.079192	.081623	.086582	.091658
	-.20	.063214	.065317	.067459	.069639	.071857	.074112	.076403	.078730	.081092	.083489	.085919	.090879	.095954
	-.30	.067510	.069614	.071756	.073936	.076153	.078408	.080699	.083026	.085388	.087785	.090215	.095175	.100211
	-.40	.071807	.073910	.076052	.078232	.080449	.082704	.084995	.087322	.089685	.092081	.094512	.099471	.104557
20	.40	.036986	.039519	.042102	.044733	.047411	.050136	.052904	.055714	.058565	.061456	.064384	.070346	.076438
	.30	.041282	.043815	.046398	.049029	.051708	.054432	.057200	.060010	.062862	.065752	.068680	.074642	.080734
	.20	.045579	.048111	.050694	.053326	.056004	.058728	.061496	.064307	.067158	.070048	.072976	.078938	.085030
	.10	.049875	.052408	.054990	.057622	.060300	.063024	.065792	.068603	.071454	.074345	.077273	.083234	.089326
	0.00	.054171	.056704	.059287	.061918	.064596	.067321	.070089	.072899	.075750	.078641	.081569	.087531	.093623
	-.10	.058467	.061000	.063583	.066215	.068893	.071617	.074385	.077195	.080047	.082937	.085865	.091827	.097919
	-.20	.062764	.065296	.067879	.070511	.073189	.075913	.078681	.081492	.084343	.087233	.090161	.096123	.102215
	-.30	.067060	.069593	.072176	.074807	.077485	.080209	.082978	.085788	.088639	.091530	.094458	.100419	.106512
	-.40	.071356	.073889	.076472	.079103	.081782	.084506	.087274	.090084	.092936	.095826	.098754	.104716	.110808
25	.40	.036726	.039507	.042339	.045221	.048150	.051124	.054139	.057193	.060283	.063408	.066564	.072961	.079457
	.30	.041023	.043803	.046636	.049518	.052447	.055420	.058435	.061489	.064580	.067704	.070860	.077258	.083753
	.20	.045319	.048100	.050932	.053814	.056743	.059716	.062731	.065785	.068876	.072001	.075157	.081554	.088050
	.10	.049615	.052396	.055228	.058110	.061039	.064013	.067028	.070082	.073172	.076297	.079453	.085850	.092346
	0.00	.053912	.056692	.059524	.062406	.065335	.068309	.071324	.074378	.077468	.080593	.083749	.090146	.096642
	-.10	.058208	.060989	.063821	.066703	.069632	.076605	.075620	.078674	.081765	.084889	.088045	.094443	.100939
	-.20	.062504	.065285	.068117	.070999	.073928	.076901	.079916	.082970	.086061	.089186	.092342	.098739	.105235
	-.30	.066800	.069581	.072413	.075295	.078224	.081198	.084213	.087267	.090357	.093482	.096638	.103035	.109531
	-.40	.071097	.073877	.076710	.079592	.082521	.085494	.088509	.091563	.094654	.097778	.100934	.107332	.113827
30	.40	.036562	.039499	.042487	.045521	.048598	.051714	.054866	.058051	.061265	.064505	.067769	.074357	.081010
	.30	.040858	.043790	.046783	.049817	.052894	.056010	.059162	.062347	.065561	.068801	.072065	.078654	.085306
	.20	.045155	.048092	.051079	.054113	.057190	.060306	.063458	.066643	.069857	.073098	.076362	.082950	.089603
	.10	.049451	.052388	.055376	.058410	.061486	.064603	.067755	.070939	.074153	.077394	.080658	.087246	.093895
	0.00	.053747	.056684	.059672	.062706	.065783	.068899	.072051	.075236	.078450	.081690	.084954	.091542	.098195
	-.10	.058043	.060981	.063968	.067002	.070079	.073195	.076347	.079532	.082746	.085987	.089251	.095839	.102491
	-.20	.062340	.065277	.068264	.071298	.074375	.077492	.080644	.083828	.087042	.090283	.093547	.100135	.106788
	-.30	.066636	.069573	.072561	.075595	.078672	.081788	.084940	.088125	.091339	.094579	.097843	.104431	.111084
	-.40	.070932	.073870	.076857	.079891	.082968	.086084	.089236	.092421	.095635	.098875	.102139	.108728	.115380

301

15.0 YEAR HOLDING PERIOD
.060 EQUITY YIELD RATE
.700 LOAN RATIO

INTEREST RATE

TERM YEARS	APPR DEP	5.0	5.5	6.0	6.5	7.0	7.5	8.0	8.5	9.0	9.5	10.0	11.0	12.0
10	.40	.038143	.039422	.040703	.041987	.043273	.044560	.045846	.047131	.048415	.049695	.050972	.053509	.056018
	.30	.042440	.043718	.044999	.046284	.047569	.048856	.050142	.051428	.052711	.053992	.055268	.057805	.060315
	.20	.046736	.048014	.049296	.050580	.051866	.053152	.054438	.055724	.057007	.058288	.059564	.062102	.064611
	.10	.051032	.052310	.053592	.054876	.056162	.057448	.058735	.060020	.061304	.062584	.063861	.066398	.068907
	0.00	.055328	.056607	.057888	.059172	.060458	.061745	.063031	.064316	.065600	.066880	.068157	.070694	.073203
	-.10	.059625	.060903	.062185	.063469	.064754	.066041	.067327	.068613	.069896	.071177	.072453	.074991	.077500
	-.20	.063921	.065199	.066481	.067765	.069051	.070337	.071624	.072909	.074192	.075473	.076749	.079287	.081796
	-.30	.068217	.069496	.070777	.072061	.073347	.074633	.075920	.077205	.078489	.079769	.081046	.083583	.086092
	-.40	.072514	.073792	.075073	.076357	.077643	.078930	.080216	.081502	.082785	.084065	.085342	.087879	.090388
15	.40	.037168	.039376	.041025	.043914	.046243	.048610	.051016	.053459	.055939	.058456	.061008	.066215	.071555
	.30	.041464	.043672	.045921	.048210	.050539	.052906	.055312	.057755	.060236	.062752	.065304	.070511	.075851
	.20	.045760	.047969	.050217	.052507	.054835	.057203	.059608	.062052	.064532	.067048	.069600	.074808	.080148
	.10	.050056	.052265	.054514	.056803	.059131	.061499	.063905	.066348	.068828	.071345	.073897	.079104	.084444
	0.00	.054353	.056561	.058810	.061099	.063428	.065795	.068201	.070644	.073124	.075641	.078193	.083400	.088740
	-.10	.058649	.060857	.063106	.065395	.067724	.070091	.072497	.074940	.077421	.079937	.082489	.087696	.093036
	-.20	.062945	.065154	.067403	.069692	.072020	.074388	.076793	.079237	.081717	.084233	.086785	.091993	.097333
	-.30	.067242	.069450	.071699	.073988	.076316	.078684	.081090	.083533	.086013	.088530	.091082	.096289	.101629
	-.40	.071538	.073746	.075995	.078284	.080613	.082980	.085386	.087829	.090310	.092826	.095378	.100585	.105925
20	.40	.036695	.039354	.042066	.044829	.047641	.050502	.053408	.056359	.059353	.062388	.065462	.071722	.078119
	.30	.040991	.043650	.046362	.049125	.051938	.054798	.057704	.060655	.063649	.066684	.069758	.076018	.082415
	.20	.045287	.047947	.050658	.053421	.056234	.059094	.062001	.064952	.067945	.070980	.074055	.080314	.086711
	.10	.049583	.052243	.054955	.057718	.060530	.063390	.066297	.069248	.072242	.075277	.078351	.084611	.091007
	0.00	.053880	.056539	.059251	.062014	.064826	.067687	.070593	.073544	.076538	.079573	.082647	.088907	.095304
	-.10	.058176	.060835	.063547	.066310	.069123	.071983	.074889	.077840	.080834	.083869	.086943	.093203	.099600
	-.20	.062472	.065132	.067844	.070607	.073419	.076279	.079186	.082137	.085130	.088165	.091240	.097500	.103896
	-.30	.066768	.069428	.072140	.074903	.077715	.080575	.083482	.086433	.089427	.092462	.095536	.101796	.108193
	-.40	.071065	.073724	.076436	.079199	.082011	.084872	.087778	.090729	.093723	.096758	.099832	.106092	.112489
25	.40	.036422	.039341	.042316	.045342	.048417	.051539	.054705	.057912	.061157	.064438	.067751	.074469	.081289
	.30	.040718	.043638	.046612	.049638	.052713	.055835	.059001	.062208	.065453	.068734	.072048	.078765	.085585
	.20	.045015	.047934	.050908	.053934	.057010	.060132	.063297	.066504	.069749	.073030	.076344	.083061	.089882
	.10	.049311	.052230	.055204	.058230	.061306	.064428	.067594	.070800	.074046	.077326	.080640	.087357	.094178
	0.00	.053607	.056527	.059501	.062527	.065602	.068724	.071890	.075097	.078342	.081623	.084936	.091654	.098474
	-.10	.057903	.060823	.063797	.066823	.069898	.073020	.076186	.079393	.082638	.085919	.089233	.095950	.102771
	-.20	.062200	.065119	.068093	.071119	.074195	.077317	.080482	.083689	.086934	.090215	.093529	.100246	.107067
	-.30	.066496	.069415	.072389	.075416	.078491	.081613	.084779	.087986	.091231	.094511	.097825	.104542	.111363
	-.40	.070792	.073712	.076686	.079712	.082787	.085909	.089075	.092282	.095527	.098808	.102122	.108839	.115659
30	.40	.036249	.039334	.042470	.045656	.048887	.052159	.055468	.058812	.062187	.065530	.069017	.075934	.082919
	.30	.040546	.043630	.046767	.049953	.053183	.056455	.059765	.063109	.066483	.069886	.073313	.080231	.087216
	.20	.044842	.047926	.051063	.054249	.057479	.060751	.064061	.067405	.070780	.074182	.077609	.084527	.091512
	.10	.049138	.052222	.055359	.058545	.061776	.065048	.068357	.071701	.075076	.078478	.081906	.088823	.095808
	0.00	.053434	.056519	.059655	.062841	.066072	.069344	.072654	.075997	.079372	.082775	.086202	.093119	.100105
	-.10	.057731	.060815	.063952	.067137	.070368	.073640	.076950	.080294	.083668	.087071	.090498	.097416	.104401
	-.20	.062027	.065111	.068248	.071434	.074664	.077936	.081246	.084590	.087965	.091367	.094794	.101712	.108697
	-.30	.066323	.069407	.072544	.075730	.078961	.082233	.085542	.088886	.092261	.095663	.099091	.106008	.112993
	-.40	.070620	.073703	.076841	.080026	.083257	.086529	.089839	.093183	.096557	.099960	.103387	.110304	.117290

302

15.0 YEAR HOLDING PERIOD
.060 EQUITY YIELD RATE
.750 LOAN RATIO

INTEREST RATE

TERM YEARS	APPR DEP	5.0	5.5	6.0	6.5	7.0	7.5	8.0	8.5	9.0	9.5	10.0	11.0	12.0
10	.40	.037810	.039179	.040552	.041928	.043306	.044684	.046062	.047440	.048815	.050187	.051554	.054273	.056961
	.30	.042106	.043476	.044849	.046224	.047602	.048980	.050359	.051736	.053111	.054483	.055851	.058569	.061258
	.20	.046402	.047772	.049145	.050521	.051898	.053277	.054655	.056032	.057407	.058779	.060147	.062866	.065554
	.10	.050699	.052068	.053441	.054817	.056195	.057573	.058951	.060328	.061704	.063076	.064443	.067162	.069850
	0.00	.054995	.056364	.057737	.059113	.060491	.061869	.063248	.064625	.066000	.067372	.068740	.071458	.074146
	-.10	.059291	.060661	.062034	.063410	.064787	.066166	.067544	.068921	.070296	.071668	.073036	.075754	.078443
	-.20	.063587	.064957	.066330	.067706	.069083	.070462	.071840	.073217	.074592	.075964	.077332	.080051	.082739
	-.30	.067884	.069253	.070626	.072002	.073380	.074758	.076136	.077514	.078889	.080261	.081628	.084347	.087035
	-.40	.072180	.073549	.074923	.076298	.077676	.079054	.080433	.081810	.083185	.084557	.085925	.088643	.091332
15	.40	.036764	.039130	.041540	.043992	.046487	.049024	.051602	.054219	.056877	.059573	.062307	.067887	.073608
	.30	.041061	.043427	.045836	.048289	.050784	.053320	.055898	.058516	.061173	.063869	.066604	.072183	.077904
	.20	.045357	.047723	.050132	.052585	.055080	.057616	.060194	.062812	.065469	.068166	.070900	.076479	.082200
	.10	.049653	.052019	.054429	.056881	.059376	.061913	.064490	.067108	.069766	.072462	.075196	.080775	.086497
	0.00	.053949	.056315	.058725	.061178	.063672	.066209	.068787	.071404	.074062	.076758	.079492	.085072	.090793
	-.10	.058246	.060612	.063021	.065474	.067969	.070505	.073083	.075701	.078358	.081054	.083789	.089368	.095089
	-.20	.062542	.064908	.067318	.069770	.072265	.074802	.077379	.079997	.082654	.085351	.088085	.093664	.099386
	-.30	.066838	.069204	.071614	.074066	.076561	.079098	.081675	.084293	.086951	.089647	.092381	.097960	.103682
	-.40	.071134	.073501	.075910	.078363	.080858	.083394	.085972	.088590	.091247	.093943	.096677	.102257	.107978
20	.40	.036257	.039107	.042012	.044973	.047986	.051051	.054165	.057326	.060534	.063786	.067080	.073787	.080640
	.30	.040554	.043403	.046309	.049269	.052282	.055347	.058461	.061623	.064830	.068082	.071376	.078083	.084937
	.20	.044850	.047699	.050605	.053565	.056579	.059643	.062757	.065919	.069127	.072378	.075672	.082379	.089233
	.10	.049146	.051996	.054901	.057862	.060875	.063939	.067053	.070215	.073423	.076675	.079969	.086676	.093529
	0.00	.053442	.056292	.059198	.062158	.065171	.068236	.071350	.074512	.077719	.080971	.084265	.090972	.097825
	-.10	.057739	.060588	.063494	.066454	.069467	.072532	.075646	.078808	.082015	.085267	.088561	.095268	.102122
	-.20	.062035	.064884	.067790	.070750	.073764	.076828	.079942	.083104	.086312	.089563	.092857	.099564	.106418
	-.30	.066331	.069181	.072086	.075047	.078060	.081125	.084239	.087400	.090608	.093860	.097154	.103861	.110714
	-.40	.070628	.073477	.076383	.079343	.082356	.085421	.088535	.091697	.094904	.098156	.101450	.108157	.115011
25	.40	.035965	.039093	.042280	.045522	.048817	.052162	.055554	.058990	.062467	.065982	.069533	.076730	.084337
	.30	.040262	.043390	.046576	.049818	.053114	.056459	.059850	.063286	.066763	.070278	.073829	.081026	.088633
	.20	.044558	.047686	.050872	.054114	.057410	.060755	.064147	.067582	.071059	.074575	.078125	.085322	.092930
	.10	.048854	.051982	.055169	.058411	.061706	.065051	.068443	.071879	.075356	.078871	.082421	.089618	.097226
	0.00	.053151	.056278	.059465	.062707	.066002	.069347	.072739	.076175	.079652	.083167	.086718	.093915	.101522
	-.10	.057447	.060575	.063761	.067004	.070299	.073644	.077035	.080471	.083948	.087463	.091014	.098211	.105819
	-.20	.061743	.064871	.068058	.071300	.074595	.077940	.081332	.084768	.088244	.091760	.095310	.102507	.110115
	-.30	.066039	.069167	.072354	.075596	.078891	.082236	.085628	.089064	.092541	.096056	.099607	.106803	.114411
	-.40	.070336	.073464	.076650	.079892	.083187	.086532	.089924	.093360	.096837	.100352	.103903	.111100	.118408
30	.40	.035780	.039085	.042446	.045859	.049320	.052826	.056372	.059955	.063571	.067216	.070888	.078300	.085784
	.30	.040077	.043381	.046742	.050155	.053617	.057122	.060669	.064251	.067867	.071513	.075185	.082596	.090080
	.20	.044373	.047677	.051038	.054452	.057913	.061419	.064965	.068548	.072163	.075809	.079481	.086892	.094377
	.10	.048669	.051974	.055335	.058748	.062209	.065715	.069261	.072844	.076460	.080105	.083777	.091189	.098673
	0.00	.052965	.056270	.059631	.063044	.066506	.070011	.073557	.077140	.080756	.084401	.088073	.095485	.102969
	-.10	.057262	.060566	.063927	.067340	.070802	.074308	.077854	.081436	.085052	.088698	.092370	.099781	.107265
	-.20	.061558	.064863	.068223	.071637	.075098	.078604	.082150	.085733	.089348	.092994	.096666	.104078	.111562
	-.30	.065854	.069159	.072520	.075933	.079394	.082900	.086446	.090029	.093645	.097290	.100962	.108374	.115858
	-.40	.070151	.073455	.076816	.080229	.083691	.087196	.090742	.094325	.097941	.101586	.105258	.112670	.120154

15.0 YEAR HOLDING PERIOD
.060 EQUITY YIELD RATE
.800 LOAN RATIO

INTEREST RATE

TERM YEARS	APPR DEP	5.0	5.5	6.0	6.5	7.0	7.5	8.0	8.5	9.0	9.5	10.0	11.0	12.0
10	.40	.037476	.038937	.040402	.041869	.043338	.044809	.046279	.047748	.049215	.050678	.052137	.055037	.057904
	.30	.041772	.043233	.044698	.046165	.047635	.049105	.050575	.052044	.053511	.054974	.056433	.059333	.062201
	.20	.046069	.047529	.048994	.050462	.051931	.053401	.054871	.056340	.057807	.059271	.060730	.063629	.066497
	.10	.050365	.051826	.053290	.054758	.056227	.057698	.059168	.060637	.062104	.063567	.065026	.067926	.070793
	0.00	.054661	.056122	.057587	.059054	.060524	.061994	.063464	.064933	.066400	.067863	.069322	.072222	.075090
	-.10	.058957	.060418	.061883	.063350	.064820	.066290	.067760	.069229	.070696	.072160	.073618	.076518	.079386
	-.20	.063254	.064715	.066179	.067647	.069116	.070586	.072057	.073526	.074992	.076456	.077915	.080815	.083682
	-.30	.067550	.069011	.070475	.071943	.073412	.074883	.076353	.077822	.079289	.080752	.082211	.085111	.087978
	-.40	.071846	.073307	.074772	.076239	.077709	.079179	.080649	.082118	.083585	.085048	.086507	.089407	.092275
15	.40	.036361	.038885	.041455	.044071	.046732	.049438	.052187	.054980	.057814	.060690	.063607	.069558	.075661
	.30	.040657	.043181	.045751	.048367	.051028	.053734	.056484	.059276	.062111	.064987	.067903	.073854	.079957
	.20	.044953	.047477	.050047	.052664	.055325	.058030	.060780	.063572	.066407	.069283	.072199	.078151	.084253
	.10	.049250	.051774	.054344	.056960	.059621	.062327	.065076	.067869	.070703	.073579	.076496	.082447	.088550
	0.00	.053546	.056070	.058640	.061256	.063917	.066623	.069373	.072165	.074999	.077875	.080792	.086743	.092846
	-.10	.057842	.060366	.062936	.065552	.068214	.070919	.073669	.076461	.079296	.082172	.085088	.091039	.097142
	-.20	.062139	.064662	.067233	.069849	.072510	.075216	.077965	.080757	.083592	.086468	.089384	.095336	.101438
	-.30	.066435	.068959	.071529	.074145	.076806	.079512	.082261	.085054	.087888	.090764	.093680	.099632	.105735
	-.40	.070731	.073255	.075825	.078441	.081102	.083808	.086557	.089350	.092184	.095060	.097977	.103928	.110031
20	.40	.035860	.038860	.041959	.045117	.048331	.051600	.054921	.058294	.061715	.065184	.068697	.075852	.083162
	.30	.040116	.043156	.046255	.049413	.052627	.055896	.059218	.062590	.066012	.069480	.072994	.080148	.087458
	.20	.044413	.047452	.050551	.053709	.056923	.060192	.063514	.066886	.070308	.073776	.077290	.084444	.091755
	.10	.048709	.051748	.054848	.058005	.061220	.064488	.067810	.071183	.074604	.078073	.081586	.088740	.096051
	0.00	.053005	.056045	.059144	.062302	.065516	.068785	.072106	.075479	.078901	.082369	.085883	.093037	.100347
	-.10	.057302	.060341	.063440	.066598	.069812	.073081	.076403	.079775	.083197	.086665	.090179	.097333	.104643
	-.20	.061598	.064637	.067737	.070894	.074108	.077377	.080699	.084072	.087493	.090962	.094475	.101629	.108940
	-.30	.065894	.068933	.072033	.075190	.078405	.081674	.084995	.088368	.091789	.095258	.098771	.105925	.113236
	-.40	.070190	.073230	.076329	.079487	.082701	.085970	.089292	.092664	.096086	.099554	.103068	.110222	.117532
25	.40	.035509	.038845	.042244	.045703	.049217	.052785	.056403	.060068	.063777	.067526	.071314	.078990	.086785
	.30	.039805	.043141	.046540	.049999	.053514	.057082	.060700	.064365	.068073	.071823	.075610	.083287	.091082
	.20	.044101	.047438	.050837	.054295	.057810	.061378	.064996	.068661	.072370	.076119	.079906	.087583	.095378
	.10	.048398	.051734	.055133	.058591	.062106	.065674	.069292	.072957	.076666	.080415	.084203	.091879	.099674
	0.00	.052694	.056030	.059429	.062888	.066403	.069971	.073588	.077253	.080962	.084712	.088499	.096176	.103971
	-.10	.056990	.060327	.063726	.067184	.070699	.074267	.077885	.081550	.085258	.089008	.092795	.100472	.108267
	-.20	.061286	.064623	.068022	.071480	.074995	.078563	.082181	.085846	.089555	.093304	.097091	.104768	.112563
	-.30	.065583	.068919	.072318	.075777	.079291	.082859	.086477	.090142	.093851	.097600	.101388	.109064	.116859
	-.40	.069879	.073215	.076614	.080073	.083588	.087156	.090774	.094438	.098147	.101897	.105684	.113361	.121156
30	.40	.035311	.038836	.042421	.046062	.049754	.053494	.057276	.061098	.064955	.068843	.072760	.080666	.088649
	.30	.039608	.043132	.046717	.050358	.054050	.057790	.061572	.065394	.069251	.073139	.077056	.084962	.092945
	.20	.043904	.047429	.051014	.054654	.058347	.062086	.065869	.069690	.073547	.077436	.081352	.089258	.097241
	.10	.048200	.051725	.055310	.058951	.062643	.066382	.070165	.073986	.077843	.081732	.085649	.093554	.101538
	0.00	.052497	.056021	.059606	.063247	.066939	.070679	.074461	.078283	.082140	.086028	.089945	.097851	.105834
	-.10	.056793	.060318	.063903	.067543	.071236	.074975	.078757	.082579	.086436	.090324	.094241	.102147	.110130
	-.20	.061089	.064614	.068199	.071840	.075532	.079271	.083054	.086875	.090732	.094621	.098537	.106443	.114426
	-.30	.065385	.068910	.072495	.076136	.079828	.083568	.087350	.091172	.095028	.098917	.102834	.110740	.118723
	-.40	.069682	.073206	.076791	.080432	.084124	.087864	.091646	.095468	.099325	.103213	.107130	.115036	.123019

15.0 YEAR HOLDING PERIOD
.060 EQUITY YIELD RATE
.900 LOAN RATIO

INTEREST RATE

TERM YEARS	APPR DEP	5.0	5.5	6.0	6.5	7.0	7.5	8.0	8.5	9.0	9.5	10.0	11.0	12.0
10	.40	.036809	.038452	.040100	.041751	.043404	.045058	.046712	.048365	.050015	.051661	.053302	.056565	.059751
	.30	.041105	.042748	.044396	.046047	.047700	.049354	.051008	.052661	.054311	.055957	.057599	.060861	.064087
	.20	.045401	.047045	.048692	.050343	.051996	.053651	.055304	.056957	.058607	.060254	.061895	.065157	.068383
	.10	.049697	.051341	.052989	.054640	.056293	.057947	.059601	.061253	.062904	.064550	.066191	.069453	.072679
	0.00	.053994	.055637	.057285	.058936	.060589	.062243	.063897	.065550	.067200	.068846	.070484	.073750	.076976
	-.10	.058290	.059934	.061581	.063232	.064885	.066539	.068193	.069846	.071496	.073685	.074784	.078046	.081272
	-.20	.062586	.064230	.065878	.067528	.069182	.070836	.072490	.074142	.075792	.077439	.079080	.082342	.085568
	-.30	.066883	.068526	.070174	.071825	.073478	.075132	.076786	.078439	.080089	.081735	.083376	.086639	.089865
	-.40	.071179	.072822	.074470	.076121	.077774	.079428	.081082	.082735	.084385	.086031	.087673	.090935	.094161
15	.40	.035554	.038393	.041285	.044228	.047222	.050266	.053359	.056500	.059689	.062925	.066206	.072901	.079767
	.30	.039851	.042690	.045581	.048524	.051518	.054562	.057655	.060797	.063985	.067221	.070502	.077197	.084063
	.20	.044147	.046986	.049877	.052821	.055814	.058858	.061951	.065093	.068282	.071517	.074798	.081493	.088359
	.10	.048443	.051282	.054174	.057117	.060111	.063155	.066248	.069389	.072578	.075814	.079095	.085790	.092655
	0.00	.052739	.055579	.058470	.061413	.064407	.067451	.070544	.073685	.076874	.080110	.083391	.090086	.096952
	-.10	.057036	.059875	.062766	.065709	.068703	.071747	.074840	.077982	.081171	.084406	.087687	.094382	.101248
	-.20	.061332	.064171	.067063	.070006	.073000	.076043	.079136	.082278	.085467	.088702	.091983	.098679	.105544
	-.30	.065628	.068467	.071359	.074302	.077296	.080340	.083433	.086574	.089763	.092999	.096280	.102975	.109840
	-.40	.069924	.072764	.075655	.078598	.081592	.084636	.087729	.090870	.094059	.097295	.100576	.107271	.114137
20	.40	.034946	.038365	.041852	.045404	.049020	.052698	.056435	.060229	.064078	.067980	.071933	.079981	.088205
	.30	.039242	.042661	.046148	.049701	.053316	.056994	.060731	.064525	.068374	.072276	.076229	.084277	.092502
	.20	.043538	.046958	.050444	.053997	.057613	.061290	.065027	.068821	.072671	.076573	.080525	.088574	.096798
	.10	.047835	.051254	.054741	.058293	.061909	.065587	.069323	.073118	.076967	.080869	.084822	.092870	.101094
	0.00	.052131	.055550	.059037	.062589	.066205	.069883	.073620	.077414	.081263	.085165	.089118	.097166	.105390
	-.10	.056427	.059847	.063333	.066886	.070502	.074179	.077916	.081710	.085559	.089461	.093414	.101462	.109637
	-.20	.060724	.064143	.067630	.071182	.074798	.078475	.082212	.086006	.089856	.093758	.097711	.105759	.113933
	-.30	.065020	.068439	.071926	.075478	.079094	.082772	.086509	.090303	.094152	.098054	.102007	.110055	.118279
	-.40	.069316	.072735	.076222	.079774	.083390	.087068	.090805	.094599	.098448	.102350	.106303	.114351	.122576
25	.40	.034596	.038349	.042173	.046064	.050018	.054032	.058102	.062225	.066397	.070615	.074876	.083512	.092282
	.30	.038892	.042645	.046469	.050360	.054314	.058328	.062398	.066521	.070694	.074912	.079172	.087809	.096578
	.20	.043188	.046942	.050765	.054656	.058610	.062624	.066695	.070817	.074990	.079208	.083469	.092105	.100874
	.10	.047484	.051238	.055062	.058952	.062907	.066921	.070991	.075114	.079286	.083504	.087765	.096401	.105171
	0.00	.051781	.055534	.059358	.063249	.067203	.071217	.075287	.079410	.083582	.087800	.092061	.100698	.109467
	-.10	.056077	.059830	.063654	.067545	.071499	.075513	.079583	.083706	.087879	.092097	.096357	.104994	.113763
	-.20	.060373	.064127	.067951	.071841	.075795	.079809	.083880	.088003	.092175	.096393	.100654	.109290	.118059
	-.30	.064669	.068423	.072247	.076138	.080092	.084106	.088176	.092299	.096471	.100689	.104950	.113586	.122356
	-.40	.068966	.072719	.076543	.080434	.084388	.088402	.092472	.096595	.100767	.104986	.109246	.117883	.126652
30	.40	.034373	.038339	.042372	.046468	.050622	.054828	.059084	.063383	.067722	.072097	.076503	.085397	.094378
	.30	.038670	.042635	.046668	.050764	.054918	.059125	.063380	.067679	.072018	.076393	.080799	.089693	.098674
	.20	.042966	.046931	.050965	.055060	.059214	.063421	.067676	.071976	.076315	.080689	.085092	.093989	.102971
	.10	.047262	.051228	.055261	.059357	.063510	.067717	.071973	.076272	.080611	.084985	.089392	.098286	.107267
	0.00	.051559	.055524	.059557	.063653	.067807	.072014	.076269	.080568	.084907	.089282	.093688	.102582	.111563
	-.10	.055855	.059820	.063853	.067949	.072103	.076310	.080565	.084864	.089203	.093578	.097984	.106878	.115859
	-.20	.060151	.064117	.068150	.072245	.076399	.080606	.084861	.089161	.093500	.097874	.102281	.111175	.120156
	-.30	.064448	.068413	.072446	.076542	.080696	.084902	.089158	.093457	.097796	.102170	.106577	.115471	.124452
	-.40	.068744	.072709	.076742	.080838	.084992	.089199	.093454	.097753	.102092	.106467	.110873	.119767	.128748

305

15.0 YEAR HOLDING PERIOD
.080 EQUITY YIELD RATE
.600 LOAN RATIO

INTEREST RATE

TERM YEARS	APPR DEP	5.0	5.5	6.0	6.5	7.0	7.5	8.0	8.5	9.0	9.5	10.0	11.0	12.0
10	.40	.055598	.056790	.057989	.059192	.060400	.061612	.062827	.064044	.065264	.066485	.067706	.070145	.072577
	.30	.059281	.060473	.061671	.062875	.064083	.065295	.066510	.067727	.068947	.070168	.071389	.073828	.076260
	.20	.062964	.064156	.065354	.066558	.067766	.068977	.070193	.071410	.072630	.073850	.075071	.077511	.079943
	.10	.066647	.067839	.069037	.070241	.071449	.072660	.073876	.075093	.076313	.077533	.078754	.081194	.083626
	0.00	.070330	.071522	.072720	.073924	.075132	.076343	.077559	.078776	.079996	.081216	.082437	.084877	.087309
	-.10	.074013	.075205	.076403	.077607	.078815	.080026	.081241	.082459	.083679	.084899	.086120	.088560	.090992
	-.20	.077696	.078888	.080086	.081290	.082497	.083709	.084924	.086142	.087362	.088532	.089803	.092243	.094675
	-.30	.081379	.082571	.083769	.084973	.086180	.087392	.088607	.089825	.091045	.092255	.093486	.095926	.098358
	-.40	.085062	.086254	.087452	.088655	.089863	.091075	.092290	.093508	.094728	.095948	.097169	.099609	.102041
15	.40	.052108	.054000	.055928	.057890	.059886	.061915	.063977	.066072	.068198	.070355	.072542	.077005	.081583
	.30	.055791	.057683	.059611	.061573	.063569	.065598	.067660	.069755	.071881	.074038	.076225	.080688	.085266
	.20	.059474	.061366	.063294	.065256	.067252	.069281	.071343	.073438	.075564	.077721	.079908	.084371	.088948
	.10	.063156	.065049	.066977	.068939	.070935	.072964	.075026	.077121	.079247	.081403	.083591	.088054	.092631
	0.00	.066839	.068732	.070660	.072622	.074618	.076646	.078709	.080804	.082929	.085086	.087274	.091737	.096314
	-.10	.070522	.072415	.074343	.076305	.078301	.080330	.082392	.084486	.086612	.088769	.090957	.095420	.099992
	-.20	.074205	.076098	.078026	.079988	.081984	.084013	.086075	.088169	.090295	.092452	.094640	.099103	.103680
	-.30	.077888	.079781	.081709	.083671	.085667	.087696	.089758	.091852	.093978	.096135	.098323	.102736	.107363
	-.40	.081571	.083464	.085392	.087354	.089350	.091379	.093441	.095535	.097661	.099828	.102006	.106459	.111046
20	.40	.050415	.052656	.054942	.057272	.059644	.062057	.064510	.067001	.069529	.072092	.074689	.079979	.085387
	.30	.054098	.056339	.058625	.060955	.063327	.065740	.068193	.070684	.073211	.075775	.078372	.083652	.089070
	.20	.057781	.060022	.062308	.064638	.067010	.069423	.071876	.074367	.076894	.079458	.082055	.087344	.092753
	.10	.061464	.063705	.065991	.068321	.070693	.073106	.075559	.078050	.080577	.083140	.085737	.091027	.096436
	0.00	.065147	.067388	.069674	.072004	.074376	.076789	.079242	.081733	.084260	.086823	.089420	.094710	.100119
	-.10	.068830	.071071	.073357	.075687	.078059	.080472	.082925	.085416	.087943	.090506	.093103	.098393	.103802
	-.20	.072513	.074754	.077040	.079370	.081742	.084155	.086608	.089099	.091626	.094169	.096786	.102076	.107485
	-.30	.076196	.078437	.080723	.083053	.085425	.087838	.090291	.092781	.095309	.097872	.100469	.105759	.111168
	-.40	.079879	.082120	.084406	.086736	.089108	.091521	.093974	.096464	.098992	.101555	.104152	.109442	.114851
25	.40	.049440	.051889	.054384	.056966	.059510	.062135	.064799	.067498	.070232	.072957	.075792	.081461	.087225
	.30	.053123	.055572	.058067	.060609	.063193	.065818	.068481	.071181	.073915	.076680	.079475	.085144	.090908
	.20	.056806	.059254	.061750	.064292	.066876	.069501	.072164	.074864	.077598	.080363	.083158	.088827	.094591
	.10	.060489	.062937	.065433	.067975	.070559	.073184	.075847	.078547	.081281	.084046	.086841	.092510	.098273
	0.00	.064172	.066620	.069116	.071657	.074242	.076867	.079530	.082230	.084964	.087729	.090524	.096193	.101956
	-.10	.067855	.070303	.072799	.075340	.077925	.080550	.083213	.085913	.088647	.091412	.094207	.099876	.105639
	-.20	.071538	.073986	.076482	.079023	.081608	.084233	.086896	.089596	.092330	.095095	.097890	.103559	.109322
	-.30	.075221	.077669	.080165	.082706	.085291	.087916	.090579	.093279	.096012	.098778	.101573	.107242	.113005
	-.40	.078904	.081352	.083848	.086389	.088974	.091599	.094262	.096962	.099695	.102461	.105255	.110925	.116688
30	.40	.048622	.051407	.054038	.056713	.059429	.062181	.064968	.067787	.070634	.073506	.076402	.082253	.088170
	.30	.052505	.055090	.057721	.060396	.063112	.065864	.068651	.071470	.074316	.077189	.080085	.085936	.091853
	.20	.056188	.058773	.061404	.064079	.066795	.069547	.072334	.075153	.077999	.080872	.083768	.089619	.095535
	.10	.059871	.062456	.065087	.067762	.070478	.073230	.076017	.078836	.081682	.084555	.087450	.093302	.099218
	0.00	.063554	.066139	.068770	.071445	.074161	.076913	.079700	.082519	.085365	.088238	.091133	.096985	.102901
	-.10	.067237	.069822	.072453	.075128	.077843	.080596	.083383	.086202	.089048	.091921	.094816	.100668	.106584
	-.20	.070920	.073505	.076136	.078811	.081526	.084279	.087066	.089885	.092731	.095604	.098499	.104351	.110267
	-.30	.074603	.077188	.079819	.082494	.085209	.087962	.090749	.093567	.096414	.099287	.102182	.108034	.113950
	-.40	.078286	.080871	.083502	.086177	.088892	.091645	.094432	.097250	.100097	.102970	.105865	.111717	.117633

15.0 YEAR HOLDING PERIOD
.080 EQUITY YIELD RATE
.667 LOAN RATIO

INTEREST RATE

TERM YEARS	APPR DEP	5.0	5.5	6.0	6.5	7.0	7.5	8.0	8.5	9.0	9.5	10.0	11.0	12.0
10	.40	.054524	.055848	.057180	.058517	.059859	.061205	.062555	.063908	.065263	.066620	.067976	.070687	.073389
	.30	.058207	.059531	.060863	.062200	.063542	.064888	.066238	.067591	.068946	.070303	.071659	.074370	.077072
	.20	.061890	.063214	.064546	.065883	.067225	.068571	.069921	.071274	.072629	.073986	.075342	.078053	.080755
	.10	.065573	.066897	.068229	.069566	.070908	.072254	.073604	.074957	.076312	.077669	.079025	.081736	.084438
	0.00	.069256	.070580	.071911	.073248	.074591	.075937	.077287	.078640	.079995	.081352	.082708	.085419	.088121
	-.10	.072939	.074263	.075594	.076931	.078274	.079620	.080970	.082323	.083678	.085035	.086391	.089102	.091804
	-.20	.076622	.077946	.079277	.080614	.081956	.083303	.084653	.086006	.087361	.088717	.090074	.092785	.095487
	-.30	.080305	.081629	.082960	.084297	.085639	.086986	.088336	.089689	.091044	.092400	.093757	.096468	.099170
	-.40	.083987	.085312	.086643	.087980	.089322	.090669	.092019	.093372	.094727	.096083	.097440	.100151	.102853
15	.40	.050645	.052748	.054890	.057070	.059288	.061543	.063834	.066161	.068523	.070920	.073350	.078310	.083395
	.30	.054328	.056431	.058573	.060753	.062971	.065226	.067517	.069844	.072206	.074603	.077033	.081993	.087078
	.20	.058011	.060114	.062256	.064436	.066654	.068909	.071200	.073527	.075889	.078286	.080716	.085676	.090761
	.10	.061694	.063797	.065939	.068119	.070337	.072592	.074883	.077210	.079572	.081969	.084399	.089359	.094444
	0.00	.065377	.067480	.069622	.071802	.074020	.076275	.078566	.080893	.083255	.085652	.088082	.093041	.098127
	-.10	.069060	.071163	.073305	.075485	.077703	.079958	.082249	.084576	.086938	.089335	.091765	.096724	.101810
	-.20	.072743	.074846	.076988	.079168	.081386	.083641	.085932	.088259	.090621	.093018	.095448	.100407	.105493
	-.30	.076426	.078529	.080671	.082851	.085069	.087323	.089615	.091942	.094304	.096701	.099131	.104090	.109176
	-.40	.080109	.082212	.084354	.086534	.088752	.091006	.093298	.095625	.097987	.100383	.102814	.107773	.112859
20	.40	.048765	.051205	.053795	.056384	.059019	.061700	.064426	.067193	.070002	.072850	.075735	.081613	.087622
	.30	.052448	.054938	.057478	.060067	.062702	.065383	.068109	.070876	.073685	.076533	.079418	.085296	.091305
	.20	.056131	.058621	.061161	.063750	.066385	.069066	.071792	.074559	.077368	.080216	.083101	.088979	.094988
	.10	.059814	.062304	.064844	.067432	.070068	.072749	.075474	.078242	.081051	.083899	.086784	.092662	.098671
	0.00	.063497	.065987	.068527	.071115	.073751	.076432	.079157	.081925	.084734	.087582	.090467	.096345	.102354
	-.10	.067180	.069670	.072210	.074798	.077434	.080115	.082840	.085608	.088417	.091265	.094150	.100028	.106037
	-.20	.070862	.073353	.075893	.078481	.081117	.083798	.086523	.089291	.092100	.094948	.097833	.103711	.109720
	-.30	.074545	.077036	.079576	.082164	.084800	.087481	.090206	.092974	.095783	.098630	.101516	.107394	.113403
	-.40	.078228	.080719	.083259	.085847	.088483	.091164	.093889	.096657	.099466	.102313	.105199	.111077	.117086
25	.40	.047682	.050402	.053175	.055999	.058870	.061787	.064746	.067746	.070783	.073856	.076961	.083261	.089664
	.30	.051365	.054085	.056858	.059682	.062553	.065470	.068429	.071429	.074466	.077539	.080644	.086944	.093347
	.20	.055048	.057768	.060541	.063365	.066236	.069153	.072112	.075112	.078149	.081222	.084327	.090627	.097030
	.10	.058730	.061451	.064224	.067048	.069919	.072836	.075795	.078795	.081832	.084905	.088010	.094310	.100713
	0.00	.062413	.065134	.067907	.070730	.073602	.076519	.079478	.082478	.085515	.088588	.091693	.097993	.104396
	-.10	.066096	.068817	.071590	.074413	.077285	.080202	.083161	.086161	.089198	.092271	.095376	.101676	.108079
	-.20	.069779	.072500	.075273	.078096	.080968	.083885	.086844	.089844	.092881	.095954	.099059	.105359	.111762
	-.30	.073462	.076183	.078956	.081779	.084651	.087568	.090527	.093527	.096564	.099637	.102742	.109042	.115445
	-.40	.077145	.079866	.082639	.085462	.088334	.091250	.094210	.097210	.100247	.103320	.106425	.112724	.119128
30	.40	.046995	.049667	.052790	.055703	.058780	.061838	.064935	.068067	.071230	.074421	.077639	.084140	.090714
	.30	.050678	.053350	.056473	.059446	.062463	.065521	.068618	.071750	.074913	.078104	.081322	.087823	.094397
	.20	.054361	.057233	.060156	.063129	.066156	.069204	.072301	.075433	.078597	.081787	.085005	.091506	.098080
	.10	.058044	.060916	.063839	.066812	.069829	.072887	.075984	.079115	.082279	.085470	.088688	.095189	.101763
	0.00	.061727	.064599	.067522	.070494	.073512	.076570	.079667	.082798	.085962	.089153	.092371	.098872	.105446
	-.10	.065410	.068281	.071205	.074177	.077195	.080253	.083350	.086481	.089644	.092836	.096054	.102555	.109129
	-.20	.069093	.071964	.074888	.077860	.080878	.083936	.087033	.090164	.093327	.096519	.099736	.106238	.112812
	-.30	.072776	.075647	.078571	.081543	.084561	.087619	.090716	.093847	.097010	.100202	.103419	.109921	.116495
	-.40	.076459	.079330	.082254	.085226	.088243	.091302	.094399	.097530	.100693	.103885	.107102	.113604	.120078

15.0 YEAR HOLDING PERIOD
.080 EQUITY YIELD RATE
.700 LOAN RATIO

INTEREST RATE

TERM YEARS	APPR DEP	5.0	5.5	6.0	6.5	7.0	7.5	8.0	8.5	9.0	9.5	10.0	11.0	12.0
10	.40	.053907	.055378	.056775	.058179	.059588	.061002	.062420	.063840	.065263	.066687	.068112	.070958	.073795
	.30	.057670	.059060	.060458	.061862	.063271	.064685	.066103	.067523	.068946	.070370	.071795	.074641	.077478
	.20	.061353	.062743	.064141	.065545	.066968	.068368	.069786	.071206	.072629	.074053	.075478	.078324	.081161
	.10	.065036	.066426	.067824	.069228	.070637	.072051	.073469	.074889	.076312	.077736	.079161	.082007	.084844
	0.00	.068718	.070109	.071507	.072911	.074320	.075734	.077152	.078572	.079995	.081419	.082844	.085690	.088527
	-.10	.072441	.073792	.075190	.076594	.078003	.079417	.080835	.082255	.083678	.085102	.086527	.089373	.092210
	-.20	.076084	.077475	.078873	.080277	.081686	.083100	.084518	.085938	.087361	.088785	.090210	.093056	.095893
	-.30	.079767	.081158	.082556	.083960	.085369	.086783	.088200	.089621	.091044	.092468	.093892	.096739	.099576
	-.40	.083450	.084841	.086239	.087643	.089052	.090466	.091883	.093304	.094727	.096151	.097575	.100422	.103259
15	.40	.049914	.052123	.054371	.056661	.058989	.061357	.063762	.066206	.068686	.071202	.073754	.078962	.084302
	.30	.053597	.055805	.058054	.060343	.062672	.065039	.067445	.069889	.072369	.074885	.077437	.082645	.087985
	.20	.057280	.059488	.061737	.064026	.066355	.068722	.071128	.073572	.076052	.078568	.081120	.086328	.091668
	.10	.060963	.063171	.065420	.067709	.070038	.072405	.074811	.077254	.079735	.082251	.084803	.090011	.095350
	0.00	.064646	.066854	.069103	.071392	.073721	.076088	.078494	.080937	.083418	.085934	.088486	.093693	.099033
	-.10	.068329	.070537	.072786	.075075	.077404	.079771	.082177	.084620	.087101	.089617	.092169	.097376	.102716
	-.20	.072012	.074220	.076469	.078758	.081087	.083454	.085860	.088303	.090784	.093300	.095852	.101059	.106399
	-.30	.075695	.077903	.080152	.082441	.084770	.087137	.089543	.091986	.094467	.096983	.099535	.104742	.110082
	-.40	.079378	.081586	.083835	.086124	.088453	.090820	.093226	.095669	.098150	.100666	.103218	.108425	.113765
20	.40	.047940	.050554	.053221	.055939	.058707	.061522	.064383	.067290	.070239	.073229	.076259	.082430	.088740
	.30	.051623	.054237	.056904	.059622	.062390	.065205	.068066	.070973	.073922	.076912	.079942	.086113	.092423
	.20	.055306	.057920	.060587	.063305	.066073	.068888	.071749	.074655	.077604	.080595	.083625	.089796	.096106
	.10	.058989	.061603	.064270	.066988	.069756	.072571	.075432	.078338	.081287	.084278	.087308	.093479	.099789
	0.00	.062671	.065286	.067953	.070671	.073439	.076254	.079115	.082021	.084970	.087961	.090990	.097162	.103472
	-.10	.066354	.068969	.071636	.074354	.077122	.079937	.082798	.085704	.088653	.091644	.094673	.100845	.107155
	-.20	.070037	.072652	.075319	.078037	.080805	.083620	.086481	.089387	.092336	.095327	.098356	.104528	.110838
	-.30	.073720	.076335	.079002	.081720	.084487	.087303	.090164	.093070	.096019	.099010	.102039	.108211	.114521
	-.40	.077403	.080018	.082685	.085403	.088170	.090986	.093847	.096753	.099702	.102692	.105722	.111894	.118204
25	.40	.046002	.049659	.052270	.055535	.058550	.061613	.064720	.067870	.071059	.074285	.077546	.084160	.090884
	.30	.050465	.053342	.056233	.059218	.062233	.065296	.068403	.071553	.074742	.077968	.081229	.087843	.094567
	.20	.054168	.057025	.059936	.062901	.065916	.068979	.072086	.075236	.078425	.081651	.084912	.091526	.098250
	.10	.057851	.060708	.063619	.066584	.069599	.072662	.075769	.078919	.082108	.085334	.088595	.095209	.101933
	0.00	.061534	.064390	.067302	.070267	.073282	.076345	.079452	.082602	.085791	.089017	.092278	.098892	.105616
	-.10	.065217	.068073	.070985	.073950	.076965	.080028	.083135	.086285	.089474	.092700	.095961	.102575	.109299
	-.20	.068900	.071756	.074668	.077633	.080648	.083711	.086818	.089968	.093157	.096383	.099644	.106258	.112982
	-.30	.072583	.075439	.078351	.081316	.084331	.087393	.090501	.093651	.096840	.100066	.103327	.109941	.116665
	-.40	.076266	.079122	.082034	.084999	.088014	.091076	.094184	.097334	.100523	.103749	.107009	.113624	.120348
30	.40	.046081	.049097	.052167	.055287	.058455	.061667	.064919	.068207	.071528	.074879	.078257	.085084	.091986
	.30	.049764	.052780	.055850	.058970	.062138	.065350	.068601	.071889	.075211	.078562	.081940	.088767	.095669
	.20	.053447	.056463	.059533	.062653	.065821	.069033	.072284	.075572	.078894	.082245	.085623	.092450	.099352
	.10	.057130	.060146	.063216	.066336	.069504	.072716	.075967	.079255	.082577	.085928	.089306	.096133	.103035
	0.00	.060813	.063829	.066898	.070019	.073187	.076399	.079650	.082938	.086260	.089611	.092989	.099816	.106718
	-.10	.064496	.067511	.070581	.073702	.076870	.080082	.083333	.086621	.089943	.093294	.096672	.103498	.110401
	-.20	.068179	.071194	.074264	.077385	.080553	.083765	.087016	.090304	.093625	.096977	.100355	.107182	.114084
	-.30	.071862	.074877	.077947	.081068	.084236	.087448	.090699	.093987	.097308	.100660	.104038	.110865	.117767
	-.40	.075545	.078560	.081630	.084751	.087919	.091131	.094382	.097670	.100991	.104343	.107721	.114547	.121450

15.0 YEAR HOLDING PERIOD
.080 EQUITY YIELD RATE
.750 LOAN RATIO

INTEREST RATE

TERM YEARS	APPR DEP	5.0	5.5	6.0	6.5	7.0	7.5	8.0	8.5	9.0	9.5	10.0	11.0	12.0
10	.40	.053181	.054671	.056169	.057673	.059183	.060697	.062216	.063738	.065263	.066789	.068315	.071365	.074404
	.30	.056864	.058354	.059852	.061356	.062866	.064380	.065899	.067421	.068946	.070472	.071998	.075048	.078087
	.20	.060547	.062037	.063535	.065039	.066549	.068063	.069582	.071104	.072629	.074155	.075681	.078731	.081770
	.10	.064230	.065720	.067217	.068722	.070231	.071746	.073265	.074787	.076312	.077838	.079364	.082414	.085453
	0.00	.067913	.069403	.070900	.072405	.073914	.075429	.076948	.078470	.079995	.081520	.083047	.086097	.089136
	-.10	.071596	.073086	.074583	.076088	.077597	.079112	.080631	.082153	.083678	.085203	.086730	.089780	.092819
	-.20	.075279	.076769	.078266	.079770	.081280	.082795	.084314	.085836	.087361	.088886	.090413	.093463	.096502
	-.30	.078962	.080452	.081949	.083453	.084963	.086478	.087997	.089519	.091044	.092569	.094096	.097145	.100185
	-.40	.082644	.084135	.085632	.087136	.088646	.090161	.091680	.093202	.094727	.096252	.097779	.100828	.103868
15	.40	.048817	.051184	.053593	.056046	.058541	.061077	.063655	.066273	.068930	.071626	.074360	.079940	.085661
	.30	.052500	.054866	.057276	.059729	.062224	.064760	.067338	.069956	.072613	.075309	.078043	.083623	.089344
	.20	.056183	.058549	.060959	.063412	.065906	.068443	.071021	.073638	.076296	.078992	.081726	.087306	.093027
	.10	.059866	.062232	.064642	.067095	.069589	.072126	.074704	.077321	.079979	.082675	.085409	.090989	.096710
	0.00	.063549	.065915	.068325	.070778	.073272	.075809	.078387	.081004	.083662	.086358	.089092	.094672	.100393
	-.10	.067232	.069598	.072008	.074460	.076955	.079492	.082069	.084687	.087345	.090041	.092775	.098355	.104076
	-.20	.070915	.073281	.075691	.078143	.080638	.083175	.085752	.088370	.091028	.093724	.096458	.102037	.107759
	-.30	.074598	.076964	.079374	.081826	.084321	.086858	.089435	.092053	.094711	.097407	.100141	.105720	.111442
	-.40	.078281	.080647	.083057	.085509	.088004	.090541	.093118	.095736	.098394	.101090	.103824	.109403	.115125
20	.40	.046702	.049503	.052362	.055273	.058238	.061254	.064320	.067434	.070594	.073797	.077044	.083656	.090417
	.30	.050385	.053186	.056045	.058956	.061921	.064937	.068003	.071117	.074277	.077480	.080727	.087339	.094100
	.20	.054068	.056869	.059728	.062639	.065604	.068620	.071686	.074800	.077960	.081163	.084410	.091022	.097782
	.10	.057751	.060552	.063411	.066322	.069287	.072303	.075369	.078483	.081643	.084846	.088093	.094705	.101465
	0.00	.061434	.064235	.067094	.070005	.072970	.075986	.079052	.082166	.085326	.088529	.091776	.098388	.105148
	-.10	.065117	.067918	.070777	.073688	.076653	.079669	.082735	.085849	.089008	.092212	.095458	.102071	.108831
	-.20	.068800	.071601	.074460	.077371	.080336	.083352	.086418	.089532	.092691	.095895	.099141	.105754	.112514
	-.30	.072484	.075284	.078143	.081054	.084019	.087035	.090101	.093215	.096374	.099578	.102824	.109437	.116197
	-.40	.076166	.078967	.081825	.084737	.087702	.090718	.093784	.096898	.100057	.103261	.106507	.113120	.119880
25	.40	.045483	.048544	.051664	.054840	.058070	.061352	.064681	.068056	.071473	.074929	.078423	.085510	.092714
	.30	.049166	.052227	.055347	.058523	.061753	.065035	.068364	.071739	.075156	.078612	.082106	.089193	.096397
	.20	.052849	.055910	.059029	.062206	.065435	.068718	.072047	.075422	.078839	.082295	.085789	.092876	.100080
	.10	.056532	.059593	.062713	.065889	.069119	.072401	.075730	.079105	.082522	.085978	.089472	.096559	.103763
	0.00	.060215	.063276	.066396	.069572	.072802	.076084	.079413	.082788	.086205	.089661	.093155	.100242	.107446
	-.10	.063898	.066958	.070079	.073255	.076485	.079766	.083096	.086470	.089888	.093344	.096838	.103925	.111128
	-.20	.067581	.070641	.073762	.076938	.080168	.083449	.086779	.090153	.093571	.097027	.100521	.107608	.114811
	-.30	.071264	.074324	.077444	.080621	.083851	.087132	.090462	.093836	.097253	.100710	.104203	.111290	.118494
	-.40	.074947	.078007	.081127	.084304	.087534	.090815	.094145	.097519	.100936	.104393	.107886	.114973	.122177
30	.40	.044711	.047942	.051231	.054575	.057959	.061410	.064894	.068416	.071975	.075565	.079185	.086499	.093895
	.30	.048394	.051625	.054914	.058258	.061642	.065093	.068577	.072099	.075658	.079248	.082868	.090182	.097578
	.20	.052077	.055308	.058597	.061940	.065325	.068776	.072259	.075782	.079341	.082931	.086551	.093865	.101261
	.10	.055760	.058991	.062280	.065623	.069008	.072459	.075942	.079465	.083024	.086614	.090234	.097548	.104944
	0.00	.059443	.062673	.065963	.069306	.072691	.076142	.079626	.083148	.086707	.090297	.093917	.101231	.108627
	-.10	.063126	.066356	.069646	.072989	.076374	.079825	.083308	.086831	.090390	.093980	.097600	.104914	.112310
	-.20	.066809	.070039	.073329	.076672	.080057	.083508	.086991	.090514	.094073	.097663	.101283	.108597	.115993
	-.30	.070492	.073722	.077011	.080355	.083740	.087190	.090674	.094197	.097756	.101346	.104966	.112280	.119676
	-.40	.074175	.077405	.080694	.084038	.087432	.090873	.094357	.097879	.101438	.105029	.108649	.115963	.123359

15.0 YEAR HOLDING PERIOD
.080 EQUITY YIELD RATE
.800 LOAN RATIO

INTEREST RATE

TERM YEARS	APPR DEP	5.0	5.5	6.0	6.5	7.0	7.5	8.0	8.5	9.0	9.5	10.0	11.0	12.0
10	.40	.052375	.053965	.055562	.057166	.058777	.060393	.062013	.063636	.065263	.066890	.068518	.071771	.075013
	.30	.056058	.057648	.059245	.060849	.062460	.064076	.065696	.067319	.068945	.070573	.072201	.075454	.078696
	.20	.059741	.061330	.062928	.064532	.066143	.067759	.069379	.071002	.072628	.074256	.075884	.079137	.082379
	.10	.063424	.065013	.066611	.068215	.069826	.071442	.073062	.074685	.076311	.077939	.079567	.082820	.086062
	0.00	.067107	.068696	.070294	.071898	.073509	.075125	.076745	.078368	.079994	.081622	.083250	.086503	.089745
	-.10	.070790	.072379	.073977	.075581	.077192	.078807	.080428	.082051	.083677	.085305	.086933	.090186	.093428
	-.20	.074473	.076062	.077660	.079264	.080875	.082490	.084111	.085734	.087360	.088988	.090616	.093869	.097111
	-.30	.078156	.079745	.081343	.082947	.084558	.086173	.087794	.089417	.091043	.092671	.094299	.097552	.100794
	-.40	.081839	.083428	.085026	.086630	.088241	.089856	.091477	.093100	.094726	.096354	.097982	.101235	.104477
15	.40	.047721	.050245	.052815	.055431	.058092	.060798	.063547	.066340	.069174	.072050	.074967	.080918	.087021
	.30	.051404	.053928	.056498	.059114	.061775	.064481	.067230	.070022	.072857	.075733	.078650	.084601	.090704
	.20	.055087	.057610	.060181	.062797	.065458	.068164	.070913	.073705	.076540	.079416	.082333	.088284	.094387
	.10	.058770	.061293	.063864	.066480	.069141	.071847	.074596	.077388	.080223	.083099	.086016	.091967	.098070
	0.00	.062453	.064976	.067547	.070163	.072824	.075530	.078279	.081071	.083906	.086782	.089698	.095650	.101752
	-.10	.066136	.068659	.071230	.073846	.076507	.079213	.081962	.084754	.087589	.090465	.093381	.099333	.105435
	-.20	.069818	.072342	.074913	.077529	.080190	.082895	.085645	.088437	.091272	.094148	.097064	.103016	.109118
	-.30	.073501	.076025	.078595	.081212	.083873	.086578	.089328	.092120	.094955	.097831	.100747	.106699	.112801
	-.40	.077184	.079708	.082278	.084894	.087556	.090261	.093011	.095803	.098638	.101514	.104430	.110381	.116484
20	.40	.045464	.048452	.051501	.054607	.057769	.060987	.064257	.067578	.070949	.074366	.077829	.084882	.092093
	.30	.049147	.052135	.055183	.058290	.061452	.064670	.067940	.071261	.074632	.078049	.081512	.088565	.095776
	.20	.052830	.055818	.058866	.061973	.065135	.068353	.071623	.074944	.078315	.081732	.085195	.092248	.099459
	.10	.056513	.059501	.062549	.065656	.068818	.072036	.075306	.078627	.081997	.085415	.088878	.095931	.103142
	0.00	.060196	.063184	.066232	.069339	.072501	.075719	.078989	.082310	.085680	.089098	.092561	.099614	.106825
	-.10	.063879	.066867	.069915	.073022	.076184	.079402	.082672	.085993	.089363	.092781	.096244	.103297	.110508
	-.20	.067562	.070550	.073598	.076704	.079867	.083085	.086355	.089676	.093046	.096464	.099926	.106980	.114191
	-.30	.071245	.074233	.077281	.080387	.083550	.086768	.090038	.093359	.096729	.100147	.103609	.110663	.117874
	-.40	.074928	.077916	.080964	.084070	.087233	.090451	.093721	.097042	.100412	.103830	.107292	.114346	.121557
25	.40	.044164	.047429	.050757	.054145	.057591	.061091	.064642	.068242	.071886	.075573	.079300	.086859	.094543
	.30	.047847	.051112	.054439	.057828	.061274	.064774	.068325	.071925	.075569	.079256	.082983	.090542	.098226
	.20	.051530	.054795	.058122	.061511	.064956	.068457	.072008	.075607	.079252	.082939	.086666	.094225	.101909
	.10	.055213	.058478	.061805	.065194	.068639	.072139	.075691	.079290	.082935	.086622	.090349	.097908	.105592
	0.00	.058896	.062161	.065488	.068877	.072322	.075822	.079374	.082973	.086618	.090305	.094032	.101591	.109275
	-.10	.062579	.065843	.069171	.072560	.076005	.079505	.083057	.086656	.090301	.093988	.097715	.105274	.112958
	-.20	.066262	.069526	.072854	.076243	.079688	.083188	.086740	.090339	.093984	.097671	.101397	.108957	.116641
	-.30	.069945	.073209	.076537	.079926	.083371	.086871	.090423	.094022	.097667	.101354	.105080	.112640	.120324
	-.40	.073628	.076892	.080220	.083608	.087054	.090554	.094106	.097705	.101350	.105037	.108763	.116323	.124007
30	.40	.043340	.046786	.050295	.053862	.057482	.061153	.064869	.068626	.072422	.076252	.080113	.087914	.095803
	.30	.047023	.050469	.053978	.057545	.061165	.064836	.068552	.072309	.076105	.079935	.083796	.091597	.099486
	.20	.050706	.054152	.057661	.061228	.064848	.068518	.072234	.075992	.079788	.083618	.087479	.095280	.103169
	.10	.054389	.057835	.061344	.064911	.068531	.072201	.075917	.079675	.083471	.087301	.091162	.098963	.106852
	0.00	.058072	.061518	.065027	.068593	.072214	.075884	.079600	.083358	.087154	.090984	.094845	.102646	.110535
	-.10	.061755	.065201	.068710	.072276	.075897	.079567	.083283	.087041	.090837	.094667	.098528	.106329	.114218
	-.20	.065438	.068884	.072393	.075959	.079580	.083250	.086966	.090724	.094520	.098350	.102211	.110012	.117901
	-.30	.069121	.072567	.076076	.079642	.083263	.086933	.090649	.094407	.098203	.102033	.105893	.113695	.121584
	-.40	.072804	.076250	.079759	.083325	.086946	.090616	.094332	.098090	.101886	.105716	.109576	.117378	.125267

15.0 YEAR HOLDING PERIOD
.080 EQUITY YIELD RATE
.900 LOAN RATIO

INTEREST RATE

TERM YEARS	APPR DEP	5.0	5.5	6.0	6.5	7.0	7.5	8.0	8.5	9.0	9.5	10.0	11.0	12.0
10	.40	.050763	.052552	.054349	.056154	.057966	.059783	.061606	.063433	.065262	.067093	.068924	.072584	.076232
	.30	.054446	.056235	.058032	.059837	.061648	.063466	.065289	.067115	.068945	.070776	.072607	.076267	.079915
	.20	.058129	.059918	.061715	.063520	.065331	.067149	.068972	.070798	.072628	.074459	.076290	.079950	.083598
	.10	.061812	.063601	.065398	.067203	.069014	.070832	.072655	.074481	.076311	.078142	.079973	.083633	.087280
	0.00	.065495	.067283	.069081	.070885	.072697	.074515	.076338	.078164	.079994	.081825	.083656	.087316	.090963
	-.10	.069178	.070966	.072763	.074568	.076380	.078198	.080021	.081847	.083677	.085508	.087339	.090999	.094646
	-.20	.072861	.074649	.076446	.078251	.080063	.081881	.083704	.085530	.087360	.089191	.091022	.094682	.098329
	-.30	.076544	.078332	.080129	.081934	.083746	.085564	.087387	.089213	.091042	.092873	.094705	.098365	.102012
	-.40	.080227	.082015	.083812	.085617	.087429	.089247	.091070	.092896	.094725	.096556	.098388	.102048	.105695
15	.40	.045527	.048367	.051258	.054201	.057195	.060239	.063332	.066473	.069662	.072898	.076179	.082874	.089740
	.30	.049210	.052050	.054941	.057884	.060878	.063922	.067015	.070156	.073345	.076581	.079862	.086557	.093423
	.20	.052893	.055733	.058624	.061567	.064561	.067605	.070698	.073839	.077028	.080264	.083545	.090240	.097106
	.10	.056576	.059415	.062307	.065250	.068244	.071288	.074381	.077522	.080711	.083947	.087228	.093923	.100789
	0.00	.060259	.063098	.065990	.068933	.071927	.074971	.078064	.081205	.084394	.087630	.090911	.097606	.104472
	-.10	.063942	.066781	.069673	.072616	.075610	.078654	.081747	.084888	.088077	.091313	.094594	.101289	.108155
	-.20	.067625	.070464	.073356	.076299	.079293	.082337	.085430	.088571	.091760	.094996	.098277	.104972	.111837
	-.30	.071308	.074147	.077039	.079982	.082976	.086020	.089113	.092254	.095443	.098679	.101960	.108655	.115520
	-.40	.074991	.077830	.080722	.083665	.086659	.089703	.092796	.095937	.099126	.102361	.105643	.112338	.119203
20	.40	.042989	.046350	.049780	.053274	.056832	.060452	.064131	.067867	.071659	.075503	.079399	.087334	.095446
	.30	.046672	.050033	.053462	.056957	.060515	.064135	.067814	.071550	.075342	.079186	.083082	.091017	.099129
	.20	.050355	.053716	.057145	.060640	.064198	.067818	.071497	.075233	.079025	.082869	.086765	.094700	.102812
	.10	.054038	.057399	.060828	.064323	.067881	.071501	.075180	.078916	.082708	.086552	.090448	.098383	.106489
	0.00	.057720	.061082	.064511	.068006	.071564	.075184	.078863	.082599	.086390	.090235	.094131	.102066	.110178
	-.10	.061403	.064765	.068194	.071689	.075247	.078866	.082545	.086282	.090073	.093918	.097814	.105749	.113861
	-.20	.065086	.068448	.071877	.075372	.078930	.082549	.086228	.089965	.093756	.097601	.101497	.109432	.117544
	-.30	.068769	.072131	.075560	.079055	.082613	.086232	.089911	.093648	.097439	.101284	.105179	.113114	.121227
	-.40	.072452	.075814	.079243	.082738	.086296	.089915	.093594	.097331	.101122	.104967	.108862	.116797	.124910
25	.40	.041526	.045199	.048943	.052754	.056631	.060568	.064564	.068613	.072714	.076862	.081054	.089558	.098203
	.30	.045209	.048882	.052626	.056437	.060314	.064251	.068247	.072296	.076397	.080544	.084737	.093241	.101886
	.20	.048892	.052565	.056308	.060120	.063997	.067934	.071930	.075979	.080080	.084227	.088420	.096924	.105569
	.10	.052575	.056248	.059991	.063803	.067680	.071617	.075613	.079662	.083762	.087910	.092103	.100607	.109252
	0.00	.056258	.059931	.063674	.067486	.071363	.075300	.079296	.083345	.087445	.091593	.095785	.104290	.112935
	-.10	.059941	.063614	.067357	.071169	.075046	.078983	.082978	.087028	.091128	.095276	.099468	.107973	.116618
	-.20	.063624	.067297	.071040	.074852	.078729	.082666	.086661	.090711	.094811	.098959	.103151	.111656	.120301
	-.30	.067307	.070979	.074723	.078535	.082412	.086349	.090344	.094394	.098494	.102642	.106834	.115339	.123983
	-.40	.070990	.074662	.078406	.082218	.086094	.090032	.094027	.098077	.102177	.106325	.110517	.119022	.127666
30	.40	.040600	.044476	.048423	.052436	.056509	.060638	.064819	.069046	.073316	.077625	.081968	.090745	.099620
	.30	.044282	.048159	.052106	.056119	.060192	.064321	.068502	.072729	.076999	.081308	.085651	.094428	.103303
	.20	.047965	.051842	.055789	.059802	.063875	.068004	.072185	.076412	.080682	.084991	.089334	.098111	.106986
	.10	.051648	.055525	.059472	.063485	.067558	.071687	.075867	.080095	.084365	.088674	.093017	.101794	.110669
	0.00	.055331	.059208	.063155	.067168	.071241	.075370	.079550	.083778	.088048	.092357	.096700	.105477	.114352
	-.10	.059014	.062891	.066838	.070851	.074924	.079053	.083233	.087461	.091731	.096040	.100383	.109160	.118035
	-.20	.062697	.066574	.070521	.074534	.078607	.082736	.086916	.091144	.095414	.099723	.104066	.112843	.121718
	-.30	.066380	.070257	.074204	.078217	.082290	.086419	.090599	.094827	.099097	.103406	.107749	.116526	.125401
	-.40	.070063	.073940	.077887	.081899	.085973	.090102	.094282	.098510	.102780	.107089	.111432	.120209	.129084

15.0 YEAR HOLDING PERIOD
.100 EQUITY YIELD RATE
.600 LOAN RATIO

INTEREST RATE

TERM YEARS	APPR DEP	5.0	5.5	6.0	6.5	7.0	7.5	8.0	8.5	9.0	9.5	10.0	11.0	12.0
10	.40	.071272	.072548	.073833	.075126	.076427	.077734	.079047	.080366	.081690	.083018	.084350	.087021	.089698
	.30	.074419	.075691	.076981	.078274	.079574	.080881	.082195	.083514	.084837	.086165	.087497	.090169	.092846
	.20	.077567	.078843	.080128	.081421	.082721	.084029	.085342	.086661	.087985	.089313	.090645	.093316	.095993
	.10	.080714	.081991	.083276	.084568	.085869	.087176	.088489	.089808	.091132	.092460	.093792	.096463	.099140
	0.00	.083861	.085138	.086423	.087716	.089016	.090323	.091637	.092956	.094279	.095508	.096939	.099611	.102288
	-.10	.087009	.088285	.089570	.090863	.092164	.093471	.094784	.096103	.097427	.098755	.100087	.102758	.105435
	-.20	.090156	.091433	.092718	.094011	.095311	.096618	.097931	.099250	.100574	.101902	.103234	.105905	.108582
	-.30	.093304	.094580	.095865	.097158	.098458	.099765	.101079	.102398	.103722	.105050	.106381	.109053	.111730
	-.40	.096451	.097727	.099012	.100305	.101606	.102913	.104226	.105545	.106869	.108197	.109529	.112200	.114877
15	.40	.065463	.067356	.069284	.071246	.073264	.075271	.077333	.079427	.081553	.083710	.085898	.090361	.094938
	.30	.068611	.070504	.072431	.074393	.076389	.078418	.080481	.082575	.084701	.086858	.089045	.093509	.098086
	.20	.071758	.073651	.075579	.077541	.079537	.081566	.083628	.085722	.087848	.090005	.092193	.096656	.101233
	.10	.074905	.076798	.078726	.080688	.082684	.084713	.086775	.088870	.089996	.093153	.095340	.099803	.104380
	0.00	.078053	.079940	.081873	.083835	.085831	.087861	.089923	.092017	.094143	.096300	.098487	.102951	.107528
	-.10	.081200	.083093	.085021	.086983	.088979	.091008	.093070	.095164	.097290	.099447	.101635	.106098	.110675
	-.20	.084348	.086240	.088168	.090130	.092126	.094155	.096217	.098312	.100438	.102595	.104782	.109245	.113823
	-.30	.087495	.089388	.091316	.093278	.095274	.097303	.099365	.101459	.103585	.105742	.107929	.112393	.116970
	-.40	.090642	.092535	.094463	.096425	.098421	.100450	.102512	.104606	.106732	.108889	.111077	.115540	.120117
20	.40	.062647	.064855	.067107	.069403	.071742	.074121	.076540	.078997	.081491	.084021	.086585	.091809	.097152
	.30	.065795	.068002	.070255	.072551	.074889	.077268	.079687	.082145	.084639	.087169	.089732	.094956	.100299
	.20	.068942	.071150	.073402	.075698	.078036	.080416	.082835	.085292	.087786	.090316	.092880	.098104	.103447
	.10	.072089	.074297	.076549	.078846	.081184	.083563	.085982	.088439	.090934	.093463	.096027	.101251	.106594
	0.00	.075237	.077444	.079697	.081993	.084331	.086711	.089130	.091587	.094081	.096611	.099174	.104398	.109742
	-.10	.078384	.080592	.082844	.085140	.087479	.089858	.092277	.094734	.097228	.099758	.102322	.107546	.112889
	-.20	.081531	.083739	.085992	.088288	.090626	.093005	.095424	.097882	.100376	.102905	.105469	.110693	.116036
	-.30	.084679	.086887	.089139	.091435	.093773	.096153	.098572	.101029	.103523	.106053	.108616	.113840	.119184
	-.40	.087826	.090034	.092286	.094582	.096921	.099300	.101719	.104176	.106670	.109200	.111764	.116988	.122331
25	.40	.061025	.063426	.065875	.068371	.070910	.073490	.076110	.078767	.081459	.084183	.086938	.092531	.098221
	.30	.064172	.066573	.069023	.071518	.074057	.076638	.079257	.081914	.084606	.087330	.090085	.095678	.101369
	.20	.067320	.069721	.072170	.074665	.077204	.079785	.082405	.085062	.087753	.090478	.093233	.098826	.104516
	.10	.070467	.072868	.075317	.077813	.080352	.082932	.085552	.088209	.090901	.093625	.096380	.101973	.107663
	0.00	.073614	.076015	.078465	.080960	.083499	.086080	.088700	.091357	.094048	.096773	.099527	.105120	.110811
	-.10	.076762	.079163	.081612	.084107	.086647	.089227	.091847	.094504	.097196	.099920	.102675	.108268	.113958
	-.20	.079909	.082310	.084760	.087255	.089794	.092374	.094994	.097651	.100343	.103067	.105822	.111415	.117106
	-.30	.083057	.085458	.087907	.090402	.092941	.095522	.098142	.100799	.103490	.106215	.108970	.114562	.120253
	-.40	.086204	.088605	.091054	.093550	.096089	.098669	.101289	.103946	.106638	.109362	.112117	.117710	.123400
30	.40	.059997	.062530	.065111	.067737	.070406	.073113	.075857	.078633	.081440	.084274	.087133	.092916	.098771
	.30	.063144	.065677	.068258	.070885	.073553	.076261	.079004	.081781	.084587	.087422	.090281	.096063	.101919
	.20	.066292	.068824	.071406	.074032	.076701	.079408	.082152	.084928	.087735	.090569	.093428	.099211	.105066
	.10	.069439	.071972	.074553	.077180	.079848	.082556	.085299	.088076	.090882	.093716	.096575	.102358	.108213
	0.00	.072586	.075119	.077700	.080327	.082995	.085703	.088446	.091223	.094030	.096364	.099723	.105506	.111361
	-.10	.075734	.078267	.080848	.083474	.086143	.088850	.091594	.094370	.097177	.100011	.102870	.108653	.114508
	-.20	.078881	.081414	.083995	.086622	.089290	.091998	.094741	.097518	.100324	.103158	.106017	.111800	.117655
	-.30	.082028	.084561	.087143	.089769	.092438	.095145	.097889	.100665	.103472	.106306	.109165	.114948	.120803
	-.40	.085176	.087709	.090290	.092916	.095585	.098292	.101036	.103812	.106619	.109453	.112312	.118095	.123950

15.0 YEAR HOLDING PERIOD
.100 EQUITY YIELD RATE
.667 LOAN RATIO

INTEREST RATE

TERM YEARS	APPR DEP	5.0	5.5	6.0	6.5	7.0	7.5	8.0	8.5	9.0	9.5	10.0	11.0	12.0
10	.40	.069479	.070897	.072325	.073761	.075206	.076659	.078118	.079583	.081054	.082530	.084010	.086978	.089952
	.30	.072626	.074044	.075472	.076909	.078354	.079806	.081265	.082731	.084202	.085677	.087157	.090125	.093100
	.20	.075773	.077192	.078620	.080056	.081501	.082953	.084413	.085878	.087349	.088825	.090304	.093273	.096247
	.10	.078921	.080339	.081767	.083204	.084648	.086101	.087560	.089026	.090496	.091972	.093452	.096420	.099395
	0.00	.082068	.083487	.084914	.086351	.087796	.089248	.090707	.092173	.093644	.095120	.096599	.099567	.102542
	-.10	.085216	.086634	.088062	.089498	.090943	.092396	.093855	.095320	.096791	.098267	.099747	.102715	.105689
	-.20	.088363	.089781	.091209	.092646	.094090	.095543	.097002	.098468	.099939	.101414	.102894	.105862	.108837
	-.30	.091510	.092929	.094356	.095793	.097238	.098690	.100150	.101615	.103086	.104562	.106041	.109010	.111384
	-.40	.094658	.096076	.097504	.098940	.100385	.101838	.103297	.104762	.106233	.107709	.109189	.112217	.115131
15	.40	.063025	.065128	.067270	.069450	.071667	.073922	.076213	.078540	.080903	.083299	.085730	.090689	.095775
	.30	.066172	.068275	.070417	.072597	.074815	.077070	.079361	.081688	.084050	.086447	.088877	.093836	.098322
	.20	.069319	.071423	.073565	.075745	.077962	.080217	.082508	.084835	.087197	.089594	.092024	.096984	.102070
	.10	.072467	.074570	.076712	.078892	.081110	.083364	.085656	.087983	.090345	.092741	.095172	.100131	.105217
	0.00	.075614	.077717	.079859	.082039	.084257	.086512	.088803	.091130	.093492	.095889	.098319	.103279	.108364
	-.10	.078762	.080865	.083006	.085187	.087404	.089659	.091950	.094277	.096639	.099036	.101467	.106426	.111512
	-.20	.081909	.084012	.086154	.088334	.090552	.092806	.095098	.097425	.099787	.102184	.104614	.109573	.114659
	-.30	.085056	.087160	.089301	.091481	.093699	.095954	.098245	.100572	.102934	.105331	.107761	.112721	.117806
	-.40	.088204	.090307	.092449	.094629	.096847	.099101	.101392	.103719	.106082	.108478	.110909	.115868	.120954
20	.40	.059896	.062349	.064851	.067402	.070001	.072644	.075332	.078062	.080834	.083645	.086493	.092238	.098234
	.30	.063043	.065496	.067999	.070547	.073148	.075792	.078480	.081210	.083981	.086972	.089640	.095544	.101382
	.20	.066190	.068643	.071146	.073697	.076295	.078939	.081627	.084357	.087129	.089939	.092788	.098592	.104529
	.10	.069338	.071791	.074293	.076845	.079443	.082087	.084774	.087505	.090276	.093087	.095935	.101740	.107677
	0.00	.072485	.074938	.077441	.079992	.082590	.085234	.087922	.090652	.093423	.096234	.099083	.104887	.110824
	-.10	.075632	.078085	.080588	.083139	.085738	.088381	.091069	.093799	.096571	.099381	.102230	.108034	.113971
	-.20	.078780	.081233	.083736	.086287	.088885	.091529	.094216	.096947	.099718	.102529	.105377	.111182	.117119
	-.30	.081927	.084380	.086883	.089434	.092032	.094676	.097364	.100094	.102865	.105676	.108525	.114329	.120266
	-.40	.085075	.087528	.090030	.092582	.095180	.097823	.100511	.103241	.106013	.108824	.111672	.117477	.123413
25	.40	.058093	.060761	.063482	.066255	.069076	.071943	.074854	.077807	.080797	.083824	.086885	.093100	.099423
	.30	.061240	.063908	.066630	.069402	.072223	.075091	.078002	.080954	.083945	.086972	.090033	.096247	.102570
	.20	.064388	.067056	.069777	.072550	.075371	.078238	.081149	.084101	.087092	.090119	.093180	.099395	.105717
	.10	.067535	.070203	.072925	.075697	.078518	.081386	.084297	.087249	.090240	.093267	.096328	.102542	.108865
	0.00	.070683	.073350	.076072	.078844	.081666	.084533	.087444	.090396	.093387	.096414	.099475	.105689	.112012
	-.10	.073830	.076498	.079219	.081992	.084813	.087680	.090591	.093543	.096534	.099561	.102622	.108837	.115160
	-.20	.076977	.079645	.082367	.085139	.087960	.090828	.093739	.096691	.099682	.102709	.105770	.111984	.118307
	-.30	.080125	.082793	.085514	.088287	.091108	.093975	.096886	.099838	.102829	.105856	.108917	.115131	.121454
	-.40	.083272	.085940	.088661	.091434	.094255	.097122	.100033	.102986	.105976	.109004	.112064	.118279	.124602
30	.40	.056951	.059765	.062633	.065551	.068516	.071525	.074573	.077658	.080777	.083926	.087102	.093528	.100034
	.30	.060098	.062912	.065780	.068699	.071664	.074672	.077720	.080805	.083924	.087073	.090250	.096675	.103181
	.20	.063245	.066060	.068928	.071846	.074811	.077820	.080868	.083953	.087071	.090220	.093397	.099823	.106328
	.10	.066393	.069207	.072075	.074994	.077959	.080967	.084015	.087100	.090219	.093368	.096544	.102970	.109476
	0.00	.069540	.072354	.075223	.078141	.081106	.084114	.087163	.090248	.093366	.096515	.099692	.106117	.112623
	-.10	.072688	.075502	.078370	.081288	.084253	.087262	.090310	.093395	.096514	.099663	.102839	.109265	.115770
	-.20	.075835	.078649	.081517	.084436	.087401	.090409	.093457	.096542	.099661	.102810	.105987	.112412	.118918
	-.30	.078982	.081797	.084665	.087583	.090548	.093556	.096605	.099690	.102808	.105957	.109134	.115560	.122065
	-.40	.082130	.084944	.087812	.090730	.093695	.096704	.099752	.102837	.105956	.109105	.112281	.118707	.125213

313

15.0 YEAR HOLDING PERIOD
.100 EQUITY YIELD RATE
.700 LOAN RATIO

INTEREST RATE

TERM YEARS	APPR DEP	5.0	5.5	6.0	6.5	7.0	7.5	8.0	8.5	9.0	9.5	10.0	11.0	12.0
10	.40	.066582	.070671	.071571	.073079	.074596	.076121	.077653	.079192	.080737	.082286	.083840	.086956	.090079
	.30	.071730	.073219	.074718	.076226	.077743	.079268	.080801	.082339	.083884	.085433	.086987	.090104	.093227
	.20	.074877	.076360	.077865	.079374	.080891	.082416	.083948	.085487	.087031	.088581	.090134	.093251	.096374
	.10	.078024	.079514	.081013	.082521	.084038	.085563	.087095	.088634	.090179	.091728	.093282	.096398	.099522
	0.00	.081172	.082661	.084160	.085669	.087186	.088711	.090243	.091782	.093326	.094876	.096429	.099546	.102669
	-.10	.084419	.085808	.087307	.088816	.090333	.091858	.093390	.094929	.096473	.098023	.099577	.102693	.105816
	-.20	.087466	.088956	.090455	.091963	.093480	.095005	.096538	.098076	.099621	.101170	.102724	.105841	.108964
	-.30	.090614	.092103	.093602	.095111	.096628	.098153	.099685	.101224	.102768	.104318	.105871	.108988	.112111
	-.40	.093761	.095250	.096750	.098258	.099775	.101300	.102832	.104371	.105916	.107465	.109019	.112135	.115258
15	.40	.061806	.064014	.066263	.068552	.070880	.073248	.075654	.078097	.080577	.083094	.085646	.090853	.096193
	.30	.064953	.067161	.069410	.071699	.074028	.076395	.078801	.081244	.083725	.086241	.088793	.094000	.099340
	.20	.068100	.070309	.072558	.074847	.077175	.079543	.081948	.084392	.086872	.089388	.091940	.097148	.102488
	.10	.071248	.073456	.075705	.077994	.080323	.082690	.085096	.087539	.090019	.092536	.095088	.100295	.105635
	0.00	.074395	.076603	.078852	.081141	.083470	.085837	.088243	.090686	.093167	.095683	.098235	.103442	.108782
	-.10	.077542	.079751	.082000	.084289	.086617	.088985	.091391	.093834	.096314	.098831	.101383	.106590	.111930
	-.20	.080690	.082898	.085147	.087436	.089765	.092132	.094538	.096981	.099462	.101978	.104530	.109737	.115077
	-.30	.083837	.086045	.088294	.090584	.092912	.095280	.097685	.100129	.102609	.105125	.107677	.112885	.118225
	-.40	.086985	.089193	.091442	.093731	.096059	.098427	.100833	.103276	.105756	.108273	.110825	.116032	.121372
20	.40	.058520	.061096	.063723	.066402	.069130	.071906	.074728	.077595	.080505	.083456	.086447	.092542	.098776
	.30	.061667	.064243	.066871	.069550	.072278	.075054	.077876	.080742	.083652	.086604	.089595	.095689	.101923
	.20	.064815	.067390	.070018	.072697	.075425	.078201	.081023	.083890	.086800	.089751	.092742	.098837	.105070
	.10	.067962	.070538	.073166	.075844	.078572	.081348	.084170	.087037	.089947	.092898	.095889	.101984	.108218
	0.00	.071109	.073685	.076313	.078992	.081720	.084496	.087318	.090185	.093094	.096046	.099037	.105131	.111365
	-.10	.074257	.076832	.079460	.082139	.084867	.087643	.090465	.093332	.096242	.099193	.102184	.108279	.114512
	-.20	.077404	.079980	.082608	.085286	.088015	.090790	.093613	.096479	.099389	.102340	.105332	.111426	.117660
	-.30	.080552	.083127	.085755	.088434	.091162	.093938	.096760	.099627	.102537	.105488	.108479	.114574	.120807
	-.40	.083699	.086275	.088903	.091581	.094309	.097085	.099907	.102774	.105684	.108635	.111626	.117721	.123955
25	.40	.056627	.059429	.062286	.065197	.068159	.071170	.074227	.077326	.080467	.083645	.086859	.093384	.100023
	.30	.059775	.062576	.065433	.068345	.071307	.074318	.077374	.080474	.083614	.086793	.090007	.096532	.103171
	.20	.062922	.065723	.068581	.071492	.074454	.077465	.080521	.083621	.086762	.089940	.093154	.099679	.106318
	.10	.066069	.068871	.071728	.074639	.077602	.080612	.083669	.086769	.089909	.093087	.096301	.102826	.109465
	0.00	.069217	.072018	.074876	.077787	.080749	.083760	.086816	.089916	.093056	.096235	.099449	.105974	.112613
	-.10	.072364	.075166	.078023	.080934	.083896	.086907	.089964	.093063	.096204	.099382	.102596	.109121	.115760
	-.20	.075512	.078313	.081170	.084082	.087044	.090054	.093111	.096211	.099351	.102529	.105743	.112268	.118907
	-.30	.078659	.081460	.084318	.087229	.090191	.093202	.096258	.099358	.102498	.105677	.108891	.115416	.122055
	-.40	.081806	.084608	.087465	.090376	.093338	.096349	.099406	.102505	.105646	.108824	.112038	.118563	.125202
30	.40	.055428	.058383	.061394	.064459	.067572	.070731	.073931	.077171	.080445	.083751	.087087	.093834	.100665
	.30	.058575	.061530	.064542	.067606	.070719	.073878	.077079	.080318	.083592	.086899	.090234	.096981	.103812
	.20	.061723	.064678	.067689	.070753	.073867	.077025	.080226	.083465	.086740	.090046	.093382	.100128	.106959
	.10	.064870	.067825	.070836	.073901	.077014	.080173	.083373	.086613	.089887	.093194	.096529	.103276	.110107
	0.00	.068017	.070972	.073984	.077048	.080161	.083320	.086521	.089760	.093034	.096341	.099676	.106423	.113254
	-.10	.071165	.074120	.077131	.080195	.083309	.086467	.089668	.092907	.096182	.099488	.102824	.109571	.116402
	-.20	.074312	.077267	.080279	.083343	.086456	.089615	.092816	.096055	.099329	.102636	.105971	.112718	.119549
	-.30	.077459	.080414	.083426	.086490	.089603	.092762	.095963	.099202	.102477	.105783	.109119	.115865	.122696
	-.40	.080607	.083562	.086573	.089638	.092751	.095910	.099110	.102350	.105624	.108930	.112266	.119013	.125844

.100 EQUITY YIELD RATE
.750 LOAN RATIO

TERM YEARS	APPR DEP	5.0	5.5	6.0	6.5	7.0	7.5	8.0	8.5	9.0	9.5	10.0	11.0	12.0
10	.40	.067237	.068833	.070439	.072055	.073681	.075315	.076956	.078605	.080260	.081920	.083585	.086924	.090270
	.30	.070385	.071980	.073587	.075203	.076828	.078462	.080104	.081752	.083407	.085067	.086732	.090071	.093417
	.20	.073532	.075128	.076734	.078350	.079976	.081609	.083251	.084900	.086555	.088215	.089879	.093219	.096565
	.10	.076679	.078275	.079881	.081497	.083123	.084757	.086399	.088047	.089702	.091362	.093027	.096366	.099712
	0.00	.079827	.081422	.083029	.084645	.086270	.087904	.089546	.091195	.092849	.094510	.096174	.099513	.102860
	-.10	.082974	.084570	.086176	.087792	.089418	.091052	.092693	.094342	.095997	.097657	.099322	.102661	.106007
	-.20	.086122	.087717	.089323	.090940	.092565	.094199	.095841	.097489	.099144	.100804	.102469	.105808	.109154
	-.30	.089269	.090865	.092471	.094087	.095712	.097346	.098988	.100637	.102291	.103952	.105616	.108955	.112302
	-.40	.092416	.094012	.095618	.097234	.098860	.100494	.102135	.103784	.105439	.107099	.108764	.112103	.115449
15	.40	.059977	.062343	.064752	.067205	.069700	.072236	.074814	.077432	.080089	.082785	.085520	.091099	.096820
	.30	.063124	.065490	.067900	.070352	.072847	.075384	.077961	.080579	.083237	.085933	.088667	.094246	.099968
	.20	.066271	.068637	.071047	.073500	.075994	.078531	.081109	.083726	.086384	.089080	.091814	.097394	.103115
	.10	.069419	.071785	.074194	.076647	.079142	.081678	.084256	.086874	.089531	.092228	.094962	.100541	.106262
	0.00	.072566	.074932	.077342	.079794	.082289	.084826	.087403	.090021	.092679	.095375	.098109	.103688	.109410
	-.10	.075713	.078080	.080489	.082942	.085437	.087973	.090551	.093169	.095826	.098522	.101257	.106836	.112557
	-.20	.078861	.081227	.083637	.086089	.088584	.091121	.093698	.096316	.098973	.101670	.104404	.109983	.115705
	-.30	.082008	.084374	.086784	.089236	.091731	.094268	.096845	.099463	.102121	.104817	.107551	.113131	.118852
	-.40	.085156	.087522	.089931	.092384	.094879	.097415	.099993	.102611	.105268	.107964	.110699	.116278	.121999
20	.40	.056456	.059216	.062032	.064902	.067825	.070799	.073822	.076894	.080012	.083174	.086378	.092908	.099587
	.30	.059604	.062363	.065179	.068049	.070972	.073946	.076970	.080041	.083159	.086361	.089526	.096056	.102735
	.20	.062751	.065511	.068326	.071196	.074119	.077093	.080117	.083189	.086306	.089469	.092673	.099203	.105882
	.10	.065898	.068658	.071474	.074344	.077267	.080241	.083265	.086336	.089454	.092616	.095821	.102351	.109030
	0.00	.069046	.071805	.074621	.077491	.080414	.083388	.086412	.089484	.092601	.095763	.098968	.105498	.112177
	-.10	.072193	.074953	.077768	.080639	.083561	.086536	.089559	.092631	.095749	.098911	.102115	.108645	.115324
	-.20	.075341	.078100	.080916	.083786	.086709	.089683	.092707	.095778	.098896	.102058	.105263	.111793	.118472
	-.30	.078488	.081248	.084063	.086933	.089856	.092830	.095854	.098926	.102043	.105205	.108410	.114940	.121619
	-.40	.081635	.084395	.087211	.090081	.093004	.095978	.099001	.102073	.105191	.108353	.111557	.118087	.124766
25	.40	.054429	.057430	.060492	.063611	.066784	.070010	.073285	.076606	.079971	.083376	.086820	.093811	.100524
	.30	.057576	.060577	.063639	.066758	.069932	.073158	.076432	.079753	.083118	.086524	.089967	.096958	.104071
	.20	.060723	.063725	.066786	.069905	.073079	.076305	.079580	.082901	.086266	.089671	.093115	.100106	.107219
	.10	.063871	.066872	.069934	.073053	.076227	.079452	.082727	.086048	.089413	.092818	.096262	.103253	.110366
	0.00	.067018	.070019	.073081	.076200	.079374	.082600	.085874	.089196	.092560	.095966	.099409	.106400	.113514
	-.10	.070165	.073167	.076228	.079347	.082521	.085747	.089022	.092343	.095708	.099113	.102557	.109548	.116661
	-.20	.073313	.076314	.079376	.082495	.085669	.088894	.092169	.095490	.098855	.102261	.105704	.112695	.119808
	-.30	.076460	.079462	.082523	.085642	.088810	.092042	.095317	.098638	.102002	.105408	.108851	.115843	.122956
	-.40	.079608	.082609	.085671	.088790	.091963	.095189	.098464	.101785	.105150	.108555	.111999	.118990	.126103
30	.40	.053143	.056309	.059536	.062819	.066155	.069539	.072969	.076439	.079947	.083490	.087064	.094293	.101611
	.30	.056291	.059457	.062683	.065966	.069302	.072687	.076116	.079586	.083095	.086637	.090211	.097440	.104759
	.20	.059438	.062604	.065831	.069114	.072450	.075834	.079263	.082734	.086242	.089785	.093359	.100587	.107906
	.10	.062585	.065752	.068978	.072261	.075597	.078981	.082411	.085881	.089390	.092932	.096506	.103735	.111054
	0.00	.065733	.068899	.072126	.075409	.078744	.082129	.085558	.089029	.092537	.096080	.099653	.106882	.114201
	-.10	.068880	.072046	.075273	.078556	.081892	.085276	.088705	.092176	.095684	.099227	.102801	.110029	.117348
	-.20	.072028	.075194	.078420	.081703	.085039	.088423	.091853	.095323	.098832	.102374	.105948	.113177	.120496
	-.30	.075175	.078341	.081568	.084851	.088186	.091571	.095000	.098471	.101979	.105522	.109095	.116324	.123643
	-.40	.078322	.081488	.084715	.087998	.091334	.094718	.098148	.101618	.105126	.108669	.112243	.119472	.126790

15.0 YEAR HOLDING PERIOD
.100 EQUITY YIELD RATE
.800 LOAN RATIO

INTEREST RATE

TERM YEARS	APPR DEP	5.0	5.5	6.0	6.5	7.0	7.5	8.0	8.5	9.0	9.5	10.0	11.0	12.0
10	.40	.065892	.067594	.069308	.071032	.072765	.074508	.076259	.078018	.079783	.081554	.083330	.086691	.090461
	.30	.069940	.070742	.072455	.074179	.075913	.077626	.079407	.081165	.082931	.084701	.086477	.090039	.093608
	.20	.072187	.073889	.075602	.077326	.079060	.080803	.082554	.084313	.086078	.087849	.089624	.093186	.096756
	.10	.075335	.077037	.078750	.080474	.082208	.083950	.085702	.087460	.089225	.090996	.092772	.096333	.099903
	0.00	.078482	.080184	.081897	.083621	.085355	.087098	.088849	.090608	.092373	.094143	.095919	.099481	.103050
	-.10	.081629	.083331	.085045	.086769	.088502	.090245	.091996	.093755	.095520	.097291	.099066	.102628	.106198
	-.20	.084777	.086479	.088192	.089916	.091650	.093393	.095144	.096902	.098667	.100438	.102214	.105776	.109345
	-.30	.087924	.089626	.091339	.093063	.094797	.096540	.098291	.100050	.101815	.103586	.105361	.108923	.112492
	-.40	.091072	.092773	.094487	.096211	.097944	.099687	.101438	.103197	.104962	.106733	.108509	.112070	.115640
15	.40	.058148	.060671	.063242	.065858	.068519	.071225	.073974	.076766	.079601	.082477	.085394	.091145	.097448
	.30	.061295	.063819	.066389	.069005	.071666	.074372	.077121	.079914	.082748	.085624	.088541	.094492	.100595
	.20	.064442	.066966	.069536	.072153	.074814	.077519	.080269	.083061	.085896	.088772	.091688	.097640	.103742
	.10	.067590	.070114	.072684	.075300	.077961	.080667	.083416	.086209	.089043	.091919	.094836	.100787	.106890
	0.00	.070737	.073261	.075831	.078447	.081108	.083814	.086564	.089356	.092191	.095067	.097983	.103934	.110037
	-.10	.073885	.076408	.078979	.081595	.084256	.086962	.089711	.092503	.095338	.098214	.101130	.107082	.113184
	-.20	.077032	.079556	.082126	.084742	.087403	.090110	.092858	.095651	.098485	.101361	.104278	.110229	.116332
	-.30	.080179	.082703	.085273	.087889	.090551	.093256	.096006	.098798	.101633	.104509	.107425	.113376	.119479
	-.40	.083327	.085851	.088421	.091037	.093698	.096404	.099153	.101945	.104780	.107656	.110573	.116524	.122627
20	.40	.054393	.057336	.060340	.063401	.066519	.069691	.072917	.076193	.079518	.082891	.086310	.093275	.100399
	.30	.057540	.060484	.063487	.066548	.069606	.072839	.076064	.079340	.082666	.086039	.089457	.096422	.103547
	.20	.060687	.063631	.066634	.069696	.072814	.075986	.079211	.082488	.085813	.089186	.092604	.099570	.106694
	.10	.063835	.066778	.069782	.072843	.075961	.079133	.082359	.085635	.088961	.092333	.095752	.102717	.109841
	0.00	.066982	.069926	.072929	.075991	.079108	.082281	.085506	.088782	.092108	.095481	.098899	.105864	.112989
	-.10	.070130	.073073	.076077	.079138	.082256	.085428	.088653	.091930	.095255	.098628	.102047	.109012	.116136
	-.20	.073277	.076221	.079224	.082285	.085403	.088575	.091801	.095077	.098403	.101776	.105194	.112159	.119283
	-.30	.076424	.079368	.082371	.085433	.088550	.091723	.094948	.098225	.101550	.104923	.108341	.115307	.122431
	-.40	.079572	.082515	.085519	.088580	.091698	.094870	.098096	.101372	.104697	.108070	.111489	.118454	.125578
25	.40	.052230	.055431	.058697	.062024	.065409	.068850	.072343	.075886	.079475	.083107	.086780	.094238	.101825
	.30	.055377	.058579	.061844	.065171	.068557	.071997	.075491	.079033	.082622	.086255	.089928	.097385	.104972
	.20	.058525	.061726	.064992	.068319	.071704	.075145	.078638	.082181	.085770	.089402	.093075	.100532	.108120
	.10	.061672	.064873	.068139	.071466	.074851	.078292	.081785	.085328	.088917	.092549	.096223	.103680	.111267
	0.00	.064819	.068021	.071286	.074613	.077999	.081440	.084933	.088475	.092064	.095697	.099370	.106827	.114414
	-.10	.067967	.071168	.074434	.077761	.081146	.084587	.088080	.091623	.095212	.098844	.102517	.109974	.117562
	-.20	.071114	.074315	.077581	.080908	.084294	.087734	.091228	.094770	.098359	.101992	.105665	.113122	.120709
	-.30	.074261	.077463	.080729	.084056	.087441	.090882	.094375	.097917	.101506	.105139	.108812	.116269	.123857
	-.40	.077409	.080610	.083876	.087203	.090588	.094029	.097522	.101065	.104654	.108236	.111959	.119417	.127004
30	.40	.050859	.054006	.057078	.061180	.064738	.068348	.072006	.075708	.079450	.083229	.087041	.094751	.102558
	.30	.054006	.057383	.060825	.064327	.067885	.071495	.075153	.078855	.082597	.086376	.090188	.097899	.105706
	.20	.057154	.060531	.063972	.067474	.071032	.074643	.078300	.082002	.085745	.089523	.093335	.101046	.108853
	.10	.060301	.063678	.067120	.070622	.074180	.077790	.081448	.085150	.088892	.092671	.096483	.104193	.112000
	0.00	.063448	.066826	.070267	.073769	.077327	.080937	.084595	.088297	.092039	.095818	.099630	.107341	.115148
	-.10	.066596	.069973	.073415	.076917	.080475	.084085	.087743	.091445	.095187	.098966	.102778	.110488	.118295
	-.20	.069743	.073120	.076562	.080064	.083622	.087232	.090890	.094592	.098334	.102113	.105925	.113636	.121442
	-.30	.072890	.076268	.079709	.083211	.086769	.090379	.094037	.097739	.101482	.105260	.109072	.116783	.124590

316

-INTEREST RATE

TERM YEARS	APPR DEP	5.0	5.5	6.0	6.5	7.0	7.5	8.0	8.5	9.0	9.5	10.0	11.0	12.0
10	.40	.063203	.065117	.067045	.068984	.070935	.072896	.074866	.076844	.078830	.080822	.082819	.086826	.090642
	.30	.066350	.068265	.070192	.072132	.074082	.076043	.078013	.079991	.081977	.083969	.085967	.089974	.093989
	.20	.069497	.071412	.073340	.075279	.077230	.079190	.081160	.083139	.085124	.087117	.089114	.093121	.097137
	.10	.072645	.074560	.076487	.078426	.080377	.082338	.084308	.086286	.088272	.090264	.092264	.096269	.100084
	0.00	.075792	.077707	.079634	.081574	.083524	.085485	.087455	.089433	.091419	.093411	.095409	.099416	.103432
	-.10	.078940	.080854	.082782	.084721	.086672	.088632	.090602	.092581	.094567	.096559	.098556	.102563	.106579
	-.20	.082087	.084002	.085929	.087869	.089819	.091780	.093750	.095729	.097714	.099706	.101704	.105711	.109926
	-.30	.085234	.087149	.089076	.091016	.092966	.094927	.096897	.098876	.100861	.102854	.104851	.108858	.112674
	-.40	.088382	.090296	.092224	.094163	.096114	.098075	.100045	.102023	.104009	.106001	.107998	.112005	.116021
15	.40	.054490	.057329	.060221	.063104	.066158	.069201	.072295	.075436	.078625	.081860	.085141	.091837	.098702
	.30	.057637	.060476	.063368	.066311	.069305	.072349	.075442	.078583	.081772	.085008	.088289	.094984	.101850
	.20	.060785	.063624	.066515	.069458	.072452	.075496	.078589	.081731	.084920	.088155	.091436	.098131	.104997
	.10	.063932	.066919	.069663	.072606	.075600	.078644	.081737	.084878	.088067	.091302	.094584	.101279	.108144
	0.00	.067079	.069919	.072810	.075753	.078747	.081791	.084884	.088025	.091214	.094450	.097731	.104426	.111292
	-.10	.070227	.073066	.075958	.078901	.081894	.084938	.088031	.091173	.094362	.097597	.100879	.107573	.114439
	-.20	.073374	.076213	.079105	.082048	.085042	.088086	.091179	.094320	.097509	.100745	.104026	.110721	.117587
	-.30	.076521	.079361	.082252	.085195	.088189	.091233	.094326	.097468	.100657	.103892	.107173	.113868	.120734
	-.40	.079669	.082508	.085400	.088343	.091337	.094380	.097474	.100615	.103804	.107039	.110320	.117016	.123881
20	.40	.050265	.053577	.056956	.060400	.063907	.067476	.071105	.074791	.078532	.082326	.086172	.094008	.102023
	.30	.053413	.056724	.060103	.063547	.067055	.070624	.074252	.077938	.081679	.085474	.089319	.097155	.105570
	.20	.056560	.059872	.063251	.066695	.070202	.073771	.077400	.081085	.084827	.088621	.092467	.100303	.108318
	.10	.059708	.063019	.066398	.069842	.073349	.076918	.080547	.084233	.087974	.091769	.095614	.103450	.111465
	0.00	.062855	.066167	.069545	.072989	.076497	.080066	.083694	.087380	.091121	.094916	.098762	.106597	.114612
	-.10	.066002	.069314	.072693	.076137	.079644	.083213	.086842	.090528	.094269	.098063	.101909	.109745	.117760
	-.20	.069150	.072461	.075840	.079284	.082792	.086361	.089989	.093675	.097416	.101211	.105056	.112892	.120907
	-.30	.072297	.075609	.078987	.082431	.085939	.089508	.093136	.096822	.100564	.104358	.108204	.116040	.124054
	-.40	.075445	.078756	.082135	.085579	.089086	.092655	.096284	.099970	.103711	.107505	.111351	.119187	.127202
25	.40	.047832	.051434	.055108	.058851	.062659	.066530	.070460	.074445	.078483	.082569	.086702	.095091	.103627
	.30	.050980	.054581	.058255	.061998	.065807	.069677	.073607	.077593	.081630	.085717	.089849	.098238	.106774
	.20	.054128	.057729	.061402	.065145	.068954	.072825	.076755	.080740	.084778	.088864	.092996	.101369	.109922
	.10	.057274	.060876	.064550	.068293	.072101	.075972	.079902	.083887	.087925	.092012	.096144	.104533	.113369
	0.00	.060422	.064023	.067697	.071440	.075249	.079120	.083049	.087035	.091072	.095159	.099291	.107680	.116216
	-.10	.063569	.067171	.070845	.074587	.078396	.082267	.086197	.090182	.094220	.098306	.102439	.110828	.119364
	-.20	.066716	.070318	.073992	.077735	.081543	.085414	.089344	.093330	.097367	.101454	.105586	.113975	.122511
	-.30	.069864	.073465	.077139	.080882	.084691	.088562	.092492	.096477	.100514	.104601	.108733	.117123	.125558
	-.40	.073011	.076613	.080287	.084030	.087838	.091709	.095639	.099624	.103662	.107748	.111881	.120270	.128306
30	.40	.046290	.050089	.053961	.057901	.061904	.065965	.070080	.074245	.078455	.082706	.086994	.095669	.104452
	.30	.049437	.053237	.057109	.061048	.065051	.069112	.073227	.077392	.081602	.085853	.090142	.098816	.107599
	.20	.052585	.056384	.060256	.064196	.068198	.072260	.076375	.080540	.084750	.089001	.093289	.101964	.110746
	.10	.055732	.059531	.063403	.067343	.071346	.075407	.079522	.083687	.087897	.092148	.096437	.105111	.113894
	0.00	.058879	.062679	.066551	.070490	.074493	.078554	.082670	.086834	.091044	.095295	.099584	.108188	.117041
	-.10	.062027	.065826	.069698	.073638	.077641	.081702	.085817	.089982	.094192	.098443	.102731	.111406	.120188
	-.20	.065174	.068974	.072845	.076785	.080788	.084849	.088964	.093129	.097339	.101590	.105879	.114553	.123336
	-.30	.068322	.072121	.075993	.079932	.083935	.087997	.092112	.096277	.100486	.104738	.109026	.117701	.126483
	-.40	.071469	.075268	.079140	.083060	.087083	.091144	.095259	.099424	.103634	.107885	.112173	.120848	.129631

317

15.0 YEAR HOLDING PERIOD
.120 EQUITY YIELD RATE
.600 LOAN RATIO

INTEREST RATE

TERM YEARS	APPR DEP	5.0	5.5	6.0	6.5	7.0	7.5	8.0	8.5	9.0	9.5	10.0	11.0	12.0
10	.40	.085934	.087283	.088644	.090015	.091395	.092785	.094184	.095591	.097005	.098426	.099854	.102726	.105617
	.30	.088016	.089966	.091326	.092697	.094078	.095468	.096866	.098273	.099687	.101209	.102537	.105409	.108299
	.20	.091299	.092648	.094009	.095379	.096760	.098150	.099549	.100955	.102370	.103791	.105219	.108091	.110981
	.10	.093961	.095331	.096691	.098062	.099442	.100832	.102231	.103638	.105052	.106474	.107901	.110771	.113664
	0.00	.096663	.098013	.099374	.100744	.102125	.103515	.104913	.106320	.107735	.109156	.110584	.113456	.116346
	-.10	.099346	.100696	.102056	.103427	.104807	.106197	.107596	.109003	.110417	.111838	.113266	.116139	.119029
	-.20	.102028	.103378	.104738	.106109	.107490	.108880	.110278	.111685	.113099	.114521	.115948	.118821	.121711
	-.30	.104711	.106060	.107421	.108792	.110172	.111562	.112961	.114367	.115782	.117203	.118631	.121503	.124393
	-.40	.107393	.108743	.110103	.111474	.112855	.114244	.115643	.117050	.118464	.119886	.121314	.124186	.127076
15	.40	.078113	.080006	.081933	.083895	.085891	.087921	.089983	.092077	.094203	.096360	.098547	.103011	.107588
	.30	.080795	.082688	.084616	.086578	.088574	.090603	.092665	.094759	.096885	.099042	.101230	.105693	.110270
	.20	.083478	.085371	.087298	.089260	.091256	.093285	.095348	.097442	.099568	.101725	.103912	.108376	.112953
	.10	.086160	.088053	.089981	.091943	.093939	.095968	.098030	.100124	.102250	.104407	.106595	.111058	.115635
	0.00	.088843	.090735	.092663	.094625	.096621	.098650	.100712	.102807	.104933	.107090	.109277	.113740	.118318
	-.10	.091525	.093418	.095346	.097308	.099304	.101333	.103395	.105489	.107615	.109772	.111959	.116423	.121000
	-.20	.094207	.096100	.098028	.099990	.101986	.104015	.106077	.108172	.110297	.112454	.114642	.119105	.123682
	-.30	.096890	.098783	.100710	.102672	.104668	.106698	.108760	.110854	.112980	.115137	.117324	.121788	.126365
	-.40	.099572	.101465	.103393	.105355	.107351	.109380	.111442	.113536	.115662	.117819	.120007	.124470	.129047
20	.40	.074321	.076500	.078723	.080990	.083299	.085649	.088039	.090467	.092932	.095432	.097967	.103134	.108421
	.30	.077004	.079182	.081406	.083672	.085981	.088331	.090721	.093149	.095614	.098115	.100650	.105816	.111103
	.20	.079686	.081865	.084088	.086355	.088664	.091014	.093404	.095832	.098297	.100797	.103332	.108499	.113786
	.10	.082368	.084547	.086770	.089037	.091346	.093696	.096086	.098514	.100979	.103480	.106015	.111181	.116468
	0.00	.085051	.087229	.089453	.091720	.094029	.096379	.098768	.101197	.103662	.106162	.108697	.113864	.119150
	-.10	.087733	.089912	.092135	.094402	.096711	.099061	.101451	.103879	.106344	.108845	.111379	.116546	.121833
	-.20	.090416	.092594	.094818	.097084	.099394	.101744	.104133	.106561	.109026	.111527	.114062	.119229	.124515
	-.30	.093098	.095277	.097500	.099767	.102076	.104426	.106816	.109244	.111709	.114209	.116744	.121911	.127198
	-.40	.095780	.097959	.100182	.102449	.104758	.107108	.109498	.111926	.114391	.116892	.119427	.124593	.129880
25	.40	.072137	.074497	.076906	.079361	.081861	.084403	.086985	.089605	.092260	.094949	.097669	.103195	.108823
	.30	.074819	.077179	.079588	.082044	.084543	.087085	.089667	.092287	.094943	.097631	.100352	.105878	.111505
	.20	.077502	.079862	.082271	.084726	.087226	.089768	.092350	.094970	.097625	.100314	.103034	.108560	.114188
	.10	.080184	.082544	.084953	.087408	.089908	.092450	.095032	.097652	.100307	.102996	.105716	.111243	.116870
	0.00	.082867	.085227	.087636	.090091	.092591	.095133	.097715	.100334	.102990	.105679	.108399	.113925	.119553
	-.10	.085549	.087909	.090318	.092773	.095273	.097815	.100397	.103017	.105672	.108361	.111081	.116608	.122235
	-.20	.088231	.090592	.093000	.095456	.097956	.100498	.103079	.105699	.108355	.111044	.113764	.119290	.124917
	-.30	.090914	.093274	.095683	.098138	.100638	.103180	.105762	.108382	.111037	.113726	.116446	.121972	.127600
	-.40	.093596	.095956	.098365	.100821	.103320	.105862	.108444	.111064	.113720	.116408	.119129	.124655	.130282
30	.40	.070753	.073241	.075778	.078363	.080991	.083659	.086364	.089105	.091876	.094677	.097504	.103228	.109030
	.30	.073435	.075923	.078461	.081045	.083673	.086341	.089047	.091787	.094559	.097360	.100187	.105911	.111712
	.20	.076117	.078605	.081143	.083728	.086355	.089024	.091729	.094469	.097241	.100042	.102869	.108593	.114395
	.10	.078800	.081288	.083826	.086410	.089038	.091706	.094412	.097152	.099924	.102725	.105552	.111275	.117077
	0.00	.081482	.083970	.086508	.089092	.091720	.094388	.097094	.099834	.102606	.105407	.108234	.113958	.119760
	-.10	.084165	.086653	.089191	.091775	.094403	.097071	.099777	.102517	.105289	.108089	.110917	.116640	.122442
	-.20	.086847	.089335	.091873	.094457	.097085	.099753	.102459	.105199	.107971	.110772	.113599	.119323	.125124
	-.30	.089529	.092018	.094555	.097140	.099768	.102436	.105141	.107882	.110653	.113454	.116281	.122005	.127807

318

.120 EQUITY YIELD RATE
.667 LOAN RATIO

INTEREST RATE

TERM YEARS	APPR DEP	5.0	5.5	6.0	6.5	7.0	7.5	8.0	8.5	9.0	9.5	10.0	11.0	12.0
10	.40	.083341	.084840	.086332	.087875	.089409	.090953	.092507	.094070	.095642	.097221	.098808	.101999	.105211
	.30	.086023	.087523	.089034	.090557	.092091	.093636	.095190	.096753	.098324	.099904	.104490	.104682	.107893
	.20	.088706	.090205	.091717	.093240	.094774	.096318	.097872	.099435	.101007	.102586	.104173	.107364	.110575
	.10	.091388	.092888	.094399	.095922	.097456	.099001	.100555	.102118	.103689	.105269	.106855	.110047	.113258
	0.00	.094070	.095570	.097082	.098605	.100139	.101683	.103237	.104800	.106372	.107951	.109538	.112729	.115940
	-.10	.096753	.098252	.099764	.101287	.102821	.104365	.105919	.107483	.109054	.110634	.112220	.115411	.118623
	-.20	.099435	.100935	.102446	.103970	.105504	.107048	.108602	.110165	.111737	.113316	.114902	.118102	.121305
	-.30	.102118	.103617	.105129	.106652	.108186	.109730	.111284	.112847	.114419	.115998	.117585	.120776	.123987
	-.40	.104800	.106300	.107811	.109334	.110868	.112413	.113967	.115530	.117101	.118681	.120267	.123459	.126670
15	.40	.074651	.076754	.078896	.081076	.083294	.085548	.087840	.090167	.092529	.094925	.097356	.102315	.107401
	.30	.077333	.079436	.081578	.083758	.085976	.088231	.090522	.092849	.095211	.097608	.100038	.104998	.110083
	.20	.080016	.082119	.084261	.086441	.088658	.090913	.093204	.095531	.097894	.100290	.102721	.107680	.112766
	.10	.082698	.084801	.086943	.089123	.091341	.093596	.095887	.098214	.100576	.102973	.105404	.110362	.115448
	0.00	.085380	.087484	.089626	.091806	.094023	.096278	.098569	.100896	.103258	.105655	.108086	.113045	.118131
	-.10	.088063	.090166	.092308	.094488	.096706	.098960	.101252	.103579	.105941	.108338	.110768	.115727	.120813
	-.20	.090745	.092849	.094990	.097170	.099388	.101643	.103934	.106261	.108623	.111020	.113450	.118410	.123495
	-.30	.093428	.095531	.097673	.099853	.102071	.104325	.106617	.108944	.111306	.113702	.116133	.121092	.126178
	-.40	.096110	.098213	.100355	.102535	.104753	.107008	.109299	.111626	.113988	.116385	.118815	.123775	.128860
20	.40	.070438	.072858	.075329	.077847	.080413	.083024	.085680	.088377	.091116	.093895	.096711	.102452	.108326
	.30	.073120	.075541	.078011	.080530	.083096	.085707	.088362	.091060	.093799	.096577	.099394	.105135	.111009
	.20	.075802	.078223	.080694	.083212	.085778	.088389	.091044	.093742	.096481	.099260	.102076	.107817	.113691
	.10	.078485	.080906	.083376	.085895	.088460	.091072	.093727	.096425	.099164	.101942	.104759	.110499	.116374
	0.00	.081167	.083588	.086058	.088577	.091143	.093754	.096409	.099107	.101846	.104625	.107441	.113182	.119056
	-.10	.083849	.086271	.088741	.091260	.093825	.096436	.099092	.101790	.104529	.107307	.110123	.115864	.121738
	-.20	.086532	.088953	.091423	.093942	.096508	.099119	.101774	.104472	.107211	.109989	.112806	.118547	.124421
	-.30	.089215	.091635	.094106	.096624	.099190	.101801	.104457	.107154	.109893	.112672	.115488	.121229	.127103
	-.40	.091897	.094318	.096788	.099307	.101873	.104484	.107139	.109837	.112576	.115354	.118171	.123912	.129786
25	.40	.068011	.070633	.073310	.076038	.078815	.081640	.084509	.087420	.090370	.093358	.096380	.102520	.108773
	.30	.070693	.073316	.075992	.078720	.081498	.084322	.087191	.090102	.093052	.096040	.099063	.105203	.111456
	.20	.073376	.075998	.078674	.081403	.084180	.087005	.089874	.092784	.095735	.098723	.101745	.107885	.114138
	.10	.076058	.078680	.081357	.084085	.086863	.089687	.092556	.095467	.098417	.101405	.104427	.110568	.116821
	0.00	.078740	.081363	.084039	.086768	.089545	.092369	.095238	.098149	.101100	.104087	.107110	.113250	.119503
	-.10	.081423	.084045	.086722	.089450	.092227	.095052	.097921	.100832	.103782	.106770	.109792	.115933	.122185
	-.20	.084105	.086728	.089404	.092132	.094910	.097734	.100603	.103514	.106465	.109452	.112475	.118615	.124868
	-.30	.086788	.089410	.092087	.094815	.097592	.100417	.103286	.106197	.109147	.112135	.115157	.121297	.127550
	-.40	.089470	.092093	.094769	.097497	.100275	.103099	.105968	.108879	.111829	.114817	.117840	.123980	.130233
30	.40	.066473	.069237	.072057	.074928	.077848	.080813	.083819	.086864	.089944	.093056	.096197	.102557	.109003
	.30	.069155	.071920	.074739	.077611	.080531	.083496	.086502	.089546	.092626	.095738	.098879	.105239	.111686
	.20	.071837	.074602	.077422	.080293	.083213	.086178	.089184	.092229	.095309	.098421	.101562	.107922	.114368
	.10	.074520	.077284	.080104	.082976	.085895	.088860	.091867	.094911	.097991	.101103	.104244	.110604	.117050
	0.00	.077202	.079967	.082787	.085658	.088578	.091543	.094549	.097594	.100673	.103785	.106927	.113287	.119733
	-.10	.079885	.082649	.085469	.088340	.091260	.094225	.097231	.100276	.103356	.106468	.109609	.115969	.122415
	-.20	.082567	.085332	.088151	.091023	.093943	.096907	.099914	.102958	.106038	.109150	.112292	.118651	.125098
	-.30	.085250	.088014	.090834	.093705	.096625	.099590	.102596	.105641	.108721	.111833	.114974	.121334	.127780
	-.40	.087932	.090697	.093516	.096388	.099308	.102272	.105279	.108323	.111403	.114515	.117656	.124016	.130462

15.0 YEAR HOLDING PERIOD
.120 EQUITY YIELD RATE
.700 LOAN RATIO

INTEREST RATE

TERM YEARS	APPR DEP	5.0	5.5	6.0	6.5	7.0	7.5	8.0	8.5	9.0	9.5	10.0	11.0	12.0
10	.40	.082044	.083619	.085206	.086805	.088416	.090038	.091669	.093311	.094961	.096619	.098285	.101636	.105008
	.30	.084727	.086301	.087889	.089488	.091098	.092720	.094352	.095993	.097643	.099301	.100967	.104318	.107690
	.20	.087409	.088984	.090571	.092170	.093781	.095402	.097034	.098675	.100326	.101984	.103650	.107001	.110372
	.10	.090092	.091666	.093253	.094853	.096463	.098085	.099717	.101358	.103008	.104666	.106332	.109683	.113055
	0.00	.092774	.094349	.095936	.097535	.099146	.100767	.102399	.104040	.105690	.107349	.109014	.112365	.115737
	-.10	.095456	.097031	.098618	.100217	.101828	.103450	.105081	.106723	.108373	.110031	.111697	.115048	.118420
	-.20	.098139	.099713	.101301	.102900	.104511	.106132	.107764	.109405	.111055	.112714	.114379	.117730	.121102
	-.30	.100821	.102396	.103983	.105582	.107193	.108815	.110446	.112088	.113738	.115396	.117062	.120413	.123785
	-.40	.103504	.105078	.106665	.108265	.109875	.111497	.113129	.114770	.116420	.118078	.119744	.123095	.126467
15	.40	.072920	.075128	.077377	.079666	.081995	.084362	.086768	.089211	.091692	.094208	.096760	.101967	.107307
	.30	.075602	.077811	.080060	.082349	.084677	.087045	.089451	.091894	.094374	.096891	.099443	.104650	.109990
	.20	.078285	.080493	.082742	.085031	.087360	.089727	.092133	.094576	.097057	.099573	.102125	.107332	.112672
	.10	.080967	.083176	.085425	.087714	.090042	.092410	.094816	.097259	.099739	.102255	.104807	.110015	.115355
	0.00	.083650	.085858	.088107	.090396	.092725	.095092	.097498	.099941	.102421	.104938	.107490	.112697	.118037
	-.10	.086332	.088540	.090789	.093078	.095407	.097774	.100180	.102624	.105104	.107620	.110172	.115380	.120720
	-.20	.089015	.091223	.093472	.095761	.098089	.100457	.102863	.105306	.107786	.110303	.112855	.118062	.123402
	-.30	.091697	.093905	.096154	.098443	.100772	.103139	.105545	.107988	.110469	.112985	.115537	.120744	.126084
	-.40	.094379	.096588	.098837	.101126	.103454	.105822	.108228	.110671	.113151	.115668	.118220	.123427	.128767
20	.40	.068496	.071038	.073632	.076276	.078970	.081712	.084500	.087333	.090209	.093126	.096083	.102111	.108279
	.30	.071179	.073720	.076314	.078959	.081653	.084395	.087183	.090015	.092891	.095809	.098766	.104794	.110961
	.20	.073861	.076403	.078997	.081641	.084335	.087077	.089865	.092698	.095574	.098491	.101448	.107476	.113644
	.10	.076543	.079085	.081679	.084324	.087018	.089759	.092547	.095380	.098256	.101173	.104131	.110159	.116326
	0.00	.079226	.081768	.084362	.087006	.089700	.092442	.095230	.098063	.100938	.103856	.106813	.112841	.119009
	-.10	.081908	.084450	.087044	.089689	.092383	.095124	.097912	.100745	.103621	.106538	.109496	.115523	.121691
	-.20	.084591	.087133	.089726	.092371	.095065	.097807	.100595	.103427	.106303	.109221	.112178	.118206	.124374
	-.30	.087273	.089815	.092409	.095053	.097747	.100489	.103277	.106110	.108986	.111903	.114860	.120888	.127056
	-.40	.089956	.092497	.095091	.097736	.100430	.103172	.105960	.108792	.111668	.114586	.117543	.123571	.129738
25	.40	.065948	.068701	.071512	.074376	.077293	.080258	.083271	.086327	.089425	.092562	.095736	.102183	.108748
	.30	.068630	.071384	.074194	.077059	.079975	.082941	.085953	.089010	.092108	.095245	.098418	.104865	.111431
	.20	.071313	.074066	.076877	.079741	.082658	.085623	.088636	.091692	.094790	.097927	.101101	.107548	.114113
	.10	.073995	.076749	.079559	.082424	.085340	.088306	.091318	.094374	.097472	.100609	.103783	.110230	.116796
	0.00	.076678	.079431	.082241	.085106	.088022	.090988	.094000	.097057	.100155	.103292	.106465	.112913	.119478
	-.10	.079360	.082114	.084924	.087788	.090705	.093671	.096683	.099739	.102837	.105974	.109148	.115595	.122161
	-.20	.082043	.084796	.087606	.090471	.093387	.096353	.099365	.102422	.105520	.108657	.111830	.118277	.124843
	-.30	.084725	.087478	.090289	.093153	.096070	.099035	.102048	.105104	.108202	.111339	.114513	.120960	.127525
	-.40	.087407	.090161	.092971	.095836	.098752	.101718	.104730	.107787	.110885	.114022	.117195	.123642	.130208
30	.40	.064333	.067236	.070196	.073211	.076277	.079390	.082547	.085744	.088977	.092245	.095543	.102221	.108990
	.30	.067015	.069918	.072879	.075894	.078960	.082073	.085229	.088426	.091660	.094928	.098226	.104904	.111672
	.20	.069698	.072601	.075561	.078576	.081642	.084755	.087912	.091109	.094342	.097610	.100908	.107586	.114355
	.10	.072380	.075283	.078244	.081259	.084325	.087437	.090594	.093791	.097025	.100292	.103591	.110268	.117037
	0.00	.075063	.077965	.080926	.083941	.087007	.090120	.093277	.096473	.099707	.102975	.106273	.112951	.119719
	-.10	.077745	.080648	.083608	.086624	.089689	.092802	.095959	.099156	.102390	.105657	.108956	.115633	.122402
	-.20	.080427	.083330	.086291	.089306	.092372	.095485	.098641	.101838	.105072	.108340	.111638	.118316	.125084
	-.30	.083110	.086013	.088973	.091988	.095054	.098167	.101324	.104521	.107754	.111022	.114320	.120998	.127767

320

.120 EQUITY YIELD RATE
.750 LOAN RATIO

INTEREST RATE

TERM YEARS	APPR DEP	5.0	5.5	6.0	6.5	7.0	7.5	8.0	8.5	9.0	9.5	10.0	11.0	12.0
10	.40	.080100	.081787	.083487	.085201	.086926	.088664	.090412	.092171	.093939	.095715	.097500	.101090	.104703
	.30	.082782	.084469	.086170	.087883	.089609	.091346	.093094	.094853	.096621	.098398	.100183	.103773	.107385
	.20	.085464	.087152	.088852	.090566	.092291	.094029	.095777	.097535	.099303	.101080	.102865	.106455	.110068
	.10	.088147	.089834	.091534	.093248	.094973	.096711	.098459	.100218	.101986	.103763	.105547	.109138	.112750
	0.00	.090829	.092516	.094217	.095930	.097656	.099393	.101142	.102900	.104668	.106445	.108230	.111820	.115433
	-.10	.093512	.095199	.096899	.098613	.100339	.102076	.103824	.105583	.107351	.109127	.110912	.114503	.118115
	-.20	.096194	.097881	.099582	.101295	.103021	.104758	.106507	.108265	.110033	.111810	.113595	.117185	.120798
	-.30	.098877	.100564	.102264	.103978	.105703	.107441	.109189	.110948	.112716	.114492	.116277	.119867	.123480
	-.40	.101559	.103246	.104947	.106660	.108386	.110123	.111871	.113630	.115398	.117175	.118960	.122550	.126162
15	.40	.070324	.072690	.075099	.077552	.080047	.082583	.085161	.087779	.090436	.093132	.095867	.101446	.107167
	.30	.073006	.075372	.077782	.080234	.082729	.085266	.087843	.090461	.093119	.095815	.098549	.104128	.109850
	.20	.075688	.078054	.080464	.082917	.085412	.087948	.090526	.093144	.095801	.098497	.101231	.106811	.112532
	.10	.078371	.080737	.083147	.085599	.088094	.090631	.093208	.095826	.098483	.101180	.103914	.109493	.115215
	0.00	.081053	.083419	.085829	.088281	.090776	.093313	.095891	.098508	.101166	.103862	.106596	.112176	.117897
	-.10	.083736	.086102	.088511	.090964	.093459	.095995	.098573	.101191	.103848	.106544	.109279	.114858	.120579
	-.20	.086418	.088784	.091194	.093646	.096141	.098678	.101255	.103873	.106531	.109227	.111961	.117541	.123262
	-.30	.089101	.091467	.093876	.096329	.098824	.101360	.103938	.106556	.109213	.111909	.114644	.120223	.125944
	-.40	.091783	.094149	.096559	.099011	.101506	.104043	.106620	.109238	.111896	.114592	.117326	.122905	.128627
20	.40	.065584	.068307	.071086	.073920	.076806	.079744	.082731	.085766	.088847	.091973	.095142	.101600	.108208
	.30	.068266	.070990	.073769	.076602	.079489	.082426	.085413	.088448	.091530	.094655	.097824	.104282	.110891
	.20	.070949	.073672	.076451	.079285	.082171	.085109	.088096	.091131	.094212	.097338	.100506	.106965	.113573
	.10	.073631	.076354	.079134	.081967	.084853	.087791	.090778	.093813	.096895	.100020	.103189	.109647	.116256
	0.00	.076313	.079037	.081816	.084649	.087536	.090473	.093461	.096496	.099577	.102703	.105871	.112330	.118938
	-.10	.078996	.081719	.084498	.087332	.090218	.093156	.096143	.099178	.102259	.105385	.108554	.115012	.121620
	-.20	.081678	.084402	.087181	.090014	.092901	.095838	.098825	.101860	.104942	.108068	.111236	.117694	.124303
	-.30	.084361	.087084	.089863	.092697	.095583	.098521	.101508	.104543	.107624	.110750	.113919	.120377	.126985
	-.40	.087043	.089767	.092546	.095379	.098266	.101203	.104190	.107225	.110307	.113432	.116601	.123059	.129668
25	.40	.062854	.065804	.068815	.071884	.075009	.078186	.081414	.084688	.088008	.091369	.094769	.101677	.108711
	.30	.065536	.068486	.071497	.074566	.077691	.080869	.084096	.087371	.090690	.094051	.097451	.104359	.111394
	.20	.068218	.071169	.074180	.077249	.080374	.083551	.086778	.090053	.093372	.096734	.100134	.107042	.114076
	.10	.070901	.073851	.076862	.079931	.083056	.086233	.089461	.092736	.096055	.099416	.102816	.109724	.116758
	0.00	.073583	.076533	.079544	.082614	.085738	.088916	.092143	.095418	.098737	.102098	.105499	.112406	.119441
	-.10	.076266	.079216	.082227	.085296	.088421	.091598	.094826	.098100	.101420	.104781	.108181	.115089	.122123
	-.20	.078948	.081898	.084909	.087978	.091103	.094281	.097508	.100783	.104102	.107463	.110863	.117771	.124806
	-.30	.081631	.084581	.087592	.090661	.093786	.096963	.100191	.103465	.106785	.110146	.113546	.120454	.127488
	-.40	.084313	.087263	.090274	.093343	.096468	.099646	.102873	.106148	.109467	.112828	.116228	.123136	.130170
30	.40	.061123	.064233	.067405	.070636	.073921	.077256	.080638	.084063	.087528	.091029	.094563	.101718	.108970
	.30	.063806	.066916	.070088	.073318	.076603	.079938	.083320	.086746	.090210	.093711	.097245	.104400	.111652
	.20	.066488	.069598	.072770	.076001	.079285	.082621	.086003	.089428	.092893	.096394	.099928	.107083	.114335
	.10	.069170	.072280	.075453	.078683	.081968	.085303	.088685	.092110	.095575	.099076	.102610	.109765	.117017
	0.00	.071853	.074963	.078135	.081366	.084650	.087986	.091368	.094793	.098258	.101759	.105293	.112447	.119699
	-.10	.074535	.077645	.080818	.084048	.087333	.090668	.094050	.097475	.100940	.104441	.107975	.115130	.122382
	-.20	.077218	.080328	.083500	.086730	.090015	.093350	.096733	.100158	.103623	.107124	.110658	.117812	.125064
	-.30	.079900	.083010	.086182	.089413	.092698	.096033	.099415	.102840	.106305	.109806	.113340	.120495	.127747
	-.40	.082582	.085693	.088865	.092095	.095380	.098715	.102097	.105523	.108987	.112488	.116022	.123177	.130429

321

15.0 YEAR HOLDING PERIOD
.120 EQUITY YIELD RATE
.800 LOAN RATIO

INTEREST RATE

TERM YEARS	APPR DEP	5.0	5.5	6.0	6.5	7.0	7.5	8.0	8.5	9.0	9.5	10.0	11.0	12.0
10	.40	.076155	.079954	.081768	.083596	.085437	.087290	.089155	.091031	.092916	.094812	.096715	.100545	.104399
	.30	.080837	.082637	.084451	.086278	.088119	.089972	.091837	.093713	.095599	.097494	.099398	.103228	.107081
	.20	.083520	.085319	.087133	.088961	.090802	.092655	.094520	.096395	.098281	.100177	.102080	.105910	.109763
	.10	.086202	.088002	.089816	.091643	.093484	.095337	.097202	.099078	.100964	.102859	.104763	.108592	.112446
	0.00	.088885	.090684	.092498	.094326	.096167	.098020	.099885	.101760	.103646	.105541	.107445	.111275	.115128
	-.10	.091567	.093367	.095180	.097008	.098849	.100702	.102567	.104443	.106329	.108224	.110128	.113957	.117811
	-.20	.094249	.096049	.097863	.099691	.101531	.103385	.105249	.107125	.109011	.110906	.112810	.116640	.120493
	-.30	.096932	.098731	.100545	.102373	.104214	.106067	.107932	.109808	.111693	.113589	.115492	.119322	.123176
	-.40	.099614	.101414	.103228	.105055	.106896	.108749	.110614	.112490	.114376	.116271	.118175	.122005	.125858
15	.40	.067727	.070251	.072821	.075437	.078098	.080804	.083554	.086346	.089181	.092056	.094973	.100924	.107027
	.30	.070410	.072933	.075504	.078120	.080781	.083487	.086236	.089028	.091863	.094739	.097655	.103607	.109709
	.20	.073092	.075616	.078186	.080802	.083463	.086169	.088918	.091711	.094545	.097421	.100338	.106289	.112392
	.10	.075774	.078298	.080868	.083484	.086145	.088851	.091601	.094393	.097228	.100104	.103020	.108971	.115074
	0.00	.078457	.080981	.083551	.086167	.088828	.091534	.094283	.097076	.099910	.102786	.105703	.111654	.117757
	-.10	.081139	.083663	.086233	.088849	.091511	.094216	.096966	.099758	.102593	.105469	.108385	.114336	.120439
	-.20	.083822	.086345	.088916	.091532	.094193	.096899	.099648	.102440	.105275	.108151	.111068	.117019	.123122
	-.30	.086504	.089028	.091598	.094214	.096875	.099581	.102330	.105123	.107957	.110833	.113750	.119701	.125804
	-.40	.089186	.091710	.094281	.096897	.099558	.102263	.105013	.107805	.110640	.113516	.116432	.122384	.128486
20	.40	.062671	.065576	.068541	.071563	.074642	.077775	.080962	.084199	.087486	.090820	.094200	.101089	.108137
	.30	.065354	.068259	.071223	.074246	.077324	.080458	.083644	.086881	.090168	.093502	.096882	.103771	.110820
	.20	.068036	.070941	.073906	.076928	.080007	.083140	.086326	.089563	.092851	.096185	.099565	.106453	.113502
	.10	.070719	.073624	.076588	.079610	.082689	.085823	.089009	.092246	.095533	.098867	.102247	.109136	.116185
	0.00	.073401	.076306	.079270	.082293	.085372	.088505	.091691	.094929	.098215	.101550	.104929	.111818	.118867
	-.10	.076083	.078988	.081953	.084975	.088054	.091187	.094374	.097611	.100898	.104232	.107612	.114501	.121550
	-.20	.078766	.081671	.084635	.087658	.090736	.093870	.097056	.100294	.103587	.106914	.110294	.117183	.124232
	-.30	.081448	.084353	.087318	.090340	.093419	.096552	.099739	.102976	.106263	.109597	.112977	.119865	.126914
	-.40	.084131	.087036	.090000	.093022	.096101	.099235	.102421	.105658	.108945	.112279	.115659	.122548	.129597
25	.40	.059759	.062906	.066118	.069392	.072725	.076114	.079556	.083050	.086590	.090175	.093802	.101170	.108674
	.30	.062442	.065588	.068800	.072074	.075407	.078796	.082239	.085732	.089273	.092358	.096485	.103853	.111356
	.20	.065124	.068271	.071483	.074756	.078089	.081479	.084921	.088414	.091955	.095540	.099167	.106535	.114039
	.10	.067806	.070953	.074165	.077439	.080772	.084161	.087604	.091097	.094637	.098223	.101849	.109218	.116721
	0.00	.070489	.073636	.076847	.080121	.083454	.086844	.090286	.093779	.097320	.100905	.104532	.111900	.119404
	-.10	.073171	.076318	.079530	.082804	.086137	.089526	.092969	.096462	.100002	.103587	.107214	.114583	.122086
	-.20	.075854	.079000	.082212	.085486	.088819	.092208	.095651	.099144	.102685	.106270	.109897	.117265	.124768
	-.30	.078536	.081683	.084895	.088168	.091502	.094891	.098333	.101827	.105367	.108952	.112579	.119947	.127451
	-.40	.081218	.084365	.087577	.090851	.094184	.097573	.101016	.104509	.108049	.111635	.115262	.122630	.130133
30	.40	.057913	.061231	.064614	.068060	.071504	.075122	.078729	.082383	.086079	.089813	.093583	.101214	.108950
	.30	.060596	.063913	.067297	.070743	.074246	.077804	.081412	.085065	.088761	.092495	.096265	.103897	.111632
	.20	.063278	.066596	.069979	.073425	.076929	.080486	.084094	.087748	.091443	.095178	.098947	.106579	.114314
	.10	.065961	.069278	.072662	.076107	.079611	.083169	.086776	.090430	.094126	.097860	.101630	.109261	.116997
	0.00	.068643	.071960	.075344	.078790	.082294	.085851	.089459	.093112	.096808	.100543	.104312	.111944	.119679
	-.10	.071325	.074643	.078027	.081472	.084976	.088534	.092141	.095795	.099491	.103225	.106995	.114626	.122362
	-.20	.074008	.077325	.080709	.084155	.087658	.091216	.094824	.098477	.102173	.105907	.109677	.117309	.125044
	-.30	.076690	.080008	.083391	.086837	.090341	.093899	.097506	.101160	.104855	.108590	.112359	.119991	.127727

322

15.0 YEAR HOLDING PERIOD
.120 EQUITY YIELD RATE
.900 LOAN RATIO

INTEREST RATE

TERM YEARS	APPR DEP	5.0	5.5	6.0	6.5	7.0	7.5	8.0	8.5	9.0	9.5	10.0	11.0	12.0
10	.40	.074266	.076290	.078331	.080387	.082458	.084542	.086640	.088751	.090872	.093004	.095146	.099454	.103790
	.30	.076948	.078972	.081013	.083069	.085140	.087225	.089323	.091433	.093555	.095687	.097829	.102137	.106472
	.20	.079630	.081655	.083695	.085752	.087823	.089907	.092005	.094115	.096237	.098369	.100511	.104819	.109154
	.10	.082313	.084337	.086378	.088434	.090505	.092590	.094688	.096798	.098920	.101052	.103193	.107502	.111837
	0.00	.084995	.087020	.089060	.091116	.093187	.095272	.097370	.099480	.101602	.103734	.105876	.110184	.114519
	-.10	.087678	.089702	.091743	.093799	.095870	.097955	.100053	.102163	.104284	.106416	.108558	.112867	.117202
	-.20	.090360	.092384	.094425	.096481	.098552	.100637	.102735	.104845	.106967	.109099	.111241	.115549	.119884
	-.30	.093042	.095067	.097108	.099164	.101235	.103319	.105417	.107528	.109649	.111781	.113923	.118231	.122567
	-.40	.095725	.097749	.099790	.101846	.103917	.106002	.108100	.110210	.112332	.114464	.116605	.120914	.125249
15	.40	.062534	.065374	.068265	.071208	.074202	.077246	.080339	.083480	.086669	.089905	.093186	.099881	.106747
	.30	.065217	.068056	.070947	.073891	.076884	.079928	.083021	.086163	.089352	.092587	.095868	.102563	.109429
	.20	.067899	.070738	.073630	.076573	.079567	.082611	.085704	.088845	.092034	.095270	.098551	.105246	.112111
	.10	.070581	.073421	.076312	.079255	.082249	.085293	.088386	.091528	.094717	.097952	.101233	.107928	.114794
	0.00	.073264	.076103	.078995	.081938	.084932	.087976	.091069	.094210	.097399	.100634	.103916	.110611	.117476
	-.10	.075946	.078786	.081677	.084620	.087614	.090658	.093751	.096892	.100081	.103317	.106598	.113293	.120159
	-.20	.078629	.081468	.084360	.087303	.090296	.093340	.096433	.099575	.102764	.105999	.109280	.115976	.122841
	-.30	.081311	.084150	.087042	.089985	.092979	.096023	.099116	.102257	.105446	.108682	.111963	.118658	.125524
	-.40	.083994	.086833	.089724	.092667	.095661	.098705	.101798	.104940	.108129	.111364	.114645	.121340	.128206
20	.40	.056846	.060114	.063449	.066850	.070313	.073838	.077423	.081065	.084763	.088514	.092316	.100066	.107996
	.30	.059529	.062797	.066132	.069532	.072996	.076521	.080105	.083748	.087445	.091196	.094998	.102748	.110678
	.20	.062211	.065479	.068814	.072215	.075678	.079203	.082788	.086430	.090127	.093878	.097681	.105431	.113361
	.10	.064894	.068162	.071497	.074897	.078361	.081886	.085470	.089112	.092810	.096561	.100363	.108113	.116043
	0.00	.067576	.070844	.074179	.077579	.081043	.084568	.088153	.091795	.095492	.099243	.103046	.110795	.118726
	-.10	.070259	.073527	.076862	.080262	.083725	.087250	.090835	.094477	.098175	.101926	.105728	.113478	.121408
	-.20	.072941	.076209	.079544	.082944	.086408	.089933	.093518	.097160	.100857	.104608	.108410	.116160	.124090
	-.30	.075623	.078891	.082226	.085627	.089090	.092615	.096200	.099842	.103540	.107291	.111093	.118843	.126773
	-.40	.078306	.081574	.084909	.088309	.091773	.095298	.098882	.102524	.106222	.109973	.113775	.121525	.129455
25	.40	.053570	.057110	.060724	.064407	.068156	.071969	.075842	.079772	.083755	.087788	.091869	.100158	.108599
	.30	.056253	.059793	.063406	.067089	.070839	.074652	.078525	.082454	.086437	.090471	.094551	.102840	.111282
	.20	.058935	.062475	.066088	.069772	.073521	.077334	.081207	.085137	.089120	.093153	.097234	.105523	.113964
	.10	.061617	.065158	.068771	.072454	.076204	.080017	.083890	.087819	.091802	.095836	.099916	.108205	.116647
	0.00	.064300	.067840	.071453	.075136	.078886	.082699	.086572	.090502	.094485	.098518	.102598	.110888	.119329
	-.10	.066982	.070523	.074136	.077819	.081568	.085381	.089254	.093184	.097167	.101200	.105281	.113570	.122011
	-.20	.069665	.073205	.076818	.080501	.084251	.088064	.091937	.095866	.099850	.103883	.107963	.116253	.124694
	-.30	.072347	.075887	.079501	.083184	.086933	.090746	.094619	.098549	.102532	.106565	.110646	.118935	.127376
	-.40	.075030	.078570	.082183	.085866	.089616	.093429	.097302	.101231	.105214	.109248	.113328	.121617	.130059
30	.40	.051494	.055226	.059032	.062909	.066851	.070853	.074912	.079022	.083180	.087381	.091622	.100207	.108910
	.30	.054176	.057908	.061715	.065591	.069533	.073535	.077594	.081704	.085862	.090063	.094304	.102880	.111592
	.20	.056858	.060591	.064397	.068274	.072216	.076218	.080276	.084387	.088544	.092746	.096986	.105572	.114274
	.10	.059541	.063273	.067080	.070956	.074898	.078900	.082959	.087069	.091227	.095428	.099669	.108254	.116957
	0.00	.062223	.065955	.069762	.073639	.077580	.081583	.085641	.089751	.093909	.098110	.102351	.110937	.119639
	-.10	.064906	.068638	.072445	.076321	.080263	.084265	.088324	.092434	.096592	.100793	.105034	.113619	.122322
	-.20	.067588	.071320	.075127	.079003	.082945	.086948	.091006	.095116	.099274	.103475	.107716	.116302	.125004
	-.30	.070271	.074003	.077809	.081686	.085628	.089630	.093688	.097799	.101957	.106158	.110398	.118984	.127687
	-.40	.072953	.076685	.080492	.084368	.088310	.092312	.096371	.100481	.104639	.108840	.113081	.121667	.130369

15.0 YEAR HOLDING PERIOD
.140 EQUITY YIELD RATE
.600 LOAN RATIO

INTEREST RATE

TERM YEARS	APPR DEP	5.0	5.5	6.0	6.5	7.0	7.5	8.0	8.5	9.0	9.5	10.0	11.0	12.0
10	.40	.099687	.101100	.102525	.103963	.105413	.106874	.108347	.109829	.111322	.112824	.114335	.117381	.120455
	.30	.101968	.103381	.104806	.106244	.107694	.109155	.110628	.112111	.113603	.115105	.116616	.119662	.122736
	.20	.104249	.105661	.107087	.108525	.109975	.111436	.112908	.114391	.115884	.117386	.118897	.121942	.125016
	.10	.106529	.107942	.109368	.110806	.112256	.113717	.115189	.116672	.118165	.119667	.121178	.124223	.127297
	0.00	.108810	.110223	.111649	.113087	.114537	.115998	.117470	.118953	.120446	.121948	.123459	.126504	.129578
	-.10	.111091	.112504	.113930	.115368	.116818	.118279	.119751	.121234	.122727	.124228	.125739	.128785	.131859
	-.20	.113372	.114785	.116211	.117649	.119098	.120560	.122032	.123515	.125007	.126509	.128020	.131066	.134140
	-.30	.115653	.117066	.118492	.119929	.121379	.122841	.124313	.125796	.127288	.128790	.130301	.133347	.136421
	-.40	.117934	.119347	.120772	.122210	.123660	.125122	.126594	.128077	.129569	.131071	.132582	.135628	.138702
15	.40	.090128	.092021	.093949	.095911	.097907	.099936	.101998	.104092	.106218	.108375	.110563	.115026	.119603
	.30	.092409	.094302	.096230	.098192	.100188	.102217	.104279	.106373	.108499	.110656	.112844	.117307	.121884
	.20	.094690	.096583	.098511	.100473	.102468	.104498	.106560	.108654	.110780	.112937	.115124	.119588	.124165
	.10	.096971	.098864	.100791	.102753	.104749	.106779	.108841	.110935	.113061	.115218	.117405	.121869	.126446
	0.00	.099252	.101145	.103072	.105034	.107030	.109060	.111122	.113216	.115342	.117499	.119686	.124150	.128727
	-.10	.101533	.103426	.105353	.107315	.109311	.111340	.113402	.115497	.117623	.119780	.121967	.126430	.131008
	-.20	.103814	.105706	.107634	.109596	.111592	.113621	.115683	.117778	.119904	.122061	.124248	.128711	.133289
	-.30	.106094	.107987	.109915	.111877	.113873	.115902	.117964	.120059	.122185	.124341	.126529	.130992	.135569
	-.40	.108375	.110268	.112196	.114158	.116154	.118183	.120245	.122339	.124465	.126622	.128810	.133273	.137850
20	.40	.085494	.087647	.089846	.092087	.094371	.096696	.099060	.101463	.103903	.106379	.108888	.114006	.119243
	.30	.087775	.089928	.092126	.094368	.096652	.098977	.101341	.103744	.106184	.108659	.111169	.116286	.121524
	.20	.090056	.092209	.094407	.096649	.098933	.101258	.103622	.106025	.108465	.110940	.113450	.118567	.123805
	.10	.092337	.094490	.096688	.098930	.101214	.103538	.105903	.108306	.110746	.113221	.115731	.120848	.126086
	0.00	.094617	.096771	.098969	.101211	.103495	.105819	.108184	.110587	.113027	.115502	.118012	.123130	.128367
	-.10	.096898	.099052	.101250	.103492	.105775	.108100	.110465	.112868	.115307	.117783	.120293	.125410	.130648
	-.20	.099179	.101333	.103531	.105773	.108056	.110381	.112746	.115148	.117588	.120064	.122574	.127691	.132929
	-.30	.101460	.103614	.105812	.108053	.110337	.112662	.115026	.117429	.119869	.122345	.124855	.129972	.135210
	-.40	.103741	.105895	.108093	.110334	.112618	.114943	.117307	.119710	.122150	.124626	.127136	.132253	.137491
25	.40	.082824	.085149	.087523	.089944	.092410	.094918	.097468	.100055	.102679	.105338	.108028	.113497	.119070
	.30	.085105	.087430	.089804	.092225	.094691	.097199	.099749	.102336	.104960	.107619	.110309	.115777	.121351
	.20	.087386	.089711	.092085	.094506	.096972	.099480	.102029	.104617	.107241	.109899	.112590	.118058	.123631
	.10	.089667	.091992	.094366	.096787	.099252	.101761	.104310	.106898	.109522	.112180	.114871	.120339	.125912
	0.00	.091948	.094273	.096647	.099067	.101533	.104042	.106591	.109179	.111803	.114461	.117151	.122520	.128193
	-.10	.094229	.096554	.098927	.101348	.103814	.106323	.108872	.111460	.114084	.116742	.119432	.124901	.130474
	-.20	.096510	.098834	.101208	.103629	.106095	.108604	.111153	.113741	.116365	.119023	.121713	.127182	.132755
	-.30	.098791	.101115	.103489	.105910	.108376	.110885	.113434	.116022	.118646	.121304	.123994	.129463	.135036
	-.40	.101072	.103396	.105770	.108191	.110657	.113166	.115715	.118303	.120927	.123585	.126275	.131744	.137317
30	.40	.081132	.083582	.086082	.088630	.091223	.093857	.096530	.099239	.101981	.104753	.107552	.113225	.118980
	.30	.083413	.085863	.088363	.090911	.093503	.096138	.098811	.101520	.104261	.107033	.109833	.115506	.121261
	.20	.085694	.088144	.090644	.093192	.095784	.098419	.101092	.103801	.106542	.109314	.112114	.117787	.123542
	.10	.087975	.090424	.092925	.095473	.098065	.100700	.103373	.106081	.108823	.111595	.114395	.120068	.125823
	0.00	.090256	.092705	.095206	.097754	.100346	.102980	.105654	.108362	.111104	.113876	.116676	.122349	.128104
	-.10	.092537	.094986	.097486	.100034	.102627	.105261	.107934	.110643	.113385	.116157	.118957	.124629	.130385
	-.20	.094818	.097267	.099767	.102315	.104908	.107542	.110215	.112924	.115666	.118438	.121238	.126910	.132666
	-.30	.097099	.099548	.102048	.104596	.107189	.109823	.112496	.115205	.117947	.120719	.123519	.129191	.134947
	-.40	.099380	.101829	.104329	.106877	.109470	.112104	.114777	.117486	.120228	.123000	.125799	.131472	.137227

INTEREST RATE

TERM YEARS	APPR DEP	5.0	5.5	6.0	6.5	7.0	7.5	8.0	8.5	9.0	9.5	10.0	11.0	12.0
10	.40	.096221	.097791	.099375	.100973	.102584	.104207	.105843	.107491	.109149	.110818	.112497	.115881	.119297
	.30	.098502	.100072	.101656	.103254	.104865	.106488	.108124	.109772	.111430	.113099	.114778	.118162	.121578
	.20	.100783	.102353	.103937	.105535	.107146	.108769	.110405	.112053	.113711	.115380	.117059	.120443	.123858
	.10	.103064	.104634	.106218	.107815	.109426	.111050	.112686	.114333	.115992	.117661	.119339	.122724	.126139
	0.00	.105345	.106915	.108499	.110096	.111707	.113331	.114967	.116614	.118273	.119942	.121620	.125005	.128420
	-.10	.107626	.109195	.110779	.112377	.113988	.115612	.117247	.118895	.120554	.122223	.123901	.127285	.130701
	-.20	.109907	.111476	.113060	.114658	.116269	.117893	.119529	.121176	.122835	.124503	.126182	.129566	.132982
	-.30	.112187	.113757	.115341	.116939	.118550	.120174	.121810	.123457	.125115	.126784	.128463	.131847	.135263
	-.40	.114468	.116038	.117622	.119220	.120831	.122455	.124090	.125738	.127396	.129065	.130744	.134128	.137544
15	.40	.085600	.087704	.089845	.092026	.094243	.096498	.098789	.101116	.103478	.105875	.108305	.113265	.118350
	.30	.087881	.089984	.092126	.094306	.096524	.098779	.101070	.103397	.105759	.108156	.110586	.115546	.120631
	.20	.090162	.092265	.094407	.096587	.098805	.101060	.103351	.105678	.108040	.110437	.112867	.117827	.122912
	.10	.092443	.094546	.096688	.098868	.101086	.103341	.105632	.107959	.110321	.112718	.115148	.120107	.125193
	0.00	.094724	.096827	.098969	.101149	.103367	.105622	.107913	.110240	.112602	.114999	.117429	.122388	.127474
	-.10	.097005	.099108	.101250	.103430	.105648	.107902	.110194	.112521	.114883	.117279	.119710	.124669	.129755
	-.20	.099286	.101389	.103531	.105711	.107929	.110183	.112474	.114801	.117164	.119560	.121991	.126950	.132036
	-.30	.101567	.103670	.105812	.107992	.110209	.112464	.114755	.117082	.119445	.121841	.124272	.129231	.134317
	-.40	.103848	.105951	.108093	.110273	.112490	.114745	.117036	.119363	.121725	.124122	.126553	.131512	.136598
20	.40	.080451	.082844	.085286	.087777	.090315	.092898	.095525	.098195	.100906	.103656	.106445	.112131	.117951
	.30	.082732	.085125	.087567	.090058	.092595	.095179	.097806	.100476	.103187	.105937	.108726	.114412	.120232
	.20	.085013	.087406	.089848	.092339	.094876	.097459	.100087	.102757	.105468	.108218	.111007	.116693	.122513
	.10	.087294	.089687	.092129	.094620	.097157	.099740	.102368	.105037	.107748	.110499	.113288	.118974	.124793
	0.00	.089575	.091968	.094410	.096901	.099438	.102021	.104648	.107318	.110029	.112780	.115569	.121254	.127074
	-.10	.091856	.094248	.096691	.099181	.101719	.104302	.106929	.109599	.112310	.115061	.117850	.123535	.129355
	-.20	.094136	.096529	.098972	.101462	.104000	.106583	.109210	.111880	.114591	.117342	.120131	.125816	.131636
	-.30	.096417	.098810	.101253	.103744	.106281	.108864	.111491	.114161	.116872	.119623	.122411	.128097	.133917
	-.40	.098698	.101091	.103534	.106024	.108562	.111145	.113772	.116442	.119153	.121904	.124692	.130378	.136198
25	.40	.077465	.080060	.082706	.085396	.088135	.090923	.093755	.096631	.099546	.102500	.105489	.111565	.117758
	.30	.079766	.082349	.084987	.087677	.090416	.093204	.096036	.098912	.101827	.104781	.107770	.113846	.120039
	.20	.082047	.084630	.087267	.089957	.092697	.095485	.098317	.101192	.104108	.107062	.110051	.116127	.122320
	.10	.084328	.086911	.089548	.092238	.094978	.097766	.100598	.103473	.106389	.109343	.112332	.118408	.124600
	0.00	.086600	.089182	.091829	.094519	.097259	.100046	.102879	.105754	.108670	.111623	.114613	.120689	.126881
	-.10	.088889	.091473	.094110	.096800	.099540	.102327	.105160	.108035	.110951	.113904	.116894	.122970	.129162
	-.20	.091170	.093753	.096391	.099081	.101821	.104608	.107441	.110316	.113232	.116185	.119174	.125251	.131443
	-.30	.093451	.096034	.098672	.101362	.104102	.106890	.109722	.112597	.115513	.118466	.121455	.127532	.133724
	-.40	.095732	.098315	.100953	.103643	.106383	.109170	.112003	.114878	.117793	.120747	.123736	.129813	.136005
30	.40	.075605	.078327	.081105	.083936	.086816	.089743	.092713	.095723	.098770	.101850	.104961	.111264	.117658
	.30	.077886	.080607	.083385	.086217	.089097	.092024	.094994	.098004	.101051	.104131	.107241	.113544	.119939
	.20	.080167	.082888	.085666	.088497	.091378	.094305	.097275	.100285	.103332	.106412	.109522	.115825	.122220
	.10	.082448	.085169	.087947	.090778	.093659	.096586	.099556	.102566	.105612	.108692	.111803	.118106	.124501
	0.00	.084729	.087450	.090228	.093059	.095940	.098867	.101837	.104847	.107893	.110973	.114084	.120387	.126793
	-.10	.087009	.089731	.092509	.095340	.098221	.101148	.104118	.107128	.110174	.113254	.116365	.122668	.129053
	-.20	.089290	.092012	.094790	.097621	.100502	.103429	.106399	.109409	.112455	.115535	.118646	.124949	.131344
	-.30	.091571	.094293	.097071	.099902	.102783	.105710	.108680	.111690	.114736	.117816	.120927	.127230	.133625
	-.40	.093652	.096574	.099352	.102183	.105064	.107991	.110961	.113970	.117017	.120097	.123208	.129511	.135936

15.0 YEAR HOLDING PERIOD
.140 EQUITY YIELD RATE
.700 LOAN RATIO

INTEREST RATE

TERM YEARS	APPR DEP	5.0	5.5	6.0	6.5	7.0	7.5	8.0	8.5	9.0	9.5	10.0	11.0	12.0
10	.40	.094489	.096137	.097800	.099478	.101169	.102874	.104592	.106322	.108063	.109815	.111578	.115131	.118718
	.30	.096769	.098418	.100081	.101759	.103450	.105155	.106873	.108602	.110344	.112096	.113859	.117442	.120999
	.20	.099050	.100699	.102362	.104039	.105731	.107436	.109154	.110883	.112625	.114377	.116140	.119693	.123279
	.10	.101331	.102980	.104643	.106320	.108012	.109717	.111434	.113164	.114906	.116658	.118421	.121974	.125560
	0.00	.103612	.105260	.106924	.108601	.110293	.111998	.113715	.115445	.117187	.118939	.120701	.124265	.127841
	-.10	.105893	.107541	.109205	.110882	.112574	.114279	.115996	.117726	.119467	.121220	.122982	.126536	.130122
	-.20	.108174	.109822	.111485	.113163	.114855	.116559	.118277	.120007	.121748	.123501	.125263	.128817	.132403
	-.30	.110455	.112103	.113766	.115444	.117136	.118840	.120558	.122288	.124029	.125782	.127544	.131098	.134684
	-.40	.112736	.114384	.116047	.117725	.119416	.121121	.122839	.124569	.126310	.128062	.129825	.133378	.136965
15	.40	.083337	.085545	.087794	.090083	.092412	.094779	.097185	.099628	.102109	.104625	.107177	.112384	.117724
	.30	.085618	.087826	.090075	.092364	.094693	.097060	.099466	.101909	.104389	.106906	.109458	.114665	.120005
	.20	.087899	.090107	.092356	.094645	.096974	.099341	.101747	.104190	.106670	.109187	.111739	.116946	.122286
	.10	.090179	.092388	.094637	.096926	.099254	.101622	.104028	.106471	.108951	.111468	.114020	.119227	.124567
	0.00	.092460	.094669	.096918	.099207	.101535	.103903	.106309	.108752	.111232	.113749	.116301	.121508	.126848
	-.10	.094741	.096950	.099199	.101488	.103816	.106184	.108589	.111033	.113513	.116029	.118581	.123789	.129129
	-.20	.097022	.099231	.101479	.103769	.106097	.108465	.110870	.113314	.115794	.118310	.120862	.126070	.131410
	-.30	.099303	.101511	.103760	.106049	.108378	.110745	.113151	.115595	.118075	.120591	.123143	.128351	.133691
	-.40	.101584	.103792	.106041	.108330	.110659	.113026	.115432	.117875	.120356	.122872	.125424	.130631	.135971
20	.40	.077930	.080443	.083007	.085622	.088287	.090999	.093758	.096561	.099407	.102296	.105224	.111194	.117305
	.30	.080211	.082723	.085288	.087903	.090568	.093280	.096038	.098842	.101688	.104576	.107505	.113475	.119585
	.20	.082492	.085004	.087569	.090184	.092849	.095561	.098319	.101123	.103969	.106857	.109785	.115756	.121866
	.10	.084773	.087285	.089850	.092465	.095130	.097842	.100600	.103404	.106250	.109138	.112066	.118036	.124147
	0.00	.087054	.089566	.092131	.094746	.097410	.100123	.102881	.105684	.108531	.111419	.114347	.120317	.126428
	-.10	.089335	.091847	.094412	.097027	.099691	.102403	.105162	.107965	.110812	.113700	.116628	.122598	.128709
	-.20	.091615	.094128	.096692	.099308	.101972	.104684	.107443	.110246	.113093	.115981	.118909	.124879	.130990
	-.30	.093896	.096409	.098973	.101589	.104253	.106965	.109724	.112527	.115374	.118262	.121190	.127160	.133271
	-.40	.096177	.098690	.101254	.103869	.106534	.109246	.112005	.114808	.117655	.120543	.123471	.129441	.135552
25	.40	.074816	.077528	.080297	.083122	.085999	.088925	.091900	.094919	.097980	.101081	.104220	.110600	.117102
	.30	.077097	.079809	.082578	.085403	.088280	.091206	.094180	.097199	.100261	.103362	.106501	.112881	.119383
	.20	.079377	.082090	.084859	.087684	.090560	.093487	.096461	.099480	.102542	.105643	.108782	.115162	.121664
	.10	.081658	.084371	.087140	.089964	.092841	.095768	.098742	.101761	.104823	.107924	.111062	.117443	.123945
	0.00	.083939	.086651	.089421	.092245	.095122	.098049	.101023	.104042	.107103	.110205	.113343	.119723	.126225
	-.10	.086220	.088932	.091702	.094526	.097403	.100330	.103304	.106323	.109384	.112486	.115624	.122004	.128506
	-.20	.088501	.091213	.093983	.096807	.099684	.102611	.105585	.108604	.111665	.114767	.117905	.124285	.130787
	-.30	.090782	.093494	.096264	.099088	.101965	.104892	.107866	.110885	.113946	.117047	.120186	.126566	.133068
	-.40	.093063	.095775	.098545	.101369	.104246	.107173	.110147	.113166	.116227	.119328	.122467	.128847	.135349
30	.40	.072842	.075699	.078616	.081589	.084614	.087687	.090806	.093966	.097165	.100399	.103665	.110283	.116998
	.30	.075123	.077980	.080897	.083870	.086895	.089968	.093086	.096247	.099445	.102680	.105946	.112564	.119279
	.20	.077403	.080261	.083178	.086151	.089175	.092249	.095367	.098528	.101726	.104960	.108227	.114845	.121559
	.10	.079684	.082542	.085459	.088432	.091456	.094530	.097648	.100808	.104007	.107241	.110508	.117126	.123840
	0.00	.081965	.084823	.087740	.090712	.093737	.096811	.099929	.103089	.106288	.109522	.112789	.119407	.126121
	-.10	.084246	.087104	.090021	.092993	.096018	.099091	.102210	.105370	.108569	.111803	.115069	.121687	.128402
	-.20	.086527	.089385	.092302	.095274	.098299	.101372	.104491	.107651	.110850	.114084	.117350	.123968	.130683
	-.30	.088808	.091666	.094583	.097555	.100580	.103653	.106772	.109932	.113131	.116365	.119631	.126249	.132964
	-.40	.091089	.093947	.096863	.099836	.102861	.105934	.109053	.112213	.115412	.118646	.121912	.128530	.135245

15.0 YEAR HOLDING PERIOD
.140 EQUITY YIELD RATE
.750 LOAN RATIO

INTEREST RATE

TERM YEARS	APPR DEP	5.0	5.5	6.0	6.5	7.0	7.5	8.0	8.5	9.0	9.5	10.0	11.0	12.0
10	.40	.091889	.093655	.095437	.097235	.099047	.100874	.102714	.104568	.106433	.108311	.110199	.114007	.117849
	.30	.094170	.095936	.097718	.099516	.101328	.103155	.104995	.106849	.108714	.110592	.112480	.116288	.120130
	.20	.096451	.098217	.099999	.101797	.103609	.105436	.107276	.109129	.110995	.112873	.114761	.118568	.122411
	.10	.098732	.100498	.102280	.104078	.105890	.107717	.109557	.111410	.113276	.115154	.117042	.120849	.124692
	0.00	.101013	.102779	.104561	.106359	.108171	.109998	.111838	.113691	.115557	.117434	.119323	.123130	.126973
	-.10	.103294	.105060	.106842	.108639	.110452	.112278	.114119	.115972	.117838	.119715	.121604	.125411	.129254
	-.20	.105575	.107341	.109123	.110920	.112733	.114559	.116400	.118253	.120119	.121996	.123885	.127692	.131535
	-.30	.107856	.109622	.111404	.113201	.115014	.116840	.118681	.120534	.122400	.124277	.126166	.129973	.133815
	-.40	.110137	.111903	.113685	.115482	.117294	.119121	.120961	.122815	.124681	.126558	.128447	.132254	.136096
15	.40	.079941	.082307	.084717	.087169	.089664	.092201	.094778	.097396	.100054	.102750	.105484	.111063	.116785
	.30	.082222	.084588	.086998	.089450	.091945	.094482	.097059	.099677	.102335	.105031	.107765	.113344	.119066
	.20	.084503	.086869	.089279	.091731	.094226	.096763	.099340	.101958	.104615	.107312	.110046	.115625	.121347
	.10	.086784	.089150	.091559	.094012	.096507	.099043	.101621	.104239	.106896	.109593	.112327	.117906	.123628
	0.00	.089065	.091431	.093840	.096293	.098788	.101324	.103902	.106520	.109177	.111873	.114608	.120187	.125908
	-.10	.091346	.093712	.096121	.098574	.101069	.103605	.106183	.108801	.111458	.114154	.116889	.122468	.128189
	-.20	.093626	.095993	.098402	.100855	.103350	.105886	.108464	.111082	.113739	.116435	.119170	.124749	.130470
	-.30	.095907	.098273	.100683	.103136	.105631	.108167	.110745	.113363	.116020	.118716	.121450	.127030	.132751
	-.40	.098188	.100554	.102964	.105417	.107911	.110448	.113026	.115643	.118301	.120997	.123731	.129311	.135032
20	.40	.074148	.076840	.079588	.082390	.085245	.088151	.091106	.094110	.097160	.100254	.103391	.109788	.116335
	.30	.076429	.079121	.081869	.084671	.087525	.090431	.093387	.096391	.099440	.102535	.105672	.112069	.118616
	.20	.078710	.081402	.084150	.086952	.089806	.092712	.095668	.098672	.101721	.104816	.107953	.114350	.120897
	.10	.080991	.083683	.086431	.089233	.092087	.094993	.097949	.100952	.104002	.107097	.110234	.116630	.123178
	0.00	.083272	.085964	.088711	.091513	.094368	.097274	.100230	.103233	.106283	.109378	.112515	.118911	.125459
	-.10	.085553	.088245	.090992	.093794	.096649	.099555	.102511	.105514	.108564	.111659	.114796	.121192	.127740
	-.20	.087834	.090526	.093273	.096075	.098930	.101836	.104792	.107795	.110845	.113939	.117077	.123473	.130021
	-.30	.090114	.092806	.095554	.098356	.101211	.104117	.107072	.110076	.113126	.116220	.119358	.125754	.132301
	-.40	.092395	.095087	.097835	.100637	.103492	.106398	.109353	.112357	.115407	.118501	.121639	.128035	.134582
25	.40	.070811	.073717	.076685	.079711	.082793	.085929	.089115	.092350	.095630	.098953	.102316	.109152	.116118
	.30	.073092	.075998	.078966	.081992	.085074	.088210	.091396	.094631	.097911	.101234	.104597	.111432	.118399
	.20	.075373	.078279	.081247	.084273	.087355	.090491	.093677	.096912	.100192	.103515	.106878	.113713	.120680
	.10	.077654	.080560	.083528	.086553	.089636	.092772	.095958	.099193	.102473	.105796	.109158	.115994	.122961
	0.00	.079935	.082841	.085808	.088834	.091917	.095052	.098239	.101474	.104754	.108076	.111439	.118275	.125242
	-.10	.082216	.085122	.088090	.091115	.094198	.097333	.100520	.103755	.107035	.110357	.113720	.120556	.127522
	-.20	.084497	.087403	.090370	.093396	.096478	.099614	.102801	.106035	.109316	.112638	.116001	.122837	.129803
	-.30	.086778	.089684	.092651	.095677	.098759	.101895	.105082	.108316	.111596	.114919	.118282	.125118	.132084
	-.40	.089058	.091964	.094933	.097958	.101040	.104176	.107363	.110597	.113877	.117200	.120563	.127399	.134365
30	.40	.068696	.071758	.074883	.078068	.081309	.084602	.087943	.091329	.094757	.098222	.101721	.108812	.116006
	.30	.070977	.074039	.077164	.080349	.083590	.086883	.090224	.093610	.097037	.100503	.104002	.111093	.118287
	.20	.073258	.076320	.079445	.082630	.085871	.089164	.092505	.095891	.099318	.102783	.106283	.113374	.120568
	.10	.075539	.078601	.081726	.084911	.088152	.091445	.094786	.098172	.101599	.105064	.108564	.115655	.122849
	0.00	.077820	.080881	.084007	.087192	.090433	.093726	.097067	.100453	.103880	.107345	.110845	.117936	.125130
	-.10	.080101	.083163	.086288	.089473	.092714	.096007	.099348	.102734	.106161	.109626	.113126	.120217	.127411
	-.20	.082382	.085443	.088569	.091754	.094994	.098287	.101629	.105015	.108442	.111907	.115407	.122497	.129692
	-.30	.084663	.087724	.090850	.094035	.097275	.100568	.103910	.107295	.110723	.114188	.117688	.124778	.131973
	-.40	.086944	.090005	.093131	.096315	.099556	.102849	.106190	.109577	.113004	.116469	.119968	.127059	.134253

327

15.0 YEAR HOLDING PERIOD
.140 EQUITY YIELD RATE
.800 LOAN RATIO

INTEREST RATE

TERM YEARS	APPR DEP	5.0	5.5	6.0	6.5	7.0	7.5	8.0	8.5	9.0	9.5	10.0	11.0	12.0
10	.40	.089290	.091174	.093075	.094992	.096925	.098874	.100837	.102814	.104804	.106807	.108821	.112882	.116981
	.30	.091571	.093455	.095356	.097273	.099206	.101155	.103118	.105095	.107085	.109087	.111102	.115163	.119262
	.20	.093852	.095736	.097637	.099554	.101487	.103436	.105399	.107376	.109366	.111368	.113383	.117444	.121543
	.10	.096133	.098017	.099918	.101835	.103768	.105716	.107679	.109656	.111647	.113649	.115664	.119725	.123823
	0.00	.098414	.100298	.102198	.104116	.106049	.107997	.109960	.111937	.113927	.115930	.117945	.122006	.126104
	-.10	.100695	.102579	.104479	.106397	.108330	.110278	.112241	.114218	.116208	.118211	.120226	.124286	.128385
	-.20	.102976	.104859	.106760	.108678	.110611	.112559	.114522	.116499	.118489	.120492	.122506	.126567	.130666
	-.30	.105257	.107140	.109041	.110958	.112892	.114840	.116803	.118780	.120770	.122773	.124787	.128848	.132947
	-.40	.107537	.109421	.111322	.113239	.115173	.117121	.119084	.121061	.123051	.125054	.127068	.131129	.135228
15	.40	.076545	.079069	.081639	.084256	.086917	.089622	.092372	.095164	.097999	.100675	.103791	.109743	.115845
	.30	.078826	.081350	.083920	.086536	.089198	.091903	.094653	.097445	.100280	.103156	.106072	.112023	.118126
	.20	.081107	.083631	.086201	.088817	.091479	.094184	.096934	.099726	.102561	.105437	.108353	.114304	.120407
	.10	.083388	.085912	.088482	.091098	.093759	.096465	.099215	.102007	.104842	.107718	.110634	.116585	.122688
	0.00	.085669	.088193	.090763	.093379	.096040	.098746	.101496	.104288	.107122	.109998	.112915	.118866	.124969
	-.10	.087950	.090474	.093044	.095660	.098321	.101027	.103776	.106569	.109403	.112279	.115196	.121147	.127250
	-.20	.090231	.092755	.095325	.097941	.100602	.103308	.106057	.108850	.111684	.114560	.117477	.123428	.129531
	-.30	.092512	.095036	.097606	.100222	.102883	.105589	.108338	.111131	.113965	.116841	.119758	.125709	.131812
	-.40	.094793	.097316	.099887	.102503	.105164	.107870	.110619	.113411	.116246	.119122	.122039	.127990	.134093
20	.40	.070366	.073238	.076169	.079157	.082202	.085302	.088455	.091659	.094912	.098213	.101559	.108382	.115366
	.30	.072647	.075519	.078450	.081438	.084483	.087583	.090736	.093939	.097193	.100493	.103840	.110663	.117647
	.20	.074928	.077800	.080730	.083719	.086764	.089864	.093017	.096220	.099474	.102774	.106121	.112944	.119928
	.10	.077209	.080080	.083011	.086000	.089045	.092145	.095297	.098501	.101754	.105055	.108402	.115225	.122208
	0.00	.079490	.082361	.085292	.088281	.091326	.094426	.097578	.100782	.104035	.107336	.110683	.117505	.124489
	-.10	.081771	.084642	.087573	.090562	.093607	.096707	.099859	.103063	.106316	.109617	.112964	.119786	.126770
	-.20	.084052	.086923	.089854	.092843	.095888	.098988	.102140	.105344	.108597	.111898	.115244	.122067	.129051
	-.30	.086333	.089204	.092135	.095124	.098169	.101268	.104421	.107625	.110878	.114179	.117525	.124348	.131332
	-.40	.088613	.091485	.094416	.097405	.100450	.103549	.106702	.109906	.113159	.116460	.119806	.126629	.133613
25	.40	.066807	.069917	.073072	.076300	.079588	.082932	.086331	.089782	.093280	.096825	.100412	.107703	.115134
	.30	.069088	.072198	.075353	.078581	.081868	.085213	.088612	.092063	.095561	.099106	.102693	.109984	.117415
	.20	.071369	.074468	.077634	.080862	.084149	.087494	.090893	.094343	.097842	.101386	.104974	.112265	.119696
	.10	.073650	.076749	.079915	.083142	.086430	.089775	.093174	.096624	.100123	.103667	.107254	.114546	.121977
	0.00	.075931	.079030	.082195	.085423	.088711	.092056	.095455	.098905	.102404	.105948	.109535	.116827	.124258
	-.10	.078211	.081311	.084476	.087704	.090992	.094337	.097736	.101186	.104685	.108229	.111816	.119108	.126539
	-.20	.080492	.083592	.086757	.089985	.093273	.096618	.100017	.103467	.106966	.110510	.114097	.121389	.128819
	-.30	.082773	.085873	.089038	.092266	.095554	.098899	.102298	.105748	.109247	.112791	.116378	.123670	.131100
	-.40	.085054	.088154	.091319	.094547	.097835	.101180	.104579	.108029	.111528	.115072	.118659	.125950	.133381
30	.40	.064551	.067817	.071150	.074548	.078005	.081517	.085081	.088693	.092349	.096045	.099778	.107341	.115015
	.30	.066832	.070098	.073431	.076829	.080286	.083798	.087362	.090974	.094629	.098326	.102058	.109622	.117296
	.20	.069113	.072379	.075712	.079110	.082566	.086079	.089643	.093255	.096910	.100506	.104339	.111903	.119577
	.10	.071394	.074660	.077993	.081390	.084847	.088360	.091924	.095536	.099191	.102887	.106620	.114184	.121858
	0.00	.073675	.076940	.080274	.083671	.087128	.090641	.094205	.097816	.101472	.105168	.108901	.116465	.124139
	-.10	.075955	.079221	.082555	.085952	.089409	.092922	.096486	.100097	.103753	.107449	.111182	.118746	.126419
	-.20	.078236	.081502	.084836	.088233	.091690	.095202	.098766	.102378	.106034	.109730	.113463	.121026	.128700
	-.30	.080517	.083783	.087117	.090514	.093971	.097483	.101047	.104659	.108315	.112011	.115744	.123307	.130981
	-.40	.082798	.086064	.089398	.092795	.096252	.099764	.103328	.106940	.110596	.114292	.118025	.125588	.133262

15.0 YEAR HOLDING PERIOD
.140 EQUITY YIELD RATE
.900 LOAN RATIO

INTEREST RATE

TERM YEARS	APPR DEP	5.0	5.5	6.0	6.5	7.0	7.5	8.0	8.5	9.0	9.5	10.0	11.0	12.0
10	.40	.084092	.086211	.088350	.090507	.092681	.094873	.097082	.099306	.101545	.103798	.106064	.110633	.115244
	.30	.086373	.088492	.090631	.092788	.094962	.097154	.099363	.101587	.103826	.106079	.108345	.112914	.117525
	.20	.088654	.090773	.092911	.095068	.097243	.099435	.101644	.103868	.106107	.108360	.110626	.115194	.119806
	.10	.090935	.093054	.095192	.097349	.099524	.101716	.103925	.106149	.108388	.110640	.112907	.117475	.122086
	0.00	.093216	.095335	.097473	.099630	.101805	.103997	.106205	.108429	.110668	.112921	.115188	.119756	.124367
	-.10	.095496	.097616	.099754	.101911	.104086	.106278	.108486	.110710	.112949	.115202	.117469	.122037	.126648
	-.20	.097777	.099897	.102035	.104192	.106367	.108559	.110767	.112991	.115230	.117483	.119749	.124318	.128929
	-.30	.100058	.102177	.104316	.106473	.108648	.110840	.113048	.115272	.117511	.119764	.122030	.126599	.131210
	-.40	.102339	.104458	.106597	.108754	.110929	.113121	.115329	.117553	.119792	.122045	.124311	.128880	.133491
15	.40	.069754	.072593	.075485	.078428	.081422	.084466	.087559	.090700	.093889	.097125	.100406	.107101	.113966
	.30	.072035	.074874	.077766	.080709	.083703	.086747	.089840	.092981	.096170	.099406	.102687	.109382	.116247
	.20	.074316	.077155	.080047	.082990	.085984	.089027	.092121	.095262	.098451	.101686	.104967	.111663	.118528
	.10	.076597	.079436	.082328	.085271	.088264	.091308	.094401	.097543	.100732	.103967	.107248	.113943	.120809
	0.00	.078878	.081717	.084608	.087552	.090545	.093589	.096682	.099824	.103013	.106248	.109529	.116224	.123090
	-.10	.081159	.083998	.086889	.089832	.092826	.095870	.098963	.102105	.105294	.108529	.111810	.118505	.125371
	-.20	.083439	.086279	.089170	.092113	.095107	.098151	.101244	.104386	.107575	.110810	.114091	.120786	.127652
	-.30	.085720	.088560	.091451	.094394	.097388	.100432	.103525	.106666	.109855	.113091	.116372	.123067	.129933
	-.40	.088001	.090841	.093732	.096675	.099669	.102713	.105806	.108947	.112136	.115372	.118653	.125348	.132214
20	.40	.062803	.066033	.069330	.072693	.076118	.079605	.083152	.086756	.090416	.094130	.097894	.105570	.113427
	.30	.065083	.068314	.071611	.074973	.078399	.081886	.085433	.089037	.092697	.096410	.100175	.107851	.115708
	.20	.067364	.070595	.073892	.077254	.080680	.084167	.087714	.091318	.094978	.098691	.102456	.110132	.117989
	.10	.069645	.072876	.076173	.079535	.082961	.086448	.089995	.093599	.097259	.100972	.104737	.112413	.120270
	0.00	.071926	.075157	.078454	.081816	.085242	.088729	.092276	.095880	.099540	.103253	.107018	.114694	.122550
	-.10	.074207	.077437	.080735	.084097	.087523	.091010	.094557	.098161	.101821	.105534	.109299	.116975	.124831
	-.20	.076488	.079718	.083016	.086378	.089804	.093291	.096837	.100442	.104102	.107815	.111580	.119255	.127112
	-.30	.078769	.081999	.085296	.088659	.092084	.095572	.099118	.102723	.106382	.110096	.113861	.121536	.129393
	-.40	.081050	.084280	.087577	.090940	.094365	.097853	.101399	.105004	.108663	.112377	.116142	.123817	.131674
25	.40	.058798	.062285	.065846	.069478	.073176	.076939	.080763	.084645	.088581	.092568	.096604	.104807	.113166
	.30	.061079	.064566	.068127	.071759	.075457	.079220	.083044	.086926	.090862	.094849	.098885	.107088	.115447
	.20	.063360	.066847	.070408	.074039	.077738	.081501	.085325	.089207	.093143	.097130	.101165	.109368	.117728
	.10	.065641	.069128	.072689	.076320	.080019	.083782	.087606	.091488	.095424	.099411	.103446	.111649	.120009
	0.00	.067922	.071409	.074970	.078601	.082300	.086063	.089887	.093768	.097704	.101692	.105727	.113930	.122290
	-.10	.070203	.073690	.077251	.080882	.084581	.088344	.092168	.096049	.099985	.103973	.108008	.116211	.124571
	-.20	.072484	.075971	.079532	.083163	.086862	.090625	.094449	.098330	.102266	.106254	.110289	.118492	.126852
	-.30	.074765	.078252	.081813	.085444	.089143	.092906	.096730	.100611	.104547	.108534	.112570	.120773	.129133
	-.40	.077045	.080533	.084093	.087725	.091424	.095187	.099010	.102892	.106828	.110815	.114851	.123054	.131413
30	.40	.056260	.059934	.063685	.067507	.071396	.075347	.079357	.083420	.087533	.091691	.095890	.104399	.113032
	.30	.058541	.062215	.065966	.069788	.073677	.077628	.081638	.085701	.089814	.093972	.098171	.106680	.115313
	.20	.060822	.064496	.068247	.072068	.075957	.079909	.083918	.087982	.092094	.096252	.100452	.108961	.117594
	.10	.063103	.066777	.070527	.074349	.078238	.082190	.086199	.090263	.094375	.098533	.102733	.111242	.119875
	0.00	.065384	.069058	.072808	.076630	.080519	.084471	.088480	.092544	.096656	.100814	.105014	.113523	.122156
	-.10	.067665	.071339	.075089	.078911	.082800	.086752	.090761	.094824	.098937	.103095	.107295	.115804	.124437
	-.20	.069946	.073620	.077370	.081192	.085081	.089033	.093042	.097105	.101218	.105376	.109576	.118085	.126718
	-.30	.072227	.075901	.079651	.083473	.087362	.091313	.095323	.099386	.103499	.107657	.111857	.120365	.128999
	-.40	.074508	.078182	.081932	.085754	.089643	.093594	.097604	.101667	.105780	.109938	.114137	.122646	.131279

15.0 YEAR HOLDING PERIOD
.150 EQUITY YIELD RATE
.600 LOAN RATIO

INTEREST RATE

TERM YEARS	APPR DEP	5.0	5.5	6.0	6.5	7.0	7.5	8.0	8.5	9.0	9.5	10.0	11.0	12.0
10	.40	.106254	.107695	.109150	.110618	.112099	.113592	.115097	.116614	.118141	.119679	.121227	.124350	.127506
	.30	.108356	.109797	.111252	.112720	.114200	.115694	.117199	.118715	.120243	.121781	.123329	.126452	.129608
	.20	.110458	.111899	.113353	.114821	.116302	.117795	.119300	.120817	.122345	.123883	.125430	.128554	.131710
	.10	.112559	.114000	.115455	.116923	.118404	.119897	.121402	.122919	.124446	.125984	.127532	.130655	.133811
	0.00	.114661	.116102	.117557	.119025	.120506	.121999	.123504	.125020	.126548	.128086	.129634	.132757	.135913
	-.10	.116763	.118204	.119658	.121126	.122607	.124100	.125606	.127122	.128650	.130188	.131735	.134859	.138015
	-.20	.118864	.120305	.121760	.123228	.124709	.126202	.127707	.129224	.130751	.132289	.133837	.136960	.140117
	-.30	.120966	.122407	.123862	.125330	.126811	.128304	.129809	.131326	.132853	.134391	.135939	.139060	.142218
	-.40	.123068	.124509	.125964	.127432	.128912	.130406	.131911	.133427	.134955	.136493	.138041	.141164	.144320
15	.40	.095920	.097813	.099741	.101703	.103699	.105728	.107790	.109884	.112010	.114167	.116355	.120818	.125395
	.30	.098022	.099915	.101842	.103804	.105800	.107830	.109892	.111986	.114112	.116269	.118456	.122922	.127457
	.20	.100123	.102016	.103944	.105906	.107902	.109931	.111993	.114088	.116214	.118371	.120558	.125021	.129558
	.10	.102225	.104118	.106046	.108008	.110004	.112033	.114095	.116189	.118315	.120472	.122660	.127123	.131700
	0.00	.104327	.106220	.108147	.110109	.112105	.114135	.116197	.118291	.120417	.122574	.124761	.129225	.133802
	-.10	.106429	.108321	.110249	.112211	.114207	.116236	.118298	.120393	.122519	.124676	.126863	.131326	.135904
	-.20	.108530	.110423	.112351	.114313	.116309	.118338	.120400	.122494	.124620	.126777	.128965	.133428	.138005
	-.30	.110632	.112525	.114453	.116415	.118411	.120440	.122502	.124596	.126722	.128879	.131066	.135523	.140107
	-.40	.112734	.114627	.116554	.118516	.120512	.122541	.124604	.126698	.128824	.130981	.133168	.137632	.142209
20	.40	.090910	.093052	.095239	.097469	.099742	.102055	.104409	.106800	.109229	.111693	.114192	.119287	.124503
	.30	.093011	.095154	.097341	.099571	.101844	.104157	.106510	.108902	.111331	.113795	.116294	.121389	.126605
	.20	.095113	.097256	.099442	.101673	.103945	.106259	.108612	.111004	.113432	.115897	.118395	.123490	.128707
	.10	.097215	.099357	.101544	.103774	.106047	.108361	.110714	.113106	.115534	.117998	.120497	.125592	.130808
	0.00	.099317	.101459	.103646	.105876	.108149	.110462	.112815	.115207	.117636	.120100	.122599	.127694	.132910
	-.10	.101418	.103561	.105748	.107978	.110250	.112564	.114917	.117309	.119737	.122202	.124700	.129796	.135012
	-.20	.103520	.105662	.107849	.110080	.112352	.114666	.117019	.119410	.121839	.124303	.126802	.131897	.137113
	-.30	.105622	.107764	.109951	.112181	.114454	.116767	.119121	.121512	.123941	.126405	.128904	.133999	.139215
	-.40	.107723	.109866	.112053	.114283	.116556	.118869	.121222	.123614	.126042	.128507	.131006	.136101	.141317
25	.40	.088024	.090333	.092691	.095096	.097547	.100041	.102576	.105149	.107759	.110404	.113081	.118523	.124072
	.30	.090125	.092434	.094793	.097198	.099649	.102143	.104677	.107251	.109861	.112505	.115182	.120625	.126174
	.20	.092227	.094536	.096894	.099300	.101751	.104244	.106779	.109352	.111962	.114507	.117284	.122727	.128276
	.10	.094329	.096638	.098996	.101403	.103852	.106346	.108881	.111454	.114064	.116709	.119386	.124829	.130377
	0.00	.096430	.098739	.101098	.103503	.105954	.108448	.110982	.113556	.116166	.118810	.121487	.126930	.132479
	-.10	.098532	.100841	.103199	.105605	.108056	.110549	.113084	.115658	.118268	.120912	.123589	.129032	.134581
	-.20	.100634	.102943	.105301	.107707	.110157	.112651	.115186	.117759	.120369	.123014	.125690	.131134	.136683
	-.30	.102736	.105045	.107403	.109808	.112259	.114753	.117288	.119861	.122471	.125116	.127792	.133235	.138784
	-.40	.104837	.107146	.109505	.111910	.114361	.116855	.119389	.121963	.124573	.127217	.129894	.135337	.140886
30	.40	.086194	.088627	.091110	.093642	.096219	.098838	.101496	.104191	.106920	.109679	.112466	.118116	.123851
	.30	.088296	.090728	.093212	.095743	.098320	.100940	.103598	.106293	.109021	.111780	.114568	.120218	.125952
	.20	.090398	.092830	.095313	.097845	.100422	.103041	.105700	.108395	.111123	.113882	.116671	.122319	.128054
	.10	.092500	.094932	.097415	.099947	.102524	.105143	.107801	.110496	.113225	.115984	.118771	.124421	.130156
	0.00	.094601	.097033	.099517	.102049	.104625	.107245	.109903	.112598	.115326	.118086	.120873	.126523	.132258
	-.10	.096703	.099135	.101619	.104150	.106727	.109346	.112005	.114700	.117428	.120187	.122975	.128625	.134359
	-.20	.098805	.101237	.103720	.106252	.108829	.111448	.114107	.116801	.119530	.122289	.125076	.130726	.136461
	-.30	.100906	.103339	.105822	.108354	.110931	.113550	.116208	.118903	.121631	.124391	.127178	.132828	.138563
	-.40	.103008	.105440	.107924	.110455	.113032	.115652	.118310	.121005	.123733	.126492	.129280	.134930	.140664

15.0 YEAR HOLDING PERIOD
.150 EQUITY YIELD RATE
.667 LOAN RATIO

INTEREST RATE

TERM YEARS	APPR DEP	5.0	5.5	6.0	6.5	7.0	7.5	8.0	8.5	9.0	9.5	10.0	11.0	12.0
10	.40	.102327	.103929	.105545	.107176	.108821	.110481	.112153	.113838	.115535	.117244	.118964	.122434	.125941
	.30	.104429	.106030	.107647	.109278	.110923	.112582	.114255	.115940	.117637	.119346	.121066	.124536	.128043
	.20	.106531	.108132	.109748	.111379	.113025	.114684	.116356	.118041	.119739	.121448	.123167	.126638	.130144
	.10	.108633	.110234	.111850	.113481	.115127	.116786	.118458	.120143	.121840	.123549	.125269	.128739	.132246
	0.00	.110734	.112335	.113952	.115583	.117228	.118887	.120560	.122245	.123942	.125651	.127371	.130841	.134348
	-.10	.112836	.114437	.116053	.117685	.119330	.120989	.122661	.124347	.126044	.127753	.129472	.132943	.136450
	-.20	.114938	.116539	.118155	.119786	.121432	.123091	.124763	.126448	.128145	.129854	.131574	.135044	.138551
	-.30	.117039	.118641	.120257	.121888	.123533	.125192	.126865	.128550	.130247	.131956	.133676	.137146	.140653
	-.40	.119141	.120742	.122359	.123990	.125635	.127294	.128967	.130652	.132349	.134058	.135778	.139248	.142755
15	.40	.090845	.092948	.095090	.097270	.099488	.101743	.104034	.106361	.108723	.111120	.113550	.118509	.123595
	.30	.092947	.095050	.097192	.099372	.101590	.103844	.106135	.108463	.110825	.113221	.115652	.120611	.125697
	.20	.095048	.097152	.099294	.101474	.103691	.105946	.108237	.110564	.112926	.115323	.117755	.122713	.127799
	.10	.097150	.099253	.101395	.103575	.105793	.108048	.110339	.112666	.115028	.117425	.119855	.124815	.129900
	0.00	.099252	.101355	.103497	.105677	.107895	.110149	.112441	.114768	.117130	.119526	.121957	.126916	.132002
	-.10	.101354	.103457	.105599	.107779	.109996	.112251	.114542	.116869	.119231	.121628	.124059	.129018	.134104
	-.20	.103455	.105558	.107700	.109880	.112098	.114353	.116644	.118971	.121333	.123730	.126160	.131120	.136205
	-.30	.105557	.107660	.109802	.111982	.114200	.116455	.118746	.121073	.123435	.125832	.128262	.133221	.138307
	-.40	.107659	.109762	.111904	.114084	.116302	.118556	.120847	.123174	.125537	.127933	.130364	.135323	.140409
20	.40	.085278	.087658	.090038	.092566	.095092	.097662	.100277	.102934	.105633	.108371	.111147	.116808	.122604
	.30	.087380	.089760	.092190	.094668	.097193	.099764	.102378	.105036	.107734	.110473	.113249	.118910	.124706
	.20	.089481	.091862	.094292	.096770	.099295	.101866	.104480	.107138	.109836	.112574	.115351	.121012	.126808
	.10	.091583	.093964	.096393	.098872	.101397	.103967	.106582	.109239	.111938	.114676	.117452	.123114	.128909
	0.00	.093685	.096065	.098495	.100973	.103498	.106069	.108684	.111341	.114039	.116778	.119554	.125215	.131011
	-.10	.095787	.098167	.100597	.103075	.105600	.108171	.110785	.113443	.116141	.118879	.121656	.127317	.133113
	-.20	.097888	.100269	.102699	.105177	.107702	.110272	.112887	.115544	.118243	.120981	.123757	.129419	.135214
	-.30	.099990	.102371	.104800	.107278	.109803	.112374	.114989	.117646	.120345	.123083	.125859	.131520	.137316
	-.40	.102092	.104472	.106902	.109380	.111905	.114476	.117090	.119748	.122446	.125184	.127961	.133622	.139418
25	.40	.082071	.084637	.087257	.089930	.092653	.095424	.098240	.101099	.104000	.106938	.109912	.115960	.122125
	.30	.084173	.086738	.089359	.092032	.094755	.097526	.100342	.103201	.106101	.109040	.112014	.118062	.124227
	.20	.086275	.088840	.091460	.094133	.096856	.099627	.102444	.105303	.108203	.111141	.114116	.120163	.126329
	.10	.088376	.090942	.093562	.096235	.098958	.101729	.104545	.107405	.110305	.113243	.116217	.122265	.128431
	0.00	.090478	.093044	.095664	.098337	.101060	.103831	.106647	.109506	.112406	.115345	.118319	.124367	.130532
	-.10	.092580	.095145	.097766	.100438	.103161	.105932	.108749	.111608	.114508	.117446	.120421	.126469	.132634
	-.20	.094681	.097247	.099867	.102540	.105263	.108034	.110850	.113710	.116610	.119548	.122523	.128570	.134736
	-.30	.096783	.099349	.101969	.104642	.107365	.110136	.112952	.115811	.118711	.121650	.124624	.130672	.136837
	-.40	.098885	.101450	.104071	.106744	.109467	.112237	.115054	.117913	.120813	.123752	.126726	.132774	.138939
30	.40	.080039	.082741	.085500	.088314	.091177	.094087	.097041	.100035	.103067	.106133	.109230	.115507	.121679
	.30	.082140	.084843	.087602	.090415	.093279	.096189	.099143	.102137	.105168	.108234	.111331	.117609	.123781
	.20	.084242	.086945	.089704	.092517	.095380	.098290	.101244	.104239	.107270	.110336	.113433	.119711	.126083
	.10	.086344	.089046	.091806	.094619	.097482	.100392	.103346	.106340	.109372	.112438	.115535	.121812	.128184
	0.00	.088446	.091148	.093907	.096720	.099584	.102494	.105448	.108442	.111474	.114539	.117637	.123914	.130286
	-.10	.090547	.093250	.096009	.098822	.101685	.104596	.107549	.110544	.113575	.116641	.119738	.126016	.132388
	-.20	.092649	.095351	.098111	.100924	.103787	.106697	.109651	.112645	.115677	.118743	.121840	.128118	.134489
	-.30	.094751	.097453	.100212	.103025	.105889	.108799	.111753	.114747	.117779	.120844	.123942	.130219	.136591
	-.40	.096852	.099555	.102314	.105127	.107990	.110901	.113855	.116849	.119880	.122946	.126043	.132321	.138693

15.0 YEAR HOLDING PERIOD
.150 EQUITY YIELD RATE
.700 LOAN RATIO

INTEREST RATE

TERM YEARS	APPR DEP	5.0	5.5	6.0	6.5	7.0	7.5	8.0	8.5	9.0	9.5	10.0	11.0	12.0
10	.40	.100364	.102046	.103743	.105455	.107183	.108925	.110681	.112450	.114233	.116027	.117833	.121476	.125159
	.30	.102466	.104147	.105844	.107557	.109285	.111027	.112783	.114552	.116334	.118128	.119934	.123578	.127260
	.20	.104568	.106249	.107946	.109659	.111386	.113128	.114884	.116654	.118436	.120230	.122036	.125680	.129362
	.10	.106670	.108351	.110048	.111760	.113488	.115230	.116986	.118756	.120538	.122332	.124138	.127781	.131464
	0.00	.108771	.110452	.112150	.113862	.115590	.117332	.119088	.120857	.122639	.124434	.126239	.129883	.133565
	-.10	.110873	.112554	.114251	.115964	.117692	.119434	.121190	.122959	.124741	.126535	.128341	.131985	.135667
	-.20	.112975	.114656	.116353	.118066	.119793	.121535	.123291	.125061	.126843	.128637	.130443	.134087	.137769
	-.30	.115076	.116758	.118455	.120167	.121895	.123637	.125393	.127162	.128944	.130739	.132545	.136188	.139870
	-.40	.117178	.118859	.120556	.122269	.123997	.125739	.127495	.129264	.131046	.132840	.134646	.138290	.141972
15	.40	.088308	.090516	.092765	.095054	.097383	.099750	.102156	.104599	.107080	.109596	.112148	.117355	.122695
	.30	.090410	.092618	.094867	.097156	.099485	.101852	.104258	.106701	.109181	.111698	.114250	.119457	.124797
	.20	.092511	.094720	.096969	.099258	.101586	.103954	.106359	.108803	.111283	.113300	.116351	.121559	.126899
	.10	.094613	.096821	.099070	.101359	.103688	.106055	.108461	.110904	.113385	.115901	.118453	.123661	.129000
	0.00	.096715	.098923	.101172	.103461	.105790	.108157	.110563	.113006	.115486	.118003	.120555	.125762	.131102
	-.10	.098816	.101025	.103274	.105563	.107891	.110259	.112665	.115108	.117588	.120105	.122657	.127864	.133204
	-.20	.100918	.103126	.105375	.107664	.109993	.112361	.114766	.117210	.119690	.122206	.124758	.129966	.135306
	-.30	.103020	.105228	.107477	.109766	.112095	.114462	.116868	.119311	.121792	.124308	.126860	.132067	.137407
	-.40	.105122	.107330	.109579	.111868	.114196	.116564	.118970	.121413	.123893	.126410	.128962	.134169	.139509
20	.40	.082463	.084962	.087513	.090115	.092767	.095466	.098211	.101001	.103835	.106710	.109625	.115569	.121655
	.30	.084564	.087064	.089615	.092217	.094868	.097567	.100313	.103103	.105936	.108312	.111727	.117671	.123756
	.20	.086666	.089165	.091717	.094319	.096970	.099669	.102415	.105205	.108038	.110313	.113829	.119773	.125858
	.10	.088768	.091267	.093818	.096421	.099072	.101771	.104516	.107306	.110140	.113015	.115930	.121874	.127960
	0.00	.090869	.093369	.095920	.098522	.101174	.103873	.106618	.109408	.112242	.115117	.118032	.123976	.130062
	-.10	.092971	.095470	.098022	.100624	.103275	.105974	.108720	.111510	.114343	.117218	.120134	.126078	.132163
	-.20	.095073	.097572	.100124	.102726	.105377	.108076	.110821	.113611	.116445	.119320	.122235	.128180	.134265
	-.30	.097174	.099674	.102225	.104827	.107479	.110178	.112923	.115713	.118547	.121422	.124337	.130281	.136367
	-.40	.099276	.101776	.104327	.106929	.109580	.112279	.115025	.117815	.120648	.123524	.126439	.132383	.138468
25	.40	.079095	.081789	.084541	.087347	.090206	.093116	.096073	.099075	.102120	.105205	.108328	.114679	.121152
	.30	.081197	.083891	.086642	.089449	.092308	.095217	.098174	.101177	.104222	.107307	.110430	.116780	.123254
	.20	.083299	.085993	.088744	.091550	.094410	.097319	.100276	.103278	.106323	.109409	.112532	.118882	.125356
	.10	.085401	.088094	.090846	.093652	.096511	.099421	.102378	.105380	.108425	.111510	.114634	.120984	.127457
	0.00	.087502	.090196	.092947	.095754	.098613	.101522	.104480	.107482	.110527	.113512	.116735	.123085	.129559
	-.10	.089604	.092298	.095049	.097856	.100715	.103624	.106581	.109584	.112629	.115714	.118837	.125187	.131661
	-.20	.091706	.094399	.097151	.099957	.102816	.105726	.108683	.111685	.114730	.117816	.120939	.127289	.133762
	-.30	.093807	.096501	.099252	.102059	.104918	.107828	.110785	.113787	.116832	.119917	.123040	.129390	.135864
	-.40	.095909	.098603	.101354	.104161	.107020	.109929	.112886	.115889	.118934	.122019	.125142	.131492	.137966
30	.40	.076961	.079799	.082696	.085650	.088656	.091712	.094814	.097957	.101141	.104360	.107612	.114203	.120894
	.30	.079063	.081901	.084798	.087752	.090758	.093814	.096915	.100059	.103242	.106461	.109713	.116305	.122995
	.20	.081165	.084002	.086900	.089853	.092860	.095915	.099017	.102161	.105344	.108563	.111815	.118407	.125097
	.10	.083266	.086104	.089001	.091955	.094961	.098017	.101119	.104263	.107446	.110665	.113917	.120508	.127199
	0.00	.085368	.088206	.091103	.094057	.097063	.100119	.103220	.106364	.109547	.112766	.116019	.122610	.129300
	-.10	.087470	.090307	.093205	.096158	.099165	.102221	.105322	.108466	.111649	.114868	.118120	.124712	.131402
	-.20	.089572	.092409	.095306	.098260	.101266	.104322	.107424	.110568	.113751	.116970	.120222	.126813	.133504
	-.30	.091673	.094511	.097408	.100362	.103368	.106424	.109525	.112669	.115853	.119072	.122324	.128915	.135606
	-.40	.093775	.096612	.099510	.102463	.105470	.108526	.111627	.114771	.117954	.121173	.124425	.131017	.137707

15.0 YEAR HOLDING PERIOD
.150 EQUITY YIELD RATE
.750 LOAN RATIO

INTEREST RATE

TERM YEARS	APPR DEP	5.0	5.5	6.0	6.5	7.0	7.5	8.0	8.5	9.0	9.5	10.0	11.0	12.0
10	.40	.097419	.099221	.101039	.102874	.104725	.106592	.108473	.110369	.112278	.114201	.116135	.120039	.123985
	.30	.099521	.101322	.103141	.104976	.106827	.108693	.110575	.112470	.114380	.116302	.118237	.122141	.126086
	.20	.101623	.103424	.105243	.107078	.108929	.110795	.112676	.114572	.116482	.118404	.120339	.124243	.128188
	.10	.103725	.105526	.107344	.109179	.111030	.112897	.114778	.116674	.118583	.120506	.122441	.126345	.130290
	0.00	.105826	.107628	.109446	.111281	.113132	.114998	.116880	.118776	.120685	.122607	.124542	.128446	.132391
	-.10	.107928	.109729	.111548	.113383	.115234	.117100	.118982	.120877	.122787	.124709	.126644	.130548	.134493
	-.20	.110030	.111831	.113649	.115484	.117335	.119202	.121083	.122979	.124888	.126811	.128746	.132650	.136595
	-.30	.112131	.113933	.115751	.117586	.119437	.121304	.123185	.125081	.126990	.128913	.130847	.134751	.138697
	-.40	.114233	.116034	.117853	.119688	.121539	.123405	.125287	.127182	.129092	.131014	.132949	.136853	.140798
15	.40	.084502	.086868	.089278	.091730	.094225	.096762	.099339	.101957	.104614	.107311	.110045	.115624	.121346
	.30	.086604	.088970	.091379	.093832	.096327	.098863	.101441	.104059	.106716	.109412	.112147	.117726	.123447
	.20	.088705	.091071	.093481	.095933	.098428	.100965	.103542	.106160	.108818	.111516	.114248	.119828	.125549
	.10	.090807	.093173	.095583	.098035	.100530	.103067	.105644	.108262	.110919	.113616	.116350	.121929	.127651
	0.00	.092909	.095275	.097684	.100137	.102632	.105168	.107746	.110364	.113021	.115717	.118452	.124031	.129752
	-.10	.095010	.097376	.099786	.102239	.104733	.107270	.109848	.112465	.115123	.117819	.120553	.126133	.131854
	-.20	.097112	.099478	.101888	.104340	.106835	.109372	.111949	.114567	.117225	.119921	.122655	.128234	.133956
	-.30	.099214	.101580	.103989	.106442	.108937	.111473	.114051	.116669	.119326	.122023	.124757	.130336	.136057
	-.40	.101315	.103682	.106091	.108544	.111039	.113575	.116153	.118771	.121428	.124124	.126858	.132438	.138159
20	.40	.078239	.080917	.083651	.086438	.089279	.092171	.095112	.098102	.101138	.104218	.107342	.113710	.120231
	.30	.080341	.083019	.085752	.088540	.091381	.094273	.097214	.100204	.103239	.106320	.109443	.115812	.122332
	.20	.082442	.085120	.087854	.090642	.093482	.096374	.099316	.102305	.105341	.108422	.111545	.117914	.124434
	.10	.084544	.087222	.089956	.092744	.095584	.098476	.101418	.104407	.107443	.110523	.113647	.120016	.126536
	0.00	.086646	.089324	.092057	.094845	.097686	.100578	.103519	.106509	.109545	.112625	.115748	.122117	.128637
	-.10	.088747	.091425	.094159	.096947	.099788	.102679	.105621	.108610	.111646	.114727	.117850	.124219	.130739
	-.20	.090849	.093527	.096261	.099049	.101889	.104781	.107723	.110712	.113748	.116828	.119952	.126321	.132841
	-.30	.092951	.095629	.098362	.101150	.103991	.106883	.109824	.112814	.115850	.118930	.122054	.128422	.134943
	-.40	.095053	.097731	.100464	.103252	.106093	.108985	.111926	.114916	.117951	.121032	.124155	.130524	.137044
25	.40	.074031	.077518	.080465	.083472	.086536	.089653	.092821	.096038	.099301	.102606	.105952	.112756	.119692
	.30	.076733	.079619	.082567	.085574	.088637	.091755	.094923	.098140	.101402	.104708	.108054	.114858	.121794
	.20	.078835	.081721	.084669	.087676	.090739	.093856	.097025	.100241	.103504	.106810	.110156	.116959	.123895
	.10	.080936	.083823	.086770	.089777	.092841	.095958	.099126	.102343	.105606	.108911	.112257	.119061	.125997
	0.00	.083038	.085924	.088872	.091879	.094943	.098060	.101228	.104445	.107707	.111013	.114359	.121163	.128099
	-.10	.085140	.088026	.090974	.093981	.097044	.100161	.103330	.106547	.109809	.113115	.116461	.123265	.130201
	-.20	.087242	.090128	.093076	.096083	.099146	.102263	.105431	.108648	.111911	.115216	.118563	.125366	.132302
	-.30	.089343	.092229	.095177	.098184	.101248	.104365	.107533	.110750	.114012	.117318	.120664	.127468	.134404
	-.40	.091445	.094331	.097279	.100286	.103349	.106467	.109635	.112852	.116114	.119420	.122766	.129570	.136506
30	.40	.072045	.075385	.078489	.081654	.084875	.088149	.091472	.094841	.098251	.101700	.105184	.112247	.119415
	.30	.074446	.077487	.080591	.083756	.086977	.090251	.093574	.096942	.100353	.103802	.107286	.114348	.121517
	.20	.076548	.079588	.082693	.085857	.089078	.092352	.095676	.099044	.102455	.105904	.109388	.116450	.123619
	.10	.078650	.081690	.084794	.087959	.091180	.094454	.097777	.101146	.104556	.108005	.111490	.118552	.125720
	0.00	.080752	.083792	.086896	.090061	.093282	.096556	.099880	.103247	.106658	.110107	.113591	.120654	.127822
	-.10	.082853	.085893	.088998	.092162	.095384	.098658	.101981	.105349	.108760	.112209	.115693	.122755	.129924
	-.20	.084955	.087995	.091099	.094264	.097485	.100759	.104082	.107451	.110861	.114310	.117795	.124857	.132025
	-.30	.087057	.090097	.093201	.096366	.099587	.102861	.106184	.109553	.112963	.116412	.119896	.126959	.134127
	-.40	.089158	.092199	.095303	.098467	.101669	.104963	.108286	.111654	.115065	.118514	.121998	.129060	.136229

15.0 YEAR HOLDING PERIOD
.150 EQUITY YIELD RATE
.800 LOAN RATIO

INTEREST RATE

TERM YEARS	APPR DEP	5.0	5.5	6.0	6.5	7.0	7.5	8.0	8.5	9.0	9.5	10.0	11.0	12.0
10	.40	.094475	.096396	.098336	.100293	.102267	.104258	.106265	.108287	.110324	.112374	.114438	.118603	.122811
	.30	.096576	.098498	.100437	.102395	.104369	.106360	.108367	.110389	.112426	.114476	.116540	.120704	.124912
	.20	.098678	.100599	.102539	.104496	.106471	.108462	.110468	.112491	.114527	.116578	.118642	.122806	.127014
	.10	.100780	.102701	.104641	.106598	.108572	.110563	.112570	.114592	.116629	.118680	.120743	.124908	.129116
	0.00	.102881	.104803	.106742	.108700	.110674	.112665	.114672	.116694	.118731	.120781	.122845	.127009	.131218
	-.10	.104983	.106904	.108844	.110801	.112776	.114767	.116774	.118796	.120832	.122883	.124947	.129111	.133319
	-.20	.107085	.109006	.110946	.112903	.114877	.116868	.118875	.120897	.122934	.124985	.127048	.131213	.135421
	-.30	.109187	.111108	.113047	.115005	.116979	.118970	.120977	.122999	.125036	.127086	.129150	.133314	.137523
	-.40	.111288	.113210	.115149	.117106	.119081	.121072	.123079	.125101	.127137	.129188	.131252	.135416	.139624
15	.40	.080696	.083220	.085790	.088406	.091067	.093773	.096522	.099315	.102149	.105025	.107942	.113893	.119996
	.30	.082797	.085321	.087691	.090508	.093169	.095874	.098624	.101416	.104251	.107127	.110043	.115995	.122097
	.20	.084899	.087423	.089993	.092609	.095270	.097976	.100726	.103518	.106353	.109229	.112145	.118096	.124199
	.10	.087001	.089525	.092095	.094711	.097372	.100078	.102827	.105620	.108454	.111330	.114247	.120198	.126301
	0.00	.089103	.091626	.094197	.096813	.099474	.102180	.104929	.107721	.110556	.113432	.116348	.122300	.128402
	-.10	.091204	.093728	.096298	.098914	.101576	.104281	.107031	.109823	.112658	.115534	.118450	.124401	.130504
	-.20	.093306	.095830	.098400	.101016	.103677	.106383	.109132	.111925	.114759	.117635	.120552	.126503	.132606
	-.30	.095408	.097931	.100502	.103118	.105779	.108485	.111234	.114026	.116861	.119737	.122654	.128605	.134708
	-.40	.097509	.100033	.102603	.105219	.107881	.110586	.113336	.116128	.118963	.121839	.124755	.130706	.136809
20	.40	.074015	.076872	.079788	.082761	.085791	.088876	.092014	.095203	.098441	.101727	.105058	.111852	.118806
	.30	.076117	.078973	.081889	.084863	.087893	.090978	.094115	.097304	.100542	.103828	.107160	.113953	.120908
	.20	.078219	.081075	.083991	.086965	.089995	.093080	.096217	.099406	.102644	.105930	.109262	.116056	.123010
	.10	.080320	.083177	.086093	.089067	.092097	.095181	.098319	.101508	.104746	.108032	.111363	.118157	.125112
	0.00	.082422	.085279	.088195	.091168	.094198	.097283	.100421	.103609	.106848	.110133	.113465	.120258	.127213
	-.10	.084524	.087380	.090296	.093270	.096300	.099385	.102522	.105711	.108949	.112235	.115567	.122360	.129315
	-.20	.086626	.089482	.092398	.095372	.098402	.101486	.104624	.107813	.111051	.114337	.117668	.124462	.131417
	-.30	.088727	.091584	.094500	.097473	.100503	.103588	.106726	.109914	.113153	.116439	.119770	.126564	.133518
	-.40	.090829	.093685	.096601	.099575	.102605	.105690	.108827	.112016	.115254	.118540	.121872	.128665	.135620
25	.40	.070167	.073246	.076390	.079598	.082865	.086190	.089570	.093001	.096481	.100007	.103576	.110834	.118232
	.30	.072269	.075348	.078492	.081699	.084967	.088292	.091671	.095103	.098583	.102109	.105678	.112935	.120334
	.20	.074371	.077449	.080594	.083801	.087069	.090394	.093773	.097204	.100684	.104210	.107780	.115037	.122435
	.10	.076472	.079551	.082695	.085903	.089170	.092495	.095875	.099306	.102786	.106312	.109881	.117139	.124537
	0.00	.078574	.081653	.084797	.088004	.091272	.094597	.097977	.101408	.104888	.108414	.111983	.119240	.126639
	-.10	.080676	.083754	.086899	.090106	.093374	.096699	.100078	.103510	.106990	.110516	.114085	.121342	.128741
	-.20	.082777	.085856	.089000	.092208	.095475	.098800	.102180	.105611	.109091	.112617	.116187	.123444	.130842
	-.30	.084879	.087958	.091102	.094310	.097577	.100902	.104282	.107713	.111193	.114719	.118288	.125546	.132944
	-.40	.086981	.090059	.093204	.096411	.099679	.103004	.106383	.109815	.113295	.116821	.120390	.127647	.135046
30	.40	.067728	.070971	.074282	.077658	.081094	.084586	.088131	.091724	.095362	.099041	.102757	.110290	.117937
	.30	.069830	.073073	.076384	.079760	.083196	.086688	.090232	.093826	.097463	.101142	.104859	.112392	.120038
	.20	.071932	.075174	.078486	.081861	.085297	.088790	.092334	.095927	.099565	.103244	.106961	.114494	.122140
	.10	.074033	.077276	.080587	.083963	.087399	.090891	.094436	.098029	.101667	.105346	.109062	.116595	.124242
	0.00	.076135	.079378	.082689	.086065	.089501	.092993	.096538	.100131	.103768	.107447	.111164	.118697	.126343
	-.10	.078237	.081480	.084791	.088166	.091602	.095095	.098639	.102232	.105870	.109549	.113266	.120799	.128445
	-.20	.080338	.083581	.086893	.090268	.093704	.097196	.100743	.104334	.107972	.111651	.115367	.122901	.130547
	-.30	.082440	.085683	.088994	.092370	.095806	.099298	.102843	.106436	.110074	.113753	.117469	.125002	.132649
	-.40	.084542	.087785	.091096	.094472	.097907	.101400	.104944	.108537	.112175	.115854	.119571	.127104	.134750

15.0 YEAR HOLDING PERIOD
.150 EQUITY YIELD RATE
.900 LOAN RATIO

INTEREST RATE

TERM YEARS	APPR DEP	5.0	5.5	6.0	6.5	7.0	7.5	8.0	8.5	9.0	9.5	10.0	11.0	12.0
10	.40	.088585	.090746	.092928	.095130	.097352	.099591	.101849	.104124	.106415	.108722	.111044	.115729	.120463
	.30	.090686	.092848	.095030	.097232	.099453	.101693	.103951	.106226	.108517	.110824	.113146	.117830	.122565
	.20	.092788	.094950	.097132	.099334	.101555	.103795	.106052	.108327	.110619	.112925	.115247	.119932	.124666
	.10	.094890	.097051	.099233	.101435	.103657	.105896	.108154	.110429	.112720	.115027	.117349	.122034	.126768
	0.00	.096992	.099153	.101335	.103537	.105758	.107998	.110256	.112531	.114822	.117129	.119451	.124136	.128870
	-.10	.099093	.101255	.103437	.105639	.107860	.110100	.112358	.114632	.116924	.119231	.121552	.126237	.130971
	-.20	.101195	.103357	.105539	.107741	.109962	.112202	.114459	.116734	.119025	.121332	.123654	.128339	.133073
	-.30	.103297	.105458	.107640	.109842	.112063	.114303	.116561	.118836	.121127	.123434	.125756	.130441	.135175
	-.40	.105398	.107560	.109742	.111944	.114165	.116405	.118663	.120938	.123229	.125536	.127858	.132542	.137277
15	.40	.073084	.075923	.078814	.081757	.084751	.087795	.090888	.094030	.097219	.100454	.103735	.110430	.117296
	.30	.075185	.078025	.080916	.083859	.086853	.089897	.092990	.096131	.099320	.102556	.105837	.112532	.119398
	.20	.077287	.080126	.083018	.085961	.088955	.091999	.095092	.098233	.101422	.104658	.107939	.114634	.121499
	.10	.079389	.082228	.085119	.088063	.091056	.094100	.097193	.100335	.103524	.106759	.110040	.116735	.123601
	0.00	.081490	.084330	.087221	.090164	.093158	.096202	.099295	.102437	.105625	.108861	.112142	.118837	.125703
	-.10	.083592	.086431	.089323	.092266	.095260	.098304	.101397	.104538	.107727	.110963	.114244	.120939	.127805
	-.20	.085694	.088533	.091425	.094368	.097362	.100405	.103498	.106640	.109829	.113064	.116345	.123041	.129906
	-.30	.087795	.090635	.093526	.096469	.099463	.102507	.105600	.108742	.111931	.115166	.118447	.125142	.132008
	-.40	.089897	.092736	.095628	.098571	.101565	.104609	.107702	.110843	.114032	.117268	.120549	.127244	.134110
20	.40	.065568	.068782	.072002	.075407	.078816	.082287	.085816	.089404	.093047	.096743	.100491	.108134	.115958
	.30	.067670	.070883	.074164	.077509	.080918	.084388	.087918	.091505	.095148	.098845	.102593	.110236	.118060
	.20	.069771	.072985	.076265	.079611	.083020	.086490	.090020	.093607	.097250	.100947	.104695	.112337	.120162
	.10	.071873	.075087	.078367	.081713	.085121	.088592	.092121	.095709	.099352	.103048	.106796	.114439	.122263
	0.00	.073975	.077188	.080469	.083814	.087223	.090693	.094223	.097811	.101454	.105150	.108898	.116541	.124365
	-.10	.076077	.079290	.082571	.085916	.089325	.092795	.096325	.099912	.103555	.107252	.111000	.118642	.126467
	-.20	.078178	.081392	.084672	.088018	.091426	.094897	.098427	.102014	.105657	.109353	.113102	.120744	.128568
	-.30	.080280	.083494	.086774	.090119	.093528	.096998	.100528	.104116	.107759	.111455	.115203	.122846	.130570
	-.40	.082382	.085595	.088876	.092221	.095630	.099100	.102630	.106217	.109860	.113557	.117305	.124948	.132772
25	.40	.061239	.064702	.068240	.071848	.075524	.079265	.083067	.086927	.090842	.094809	.098824	.106989	.115312
	.30	.063341	.066804	.070342	.073950	.077626	.081367	.085169	.089029	.092944	.096910	.100926	.109090	.117414
	.20	.065442	.068906	.072443	.076052	.079728	.083468	.087270	.091130	.095045	.099012	.103028	.111192	.119515
	.10	.067544	.071007	.074545	.078153	.081829	.085570	.089372	.093232	.097147	.101114	.105129	.113294	.121617
	0.00	.069646	.073109	.076647	.080255	.083931	.087672	.091474	.095334	.099249	.103216	.107231	.115395	.123719
	-.10	.071747	.075211	.078748	.082357	.086033	.089773	.093575	.097435	.101351	.105317	.109333	.117497	.125820
	-.20	.073849	.077313	.080850	.084458	.088134	.091875	.095677	.099537	.103452	.107419	.111434	.119599	.127922
	-.30	.075951	.079414	.082952	.086560	.090236	.093977	.097779	.101639	.105554	.109521	.113536	.121701	.130024
	-.40	.078053	.081516	.085053	.088662	.092338	.096078	.099880	.103741	.107656	.111622	.115638	.123802	.132125
30	.40	.058495	.062143	.065868	.069606	.073531	.077460	.081448	.085490	.089583	.093722	.097903	.106377	.114980
	.30	.060597	.064245	.067970	.071768	.075633	.079562	.083550	.087592	.091684	.095823	.100004	.108479	.117081
	.20	.062698	.066347	.070072	.073869	.077735	.081664	.085651	.089694	.093786	.097925	.102106	.110581	.119183
	.10	.064800	.068448	.072174	.075971	.079837	.083766	.087753	.091795	.095888	.100027	.104208	.112683	.121286
	0.00	.066902	.070550	.074275	.078073	.081938	.085867	.089855	.093897	.097990	.102128	.106310	.114784	.123386
	-.10	.069004	.072652	.076377	.080175	.084040	.087969	.091956	.095998	.100091	.104230	.108411	.116886	.125488
	-.20	.071105	.074753	.078478	.082276	.086142	.090070	.094058	.098100	.102193	.106332	.110513	.118988	.127590
	-.30	.073207	.076855	.080580	.084378	.088243	.092172	.096160	.100202	.104295	.108433	.112615	.121089	.129691
	-.40	.075309	.078957	.082682	.086480	.090345	.094274	.098262	.102304	.106396	.110535	.114716	.123191	.131793

15.0 YEAR HOLDING PERIOD
.180 EQUITY YIELD RATE
.600 LOAN RATIO

INTEREST RATE

TERM YEARS	APPR DEP	5.0	5.5	6.0	6.5	7.0	7.5	8.0	8.5	9.0	9.5	10.0	11.0	12.0
10	.40	.124865	.126379	.127909	.129495	.131014	.132590	.134179	.135783	.137401	.139131	.140674	.143997	.147365
	.30	.126506	.128019	.129549	.131194	.132655	.134230	.135820	.137424	.139041	.140571	.142315	.145637	.149005
	.20	.128146	.129660	.131189	.132734	.134295	.135870	.137460	.139064	.140681	.142312	.143955	.147278	.150645
	.10	.129786	.131300	.132830	.134375	.135935	.137511	.139100	.140704	.142321	.143952	.145595	.148918	.152285
	0.00	.131427	.132940	.134470	.136015	.137576	.139151	.140741	.142344	.143962	.145592	.147236	.150558	.153926
	-.10	.133067	.134581	.136110	.137655	.139216	.140791	.142381	.143985	.145602	.147233	.148876	.152198	.155566
	-.20	.134707	.136221	.137750	.139296	.140856	.142431	.144021	.145625	.147242	.148873	.150516	.153839	.157206
	-.30	.136347	.137861	.139391	.140936	.142496	.144072	.145661	.147265	.148883	.150513	.152156	.155479	.158847
	-.40	.137988	.139501	.141031	.142576	.144137	.145712	.147302	.148905	.150523	.152153	.153797	.157119	.160487
15	.40	.112534	.114427	.116355	.118317	.120313	.122342	.124404	.126498	.128624	.130781	.132969	.137432	.142009
	.30	.114175	.116068	.117995	.119957	.121953	.123982	.126044	.128139	.130265	.132422	.134609	.139072	.143650
	.20	.115815	.117708	.119635	.121598	.123593	.125623	.127685	.129779	.131905	.134062	.136249	.140713	.145290
	.10	.117455	.119348	.121276	.123238	.125234	.127263	.129325	.131419	.133545	.135702	.137890	.142353	.146930
	0.00	.119095	.120988	.122916	.124878	.126874	.128903	.130965	.133060	.135186	.137343	.139530	.143993	.148570
	-.10	.120736	.122629	.124556	.126518	.128514	.130543	.132606	.134700	.136826	.138983	.141170	.145634	.150211
	-.20	.122376	.124269	.126197	.128159	.130155	.132184	.134246	.136340	.138466	.140623	.142810	.147274	.151851
	-.30	.124016	.125909	.127837	.129799	.131795	.133824	.135886	.137980	.140106	.142263	.144451	.148914	.153491
	-.40	.125657	.127549	.129477	.131439	.133435	.135464	.137526	.139621	.141747	.143904	.146091	.150554	.155132
20	.40	.106556	.108669	.110827	.113029	.115272	.117557	.119881	.122243	.124643	.127079	.129549	.134587	.139747
	.30	.108196	.110310	.112468	.114669	.116912	.119197	.121521	.123884	.126283	.128719	.131189	.136227	.141387
	.20	.109836	.111950	.114108	.116309	.118553	.120837	.123161	.125524	.127924	.130359	.132829	.137868	.143028
	.10	.111477	.113590	.115748	.117950	.120193	.122477	.124802	.127164	.129564	.132000	.134470	.139508	.144668
	0.00	.113117	.115230	.117388	.119590	.121833	.124118	.126442	.128805	.131204	.133640	.136110	.141148	.146308
	-.10	.114757	.116871	.119029	.121230	.123474	.125758	.128082	.130445	.132845	.135280	.137750	.142788	.147948
	-.20	.116397	.118511	.120669	.122870	.125114	.127398	.129722	.132085	.134485	.136920	.139390	.144429	.149589
	-.30	.118038	.120151	.122309	.124511	.126754	.129039	.131363	.133725	.136125	.138561	.141031	.146069	.151229
	-.40	.119678	.121792	.123950	.126151	.128394	.130679	.133003	.135366	.137765	.140201	.142671	.147709	.152869
25	.40	.103112	.105380	.107698	.110064	.112476	.114932	.117429	.119965	.122539	.125149	.127791	.133168	.138654
	.30	.104752	.107021	.109339	.111705	.114116	.116572	.119069	.121606	.124180	.126789	.129431	.134808	.140294
	.20	.106393	.108661	.110979	.113345	.115757	.118212	.120709	.123246	.125820	.128429	.131072	.136448	.141935
	.10	.108033	.110301	.112619	.114985	.117397	.119852	.122350	.124886	.127460	.130069	.132712	.138089	.143575
	0.00	.109673	.111941	.114260	.116626	.119037	.121493	.123990	.126526	.129100	.131710	.134352	.139729	.145215
	-.10	.111313	.113582	.115900	.118266	.120678	.123133	.125630	.128167	.130741	.133350	.135992	.141369	.146856
	-.20	.112954	.115222	.117540	.119906	.122318	.124773	.127270	.129807	.132381	.134990	.137633	.143010	.148496
	-.30	.114594	.116862	.119180	.121546	.123958	.126414	.128911	.131447	.134021	.136630	.139273	.144650	.150136
	-.40	.116234	.118503	.120821	.123187	.125598	.128054	.130551	.133087	.135661	.138271	.140913	.146290	.151776
30	.40	.100929	.103317	.105757	.108247	.110784	.113364	.115985	.118644	.121337	.124064	.126820	.132411	.138092
	.30	.102569	.104957	.107398	.109887	.112424	.115004	.117625	.120284	.122978	.125704	.128460	.134051	.139732
	.20	.104210	.106598	.109038	.111528	.114064	.116644	.119265	.121924	.124618	.127344	.130100	.135691	.141373
	.10	.105850	.108238	.110678	.113168	.115705	.118285	.120906	.123564	.126258	.128984	.131740	.137331	.143013
	0.00	.107490	.109878	.112318	.114808	.117345	.119925	.122546	.125205	.127899	.130625	.133381	.138972	.144653
	-.10	.109131	.111518	.113959	.116449	.118985	.121565	.124186	.126845	.129539	.132265	.135021	.140612	.146294
	-.20	.110771	.113159	.115599	.118089	.120625	.123206	.125827	.128485	.131179	.133905	.136661	.142252	.147934
	-.30	.112411	.114799	.117239	.119729	.122266	.124846	.127467	.130126	.132819	.135546	.138301	.143893	.149574
	-.40	.114052	.116439	.118879	.121369	.123906	.126486	.129107	.131766	.134460	.137186	.139942	.145533	.151214

15.0 YEAR HOLDING PERIOD
.180 EQUITY YIELD RATE
.667 LOAN RATIO

INTEREST RATE

TERM YEARS	APPR DEP	5.0	5.5	6.0	6.5	7.0	7.5	8.0	8.5	9.0	9.5	10.0	11.0	12.0
10	.40	.119468	.121150	.122850	.124566	.126300	.128051	.129817	.131599	.133396	.135208	.137034	.140726	.144467
	.30	.121108	.122790	.124490	.126207	.127941	.129691	.131457	.133239	.135036	.136848	.138674	.142366	.146108
	.20	.122749	.124431	.126130	.127847	.129581	.131331	.133098	.134880	.136677	.138488	.140314	.144006	.147748
	.10	.124389	.126071	.127770	.129487	.131221	.132972	.134738	.136520	.138317	.140129	.141955	.145646	.149388
	0.00	.126029	.127711	.129411	.131128	.132861	.134612	.136378	.138160	.139957	.141769	.143595	.147287	.151028
	-.10	.127670	.129351	.131051	.132768	.134502	.136252	.138018	.139800	.141598	.143409	.145235	.148927	.152669
	-.20	.129310	.130992	.132691	.134408	.136142	.137892	.139659	.141441	.143238	.145050	.146875	.150567	.154309
	-.30	.130950	.132632	.134332	.136048	.137782	.139533	.141299	.143081	.144878	.146690	.148516	.152208	.155949
	-.40	.132590	.134272	.135972	.137689	.139423	.141173	.142939	.144721	.146518	.148330	.150156	.153848	.157590
15	.40	.105767	.107870	.110012	.112192	.114410	.116664	.118956	.121283	.123645	.126041	.128472	.133431	.139517
	.30	.107407	.109510	.111652	.113832	.116050	.118305	.120596	.122923	.125285	.127682	.130112	.135072	.141157
	.20	.109047	.111151	.113292	.115473	.117690	.119945	.122236	.124563	.126925	.129322	.131752	.136712	.142798
	.10	.110688	.112791	.114933	.117113	.119330	.121585	.123876	.126203	.128566	.130962	.133393	.138352	.144438
	0.00	.112328	.114431	.116573	.118753	.120971	.123226	.125517	.127844	.130206	.132603	.135033	.139992	.146078
	-.10	.113968	.116071	.118213	.120393	.122611	.124866	.127157	.129484	.131846	.134243	.136673	.141633	.147718
	-.20	.115609	.117712	.119854	.122034	.124251	.126506	.128797	.131124	.133486	.135883	.138314	.143273	.149359
	-.30	.117249	.119352	.121494	.123674	.125892	.128146	.130438	.132765	.135127	.137523	.139954	.144913	.150999
	-.40	.118889	.120992	.123134	.125314	.127532	.129787	.132078	.134405	.136767	.139164	.141594	.146553	.152639
20	.40	.099124	.101472	.103870	.106316	.108809	.111347	.113930	.116555	.119221	.121927	.124672	.130270	.136003
	.30	.100764	.103113	.105510	.107956	.110449	.112987	.115570	.118195	.120861	.123568	.126312	.131910	.137644
	.20	.102405	.104753	.107151	.109597	.112089	.114628	.117210	.119835	.122502	.125208	.127952	.133550	.139284
	.10	.104045	.106393	.108791	.111237	.113730	.116268	.118850	.121476	.124142	.126848	.129593	.135191	.140924
	0.00	.105685	.108034	.110431	.112877	.115370	.117908	.120491	.123116	.125782	.128488	.131233	.136831	.142564
	-.10	.107325	.109674	.112072	.114517	.117010	.119549	.122131	.124756	.127423	.130129	.132873	.138471	.144205
	-.20	.108966	.111314	.113712	.116158	.118651	.121189	.123771	.126396	.129063	.131769	.134514	.140112	.145845
	-.30	.110606	.112954	.115352	.117798	.120291	.122829	.125412	.128037	.130703	.133409	.136154	.141752	.147485
	-.40	.112246	.114595	.116992	.119438	.121931	.124469	.127052	.129677	.132343	.135050	.137794	.143392	.149125
25	.40	.095298	.097818	.100394	.103022	.105702	.108430	.111205	.114023	.116883	.119783	.122719	.128693	.134789
	.30	.096938	.099458	.102034	.104663	.107342	.110071	.112845	.115664	.118524	.121423	.124359	.130333	.136429
	.20	.098578	.101098	.103674	.106303	.108983	.111711	.114486	.117304	.120164	.123063	.125999	.131974	.138070
	.10	.100218	.102739	.105314	.107943	.110623	.113351	.116126	.118944	.121804	.124703	.127640	.133614	.139710
	0.00	.101859	.104379	.106955	.109584	.112263	.114992	.117766	.120585	.123445	.126344	.129280	.135254	.141350
	-.10	.103499	.106019	.108595	.111224	.113904	.116632	.119406	.122225	.125085	.127984	.130920	.136894	.142990
	-.20	.105139	.107660	.110235	.112864	.115544	.118272	.121047	.123865	.126725	.129624	.132560	.138535	.144631
	-.30	.106779	.109300	.111876	.114504	.117184	.119912	.122687	.125505	.128365	.131265	.134201	.140175	.146271
	-.40	.108420	.110940	.113516	.116145	.118824	.121553	.124327	.127146	.130006	.132905	.135841	.141815	.147911
30	.40	.092872	.095525	.098237	.101003	.103822	.106669	.109601	.112555	.115548	.118577	.121639	.127852	.134165
	.30	.094513	.097166	.099877	.102644	.105462	.108329	.111241	.114195	.117188	.120218	.123280	.129492	.135805
	.20	.096153	.098806	.101517	.104284	.107102	.109969	.112881	.115836	.118829	.121858	.124920	.131132	.137445
	.10	.097793	.100446	.103158	.105924	.108742	.111609	.114522	.117476	.120469	.123498	.126560	.132772	.139085
	0.00	.099433	.102086	.104798	.107564	.110383	.113250	.116162	.119116	.122109	.125138	.128200	.134413	.140726
	-.10	.101074	.103727	.106438	.109205	.112023	.114890	.117802	.120756	.123750	.126779	.129841	.136053	.142366
	-.20	.102714	.105367	.108078	.110845	.113663	.116530	.119442	.122397	.125390	.128419	.131481	.137693	.144006
	-.30	.104354	.107007	.109719	.112485	.115304	.118171	.121083	.124037	.127030	.130059	.133121	.139334	.145647
	-.40	.105994	.108647	.111359	.114125	.116944	.119811	.122723	.125677	.128670	.131699	.134762	.140974	.147287

15.0 YEAR HOLDING PERIOD
.180 EQUITY YIELD RATE
.700 LOAN RATIO

INTEREST RATE

TERM YEARS	APPR DEP	5.0	5.5	6.0	6.5	7.0	7.5	8.0	8.5	9.0	9.5	10.0	11.0	12.0
10	.40	.116770	.118536	.120320	.122123	.123944	.125782	.127636	.129507	.131394	.133297	.135214	.139090	.143019
	.30	.118410	.120176	.121961	.123763	.125584	.127422	.129277	.131148	.133035	.134937	.136854	.140730	.144659
	.20	.120050	.121816	.123601	.125404	.127224	.129062	.130917	.132788	.134675	.136577	.138494	.142371	.146299
	.10	.121691	.123457	.125242	.127044	.128864	.130702	.132557	.134428	.136315	.138217	.140134	.144011	.147940
	0.00	.123331	.125097	.126881	.128684	.130505	.132343	.134197	.136068	.137955	.139858	.141775	.145651	.149580
	-.10	.124971	.126737	.128522	.130324	.132145	.133983	.135838	.137709	.139596	.141498	.143415	.147291	.151220
	-.20	.126612	.128377	.130162	.131965	.133785	.135623	.137478	.139349	.141236	.143138	.145055	.148932	.152861
	-.30	.128252	.130018	.131802	.133605	.135426	.137263	.139118	.140989	.142876	.144779	.146696	.150572	.154501
	-.40	.129892	.131658	.133443	.135245	.137066	.138904	.140758	.142630	.144516	.146419	.148336	.152212	.156141
15	.40	.102384	.104592	.106841	.109130	.111459	.113826	.116232	.118675	.121155	.123672	.126224	.131431	.136771
	.30	.104024	.106232	.108481	.110770	.113099	.115466	.117872	.120315	.122796	.125312	.127864	.133071	.138411
	.20	.105664	.107873	.110121	.112411	.114739	.117107	.119513	.121956	.124436	.126952	.129504	.134712	.140052
	.10	.107304	.109513	.111762	.114051	.116379	.118747	.121153	.123596	.126076	.128593	.131145	.136352	.141692
	0.00	.108945	.111153	.113402	.115691	.118020	.120387	.122793	.125236	.127716	.130233	.132785	.137992	.143332
	-.10	.110585	.112793	.115042	.117331	.119660	.122027	.124433	.126876	.129357	.131873	.134425	.139632	.144972
	-.20	.112225	.114434	.116683	.118972	.121300	.123668	.126073	.128517	.130997	.133513	.136065	.141273	.146613
	-.30	.113866	.116074	.118323	.120612	.122940	.125308	.127714	.130157	.132637	.135154	.137706	.142913	.148253
	-.40	.115506	.117714	.119963	.122252	.124581	.126948	.129354	.131797	.134278	.136794	.139346	.144553	.149893
20	.40	.095409	.097874	.100392	.102960	.105578	.108243	.110954	.113711	.116511	.119352	.122234	.128112	.134132
	.30	.097049	.099515	.102032	.104601	.107218	.109883	.112595	.115351	.118151	.120992	.123874	.129752	.135772
	.20	.098689	.101155	.103672	.106241	.108858	.111523	.114235	.116991	.119791	.122633	.125514	.131392	.137412
	.10	.100329	.102795	.105313	.107881	.110499	.113164	.115875	.118632	.121431	.124273	.127155	.133032	.139053
	0.00	.101970	.104436	.106953	.109521	.112139	.114804	.117516	.120272	.123072	.125913	.128795	.134673	.140693
	-.10	.103610	.106076	.108593	.111162	.113779	.116444	.119156	.121912	.124712	.127553	.130435	.136313	.142333
	-.20	.105250	.107716	.110234	.112802	.115419	.118085	.120796	.123552	.126352	.129194	.132075	.137953	.143973
	-.30	.106891	.109356	.111874	.114442	.117060	.119725	.122436	.125193	.127992	.130834	.133716	.139594	.145614
	-.40	.108531	.110997	.113514	.116083	.118700	.121365	.124077	.126833	.129633	.132474	.135356	.141234	.147254
25	.40	.091391	.094037	.096742	.099502	.102316	.105180	.108094	.111053	.114056	.117100	.120183	.126456	.132857
	.30	.093031	.095678	.098382	.101142	.103956	.106821	.109734	.112693	.115696	.118740	.121823	.128096	.134497
	.20	.094671	.097318	.100022	.102783	.105596	.108461	.111374	.114334	.117337	.120381	.123464	.129737	.136137
	.10	.096312	.098958	.101663	.104423	.107237	.110101	.113014	.115974	.118977	.122021	.125104	.131377	.137778
	0.00	.097952	.100598	.103303	.106063	.108877	.111742	.114655	.117614	.120617	.123661	.126744	.133017	.139418
	-.10	.099592	.102239	.104943	.107703	.110517	.113382	.116295	.119254	.122257	.125301	.128384	.134657	.141058
	-.20	.101233	.103879	.106583	.109344	.112157	.115022	.117935	.120895	.123898	.126942	.130025	.136298	.142698
	-.30	.102873	.105519	.108224	.110984	.113798	.116662	.119576	.122535	.125538	.128582	.131665	.137938	.144339
	-.40	.104513	.107159	.109864	.112624	.115438	.118303	.121216	.124175	.127178	.130222	.133305	.139578	.145979
30	.40	.088844	.091630	.094477	.097382	.100341	.103351	.106409	.109511	.112654	.115834	.119050	.125573	.132201
	.30	.090485	.093271	.096117	.099022	.101981	.104992	.108049	.111151	.114294	.117475	.120690	.127213	.133841
	.20	.092125	.094911	.097758	.100662	.103622	.106632	.109690	.112792	.115934	.119115	.122330	.128853	.135482
	.10	.093765	.096551	.099398	.102303	.105262	.108272	.111330	.114432	.117575	.120755	.123970	.130493	.137122
	0.00	.095405	.098191	.101038	.103943	.106902	.109913	.112970	.116072	.119215	.122396	.125611	.132134	.138762
	-.10	.097046	.099831	.102678	.105583	.108543	.111553	.114611	.117713	.120855	.124036	.127251	.133774	.140402
	-.20	.098686	.101472	.104319	.107224	.110183	.113193	.116251	.119353	.122496	.125676	.128891	.135414	.142043
	-.30	.100326	.103112	.105959	.108864	.111823	.114833	.117891	.120993	.124136	.127316	.130532	.137056	.143683
	-.40	.101967	.104752	.107599	.110504	.113463	.116474	.119531	.122633	.125776	.128957	.132172	.138695	.145323

15.0 YEAR HOLDING PERIOD
.180 EQUITY YIELD RATE
.750 LOAN RATIO

INTEREST RATE

TERM YEARS	APPR DEP	12.0	11.0	10.0	9.5	9.0	8.5	8.0	7.5	7.0	6.5	6.0	5.5	5.0
10	.40	.143846	.136637	.132483	.130429	.128391	.126369	.124365	.122377	.120408	.118458	.116520	.114614	.112722
	.30	.142486	.138277	.134424	.132070	.130031	.128010	.126005	.124018	.122049	.120098	.118166	.116254	.114362
	.20	.144127	.139917	.135764	.133710	.131672	.129650	.127645	.125658	.123689	.121738	.119807	.117895	.116003
	.10	.145767	.141557	.137404	.135350	.133312	.131290	.129285	.127298	.125329	.123379	.121447	.119535	.117643
	0.00	.147407	.143198	.139044	.136990	.134952	.132930	.130926	.128939	.126969	.125019	.123087	.121175	.119283
	-.10	.149047	.144838	.140685	.138631	.136592	.134571	.132566	.130579	.128610	.126659	.124728	.122816	.120924
	-.20	.150688	.146478	.142325	.140271	.138233	.136211	.134206	.132219	.130250	.128299	.126368	.124456	.122564
	-.30	.152328	.148119	.143965	.141911	.139873	.137851	.135847	.133859	.131890	.129940	.128008	.126096	.124204
	-.40	.153968	.149759	.145606	.143551	.141513	.139492	.137487	.135500	.133530	.131580	.129648	.127736	.125844
15	.40	.134152	.128431	.122851	.120117	.117421	.114763	.112145	.109568	.107031	.104536	.102084	.099674	.097308
	.30	.135792	.130071	.124492	.121757	.119061	.116404	.113786	.111208	.108672	.106177	.103724	.101315	.098949
	.20	.137432	.131711	.126132	.123398	.120701	.118044	.115426	.112848	.110312	.107817	.105364	.102955	.100589
	.10	.139073	.133351	.127772	.125038	.122342	.119684	.117066	.114489	.111952	.109457	.107005	.104595	.102229
	0.00	.140713	.134992	.129412	.126678	.123982	.121324	.118707	.116129	.113592	.111098	.108645	.106235	.103869
	-.10	.142353	.136632	.131053	.128318	.125622	.122965	.120347	.117769	.115233	.112738	.110285	.107876	.105510
	-.20	.143994	.138272	.132693	.129959	.127262	.124605	.121987	.119410	.116873	.114378	.111926	.109516	.107150
	-.30	.145634	.139912	.134333	.131599	.128903	.126245	.123627	.121050	.118513	.116018	.113566	.111156	.108790
	-.40	.147274	.141553	.135973	.133239	.130543	.127886	.125268	.122690	.120154	.117659	.115206	.112797	.110430
20	.40	.131324	.124874	.118576	.115489	.112444	.109445	.106491	.103586	.100730	.097926	.095474	.092477	.089835
	.30	.132964	.126514	.120216	.117129	.114084	.111085	.108132	.105226	.102371	.099566	.096815	.094117	.091475
	.20	.134605	.128155	.121857	.118769	.115725	.112725	.109772	.106867	.104011	.101207	.098455	.095758	.093116
	.10	.136245	.129795	.123497	.120410	.117365	.114365	.111412	.108507	.105651	.102847	.100095	.097398	.094756
	0.00	.137885	.131435	.125137	.122050	.119005	.116006	.113052	.110147	.107292	.104487	.101736	.099038	.096396
	-.10	.139525	.133075	.126778	.123690	.120646	.117646	.114693	.111787	.108932	.106128	.103376	.100678	.098036
	-.20	.141166	.134716	.128418	.125330	.122286	.119286	.116333	.113428	.110572	.107768	.105016	.102319	.099677
	-.30	.142806	.136356	.130058	.126971	.123926	.120926	.117973	.115068	.112212	.109408	.106656	.103959	.101317
	-.40	.144446	.137996	.131698	.128611	.125566	.122567	.119613	.116708	.113853	.111048	.108297	.105599	.102957
25	.40	.129958	.123100	.116379	.113076	.109814	.106597	.103426	.100305	.097235	.094221	.091263	.088366	.085530
	.30	.131598	.124740	.118019	.114716	.111455	.108237	.105066	.101945	.098876	.095861	.092904	.090006	.087171
	.20	.133239	.126381	.119660	.116356	.113095	.109877	.106707	.103585	.100516	.097501	.094544	.091646	.088811
	.10	.134879	.128021	.121300	.117997	.114735	.111518	.108347	.105226	.102156	.099142	.096184	.093287	.090451
	0.00	.136519	.129661	.122940	.119637	.116375	.113158	.109987	.106866	.103797	.100782	.097824	.094927	.092091
	-.10	.138159	.131301	.124580	.121277	.118016	.114798	.111628	.108506	.105437	.102422	.099465	.096567	.093732
	-.20	.139800	.132942	.126221	.122918	.119656	.116439	.113268	.110146	.107077	.104062	.101105	.098207	.095372
	-.30	.141440	.134582	.127861	.124558	.121296	.118079	.114908	.111787	.108717	.105703	.102745	.099848	.097012
	-.40	.143080	.136222	.129501	.126198	.122937	.119719	.116548	.113427	.110358	.107343	.104386	.101488	.098653
30	.40	.129256	.122153	.115165	.111720	.108312	.104945	.101621	.098345	.095120	.091949	.088837	.085786	.082602
	.30	.130896	.123794	.116805	.113360	.109952	.106585	.103262	.099985	.096760	.093589	.090477	.087427	.084442
	.20	.132536	.125434	.118445	.115000	.111593	.108225	.104902	.101626	.098400	.095230	.092117	.089067	.086082
	.10	.134176	.127074	.120086	.116641	.113233	.109866	.106542	.103266	.100041	.096870	.093758	.090707	.087723
	0.00	.135817	.128715	.121726	.118281	.114873	.111506	.108182	.104906	.101681	.098510	.095398	.092348	.089363
	-.10	.137457	.130355	.123366	.119921	.116514	.113146	.109823	.106547	.103321	.100151	.097038	.093988	.091003
	-.20	.139097	.131995	.125006	.121562	.118154	.114787	.111463	.108187	.104962	.101791	.098679	.095628	.092644
	-.30	.140737	.133635	.126646	.123202	.119794	.116427	.113103	.109827	.106602	.103431	.100319	.097268	.094284
	-.40	.142378	.135276	.128287	.124842	.121434	.118067	.114744	.111467	.108242	.105071	.101959	.098909	.095924

15.0 YEAR HOLDING PERIOD
.180 EQUITY YIELD RATE
.800 LOAN RATIO

INTEREST RATE

TERM YEARS	APPR DEP	5.0	5.5	6.0	6.5	7.0	7.5	8.0	8.5	9.0	9.5	10.0	11.0	12.0
10	.40	.108674	.110693	.112732	.114792	.116873	.118973	.121093	.123231	.125388	.127562	.129753	.134183	.138673
	.30	.110315	.112333	.114372	.116433	.118513	.120614	.122733	.124872	.127028	.129202	.131393	.135823	.140313
	.20	.111955	.113973	.116013	.118073	.120153	.122254	.124374	.126512	.128668	.130842	.133033	.137464	.141954
	.10	.113595	.115613	.117653	.119713	.121794	.123894	.126014	.128152	.130309	.132483	.134674	.139104	.143594
	0.00	.115235	.117254	.119293	.121353	.123434	.125534	.127654	.129792	.131949	.134123	.136314	.140744	.145234
	-.10	.116876	.118894	.120933	.122994	.125074	.127175	.129294	.131433	.133589	.135763	.137954	.142384	.146875
	-.20	.118516	.120534	.122574	.124634	.126715	.128815	.130935	.133073	.135230	.137404	.139595	.144025	.148515
	-.30	.120156	.122174	.124214	.126274	.128355	.130455	.132575	.134713	.136870	.139044	.141235	.145665	.150156
	-.40	.121797	.123815	.125854	.127915	.129995	.132096	.134215	.136354	.138510	.140684	.142875	.147305	.151795
15	.40	.092233	.094757	.097327	.099943	.102604	.105310	.108059	.110852	.113686	.116562	.119479	.125430	.131533
	.30	.093873	.096397	.098967	.101583	.104244	.106950	.109700	.112492	.115327	.118203	.121119	.127070	.133173
	.20	.095513	.098037	.100607	.103224	.105885	.108590	.111340	.114132	.116967	.119843	.122759	.128711	.134813
	.10	.097154	.099678	.102248	.104864	.107525	.110231	.112980	.115772	.118607	.121483	.124399	.130351	.136454
	0.00	.098794	.101318	.103888	.106504	.109165	.111871	.114620	.117413	.120247	.123123	.126040	.131991	.138094
	-.10	.100434	.102958	.105528	.108144	.110806	.113511	.116261	.119053	.121888	.124764	.127680	.133631	.139734
	-.20	.102075	.104598	.107169	.109785	.112446	.115152	.117901	.120693	.123528	.126404	.129320	.135272	.141374
	-.30	.103715	.106239	.108809	.111425	.114086	.116792	.119541	.122334	.125168	.128044	.130961	.136912	.143015
	-.40	.105355	.107879	.110449	.113065	.115726	.118432	.121181	.123974	.126808	.129684	.132601	.138552	.144655
20	.40	.084261	.087080	.089957	.092892	.095883	.098929	.102028	.105178	.108378	.111625	.114919	.121636	.128516
	.30	.085902	.088720	.091597	.094532	.097524	.100569	.103668	.106819	.110018	.113266	.116559	.123277	.130157
	.20	.087542	.090360	.093237	.096172	.099164	.102210	.105309	.108459	.111658	.114906	.118199	.124917	.131797
	.10	.089182	.092000	.094878	.097813	.100804	.103850	.106949	.110099	.113299	.116546	.119840	.126557	.133437
	0.00	.090823	.093641	.096518	.099453	.102444	.105490	.108589	.111739	.114939	.118186	.121480	.128197	.135077
	-.10	.092463	.095281	.098158	.101093	.104085	.107131	.110229	.113380	.116579	.119827	.123120	.129838	.136718
	-.20	.094103	.096921	.099799	.102734	.105725	.108771	.111870	.115020	.118220	.121467	.124760	.131478	.138358
	-.30	.095743	.098561	.101439	.104374	.107365	.110411	.113510	.116660	.119860	.123107	.126401	.133118	.139998
	-.40	.097384	.100202	.103079	.106014	.109005	.112051	.115150	.118300	.121500	.124748	.128041	.134759	.141639
25	.40	.079670	.082694	.085785	.088940	.092155	.095429	.098759	.102141	.105573	.109052	.112575	.119744	.127059
	.30	.081310	.084334	.087425	.090580	.093796	.097069	.100399	.103781	.107213	.110692	.114215	.121384	.128700
	.20	.082950	.085975	.089066	.092220	.095436	.098710	.102039	.105421	.108853	.112332	.115856	.123025	.130340
	.10	.084591	.087615	.090706	.093860	.097076	.100350	.103679	.107062	.110494	.113973	.117496	.124665	.131980
	0.00	.086231	.089255	.092346	.095501	.098716	.101990	.105320	.108702	.112134	.115613	.119136	.126305	.133620
	-.10	.087871	.090896	.093986	.097141	.100357	.103631	.106960	.110342	.113774	.117253	.120776	.127946	.135261
	-.20	.089511	.092536	.095627	.098781	.101997	.105271	.108600	.111982	.115414	.118893	.122417	.129586	.136901
	-.30	.091152	.094176	.097267	.100422	.103637	.106911	.110241	.113623	.117055	.120534	.124057	.131226	.138541
	-.40	.092792	.095816	.098907	.102062	.105277	.108551	.111881	.115263	.118695	.122174	.125697	.132866	.140181
30	.40	.076759	.079943	.083197	.086517	.089899	.093339	.096834	.100379	.103970	.107605	.111280	.118734	.126310
	.30	.078400	.081583	.084837	.088157	.091539	.094979	.098474	.102019	.105611	.109246	.112920	.120375	.127950
	.20	.080040	.083224	.086477	.089797	.093179	.096619	.100114	.103659	.107251	.110886	.114560	.122015	.129591
	.10	.081680	.084864	.088118	.091437	.094819	.098260	.101754	.105299	.108891	.112526	.116201	.123655	.131231
	0.00	.083321	.086504	.089758	.093078	.096460	.099900	.103395	.106940	.110531	.114166	.117841	.125296	.132871
	-.10	.084961	.088144	.091398	.094718	.098100	.101540	.105035	.108580	.112172	.115807	.119481	.126936	.134511
	-.20	.086601	.089785	.093038	.096358	.099740	.103181	.106675	.110220	.113812	.117447	.121121	.128576	.136152
	-.30	.088241	.091425	.094679	.097999	.101381	.104821	.108315	.111861	.115452	.119087	.122762	.130216	.137792
	-.40	.089882	.093065	.096319	.099639	.103021	.106461	.109956	.113501	.117093	.120727	.124402	.131857	.139432

15.0 YEAR HOLDING PERIOD
.180 EQUITY YIELD RATE
.900 LOAN RATIO

INTEREST RATE

TERM YEARS	APPR DEP	5.0	5.5	6.0	6.5	7.0	7.5	8.0	8.5	9.0	9.5	10.0	11.0	12.0
10	.40	.105579	.102849	.105144	.107461	.109802	.112165	.114550	.116955	.119382	.121827	.124292	.129276	.134327
	.30	.102219	.104490	.106784	.109102	.111442	.113805	.116190	.118596	.121022	.123468	.125932	.130916	.135968
	.20	.103859	.106130	.108424	.110742	.113083	.115446	.117830	.120236	.122662	.125108	.127573	.132557	.137608
	.10	.105500	.107770	.110064	.112382	.114723	.117086	.119471	.121876	.124302	.126748	.129213	.134197	.139248
	0.00	.107140	.109410	.111705	.114023	.116363	.118726	.121111	.123517	.125943	.128388	.130853	.135837	.140889
	-.10	.108780	.111051	.113345	.115663	.118004	.120367	.122751	.125157	.127583	.130029	.132494	.137478	.142529
	-.20	.110420	.112691	.114985	.117303	.119644	.122007	.124391	.126797	.129223	.131669	.134134	.139118	.144169
	-.30	.112061	.114331	.116626	.118943	.121284	.123647	.126032	.128437	.130863	.133309	.135774	.140758	.145809
	-.40	.113701	.115971	.118266	.120584	.122924	.125287	.127672	.130078	.132504	.134950	.137414	.142398	.147450
15	.40	.082082	.084921	.087813	.090756	.093750	.096794	.099887	.103028	.106217	.109453	.112734	.119429	.126295
	.30	.083722	.086562	.089453	.092396	.095390	.098434	.101527	.104669	.107857	.111093	.114374	.121069	.127935
	.20	.085363	.088202	.091093	.094037	.097030	.100074	.103167	.106309	.109498	.112733	.116014	.122709	.129575
	.10	.087003	.089842	.092734	.095677	.098671	.101715	.104808	.107949	.111138	.114373	.117655	.124350	.131215
	0.00	.088643	.091483	.094374	.097317	.100311	.103355	.106448	.109589	.112778	.116014	.119295	.125990	.132856
	-.10	.090283	.093123	.096014	.098957	.101951	.104995	.108088	.111230	.114419	.117654	.120935	.127630	.134496
	-.20	.091924	.094763	.097655	.100598	.103592	.106635	.109728	.112870	.116059	.119294	.122575	.129271	.136136
	-.30	.093564	.096403	.099295	.102238	.105232	.108276	.111369	.114510	.117699	.120935	.124216	.130911	.137776
	-.40	.095204	.098044	.100935	.103878	.106872	.109916	.113009	.116150	.119339	.122575	.125856	.132551	.139417
20	.40	.073114	.076285	.079522	.082824	.086189	.089615	.093102	.096646	.100245	.103899	.107604	.115161	.122901
	.30	.074755	.077925	.081162	.084464	.087829	.091256	.094742	.098286	.101886	.105539	.109244	.116801	.124541
	.20	.076395	.079565	.082802	.086104	.089469	.092896	.096382	.099926	.103526	.107179	.110884	.118442	.126182
	.10	.078035	.081205	.084442	.087744	.091110	.094536	.098023	.101566	.105166	.108819	.112525	.120082	.127822
	0.00	.079675	.082846	.086083	.089385	.092750	.096177	.099663	.103207	.106806	.110460	.114165	.121722	.129462
	-.10	.081316	.084486	.087723	.091025	.094390	.097817	.101303	.104847	.108447	.112100	.115805	.123362	.131102
	-.20	.082956	.086126	.089363	.092665	.096030	.099457	.102943	.106487	.110087	.113740	.117446	.125003	.132743
	-.30	.084596	.087767	.091004	.094306	.097671	.101097	.104584	.108128	.111727	.115381	.119086	.126643	.134383
	-.40	.086237	.089407	.092644	.095946	.099311	.102738	.106224	.109768	.113367	.117021	.120726	.128283	.136023
25	.40	.067949	.071351	.074628	.078377	.081995	.085678	.089424	.093228	.097089	.101003	.104967	.113032	.121262
	.30	.069589	.072991	.076469	.080017	.083635	.087318	.091064	.094869	.098730	.102644	.106607	.114673	.122902
	.20	.071229	.074632	.078109	.081658	.085275	.088959	.092704	.096509	.100370	.104284	.108248	.116313	.124542
	.10	.072869	.076272	.079749	.083298	.086916	.090599	.094344	.098149	.102010	.105924	.109888	.117953	.126183
	0.00	.074510	.077912	.081389	.084938	.088556	.092239	.095985	.099790	.103651	.107564	.111528	.119593	.127823
	-.10	.076150	.079552	.083030	.086578	.090196	.093879	.097625	.101431	.105291	.109205	.113169	.121234	.129462
	-.20	.077790	.081193	.084670	.088219	.091836	.095520	.099265	.103070	.106931	.110845	.114809	.122874	.131103
	-.30	.079431	.082833	.086310	.089859	.093477	.097160	.100906	.104710	.108571	.112485	.116449	.124514	.132744
	-.40	.081071	.084473	.087950	.091499	.095117	.098800	.102546	.106351	.110212	.114126	.118089	.126155	.134384
30	.40	.064674	.068256	.071916	.075651	.079456	.083326	.087258	.091246	.095287	.099376	.103510	.111896	.120419
	.30	.066315	.069896	.073557	.077292	.081096	.084967	.088898	.092886	.096927	.101016	.105150	.113537	.122059
	.20	.067955	.071537	.075197	.078932	.082737	.086607	.090538	.094527	.098567	.102657	.106790	.115177	.123699
	.10	.069595	.073177	.076837	.080572	.084377	.088247	.092179	.096167	.100208	.104297	.108431	.116817	.125340
	0.00	.071236	.074817	.078478	.082212	.086017	.089888	.093819	.097807	.101848	.105937	.110071	.118458	.126980
	-.10	.072876	.076457	.080118	.083853	.087657	.091528	.095459	.099447	.103488	.107577	.111711	.120098	.128620
	-.20	.074516	.078098	.081758	.085493	.089298	.093168	.097100	.101088	.105128	.109218	.113352	.121738	.130261
	-.30	.076156	.079738	.083398	.087133	.090938	.094808	.098740	.102728	.106769	.110858	.114992	.123378	.131901
	-.40	.077797	.081378	.085039	.088773	.092578	.096449	.100380	.104368	.108409	.112498	.116632	.125019	.133541

15.0 YEAR HOLDING PERIOD
.200 EQUITY YIELD RATE
.600 LOAN RATIO

INTEREST RATE

TERM YEARS	APPR DEP	5.0	5.5	6.0	6.5	7.0	7.5	8.0	8.5	9.0	9.5	10.0	11.0	12.0
10	.40	.136477	.138030	.139601	.141188	.142792	.144412	.146048	.147700	.149366	.151047	.152743	.156174	.159657
	.30	.137865	.139419	.140989	.142576	.144180	.145801	.147437	.149088	.150755	.152436	.154131	.157563	.161046
	.20	.139253	.140807	.142377	.143965	.145569	.147189	.148825	.150476	.152143	.153824	.155519	.158951	.162434
	.10	.140642	.142195	.143766	.145353	.146957	.148577	.150213	.151864	.153531	.155212	.156907	.160339	.163822
	0.00	.142030	.143563	.145154	.146741	.148345	.149965	.151601	.153253	.154919	.156600	.158296	.161727	.165210
	-.10	.143418	.144971	.146542	.148129	.149733	.151353	.152989	.154641	.156307	.157988	.159684	.163115	.166598
	-.20	.144806	.146360	.147930	.149518	.151122	.152742	.154378	.156029	.157696	.159377	.161072	.164504	.167987
	-.30	.146195	.147748	.149318	.150906	.152510	.154130	.155766	.157417	.159084	.160765	.162460	.165892	.169375
	-.40	.147583	.149136	.150707	.152294	.153898	.155518	.157154	.158806	.160472	.162153	.163848	.167280	.170763
15	.40	.123055	.124948	.126876	.128838	.130834	.132863	.134925	.137019	.139145	.141302	.143489	.147953	.152530
	.30	.124443	.126336	.128264	.130226	.132222	.134251	.136313	.138407	.140533	.142690	.144878	.149341	.153918
	.20	.125831	.127724	.129652	.131614	.133610	.135639	.137701	.139796	.141921	.144078	.146266	.150729	.155306
	.10	.127220	.129113	.131040	.133002	.134998	.137027	.139089	.141184	.143310	.145467	.147654	.152117	.156695
	0.00	.128608	.130501	.132428	.134390	.136386	.138416	.140478	.142572	.144698	.146855	.149042	.153506	.158083
	-.10	.129996	.131889	.133817	.135779	.137775	.139804	.141866	.143960	.146086	.148243	.150431	.154894	.159471
	-.20	.131384	.133277	.135205	.137167	.139163	.141192	.143254	.145348	.147474	.149631	.151819	.156282	.160859
	-.30	.132773	.134665	.136593	.138555	.140551	.142580	.144642	.146737	.148863	.151020	.153207	.157670	.162247
	-.40	.134161	.136054	.137981	.139943	.141939	.143968	.146031	.148125	.150251	.152408	.154595	.159059	.163636
20	.40	.116548	.118645	.120788	.122973	.125201	.127469	.129778	.132124	.134508	.136928	.139383	.144390	.149519
	.30	.117936	.120034	.122176	.124361	.126589	.128857	.131166	.133513	.135897	.138316	.140771	.145778	.150907
	.20	.119324	.121422	.123564	.125749	.127977	.130246	.132554	.134901	.137285	.139705	.142159	.147166	.152295
	.10	.120712	.122810	.124952	.127138	.129365	.131634	.133942	.136289	.138673	.141093	.143547	.148554	.153684
	0.00	.122100	.124198	.126340	.128526	.130754	.133022	.135330	.137677	.140061	.142481	.144935	.149942	.155072
	-.10	.123489	.125586	.127729	.129914	.132142	.134410	.136719	.139065	.141449	.143869	.146324	.151331	.156460
	-.20	.124877	.126975	.129117	.131302	.133530	.135799	.138107	.140454	.142838	.145257	.147712	.152719	.157848
	-.30	.126265	.128363	.130505	.132691	.134918	.137187	.139495	.141842	.144226	.146646	.149100	.154107	.159237
	-.40	.127653	.129751	.131893	.134079	.136306	.138575	.140883	.143230	.145614	.148034	.150488	.155495	.160625
25	.40	.112799	.115045	.117341	.119686	.122076	.124511	.126987	.129504	.132058	.134648	.137272	.142612	.148065
	.30	.114187	.116433	.118730	.121074	.123464	.125899	.128375	.130892	.133446	.136036	.138660	.144001	.149453
	.20	.115576	.117822	.120118	.122462	.124853	.127287	.129764	.132280	.134834	.137424	.140048	.145389	.150841
	.10	.116964	.119210	.121506	.123850	.126241	.128675	.131152	.133668	.136223	.138813	.141437	.146777	.152229
	0.00	.118352	.120598	.122894	.125239	.127629	.130064	.132540	.135057	.137611	.140201	.142825	.148165	.153617
	-.10	.119740	.121986	.124282	.126627	.129017	.131452	.133928	.136445	.138999	.141589	.144213	.149553	.155006
	-.20	.121128	.123375	.125671	.128015	.130405	.132840	.135317	.137833	.140387	.142977	.145601	.150942	.156394
	-.30	.122517	.124763	.127059	.129403	.131794	.134228	.136705	.139221	.141775	.144365	.146989	.152330	.157782
	-.40	.123905	.126151	.128447	.130791	.133182	.135616	.138093	.140609	.143164	.145754	.148377	.153718	.159170
30	.40	.110423	.112787	.115203	.117670	.120185	.122744	.125344	.127983	.130658	.133366	.136105	.141664	.147317
	.30	.111811	.114175	.116592	.119059	.121573	.124132	.126732	.129372	.132047	.134755	.137493	.143052	.148705
	.20	.113200	.115563	.117980	.120447	.122961	.125520	.128121	.130760	.133435	.136143	.138882	.144440	.150093
	.10	.114588	.116951	.119368	.121835	.124350	.126908	.129509	.132148	.134823	.137531	.140270	.145829	.151481
	0.00	.115976	.118340	.120756	.123223	.125738	.128297	.130897	.133536	.136211	.138919	.141658	.147217	.152869
	-.10	.117364	.119728	.122144	.124611	.127126	.129685	.132285	.134924	.137599	.140308	.143046	.148605	.154258
	-.20	.118753	.121116	.123533	.126000	.128514	.131073	.133674	.136313	.138988	.141696	.144434	.149993	.155646
	-.30	.120141	.122504	.124921	.127388	.129902	.132461	.135062	.137701	.140376	.143084	.145823	.151382	.157034
	-.40	.121529	.123892	.126309	.128776	.131291	.133850	.136450	.139089	.141764	.144472	.147211	.152770	.158422

342

15.0 YEAR HOLDING PERIOD
.200 EQUITY YIELD RATE
.667 LOAN RATIO

INTEREST RATE

TERM YEARS	APPR DEP	5.0	5.5	6.0	6.5	7.0	7.5	8.0	8.5	9.0	9.5	10.0	11.0	12.0
10	.40	.130036	.131762	.133507	.135270	.137053	.138853	.140670	.142505	.144357	.146225	.148109	.151922	.155792
	.30	.131424	.133150	.134895	.136659	.138441	.140241	.142059	.143894	.145745	.147613	.149497	.153310	.157180
	.20	.132812	.134538	.136283	.138047	.139829	.141629	.143447	.145282	.147133	.149001	.150885	.154698	.158568
	.10	.134200	.135926	.137671	.139435	.141217	.143017	.144835	.146670	.148522	.150390	.152273	.156086	.159956
	0.00	.135588	.137314	.139059	.140823	.142605	.144406	.146223	.148058	.149910	.151778	.153662	.157474	.161344
	-.10	.136977	.138703	.140448	.142211	.143994	.145794	.147612	.149446	.151298	.153166	.155050	.158863	.162733
	-.20	.138365	.140091	.141836	.143600	.145382	.147182	.149000	.150835	.152686	.154554	.156438	.160251	.164121
	-.30	.139753	.141479	.143224	.144988	.146770	.148570	.150388	.152223	.154075	.155942	.157826	.161639	.165509
	-.40	.141141	.142867	.144612	.146376	.148158	.149958	.151776	.153611	.155463	.157331	.159214	.163027	.166897
15	.40	.115122	.117225	.119367	.121547	.123765	.126020	.128311	.130638	.133000	.135397	.137827	.142787	.147872
	.30	.116510	.118614	.120755	.122936	.125153	.127408	.129699	.132026	.134388	.136785	.139215	.144175	.149260
	.20	.117899	.120002	.122144	.124324	.126541	.128796	.131087	.133414	.135777	.138173	.140604	.145563	.150649
	.10	.119287	.121390	.123532	.125712	.127930	.130184	.132476	.134803	.137165	.139561	.141992	.146951	.152037
	0.00	.120675	.122778	.124920	.127100	.129318	.131573	.133864	.136191	.138553	.140950	.143380	.148339	.153425
	-.10	.122063	.124166	.126308	.128488	.130706	.132961	.135252	.137579	.139941	.142338	.144768	.149728	.154813
	-.20	.123451	.125555	.127697	.129877	.132094	.134349	.136640	.138967	.141329	.143726	.146156	.151116	.156202
	-.30	.124840	.126943	.129085	.131265	.133482	.135737	.138028	.140355	.142718	.145114	.147545	.152504	.157590
	-.40	.126228	.128331	.130473	.132653	.134871	.137125	.139417	.141744	.144106	.146502	.148933	.153892	.158978
20	.40	.107892	.110223	.112603	.115031	.117506	.120027	.122592	.125199	.127848	.130537	.133264	.138827	.144527
	.30	.109280	.111611	.113991	.116419	.118894	.121415	.123980	.126587	.129236	.131925	.134652	.140216	.145915
	.20	.110668	.112999	.115379	.117807	.120283	.122803	.125368	.127976	.130625	.133313	.136040	.141604	.147303
	.10	.112056	.114387	.116767	.119196	.121671	.124192	.126756	.129364	.132013	.134701	.137429	.142992	.148691
	0.00	.113444	.115775	.118156	.120584	.123059	.125580	.128145	.130752	.133401	.136090	.138817	.144380	.150080
	-.10	.114833	.117164	.119544	.121972	.124447	.126968	.129533	.132140	.134789	.137478	.140205	.145768	.151468
	-.20	.116221	.118552	.120932	.123360	.125835	.128356	.130921	.133528	.136177	.138866	.141593	.147157	.152856
	-.30	.117609	.119940	.122320	.124749	.127224	.129744	.132309	.134917	.137566	.140254	.142981	.148545	.154244
	-.40	.118997	.121328	.123708	.126137	.128612	.131133	.133697	.136305	.138954	.141643	.144370	.149933	.155632
25	.40	.103727	.106222	.108774	.111379	.114035	.116740	.119491	.122287	.125125	.128003	.130919	.136853	.142911
	.30	.105115	.107611	.110162	.112767	.115423	.118128	.120880	.123676	.126514	.129392	.132307	.138241	.144299
	.20	.106503	.108999	.111550	.114155	.116811	.119516	.122268	.125064	.127902	.130780	.133695	.139629	.145687
	.10	.107891	.110387	.112938	.115543	.118199	.120904	.123656	.126452	.129290	.132168	.135083	.141017	.147075
	0.00	.109280	.111775	.114327	.116931	.119587	.122292	.125044	.127840	.130678	.133556	.136471	.142406	.148464
	-.10	.110668	.113163	.115715	.118320	.120976	.123681	.126432	.129228	.132067	.134944	.137860	.143794	.149852
	-.20	.112056	.114552	.117103	.119708	.122364	.125069	.127821	.130617	.133455	.136333	.139248	.145182	.151240
	-.30	.113444	.115940	.118491	.121096	.123752	.126457	.129209	.132005	.134843	.137721	.140636	.146570	.152628
	-.40	.114832	.117328	.119879	.122484	.125140	.127845	.130597	.133393	.136231	.139109	.142024	.147958	.154016
30	.40	.101087	.103713	.106398	.109139	.111933	.114776	.117666	.120598	.123570	.126579	.129622	.135799	.142080
	.30	.102475	.105101	.107786	.110527	.113321	.116165	.119054	.121986	.124959	.127968	.131011	.137187	.143468
	.20	.103863	.106489	.109174	.111916	.114710	.117553	.120442	.123375	.126347	.129356	.132399	.138575	.144856
	.10	.105251	.107877	.110563	.113304	.116098	.118941	.121830	.124763	.127735	.130744	.133787	.139964	.146244
	0.00	.106640	.109266	.111951	.114692	.117486	.120329	.123219	.126151	.129123	.132132	.135175	.141352	.147633
	-.10	.108028	.110654	.113339	.116080	.118874	.121717	.124607	.127539	.130511	.133520	.136563	.142740	.149021
	-.20	.109416	.112042	.114727	.117469	.120262	.123106	.125995	.128927	.131900	.134909	.137952	.144128	.150409
	-.30	.110804	.113430	.116116	.118857	.121651	.124494	.127383	.130316	.133288	.136297	.139340	.145516	.151797
	-.40	.112193	.114819	.117504	.120245	.123039	.125882	.128771	.131704	.134676	.137685	.140728	.146905	.153185

15.0 YEAR HOLDING PERIOD
.200 EQUITY YIELD RATE
.700 LOAN RATIO

INTEREST RATE

TERM YEARS	APPR DEP	5.0	5.5	6.0	6.5	7.0	7.5	8.0	8.5	9.0	9.5	10.0	11.0	12.0
10	.40	.126815	.128628	.130460	.132312	.134183	.136073	.137982	.139909	.141853	.143814	.145792	.149796	.153859
	.30	.128204	.130016	.131848	.133700	.135571	.137461	.139370	.141297	.143241	.145202	.147180	.151184	.155247
	.20	.129596	.131404	.133236	.135088	.136960	.138850	.140758	.142685	.144629	.146591	.148568	.152572	.156635
	.10	.130980	.132792	.134624	.136476	.138348	.140238	.142147	.144073	.146017	.147979	.149957	.153960	.158024
	0.00	.132368	.134180	.136013	.137865	.139736	.141626	.143535	.145461	.147406	.149367	.151345	.155348	.159412
	-.10	.133756	.135569	.137401	.139253	.141124	.143014	.144923	.146850	.148794	.150755	.152733	.156737	.160800
	-.20	.135145	.136957	.138789	.140641	.142512	.144403	.146311	.148238	.150182	.152143	.154121	.158125	.162188
	-.30	.136533	.138345	.140177	.142029	.143901	.145791	.147699	.149626	.151570	.153532	.155510	.159513	.163577
	-.40	.137921	.139733	.141566	.143417	.145289	.147179	.149088	.151014	.152959	.154920	.156898	.160901	.164965
15	.40	.111156	.113365	.115614	.117903	.120231	.122599	.125004	.127448	.129928	.132445	.134996	.140204	.145544
	.30	.112545	.114753	.117002	.119291	.121619	.123987	.126393	.128836	.131316	.133833	.136385	.141592	.146932
	.20	.113933	.116141	.118390	.120679	.123008	.125375	.127781	.130224	.132704	.135221	.137773	.142980	.148320
	.10	.115321	.117529	.119778	.122067	.124396	.126763	.129169	.131612	.134093	.136609	.139161	.144368	.149708
	0.00	.116709	.118918	.121166	.123456	.125784	.128152	.130557	.133001	.135481	.137997	.140549	.145757	.151097
	-.10	.118097	.120306	.122555	.124844	.127172	.129540	.131946	.134389	.136869	.139386	.141938	.147145	.152485
	-.20	.119486	.121694	.123943	.126232	.128561	.130928	.133334	.135777	.138257	.140774	.143326	.148533	.153873
	-.30	.120874	.123082	.125331	.127620	.129949	.132316	.134722	.137165	.139646	.142162	.144714	.149921	.155261
	-.40	.122262	.124470	.126719	.129008	.131337	.133704	.136110	.138553	.141034	.143550	.146102	.151310	.156649
20	.40	.103564	.106012	.108511	.111061	.113660	.116306	.118999	.121737	.124518	.127342	.130205	.136047	.142031
	.30	.104953	.107400	.109899	.112449	.115048	.117694	.120387	.123125	.125907	.128730	.131593	.137435	.143419
	.20	.106341	.108788	.111287	.113837	.116436	.119083	.121776	.124514	.127295	.130118	.132982	.138823	.144807
	.10	.107729	.110176	.112676	.115225	.117824	.120471	.123164	.125902	.128683	.131506	.134370	.140211	.146196
	0.00	.109117	.111565	.114064	.116614	.119212	.121859	.124552	.127290	.130071	.132894	.135758	.141600	.147584
	-.10	.110505	.112953	.115452	.118002	.120601	.123247	.125940	.128678	.131460	.134283	.137146	.142988	.148972
	-.20	.111894	.114341	.116840	.119390	.121989	.124636	.127329	.130066	.132848	.135671	.138534	.144376	.150360
	-.30	.113282	.115729	.118228	.120778	.123377	.126024	.128717	.131455	.134236	.137059	.139923	.145764	.151748
	-.40	.114670	.117117	.119617	.122166	.124765	.127412	.130105	.132843	.135624	.138447	.141311	.147152	.153137
25	.40	.099191	.101812	.104490	.107226	.110014	.112855	.115744	.118680	.121660	.124681	.127743	.133973	.140334
	.30	.100579	.103200	.105879	.108614	.111403	.114243	.117132	.120068	.123048	.126070	.129131	.135362	.141722
	.20	.101968	.104588	.107267	.110002	.112791	.115631	.118520	.121456	.124436	.127458	.130519	.136750	.143111
	.10	.103356	.105976	.108655	.111390	.114179	.117019	.119909	.122846	.125824	.128846	.131907	.138138	.144499
	0.00	.104744	.107364	.110043	.112778	.115567	.118408	.121297	.124233	.127213	.130234	.133295	.139526	.145887
	-.10	.106132	.108753	.111432	.114167	.116955	.119796	.122685	.125621	.128601	.131623	.134684	.140914	.147275
	-.20	.107520	.110141	.112820	.115555	.118344	.121184	.124073	.127009	.129989	.133011	.136072	.142303	.148663
	-.30	.108909	.111529	.114208	.116943	.119732	.122572	.125461	.128397	.131377	.134399	.137460	.143691	.150052
	-.40	.110297	.112917	.115596	.118331	.121120	.123960	.126850	.129785	.132765	.135787	.138848	.145079	.151440
30	.40	.096419	.099177	.101996	.104874	.107808	.110793	.113827	.116906	.120027	.123186	.126381	.132867	.139462
	.30	.097808	.100565	.103384	.106263	.109196	.112181	.115215	.118294	.121415	.124575	.127770	.134255	.140850
	.20	.099196	.101953	.104772	.107651	.110584	.113570	.116604	.119683	.122803	.125963	.129158	.135643	.142238
	.10	.100584	.103341	.106161	.109039	.111972	.114958	.117992	.121071	.124192	.127351	.130546	.137031	.143626
	0.00	.101972	.104729	.107549	.110427	.113361	.116346	.119380	.122459	.125580	.128739	.131934	.138420	.145014
	-.10	.103360	.106118	.108937	.111815	.114749	.117734	.120768	.123847	.126968	.130127	.133322	.139808	.146403
	-.20	.104749	.107506	.110325	.113204	.116137	.119123	.122156	.125235	.128356	.131516	.134711	.141196	.147791
	-.30	.106137	.108894	.111714	.114592	.117525	.120511	.123545	.126624	.129744	.132904	.136099	.142584	.149179
	-.40	.107525	.110282	.113102	.115980	.118914	.121899	.124933	.128012	.131133	.134292	.137487	.143973	.150567

15.0 YEAR HOLDING PERIOD
.200 EQUITY YIELD RATE
.750 LOAN RATIO

INTEREST RATE

TERM YEARS	APPR DEP	12.0	11.0	10.0	9.5	9.0	8.5	8.0	7.5	7.0	6.5	6.0	5.5	5.0
10	.40	.150960	.146606	.142317	.140197	.138096	.136013	.133949	.131904	.129879	.127874	.125889	.123926	.121985
	.30	.152348	.147994	.143705	.141586	.139484	.137401	.135337	.133292	.131267	.129262	.127278	.125314	.123373
	.20	.153736	.149383	.145093	.142974	.140873	.138789	.136725	.134680	.132655	.130650	.128666	.126703	.124761
	.10	.155125	.150771	.146482	.144362	.142261	.140178	.138113	.136068	.134043	.132038	.130054	.128091	.126149
	0.00	.156513	.152159	.147870	.145750	.143649	.141566	.139502	.137457	.135431	.133426	.131442	.129479	.127537
	-.10	.157901	.153547	.149258	.147139	.145037	.142954	.140890	.138845	.136820	.134815	.132830	.130867	.128920
	-.20	.159289	.154935	.150646	.148527	.146425	.144342	.142278	.140233	.138208	.136203	.134219	.132255	.130314
	-.30	.160678	.156324	.152034	.149915	.147814	.145730	.143666	.141621	.139596	.137591	.135607	.133644	.131702
	-.40	.162066	.157712	.153422	.151303	.149202	.147119	.145054	.143009	.140984	.138979	.136995	.135032	.133090
15	.40	.142051	.136329	.130750	.128016	.125320	.122662	.120044	.117467	.114930	.112435	.109983	.107573	.105207
	.30	.143439	.137717	.132138	.129404	.126708	.124050	.121432	.118855	.116318	.113823	.111371	.108961	.106595
	.20	.144827	.139106	.133526	.130792	.128096	.125439	.122821	.120243	.117707	.115212	.112759	.110349	.107983
	.10	.146215	.140494	.134915	.132180	.129484	.126827	.124209	.121631	.119095	.116600	.114147	.111738	.109372
	0.00	.147604	.141882	.136303	.133569	.130872	.128215	.125597	.123020	.120483	.117988	.115536	.113126	.110760
	-.10	.148992	.143270	.137691	.134957	.132261	.129603	.126985	.124408	.121871	.119376	.116924	.114514	.112148
	-.20	.150380	.144659	.139079	.136345	.133649	.130991	.128374	.125796	.123259	.120764	.118312	.115902	.113536
	-.30	.151768	.146047	.140468	.137733	.135037	.132380	.129762	.127184	.124648	.122153	.119700	.117291	.114924
	-.40	.153156	.147435	.141856	.139121	.136425	.133768	.131150	.128572	.126036	.123541	.121088	.118679	.116313
20	.40	.138287	.131875	.125616	.122548	.119524	.116544	.113610	.110725	.107889	.105105	.102373	.099695	.097073
	.30	.139675	.133263	.127005	.123937	.120912	.117932	.114998	.112113	.109277	.106493	.103761	.101083	.098461
	.20	.141063	.134652	.128393	.125325	.122300	.119320	.116387	.113501	.110665	.107881	.105149	.102471	.099849
	.10	.142452	.136040	.129781	.126713	.123688	.120708	.117775	.114889	.112053	.109269	.106537	.103860	.101237
	0.00	.143840	.137428	.131169	.128101	.125076	.122096	.119163	.116278	.113442	.110657	.107926	.105248	.102626
	-.10	.145228	.138816	.132557	.129489	.126465	.123485	.120551	.117666	.114830	.112046	.109314	.106636	.104014
	-.20	.146616	.140205	.133946	.130878	.127853	.124873	.121939	.119054	.116218	.113434	.110702	.108024	.105402
	-.30	.148004	.141593	.135334	.132266	.129241	.126261	.123328	.120442	.117607	.114822	.112090	.109412	.106790
	-.40	.149393	.142981	.136722	.133654	.130629	.127649	.124716	.121830	.118995	.116210	.113478	.110801	.108178
25	.40	.136469	.129654	.122978	.119698	.116461	.113268	.110122	.107027	.103983	.100995	.098065	.095195	.092387
	.30	.137857	.131042	.124366	.121086	.117849	.114656	.111510	.108415	.105372	.102384	.099453	.096583	.093775
	.20	.139245	.132430	.125754	.122475	.119237	.116044	.112899	.109803	.106760	.103772	.100841	.097971	.095163
	.10	.140634	.133818	.127143	.123863	.120625	.117432	.114287	.111191	.108148	.105160	.102230	.099359	.096552
	0.00	.142022	.135207	.128531	.125251	.122014	.118821	.115675	.112579	.109536	.106548	.103618	.100748	.097940
	-.10	.143410	.136595	.129919	.126639	.123402	.120209	.117063	.113968	.110925	.107936	.105006	.102136	.099328
	-.20	.144798	.137983	.131307	.128027	.124790	.121597	.118452	.115356	.112313	.109325	.106394	.103524	.100716
	-.30	.146186	.139371	.132695	.129416	.126178	.122985	.119840	.116744	.113701	.110713	.107782	.104912	.102105
	-.40	.147575	.140759	.134084	.130804	.127566	.124374	.121228	.118132	.115089	.112101	.109171	.106300	.103493
30	.40	.135534	.128468	.121520	.118096	.114711	.111367	.108069	.104818	.101619	.098476	.095392	.092372	.089417
	.30	.136922	.129856	.122908	.119485	.116099	.112756	.109457	.106206	.103008	.099864	.096781	.093760	.090806
	.20	.138310	.131245	.124296	.120873	.117488	.114144	.110845	.107594	.104396	.101253	.098169	.095148	.092194
	.10	.139699	.132633	.125684	.122261	.118876	.115532	.112233	.108983	.105784	.102641	.099557	.096536	.093582
	0.00	.141087	.134021	.127072	.123649	.120264	.116920	.113621	.110371	.107172	.104029	.100945	.097924	.094970
	-.10	.142475	.135409	.128461	.125037	.121652	.118309	.115010	.111759	.108560	.105417	.102333	.099313	.096358
	-.20	.143863	.136798	.129849	.126426	.123040	.119697	.116398	.113147	.109949	.106806	.103722	.100701	.097747
	-.30	.145252	.138186	.131237	.127814	.124429	.121085	.117786	.114535	.111337	.108194	.105110	.102089	.099135
	-.40	.146640	.139574	.132625	.129202	.125817	.122473	.119174	.115924	.112725	.109582	.106498	.103477	.100523

15.0 YEAR HOLDING PERIOD
.200 EQUITY YIELD RATE
.800 LOAN RATIO

INTEREST RATE

TERM YEARS	APPR DEP	5.0	5.5	6.0	6.5	7.0	7.5	8.0	8.5	9.0	9.5	10.0	11.0	12.0
10	.40	.117154	.119225	.121319	.123435	.125574	.127734	.129915	.132117	.134339	.136581	.138841	.143417	.148061
	.30	.118542	.120603	.122707	.124824	.126962	.129122	.131304	.133506	.135728	.137969	.140230	.144805	.149445
	.20	.119930	.122001	.124095	.126212	.128350	.130511	.132692	.134894	.137116	.139357	.141618	.146193	.150837
	.10	.121318	.123389	.125483	.127600	.129739	.131899	.134080	.136282	.138504	.140745	.143006	.147581	.152225
	0.00	.122707	.124778	.126872	.128998	.131127	.133287	.135468	.137670	.139892	.142134	.144394	.148970	.153614
	-.10	.124095	.126166	.128260	.130376	.132515	.134675	.136857	.139058	.141280	.143522	.145782	.150358	.155002
	-.20	.125483	.127554	.129648	.131765	.133903	.136063	.138245	.140447	.142669	.144910	.147171	.151746	.156390
	-.30	.126871	.128942	.131036	.133153	.135291	.137452	.139633	.141835	.144057	.146298	.148559	.153134	.157778
	-.40	.128259	.130330	.132424	.134541	.136680	.138840	.141021	.143223	.145445	.147687	.149947	.154522	.159166
15	.40	.099258	.101781	.104352	.106968	.109629	.112335	.115084	.117876	.120711	.123587	.126504	.132455	.138558
	.30	.100646	.103170	.105740	.108356	.111017	.113723	.116472	.119265	.122099	.124975	.127892	.133843	.139946
	.20	.102034	.104558	.107128	.109744	.112405	.115111	.117860	.120653	.123487	.126363	.129280	.135231	.141334
	.10	.103422	.105946	.108516	.111132	.113794	.116499	.119249	.122041	.124876	.127752	.130668	.136619	.142722
	0.00	.104810	.107334	.109905	.112521	.115182	.117887	.120637	.123429	.126264	.129140	.132056	.138008	.144110
	-.10	.106199	.108723	.111293	.113909	.116570	.119276	.122025	.124818	.127652	.130528	.133445	.139396	.145499
	-.20	.107587	.110111	.112681	.115297	.117958	.120664	.123413	.126206	.129040	.131916	.134833	.140784	.146887
	-.30	.108975	.111499	.114069	.116685	.119346	.122052	.124802	.127594	.130429	.133305	.136221	.142172	.148275
	-.40	.110363	.112887	.115457	.118073	.120735	.123440	.126190	.128982	.131817	.134693	.137609	.143560	.149663
20	.40	.090581	.093376	.096234	.099148	.102118	.105143	.108221	.111350	.114529	.117755	.121028	.127704	.134543
	.30	.091969	.094766	.097623	.100537	.103507	.106531	.109609	.112738	.115917	.119143	.122416	.129092	.135931
	.20	.093357	.096155	.099011	.101925	.104895	.107920	.110997	.114126	.117305	.120532	.123804	.130480	.137319
	.10	.094746	.097543	.100399	.103313	.106283	.109308	.112386	.115515	.118693	.121920	.125192	.131868	.138708
	0.00	.096134	.098931	.101787	.104701	.107671	.110696	.113774	.116903	.120082	.123308	.126580	.133257	.140096
	-.10	.097522	.100319	.103175	.106089	.109060	.112084	.115162	.118291	.121470	.124696	.127969	.134645	.141484
	-.20	.098910	.101707	.104564	.107478	.110448	.113473	.116550	.119679	.122858	.126084	.129357	.136033	.142872
	-.30	.100299	.103096	.105952	.108866	.111836	.114861	.117938	.121068	.124246	.127473	.130745	.137421	.144260
	-.40	.101687	.104484	.107340	.110254	.113224	.116249	.119327	.122456	.125634	.128861	.132133	.138809	.145649
25	.40	.085583	.088578	.091640	.094765	.097953	.101199	.104501	.107856	.111262	.114715	.118213	.125334	.132604
	.30	.086971	.089966	.093028	.096154	.099341	.102587	.105889	.109244	.112650	.116103	.119601	.126722	.133992
	.20	.088360	.091354	.094416	.097542	.100729	.103975	.107277	.110632	.114038	.117491	.120990	.128111	.135380
	.10	.089748	.092743	.095804	.098930	.102117	.105363	.108665	.112021	.115426	.118880	.122378	.129499	.136768
	0.00	.091136	.094131	.097192	.100318	.103505	.106751	.110053	.113409	.116814	.120268	.123766	.130887	.138157
	-.10	.092524	.095519	.098581	.101706	.104894	.108140	.111442	.114797	.118203	.121656	.125154	.132275	.139545
	-.20	.093912	.096907	.099969	.103095	.106282	.109528	.112830	.116185	.119591	.123044	.126543	.133663	.140933
	-.30	.095301	.098295	.101357	.104483	.107670	.110916	.114218	.117573	.120979	.124432	.127931	.135052	.142321
	-.40	.096689	.099684	.102745	.105871	.109058	.112304	.115606	.118962	.122367	.125821	.129319	.136440	.143709
30	.40	.082415	.085567	.088789	.092078	.095431	.098843	.102310	.105829	.109395	.113006	.116658	.124070	.131606
	.30	.083804	.086955	.090177	.093466	.096819	.100231	.103698	.107217	.110784	.114394	.118046	.125458	.132995
	.20	.085192	.088343	.091565	.094855	.098207	.101619	.105086	.108605	.112172	.115783	.119434	.126846	.134383
	.10	.086580	.089731	.092953	.096243	.099595	.103007	.106475	.109993	.113560	.117171	.120822	.128234	.135771
	0.00	.087968	.091119	.094342	.097631	.100984	.104396	.107863	.111382	.114948	.118559	.122211	.129623	.137159
	-.10	.089356	.092508	.095730	.099019	.102372	.105784	.109251	.112770	.116336	.119947	.123599	.131011	.138548
	-.20	.090745	.093896	.097118	.100407	.103760	.107172	.110639	.114158	.117725	.121336	.124987	.132399	.139936
	-.30	.092133	.095284	.098506	.101796	.105148	.108560	.112027	.115546	.119113	.122724	.126375	.133787	.141324
	-.40	.093521	.096672	.099894	.103184	.106537	.109948	.113416	.116934	.120501	.124112	.127763	.135175	.142712

15.0 YEAR HOLDING PERIOD
.200 EQUITY YIELD RATE
.900 LOAN RATIO

INTEREST RATE

TERM YEARS	APPR DEP	5.0	5.5	6.0	6.5	7.0	7.5	8.0	8.5	9.0	9.5	10.0	11.0	12.0
10	.40	.107492	.109822	.112178	.114559	.116965	.119395	.121849	.124326	.126826	.129348	.131891	.137038	.142262
	.30	.108880	.111210	.113566	.115947	.118353	.120783	.123237	.125714	.128214	.130736	.133279	.138426	.143651
	.20	.110268	.112598	.114954	.117335	.119741	.122171	.124625	.127103	.129602	.132124	.134667	.139814	.145039
	.10	.111657	.113987	.116342	.118723	.121129	.123560	.126014	.128491	.130991	.133512	.136055	.141203	.146427
	0.00	.113045	.115375	.117731	.120112	.122518	.124948	.127402	.129879	.132379	.134900	.137443	.142591	.147815
	-.10	.114433	.116763	.119119	.121500	.123906	.126336	.128790	.131267	.133767	.136289	.138832	.143979	.149204
	-.20	.115821	.118151	.120507	.122888	.125294	.127724	.130178	.132655	.135155	.137677	.140220	.145367	.150592
	-.30	.117210	.119539	.121895	.124276	.126682	.129113	.131566	.134044	.136543	.139065	.141608	.146755	.151980
	-.40	.118598	.120928	.123283	.125665	.128070	.130501	.132955	.135432	.137932	.140453	.142996	.148144	.153368
15	.40	.087359	.090198	.093090	.096033	.099027	.102071	.105164	.108305	.111494	.114730	.118011	.124706	.131571
	.30	.088747	.091586	.094478	.097421	.100415	.103459	.106552	.109693	.112882	.116118	.119399	.126094	.132960
	.20	.090135	.092975	.095866	.098809	.101803	.104847	.107940	.111082	.114270	.117506	.120787	.127482	.134348
	.10	.091524	.094363	.097254	.100197	.103191	.106235	.109328	.112470	.115659	.118894	.122175	.128870	.135736
	0.00	.092912	.095751	.098643	.101586	.104580	.107623	.110717	.113858	.117047	.120282	.123563	.130259	.137124
	-.10	.094300	.097139	.100031	.102974	.105968	.109012	.112105	.115246	.118435	.121671	.124952	.131647	.138512
	-.20	.095688	.098528	.101419	.104362	.107356	.110400	.113493	.116634	.119823	.123059	.126340	.133035	.139901
	-.30	.097076	.099916	.102807	.105750	.108744	.111788	.114881	.118023	.121212	.124447	.127728	.134423	.141289
	-.40	.098465	.101304	.104195	.107139	.110132	.113176	.116269	.119411	.122600	.125835	.129116	.135811	.142677
20	.40	.077598	.080744	.083958	.087236	.090577	.093980	.097443	.100963	.104539	.108169	.111850	.119361	.127055
	.30	.078986	.082133	.085346	.088624	.091966	.095368	.098831	.102351	.105927	.109557	.113238	.120749	.128443
	.20	.080374	.083521	.086734	.090012	.093354	.096757	.100219	.103739	.107315	.110945	.114627	.122137	.129831
	.10	.081762	.084909	.088122	.091401	.094742	.098145	.101607	.105128	.108703	.112333	.116015	.123526	.131220
	0.00	.083151	.086297	.089511	.092789	.096130	.099533	.102996	.106516	.110092	.113721	.117403	.124914	.132608
	-.10	.084539	.087686	.090899	.094177	.097518	.100921	.104384	.107904	.111480	.115110	.118791	.126302	.133996
	-.20	.085927	.089074	.092287	.095565	.098907	.102310	.105772	.109292	.112868	.116498	.120179	.127690	.135384
	-.30	.087315	.090462	.093675	.096953	.100295	.103698	.107160	.110680	.114256	.117886	.121568	.129078	.136772
	-.40	.088703	.091850	.095063	.098342	.101683	.105086	.108548	.112069	.115645	.119274	.122956	.130467	.138161
25	.40	.071975	.075344	.078789	.082305	.085891	.089543	.093257	.097032	.100863	.104748	.108684	.116695	.124873
	.30	.073363	.076732	.080177	.083693	.087279	.090931	.094646	.098420	.102252	.106137	.110072	.118083	.126261
	.20	.074752	.078121	.081565	.085081	.088667	.092319	.096034	.099808	.103640	.107525	.111460	.119471	.127650
	.10	.076140	.079509	.082953	.086470	.090055	.093707	.097422	.101197	.105028	.108913	.112849	.120860	.129038
	0.00	.077528	.080897	.084341	.087858	.091444	.095095	.098810	.102585	.106416	.110301	.114237	.122248	.130426
	-.10	.078916	.082285	.085730	.089246	.092832	.096484	.100198	.103973	.107804	.111689	.115625	.123636	.131814
	-.20	.080304	.083674	.087118	.090634	.094220	.097872	.101587	.105361	.109193	.113078	.117013	.125024	.133203
	-.30	.081693	.085062	.088506	.092023	.095608	.099260	.102975	.106749	.110581	.114466	.118402	.126413	.134591
	-.40	.083081	.086450	.089894	.093411	.096996	.100648	.104363	.108138	.111969	.115854	.119790	.127801	.135979
30	.40	.068411	.071956	.075581	.079282	.083054	.086892	.090793	.094752	.098764	.102826	.106934	.115272	.123751
	.30	.069800	.073345	.076970	.080670	.084442	.088280	.092181	.096140	.100152	.104214	.108322	.116661	.125140
	.20	.071188	.074733	.078358	.082058	.085830	.089669	.093569	.097528	.101540	.105603	.109710	.118049	.126528
	.10	.072576	.076121	.079746	.083447	.087218	.091057	.094957	.098916	.102929	.106991	.111099	.119437	.127916
	0.00	.073964	.077509	.081134	.084835	.088607	.092445	.096346	.100304	.104317	.108379	.112487	.120825	.129304
	-.10	.075352	.078897	.082523	.086223	.089995	.093833	.097734	.101693	.105705	.109767	.113875	.122214	.130692
	-.20	.076741	.080286	.083911	.087611	.091383	.095221	.099122	.103081	.107093	.111155	.115263	.123602	.132081
	-.30	.078129	.081674	.085299	.089000	.092771	.096610	.100510	.104469	.108481	.112544	.116652	.124990	.133469
	-.40	.079517	.083062	.086687	.090388	.094159	.097998	.101899	.105857	.109870	.113932	.118040	.126378	.134857

347

15.0 YEAR HOLDING PERIOD
.250 EQUITY YIELD RATE
.600 LOAN RATIO

INTEREST RATE

TERM YEARS	APPR DEP	5.0	5.5	6.0	6.5	7.0	7.5	8.0	8.5	9.0	9.5	10.0	11.0	12.0
10	.40	.163305	.164933	.166581	.168248	.169934	.171639	.173363	.175104	.176863	.178640	.180434	.184071	.187773
	.30	.164216	.165845	.167492	.169160	.170846	.172551	.174274	.176016	.177775	.179552	.181346	.184983	.188684
	.20	.165128	.166756	.168404	.170071	.171758	.173463	.175186	.176927	.178687	.180463	.182257	.185895	.189596
	.10	.166040	.167668	.169316	.170983	.172669	.174374	.176098	.177839	.179598	.181375	.183169	.186806	.190508
	0.00	.166951	.168580	.170228	.171895	.173581	.175286	.177009	.178751	.180510	.182287	.184081	.187718	.191420
	-.10	.167863	.169491	.171139	.172806	.174493	.176198	.177921	.179662	.181422	.183198	.184992	.188630	.192331
	-.20	.168775	.170403	.172051	.173718	.175404	.177109	.178833	.180574	.182333	.184110	.185904	.189542	.193243
	-.30	.169686	.171315	.172963	.174630	.176316	.178021	.179744	.181486	.183245	.185022	.186816	.190453	.194155
	-.40	.170598	.172226	.173874	.175541	.177228	.178933	.180656	.182398	.184157	.185934	.187727	.191365	.195066
15	.40	.147620	.149713	.151641	.153603	.155599	.157628	.159690	.161784	.163910	.166067	.168255	.172718	.177295
	.30	.148732	.150625	.152553	.154515	.156510	.158540	.160602	.162696	.164822	.166979	.169166	.173630	.178207
	.20	.149644	.151537	.153464	.155426	.157422	.159451	.161513	.163608	.165734	.167891	.170078	.174541	.179119
	.10	.150555	.152448	.154376	.156338	.158334	.160363	.162425	.164519	.166645	.168802	.170990	.175453	.180030
	0.00	.151467	.153360	.155288	.157250	.159246	.161275	.163337	.165431	.167557	.169714	.171901	.176365	.180942
	-.10	.152379	.154272	.156199	.158161	.160157	.162186	.164249	.166343	.168469	.170626	.172813	.177277	.181854
	-.20	.153290	.155183	.157111	.159073	.161069	.163098	.165160	.167255	.169380	.171537	.173725	.178188	.182765
	-.30	.154202	.156095	.158023	.159985	.161981	.164010	.166072	.168166	.170292	.172449	.174637	.179100	.183677
	-.40	.155114	.157007	.158934	.160896	.162892	.164922	.166984	.169078	.171204	.173361	.175548	.180012	.184589
20	.40	.140313	.142381	.144493	.146649	.148846	.151085	.153363	.155680	.158034	.160424	.162849	.167798	.172869
	.30	.141225	.143293	.145405	.147560	.149758	.151997	.154275	.156592	.158946	.161336	.163761	.168709	.173781
	.20	.142136	.144204	.146317	.148472	.150670	.152908	.155187	.157504	.159858	.162248	.164673	.169621	.174692
	.10	.143048	.145116	.147228	.149384	.151581	.153820	.156098	.158415	.160769	.163159	.165584	.170533	.175604
	0.00	.143960	.146028	.148140	.150296	.152493	.154732	.157010	.159327	.161681	.164071	.166496	.171444	.176516
	-.10	.144871	.146939	.149052	.151207	.153405	.155643	.157922	.160239	.162593	.164983	.167408	.172356	.177427
	-.20	.145783	.147851	.149963	.152119	.154317	.156555	.158833	.161150	.163504	.165895	.168319	.173268	.178339
	-.30	.146695	.148763	.150875	.153031	.155228	.157467	.159745	.162062	.164416	.166806	.169231	.174179	.179251
	-.40	.147606	.149674	.151787	.153942	.156140	.158379	.160657	.162974	.165328	.167718	.170143	.175091	.180163
25	.40	.135989	.138193	.140447	.142751	.145101	.147496	.149934	.152412	.154929	.157483	.160071	.165343	.170731
	.30	.136900	.139104	.141359	.143663	.146013	.148408	.150845	.153324	.155841	.158394	.160983	.166255	.171643
	.20	.137812	.140016	.142271	.144574	.146924	.149319	.151757	.154235	.156752	.159306	.161894	.167167	.172554
	.10	.138724	.140928	.143182	.145486	.147836	.150231	.152669	.155147	.157664	.160218	.162806	.168078	.173466
	0.00	.139635	.141839	.144094	.146398	.148748	.151143	.153580	.156059	.158576	.161129	.163718	.168990	.174378
	-.10	.140547	.142751	.145006	.147309	.149659	.152054	.154492	.156970	.159488	.162041	.164629	.169902	.175289
	-.20	.141459	.143663	.145918	.148221	.150571	.152966	.155404	.157882	.160399	.162953	.165541	.170813	.176201
	-.30	.142370	.144574	.146829	.149133	.151483	.153878	.156315	.158794	.161311	.163865	.166453	.171725	.177113
	-.40	.143282	.145486	.147741	.150044	.152395	.154789	.157227	.159706	.162223	.164776	.167364	.172637	.178024
30	.40	.133248	.135565	.137937	.140361	.142834	.145353	.147914	.150516	.153155	.155829	.158535	.164034	.169631
	.30	.134159	.136477	.138849	.141273	.143746	.146264	.148826	.151428	.154067	.156741	.159447	.164945	.170543
	.20	.135071	.137388	.139761	.142184	.144657	.147176	.149738	.152340	.154979	.157653	.160359	.165857	.171455
	.10	.135983	.138300	.140672	.143096	.145569	.148088	.150649	.153251	.155890	.158564	.161270	.166769	.172367
	0.00	.136894	.139212	.141584	.144008	.146481	.148999	.151561	.154163	.156802	.159476	.162182	.167680	.173278
	-.10	.137806	.140124	.142496	.144920	.147392	.149911	.152473	.155075	.157714	.160388	.163094	.168592	.174190
	-.20	.138718	.141035	.143407	.145831	.148304	.150823	.153384	.155986	.158626	.161300	.164006	.169504	.175102
	-.30	.139629	.141947	.144319	.146743	.149216	.151734	.154296	.156898	.159537	.162211	.164917	.170415	.176013
	-.40	.140541	.142859	.145231	.147655	.150127	.152646	.155208	.157810	.160449	.163123	.165829	.171327	.176925

15.0 YEAR HOLDING PERIOD
.250 EQUITY YIELD RATE
.667 LOAN RATIO

INTEREST RATE

TERM YEARS	APPR DEP	5.0	5.5	6.0	6.5	7.0	7.5	8.0	8.5	9.0	9.5	10.0	11.0	12.0
10	.40	.154077	.155886	.157717	.159569	.161443	.163337	.165252	.167187	.169142	.171116	.173109	.177151	.181263
	.30	.154988	.156797	.158628	.160481	.162354	.164249	.166164	.168099	.170054	.172028	.174021	.178063	.182175
	.20	.155900	.157709	.159540	.161393	.163266	.165161	.167075	.169010	.170965	.172939	.174933	.178974	.183087
	.10	.156812	.158621	.160452	.162304	.164178	.166072	.167987	.169922	.171877	.173851	.175844	.179886	.183999
	0.00	.157723	.159533	.161363	.163216	.165089	.166984	.168899	.170834	.172789	.174763	.176756	.180798	.184910
	-.10	.158635	.160444	.162275	.164128	.166001	.167896	.169810	.171745	.173700	.175674	.177668	.181709	.185822
	-.20	.159547	.161356	.163187	.165039	.166913	.168807	.170722	.172657	.174612	.176586	.178579	.182621	.186734
	-.30	.160458	.162268	.164099	.165951	.167825	.169719	.171634	.173569	.175524	.177498	.179491	.183533	.187645
	-.40	.161370	.163179	.165010	.166863	.168736	.170631	.172546	.174481	.176435	.178409	.180403	.184444	.188557
15	.40	.136872	.138975	.141117	.143297	.145514	.147769	.150060	.152387	.154750	.157146	.159577	.164536	.169622
	.30	.137783	.139887	.142028	.144208	.146426	.148681	.150972	.153299	.155661	.158058	.160488	.165448	.170533
	.20	.138695	.140798	.142940	.145120	.147338	.149593	.151884	.154211	.156573	.158970	.161400	.166359	.171445
	.10	.139607	.141710	.143852	.146032	.148249	.150504	.152795	.155122	.157485	.159881	.162312	.167271	.172357
	0.00	.140518	.142622	.144763	.146943	.149161	.151416	.153707	.156034	.158396	.160793	.163223	.168183	.173268
	-.10	.141430	.143533	.145675	.147855	.150073	.152328	.154619	.156946	.159308	.161705	.164135	.169094	.174180
	-.20	.142342	.144445	.146587	.148767	.150985	.153239	.155530	.157857	.160220	.162616	.165047	.170006	.175092
	-.30	.143253	.145357	.147499	.149679	.151896	.154151	.156442	.158769	.161131	.163528	.165958	.170918	.176004
	-.40	.144165	.146268	.148410	.150590	.152808	.155063	.157354	.159681	.162043	.164440	.166870	.171830	.176915
20	.40	.128530	.130828	.133175	.135570	.138012	.140499	.143031	.145605	.148221	.150876	.153570	.159069	.164704
	.30	.129442	.131740	.134087	.136482	.138923	.141411	.143942	.146517	.149132	.151788	.154482	.159980	.165615
	.20	.130353	.132651	.134998	.137393	.139835	.142323	.144854	.147428	.150044	.152700	.155394	.160892	.166527
	.10	.131265	.133563	.135910	.138305	.140747	.143234	.145766	.148340	.150956	.153611	.156306	.161804	.167439
	0.00	.132177	.134475	.136822	.139217	.141659	.144146	.146677	.149252	.151867	.154523	.157217	.162715	.168350
	-.10	.133089	.135386	.137733	.140128	.142570	.145058	.147589	.150163	.152779	.155435	.158129	.163627	.169262
	-.20	.134000	.136298	.138645	.141040	.143482	.145969	.148501	.151075	.153691	.156346	.159041	.164539	.170174
	-.30	.134912	.137210	.139557	.141952	.144394	.146881	.149412	.151987	.154602	.157258	.159952	.165451	.171085
	-.40	.135824	.138121	.140468	.142863	.145305	.147793	.150324	.152898	.155514	.158170	.160864	.166362	.171997
25	.40	.123725	.126174	.128679	.131239	.133850	.136511	.139220	.141974	.144770	.147608	.150484	.156342	.162328
	.30	.124637	.127086	.129591	.132151	.134762	.137423	.140132	.142885	.145682	.148519	.151395	.157253	.163240
	.20	.125549	.127998	.130503	.133063	.135674	.138335	.141043	.143797	.146594	.149431	.152307	.158165	.164151
	.10	.126460	.128909	.131415	.133974	.136585	.139246	.141955	.144709	.147505	.150343	.153219	.159077	.165063
	0.00	.127372	.129821	.132326	.134886	.137497	.140158	.142867	.145620	.148417	.151254	.154130	.159989	.165975
	-.10	.128284	.130733	.133238	.135797	.138409	.141070	.143778	.146532	.149329	.152166	.155042	.160900	.166886
	-.20	.129195	.131644	.134150	.136709	.139320	.141981	.144690	.147444	.150240	.153078	.155954	.161812	.167798
	-.30	.130107	.132556	.135061	.137621	.140232	.142893	.145602	.148355	.151152	.153990	.156865	.162724	.168710
	-.40	.131019	.133468	.135973	.138532	.141144	.143805	.146513	.149267	.152064	.154901	.157777	.163635	.169621
30	.40	.120680	.123255	.125890	.128584	.131331	.134130	.136976	.139867	.142800	.145771	.148777	.154887	.161106
	.30	.121591	.124166	.126802	.129497	.132243	.135041	.137888	.140779	.143711	.146682	.149689	.155798	.162018
	.20	.122503	.125078	.127714	.130407	.133154	.135953	.138799	.141690	.144623	.147594	.150601	.156710	.162930
	.10	.123415	.125990	.128625	.131319	.134066	.136865	.139711	.142602	.145535	.148506	.151512	.157622	.163841
	0.00	.124326	.126901	.129537	.132230	.134978	.137776	.140623	.143514	.146446	.149417	.152424	.158533	.164763
	-.10	.125238	.127813	.130449	.133142	.135890	.138688	.141534	.144425	.147358	.150329	.153336	.159445	.165665
	-.20	.126150	.128725	.131361	.134054	.136801	.139600	.142446	.145337	.148270	.151241	.154248	.160357	.166576
	-.30	.127062	.129637	.132272	.134965	.137713	.140511	.143358	.146249	.149181	.152153	.155159	.161268	.167488
	-.40	.127973	.130548	.133184	.135877	.138625	.141423	.144270	.147161	.150093	.153064	.156071	.162180	.168400

15.0 YEAR HOLDING PERIOD
.250 EQUITY YIELD RATE
.700 LOAN RATIO

INTEREST RATE

TERM YEARS	APPR DEP	5.0	5.5	6.0	6.5	7.0	7.5	8.0	8.5	9.0	9.5	10.0	11.0	12.0
10	.40	.149463	.151363	.153285	.155230	.157198	.159187	.161197	.163229	.165282	.167355	.169447	.173691	.178009
	.30	.150375	.152275	.154187	.156142	.158109	.160098	.162109	.164141	.166193	.168266	.170359	.174603	.178921
	.20	.151287	.153186	.155109	.157054	.159021	.161010	.163021	.165053	.167105	.169178	.171271	.175514	.179833
	.10	.152198	.154098	.156020	.157965	.159933	.161922	.163932	.165964	.168017	.170090	.172182	.176426	.180744
	0.00	.153110	.155010	.156932	.158877	.160844	.162834	.164844	.166876	.168928	.171001	.173094	.177338	.181656
	-.10	.154022	.155921	.157844	.159789	.161756	.163745	.165756	.167788	.169840	.171913	.174006	.178250	.182568
	-.20	.154933	.156833	.158756	.160701	.162668	.164657	.166668	.168699	.170752	.172825	.174917	.179161	.183479
	-.30	.155845	.157745	.159667	.161612	.163579	.165569	.167579	.169611	.171663	.173736	.175829	.180073	.184391
	-.40	.156757	.158656	.160579	.162524	.164491	.166480	.168491	.170523	.172575	.174648	.176741	.180985	.185303
15	.40	.131398	.133606	.135855	.138144	.140473	.142840	.145246	.147690	.150170	.152686	.155238	.160446	.165786
	.30	.132310	.134518	.136767	.139056	.141385	.143752	.146158	.148601	.151082	.153598	.156150	.161357	.166697
	.20	.133221	.135430	.137679	.139968	.142296	.144664	.147070	.149513	.151993	.154510	.157062	.162269	.167609
	.10	.134133	.136342	.138590	.140880	.143208	.145576	.147981	.150425	.152905	.155421	.157973	.163181	.168521
	0.00	.135045	.137253	.139502	.141791	.144120	.146487	.148893	.151336	.153817	.156333	.158885	.164092	.169432
	-.10	.135957	.138165	.140414	.142703	.145031	.147399	.149805	.152248	.154728	.157245	.159797	.165004	.170344
	-.20	.136868	.139077	.141326	.143615	.145943	.148311	.150716	.153160	.155640	.158156	.160708	.165916	.171256
	-.30	.137780	.139988	.142237	.144526	.146855	.149222	.151628	.154071	.156552	.159068	.161620	.166827	.172167
	-.40	.138692	.140900	.143149	.145438	.147767	.150134	.152540	.154983	.157463	.159980	.162532	.167739	.173079
20	.40	.122640	.125052	.127517	.130031	.132595	.135207	.137865	.140568	.143314	.146103	.148932	.154705	.160622
	.30	.123551	.125964	.128428	.130943	.133507	.136119	.138777	.141480	.144226	.147015	.149844	.155617	.161533
	.20	.124463	.126876	.129340	.131855	.134419	.137030	.139688	.142391	.145138	.147926	.150755	.156528	.162445
	.10	.125375	.127787	.130252	.132766	.135330	.137942	.140600	.143303	.146050	.148838	.151667	.157440	.163357
	0.00	.126286	.128699	.131163	.133678	.136242	.138854	.141512	.144215	.146961	.149750	.152579	.158352	.164268
	-.10	.127198	.129611	.132075	.134590	.137154	.139765	.142423	.145126	.147873	.150661	.153490	.159263	.165180
	-.20	.128110	.130522	.132987	.135502	.138065	.140677	.143335	.146038	.148785	.151573	.154402	.160175	.166092
	-.30	.129021	.131434	.133898	.136413	.138977	.141589	.144247	.146950	.149696	.152485	.155314	.161087	.167003
	-.40	.129933	.132346	.134810	.137325	.139889	.142500	.145159	.147862	.150608	.153396	.156225	.161998	.167915
25	.40	.117594	.120166	.122796	.125484	.128226	.131020	.133864	.136755	.139692	.142671	.145691	.151842	.158127
	.30	.118506	.121078	.123708	.126395	.129137	.131931	.134775	.137667	.140603	.143583	.146602	.152753	.159039
	.20	.119418	.121989	.124620	.127307	.130049	.132843	.135687	.138579	.141515	.144494	.147514	.153665	.159951
	.10	.120329	.122901	.125531	.128219	.130961	.133755	.136599	.139490	.142427	.145406	.148426	.154577	.160862
	0.00	.121241	.123813	.126443	.129131	.131872	.134667	.137510	.140402	.143338	.146318	.149337	.155488	.161774
	-.10	.122153	.124724	.127355	.130042	.132784	.135578	.138422	.141314	.144250	.147229	.150249	.156400	.162686
	-.20	.123065	.125636	.128267	.130954	.133696	.136490	.139334	.142225	.145162	.148141	.151161	.157312	.163597
	-.30	.123976	.126548	.129178	.131866	.134607	.137402	.140246	.143137	.146074	.149053	.152072	.158224	.164509
	-.40	.124888	.127459	.130090	.132777	.135519	.138313	.141157	.144049	.146985	.149964	.152984	.159135	.165421
30	.40	.114397	.117100	.119868	.122696	.125581	.128519	.131508	.134543	.137622	.140742	.143899	.150314	.156844
	.30	.115308	.118012	.120780	.123607	.126492	.129431	.132419	.135455	.138534	.141654	.144811	.151225	.157756
	.20	.116220	.118924	.121691	.124519	.127404	.130342	.133331	.136367	.139446	.142565	.145723	.152137	.158668
	.10	.117132	.119835	.122603	.125431	.128316	.131254	.134243	.137278	.140358	.143477	.146634	.153049	.159580
	0.00	.118043	.120747	.123515	.126342	.129227	.132166	.135154	.138190	.141269	.144389	.147546	.153960	.160491
	-.10	.118955	.121659	.124426	.127254	.130139	.133077	.136066	.139102	.142181	.145301	.148458	.154872	.161403
	-.20	.119867	.122571	.125338	.128166	.131051	.133989	.136978	.140013	.143093	.146212	.149369	.155784	.162315
	-.30	.120778	.123482	.126250	.129078	.131962	.134901	.137890	.140925	.144004	.147124	.150281	.156696	.163226
	-.40	.121690	.124394	.127161	.129989	.132874	.135813	.138801	.141837	.144916	.148036	.151193	.157607	.164138

15.0 YEAR HOLDING PERIOD
.250 EQUITY YIELD RATE
.750 LOAN RATIO

INTEREST RATE

TERM YEARS	APPR DEP	5.0	5.5	6.0	6.5	7.0	7.5	8.0	8.5	9.0	9.5	10.0	11.0	12.0
10	.40	.142543	.144578	.146638	.148722	.150829	.152961	.155115	.157292	.159491	.161712	.163954	.168501	.173128
	.30	.143454	.145490	.147549	.149633	.151741	.153872	.156027	.158203	.160403	.162623	.164866	.169413	.174039
	.20	.144366	.146401	.148461	.150545	.152663	.154784	.156938	.159115	.161314	.163535	.165777	.170324	.174951
	.10	.145278	.147313	.149373	.151457	.153564	.155696	.157850	.160027	.162226	.164447	.166689	.171236	.175863
	0.00	.146189	.148225	.150284	.152368	.154476	.156607	.158762	.160938	.163138	.165359	.167601	.172148	.176774
	-.10	.147101	.149136	.151196	.153280	.155388	.157519	.159673	.161850	.164049	.166270	.168512	.173059	.177686
	-.20	.148013	.150048	.152108	.154192	.156300	.158431	.160585	.162762	.164961	.167182	.169424	.173971	.178598
	-.30	.148924	.150960	.153019	.155103	.157211	.159342	.161497	.163674	.165873	.168094	.170336	.174883	.179509
	-.40	.149836	.151871	.153931	.156015	.158123	.160254	.162408	.164585	.166784	.169005	.171248	.175794	.180421
15	.40	.123187	.125553	.127963	.130415	.132910	.135447	.138024	.140642	.143300	.145996	.148730	.154309	.160031
	.30	.124099	.126465	.128874	.131327	.133822	.136358	.138936	.141554	.144211	.146908	.149642	.155221	.160942
	.20	.125010	.127376	.129786	.132239	.134734	.137270	.139848	.142466	.145123	.147819	.150553	.156133	.161854
	.10	.125922	.128288	.130698	.133150	.135645	.138182	.140759	.143377	.146035	.148731	.151465	.157044	.162766
	0.00	.126834	.129200	.131609	.134062	.136557	.139093	.141671	.144289	.146946	.149643	.152377	.157956	.163677
	-.10	.127745	.130112	.132521	.134974	.137469	.140005	.142583	.145201	.147858	.150554	.153288	.158869	.164589
	-.20	.128657	.131023	.133433	.135885	.138380	.140917	.143494	.146112	.148770	.151466	.154200	.159779	.165501
	-.30	.129569	.131935	.134345	.136797	.139292	.141829	.144406	.147024	.149681	.152378	.155112	.160691	.166413
	-.40	.130481	.132847	.135256	.137709	.140204	.142740	.145318	.147936	.150593	.153289	.156024	.161603	.167324
20	.40	.113803	.116388	.119028	.121723	.124470	.127268	.130116	.133012	.135955	.138942	.141973	.148159	.154498
	.30	.114715	.117300	.119940	.122634	.125381	.128180	.131028	.133924	.136866	.139854	.142885	.149070	.155410
	.20	.115626	.118211	.120852	.123546	.126293	.129091	.131939	.134835	.137778	.140766	.143797	.149982	.156321
	.10	.116538	.119123	.121763	.124458	.127205	.130003	.132851	.135747	.138690	.141677	.144708	.150894	.157233
	0.00	.117450	.120035	.122675	.125369	.128116	.130915	.133763	.136659	.139601	.142589	.145620	.151805	.158145
	-.10	.118361	.120946	.123587	.126281	.129028	.131826	.134674	.137570	.140513	.143501	.146532	.152717	.159056
	-.20	.119273	.121858	.124498	.127193	.129940	.132738	.135586	.138482	.141425	.144412	.147443	.153629	.159968
	-.30	.120185	.122770	.125410	.128104	.130852	.133650	.136498	.139394	.142336	.145324	.148355	.154540	.160880
	-.40	.121096	.123681	.126322	.129016	.131763	.134561	.137409	.140305	.143248	.146236	.149267	.155452	.161791
25	.40	.108397	.111153	.113971	.116850	.119786	.122782	.125829	.128927	.132073	.135265	.138500	.145091	.151825
	.30	.109309	.112064	.114883	.117762	.120700	.123693	.126740	.129838	.132985	.136177	.139412	.146003	.152737
	.20	.110221	.112976	.115794	.118673	.121611	.124605	.127652	.130750	.133886	.137088	.140324	.146914	.153649
	.10	.111132	.113888	.116706	.119585	.122523	.125517	.128564	.131662	.134808	.138000	.141235	.147826	.154560
	0.00	.112044	.114799	.117618	.120497	.123435	.126428	.129476	.132574	.135720	.138912	.142147	.148738	.155472
	-.10	.112956	.115711	.118529	.121409	.124346	.127340	.130387	.133485	.136631	.139824	.143059	.149649	.156384
	-.20	.113867	.116623	.119441	.122320	.125258	.128252	.131299	.134397	.137543	.140735	.143971	.150561	.157295
	-.30	.114779	.117534	.120353	.123232	.126170	.129163	.132211	.135309	.138455	.141647	.144882	.151473	.158207
	-.40	.115691	.118446	.121264	.124143	.127081	.130075	.133122	.136220	.139367	.142559	.145794	.152384	.159119
30	.40	.104971	.107868	.110833	.113863	.116956	.120102	.123304	.126557	.129856	.133198	.136581	.143454	.150451
	.30	.105883	.108780	.111745	.114775	.117866	.121014	.124216	.127469	.130768	.134110	.137493	.144365	.151363
	.20	.106795	.109691	.112657	.115686	.118777	.121926	.125128	.128380	.131679	.135022	.138404	.145277	.152274
	.10	.107706	.110603	.113568	.116598	.119689	.122837	.126040	.129292	.132591	.135934	.139316	.146189	.153186
	0.00	.108618	.111515	.114480	.117510	.120601	.123749	.126951	.130204	.133503	.136845	.140228	.147101	.154098
	-.10	.109530	.112427	.115392	.118421	.121512	.124661	.127863	.131115	.134414	.137757	.141139	.148012	.155010
	-.20	.110441	.113338	.116303	.119333	.122424	.125572	.128775	.132027	.135326	.138669	.142051	.148924	.155921
	-.30	.111353	.114250	.117215	.120245	.123336	.126484	.129686	.132939	.136238	.139580	.142963	.149836	.156833
	-.40	.112265	.115162	.118127	.121157	.124247	.127396	.130598	.133850	.137149	.140492	.143874	.150747	.157744

15.0 YEAR HOLDING PERIOD
.250 EQUITY YIELD RATE
.800 LOAN RATIO

INTEREST RATE

TERM YEARS	APPR DEP	5.0	5.5	6.0	6.5	7.0	7.5	8.0	8.5	9.0	9.5	10.0	11.0	12.0
10	.40	.135622	.137793	.139990	.142213	.144461	.146734	.149032	.151354	.153700	.156069	.158461	.163311	.168246
	.30	.136533	.138705	.140902	.143125	.145373	.147646	.149944	.152266	.154612	.156981	.159372	.164222	.169158
	.20	.137445	.139616	.141813	.144036	.146285	.148558	.150856	.153178	.155523	.157892	.160284	.165134	.170069
	.10	.138357	.140528	.142725	.144948	.147196	.149469	.151767	.154089	.156435	.158804	.161196	.166046	.170981
	0.00	.139269	.141440	.143637	.145860	.148108	.150381	.152679	.155001	.157347	.159716	.162108	.166958	.171893
	-.10	.140180	.142351	.144548	.146771	.149020	.151293	.153591	.155913	.158258	.160627	.163019	.167869	.172804
	-.20	.141092	.143263	.145460	.147683	.149931	.152205	.154502	.156824	.159170	.161539	.163931	.168781	.173716
	-.30	.142004	.144175	.146372	.148595	.150843	.153116	.155414	.157736	.160082	.162451	.164843	.169693	.174628
	-.40	.142915	.145086	.147283	.149506	.151755	.154028	.156326	.158648	.160993	.163362	.165754	.170604	.175539
15	.40	.114976	.117500	.120070	.122686	.125347	.128053	.130802	.133595	.136429	.139305	.142222	.148173	.154276
	.30	.115888	.118411	.120982	.123598	.126259	.128965	.131714	.134506	.137341	.140217	.143134	.149085	.155188
	.20	.116799	.119323	.121893	.124509	.127171	.129876	.132626	.135418	.138253	.141129	.144045	.149996	.156099
	.10	.117711	.120235	.122805	.125421	.128082	.130788	.133537	.136330	.139164	.142040	.144957	.150908	.157011
	0.00	.118623	.121147	.123717	.126333	.128994	.131700	.134449	.137242	.140076	.142952	.145869	.151820	.157923
	-.10	.119534	.122058	.124628	.127245	.129906	.132611	.135361	.138153	.140988	.143864	.146780	.152732	.158834
	-.20	.120446	.122970	.125540	.128156	.130817	.133523	.136272	.139065	.141899	.144775	.147692	.153643	.159746
	-.30	.121358	.123882	.126452	.129068	.131729	.134435	.137184	.139977	.142811	.145687	.148604	.154555	.160658
	-.40	.122269	.124793	.127364	.129980	.132641	.135346	.138096	.140888	.143723	.146599	.149515	.155467	.161569
20	.40	.104960	.107724	.110540	.113414	.116344	.119329	.122367	.125456	.128595	.131781	.135014	.141612	.148374
	.30	.105878	.108635	.111452	.114326	.117256	.120241	.123278	.126368	.129506	.132693	.135926	.142524	.149286
	.20	.106790	.109547	.112363	.115237	.118168	.121152	.124190	.127279	.130418	.133605	.136838	.143436	.150198
	.10	.107701	.110459	.113275	.116149	.119079	.122064	.125102	.128191	.131330	.134517	.137750	.144347	.151109
	0.00	.108613	.111370	.114187	.117061	.119991	.122976	.126013	.129103	.132241	.135428	.138661	.145259	.152021
	-.10	.109525	.112282	.115098	.117972	.120903	.123887	.126925	.130014	.133153	.136340	.139573	.146171	.152933
	-.20	.110436	.113194	.116010	.118884	.121814	.124799	.127837	.130926	.134065	.137252	.140485	.147082	.153844
	-.30	.111348	.114105	.116922	.119796	.122726	.125711	.128749	.131838	.134976	.138163	.141396	.147994	.154756
	-.40	.112260	.115017	.117833	.120707	.123638	.126622	.129660	.132749	.135888	.139075	.142308	.148906	.155668
25	.40	.099200	.102139	.105145	.108217	.111350	.114544	.117794	.121098	.124454	.127859	.131310	.138340	.145523
	.30	.100112	.103051	.106057	.109128	.112262	.115455	.118706	.122010	.125366	.128771	.132222	.139252	.146435
	.20	.101024	.103963	.106969	.110040	.113174	.116367	.119617	.122922	.126278	.129683	.133134	.140163	.147347
	.10	.101935	.104874	.107880	.110952	.114085	.117279	.120529	.123833	.127189	.130594	.134045	.141075	.148259
	0.00	.102847	.105786	.108792	.111863	.114997	.118190	.121441	.124745	.128101	.131506	.134957	.141987	.149170
	-.10	.103759	.106698	.109704	.112775	.115909	.119102	.122352	.125657	.129013	.132418	.135869	.142898	.150082
	-.20	.104670	.107609	.110616	.113687	.116820	.120014	.123264	.126568	.129924	.133329	.136780	.143810	.150994
	-.30	.105582	.108521	.111527	.114598	.117732	.120925	.124176	.127480	.130836	.134241	.137692	.144722	.151905
	-.40	.106494	.109433	.112439	.115510	.118644	.121837	.125087	.128392	.131748	.135153	.138604	.145634	.152817
30	.40	.095546	.098636	.101799	.105030	.108327	.111686	.115101	.118570	.122089	.125655	.129263	.136594	.144058
	.30	.096457	.099547	.102710	.105942	.109239	.112597	.116013	.119482	.123001	.126566	.130175	.137506	.144969
	.20	.097369	.100459	.103622	.106854	.110151	.113509	.116925	.120394	.123913	.127478	.131086	.138417	.145881
	.10	.098281	.101371	.104534	.107765	.111062	.114421	.117836	.121305	.124825	.128390	.131998	.139329	.146793
	0.00	.099192	.102282	.105445	.108677	.111974	.115332	.118748	.122217	.125736	.129302	.132910	.140241	.147704
	-.10	.100104	.103194	.106357	.109589	.112886	.116244	.119660	.123129	.126648	.130213	.133821	.141152	.148616
	-.20	.101016	.104106	.107269	.110501	.113797	.117156	.120571	.124041	.127560	.131125	.134733	.142064	.149528
	-.30	.101928	.105018	.108180	.111412	.114709	.118067	.121483	.124952	.128471	.132037	.135645	.142976	.150439
	-.40	.102839	.105929	.109092	.112324	.115621	.118979	.122395	.125864	.129383	.132948	.136556	.143887	.151351

15.0 YEAR HOLDING PERIOD
.250 EQUITY YIELD RATE
.900 LOAN RATIO

INTEREST RATE

TERM YEARS	APPR DEP	5.0	5.5	6.0	6.5	7.0	7.5	8.0	8.5	9.0	9.5	10.0	11.0	12.0
10	.40	.121780	.124223	.126695	.129195	.131725	.134282	.136867	.139479	.142118	.144783	.147474	.152930	.158483
	.30	.122692	.125134	.127606	.130107	.132636	.135194	.137779	.140391	.143030	.145695	.148386	.153842	.159394
	.20	.123604	.126046	.128518	.131019	.133548	.136105	.138691	.141303	.143942	.146607	.149298	.154754	.160306
	.10	.124515	.126958	.129430	.131930	.134460	.137017	.139602	.142214	.144853	.147519	.150209	.155666	.161218
	0.00	.125427	.127870	.130341	.132842	.135371	.137929	.140514	.143126	.145765	.148430	.151121	.156577	.162129
	-.10	.126339	.128781	.131253	.133754	.136283	.138841	.141426	.144038	.146677	.149342	.152033	.157489	.163041
	-.20	.127250	.129693	.132165	.134665	.137195	.139752	.142337	.144950	.147588	.150254	.152944	.158401	.163952
	-.30	.128162	.130605	.133076	.135577	.138106	.140664	.143249	.145861	.148500	.151165	.153856	.159312	.164664
	-.40	.129074	.131516	.133988	.136489	.139018	.141576	.144161	.146773	.149412	.152077	.154768	.160224	.165776
15	.40	.098554	.101393	.104285	.107228	.110222	.113265	.116359	.119500	.122689	.125924	.129205	.135901	.142766
	.30	.099465	.102305	.105196	.108139	.111133	.114177	.117270	.120412	.123601	.126836	.130117	.136812	.143678
	.20	.100377	.103216	.106108	.109051	.112045	.115089	.118182	.121323	.124512	.127748	.131029	.137724	.144590
	.10	.101289	.104128	.107020	.109963	.112957	.116000	.119094	.122235	.125424	.128659	.131940	.138636	.145501
	0.00	.102201	.105040	.107931	.110874	.113868	.116912	.120005	.123147	.126336	.129571	.132852	.139547	.146413
	-.10	.103112	.105952	.108843	.111786	.114780	.117824	.120917	.124058	.127247	.130483	.133764	.140459	.147325
	-.20	.104024	.106863	.109755	.112698	.115692	.118736	.121829	.124970	.128159	.131394	.134676	.141371	.148236
	-.30	.104936	.107775	.110666	.113609	.116603	.119647	.122740	.125882	.129071	.132306	.135587	.142282	.149148
	-.40	.105847	.108687	.111578	.114521	.117515	.120559	.123652	.126793	.129982	.133218	.136499	.143194	.150060
20	.40	.087293	.090395	.093563	.096797	.100093	.103451	.106868	.110344	.113875	.117460	.121097	.128520	.136127
	.30	.088204	.091307	.094475	.097708	.101005	.104363	.107780	.111255	.114787	.118372	.122009	.129431	.137039
	.20	.089116	.092218	.095387	.098620	.101916	.105274	.108692	.112167	.115698	.119283	.122832	.130343	.137950
	.10	.090028	.093130	.096298	.099532	.102828	.106186	.109603	.113079	.116610	.120195	.123832	.131255	.138862
	0.00	.090940	.094042	.097210	.100443	.103740	.107098	.110515	.113990	.117522	.121107	.124744	.132166	.139774
	-.10	.091851	.094953	.098122	.101355	.104651	.108009	.111427	.114902	.118433	.122018	.125656	.133078	.140685
	-.20	.092763	.095865	.099033	.102267	.105563	.108921	.112338	.115814	.119345	.122930	.126567	.133990	.141597
	-.30	.093675	.096777	.099945	.103178	.106475	.109833	.113250	.116725	.120257	.123842	.127479	.134902	.142509
	-.40	.094586	.097688	.100857	.104090	.107387	.110744	.114162	.117637	.121168	.124753	.128391	.135813	.143420
25	.40	.080806	.084112	.087494	.090950	.094475	.098067	.101724	.105441	.109217	.113047	.116930	.124828	.132320
	.30	.081718	.085024	.088406	.091861	.095387	.098979	.102636	.106353	.110129	.113959	.117842	.125750	.133331
	.20	.082630	.085936	.089318	.092773	.096298	.099891	.103547	.107265	.111040	.114871	.118753	.126662	.134343
	.10	.083541	.086847	.090230	.093685	.097210	.100802	.104459	.108177	.111952	.115783	.119665	.127573	.135555
	0.00	.084453	.087759	.091141	.094596	.098122	.101714	.105371	.109088	.112864	.116694	.120577	.128485	.135666
	-.10	.085365	.088671	.092053	.095508	.099033	.102626	.106282	.110000	.113775	.117606	.121488	.129397	.137478
	-.20	.086276	.089582	.092965	.096420	.099945	.103537	.107194	.110912	.114687	.118518	.122400	.130309	.138390
	-.30	.087188	.090494	.093876	.097331	.100857	.104449	.108106	.111823	.115599	.119429	.123312	.131220	.139302
	-.40	.088100	.091406	.094788	.098243	.101768	.105361	.109017	.112735	.116511	.120341	.124223	.132132	.140213
30	.40	.076695	.080171	.083729	.087365	.091074	.094852	.098695	.102598	.106557	.110567	.114627	.122874	.131271
	.30	.077606	.081083	.084641	.088277	.091986	.095764	.099606	.103509	.107468	.111479	.115538	.123786	.132182
	.20	.078518	.081994	.085553	.089189	.092897	.096676	.100518	.104421	.108380	.112391	.116450	.124697	.133094
	.10	.079430	.082906	.086464	.090100	.093809	.097587	.101430	.105333	.109292	.113303	.117362	.125609	.134006
	0.00	.080342	.083818	.087376	.091012	.094721	.098499	.102341	.106244	.110203	.114214	.118273	.126521	.134917
	-.10	.081253	.084729	.088288	.091923	.095633	.099411	.103253	.107156	.111115	.115126	.119185	.127432	.135829
	-.20	.082165	.085641	.089199	.092835	.096544	.100322	.104165	.108068	.112027	.116038	.120097	.128344	.136741
	-.30	.083077	.086553	.090111	.093747	.097456	.101234	.105077	.108979	.112938	.116949	.121008	.129256	.137652
	-.40	.083988	.087465	.091023	.094659	.098368	.102146	.105988	.109891	.113850	.117861	.121920	.130167	.138564

353

15.0 YEAR HOLDING PERIOD
.300 EQUITY YIELD RATE
.600 LOAN RATIO

INTEREST RATE

TERM YEARS	APPR DEP	5.0	5.5	6.0	6.5	7.0	7.5	8.0	8.5	9.0	9.5	10.0	11.0	12.0
10	.40	.187802	.189480	.191179	.192899	.194639	.196400	.198181	.199982	.201802	.203642	.205500	.209274	.213119
	.30	.188400	.190078	.191777	.193499	.195237	.196997	.198778	.200579	.202400	.204239	.206098	.209871	.213717
	.20	.188998	.190676	.192374	.194094	.195834	.197595	.199376	.201177	.202997	.204837	.206696	.210469	.214314
	.10	.189596	.191273	.192972	.194692	.196432	.198193	.199974	.201775	.203595	.205435	.207294	.211067	.214912
	0.00	.190193	.191871	.193570	.195290	.197030	.198791	.200572	.202373	.204193	.206033	.207891	.211665	.215510
	-.10	.190791	.192469	.194168	.195887	.197628	.199389	.201170	.202970	.204791	.206631	.208489	.212262	.216108
	-.20	.191389	.193067	.194765	.196485	.198226	.199986	.201767	.203568	.205389	.207228	.209087	.212860	.216705
	-.30	.191987	.193664	.195363	.197083	.198823	.200584	.202365	.204166	.205986	.207826	.209685	.213458	.217303
	-.40	.192585	.194262	.195961	.197681	.199421	.201182	.202963	.204764	.206584	.208424	.210283	.214056	.217901
15	.40	.170959	.172852	.174780	.176742	.178738	.180767	.182829	.184923	.187049	.189206	.191394	.195357	.200434
	.30	.171557	.173450	.175378	.177340	.179336	.181365	.183427	.185521	.187647	.189804	.191992	.196455	.201032
	.20	.172155	.174048	.175975	.177938	.179933	.181963	.184025	.186119	.188245	.190402	.192589	.197053	.201630
	.10	.172753	.174646	.176573	.178535	.180531	.182560	.184623	.186717	.188843	.191000	.193187	.197651	.202228
	0.00	.173350	.175243	.177171	.179133	.181128	.183158	.185220	.187315	.189441	.191598	.193785	.198248	.202825
	-.10	.173948	.175841	.177769	.179731	.181727	.183756	.185818	.187912	.190038	.192195	.194383	.198846	.203423
	-.20	.174546	.176439	.178367	.180329	.182325	.184354	.186416	.188510	.190636	.192793	.194980	.199444	.204021
	-.30	.175144	.177037	.178964	.180926	.182922	.184952	.187014	.189108	.191234	.193391	.195578	.200042	.204619
	-.40	.175742	.177634	.179562	.181524	.183520	.185549	.187611	.189706	.191832	.193989	.196176	.200639	.205217
20	.40	.162793	.164842	.166934	.169070	.171248	.173467	.175725	.178023	.180357	.182728	.185133	.190043	.195076
	.30	.163391	.165440	.167532	.169668	.171846	.174065	.176323	.178620	.180955	.183325	.185731	.190640	.195674
	.20	.163989	.166037	.168130	.170266	.172444	.174662	.176921	.179218	.181553	.183923	.186328	.191238	.196271
	.10	.164587	.166635	.168728	.170864	.173041	.175260	.177519	.179816	.182150	.184521	.186926	.191836	.196869
	0.00	.165184	.167233	.169326	.171461	.173639	.175858	.178117	.180414	.182748	.185119	.187524	.192434	.197467
	-.10	.165782	.167831	.169923	.172059	.174237	.176456	.178714	.181011	.183346	.185716	.188122	.193031	.198065
	-.20	.166380	.168428	.170521	.172657	.174835	.177054	.179312	.181609	.183944	.186314	.188719	.193629	.198662
	-.30	.166978	.169026	.171119	.173255	.175433	.177651	.179910	.182207	.184541	.186912	.189317	.194227	.199260
	-.40	.167576	.169624	.171717	.173852	.176030	.178249	.180508	.182805	.185139	.187510	.189915	.194825	.199858
25	.40	.158090	.160266	.162493	.164770	.167094	.169463	.171875	.174328	.176820	.179350	.181915	.187142	.192487
	.30	.158687	.160864	.163091	.165368	.167691	.170060	.172472	.174926	.177418	.179948	.182513	.187740	.193085
	.20	.159285	.161462	.163689	.165965	.168289	.170658	.173070	.175523	.178016	.180546	.183111	.188338	.193683
	.10	.159883	.162059	.164287	.166563	.168887	.171256	.173668	.176121	.178614	.181143	.183708	.188936	.194281
	0.00	.160481	.162657	.164885	.167161	.169485	.171854	.174266	.176719	.179212	.181741	.184306	.189533	.194878
	-.10	.161078	.163255	.165482	.167759	.170083	.172451	.174864	.177317	.179809	.182339	.184904	.190131	.195476
	-.20	.161676	.163853	.166080	.168357	.170680	.173049	.175461	.177915	.180407	.182937	.185502	.190729	.196074
	-.30	.162274	.164450	.166678	.168954	.171278	.173647	.176059	.178512	.181005	.183535	.186099	.191327	.196672
	-.40	.162872	.165048	.167276	.169552	.171876	.174245	.176657	.179110	.181603	.184132	.186697	.191925	.197270
30	.40	.155108	.157395	.159738	.162134	.164579	.167071	.169607	.172185	.174800	.177452	.180136	.185595	.191156
	.30	.155706	.157993	.160336	.162731	.165177	.167669	.170205	.172782	.175398	.178050	.180734	.186192	.191754
	.20	.156304	.158591	.160934	.163329	.165774	.168267	.170803	.173380	.175996	.178647	.181332	.186790	.192352
	.10	.156901	.159189	.161531	.163927	.166372	.168864	.171401	.173978	.176594	.179245	.181930	.187388	.192950
	0.00	.157499	.159787	.162129	.164525	.166970	.169462	.171998	.174576	.177191	.179843	.182528	.187986	.193547
	-.10	.158097	.160384	.162727	.165122	.167568	.170060	.172596	.175173	.177789	.180441	.183125	.188584	.194145
	-.20	.158695	.160982	.163325	.165720	.168166	.170658	.173194	.175771	.178387	.181039	.183723	.189181	.194743
	-.30	.159293	.161580	.163923	.166318	.168763	.171255	.173792	.176369	.178985	.181636	.184321	.189779	.195341
	-.40	.159890	.162178	.164520	.166916	.169361	.171853	.174389	.176967	.179583	.182234	.184919	.190377	.195939

15.0 YEAR HOLDING PERIOD
.300 EQUITY YIELD RATE
.667 LOAN RATIO

INTEREST RATE

TERM YEARS	APPR DEP	5.0	5.5	6.0	6.5	7.0	7.5	8.0	8.5	9.0	9.5	10.0	11.0	12.0
10	.40	.175601	.177465	.179353	.181263	.183197	.185154	.187133	.189133	.191156	.193200	.195266	.199458	.203730
	.30	.176199	.178063	.179950	.181861	.183795	.185751	.187730	.189731	.191754	.193798	.195863	.200056	.204328
	.20	.176797	.178661	.180548	.182459	.184393	.186349	.188328	.190329	.192352	.194396	.196461	.200654	.204926
	.10	.177394	.179258	.181146	.183057	.184991	.186947	.188926	.190927	.192950	.194994	.197059	.201251	.205524
	0.00	.177992	.179856	.181744	.183655	.185588	.187545	.189524	.191525	.193547	.195591	.197657	.201849	.206122
	-.10	.178590	.180454	.182342	.184252	.186186	.188143	.190121	.192122	.194145	.196189	.198254	.202447	.206719
	-.20	.179188	.181052	.182939	.184850	.186784	.188740	.190719	.192720	.194743	.196787	.198852	.203045	.207317
	-.30	.179785	.181649	.183537	.185448	.187382	.189338	.191317	.193318	.195341	.197385	.199450	.203642	.207915
	-.40	.180383	.182247	.184135	.186046	.187979	.189936	.191915	.193916	.195938	.197983	.200048	.204240	.208513
15	.40	.156886	.158990	.161132	.163312	.165529	.167784	.170075	.172402	.174764	.177161	.179592	.184551	.189637
	.30	.157484	.159587	.161729	.163909	.166127	.168382	.170673	.173000	.175362	.177759	.180189	.185149	.190234
	.20	.158082	.160185	.162327	.164507	.166725	.168980	.171271	.173598	.175960	.178357	.180787	.185746	.190832
	.10	.158680	.160783	.162925	.165105	.167323	.169578	.171869	.174196	.176558	.178954	.181385	.186344	.191430
	0.00	.159276	.161381	.163523	.165703	.167921	.170175	.172466	.174793	.177156	.179552	.181983	.186942	.192028
	-.10	.159875	.161979	.164120	.166301	.168518	.170773	.173064	.175391	.177753	.180150	.182580	.187540	.192625
	-.20	.160473	.162576	.164718	.166898	.169116	.171371	.173662	.175989	.178351	.180748	.183178	.188138	.193223
	-.30	.161071	.163174	.165316	.167496	.169714	.171968	.174260	.176587	.178949	.181346	.183776	.188735	.193821
	-.40	.161669	.163772	.165914	.168094	.170312	.172566	.174857	.177184	.179547	.181943	.184374	.189333	.194419
20	.40	.147813	.150089	.152414	.154787	.157207	.159673	.162182	.164735	.167328	.169362	.172635	.178090	.183683
	.30	.148411	.150687	.153012	.155385	.157805	.160270	.162780	.165332	.167926	.170560	.173233	.178688	.184280
	.20	.149009	.151285	.153610	.155983	.158403	.160868	.163378	.165930	.168524	.171158	.173830	.179286	.184878
	.10	.149600	.151882	.154208	.156581	.159001	.161466	.163976	.166528	.169122	.171756	.174428	.179883	.185476
	0.00	.150204	.152480	.154805	.157179	.159598	.162064	.164573	.167126	.169720	.172353	.175026	.180481	.186074
	-.10	.150802	.153078	.155403	.157776	.160196	.162662	.165171	.167723	.170317	.172951	.175624	.181079	.186672
	-.20	.151400	.153676	.156001	.158374	.160794	.163259	.165769	.168321	.170915	.173549	.176222	.181677	.187265
	-.30	.151998	.154274	.156599	.158972	.161392	.163857	.166367	.168919	.171513	.174147	.176819	.182275	.187867
	-.40	.152595	.154871	.157197	.159570	.161990	.164455	.166964	.169517	.172111	.174745	.177417	.182872	.188465
25	.40	.142587	.145005	.147480	.150009	.152591	.155223	.157903	.160629	.163399	.166210	.169059	.174868	.180807
	.30	.143184	.145603	.148078	.150607	.153189	.155821	.158501	.161227	.163997	.166807	.169657	.175465	.181404
	.20	.143782	.146200	.148675	.151205	.153787	.156419	.159099	.161825	.164594	.167405	.170255	.176063	.182000
	.10	.144380	.146798	.149273	.151803	.154385	.157017	.159697	.162423	.165192	.168003	.170853	.176661	.182600
	0.00	.144978	.147396	.149871	.152400	.154982	.157614	.160295	.163020	.165790	.168601	.171451	.177259	.183198
	-.10	.145575	.147994	.150469	.152998	.155580	.158212	.160892	.163618	.166388	.169198	.172048	.177857	.183795
	-.20	.146173	.148592	.151067	.153596	.156178	.158810	.161490	.164216	.166985	.169796	.172646	.178454	
	-.30	.146771	.149189	.151664	.154194	.156776	.159408	.162088	.164814	.167583	.170394	.173244	.179052	
	-.40	.147369	.149787	.152262	.154792	.157373	.160006	.162686	.165412	.168181	.170992	.173842		
30	.40	.139274	.141815	.144418	.147080	.149797	.152566	.155384	.158248	.161154	.16410			
	.30	.133872	.142413	.145016	.147678	.150395	.153164	.155982	.158846	.161752				
	.20	.140469	.143011	.145614	.148276	.150993	.153762	.156580	.159443	.162?				
	.10	.141067	.143609	.146212	.148873	.151590	.154359	.157177	.160041					
	0.00	.141665	.144206	.146810	.149471	.152188	.154957	.157775	.15837?					
	-.10	.142263	.144804	.147407	.150069	.152786	.155555	.15837?						
	-.20	.142861	.145402	.148005	.150667	.153384	.156153	.156?						
	-.30	.143458	.146000	.148603	.151264	.153981	.1563							
	-.40	.144056	.146598	.149201	.151862	.154579								

15.0 YEAR HOLDING PERIOD
.300 EQUITY YIELD RATE
.700 LOAN RATIO

INTEREST RATE

TERM YEARS	APPR DEP	5.0	5.5	6.0	6.5	7.0	7.5	8.0	8.5	9.0	9.5	10.0	11.0	12.0
10	.40	.169501	.171458	.173440	.175447	.177477	.179532	.181609	.183710	.185834	.187980	.190149	.194551	.199037
	.30	.170099	.172056	.174038	.176045	.178075	.180129	.182207	.184308	.186432	.188578	.190747	.195149	.199635
	.20	.170697	.172654	.174636	.176642	.178673	.180727	.182805	.184906	.187030	.189176	.191345	.195747	.200233
	.10	.171295	.173252	.175234	.177240	.179271	.181325	.183403	.185504	.187627	.189774	.191942	.196344	.200830
	0.00	.171892	.173850	.175832	.177838	.179868	.181923	.184000	.186101	.188225	.190372	.192540	.196942	.201428
	-.10	.172490	.174447	.176429	.178436	.180466	.182520	.184598	.186699	.188823	.190969	.193138	.197540	.202026
	-.20	.173088	.175045	.177027	.179033	.181064	.183118	.185196	.187297	.189421	.191567	.193736	.198138	.202624
	-.30	.173686	.175643	.177625	.179631	.181662	.183716	.185794	.187895	.190019	.192165	.194333	.198735	.203221
	-.40	.174283	.176241	.178223	.180229	.182259	.184314	.186392	.188492	.190616	.192763	.194931	.199333	.203819
15	.40	.149851	.152059	.154308	.156597	.158926	.161293	.163699	.166143	.168623	.171139	.173691	.178899	.184239
	.30	.150449	.152657	.154906	.157195	.159524	.161891	.164297	.166740	.169221	.171737	.174289	.179496	.184836
	.20	.151047	.153255	.155504	.157793	.160122	.162489	.164895	.167338	.169818	.172335	.174887	.180094	.185434
	.10	.151644	.153853	.156102	.158391	.160719	.163087	.165493	.167936	.170416	.172933	.175485	.180692	.186032
	0.00	.152242	.154451	.156700	.158989	.161317	.163685	.166090	.168534	.171014	.173530	.176082	.181290	.186630
	-.10	.152840	.155048	.157297	.159586	.161915	.164282	.166688	.169131	.171612	.174128	.176680	.181887	.187227
	-.20	.153438	.155646	.157895	.160184	.162513	.164880	.167286	.169729	.172210	.174726	.177278	.182485	.187825
	-.30	.154036	.156244	.158493	.160782	.163111	.165478	.167884	.170327	.172807	.175324	.177876	.183083	.188423
	-.40	.154633	.156842	.159091	.161380	.163708	.166076	.168481	.170925	.173405	.175922	.178473	.183681	.189021
20	.40	.140324	.142714	.145155	.147647	.150188	.152777	.155412	.158092	.160815	.163581	.166387	.172115	.177987
	.30	.140922	.143312	.145753	.148245	.150786	.153374	.156009	.158689	.161413	.164178	.166985	.172713	.178585
	.20	.141520	.143909	.146351	.148843	.151383	.153972	.156607	.159287	.162011	.164776	.167582	.173310	.179183
	.10	.142117	.144507	.146949	.149440	.151981	.154570	.157205	.159885	.162608	.165374	.168180	.173908	.179780
	0.00	.142715	.145105	.147546	.150038	.152579	.155168	.157803	.160483	.163206	.165972	.168778	.174506	.180378
	-.10	.143313	.145703	.148144	.150636	.153177	.155765	.158400	.161080	.163804	.166570	.169376	.175104	.180976
	-.20	.143911	.146301	.148742	.151234	.153775	.156363	.158998	.161678	.164402	.167167	.169973	.175701	.181574
	-.30	.144509	.146898	.149340	.151832	.154372	.156961	.159596	.162276	.165000	.167765	.170571	.176299	.182171
	-.40	.145106	.147496	.149938	.152429	.154970	.157559	.160194	.162874	.165597	.168363	.171169	.176897	.182769
25	.40	.134836	.137376	.139974	.142630	.145341	.148105	.150919	.153781	.156689	.159640	.162633	.168731	.174567
	.30	.135434	.137973	.140572	.143228	.145939	.148703	.151517	.154379	.157287	.160238	.163230	.169329	.175165
	.20	.136032	.138571	.141170	.143826	.146537	.149300	.152114	.154977	.157885	.160836	.163828	.169927	.175763
	.10	.136630	.139169	.141768	.144424	.147134	.149898	.152712	.155574	.158482	.161434	.164426	.170525	.176361
	0.00	.137227	.139767	.142365	.145021	.147732	.150496	.153310	.156172	.159080	.162031	.165024	.171122	.176958
	-.10	.137825	.140364	.142963	.145619	.148330	.151094	.153908	.156770	.159678	.162629	.165622	.171720	.177556
	-.20	.138423	.140962	.143561	.146217	.148928	.151691	.154506	.157368	.160276	.163227	.166219	.172318	.178154
	-.30	.139021	.141560	.144159	.146815	.149526	.152289	.155103	.157966	.160873	.163825	.166817	.172916	.178752
	-.40	.139619	.142158	.144756	.147412	.150123	.152887	.155701	.158563	.161471	.164423	.167415	.173513	.179349
30	.40	.131358	.134026	.136760	.139554	.142407	.145315	.148274	.151281	.154332	.157426	.160558	.166926	.173414
	.30	.131956	.134624	.137357	.140152	.143005	.145912	.148871	.151878	.154930	.158023	.161155	.167523	.174012
	.20	.132554	.135222	.137955	.140750	.143603	.146510	.149469	.152476	.155528	.158621	.161753	.168121	.174610
	.10	.133151	.135820	.138553	.141348	.144200	.147108	.150067	.153074	.156126	.159219	.162351	.168719	.175208
	0.00	.133749	.136418	.139151	.141945	.144798	.147706	.150665	.153672	.156723	.159817	.162949	.169317	.175805
	-.10	.134347	.137015	.139749	.142543	.145396	.148304	.151262	.154269	.157321	.160415	.163547	.169915	.176403
	-.20	.134945	.137613	.140346	.143141	.145994	.148901	.151860	.154867	.157919	.161012	.164144	.170512	.177001
	-.30	.135542	.138211	.140944	.143739	.146592	.149499	.152458	.155465	.158517	.161610	.164742	.171110	.177599
	-.40	.136140	.138809	.141542	.144337	.147189	.150097	.153056	.156063	.159115	.162208	.165340	.171708	.178196

15.0 YEAR HOLDING PERIOD
.300 EQUITY YIELD RATE
.750 LOAN RATIO

INTEREST RATE

TERM YEARS	APPR DEP	5.0	5.5	6.0	6.5	7.0	7.5	8.0	8.5	9.0	9.5	10.0	11.0	12.0
10	.40	.160351	.162448	.164571	.166721	.168896	.171097	.173324	.175575	.177850	.180150	.182473	.187190	.191996
	.30	.160948	.163046	.165169	.167319	.169494	.171695	.173921	.176172	.178448	.180748	.183071	.187787	.192593
	.20	.161546	.163643	.165767	.167916	.170092	.172293	.174519	.176770	.179046	.181345	.183669	.188385	.193192
	.10	.162144	.164241	.166365	.168514	.170690	.172891	.175117	.177368	.179644	.181943	.184267	.188983	.193790
	0.00	.162742	.164839	.166962	.169112	.171288	.173489	.175715	.177966	.180241	.182541	.184864	.189581	.194385
	-.10	.163340	.165437	.167560	.169710	.171885	.174086	.176312	.178564	.180839	.183139	.185462	.190178	.194985
	-.20	.163937	.166034	.168158	.170308	.172483	.174684	.176910	.179161	.181437	.183737	.186060	.190776	.195583
	-.30	.164535	.166632	.168756	.170905	.173081	.175282	.177508	.179759	.182035	.184334	.186658	.191374	.196181
	-.40	.165133	.167230	.169353	.171503	.173679	.175880	.178106	.180357	.182632	.184932	.187255	.191972	.196778
15	.40	.139297	.141663	.144073	.146525	.149020	.151557	.154134	.156752	.159410	.162106	.164840	.170419	.176141
	.30	.139895	.142261	.144670	.147123	.149618	.152154	.154732	.157350	.160007	.162704	.165438	.171017	.176738
	.20	.140493	.142859	.145268	.147721	.150216	.152752	.155330	.157948	.160605	.163301	.166036	.171615	.177336
	.10	.141090	.143456	.145866	.148319	.150813	.153350	.155928	.158545	.161203	.163899	.166633	.172213	.177934
	0.00	.141688	.144054	.146464	.148916	.151411	.153948	.156525	.159143	.161801	.164497	.167231	.172810	.178532
	-.10	.142286	.144652	.147062	.149514	.152009	.154546	.157123	.159741	.162398	.165095	.167829	.173408	.179130
	-.20	.142884	.145250	.147659	.150112	.152607	.155143	.157721	.160339	.162996	.165692	.168427	.174006	.179727
	-.30	.143481	.145848	.148257	.150710	.153205	.155741	.158319	.160937	.163594	.166290	.169024	.174604	.180325
	-.40	.144079	.146445	.148855	.151307	.153802	.156339	.158916	.161534	.164192	.166888	.169622	.175202	.180923
20	.40	.129089	.131650	.134266	.136936	.139658	.142431	.145255	.148126	.151044	.154007	.157014	.163151	.169443
	.30	.129687	.132248	.134864	.137533	.140256	.143029	.145852	.148724	.151642	.154605	.157612	.163749	.170040
	.20	.130285	.132846	.135461	.138131	.140853	.143627	.146450	.149322	.152240	.155203	.158209	.164346	.170638
	.10	.130883	.133443	.136059	.138729	.141451	.144225	.147048	.149919	.152837	.155801	.158807	.164944	.171236
	0.00	.131481	.134041	.136657	.139327	.142049	.144823	.147646	.150517	.153435	.156398	.159405	.165542	.171834
	-.10	.132078	.134639	.137255	.139924	.142647	.145420	.148244	.151115	.154033	.156996	.160003	.166140	.172431
	-.20	.132676	.135237	.137852	.140522	.143245	.146018	.148841	.151713	.154631	.157594	.160600	.166738	.173029
	-.30	.133274	.135834	.138450	.141120	.143842	.146616	.149439	.152310	.155229	.158192	.161198	.167335	.173627
	-.40	.133872	.136432	.139048	.141718	.144440	.147214	.150037	.152908	.155826	.158789	.161796	.167933	.174225
25	.40	.123210	.125930	.128715	.131560	.134465	.137426	.140441	.143508	.146623	.149785	.152991	.159526	.166207
	.30	.123807	.126528	.129312	.132158	.135063	.138024	.141039	.144105	.147221	.150383	.153589	.160123	.166805
	.20	.124405	.127126	.129910	.132756	.135660	.138621	.141637	.144703	.147819	.150981	.154187	.160721	.167403
	.10	.125003	.127724	.130508	.133354	.136258	.139219	.142234	.145301	.148417	.151579	.154785	.161319	.168000
	0.00	.125601	.128321	.131106	.133951	.136856	.139817	.142832	.145899	.149014	.152177	.155383	.161917	.168598
	-.10	.126199	.128919	.131703	.134549	.137454	.140415	.143430	.146497	.149612	.152774	.155980	.162515	.169196
	-.20	.126796	.129517	.132301	.135147	.138051	.141013	.144028	.147094	.150210	.153372	.156578	.163112	.169794
	-.30	.127394	.130115	.132899	.135745	.138649	.141610	.144625	.147692	.150808	.153970	.157176	.163710	.170391
	-.40	.127992	.130713	.133497	.136342	.139247	.142208	.145223	.148290	.151406	.154568	.157774	.164308	.170989
30	.40	.119483	.122342	.125270	.128265	.131321	.134436	.137607	.140828	.144098	.147413	.150768	.157591	.164543
	.30	.120081	.122940	.125868	.128863	.131919	.135034	.138205	.141426	.144696	.148010	.151366	.158189	.165141
	.20	.120679	.123538	.126466	.129460	.132517	.135632	.138802	.142024	.145294	.148608	.151964	.158787	.165739
	.10	.121276	.124135	.127064	.130058	.133115	.136230	.139400	.142622	.145892	.149206	.152562	.159384	.166336
	0.00	.121874	.124733	.127662	.130656	.133712	.136828	.139998	.143220	.146489	.149804	.153159	.159982	.166934
	-.10	.122472	.125331	.128259	.131254	.134310	.137425	.140596	.143817	.147087	.150401	.153757	.160580	.167532
	-.20	.123070	.125929	.128857	.131851	.134908	.138023	.141193	.144415	.147685	.150999	.154355	.161178	.168130
	-.30	.123667	.126526	.129455	.132449	.135506	.138621	.141791	.145013	.148283	.151597	.154953	.161776	.168728
	-.40	.124265	.127124	.130053	.133047	.136104	.139219	.142389	.145611	.148880	.152195	.155551	.162373	.169325

15.0 YEAR HOLDING PERIOD
.300 EQUITY YIELD RATE
.800 LOAN RATIO

INTEREST RATE

TERM YEARS	APPR DEP	5.0	5.5	6.0	6.5	7.0	7.5	8.0	8.5	9.0	9.5	10.0	11.0	12.0
10	.40	.151200	.153437	.155702	.157995	.160316	.162663	.165038	.167439	.169866	.172319	.174798	.179828	.184955
	.30	.151798	.154035	.156300	.158593	.160913	.163261	.165636	.168037	.170464	.172917	.175395	.180426	.185553
	.20	.152396	.154633	.156898	.159191	.161511	.163859	.166233	.168635	.171062	.173515	.175993	.181024	.186151
	.10	.152993	.155230	.157495	.159788	.162109	.164457	.166831	.169232	.171660	.174113	.176591	.181622	.186749
	0.00	.153591	.155828	.158093	.160386	.162707	.165054	.167429	.169830	.172257	.174710	.177189	.182219	.187346
	-.10	.154189	.156426	.158691	.160984	.163304	.165652	.168027	.170428	.172855	.175308	.177736	.182817	.187944
	-.20	.154787	.157024	.159289	.161582	.163902	.166250	.168625	.171026	.173453	.175906	.178334	.183415	.188542
	-.30	.155385	.157621	.159887	.162179	.164500	.166848	.169222	.171623	.174051	.176504	.178934	.184013	.189140
	-.40	.155982	.158219	.160484	.162777	.165098	.167446	.169820	.172221	.174649	.177101	.179580	.184611	.189738
15	.40	.128743	.131267	.133837	.136453	.139114	.141820	.144569	.147362	.150196	.153072	.155989	.161940	.168043
	.30	.129341	.131864	.134435	.137051	.139712	.142418	.145167	.147959	.150794	.153670	.156587	.162538	.168641
	.20	.129938	.132462	.135032	.137649	.140310	.143015	.145765	.148557	.151392	.154268	.157184	.163136	.169238
	.10	.130536	.133060	.135630	.138246	.140908	.143613	.146363	.149155	.151990	.154866	.157782	.163733	.169836
	0.00	.131134	.133658	.136228	.138844	.141505	.144211	.146960	.149753	.152587	.155463	.158380	.164331	.170434
	-.10	.131732	.134256	.136826	.139442	.142103	.144809	.147558	.150351	.153185	.156061	.158978	.164929	.171032
	-.20	.132330	.134853	.137424	.140040	.142701	.145407	.148156	.150948	.153783	.156659	.159575	.165527	.171629
	-.30	.132927	.135451	.138021	.140637	.143299	.146004	.148754	.151546	.154381	.157257	.160173	.166124	.172227
	-.40	.133525	.136049	.138619	.141235	.143896	.146602	.149351	.152144	.154978	.157854	.160771	.166722	.172825
20	.40	.117855	.120586	.123376	.126224	.129128	.132086	.135098	.138161	.141273	.144434	.147641	.154187	.160898
	.30	.118453	.121184	.123974	.126822	.129726	.132684	.135695	.138758	.141871	.145032	.148239	.154785	.161496
	.20	.119050	.121782	.124572	.127420	.130323	.133282	.136293	.139356	.142469	.145629	.148836	.155383	.162094
	.10	.119648	.122379	.125170	.128017	.130921	.133880	.136891	.139954	.143066	.146227	.149434	.155980	.162691
	0.00	.120246	.122977	.125767	.128615	.131519	.134477	.137489	.140552	.143664	.146825	.150032	.156578	.163289
	-.10	.120844	.123575	.126365	.129213	.132117	.135075	.138087	.141149	.144262	.147423	.150630	.157176	.163887
	-.20	.121442	.124173	.126963	.129811	.132714	.135673	.138684	.141747	.144860	.148020	.151227	.157774	.164485
	-.30	.122039	.124771	.127561	.130408	.133312	.136271	.139282	.142345	.145458	.148618	.151825	.158371	.165082
	-.40	.122637	.125368	.128158	.131006	.133910	.136868	.139880	.142943	.146055	.149216	.152423	.158969	.165680
25	.40	.111583	.114485	.117455	.120490	.123589	.126747	.129963	.133234	.136558	.139931	.143350	.150320	.157447
	.30	.112181	.115083	.118053	.121088	.124186	.127345	.130561	.133832	.137155	.140528	.143948	.150918	.158045
	.20	.112779	.115681	.118650	.121686	.124784	.127943	.131159	.134430	.137753	.141126	.144546	.151516	.158642
	.10	.113376	.116278	.119248	.122283	.125382	.128540	.131757	.135028	.138351	.141724	.145144	.152113	.159240
	0.00	.113974	.116876	.119846	.122881	.125980	.129138	.132354	.135625	.138949	.142322	.145741	.152711	.159838
	-.10	.114572	.117474	.120444	.123479	.126577	.129736	.132952	.136223	.139547	.142919	.146339	.153309	.160436
	-.20	.115170	.118072	.121042	.124077	.127175	.130334	.133550	.136821	.140144	.143517	.146937	.153907	.161033
	-.30	.115768	.118669	.121639	.124675	.127773	.130931	.134148	.137419	.140742	.144115	.147535	.154505	.161631
	-.40	.116365	.119267	.122237	.125272	.128371	.131529	.134745	.138017	.141340	.144713	.148133	.155102	.162229
30	.40	.107608	.110658	.113781	.116975	.120235	.123558	.126940	.130376	.133864	.137400	.140979	.148257	.155672
	.30	.108206	.111255	.114379	.117573	.120833	.124156	.127538	.130974	.134462	.137997	.141577	.148854	.156270
	.20	.108803	.111853	.114977	.118171	.121431	.124754	.128135	.131572	.135060	.138595	.142174	.149452	.156868
	.10	.109401	.112451	.115575	.118768	.122029	.125352	.128733	.132170	.135658	.139193	.142772	.150050	.157465
	0.00	.109999	.113049	.116172	.119366	.122627	.125949	.129331	.132768	.136255	.139791	.143370	.150648	.158063
	-.10	.110597	.113646	.116770	.119964	.123224	.126547	.129929	.133365	.136853	.140388	.143968	.151245	.158661
	-.20	.111195	.114244	.117368	.120562	.123822	.127145	.130527	.133963	.137451	.140986	.144566	.151843	.159259
	-.30	.111792	.114842	.117966	.121160	.124420	.127743	.131124	.134561	.138049	.141584	.145163	.152441	.159857
	-.40	.112390	.115440	.118563	.121757	.125018	.128341	.131722	.135159	.138646	.142182	.145761	.153039	.160454

15.0 YEAR HOLDING PERIOD
.300 EQUITY YIELD RATE
.900 LOAN RATIO

INTEREST RATE

TERM YEARS	APPR DEP	5.0	5.5	6.0	6.5	7.0	7.5	8.0	8.5	9.0	9.5	10.0	11.0	12.0
10	.40	.132899	.135416	.137964	.140543	.143154	.145795	.148467	.151168	.153898	.156658	.159446	.165106	.170874
	.30	.133497	.136013	.138562	.141141	.143752	.146393	.149064	.151766	.154496	.157256	.160044	.165704	.171471
	.20	.134095	.136611	.139159	.141739	.144349	.146991	.149662	.152363	.155094	.157854	.160642	.166301	.172065
	.10	.134692	.137209	.139757	.142337	.144947	.147588	.150260	.152961	.155692	.158451	.161239	.166899	.172567
	0.00	.135290	.137807	.140355	.142934	.145545	.148186	.150858	.153559	.156290	.159049	.161837	.167497	.173265
	-.10	.135888	.138404	.140953	.143532	.146143	.148784	.151455	.154157	.156887	.159647	.162435	.168095	.173863
	-.20	.136486	.139002	.141550	.144130	.146741	.149382	.152053	.154754	.157485	.160245	.163033	.168693	.174460
	-.30	.137083	.139600	.142148	.144728	.147338	.149980	.152651	.155352	.158083	.160842	.163631	.169290	.175058
	-.40	.137681	.140198	.142746	.145326	.147936	.150577	.153249	.155950	.158681	.161440	.164228	.169888	.175656
15	.40	.107635	.110474	.113365	.116308	.119302	.122346	.125439	.128581	.131770	.135005	.138286	.144981	.151847
	.30	.108232	.111072	.113963	.116906	.119900	.122944	.126037	.129179	.132367	.135603	.138884	.145579	.152445
	.20	.108830	.111669	.114561	.117504	.120498	.123542	.126635	.129776	.132965	.136201	.139482	.146177	.153043
	.10	.109428	.112267	.115159	.118102	.121096	.124140	.127233	.130374	.133563	.136798	.140080	.146775	.153640
	0.00	.110026	.112865	.115757	.118700	.121693	.124737	.127830	.130972	.134161	.137396	.140677	.147372	.154238
	-.10	.110623	.113463	.116354	.119297	.122291	.125335	.128428	.131570	.134759	.137994	.141275	.147970	.154836
	-.20	.111221	.114061	.116952	.119895	.122889	.125933	.129026	.132167	.135356	.138592	.141873	.148568	.155434
	-.30	.111819	.114658	.117550	.120493	.123487	.126531	.129624	.132765	.135954	.139190	.142471	.149166	.156031
	-.40	.112417	.115256	.118148	.121091	.124085	.127128	.130222	.133363	.136552	.139787	.143068	.149764	.156629
20	.40	.095386	.098458	.101597	.104801	.108068	.111396	.114784	.118229	.121731	.125287	.128895	.136259	.143309
	.30	.095983	.099056	.102195	.105399	.108665	.111994	.115382	.118827	.122329	.125885	.129493	.136857	.144407
	.20	.096581	.099654	.102793	.105996	.109263	.112591	.115979	.119425	.122927	.126482	.130090	.137455	.145005
	.10	.097179	.100252	.103390	.106594	.109861	.113189	.116577	.120023	.123524	.127080	.130688	.138053	.145603
	0.00	.097777	.100849	.103988	.107192	.110459	.113787	.117175	.120621	.124122	.127678	.131286	.138650	.146200
	-.10	.098374	.101447	.104586	.107790	.111057	.114385	.117773	.121218	.124720	.128276	.131884	.139248	.146798
	-.20	.098972	.102045	.105184	.108388	.111654	.114983	.118370	.121816	.125318	.128874	.132481	.139846	.147396
	-.30	.099570	.102643	.105782	.108985	.112252	.115580	.118968	.122414	.125916	.129471	.133079	.140444	.147994
	-.40	.100168	.103240	.106379	.109583	.112850	.116178	.119566	.123012	.126513	.130069	.133677	.141042	.148591
25	.40	.088330	.091595	.094936	.098350	.101836	.105389	.109007	.112687	.116426	.120221	.124068	.131909	.139927
	.30	.088928	.092192	.095533	.098948	.102434	.105987	.109605	.113285	.117024	.120819	.124666	.132507	.140524
	.20	.089525	.092790	.096131	.099546	.103032	.106585	.110203	.113883	.117622	.121416	.125264	.133105	.141122
	.10	.090123	.093388	.096729	.100144	.103629	.107183	.110801	.114481	.118220	.122014	.125861	.133702	.141720
	0.00	.090721	.093986	.097327	.100742	.104227	.107780	.111399	.115079	.118817	.122612	.126459	.134300	.142318
	-.10	.091319	.094583	.097925	.101339	.104825	.108378	.111996	.115676	.119415	.123210	.127057	.134898	.142915
	-.20	.091917	.095181	.098522	.101937	.105423	.108976	.112594	.116274	.120013	.123807	.127655	.135496	.143513
	-.30	.092514	.095779	.099120	.102535	.106020	.109574	.113192	.116872	.120611	.124405	.128252	.136094	.144111
	-.40	.093112	.096377	.099718	.103133	.106618	.110172	.113790	.117470	.121208	.125003	.128850	.136691	.144709
30	.40	.083858	.087289	.090803	.094396	.098064	.101802	.105606	.109472	.113396	.117373	.121400	.129588	.137630
	.30	.084456	.087886	.091401	.094994	.098662	.102400	.106204	.110070	.113994	.117971	.121998	.130185	.138228
	.20	.085053	.088484	.091998	.095591	.099259	.102998	.106802	.110668	.114592	.118569	.122596	.130783	.138826
	.10	.085651	.089082	.092596	.096189	.099857	.103595	.107400	.111266	.115189	.119167	.123194	.131381	.139423
	0.00	.086249	.089680	.093194	.096787	.100455	.104193	.107997	.111864	.115787	.119764	.123791	.131979	.140021
	-.10	.086847	.090278	.093792	.097385	.101053	.104791	.108595	.112461	.116385	.120362	.124389	.132576	.140619
	-.20	.087444	.090875	.094389	.097983	.101650	.105389	.109193	.113059	.116983	.120960	.124987	.133174	.141217
	-.30	.088042	.091473	.094987	.098580	.102248	.105986	.109791	.113657	.117581	.121558	.125585	.133772	.141814
	-.40	.088640	.092071	.095585	.099178	.102846	.106584	.110389	.114255	.118178	.122156	.126182	.134370	.142412

15.0 YEAR HOLDING PERIOD
.400 EQUITY YIELD RATE
.600 LOAN RATIO

INTEREST RATE

TERM YEARS	APPR DEP	5.0	5.5	6.0	6.5	7.0	7.5	8.0	8.5	9.0	9.5	10.0	11.0	12.0
10	.40	.232659	.234390	.236144	.237921	.239720	.241541	.243384	.245249	.247135	.249043	.250972	.254891	.258892
	.30	.232918	.234649	.236403	.238179	.239978	.241799	.243643	.245508	.247394	.249302	.251231	.255150	.259151
	.20	.233177	.234908	.236662	.238438	.240237	.242058	.243901	.245766	.247653	.249561	.251489	.255409	.259409
	.10	.233436	.235167	.236921	.238697	.240496	.242317	.244160	.246025	.247912	.249819	.251748	.255668	.259668
	0.00	.233694	.235425	.237179	.238956	.240755	.242576	.244419	.246284	.248170	.250078	.252007	.255927	.259927
	-.10	.233953	.235684	.237438	.239215	.241013	.242835	.244678	.246543	.248429	.250337	.252266	.256185	.260186
	-.20	.234212	.235943	.237697	.239473	.241272	.243093	.244937	.246801	.248688	.250596	.252524	.256444	.260445
	-.30	.234471	.236202	.237956	.239732	.241531	.243352	.245195	.247060	.248947	.250854	.252783	.256703	.260703
	-.40	.234730	.236461	.238214	.239991	.241790	.243611	.245454	.247319	.249205	.251113	.253042	.256962	.260962
15	.40	.214349	.216242	.218170	.220132	.222128	.224157	.226219	.228313	.230439	.232596	.234784	.239247	.243824
	.30	.214608	.216501	.218429	.220391	.222387	.224416	.226478	.228572	.230698	.232855	.235042	.239506	.244083
	.20	.214867	.216760	.218687	.220649	.222645	.224675	.226737	.228831	.230957	.233114	.235301	.239765	.244342
	.10	.215126	.217019	.218946	.220908	.222904	.224933	.226996	.229090	.231216	.233373	.235560	.240023	.244601
	0.00	.215384	.217277	.219205	.221167	.223163	.225192	.227254	.229349	.231474	.233631	.235819	.240282	.244859
	-.10	.215643	.217536	.219464	.221426	.223422	.225451	.227513	.229607	.231733	.233890	.236078	.240541	.245118
	-.20	.215902	.217795	.219723	.221685	.223680	.225710	.227772	.229866	.231992	.234149	.236336	.240800	.245377
	-.30	.216161	.218054	.219981	.221943	.223939	.225969	.228031	.230125	.232251	.234408	.236595	.241059	.245636
	-.40	.216420	.218312	.220240	.222202	.224198	.226227	.228289	.230384	.232510	.234667	.236854	.241317	.245895
20	.40	.205472	.207499	.209571	.211685	.213842	.216039	.218276	.220552	.222865	.225215	.227599	.232467	.237459
	.30	.205731	.207758	.209829	.211944	.214100	.216298	.218535	.220811	.223124	.225474	.227858	.232726	.237718
	.20	.205990	.208017	.210088	.212203	.214359	.216557	.218794	.221070	.223383	.225732	.228117	.232984	.237977
	.10	.206248	.208276	.210347	.212461	.214618	.216815	.219053	.221329	.223642	.225991	.228375	.233243	.238235
	0.00	.206507	.208534	.210606	.212720	.214877	.217074	.219311	.221587	.223901	.226250	.228634	.233502	.238494
	-.10	.206766	.208793	.210865	.212979	.215136	.217333	.219570	.221846	.224159	.226509	.228893	.233761	.238753
	-.20	.207025	.209052	.211123	.213238	.215394	.217592	.219829	.222105	.224418	.226767	.229152	.234020	.239012
	-.30	.207283	.209311	.211382	.213497	.215653	.217851	.220088	.222364	.224677	.227026	.229410	.234278	.239270
	-.40	.207542	.209569	.211641	.213755	.215912	.218109	.220347	.222622	.224936	.227285	.229669	.234537	.239529
25	.40	.200358	.202505	.204703	.206950	.209245	.211586	.213971	.216397	.218863	.221367	.223906	.229085	.234384
	.30	.200617	.202764	.204962	.207209	.209504	.211845	.214229	.216656	.219122	.221625	.224165	.229344	.234643
	.20	.200876	.203023	.205221	.207468	.209763	.212104	.214488	.216914	.219380	.221884	.224424	.229603	.234902
	.10	.201135	.203281	.205479	.207727	.210022	.212363	.214747	.217173	.219639	.222143	.224683	.229861	.235160
	0.00	.201394	.203540	.205738	.207986	.210280	.212621	.215006	.217432	.219898	.222402	.224941	.230120	.235419
	-.10	.201652	.203799	.205997	.208244	.210539	.212880	.215265	.217691	.220157	.222661	.225200	.230379	.235678
	-.20	.201911	.204058	.206256	.208503	.210798	.213139	.215523	.217950	.220416	.222919	.225459	.230638	.235937
	-.30	.202170	.204317	.206514	.208762	.211057	.213398	.215782	.218208	.220674	.223178	.225718	.230897	.236196
	-.40	.202429	.204575	.206773	.209021	.211316	.213656	.216041	.218467	.220933	.223437	.225977	.231155	.236454
30	.40	.197117	.199372	.201683	.204048	.206463	.208927	.211435	.213986	.216577	.219204	.221865	.227280	.232803
	.30	.197376	.199631	.201942	.204306	.206722	.209186	.211694	.214245	.216836	.219463	.222124	.227539	.233062
	.20	.197635	.199889	.202201	.204565	.206981	.209444	.211953	.214504	.217094	.219722	.222383	.227798	.233321
	.10	.197894	.200148	.202459	.204824	.207240	.209703	.212212	.214763	.217353	.219980	.222642	.228057	.233579
	0.00	.198152	.200407	.202718	.205083	.207498	.209962	.212471	.215021	.217612	.220239	.222900	.228316	.233838
	-.10	.198411	.200666	.202977	.205342	.207757	.210221	.212729	.215280	.217871	.220498	.223159	.228574	.234097
	-.20	.198670	.200925	.203236	.205600	.208016	.210479	.212988	.215539	.218129	.220757	.223418	.228833	.234356
	-.30	.198929	.201183	.203494	.205859	.208275	.210738	.213247	.215798	.218388	.221015	.223677	.229092	.234615
	-.40	.199188	.201442	.203753	.206118	.208534	.210997	.213506	.216057	.218647	.221274	.223936	.229351	.234873

15.0 YEAR HOLDING PERIOD
.400 EQUITY YIELD RATE
.667 LOAN RATIO

INTEREST RATE

TERM YEARS	APPR DEP	5.0	5.5	6.0	6.5	7.0	7.5	8.0	8.5	9.0	9.5	10.0	11.0	12.0
10	.40	.214180	.216103	.218052	.220026	.222025	.224048	.226096	.228168	.230264	.232384	.234527	.238882	.243327
	.30	.214439	.216362	.218311	.220285	.222284	.224307	.226355	.228427	.230523	.232643	.234786	.239141	.243586
	.20	.214698	.216621	.218570	.220544	.222542	.224566	.226614	.228686	.230782	.232902	.235045	.239400	.243845
	.10	.214956	.216880	.218828	.220802	.222801	.224825	.226873	.228945	.231041	.233160	.235304	.239659	.244104
	0.00	.215215	.217139	.219087	.221061	.223060	.225083	.227131	.229203	.231300	.233419	.235562	.239918	.244363
	-.10	.215474	.217397	.219346	.221320	.223319	.225342	.227390	.229462	.231558	.233678	.235821	.240176	.244621
	-.20	.215733	.217656	.219605	.221579	.223577	.225601	.227649	.229721	.231817	.233937	.236080	.240435	.244880
	-.30	.215992	.217915	.219864	.221837	.223836	.225860	.227908	.229980	.232076	.234196	.236339	.240694	.245139
	-.40	.216250	.218174	.220122	.222096	.224095	.226119	.228166	.230239	.232335	.234454	.236598	.240953	.245398
15	.40	.193835	.195939	.198080	.200261	.202478	.204733	.207024	.209351	.211713	.214110	.216540	.221500	.226586
	.30	.194094	.196197	.198339	.200519	.202737	.204992	.207283	.209610	.211972	.214369	.216798	.221759	.226844
	.20	.194353	.196456	.198598	.200778	.202996	.205251	.207542	.209869	.212231	.214628	.217058	.222017	.227103
	.10	.194612	.196715	.198857	.201037	.203255	.205509	.207801	.210128	.212490	.214886	.217317	.222276	.227362
	0.00	.194871	.196974	.199116	.201296	.203513	.205768	.208059	.210386	.212748	.215145	.217576	.222535	.227621
	-.10	.195129	.197233	.199374	.201554	.203772	.206027	.208318	.210645	.213007	.215404	.217834	.222793	.227879
	-.20	.195388	.197491	.199633	.201813	.204031	.206286	.208577	.210904	.213266	.215663	.218093	.223053	.228138
	-.30	.195647	.197750	.199892	.202072	.204290	.206544	.208836	.211163	.213525	.215922	.218352	.223311	.228397
	-.40	.195906	.198009	.200151	.202331	.204549	.206803	.209094	.211421	.213784	.216180	.218611	.223570	.228656
20	.40	.183972	.186224	.188526	.190875	.193271	.195713	.198199	.200728	.203298	.205908	.208557	.213966	.219505
	.30	.184230	.186483	.188785	.191134	.193530	.195972	.198458	.200987	.203557	.206167	.208816	.214225	.219764
	.20	.184489	.186742	.189043	.191393	.193789	.196231	.198716	.201245	.203815	.206426	.209075	.214484	.220023
	.10	.184748	.187001	.189302	.191652	.194048	.196489	.198975	.201504	.204074	.206685	.209334	.214742	.220281
	0.00	.185007	.187259	.189561	.191910	.194306	.196748	.199234	.201763	.204333	.206943	.209592	.215001	.220540
	-.10	.185266	.187518	.189820	.192169	.194565	.197007	.199493	.202022	.204592	.207202	.209851	.215260	.220799
	-.20	.185524	.187777	.190078	.192428	.194824	.197266	.199752	.202280	.204851	.207461	.210110	.215519	.221058
	-.30	.185783	.188036	.190337	.192687	.195083	.197524	.200010	.202539	.205109	.207720	.210369	.215778	.221317
	-.40	.186042	.188294	.190596	.192945	.195342	.197783	.200269	.202798	.205368	.207978	.210628	.216036	.221575
25	.40	.178290	.180675	.183117	.185614	.188164	.190765	.193415	.196111	.198851	.201633	.204454	.210209	.216096
	.30	.178549	.180934	.183376	.185873	.188423	.191024	.193674	.196369	.199109	.201891	.204713	.210467	.216355
	.20	.178808	.181193	.183635	.186132	.188682	.191283	.193932	.196628	.199368	.202150	.204972	.210726	.216614
	.10	.179066	.181451	.183894	.186391	.188941	.191542	.194191	.196887	.199627	.202409	.205231	.210985	.216873
	0.00	.179325	.181710	.184152	.186650	.189200	.191800	.194450	.197146	.199886	.202668	.205489	.211244	.217132
	-.10	.179584	.181969	.184411	.186908	.189458	.192059	.194709	.197404	.200145	.202927	.205748	.211503	.217390
	-.20	.179843	.182228	.184670	.187167	.189717	.192318	.194967	.197663	.200403	.203185	.206007	.211761	.217649
	-.30	.180101	.182487	.184929	.187426	.189976	.192577	.195226	.197922	.200662	.203444	.206266	.212020	.217908
	-.40	.180360	.182745	.185188	.187685	.190235	.192836	.195485	.198181	.200921	.203703	.206525	.212279	.218167
30	.40	.174689	.177194	.179762	.182389	.185073	.187810	.190598	.193432	.196310	.199230	.202187	.208203	.214340
	.30	.174948	.177453	.180020	.182648	.185332	.188069	.190857	.193691	.196569	.199488	.202445	.208462	.214598
	.20	.175206	.177711	.180279	.182907	.185591	.188328	.191115	.193950	.196828	.199747	.202704	.208721	.214857
	.10	.175465	.177970	.180538	.183166	.185849	.188587	.191374	.194209	.197087	.200006	.202963	.208980	.215116
	0.00	.175724	.178229	.180797	.183424	.186108	.188845	.191633	.194467	.197346	.200265	.203222	.209239	.215375
	-.10	.175983	.178488	.181056	.183683	.186367	.189104	.191892	.194726	.197604	.200523	.203481	.209497	.215634
	-.20	.176241	.178747	.181314	.183942	.186626	.189363	.192150	.194985	.197863	.200782	.203739	.209756	.215892
	-.30	.176500	.179005	.181573	.184201	.186885	.189622	.192409	.195244	.198122	.201041	.203998	.210015	.216151
	-.40	.176759	.179264	.181832	.184459	.187143	.189881	.192668	.195502	.198381	.201300	.204257	.210274	.216410

15.0 YEAR HOLDING PERIOD
.400 EQUITY YIELD RATE
.700 LOAN RATIO

INTEREST RATE

TERM YEARS	APPR DEP	5.0	5.5	6.0	6.5	7.0	7.5	8.0	8.5	9.0	9.5	10.0	11.0	12.0
10	.40	.204942	.206961	.209007	.211080	.213179	.215303	.217454	.219629	.221830	.224056	.226306	.230879	.235546
	.30	.205201	.207220	.209266	.211339	.213437	.215562	.217712	.219888	.222089	.224315	.226565	.231138	.235805
	.20	.205459	.207479	.209525	.211598	.213696	.215821	.217971	.220147	.222348	.224574	.226824	.231397	.236064
	.10	.205718	.207738	.209784	.211856	.213955	.216080	.218230	.220406	.222607	.224832	.227083	.231655	.236323
	0.0	.205977	.207996	.210043	.212115	.214214	.216338	.218489	.220665	.222865	.225091	.227341	.231914	.236582
	-.10	.206236	.208255	.210301	.212374	.214473	.216597	.218748	.220923	.223124	.225350	.227600	.232173	.236840
	-.20	.206494	.208514	.210560	.212633	.214731	.216856	.219006	.221182	.223383	.225609	.227859	.232432	.237099
	-.30	.206753	.208773	.210819	.212891	.214990	.217115	.219265	.221441	.223642	.225867	.228118	.232691	.237358
	-.40	.207012	.209032	.211078	.213150	.215249	.217374	.219524	.221700	.223901	.226126	.228376	.232949	.237617
15	.40	.183580	.185788	.188037	.190326	.192655	.195022	.197428	.199871	.202352	.204868	.207420	.212628	.217967
	.30	.183839	.186047	.188296	.190585	.192914	.195281	.197687	.200130	.202611	.205127	.207679	.212886	.218226
	.20	.184098	.186306	.188555	.190844	.193173	.195540	.197946	.200389	.202869	.205386	.207938	.213145	.218485
	.10	.184356	.186565	.188814	.191103	.193431	.195799	.198204	.200648	.203128	.205645	.208197	.213404	.218744
	0.0	.184615	.186824	.189072	.191362	.193690	.196058	.198463	.200907	.203387	.205903	.208455	.213663	.219003
	-.10	.184874	.187082	.189331	.191620	.193949	.196316	.198722	.201165	.203646	.206162	.208714	.213921	.219261
	-.20	.185133	.187341	.189590	.191879	.194208	.196575	.198981	.201424	.203904	.206421	.208973	.214180	.219520
	-.30	.185392	.187600	.189849	.192138	.194466	.196834	.199240	.201683	.204163	.206680	.209232	.214439	.219779
	-.40	.185650	.187859	.190108	.192397	.194725	.197093	.199498	.201942	.204422	.206939	.209490	.214698	.220038
20	.40	.173223	.175588	.178005	.180472	.182988	.185551	.188162	.190817	.193515	.196256	.199038	.204717	.210541
	.30	.173482	.175847	.178264	.180731	.183247	.185810	.188420	.191076	.193774	.196515	.199297	.204976	.210800
	.20	.173741	.176106	.178522	.180989	.183505	.186069	.188679	.191334	.194033	.196774	.199556	.205235	.211059
	.10	.174000	.176365	.178781	.181248	.183764	.186328	.188938	.191593	.194291	.197033	.199815	.205494	.211318
	0.0	.174258	.176623	.179040	.181507	.184023	.186587	.189197	.191852	.194551	.197292	.200073	.205752	.211576
	-.10	.174517	.176882	.179299	.181766	.184282	.186845	.189456	.192111	.194809	.197550	.200332	.206011	.211835
	-.20	.174776	.177141	.179558	.182024	.184540	.187104	.189714	.192369	.195068	.197809	.200591	.206270	.212094
	-.30	.175035	.177400	.179816	.182283	.184799	.187363	.189973	.192628	.195327	.198068	.200849	.206529	.212353
	-.40	.175293	.177659	.180075	.182542	.185058	.187622	.190232	.192887	.195586	.198327	.201108	.206787	.212612
25	.40	.167257	.169762	.172326	.174948	.177626	.180356	.183138	.185969	.188846	.191767	.194730	.200772	.206954
	.30	.167516	.170021	.172585	.175207	.177884	.180615	.183397	.186228	.189105	.192026	.194989	.201031	.207213
	.20	.167775	.170279	.172844	.175466	.178143	.180874	.183656	.186486	.189363	.192285	.195247	.201289	.207472
	.10	.168034	.170538	.173102	.175724	.178402	.181133	.183915	.186745	.189622	.192543	.195506	.201548	.207730
	0.0	.168292	.170797	.173361	.175983	.178661	.181392	.184173	.187004	.189881	.192802	.195765	.201807	.207989
	-.10	.168551	.171056	.173620	.176242	.178919	.181650	.184432	.187263	.190140	.193061	.196024	.202066	.208248
	-.20	.168810	.171314	.173879	.176501	.179178	.181909	.184691	.187522	.190399	.193320	.196283	.202324	.208507
	-.30	.169069	.171573	.174137	.176759	.179437	.182168	.184950	.187780	.190657	.193579	.196541	.202583	.208766
	-.40	.169328	.171832	.174396	.177018	.179696	.182427	.185209	.188039	.190916	.193837	.196800	.202842	.209024
30	.40	.163476	.166106	.168803	.171561	.174380	.177254	.180180	.183157	.186179	.189244	.192349	.198666	.205105
	.30	.163735	.166365	.169061	.171820	.174638	.177513	.180439	.183415	.186438	.189503	.192608	.198925	.205368
	.20	.163994	.166624	.169320	.172079	.174897	.177771	.180698	.183674	.186696	.189761	.192866	.199184	.205627
	.10	.164252	.166883	.169579	.172338	.175156	.178030	.180957	.183933	.186955	.190020	.193125	.199443	.205886
	0.0	.164511	.167142	.169838	.172597	.175415	.178289	.181216	.184192	.187214	.190279	.193384	.199701	.206145
	-.10	.164770	.167400	.170097	.172855	.175674	.178548	.181474	.184450	.187473	.190538	.193643	.199960	.206403
	-.20	.165029	.167659	.170355	.173114	.175932	.178806	.181733	.184709	.187731	.190797	.193902	.200219	.206662
	-.30	.165288	.167918	.170614	.173373	.176191	.179065	.181992	.184968	.187990	.191055	.194160	.200478	.206921
	-.40	.165546	.168177	.170873	.173632	.176450	.179324	.182251	.185227	.188249	.191314	.194419	.200737	.207180

362

15.0 YEAR HOLDING PERIOD
.400 EQUITY YIELD RATE
.750 LOAN RATIO

INTEREST RATE

TERM YEARS	APPR DEP	5.0	5.5	6.0	6.5	7.0	7.5	8.0	8.5	9.0	9.5	10.0	11.0	12.0
10	.40	.191083	.193247	.195439	.197660	.199908	.202185	.204489	.206820	.209178	.211562	.213973	.218873	.223874
	.30	.191342	.193506	.195698	.197918	.200167	.202443	.204747	.207078	.209437	.211821	.214232	.219132	.224132
	.20	.191601	.193764	.195957	.198177	.200426	.202702	.205006	.207337	.209695	.212080	.214491	.219391	.224391
	.10	.191859	.194023	.196215	.198436	.200685	.202961	.205265	.207596	.209954	.212339	.214750	.219649	.224650
	0.00	.192118	.194282	.196474	.198695	.200943	.203220	.205524	.207855	.210213	.212598	.215009	.219908	.224908
	-.10	.192377	.194541	.196733	.198954	.201202	.203479	.205782	.208114	.210472	.212856	.215267	.220167	.225168
	-.20	.192636	.194799	.196992	.199212	.201461	.203737	.206041	.208372	.210730	.213115	.215526	.220426	.225426
	-.30	.192894	.195058	.197251	.199471	.201720	.203996	.206300	.208631	.210989	.213374	.215785	.220684	.225685
	-.40	.193153	.195317	.197509	.199730	.201979	.204255	.206559	.208890	.211248	.213633	.216044	.220943	.225943
15	.40	.168195	.170561	.172971	.175424	.177919	.180455	.183033	.185651	.188308	.191004	.193738	.199318	.205039
	.30	.168454	.170820	.173230	.175682	.178177	.180714	.183291	.185909	.188567	.191263	.193997	.199576	.205298
	.20	.168713	.171079	.173489	.175941	.178436	.180973	.183550	.186168	.188826	.191522	.194256	.199835	.205557
	.10	.168972	.171338	.173747	.176200	.178695	.181231	.183809	.186427	.189084	.191781	.194515	.200094	.205815
	0.00	.169231	.171597	.174006	.176459	.178954	.181490	.184068	.186686	.189343	.192039	.194774	.200353	.206074
	-.10	.169489	.171855	.174265	.176718	.179212	.181749	.184327	.186944	.189602	.192298	.195032	.200612	.206333
	-.20	.169748	.172114	.174524	.176976	.179471	.182008	.184585	.187203	.189861	.192557	.195291	.200870	.206592
	-.30	.170007	.172373	.174783	.177235	.179730	.182267	.184844	.187462	.190119	.192816	.195550	.201129	.206851
	-.40	.170266	.172632	.175041	.177494	.179989	.182525	.185103	.187721	.190378	.193074	.195809	.201388	.207109
20	.40	.157099	.159633	.162222	.164865	.167561	.170308	.173104	.175949	.178841	.181777	.184757	.190842	.197082
	.30	.157358	.159892	.162481	.165124	.167820	.170566	.173363	.176208	.179099	.182036	.185016	.191101	.197341
	.20	.157616	.160150	.162740	.165383	.168078	.170825	.173622	.176467	.179358	.182295	.185275	.191360	.197600
	.10	.157875	.160409	.162998	.165641	.168337	.171084	.173881	.176725	.179617	.182554	.185534	.191619	.197859
	0.00	.158134	.160668	.163257	.165900	.168596	.171343	.174139	.176984	.179876	.182812	.185793	.191877	.198118
	-.10	.158393	.160927	.163516	.166159	.168855	.171602	.174398	.177243	.180134	.183071	.186051	.192136	.198376
	-.20	.158651	.161186	.163775	.166418	.169114	.171860	.174657	.177502	.180393	.183330	.186310	.192395	.198635
	-.30	.158910	.161444	.164034	.166677	.169372	.172119	.174916	.177761	.180652	.183589	.186569	.192654	.198894
	-.40	.159169	.161703	.164292	.166935	.169631	.172378	.175175	.178019	.180911	.183847	.186828	.192913	.199153
25	.40	.150707	.153390	.156137	.158947	.161816	.164741	.167722	.170755	.173837	.176967	.180142	.186615	.193239
	.30	.150966	.153649	.156396	.159206	.162074	.165000	.167981	.171014	.174096	.177226	.180400	.186874	.193498
	.20	.151224	.153908	.156655	.159464	.162333	.165259	.168240	.171272	.174355	.177485	.180659	.187133	.193757
	.10	.151483	.154166	.156913	.159723	.162592	.165518	.168498	.171531	.174614	.177744	.180918	.187391	.194015
	0.00	.151742	.154425	.157173	.159982	.162851	.165777	.168757	.171790	.174873	.178002	.181177	.187650	.194274
	-.10	.152001	.154684	.157431	.160241	.163109	.166035	.169016	.172049	.175131	.178261	.181436	.187909	.194533
	-.20	.152260	.154943	.157690	.160499	.163368	.166294	.169275	.172308	.175390	.178520	.181694	.188168	.194792
	-.30	.152518	.155202	.157949	.160758	.163627	.166553	.169534	.172566	.175649	.178779	.181953	.188427	.195050
	-.40	.152777	.155460	.158208	.161017	.163886	.166812	.169792	.172825	.175908	.179037	.182212	.188685	.195309
30	.40	.146655	.149474	.152362	.155318	.158338	.161417	.164553	.167742	.170980	.174264	.177590	.184359	.191263
	.30	.146914	.149732	.152621	.155577	.158597	.161676	.164812	.168000	.171239	.174523	.177849	.184618	.191521
	.20	.147173	.149991	.152880	.155836	.158855	.161935	.165071	.168259	.171497	.174781	.178108	.184877	.191780
	.10	.147432	.150250	.153139	.156095	.159114	.162194	.165329	.168518	.171756	.175040	.178367	.185136	.192039
	0.00	.147691	.150509	.153398	.156354	.159373	.162452	.165588	.168777	.172015	.175299	.178626	.185394	.192298
	-.10	.147949	.150768	.153656	.156612	.159632	.162711	.165847	.169036	.172274	.175558	.178884	.185653	.192556
	-.20	.148208	.151026	.153915	.156871	.159891	.162970	.166106	.169294	.172532	.175816	.179143	.185912	.192815
	-.30	.148467	.151285	.154174	.157130	.160149	.163229	.166365	.169553	.172791	.176075	.179402	.186171	.193074
	-.40	.148726	.151544	.154433	.157389	.160408	.163488	.166623	.169812	.173050	.176334	.179661	.186430	.193333

15.0 YEAR HOLDING PERIOD
.400 EQUITY YIELD RATE
.800 LOAN RATIO

INTEREST RATE

TERM YEARS	APPR DEP	5.0	5.5	6.0	6.5	7.0	7.5	8.0	8.5	9.0	9.5	10.0	11.0	12.0
10	.40	.177224	.179532	.181871	.184239	.186638	.189066	.191523	.194010	.196525	.199069	.201641	.206867	.212201
	.30	.177483	.179791	.182129	.184498	.186897	.189325	.191782	.194269	.196784	.199328	.201899	.207126	.212460
	.20	.177742	.180050	.182388	.184757	.187155	.189584	.192040	.194528	.197043	.199587	.202158	.207384	.212718
	.10	.178001	.180309	.182647	.185016	.187414	.189842	.192300	.194786	.197302	.199845	.202417	.207643	.212977
	0.00	.178259	.180567	.182906	.185274	.187673	.190101	.192559	.195045	.197560	.200104	.202676	.207902	.213236
	-.10	.178518	.180826	.183165	.185533	.187932	.190360	.192817	.195304	.197819	.200363	.202935	.208161	.213495
	-.20	.178777	.181085	.183423	.185792	.188190	.190619	.193076	.195563	.198078	.200622	.203193	.208420	.213754
	-.30	.179036	.181344	.183682	.186051	.188449	.190877	.193335	.195822	.198337	.200880	.203452	.208678	.214012
	-.40	.179294	.181602	.183941	.186310	.188708	.191136	.193594	.196080	.198596	.201139	.203711	.208937	.214271
15	.40	.152811	.155335	.157905	.160521	.163182	.165888	.168637	.171430	.174264	.177140	.180057	.186008	.192111
	.30	.153070	.155593	.158164	.160780	.163441	.166147	.168896	.171688	.174523	.177399	.180315	.186267	.192369
	.20	.153328	.155852	.158422	.161038	.163700	.166405	.169155	.171947	.174782	.177658	.180574	.186525	.192628
	.10	.153587	.156111	.158681	.161297	.163958	.166664	.169414	.172206	.175041	.177916	.180833	.186784	.192887
	0.00	.153846	.156370	.158940	.161556	.164217	.166923	.169672	.172465	.175299	.178175	.181092	.187043	.193146
	-.10	.154105	.156629	.159199	.161815	.164476	.167182	.169931	.172723	.175558	.178434	.181351	.187302	.193405
	-.20	.154363	.156887	.159458	.162074	.164735	.167440	.170190	.172982	.175817	.178693	.181609	.187561	.193663
	-.30	.154622	.157146	.159716	.162332	.164994	.167699	.170449	.173241	.176076	.178952	.181868	.187819	.193922
	-.40	.154881	.157405	.159975	.162591	.165252	.167958	.170707	.173500	.176334	.179210	.182127	.188078	.194181
20	.40	.140974	.143677	.146439	.149258	.152134	.155064	.158047	.161081	.164166	.167298	.170477	.176967	.183624
	.30	.141233	.143936	.146698	.149517	.152393	.155323	.158306	.161340	.164424	.167557	.170736	.177226	.183882
	.20	.141491	.144195	.146957	.149776	.152652	.155581	.158564	.161599	.164683	.167816	.170995	.177485	.184141
	.10	.141751	.144454	.147216	.150035	.152910	.155840	.158823	.161858	.164942	.168074	.171253	.177744	.184400
	0.00	.142009	.144712	.147474	.150294	.153169	.156099	.159082	.162116	.165201	.168333	.171512	.178003	.184659
	-.10	.142268	.144971	.147733	.150552	.153428	.156358	.159341	.162375	.165460	.168592	.171771	.178261	.184918
	-.20	.142527	.145230	.147992	.150811	.153687	.156617	.159600	.162634	.165718	.168851	.172030	.178520	.185176
	-.30	.142786	.145489	.148251	.151070	.153945	.156875	.159858	.162893	.165977	.169110	.172288	.178779	.185435
	-.40	.143045	.145748	.148509	.151329	.154204	.157134	.160117	.163152	.166236	.169368	.172547	.179038	.185694
25	.40	.134156	.137018	.139949	.142946	.146006	.149127	.152306	.155541	.158829	.162167	.165553	.172458	.179524
	.30	.134415	.137277	.140208	.143204	.146264	.149385	.152565	.155808	.159088	.162426	.165812	.172717	.179783
	.20	.134674	.137536	.140467	.143463	.146523	.149644	.152823	.156058	.159347	.162685	.166071	.172976	.180041
	.10	.134933	.137795	.140725	.143722	.146782	.149903	.153082	.156317	.159605	.162944	.166330	.173235	.180300
	0.00	.135191	.138054	.140984	.143981	.147041	.150162	.153341	.156576	.159864	.163202	.166589	.173494	.180559
	-.10	.135450	.138312	.141243	.144239	.147300	.150421	.153600	.156834	.160123	.163461	.166847	.173752	.180818
	-.20	.135709	.138571	.141502	.144498	.147558	.150679	.153859	.157094	.160382	.163720	.167106	.174011	.181077
	-.30	.135968	.138830	.141760	.144757	.147817	.150938	.154117	.157352	.160640	.163979	.167365	.174270	.181335
	-.40	.136227	.139089	.142019	.145016	.148076	.151197	.154376	.157611	.160899	.164238	.167624	.174529	.181594
30	.40	.129835	.132841	.135922	.139075	.142296	.145581	.148926	.152327	.155781	.159284	.162832	.170052	.177416
	.30	.130094	.133100	.136181	.139334	.142555	.145839	.149184	.152586	.156039	.159542	.163091	.170311	.177675
	.20	.130352	.133359	.136440	.139593	.142814	.146098	.149443	.152844	.156298	.159801	.163350	.170570	.177933
	.10	.130611	.133617	.136699	.139852	.143072	.146357	.149702	.153103	.156557	.160060	.163608	.170829	.178192
	0.00	.130870	.133876	.136958	.140110	.143331	.146616	.149961	.153362	.156816	.160319	.163867	.171087	.178451
	-.10	.131129	.134135	.137216	.140369	.143590	.146875	.150219	.153621	.157075	.160578	.164126	.171346	.178710
	-.20	.131388	.134394	.137475	.140628	.143849	.147133	.150478	.153880	.157333	.160836	.164385	.171605	.178968
	-.30	.131646	.134652	.137734	.140887	.144108	.147392	.150737	.154138	.157592	.161095	.164644	.171864	.179227
	-.40	.131905	.134911	.137993	.141146	.144366	.147651	.150996	.154397	.157851	.161354	.164902	.172123	.179486

15.0 YEAR HOLDING PERIOD
.400 EQUITY YIELD RATE
.900 LOAN RATIO

INTEREST RATE

TERM YEARS	APPR DEP	5.0	5.5	6.0	6.5	7.0	7.5	8.0	8.5	9.0	9.5	10.0	11.0	12.0
10	.40	.149507	.152103	.154734	.157399	.160097	.162829	.165593	.168391	.171220	.174082	.176975	.182855	.188855
	.30	.149765	.152362	.154993	.157657	.160356	.163087	.165852	.168649	.171479	.174341	.177234	.183113	.189014
	.20	.150024	.152621	.155251	.157916	.160616	.163346	.166111	.168908	.171738	.174600	.177493	.183372	.189373
	.10	.150283	.152879	.155510	.158175	.160873	.163605	.166370	.169167	.171997	.174858	.177752	.183631	.189632
	0.00	.150542	.153138	.155769	.158434	.161132	.163864	.166628	.169426	.172255	.175117	.178010	.183890	.189891
	-.10	.150800	.153397	.156028	.158692	.161391	.164123	.166887	.169685	.172514	.175376	.178269	.184149	.190149
	-.20	.151059	.153656	.156287	.158951	.161650	.164381	.167146	.169943	.172773	.175635	.178528	.184407	.190408
	-.30	.151318	.153915	.156545	.159210	.161908	.164640	.167405	.170202	.173032	.175893	.178787	.184666	.190667
	-.40	.151577	.154173	.156804	.159469	.162167	.164899	.167664	.170461	.173291	.176152	.179045	.184925	.190926
15	.40	.122041	.124881	.127772	.130715	.133709	.136753	.139846	.142988	.146177	.149412	.152693	.159388	.166254
	.30	.122300	.125140	.128031	.130974	.133968	.137012	.140105	.143246	.146435	.149671	.152952	.159647	.166513
	.20	.122559	.125398	.128290	.131233	.134227	.137271	.140364	.143505	.146694	.149930	.153211	.159906	.166772
	.10	.122818	.125657	.128549	.131492	.134486	.137529	.140623	.143764	.146953	.150188	.153469	.160165	.167030
	0.00	.123077	.125916	.128807	.131751	.134744	.137788	.140881	.144023	.147212	.150447	.153728	.160423	.167289
	-.10	.123335	.126175	.129066	.132010	.135003	.138047	.141140	.144282	.147471	.150706	.153987	.160682	.167548
	-.20	.123594	.126434	.129325	.132268	.135262	.138306	.141399	.144540	.147729	.150965	.154246	.160941	.167807
	-.30	.123853	.126692	.129584	.132527	.135521	.138565	.141658	.144799	.147988	.151224	.154505	.161200	.168065
	-.40	.124112	.126951	.129843	.132786	.135780	.138823	.141916	.145058	.148247	.151482	.154763	.161459	.168324
20	.40	.108726	.111766	.114873	.118045	.121280	.124576	.127932	.131346	.134816	.138340	.141916	.149218	.156706
	.30	.108984	.112025	.115132	.118304	.121539	.124835	.128191	.131604	.135074	.138598	.142175	.149477	.156965
	.20	.109243	.112284	.115391	.118563	.121798	.125094	.128450	.131863	.135333	.138857	.142434	.149735	.157224
	.10	.109502	.112543	.115650	.118822	.122056	.125353	.128708	.132122	.135592	.139116	.142692	.149994	.157482
	0.00	.109761	.112802	.115909	.119080	.122315	.125611	.128967	.132381	.135851	.139375	.142951	.150253	.157741
	-.10	.110019	.113060	.116167	.119339	.122574	.125870	.129226	.132640	.136110	.139634	.143210	.150512	.158000
	-.20	.110278	.113319	.116426	.119598	.122833	.126129	.129485	.132899	.136368	.139892	.143469	.150771	.158259
	-.30	.110537	.113578	.116685	.119857	.123091	.126388	.129744	.133157	.136627	.140151	.143727	.151029	.158517
	-.40	.110796	.113837	.116944	.120115	.123350	.126647	.130002	.133416	.136886	.140410	.143986	.151288	.158776
25	.40	.101055	.104275	.107572	.110943	.114386	.117897	.121474	.125113	.128812	.132568	.136377	.144145	.152094
	.30	.101314	.104534	.107831	.111202	.114644	.118156	.121732	.125372	.129071	.132826	.136636	.144404	.152353
	.20	.101573	.104793	.108090	.111461	.114903	.118414	.121991	.125631	.129330	.133085	.136895	.144663	.152611
	.10	.101832	.105051	.108348	.111719	.115162	.118673	.122250	.125889	.129588	.133344	.137153	.144922	.152870
	0.00	.102090	.105310	.108607	.111978	.115421	.118932	.122509	.126148	.129847	.133603	.137412	.145180	.153129
	-.10	.102349	.105569	.108866	.112237	.115680	.119191	.122767	.126407	.130106	.133862	.137671	.145439	.153388
	-.20	.102608	.105828	.109125	.112496	.115938	.119450	.123026	.126666	.130365	.134120	.137930	.145698	.153646
	-.30	.102867	.106087	.109384	.112755	.116197	.119708	.123285	.126924	.130623	.134379	.138188	.145957	.153905
	-.40	.103125	.106345	.109642	.113013	.116456	.119967	.123544	.127183	.130882	.134638	.138447	.146215	.154164
30	.40	.096194	.099575	.103042	.106589	.110212	.113908	.117671	.121497	.125383	.129324	.133316	.141438	.149722
	.30	.096452	.099834	.103301	.106848	.110471	.114166	.117929	.121756	.125641	.129582	.133574	.141697	.149981
	.20	.096711	.100093	.103560	.107107	.110730	.114425	.118188	.122015	.125900	.129841	.133833	.141956	.150240
	.10	.096970	.100352	.103818	.107365	.110989	.114684	.118447	.122274	.126159	.130100	.134092	.142215	.150499
	0.00	.097229	.100611	.104077	.107624	.111248	.114943	.118706	.122532	.126418	.130359	.134351	.142473	.150757
	-.10	.097488	.100869	.104336	.107883	.111506	.115202	.118965	.122791	.126677	.130617	.134609	.142732	.151016
	-.20	.097746	.101128	.104595	.108142	.111765	.115460	.119223	.123050	.126935	.130876	.134868	.142991	.151275
	-.30	.098005	.101387	.104854	.108401	.112024	.115719	.119482	.123309	.127194	.131135	.135127	.143250	.151534
	-.40	.098264	.101646	.105112	.108659	.112283	.115978	.119741	.123567	.127453	.131394	.135386	.143508	.151792

15.0 YEAR HOLDING PERIOD
.500 EQUITY YIELD RATE
.600 LOAN RATIO

INTEREST RATE

TERM YEARS	APPR DEP	5.0	5.5	6.0	6.5	7.0	7.5	8.0	8.5	9.0	9.5	10.0	11.0	12.0
10	.40	.274727	.276481	.278258	.280059	.281883	.283730	.285599	.287491	.289406	.291343	.293301	.297283	.301350
	.30	.274842	.276596	.278373	.280174	.281997	.283844	.285714	.287606	.289520	.291457	.293416	.297398	.301465
	.20	.274956	.276710	.278487	.280288	.282112	.283959	.285828	.287720	.289635	.291572	.293530	.297512	.301579
	.10	.275071	.276825	.278602	.280402	.282226	.284073	.285943	.287835	.289749	.291686	.293645	.297627	.301693
	0.00	.275185	.276939	.278716	.280517	.282341	.284187	.286057	.287949	.289864	.291801	.293759	.297741	.301808
	-.10	.275300	.277053	.278831	.280631	.282455	.284302	.286172	.288064	.289978	.291915	.293874	.297856	.301922
	-.20	.275414	.277168	.278945	.280746	.282570	.284416	.286286	.288178	.290093	.292029	.293988	.297970	.302037
	-.30	.275529	.277282	.279060	.280860	.282684	.284531	.286400	.288293	.290207	.292144	.294103	.298085	.302151
	-.40	.275643	.277397	.279174	.280975	.282798	.284645	.286515	.288407	.290322	.292258	.294217	.298199	.302266
15	.40	.255793	.257686	.259613	.261575	.263571	.265600	.267663	.269757	.271883	.274040	.276227	.280691	.285268
	.30	.255907	.257800	.259728	.261690	.263686	.265715	.267777	.269871	.271997	.274154	.276342	.280805	.285382
	.20	.256022	.257914	.259842	.261804	.263800	.265829	.267891	.269986	.272112	.274269	.276456	.280919	.285497
	.10	.256136	.258029	.259957	.261919	.263915	.265944	.268006	.270100	.272226	.274383	.276570	.281034	.285611
	0.00	.256250	.258143	.260071	.262033	.264029	.266058	.268120	.270215	.272341	.274498	.276685	.281148	.285725
	-.10	.256365	.258258	.260185	.262148	.264143	.266173	.268235	.270329	.272455	.274612	.276799	.281263	.285840
	-.20	.256479	.258372	.260300	.262262	.264258	.266287	.268349	.270443	.272569	.274726	.276914	.281377	.285954
	-.30	.256594	.258487	.260414	.262376	.264372	.266402	.268464	.270558	.272684	.274841	.277028	.281492	.286069
	-.40	.256708	.258601	.260529	.262491	.264487	.266516	.268578	.270672	.272798	.274955	.277143	.281606	.286183
20	.40	.246613	.248631	.250693	.252798	.254946	.257134	.259363	.261629	.263933	.266274	.268649	.273499	.278474
	.30	.246727	.248745	.250808	.252913	.255060	.257249	.259477	.261744	.264048	.266388	.268763	.273614	.278588
	.20	.246841	.248860	.250922	.253027	.255175	.257363	.259591	.261858	.264162	.266503	.268878	.273728	.278703
	.10	.246956	.248974	.251036	.253142	.255289	.257478	.259706	.261973	.264277	.266617	.268992	.273842	.278817
	0.00	.247070	.249089	.251151	.253256	.255404	.257592	.259820	.262087	.264391	.266732	.269107	.273957	.278931
	-.10	.247185	.249203	.251265	.253371	.255518	.257707	.259935	.262202	.264506	.266846	.269221	.274071	.279046
	-.20	.247299	.249317	.251380	.253485	.255633	.257821	.260049	.262316	.264620	.266960	.269336	.274186	.279160
	-.30	.247414	.249432	.251494	.253600	.255747	.257935	.260164	.262430	.264735	.267075	.269450	.274300	.279275
	-.40	.247528	.249546	.251609	.253714	.255861	.258050	.260278	.262545	.264849	.267189	.269565	.274415	.279389
25	.40	.241325	.243458	.245644	.247879	.250162	.252490	.254863	.257278	.259733	.262225	.264754	.269912	.275192
	.30	.241439	.243573	.245758	.247993	.250276	.252605	.254978	.257392	.259847	.262340	.264869	.270027	.275306
	.20	.241553	.243687	.245873	.248108	.250391	.252719	.255092	.257507	.259961	.262454	.264983	.270141	.275421
	.10	.241668	.243802	.245987	.248222	.250505	.252834	.255206	.257621	.260076	.262569	.265098	.270256	.275535
	0.00	.241782	.243916	.246102	.248337	.250619	.252948	.255321	.257736	.260190	.262683	.265212	.270370	.275650
	-.10	.241897	.244031	.246216	.248451	.250734	.253063	.255435	.257850	.260305	.262798	.265326	.270484	.275764
	-.20	.242011	.244145	.246330	.248566	.250848	.253177	.255550	.257965	.260419	.262912	.265441	.270599	.275878
	-.30	.242126	.244260	.246445	.248680	.250963	.253292	.255664	.258079	.260534	.263026	.265555	.270713	.275993
	-.40	.242240	.244374	.246559	.248794	.251077	.253406	.255779	.258193	.260648	.263141	.265670	.270828	.276107
30	.40	.237973	.240214	.242511	.244863	.247266	.249717	.252214	.254753	.257333	.259950	.262601	.267998	.273504
	.30	.238087	.240328	.242626	.244977	.247380	.249831	.252328	.254868	.257448	.260064	.262716	.268113	.273619
	.20	.238202	.240442	.242740	.245092	.247494	.249946	.252443	.254982	.257562	.260179	.262830	.268227	.273733
	.10	.238316	.240557	.242854	.245206	.247609	.250060	.252557	.255097	.257676	.260293	.262945	.268342	.273848
	0.00	.238431	.240671	.242969	.245320	.247723	.250175	.252672	.255211	.257791	.260408	.263059	.268456	.273962
	-.10	.238545	.240786	.243083	.245435	.247838	.250289	.252786	.255326	.257905	.260522	.263174	.268570	.274076
	-.20	.238660	.240900	.243198	.245549	.247952	.250404	.252901	.255440	.258020	.260637	.263288	.268685	.274191
	-.30	.238774	.241015	.243312	.245664	.248067	.250518	.253015	.255555	.258134	.260751	.263403	.268799	.274305
	-.40	.238888	.241129	.243427	.245778	.248181	.250632	.253129	.255669	.258249	.260866	.263517	.268914	.274420

366

15.0 YEAR HOLDING PERIOD
.500 EQUITY YIELD RATE
.667 LOAN RATIO

INTEREST RATE

TERM YEARS	APPR DEP	5.0	5.5	6.0	6.5	7.0	7.5	8.0	8.5	9.0	9.5	10.0	11.0	12.0
10	.40	.249747	.251695	.253670	.255671	.257697	.259749	.261827	.263929	.266056	.268208	.270385	.274809	.279328
	.30	.249861	.251810	.253785	.255785	.257812	.259864	.261941	.264044	.266171	.268323	.270499	.274924	.279442
	.20	.249976	.251924	.253899	.255900	.257926	.259978	.262056	.264158	.266285	.268437	.270613	.275038	.279556
	.10	.250090	.252039	.254013	.256014	.258041	.260093	.262170	.264272	.266400	.268552	.270728	.275152	.279671
	0.00	.250205	.252153	.254128	.256129	.258155	.260207	.262284	.264387	.266514	.268666	.270842	.275267	.279785
	-.10	.250319	.252268	.254242	.256243	.258270	.260322	.262399	.264501	.266629	.268781	.270957	.275381	.279900
	-.20	.250433	.252382	.254357	.256357	.258384	.260436	.262513	.264616	.266743	.268895	.271071	.275496	.280014
	-.30	.250548	.252496	.254471	.256472	.258498	.260550	.262628	.264730	.266858	.269009	.271186	.275610	.280129
	-.40	.250662	.252611	.254586	.256586	.258613	.260665	.262742	.264845	.266972	.269124	.271300	.275725	.280243
15	.40	.228708	.230811	.232953	.235133	.237351	.239606	.241897	.244224	.246586	.248983	.251413	.256372	.261458
	.30	.228823	.230926	.233068	.235248	.237465	.239720	.242011	.244338	.246700	.249097	.251528	.256487	.261573
	.20	.228937	.231040	.233182	.235362	.237580	.239835	.242126	.244453	.246815	.249212	.251642	.256601	.261687
	.10	.229051	.231155	.233296	.235477	.237694	.239949	.242240	.244567	.246929	.249326	.251756	.256716	.261802
	0.00	.229166	.231269	.233411	.235591	.237809	.240063	.242355	.244682	.247044	.249440	.251871	.256830	.261916
	-.10	.229280	.231383	.233525	.235705	.237923	.240178	.242469	.244796	.247158	.249555	.251985	.256945	.262030
	-.20	.229395	.231498	.233640	.235820	.238038	.240292	.242583	.244910	.247273	.249669	.252100	.257059	.262145
	-.30	.229509	.231612	.233754	.235934	.238152	.240407	.242698	.245025	.247387	.249784	.252214	.257174	.262259
	-.40	.229624	.231727	.233869	.236049	.238266	.240521	.242812	.245139	.247502	.249898	.252329	.257288	.262374
20	.40	.218508	.220750	.223041	.225381	.227767	.230199	.232675	.235193	.237753	.240354	.242993	.248382	.253909
	.30	.218622	.220865	.223156	.225496	.227882	.230313	.232789	.235308	.237868	.240468	.243107	.248496	.254024
	.20	.218737	.220979	.223271	.225610	.227996	.230428	.232903	.235422	.237982	.240583	.243222	.248611	.254138
	.10	.218851	.221094	.223385	.225724	.228111	.230542	.233018	.235537	.238097	.240697	.243336	.248725	.254253
	0.00	.218966	.221208	.223500	.225839	.228225	.230657	.233132	.235651	.238211	.240812	.243451	.248840	.254367
	-.10	.219080	.221323	.223614	.225953	.228339	.230771	.233247	.235765	.238326	.240926	.243565	.248954	.254481
	-.20	.219194	.221437	.223728	.226068	.228454	.230885	.233361	.235880	.238440	.241040	.243680	.249069	.254596
	-.30	.219309	.221551	.223843	.226182	.228568	.231000	.233476	.235994	.238554	.241155	.243794	.249183	.254710
	-.40	.219423	.221666	.223957	.226297	.228683	.231114	.233590	.236109	.238669	.241269	.243908	.249298	.254825
25	.40	.212632	.215003	.217431	.219915	.222451	.225039	.227675	.230358	.233086	.235855	.238665	.244397	.250263
	.30	.212747	.215118	.217546	.220029	.222566	.225153	.227790	.230473	.233200	.235970	.238780	.244511	.250377
	.20	.212861	.215232	.217660	.220144	.222680	.225268	.227904	.230587	.233315	.236084	.238894	.244625	.250492
	.10	.212976	.215347	.217775	.220258	.222795	.225382	.228019	.230702	.233429	.236199	.239009	.244740	.250606
	0.00	.213090	.215461	.217889	.220373	.222909	.225497	.228133	.230816	.233544	.236313	.239123	.244854	.250720
	-.10	.213204	.215575	.218004	.220487	.223024	.225611	.228247	.230930	.233658	.236428	.239238	.244969	.250835
	-.20	.213319	.215690	.218118	.220601	.223138	.225726	.228362	.231045	.233772	.236542	.239352	.245083	.250949
	-.30	.213433	.215804	.218232	.220716	.223253	.225840	.228476	.231159	.233887	.236657	.239466	.245198	.251064
	-.40	.213548	.215919	.218347	.220830	.223367	.225954	.228591	.231274	.234001	.236771	.239581	.245312	.251178
30	.40	.208908	.211398	.213951	.216564	.219233	.221957	.224732	.227553	.230420	.233327	.236273	.242270	.248388
	.30	.209023	.211512	.214065	.216678	.219348	.222072	.224846	.227668	.230534	.233442	.236388	.242384	.248502
	.20	.209137	.211627	.214180	.216792	.219462	.222186	.224960	.227782	.230649	.233556	.236502	.242499	.248616
	.10	.209251	.211741	.214294	.216907	.219577	.222301	.225075	.227897	.230763	.233671	.236617	.242613	.248731
	0.00	.209366	.211856	.214408	.217021	.219691	.222415	.225189	.228011	.230877	.233785	.236731	.242728	.248845
	-.10	.209480	.211970	.214523	.217136	.219806	.222529	.225304	.228126	.230992	.233900	.236846	.242842	.248960
	-.20	.209595	.212084	.214637	.217250	.219920	.222644	.225418	.228240	.231106	.234014	.236960	.242956	.249074
	-.30	.209709	.212199	.214752	.217365	.220035	.222758	.225533	.228354	.231221	.234128	.237075	.243071	.249189
	-.40	.209824	.212313	.214866	.217479	.220149	.222873	.225647	.228469	.231335	.234243	.237189	.243185	.249303

15.0 YEAR HOLDING PERIOD
.500 EQUITY YIELD RATE
.700 LOAN RATIO

INTEREST RATE

TERM YEARS	APPR DEP	5.0	5.5	6.0	6.5	7.0	7.5	8.0	8.5	9.0	9.5	10.0	11.0	12.0
10	.40	.237258	.239304	.241378	.243479	.245606	.247761	.249942	.252150	.254383	.256643	.258928	.263574	.268318
	.30	.237373	.239419	.241492	.243593	.245721	.247875	.250057	.252264	.254498	.256757	.259042	.263688	.268432
	.20	.237487	.239533	.241607	.243707	.245835	.247990	.250171	.252379	.254612	.256872	.259157	.263803	.268547
	.10	.237602	.239648	.241721	.243822	.245950	.248104	.250285	.252493	.254727	.256986	.259271	.263917	.268661
	0.00	.237716	.239762	.241836	.243936	.246064	.248219	.250400	.252607	.254841	.257101	.259386	.264031	.268776
	-.10	.237831	.239877	.241950	.244051	.246179	.248333	.250514	.252722	.254956	.257215	.259500	.264146	.268890
	-.20	.237945	.239991	.242064	.244165	.246293	.248448	.250629	.252836	.255070	.257330	.259615	.264260	.269005
	-.30	.238059	.240105	.242179	.244280	.246407	.248562	.250743	.252951	.255184	.257444	.259729	.264375	.269119
	-.40	.238174	.240220	.242293	.244394	.246522	.248676	.250858	.253065	.255299	.257558	.259843	.264489	.269234
15	.40	.215168	.217376	.219625	.221914	.224243	.226610	.229016	.231459	.233940	.236456	.239008	.244215	.249555
	.30	.215282	.217491	.219740	.222029	.224357	.226725	.229130	.231574	.234054	.236570	.239122	.244330	.249670
	.20	.215397	.217605	.219854	.222143	.224472	.226839	.229245	.231688	.234168	.236685	.239237	.244444	.249784
	.10	.215511	.217719	.219968	.222257	.224586	.226953	.229359	.231803	.234283	.236799	.239351	.244559	.249899
	0.00	.215626	.217834	.220083	.222372	.224700	.227068	.229474	.231917	.234397	.236914	.239466	.244673	.250013
	-.10	.215740	.217948	.220197	.222486	.224815	.227182	.229588	.232031	.234512	.237028	.239580	.244787	.250127
	-.20	.215854	.218063	.220312	.222601	.224929	.227297	.229703	.232146	.234626	.237143	.239695	.244902	.250242
	-.30	.215969	.218177	.220426	.222715	.225044	.227411	.229817	.232260	.234741	.237257	.239809	.245016	.250356
	-.40	.216083	.218292	.220541	.222830	.225158	.227526	.229931	.232375	.234855	.237372	.239923	.245131	.250471
20	.40	.204458	.206812	.209218	.211675	.214180	.216733	.219333	.221977	.224665	.227396	.230167	.235825	.241629
	.30	.204572	.206927	.209333	.211789	.214294	.216847	.219447	.222092	.224780	.227510	.230281	.235940	.241743
	.20	.204686	.207041	.209447	.211903	.214409	.216962	.219561	.222206	.224894	.227625	.230396	.236054	.241858
	.10	.204801	.207155	.209562	.212018	.214523	.217076	.219676	.222320	.225009	.227739	.230510	.236169	.241972
	0.00	.204915	.207270	.209676	.212132	.214638	.217191	.219790	.222435	.225123	.227853	.230625	.236283	.242087
	-.10	.205030	.207384	.209790	.212247	.214752	.217305	.219905	.222549	.225238	.227968	.230739	.236397	.242201
	-.20	.205144	.207499	.209905	.212361	.214867	.217420	.220019	.222664	.225352	.228082	.230853	.236512	.242316
	-.30	.205259	.207613	.210019	.212476	.214981	.217534	.220134	.222778	.225466	.228197	.230968	.236626	.242430
	-.40	.205373	.207728	.210134	.212590	.215095	.217649	.220248	.222893	.225581	.228311	.231082	.236741	.242544
25	.40	.198288	.200778	.203327	.205935	.208598	.211315	.214083	.216900	.219764	.222673	.225623	.231641	.237800
	.30	.198403	.200892	.203442	.206049	.208713	.211430	.214198	.217015	.219879	.222787	.225737	.231755	.237914
	.20	.198517	.201007	.203556	.206164	.208827	.211544	.214312	.217129	.219993	.222901	.225852	.231870	.238029
	.10	.198632	.201121	.203671	.206278	.208942	.211658	.214427	.217244	.220108	.223016	.225966	.231984	.238143
	0.00	.198746	.201236	.203785	.206393	.209056	.211773	.214541	.217358	.220222	.223130	.226081	.232098	.238258
	-.10	.198860	.201350	.203900	.206507	.209170	.211887	.214656	.217473	.220337	.223245	.226195	.232213	.238372
	-.20	.198975	.201464	.204014	.206622	.209285	.212002	.214770	.217587	.220451	.223359	.226310	.232327	.238487
	-.30	.199089	.201579	.204128	.206736	.209399	.212116	.214884	.217702	.220565	.223474	.226424	.232442	.238601
	-.40	.199204	.201693	.204243	.206850	.209514	.212231	.214999	.217816	.220680	.223588	.226538	.232556	.238716
30	.40	.194378	.196996	.199673	.202416	.205219	.208079	.210992	.213955	.216965	.220018	.223111	.229408	.235831
	.30	.194492	.197107	.199787	.202531	.205334	.208194	.211107	.214070	.217079	.220132	.223226	.229522	.235946
	.20	.194607	.197221	.199901	.202645	.205448	.208308	.211221	.214184	.217194	.220247	.223340	.229636	.236060
	.10	.194721	.197335	.200016	.202759	.205563	.208423	.211336	.214299	.217308	.220361	.223455	.229751	.236175
	0.00	.194836	.197450	.200130	.202874	.205677	.208537	.211450	.214413	.217423	.220476	.223569	.229865	.236289
	-.10	.194950	.197564	.200245	.202988	.205792	.208652	.211565	.214528	.217537	.220590	.223684	.229980	.236403
	-.20	.195065	.197679	.200359	.203103	.205906	.208766	.211679	.214642	.217652	.220705	.223798	.230094	.236518
	-.30	.195179	.197793	.200474	.203217	.206021	.208880	.211794	.214756	.217766	.220819	.223912	.230209	.236632
	-.40	.195294	.197908	.200588	.203332	.206135	.208995	.211908	.214871	.217880	.220934	.224027	.230323	.236747

15.0 YEAR HOLDING PERIOD
.500 EQUITY YIELD RATE
.750 LOAN RATIO

INTEREST RATE

TERM YEARS	APPR DEP	5.0	5.5	6.0	6.5	7.0	7.5	8.0	8.5	9.0	9.5	10.0	11.0	12.0
10	.40	.218524	.220716	.222937	.225188	.227468	.229777	.232114	.234479	.236872	.239293	.241741	.246719	.251802
	.30	.218638	.220830	.223052	.225303	.227582	.229891	.232228	.234593	.236986	.239407	.241856	.246833	.251916
	.20	.218753	.220945	.223166	.225417	.227697	.230005	.232342	.234708	.237101	.239522	.241970	.246948	.252031
	.10	.218867	.221059	.223281	.225532	.227811	.230120	.232457	.234822	.237215	.239636	.242085	.247062	.252145
	0.00	.218982	.221174	.223395	.225646	.227926	.230234	.232571	.234937	.237330	.239751	.242199	.247176	.252260
	-.10	.219096	.221288	.223510	.225760	.228040	.230349	.232686	.235051	.237444	.239865	.242313	.247291	.252374
	-.20	.219210	.221403	.223624	.225875	.228155	.230463	.232800	.235165	.237559	.239980	.242428	.247405	.252489
	-.30	.219325	.221517	.223739	.225989	.228269	.230578	.232915	.235280	.237673	.240094	.242542	.247520	.252603
	-.40	.219439	.221631	.223853	.226104	.228384	.230692	.233029	.235394	.237788	.240208	.242657	.247634	.252718
15	.40	.194855	.197221	.199631	.202084	.204578	.207115	.209693	.212310	.214968	.217664	.220398	.225978	.231699
	.30	.194970	.197336	.199745	.202198	.204693	.207229	.209807	.212425	.215082	.217779	.220513	.226092	.231813
	.20	.195084	.197450	.199860	.202312	.204807	.207344	.209921	.212539	.215197	.217893	.220627	.226207	.231928
	.10	.195199	.197565	.199974	.202427	.204922	.207458	.210036	.212654	.215311	.218007	.220742	.226321	.232042
	0.00	.195313	.197679	.200089	.202541	.205036	.207573	.210150	.212768	.215426	.218122	.220856	.226435	.232157
	-.10	.195428	.197794	.200203	.202656	.205151	.207687	.210265	.212883	.215540	.218236	.220971	.226550	.232271
	-.20	.195542	.197908	.200318	.202770	.205265	.207802	.210379	.212997	.215655	.218351	.221085	.226664	.232386
	-.30	.195656	.198023	.200432	.202885	.205380	.207916	.210494	.213112	.215769	.218465	.221199	.226779	.232500
	-.40	.195771	.198137	.200547	.202999	.205494	.208031	.210608	.213226	.215883	.218580	.221314	.226893	.232615
20	.40	.183380	.185903	.188481	.191113	.193797	.196532	.199318	.202151	.205031	.207957	.210926	.216988	.223207
	.30	.183495	.186017	.188595	.191227	.193911	.196647	.199432	.202265	.205146	.208071	.211040	.217103	.223321
	.20	.183609	.186132	.188710	.191341	.194026	.196761	.199546	.202380	.205260	.208186	.211155	.217217	.223435
	.10	.183723	.186246	.188824	.191456	.194140	.196876	.199661	.202494	.205375	.208300	.211269	.217332	.223550
	0.00	.183838	.186361	.188939	.191570	.194255	.196990	.199775	.202609	.205489	.208414	.211383	.217446	.223664
	-.10	.183952	.186475	.189053	.191685	.194369	.197105	.199890	.202723	.205603	.208529	.211498	.217561	.223779
	-.20	.184067	.186590	.189167	.191799	.194484	.197219	.200004	.202838	.205718	.208643	.211612	.217675	.223893
	-.30	.184181	.186704	.189282	.191914	.194598	.197333	.200119	.202952	.205832	.208758	.211727	.217789	.224008
	-.40	.184296	.186818	.189396	.192028	.194712	.197448	.200233	.203067	.205947	.208872	.211841	.217904	.224122
25	.40	.176770	.179437	.182169	.184963	.187817	.190727	.193693	.196712	.199780	.202896	.206057	.212505	.219104
	.30	.176885	.179552	.182284	.185077	.187931	.190842	.193808	.196826	.199895	.203011	.206172	.212619	.219219
	.20	.176999	.179666	.182398	.185192	.188045	.190956	.193922	.196941	.200009	.203125	.206286	.212734	.219333
	.10	.177113	.179781	.182512	.185306	.188160	.191071	.194037	.197055	.200124	.203239	.206401	.212848	.219448
	0.00	.177228	.179895	.182627	.185421	.188274	.191185	.194151	.197170	.200238	.203354	.206515	.212963	.219562
	-.10	.177342	.180010	.182741	.185535	.188389	.191300	.194266	.197284	.200352	.203468	.206629	.213077	.219676
	-.20	.177457	.180124	.182856	.185650	.188503	.191414	.194380	.197398	.200467	.203583	.206744	.213191	.219791
	-.30	.177571	.180239	.182970	.185764	.188618	.191529	.194494	.197513	.200581	.203697	.206858	.213306	.219905
	-.40	.177686	.180353	.183085	.185878	.188732	.191643	.194609	.197627	.200696	.203812	.206973	.213420	.220020
30	.40	.172581	.175381	.178253	.181193	.184196	.187261	.190382	.193556	.196781	.200052	.203366	.210112	.216995
	.30	.172695	.175496	.178368	.181307	.184311	.187375	.190496	.193671	.196895	.200166	.203481	.210227	.217109
	.20	.172809	.175610	.178482	.181422	.184425	.187489	.190611	.193785	.197010	.200281	.203595	.210341	.217224
	.10	.172924	.175725	.178597	.181536	.184540	.187604	.190725	.193900	.197124	.200395	.203710	.210456	.217338
	0.00	.173038	.175839	.178711	.181651	.184654	.187718	.190840	.194014	.197239	.200510	.203824	.210570	.217452
	-.10	.173153	.175954	.178825	.181765	.184769	.187833	.190954	.194129	.197353	.200624	.203939	.210684	.217567
	-.20	.173267	.176068	.178940	.181879	.184883	.187947	.191068	.194243	.197468	.200739	.204053	.210799	.217681
	-.30	.173382	.176182	.179054	.181994	.184998	.188062	.191183	.194357	.197582	.200853	.204167	.210913	.217796
	-.40	.173496	.176297	.179169	.182108	.185112	.188176	.191297	.194472	.197696	.200967	.204282	.211028	.217910

15.0 YEAR HOLDING PERIOD
.500 EQUITY YIELD RATE
.800 LOAN RATIO

INTEREST RATE

TERM YEARS	APPR DEP	5.0	5.5	6.0	6.5	7.0	7.5	8.0	8.5	9.0	9.5	10.0	11.0	12.0
10	.40	.199789	.202127	.204497	.206898	.209330	.211792	.214285	.216808	.219361	.221943	.224554	.229864	.235286
	.30	.199904	.202242	.204612	.207012	.209444	.211907	.214399	.216922	.219475	.222057	.224669	.229978	.235400
	.20	.200018	.202356	.204726	.207127	.209559	.212021	.214514	.217037	.219590	.222172	.224783	.230093	.235515
	.10	.200132	.202471	.204841	.207241	.209673	.212135	.214628	.217151	.219704	.222286	.224898	.230207	.235629
	0.00	.200247	.202585	.204955	.207356	.209788	.212250	.214743	.217266	.219818	.222401	.225012	.230322	.235744
	-.10	.200361	.202700	.205069	.207470	.209902	.212364	.214857	.217380	.219933	.222515	.225127	.230436	.235858
	-.20	.200476	.202814	.205184	.207585	.210016	.212479	.214972	.217495	.220047	.222630	.225241	.230550	.235973
	-.30	.200590	.202929	.205298	.207699	.210131	.212593	.215086	.217609	.220162	.222744	.225356	.230665	.236087
	-.40	.200705	.203043	.205413	.207814	.210245	.212708	.215201	.217723	.220276	.222859	.225470	.230779	.236202
15	.40	.174543	.177067	.179637	.182253	.184914	.187620	.190369	.193162	.195996	.198872	.201789	.207740	.213843
	.30	.174657	.177181	.179751	.182367	.185029	.187734	.190484	.193276	.196111	.198987	.201903	.207854	.213957
	.20	.174772	.177296	.179866	.182482	.185143	.187849	.190598	.193391	.196225	.199101	.202018	.207969	.214072
	.10	.174886	.177410	.179980	.182596	.185258	.187963	.190713	.193505	.196340	.199216	.202132	.208083	.214186
	0.00	.175001	.177524	.180095	.182711	.185372	.188078	.190827	.193619	.196454	.199330	.202247	.208198	.214301
	-.10	.175115	.177639	.180209	.182825	.185486	.188192	.190941	.193734	.196568	.199444	.202361	.208312	.214415
	-.20	.175230	.177753	.180324	.182940	.185601	.188307	.191056	.193848	.196683	.199559	.202475	.208427	.214529
	-.30	.175344	.177868	.180438	.183054	.185715	.188421	.191170	.193963	.196797	.199673	.202590	.208541	.214644
	-.40	.175458	.177982	.180552	.183169	.185830	.188535	.191285	.194077	.196912	.199788	.202704	.208656	.214758
20	.40	.162303	.164994	.167743	.170551	.173414	.176332	.179303	.182325	.185397	.188518	.191685	.198151	.204784
	.30	.162417	.165108	.167858	.170665	.173528	.176446	.179417	.182439	.185512	.188632	.191799	.198266	.204899
	.20	.162531	.165222	.167972	.170779	.173643	.176561	.179531	.182554	.185626	.188747	.191913	.198380	.205013
	.10	.162646	.165337	.168087	.170894	.173757	.176675	.179646	.182668	.185741	.188861	.192028	.198495	.205127
	0.00	.162760	.165451	.168201	.171008	.173872	.176789	.179760	.182783	.185855	.188975	.192142	.198609	.205242
	-.10	.162875	.165566	.168316	.171123	.173986	.176904	.179875	.182897	.185969	.189090	.192257	.198724	.205356
	-.20	.162989	.165680	.168430	.171237	.174101	.177018	.179989	.183012	.186084	.189204	.192371	.198838	.205471
	-.30	.163104	.165795	.168544	.171352	.174215	.177133	.180104	.183126	.186198	.189319	.192486	.198953	.205585
	-.40	.163218	.165909	.168659	.171466	.174329	.177247	.180218	.183241	.186313	.189433	.192600	.199067	.205700
25	.40	.155252	.158097	.161011	.163991	.167035	.170140	.173303	.176523	.179796	.183120	.186491	.193369	.200408
	.30	.155366	.158212	.161125	.164105	.167149	.170254	.173418	.176638	.179910	.183234	.186606	.193483	.200523
	.20	.155481	.158326	.161240	.164220	.167264	.170369	.173532	.176752	.180025	.183349	.186720	.193598	.200637
	.10	.155595	.158440	.161354	.164334	.167378	.170483	.173647	.176866	.180139	.183463	.186835	.193712	.200752
	0.00	.155710	.158555	.161469	.164449	.167493	.170598	.173761	.176981	.180254	.183578	.186949	.193827	.200866
	-.10	.155824	.158669	.161583	.164563	.167607	.170712	.173876	.177095	.180368	.183692	.187064	.193941	.200981
	-.20	.155939	.158784	.161698	.164678	.167721	.170826	.173990	.177210	.180483	.183806	.187178	.194056	.201095
	-.30	.156053	.158898	.161812	.164792	.167836	.170941	.174105	.177324	.180597	.183921	.187293	.194170	.201209
	-.40	.156167	.159013	.161926	.164907	.167950	.171055	.174219	.177439	.180712	.184035	.187407	.194285	.201324
30	.40	.150783	.153771	.156834	.159970	.163173	.166442	.169771	.173157	.176597	.180086	.183621	.190817	.198158
	.30	.150898	.153885	.156948	.160084	.163288	.166556	.169885	.173272	.176711	.180200	.183736	.190931	.198273
	.20	.151012	.154000	.157063	.160198	.163402	.166671	.170000	.173386	.176826	.180315	.183850	.191046	.198387
	.10	.151126	.154114	.157177	.160313	.163517	.166785	.170114	.173501	.176940	.180429	.183965	.191160	.198501
	0.00	.151241	.154228	.157292	.160427	.163631	.166900	.170229	.173615	.177055	.180544	.184079	.191275	.198616
	-.10	.151355	.154343	.157406	.160542	.163746	.167014	.170343	.173730	.177169	.180658	.184193	.191389	.198730
	-.20	.151470	.154457	.157521	.160656	.163860	.167128	.170458	.173844	.177283	.180773	.184308	.191503	.198845
	-.30	.151584	.154572	.157635	.160771	.163975	.167243	.170572	.173958	.177398	.180887	.184422	.191618	.198959
	-.40	.151699	.154686	.157750	.160885	.164089	.167357	.170687	.174073	.177512	.181001	.184537	.191732	.199074

15.0 YEAR HOLDING PERIOD
.500 EQUITY YIELD RATE
.900 LOAN RATIO

INTEREST RATE

TERM YEARS	APPR DEP	5.0	5.5	6.0	6.5	7.0	7.5	8.0	8.5	9.0	9.5	10.0	11.0	12.0
10	.40	.162320	.164951	.167617	.170317	.173053	.175823	.178628	.181466	.184338	.187243	.190181	.196154	.202254
	.30	.162434	.165065	.167731	.170432	.173168	.175938	.178742	.181581	.184452	.187357	.190295	.196268	.202368
	.20	.162549	.165180	.167845	.170546	.173282	.176052	.178857	.181695	.184567	.187471	.190410	.196383	.202483
	.10	.162663	.165294	.167960	.170661	.173397	.176167	.178971	.181809	.184681	.187586	.190524	.196497	.202597
	0.00	.162778	.165408	.168074	.170775	.173511	.176281	.179086	.181924	.184796	.187701	.190639	.196612	.202712
	-.10	.162892	.165523	.168189	.170890	.173625	.176396	.179200	.182038	.184910	.187815	.190753	.196726	.202826
	-.20	.163007	.165637	.168303	.171004	.173740	.176510	.179314	.182153	.185025	.187930	.190868	.196841	.202941
	-.30	.163121	.165752	.168418	.171119	.173854	.176625	.179429	.182267	.185139	.188044	.190982	.196955	.203055
	-.40	.163236	.165866	.168532	.171233	.173969	.176739	.179543	.182382	.185254	.188159	.191097	.197070	.203170
15	.40	.133918	.136757	.139649	.142592	.145586	.148630	.151723	.154864	.158053	.161288	.164570	.171265	.178130
	.30	.134032	.136872	.139763	.142706	.145700	.148744	.151837	.154979	.158167	.161403	.164684	.171379	.178245
	.20	.134147	.136986	.139878	.142821	.145815	.148858	.151952	.155093	.158282	.161517	.164798	.171494	.178359
	.10	.134261	.137101	.139992	.142935	.145929	.148973	.152066	.155207	.158396	.161632	.164913	.171608	.178474
	0.00	.134376	.137215	.140107	.143050	.146043	.149087	.152180	.155322	.158511	.161746	.165027	.171722	.178588
	-.10	.134490	.137329	.140221	.143164	.146158	.149202	.152295	.155436	.158625	.161861	.165142	.171837	.178703
	-.20	.134605	.137444	.140335	.143278	.146272	.149316	.152409	.155551	.158740	.161975	.165256	.171951	.178817
	-.30	.134719	.137558	.140450	.143393	.146387	.149431	.152524	.155665	.158854	.162090	.165371	.172066	.178931
	-.40	.134833	.137673	.140564	.143507	.146501	.149545	.152638	.155780	.158969	.162204	.165485	.172180	.179046
20	.40	.120148	.123175	.126268	.129427	.132648	.135930	.139273	.142673	.146129	.149640	.153202	.160478	.167939
	.30	.120262	.123289	.126383	.129541	.132762	.136045	.139387	.142787	.146244	.149754	.153317	.160592	.168054
	.20	.120377	.123404	.126497	.129655	.132877	.136159	.139502	.142902	.146358	.149868	.153431	.160706	.168168
	.10	.120491	.123518	.126612	.129770	.132991	.136274	.139616	.143016	.146472	.149983	.153546	.160821	.168283
	0.00	.120605	.123633	.126726	.129884	.133106	.136388	.139730	.143131	.146587	.150097	.153660	.160935	.168397
	-.10	.120720	.123747	.126841	.129999	.133220	.136503	.139845	.143245	.146701	.150212	.153775	.161050	.168512
	-.20	.120834	.123862	.126955	.130113	.133334	.136617	.139959	.143359	.146816	.150326	.153889	.161164	.168626
	-.30	.120949	.123976	.127070	.130228	.133449	.136731	.140074	.143474	.146930	.150441	.154003	.161279	.168740
	-.40	.121063	.124091	.127184	.130342	.133563	.136846	.140188	.143588	.147045	.150555	.154118	.161393	.168855
25	.40	.112216	.115416	.118695	.122047	.125471	.128965	.132524	.136146	.139828	.143567	.147360	.155097	.163017
	.30	.112330	.115531	.118809	.122162	.125586	.129079	.132638	.136260	.139942	.143681	.147475	.155212	.163131
	.20	.112445	.115645	.118923	.122276	.125700	.129193	.132752	.136375	.140057	.143796	.147589	.155326	.163245
	.10	.112559	.115760	.119038	.122390	.125815	.129308	.132867	.136489	.140171	.143910	.147703	.155441	.163360
	0.00	.112673	.115874	.119152	.122505	.125929	.129422	.132981	.136603	.140286	.144025	.147818	.155555	.163474
	-.10	.112788	.115989	.119267	.122619	.126044	.129537	.133096	.136718	.140400	.144139	.147932	.155670	.163589
	-.20	.112902	.116103	.119381	.122734	.126158	.129651	.133210	.136832	.140514	.144254	.148047	.155784	.163703
	-.30	.113017	.116218	.119496	.122848	.126272	.129766	.133325	.136947	.140629	.144368	.148161	.155898	.163818
	-.40	.113131	.116332	.119610	.122963	.126387	.129880	.133439	.137061	.140743	.144482	.148276	.156013	.163932
30	.40	.107188	.110549	.113995	.117523	.121127	.124804	.128550	.132359	.136229	.140154	.144131	.152226	.160485
	.30	.107303	.110664	.114110	.117637	.121242	.124919	.128664	.132474	.136343	.140268	.144246	.152341	.160600
	.20	.107417	.110778	.114224	.117752	.121356	.125033	.128779	.132588	.136457	.140383	.144360	.152455	.160714
	.10	.107531	.110893	.114339	.117866	.121471	.125148	.128893	.132702	.136572	.140497	.144474	.152569	.160828
	0.00	.107646	.111007	.114453	.117981	.121585	.125262	.129007	.132817	.136686	.140612	.144589	.152684	.160943
	-.10	.107760	.111121	.114568	.118095	.121700	.125377	.129122	.132931	.136801	.140726	.144703	.152798	.161057
	-.20	.107875	.111236	.114682	.118210	.121814	.125491	.129236	.133046	.136915	.140841	.144818	.152913	.161172
	-.30	.107989	.111350	.114797	.118324	.121928	.125605	.129351	.133160	.137030	.140955	.144932	.153027	.161286
	-.40	.108104	.111465	.114911	.118438	.122043	.125720	.129465	.133275	.137144	.141069	.145047	.153142	.161401

Index

About the Author

Irvin E. Johnson teaches advanced real estate appraisal at Ventura College, California, and is administrative assistant to the Ventura County Assessor. A native of California, he received the BA at Pacific Union College in 1932 and later did graduate work at the University of the Pacific. In 1971 he was awarded the Bernard L. Barnard Award by the International Association of Assessing Officers for an article in the April 1971 *Assessors' Journal* entitled "Compound Interest Tables Made Simple." Subsequent to his development of the simplified method of capitalization, he has been conducting seminars in mortgage-equity for the Society of Real Estate Appraisers and other professional organizations throughout the United States.

34567890